DIGITAL IMAGE PROCESSING

Kenneth R. Castleman

Perceptive Scientific Instruments, Inc.

PRENTICE HALL, Upper Saddle River, New Jersey 07458

Library of Congress Cataloging-in-Publication Data

Castleman, Kenneth R.
Digital image processing / Kenneth R. Castleman.
p. cm.
Includes bibliographical references and index.
ISBN 0-13-211467-4
1. Image processing--Digital techniques. I. Title.
TA1632.C37 1996
621.367--dc20 95-11113
CIP

Acquisitions editor: *Tom Robbins*
Editorial production supervision: *Barbara Marttine Cappuccio*
Copyeditor: *Brian Baker*
Cover design: *Bruce Kenselaar*
Manufacturing buyer: *Donna Sullivan*
Editorial assistant: *Phyllis Morgan*

Upper Saddle River, NJ 07458

Printed in the United States of America

10 9 8 7

ISBN 0-13-211467-4

Prentice-Hall International (UK) Limited, *London*
Prentice-Hall of Australia Pty. Limited, *Sydney*
Prentice-Hall of Canada, Inc., *Toronto*
Prentice-Hall Hispanoamericana, S. A., *Mexico*
Prentice-Hall of India Private Limited, *New Delhi*
Prentice-Hall of Japan, Inc., *Tokyo*
Pearson Education Asia Pte. Ltd., *Singapore*
Editora Prentice-Hall do Brasil, Ltda., *Rio de Janeiro*

To
Betty, Scotty, and Princess
who enhance my image of this planet

Contents

Preface

In the 16 years since the publication of my first book on this topic, there has been a major expansion in the utilization of digital image processing. Algorithms that could run only on mainframe computers in the 1960s and minicomputers in the 1970s migrated to the desktop in the 1980s. Personal computers transformed from something a few dedicated hobbyists built in the mid-1970s into a common home office component. The jargon of personal computers became a universal language that bridged the oceans between the United States, Europe, and Asia.

Public awareness of digital image processing has been greatly increased by video games, digital video special effects used in the entertainment industry, and articles in the popular press. Present trends indicate a continuation of the explosive growth of digital image-processing applications well into the next century.

Perhaps the most significant impact of digital image processing in the 1990s will be in the area of applications to real-world problems. This book is aimed at the reader who intends to use the technology for research or commercial purposes. It also provides a foundation for those who seek to advance the state of the art.

While the scope and scale of digital image-processing applications have changed dramatically, other aspects of the field have not. For example, many of the basic techniques that perform reliably in practice today are those that were first applied in the early days of digital imaging. While several exciting new theoretical areas have opened up, generally they build upon, rather than replace, what has served well in the past.

With the recent advances in computer technology, some of the issues treated in the earlier work are no longer of major concern. These are deemphasized in this book, while several relevant new topics have been included. New examples serve to illustrate further how the theory can be applied to the type of problems that commonly occur in industry and research.

Perhaps most significantly, a set of exercises and suggestions for projects completes each chapter. These have been selected to build the insight and understanding that are most useful to one endeavoring to apply the technology to problems of the real world. The majority of the exercises and projects emulate actual situations a professional faces working in the field of digital image processing. They are intended to give the reader a head start in gaining the insight that supplements a theoretical knowledge and can come only from the experience of solving real problems. In my own estimation, one who not only knows how to solve the problems and carry out the projects, but has actually done most of them, will be ready to take his or her place on the most productive image-processing applications team.

For about 25 years, I have had the opportunity to observe the efforts of many individuals applying digital image-processing techniques to problems offered by the real world. A few of these individuals have established an enduring track record of solid success on almost every attempt. They have consistently contributed innovative and effective solutions that creatively employ the tools of the discipline.

These highly productive individuals demonstrably hold several characteristics in common. One can venture to assume that these characteristics constitute a formula for success, to whatever extent such a thing can exist in this field.

Uniformly, these successful persons have (1) a genuine interest in—even a fascination with—the technology involved, (2) a thorough understanding of the fundamentals of this highly multidisciplinary technology, (3) a conceptual type of understanding (as opposed to rote memorization of totally abstract theory), and (4) a knack for seeing problems visually, graphically, and from more than one viewpoint. In line with this last point, they often find themselves hard pressed to explain their ideas without the aid of a graph or drawing.

This book is designed to help the reader develop the last three of these traits and perhaps enhance the first as well. The selection of materials for inclusion (and, equally important, for omission), the examples used, the references cited, and the exercises and suggestions for projects are all directed toward this goal.

In the field of digital image processing, mathematical analysis forms the stable basis upon which one can make definite predictions regarding the performance of a digital imaging system. In this treatment, however, mathematics is employed more as a faithful servant than as a ruthless master. The emphasis is on developing a conceptual understanding, and the analysis is used to support this goal.

The organization of this book generally follows that of the earlier text, simply because that particular flow of development proved to serve its purpose well. The level of mathematical complexity increases gradually through the first two parts of the book. While many readers have the background in mathematics required to begin the discussion with sampling theory and the Fourier transform, others do not.

More importantly, though, many of the most important concepts can be presented without the aid of advanced mathmatics. Thus, we are able to avoid an additional element of complexity in the interest of making the learning process less burdensome and more appealing to all readers. As a general rule, topics receive attention in relation to their importance, rather than their complexity.

The field of digital image processing has now become so rich with technology that it is impossible to cover all aspects of it in a single volume of reasonable size. Hence, we concentrate upon those techniques that prove most useful in practice and leave most of the mathematical proofs to the references. Constraints of paper and ink further make it impossible to include nearly as many examples of images as would be desirable. (See [1] for an excellent source of these.)

Part 1 presents several important concepts that do not require detailed mathematical analysis for a basic understanding of them. Part 2 addresses techniques that rely more heavily upon their mathematical underpinning and elaborates analytically upon certain concepts introduced in Part 1. Part 3 addresses applications more specifically than they are addressed in earlier chapters.

A Note to Instructors. The development of this text has been accompanied by an accumulation of example digital images and problem solutions worked out in MathCAD™ [2] and WiT™ [3]. These are available from the World Wide Web site that supports this book (http://www.phoenix.net/~castlman/). The author can be reached via the publisher, through Compuserve (70214,1275), on the Internet (castleman@persci.com or castlman@phoenix.net) or Usenet (sci.image.processing).

A Note to Students. Digital imaging is a merger of several disciplines, and its nomenclature comes from many diverse fields. Often ordinary words are pressed into special new usage without warning. This can be quite confusing when it catches the reader unaware. Many of these specialized words are defined in Appendix 1. If the concept presented in a paragraph is not clear, check for a word that doesn't seem to fit. If there is one, look in the glossary or a dictionary for clarification. Frequent reference to the glossary and a dictionary is good insurance against difficulties in understanding the subject.

Image processing is best learned by a combination of study and application. One develops considerable insight by *using* the theory, working with actual imaging problems and image processing equipment. A balance between theory and practice keeps the subject interesting. Problems and projects are included at the end of each chapter for this purpose.

REFERENCES

1. G. A. Baxes, *Digital Image Processing: Principles and Applications,* Wiley, New York, 1994.
2. MathSoft, Inc., 201 Broadway, Cambridge, MA 02139.
3. Logical Vision, Ltd., 4299 Canada Way, Ste. 265, Bunaby, B.C., Canada V5G 1H3.

Acknowledgments

The author wishes to thank the following people who have contributed significantly to the publication of this book: Dr. Henry Fuchs, Dr. Michael Shantz and Dr. Meir Weinstein collaborated in the work on three-dimensional reconstruction from optical sections in Chapter 22. Terry Riopka of Perceptive Scientific Instruments, Inc. (PSII) contributed to the discussion of neural networks in Chapter 20. Robert Selzer and Nancy Cornelius of the Jet Propulsion Laboratory (NASA/JPL) contributed to the discussion of curve and surface fitting in Chapter 19. Dr. Qiang Wu (PSII) contributed to the chapter on wavelet transforms.

Figures were generously supplied by Prof I. T. Young of the Delft Institute of Technology, The Netherlands; Henry Hui Li of HNC Software, Inc., in San Diego; Dr. Jian Lu of the University of California, Davis; Mr. Shishir Shah and Dr. J. K. Aggarwal of The University of Texas at Austin; Marcus Gross and Lars Lippert of the Swiss Federal Institute of Technology, Zurich; Dr. James Blinn of NASA/JPL; Luc Nocente of Noesis Vision; Dr. Bruce Cameron and Dr. Qiang Wu of PSII; and NASA/JPL.

Several reviewers made valuable comments and suggestions that improved the presentation considerably. These include Dr. Stuart Taylor (Mayo Foundation) and Dr. David Shotton (Oxford University). Also among them are Dr. Bruce F. Cameron, Steve Clarner, Chuck Johnson, Robert McGill, Robert S. Rosser, and Dr. Qiang Wu, all of PSII. Special thanks go to the four publishers' reviewers whose thoughtful comments on an early manuscript resulted in considerable improvement thereto, and to Mr. Brian Baker, publisher's copy editor, whose thoughtful comments significantly improved the clarity of the text.

Preparation of the manuscript and figures was transformed from a burdensome task to an enjoyable journey by the competent and tireless assistance of Deborah K. Cate, Sheri D.

Breaux, and Donna Call of PSII. I would also like to thank Mr. Robin Downes, Director of University Libraries, the University of Houston, and his staff at the M. D. Anderson Library for making available their excellent research facilities.

Luc Nocente of Noesis Vision made available Visilog 4.3, which was used in the preparation of several of the figures. The manuscript was prepared in Word 6.0 (Microsoft). The numerical examples were computed in MathCAD+ 5.0 (MathSoft, Inc.), and many of the drawings were done in Visio 3.0 (Shapeware Corporation).

The author has benefited significantly over the years from discussions with gifted colleagues. These include Dr. Robert Nathan, Dr. Ray Wall, and Robert Selzer (all of NASA/JPL), Dr. Benjamin S. White (Exxon Research Laboratory), Dr. Kenneth Price (Stephen F. Austin State University), and Donald Winkler (PSII), as well as many of the authors whose work is cited herein. Also of note in this regard are Prof. I. T. Young (Delft Institute of Technology), Dr. M. Don Graham (Coulter Corp.), Dr. David Zahniser (Cytyc Corp.), Dr. Jeff Brenner (Tufts New England Medical Center), Dr. James Baccus (Cell Analysis Systems) Dr. Mortimer Mendelsohn (Lawrence Livermore Laboratory) and Dr. Brian Mayall (University of California, San Francisco).

Part One

CHAPTER 1

Images and Digital Processing

1.1 INTRODUCTION

Digital image processing—the manipulation of images by computer—is a relatively recent development in terms of humans' ancient fascination with visual stimuli. In its short history, it has been applied to practically every type of imagery, with varying degrees of success. The inherent subjective appeal of pictorial displays attracts perhaps a disproportionate amount of attention from scientist and lay person alike.

Like other multidisciplinary fields, digital image processing suffers from myths, misunderstandings, misconceptions, and misinformation. It is a broad umbrella under which fall diverse aspects of optics, electronics, mathematics, photography, and computer technology. It is plagued with imprecise and often contradictory jargon taken from many different fields. This book attempts to collect the fundamental concepts of digital image processing into a self-consistent package for a relatively easily digested introduction to the field.

Several factors indicate continued growth for the field. A major one is the perpetually declining cost of the computer equipment required. Both processing units and bulk storage devices continue to become less expensive year by year. A second factor is the increasing availability of equipment for digitizing and displaying images. There are indications that the cost of computer equipment will continue to decline.

Several new technological trends promise to further stimulate the growth of the field. Among these are parallel processing, made practical by low-cost microprocessors; inexpensive charge-coupled devices (CCDs) for digitizing; new memory technologies for large, low-cost image storage arrays; and inexpensive, high-resolution color display systems.

Another impetus for development stems from a steady flow of new applications. The usage of digital imaging in commercial, industrial, and medical applications and in scientific research continues to grow. Even with the scaling down of military expenditures comes increased use of remote sensing with digital imaging techniques. Thus, with increasing availability of reasonably inexpensive hardware and some very important applications on the horizon, one can expect digital image processing to play an important role in the future.

1.2 THE ELEMENTS OF DIGITAL IMAGE PROCESSING

At its most basic level, digital image processing requires a computer upon which to process images and two pieces of special input/output equipment: an image digitizer and an image display device.

In their naturally occurring form, images are not directly amenable to computer analysis. Since computers work with numerical (rather than pictorial) data, an image must be converted to numerical form before processing by computer can commence.

Figure 1–1 illustrates how a rectangular array of numbers can represent a physical image. The physical image is divided into small regions called *picture elements,* or *pixels.* The most common subdivision scheme is the rectangular sampling grid shown in the figure. The image is divided into horizontal lines of adjacent pixels. The number inserted into the digital image at each pixel location reflects the brightness of the image at the corresponding point.

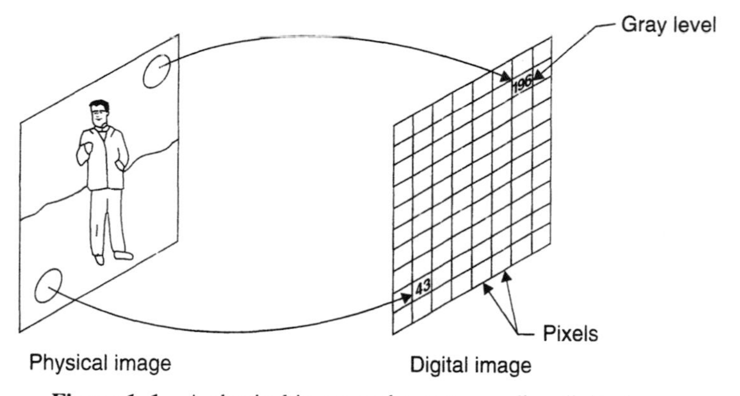

Figure 1–1 A physical image and a corresponding digital image

The conversion process itself is called *digitization,* and a common form is illustrated in Figure 1–2. At each pixel location, the brightness of the image is sampled and quantized. This step generates, for each pixel, an integer representing the brightness or darkness of the image at that point. When this has been done for all of the pixels, the image is represented by a rectangular array of integers. Each pixel has an integer location or address (line or row number and sample or column number) and an integer value called the *gray level.* This array of digital data is now a candidate for computer processing.

Figure 1–3 shows a complete system for image processing. The digital image produced by the digitizer goes into temporary storage on a suitable device. In response to instructions from the operator, the computer calls up and executes image-processing

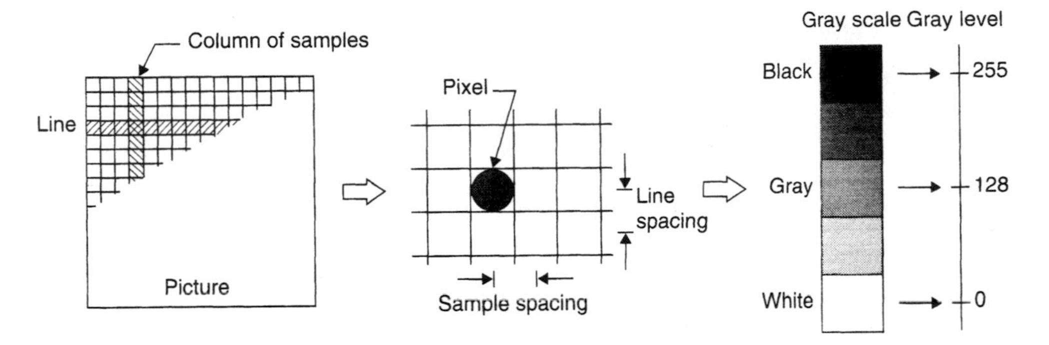

Figure 1–2 Digitizing an image

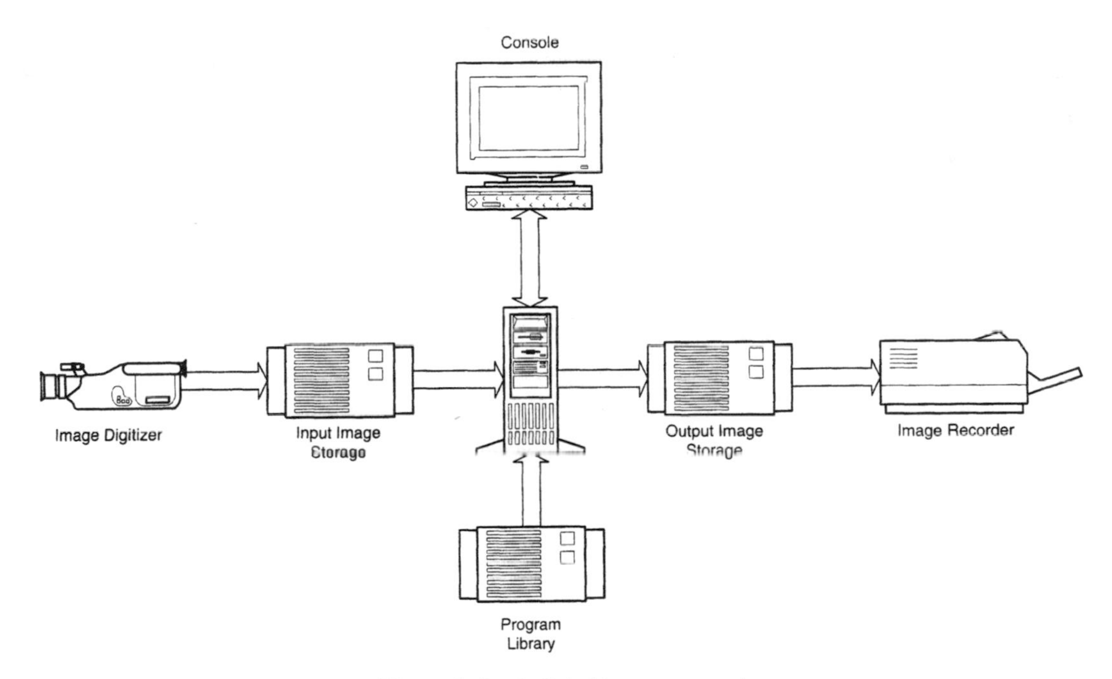

Figure 1–3 A digital image-processing system

programs from a library. During execution, the input image is read into the computer line by line. Operating upon one or several lines, the computer generates the output image, pixel by pixel, and stores it on the output data storage device, line by line.

During the processing, the pixels may be modified at the programmer's discretion. The processing steps are limited only by the programmer's imagination and patience, and the computing budget. After processing, the final product is displayed by a process that is the reverse of digitization: The gray level of each pixel is used to determine the brightness of the corresponding point on a display screen. The processed image is thereby made visible, and once again amenable to human interpretation.

1.2.1 The Terminology of Digital Image Processing

Images occur in various forms, some visible and others not, some abstract and others physical, some suitable for computer analysis and others not. It is thus important to have an awareness of the different types of images. A lack of this awareness can lead to considerable confusion, particularly when people are communicating ideas about images when they have different concepts of what an image is.

Since images form an overwhelming part of our experience from birth, there is a tendency to take them for granted. This section is intended to establish a foundation upon which images of all forms can be discussed with minimal confusion. Our definitions neither conform to nor establish a standard for the field, but are introduced to make the text self-consistent. Further definitions appear in the glossary in Appendix 1. The reader may wish to compare this section with other discussions of nomenclature [1–3].

Before we can define digital image processing, we must agree upon a definition for the word *image*. While most people have a notion of what an image is, a precise definition is elusive. Among the definitions of the word in several of Webster's dictionaries [4–6] are the following: "A representation, likeness, or imitation of an object or thing, . . . a vivid or graphic description, . . . something introduced to represent something else." Thus, in a general sense, an image is a representation of something else. A photograph of Abraham Lincoln, for instance, is a representation of an American president as he once appeared before a camera.

An image contains descriptive information about the object it represents. A photograph displays this information in a manner that allows the viewer to visualize the subject itself. Notice that under this relatively broad definition of *image* fall many "representations" that are not perceivable by the eye.

Images can be classified into several types based upon their form or their method of generation. In this regard, it is instructive to employ a set-theoretical approach. If we consider the set of all objects (Figure 1–4), the images form a subset thereof, and there is a correspondence between each image in the subset and the object that it represents. Within the set of images itself, there is a very important subset containing all the *visible* images—those that can be seen and perceived by the eye. Within this set again, there are several subsets representing the various methods of generation of the image. These include photographs, drawings, and paintings. Another subset contains the *optical* images, that is, those formed with lenses, gratings, and holograms.

The physical images are actual distributions of matter or energy. For example, optical images are spatial distributions of light intensity. These can be seen by the human eye and are thus visible images as well. Examples of nonvisible physical images are temperature, pressure, elevation, and population density maps. A subset of the physical images is *multispectral* images—those having more than one local property defined at each point. An example is the trispectral (red, green, blue) image, as it is reproduced in color photography and color television practice. Whereas the black-and-white image has one value of brightness at each point, the color image has three values of brightness, one each for red, green, and blue. The three values represent intensity in different spectral bands, which the eye perceives as different colors.

Another subset of images contains the abstract images of mathematics, which consists of the continuous functions and the discrete functions, or digital images. Only the digital images can be processed by computer.

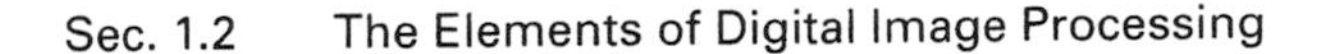

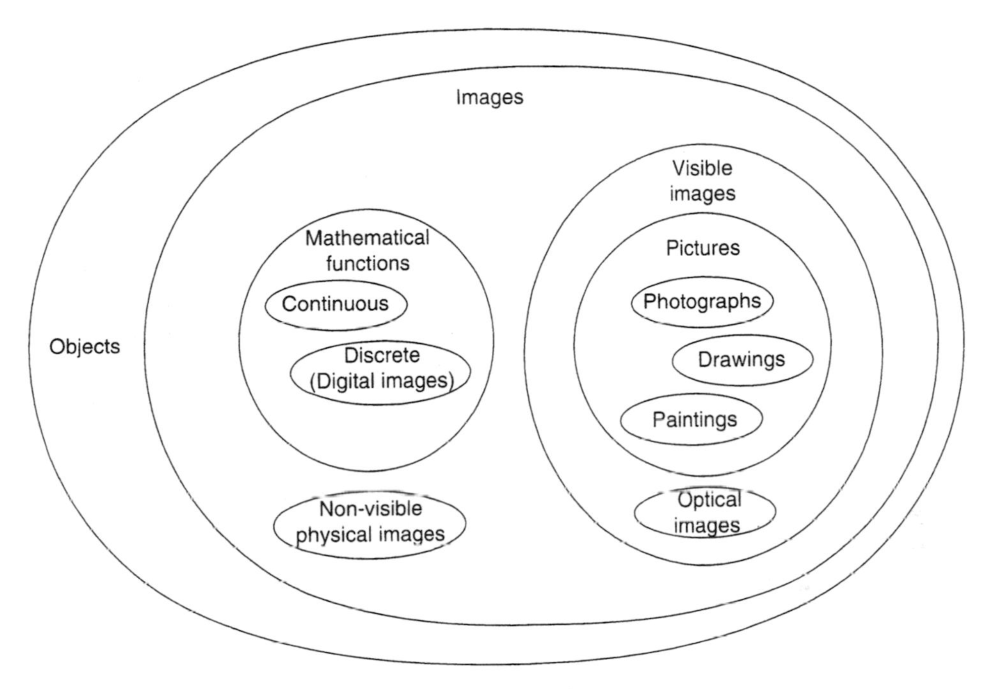

Figure 1–4 Types of images

A *picture* is a restricted type of image. Webster [5,6] defines a picture as "a representation made by painting, drawing, or photography, . . . a vivid, graphic, accurate description of an object or thing so as to suggest a mental image or give an accurate idea of the thing itself." For our purposes, we take the word *picture* to mean a distribution of matter that is visible when properly illuminated. In the vernacular of image processing, however, the word is sometimes used as equivalent to the word *image.*

The word *digital* relates to calculation by numerical methods or by discrete units. If we now define a *digital image* to be a numerical representation of an object (which may itself be an image), the pixels are the discrete units, and the quantized (integer) gray scale supplies the numerical component.

Processing is the act of subjecting something to a process. A *process* is a series of actions or operations leading to a desired result. Thus, a series of actions is performed upon an object to alter its form in a desired manner. An example is a car wash, wherein automobiles are processed to change them from dirty to clean.

Now we can define *digital image processing* as subjecting a numerical representation of an object to a series of operations in order to obtain a desired result. In the case of pictures, the processing changes their form to make them more desirable or attractive, or to accomplish some other predefined goal.

For purposes of discussion, it is convenient to restrict the general definition of a digital image. Unless otherwise stated, then, in this text we use the restricted definition of a digital image, which is *a sampled, quantized function of two dimensions that has been generated by optical means, sampled in an equally spaced rectangular grid pattern, and quantized in equal intervals of amplitude.* Thus, a digital image is now a two-dimensional rectangular array of quantized sample values.

In discussing images that are less restricted, we shall make use of the following four generalized images and processes: (1) nonoptical digital images generated from other than optical images; (2) higher dimensional digital images defined in three or more dimensions (this includes multispectral images in which there is more than one gray level value at each point); (3) nonstandard sampling, in which the domain of the image is sampled by a scheme other than the equally spaced rectangular grid; and (4) nonstandard quantization, where the quantizing levels are not equally spaced.

An image is usually a condensation or a summary of the information in the object that it represents. Ordinarily, an image contains considerably less information than the original object; thus, an image is an incomplete and inexact, yet in some sense adequate, representation of the object.

Digital image processing starts with one image and produces a modified version of that image. It is therefore a process that takes an image into an image. *Digital image analysis* is taken to mean a process that takes a digital image into something other than a digital image, such as a set of measurement data or a decision. For example, if a digital image contains a number of objects, a program might analyze the image and extract measurements of the objects. The term *digital image processing,* however, is loosely used to cover both processing and analysis.

Computer graphics is concerned with the processing and display of images of things that exist conceptually or as mathematical descriptions rather than as solid objects. The emphasis is often on the generation of an image, given a model that describes the object, its illumination, and the geometry of an imaginary camera. Computer graphics also includes *"computer art,"* the use of a digital imaging system as a medium for artistic expression.

Computer vision is concerned with developing systems that can interpret the content of natural scenes. In the field of robotics, computer vision supplies the eyes of the robot.

On a broader scale, we use the term *digital imaging* to encompass any manipulation of image-related data by computer. This includes computer graphics and computer vision, as well as digital image processing and analysis.

Digitizing is the process of converting an image from its original form into digital form. The term *conversion* is used in a nondestructive sense because the original image is not destroyed. Instead, it is used to guide the generation of the digital image. The reverse operation is *display,* that is, the generation of a visible image from a digital image. Commonly used equivalents are the terms *playback, image reconstruction, hardcopy,* and *image recording.* This process is nondestructive as well, since displaying a digital image does not destroy the data. There are both *volatile* and *permanent* displays. The latter produce hardcopy output.

We take *scanning* to mean the selective addressing of specific locations within the domain of an image. Each of the small subregions addressed in the scanning process is called a *picture element,* which is abbreviated by the word *pixel.* In digitizing photographic images, *scanning* is the process of sequentially addressing small spots on the film. The term is loosely taken as equivalent to the term *digitizing.* The rectangular grid scanning pattern is known as a *raster.*

Sampling means measuring the gray level of an image at each pixel location. Sampling is usually done by an image-sensing device that produces a voltage proportional to the light intensity at each pixel in an image.

Quantization is the representation of a measured value by an integer. Since digital computers process numbers, it is necessary to reduce the continuous measurement values to discrete units and represent them by integers. The image sensor, then, is usually followed by an *analog-to-digital converter,* an electronic circuit that generates a number proportional to a voltage.

The steps of scanning, sampling, and quantization are sufficient to generate a numerical representation of an image, and they comprise the steps of digitization. One can reverse this process to *display* a digital image. With the ability to convert images into digital form and back into visible form, one is able to define and execute digital processing steps on selected images and observe the results.

When a process generates an output image from an input image, there must exist a correspondence between points in the two images. Each pixel in the output image corresponds to one pixel in the input image. Thus, when the operation is applied to one point or a neighborhood centered upon one point in the input image, the resulting gray-level value is stored in the *corresponding point* in the output image.

The operations that can be performed on digital images fall into several classes. An operation is *global* if it is applied equally throughout the entire digital image. A *point* operation is an operation in which the value of the output pixel depends only on the value of the corresponding input pixel. The use of point operations is sometimes called *contrast manipulation* or *contrast stretching.* A *local* operation is an operation in which the gray level of each output pixel is computed from the gray levels of several pixels in a neighborhood of the corresponding input pixel.

The notion of *contrast* refers to the amplitude of gray-level differences within an image. Noise is broadly defined as an additive (or possibly multiplicative) contamination of an image.

Gray-scale resolution is the number of gray levels per unit of measure of image amplitude. Storing a digital image in 8-bit bytes, for example, yields a 256-level gray scale.

The *sampling density* of a digital image is the number of sample points per unit of measure (e.g., pixels per millimeter, etc.) in the domain of the image. The reciprocal of the sampling density is the *pixel spacing.*

Magnification refers to the size relationship between the objects in an image and the objects in the scene it represents. It is defined only for linear geometrical relations in which one can define the same metric in the domains of both image and scene, and in which the relationship is uniform over the entire image. Magnification is a meaningful relationship between the input and output digital images in a processing step. However, the "magnification" from a physical image to a digital image is not a meaningful concept. Sampling density (or pixel spacing) is the concept that proves useful in this regard.

1.3 PHILOSOPHICAL CONSIDERATIONS

One cannot approach a subject such as digital image processing without bringing to it a set of notions and attitudes—in other words, a viewpoint or a philosophy. In this section, we discuss two topics that are constructive in this regard.

1.3.1 Continuous and Discrete Approaches

There are two viewpoints from which one can approach the design and implementation of digital image-processing operations. One can think of the digital image as a set of discrete sample points (which it actually is), each having its own individual identity. Then the processing operation becomes the manipulation of these discrete units, much as one might handle the individual components when assembling a machine. The process is described in terms of what is done to the pixels, rather than what is done to the image or the objects therein.

On the other hand, images of interest commonly originate in the physical universe, which obeys principles well described by continuous mathematics (quantum mechanics excepted). For this reason, the image and its content are often better described by continuous functions. Thus, when manipulating an array of integers, one can think of the processing steps as they affect the underlying continuous function that the digital image temporarily represents.

The theory behind many of the processing operations is based on the analysis of continuous functions, and this approach serves the analyst well. Other processes are more productively thought of as logical operations performed on individual pixels, and the discrete approach serves better there. Often, either approach can describe the process, and we are left with a choice. In many cases we find that two developments, one based on the analysis of continuous functions and the other employing discrete techniques, lead us to the same solution. The insight gained along the way, however, may be significantly different.

Since the digital image is fundamentally discrete, it is dangerous to hold solidly to the continuous philosophy and overlook this basic characteristic. Sometimes, while thinking in the continuous mode, one can be surprised by an unexpected characteristic of the processed image, something brought about by its discrete nature. This can be a visible artifact (e.g., a moiré pattern) or a particularly inaccurate measurement. When the processing result differs markedly from that predicted by the analysis of continuous functions, we call this a *sampling effect.*

Since the objects in the scene to which the image corresponds, as well as the devices that formed the image, are better described by continuous functions, it is similarly unwise to restrict one's thinking to discrete mathematics and logical operations alone. In image restoration, for example, one uses digital (discrete) methods to improve an image that originated, became degraded, and will be displayed and viewed in analog (continuous) form. Thus, to regard digital imaging as strictly an exercise in discrete mathematics is to ignore the bulk of the process. Only when the image originates and culminates in digital form is an all-discrete approach justified.

Most commonly, we use discrete techniques to process images of a continuous world. The native state of the image is continuous, and the results of our processing normally will be interpreted in analog form as well. The image only becomes discrete for a brief time so that we can use the digital computer as a tool to implement our algorithms. Even if the image is presented to us in digital form, we usually cannot ignore its origin in the continuous domain.

> The term *digital image processing,* then, does not mean *processing digital images;* rather it means *digital processing of images.* This distinction, albeit rather subtle, is fundamental to our approach to the subject.

The Approach. We can summarize the approach taken here as follows. First, we expect to be able to characterize the effects digitization has upon an image that originates in continuous form. Second, we seek means to convert an image into digital form, and back into analog form, in such a way that the content of interest is not lost or significantly damaged. Third, we expect to be able to predict sampling effects, to recognize them when they occur, and to take steps to eliminate them or reduce them to tolerable levels. This unifies continuous and discrete processing into a more general approach to the problem. Chapters 12 and 15 discuss what is required to establish and maintain this approach.

When the unified approach is followed, the digital image that we process becomes essentially equivalent to the continuous original it represents. This is because (1) we can, at any time, recover the underlying continuous image from the discrete array by a properly conducted image display or printing process, and (2) we can implement digitally a process that produces the same effect that the equivalent physical process conducted in the continuous domain would produce. Under these conditions we are free to choose between continuous and discrete analysis, at each step and as it is convenient, because they produce the same result. Thus, ideally, one should be able to look at digital image processing from either viewpoint, as appropriate and without confusion.

1.3.2 Correspondence between Images

In most digital image-processing applications, we process the image of an object in order to derive information about the object itself. Since it is only digital images that can be processed by the computer, such images act as temporary substitutes for the objects they represent. Thus, we establish a correspondence between an object and the image that is used to represent it. Since we cannot digitally process an object, or even a nondigital image, we are restricted to processing its corresponding digital image.

Figure 1–5 views an image-processing sequence in terms of a chain of corresponding images. The camera forms an optical image that corresponds to the subject. The developed

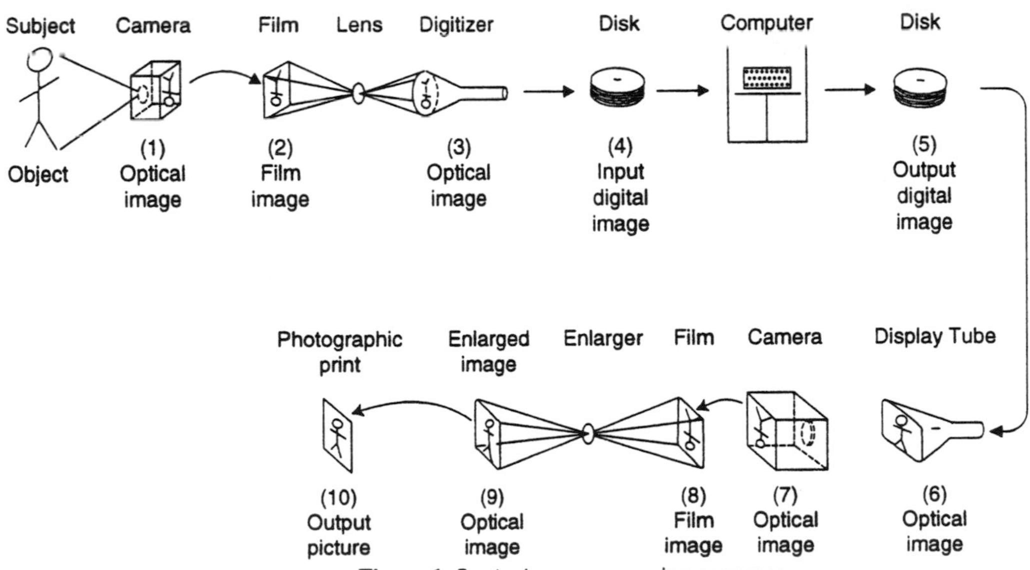

Figure 1–5 An image-processing sequence

film has on it a negative image corresponding to the optical image. The film forms a corresponding optical image on the digitizer faceplate, and that produces an input digital image that gives rise to a series of 6 corresponding images, the last of which is the desired output picture. Even if the actual processing is a simple one-step operation, there is still a series of 10 corresponding images between the subject and the output picture. Although our casual parlance belies this fact, it is important to remember how many corresponding images are involved.

Each step in the process provides an opportunity for the image to be degraded. To minimize degradation, each step should be well designed and properly controlled. One goal of this book is to develop means to analyze quantitatively the performance of each step and of the process as a whole.

1.4 DIGITAL IMAGE PROCESSING IN PRACTICE

Digital image processing requires knowledge from a varied background for its successful use. Practitioners in the field are called upon for both theoretical analysis and practical application. The technique requires a balanced knowledge of mathematics, optics, and computer technology, as well as the use of intuition and common sense.

1.4.1 Functional Requirements for Digital Image Processing

The following is a list of requirements an effective general-purpose image-processing system should meet:

1. The hardware must be adequate for the problems attempted. Inadequate sampling in the spatial domain and inadequate gray scale quantization may not preclude success, but can render the reason for failure inconclusive. Processing algorithms often assume that the image function is continuous. If the sampling and quantization in use do not justify this assumption, performance may suffer considerably. Thus, inadequate data-handling capability can be a threat to a successful solution to a problem.
2. High-quality equipment is required. When system noise levels degrade the image, success is once again in jeopardy.
3. While image analysis requires a high-quality image digitizer, image processing requires a high-quality image display device as well.
4. For general-purpose work, the software system should allow simple and logical menu selection of processing and analysis programs. Convenient storage of, and quick access to, input and output digital images and library programs is a practical requirement.
5. The tasks in the image-processing library should be maintained with an eye toward versatility. The power of the system is greatly enhanced if existing programs can be used to try out new approaches to old or new problems without the need for reprogramming.
6. The program library should be easily expandable to include new modules as they are developed, so that the system undergoes continual growth.

PROBLEMS

1. Watch a television news program, and make a log of all the uses of digital imaging and what each contributes to the overall image the producers are seeking for the program.
2. Watch someone play an arcade video game, and write an short paper describing how digital imaging is used to create the illusion.
3. Watch a motion picture that uses a substantial amount of computer-generated animation (e.g., *The Last Starfighter*), and write a short paper describing what digital imaging techniques are used and how each contributes to the story line.
4. Tour the medical imaging facility of a hospital, and write a short paper describing which digital imaging techniques are used in the equipment and how each contributes to health care delivery in terms of accuracy, throughput, and cost savings.
5. Interview a police officer, prosecuting attorney, or defense attorney about cases involving photographic evidence, and write a short paper describing how digital image processing could be used to solve, prosecute, or defend one such case.
6. Use a computer painting or drawing program to generate a picture for some purpose, and write a short paper describing what digital imaging techniques are used and how each contributes to the creation of the picture and to the purpose the picture serves.
7. A certain graphical environment uses icons that are 32 by 32 pixel images, and each pixel is one of 16 colors. How many different icons are there? Assuming that one in a million of the possible icons is potentially useful, how large a piece of paper would be required to print them all side by side at 100 pixels per inch? If this turns out to be impractical, how many 8-by-10 prints would it take to catalogue them? If the paper is 0.01 inch thick, how tall will the stack of prints be?
8. How long would it take to flip through a catalogue containing all the recognizable images that are 200 by 200 pixels with 40 gray levels? Assume that one out of every billion of the possible images is recognizable and that it takes one second to peruse each image.

REFERENCES

For additional reading, see Appendix 2.

1. R. M. Haralick, "Glossary and Index to Remotely Sensed Image Pattern Recognition Concepts," *Pattern Recognition,* **5**:391–403, 1973.
2. R. M. Haralick and L. G. Shapiro, "Glossary of Computer Vision Terms," *Pattern Recognition,* **24**:69–93, 1991.
3. IEEE Std 610.4-1990, *IEEE Standard Glossary of Image Processing and Pattern Recognition Terminology,* IEEE, New York 1990.
4. *Webster's New World Dictionary of Computer Terms* (3d ed.), Prentice-Hall, New York, 1988.
5. *Webster Illustrated Contemporary Dictionary,* Doubleday & Company, Garden City, NY, 1982.
6. *Webster's New Ideal Dictionary,* G. & C. Merriam Co., Springfield, MA, 1978.

CHAPTER 2

Digitizing Images

2.1 INTRODUCTION

Since computers can process only digital images, and nature affords images in other forms, a prerequisite for digital image processing is the conversion of images into digital form. The specialized equipment for digitizing images is, by and large, what transforms an ordinary computer system into an image-processing workstation. An image-recording device may also be required, although a dot matrix (graphics) printer can produce hard copy of limited quality.

In the early days of digital image processing, image-digitizing equipment was so expensive and complex that only a relatively few research centers could afford such a capability. Advances in technology, however, have made image digitizers inexpensive and their use widespread.

Widely diverse configurations of apparatus have been used to convert images into digital form. In this chapter, we discuss the elements of an image digitizer and some of the physical phenomena that are often employed in the process, and we examine several implementations. The aim is to develop an insight into the capabilities and limitations of these different approaches to image digitization and a feeling for the noise and distortion that can be introduced by each. The reduction or removal of digitizer noise and distortion is one of the major functions of digital image processing.

2.1.1 The Elements of a Digitizer

An image digitizer must be able to divide an image into picture elements (pixels) and address each individually, to measure the gray level of the image at each pixel, to quantize the continuous measurements to produce a set of integers, and to write that set of integers on a data storage device. To accomplish this, a digitizer must have five elements.

The first element of the digitizer is a sampling aperture—something that allows the digitizer to access picture elements individually while ignoring the remainder of the image.

The second element is a mechanism for scanning the image. This process consists of moving the sampling aperture over the image in a predetermined pattern. Scanning allows the sampling aperture to address the pixels in order, one at a time.

The third element is a light sensor, which can measure the brightness of the image at each pixel through the sampling aperture. The sensor is commonly a transducer that converts light intensity into an electrical voltage or current.

The fourth element, a quantizer, converts the continuous output of the sensor into an integer value. Typically, the quantizer is an electronic circuit called an *analog-to-digital converter.* This unit produces a number that is proportional to the input voltage or current.

The fifth element of an image digitizer is the output storage medium. The gray-level values produced by the quantizer must be stored in an appropriate format for subsequent computer processing. The output medium can be solid-state memory, magnetic disk, or some other suitable device.

2.2 CHARACTERISTICS OF AN IMAGE DIGITIZER

While image digitizers differ in the apparatus they use to perform their function, they may be compared on the basis of their relevant characteristics.

Pixel Size. Two important characteristics are the size of the sampling aperture and the spacing between adjacent pixels. If the digitizer is mounted on an optical system with variable magnification, the sample size and spacing at the input image plane are variable, and it is the range that is of interest.

Image Size. Another important parameter is the input image size capability of the instrument. In the case of a film scanner, the maximum input size might be 35 mm film or, perhaps, 11-by-14-inch X rays. At the output, image size is specified by the maximum number of lines and of pixels per line.

Local Property Measured. A third significant characteristic of an image digitizer is the physical parameter that it actually measures and quantizes. In the case of film scanners, for example, the instrument could measure and quantize either the transmittance or the optical density of the film. Both are functions of the darkness or lightness of the film, but in certain applications one may be more useful than the other.

Linearity. The degree of linearity of the digitization is also an important factor. For instance, if the instrument digitizes light intensity, one should know to what degree of accuracy the gray levels are, in fact, proportional to the actual brightness of the image. The validity of subsequent processing may be jeopardized by a nonlinear digitizer. Of interest, as well, is the number of gray levels to which the instrument can quantize the image. Early image digitizers had only two gray levels: black and white. In current monochrome digitizing practice, eight-bit (256-level) data is commonplace, and considerably higher resolution is possible with available instrumentation.

Noise. Finally, one of the most important characteristics of a digitizer is its noise level. If a uniformly gray image is presented to a digitizer, the noise inherent in the system will cause variations in the output gray level across the image, even though the input brightness is constant. Noise introduced by the digitizer is a source of image degradation, and this should be small relative to the contrast within the image.

These characteristics constitute a brief specification sheet for an image digitizer. They provide a basis upon which to compare different instruments or to decide whether a particular digitizer is adequate for a specific job. In some applications, digitizing images with relatively few lines, pixels per line, and gray levels, and with appreciable nonlinearity and a high noise level, may be adequate. Many of the important applications of digital image processing, however, require a high-quality image digitizer—one capable of digitizing large images to many gray levels with good linearity and a low noise level. In later sections, we discuss image digitizer requirements in light of processing applications.

2.3 TYPES OF IMAGE DIGITIZERS

An important and highly versatile type of image digitizer is the digitizing camera, which has a lens system and can digitize an image of any object presented to it. An example is a television camera interfaced to a computer. Such a device can digitize not only physical objects, but also images such as photographic film.

A restricted, but nonetheless important, type of image digitizer is the film scanner. This is an instrument made specifically for scanning photographic images on film. Film scanners can digitize an image of an object only after it has been photographed initially by a film camera. Historically, film scanners have played a predominant role in image processing, but current practice tends to favor direct digitizing cameras.

2.3.1 Scan-In and Scan-Out Digitizing

There are two general digitizing approaches, called *scan-in* digitizing and *scan-out* digitizing. In a scan-out system (Figure 2–1), the entire object, or film image, is illuminated continuously, and the sampling aperture allows the light sensor to "see" only one pixel at a time. In a scan-in system (Figure 2–2), only one small spot of the object is illuminated at any time, and all the transmitted light is collected for the sensor. In this case, the object is scanned with the illuminating beam, and the sensor is spatially nonspecific.

There is a third philosophy that is a combination of the previous two. In a *scan-in/scan-out* system, the object is illuminated by a moving spot and sampled through a moving

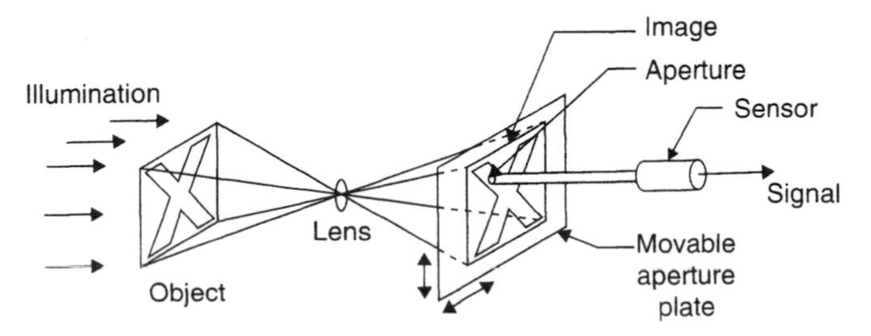

Figure 2–1 A scan-out digitizer

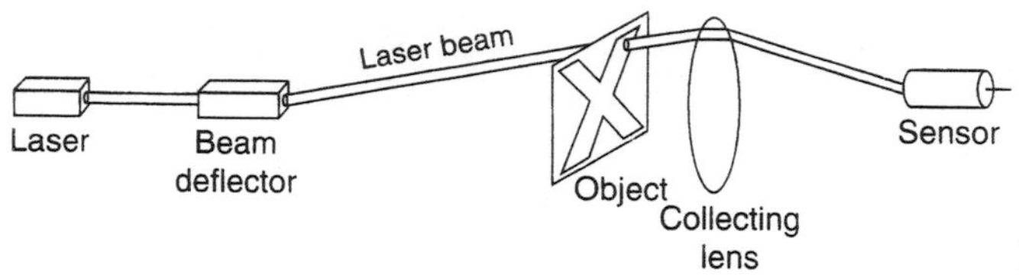

Figure 2–2 A scan-in digitizer

aperture that follows the spot. Such a system reduces the effects of glare and has found some application in digitizing microscope images. Their complexity, however, particularly in tracking the illuminating spot with the sampling spot, has somewhat limited the application of scan-in/scan-out systems.

2.4 IMAGE-DIGITIZING COMPONENTS

As discussed before, an image digitizer must have a light source, a light sensor, and a scanning system. Furthermore, either the light source or the light sensor (or both) must be behind a sampling aperture. In this section, we discuss various types of discrete light sources, light sensors, and scanning systems. In the next section, we put them together to form complete image digitizers.

2.4.1 Light Sources

Incandescent Bulbs. The most common artificial light source is the incandescent bulb. For scan-out systems, incandescent lighting is convenient for general illumination of the object or image being digitized. For scan-in work, the filament of a small bulb or a light-emitting diode (LED) can be imaged with a lens to form a small bright spot.

Lasers. Highly concentrated beams of light can be produced with a laser. The laser generates a narrow, intense, coherent beam of light by first raising the atoms of an active material (argon, helium, neon, etc.) to a high-energy state and then stimulating a simultaneous transition back to the normal state. This transition gives rise to a high-intensity beam of coherent light that is easily focused and deflected. While the laser could be used for general illumination in a scan-out system, its principal advantage lies in producing small high-intensity spots for scan-in digitizers.

Phosphors. Certain phosphors emit light when irradiated with electrons. If an electron beam is focused to a small spot on the face of a phosphor-coated glass plate (Figure 2–3), light is emitted from that spot. The phosphor that coats the face of the cathode-ray tube (CRT) is a crystalline compound doped with certain impurities. The phosphor is deposited on the face of the tube over a transparent aluminum film. This film is positively charged and forms an anode that attracts the electron beam.

The impact of the energetic electrons in the beam excites the atoms of the host phosphor, raising some of their electrons to high-energy states. As each of these electrons decays back to its normal state, it emits a photon. The spectrum (color) and persistence (decay rate) of the light generated can be controlled in the manufacture of the phosphor. A wide variety of emission spectra and persistence times, from less than 1 microsecond to several seconds, is available.

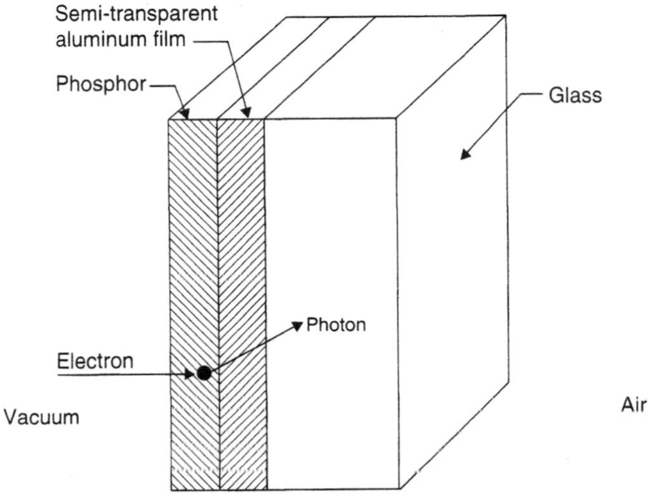

Figure 2–3 CRT target construction

The brightness of the light spot produced by the electron beam is roughly proportional to the average beam current density. The phosphor is made up of granules and is therefore subject to graininess and scattering of light within the phosphor layer. Cathode-ray tubes have a resolution limit of 30 to 70 line pairs (cycles) per millimeter.

LEDs. Solid-state LEDs also form compact and convenient light sources. LEDs are typically made of gallium arsenide semiconductor. They emit light at controlled intensity from a spatially small source. This also makes them useful for scan-in systems.

2.4.2 Light Sensors

Light sensors produce an electrical signal proportional to the intensity of light falling upon them. Five different physical phenomena are employed, and these give rise to five types of light sensors: photoemissive devices, photovoltaic cells, photoconductors, silicon sensors, and junction devices. Photoemissive substances emit electrons when irradiated with light. Photovoltaic substances, such as silicon solar cells, generate an electrical potential when exposed to light. Photoconductors, such as cadmium sulfide, show a drop in their electrical resistance when exposed to light. Silicon devices exploit the light-sensing properties of silicon in pure crystal form. Photodiodes and phototransistors change their junction characteristics under the influence of incident light.

Photoemissive Devices. The photomultiplier tube (Figure 2–4) has a photoemissive face that forms a semitransparent photocathode. The tube is coated with oxides of the alkaline metals (silver, cesium, antimony, sodium, bismuth, and rubidium). When photons of sufficient energy ($\lambda < 1$ micron or so) strike the negatively charged photocathode, electrons are freed from the surface.

Behind the photocathode is a series of *dynodes* held at progressively higher positive voltages. Primary electrons that have been freed from the photocathode by incident photons accelerate toward the first dynode. The impact of each frees several secondary electrons, producing a multiplying effect. The resulting electrons are then attracted toward the second dynode, where the same effect takes place. The process continues until the electrons from

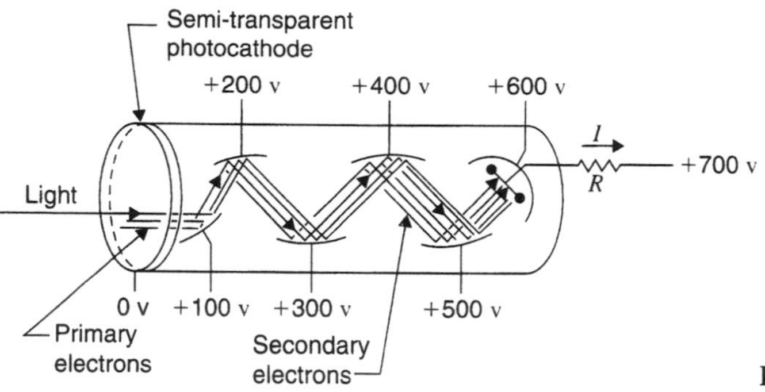

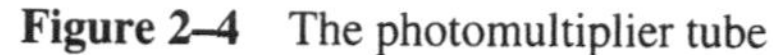
Figure 2–4 The photomultiplier tube

the last dynode are collected by the anode, producing a current in the external circuit. This current is proportional to the photon flux incident on the photocathode. It is sensed by the external circuit and may be sampled and quantized.

The photomultiplier tube is quite sensitive because of the multiplying effect of the dynodes. One primary electron may give rise to as many as a million electrons in the external circuit. This high sensitivity makes the photomultiplier tube useful for digitizing at low light levels.

Silicon Sensors. Prepared to a very high degree of purity, silicon can be grown in large crystals. Each silicon atom is covalently bonded to its six neighbors in a three-dimensional rectangular crystal lattice. Incident photons of sufficient energy ($\lambda < 1$ μm) will break such a bond, freeing an electron and leaving a "hole" where the electron was.

A thin metal layer deposited on the surface of the silicon and charged with a positive voltage creates a *potential well* that collects and holds the *photoelectrons* that have been freed by photons in the local area. Each potential well corresponds to one pixel in an array of sensors. A potential well can hold about 800 electrons per square micron of area, or 10^5 to 10^6 electrons per pixel on typical chips.

The dynamic range of a well is the ratio of its capacity in electrons to the readout noise level, also in electrons. Readout noise can be as low as 5–10 electrons for high-quality devices. Overexposure of a well generates excess electrons that can spread to adjacent wells, causing *blooming* of the image.

Thermal energy also causes random bond breakage, creating occasional *thermal electrons* that are indistinguishable from photoelectrons. This gives rise to the *dark current* of a silicon sensor—that is, the current it produces even in the absence of light. The dark current is temperature sensitive, doubling for each 6°C increase in temperature. At the long integration times that are required for low-light-level image sensing, the wells can fill with thermal electrons rather than photoelectrons.

Cooling is often employed to reduce dark current and thereby extend the usable integration time. Cooling a silicon sensor well reduces its dark current from several thousand electrons per second at room temperature to a number on the order of one electron per second at –60°C.

Photodiodes. The photodiode (Figure 2–5) is a solid-state P-N junction device. An electric field forms in the vicinity of the junction of two semiconductor materials of opposite polarity. This field sweeps the charge carriers (electrons and holes) out of the

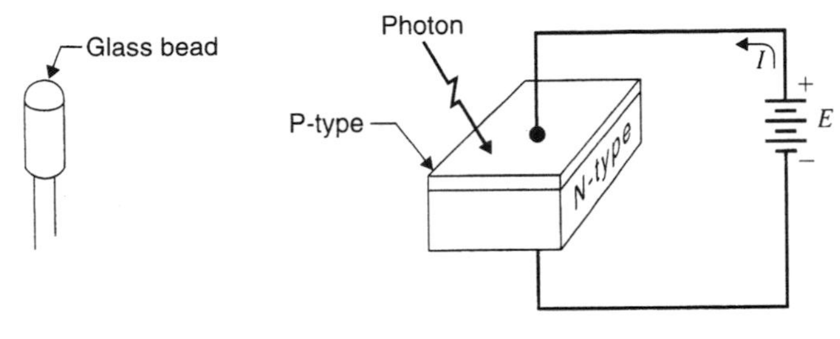

Figure 2–5 The photodiode

junction region, creating a depletion layer that impedes current flow. Such a device normally allows current flow in only one direction. In photodiodes, one side of the device (e.g., the P-layer) is made very thin so that light can penetrate to the junction.

In operation, the junction is supplied with a reverse-polarity voltage, and it thus conducts very little current. Impinging photons, however, release electron-hole pairs inside the material. In the depletion layer, where the electric field is strong, most of these mobilized carriers drift apart under the influence of the field before they can recombine. Their migration creates, in the external circuit, a current that is proportional to the incident photon flux.

Since the P-N junction presents a high resistance to current flow in the reverse direction, what current does flow is controlled by the light intensity and is relatively independent of the externally applied voltage. The depletion layer can be made comparatively thick to capture long-wavelength photons.

The *avalanche photodiode* achieves higher sensitivity than the ordinary photodiode through an electron multiplication effect reminiscent of the photomultiplier tube. The avalanche photodiode is subjected to a very high reverse-polarity voltage. Electrons that are freed by impinging photons are accelerated by the intense field in the depletion layer. They attain such high velocities that they have ionizing collisions within the material, freeing more electrons. This effect can produce gain factors as high as 1,000, considerably increasing the sensitivity of the device.

In the previous discussion, photodiodes were said to produce a steady-state current proportional to the incident photon flux. Alternatively, they can operate in the *integrating mode*. Since the photodiode junction exhibits capacitance, it will hold a charge of the reverse-biased polarity. Subsequently, photoconduction bleeds off the charge at a rate proportional to incident photo flux. If the photodiode is periodically recharged to some reference voltage, the required charge (number of electrons) is proportional to the integral of the incident photon flux over the period between recharges. Thus, in the integrating mode, the photodiode senses not instantaneous photon flux, but photon flux integrated over a certain period of time.

Two factors limit the dynamic range of photodiodes operating in the integrating mode. First, the small junction capacitance limits the initial charge that can be stored. Second, the dark current, which flows even without incident light, gradually discharges the photodiode. These factors limit the integration period to a few milliseconds and the dynamic range to about 100 to 1 at room temperature. Since the dark current is temperature sensitive, cooling the photodiode significantly increases practical integration times.

Phototransistors. The phototransistor is a three-layer semiconductor device mounted in clear plastic or in a can with a lens on top to permit light to access the transistor

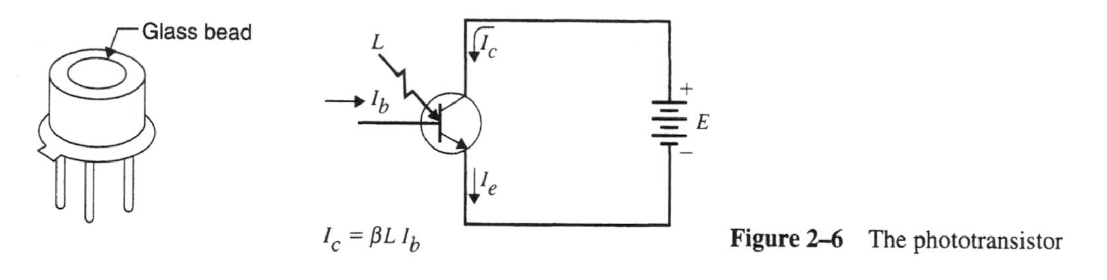

Figure 2–6 The phototransistor

junction (Figure 2–6). Impinging photons release electron-hole pairs in the collector-base junction. The movement of these carriers constitutes base current in the transistor. The collector current is proportional to the base current multiplied by the current gain factor (the *beta*) of the transistor. Externally, the phototransistor behaves like the photodiode, except with higher sensitivity. Design requirements for speed and linearity, however, dictate compromises in transistor design that place limits on achievable current gains. Both the photodiode and the phototransistor have a fast and stable response to light intensity variations, and they make excellent point sensors for digitizing images.

2.4.3 Scanning Mechanisms

In this section, we discuss techniques that may be used to move the scanning or illuminating spot about the image. In the next section, we consider light sources, sensors, and scanning mechanisms operating together in complete image-digitizing systems.

Mechanical Scanning Devices. Figure 2–7 shows two mechanical methods for image scanning: the rotating drum and the lead screw. A photographic image is wrapped, partially or completely, around a cylindrical drum, and the drum is rotated to pull the image past a stationary aperture. This effects scanning in one direction. The scanning aperture may be mounted on a lead screw that rotates to move the aperture across the image. In the figure, a rotating drum and lead screw have been combined to produce a two-dimensional image scanner. If the lead screw turns continuously rather than in steps, the scan is helical, but this is normally an adequate approximation to a rectilinear scan.

Mechanical scanning devices such as these are limited in speed of operation, but can provide good geometric stability on large images at relatively low cost.

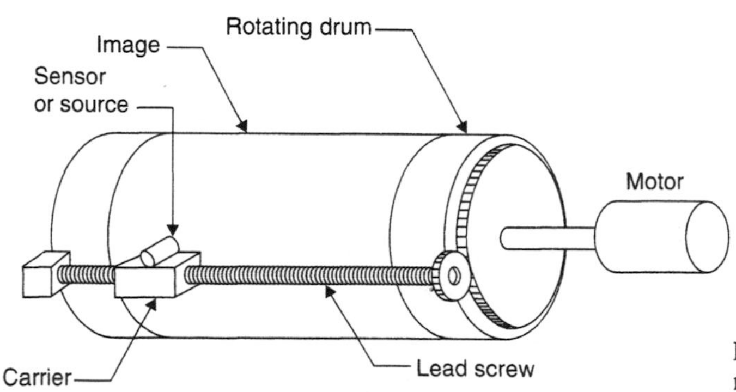

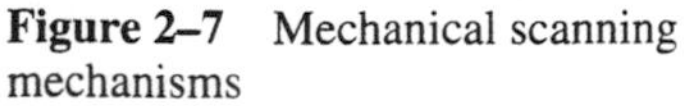
Figure 2–7 Mechanical scanning mechanisms

Electron Beam Scanning. Several electronic devices that are useful in digitizing and displaying images scan the images with an electron beam. Figure 2–8 illustrates two means of deflecting an electron beam to scan a target.

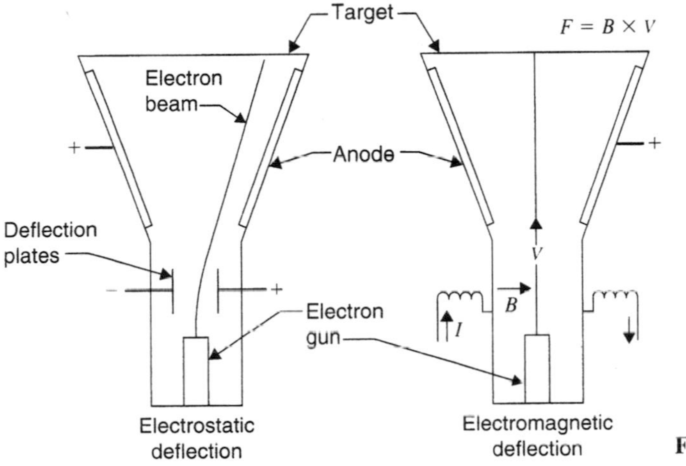

Figure 2–8 Electron beam deflection

Electrostatic Deflection. An electron beam, generated by an electron gun in the base of the tube, is attracted toward the target by the positively charged anode. As the electron beam passes between the electrostatic deflection plates, the electric field there exerts a force on the electrons, changing their direction of travel. The deflection angle is dependent on the beam velocity and the electrical potential between the plates. By controlling the potential, one can cause the electron beam to impact any point on the target.

Magnetic Deflection. A transverse magnetic field can also be used to deflect an electron beam. The force on a moving charged particle in a magnetic field is the vector cross product of the particle velocity and the magnetic field. The deflecting force acts at right angles to both the beam direction and the magnetic field. Thus, in Figure 2–8, the negatively charged electrons will be deflected downward.

Beam Focus. Electron beams must also be focused to a small spot on the target. Like deflection, this can be done by electrostatic or electromagnetic means. Poor convergence of the electron beam leads to large scanning spots and low resolution.

2.5 ELECTRONIC IMAGE TUBE CAMERAS

Electronic imaging tubes were the first devices to see widespread usage in television image sensing [1–4]. While they still play an important part in image digitization, they are losing out to solid-state devices.

2.5.1 The Vidicon Camera Tube

Figure 2–9 illustrates the construction of the vidicon, a common type of television image-sensing tube. The vidicon is a cylindrical glass envelope containing an electron gun at one

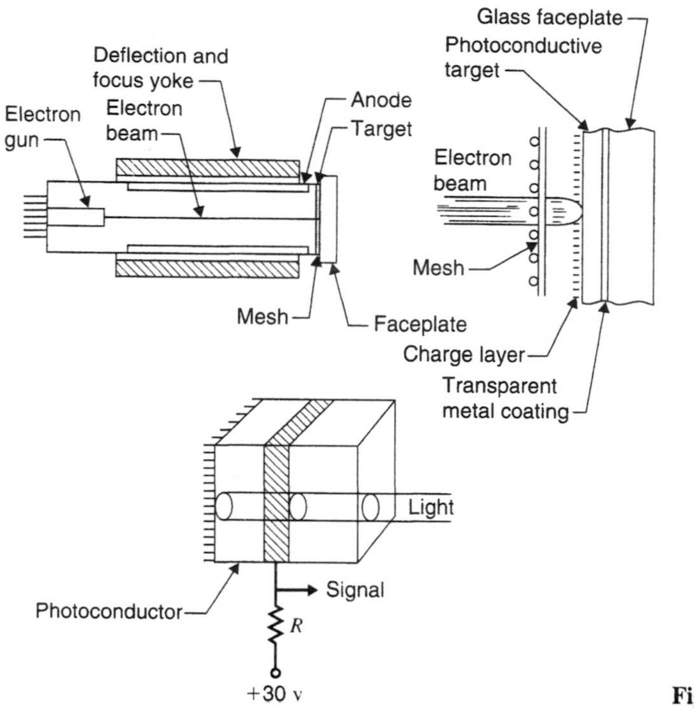

Figure 2–9 The vidicon camera tube

end and a target and faceplate at the other. The tube is surrounded by a yoke containing electromagnetic focus and beam deflection coils. The faceplate is coated on the inside with a thin layer of photoconductor over a thin transparent metal film. This double layer forms the *target.* A small positive charge is applied to the metal coating of the target, behind which is a positively charged fine wire screen called the *mesh.*

Arriving electrons decelerate after passing through the mesh, and they reach the target with approximately zero velocity. In darkness, the photoconductor behaves as an insulator, not allowing electrons to flow through to the positively charged film. The effect of the electron beam is to deposit a layer of electrons on the inner surface of the photoconductor to balance the positive charge on the metal coating. Thus, after a complete scan by the electron beam, the photoconductor appears as a capacitor with a positively charged plate on one side and a surface charge of electrons on the other side.

When light strikes a small area of the photoconductor, electrons begin to flow through, locally depleting the surface charge layer. Thus, if an optical image is formed on the target, the photoconductor will leak electrons until an identical electron image is formed on the back of the target. That is, electrons will be present in dark areas and absent in light areas.

As the electron beam scans the target, it replaces the lost electrons, restoring the uniform surface charge. As the electrons are replaced, a current flows in the external circuit of the target. This current is proportional to the number of electrons required to restore the charge and, therefore, to the light intensity at that point. It is also proportional to the scanning beam velocity, which, in turn, determines the time available for the charge to flow.

Current variations in the target circuit produce the video signal. The electron beam repeatedly scans the surface of the target, replacing the charge that bleeds away. The vidicon target is thus an integrating sensor, with the period of integration set by the scanning rate.

Scanning Convention. Figure 2–10 illustrates the Electronic Industries Association (EIA) RS–170 scanning convention, which is the standard for monochrome broadcast television in the United States [2–8]. The beam scans the entire surface of the target in 525 horizontal scan lines, 30 times each second. The lines are not scanned in sequential order, however, because if the TV screen were to be refreshed at only a 30-per-second rate, the eye would perceive an annoying flicker. Instead, an *interlaced* scanning convention is used to yield a 60-per-second refresh rate on the monitor.

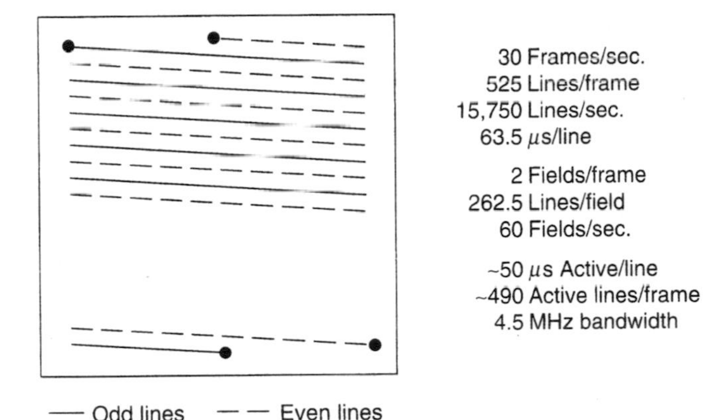

Figure 2–10 The RS–170 scanning convention

Each frame is made up of two interlaced fields, each consisting of 262.5 lines. The first field of the frame scans all the odd lines, while the second scans the intervening even lines. Interlacing yields a 60-per-second field rate to minimize perceived flicker, while the 30-per-second frame rate reduces the frequency bandwidth requirement of the transmitted signal.

Each horizontal line scan requires 63.5 μs, of which 83 percent, or approximately 50 μs, are active. Of the 525 lines per frame, 21 are lost in the vertical retrace of each field, leaving 483 active lines per frame. The bandwidth of the standard video signal extends up to 4.5 megahertz (MHz), which allows 225 cycles, or about 550 pixels worth of information, across the active portion of each line. The topics of sampling and resolution are addressed in Chapter 15.

Color Scanning Conventions. The National Television Standards Committee (NTSC) RS-170A timing standard for color television differs only very slightly from the RS-170 convention. It was designed to accommodate color transmission while maintaining compatibility with existing monochrome receivers. Different scanning conventions are used in other countries. The Comité Consultatif International des Radiocommunications (CCIR) standard, for example, used in much of Europe, employs a frame of 625 interlaced scan lines of about 768 pixels each. It runs at 25 frames per second.

One can use the vidicon camera as an image digitizer simply by sampling the video signal with a fast analog-to-digital converter. To obtain approximately 500 points per line, however, one must sample the video every 100 nanoseconds. A *frame grabber* is a digitizer that stores this high-speed data stream in a solid-state memory and then feeds it out at a slower rate to a more permanent storage device.

The Vidicon Family. The target of the standard vidicon is made of selenium photoconductor material. A similar tube, the plumbicon, has a lead oxide target. Other relatives of the vidicon, having similar sounding names, differ mainly in the composition of the photoconductive material used in the target. The plumbicon is somewhat more sensitive than the vidicon and has faster response to a rapidly changing image, but slightly lower resolution. The other members of the family excel in various imaging characteristics, depending upon the nature of the target material.

2.6 SOLID-STATE CAMERAS

A more recently developed type of image sensor is the electronic self-scanning solid-state sensor array. The three principal types are the charge-coupled device (CCD) array, the charge injection device (CID) array, and the photodiode array. All of these devices have a linear or rectangular array of light sensor sites on a single integrated circuit chip, complete with the circuitry necessary to read out the electron charge generated by the incident image.

2.6.1 Photodiode Arrays

The self-scanning photodiode array (Figure 2–11) contains, on one chip, an array of photodiode sensors and a series of switches with associated control circuitry. The photodiodes operate in the light-integrating mode. Responding to externally supplied clock pulses, the circuitry closes the switches, one at a time, to allow the junction capacitance to be recharged by the external circuit. The pulse of charging current, I_c, is proportional to the total amount of light that has fallen on the diode during the period between scans. The rather large amount of associated circuitry that must be manufactured on the chip places practical limitations on the size of photodiode arrays. They are most commonly made in long, one-dimensional arrays such as those used in facsimile scanners.

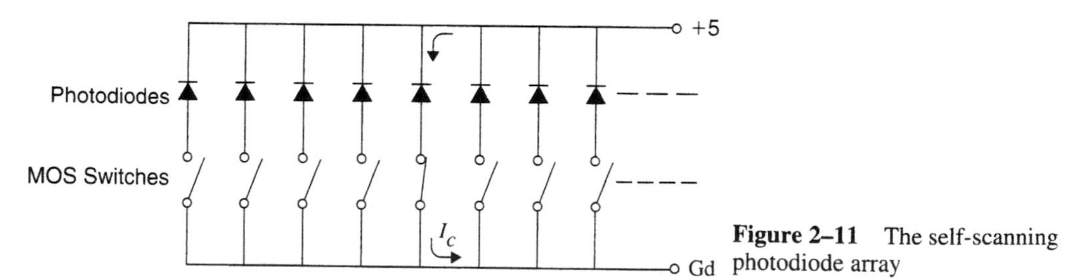

Figure 2–11 The self-scanning photodiode array

2.6.2 Charge-Coupled Devices

CCD chips [9–12] are manufactured on a light-sensitive crystalline silicon chip, as discussed earlier. A rectangular array of photodetector sites (potential wells) is built into the silicon substrate. The photoelectrons produced in a local area are held in the nearest potential well and are shifted as a *charge packet* down a series of wells until they reach an external terminal.

Three different architectures can be employed for reading the accumulated charge out of CCD image-sensing devices: the classical or full-frame architecture, the interline-transfer architecture, and the frame-transfer architecture (Figure 2–12).

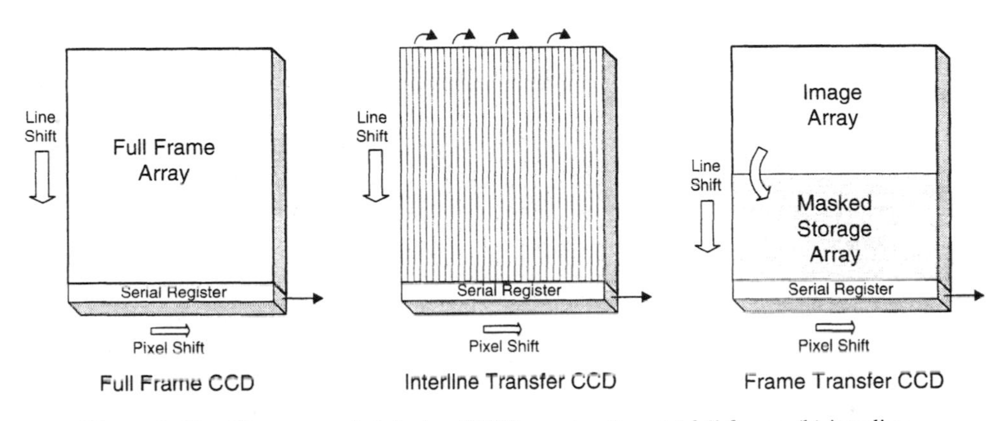

Figure 2–12 Charge-coupled device (CCD) construction: (a) full frame; (b) interline transfer; (c) frame transfer

Full-Frame CCD. Following exposure, the full-frame CCD must be shuttered to keep it in the dark during the readout process. It then shifts the charge image out of the bottom row of sensor wells, one pixel at a time. After the bottom row is empty, the charge in all of the rows is shifted down one row, and the bottom row is again shifted out. This process repeats until the top row has at last been shifted down and out of the bottom row of sensor wells. Then the device is ready to integrate another image.

Interline-Transfer CCD. In an interline transfer CCD every second column of sensors is covered by an opaque mask. These columns of masked wells are used only in the readout process. After exposure, the charge packet in each exposed well is shifted into the adjacent masked well. This transfer requires very little time since all charge packets are shifted at once. While the exposed wells are accumulating the next image, the charge in the masked columns is being shifted down and out in the same way as the classical CCD. In a sensor of this type, the number of pixels per line is half the actual number of wells per row on the chip. No more than 50% of the chip area is light-sensitive since the masked columns occupy half of its surface.

Frame-Transfer CCD. A frame-transfer CCD chip has a doubly long sensor array. The top half senses the image in the standard manner. The bottom half—the storage array—is protected from incident light by an opaque mask. At the end of the integration period, the entire charge image that has accumulated in the sensing array is shifted rapidly, row by row, into the storage array. From there it is shifted out, pixel by pixel in the standard manner, while the sensing array integrates the next image. Like interline transfer, this technique employs simultaneous integration and readout, making video-rate image sensing possible.

CCD Performance. Available in a variety of configurations, CCDs give rise to a line of compact and rugged solid-state cameras for both television usage and image-digitizing applications. These cameras are free of geometric distortion and highly linear in their response to light. CCDs are emerging as the device of choice for a variety of image-sensing applications.

CCDs can be scanned at television rates (30 frames per second) or much more slowly. Since they can integrate for periods from seconds to hours to capture low-light-level images, they are used in astronomy and fluorescence microscopy, for example. The long integration times require that the sensor be cooled well below room temperature to reduce dark current effects. Dark current can fill the wells with thermal electrons before the photoelectrons have a chance to build up. Due to imperfections in the crystal lattice, dark current can vary significantly from pixel to pixel, particularly in the less expensive chips. In long-exposure images, this leaves a fixed noise pattern that looks like a star field. The effect is due to a few pixels with abnormally high dark current. Since the pattern is stationary, it can be recorded and subtracted out, unless dark current has been allowed to saturate the well with thermal electrons.

Readout noise is random noise generated by the on-chip electronics. It ranges from a few to many electrons per pixel, depending on the chip design. It gets worse as the charge is read out at a faster rate. Readout noise is usually the dominant noise factor under short-exposure, low-light conditions, where the dark current and photon noise components are small.

Photon noise results from the quantum nature of light. If a CCD is illuminated with, for example, 100 photons per pixel per second on the average, the actual number of photons striking any particular pixel in any one second will be a random number. Statistically, that number has a Poisson distribution, so its standard deviation is equal to the square root of its mean. In the foregoing example, the average number of photons incident upon pixels would be 100, with a standard deviation of 10. In general, the photon noise component is the square root of the number of electrons that accumulate in a well (i.e., photoelectrons plus thermal electrons). This usually becomes the dominant noise source under high exposure or high dark current conditions.

The charge developed in a pixel must be shifted from well to well as many as a thousand times or more (depending upon its location and the array size) before leaving the chip. This requires the charge-transfer efficiency to be extremely high, or significant numbers of photoelectrons will be lost in the readout process.

Often, half or more of the available area of the sensor is covered by opaque charge-transfer circuitry, leaving gaps between the pixels. Overexposure of a CCD sensor can cause blooming of the image as excess photoelectrons spread to adjacent pixels. Defects in the crystal lattice can cause a *dead pixel,* which will not hold photoelectrons. Since charge is shifted through the pixels on its way out of the chip, one dead pixel can wipe out all or part of an entire column.

2.6.3 Charge Injection Devices

CID sensors [13–17] exploit the photoelectronic properties of silicon as do CCDs. Their readout method, however, is considerably different, and this yields distinctly different image sensing properties.

CID Operation. At each pixel site, the CID has two adjacent potential-well-producing electrodes (Figure 2–13). These are separated from the silicon surface by a thin, metal-oxide insulating layer. One electrode is electrically connected to one electrode of all

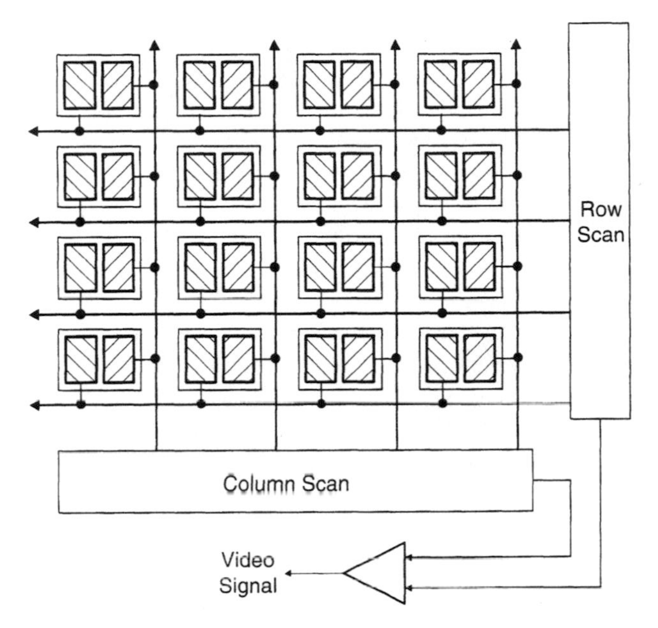

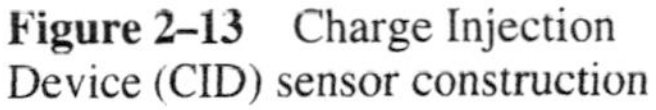

Figure 2–13 Charge Injection Device (CID) sensor construction

the other pixels in its column, while the other electrode is connected to all the pixels in its row. Thus, a single pixel can be addressed by selecting its row and column address.

When both electrodes at a pixel site are held at a positive voltage, photoelectrons will accumulate under them. This is the integrating mode. If all rows and columns are held positive, the entire chip accumulates an image.

When one electrode is driven to (or below) zero volts, the accumulated photoelectrons will shift to a position underneath the second (still positive) electrode. This shift creates a current pulse in the external circuitry connected to the second electrode. The size of the current pulse reflects the amount of accumulated photoelectronic charge. The accumulated photoelectrons remain in the well after the shift. This is the nondestructive readout mode. The pixel can be read repeatedly by shifting the charge back and forth without losing it.

When the second electrode is also driven to (or below) zero, the accumulated photoelectrons are flushed, or *injected,* into the underlying substrate, producing a current flow in the external circuitry. Again, the size of the current pulse reflects the amount of accumulated photoelectronic charge. This process, however, leaves the well empty of electrons. Hence, it is called the destructive readout mode. It is used to prepare the chip for integrating another image.

The circuitry built into the chip controls the voltages on the row and column electrodes as required to integrate an image and read it out destructively or nondestructively. This allows the CID to address individual pixels in any order, so that subimages of any size can be read out at any speed. The nondestructive readout capability allows one to watch the image as it accumulates on the chip, rereading it continuously (for hours) without erasing it. This is useful when the proper length of the integration period is not known. One can also average together several nondestructive readouts of the same image to reduce the effects of the random noise generated by the readout circuitry.

CID Performance. CIDs are less susceptible to blooming and radiation damage than CCDs and are thus useful under severe lighting and environmental conditions. Blooming is avoided because there is no built-in pathway connecting adjacent wells (as there is in the CCD) and excess photoelectrons are captured by the underlying substrate rather than spreading to neighboring pixels. Also, with nondestructive readout, the control program can monitor the filling of the wells and flush individual pixels that become full before the integration period is over.

Since CIDs do not shift their charge across the array, there is no concern about charge-transfer efficiency. Unlike the situation with the CCD, a defect in the crystal lattice affects only the pixel in the immediate area. Also, essentially the entire surface area is light sensitive, leaving virtually no gaps between pixels.

CIDs are considerably less light sensitive than corresponding CCDs. They are used in specialized applications in which their random access, nondestructive readout and anti-blooming characteristics are particularly valuable.

(*Note:* The foregoing explanations of CCDs and CIDs assume that the silicon is prepared as an N-type semiconductor, having electrons as the majority charge carriers. In actual practice, CIDs are commonly made of P-type silicon, in which the charge carriers are [positive] holes, and the row and column electrodes are held at negative, rather than positive, voltages during integration.)

2.7 FILM SCANNING

Photography [18] often plays an important role in digital image processing, both before digitizing and after display. In this section, we discuss the photographic process and some considerations that apply to film scanners.

2.7.1 Transmittance and Density

When an object passes some, but not all, of the light that is incident upon it, it is neither transparent nor opaque. There are two ways this partial light-transmitting property is commonly measured: in terms of transmittance and in terms of optical density (OD). The transmittance of the left-hand object in Figure 2–14 is given by

$$T_1 = \frac{I_2}{I_1} \qquad 0 \le T_1 \le 1 \tag{1}$$

where I_1 is the incident and I_2 the transmitted photon flux density. Transmittance is merely the factor by which an object attenuates light intensity, and it is confined to the range from zero to one. The optical density of the left-hand object is

$$D_1 = \log\frac{I_1}{I_2} = \log\frac{1}{T_1} = -\log T_1 \qquad 0 \le D_1 \le \infty \tag{2}$$

and is not confined to a convenient range, since it approaches infinity for opaque objects.

The two objects in Figure 2–14 are serially arranged in the light path and thus superimposed. The transmittance of the combination is

$$T_3 = \frac{I_3}{I_1} = \frac{I_3 I_2}{I_2 I_1} = T_1 T_2 \tag{3}$$

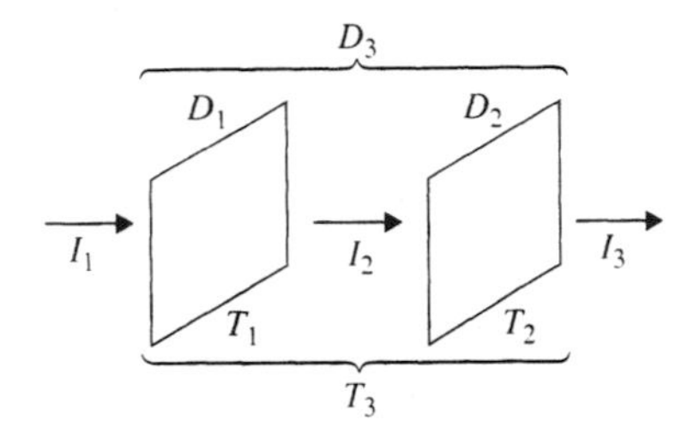

Figure 2–14 Density, transmittance, and superimposition

whereas the optical density of the combination is

$$D_3 = \log\frac{I_1}{I_3} = \log\frac{1}{T_1T_2} = \log\frac{1}{T_1} + \log\frac{1}{T_2} = D_1 + D_2 \tag{4}$$

Thus, when light-absorbing objects are superimposed, their optical densities add and their transmittances multiply. In Chapter 7, we use these properties to remove undesirable superimposed information by computer processing.

2.7.2 The Photographic Process

Photographic Film. The construction of photographic film is illustrated in Figure 2–15. The film base is either glass or a flexible, transparent acetate sheet that gives the film its mechanical stability. The base is coated with a 5- to 25-micron-thick emulsion made up of silver salt grains embedded in gelatin. The grains are halides of silver—silver chloride, silver bromide, or silver iodide crystals.

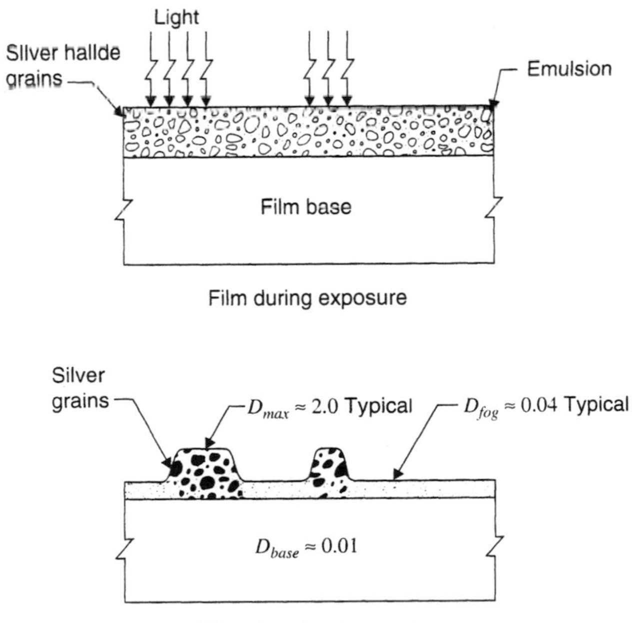

Figure 2–15 The photographic process

During the manufacturing of the film, the silver halide grains are activated to make them photosensitive. During exposure, different parts of the emulsion receive light at varying intensities. When a silver halide grain absorbs a photon, one or more molecules are reduced to silver, and the grain becomes *exposed.*

Film Development. The development process reduces the silver halide grains to silver. The reduction reaction, however, proceeds much more rapidly on exposed than on unexposed grains. After a suitable period of time, most of the exposed grains and only a few of the unexposed grains have been reduced. As a final step, the unreduced grains are washed off the base. Thus, the developed film has a granular silver coating of varying thickness. In areas that have been heavily exposed, the entire emulsion thickness is maintained, giving a maximum density. In unexposed areas, the silver halide grains are almost completely removed, leaving only a *fog level* of approximately 0.04 optical density.

Emulsion Response to Light. Figure 2–16 shows a convenient means for characterizing the light response of the emulsion. The response is called the D–*log* E *curve* or the *H and D curve,* after its original proponents, Hurter and Driffield. It shows the density of the developed film as a function of the logarithm of exposure. For reasonable exposure times—that is, from milliseconds to seconds—the exposure may be taken as the product of incident radiant energy flux density times duration. This equivalence between intensity and exposure time is called the *reciprocity law.* The breakdown of the law at extremely long or short exposure durations is called *reciprocity failure.*

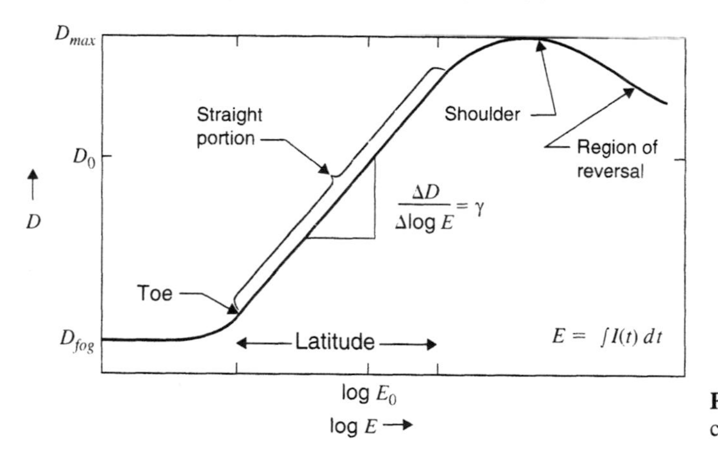

Figure 2–16 The emulsion characteristic curve

The gross fog level (emulsion fog level plus base density) sets the minimum density for unexposed film. The maximum density is limited by the emulsion thickness and grain size. Over a relatively wide range of exposure, the relationship between density and the logarithm of exposure is approximately linear. This is the normal working range of a photographic emulsion. The length of the abscissa in the linear portion is the latitude of the emulsion. The slope of the curve in the straight portion is called *gamma* (γ) and represents the contrast of the emulsion. Beyond the shoulder of the curve is a region of reversal, where continued exposure brings about a decrease in density.

Emulsion Characteristics. The emulsion thickness and grain size determine several important characteristics of the film. For example, a high maximum density is possible only with a thick emulsion. High resolution, however, requires small grains in a thin emulsion to avoid light scatter within the emulsion. Highly sensitive films that must work at low light levels require a thin emulsion containing relatively few grains. Thus, any film is a compromise among the opposing constraints of resolution, sensitivity, and maximum density. So many different emulsions are available, however, that a suitable compromise usually can be found. In general, the lower the speed rating (sensitivity) of an emulsion, the higher its resolution and gamma will be, while its granularity and latitude will be lower. Granularity is due to the random grain distribution within the emulsion. It results in the subjective phenomenon of graininess and becomes more pronounced as density increases.

Maximum resolution of a low-contrast image is obtained when the image is exposed and developed to lie between about 0.8 and 1.2 optical density on the film. Below that range, the toe of the H and D curve reduces the contrast, while granularity becomes more of a problem at higher densities.

The H and D curve for a particular emulsion varies with the parameters of the development process. For example, overdevelopment tends to shift the curve to the left and increase gamma. Obtaining predictable, reproducible results requires careful control of the exposure and development parameters.

Film Resolution. While the H and D curve illustrates an emulsion's response to light, it says nothing about the resolution of the film. The modulation transfer function (MTF) (Figure 2–17) is a common way to specify the resolution characteristics of an emulsion. Suppose we expose an emulsion with a spatially periodic pattern of light intensity given by

$$\log E = \log E_0 + \sin(2\pi f x) \tag{5}$$

where $\log E_0$ falls in the central part of the straight portion of the H and D curve. From the H and D curve, one would expect the density to be

$$D(x) = D_0 + \gamma \sin(2\pi f x) \tag{6}$$

When the spatial frequency f is high, however, grain size and light scatter within the emulsion reduce the contrast of the sinusoidal density variations. Thus, the observed density is

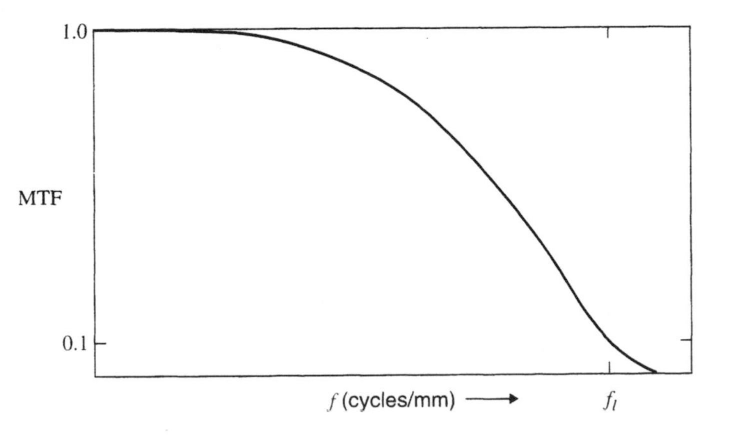

Figure 2–17 The modulation transfer function

$$D(x) = D_0 + \gamma M(f)\sin(2\pi f x) \qquad 0 \le M(f) \le 1 \tag{7}$$

where $M(f)$ represents the loss of image contrast as a function of spatial frequency. To further simplify the specification of film resolution, manufacturers often refer to the *frequency of limiting resolution*, f_L. This is the spatial frequency at which the modulation transfer function falls to 0.1, and it corresponds roughly to the limit of visibility.

2.7.3 Photocopying

Often, one must work with film images that are not originals, but photographic copies of other film images. Figure 2–18 illustrates the setup for photocopying and photomicrography. Let the density of the original image be $D_s(x, y)$, and assume that the copy film has the characteristic shown in Figure 2–19. Suppose the specimen is illuminated from behind with intensity l_0 for duration T. This means that the amount of exposure coming from (x, y) and reaching point (x', y') on the film is

$$E(x', y') = l_0 T 10^{-D_s(x, y)} \tag{8}$$

Letting $E_0 = l_0 T$ and taking the log of both sides yields

$$\log[E(x', y')] = \log E_0 - D_s(x, y) \tag{9}$$

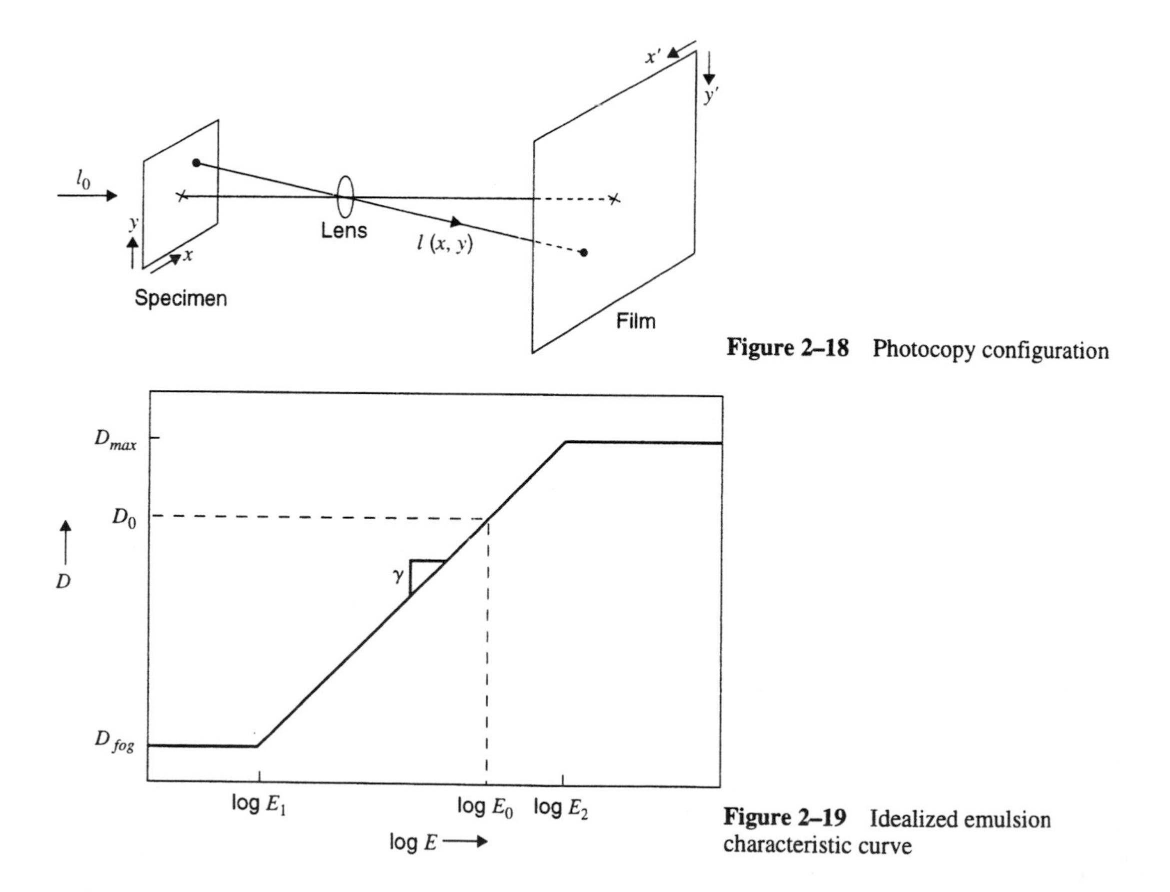

Figure 2–18 Photocopy configuration

Figure 2–19 Idealized emulsion characteristic curve

In the linear region of Figure 2–19, the density is given by

$$D(\log E) = D_{\text{fog}} + \gamma(\log E - \log E_1) \tag{10}$$

Combining this with Eq. (9) produces

$$D(x', y') = D_{\text{fog}} + \gamma[\log E_0 - D_s(x, y) - \log E_1] = D_0 - \gamma D_s(x, y) \tag{11}$$

where

$$D_0 = D_{\text{fog}} + \gamma(\log E_0 - \log E_1) = D(\log E_0) \tag{12}$$

Eq. (11) illustrates that the copy is a negative image with density falling below D_0 and with contrast modified by the factor γ.

2.8 SUMMARY OF IMPORTANT POINTS

1. The necessary elements of an image digitizer include (1) the sampling aperture, (2) a means of scanning, (3) a light sensor, (4) a quantizer, and (5) an output medium.
2. The important characteristics of an image digitizer include (1) the pixel size, (2) the spacing between pixels, (3) the number of pixels per column and per line, (4) the number of gray levels, (5) the photometric parameter the digitizer measures, (6) the linearity of that measurement, and (7) the noise level.
3. Light sources include incandescent bulbs, arc lamps, LEDs, lasers, and phosphors.
4. Light sensors include photomultiplier tubes, photodiodes, phototransistors, and solid-state sensors.
5. Scanning can be done with mechanical means, electron beams, and integrated circuitry.
6. Electronic imaging tubes produce a video signal that can be sampled and digitized.
7. Solid-state image sensors include photodiode arrays, charge-coupled devices (CCDs), and charge injection devices (CIDs).
8. Commonly used CCD architectures are full frame, interline transfer, and frame transfer.
9. The major CCD noise sources are readout, which produces noise that increases with readout rate; dark current, which doubles with each 6°C temperature increase, and photon noise, which increases as the square root of electron count.
10. Cooled CCDs can integrate for long periods of time to record low-light-level images.
11. CIDs are less light sensitive than CCDs, but are less subject to blooming and radiation damage, and they can be read out nondestructively and with random access.
12. When partially transparent objects are superimposed, their transmittances multiply, but their optical densities add.
13. Developing a photographic emulsion produces optical density approximately proportional to the logarithm of exposure intensity multiplied by exposure time.
14. The contrast of a photographic emulsion can be specified by gamma, the slope of the curve of its density vs. the logarithm of its exposure (its H and D curve).

PROBLEMS

1. A certain 480-by-640 pixel frame-transfer CCD image-sensing chip is used at video rates (16.7 msec exposure time, 14 MHz readout frequency). It has 6.3- × 9.3-micron pixels and a pixel well capacity of 20,000 electrons. How does its charge storage density compare with the 800 electrons per square micron of well area mentioned in the text? The chip has readout noise of 80 electrons per pixel at a 10-MHz readout rate and 180 electrons per pixel at 20 MHz. Assuming a linear relationship, what is its readout noise at 14 MHz? What is its dynamic range? The chip has a quantum efficiency of 0.35 at visible wavelengths and dark current of 6,000 electrons per second per pixel at 25°C. What would its dark current be if it were cooled to 0°C? Assuming that the incident light flux is 2×10^6 photons per second per pixel, to what percent of capacity will the wells fill during the 16.7-msec exposure time? What exposure time would saturate the wells (fill them completely)? At 25°C, what is the chip's signal-to-noise ratio (SNR)? What is its photon noise level? What is its total noise level?
2. A certain 384-by 576-pixel full-frame CCD image-sensing chip has 23- × 23-micron pixels and a pixel well capacity of 175,000 electrons. How does its charge storage density compare with the 800 electrons per square micron of well area mentioned in the text? The chip has readout noise of 8 electrons per pixel at a 40-Hz readout rate and 24 electrons per pixel at 200 kHz. Assuming a linear relationship, at what readout frequency will it have a dynamic range of 10,000? 20,000? The chip has a quantum efficiency of 0.40 at visible wavelengths and dark current of 6.5 electrons per second per pixel at –45°C. What is its dark current at 0°C? Assuming that the incident light flux is 10,000 photons per second per pixel, to what percent of capacity will the wells fill with a 20-sec exposure time? What exposure time would saturate the wells (fill them completely)? At a 50-kHz readout rate and 0°C, what exposure time would make the chip's SNR 300? What would be the filling percentage of the wells at this exposure time?
3. A certain 1317- by 1,035-pixel full-frame CCD image-sensing chip has 6.8- × 6.8-micron pixels and a pixel well capacity of 45,000 electrons. How does its charge storage density compare with the 800 electrons per square micron of well area mentioned in the text? The chip has readout noise of 5 electrons per pixel at a 50-kHz readout rate and 13 electrons per pixel at 500 kHz. Assuming a linear relationship, at what readout frequency will it have a dynamic range of 4,000? The chip has a quantum efficiency of 0.41 at visible wavelengths and dark current of 0.02 electron per second per pixel at –40°C. What is its dark current at 25°C? Assuming that the incident light flux is 2,000 photons per second per pixel, what exposure time would saturate the wells (fill them completely)? At a 400-kHz readout rate and 0°C, what exposure time would make the chip's SNR 200? What would be the filling percentage of the wells at this exposure time? What exposure time would make the SNR 100? What would be the filling percentage of the wells at this exposure time?
4. A certain 2,048- by 2,048-pixel full-frame CCD image-sensing chip has 9- × 9-micron pixels and a pixel well density of 1,049 electrons per square micron. What is its well capacity? The chip has readout noise of 13 electrons per pixel at a 200-kHz readout rate and at 500 kHz. What is its dynamic range? The chip has a quantum efficiency of 0.45 at visible wavelengths and dark current of 0.25 electron per second per pixel at –20°C. What is its dark current at 25°C? Assuming that the incident light flux is 20,000 photons per second per pixel, what exposure time would saturate the wells (fill them completely)? At a 400-kHz readout rate and –30°C, what exposure time would make the chip's SNR 150? What would be the filling percentage of the wells at this exposure time? What is the total noise level?
5. A certain 3,072- by 2,028-pixel full-frame CCD image-sensing chip has 9- × 9-micron pixels, and a pixel well capacity of 85,000 electrons per pixel. It has readout noise of 9 electrons per pixel

at a 500-kHz readout rate and 20 electrons per pixel at 2 mHz. What frequency gives it a dynamic range of 5,000? The chip has a quantum efficiency of 0.45 at visible wavelengths, and dark current of 0.05 electron per second per pixel at –40°C. What is its dark current at 25°C? Assuming that the incident light flux is 8,000 photons per second per pixel, what exposure time would saturate the wells (fill them completely)? At a 1-MHz readout rate and –30°C, what exposure time would make the chip's SNR 256? What would be the filling percentage of the wells at this exposure time?

6. Under what general conditions of illumination, temperature, and exposure time would you expect to see predominantly readout noise in an image digitized from a CCD sensor? Under what conditions of illumination, temperature, and exposure time would you expect to see predominantly dark current noise? Under what conditions of illumination, temperature and exposure time would you expect to see predominantly photon noise?
7. A vidicon camera has a target 25 mm in diameter and a sensing spot 35 microns in diameter. What is the maximum number of rows and columns it can digitize in a square image if its pixel spacing is set equal to the spot diameter? If the digitized image is 480 by 640 pixels, what is the maximum pixel spacing on the target?

PROJECTS

1. Referring to problem 6 above, digitize flat field images from a CCD video camera under light and dark conditions, and analyze them to determine the qualitative and quantitative nature of the readout and photon noise components. Use the standard deviation of the gray level or the width of the gray level histogram (see Chapter 5) to quantify the noise level. Account for any unflatness of the test image.
2. Referring to problem 6 above, digitize flat field images from a cooled integrating CCD camera under light and dark conditions, at short and long exposures at high and low temperatures. Analyze the images to determine the qualitative and quantitative nature of the readout, dark current, and photon noise components. Use the standard deviation of the gray level or the width of the gray level histogram (see Chapter 5) to quantify the noise level. Account for any unflatness of the test image.
3. Digitize an image from film, and characterize the resolution, noise level, and linearity of the process. Use areas of constant gray level to estimate the noise level and sharp edges to estimate the resolution. If the scene contains areas of different known brightnesses, plot the photometric response of the process.

REFERENCES

1. I. P. Csorba, ed. *Selected Papers on Image Tubes,* SPIE Press, Bellingham, WA, 1990.
2. D. G. Fink, ed., *Television Engineering Handbook,* McGraw-Hill Book Company, New York, 1957.
3. D. G. Fink and D. Christiansen, *Electronics Engineers Handbook,* McGraw-Hill, New York, 1989.
4. K. B. Benson, *Television Engineering Handbook: Featuring HDTV Systems* (rev. ed.), McGraw-Hill, New York, 1992.
5. G. Hutson, P. Shepherd, and J. Brice, *Colour Television Theory: System Principles, Engineering Practice & Applied Technology,* McGraw-Hill, New York, 1990.

6. W. Wharton, S. Metcalfe, and G. C. Platts, *Broadcast Transmission Engineering Practice,* Focal Press, London, 1992.
7. A. F. Inglis, *Video Engineering: NTSC, EDTV, & HDTV Systems,* McGraw-Hill, New York, 1992.
8. P. Neidhardt, *Technical Dictionary of TV Engineering: TV Electronics in Four Languages,* Franklin Book Company, New York, 1964.
9. J. R. Janesic, S. T. Elliot, A. S. Collins, H. H. Marsh, M. M. Blouke, and J. Freeman, "Scientific Charge-Coupled Devices," *Optical Engineering,* **26**(8):692–714, 1987.
10. M. M. Blouke, B. Corrie, D. L. Heidtmann, F. H. Yang, M. Winzenread, M. L. Lust, H. H. Marsh, and J. R. Janesic, "Large Format, High Resolution Image Sensors," *Optical Engineering,* **26**(9):837–43, 1987.
11. M. Razeghi, ed., *Optoelectronic Materials & Device Concepts,* SPIE Press, Bellingham, WA, 1991.
12. Y. Hiraoka, J. W. Sedat, and D. A. Agard, "The Use of a Charge-Coupled Device for Quantitative Optical Microscopy of Biological Structures," *Science,* **238:**36–41, 1987.
13. B. Williams and D. Carta, "CID Cameras: More than an Alternative to CCDs," *Advanced Imaging,* 2–13, Jan., 1989.
14. H. Kaplan, "New Jobs for Charge-Transfer Devices," *Photonics Spectra, 86–87,* Nov. 1990.
15. J. Carbone, "Sub-Pixel Interpolation with Charge Injection Devices," *Proc. SPIE,* **1071:**80–89, 1989.
16. G. R. Sims and M. B. Denton, "Multielement Emission Spectroscopy Using a Charge-Injection Device Detector," in Y. Talmi, ed., *Multichannel Image Detectors,* **2:**117–132, American Chemical Society, Washington, D.C., 1983.
17. H. A. Lewis and M. B. Denton, "Determination of the Ultraviolet and Visible Spectral Response of a Charge-Injection Device Array Detector," *Journal of Automatic Chemistry,* **3:**9–12, 1981.
18. C. E. K. Mees and T. N. James, *The Theory of the Photographic Process,* MacMillan, New York, 1966.

CHAPTER 3

Digital Image Display

3.1 INTRODUCTION

Image display is the final link in the digital image-processing chain. After all processing is completed, the display transforms the digital image into a form suitable for human consumption. While it is required for digital image processing, image display is not, strictly speaking, required for digital image analysis—something that produces its output in the form of numerical data or decisions. Display is useful in image analysis, however, for monitoring and interactive control of the process.

In this chapter, we consider the construction and characteristics of digital image display systems and, in particular, the factors that determine the quality of displayed images [1–6]. There are several display-related pitfalls that should be avoided if one is to produce images that do not call attention to themselves as having been processed by computer. Consistent with the philosophy that computer processing, *per se*, should not degrade image quality, we wish to avoid allowing a clearly imaged, properly digitized, and accurately processed digital image to be degraded by a noisy or inaccurate display system.

3.1.1 Image Quality

The eye is capable of resolving only about 40 gray levels. This means that if the range between black and white were divided into more than 40 equal intervals, adjacent gray levels would appear identical to the human eye. There is, however, a built-in edge enhancement process on the retina that makes it possible for the eye to detect gray-level transitions much smaller than 1/40 of the total range.

For example, consider a gray-scale target consisting of an array of 256 squares ranging in gray level from black to white (Figure 3–1). The normal human observer can easily see the boundary between adjacent squares, even though the difference in gray levels is only 1 step in a range of 256 steps. However, if the boundary between adjacent squares is obscured by a narrow strip, then adjacent squares appear to have equal brightness. Thus, it is the edge, not the difference in gray levels, that is perceived.

There are two basic types of displays: permanent and volatile. Permanent displays produce a *hard-copy* image on paper, film, or other permanent recording medium by permanently altering the light-absorbing characteristics of the recording medium. Volatile displays produce a temporary image on a display screen.

The basic components of a CRT display system are similar to those discussed in Chapter 2. The scanning spot intensity is controlled by the gray-level values of the digital image being displayed. Some CRT devices can be used as both film scanners and film recorders.

Ordinarily, a display system produces an image in which the brightness of each display pixel is controlled directly by the gray level of the corresponding pixel in the digital image. However, the primary function of the display is to allow the human observer to understand and interpret the content of the image. In some cases, then, it is helpful to match the display process to the characteristics of the human eye. For example, the human eye has considerable acuity in discriminating fine detail (high-spatial-frequency information), although it is not particularly sensitive to low-frequency (slowly varying) information in the image. Some images may be more easily understood if they are displayed indirectly by using contour lines, shading, color, or some other graphical representation. Examples of such displays appear later in the book.

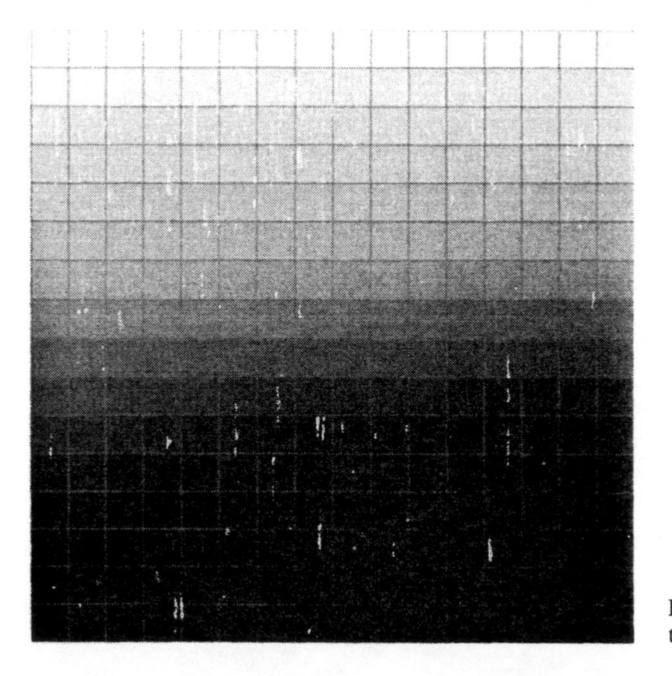

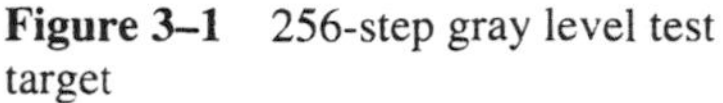

Figure 3–1 256-step gray level test target

3.2 DISPLAY CHARACTERISTICS

In this section, we discuss those characteristics which, taken together, determine the quality of a digital image display system and its suitability for particular applications. The primary characteristics of interest are the size, photometric and spatial resolution, low-frequency response, and noise characteristics of the display.

3.2.1 Displayed Image Size

The image size capability of a display system has two components. First is the physical size of the display itself, which should be large enough to permit convenient examination and interpretation of the displayed images. The second characteristic is the size of the largest digital image that the display system can handle. The display must be adequate for the number of lines and the number of pixels per line in the largest image to be displayed. The trend is toward processing larger images. Inadequate display size can reduce the effectiveness of an image-processing installation.

3.2.2 Photometric Resolution

For display systems, photometric resolution refers to the accuracy with which the system produces the correct brightness or density value at each pixel position. Of particular interest is the number of discrete gray levels that the system can produce. This is partially dependent on the number of bits used to control the brightness of each pixel.

Some displays are capable of handling only four-bit data, therefore producing only 16 distinct gray levels, while others handle eight-bit data producing 256 gray levels. However, it is one thing to design a display that can accept eight-bit data and quite another to produce a system that can reliably display 256 distinct levels of gray. The effective number of gray levels is never more than the number of gray levels in the digital data, but it may well be less.

If electronic noise generated within the display system occupies more than one gray level, then the effective number of gray levels is reduced. As a rule of thumb, the root-mean-square (RMS) noise level represents a practical lower limit for gray-scale resolution. For example, if the RMS noise level is 1 percent of the total display range from black to white, then the display can be assumed to have a photometric resolution of 100 shades of gray. If the display system accepts eight-bit data, it still has only 100 effective gray levels. If it is a six-bit display system, then it has 64 gray levels. The RMS noise level is used because, if the noise can be assumed to have a normal distribution, then it will stay within one standard deviation about 68 percent of the time.

3.2.3 Gray-Scale Linearity

Another important display characteristic is the linearity of the gray scale. By this, we mean the degree to which brightness or density is proportional to input gray level. Any display device has an input-gray-level to output-brightness transfer curve. For proper operation, this curve should be reasonably linear and constant from one usage to the next. With permanent displays involving a film recorder followed by development and enlargement, careful quality control is required for reproducible results.

Fortunately, the human eye is not a very accurate photometer. Slight nonlinearities in the transfer curve, as well as 10- to 20-percent intensity shading across the image, are hardly noticed. If the transfer curve has a definite shoulder or toe at one end or the other, however, information may be lost or degraded in the light or the dark areas.

3.2.4 Display Calibration

On volatile displays using television monitors, the transfer curve depends in part on the brightness and contrast control settings on the monitor. Hard-copy printers often have one or more adjustments on the front or rear panels as well. Sometimes these include a *gamma* setting that affects the shape of the nonlinear transfer curve. Thus, it is possible for the user to alter the transfer curve to suit his or her particular image and personal taste. In most cases, however, it is most satisfactory to allow the processing to be done by the software and not the display system, which should merely present the data to the operator without additional "enhancement."

A display calibration procedure can ensure that the displayed image properly renders the digital image. A gray-scale test target, containing bars or squares of all different gray levels, is displayed on the monitor or sent to the image recorder. Then the various adjustments are set so that the full range of brightness is visible, but with no gray levels lost at either end.

When an image-processing system is in proper calibration, a print from the hard-copy recorder looks just like the image displayed on the screen, and this, in turn, is an accurate rendering of the digital image data.

3.2.5 Low-Frequency Response

In this section, we consider the ability of a display system to reproduce large areas of constant gray level, or *flat fields*. This ability depends primarily on the shape of the display spot, the spacing between the spots, and the amplitude and position noise characteristics of the display system. Since our goal is to minimize the visible effects of digital processing, we prefer flat fields to be displayed with uniform intensity.

Pixel Polarity. A flat field can, of course, be displayed at any shade of gray between black and white. On a cathode-ray tube display, for example, a high-intensity pixel is displayed as a bright spot on an otherwise dark tube face. Zero-intensity pixels leave the tube face in its intrinsic dark state. In a CRT film recorder, a high-intensity pixel leaves a black spot on otherwise transparent film. Zero-intensity pixels leave the film transparent. Thus, any display system has a characteristic pixel polarity. No matter what the polarity, however, zero-intensity fields are displayed uniformly flat. Therefore, flat field performance becomes a problem only at intermediate- and high-intensity gray levels. These may be either black or white, depending on the display system polarity.

Pixel Interaction. Flat field performance depends primarily upon how well the pixels "fit" together. Certain-rotating drum film recorders image a rectangular aperture on the sensitized film, producing sharp-edged rectangular pixels that fit together accurately, creating excellent field flatness. However, CRT devices, which are common for digital image display, use a rectangular array of circular spots.

In the rest of this section, we examine the factors that affect field flatness with circular spots. We model these circular display spots with the Gaussian function, which provides a reasonable model for the study of display spot interaction. We address the problem of selecting display spot spacing in terms of the spot radius.

3.2.5.1 The Gaussian Display Spot

Assume that the display spot has a two-dimensional Gaussian intensity distribution of the form

$$p(x, y) = e^{-(x^2+y^2)} = e^{-r^2} \tag{1}$$

where r is the radial distance measured from the center of the spot. If we define R as the radius at which the intensity drops to one-half its maximum value, we can write the spot profile function as

$$p(r) = e^{-(r/R)^2 \ln(2)} \tag{2}$$

Rearranging the exponent yields

$$p(r) = e^{\ln(2^{-r^2/R^2})} \tag{3}$$

which is simply

$$p(r) = 2^{-(r/R)^2} \tag{4}$$

as illustrated in Figure 3–2. The intensity distribution of a single spot then becomes

$$p(x, y) = 2^{-[(x^2+y^2)/R^2]} \tag{5}$$

which is depicted in Figure 3–3. We denote the display intensity by $D(x, y)$, which reflects the contributions of all the spots.

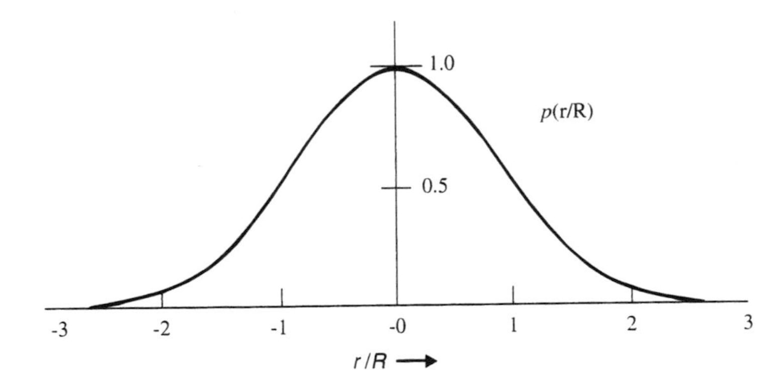

Figure 3–2 The Gaussian spot profile

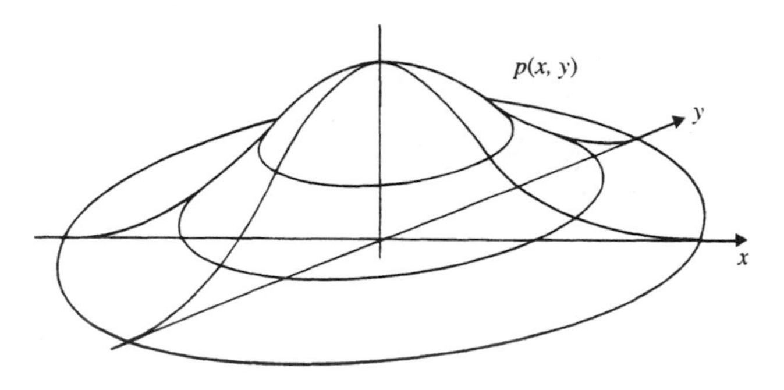

Figure 3–3 The intensity distribution of the Gaussian spot

3.2.5.2 Display Spot Interaction

Since the Gaussian spot does not fall below 1 percent of its peak amplitude until a distance of about 2 radii from the center, display spots overlap unless they are rather widely spaced. Figure 3–4 illustrates the density distribution along a line connecting two adjacent equal-amplitude Gaussian spots separated by a distance $d = 2R$. Notice that there is a 12.5-percent variation in intensity between the spot centers and the midway position. Thus, $d = 2R$ cannot yield microscopically flat fields.

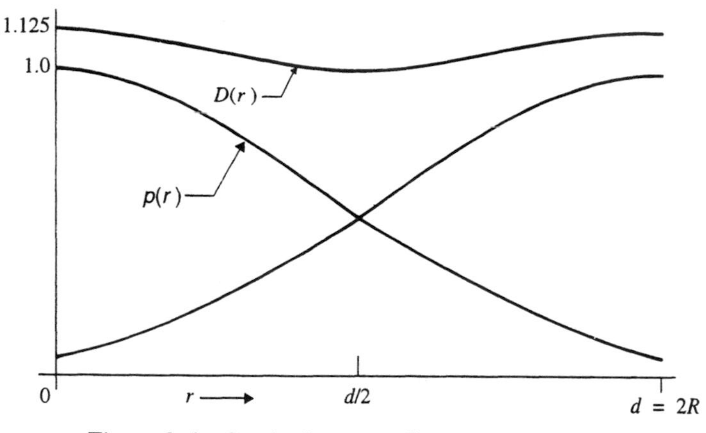

Figure 3–4 Overlap between adjacent Gaussian spots

In selecting display spot spacing for flat field performance, we are concerned with the three "worst case" positions shown in Figure 3–5. These positions are the pixel center, mid-pixel (midway between two pixels), and middiagonal (midway between four pixels). Ideally, the pixel spacing would be chosen to make $D(x, y)$ equal at all three positions. We can write the display density at pixel center in a flat field of unit-amplitude spots as

$$D(0, 0) \approx 1 + 4p(d) + 4p(\sqrt{2}d) \tag{6}$$

since only the eight nearest neighbor spots contribute 1 percent or more to the density for $d \geq \sqrt{2}R$. Similarly, we can write

$$D\left(\frac{1}{2}, 0\right) \approx 2p\left(\frac{d}{2}\right) + 4p\left(\sqrt{5}\frac{d}{2}\right) \tag{7}$$

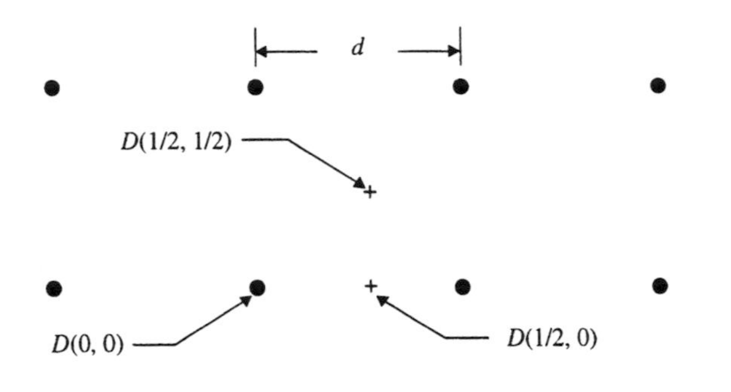

Figure 3–5 Critical positions for flat field display

for the midpixel position, accounting for six neighbors. Finally,

$$D\left(\frac{1}{2}, \frac{1}{2}\right) \approx 4p\left(\sqrt{2}\frac{d}{2}\right) + 8p\left(\sqrt{10}\frac{d}{2}\right) \tag{8}$$

accounts for 12 spots surrounding the middiagonal position.

Figure 3–6 shows a plot of Eq. (6), (7), and (8) in the range $2R \leq d \leq 3R$ for the Gaussian spot. Notice that no choice of d makes the density equal at all three points. The best field flatness falls in the range $1.55R \leq d \leq 1.65R$. At the intuitive choice of $d = 2R$, there is a 26 percent variation in intensity. At $d = 3R$, the pixels are clearly visible in high-intensity areas of the displayed image.

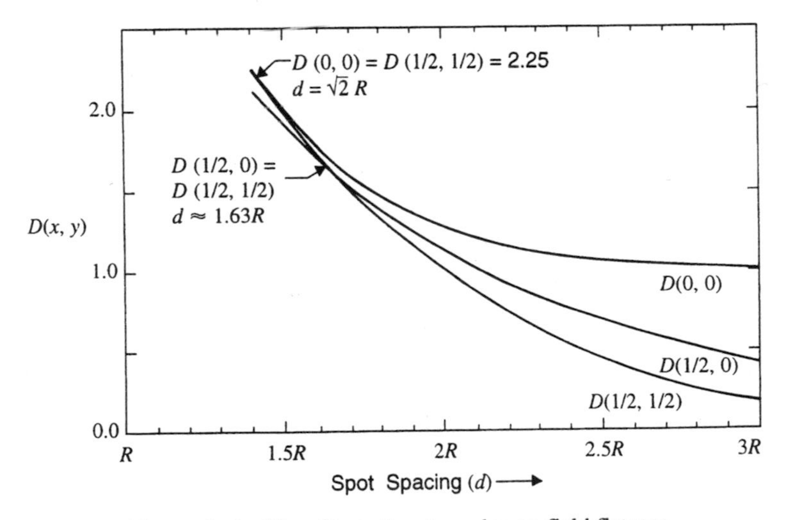

Figure 3–6 The effect of spot overlap on field flatness

3.2.6.1 The High-Frequency Line Pattern

A common high-frequency test pattern consists of alternating light and dark vertical (or horizontal) lines spaced one pixel apart. These are sometimes referred to as *line pairs,* where a pair consists of one dark and one adjacent light line. Every second column contains high-intensity pixels, while the columns in between contain zero-intensity pixels. How well a display system can reproduce a line pattern gives an indication about its performance on fine image detail.

Figure 3–7 shows the positions of interest in a high-frequency vertical line pattern. Bold dots represent pixels of unit amplitude, small dots pixels of zero amplitude. We can write the pixel center density on the lines as

$$D(0, 0) \approx 1 + 2p(d) + 2p(2d) \tag{9}$$

and between the lines as

$$D(1, 0) \approx 2p(d) + 4p(\sqrt{2}d) \tag{10}$$

Subtracting Eq. (10) from Eq. (9) yields

$$D(0, 0) - D(1, 0) \approx 1 + 2p(2d) - 4p(\sqrt{2}d) \tag{11}$$

which is the contrast of the displayed line pattern. The modulation factor

$$M = \frac{D(0, 0) - D(1, 0)}{D(0, 0)} \tag{12}$$

is shown in Figure 3–8 as a function of spot spacing. Notice that the modulation depth falls off rapidly as spot spacing decreases below $2R$.

3.2.6.2 The Checkerboard Pattern

Another "worst case" high-frequency display pattern is the single-pixel checkerboard. Here, pixel intensity alternates both horizontally and vertically. The critical positions for this pattern are shown in Figure 3–9. The maximum density is given by

$$D(0, 0) \approx 1 + 4p(\sqrt{2}d) \tag{13}$$

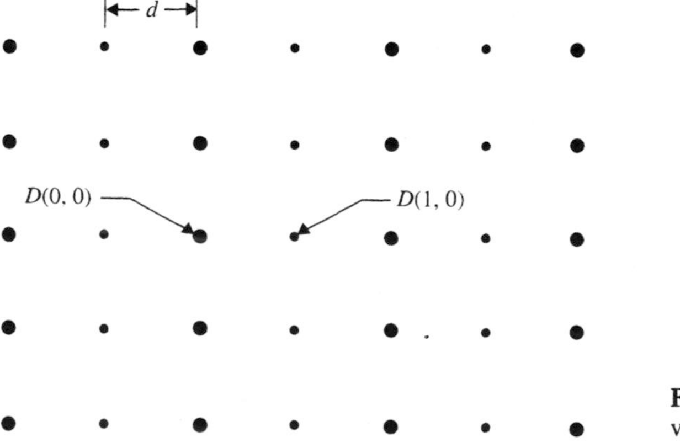

Figure 3–7 Critical positions for the vertical line pattern

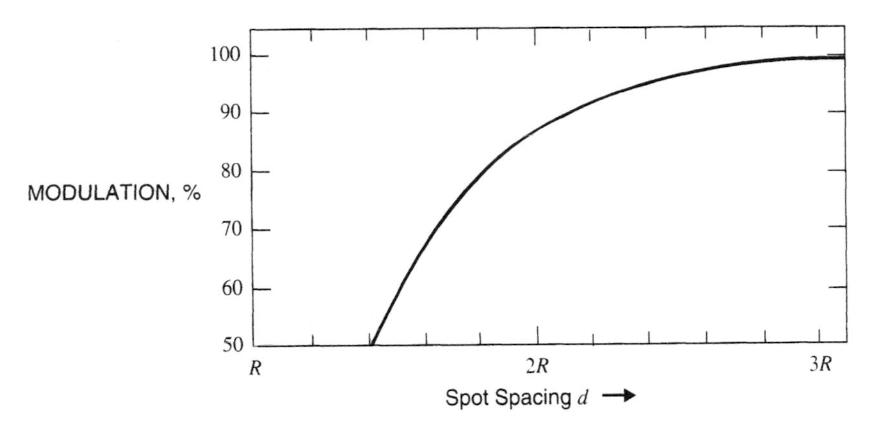

Figure 3–8 Spot spacing effect on the vertical line pattern

and the minimum density by

$$D(1,0) \approx 4p(d) + 8p(\sqrt{5}d) \tag{14}$$

The modulation factor, again given by Eq. (12), is plotted in Figure 3–10. The loss of modulation depth with decreasing spot spacing in the checkerboard pattern is even worse than in the line pattern.

The Spot Spacing Compromise. The goals of field flatness and high-frequency response place conflicting constraints upon the selection of spot spacing. The actual compromise between the two depends on the relative importance of high- and low-frequency information in each individual image. Spot spacing can be considered a display variable that must be tailored to the image-processing application.

3.2.7 Sampling for Display Purposes

We show in Chapter 12 that displaying a digital image is actually a process of interpolation, in that it reconstructs a continuous image from a set of discrete samples. We also see that the

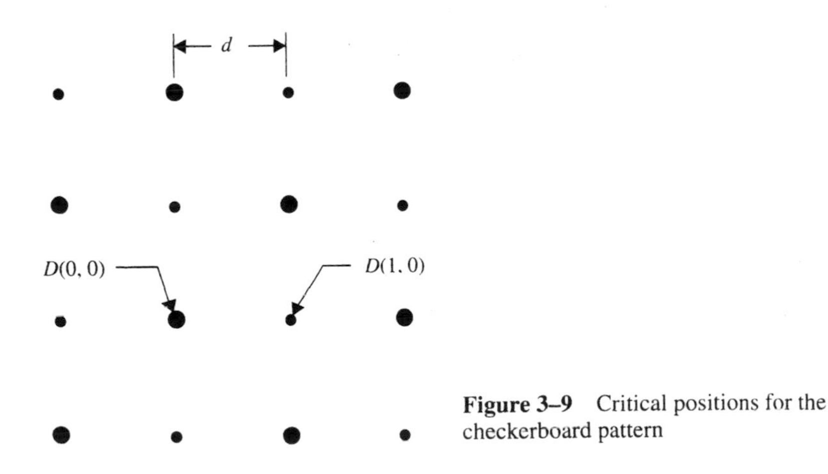

Figure 3–9 Critical positions for the checkerboard pattern

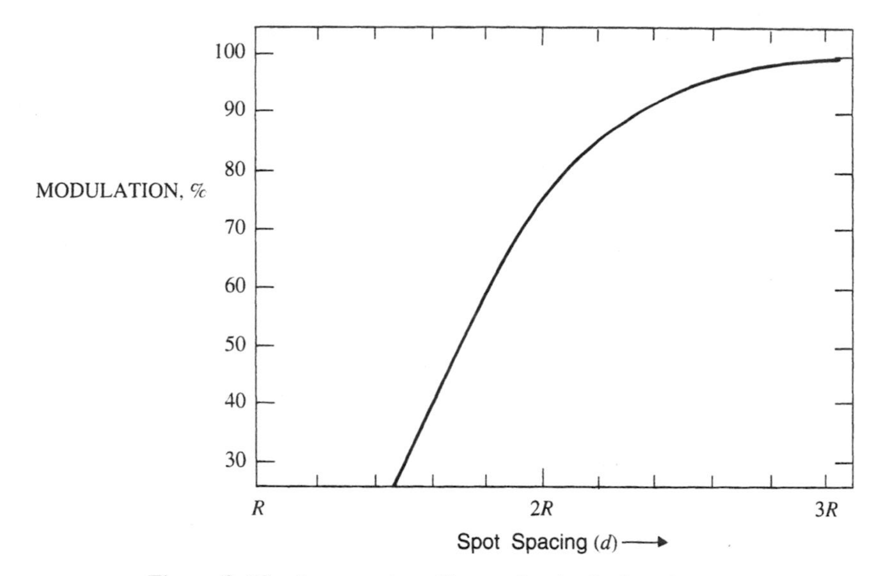

Figure 3–10 Spot spacing effect on the checkerboard pattern

proper interpolation function (i.e., the shape of the display spot) has the form $\text{sinc}(\alpha x) = \sin(\alpha x)/\alpha x$, which is, in fact, quite different from the Gaussian.

Figure 3–11(a) shows, in one dimension, the example of a cosine function that is sampled at a rate of 3.3 sample points per cycle of the cosine. That is, the sample spacing is 30 percent of the period of the cosine. In Chapter 12, we shall see that this sample spacing is small enough to preserve the cosine and that proper interpolation will reconstruct the cosine from its samples without error. When this sampled function is interpolated with the Gaussian, however, the distorted waveform in Figure 3–11(b) results. This illustrates that the display process itself can degrade an image—even one that has survived digitization without damage.

The difficulties encountered in the foregoing sections illustrate that image display using a Gaussian-shaped spot is a suboptimal process. While it is impractical to implement display devices with $\sin(\alpha x)/\alpha x$- shaped display spots, there are things that can be done to improve the situation.

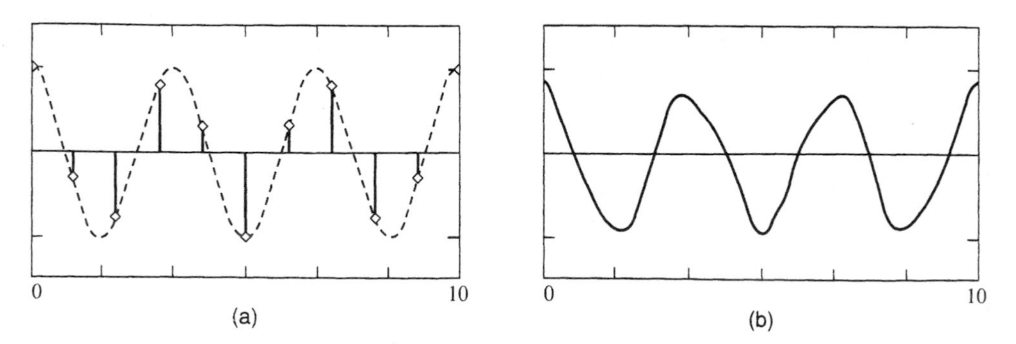

Figure 3–11 Sampling and interpolation: (a) the cosine sampled at 3.3 samples per cycle; (b) the sampled cosine interpolated with a Gaussian display spot

3.2.7.1 Oversampling

The inappropriate shape of the Gaussian display spot has less effect when there are more sample points per cycle of the cosine. Thus, one can improve the situation by arranging to have many pixels that are small in relation to the detail in the image. This is called *oversampling*. It requires more expensive cameras and produces more image data than other system design considerations would dictate.

3.2.7.2 Resampling

Another way to improve the appearance of an image displayed with a Gaussian spot is by *resampling*. This is the process of increasing the size of the image by digitally implemented interpolation prior to displaying it. For example, a 512-by-512 image might be interpolated up to 1,024 by 1,024 and then displayed on a monitor with a Gaussian display spot. If the interpolation is properly done, the displayed result will be more satisfactory.

Figure 3–12 shows what happens when two extra sample points are inserted between each pair in Figure 3–11(a). The value at each new sample point is determined by placing a $\sin(\alpha x)/\alpha x$ function at each of the original sample points and summing their values at each new sample position. Here, $\alpha = \pi/\tau$, where τ is the original sample spacing. This is digitally implemented interpolation using the correct interpolation function. Figure 3–12(b) shows that when the new (three times larger) sampled function is interpolated with a Gaussian function, the result is more satisfactory.

Resampling a digital image by a factor of two or three increases its size by a factor of four or nine, respectively, and this requires a display device that can accommodate the resulting larger image size. It needs to be done only as the last step prior to display, however, so the burden is not felt until that stage. Some high-quality display systems have resampling built into them.

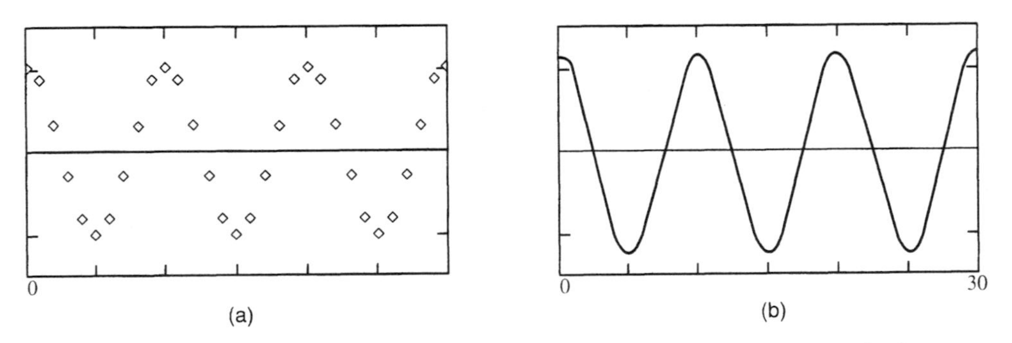

Figure 3–12 Resampling with sinc interpolation: (a) resampling; (b) reconstruction by Gaussian interpolation

3.2.8 Noise Considerations

Electronic noise in a display system produces variations in both the intensity and position of the display spot.

3.2.8.1 Amplitude Noise

Random noise in the intensity channel can produce a salt-and-pepper effect that is particularly visible in flat fields. The previously stated rule of thumb indicates that the effective quantizing level is roughly equal to the RMS noise amplitude. If the noise is periodic and of reasonably high intensity, it can produce a herringbone pattern superimposed on the displayed image.

If the noise is periodic and synchronized with the horizontal or vertical deflection signals, it can produce a pattern of bars. The general display quality is adequate if all noise, random and periodic, is kept at or below one gray level in amplitude. In many systems, it is much worse than that.

3.2.8.2 Spot Position Noise

A more serious effect results from noise in the display spot deflection circuits: nonuniformity in the display spot spacing. Display position noise, unless extremely severe, will not have a noticeable geometric effect upon the image. However, the effects of spot interaction combine with position noise to produce considerable variation in amplitude. Because spot interaction effects amplify position noise, careful display design requires precise pixel position control.

Recall from Figure 3–6 that variations in spot spacing cause considerable change in the midpixel, pixel center, and middiagonal intensities of flat fields. As an example, suppose that a 1,000- by-1,000-pixel display uses a spot spacing equal to twice the spot radius. Notice in the figure that, as spot spacing goes from $1.9R$ to $2.1R$, middiagonal intensity increases from about 0.87 to 1.16. This reflects a 29-percent change using 1.0 as an intensity reference. However, a spot spacing variation of $0.2R$ is only 0.01 percent of full-scale deflection. Thus 0.01-percent peak-to-peak noise in the deflection circuit produces a 29-percent variation in the middiagonal amplitude. The pixel center and midpixel amplitudes are also affected, but to a lesser degree. At spot spacings less than $2R$, the effect of position noise is even more pronounced.

When position noise is random, it produces a salt-and-pepper effect throughout the displayed image. Position noise is most visible in high-intensity flat fields, where spot interaction is most obvious. Frequently, nonrandom position noise is introduced by inaccurate digital-to-analog converters. The analog deflection signal is often produced by digitally switching resistances into and out of a resistive voltage divider network. If these resistance values are not precise, the conversion, and thus the deflection signal, will be inaccurate. Digital-to-analog converter noise produces fine vertical and/or horizontal lines at regular intervals throughout the image.

Numerous other techniques exist to improve the flat field and high-frequency response of display systems. For example, a hexagonal sampling grid may be used for some improvement of flat field response. In some cases, it is possible to control the pixel shape for better overlap characteristics. In many systems, however, the pixel shape is beyond the operator's control. In Part 2, we develop analytical techniques to describe the effects of pixel shape and spot spacing.

3.3 VOLATILE DISPLAYS

The most common type of volatile display uses a cathode-ray tube, scanned in a raster fashion, while the pixel spot intensity varies with position to produce the image [7–12]. An ordinary television monitor can act as a digital image display if it is provided with a suitable video signal. Since the display spot scans the image continuously, the display must be continually *refreshed* from a stored digital image. Volatile displays can be refreshed from a digital image stored in a dedicated random-access memory.

Laser displays can be built using moving mirrors or other means for beam deflection and a Kerr cell for intensity modulation of the beam. Gas discharge displays are made by sandwiching a fine mesh between two sheets of glass, leaving a rectangular array of cells containing an ionizable gas. By using coincident horizontal and vertical addressing techniques, the cells can be made to glow under the influence of a permanent sustaining electrical potential.

Several new types of solid-state displays are on the horizon. These promise to be compact and relatively inexpensive, using liquid crystal and light-emitting diode technology.

3.4 PERMANENT DISPLAYS

Devices that record a permanent image on paper or film are called image recorders or hard-copy devices. This section addresses the various technologies upon which these units are based.

Dithering. Some printing technologies are able to print each pixel with any desired shade of gray, from white to black. Others, however, can print only a solid dot or nothing, leaving the paper in its native (white) state.

The *halftone* process used in newspaper printing simulates shades of gray by varying the sizes of tiny black dots arranged in a regular pattern. In light areas of the picture, the dots are quite small relative to their spacing. The dot diameter grows where the image takes on darker shades, until the dots merge to form solid black.

The process of using a pattern of solid dots to simulate shades of gray is called *dithering* or halftoning. Different shapes and patterns of dots have been employed in this process, but the effect is the same. When viewed from a great enough distance that the dots themselves are not discernible, the pattern appears as a solid shade of gray.

Color Printing. The human visual system can independently sense three spectral bands of light: red, green, and blue. (See also Chapter 21.) These are called the *primary colors* because any perceived color can be duplicated by a proper mixture of red, green, and blue light. Color CRTs exploit this property by using thousands of tiny red, green, and blue light-emitting dots to re-create a picture on the face of the tube.

A hard-copy print, however, is viewed in reflected light. Thus, the primary elements for its image construction are three dyes, each of which absorbs red, green, or blue. Mixed in the proper proportion, three such dyes can theoretically reproduce any visible color.

A dye that absorbs blue light appears yellow when viewed in white light. Likewise, a green-absorbing dye appears magenta (purple), and a red-absorbing dye appears cyan (blue-green). Cyan, magenta, and yellow, called the *secondary colors,* are thus the three basic colors used in color printing and constitute what is called the *CMY system.*

Theoretically, an equal mixture of cyan, magenta, and yellow dyes will appear black, since red, green, and blue are each absorbed. A dilute mixture will appear gray, since it can absorb only a portion of the incident light. The black that results from mixing the three secondaries is called *composite black.*

In practice, however, available dyes are often unable to produce visually pleasing shades of gray. For this reason, color printing practice commonly uses a fourth ink, black, to ensure that the gray scale is properly rendered. Such a system is called the *CMYK system,* or the *four-color* printing process.

3.4.1 CRT and Laser Image Recorders

A common permanent display technology is the CRT film recorder. This is basically a film camera, mounted in front of a CRT display. With the shutter open, the entire image is displayed, pixel by pixel, to expose the film. Since only one pass is needed, no refreshing is required.

The pixel intensity can be modulated by controlling either the brightness of the spot or the duration for which each pixel is displayed. The pixel exposure on the film is nominally proportional to the product of the exposure intensity and exposure time. If spot intensity modulation is used, nonlinearities in the phosphor brightness versus beam current curve must be compensated for.

Drum-feed display devices use a slowly rotating drum to pull paper or film past a linear scanning mechanism operating perpendicular to the direction of motion of the paper or film. The linear scanning element can be a cathode-ray tube performing a single line scan. The scan line is imaged on the paper to effect exposure. The scanning mechanism might also be a laser beam exposing photosensitive paper or an electric current exposing electrolytic paper.

Electrolytic paper is sensitized so that a localized current through the paper causes the portion affected to darken. In general, the degree of darkening is proportional to the current, and this provides a means of modulating the pixel intensity. Better results are obtained by dithering with solid black pixels, however, since the electrolytic process is considerably more repeatable when carried to saturation.

Finally, an electrostatic charge image can be written on the paper and used to attract a powdered toner. Heat is then used to fuse the toner permanently into the paper. This technology is similar to that commonly used in photocopy machines.

The rotating-drum film recorder uses a rotating drum and lead screw arrangement similar to Figure 2–7 to expose a single sheet of film. It uses an objective lens to image the aperture upon the unexposed film. The aperture is illuminated by a light source, typically a light-emitting diode. The intensity of the light source is modulated by the gray level of the digital image. Frequently, the size and shape of the aperture, as well as the horizontal and vertical pixel spacing, are adjustable.

3.4.2 Ink-Jet Printers

Whether monochrome or color, liquid ink-jet printers operate by spraying a stream of ink through a set of fine nozzles mounted in a disposable cartridge [13]. When the ink (an opaque dye dissolved in water) hits the medium (paper or film), it dries, leaving a small spot. Sometimes heat is applied to speed the drying process and prevent the ink from smearing before it dries.

When ordinary paper is used, the ink spreads out through the paper before it dries, making the printed pixels somewhat larger and more diffuse than they would otherwise be. Special (more expensive) paper controls this phenomenon, producing sharper images. Dot densities commonly range from 300 to 600 dots per inch (dpi). Since the ink is opaque, dithering is required to reproduce shades of gray.

A liquid ink-jet color printer uses either three (CMY) or four (CMYK) colored inks. Gradations of color are produced by dithering. The process can result in visible contour lines in areas of an image that change color or brightness gradually.

Solid ink-jet color printers use three or four sticks of ink in solid form. Each ink is a mixture of wax, adhesives, and non-water-soluble dye. It is melted by heat and sprayed onto the recording medium the same as with a liquid ink-jet printer. The ink cools and solidifies quickly, however, minimizing absorption into the paper and leaving a sharper image. The colors are more brilliant, particularly on plain paper. Since the ink is not water soluble, the prints are more water resistant. Transparencies are less successful, however, since the beads of ink that are deposited on the film scatter light, giving a washed-out appearance to the projected image.

Ink-jet printers are reasonably inexpensive to buy and operate, particularly if plain paper is used. The cost of ink cartridges can be substantial, however, particularly if the images printed have a large portion of their area covered with color. Compared to the other technologies discussed here, the image quality of ink-jet printers is somewhat limited.

3.4.3 Thermal Wax Transfer Printers

The *thermal wax transfer* printing process uses a roll of plastic film that is coated with pigment-impregnated wax [14]. This *ribbon* has rectangular panels, each the size of a printed sheet, that are coated with ink. The panels alternate through the colors cyan, magenta, yellow, and black.

In operation, the colors are applied, one at a time, by placing the appropriate panel of the ribbon in contact with the print medium and drawing this past the print head. The print head has thousands of tiny heating elements that turn on as required to melt the wax and transfer it to the paper, leaving a dot. Dot densities go up to 300 dpi or more. As with the ink-jet printer, dithering is required to produce shades of color.

Thermal wax prints are more vivid than ink-jet prints, particularly on projected transparencies. They can use plain paper, but special (more expensive) thermal transfer paper accepts the wax transfer more reliably, yielding better results. Prints appear glossy, except in areas where no ink is applied. Dithering can produce visible contours where colors change gradually.

3.4.4 Dye Sublimation Printers

The construction of a dye sublimation printer is similar to that of a wax transfer printer, with a ribbon of alternating CMYK ink panels and a thermal print head. The difference is in the method of color transfer to the print medium [15].

Unlike inks, which are opaque and make a solid dot, dyes are transparent and merely tint the print medium. Under the influence of the heat from the print head, the dye on the ribbon sublimates; that is, it changes directly from the solid phase into a gas. It is then immediately absorbed by the polyester coating of the medium, producing a small colored dot.

Varying the temperature of the print head element controls the intensity of the resulting dot. Since the dyes are transparent, overlying dots mix, forming intermediate colors. Thus, there is no requirement for dithering to produce intermediate shades. This gives dye sublimation prints almost photographic quality. Diffusion of the gas gives the dots soft edges, making flat areas appear quite smooth. However, it also reduces the printer's ability to reproduce sharp-edged graphics. Dot densities go up to 300 dpi.

Of the three most commonly used printing technologies, dye sublimation printers are the most expensive to buy and operate, but they deliver the best image quality. Thermal wax printers are intermediate in price and image quality, except that they are particularly well suited for transparencies. Ink-jet printers are lowest in price and image quality.

3.4.5 Other Printing Technologies

Other display technologies can be combined to produce systems not enumerated here. We have, however, covered the most important digital image display technologies at the current state of the art. This should provide a basis upon which to evaluate the adequacy of individual systems for particular image display tasks.

Continuing development in the rapidly expanding field of solid-state electronics and color printing technology promises to improve display quality and reduce cost in the future. We can look forward to more compact and efficient, high-quality digital image display devices at reduced cost.

3.5 SUMMARY OF IMPORTANT POINTS

1. The quality of an image-processing solution is usually judged by the subjective quality of its displayed images.
2. A poorly designed, adjusted, or maintained display system can degrade, in the final step, an image that has been otherwise properly digitized and processed.
3. Smaller display spot spacing produces better flatness of uniform fields, while larger spot spacing better reproduces the contrast of fine detail.
4. Displaying a digital image is an interpolation process that reconstructs a continuous function from a set of discrete samples.
5. The proper form for the interpolation function is $\sin(\alpha x)/\alpha x$, where $\alpha = \pi/\tau$, and τ is the sample spacing.

6. Most display devices have a display spot that is approximately Gaussian in shape and is thus less than ideal for the interpolation process.
7. Image degradation due to spot shape can be reduced by oversampling the image when digitizing, or by digital resampling to increase the number of pixels, prior to display.
8. Digital resampling should be done with the $\sin(\alpha x)/\alpha x$ function.
9. Some high-quality display systems have resampling built in.

PROBLEMS

1. A particular display system has its Gaussian spot spacing adjusted to $1.6R$ for good flat field rendition. What will be the modulation factor of a horizontal pattern of one-pixel-wide black-and-white lines displayed on that system? Of a one-pixel checkerboard? Sketch the profile of displayed brightness across four pixels.
2. If you adjust the spot spacing of a display system with a Guassian spot so that a one-pixel-wide line pattern has no less than 85-percent modulation and a one-pixel checkerboard has no less than 75-percent modulation, what is the least variation in intensity you can get in a flat field? What pixel spacing (in terms of spot radius) should you use? Plot what the profile of a flat field will look like.
3. Suppose you have a rotating-drum of type film recorder that lays down a square display spot with steep sides. Plot the profile of the flat field that would result from using spot spacing values of (a) 0.85, (b) 1.0, and (c) 1.15 times the width of the spot. What instructions would you give the operator regarding adjustment of the spot spacing prior to printing your images?

PROJECTS

1. Resample a digital image, making it larger by a factor of two using (a) pixel replication (nearest neighbor interpolation), (b) bilinear interpolation (see Chapter 8), and (c) sinc interpolation (see also Chapter 12). Display all three images, and survey 10 people from other departments on what they like and dislike about each. Write a report comparing the computational complexity of and image quality produced by the three methods. In particular, discuss how the type of image (i.e., graphics vs. natural scene, etc.) and the display hardware used contribute to the result.
2. Generate a test image having flat field, line, and checkerboard patterns, and use it, in combination with a magnifying glass, to estimate the spot spacing (in units of spot radius) of at least two color and at least two black-and-white CRT display systems.
3. Generate a test image that shades linearly from white to black and use it to evaluate the dither patterns produced by at least two gray-scale or color printers. Using a magnifying glass, determine what the dithering scheme is, and explain why the best scheme is better and the worst scheme is worse.

REFERENCES

For additional reading, see Appendix 2.

1. J. I. Pankove, ed., *Display Devices* (Topics in Applied Physics Series, Vol. 40), Springer-Verlag, New York, 1980.

2. H. Poole, *Fundamentals of Display Systems,* MacMillan, London, 1966.
3. H. R. Luxenberg and R. L. Kuehn, eds., *Display Systems Engineering,* McGraw-Hill, New York, 1968.
4. A. Cox and R. Hartmann, eds., *Display System Optics,* SPIE Press, Bellingham, WA, 1987.
5. H. M. Assenheim, ed., *Display System Optics II,* SPIE Press, Bellingham, WA, 1989.
6. T. R. Hsing and A. G. Tescher, eds., *Selected Papers on Visual Communication: Technology & Applications,* SPIE Press, Bellingham, WA, 1990.
7. K. B. Benson, *Television Engineering Handbook: Featuring HDTV Systems* (rev. ed.), McGraw-Hill, New York, 1992.
8. D. Fink, ed., *Television Engineering Handbook,* McGraw-Hill, New York, 1957.
9. D. G. Fink and D. Christiansen, *Electronics Engineer's Handbook,* McGraw-Hill, New York, 1989.
10. G. Hutson, P. Shepherd, and J. Brice, *Colour Television Theory: System Principles, Engineering Practice & Applied Technology,* McGraw-Hill, New York, 1990.
11. A. F. Inglis, *Video Engineering: NTSC, EDTV, & HDTV Systems,* McGraw-Hill, New York, 1992.
12. W. Wharton, S. Metcalfe, and G. C. Platts, *Broadcast Transmission Engineering Practice,* Focal Press, London, 1992.
13. J. Heid, "Ink-Jet," *Macworld* **10**(5):94–99, May 1993.
14. J. Heid, "Thermal-Wax," *Macworld* **10**(5):100–105, May 1993.
15. J. Heid, "Dye-Sublimation," *Macworld* **10**(5):106–111, May 1993.

CHAPTER 4

Image-Processing Software

4.1 INTRODUCTION

Other sections of this book address the algorithms used in digital image processing and the hardware components upon which these techniques are implemented. In this chapter, we address the organization of the computer programs that implement the operations. In particular, we consider how the software is designed, developed, and presented to the user. A knowledge of this process is useful to image-processing software developers and users alike. For developers, it can save wasted effort and disappointing performance. For users, it can aid software evaluation and project execution.

The chapter provides an overview of these vital topics. We note the importance of those issues that are particularly relevant to digital imaging and point to the substantial body of literature on the subject.

In its most complete form, as with a commercially available software product, the software development process involves several stages. The conceptual design phase establishes the basic functional and operational characteristics, and then an algorithm research activity identifies and qualifies workable techniques. Next, the coding phase produces the first version of the complete software package. In the testing and revision phase, bugs are fixed and new ideas are incorporated into the program. User documentation describing how to operate the system and technical documentation explaining its physical and logical structure come next. Finally, the software is released and supported in the field. The latter activity includes customer training, technical support, and ongoing maintenance of the software.

An applications project is different from a development project in that one uses existing hardware and software to solve a particular problem. This begins with the selection of the hardware platform and software packages to be used. There is again a conceptual design phase, followed by the collection of a set of images for use in development and testing. The actual algorithm development is followed by performance testing, and then the technique goes into routine use. This might involve demonstrating and publishing the technique, conducting a research study of finite duration, or installing the system in some production-oriented activity.

4.2 IMAGE-PROCESSING SYSTEMS

The computer systems that are most commonly used for digital image processing fall into four categories: (1) the Apple Macintosh, with its built-in operating system software and user interface; (2) IBM PC-compatible computers, using a disk operating system (DOS, PS/2, etc.) and frequently Microsoft Windows™ or IBM OS/2™ as well; (3) graphics workstations, typically using the UNIX operating system and often the XWINDOWS environment; and (4) mainframe computer systems, with vast resources shared by multiple users located at remote workstations. Groups of nearby systems often share resources and data through a *local area network* (LAN). They frequently have access to a wide-area network as well.

4.2.1 Image Data File Format

As an activity, digital image processing generally creates large numbers of relatively large data files containing digital images. These must be archived, and often they need to be exchanged between different users and systems. This calls for some standard format for the storage and transfer of digital image files.

Many digital image file formats have been defined and used [1]. A few have gained wide enough usage to become more or less *de facto* standards. (See Table 4–1 for examples.) Most commercially available image-processing programs can read and write several of the popular image file formats. Other programs exist simply to read and display images stored in a variety of file formats and convert them from one format to another. Such programs automatically sense the format of the specified input file, either from its filename extension or from identifying information in the file itself. When saving a displayed image to a file, the user can specify the desired file format.

TABLE 4–1 IMAGE DATA FILE FORMATS

Name	Type	Usage
Tagged image file format	*.TIF	DOS, UNIX, and Macintosh images
Encapsulated PostScript	*.EPS	Publishing industry format
Graphical interchange format	*.GIF	CompuServe graphics format
Bit-mapped format	*.BMP	Microsoft Windows format
Presentation manager	*.BMP	IBM OS/2 bit-mapped format
Macintosh	*.PICT	Apple Macintosh images

Most image file formats store label annotation in addition to the image data. This can include data about the creation and format of the image, as well as annotation supplied by the user.

Monochrome display devices commonly employ an eight-bit digital-to-analog converter circuit to generate the video signal that controls the brightness of the displayed pixels on the screen. This provides the capability for 256 shades of gray. Color display devices use three eight-bit digital-to-analog converters to generate the three video signals that control the brightness of the red, green, and blue components of the displayed image. Thus, these have the inherent ability to display 2^{24}, or over 16 million, different colors. Given the imperfections common in display tubes and the limitations of the human eye, the actual number of discernible colors is considerably less.

Digital images occur not only in both monochrome and color format, but in different degrees of photometric resolution (numbers of colors or shades of gray) as well. For monochrome images, the number of shades of gray in the gray scale is most commonly either 2, 16, or 256, corresponding to 1, 4, and 8 bits per pixel, respectively. These particular resolutions are easily packed into eight-bit bytes in memory and disk files. Different resolutions are also used in certain applications.

The *palette* is a look-up table that relates each pixel value in the image to the corresponding displayed color. A four-bit color image, then, is displayed using 16 specific colors selected by the palette from the 16 million of which the display is ideally capable.

For color images, a fixed number of colors is represented by the different pixel values. A 4-bit color image can show only 16 distinct colors on the display. A palette defines the mapping from the 16 possible pixel values to the much larger number of display colors. The choice of the 16 particular colors is at the discretion of the programmer and is often passed on to the user. Eight-bit color images are displayed with 256 separate colors, and 24-bit color images have a range that includes 16 million colors. The palette that specifies the mapping for a particular image is commonly included in the image data file, and it controls the display device when the image is being viewed or printed.

4.3 THE USER INTERFACE

In the early days of computing, the user's primary interface with the system was the manufacturer's operating system software. Although flexible, these packages were necessarily cumbersome in routine use. More recently, the trend has been toward making the software interface quite user friendly. This affords the operator a convenient and comfortable environment in which to develop and use digital image-processing software. Such a user interface makes the required tools conveniently available, with a minimum of burden. Modern software packages for digital image processing put processing power and flexibility in the hands of the user quickly and easily. Their design caters to the user's intuition, and this makes them easy to learn and to use. Although usually well documented, they approach the ideal of being self-explanatory.

4.3.1 Command-Line Interpreter

The oldest and simplest type of user interface is the command-line interpreter (Figure 4–1). Using textual language exclusively, it requires the user to know the available options, either from memory or from documentation open on the desk. It greets the user with an on-screen prompting character indicating that it is ready to proceed, but it offers no assistance

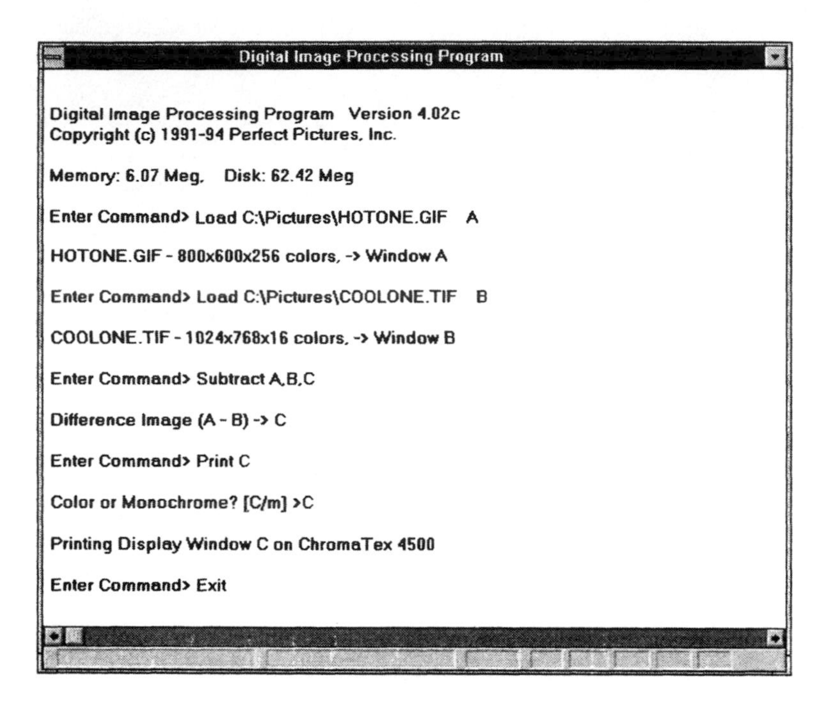

Figure 4–1 A command-line interpreter interface

regarding what is possible or advisable. This requires a heavy reliance on the written documentation, particularly in the learning phase. The situation is improved significantly by the use of *batch files* or *script files,* which specify a series of processing steps and can be invoked with a single command. A rich set of script files can make a command-line interpreter bearable to deal with.

4.3.2 Menu-Driven Interface

The second generation, the menu-driven interface, offers an on-screen list of choices, the selection of which can be accomplished by one or two keystrokes (Figure 4–2). This greatly reduces the operator's memorization burden and reliance on written documentation, as well as the effort required to launch a particular process into action.

In its more advanced incarnation, the menu-driven user interface operates in response to a graphical pointer device (mouse, trackball, etc.). This is the *point-and-click* interface, with which the user moves the on-screen pointer to an appropriately labeled area and presses a button on the device. The user can *pull down* one of several menus from a menu bar at the top of the display as needed, thus reducing clutter on the screen. The user then clicks on the option chosen, and the menu disappears.

Menus can exist in a hierarchical structure. Selecting an item in one menu displays a submenu of more specific choices. Each menu or menu item may also have an associated *help message* explaining the option and its use. This also pops up on the screen at the operator's request.

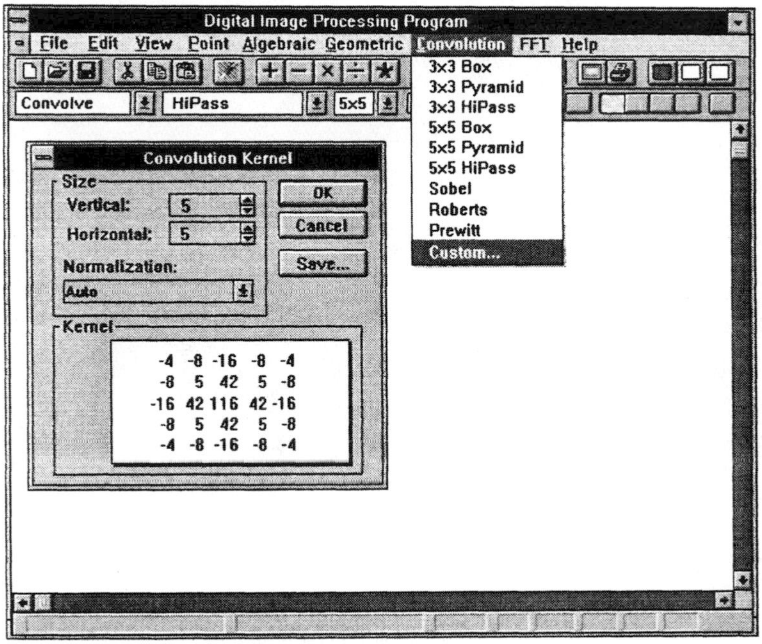

Figure 4–2 A menu-driven interface in a window environment

4.3.3 Graphical User Interface

The third generation is the *graphical user interface* (GUI, pronounced "gooey"). The operator controls the system in part via a *visual language* rather than a strictly textual language, as with the command-line interpreter. The GUI represents the available options not with text, as in a menu, but with graphical symbols displayed on the screen. These *icons* can represent not only processes, but also data (such as digital images) and hardware devices (disk drives, printers, etc.).

With a GUI implementation, one can initiate an action—for example, the printing of a stored image—by the *drag-and-drop* technique. Using the pointer device, the operator picks up the icon representing the image, moves it to another icon representing the printer, and releases it, and the printing process begins. This is not only faster than typing a command line, but more entertaining as well.

4.3.4 Data Flow Interface

Another type of GUI uses a graphical *network,* or *data-flow diagram,* symbology (Figure 4–3) [2]. Here, visual language is used almost exclusively. One again has available a menu of symbols (*glyphs*) representing devices, data, and processes. In this case, however, by dragging glyphs with the pointer, one composes an on-screen flowchart describing the intended series of processing steps. Each glyph has one or more input and/or output *pads* (connection points), as appropriate. The user specifies the processing flow by interconnecting the pads with lines drawn using the pointer device.

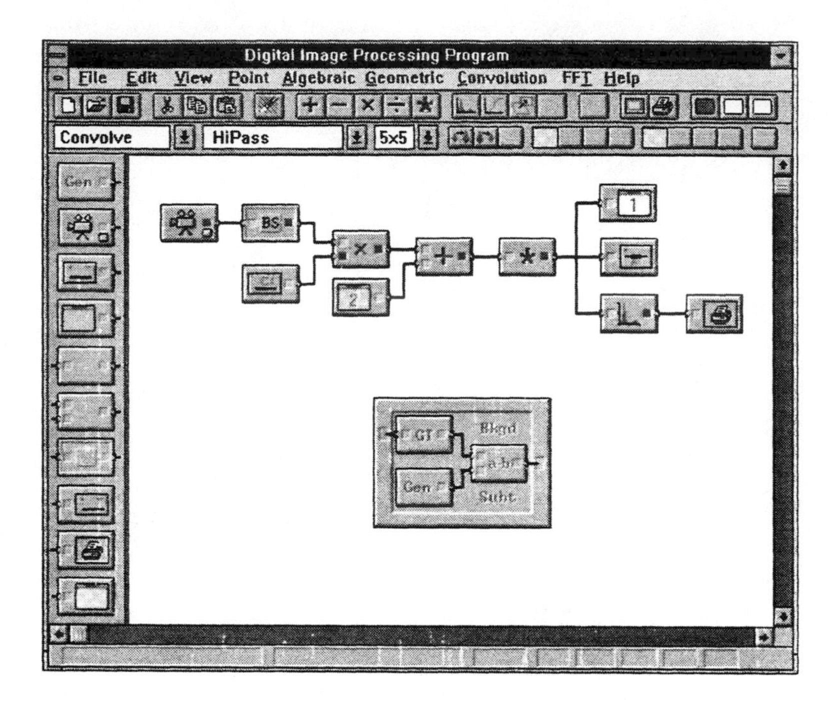

Figure 4–3 Example of a data-flow diagram GUI

Each glyph also has control pads which, when selected by the pointer, either initiate execution of the process or cause menus to pop up, thereby allowing the user to define the specifics of the process. Each glyph typically displays a state indicator that shows whether it (1) is incompletely defined, (2) is ready to be activated, or (3) has already completed its action.

4.3.5 Windows

In the early days of image processing, well-funded users discovered that having multiple display monitors available on the system greatly increased its usability. It is convenient to use separate displays for the user interface and for image display, for example. A modern (and less expensive) alternative is to use a single large-format display for several functions at once.

A *window-oriented environment* is a software package that uses the display screen efficiently to show several independent objects at the same time. The user can *open* (i.e., establish or define) several display windows on the screen and use each for a different display purpose, much as one might use multiple display screens. Each window can be relocated and resized at will on the screen, typically by dragging its borders with the pointer device. Where windows overlap, one (the *active window*) hides part or all of the window or windows "beneath" it, as with overlapping photographs on a desktop.

The trend in user interface design is toward more use of visual language, at the expense of textual language. The feeling is that a visual interface is easier for the beginner to learn and faster for the expert to use than one that requires typing text at a keyboard. Voice input is also a useful adjunct to the mouse and keyboard. Synthesized speech allows the system to respond in kind to the operator. Such a verbal interface is particularly useful when the operator's attention is divided between the display and other tasks. In some cases, digitized video sequences can supply valuable on-line help when needed.

4.4 THE SOFTWARE DEVELOPMENT PROCESS

In the pioneering days of computer programming in general, and digital image processing in particular, the software development process was, in today's parlance, *unstructured.* Computer programmers were not only rare, but, like other types of pioneers, individualistic as well.

Perhaps having only a vague concept of what the new software was required to do, the programmer simply started writing code, synthesizing a complex whole from simpler parts in the process. The overall design, then, developed in parallel with the implementation. Major design decisions were made all along the way. The modules commonly developed from the bottom up, with the most basic routines written first and higher level routines then built upon those. Early programmers creatively exploited the richness of the high-level languages of the day by writing code that was fast, compact, and essentially undecipherable.

By 1970, several problems with this approach had become apparent. First, the complexity of software projects advanced to the point that it was difficult for the programmer to keep all aspects of the program in mind at once. Research in psychology suggests that a human is uncomfortable trying to keep track of more than five to nine different pieces of information at one time [3]. This limitation repeatedly took its toll on the cost and budget of large software development projects.

Second, on projects involving groups of programmers, coordination of effort became a major problem. Modules written by different individuals failed to mesh together smoothly. Third, as personnel changes occurred, it became quite wasteful for new programmers to decipher existing source code in the absence of some commonly agreed-upon structure, particularly when accompanied by a lack of written documentation. In a university setting, for example, the departure of one student or staff programmer could render unusable all the software he or she had developed while working on research projects.

Modern commercial software development projects require considerable interaction among many individuals to ensure that the final product meets all the (often competing) requirements. Figure 4–4 is an example of a flowchart used in a commercial software development project.

The major steps in the software development cycle are listed in Table 4–2. These can be done sequentially, with overlap, or iteratively. By definition, *analysis* is the process of studying the problem and specifying the operational characteristics of the solution in terms of its externally observed behavior. The result is a functional specification of the software that is to be written. *Design* is taking this specification and adding the details required for implementation on a particular platform. *Programming,* of course, is writing, testing, debugging, and documenting computer programs.

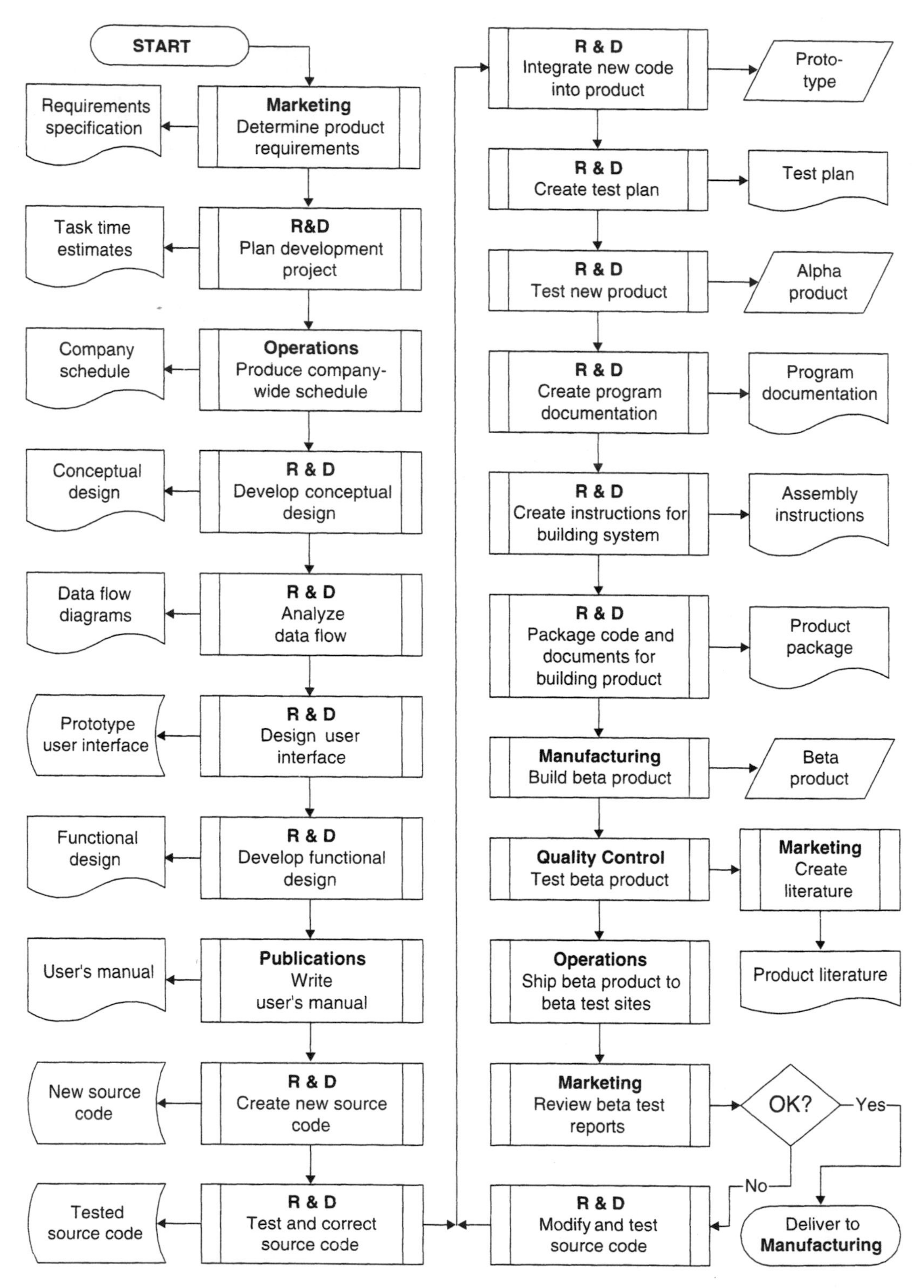

Figure 4–4 Example of a software development flowchart (courtesy Perceptive Scientific Instruments, Inc.)

TABLE 4–2 THE SOFTWARE DEVELOPMENT CYCLE

1. Requirements analysis
2. Preliminary design
3. Prototyping (if required)
4. Detailed design
5. Implementation (coding)
6. Testing
7. Maintenance

While this approach may appear overly complex, experience has shown that it is less expensive to do the job right the first time than to spend extra time modifying and debugging a program because it was done poorly the first time.

4.4.1 Program Operation

An application program can operate in one of three modes, depending on what role time plays in the computation. In *batch mode,* the program is placed in a queue and executed whenever the computer becomes free of prior tasks. While the instructions must be executed in sequence, it makes no difference whether nanoseconds or minutes pass between instruction executions. Some image-processing programs fall into this category.

An *event-driven* program sits in an *event loop,* waiting for something to happen. Normally, an action by the operator (pressing a key, clicking the mouse, etc.) constitutes an event. The program continually polls the input devices and detects and identifies each event when it occurs. Then it executes the appropriate routine and returns to the event loop. Interactive image-processing programs normally fall into this category.

A *real-time* program monitors an ongoing process, such as a manufacturing operation. Time itself plays an important role in the computations. Often, the program is monitoring the output of a process while adjusting the parameters that control the process. This can involve image processing.

4.4.2 Top-Down Design

In the early 1970s, the concepts of *structured programming* and *top-down design* arose in response to the problems created by unstructured programming. Top-down design calls for writing and debugging the highest level of software (typically the user interface) first and then progressively adding lower level routines, with hardware driver routines usually written last. This contrasts with *bottom-up* design, wherein one writes the most basic routines first and then builds progressively upon them, sometimes only to discover that a needed function has been omitted from the lower level routines.

Top-down design has two significant advantages. One concerns the interfaces between modules. The top level is designed directly from the functional specifications of the system. Then each interface between modules is worked out using *stubs* (dummy routines that simply return control to the upper-level routine without taking any action). It then becomes much less likely that some critical variable will be left out of the interface.

The second advantage is that the system becomes partially demonstrable very early in the development process. The user interface can be shown and evaluated early on, giving potential users a preview of things to come. Stubs stand in for the unwritten lower level routines. Functional routines gradually replace the stubs, from the top down, as the project unfolds.

4.4.3 Structured Development

The *structured* approach to software development became prominent in the 1970s. It was an effort to make the process more efficient by formalizing it, imposing discipline on it, and using design tools that tend to prevent the problems that otherwise plague the process. Structured development primarily decomposes the problem along functional lines. It is well suited for batch-mode programs.

4.4.3.1 Structured Analysis

Structured analysis decomposes the problem that is to be solved along functional lines. It results in a *structured specification.* This consists of (1) *data flow diagrams* (DFDs) showing the decomposition of the overall function into *processes* and the data flow and interfaces between the processes; (2) a *data dictionary* that documents the data and interfaces in the DFDs; and (3) *transform descriptions* that document the function of each process on the DFDs. The structured specification, then, shows the various structural components of the system and how information flows between, and is transformed by, each of them. [4,5].

4.4.3.2 Structured Design

The goal of structured design is an organized methodology that distinguishes between good and bad designs and proceeds to an optimal solution. It is a collection of strategies and techniques that lead to designs that satisfy the technical objectives and constraints that are common to commercial and scientific computing environments. Structured design develops a design consisting of *black-box* components whose function is specified, but whose internal workings are not. It shares several principles with the techniques that are used to develop organization charts for corporations [6].

4.4.3.3 Structured Programming

Structured programming establishes standardized coding techniques and removes from the programming languages certain commands that tend to encourage poor programming habits. Structured programs conform to a flowchart that is built up from a restricted set of single-entry, single-exit subfunctions. Programming then becomes a much more disciplined endeavor, avoiding cleverly creative constructs in favor of adherence to standards. The resulting code is much easier to read, test, modify, document, and debug [7–9].

Structured programming languages, such as Pascal, Ada, and C, emerged to compete with unstructured languages, such as FORTRAN and BASIC. Structured languages provide capabilities that encourage and support the discipline of structured programming, while avoiding those that encourage poor programming practice. More recent versions of the earlier languages now incorporate some of the concepts of structure as well.

In an unstructured language, the *thread of control* is free to jump about throughout the entire program. An example is the infamous *computed GOTO* statement in FORTRAN.

Control is transferred to one of several different locations in the code, depending upon the value of a specified variable at the time the statement is executed. A listing of a routine containing these constructs can be extremely difficult to read and understand—even by the author of the routine—if the code is more than 60 days old.

In a structured language, the flow of control is restricted to a *single-thread* construction, and code and data are easily compartmentalized. Subroutines using only local (temporary) variables cannot create inadvertent side effects in other parts of the program.

4.4.4 Object-Oriented Development

The *object-oriented* approach to software development decomposes the problem along data-related lines. Conceptually, a program is decomposed into *objects,* each of which is a combination of the data that relate to a particular aspect of the problem and the corresponding code that performs a set of well-defined functions using those data. Data and program code are *encapsulated* into a seamless package whose inner workings are concealed from the outside world. This approach is particularly well suited to event-driven applications.

Each object behaves like a *black box,* performing predefined functions on demand, but revealing little about its inner workings. It is activated by receiving a message, and, when finished, it responds with a message. Each object is self-contained and handles program control and data flow simultaneously while it is active. This makes the program exceedingly modular and avoids a situation wherein changes made in one routine create unexpected effects in other parts of the program.

4.4.4.1 Object-Oriented Analysis

An object-oriented analysis of a problem results in a list of the objects that will work together to solve the problem. This includes a specification of the data (*attributes*) and functions (*services*) of each object. Object-oriented analysis is done without regard to the hardware, operating system, or software development tools that will be employed in the implementation [10].

4.4.4.2 Object-Oriented Design

The object-oriented design phase works out how the logical design that resulted from the analysis will be implemented on a particular platform—that is, a combination of hardware, operating system, and software development tools (compiler, etc.). Often, considerable modification of the initial design is necessitated by the realities of the platform [11].

4.4.4.3 Object-Oriented Programming

In object-oriented programming, the programmer often starts with an *application framework.* This is a program that already has many generic functions that are common to most programs. It serves as a skeleton upon which to build a complete unit. The application framework normally handles the event loop and event identification. The programmer then has only to add the objects that are required for the application at hand. Each object is written with data and program control encapsulated into an independent, more or less sealed unit [12].

New objects need not be designed and written from scratch; they can *inherit* the properties of existing objects. Thus, if, for example, one type of display window object already exists, it needs only to be modified to form a different type of display window.

4.4.5 CASE Tools

In practice, a considerable portion of a programmer's time is spent performing noncreative work—tasks that, strictly speaking, are mechanical and require no creative input of knowledge. Software tools have arisen to take over much of this part of the development activity. These are commonly called *computer-aided software engineering* (CASE) tools. They take over many documentation and error-checking functions.

It is, of course, necessary for the programmer or software designer to contribute design-related information into the system at the outset, but considerable human effort can be avoided by programs that compile and format that information in specific ways. Effective use of CASE tools requires additional discipline in the software design and programming effort, such as the inclusion of standardized descriptive headers at the beginning of each code module.

An example of a CASE tool is a program that combines the header information from all the source code modules to produce a software documentation manual. Other programs can read the source code files, compiling a linkage map of dependencies and communication among the modules, and pointing out potential problems along the way.

In the past, only the conceptual design was completed at the beginning of the project, with many details of the design filled in as coding progressed. Now the trend is toward concentrating the entire design effort at the beginning of the project. This means that the actual programming effort is largely a mechanical process, working from a completely specific design document.

The ramifications of this new trend are twofold. First, software development teams tend to subdivide into software designers and programmers. Second, the actual code generation part of the effort can be taken over by CASE tools. A software designer, sitting at a workstation, can develop a complete specification for a software package. CASE tools can then use this specification to produce both source code (that is free of coding errors) and technical documentation (though not user documentation).

A potential drawback of this approach is the risk that the design effort, done in the sterile preimplementation environment, will not be as creative as it would be if it had been done on the fly. Ideas that might have occurred during implementation are lost, or at least delayed until the system is put into use.

4.4.6 Platform Independence

The development of complex digital image-processing software packages is an expensive and time-consuming task. There are several different computer systems that lend themselves to digital image processing. Different platforms have relative advantages and disadvantages in performance and cost. Hardware advances occur so rapidly that obsolescence is never distant. Thus, there is a need to avoid partial or total rewriting of software for each new peripheral device or hardware platform.

Today's trend is toward software development methodologies that are, in the main, independent of the particular hardware they are to run on. A *portability tool kit* is a software interface that sits between the platform-independent application program and the *native system* (Figure 4–5). The application program is written according to standard rules as if the tool kit were the platform. The tool kit provides the interface between the application program and the native system's operating system, GUI, and memory resources. It translates communications between the application and the native system.

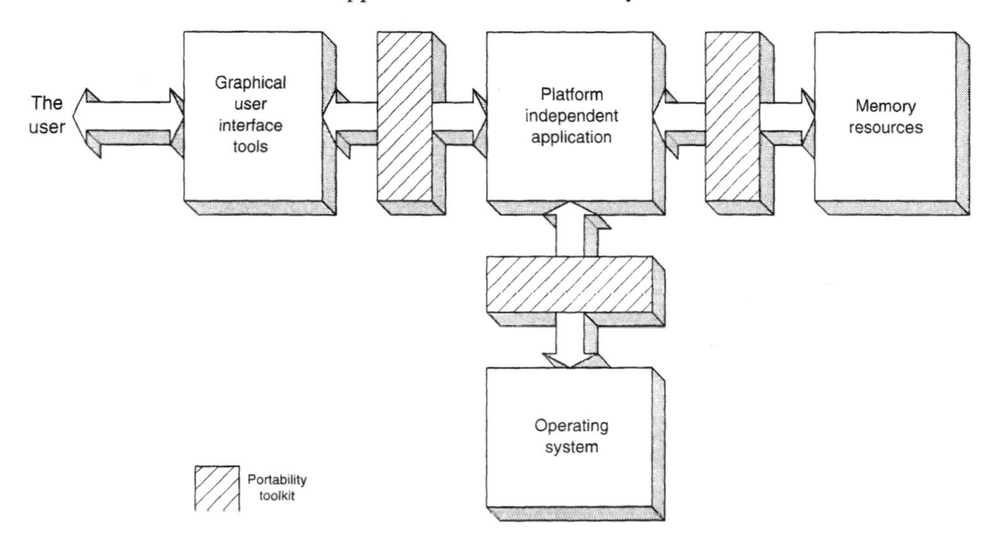

Figure 4–5 Platform-independent software organization

Each different native system (e.g., UNIX workstation, Macintosh, etc.) has a different version of the portability tool kit, but each version looks the same to the application program. That way, an application program developed on one native system will run (theoretically) without modification on another native system. In most cases, only a checkout of functionality is required after porting an application program to a different native system.

A well-designed portability tool kit will give the programmer direct access (through a thin software interface) to most, if not all, of the features and resources of the native system. Those features that do not exist on the native system, but do exist on other native systems in the supported set, are emulated in software by the tool kit. A good portability tool kit will give the programmer access to essentially all the features available on all the supported native systems and, frequently, additional features as well.

When a platform-independent program is ported to a different native system, its functionality is unchanged on the second system. Its "look and feel," however, will be that of its new host. Running on a Macintosh, it will look like it was written for that machine, and likewise for other platforms.

Platform-independent programming makes it easier for programmers to move between platforms. They don't have to learn a new set of features and resources each time they make the switch, provided the same portability tool kit is used.

4.4.7 Software Documentation

The documentation that should accompany the development and use of an image-processing software package falls into five categories. First is the design documentation, which specifies what the package is intended to do. Next is the documentation of the code itself, including the algorithms and the details of the modular structure. Third is the operator's manual, which may include tutorial exercises for beginning users. Fourth is a reference manual, which concisely organizes specific information for the experienced operator's occasional use. Fifth is on-line help, which the user can call up on the screen (often in a separate *help window*) while the program is running.

Sometimes the documentation effort suffers in the haste that precedes completion and release of the software. The delayed cost, in time and money, of inadequate documentation is often quite high. Trying to decipher the operation of poorly documented software can be so frustrating that the new user may give up before becoming competent. Upgrading poorly documented code is likewise time consuming and expensive.

The ideal is a software package with so clear and intuitive a user interface that its complete and well-written documentation package is seldom used. After a brief introduction to the program, the user requires only occasional assistance from on-line help and the reference manual.

4.5 SUMMARY OF IMPORTANT POINTS

1. A convenient user interface and good user documentation are as important as functionality and accuracy in the acceptance of software.
2. For most users, the menu-driven graphical user interface is easier to learn and to operate than a textual interface.
3. The trend in user interfaces is from textual toward verbal and visual interfaces.
4. A program can run in batch mode, be event driven, or operate in real time.
5. Structured software development decomposes a problem along functional lines and emphasizes data flow and the interfaces between components.
6. Structured programs are built up of single-entry, single-exit subfunctions and avoid constructs that make the sequence of program control difficult to follow.
7. Object-oriented development encapsulates the data and functions related to each component of the system into *objects* that communicate via messages.
8. Platform-independent programming permits software developed on one type of system to be moved easily to other types of system.

PROBLEMS

1. Develop a two-level menu structure for a program designed to import, process, and export images taken from spacecraft. The program must be able to import images from satellite downlink, the Internet, modems, and optical disk, and export images to the Internet, modems, optical disk, and hard-copy printers. For processing, choose six processes from Part 1 of the book. Explain how your chosen number of menu levels is optimal for user convenience.

2. Develop a software development flowchart for a project to produce a commercial interactive image-processing program for the integrated circuit chip-inspection industry. The program will enhance digitized microscope images of chips and display stored images of good chips for comparison. Include in your plan adequate allowance for input from potential users, salespersons, and marketing and financial people, as well as for alpha and beta testing prior to release for manufacturing.

PROJECTS

1. Design a graphical user interface for a specific type of image processing (e.g., astronomy, medical, mapping) complete with menus, icons, etc.
2. Implement a prototype (nonfunctional) graphical user interface for a specific type of image processing, and have it reviewed by potential users.
3. Using a paint program, develop a suitable 16-color palette, and use it to color a digitized line drawing. Document the palette, giving the hue, saturation, and intensity of each color and what the color is used for in the image.
4. Prepare a detailed outline for a technical documentation package for an existing software package.
5. Prepare a detailed outline for a user documentation package for an existing software package.
6. Write a program to read images stored in one file format and display them and store them in another format (see Ref. 1).

REFERENCES

For additional reading, see Appendix 2.

1. D. C. Kay and J. R. Levine, *Graphics File Formats,* Windcrest/McGraw-Hill, Blue Ridge Summit, PA, 1992.
2. C. Balasubramaniam, "Dataflow Image Processing," *IEEE Computer*, 82–84, Nov., 1994.
3. G. Miller, "The Magic Number Seven, Plus or Minus Two: Some Limits on our Capacity for Processing Information," *Psychological Review,* **63**(2):86, March 1956.
4. T. DeMarco, *Structured Analysis and System Specification,* Prentice Hall, Englewood Cliffs, NJ, 1978.
5. C. Gane and T. Sarson, *Structured Systems Analysis,* Prentice Hall, Englewood Cliffs, NJ, 1979.
6. E. Yourdon and L. L. Constantine, *Structured Design,* Prentice Hall, Englewood Cliffs, NJ, 1979.
7. N. Wirth, *Systematic Programming: An Introduction,* Prentice Hall, Englewood Cliffs, NJ, 1973.
8. C. L. McGowan and J. R. Kelley, *Top-Down Structured Programming Techniques,* Van Nostrand Reinhold, New York, 1975.
9. O. J. Dahl, E. W. Dijkstra, and C. A. R. Hoare, *Structured Programming,* Academic Press, London, 1972.
10. P. Coad and E. Yourdon, *Object-Oriented Analysis* (2d ed.), Prentice Hall, Englewood Cliffs, NJ, 1991.
11. P. Coad and E. Yourdon, *Object-Oriented Design,* Prentice Hall, Englewood Cliffs, NJ, 1991.
12. P. Coad and J. Nicola, *Object-Oriented Programming,* Prentice Hall, Englewood Cliffs, NJ, 1993.

CHAPTER 5

The Gray-Level Histogram

5.1 INTRODUCTION

One of the simplest and most useful tools in digital image processing is the gray-level histogram. This function summarizes the gray-level content of an image. While the histogram of any image contains considerable information, certain types of images are completely specified by their histograms. Computation of the histogram is simple and may be done at little apparent cost when an image is copied from one place to another.

5.1.1 Definition

The gray-level histogram is a function showing, for each gray level, the number of pixels in the image that have that gray level. The abscissa is gray level and the ordinate is frequency of occurrence (number of pixels). Figure 5–1 shows an example.

There is another way to define the gray-level histogram [1], and the following exercise yields insight into the usefulness of this function. Suppose we have a continuous image, defined by the function $D(x, y)$, that varies smoothly from high gray level at the center to low gray level at the borders. We can select some gray level D_1 and define a set of contour lines connecting all points in the image with value D_1. The resulting contour lines form closed curves that surround regions in which the gray level is greater than or equal to D_1.

Figure 5–2 shows an image containing one contour line at the gray level D_1. A second contour line has been drawn at a higher gray level D_2. A_1 is the area of the region inside the first contour line, and similarly, A_2 is the area inside the second line.

The threshold area function $A(D)$ of a continuous image is the area enclosed by all contour lines of gray level D. Now the histogram may be defined as

$$H(D) = \lim_{\Delta D \to 0} \frac{A(D) - A(D + \Delta D)}{\Delta D} = -\frac{d}{dD}A(D) \tag{1}$$

Thus, the histogram of a continuous image is the negative of the derivative of its area function. The minus sign results from the fact that $A(D)$ decreases with increasing D. If the image is considered a random variable of two dimensions, the area function is proportional to its cumulative distribution function and the gray level histogram to its probability density function.

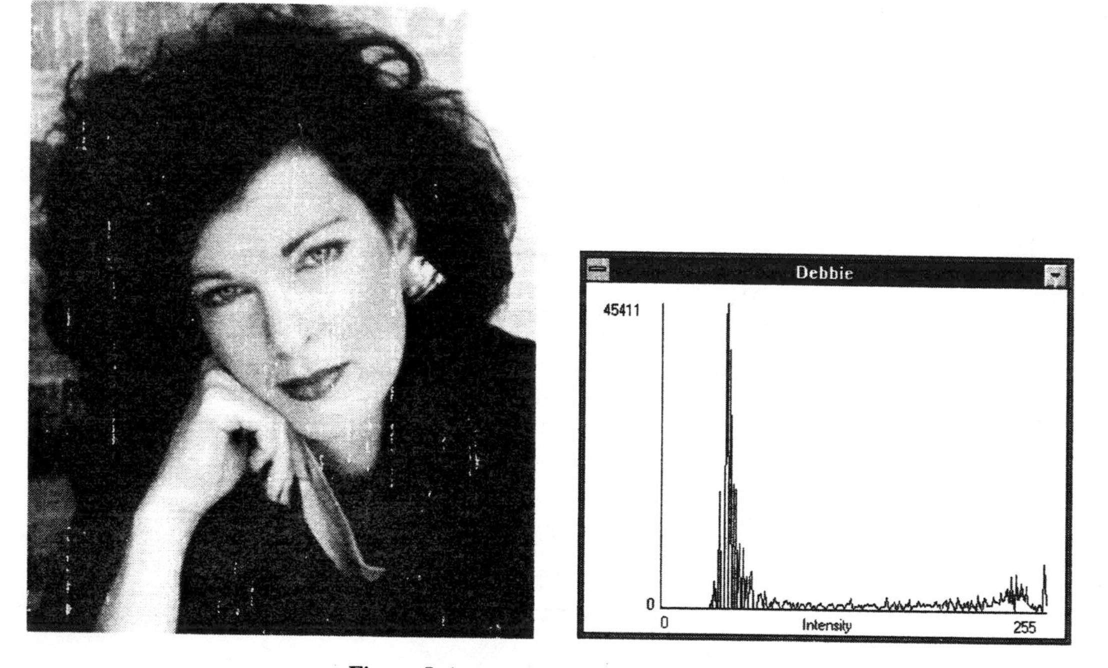

Figure 5–1 An image and its gray-level histogram

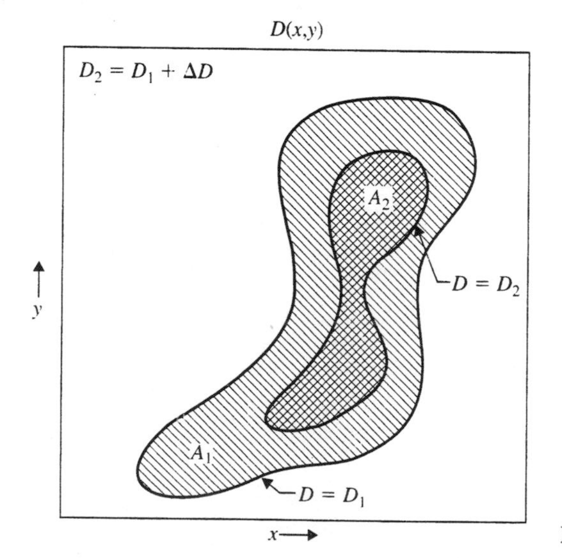

Figure 5–2 Contour lines in an image

For the case of discrete functions, we fix ΔD at unity, and E. (1) becomes

$$H(D) = A(D) - A(D+1) \tag{2}$$

The area function of a digital image is merely the number of pixels having gray level greater than or equal to D for any gray level D.

5.1.2 The Two-Dimensional Histogram

Frequently, one finds it useful to construct histograms of higher dimension than one. This is particularly useful for color images [2], as discussed in Chapter 21. Figure 5–3 shows images digitized from a microscope field containing a white blood cell and several red blood cells. The field was digitized in white light and, through colored filters, in red and blue light. At the lower right is the two-dimensional *red-versus-blue* histogram of the latter two images.

The two-dimensional histogram is a function of two variables: gray level in the red image and gray level in the blue image. Its value at the coordinate (D_R, D_B) is the number of corresponding pixel pairs having gray level D_R in the red image and gray level D_B in the blue image. Recall that a multispectral digital image such as this can be thought of as having a single pixel at each sample point, but each pixel has multiple values—in this case, two. The two-dimensional histogram shows how the pixels are distributed among combinations of two gray levels. If the red and blue component images were identical, the histogram would have zero value except on the 45° diagonal. Pixels having higher red than blue gray level, and vice versa, contribute to the histogram above and below the diagonal line, respectively.

In white light, the microscope field of Figure 5–3 shows considerable information in color. The red blood cells appear pinkish, while the white blood cell is gray with a dark blue nucleus due to the staining treatment. Thus, the red cells appear dark in blue light, which they absorb, and light in red light, which they transmit. Similarly, the nucleus is much denser in red light. The red-versus-blue histogram therefore has four distinct peaks, one each due to the background (B), the red blood cells (R), and the nucleus (N) and cytoplasm (C) of the white cell. The analysis of two-dimensional histograms is discussed further in Chapter 21.

5.1.3 Properties of the Histogram

When an image is condensed into a histogram, all spatial information is discarded. The histogram specifies the number of pixels having each gray level, but gives no hint as to where those pixels are located within the image. Thus, the histogram is unique for any particular image, but the reverse is not true: Vastly different images could have identical histograms. Such operations as moving objects around within an image typically have no effect on the histogram. The histogram does, nevertheless, possess some useful properties.

If we change variables in Eq. (1) and integrate both sides from D to infinity, we find that

$$\int_D^\infty H(P)dP = -\Big[A(P)\Big]_D^\infty = A(D) \tag{3}$$

the area function. If we then set $D = 0$, assuming nonnegative gray levels, we obtain

$$\int_0^\infty H(P)dP = \text{area of image} \tag{4}$$

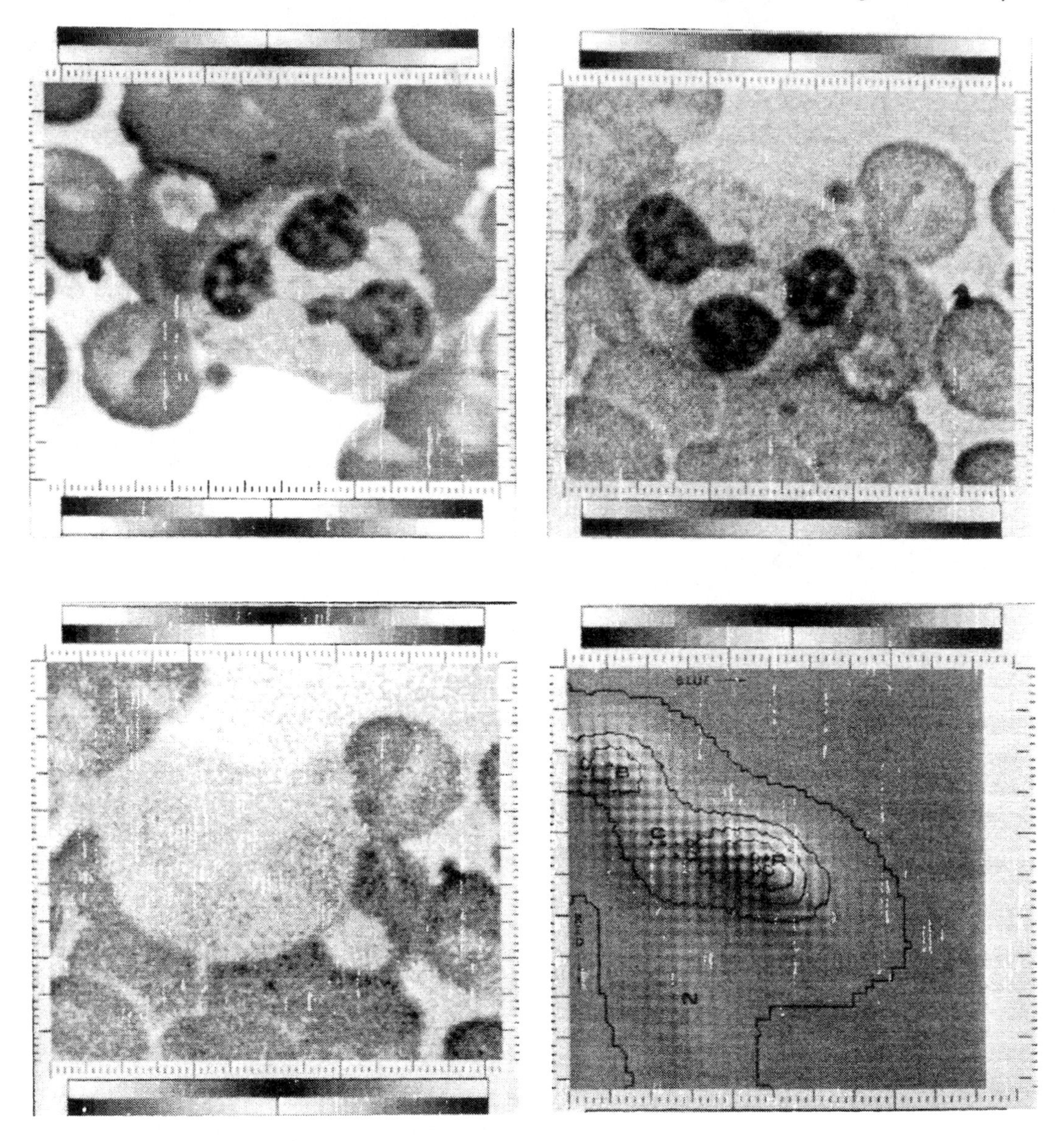

Figure 5–3 Example of a two-dimensional histogram: (a) white-light image; (b) red-light image; (c) blue-light image; (d) red-versus-blue histogram.

or, in the discrete case,

$$\sum_{D=0}^{255} H(D) = NL \times NS \tag{5}$$

where *NL* and *NS* are the numbers of rows and columns, respectively, in the image.

If an image contains a single uniformly gray object on a contrasting background, and we stipulate that the boundary of that object is the contour line defined by gray level D_1, then

$$\int_{D_1}^{\infty} H(D)dD = \text{area of object} \tag{6}$$

If the image contains multiple objects, all of whose boundaries are contour lines at gray level D_1, then Eq. (6) gives the aggregate area of all the objects.

Normalizing the gray-level histogram by dividing by the area of the image produces the probability density function (PDF) of the image. A similar normalization of the area function produces the cumulative distribution function (CDF) of the image. These functions are useful in the statistical treatment of images, as illustrated in Chapter 6.

The histogram has another useful property, which follows directly from its definition as the number of pixels having each gray level: If an image consists of two disjoint regions, and the histogram of each region is known, then the histogram of the entire image is the sum of the two regional histograms. Clearly, this can be extended to any number of disjoint regions.

5.2 USES OF THE HISTOGRAM

5.2.1 Digitizing Parameters

The histogram gives a simple visual indication as to whether or not an image is properly scaled within the available range of gray levels. Ordinarily, a digital image should make use of all or almost all of the available gray levels, as in Figure 5–1. Failure to do so increases the effective quantizing interval. Once the image has been digitized to fewer than 256 gray levels, the lost information cannot be restored without redigitizing.

Likewise, if the image has a greater brightness range than the digitizer is set to handle, then the gray levels will be *clipped* at 0 and/or 255, producing spikes at one or both ends of the histogram. It is a good practice routinely to review the histogram when digitizing. A quick check of the histogram can bring digitizing problems into the open before much time has been wasted.

5.2.2 Boundary Threshold Selection

As mentioned earlier, contour lines provide an effective way to establish the boundary of a simple object within an image. The technique of using contour lines as boundaries is called *thresholding*. The use of optimal techniques for selecting threshold gray levels is a subject of considerable discussion in the literature and is treated in Chapter 18.

Suppose an image contains a dark object on a light background. Figure 5–4 illustrates the appearance of the histogram of such an image. The dark pixels inside the object produce the rightmost peak in the histogram. The leftmost peak is due to the large number of gray levels in the background. The relatively few midlevel gray pixels around the edge of the object produce the dip between the two peaks. A threshold gray level chosen in the area of the dip will produce a reasonable boundary for the object [3,4].

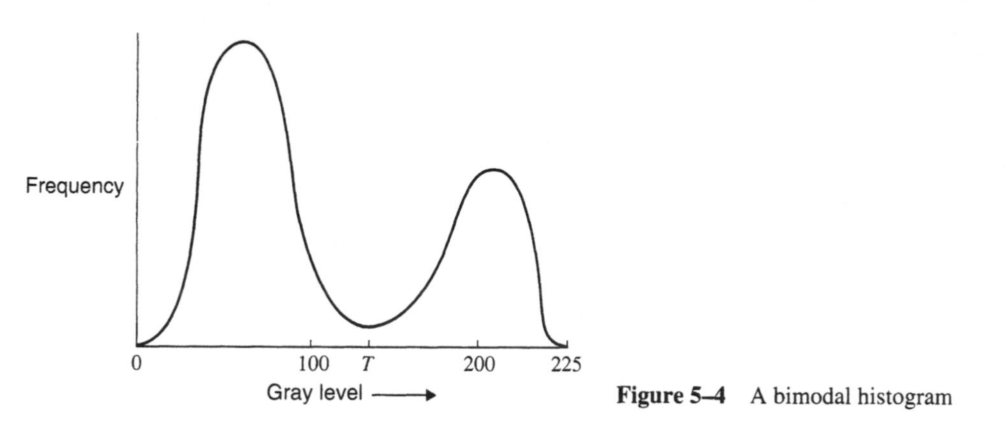

Figure 5–4 A bimodal histogram

In one sense, the gray level corresponding to the minimum between the two peaks is optimal for defining the boundary. Recall from Eq. (1) that the histogram is the derivative of the area function. In the vicinity of the dip, the histogram takes on relatively small values, implying that the area function changes slowly with threshold gray level. If we place the threshold gray level at the dip, we minimize its effect upon the boundary of the object. If we are concerned with measuring the object's area, selecting a threshold at the dip in the histogram minimizes the sensitivity of the area measurement to variations in threshold gray level.

5.2.3 Integrated Optical Density

Given the histogram in Figure 5–4, we could determine an optimal threshold gray level for the object and compute its area [Eq. (6)] without ever seeing the image. Another measurement that can be computed directly from the histogram of simple images is the *integrated optical density* (IOD). A useful measure of the "mass" of an image, it is defined as

$$IOD = \int_0^a \int_0^b D(x, y)\,dx\,dy \tag{7}$$

where a and b delimit the region of the image. When the image consists of a dark object situated on a background of zero gray level, the IOD reflects a combination of the area and density of that object.

For a digital image

$$IOD = \sum_{i=1}^{NL} \sum_{j=1}^{NS} D(i, j) \tag{8}$$

where $D(i, j)$ is the gray level of the pixel at line i, sample j. Let N_k be the number of pixels in the image with gray level equal to k. Then Eq. (8) can be written as

$$IOD = \sum_{k=0}^{255} kN_k \tag{9}$$

since, clearly, this adds up the gray levels of all pixels within the image. However, N_k is merely the histogram evaluated at gray level k. Thus Eq. (9) can be written as

$$IOD = \sum_{k=0}^{255} kH(k) \tag{10}$$

that is, a gray-level-weighted summation of the histogram. By equating Eqs. (8) and (10) and taking a limit as the increment between gray levels approaches zero, we derive similar expressions for continuous images:

$$IOD = \int_0^{\infty} DH(D)dD \tag{11}$$

and

$$\int_0^a \int_0^b D(x, y)dx\,dy = \int_0^{\infty} DH(D)dD \tag{12}$$

If an object within the image is delineated by a threshold boundary at gray level T, the IOD within the object boundary is given by

$$IOD(T) = \int_T^{\infty} DH(D)dD \tag{13}$$

The mean interior gray level is the ratio of IOD to area:

$$MGL = \frac{IOD(T)}{A(T)} = \frac{\int_T^{\infty} DH(D)dD}{\int_T^{\infty} H(D)dD} \tag{14}$$

5.3 RELATIONSHIP BETWEEN HISTOGRAM AND IMAGE

Since the histogram of a particular image is unique, it is possible to derive the histogram of simple images whose functional form is known. While this technique is perhaps seldom used, it does yield insight into the histogram, and it establishes a basis for further study of threshold selection in Chapter 18.

Suppose we have an image of given functional form, and we desire to compute its histogram. We know that this is the negative of the derivative with respect to gray level of the area function [Eq. (1)]. Thus, we may derive the histogram if we first derive the area function from the expression for the image itself. Sometimes this can be done simply by observation.

5.3.1 One Dimension

For simplicity, we first address the one-dimensional case. Here the "area" is actually a length, but it demonstrates the relationship between a histogram and its image.

Consider the one-dimensional Gaussian pulse (Figure 5–5) given by

$$D(x) = e^{-x^2} \qquad -\infty \le x \le \infty \tag{15}$$

Notice that for nonnegative x, the function is monotonic. Furthermore, the area is merely the inverse of the image function. Thus, for nonnegative values of x, we may solve Eq. (15) for x as a function of gray level to yield

$$x(D) = \sqrt{-\ln(D)} \qquad x \ge 0 \tag{16}$$

which is the area function for the right half of the image. Since the two halves of the image

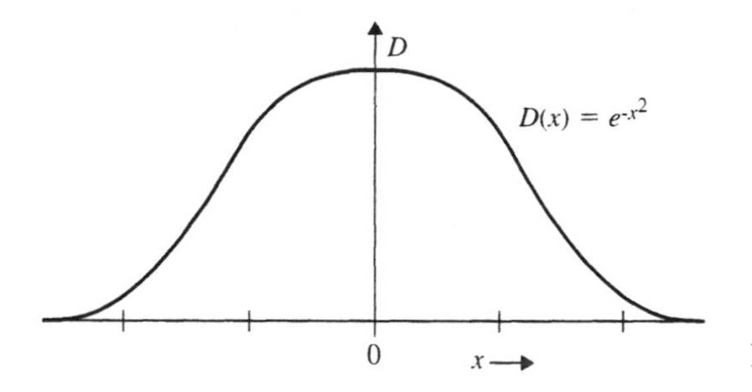

Figure 5–5 The Gaussian pulse

are symmetrical, the overall area function is twice that of Eq. (16). The histogram is given by

$$H(D) = -\frac{d}{dD}\left[2\sqrt{-\ln(D)}\right] = \frac{1}{D\sqrt{-\ln(D)}} \tag{17}$$

and is shown in Figure 5–6. The histogram builds up to a spike at $D = 0$ because of the large areas of low gray level at large positive and negative values of x. The small spike at $D = 1$ results from the image having zero slope at $x = 0$ (i.e., the Gaussian is locally "flat" at the very top).

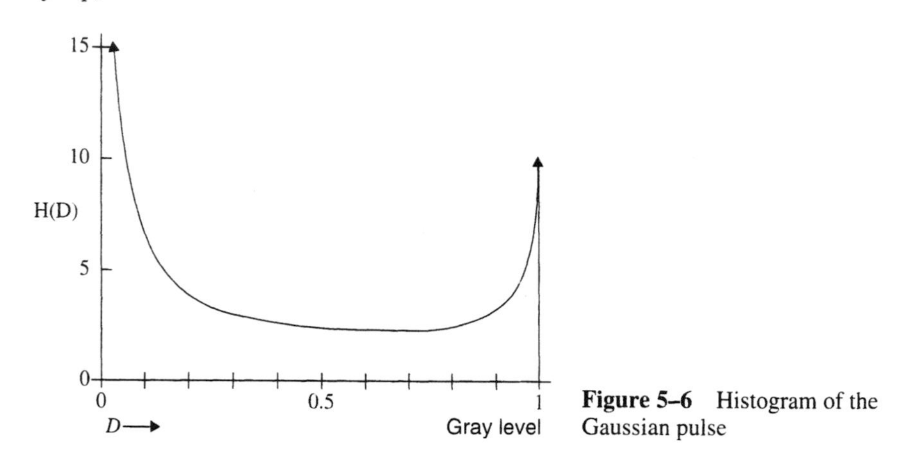

Figure 5–6 Histogram of the Gaussian pulse

5.3.2 Two Dimensions

The same procedure may be extended to two-dimensional images by judicious use of symmetry within the image. For example, suppose that the one-dimensional Gaussian pulse of Eq. (15) is actually one line of a two-dimensional image. Then if all lines are identical, the histogram will have the same shape as that in Figure 5–6, differing only in ordinate scale.

One may take advantage of circular symmetry in the following way. Suppose the image is a circularly symmetric Gaussian pulse centered on the origin (Figure 5–7). The image function in polar coordinates is given by

$$D(r, \theta) = e^{-r^2} \qquad 0 \le r \le \infty, 0 \le \theta < 2\pi \tag{18}$$

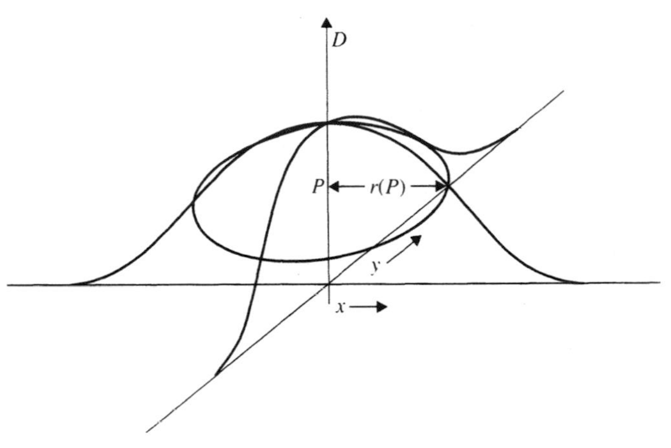

Figure 5–7 The circular Gaussian spot

A contour of constant gray level P is a circle of radius

$$r(P) = \sqrt{-\ln(P)} \tag{19}$$

Such a contour encloses an area

$$A(P) = \pi[r(P)]^2 = -\pi \ln(P) \tag{20}$$

The area function of Eq. (20) may now be differentiated to yield the histogram [1]

$$H(P) = \frac{d}{dP}A(P) = \frac{\pi}{P} \tag{21}$$

shown in Figure 5–8. Notice that the point of zero slope at the origin is not powerful enough to produce a spike at $D = 1$, as it did in the one-dimensional case.

For more complex images, the histogram may be derived by first partitioning the image into disjoint regions over which the area function may be determined. The histogram of the complete image is then the sum of the histograms of all the disjoint regions.

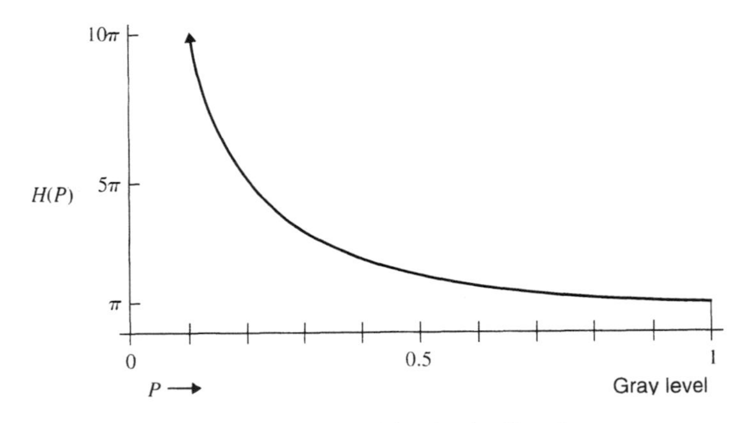

Figure 5–8 Histogram of the circular Gaussian spot

5.4 SUMMARY OF IMPORTANT POINTS

1. The gray-level histogram is the negative of the derivative of the threshold area function.
2. The histogram shows how many pixels occur at each gray level.
3. Inspection of the histogram points out improper digitization.
4. The area and IOD of a simple object can be computed from the histogram of its image.
5. The histogram of an image of specified functional form can be derived with the aid of the area function.

PROBLEMS

1. A film image shows a dark-colored barn with a light colored roof against a bright sky. Sketch what its histogram might look like if it were (a) properly digitized, (b) digitized with gain set too low, (c) digitized with gain set too high, (d) digitized with too much offset, (e) digitized with too little offset, and (f) digitized with too much gain and offset. Assume that 0 is dark and 255 is light.
2. A television camera is pointed at a news anchor man wearing a dark jacket and standing in front of a gray background. Sketch what the histogram of a digitized frame might look like if it were (a) properly digitized, (b) digitized with gain set too low, (c) digitized with gain set too high, (d) digitized with too much (positive) offset (from zero), (e) digitized with too little offset, and (f) digitized with too much gain and offset. Make reasonable assumptions about the coloring of the man's hair and skin.
3. An eight-bit image of a bright object on a dark background has a histogram given by

$$H(D) = 100G(60, 5, D) + 20G(180, 20, D) \qquad G(\mu, \sigma, x) = e^{-(x-\mu)^2/(2\sigma^2)}$$

where zero is black and the pixel spacing is 0.2 mm. Where would you put the threshold gray level? What are the area and the IOD of the object?
4. Below is the histogram of an image of a black-and-white soccer ball on a gray background. This soccer ball is 230 mm in diameter. What is the pixel spacing?

[0 520 920 490 30 40 5910 24040 6050 80 20 80 440 960 420 0]

PROJECTS

1. Develop a program to display histogram plots of digital images. Test the program on suitable images.
2. Develop a program to determine the minimum, maximum, and modal gray level from the gray-level histogram of an image. Test the program on suitable images.
3. Develop a program that can display an input image and its histogram, allow interactive selection of a threshold gray level, and generate a binary output image by thresholding the input image. Test the program on suitable images.
4. Develop a program that can compute the histogram of an input image, automatically locate the dip in the histogram and threshold the image to produce a binary output image. Test the program on suitable images.
5. Develop a program that can display the histogram of a television camera image in real time and use the histogram to assist in the focusing of a camera, telescope, or microscope.
6. Develop a program that can calculate the histogram of an image of an object on a contrasting background and, from that, the area and IOD of the object. Test the program on suitable objects.

REFERENCES

For additional reading, see Appendix 2.

1. R. J. Wall, A. Klinger, and K. R. Castleman, "Analysis of Image Histograms," *Proc. Second Int. Cong. on Pattern Recognition,* Copenhagen, 1974.
2. C. L. Novak and S. A. Shafer, "Anatomy of a Color Histogram," *Proceedings of the 1992 IEEE Computer Society Conference on Computer Vision and Pattern Recognition,* 599–605, IEEE Computer Society Press, Los Alamitos, CA, 1992.
3. J. Prewitt and M. Mendelsohn, "The Analysis of Cell Images," *Annals of the New York Academy of Sciences,* 128, 1035–1053, January 1966.
4. M. Mendelsohn, B. Mayall, J. Prewitt, R. Bostrom, and R. Holcomb, "Digital Transformation and Computer Analysis of Microscope Images," in R. Barer and V. Cosslet, eds., *Advances in Optical and Electron Microscopy,* **2,** Academic Press, London, 1968.

CHAPTER 6

Point Operations

6.1 INTRODUCTION

Point operations constitute a simple but important class of image-processing techniques. They allow the user to modify the way in which the image data fills the available range of gray levels. This particularly affects how the image will appear when displayed.

A *point operation* takes a single input image into a single output image in such a way that each output pixel's gray level depends only upon the gray level of the corresponding input pixel. This contrasts with *local operations,* in which a neighborhood of input pixels determines the gray level of each output pixel. Furthermore, in a point operation, each output pixel corresponds directly to the input pixel having the same coordinates. Thus, a point operation cannot modify the spatial relationships within an image.

Point operations are sometimes called by other names, including *contrast enhancement, contrast stretching,* and *gray-scale transformations.* They are often built in as an integral part of image digitizing and image display software.

Point operations modify the gray-level histogram of an image in a predictable way. They may be viewed as pixel-by-pixel copying operations, except that the gray levels are modified according to the specified gray-scale transformation function. A point operation that takes an input image $A(x, y)$ into an output image $B(x, y)$ may be expressed as

$$B(x, y) = f[A(x, y)] \tag{1}$$

The point operation is completely specified by the *gray-scale transformation (GST) function, $f(D)$,* which specifies the mapping of input gray level to output gray level.

6.1.1 Applications of Point Operations

Point operations are sometimes used to overcome image digitizer limitations before the actual processing begins. Equally important are point operations used to improve the image display process.

Photometric Calibration. It is often desirable to have the gray levels of a digitized image reflect some physical property, such as light intensity or optical density. Point operations can do this by removing the effects of image sensor nonlinearity. As an example, suppose an image has been digitized by an instrument with a nonlinear response to light intensity. A point operation can transform the gray scale so that the gray levels represent equal increments in light intensity. This is an example of *photometric calibration.*

Another use for the point operation is to transform the units of the gray scale. Suppose a microscope image has been digitized by an instrument that produces gray-level values that are linear with the specimen's transmittance. A point operation can be used to create an image in which the gray levels represent equal steps in optical density. We can consider photometric calibration as the software side of image digitizing.

Contrast Enhancement. In some digital images, the features of interest occupy only a relatively narrow range of the gray scale. One might use a point operation to expand the contrast of the features of interest so that they occupy a larger portion of the displayed gray-level range. This is sometimes called *contrast enhancement,* or *contrast stretching.*

Display Calibration. Some display devices have a preferred range of gray levels over which they make image features most visible. Darker and lighter features, having the same contrast in the digital image, do not show up as well on such a display. In this case, the user may employ a point operation to ensure that the features of interest fall into the *maximum-visibility range* of the display.

Many display devices do not maintain a linear relationship between the gray level of a pixel in the digital image and the brightness of the corresponding point on the display screen. Similarly, many film recorders are unable to transform gray levels linearly into optical density. These shortcomings may be overcome by a suitably designed point operation prior to displaying the image. Taken together, the point operation and the display nonlinearities combine to cancel each other, and this preserves linearity in the displayed image. The procedure is called *display calibration.*

Sometimes a particular nonlinear display relationship is desired for proper presentation of the image. This deliberate nonlinearity is specified by the *gamma* of television and CRT monitors. Point operations can correct or adjust the gamma of image displays.

Point operations are sometimes viewed as image-processing steps that bring out detail or increase the contrast of components of an image. What is really being done, however, is matching the gray levels of interesting portions of the image to the contrast range of the display device, since that information was present in the digital image all along. Thus, we can consider display calibration and contrast enhancement as the software side of digital image display.

Contour Lines. A point operation can add contour lines to an image. One can also accomplish thresholding with a point operation that divides an image into disjoint regions on the basis of gray level. This is useful for defining boundaries or for making masks for subsequent operations.

Clipping. Since digital images are commonly stored in integer (often byte) format, the range of available gray levels is necessarily limited. For eight-bit images, the output gray level must be clipped to the range 0–255 before each pixel value is stored. In this chapter, we assume that each point operation is followed by a step that sets negative values to zero and limits positive values to D_m, the maximum gray level.

6.1.2 Types of Point Operations

It is convenient to divide point operations into different categories.

6.1.2.1 Linear Point Operations

We first consider point operations in which the output gray level is a linear function of the input gray level. In this case, the gray scale transformation function of Eq. (1) takes the form

$$D_B = f(D_A) = aD_A + b \tag{2}$$

where D_B is the gray level of the output point corresponding to an input point having gray level D_A (Figure 6–1). Obviously, if $a = 1$ and $b = 0$, we have the identity operation that merely copies $A(x, y)$ into $B(x, y)$. If a is greater than 1, the contrast will be increased in the output image. For $a < 1$, the contrast is reduced. If $a = 1$ and b is nonzero, the operation merely shifts the gray level values of all pixels up or down. The effect of this is to make the entire image appear darker or lighter when displayed. If a is negative, dark areas become light, light areas become dark, and the image is *complemented* by the operation.

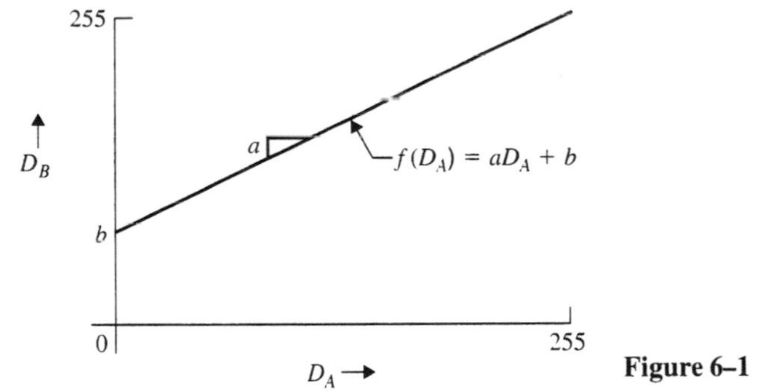

Figure 6–1 The linear point operation

6.1.2.2 Nonlinear Monotonic Point Operations

We next consider nondecreasing gray-scale transformation functions—those that have a finite positive slope everywhere. These functions preserve the basic appearance of an image, but are not as constrained as the linear operation.

Nonlinear point operations can be classified by what they do to the midrange gray levels. Figure 6–2 shows a gray-scale transformation function that boosts the gray level of midrange pixels while leaving dark and light pixels little changed. An example of such a gray-scale transformation function is

$$f(x) = x + Cx(D_m - x) \tag{3}$$

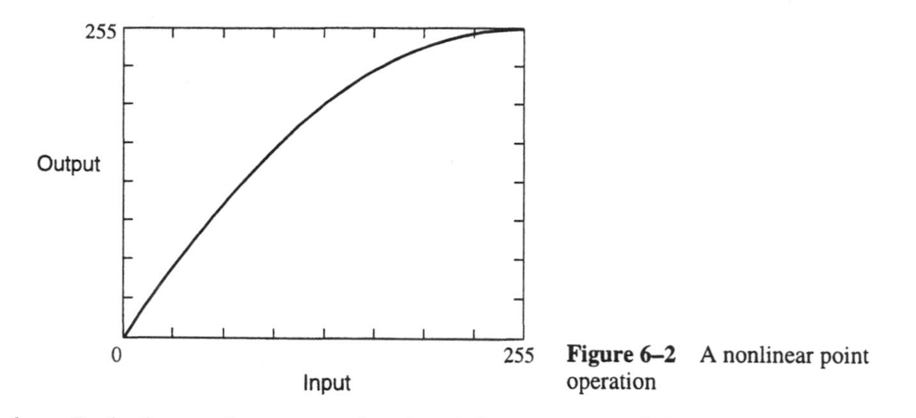

Figure 6–2 A nonlinear point operation

where D_m is the maximum gray level and the parameter C determines the amount of increase ($C > 0$) or decrease ($C < 0$) in the medieval gray range.

A second type of nonlinear monotonic point operation increases the contrast within migraine objects at the expense of light and dark objects. Such a *signed* (S-shaped) gray-scale transformation function has slope greater than 1 in the migraine and less than 1 toward the ends. An example based on the sine function is

$$f(x) = 0\frac{D_m}{2}\left\{1 + \frac{1}{\sin\left(\alpha\frac{\pi}{2}\right)}\sin\left[\alpha\pi\left(\frac{x}{D_m} - \frac{1}{2}\right)\right]\right\} \# 0 < \alpha < 1 \tag{4}$$

where zero to D_m is the gray-level range over which the histogram is nonzero. The larger the parameter α is, the more seriously the migraine is affected.

A third type of nonlinear monotonic point operation decreases the contrast in the migraine and increases it within light and dark objects. Such a gray scale transformation function has slope less than 1 in the migraine and greater than 1 near the ends. An example based on the tangent function is

$$f(x) = \frac{D_m}{2}\left\{1 + \frac{1}{\tan\left(\alpha\frac{\pi}{2}\right)}\tan\left[\alpha\pi\left(\frac{x}{D_m} - \frac{1}{2}\right)\right]\right\} \# 0 < \alpha < 1 \tag{5}$$

Again, the parameter α determines how serious the effect of the point operation will be.

6.2 POINT OPERATIONS AND THE HISTOGRAM

The foregoing discussion suggests that a point operation modifies the gray-level histogram in a predictable way. We now address the question of predicting the output image histogram, given the input image histogram and the functional form of the gray-scale transformation.

Having this capability is useful for two reasons. First, one may wish to design a point operation to scale the output gray levels into a predetermined range or to produce an output histogram of a particular form. Second, this exercise develops one's insight into the effects that point operations can have on an image. Such an understanding proves useful when one is designing point operations.

6.2.1 The Output Histogram

Suppose a point operation defined by a gray-scale transformation function $f(D)$ takes an input image $A(x, y)$ into an output image $B(x, y)$. Given $H_A(D)$, the histogram of the input image, we wish to derive an expression for the output image histogram. The gray level of an arbitrary output pixel is given by

$$D_B = f(D_A) \tag{6}$$

where D_A is the gray level of the corresponding input pixel. For the present, let us assume that $f(D)$ is a nondecreasing function with finite slope. Thus, its inverse function exists, and we can write

$$D_A = f^{-1}(D_B) \tag{7}$$

We shall later find ways around this restriction.

Figure 6–3 illustrates the relationship between the input histogram, the gray-scale transformation function, and the output histogram. The gray level D_A transforms to D_B; similarly, the gray level $D_A + \Delta D_A$ transforms to $D_B + \Delta D_B$. Furthermore, all pixels with gray levels between D_A and $D_A + \Delta D_A$ will transform to gray levels between D_B and $D_B + \Delta D_B$. Thus, the number of output pixels having gray levels between D_B and $D_B + \Delta D_B$ equals the number of input pixels with gray levels between D_A and $D_A + \Delta D_A$. This implies that the area under $H_B(D)$ between D_B and $D_B + \Delta D_B$ is the same as that under $H_A(D)$ between D_A and $D_A + \Delta D_A$, or

$$\int_{D_B}^{D_B + \Delta D_B} H_B(D)dD = \int_{D_A}^{D_A + \Delta D_A} H_A(D)dD \tag{8}$$

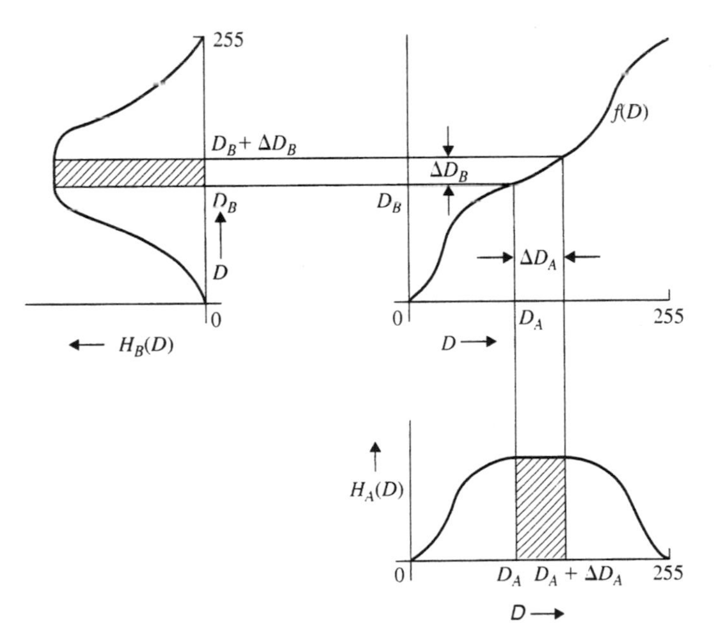

Figure 6–3 Effect of a point operation on the histogram

If we make ΔD_A suitably small, ΔD_B will also be small, and we can write a rectangular approximation to the integral:

$$H_B(D_B)\Delta D_B = H_A(D_A)\Delta D_A \tag{9}$$

We now solve for the value of the output histogram to obtain

$$H_B(D_B) = \frac{H_A(D_A)}{\Delta D_B / \Delta D_A} \tag{10}$$

and take the limit as ΔD_A approaches zero. Since $f(D)$ has nonzero slope everywhere, ΔD_B also approaches zero, to yield

$$H_B(D_B) = \frac{H_A(D_A)}{dD_B / dD_A} \tag{11}$$

But since D_B is given by Eq. (6), we can substitute to find

$$H_B(D_B) = \frac{H_A(D_A)}{(d/dD_A)f(D_A)} \tag{12}$$

We now have a mixture of independent variables in this equation: D_B on the left and D_A on the right. We can overcome this by substituting the inverse function given in Eq. (7). This yields the general form

$$H_B(D) = \frac{H_A\left[f^{-1}(D)\right]}{f'\left[f^{-1}(D)\right]} \tag{13}$$

where

$$f' = df/dD \tag{14}$$

and the subscript has been dropped.

6.2.2 Examples

6.2.2.1 Linear Point Operation

Consider the linear point operation given by Eq. (2). We note that its derivative is a and its inverse is

$$D_A = f^{-1}(D_B) = (D_B - b)/a \tag{15}$$

Substituting into Eq. (13) yields

$$H_B(D) = \frac{1}{a} H_A\left(\frac{D-b}{a}\right) \tag{16}$$

Notice that $b > 0$ shifts the histogram to the right, while $b < 0$ shifts it left. Also, $a > 1$ broadens the histogram while reducing its amplitude, to keep the area under the histogram constant. The effect of $a < 1$ is the opposite.

To illustrate the effect of a linear point operation, let us assume that the input histogram has a Gaussian form, given by

$$H_A(D) = e^{-(D-c)^2} \tag{17}$$

and shown in Figure 6–4. Substituting into Eq. (16) yields

$$H_B(D) = \frac{1}{a} e^{-[D/a - (c + b/a)]^2} \tag{18}$$

as shown in the figure. The output histogram is also Gaussian, but the peak is moved to $c + b/a$. Also, the width (at the $1/e$ point) goes from unity to a, while the height goes from unity to $1/a$.

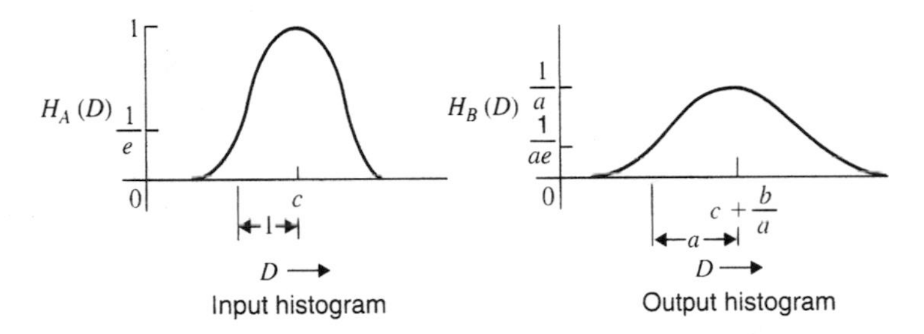

Figure 6–4 Effect of a linear point operation on a Gaussian histogram

6.2.2.2 Second-Order Point Operation

As a second example, consider a square-law point operation

$$D_B = f(D_A) = D_A^2 \tag{19}$$

operating upon an image whose histogram

$$H_A(D_A) = e^{-D_A^2} \tag{20}$$

is the right-hand half of a Gaussian pulse. Both of these appear in Figure 6–5.

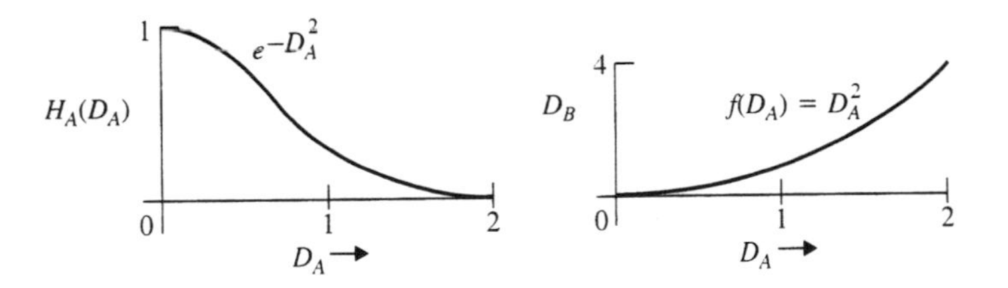

Figure 6–5 A square-law point operation

Using Eq. (13), we obtain the output histogram

$$H_B(D_B) = \frac{e^{-D_B}}{2\sqrt{D_B}} \tag{21}$$

which is shown in Figure 6–6.

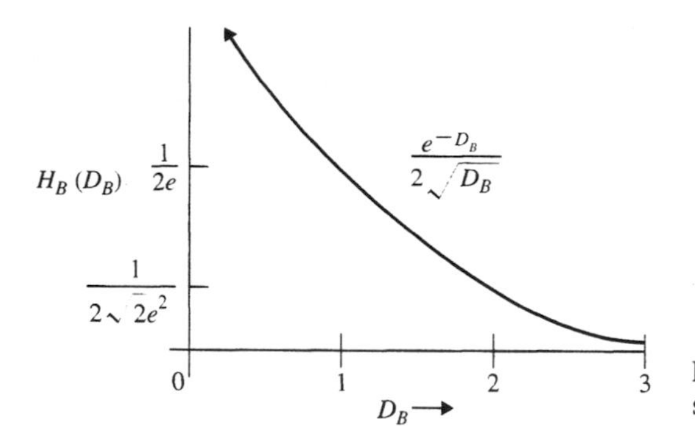

Figure 6–6 Output histogram from square-law point operation

6.2.2.3 A Sigmoid Transformation

As a third example, consider the sine stretch of Eq. (4) operating on an image with the bimodal histogram

$$H_A(D_A) = G(\sigma_1, \mu_1, D_A) + G(\sigma_2, \mu_2, D_A) \tag{22}$$

shown in Figure 6–7b. This is typical of images of high-gray-level objects on a low-gray-level background.

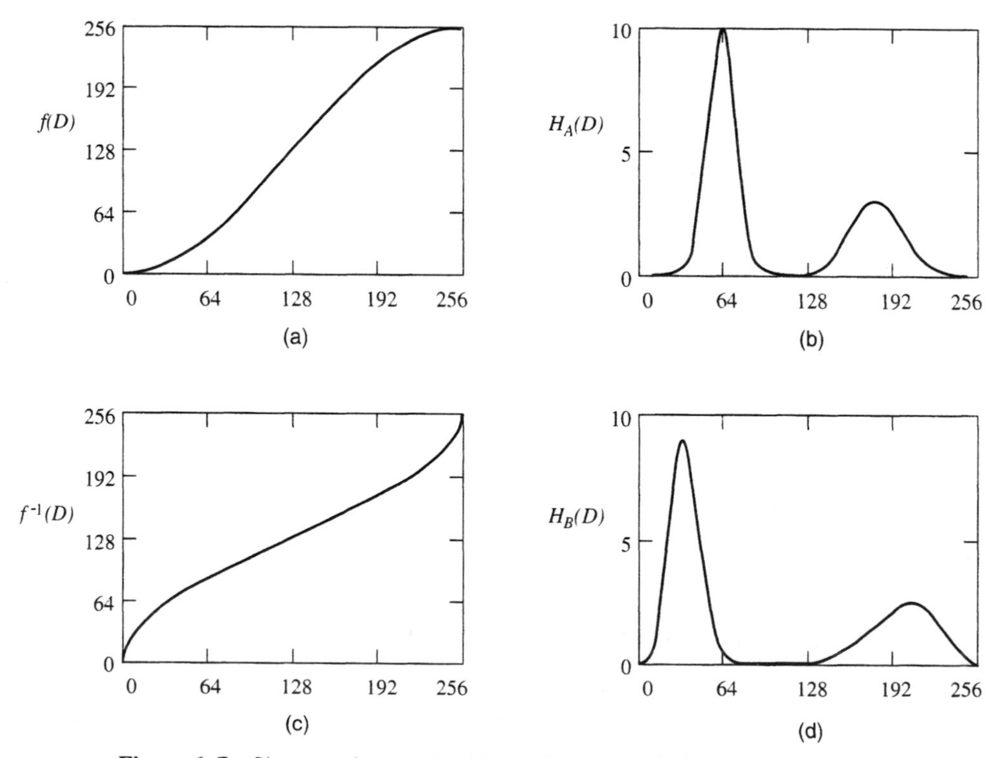

Figure 6–7 Sine stretch example: (a) transformation; (b) input histogram; (c) inverse transformation; (d) output histogram

Solving Eq. (4) for its inverse leads to

$$f^{-1}(D) = \frac{D_m}{2} + \frac{D_m}{\alpha\pi}\sin^{-1}\left[\left(\frac{2D}{D_m} - 1\right)\sin\left(\alpha\frac{\pi}{2}\right)\right] \tag{23}$$

while the derivative of the transformation function is

$$\frac{df}{dx} = \frac{\alpha\pi}{2\sin\left(\alpha\frac{\pi}{2}\right)}\cos\left[\alpha\pi\left(\frac{x}{D_m} - \frac{1}{2}\right)\right] \tag{24}$$

Substituting these into Eq. (13) produces the output histogram shown in Figure 6–7d. Notice that the separation between the peaks is increased by this point operation.

6.2.3 The General Case

In the derivation that led to Eq. (13), we assumed that $f(D)$ had finite, nonzero slope everywhere. If, instead, $f(D)$ has zero slope over some interval, then the finite area under H_A will be forced into a strip of infinitesimal width in H_B, producing a spike, as Eq. (13) suggests. If, on the other hand, $f(D)$ has infinite slope, the opposite is the case: An infinitesimally wide strip under H_A is expanded throughout a finite interval in H_B, producing a vanishingly small value for the output histogram there. Thus, the construction of Figure 6–3 is valid in these two extreme cases, and the output histograms behave as Eq. (13) suggests.

If the gray-scale transformation $f(D)$ is not a monotonic function, its inverse does not exist, and Eq. (13) cannot be used directly. The input gray-level range may be divided into disjoint intervals, however, over which the previously developed technique can be used. This partitions the input image into contiguous disjoint regions, and the output histogram is the sum of the transformed regional histograms.

6.3 APPLICATIONS OF POINT OPERATIONS

6.3.1 Histogram Equalization

Suppose we desire a point operation to take a given input image into an output image with equally many pixels at every gray level (a flat histogram). This can be useful for putting images into a consistent format prior to comparison or segmentation. The number of pixels at each gray level will be A_0/D_m, where D_m is the maximum gray level and A_o is the area of the image. Figure 6–8 shows three images with their normalized histograms and normalized area functions. The left and center images illustrate histogram flattening.

Notice from Eq. (13) that the output histogram is the ratio of two functions of the same argument. Clearly, this will be a constant if the numerator and denominator are the same function, scaled by a constant—that is, if

$$f'(D) = \frac{D_m}{A_o}H(D) \tag{25}$$

Integrating both sides of Eq. (25), we find this condition to be satisfied if

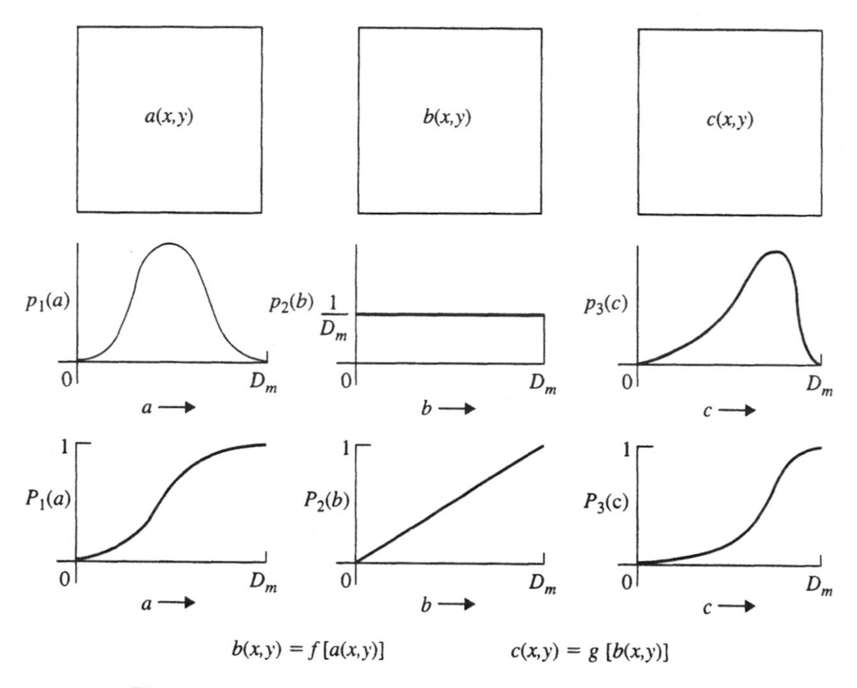

Figure 6–8 Histogram equalization and histogram matching

$$f(D) = \frac{D_m}{A_o} \int_0^D H(u)du \tag{26}$$

Recall from Chapter 5 that the probability density function (PDF) of an image is its histogram normalized to unit area; that is,

$$p(D) = \frac{1}{A_o} H(D) \tag{27}$$

where $H(D)$ is the histogram and A_o is the area of the image. Recall also that the cumulative distribution function (CDF) of an image is its area-normalized threshold area function:

$$P(D) = \int_0^D p(u)du = \frac{1}{A_o} \int_0^D H(u)du \tag{28}$$

Thus, the CDF is the point operation that flattens the histogram, i.e.,

$$f(D) = D_m P(D) \tag{29}$$

and the histogram equalization GST function for Figure 6–8 is

$$B(x, y) = f[A(x, y)] = D_m P [A(x.y)] \tag{30}$$

The CDF is a particularly well-behaved function, since it is always nonnegative with finite, nonnegative slope.

After a histogram equalization point operation, the actual histogram will usually take on a rather ragged appearance due to the finite number of available gray levels. Some gray levels will be unoccupied and others highly populated. On the average, however, the histogram will be approximately flat. Figure 6–9 shows an example of histogram equalization.

6.3.2 Histogram Matching

Sometimes it is desirable to transform an image so that its histogram matches that of another image or a specified functional form. This could be used, for example, before comparing two images of the same scene when they have been digitized under different lighting conditions.

In Figure 6–8, suppose we desire to transform $A(x, y)$ into $C(x, y)$ with histogram $H_3(D)$ specified. We can do this in two steps, first using $f(D)$ to transform $A(x, y)$ into $B(x, y)$ with a flat histogram as before, and then taking $B(x, y)$ through a second point operation, $g(D)$, to produce $C(x, y)$, that is,

$$C(x, y) = g[B(x, y)] \tag{31}$$

We know from Eq. (30) what is required to produce $B(x, y)$. Furthermore, we know that the point operation

$$B(x, y) = D_m P_3[C(x, y)] \tag{32}$$

would take $C(x, y)$ into an image with a flat histogram and is thus the opposite of what we require.

Expressing $B(x, y)$ as in Eq. (32), we can write the second point operation, Eq. (31), as

$$C(x, y) = g\{D_m P_3[C(x, y)]\} \tag{33}$$

This says that the sequential application of $D_m P_3(D)$ followed by $g(D)$ produces no net effect. Thus, $g(D)$ is the inverse function of $D_m P_3(D)$; that is,

$$g(D) = P_3^{-1}(D/D_m) \tag{34}$$

Now, if we desire to take $A(x, y)$ to $C(x, y)$ in one step, we can concatenate the two point operations, and then,

$$C(x, y) = g\{f[A(x, y)]\} = P_3^{-1}\{P_1[A(x, y)]\} \tag{35}$$

Notice that in substituting Eqs. (30) and (34) into Eq. (35), the D_m's cancel.

6.3.3 Photometric Calibration

Historically, one of the most important uses of point operations has been the removal of digitizer-induced photometric nonlinearity. Suppose a certain film digitizer has a nonlinear relationship between its input film density and output gray level. We may think of this as an ideal digitizer followed by a nonlinear point operation. We wish to design a second point operation that will restore linearity by reproducing the image as it would have come from the ideal digitizer. This process is shown in Figure 6–10. The gray-scale transformation of the digitizer either is known in functional form or can be measured. We wish to select $g(D)$ so that the net effect of the two cascaded point operations is zero; that is,

$$C(x, y) = g\{f[A(x, y)]\} = A(x, y) \tag{36}$$

This is satisfied by

$$g(D) = f^{-1}(D) \tag{37}$$

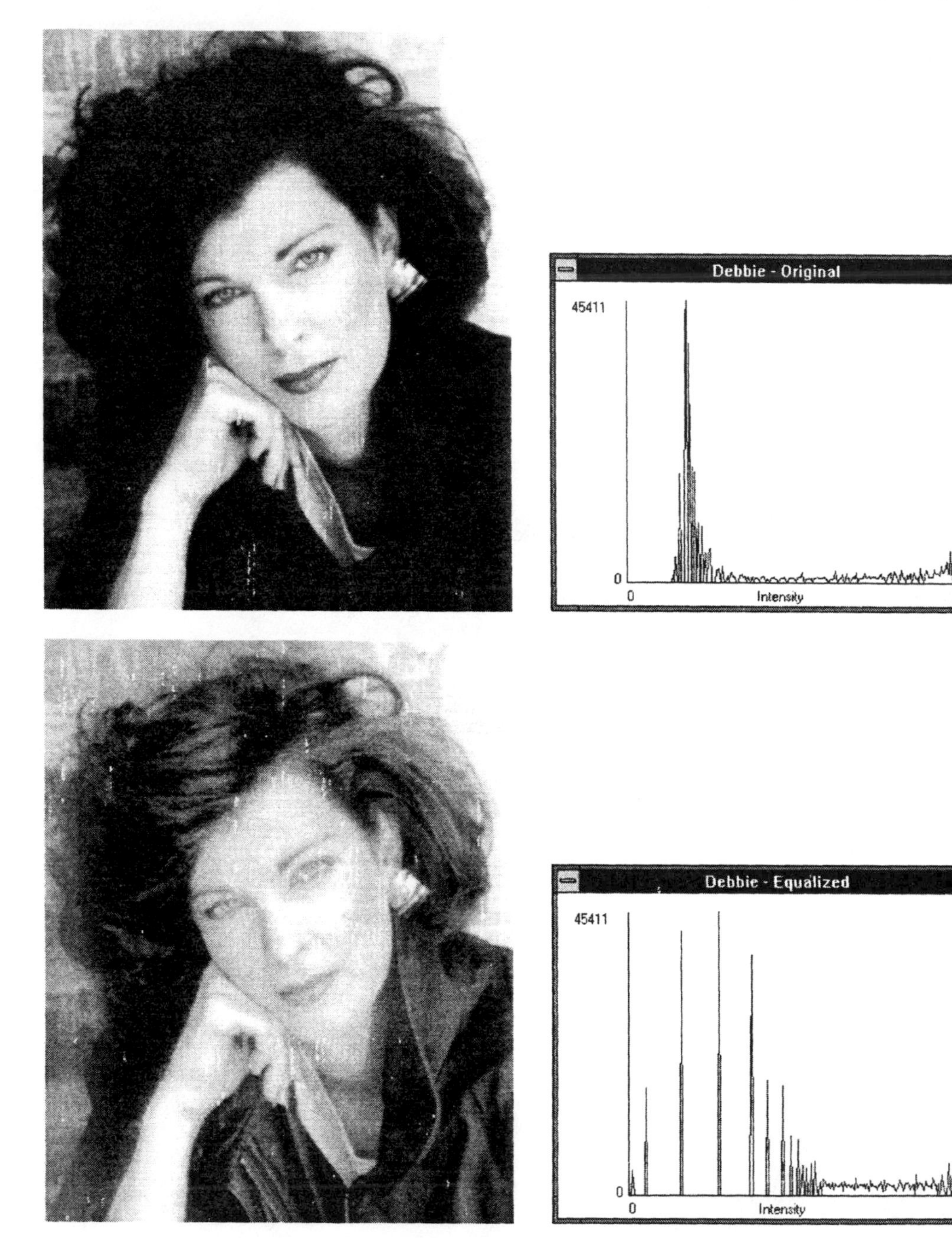

Figure 6–9 Histogram equalization

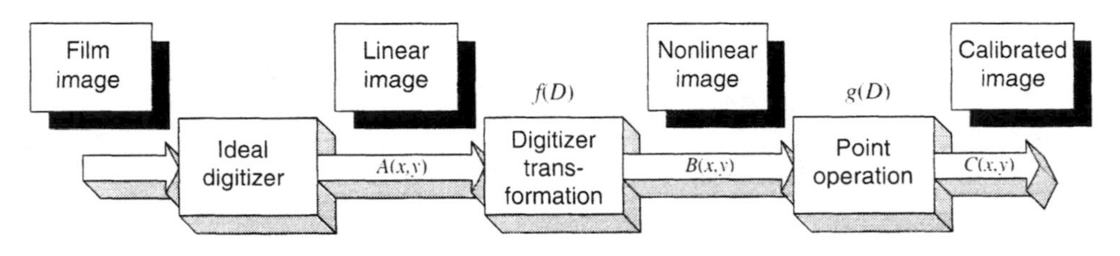

Figure 6–10 Photometric calibration

since the effect of a point operation is undone by its inverse function.

The digitizer's gray-scale transfer curve $f(D)$ can be measured by digitizing a linear gray-wedge test image. This function is normally nondecreasing and easily inverted numerically to produce the required gray-scale transformation. Difficulty may be encountered if digitizer saturation drives the slope of $f(D)$ to zero.

As an example of photometric calibration, consider the digitizer transfer curve

$$D_B = f(D_A) = aD_A^2 + b \tag{38}$$

We can solve Eq. (38) for D_A, and the required transformation is

$$g(D_B) = \sqrt{\frac{D_B - b}{a}} \tag{39}$$

Substituting Eq. (38) into Eq. (39) produces

$$D_C = g(D_B) = D_A \tag{40}$$

as expected.

Spatial Variation. Digitizers that measure each pixel with the same sensing device generally have a gray-scale sensitivity function that is constant throughout the image. Other digitizers, such as the vidicon or CCD, may have spatially variant sensitivity, different from one pixel to the next. In this case, a simple point operation is not sufficient, and an algebraic operation may be required, as discussed in the next chapter. It may be necessary to use a spatially variant point operation, implemented by dividing the image into regions and performing a separate point operation in each region. It might be practical to specify the functional form of a spatially variant gray-scale transformation. While a spatially variant point operation does not fit the definition offered at the beginning of this chapter, we may consider it a generalization of the original concept.

In extreme cases, it may be necessary to specify a unique point operation for each picture element. For the Mariner Venus/Mercury 1973 mission, for example, nine different flat field calibration images were taken at different illumination levels before the cameras were flown. This defined, for each pixel, a nine-point piecewise-linear digitizer transfer curve. These were inverted to form individual piecewise-linear gray-level transformations for each pixel. While the method required storing a considerable amount of data, it produced previously unattained photometric accuracy.

Figure 6–11(a) shows a flat-field image taken by the B camera of Mariner 10, after contrast enhancement by a factor of ten. The shading pattern occupies about 25 of the 256 gray levels. After calibration the shading pattern occupies only about 5 gray levels. Figure 6–11(b) shows the calibrated flat field after a contrast enhancement by a factor of 50.

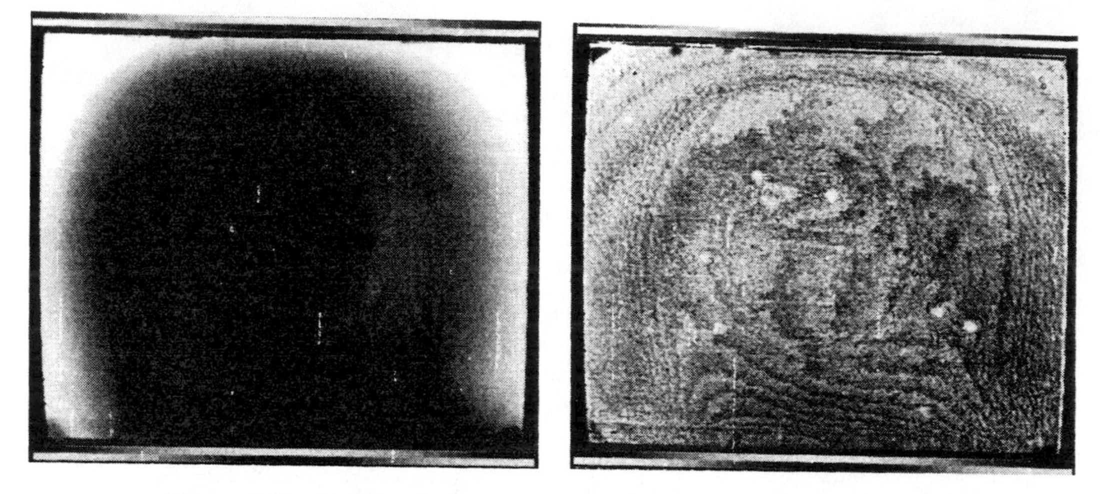

Figure 6–11 MVM'73 photometric calibration example: (a) flat field image before calibration, contrast × 10; (b) after calibration, contrast × 50 (Courtesy NASA/JPL)

6.3.4 Display Calibration

One can use an approach similar to the preceding to design a point operation that compensates for display nonlinearity. In this case, one would model the imperfect display as an ideal display preceded by a nonlinear point operation, as shown in Figure 6–12. The transformation $g(D)$ would be given, and $f(D)$ would have to be determined. Since we wish to undo $g(D)$ in advance, the desired gray-scale transformation is given by

$$f(D) = g^{-1}(D) \tag{41}$$

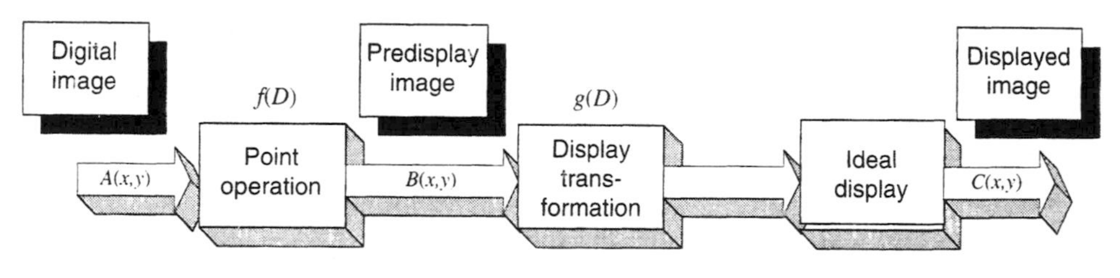

Figure 6–12 Display calibration

6.4 SUMMARY OF IMPORTANT POINTS

1. Point operations transform the gray scale of an image.
2. Point operations are useful for photometric calibration, display calibration, enhancement, and histogram modification.
3. A point operation is specified by the gray-scale transformation function that expresses the mapping between input and output gray-level values.

4. The histogram of an image following a specified point operation can be computed from Eq. (13).
5. A linear point operation can only stretch or compress the histogram and shift it right or left.
6. The cumulative distribution function (normalized area function) is the point operation that flattens the histogram.
7. The histogram of an image can be brought into a desired form by the concatenation of a point operation that flattens the original histogram, followed by the inverse of one that flattens the desired histogram (Eq. 35).
8. Photometric calibration of a digitized image is accomplished by a gray-scale transformation that is the inverse of the digitizer's nonlinear sensitivity curve (Eq. 37).
9. Display calibration for a digital image is accomplished by a gray-scale transformation that is the inverse of the display device's nonlinear response curve (Eq. 41).

PROBLEMS

1. What values of a and b in a linear stretch will move the two peaks of a bimodal histogram from 23 and 155 to 16 and 240, respectively? Sketch the gray-scale transformation (GST) function and the two histograms.
2. What values of a and b in a linear stretch will move A and B, where $0 \le A < B \le 255$, to zero and D_m, respectively? Sketch the GST function for $A = 32$, $B = 200$, and $D_m = 255$.
3. Develop a function based on the hyperbolic tangent function. Express it in a form similar to Eq. (4). Assume that $D_{max} = 63$. If the histogram of the input image is $5G[2,20,D] + G[5,35,D]$, sketch the histogram of the output image when $\alpha = 1.0$. What does this point operation do to the midrange? $G(\mu, \sigma, x)$ = Gaussian
4. Develop a GST function based on the hyperbolic sine function. Express it in a form similar to Eq. (4). Assume that $D_{max} = 63$. If the histogram of the input image is $5G[2,20,D] + G[5,35,D]$, sketch the histogram of the output image when $\alpha = 1.0$. What does this point operation do to the midrange?
5. An eight-bit image has a histogram given by $H(D) = 1{,}704\sin(\pi D/255)$. Derive an expression for the GST function that will flatten that histogram. Sketch the histogram and the GST function. Use Eq. (13) to show that the GST function derived in this problem actually produces a flat output histogram.
6. If $H_1(D) = 12A_o[(D/D_m)^2 - (D/D_m)^3]$, sketch the GST function that will flatten H_1.
7. Suppose you have two photographs of a building taken by different persons standing in the same spot four hours apart on the same day. During the time between the photos, three shots were fired from one of the windows. Detectives investigating the shooting do not know which office was used. Visual examination of the film failed to show whether any of the windows was either opened or closed during the time in question. The detectives want to know, however, whether the position of any of the windows may have changed slightly during that period.

   You carefully digitized, aligned, and subtracted the two images (more on that in Chapter 7). Differences in cameras, film, and lighting, however, rendered your difference image inconclusive. To a good approximation, the histograms of the two images are given by the beta distribution

$$H(D) = A_o C\left(\frac{D}{D_m}\right)^{\alpha}\left(1 - \frac{D}{D_m}\right)^{\beta} \qquad C = \frac{(\alpha + \beta + 1)!}{\alpha!\,\beta!}$$

where $D_m = 63$, $\alpha = 1$ and $\beta = 1$ for the first image, and $\alpha = 2$ and $\beta = 1$ for the second image. What GST function would: (a) flatten the histogram of the first image? Sketch the function. (b) flatten the histogram of the second image? Sketch the function. (c) make the histogram of the second image match that of the first? Sketch the function. (d) make the histogram of the first image match that of the second? Sketch the function. If the result were conclusive, how much do you think the FBI would pay you for your work? If the result were inconclusive, how much do you think one of the supermarket tabloids would pay you for your processed image?

8. Suppose you have two X-ray films taken immediately before and after injection of contrast medium (dye) into the arteries of a patient's heart. Radiologists are studying the films to determine whether coronary bypass surgery or heart valve replacement is required. Normally they use digital image subtraction to visualize the dye as it fills the arterial passageways. In this case, however, problems in exposure and development of the two films make a direct comparison inconclusive. The patient is too weak to undergo the angiography procedure again. Only digital subtraction (Chapter 7) of the two images will reveal the extent of coronary disease.

To a good approximation, the histograms of the two images are given by the Rayleigh distribution

$$H(D) = \frac{DD_m}{\alpha^2} e^{-\frac{D^2}{2\alpha^2}}$$

where $D_m = 63$, $\alpha = 16$ for the first image, and $\alpha = 24$ for the second image. What GST function would: (a) flatten the histogram of the preinjection image? Sketch the function. (b) flatten the histogram of the postinjection image? Sketch the function. (c) make the histogram of the postinjection image match that of the preinjection image? Sketch the function. (d) make the histogram of the preinjection image match that of the postinjection image? Sketch the function.

9. Suppose you have two aerial reconnaissance photos taken immediately before and after an air strike against a surface-to-air missile site. The generals are studying the films to determine the extent of damage to the enemy's radar control facilities. Cloud movement over the battlefield, combined with an accidental exposure of the film to light in the darkroom, make a direct comparison inconclusive. It is dangerous to risk another reconnaissance flight because the missiles may not have been knocked out. Only digital subtraction (Chapter 7) of the two images will reveal the extent of the damage.

To a good approximation, the histograms of the two images are given by the gamma distribution

$$H(D) = \frac{DD_m}{\beta^2} e^{-\frac{D}{\beta}}$$

where $D_m = 63$, $\beta = 8$ for the first image, and $\beta = 12$ for the second image. What GST function would: (a) flatten the histogram of the preattack image? Sketch the function. (b) flatten the histogram of the postattack image? Sketch the function. (c) make the histogram of the postattack image match that of the preattack image? Sketch the function. (d) make the histogram of the preattack image match that of the postattack image? Sketch the function.

10. A digitizer produces gray levels that are related to the brightness of a scene by

$$f(x) = \frac{D_m}{2}\left[1 - \cos\left(\frac{\pi x}{D_m}\right)\right]$$

Derive an expression for the GST function of a point operation that will linearize the relation between brightness and gray level.

11. A CCD camera mounted on a microscope produces, in digitized images, gray levels that are proportional to image brightness. Derive an expression for the GST function of a point operation that will linearize the relation between gray level and the optical density (Sec. 2.7.1) of the specimen.

12. An image display monitor has a gamma of 0.8. Derive an expression for the GST function of a point operation that will display images (on that same monitor) so that it appears to have a gamma of 1.4. Note: $f(x) = D_m (x/D_m)^{\gamma}$

13. If $H_1(D) = 5G(2,10,D) + G(5,45,D)$, $D_m = 63$ and $f(D)$ is given by Eq. (5), sketch $H_1(D)$, $f(D)$, $f'(D)$, f^{-1}, and the output histogram $H_2(D)$ for $\alpha = 0.7$. What value of α will move the left-hand peak to a gray level of 15?

PROJECTS

1. Implement a computer program that, given an input histogram as an array, will show, in real time, a graph of what the output histogram of a linear stretch will be, as you adjust the parameters A and B. (See Problem 2.)
2. Implement a computer program that, given an input histogram as an array, will show, in real time, a graph of what the output histogram of a nonlinear stretch will be as you adjust the parameter α. Base the GST function on either the sine, arc sine, tangent, arc tangent, hyperbolic sin (sinh), or hyperbolic tangent (tanh) function.
3. Implement a computer program that (1) allows you to design a GST function graphically, (2) performs the point operation, and (3) displays the input and output images and histograms simultaneously. Use a monotonic functional form (linear, sine, tanh, etc.) for the transformation, leaving at least one adjustable parameter.
4. Implement a point operation program for histogram flattening and test the program on several images. Use numerical methods rather than assuming a functional form for the input histogram.
5. Implement a point operation program that will output an image with a Gaussian histogram with specified μ and σ, and test the program on several images. Use numerical methods on the actual input histogram rather than assuming a functional form.
6. Implement a point operation program that will stretch one image to match the histogram of another, and test the program on several images. Use numerical methods based on the actual histograms rather than assuming a functional form for the two histograms.

CHAPTER 7

Algebraic Operations

7.1 INTRODUCTION

Algebraic operations are operations that produce an output image which is the pixel-by-pixel sum, difference, product, or quotient of two input images. In the case of sums and products, more than two input images may be involved. In general, one of the input images may be a constant. However, addition, subtraction, multiplication, and division by a constant can be treated as a linear point operation, as discussed in Chapter 6. The same is true for cases where the input images are identical.

7.1.1 Definitions

The four algebraic image-processing operations are expressed mathematically as

$$C(x, y) = A(x, y) + B(x, y) \tag{1}$$

$$C(x, y) = A(x, y) - B(x, y) \tag{2}$$

$$C(x, y) = A(x, y) \times B(x, y) \tag{3}$$

$$C(x, y) = A(x, y) \div B(x, y) \tag{4}$$

where $A(x, y)$ and $B(x, y)$ are the input images and $C(x, y)$ is the output image. By making suitable combinations, one may form complex algebraic equations involving several images.

7.1.2 Uses of Algebraic Operations

An important application of image addition is averaging together multiple images of the same scene. This is used frequently and successfully to reduce the effects of additive random noise. Image addition may also be used to superimpose the contents of one image upon another, producing a *double-exposure* effect.

Image subtraction can be used to remove an undesired additive pattern from an image. This may be a slowly varying background shading pattern, a periodic noise pattern, or any other additive contamination that is known at every point in the image. Subtraction is also useful in detecting changes between two images of the same scene. For example, one could detect motion by subtracting sequential images of a scene. Image subtraction is also required to compute the gradient, a useful function for locating edges.

Multiplication and division find less application in digital image processing, but they do have important uses. Both can be used to correct for the effects of a digitizer in which the sensitivity of the light sensor varies from point to point within the image. Division can produce ratio images that are important in color and multispectral image analysis (Chapter 21). Multiplication by a *mask image* can blot out certain portions of an image, leaving only the objects of interest.

7.2 ALGEBRAIC OPERATIONS AND THE HISTOGRAM

In this section, we examine the output histogram of sum and difference operations. This yields insight into the operations and the scaling necessary to keep the output gray levels within range. We also present a technique for determining the integrated optical density (IOD) of an image contaminated by additive random noise.

7.2.1 Histograms of Sum Images

Suppose, for the operation in Eq. (1), that the input images $A(x, y)$ and $B(x, y)$ have gray-level histograms $H_A(D)$ and $H_B(D)$, respectively. We wish to determine the output histogram $H_C(D)$. If the input images are identical, or if one is constant, the process reduces to a point operation, and the results of Chapter 6 apply. In this section, we address the case where the images are uncorrelated.

The two input images are uncorrelated if their joint two-dimensional histogram is

$$H_{AB}(D_A, D_B) = H_A(D_A)H_B(D_B) \tag{5}$$

the product of the two individual image histograms. In practical terms, this means that the images are unrelated.

Note that Eq. (5) is not satisfied if the input images are identical, but it is satisfied if at least one image is random and statistically independent of the other.

We can reduce a two-dimensional histogram to a one-dimensional marginal histogram by integrating over one of the independent variables; that is,

$$H(D_A) = \int_{-\infty}^{\infty} H_{AB}(D_A, D_B)dD_B \tag{6}$$

Thus, given Eq. (5), we may produce a one-dimensional histogram by

$$H(D) = \int_{-\infty}^{\infty} H_A(D_A)H_B(D_B)dD_B \tag{7}$$

Eq. (1) implies, however, that at every point,

$$D_A = D_C - D_B \tag{8}$$

Substituting this into the right side of Eq. (7) yields

$$H(D) = \int_{-\infty}^{\infty} H_A(D_C - D_B)H_B(D_B)dD_B \tag{9}$$

This one-dimensional histogram is a function of output gray level and thus is the output histogram. We may now write the output histogram of an operation that sums uncorrelated images as

$$H_C(D_C) = H_A(D_A) * H_B(D_B) \tag{10}$$

where the $*$ indicates the convolution operation defined by the integral in Eq. (9).

The convolution integral is discussed in more detail in Chapter 9, but the following development illustrates its operation. Suppose we wish to convolve two identical Gaussian functions, each given by e^{-x^2}. Then

$$e^{-x^2} * e^{-x^2} = \int_{-\infty}^{\infty} e^{-y^2} e^{-(x-y)^2} dy \tag{11}$$

Expanding the exponent and collecting terms produces

$$e^{-x^2} * e^{-x^2} = \int_{-\infty}^{\infty} e^{-(x^2 - 2xy - 2y^2)} dy \tag{12}$$

We now insert a product that is unity, yielding

$$e^{-x^2} * e^{-x^2} = \int_{-\infty}^{\infty} e^{-(x^2 - 2xy - 2y^2)} e^{+x^2/2} e^{-x^2/2} dy \tag{13}$$

which may be rearranged as

$$e^{-x^2} * e^{-x^2} = \int_{-\infty}^{\infty} e^{-2(x^2/4 - xy + y^2)} e^{-x^2/2} dy \tag{14}$$

This may be factored in the exponent to yield

$$e^{-x^2} * e^{-x^2} = \int_{-\infty}^{\infty} e^{-2(y - x/2)^2} e^{-x^2/2} dy \tag{15}$$

which may be rearranged to produce

$$e^{-x^2} * e^{-x^2} = e^{-x^2/2} \int_{-\infty}^{\infty} e^{-(y - x/2)^2/[2(1/4)]} dy \tag{16}$$

We now use a property of the Gaussian function, namely, that

$$\int_{-\infty}^{\infty} e^{-(x-\mu)^2/2\sigma^2} dx = \sqrt{2\pi\sigma^2} \tag{17}$$

and Eq. (16) becomes

$$e^{-x^2} * e^{-x^2} = \sqrt{2\pi\left(\frac{1}{4}\right)} e^{-x^2/2} \tag{18}$$

A similar but more general development shows that

$$A_1 e^{-(x-\mu_1)^2/2\sigma_1^2} * A_2 e^{-(x-\mu_2)^2/2\sigma_2^2} = A_1 A_2 \sqrt{2\pi\sigma_1\sigma_2} e^{-(x-\mu_3)^2/2\sigma_3^2} \tag{19}$$

where

$$\mu_3 = \mu_1 + \mu_2 \tag{20}$$

and

$$\sigma_3^2 = \sigma_1^2 + \sigma_2^2 \tag{21}$$

This means that convolving two Gaussians produces a third Gaussian that is shifted and broader, as Eq. (21) indicates.

In general, convolution "smears" a function. Since adding uncorrelated images convolves their histograms, we can expect the sum of uncorrelated images to occupy a broader gray level range than that of its component images. Further discussion of the convolution operation is reserved for Chapter 9.

7.2.2 Histograms of Difference Images

For subtraction of uncorrelated images, Eq. (10) holds after redefinition of one image as its negative. Thus, addition and subtraction of uncorrelated images behave similarly. There is, however, one case of image subtraction that bears further consideration: the subtraction of near-identical images that are slightly misaligned. This situation arises when sequential images of a scene are subtracted to detect motion or other change, and exact registration is not maintained.

Suppose the difference image is given by

$$C(x, y) = A(x, y) - A(x + \Delta x, y) \tag{22}$$

which may be approximated by

$$C(x, y) \approx \frac{\partial}{\partial x} A(x, y)\Delta x \tag{23}$$

if Δx is small.

Notice that $\partial A/\partial x$ is itself an image with a histogram we may denote by $H_A'(D)$. Thus, the histogram of the displaced difference image is

$$H_C(D) \approx \frac{1}{\Delta x} H_A'(D/\Delta x) \tag{24}$$

(Recall, from Chapter 6, the effect of a multiplicative constant.) Hence, subtracting slightly misaligned copies of an image produces a partial derivative image. The direction of the partial derivative is the same as that of the displacement.

7.2.3 IOD of a Noisy Image

Suppose we have an image containing a spot on a uniform, contrasting background. Suppose also that the image has been contaminated by additive random noise, and we wish to determine the IOD of the spot. We model the situation as follows: Let $S(x, y)$ represent the noise-free image of the spot and $N(x, y)$ the noise image defined on the same region. Then the observed image is

$$M(x, y) = S(x, y) + N(x, y) \tag{25}$$

The histograms of the three images are shown in Figure 7–1. We assume that the noise has a symmetrical histogram centered on the unknown mean value N_0 and that the spot histogram has a sharp spike at the origin due to the uniform background surrounding the spot.

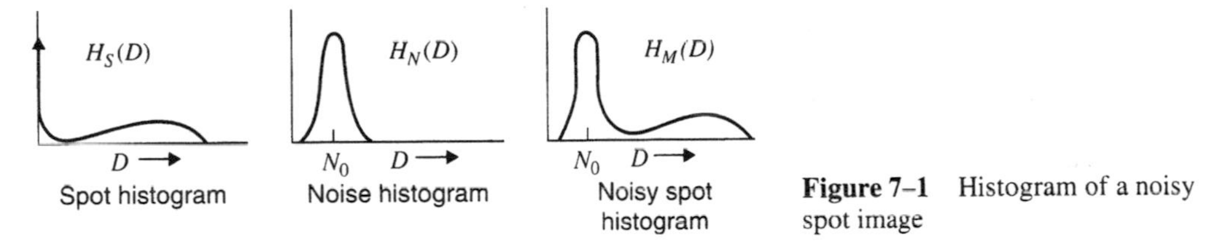

Figure 7–1 Histogram of a noisy spot image

We wish to determine

$$IOD_S = \int_0^a \int_0^b S(x, y)dx\,dy = \int_0^a \int_0^b M(x, y)dx\,dy - \int_0^a \int_0^b N(x, y)dx\,dy \tag{26}$$

Substituting the property of Chapter 5, Eq. (12), produces

$$IOD_S = \int_0^\infty DH_M(D)dD - N_0A \tag{27}$$

where A is the area of the region of definition. Now, recalling Eq. (4) of Chapter 5, we can write

$$A = \int_0^\infty H_M(D)dD \tag{28}$$

since the total areas of the noise and observed images are the same. Now

$$IOD_S = \int_0^\infty DH_M(D)dD - N_0 \int_0^\infty H_M(D)dD \tag{29}$$

and rearrangement yields

$$IOD_S = \int_0^\infty (D - N_0)H_M(D)dD \tag{30}$$

This is a simple expression for IOD, provided that N_0 can be determined. One could estimate N_0 by averaging the gray level of a small area distant from the spot.

Under a set of reasonable assumptions, however, we can argue that the leftmost peak of the histogram $H_M(D)$ occurs at N_0. Assume that the noise histogram $H_N(D)$ is symmetrical, so that its peak occurs at the mean value N_0. Since $N(x, y)$ is random, the two images are uncorrelated. Eq. (10) states that the sum of uncorrelated images has a histogram that is the convolution of the histograms of the two original images. Furthermore, $H_S(D)$ is dominated by the spike at $D = 0$.

We show in Chapter 9 that the spike (impulse) is the identity function under convolution [Chapter 9, Eq. (67)]. Thus, the histogram $H_M(D)$ will be dominated by a peak at N_0, as shown in Figure 7–1. The asymmetry of $H_S(D)$ will skew the peak slightly to the right, but the location of the peak remains a good estimate of N_0 if the spot is surrounded by a reasonable amount of background. Thus, the histogram of a noisy spot image yields an easily computed estimate of the noise-free IOD.

7.3 APPLICATIONS OF ALGEBRAIC OPERATIONS

In this section, we illustrate several situations in which algebraic operations are useful.

7.3.1 Averaging for Noise Reduction

In many applications, it is possible to obtain multiple images of a stationary scene. If these images are contaminated by an additive random noise source, the multiple images may be averaged to reduce the noise. In the averaging process, the stationary component of the image is unchanged, whereas the noise pattern, different from one image to the next, builds up more slowly in the summation.

Suppose we have a set of M images of the form

$$D_i(x, y) = S(x, y) + N_i(x, y) \tag{31}$$

where $S(x, y)$ is the image of interest and the $N_i(x, y)$ are noise images such as those introduced by film grain or electronic noise in a digitizing system. Each image in the set is degraded by a different noise image. While we do not know these noise images exactly, we assume that each comes from an ensemble of uncorrelated random noise images, all having zero mean value. This means that

$$\varepsilon\{N_i(x, y)\} = 0 \tag{32}$$

$$\varepsilon\{N_i(x, y) + N_j(x, y)\} = \varepsilon\{N_i(x, y)\} + \varepsilon\{N_j(x, y)\} \qquad (i \neq j) \tag{33}$$

and

$$\varepsilon\{N_i(x, y)N_j(x, y)\} = \varepsilon\{N_i(x, y)\}\varepsilon\{N_j(x, y)\} \qquad (i \neq j) \tag{34}$$

where $\varepsilon\{\ \}$ indicates the expectation operator; that is, $\varepsilon\{N_i(x, y)\}$ is the average of the points at x, y of all the noise images in the ith ensemble. Expectation and random variables are discussed in more detail in Chapter 11.

For any point in the image, we may define the signal-to-noise power ratio as

$$P(x, y) = \frac{S^2(x, y)}{\varepsilon\{N^2(x, y)\}} \tag{35}$$

If we average M images to form

$$\bar{D}(x, y) = \frac{1}{M}\sum_{i=1}^{M}[S(x, y) + N_i(x, y)] \tag{36}$$

the signal-to-noise power ratio becomes

$$\bar{P}(x, y) = \frac{S^2(x, y)}{\varepsilon\left\{\left[\left(\frac{1}{M}\right)\sum_{i=1}^{M} N_i(x, y)\right]^2\right\}} \tag{37}$$

The numerator is unchanged because averaging does not affect the signal component.

We may factor $1/M$ out of the denominator to obtain

$$\bar{P}(x, y) = \frac{S^2(x, y)}{\frac{1}{M^2}\varepsilon\left\{\sum_{i=1}^{M} N_i(x, y)^2\right\}} \tag{38}$$

or

$$\bar{P}(x, y) = \frac{M^2 S^2(x, y)}{\varepsilon\left\{\sum_{i=1}^{M}\sum_{j=1}^{M} N_i(x, y)N_j(x, y)\right\}} \tag{39}$$

Using the property of Eq. (33), we may separate the denominator into two terms, producing

$$\bar{P}(x, y) = \frac{M^2 S^2(x, y)}{\varepsilon\left\{\sum_{i=1}^{M} N_i^2(x, y)\right\} + \varepsilon\left\{\underbrace{\sum_{i=1}^{M}\sum_{j=1}^{M}}_{i \neq j} N_i(x, y)N_j(x, y)\right\}} \tag{40}$$

The second term may be factored according to Eq. (34) while the first term may be written as a sum of expectations, yielding

$$\bar{P}(x, y) = \frac{M^2 S^2(x, y)}{\sum_{i=1}^{M}\varepsilon\{N_i^2(x, y)\} + \underbrace{\sum_{i=1}^{M}\sum_{j=1}^{M}}_{i \neq j}\varepsilon\{N_i(x, y)\}\varepsilon\{N_j(x, y)\}} \tag{41}$$

Now, Eq. (32) implies that the second term in the denominator is zero. Furthermore, since the M noise samples come from the same ensemble, all terms in the first summation are identical. Therefore,

$$\bar{P}(x, y) = \frac{M^2 S^2(x, y)}{M\varepsilon\{N^2(x, y)\}} = MP(x, y) \tag{42}$$

Thus, averaging M images increases the signal-to-noise power ratio by the factor M at all points in the image. The signal-to-noise amplitude ratio is the square root of the power ratio, i.e.,

$$\overline{\text{SNR}} = \sqrt{\overline{P}(x, y)} = \sqrt{M}\sqrt{P(x, y)} \tag{43}$$

and it goes up by the square root of the number of images averaged.

Figure 7–2 illustrates the effect of image averaging. Part (a) shows a telescope photograph of a star cluster, and the image is contaminated by film grain noise. The images in parts (b), (c), and (d) are the averages of two, four, and eight consecutive photographs of the star cluster, respectively. The improvement in the image results because the film grain pattern builds up in the summation more slowly than does the image of the stationary star cluster.

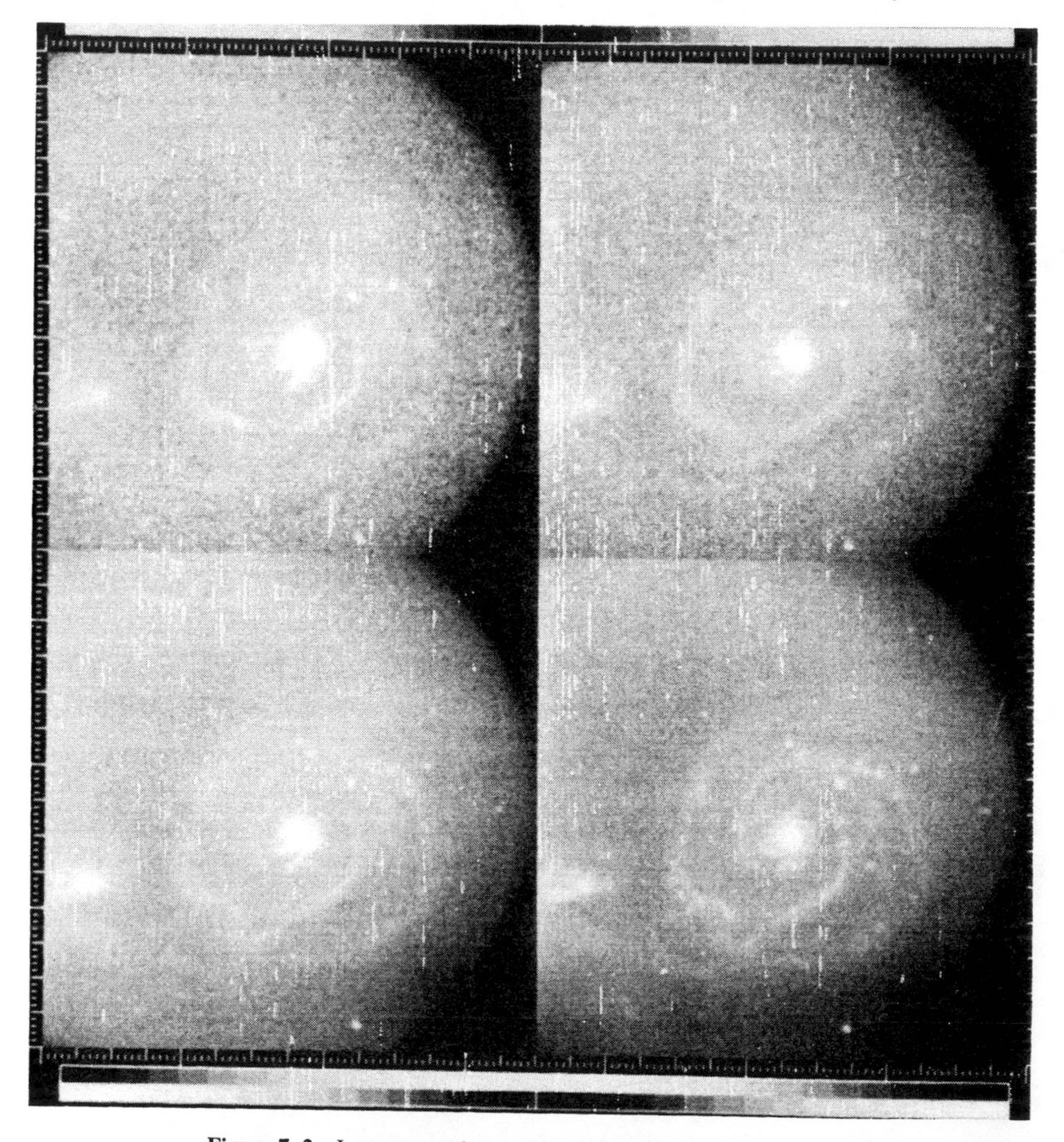

Figure 7–2 Image averaging to reduce film grain noise (Courtesy NASA-JPL)

7.3.2 Image Subtraction

7.3.2.1 Background Subtraction

The technique of subtracting a superimposed noise pattern is illustrated in Figure 7–3. Part (a) shows a digitized light microscope image containing two human metaphase chromosome spreads. The image is contaminated by a slowly varying background shading pattern. In part (b), the microscope stage is moved to bring an empty field beneath the objective lens. Thus, (b) contains only the background shading pattern. In part (c), the background is subtracted from the original image of part (a), thus removing the shading. A constant value of 64 is added to each pixel after the subtraction. Below each image appears its gray-level histogram. Notice the complexity of the background histogram, how it affects the histogram of part (a), and how the histogram of part (c) resembles the ideal histogram of dark objects on a uniform, white background.

The background subtraction technique works well in Figure 7–3 because the image comes from an optical density digitizer used in a case in which the background is superimposed. If some parameter other than optical density had been digitized, the subtraction would have been mathematically invalid and the removal of the background probably less effective.

The histogram in part (c) departs slightly from the ideal histogram. In particular, it has some pixels with gray level less than 64, which is the theoretical minimum. This results from noise in the digitizing process. Digitizer noise prevents background pixels in parts (a) and (b) from having identical gray level values.

7.3.2.2 Motion Detection

Figure 7–4 illustrates subtraction for motion detection. Parts (a) and (b) show sequential aerial photographs of a freeway. Part (c) is the difference image. The freeway and stationary

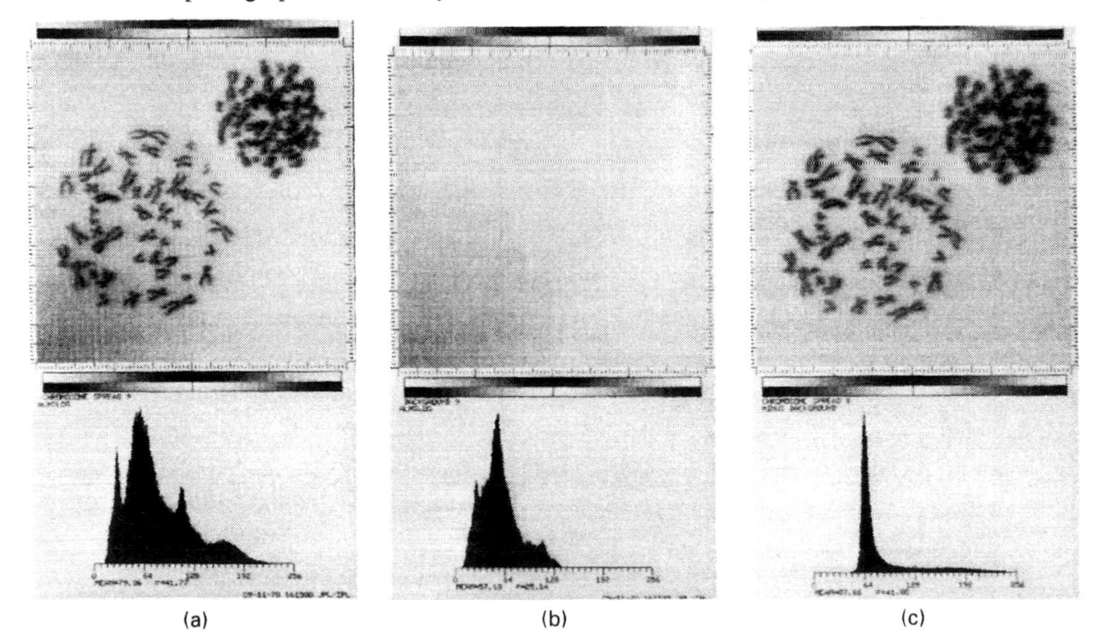

(a) (b) (c)

Figure 7–3 Background subtraction: (a) original image; (b) background; (c) difference image

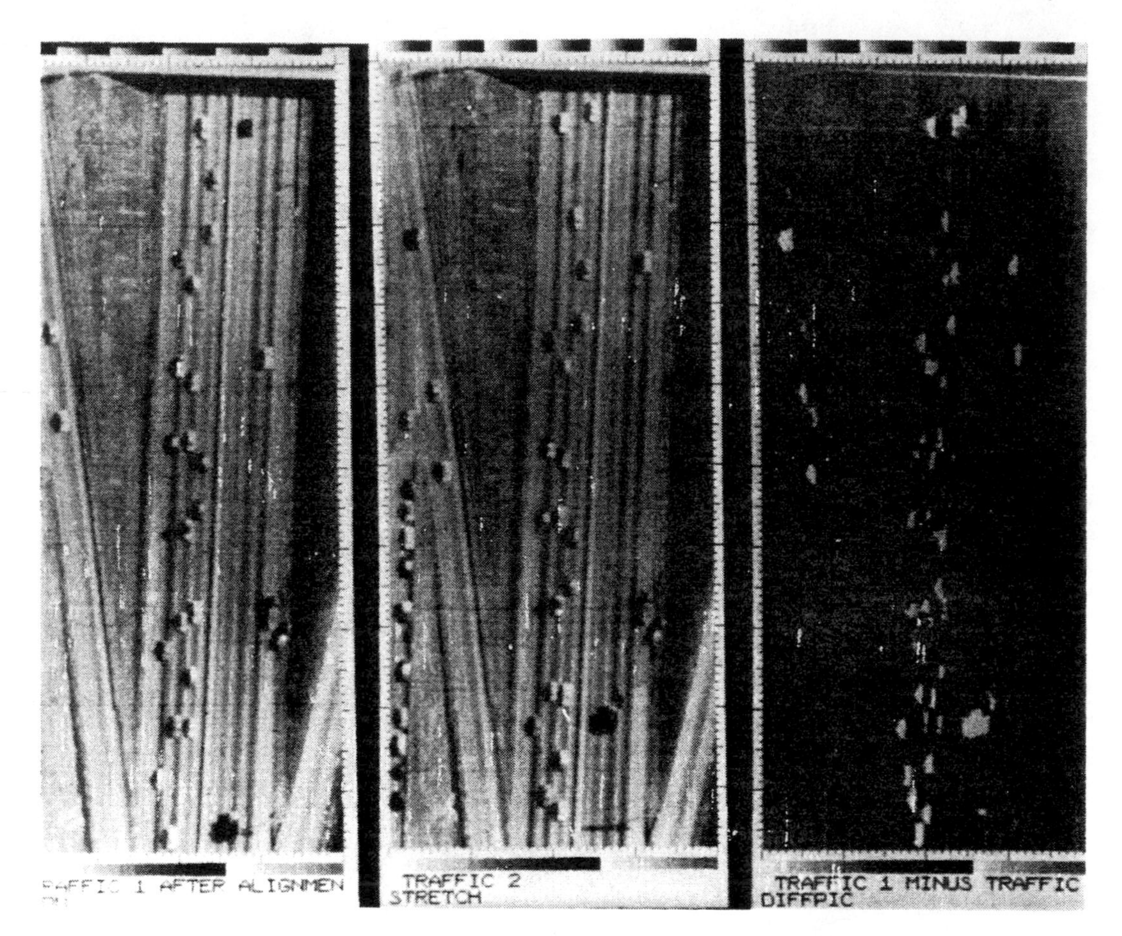

Figure 7–4 Motion detection in an aerial photograph (Courtesy NASA-JPL)

vehicles subtract out, while movement of the vehicles is apparent in the difference image. Part (c) is considerably easier to analyze for the detection of moving vehicles than are parts (a) and (b). Imperfect registration between the two frames causes some of the stationary structures to produce low-contrast, residual *derivative edges* in the difference image. [Recall Eq. (23).]

7.3.2.3 Gradient Magnitude

Image subtraction can also be used to produce an important derivative of the image, the gradient magnitude function. The gradient is defined as follows: Given a scalar function $f(x, y)$ and a coordinate system with unit vectors $\mathbf{i}$ in the x-direction and $\mathbf{j}$ in the y-direction, the gradient is the vector function

$$\nabla f(x, y) = \mathbf{i}\frac{\partial f(x, y)}{\partial x} + \mathbf{j}\frac{\partial f(x, y)}{\partial y} \tag{44}$$

where ∇ indicates the vector gradient operator. The vector $\nabla f(x, y)$ points in the direction of maximum upward slope, and its magnitude (length) is equal to the value of the slope. An important scalar function is the gradient magnitude, given by

$$|\nabla f(x, y)| = \sqrt{\left(\frac{\partial f}{\partial x}\right)^2 + \left(\frac{\partial f}{\partial y}\right)^2} \tag{45}$$

This represents the steepness of the slope at every point, but directional information is lost. Also, since the square root operation is computationally expensive, Eq. (45) is often approximated by the form

$$|\nabla f(x, y)| \approx \max\left[|f(x, y) - f(x + 1, y)|, |f(x, y) - f(x, y + 1)|\right] \tag{46}$$

that is, the maximum of the absolute vertical and horizontal neighboring pixel differences.

The gradient magnitude takes on large values in areas of steep slope, such as at the edges of objects. Figure 7–5 illustrates the gradient magnitude of a microscope image of a muscle biopsy specimen. The gradient magnitude is high at the edges and low in the interior of the uniformly gray fibers.

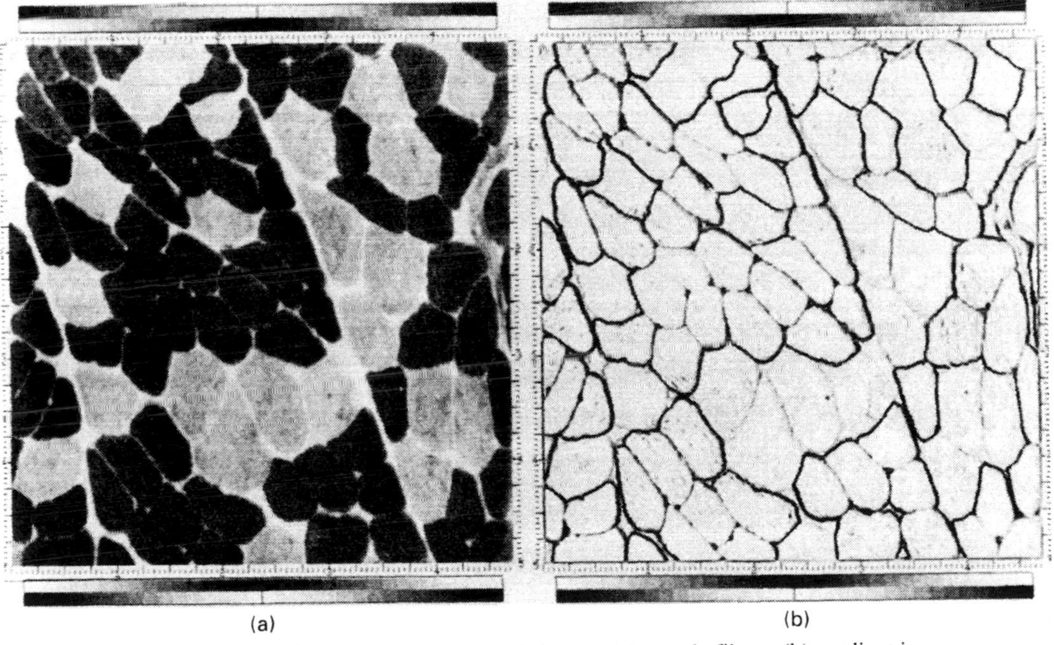

(a) (b)

Figure 7–5 A gradient magnitude image: (a) muscle fibers; (b) gradient image

7.3.3 Multiplication and Division

The multiplication operation can be used for masking portions of an image. The mask image is unity in areas to be left intact and zero in areas where the image content is to be suppressed. Multiplying an image by the mask will blot out, or drive to zero, the specified area. One may then produce a complementary mask for a second image that will blot out those areas retained in the first image. The two masked images may be added to compose the final product.

Division may be used to remove effects of a spatially varying digitizer sensitivity function. Division also can be used to generate ratio images that are useful in multispectral analysis. This technique is discussed in Chapter 21.

7.4 SUMMARY OF IMPORTANT POINTS

1. The histogram of the sum of two uncorrelated images is given by the convolution of the two input histograms.
2. Averaging N images of a stationary scene contaminated by random noise increases the signal-to-noise amplitude ratio by $\sqrt{N}$.
3. Subtracting slightly displaced identical images produces a partial derivative image.
4. The convolution of two Gaussian functions produces another, broader Gaussian.
5. In the convolution of two Gaussians, their means and variances add.
6. The IOD of a noisy image can be computed from the histogram of the image [Eq. (30)].
7. Image subtraction is useful for background removal and motion detection.
8. Image multiplication is useful for masking out a portion of an image.
9. Image division is useful for generating ratio images to extract color and spectral information from, and identify regions of different color in, an image.

PROBLEMS

1. Suppose you have two chest X rays from a patient taken eight months apart. Both films show a nodule that may or may not be malignant. Both the size and density of the nodule have changed during the period, but radiologists are unsure, after visual examination, if the nodule is getting better or worse. Below are histograms from a small region of each image containing the nodule. Low gray level represents dark on the film. Compute the area, IOD, and mean density of the nodule from each film. Is the nodule getting larger or smaller? Is it getting more or less dense? *Recommend* (but do not *prescribe,* unless you are licensed to practice medicine) the proper treatment—either surgery or a low-fat diet. Remember that the X ray is a negative image; that is, denser objects appear lighter.

   FEBRUARY:

   [0 500 8000 500 100 100 200 300 200 100 0 0 0 0 0 0]

   OCTOBER:

   [0 500 8000 500 100 0 0 100 200 300 200 100 0 0 0 0]

2. Suppose you have another patient with the following histograms:

   APRIL:

   [0 0 0 500 5000 500 200 100 100 200 300 200 100 0 0 0]

   NOVEMBER:

   [0 0 0 500 5250 500 200 100 100 150 200 150 50 0 0 0]

   Repeat the exercise in Problem 1 for this patient.

3. Below are the histograms of two 100- by 100-pixel, 16-gray level (0–15) images. What will be the histogram of their sum image?

   [0 0 0 10,000 0 0 0 0 0 0 0 0 0 0 0 0]

   [600 1000 1800 2500 1900 1100 800 200 0 0 0 0 0 0 0 0]

4. Suppose you have two diskettes, each containing a four-bit digitized image of a billiard table. (White is 15.) Both images were taken from the same camera position, one just prior to the final, game-winning shot (which sank the last three white balls) and the other immediately after the table had been cleared. Each diskette is accompanied by a histogram of its image. (See below.) Which image has balls in it? Sketch the two histograms and what the difference image histogram will look like if you subtract the image of the table only from the other image to produce an unshaded picture of the setup prior to the last shot.

   DISKETTE 1:

   [0 100 400 700 800 600 500 600 500 400 400 600 400 100 0 0]

   DISKETTE 2:

   [0 100 300 700 700 600 500 600 500 400 400 600 500 200 0 0]

5. Plot the two 16-level histograms below. Which one corresponds to a gradient magnitude image (possibly with a constant added)?

   [0 0 0 100 200 300 500 800 500 300 200 100 0 0 0 0]

   [0 0 0 100 300 500 400 200 300 500 300 200 100 100 0 0]

PROJECTS

1. Digitize an image of a street scene with and without cars in it. Subtract the image without cars from the image with cars to show the cars floating in space.
2. Digitize an image of a group of your friends and the same scene without the people. Subtract the latter image from the former image to show your friends floating in space.
3. Repeat Project 1 or 2, but shift the camera position slightly between images and compare the result.
4. Repeat Project 1 or 2, but change the lighting conditions slightly (e.g., take the picture after the sun goes behind a cloud, don't use a flash, etc.) and compare the result.
5. Subtract digital images of two frames of movie film or videotape, and use the subtracted image to count the number of moving objects there are.
6. Subtract digital images of two frames of movie film or videotape, and use the subtracted image to determine the velocity of a moving object that is shown. Specify how the pixel spacing and time interval were determined.
7. Digitize successive movie or video frames of a predominantly stationary scene, and use image averaging to cut the noise level in half. Point out the result of any movement in the images.
8. Develop (or obtain) a program that can compute the gradient magnitude image, and use the program to convert a photograph of a friend into a cartoon (black-on-white line drawing).
9. Digitize a scene through first a red and then a green filter, and use image division to produce ratio images that will isolate the different colored objects (e.g., fruit, flowers, toys, cars, etc.). Include a test target with black, white, and gray in the scene. Compute gray-level histograms of the test target in both images, and use the histograms for any photometric calibration required prior to generating the ratios. Comment on the effects of photometric calibration and motion of the camera.

CHAPTER 8

Geometric Operations

8.1 INTRODUCTION

Geometric operations change the spatial relationships among the objects in an image. Such operations may be thought of as moving things around within the image. The effect is the same as printing the image on a rubber sheet, stretching the rubber sheet, and tacking it down at various points. Actually, a geometric operation is much more general than that, since any point in the input image may move to any position in the output image. Such an unconstrained geometric operation would almost certainly scramble the image content, so geometric operations are generally constrained to preserve some semblance of order.

Two separate algorithms are required for a geometric operation. First, there must be an algorithm that defines the spatial transformation itself. This specifies the "motion" of each pixel as it "moves" from its initial to its final position in the image. Also required is an algorithm for gray-level interpolation. This is necessary because, in general, integer x, y positions in the input image map to fractional (noninteger) positions in the output image and conversely.

8.1.1 The Spatial Transformation

In most applications, it is desirable to preserve the continuity of curvilinear features and the connectivity of objects within the image. A less constrained spatial transformation algorithm would break up lines and objects and tend to "splatter" the contents of the image.

One could exhaustively specify the motion of each pixel in the image, but this would quickly become unwieldy, even for small images. It is more convenient to specify mathematically the spatial relationship between points in the input image and points in the output image. The general definition for a geometric operation is

$$g(x, y) = f(x', y') = f[a(x, y), b(x, y)] \qquad (1)$$

where $f(x, y)$ is the input image and $g(x, y)$ is the output image. The functions $a(x, y)$ and $b(x, y)$ uniquely specify the spatial transformation. If they are continuous, connectivity will be preserved within the image.

8.1.2 Gray-Level Interpolation

The second requirement for a geometric operation is an algorithm for the interpolation of gray-level values. In the input image $f(x, y)$, the gray-level values are defined only at integral values of x and y. Eq. (1), however, will in general dictate that the gray-level value for $g(x, y)$ be taken from $f(x, y)$ at fractional (nonintegral) coordinate positions. If the geometric operation is considered a mapping from f to g, pixels in f can map to positions between pixels in g and vice versa. For the purposes of this discussion, we stipulate that pixels be located exactly at integral coordinates of the sampling grid.

Armed with a spatial transformation and an algorithm for gray-level interpolation, we are prepared to perform a geometric operation. Usually, the gray-level interpolation algorithm is permanently established in the computer program. The algorithm defining the spatial transformation, however, is specified uniquely for the task at hand. Since the gray-level interpolation algorithm is always the same, or one of several options, it is the spatial transformation that defines a particular geometric operation.

8.1.3 Implementation

One can adopt either of two approaches when implementing a geometric operation. One can think of the operation as transferring the gray levels from the input image to the output image, pixel by pixel. If an input pixel maps to a position between four output pixels, then its gray level is divided among the four output pixels according to the interpolation rule. We call this the *pixel carry-over* or *forward-mapping* approach. (See Figure 8–1.)

An alternative, and more effective, implementation is achieved by the *pixel-filling* or *backward-mapping* algorithm. In this case, the output pixels are mapped back into the input image, one at a time, to establish their gray levels. If an output pixel falls between four input pixels, its gray level is determined by gray-level interpolation (Figure 8–1). The backward spatial transformation is the inverse of the forward transformation.

The forward-mapping algorithm is somewhat wasteful, since many input pixels might map to positions outside the border of the output image. Furthermore, each output pixel might be addressed several times, with many input pixels contributing to its final gray-level value. If the spatial transformation involves demagnification, more than four input pixels would contribute. If magnification were involved, certain of the output pixels might be missed when no input pixels mapped to positions near their location.

The backward-mapping algorithm, however, generates the output image pixel by pixel, line by line. The gray level of each pixel is uniquely determined by one interpolation step between, at most, four input pixels. The input image, of course, must be accessed randomly in a manner defined by the spatial transformation, and this can be quite complex. Nevertheless, the pixel-filling approach is the more practical algorithm for general use.

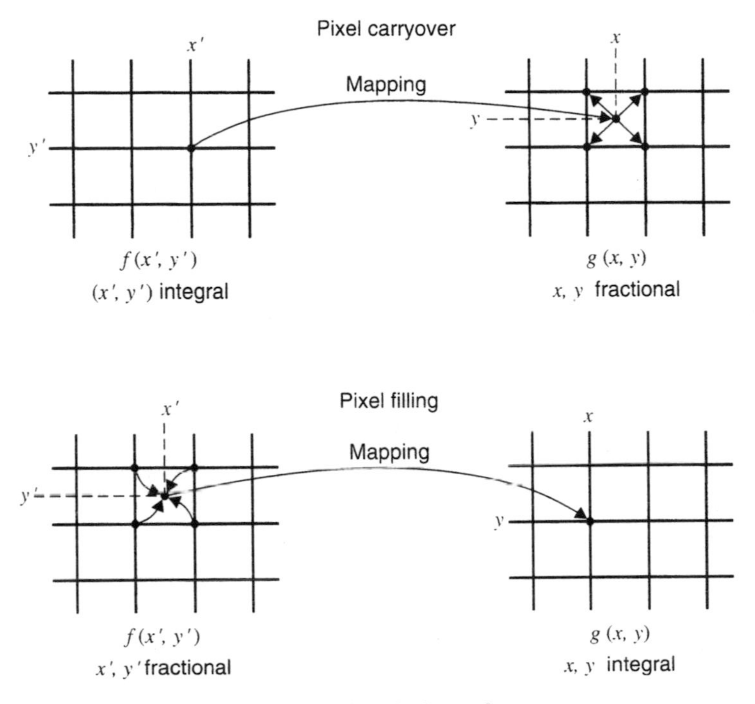

Figure 8–1 Pixel transfer

8.2 GRAY-LEVEL INTERPOLATION

Since output pixels map to fractional positions in the input image, they generally fall into the space between four input pixels. Interpolation is then necessary to determine what gray level corresponds to that position.

8.2.1 Nearest Neighbor Interpolation

The simplest interpolation scheme is the so-called zero-order, or *nearest neighbor,* interpolation. In this case, the gray level of the output pixel is taken to be that of the input pixel nearest the location to which the output pixel maps. This is computationally simple and produces acceptable results in many cases. However, nearest neighbor interpolation can introduce artifacts in images containing fine structure whose gray level changes significantly from one pixel to the next. Figure 8–2 shows an example of rotating images with nearest neighbor interpolation, with the resulting sawtooth effect at some of the edges.

8.2.2 Bilinear Interpolation

First-order, or *bilinear,* interpolation produces more desirable results than does zero-order interpolation, with only a slight increase in programming complexity and execution time. Since fitting a plane through four points is an overconstrained problem, first-order interpolation on a rectangular grid requires the bilinear function.

Let $f(x, y)$ be a function of two variables that is known at the vertices of the unit square. Suppose we desire to establish by interpolation the value of $f(x, y)$ at an arbitrary

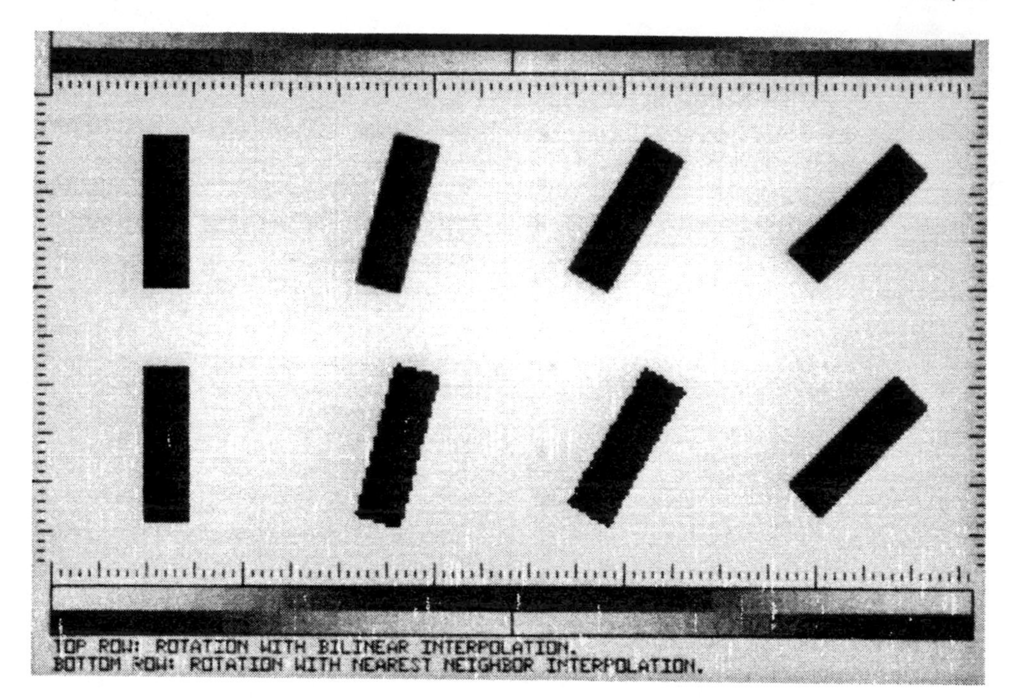

Figure 8–2 Comparison of zero-order and first-order gray level interpolation

point inside the square (Figure 8–3). We can do so by fitting a hyperbolic paraboloid, defined by the bilinear equation

$$f(x, y) = ax + by + cxy + d \tag{2}$$

through the four known values.

The four coefficients, a through d, are to be chosen so that $f(x, y)$ fits the known values at the four corners. There is a simple algorithm that produces a bilinear interpolation function

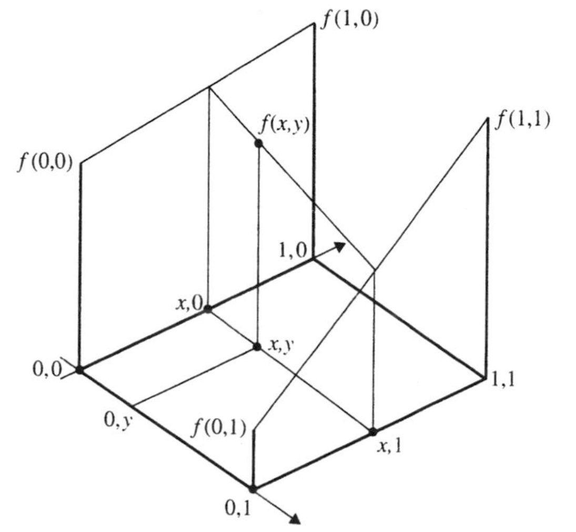

Figure 8–3 Bilinear interpolation

which fits $f(x, y)$ at the corners. First, we linearly interpolate between the upper two points to establish the value of

$$f(x, 0) = f(0, 0) + x[f(1, 0) - f(0, 0)] \tag{3}$$

Similarly, for the two lower points,

$$f(x, 1) = f(0, 1) + x[f(1, 1) - f(0, 1)] \tag{4}$$

Finally, we linearly interpolate vertically to determine the value of

$$f(x, y) = f(x, 0) + y[f(x, 1) - f(x, 0)] \tag{5}$$

Substituting Eqs. (3) and (4) into Eq. (5), expanding, and collecting terms produces

$$\begin{aligned} f(x, y) = {} & [f(1, 0) - f(0, 0)]\, x + [f(0, 1) - f(0, 0)]\, y \\ & + [f(1, 1) + f(0, 0) - f(0, 1) - f(1, 0)]\, xy + f(0, 0) \end{aligned} \tag{6}$$

which is in the form of Eq. (2) and is thus bilinear. Upon inspection, it is clear that Eq. (6) fits the four known values of $f(x, y)$ at the corners of the unit square.

Notice that if we hold either x or y constant, Eq. (2) becomes linear in the other variable. This illustrates that the hyperbolic paraboloid is a two-way ruled surface; that is, it intersects all planes parallel to the xz-plane and all planes parallel to the yz-plane in a straight line.

Bilinear interpolation can be implemented either directly, by Eq. (6), or by performing the triple linear interpolation given by Eqs. (3), (4), and (5). Since Eq. (6) involves four multiplications and eight additions or subtractions, geometric transformation programs typically do the latter, which requires only three multiplications and six additions or subtractions.

Although the foregoing development was performed on the unit square, it is easily generalized by an integer translation, after which x and y represent the fractional pixel position. Figure 8–2 compares bilinear with nearest neighbor interpolation.

When adjacent four-pixel neighborhoods are interpolated with the bilinear equation, the resulting surfaces match in amplitude at the neighborhood boundaries, but do not match in slope. Thus, a surface generated by piecewise bilinear interpolation is continuous, but its derivatives, in general, are discontinuous at the neighborhood boundaries.

8.2.3 Higher Order Interpolation

In geometric operations, the smoothing effect of bilinear gray level interpolation may degrade fine detail in the image, particularly if magnification is involved. In other applications, the slope discontinuities of bilinear interpolation may produce undesirable effects. In either of these cases, the extra computational efforts of higher order interpolation may be justified. A function similar to, but more complex than, Eq. (2) and having more than four coefficients is made to fit through a neighborhood of more than four points.

If the number of coefficients equals the number of points, the interpolating surface can be made to fit at every point. If the points outnumber the coefficients, a curve-fitting or error-minimizing procedure can be used. Examples of higher order interpolating functions are cubic splines, Legendre centered functions, and the function $\sin(\alpha x)/\alpha x$. The latter is discussed in later chapters. Higher order interpolation is usually implemented by convolution. A discussion of this is reserved for Part 2 of the text.

8.3 THE SPATIAL TRANSFORMATION

Eq. (1) gives the general expression for the spatial transformation. It is instructive to consider some less complex special cases before going on to general geometric operations.

8.3.1 Simple Transformations

If we let

$$a(x, y) = x \qquad b(x, y) = y \tag{7}$$

in Eq. (1), we have the identity operation, which merely copies f into g without modification.

If we let

$$a(x, y) = x + x_0 \qquad b(x, y) = y + y_0 \tag{8}$$

we have the translation operation, in which the point x_0,y_0 is translated to the origin, and features within the image are moved by an amount $\sqrt{x_0^2 + y_0^2}$. Using the formulation called *homogeneous coordinates* [1–9] we can consider the x–y plane to be the $z = 1$ plane of three-dimensional x, y, z space and write Eq. (8) compactly in matrix form as

$$\begin{bmatrix} a(x, y) \\ b(x, y) \\ 1 \end{bmatrix} = \begin{bmatrix} 1 & 0 & x_0 \\ 0 & 1 & y_0 \\ 0 & 0 & 1 \end{bmatrix} \begin{bmatrix} x \\ y \\ 1 \end{bmatrix} \tag{9}$$

Letting

$$a(x, y) = x/c \qquad b(x, y) = y/d \tag{10}$$

will magnify the image by the factors c in the x-direction and d in the y-direction. The origin of the image (typically the upper left-hand corner) remains stationary as the image "expands." In homogeneous coordinates Eq. (10) is written as

$$\begin{bmatrix} a(x, y) \\ b(x, y) \\ 1 \end{bmatrix} = \begin{bmatrix} \frac{1}{c} & 0 & 0 \\ 0 & \frac{1}{d} & 0 \\ 0 & 0 & 1 \end{bmatrix} \begin{bmatrix} x \\ y \\ 1 \end{bmatrix} \tag{11}$$

Letting $c = -1$ produces a reflection about the y-axis,

$$a(x, y) = -x \qquad b(x, y) = y \tag{12}$$

and similarly for d and the x-axis.

Finally, letting

$$a(x, y) = x \cos(\theta) - y \sin(\theta) \tag{13}$$

and

$$b(x, y) = x \sin(\theta) + y \cos(\theta) \tag{14}$$

produces a cw rotation through an angle θ about the origin. This equation can be written in homogeneous coordinates as

$$\begin{bmatrix} a(x, y) \\ b(x, y) \\ 1 \end{bmatrix} = \begin{bmatrix} \cos(\theta) & -\sin(\theta) & 0 \\ \sin(\theta) & \cos(\theta) & 0 \\ 0 & 0 & 1 \end{bmatrix} \begin{bmatrix} x \\ y \\ 1 \end{bmatrix} \tag{15}$$

Clearly, we can combine translation with magnification to cause the image to "grow" about a point other than the origin. Likewise, we can combine translation with rotation to produce rotation about an arbitrary point.

Homogeneous coordinates provide a simple way to determine the formulas for compound transformations. For example, rotation about the point x_0, y_0 is accomplished by

$$\begin{bmatrix} a(x, y) \\ b(x, y) \\ 1 \end{bmatrix} = \begin{bmatrix} 1 & 0 & x_0 \\ 0 & 1 & y_0 \\ 0 & 0 & 1 \end{bmatrix} \begin{bmatrix} \cos(\theta) & -\sin(\theta) & 0 \\ \sin(\theta) & \cos(\theta) & 0 \\ 0 & 0 & 1 \end{bmatrix} \begin{bmatrix} 1 & 0 & -x_0 \\ 0 & 1 & -y_0 \\ 0 & 0 & 1 \end{bmatrix} \begin{bmatrix} x \\ y \\ 1 \end{bmatrix} \tag{16}$$

The image is first translated so that the point x_0, y_0 is at the origin, then rotated through the angle θ, and then translated back to its origin. Multiplying out Eq. 16 yields the appropriate transformation equations. Other compound transformations can be constructed similarly. In the construction of the right-hand side of the equation, the sequence of operations is from left to right.

Separable Implementations. If an image is subjected to translation [Eq. (8)] or magnification [Eq. (11)], the output pixel addresses, $a(x, y)$ and $b(x, y)$, depend only on x and y, respectively. Thus, it is possible, and sometimes more efficient, to perform the operation in two steps. First it is done, for example, in the horizontal direction, producing an intermediate image. Then the vertical part of the operation proceeds, using the intermediate image as its input and producing the final result.

Catmull and Smith [10] have shown that it is possible to perform a rotation in the same type of two-step procedure. Solving for x in Eq. (13) yields

$$x = \frac{a(x, y) + y \sin(\theta)}{\cos(\theta)} \tag{17}$$

and substituting this into Eq. (14) leads to

$$b(x, y) = \frac{a(x, y) \sin(\theta) + y}{\cos(\theta)} \tag{18}$$

Thus, we can use Eq. (13), which is linear in x along any scan line, in combination with $b(x, y) = y$ in the first (horizontal-only) part of the operation. Then we can use Eq. (18), which is linear in y along any column, along with $a(x, y) = x$ in the second (vertical-only) part of the operation.

In this type of rotation, image features are "compressed" in the x-direction by the factor $\cos(\theta)$ in the first step, and then "expanded" in the y-direction in the second step. The technique fails at multiples of 90 degrees, where the cosine goes through zero, and inaccuracy restricts it to smaller angles.

For image registration applications, the required rotation angles are normally small. Even if this is not the case, rotation through multiples of 90 degrees can be done with simple row and column swapping. Thus, it is possible to rotate an image through any angle while keeping the actual rotation angle between plus and minus 45 degrees and the compression factor no less than 0.707. With this restriction, then, translation, magnification and rotation have one-dimensional implementations.

8.3.2 General Transformations

For relatively simple spatial transformations, it may be practical to use an analytic expression for Eq. (1). In many image-processing applications, however, the desired spatial transformation is relatively complex and not amenable to convenient mathematical expression. Furthermore, the desired pixel translations are frequently obtained from measurement of actual images, and it is desirable to specify the geometric transformation in these terms rather than in functional form.

An example of this is the geometric calibration of an image taken with a camera having geometric distortion. First, a rectangular grid target is digitized and displayed. Because of geometric distortion in the camera, the displayed grid pattern will not be exactly rectangular. (See Figure 8–4.) The desired spatial transformation is that which makes the grid pattern rectangular again, thereby correcting the distortion introduced by the camera. This same spatial transformation can then be used on subsequent images digitized by the same camera (assuming that the distortion is not scene dependent), thereby producing undistorted images.

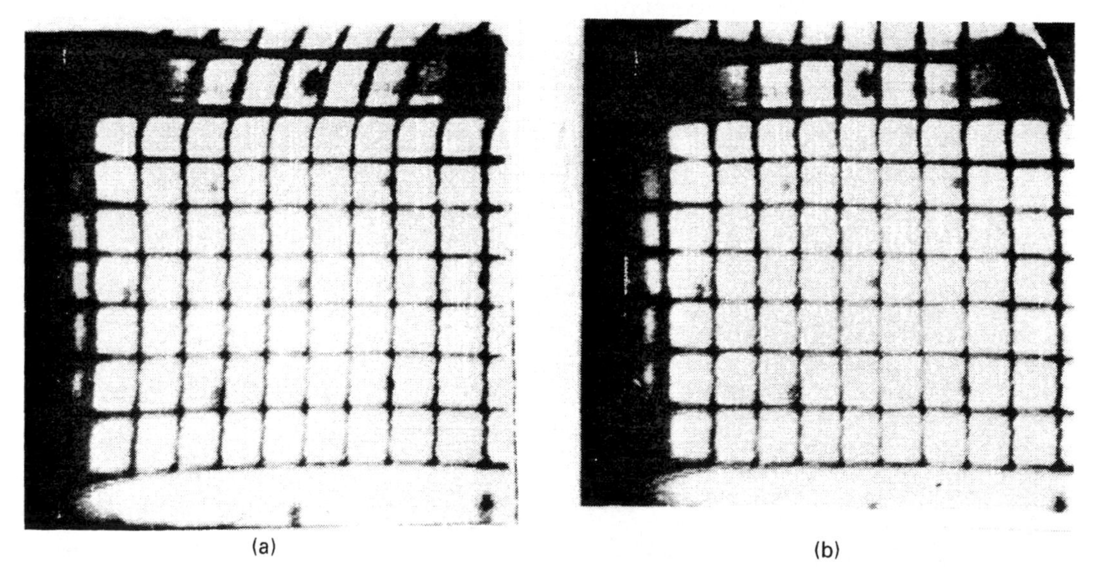

Figure 8–4 Geometric calibration of an early Ranger spacecraft camera: (a) before, (b) after (Courtesy NASA-JPL, from [19])

8.3.3 Specification by Control Points

It is convenient to specify the spatial transformation as a series of displacement values for selected *control points* in the image. Since only a small fraction of the pixels are actually specified, the displacements of noncontrol points must be determined by interpolation.

One way to do this is to develop functional expressions for $a(x, y)$ and $b(x, y)$ in Eq. (1). Commonly, a polynomial is used as the general form of the transformation expression. Its parameters are selected to make it fit the control points and their specified displacements. This is called *polynomial warping*. It is practical to use polynomials up to the fifth order for the transformation function [11].

In many cases, the limitations of polynomial warping will not accommodate the complex transformation required. Thus, some programs for geometric operations break the image up into polygonal regions and use piecewise bilinear mapping functions. The user specifies an input *control grid* made up of control points that form the vertices of contiguous quadrilaterals in the input image [11–16]. The input control grid maps to a grid of contiguous, horizontally oriented rectangles in the output image (Figure 8–5). The vertices (input control points) of the quadrilateral map directly to the corresponding vertices of the rectangle. Similarly, points inside an input quadrilateral map to points within the corresponding output rectangle.

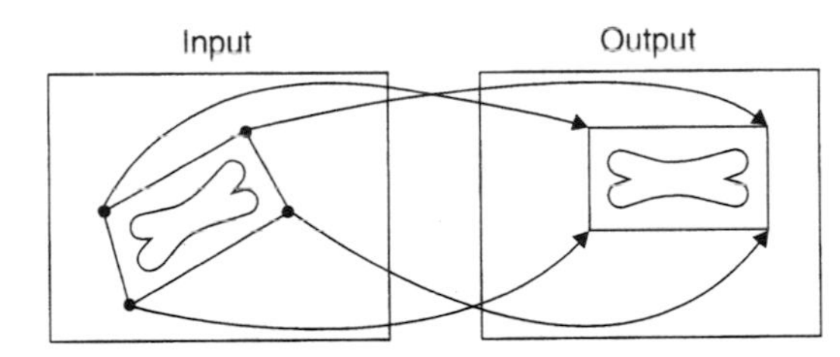

Figure 8–5 Spatial mapping of control points

8.3.4 Polynomial Warping

If the number of terms in the polynomial matches the number of control points, then the transformation can be designed to map the control points exactly as specified. Solving for the coefficients of the polynomial becomes an exercise in simultaneous linear equations, and a matrix inversion will normally produce the required result. (See Sec. 19.5.2.)

If there are more control points than terms in the polynomial, however, a fitting procedure must be used to determine the coefficients of the polynomial. In this case, the spatial transformation is a *best fit* to the control point specifications, and the mapping of individual control points does not occur exactly as specified.

Techniques for fitting one- and two-dimensional functions to a set of given data points are discussed in Section 19.5. The *pseudoinverse* technique (Sec. 19.5.2, Appendix 3) for determining the coefficients of the best fitting function is commonly used for polynomial warping. Other numerical methods, such as singular value decomposition ([17], Appendix 3) and orthonormal decomposition [11] may prove superior in practice.

Once the coefficients of the polynomial have been determined, the implementation is the same as before. There are numerical methods, however, such as Horner's nesting scheme [11,18], that can reduce the required number of computational steps. Even so, the task can be formidable when performing higher order warps on large images.

8.3.5 Control Grid Interpolation

If polynomial warping is impractical, the image must be warped in pieces. In the most common implementation, the input control points form a grid that maps to a grid of contiguous, horizontally oriented rectangles in the output image, as in Figure 8–5. The input control points map to the vertices of the corresponding rectangles, while points inside each input polygon map to points within the corresponding output rectangle.

Bilinear interpolation is a common choice for control grid interpolation, because it is computationally simple and produces a smooth mapping that preserves continuity and connectivity. The general expression for the bilinear spatial transformation is

$$G(x, y) = F(x', y') = F(ax + by + cxy + d, ex + fy + gxy + h) \tag{19}$$

The bilinear transformation is defined by the values of the eight coefficients a through h. By specifying that the four vertices of a quadrilateral map to the four vertices of the corresponding rectangle, we create two sets of four linear equations in four unknowns. The mapping from x' to x generates four equations in a, b, c, and d, and likewise for the mapping from y' to y and the coefficients e, f, g, and h. These sets of equations may be solved for a through h [recall Eq. (6)] to specify the bilinear spatial transformation algorithm that applies to all output points falling inside the rectangle.

While the spatial transformation algorithm could be implemented as Eq. (19), there is a more convenient and computationally efficient way of implementing it. By redefining the coefficients a and e, we can write Eq. (19) as

$$G(x, y) = F\,[x + dx(x, y), y + dy(x, y)] \tag{20}$$

where $dx(x, y)$ and $dy(x, y)$ are pixel displacements that are bilinear functions of x and y. Figure 8–6 shows these displacements with the input quadrilateral superimposed upon the output rectangle to which it maps. The problem now reduces to specifying dx and dy for all points inside the rectangle. Since $dx(x, y)$ and $dy(x, y)$ are bilinear in x and y, they become linear in x along each output line. Thus, for each line, we can define an increment, Δx, such that, assuming unit pixel spacing,

$$dx(x + 1, y) = dx(x, y) + \Delta x \tag{21}$$

and similarly for dy. The increment Δx changes from line to line, but is easily computed from the displacement values at the ends of the output rectangle. These can be interpolated between the given displacements at the vertices. Implementing Eq. (21) requires only two additions, one for dx and one for dy, at each output pixel to compute the coordinates of the corresponding input point.

The foregoing procedure specifies the spatial transformation for points falling inside the output rectangle. Frequently, a single quadrilateral-to-rectangle mapping is inadequate to specify the desired spatial transformations, and one can designate contiguous sets of quadrilaterals in the input image that map into contiguous sets of rectangles in the output image. It is not necessary, however, for the rectangles to cover the output image completely.

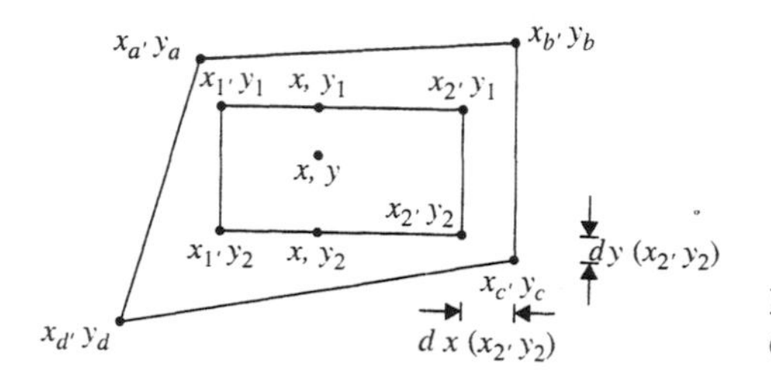

Figure 8–6 Control point displacements

Figure 8–7 shows an output image in which six contiguous rectangles are defined. Inside each of the rectangles, the spatial transformation is defined as described above. The figure also shows how the spatial transformation can be extrapolated outside the rectangles by which it is defined. The numbers inside the unspecified (dotted) rectangles indicate the control rectangles from which the bilinear coefficients are used [12]. For example, the spatial transformation used in the upper left-hand rectangle of the output image uses the bilinear coefficients for rectangle 1.

It is clear from the previous discussion that the bilinear transformation is continuous and unique at the vertices and boundaries of output rectangles. At each boundary, bilinear interpolation degenerates into linear interpolation between the two end points.

When specifying adjacent rectangles in the output image, one must make their vertices coincident. Similarly, adjacent quadrilaterals in the input image must have coincident vertices. Nonadjacent quadrilaterals, however, are not so constrained and may even overlap. Objects inside areas where input quadrilaterals overlap become duplicated in the output image.

1	1	2	3	3
1	1	2	3	3
4	4	5	6	6
4	4	5	6	6

Figure 8–7 Control grid extrapolation

8.4 APPLICATIONS OF GEOMETRIC OPERATIONS

8.4.1 Geometric Calibration

An important application of geometric operations is the removal of camera-induced geometric distortion from digital images [13–16,19]. An example appears in Figure 8–4. Geometric calibration has proved important in extracting quantitative spatial measurements from a wide variety of digitized images. Certain images, such as those from satellites and airborne side-looking radar, are subject to rather severe geometric distortions. These images often require geometric correction prior to interpretation.

8.4.2 Image Rectification

Some imaging systems use non-rectangular pixel coordinates. Before images digitized with such a system can be viewed properly on ordinary display systems, they must be rectified, that is, transformed into rectangular pixel coordinates.

The Viking Lander spacecraft, for example, used an angle-scanning camera designed for digitizing Martian panoramas. It used a spherical coordinate system with scan lines spaced at equal angles of elevation, and its pixel spacing represented equal increments of azimuth angle. Figure 8–8(a) shows the distortion this design produced on rectangular displays, particularly for objects located near the camera.

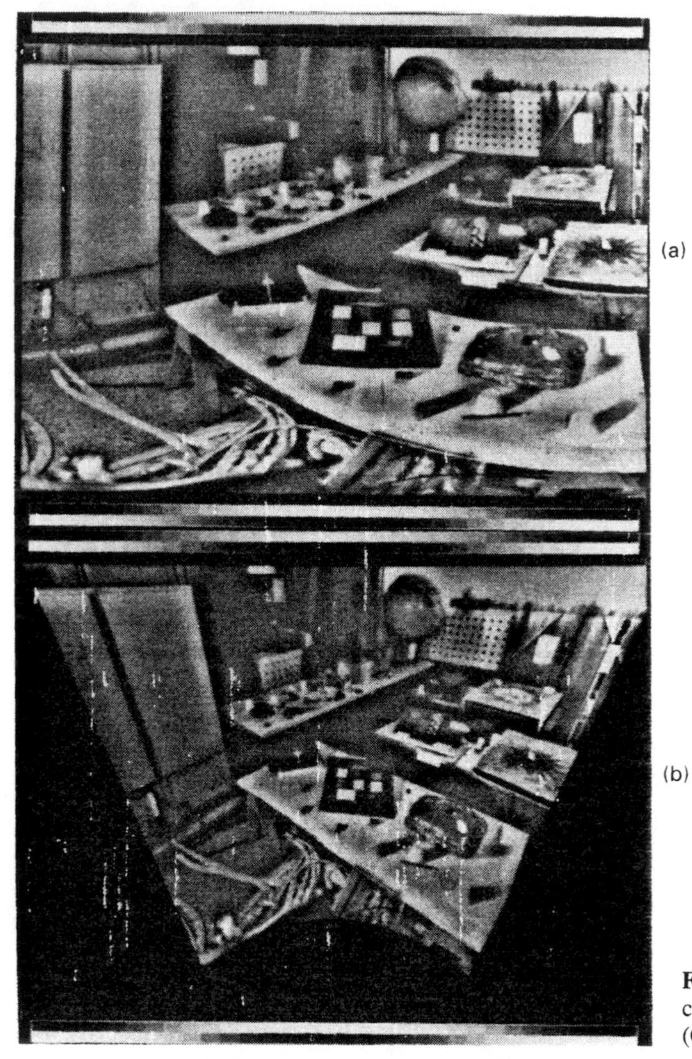

Figure 8–8 Viking Lander camera correction: (a) before, (b) after (Courtesy NASA-JPL)

Rectification of angle-scanned images for rectangular display involves the projection of a spherical surface onto a tangent plane. The projection lines emanate from the center of the sphere and carry points on its surface out to the plane. The relationship between input and output pixel location is derived in [14]. Figure 8–8(a) was rectified for rectangular display in Figure 8–8(b). Notice that the table edges appear straight, as they should, in the rectified image.

A free-roaming robot, like a human, requires wide-angle stereoscopic vision in order to navigate among obstacles, such as passing through doorways. A *fish-eye* lens can image a field of view approximately 180 degrees wide, but it does so with considerable distortion (Figure 8–9a,b). A properly designed geometric operation can rectify such an image into a rectangular coordinate system (Figure 8–9c,d) so that stereoscopic ranging techniques (discussed in Chapter 22) can locate the surrounding objects in three dimensions. In this example, a fifth-order polynomial warp, implemented in a polar coordinate system, rectified the images [20,21].

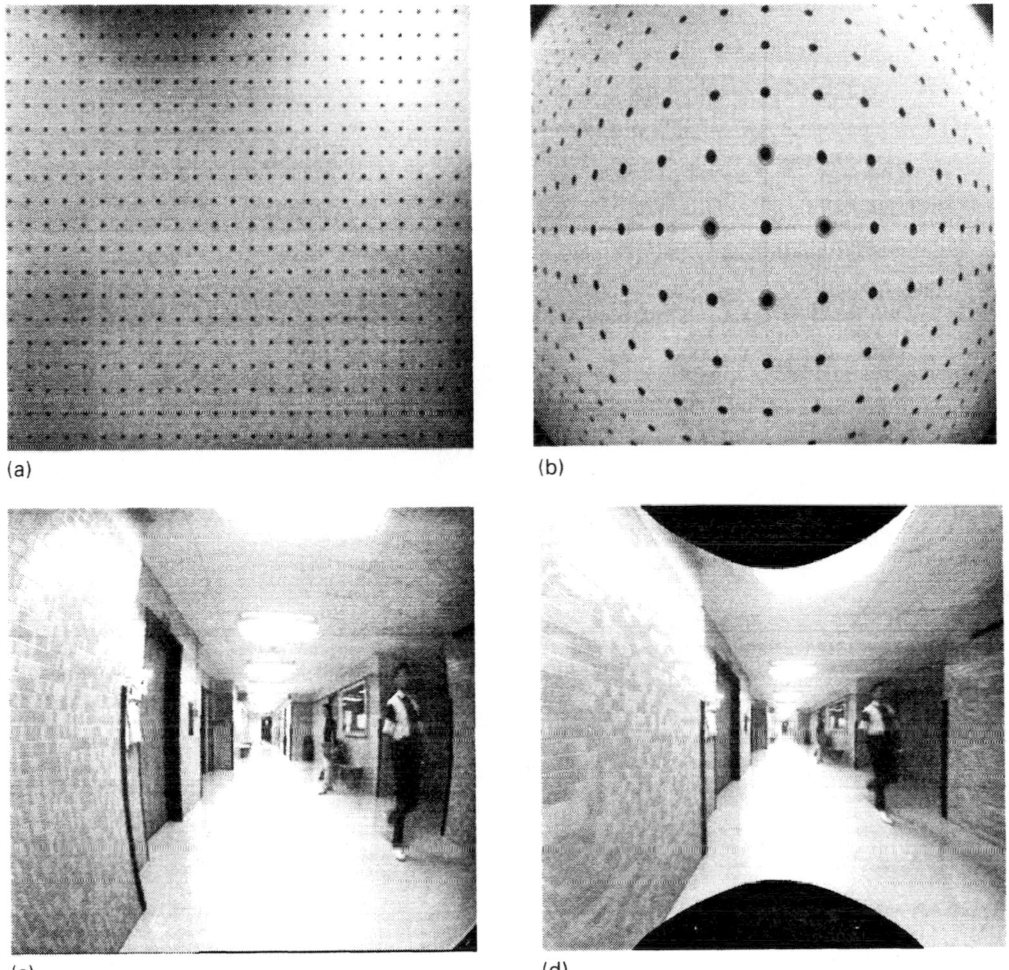

(a) (b) (c) (d)

Figure 8–9 Geometric rectification of an image taken with a fish-eye lens: (a) test target, (b) fisheye image; (c) original, (d) rectified hallway image (Courtesy Shishir Shah, The University of Texas at Austin, from [20])

8.4.3 Image Registration

Another application of geometric operations is registering similar images for purposes of comparison. This is typified by image subtraction to detect motion or change. As pointed out in Chapter 7, if similar images are displaced slightly and subtracted, the difference image has a strong partial derivative component. This could easily mask the image differences of interest. If images of a stationary object can be digitized from a fixed camera position, they can be obtained in register. If this is not the case, however, it is likely that the images will have to be registered prior to subtraction.

While simple translation is easily accomplished, rotation or more complex distortion requires a geometric operation. Registration of film scan images is likely to involve translation and rotation. Serial sections of biological tissue, sliced on a microtome and photographed through a microscope, for example, are subject to rather severe geometric distortion. In such cases, simple translation and rotation are inadequate. Instead, one such image can be taken as a standard of reference and the others distorted to match it. Small features are located throughout the images and used to define control points. Chapter 7 shows examples of image subtraction in which careful registration is required.

8.4.4 Image Format Conversion

Geometric operations are sometimes useful simply for placing images into a format more convenient for interpretation. Figure 8–10(a) shows a photographic map of the chromo-

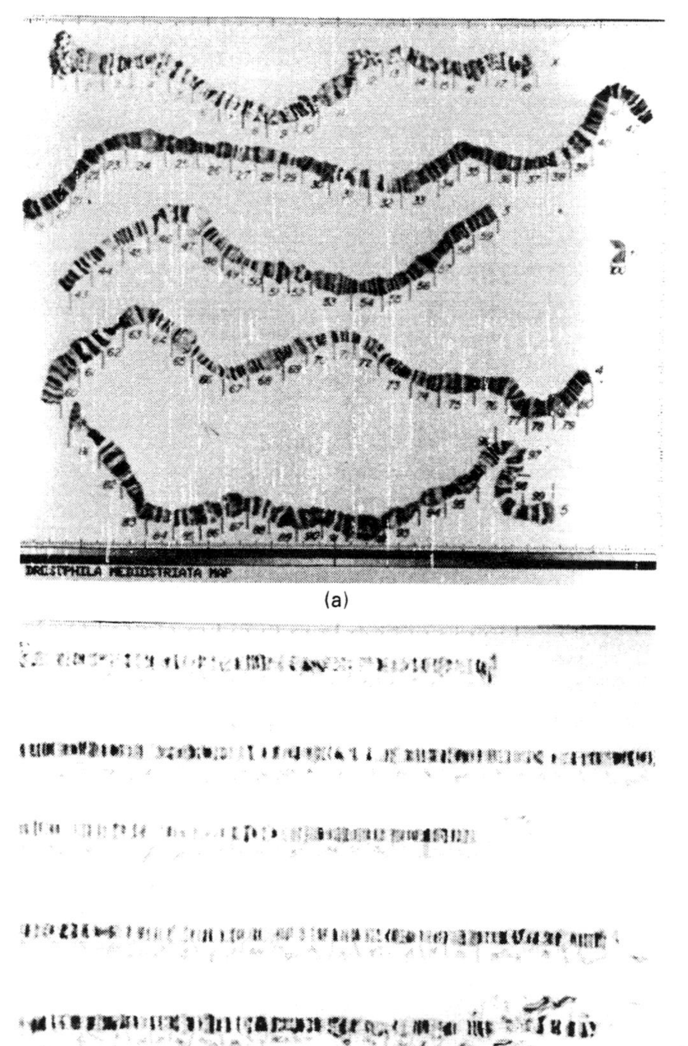

Figure 8–10 *Drosophila* chromosome map: (a) original, (b) straightened (Courtesy NASA-JPL)

somes of one species of the fruit fly *Drosophila.* The map is made by pasting up photographs of chromosomes taken through a microscope. Geneticists analyze the pattern of bands on the chromosomes to deduce patterns of evolution. The areas are numbered for reference.

Figure 8–10(b) shows the result of using a geometric operation to produce a map in which the chromosomes appear straight. In the input image, each chromosome was overlaid with a control grid of quadrilaterals, each with two sides parallel to the chromosome axis. These were mapped into horizontal strings of rectangles in the output image. In order to prevent axial distortion of the chromosome, the horizontal length of each rectangle was made equal to the mean of the two axial sides of the corresponding quadrilateral.

The numbers below chromosome 3 suffered less distortion than the others because a second row of quadrilaterals was defined below this chromosome. These were actually parallelograms with vertical ends and sides parallel to the chromosome axis. They mapped into a second row of rectangles falling beneath those that defined the straightened chromosome.

8.4.5 Map Projection

Another major application of geometric operations is projecting images for purposes of mapping. For example, it is necessary to produce photomosaic maps of the Earth, moon, and planets using images transmitted back from spacecraft. The borders of the spacecraft camera image project onto the planet's surface, forming a "footprint" with four curvilinear sides [Figure 8–11(a)]. The spherical surface of the planet is projected onto a flat surface to make a map [Figure 8–11(b)]. The "footprint" also projects onto the map, producing a further distorted four-sided figure.

A geometric operation can transform the spacecraft camera image into the form it should assume on the map. Multiple images processed in this way can be combined into a mosaic to form a photographic map of the planet. The task of determining the control points for projecting a given image is somewhat involved. The program must take the spacecraft viewing geometry and the desired cartographic projection parameters and generate input and output control grids.

Determining the spatial transformation between the input and the projected image is a two-step process. Software used in the space program solves this problem by working backward from the output image to the input image. The specified cartographic projection technique defines the relationship between points in the output image and points on the planet's surface. The spacecraft viewing geometry determines the spatial relationship between points on the surface of the planet and pixel positions in the camera image. The program overlays a rectangular control grid on the output image and maps it back through the cartographic projection and the spacecraft viewing geometry to overlay it on the input image. The following section outlines this technique.

Cartography. The science of cartography is concerned with producing two-dimensional maps of spherical or ellipsoidal bodies. This is not a simple matter, because spherical surfaces cannot be flattened without distortion. Cartographers solve the problem by projecting the spherical surface onto a plane or onto a cylinder or cone that can be "unrolled" to form a flat surface [22,23].

Map Properties. There are three important properties that a particular map may or may not have, depending on its method of generation. A map is said to be *equidistant* if

(a)

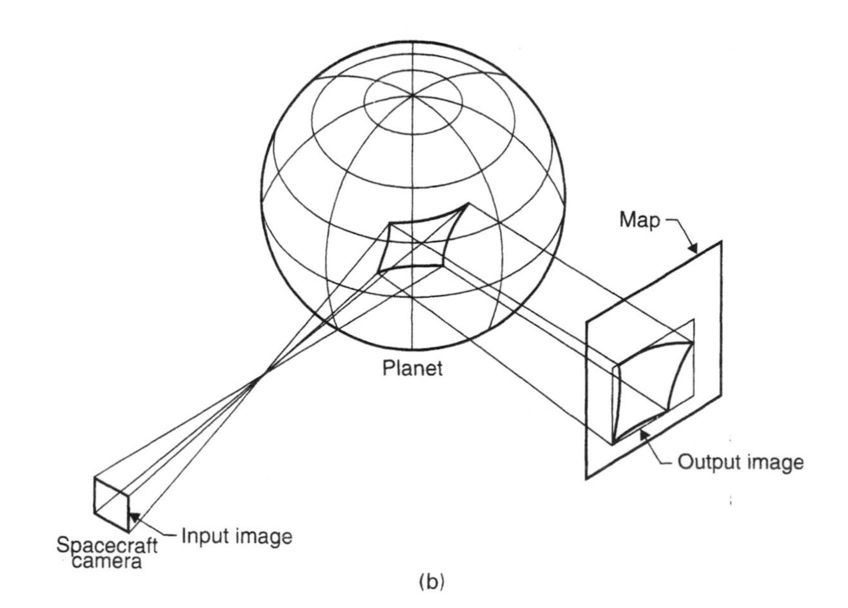

(b)

Figure 8–11 Photographic mapping: (a) spacecraft camera "footprint," (b) map projection (Courtesy NASA-JPL)

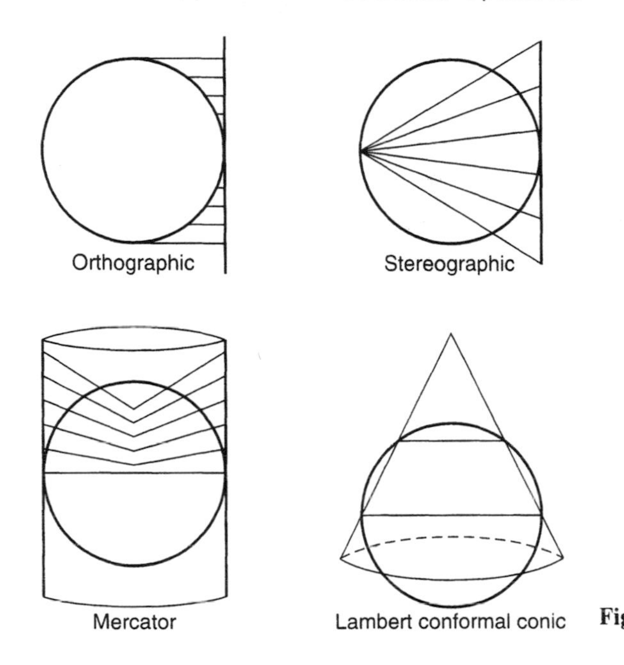

Figure 8–12 Cartographic projections

scale is preserved along certain lines. This means distances along those lines are proportional to the distance between corresponding points on the planet. A map has the property of *equivalence* if the area of a region is preserved in the projection. Such maps may be used for comparing the areas of different features. A map is *conformal* or *orthomorphic* if angles are preserved in the projection—that is, if lines on the surface intersect at the same angle as their projections on the map. A conformal map also preserves shape at a point. This means that the shape of small features is distorted only very slightly. The distortion of shapes becomes progressively more significant as the size of the features increases.

Cartographic Projections. There are three types of surfaces onto which surface features may be projected to form a two-dimensional map: the plane, the cylinder, and the cone. The last two must be cut along a line parallel to the axis and "unrolled" to form a flat map. The cone may be considered the general case, since the plane can be thought of as a cone with apex angle 180° and the cylinder a cone with apex angle 0°.

While many types of projections have been defined and used throughout cartographic history, four of the most important are the *orthographic*, the *stereographic*, the *Mercator*, and the *Lambert conformal conic* projections [24]. These projections differ in the techniques by which they are generated and in their properties. They are described next, with reference to Figure 8–12.

In the orthographic projection, surface features are projected onto a plane tangent to the sphere at a point called the *center of projection.* Features are projected along parallel lines normal to the plane. When the center of projection is a pole, the scale along parallels of latitude is constant. By contrast, the radial scale decreases away from the center of projection. There is little distortion of features near the center of projection. Parallels of latitude project as concentric circles centered on the pole, and meridians project as straight lines intersecting at the pole.

The orthographic projection is useful because it approximates viewing the planet from a large distance, and the eye is able to visualize the spherical shape of the planet. Because scale and shape are distorted, however, orthographic maps are of restricted quantitative use, except for small features near the center of projection.

The stereographic projection is similar to the orthographic projection, except that the projection rays emanate from a *perspective point* located directly opposite the center of projection. In the polar case, parallels of latitude project as concentric circles centered on the pole, and meridians project as radial lines intersecting at the pole. The scale along parallels and that along meridians increase away from the pole. They increase proportionately, however, so that at any point the longitude and latitude scales are the same. This makes the stereographic projection conformal, and shape is preserved locally. There is little distortion of features near the center of projection. Coupled with conformality, this property makes the stereographic projection quite useful.

The Mercator projection maps surface features onto a right circular cylinder that is tangent to the sphere at the equator. The cylinder axis is colinear with the polar axis of the sphere. Meridians map to equidistant vertical lines, and parallels map to circles on the cylinder, which open up to form horizontal lines on the map. Scale along latitude lines increases with distance from the equator. The projection is designed so that the perspectival point moves up the axis with increasing latitude, keeping the latitude and longitude scales equal and thus making the map conformal. Scale is exaggerated away from the equator, and features near the poles become quite large. The poles themselves cannot be mapped.

The vertical position of latitude lines is given by

$$y = R \ln\left[\tan\left(45 + \frac{\phi}{2}\right)\right] \tag{22}$$

where R is the planet's radius on the map and ϕ is latitude.

Historically, the Mercator projection has been used for navigation because a course of constant compass heading projects to a straight line on the map.

In the Lambert conformal conic projection, surface features are projected onto a cone having the same axis as the planet. The cone intersects the sphere at two parallels called the standard parallels. Meridians map to straight lines, and parallels map to circles inside the cone. When the cone is unrolled, the parallels become arcs and the meridians merge at the pole. The spacing of the parallels is adjusted to achieve conformality. The two standard parallels project at true scale: Scale decreases between them and is exaggerated outside of them.

8.4.5.1 Implementation

The steps necessary to project a spacecraft image for mapping purposes are the following:

1. Establish the spacecraft camera viewing geometry.
2. Determine an expression giving camera position as a function of the latitude and longitude of the corresponding point on the planet's surface.
3. Select the map projection parameters (type of projection, center of projection, etc.), and establish the borders of the output image on the map.
4. Determine an expression giving the latitude and longitude of a point on the planet's surface in terms of the pixel coordinates of the corresponding point on the map.

5. Combine the results of steps 2 and 4 to yield an expression giving camera pixel position as a function of position on the output map.
6. Overlay a rectilinear control grid on the output picture.
7. Use the expression of step 5 to map the output control points into the input image, thus establishing the input control grid.
8. Use the results of step 7 in a geometric operation to effect the projection.

The spacecraft viewing geometry may be established with reference to Figure 8–13. In this figure, the spacecraft is located at a distance R_s from the center of the planet, directly above the point at latitude ϕ_s and longitude λ_s. Point C is the perspective point that represents the nodal point (center) of the camera lens. Point p is in the camera image and corresponds to point p', which has longitude λ and latitude ϕ on the surface. The distance f represents the focal length of the lens and is exaggerated for clarity in the figure. The vector **Q** extends from C to p'. Notice that the vector

$$\mathbf{P} = \begin{bmatrix} x_p \\ y_p \\ f \end{bmatrix} \tag{23}$$

has components x_p and y_p, which are the camera pixel position coordinates. Since **P** and **Q** are colinear, they are related by a scale factor:

$$\mathbf{P} = \left(\frac{f}{Q_z}\right)\mathbf{Q} \tag{24}$$

From Figure 8–13, we see that

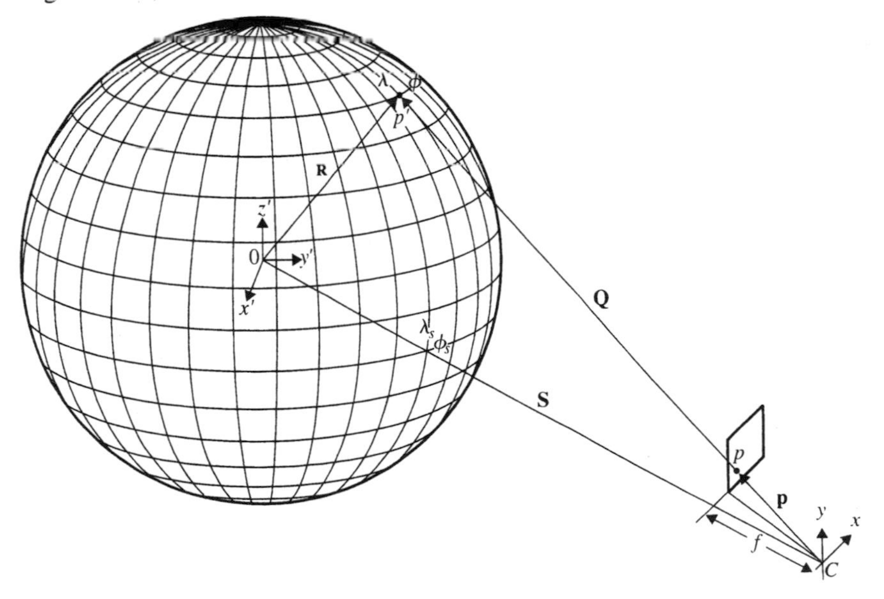

Figure 8–13 Spacecraft viewing geometry

$$\mathbf{Q} = \mathbf{R} - \mathbf{S} \tag{25}$$

which we can write in matrix notation as

$$\begin{bmatrix} Q_x \\ Q_y \\ Q_z \end{bmatrix} = [M] \begin{bmatrix} R\cos\phi\cos\lambda - R_s\cos\phi_s\cos\lambda_s \\ R\cos\phi\sin\lambda - R_s\cos\phi_s\sin\lambda_s \\ R\sin\phi - R_s\sin\phi_s \end{bmatrix} \tag{26}$$

where $[M]$ is the three-by-three matrix that transforms from planet-centered to spacecraft coordinates.

Finally, Eq. (24) implies that

$$x_p = \left(\frac{f}{Q_z}\right)Q_x \quad \text{and} \quad y_p = \left(\frac{f}{Q_z}\right)Q_y \tag{27}$$

Several cartography texts develop equations that give map position in terms of latitude and longitude on the surface. Since we must work backward from map to planet, however, inverse forms of the equations are required. These are developed in [24] for the four projections mentioned above.

Spacecraft images often require both geometric correction and map projection, suggesting two sequential geometric operations. Pixel interpolation done twice, however, would reduce detail in the image, so the two geometric operations are usually combined into one execution that both corrects and projects the image.

8.4.5.2 Examples of Map Projection

Figure 8–14 illustrates the steps used in producing a photographic map. Part (a) is a Mariner 10 image of Mercury prior to correction for photometric and geometric distortion. In (b), the image has been subjected to a geometric operation to produce an orthographic projection. In (c), several neighboring orthographic projections have been combined to form a mosaic. Finally, in (d), a latitude and longitude grid has overlaid the orthographic mosaic.

Figure 8–15 shows a polar orthographic projection of images of Mars taken from Mariner 6 and Mariner 7 [25]. A mosaic of high-resolution, narrow-angle images has been inserted into a mosaic of wide-angle, low-resolution pictures of the entire polar area. Figure 8–16 shows a four-foot-diameter globe covered with 2,000 orthographic projections of Mariner 9 images of Mars [15].

8.4.6 Morphing

Several special effects that have become popular in the motion picture and television industries are based on geometric operations. *Morphing* is a technique that allows one object to transform gradually into another [26].

Suppose we have two images from which we wish to create a sequence of movie frames. That sequence is to depict the transformation of the object in the first scene into the object in the second scene. An example would be transforming the face of a cat into the face of a tiger. In a *dissolve,* the first image gradually fades out as the second fades in. This technique rarely produces a realistic looking transformation. With a morph, however, during a

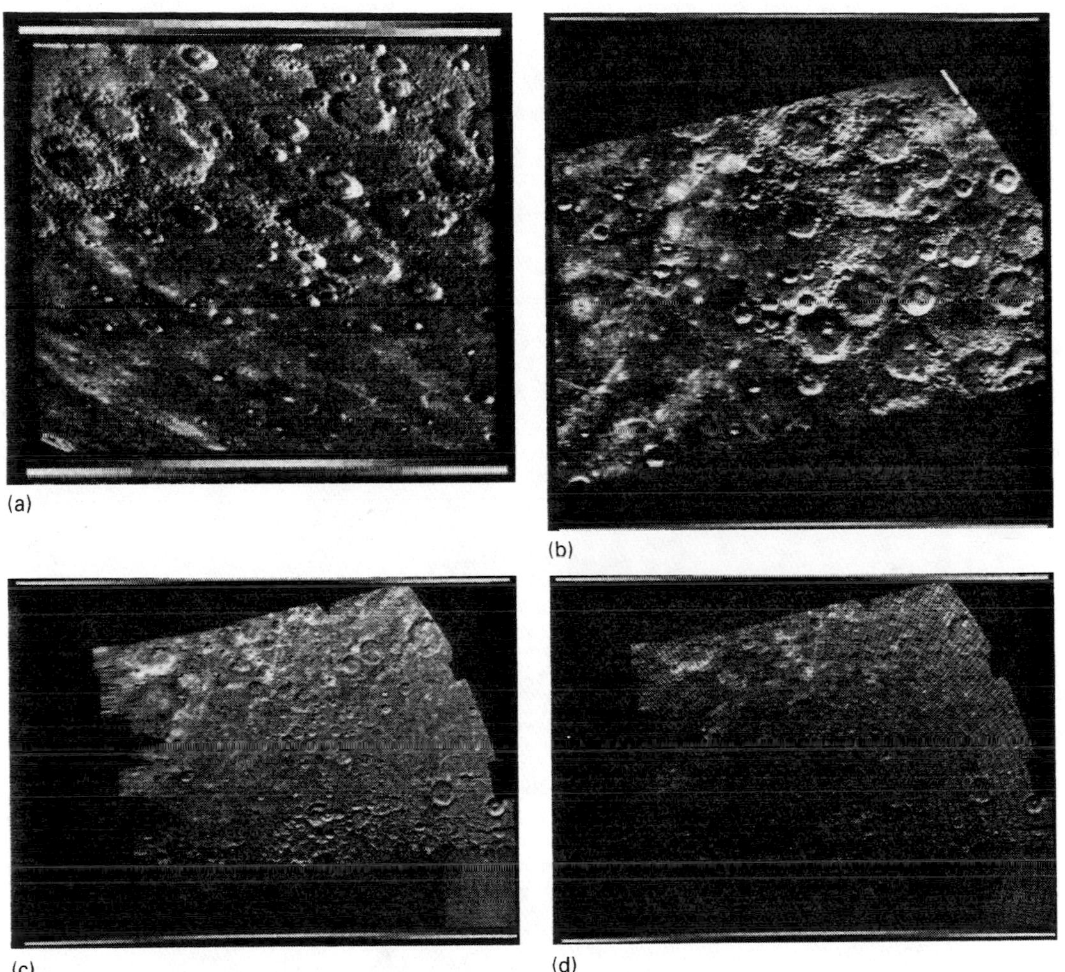

(a) (b) (c) (d)

Figure 8–14 Example of Mariner 10 map projection: (a) original image; (b) orthographic projection; (c) mosaic of several projections; (d) map grid overlay (Courtesy NASA-JPL)

dissolve points on the object are incrementally warped from their initial position to their final position, creating a more impressive result.

Figure 8–17 shows four frames from a morph sequence. Figures 8–17a and 8–17d are the initial and final images, respectively. Figure 8–17b and 8–17c represent the 40% and 70% points, respectively, in the sequence.

At each step in the sequence, both the initial and final images are warped so that their control points map to positions intermediate between their initial and final positions. This produces two sequences in which the marked features move gradually from their initial to their final positions. A dissolve between these two sequences completes the morph operation.

Morphing can also be done between two movie sequences. Here, since the objects are moving, the corresponding control points must be designated in each frame of each sequence. Most commonly, the control points are specified for only a few of the frames, and

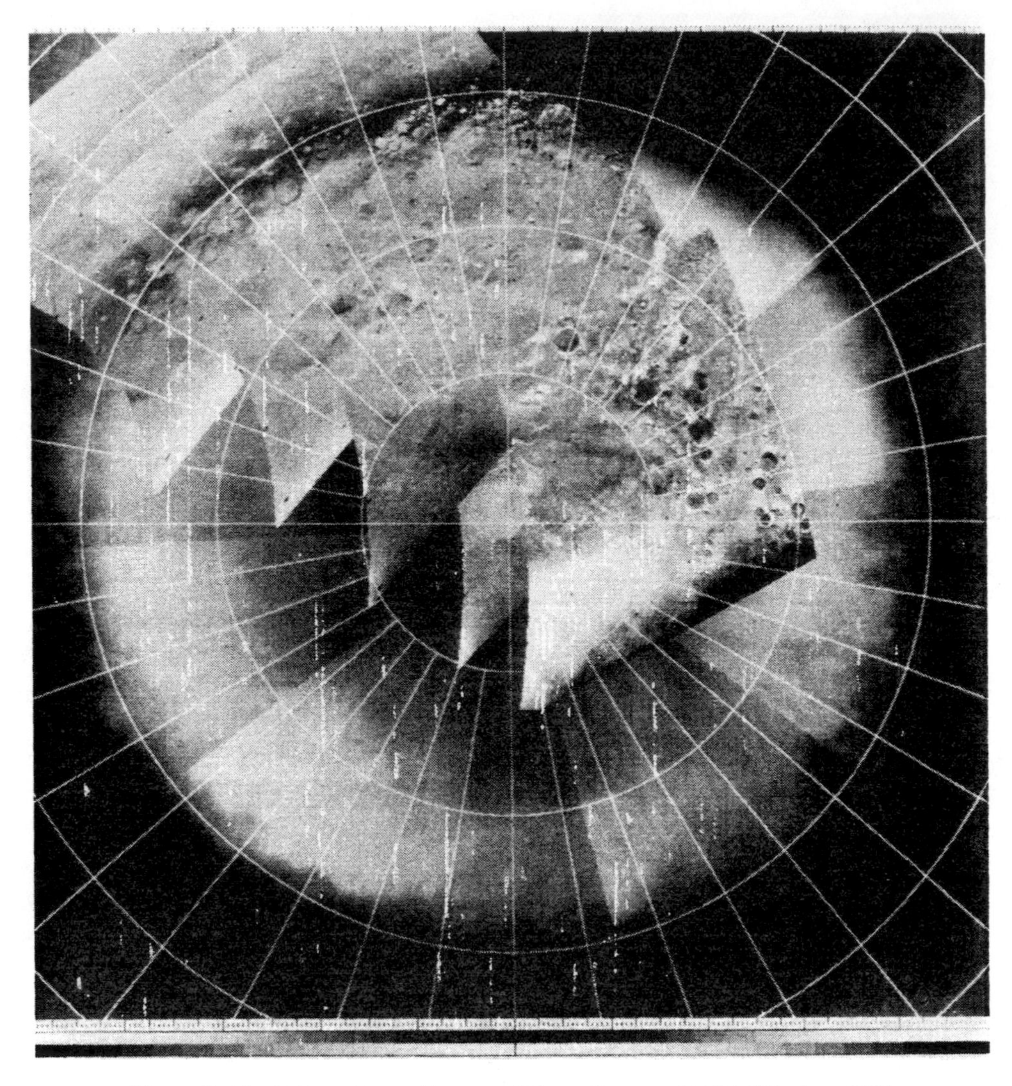

Figure 8–15 Polar orthographic map of Mars (Courtesy NASA-JPL, from [23])

spatial interpolation supplies the rest. At each frame in the sequence, the two images are warped so that their control points align. The position to which a pair of control points is mapped starts near the initial image position and gradually moves toward the final image position as the sequence progresses.

In practice, it is often only one object in the scene that is actually transformed, with the background remaining stationary. The object of interest is filmed against a black background. The finished morph sequence is then inserted into a scene containing the appropriate background.

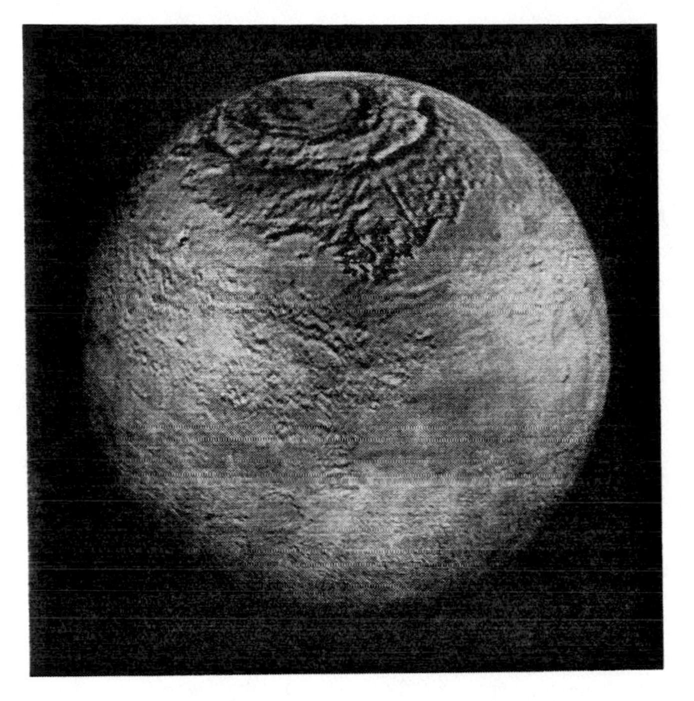

Figure 8–16 Mariner 9 photomosaic globe of Mars (Courtesy NASA-JPL)

Figure 8–17 Image morphing sequence: (a) initial image, (b) 40% point, (c) 70% point, (d) final image.

8.5 SUMMARY OF IMPORTANT POINTS

1. A geometric operation requires a means for specifying its spatial transformation and an algorithm for gray-level interpolation.
2. A geometric operation can be thought of as mapping each output image pixel into the input image, where the ouput gray-level value is determined by interpolation.
3. Bilinear gray-level interpolation is generally superior to nearest neighbor interpolation, and it produces only a modest increase in program complexity and execution time.
4. A spatial transformation can be specified by a pair of control grids, one defined in the input image and one in the output image.
5. The input control points map to the corresponding output control points.
6. Between control points, a spatial transformation is obtained by interpolation.
7. Bilinear interpolation is useful for non-control-point interpolation.
8. Geometric operations are useful for digitizer calibration, display rectification, image registration, map projection, image reformatting for display, and visual special effects.

PROBLEMS

1. Let $F(221,396) = 18$, $F(221,397) = 45$, $F(222,396) = 52$, and $F(222,397) = 36$. What is $F(221.3,396.7)$, obtained by nearest neighbor interpolation? By bilinear interpolation? Write the bilinear equation (Eq. 2), showing the values of the coefficients. Draw a graph similar to Figure 8–3.
2. Let $F(109,775) = 113$, $F(109,776) = 109$, $F(110,775) = 105$, and $F(110,776) = 103$. What is $F(110.27,776.44)$, obtained by nearest neighbor interpolation? By bilinear interpolation? Write the bilinear equation (Eq. 2), showing the values of the coefficients. Draw a graph similar to Figure 8–3.
3. Write the geometric transformation required to rotate an image 33° counterclockwise about the point $x, y = 207,421$. Assume that 0,0 is at the upper left.
4. Suppose you have two digitized images of a canyon wall taken 100 years apart and you wish to detect changes due to erosion by image subtraction. You find a rock that is located at 303,467 in the first image and at 316,440 in the second image, and a stump that is located at 298,227 in the first image and at 311,200 in the second image. Has there been any (a) translation? (b) rotation? (c) change in scale? How much? Write the geometric transformation required to register the second image with the first prior to subtraction. Assume that there has been no geometric distortion beyond translation, rotation, and change in scale.
5. Suppose you have two digitized images of a section of a city taken from the top of a tall building 25 years apart and you wish to display changes by projecting an overlay of the two images. You find a corner of a building that is located at 103,84 in the first image and at 107,94 in the second image, and a window that is located at 433,504 in the first image and at 377,439 in the second image. Has there been any (a) translation? (b) rotation? (c) change in scale? How much? Write the geometric transformation required to register the second image with the first. Assume that there has been no geometric distortion beyond translation, rotation, and change in scale.
6. Suppose you have two digitized images of a movie star's face taken 30 years apart and you wish to include a fade between the two portraits in an upcoming documentary. You find that the cen-

ters of the film idol's pupils are located at 83,231 and 437,244 in the first image and at 64,281 and 479,370 in the second image. Has there been any (a) translation? (b) rotation? (c) change in scale? How much? Write the geometric transformation required to register the second image with the first. Assume that there has been no geometric distortion beyond translation, rotation, and change in scale.

7. Suppose you have a digitized photograph of the ground taken at an angle from behind the window of an airplane. You want to rectify the image so that it appears as if you are looking straight down. A square cotton field has corners at pixel coordinates (62, 85), (77, 128), (125, 134), and (140, 106). Derive the geometric transformation that will rectify the image. Plot the cotton field in the image before and after rectification.
8. Suppose you have film that was taken by a security camera during a daring daylight holdup of a bank. At one point in the series of images, one of the bandits ducks behind a counter and briefly removes his mask. Beside him is a chrome-plated vertical column 24 inches in diameter. The reflection of his face is visible in the shiny column, but is too distorted for identification. Derive the equation for a geometric transformation that will rectify the image of the bad guy. Assume that the column is parallel to the y-axis in the digitized image and the pixel spacing corresponds to 10 pixels per inch at the column. You may also assume that the radius of the column is negligible compared to its distance from the camera and from the villain.
9. The police have a photograph taken during the commission of a crime. Unfortunately, the robbery took place behind the tourist with the camera. You notice in the photo a large chrome-plated sphere that appears to be acting like a mirror. You use a film digitizer with 25-μ pixel spacing and find that the image of the ball measures 360 pixels in diameter. The actual ball is 3 feet in diameter, and it was 27 feet from the camera position. Develop an equation for the geometric transformation that will rectify the image of the robbers. You may assume that the radius of the ball is negligible compared to its distance from the camera and from the crime.
10. Suppose you have a photograph of a bite mark on the arm of a murder victim. The photo was taken at the autopsy of the victim. The body has since been cremated, but the district attorney needs a rectified picture of the bite mark to match against the bite of the suspect in order to get a conviction. Assume that the arm is a cylinder 80 mm in diameter lying parallel to the x-axis. Develop the equation for a geometric transformation that will "unroll" the bite mark for comparison with bites made on wax sheets by the suspect.
11. Develop the geometric transformation equations required to rotate an image 60 degrees counterclockwise about the point $x, y = 120,210$.
12. Develop the geometric transformation equations required to scale an image by 130 percent about the point $x, y = 64,120$ along a line 30 degrees counterclockwise from the x-axis and by 85 percent along a line 30 degrees counterclockwise from the y-axis.
13. Derive Eq. (18).

PROJECTS

These projects require access to an image-processing workstation with digitization and general geometric transformation capabilities.

1. Digitize an image of a friend taken with a wide-angle "fish-eye" lens. Develop equations that describe the distortion and use polynomial warping to correct it.
2. Digitize an image of a friend taken with a fish-eye lens. Use linear objects in the image as fiducial marks, and use a geometric transformation to correct the image.

3. Digitize an image of a friend taken with a fish-eye lens. Take a second image of a grid from the same camera position, and use a geometric transformation to correct the image
4. Digitize an image of a spherical hallway safety mirror, and use a geometric transformation to rectify the image. Use linear objects in the image as fiducial marks.
5. Digitize an image of a person reflected in a fun house mirror and then a second image containing a large grid. Use the same camera position both times. Use a geometric transformation to rectify the image of the person. Write a report, commenting on the accuracy of the results and any difficulties encountered.
6. Digitize an image of a large grid in a fun house mirror. Digitize an ordinary image of a friend of yours, and use a geometric operation to show what he or she would look like if seen in the mirror.
7. Digitize an image of a structure such as a house or building taken from an odd angle. Use a geometric operation to develop elevation (90 degree) views of the structure.
8. Develop an image-processing program that can be used to predict the effects of cosmetic and reconstructive surgery (a "nose job," chin augmentation, etc.). Use the program to determine what, if any, cosmetic surgery might improve your appearance or that of a friend or a celebrity.
9. Develop a geometric transformation program that will warp one facial photograph to match the features in another. Digitize a picture of a famous personality, digitize a picture of yourself in the same pose, and warp your picture to look like the other person.
10. Use a geometric transformation to "unroll" a picture of a poster wrapped around a pole.
11. Develop a geometric transformation program that will rotate, translate, and scale an image by specified amounts. Evaluate your implementation in terms of speed and accuracy.
12. Develop a geometric transformation program that will rotate, translate, and scale an image by specified amounts when the rotation angle is small (say, $\theta \leq 6°$). Use approximations to make execution of the program as fast as possible. Evaluate your implementation in terms of speed and accuracy.
13. Develop an image sequence that morphs an image of your face into that of a famous person.
14. View a movie containing morph operations (e.g., *Terminator 2*) on a video player with stop-motion capability. Examine the morph sequences in slow motion, and estimate how many control points were required and where they were located. Write a brief paper outlining your estimates, along with the digitizing, processing and display requirements for this project, as well as on the financial impact of these scenes on the producers.

REFERENCES

For additional reading, see Appendix 2.

1. L. G. Roberts, "Machine Perception of Three-Dimensional Solids," in J. D. Tippet et al, eds., *Optical and Electro-Optical Information Processing,* MIT Press, Cambridge, MA, 1965.
2. D. F. Rogers and J. A. Adams, *Mathematical Elements for Computer Graphics,* McGraw-Hill, New York, 1976.
3. J. D. Foley and A. van Dam, *Fundamentals of Interactive Computer Graphics,* Addison-Wesley, Reading, MA, 1982.
4. W. M. Newman and R. F. Sproul, *Principles of Interactive Computer Graphics* (2d ed.), McGraw-Hill, New York, 1979, Sec. 4.3.
5. D. H. Ballard and C. M. Brown, *Computer Vision,* Prentice-Hall, Englewood Cliffs, NJ, 1982, Sec. A1.7.

6. R. Nevatia, *Machine Perception,* Prentice-Hall, Englewood Cliffs, NJ, 1982, Sec. 3.2.
7. W. K. Pratt, *Digital Image Processing,* John Wiley and Sons, New York, 1991, Sec. 14.1.
8. R. C. Gonzales and R. C. Woods, *Digital Image Processing,* Addison-Wesley, Reading, MA, 1992, Sec. 2.5.
9. K. S. Fu, R. C. Gonzalez, and C. S. G. Lee, *Robotics: Control, Sensing, Vision, and Intelligence,* McGraw-Hill, New York, 1987.
10. E. Catmull and A. R. Smith, "3-D Transformation of Images in Scanline Order," *Computer Graphics,* **14**(3):279–285, 1980.
11. Z. Jericevic, D. M. Benson, J. Bryan, and L. C. Smith, "Geometric Correction of Digital Images Using Orthonormal Decomposition," *Journal of Microscopy,* **149**(3):233–245, 1987.
12. H. Frieden, "GEOM and LGEOM," in *Image Processing Laboratory Users Documentation of Applications Programs,* Jet Propulsion Laboratory Internal Document No. 900-670, Pasadena, CA, October 11, 1975.
13. J. E. Kreznar, *User and Programmer Guide to the MM'71 Geometric Calibration and Decalibration Programs,* Jet Propulsion Laboratory Internal Document No. 900-575, Pasadena, CA, March 1, 1973.
14. M. Girard, *Viking 75 Project Software Requirements Document for the GEOTRAN Program,* Jet Propulsion Laboratory Internal Document No. 620-52, Pasadena, CA, January 12, 1975.
15. W. B. Green, P. L. Jepsen, J. E. Kreznar, R. M. Ruiz, A. A. Schwartz, and J. B. Seidman, "Removal of Instrument Signature from Mariner 9 Television Images of Mars," *Applied Optics,* **14:**105–114, 1975.
16. D. A. O'Handley and W. B. Green, "Recent Developments in Digital Image Processing at the Image Processing Laboratory of the Jet Propulsion Laboratory," *Proc. IEEE,* **60**(7):821–828, July 1972.
17. C. L. Lawson and R. J. Hanson, *Solving Least Squares Problems,* Prentice-Hall, Englewood Cliffs, NJ, 1974.
18. W. H. Press, S. A. Teukolsky, W. T. Vetterling, and B. P. Flannery, *Numerical Recipes in C* (2d ed.), Cambridge University Press, Cambridge, U.K., 1992.
19. R. Nathan, *Digital Video Data Handling,* JPL Tech. Report 32-877, Pasadena, CA, January 5, 1966.
20. S. Shah and J. K. Aggarwal, "A Simple Calibration Procedure for Fish-Eye (High-Distortion) Lens Camera," *Proc. IEEE Int. Conf. on Robotics and Automation,* 3422–3427, 1994.
21. S. Shah and J. K. Aggarwal, "Depth Estimation Using Stereo Fish-Eye Lenses," *ICIP-94, Proc. IEEE Int. Conf. on Image Processing,* **2:** 740–744, 1994.
22. G. P. Keloway, *Map Projections,* Methuen and Co., London, 1946.
23. P. Richardis and R. K. Adler, *Map Projections,* American Elsevier, New York, 1972.
24. C. A. Rofer, A. A. Schwartz, J. B. Seidman, and W. B. Green, *Computer Cartographic Projections for Planetary Mosaics—Final Report* (three volumes), Jet Propulsion Laboratory Internal Document No. 900-636, Pasadena, CA, November 15, 1973.
25. A. R. Gillespie and J. M. Soha, "An Orthographic Photomap of the South Pole of Mars," *Icarus,* **16:**522, 1972.
26. G. Wolberg, *Digital Image Warping,* IEEE Computer Society Press, Los Alamitos, CA, 1990.

Part Two

CHAPTER 9

Linear System Theory

9.1 INTRODUCTION

In preceding chapters, we examined some effects that certain image-processing operations have on images. These effects can be explained by relatively simple mathematics. Thus far, we have not discussed sampling effects, spatial resolution, or the operations commonly referred to as *image enhancement*. In Part 2, we address questions of sampling, resolution, and linear filtering, an approach commonly used for image enhancement. In this chapter and the next, we develop the analytical tools required to approach these questions.

Linear system theory is a well-developed field commonly used to describe the behavior of electrical circuits and optical systems [1–5]. It provides a firm mathematical basis upon which to examine the effects of sampling, filtering, and spatial resolution. Linear system theory is also helpful in a variety of other applications, and it makes a useful addition to one's technical background.

9.1.1 Definitions

In the context of this book, we consider a *system* to be anything that accepts an input and produces an output in response. Since we are concerned only with the relationship between input and output, we have little interest in what is inside the system. The input and output can be one dimensional, two dimensional, or higher dimensional.

In the initial development, however, we restrict our examples to two cases: one-dimensional functions of time and two-dimensional functions of two spatial variables. This keeps the notation simpler and makes the analysis somewhat less abstract, since the development is tied to real physical processes. It also avoids a burden of excess generality. The analysis can be easily generalized to higher dimensions when necessary. In the first part of the chapter, the development is done for one-dimensional functions of time and generalized to two-dimensional images.

Figures 9–1 and 9–2 show the conventional notation for one- and two-dimensional linear systems. In each case, the input to the system is a function of one or two variables, and it produces a response from the system that is another function of the same variable or variables.

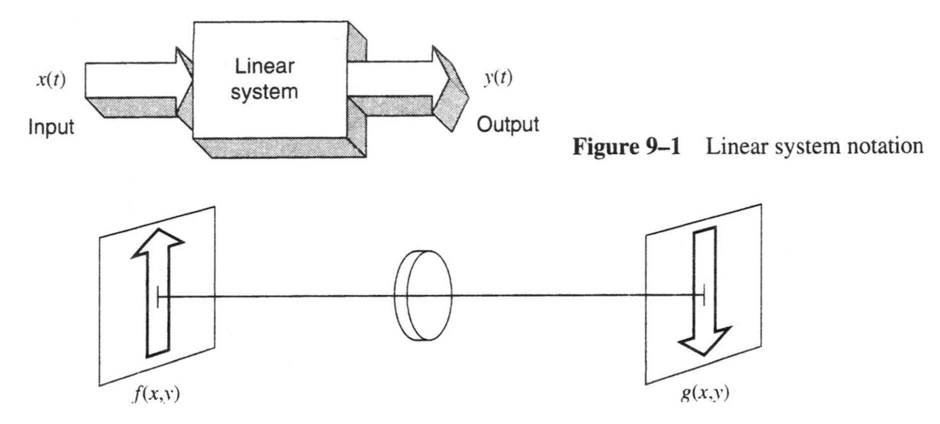

Figure 9–1 Linear system notation

Figure 9–2 Two-dimensional linear system

Linearity. Linear systems have a property that gives rise to their name. Suppose that, for a particular system, an input $x_1(t)$ gives rise to an output $y_1(t)$:

$$x_1(t) \rightarrow y_1(t) \tag{1}$$

(The arrow is read as "produces.") Suppose also that a second input $x_2(t)$ gives rise to an output $y_2(t)$:

$$x_2(t) \rightarrow y_2(t) \tag{2}$$

The system is linear if and only if it has the property

$$x_1(t) + x_2(t) \rightarrow y_1(t) + y_2(t) \tag{3}$$

That is, a third input signal which is the sum of the first two produces an output signal that is the sum of the original two output signals. Any system that does not obey this constraint is nonlinear. Nonlinear system analysis has produced many useful results in a variety of areas. However, the analysis of nonlinear systems is considerably more complex than that of linear systems, and that additional complexity is not required for our purposes. Therefore, we shall restrict our discussion to the analysis of linear systems.

The definition of a linear system states that an input which is the sum of two signals produces an output which is the sum of the outputs produced by each of the individual input signals acting alone. From this it follows that, if an input signal is multiplied by a rational number, the output is increased or decreased by the same factor; that is,

$$ax_1(t) \rightarrow ay_1(t) \tag{4}$$

We take it as an axiom that Eq. (4) also holds for irrational numbers.

The property defined in Eqs. (1), (2), and (3), and its corollary in Eq. (4), serve to define a linear system. When using linear system theory to analyze a process, it is imperative that the process being modeled is, at least approximately, linear. If the system under study does not satisfy the criteria for linearity, then it is nonlinear, and linear system theory will produce inaccurate and possibly misleading results. If the system is only slightly nonlinear, it may be assumed linear for purposes of analysis, but the results of the analysis will be only as good as the assumption.

Frequently, systems known to be slightly nonlinear are studied with linear system theory because this approach is mathematically tractable. However, one must be cautious when dealing with nonlinear systems because the protective canopy of linear system theory disintegrates as the assumption of linearity breaks down. The analyst has the responsibility not only for the mathematics, but for the validity of the underlying assumptions as well.

Shift Invariance. A useful property that certain systems exhibit is called *shift invariance.* It is illustrated by the following. Assume, for a particular linear system, that

$$x(t) \rightarrow y(t) \tag{5}$$

Suppose we now shift the input signal in time by an amount T. The system is shift invariant if

$$x(t-T) \rightarrow y(t-T) \tag{6}$$

that is, the output is shifted by the same amount as the input, but is otherwise unchanged. Thus, for a shift-invariant system, shifting the input merely shifts the output by the same amount. The important point is that the nature of the output is not changed by a shift of the input signal. Spatial shift invariance is the two-dimensional analog of time shift invariance: If the input image is shifted relative to its origin, the output image is the same as before, except for an identical shift.

Most of the analysis in the next few chapters is directed toward shift-invariant linear systems. The assumptions of linearity and shift invariance are valid to a very good approximation for electrical networks, well-designed linear electronic networks, and optical systems—the principal components of image-processing systems.

9.2 HARMONIC SIGNALS AND COMPLEX SIGNAL ANALYSIS

In ordinary usage, signals and images can be represented by real-valued functions of one and two variables, respectively. The value of the function represents the magnitude of some physical parameter, such as voltage, as a function of time or light intensity as a function of two spatial coordinates. The development of linear system properties proceeds much more smoothly, however, if we allow the inputs and outputs to be complex-valued functions. Since real-valued functions can be considered a special case of complex-valued functions, we lose nothing by this generalization. The advantages become clear during the course of the development.

9.2.1 Harmonic Signals

Consider a complex-valued signal of the form

$$x(t) = e^{j\omega t} = \cos(\omega t) + j\sin(\omega t) \tag{7}$$

where $j^2 = -1$. This is called a *harmonic signal.* It is a complex-valued function of time that can be viewed as a unit length vector rotating in the complex plane with an angular velocity ω (Figure 9–3). The angular frequency ω, in radians per second, is related to f, the frequency in revolutions or cycles per second (Hertz) by $\omega = 2\pi f$.

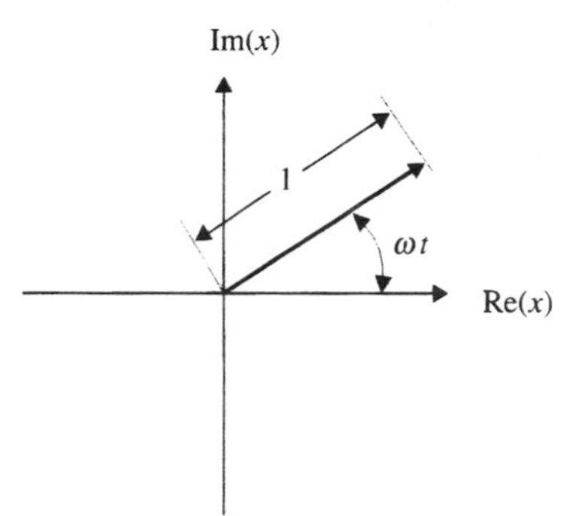

Figure 9–3 Harmonic signal-generating vector

9.2.2 Response to a Harmonic Input

Suppose a shift-invariant linear system is presented with a harmonic input

$$x_1(t) = e^{j\omega t} \tag{8}$$

We can express the response of the system as

$$y_1(t) = K(\omega, t)e^{j\omega t} \tag{9}$$

where

$$K(\omega, t) = \frac{y_1(t)}{e^{j\omega t}} \tag{10}$$

is a complex function of ω and t selected so that, when multiplied by $e^{j\omega t}$, it yields $y_1(t)$. Thus, there is always a $K(\omega, t)$ that will work.

Now suppose we generate a second input signal by time shifting $x_1(t)$. We then have

$$x_2(t) = e^{-j\omega(t-T)} = e^{-j\omega T}e^{j\omega t} = e^{-j\omega T}x_1(t) \tag{11}$$

Notice that $x_2(t)$ is merely $x_1(t)$ multiplied by a complex constant. This results because $x_1(t)$ is a harmonic signal.

The linear system's response to $x_2(t)$ is now

$$y_2(t) = K(\omega, t-T)e^{j\omega(t-T)} \tag{12}$$

which is

$$y_2(t) = K(\omega, t-T)e^{-j\omega T}e^{j\omega t} \tag{13}$$

or

$$y_2(t) = K(\omega, t-T)e^{-j\omega T}x_1(t) \tag{14}$$

Recalling Eq. (4), we can write

$$x_2(t) = e^{-j\omega T}x_1(t) \rightarrow e^{-j\omega T}y_1(t) = e^{-j\omega T}K(\omega, t)e^{j\omega t} \tag{15}$$

From Eq. (8), we recognize the exponential factor on the right as $x_1(t)$. Also, we know that the response side of Eq. (15) has to be $y_2(t)$, since it is the system's response to $x_2(t)$. Therefore, we can write

$$y_2(t) = e^{-j\omega T}K(\omega, t)x_1(t) \tag{16}$$

which is a second expression for the system's response to the shifted harmonic input.

Eq. (14) was obtained by inserting a time shift into Eq. (9). Eq. (16) resulted from the linearity property of Eq. (4). Both equations, however, are expressions for the linear system's response to the time-shifted harmonic input; thus, they must be equal. Combining Eqs. (14) and (16) produces

$$K(\omega, t-T)e^{-j\omega T}x_1(t) = K(\omega, t)e^{-j\omega T}x_1(t) \tag{17}$$

and it is clear that

$$K(\omega, t-T) = K(\omega, t) \tag{18}$$

must be true for any amount of shift T. Eq. (18) can be true, however, only if $K(\omega, t)$ is independent of t. So Eq. (9) can be rewritten in general form as

$$y(t) = K(\omega)x(t) \tag{19}$$

The general function whose form was assumed in Eq. (10) turns out to be a function of only the frequency variable, ω. Eq. (19) states the important property that the response of a shift-invariant linear system to a harmonic input is simply that input multiplied by a frequency-dependent complex number. Notice that a harmonic input always produces a harmonic output at the same frequency.

9.2.3 Harmonic Signals and Sinusoids

When we use a linear system to model the behavior of a physical (electronic or optical) system, the inputs and outputs are conveniently represented by real-valued functions. Thus, we can add another restriction to shift-invariant linear systems, namely, that they preserve realness. By definition, this means that a real-valued input can produce only a real-valued output. From this, it can be shown that such a system also preserves imaginariness and that removing the imaginary part of a complex input merely removes the imaginary part of the corresponding complex output; that is,

$$x(t) \rightarrow y(t) \Rightarrow \Re e\{x(t)\} \rightarrow \Re e\{y(t)\} \tag{20}$$

In a sense, the real and imaginary parts of a harmonic input go through the system independently of each other.

The real-preserving restriction on linear systems allows us to simplify the analysis. For example, if the input is a cosine, we can add an imaginary sine component to form a harmonic signal [recall Eq. (7)], determine the system's response to that harmonic input, and then discard the imaginary part of the complex output. This indirect approach is justified by a significant simplification of the analysis.

Any sinusoidal signal can be thought of as the real part of a (unique) harmonic signal. This approach allows us to derive a linear system's response to a sinusoid by (1) representing the input sinusoid by a harmonic signal, (2) deriving the linear system's response to the harmonic input, and (3) taking the real part of the harmonic output to yield the actual output.

In so doing, we are using a transform method of solution; that is, we transform from sinusoids to harmonic signals, solve the problem in terms of harmonics, and then transform the harmonic output back into a sinusoid.

The technique is analogous to using logarithms for multiplication: One transforms the multiplier and multiplicand into logarithms, adds them to effect the multiplication, and then transforms the result back from logarithms to ordinary numbers to obtain the desired product. As with logarithms, the transformation to harmonic signals simplifies the analysis of linear systems considerably.

9.2.4 The Transfer Function

The function $K(\omega)$ is called the *transfer function* of the linear system and is sufficient to specify the system completely. For a shift-invariant linear system, the transfer function contains all the information that exists about the system.

We can convert $K(\omega)$ to polar form to obtain

$$K(\omega) = A(\omega)e^{j\phi(\omega)} \tag{21}$$

where $A(\omega)$ is real-valued function of frequency and the complex exponential is a unit vector in the complex plane—that is, a complex number having unit magnitude.

The effect of the transfer function is illustrated by the following. Suppose the input is a cosine, taken to be the real part of a harmonic signal:

$$x(t) = \cos(\omega t) = \Re e\{e^{j\omega t}\} \tag{22}$$

The system's response to the harmonic input is

$$K(\omega)e^{j\omega t} = A(\omega)e^{j\phi}e^{j\omega t} = A(\omega)e^{j(\omega t + \phi)} \tag{23}$$

Finally, the actual output signal is

$$\begin{aligned} y(t) = \Re e\{A(\omega)e^{j(\omega t + \phi)}\} &= \Re e\{A(\omega)[\cos(\omega t + \phi) + j\sin(\omega t + \phi)]\} \\ &= A(\omega)\cos(\omega t + \phi) \end{aligned} \tag{24}$$

$A(\omega)$ is a multiplicative gain factor and represents the degree to which the system amplifies or attenuates the input signal. $\phi(\omega)$ is the phase shift angle. Its only effect is to shift the time origin of the harmonic input function.

In the remainder of this book, the analysis will be done in terms of harmonic signals, with the conversion to sinusoids left as a step of interpretation.

In sum, we have developed three important properties of shift-invariant linear systems: (1) A harmonic input always produces a harmonic output at the same frequency. (2) The system is completely specified by its transfer function, a complex-valued function of frequency alone. (3) The transfer function produces only two effects upon a harmonic input—a change in amplitude and a phase shift (a shift of the time origin).

9.3 THE CONVOLUTION OPERATION

Consider again the linear system shown in Figure 9–1. It would be useful to have a general expression that relates the output signal, $y(t)$, to the input signal, $x(t)$. We can obtain such a relation in the following way. The linear functional expression (superposition integral)

$$y(t) = \int_{-\infty}^{\infty} f(t, \tau)x(\tau)d\tau \tag{25}$$

is general enough to express the relationship between $x(t)$ and $y(t)$ for any linear system. A function $f(t,\tau)$ of two variables can be chosen to make Eq. (25) hold for any linear system; but we would prefer to characterize a linear system with a function of only one variable.

We now impose the shift invariance constraint in an effort to simplify Eq. (25). Substituting Eq. (6) into Eq. (25) produces

$$y(t-T) = \int_{-\infty}^{\infty} f(t, \tau)x(t-T)d\tau \tag{26}$$

We make a change of variables by adding T to both t and τ. This produces

$$y(t) = \int_{-\infty}^{\infty} f(t+T, \tau+T)x(\tau)d\tau \tag{27}$$

If we compare Eqs. (25) and (27), we see that

$$f(t, \tau) = f(t+T, \tau+T) \tag{28}$$

must be true for all values of T. This means that $f(t,\tau)$ does not change if we add the same constant to both of its arguments. In other words, $f(t,\tau)$ is constant as long as the difference between t and τ is constant. Thus we can define a new function of only this difference, namely,

$$g(t-\tau) = f(t, \tau) \tag{29}$$

and Eq. (25) becomes

$$y(t) = \int_{-\infty}^{\infty} g(t-\tau)x(\tau)d\tau \tag{30}$$

This is the familiar *convolution integral.* It states that the output of a shift-invariant linear system is given by the convolution of the input signal with a function $g(t)$ which is characteristic of that system (Figure 9–4). This characteristic function is called the *impulse response* of the system for reasons pointed out later. Notice that the system preserves realness if and only if $g(t)$ is a real-valued function.

We now have two ways to specify the relationship between the input and output of a shift-invariant linear system: (1) Every such system has a complex transfer function that, when multiplied by a harmonic input, yields the harmonic output; and (2) every such system has a real impulse response that, when convolved with the input signal, yields the output signal.

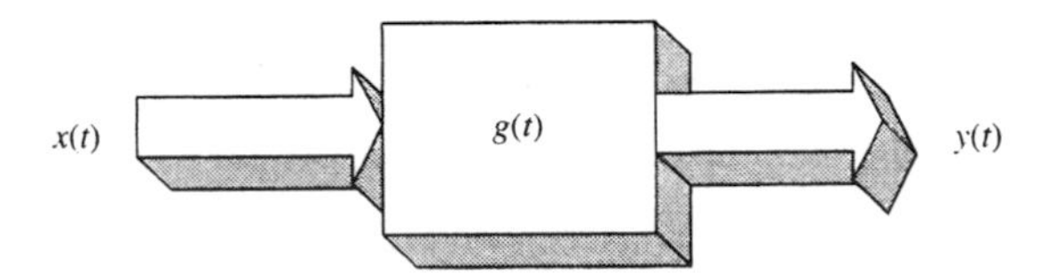

Figure 9–4 A linear system

Since the transfer function and the impulse response of a shift-invariant linear system are each unique and adequate to specify the system completely, we suspect that the two functions may be related. This relationship is developed in the next chapter.

9.3.1 Convolution in One Dimension

The convolution integral in Eq. (30) may be abbreviated by the shorthand notation

$$y = g * x \tag{31}$$

where $*$ is used to indicate the convolution of two functions. Figure 9–5 presents a graphic illustration of the convolution operation. One point on the curve $y(t)$ is obtained in the following way. One function g is reflected about its origin and shifted by an amount t to the right. The point-by-point product of x and the reflected, shifted g is formed, and that product is integrated to produce the value of the output at t. This process is repeated for all values of t to produce other points on the output curve. As t is varied, the reflected function is shifted past the stationary function, and the value of $y(t)$ depends on the amount of overlap of the two functions.

The convolution operation has several useful properties. First, convolution is commutative; that is,

$$f * g = g * f \tag{32}$$

and we may reflect either function and obtain the same result. This can be shown by writing

$$f * g = \int_{-\infty}^{\infty} f(\tau)g(t-\tau)d\tau \tag{33}$$

making the change of variables

$$x = t - \tau \qquad \tau = t - x \qquad dx = -d\tau \tag{34}$$

and rearranging to produce

$$f * g = \int_{-\infty}^{\infty} f(t-x)g(x)dx = g * f \tag{35}$$

In Eq. (35), the limits had to be interchanged, and this compensated for the minus sign on $d\tau$.

The convolution operation is also distributive over addition; that is,

$$f * (g + h) = f * g + f * h \tag{36}$$

This can be shown by writing

$$f * (g + h) = \int_{-\infty}^{\infty} f(t-\tau)\,[g(\tau) + h(\tau)]\,d\tau \tag{37}$$

and rearranging to yield

$$f * (g + h) = \int_{-\infty}^{\infty} f(t-\tau)g(\tau)d\tau + \int_{-\infty}^{\infty} f(t-\tau)h(\tau)d\tau = f * g + f * h \tag{38}$$

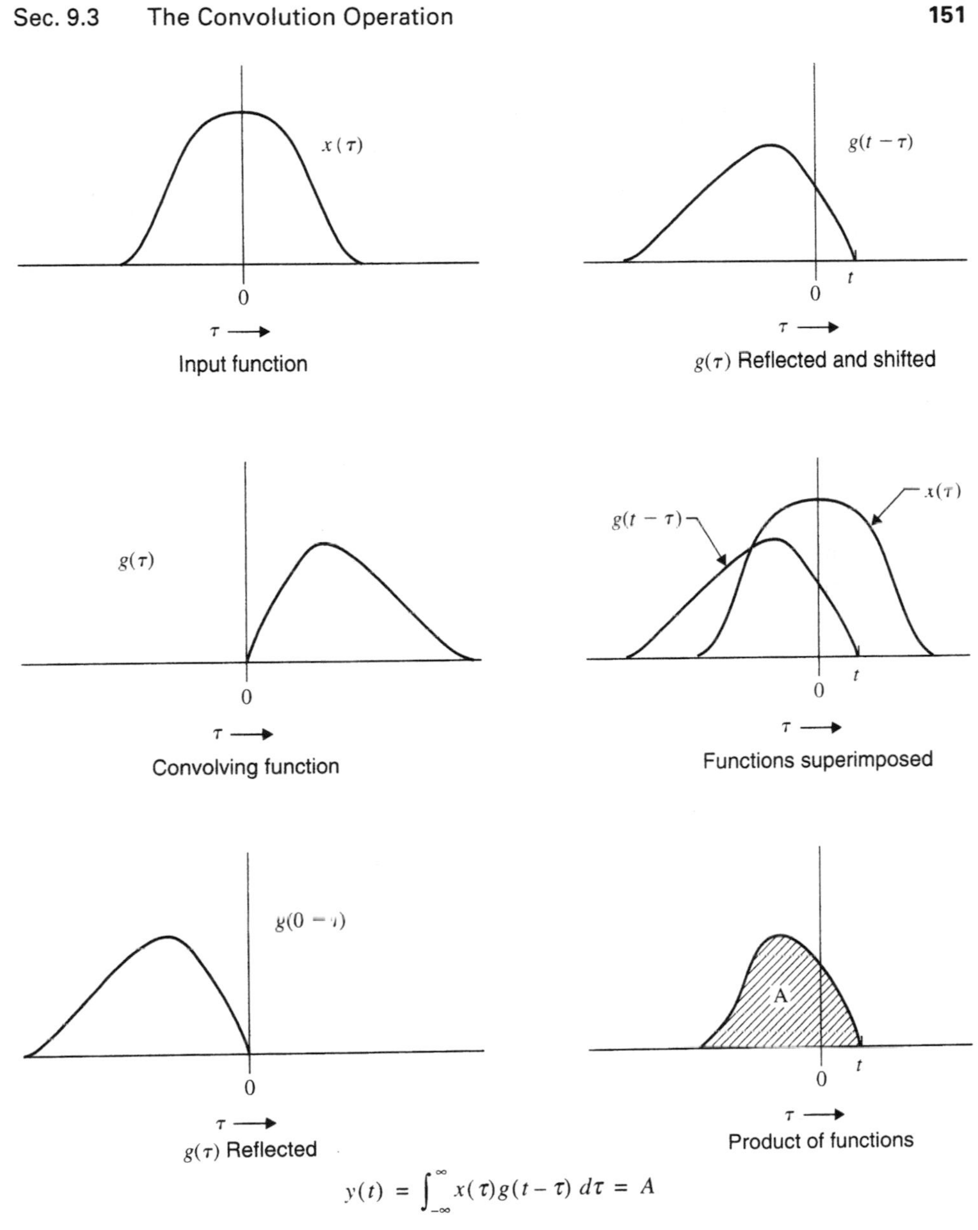

$$y(t) = \int_{-\infty}^{\infty} x(\tau)g(t-\tau)\,d\tau = A$$

Figure 9–5 Convolution

Convolution is also associative, which means that

$$f * (g * h) = (f * g) * h \tag{39}$$

This equation may be verified by the reader. Under differentiation,

$$\frac{d}{dt}[f * g] = f' * g = f * g' \tag{40}$$

9.3.2 Discrete One-Dimensional Convolution

Discrete sequences can be convolved in a manner similar to the convolution of continuous functions. The independent variable becomes an index, and the integral is replaced by a summation. Thus, for two sequences $f(i)$ and $g(i)$ of length m and n, respectively, the analog of Eq. (33) is

$$h(i) = f(i) * g(i) = \sum_j f(j)g(i-j) \tag{41}$$

which produces an output sequence of length $N = m + n - 1$.

While discrete and continuous convolution are quite different operations, they hold many properties in common. It is our good fortune that discrete convolution, which we can readily implement on digital images, closely parallels continuous convolution, which describes many of the things that happen to our images before (and after) they are in digital form. This is exploited in image restoration, which seeks to reverse the effects of degrading influences that have already acted upon the image.

9.3.2.1 Matrix Formulation

It is convenient to represent discrete sequences as vectors and take advantage of the compact notation and well-developed properties afforded by linear algebra. Although Eq. (41) is a summation of products, the convolution of two sequences cannot be effected by a simple vector multiplication. It can be described by a matrix multiplication, however, if the situation is set up properly.

First we assume that $f(i)$ is actually a portion of an infinite-length sequence that is periodic with a period of at least N, the length of the convolution output sequence of Eq. (41). Since $f(i)$ is shorter than N, it is necessary to pad the additional elements with zeros. The word *pad* was chosen to describe such a process probably because the process resembles sewing padding into one's clothing to make oneself look larger.

One period of the infinite sequence that results from this manipulation is given by

$$f_p(i) = \begin{cases} f(i) & 1 \le i \le m \\ 0 & m < i \le N \end{cases} \tag{42}$$

We repeat this construction with $g(i)$ and $h(i)$ as well. Now all three sequences have the same length. While the benefits of this complication may not yet be apparent, at least it can be done without loss of generality.

Next we let **f** be an N-by-1 column vector whose elements are $f_p(i)$, one period of the infinite sequence formed from $f(i)$. We also let **G** be a matrix whose first row is the zero-padded sequence $g_p(i)$ stored in reverse order. Subsequent rows of **G** are formed by a circular right shift of the elements of the previous row. Now we can write

$$\mathbf{h} = \mathbf{G} \cdot \mathbf{f} = \begin{bmatrix} g_p(1) & g_p(N) & \cdots & g_p(2) \\ g_p(2) & g_p(1) & \cdots & g_p(3) \\ \vdots & \vdots & & \vdots \\ g_p(N) & g_p(N-1) & \cdots & g_p(1) \end{bmatrix} \cdot \begin{bmatrix} f_p(1) \\ f_p(2) \\ \vdots \\ f_p(N) \end{bmatrix} \tag{43}$$

where **h** is an N-by-1 vector containing the output sequence. The discrete convolution is now expressed as the product of an N-by-N matrix and an N-by-1 vector. Recall that N is the length of the output sequence that results from Eq. (41).

The matrix **G** in Eq. (43) is called a *circulant* matrix because each row is a circular, right-shifted version of the previous row. It is this structure that allows us to write convolution as a matrix product. Each row of **G** serves to generate one element of the output sequence.

9.3.3 Convolution in Two Dimensions

The convolution of continuous functions of two variables is similar to one-dimensional convolution. Note that as the discussion extends to the case of two dimensions, we shall use x and y as the two independent variables. The equation for two-dimensional convolution is

$$h(x, y) = f * g = \int_{-\infty}^{\infty}\int_{-\infty}^{\infty} f(u, v)g(x-u, y-v)du\, dv \tag{44}$$

illustrated graphically in Figure 9–6. Notice that $g(0-u, 0-v)$ is merely $g(u, v)$ rotated 180° about its origin and that $g(x-u, y-v)$ is translated so as to move the origin of the

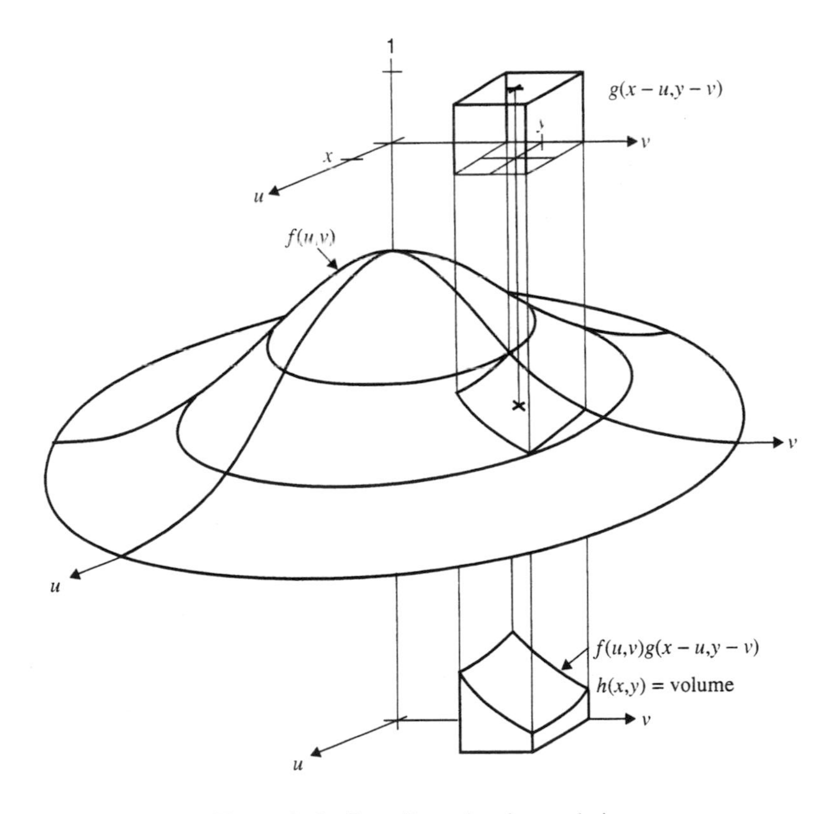

Figure 9–6 Two-dimensional convolution

rotated g to the point x, y. The functions are then multiplied pointwise, and the product function is integrated over two dimensions. As an example, suppose that

$$f(x, y) = Ae^{-(x^2+y^2)/2\sigma^2} \tag{45}$$

and

$$g(x, y) = \begin{cases} 1, & -1 \le x \le 1, -1 \le y \le 1 \\ 0, & \text{elsewhere} \end{cases} \tag{46}$$

as shown in Figure 9–6. In this case, a two-dimensional rectangular pulse is convolved with a larger two-dimensional Gaussian. Since $g(x, y)$ is symmetric about the origin, the 180° rotation has no effect. The value of $h(x, y)$ is merely the volume of the product function when the rectangular pulse is shifted to the position x, y.

9.3.3.1 Example: Sampling with a Finite Spot

Suppose a particular image digitizer (e.g., a CCD sensor) samples an image with a square sampling spot. At each pixel location, the digitized gray level is the local average of a small square section of the image. In Figure 9–6, $f(x, y)$ could represent the image and $g(x, y)$ the spatial sensitivity function of the sampling spot. Then $h(x, y)$, the convolution of $f(x, y)$ with $g(x, y)$, is the same local average that the digitizer "sees." Thus, convolution is a valid way to model the action of a sampling spot on an image. The function $g(x, y)$ can be chosen to model the spatial sensitivity function of whatever sampling aperture is used.

9.3.4 Discrete Two-Dimensional Convolution

The convolution of digital images is similar to that of continuous functions, except that the variables take on integer values and the double integral becomes a double summation. Thus, for a digital image,

$$\mathbf{H} = \mathbf{F} * \mathbf{G} \qquad H(i, j) = \sum_m \sum_n F(m, n)G(i-m, j-n) \tag{47}$$

Since both **F** and **G** are nonzero only over a finite domain, the summations need to be taken only over the region of nonzero overlap.

Discrete convolution is illustrated in Figure 9–7. The array **G** is rotated 180°, and its origin is shifted to the coordinates (i, j). The two arrays are multiplied together, element by element, and the resulting products are summed to give the output value.

In the figure, a 3×3 array **G** (called the *convolution kernel*) is convolved with a larger digital image, **F**. Clearly, the required number of multiplication and addition operations is equal to the number of pixels in **G** times the number of pixels in **F** (ignoring effects near the borders of the image). Unless the kernel is small (or has a relatively small nonzero domain and thus can be trimmed), convolution becomes a computationally expensive operation.

Pixels near the border of the image lack a full set of neighbors, and convolution cannot proceed smoothly through these areas. In implementing digital convolution, four options are commonly used regarding pixels near the edge. One can (a) *extend* the input image by repeating the border rows and columns of the array to allow convolution to proceed to the border of the output image, (b) *wrap* the input image (thereby making it periodic) by

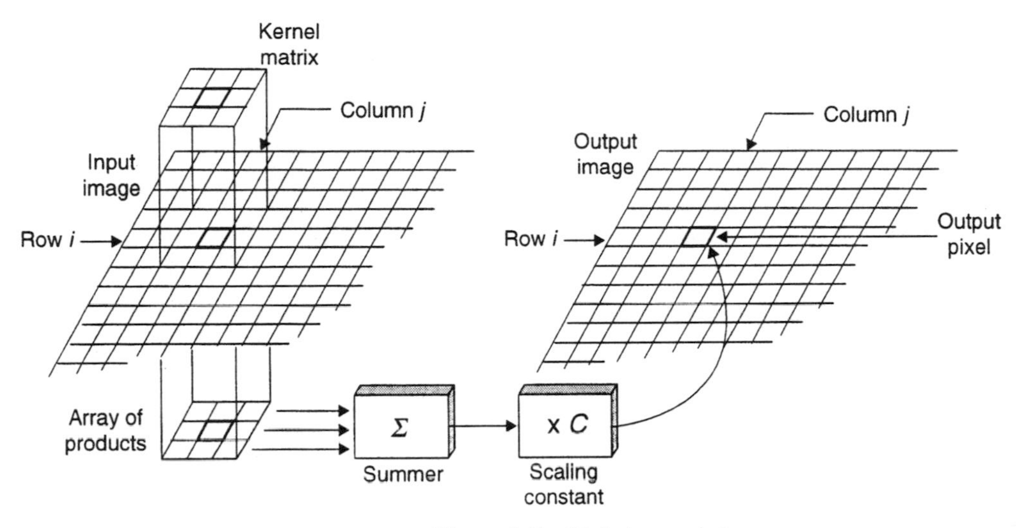

Figure 9–7 Digital convolution

assuming the first column comes immediately after the last, etc., (c) fill in a constant (e.g., zero) for output pixels too near the border; or (d) compute an output image of reduced size, by eliminating output rows and columns that cannot be computed by convolution.

The first and third of these options are often the most workable solutions. The best approach is to digitize the image in such a way that no important information falls closer to the border than half the width of the kernel. Then the choice is not critical.

9.3.4.1 Matrix Formulation

As with one dimensional discrete sequences, it is convenient to represent digital images as matrices and exploit the benefits of linear algebra. Again, matrix multiplication will not implement convolution directly, but a suitable construction can produce the desired effect [6,7]. The process is illustrated in Figure 9–8.

As before, we assume that the arrays **F** and **G** are periodic in the x-direction with a period of at least the sum of their horizontal extents, and similarly for the y-direction. Thus, if **F** is m_1 by n_1 and **G** is m_2 by n_2, we pad both with zeros to bring them up to a size $M \geq m_1 + m_2 - 1$ by $N \geq n_1 + n_2 - 1$. We call these new (larger) arrays $\mathbf{F_p}$ and $\mathbf{G_p}$, respectively. For the remainder of this development, we assume the common case of $M = N$.

Next, we form an N^2-by-1 column vector $\mathbf{f_p}$ from the matrix $\mathbf{F_p}$ by *row stacking*: The first row of $\mathbf{F_p}$, transposed to the vertical, becomes the top N elements of $\mathbf{f_p}$, and similarly as subsequent rows are transposed and placed underneath.

Each row of $\mathbf{G_p}$ is then used to form an N-by-N circulant matrix in the manner described in Sec. 9.3.2. This produces a set of N such matrices $\mathbf{G_i}$ ($1 \leq i \leq N$), one for each row of $\mathbf{G_p}$.

A *block matrix* is a matrix, each element of which is itself a matrix. Thus, a block matrix is a larger matrix that is actually an array of smaller matrices. A *block circulant matrix* is a matrix, each element of which is a circulant matrix. We can use a block circulant matrix to extend the approach used in Sec. 9.3.2 to two dimensions.

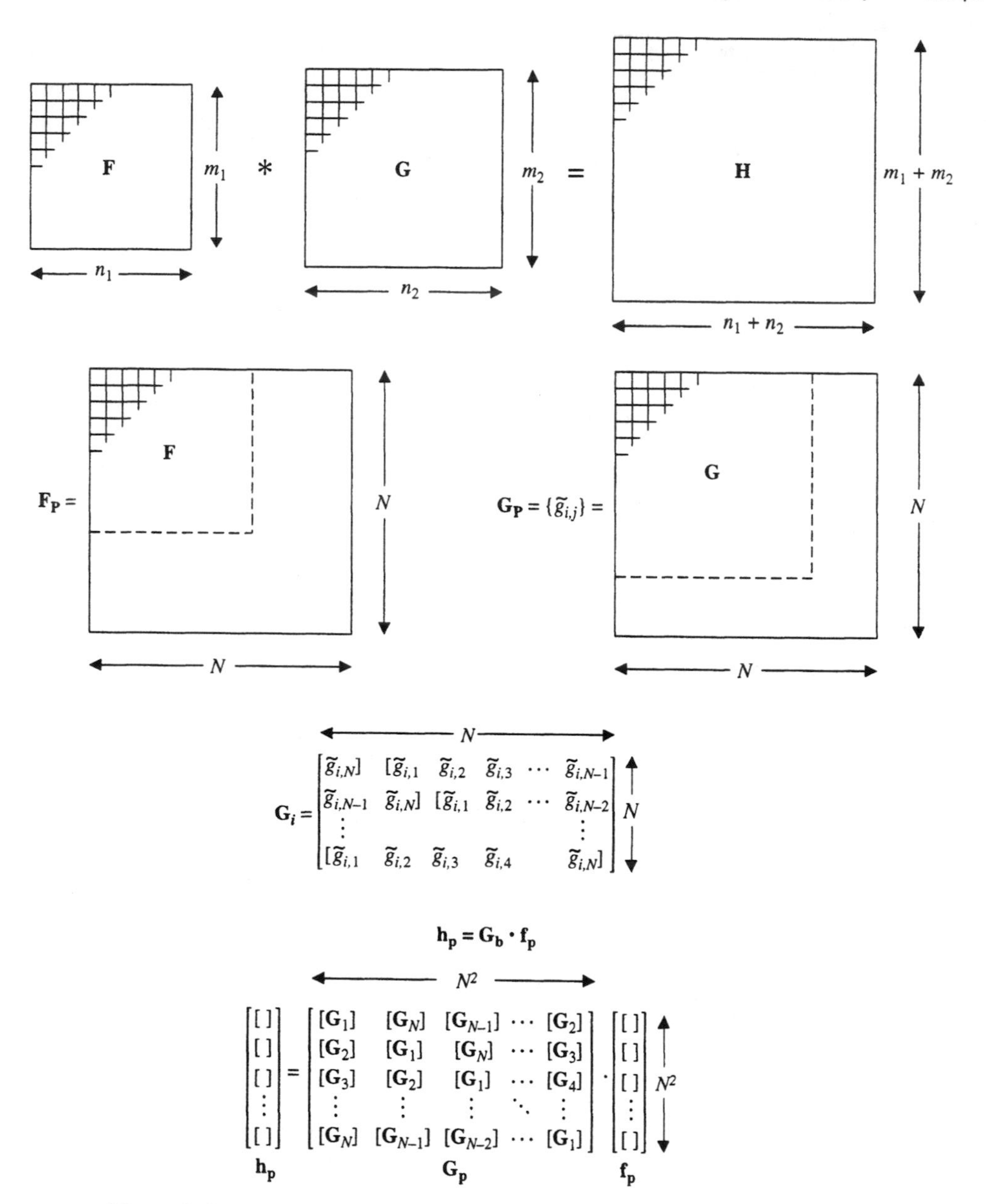

Figure 9–8 The matrix formulation for two-dimensional convolution: **F** and **G** are padded with zeros to form $\mathbf{F_p}$ and $\mathbf{G_p}$. Each row of $\mathbf{G_p}$ gives rise to a circulant matrix, $\mathbf{G}_i$, in the manner shown. $\mathbf{G_b}$ is a block circulant matrix formed from the $\mathbf{G}_i$ matrices, and $\mathbf{f_p}$ is a row-stacked column vector formed from $\mathbf{F_p}$. $\mathbf{h_p}$ is the convolution result in row-stacked format.

We form the N^2-by-N^2 block circulant matrix $\mathbf{G_b}$ as follows: $\mathbf{G_b}$ is composed of N-by-N blocks, each of which is one of the N-by-N circulant matrices $\mathbf{G}_i$ formed from the ith row of $\mathbf{G_p}$. That is,

$$\mathbf{G_b} = \begin{bmatrix} [\mathbf{G}_1] & [\mathbf{G}_N] & \cdots & [\mathbf{G}_2] \\ [\mathbf{G}_2] & [\mathbf{G}_1] & \cdots & [\mathbf{G}_3] \\ \vdots & \vdots & \ddots & \vdots \\ [\mathbf{G}_N] & [\mathbf{G}_{N-1}] & \cdots & [\mathbf{G}_1] \end{bmatrix} \tag{48}$$

The upper left block, $\mathbf{G}_1$, has as its first row the elements of the first row of $\mathbf{G_p}$, transposed and reversed, as in Sec. 9.3.2. Subsequent rows of $\mathbf{G}_1$ are formed by a circular right shift of the previous row. The other blocks of $\mathbf{G_b}$ are formed similarly from the other rows of $\mathbf{G_p}$. Thus, $\mathbf{G_b}$ is an N-by-N circulant array of N-by-N circulant matrices, each of which computes one pixel in the output image.

Now we are in a position to write the two-dimensional convolution of Eq. (47) simply as the matrix product

$$\mathbf{h_p} = \mathbf{G_b} \cdot \mathbf{f_p} \tag{49}$$

where $\mathbf{h_p}$ is the output image in padded, row-stacked, column vector form. This construct, then, generalizes the matrix formulation of convolution to two dimensions.

Notice that $\mathbf{G_b}$ has N^4 elements. If, for example, $N = 1{,}000$, then $\mathbf{G_b}$ has 10^{12} (one trillion) elements. Thus, the utility of the matrix formulation lies elsewhere than in efficiency of implementation. What it does, in fact, is allow us to use the extremely compact notation of linear algebra in image-restoration filter design. Also, by taking advantage of the significant amount of symmetry in these matrices, one can sometimes simplify the computations into a manageable range.

An Example. Figure 9–9 shows a numerical example of using the matrix formulation to convolve two 2-by-2 arrays.

$$\mathbf{F} = \begin{bmatrix} 1 & 2 \\ 3 & 4 \end{bmatrix} \quad \mathbf{F}_p = \begin{bmatrix} 1 & 2 & 0 \\ 3 & 4 & 0 \\ 0 & 0 & 0 \end{bmatrix} \quad \mathbf{G} = \begin{bmatrix} -1 & 1 \\ -2 & 2 \end{bmatrix} \quad \mathbf{G}_p = \begin{bmatrix} -1 & 1 & 0 \\ -2 & 2 & 0 \\ 0 & 0 & 0 \end{bmatrix}$$

$$\mathbf{h}_p = \mathbf{G}_b \cdot \mathbf{f}_p = \left[\begin{array}{ccc|ccc|ccc} -1 & 0 & 1 & 0 & 0 & 0 & -2 & 0 & 2 \\ 1 & -1 & 0 & 0 & 0 & 0 & 2 & -2 & 0 \\ 0 & 1 & -1 & 0 & 0 & 0 & 0 & 2 & -2 \\ \hline 2- & 0 & 2 & -1 & 0 & 1 & 0 & 0 & 0 \\ 2 & -2 & 0 & 1 & -1 & 0 & 0 & 0 & 0 \\ 0 & 2 & -2 & 0 & 1 & -1 & 0 & 0 & 0 \\ \hline 0 & 0 & 0 & -2 & 0 & 2 & -1 & 0 & 1 \\ 0 & 0 & 0 & 2 & -2 & 0 & 1 & -1 & 0 \\ 0 & 0 & 0 & 0 & 2 & -2 & 0 & 1 & -1 \end{array}\right] \cdot \begin{bmatrix} 1 \\ 2 \\ 0 \\ 3 \\ 4 \\ 0 \\ 0 \\ 0 \\ 0 \end{bmatrix} = \begin{bmatrix} -1 \\ -1 \\ 2 \\ -5 \\ -3 \\ 8 \\ -6 \\ -2 \\ 8 \end{bmatrix} \qquad \mathbf{H} = \mathbf{F} * \mathbf{G} = \begin{bmatrix} -1 & -1 & 2 \\ -5 & -3 & 8 \\ -6 & -2 & 8 \end{bmatrix}$$

Figure 9–9 Two-by-two convolution example using the matrix formulation

9.3.5 Applications of Convolution

Digitally implemented linear filtering is useful for three major classes of image-processing applications:

1. *Deconvolution,* i.e., removing the effects of unwanted but previously applied linear systems that have operated on the image. An example of this is using convolution to restore the detail lost by a lens system or by motion blur, both of which can be assumed to be linear operations.

2. *Noise removal,* i.e, reducing the effects of undesirable, contaminative signals that have been linearly added to the image. Examples are:

(a) Estimating what the signal was before the noise was added.
(b) Detecting the presence of known features embedded in a noisy background.
(c) Coherent (periodic) noise removal.

3. *Feature enhancement,* i.e., increasing the contrast of specific features (edges, spots, etc.) at the expense of other objects in the scene.

9.4 SOME USEFUL FUNCTIONS

In the development of linear system theory and its application to image processing, we shall make particular use of five functions. At this point, we introduce these five functions and derive some of their properties. This will greatly simplify the development and examples in the chapters that follow. In the remainder of this chapter, we continue to use x as an independent variable, even for one-dimensional functions.

9.4.1 The Rectangular Pulse

Following the notation of [1], we denote the rectangular pulse by

$$\Pi(x) = \begin{cases} 1, & -\frac{1}{2} < x < \frac{1}{2} \\ \frac{1}{2}, & x = \pm\frac{1}{2} \\ 0, & \text{elsewhere} \end{cases} \tag{50}$$

The rectangular pulse of height A and width a is shown in Figure 9–10. This function is useful for modeling rectangular sampling windows and smoothing functions.

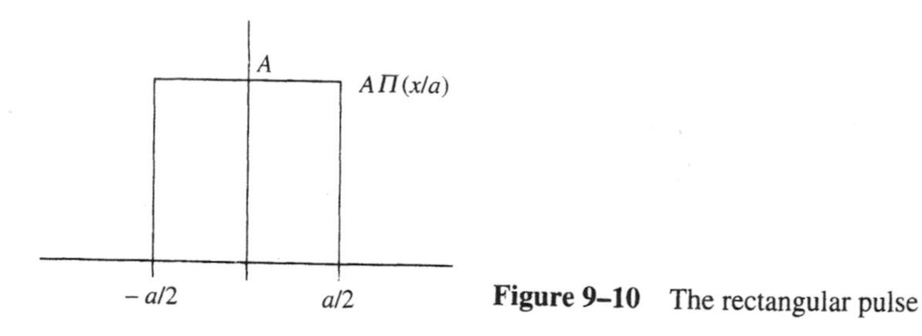

Figure 9–10 The rectangular pulse

9.4.2 The Triangular Pulse

We denote the triangular pulse by

$$\Lambda(x) = \begin{cases} 1 - |x|, & |x| \leq 1 \\ 0, & |x| > 1 \end{cases} \tag{51}$$

This function is shown in Figure 9–11. Its applications are similar to those of the rectangular pulse. Convolving two identical rectangular pulses produces a triangular pulse.

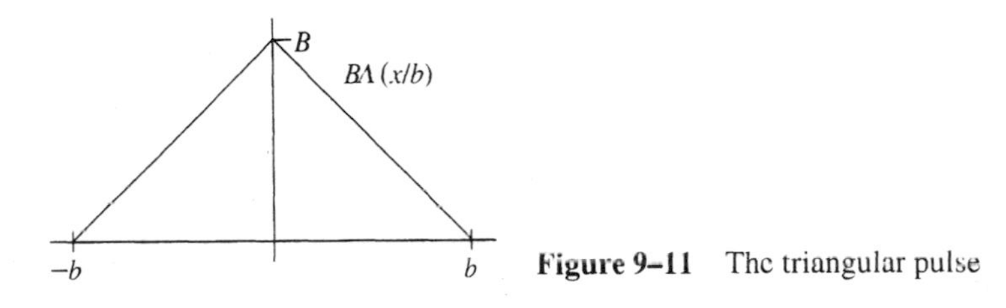

Figure 9–11 The triangular pulse

9.4.3 The Gaussian Function

The Gaussian function is given by

$$e^{-x^2/2\sigma^2} \tag{52}$$

and is shown in Figure 9–12. The area under the Gaussian function is

$$\int_{-\infty}^{\infty} e^{-x^2/2\sigma^2} dx = \frac{1}{\sqrt{2\pi\sigma^2}} \tag{53}$$

In probability theory, the normal distribution with mean x_0 is given by

$$p(x) = \frac{1}{\sqrt{2\pi\sigma^2}} e^{-(x-x_0)^2/2\sigma^2} \tag{54}$$

which is a Gaussian function adjusted to unit area. The term σ^2 is called the *variance,* and σ itself is known as the *standard deviation.* Table 9–1 lists the values of the Gaussian at several points.

The Gaussian has a very useful property, mentioned in Chapter 7: The convolution of two Gaussian functions always produces another Gaussian. In particular,

$$Ae^{-(x-a)^2/2\sigma_1^2} * Be^{-(x-b)^2/2\sigma_2^2} = ABe^{-(x-c)^2/2\sigma_3^2} \tag{55}$$

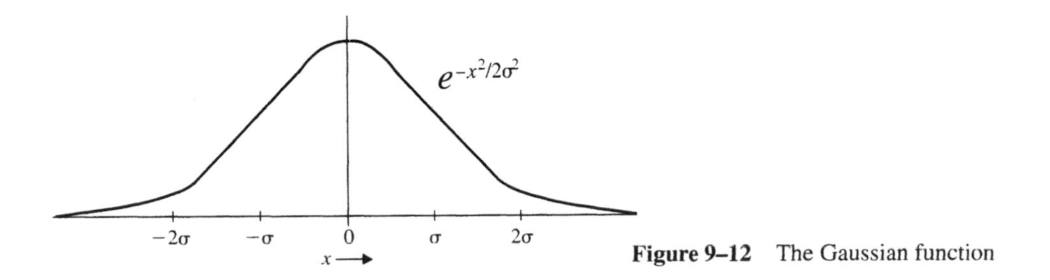

Figure 9–12 The Gaussian function

TABLE 9–1 VALUES OF THE GAUSSIAN FUNCTION

x	$e^{-x^2/2\sigma^2}$
0	1
0.5σ	0.8825
1.0σ	0.6065
1.177σ	0.5000
1.5σ	0.3247
$1.177\sigma\sqrt{2}$	0.2500
2.0σ	0.1353
3.0σ	0.0111

where

$$c = a + b \text{ and } \sigma_3^2 = \sigma_1^2 + \sigma_2^2 \tag{56}$$

Thus, the resulting Gaussian is broadened: Its standard deviation is the root mean square of the two original standard deviations, and its offset from the origin is the sum of the two original offsets. The amplitude of the peak is the product of the amplitudes of the two original peaks.

This convolution property of the Gaussian is quite useful for studying linear systems. Furthermore, the smooth, unimodal shape of the Gaussian makes it appropriate for modeling sampling spots, display spots, and a variety of other entities encountered in digital image processing and the analysis of optical systems. Several more useful properties of the Gaussian are developed in subsequent chapters. Taken together, these properties explain the frequent usage of the Gaussian function in linear system analysis.

9.4.4 The Impulse

The impulse, or Dirac delta function $\delta(x)$, is not a function by the traditional definition of the term. Instead, it is a symbolic function defined by its integral property,

$$\int_{-\infty}^{\infty} \delta(x)dx = \int_{-\varepsilon}^{\varepsilon} \delta(x)dx = 1 \tag{57}$$

where ε is an arbitrarily small number greater than 0. Notice that $\delta(x) = 0$ for $x \neq 0$; the impulse is undefined at the origin.

Since $\delta(x)$ is not a function, its use as such somewhat undermines our level of mathematical rigor. There is a mathematically rigorous approach treating the impulse as a concept in the theory of distributions [2–4], but its use here would only complicate the notation while producing the same results. We shall adhere to common engineering practice and treat $\delta(x)$ as if it were a function, but take note of its special properties.

The impulse can be modeled as the limit of a narrow rectangular pulse

$$\delta(x) = \lim_{a \to 0} \frac{1}{a} \Pi\left(\frac{x}{a}\right) \tag{58}$$

as shown in Figure 9–13. As a becomes smaller, the pulse becomes narrower, but taller, to maintain unit area. In the limit, the pulse becomes infinitely tall with infinitesimal width. The symbol for the shifted impulse of nonunit area is shown in Figure 9–14.

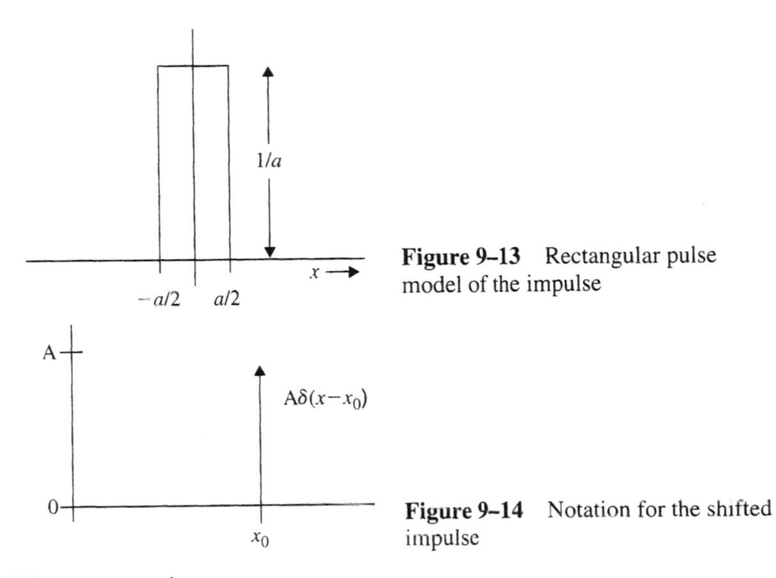

Figure 9–13 Rectangular pulse model of the impulse

Figure 9–14 Notation for the shifted impulse

From Eq. (57), we can write

$$\int_{-\infty}^{\infty} A\delta(x)dx = A \tag{59}$$

and furthermore,

$$\int_{-\infty}^{\infty} f(x)\delta(x)dx = f(0) \tag{60}$$

since the impulse is zero for nonzero x. This more general integral property is commonly taken as the definition of the impulse.

9.4.4.1 Properties of the Impulse

The impulse has a *sifting property* because of its ability to isolate a single point on a curve. This is expressed by

$$\int_{-\infty}^{\infty} f(x)\delta(x-x_0)dx = \int_{-\infty}^{\infty} f(x+x_0)\delta(x)dx = f(x_0) \tag{61}$$

When we multiply a function by a shifted impulse and integrate the product, we are left with only the value of the function at the location of the impulse. We can prove Eq. (61) by substituting $x - x_0 = \tau$, which implies $dx = d\tau$. Substituting these into Eq. (61) produces

$$\int_{-\infty}^{\infty} f(x)\delta(x-x_0)dx = \int_{-\infty}^{\infty} f(\tau+x_0)\delta(\tau)d\tau \tag{62}$$

which, from Eq. (60), becomes

$$\int_{-\infty}^{\infty} \delta(\tau)f(\tau+x_0)\,d\tau = f(\tau+x_0)\big|_{\tau=0} = f(x_0) \tag{63}$$

completing the proof.

The delta function exhibits rather curious behavior under changes of scale of the abscissa, namely,

$$\delta(ax) = \frac{1}{|a|}\delta(x) \tag{64}$$

Eq. (64) says that a change in scale of the abscissa actually produces a change in scale of the ordinate. This property must be kept in mind while performing algebraic manipulations with the impulse. We can prove Eq. (64) by letting $f(x)$ be an arbitrary function and writing

$$\int_{-\infty}^{\infty} \delta(ax)f(x)dx = \frac{1}{a}\int_{-\infty}^{\infty} \delta(\tau)f\left(\frac{\tau}{a}\right)d\tau = \frac{1}{|a|}f(0) \tag{65}$$

where $ax = \tau$, $x = \tau/a$, and $dx = (1/a)d\tau$. For $a < 0$, the required interchanging of the limits counteracts the minus sign and, hence, requires the absolute-value bars. Now we can write

$$\int_{-\infty}^{\infty} \delta(ax)f(x)dx = \frac{1}{|a|}f(0) = \frac{1}{a}\int_{-\infty}^{\infty} \delta(x)f(x)dx = \int_{-\infty}^{\infty} \left[\frac{1}{|a|}\delta(x)\right]f(x)dx \tag{66}$$

which, since $f(x)$ is an arbitrary function, can be true only if Eq. (64) is true. Notice that setting $a = -1$ proves that the delta function is symmetric about the origin.

9.4.4.2 Impulse Response of a Linear System

Notice that

$$\delta(x) * f(x) = \int_{-\infty}^{\infty} \delta(\tau)f(x-\tau)d\tau = f(x-\tau)\big|_{\tau=0} = f(x) \tag{67}$$

which means that the impulse is the identity function under convolution. For this reason, the characteristic function of the linear system [recall the discussion surrounding Eq. (30)] is called the *impulse response* of the system. The impulse response is the system output that results from an impulse at the input.

9.4.5 The Step Function

The step function is a symbolic function that is discontinuous at $x = 0$. It is given by

$$u(x) = \begin{cases} 1, & x > 0 \\ \frac{1}{2}, & x = 0 \\ 0, & x < 0 \end{cases} \tag{68}$$

and its integral property by

$$\int_{-\infty}^{\infty} u(x)f(x)dx = \int_{0}^{\infty} f(x)dx \tag{69}$$

where $f(x)$ is an arbitrary function. The shifted step function $u(x - x_0)$ is shown in Figure 9–15. Notice that the step function is the integral of the impulse:

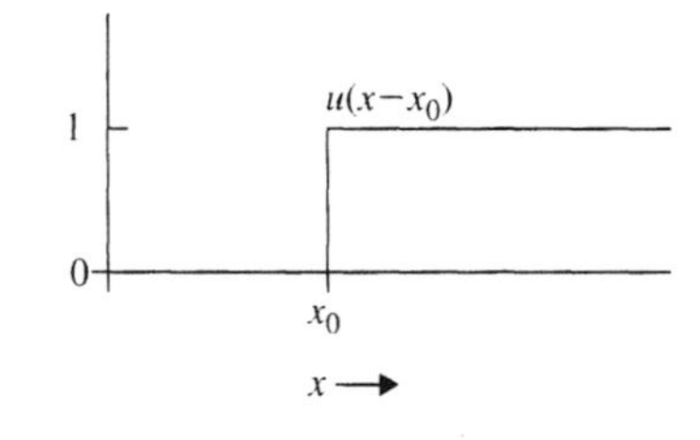

Figure 9–15 The step function

$$u(x - x_0) = \int_{-\infty}^{x} \delta(\tau - x_0)d\tau = \begin{cases} 1, & x > x_0 \\ 0, & x < x_0 \end{cases} \tag{70}$$

Also, as one might expect, the impulse is the derivative of the step function:

$$u'(x) = \frac{du(x)}{dx} = \delta(x) \tag{71}$$

We can prove Eq. (71) in the following way. First we integrate by parts the expression

$$\int_{-\infty}^{\infty} u'(x)f(x)dx = u(x)f(x)\Big|_{-\infty}^{\infty} - \int_{-\infty}^{\infty} u(x)f'(x)dx \tag{72}$$

where $f(x)$ is an arbitrary function that goes to zero at $x = \pm\infty$. With this restriction, Eq. (72) reduces to

$$\int_{-\infty}^{\infty} u'(x)f(x)dx = -\int_{-\infty}^{\infty} u(x)f'(x)dx \tag{73}$$

Making use of the definition of the step function [Eq. (69)], we can write

$$\int_{-\infty}^{\infty} u(x)f'(x)dx = \int_{0}^{\infty} f'(x)dx = [f(\infty) - f(0)] = -f(0) \tag{74}$$

since $f(\infty) = 0$. Now, using the definition of the impulse [Eq. (60)], we can write

$$\int_{-\infty}^{\infty} u'(x)f(x)dx = f(0) = \int_{-\infty}^{\infty} \delta(x)f(x)dx \tag{75}$$

which must be true for arbitrarily selected $f(x)$. But this can be the case only if Eq. (71) is true.

9.5 CONVOLUTION FILTERING

Convolution is commonly used to implement linear operations on signals and images. This section illustrates the concept with a few examples.

9.5.1 Smoothing

Figure 9–16 shows the use of convolution for smoothing a noisy function $f(x)$. A rectangular pulse $g(x)$ is the impulse response of the smoothing filter. As the convolution proceeds, the rectangular pulse moves from left to right, producing $h(x)$, which is, at every point, a local

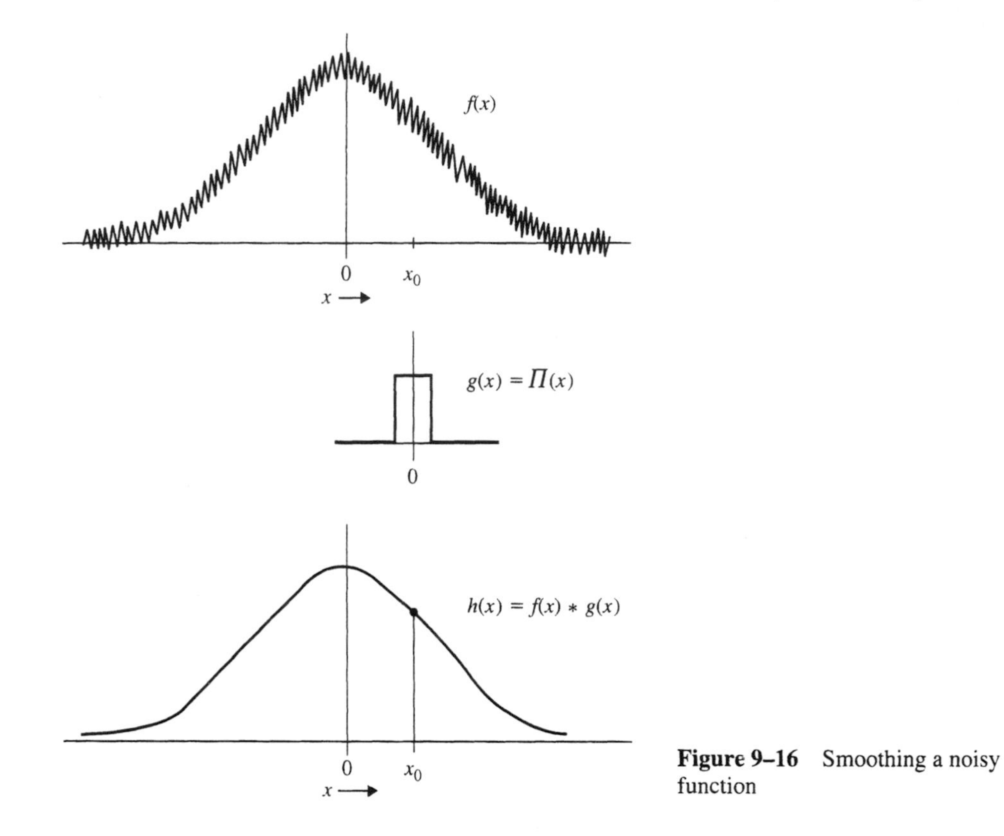

Figure 9–16 Smoothing a noisy function

average of $f(x)$ over a unit width interval. The local averaging has the effect of suppressing the high-frequency variations while preserving the basic shape of the input function. This application is typical of the use of filters with nonnegative impulse responses to smooth noisy data. We could equally well use the triangular pulse or the Gaussian pulse as the smoothing function.

9.5.2 Edge Enhancement

Figure 9–17 illustrates another type of filtering, this time for edge enhancement. The edge function $f(x)$ is a rather slowly varying transition from low to high amplitude. The impulse response $g(x)$ is a positive peak with negative side lobes. As the convolution proceeds, $g(x)$ moves from left to right, with the side lobes and main lobe progressively encountering the transition of the edge. The filter output is shown as $h(x)$.

The edge enhancement filter in the figure has two effects. First, it tends to increase the slope of the transition at the edge. Second, it produces overshoot, or *ringing,* on either side of the edge. This behavior is typical of commonly-used edge enhancement filters.

As a second example of edge enhancement, consider the impulse response given by

$$g(x) = 2\delta(x) - e^{-x^2/2\sigma^2} \tag{76}$$

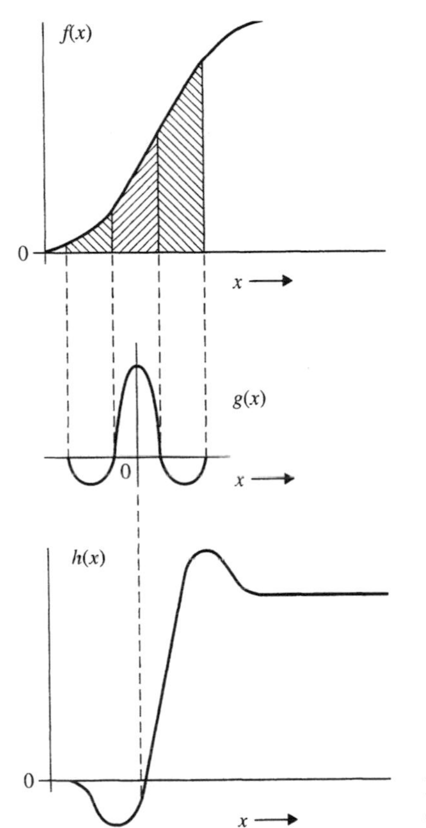

Figure 9–17 Edge enhancement, example 1

and shown in Figure 9–18. Notice that

$$h = f * g = f(x) * 2\delta(x) - f(x) * e^{-x^2/2\sigma^2} = 2f(x) - f(x) * e^{-x^2/2\sigma^2} \tag{77}$$

So the output is merely twice the input, minus the input convolved with a Gaussian. Convolving with the Gaussian blurs the edge, as illustrated in the figure. By contrast, the output has the enhanced edge form shown in the figure. Again, there is sharpening of the edge with overshoot.

This exercise points out that subtracting a blurred image from the original image has the effect of edge enhancement. The operation is reminiscent of the photographic darkroom technique called *unsharp masking.*

9.5.3 Deconvolution

Often, when an image is obtained, it has already been acted upon by one or more linear systems over which we have no control. Many of the degradations that result from less than perfect optics, sensors, recorders, and displays can be modeled as convolution operations. The technique of designing one convolution to *undo* the effects of another convolution is called *deconvolution.* This topic is addressed in Chapter 16.

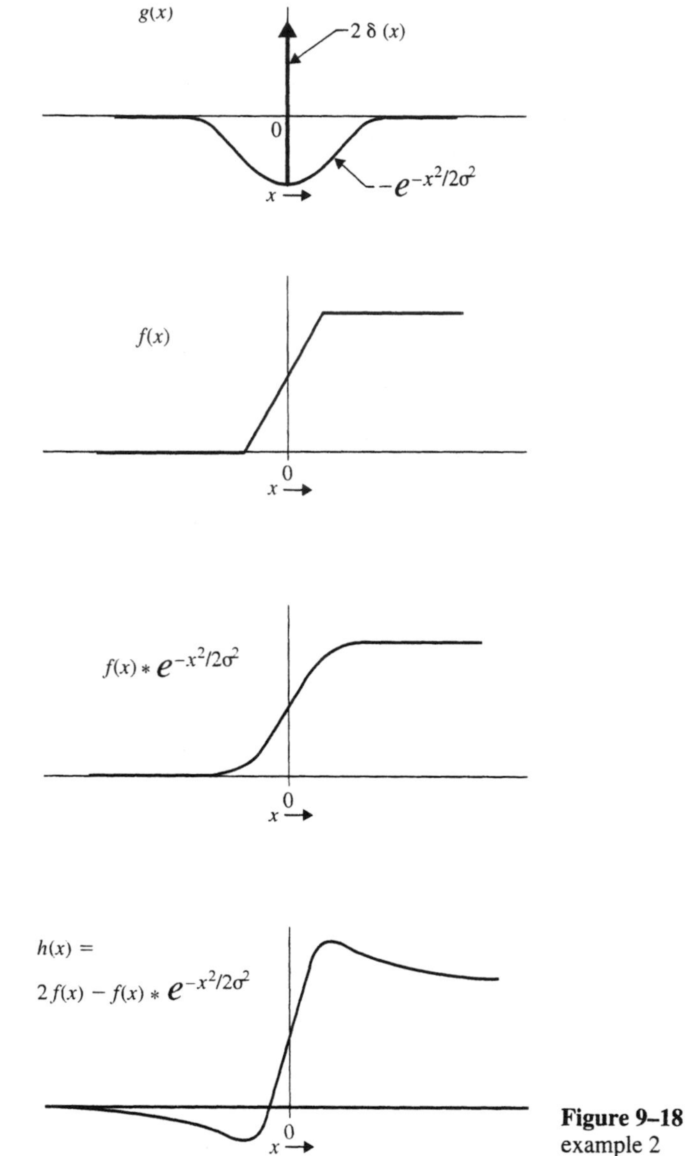

Figure 9–18 Edge enhancement, example 2

9.6 CONCLUSION

In this chapter, we have established a framework within which to analyze the behavior of optical systems, image sensors, electronic circuits, and digital filtering operations. This almost completely covers the components encountered in image processing systems. In Chapter 10, we develop another powerful tool for linear system analysis: the Fourier transform. In the remainder of Part 2, we apply these tools to develop concise methods for expressing the effects that digitizing systems, display systems, and image-processing operations can have on an image.

9.7 SUMMARY OF IMPORTANT POINTS

1. When the input into a linear system is the sum of two signals, the output is the sum of the outputs produced by each of those signals acting alone.
2. Changing the temporal (or spatial) origin of the input to a shift-invariant system merely shifts the output by the same amount.
3. Harmonic signals are used to represent sinusoidal signals because they simplify the analysis of linear systems.
4. Harmonic (sinusoidal) inputs into a shift-invariant, linear system produce harmonic outputs.
5. A linear, shift-invariant system is completely specified by its transfer function.
6. The transfer function is a complex-valued function of frequency that relates the amplitude and phase of harmonic inputs and outputs.
7. The harmonic input multiplied by the value of the transfer function at the input frequency yields the output of a shift invariant, linear system.
8. The convolution of two functions consists of reflecting and shifting one function and then integrating their product. The output is the value of the integral as a function of the amount of shift.
9. The output of a shift-invariant, linear system is given by the convolution of the input with a function called the impulse response of that system.
10. The impulse response of a particular shift-invariant, linear system is unique and completely specifies the system.
11. The convolution operation models the effect a sampling spot has on an image.
12. Convolution may be implemented digitally to perform linear filtering on digitized signals and images.
13. Digitally implemented linear filtering may be used for deconvolution, noise reduction, and feature enhancement.
14. Since convolution cannot proceed all the way to the border of an image, it is important to avoid having important information located there.
15. Convolving two Gaussian functions produces another Gaussian, broader than either of the inputs.
16. The impulse $\delta(x)$ is the identity function under convolution [Eq. (67)].
17. Changes of scale in the abscissa affect the strength of the impulse [Eq. (64)].
18. The impulse is the derivative of the step function.
19. The impulse response of an edge enhancement filter typically has a positive peak at the origin surrounded by negative side lobes.
20. Edge enhancement filters often produce the artifact called overshoot or ringing.

PROBLEMS

1. Prove Eq. (4).
2. Verify Eq. (39).

3. Verify Eq. (40).
4. Show that $\Pi(t) * \Pi(t) = \Lambda(t)$.
5. Verify Eq. (55) and (56).
6. In a particular system, $f_1(t) \rightarrow \cos^2(2\pi f_0 t)$ and $2f_1(t) \rightarrow 1 + \cos(4\pi f_0 t)$. Is this system linear? Why or why not?
7. In a particular system, $\Pi(\pi t) \rightarrow \text{cosech}(2\pi t)$ and $\Pi(\pi(t-a)] \rightarrow \text{cosech}(2\pi a t)$. Is this system shift invariant? Why or why not?
8. In a particular system, $\Lambda(\alpha t) \rightarrow \text{sech}^2(2\pi t)$ and $\Lambda[\alpha(t-a)] \rightarrow \text{sech}^2[2\pi(t-a)]$. Is this system shift invariant? Why or why not?
9. In a particular system, $f_2(t) \rightarrow \delta(2t)$ and $2f_2(t) \rightarrow \delta(t)$. Is this system linear? Why or why not?
10. In a particular system, $f_3(t) \rightarrow \cos(2\pi t)$ and $f_3(t - \pi/2) \rightarrow \sin(2\pi t)$. Is this system shift invariant? Why or why not?
11. In a particular system, $\delta(\text{t}) \rightarrow 1/[1 + (t/2)^2]$ and $\delta[4(t-2)] \rightarrow 1/(t^2 - 4t + 8)$. Is this system linear? Shift invariant? Why or why not?
12. In a particular system, $u(t)$ is the step function, $2u(t) - 1 \rightarrow [1/\sqrt{2}]\tanh[2\pi(t-2)]$, and $4u(t-9) - 2 \rightarrow \sqrt{2}\tanh[2\pi(t-11)]$. Is this system linear? Shift invariant? Why or why not?
13. Show that $\text{sech}(\pi t) * \text{sech}(\pi t) = 2t\,\text{cosech}(\pi t)$.
14. What will be the output if a Gaussian of amplitude 100 and standard deviation 4 and centered on $t = 8$ is put into a shift-invariant, linear system having an impulse response that is a Gaussian of amplitude 2 and standard deviation 3 centered on the origin? Sketch the input and output on the same graph.
15. A shift-invariant, linear system has an impulse response

$$g(t) = 2\delta(t) - \frac{1}{\sqrt{2\pi}} e^{-\frac{t^2}{2}}$$

and its input is

$$x(t) = 10e^{-\frac{t^2}{8}}$$

Sketch its input and output on the same graph.

16. If you needed to reduce the random noise in a signal, which impulse response would you use, the one in Problem 14 or the one in Problem 15? Why? If you needed to sharpen edges, which one would you use? Why?

PROJECTS

1. Using a computer system and software package with image convolution and display capability, process a noisy image of a person's face to reduce the noise. Experiment with the size and shape of the convolution kernel to obtain the most pleasing overall result. Write a brief report discussing what happens when the kernel is too small, what happens when it is too large, and how you arrived at the proper size. Include hard-copy images of the processing results in the report.
2. Develop a program that can create convolution kernels from specified parameters and write them in a form that can be read by one of the image-processing software packages. Test the program on digitized images to verify that it works.

REFERENCES

For additional reading, see Appendix 2.

1. R. Bracewell, *The Fourier Transform and Its Applications* (2d ed.), McGraw-Hill, New York, 1986.
2. E. O. Brigham, *The Fast Fourier Transform and Its Applications,* Prentice-Hall, Englewood Cliffs, New Jersey, 1988.
3. A. Papoulis, *The Fourier Integral and Its Applications,* McGraw-Hill, New York, 1962.
4. S. C. Gupta, *Transform and State Variable Methods in Linear Systems,* John Wiley & Sons, New York, 1966.
5. T. Kailath, *Linear Systems,* Prentice-Hall, Englewood Cliffs, NJ, 1980.
6. B. R. Hunt, "A Matrix Theory Proof of the Discrete Convolution Theorem," *IEEE Trans.* **AU-19**(4):285–288, 1971.
7. H. C. Andrews and B. R. Hunt, *Digital Image Restoration,* Prentice-Hall, Englewood Cliffs, New Jersey, 1977.

CHAPTER 10

The Fourier Transform

10.1 INTRODUCTION

The Fourier transform is a powerful tool in linear system analysis. It allows us to quantify the effects of digitizing systems, sampling spots, electronic amplifiers, convolution filters, noise, and display spots. Those who combine a theoretical knowledge of Fourier transform properties with a practical knowledge of their physical interpretation are well prepared to approach most image-processing problems. Usually, those who develop this combination of skills are students of electrical engineering and physical optics, and they do so in the course of their studies. For anyone who intends to use digital image processing seriously in their work, however, the time spent becoming familiar with the Fourier transform is well invested.

In a sense, the Fourier transform is like a second language for describing functions. Bilingual persons frequently find one language better than another for expressing certain ideas. Similarly, the image-processing analyst may move back and forth between the spatial domain and the frequency domain while proceeding through a problem.

When first learning a new language, one tends to think in his or her native tongue and mentally translate before speaking. After becoming fluent, however, one can think in either language. Similarly, once familiar with the Fourier transform, the analyst can think in either the spatial or the frequency domain, and this ability is quite useful.

In the first part of the chapter, we develop the properties of the Fourier transform using one-dimensional functions for simplicity of notation. Later we generalize the results to two dimensions. The convention in Part 2 of the text is first to consider one-dimensional functions as simple examples and then to extend the discussion to functions of two spatial variables as image-processing examples.

In our study of linear system analysis, we shall restrict our discussion to only one part of this well-developed field. For example, we use only the Fourier transform and not the LaPlace transform or the Z-transform, because they are not required for our purposes. This restriction allows us to develop the techniques we need for the analysis of digital image-processing systems with a minimum of mathematical complexity.

One reason we do not require the generality of the LaPlace transform, and other techniques from the field of linear system analysis, is that we are working with recorded data. This relieves us of the burden of dealing with physical realizability (*causality*) and its implications for the analysis.

Causality. Linear systems implemented with electronic hardware are referred to as *causal* because the input signal causes the output signal to occur. In particular, this means that if the input is zero for all negative time, then the output must likewise be zero for $t < 0$. While this is intuitively obvious, consider the constraint it places upon the impulse response of a linear system: If the input is an impulse at $t = 0$, the impulse response must be zero for all negative t. Thus, with physically realizable systems, the impulse response is always one sided. This means that it can be neither even nor odd, except in the trivial case. Such a condition considerably complicates the linear system analysis of physically realizable systems.

Working with recorded data leaves us not so constrained. Digitally implemented convolution can easily deal with even and odd functions, as well as those that are zero for negative time. Furthermore, in the spatial domain of image processing, the coordinate origin is arbitrary, and negative values of x and y have no special significance. Readers who find the mathematics in the following chapters burdensome should be thankful that we are working with recorded data and do not have to impose the causality condition upon the analysis.

10.1.1 The Continuous Fourier Transform

The Fourier transform of a one-dimensional function $f(t)$ is defined as [1]

$$\mathfrak{F}\{f(t)\} = F(s) = \int_{-\infty}^{\infty} f(t)e^{-j2\pi st}dt \qquad (1)$$

where $j^2 = -1$. The Fourier transform is a linear integral transformation that, in the general case, takes a complex function of n real variables into another complex function of n real variables. The inverse Fourier transform of $F(s)$ is defined as

$$\mathfrak{F}^{-1}\{F(s)\} = \int_{-\infty}^{\infty} F(s)e^{j2\pi st}ds \qquad (2)$$

The only difference between the direct and inverse Fourier transformations is the sign of the exponent.

Fourier's integral theorem states that

$$f(t) = \int_{-\infty}^{\infty} \left[\int_{-\infty}^{\infty} f(t) e^{-j2\pi st} dt \right] e^{j2\pi st} ds \tag{3}$$

This means that the transformation is reciprocal, and

$$\mathfrak{F}\{f(t)\} = F(s) \Rightarrow \mathfrak{F}^{-1}\{F(s)\} = f(t) \tag{4}$$

The functions $f(t)$ and $F(s)$ are called a *Fourier transform pair.* For any function $f(t)$, the Fourier transform $F(s)$ is unique, and vice versa.

There are alternative ways of writing Eqs. (1), (2), and (3), depending on where the factor 2π is placed in the equations. The convention used here corresponds to system 1 in [1]. In this convention, the frequency variable is measured in whole cycles (rather than radians) per unit of t.

10.1.1.1 Example: The Fourier Transform of a Gaussian

As an illustrative exercise, we now derive the Fourier transform of the Gaussian function

$$f(t) = e^{-\pi t^2} \tag{5}$$

From Eq. (1), we can write

$$F(s) = \int_{-\infty}^{\infty} e^{-\pi t^2} e^{-j2\pi st} dt$$

or

$$F(s) = \int_{-\infty}^{\infty} e^{-\pi(t^2 + j2st)} dt \tag{6}$$

We multiply the right-hand side by

$$e^{-\pi s^2} e^{+\pi s^2} = 1$$

which yields

$$F(s) = e^{-\pi s^2} \int_{-\infty}^{\infty} e^{-\pi(t + js)^2} dt \tag{7}$$

We now make the variable substitution

$$u = t + js \qquad du = dt \tag{8}$$

and Eq. (7) becomes

$$F(s) = e^{-\pi s} \int_{-\infty}^{\infty} e^{-\pi u^2} du \tag{9}$$

The integral in Eq. (9) is known to equal unity, so Eq. (9) reduces to

$$F(s) = e^{-\pi s^2} \tag{10}$$

Thus, the functions in Eqs. (5) and (10) are a Fourier transform pair, and the Fourier transform of a Gaussian is also a Gaussian. This property makes the Gaussian function quite useful in later analysis.

10.1.2 Existence of the Fourier Transform

Since the Fourier transform is an integral transformation, we must address the question of the existence of the integrals in Eqs. (1) and (2).

10.1.2.1 Transient Functions

Some functions go to zero for large positive and negative arguments rapidly enough that the integrals in Eqs. (1) and (2) exist. For our purposes, if the integral of the absolute value of a function exists, i.e., if

$$\int_{-\infty}^{\infty} |f(t)|\,dt < \infty \tag{11}$$

and the function either is continuous or has only finite discontinuities, then the Fourier transform of the function exists for all values of s. We call these functions *transient functions,* since the useful ones characteristically die out at large $|t|$.

In a sense, these are the only functions we shall ever process. Any digitized signal or image is necessarily truncated to finite duration and bounded. Thus, the transform exists for any function we shall ever be required to use. Nevertheless, it is convenient to be able to discuss other functions whose transforms do not exist in the strict sense.

10.1.2.2 Periodic and Constant Functions

Clearly, the Fourier transform does not exist for all values of s if $f(t) = \cos(2\pi t)$ or if $f(t) = 1$. However, the impulse $\delta(t)$, introduced in Chapter 9, allows us to handle these cases conveniently.

Consider the inverse transform of a pair of impulses

$$f(t) = \mathfrak{F}^{-1}\{\delta(s-f_0) + \delta(s+f_0)\} = \int_{-\infty}^{\infty} [\delta(s-f_0) + \delta(s+f_0)]e^{j2\pi st}ds$$

which, by the sifting property of the impulse, is

$$f(t) = \int_{-\infty}^{\infty} \delta(s-f_0)e^{j2\pi st}ds + \int_{-\infty}^{\infty} \delta(s+f_0)e^{j2\pi st}ds$$

$$= e^{-j2\pi f_0 t} + e^{+j2\pi f_0 t} = 2\cos(2\pi f_0 t)$$

where we have used the Euler relation (Chapter 9, Eq. 7). Dividing by 2, we can write

$$\mathfrak{F}\{\cos(2\pi f_0 t)\} = \frac{1}{2}[\delta(s-f_0) + \delta(s+f_0)] \tag{12}$$

This means that the Fourier transform of a cosine of frequency f_0 is a pair of impulses located at $s = \pm f_0$ in the frequency domain. A similar development yields

$$\mathfrak{F}\{\sin(2\pi f_0 t)\} = \frac{j}{2}[\delta(s+f_0) - \delta(s-f_0)] \tag{13}$$

If we let $f_0 = 0$ in Eq. (12), we can show that

$$\mathfrak{F}\{1\} = \delta(s) \tag{14}$$

That is, the Fourier transform of a constant is an impulse at the origin.

We now have usable expressions for the Fourier transform of constant and sinusoidal functions. It is well known in the theory of Fourier series that any periodic function of frequency f can be expressed as a summation of sinusoids having frequencies nf, where n takes on integer values. By the addition theorem [see Eq. (40)], this means that the Fourier transform of a periodic function is a series of equally spaced impulses in the frequency domain.

10.1.2.3 Random Functions

We lump nonconstant aperiodic functions of infinite extent whose absolute integral [Eq. (11)] does not exist into a class called *random functions.* In later chapters, we use these to model the output of a random process.

In most cases, we require only the autocorrelation function of a random function. This is given by

$$R_f(\tau) = \lim_{T\to\infty} \frac{1}{2T} \int_{-T}^{T} f(t)f(t+\tau)dt \tag{15}$$

and it exists for the functions that are of interest to us. The autocorrelation function is real and even, and its Fourier transform is the power spectrum of $f(t)$, as is shown later.

If it becomes necessary to transform a random function, we can redefine the Fourier transform of Eq. (1) as

$$F(s) = \lim_{T\to\infty} \frac{1}{2T} \int_{-T}^{T} f(t)e^{-j2\pi st}dt \tag{16}$$

and similarly for the inverse transform. We can then work with a class of functions for which these redefined transforms exist. In this book, however, we shall stay with the definitions set forth in Eqs. (1) and (2), since they are appropriate for bounded signals of finite duration. Any development carried out with this convention could be redone with the convention suggested by Eq. (16), thereby extending the result to random functions for which $R_f(\tau)$ exists.

We conclude this discussion by taking the position that, for our purposes, the existence of the Fourier transform is not a major problem.

10.1.3 The Fourier Series Expansion

Suppose $g(t)$ is a transient function that is zero outside the interval $[-T/2,T/2]$. This also can be considered to be one cycle of a periodic function. We can obtain a sequence of coefficients by making s a discrete variable in Eq. (1) and integrating only over the interval, so that

$$G_n = G(n\Delta s) = \int_{-T/2}^{T/2} g(t)e^{-j2\pi(n\Delta st)}dt \tag{17}$$

where T is the period and $\Delta s = 1/T$. This expansion represents $g(t)$ by an infinite sequence of (complex-valued) coefficients, although, for many interesting functions, only finitely many of the coefficients are nonzero.

The inverse transform becomes

$$g(t) = \sum_{n=0}^{\infty} G(n\Delta s)e^{j2\pi(n\Delta st)}\Delta s = \frac{1}{T}\sum_{n=0}^{\infty} G_n e^{j2\pi\left(\frac{n}{T}t\right)} \tag{18}$$

It reconstructs $g(t)$ within the interval by adding together sinusoids of different frequencies. The amplitudes of these sinusoids are the coefficients G_n.

The *Fourier series expansion* of the function $f(t)$ is [1]

$$f(t) = \frac{a_0}{2} + \sum_{n=1}^{\infty} a_n \cos\left(2\pi\frac{n}{T}t\right) + \sum_{n=1}^{\infty} b_n \sin\left(2\pi\frac{n}{T}t\right) \tag{19a}$$

where

$$a_n = \frac{2}{T}\int_{-T/2}^{T/2} f(x)\cos\left(2\pi\frac{n}{T}x\right)dx \quad \text{and} \quad b_n = \frac{2}{T}\int_{-T/2}^{T/2} f(x)\sin\left(2\pi\frac{n}{T}x\right)dx \tag{19b}$$

It represents a periodic function of period T by two infinite sequences of real coefficients.

10.1.4 The Discrete Fourier Transform

If we discretize both time and frequency the Fourier transform of Eq. (19a) becomes

$$G_n = G(n\Delta s) = \sum_{i=-N/2}^{N/2} g(i\Delta t)e^{-j2\pi(n\Delta s)i\Delta t}\Delta t = \frac{T}{N}\sum_{i=-N/2}^{N/2} g_i e^{-j2\pi\left(\frac{n}{N}\right)i} \tag{20a}$$

where $T = N\Delta t$. The inverse transform takes the form

$$g_i = g(i\Delta t) = \sum_{n=-\infty}^{\infty} G(n\Delta s)e^{j2\pi(n\Delta s)i\Delta t}\Delta s = \frac{1}{T}\sum_{n=-\infty}^{\infty} G_n e^{j2\pi\left(\frac{i}{N}\right)n} \tag{20b}$$

Again, for many interesting functions, $g(i\Delta t)$, the coefficients $\{G_n\}$ are nonzero only for relatively small n.

If $\{f_i\}$ is a sequence of length N, such as that obtained by taking samples of a continuous function at equal intervals, then its *discrete Fourier transform* (DFT) is the sequence $\{F_n\}$ given by

$$F_n = \frac{1}{\sqrt{N}}\sum_{i=0}^{N-1} f_i e^{-j2\pi\frac{n}{N}i} \tag{21}$$

and the inverse DFT is

$$f_i = \frac{1}{\sqrt{N}}\sum_{n=0}^{N-1} F_n e^{j2\pi\frac{i}{N}n} \tag{22}$$

where $0 \le i, n \le N-1$ are indices.

10.1.4.1 Relationship to the Continuous Transform

The similarity the DFT holds with Eqs. (1) and (2) and with Eqs. (20a) and (20b) suggests that the DFT might have many of the same properties as the integral transform. For the types of functions we work with in digital image processing, the differences are slight indeed. In fact, if $\{f_i\}$ is obtained by properly sampling a certain common type of continuous function, then the DFT can be shown to be a special case of the continuous Fourier transform [2]. Properly sampling these so-called *bandlimited* functions, and using the DFT to compute Fourier transforms are discussed in Chapters 12 and 13. Using the DFT to implement linear filtering is addressed in Chapter 16.

It is our good fortune that the DFT is so closely related to the continuous Fourier transform. As long as we abide by the sampling rules laid out in Chapter 12 we can view them as essentially equivalent. This flexibility affords us considerable latitude in the design process. It means, for example, that we can employ the continuous approach when formulating a solution to an image processing problem, and then implement that solution with the discrete approach.

10.1.5 The Fast Fourier Transform

When it is necessary to actually compute the Fourier transform of a sampled signal or image, we normally use the DFT. The number of multiplication and addition operations required to implement Eqs. (21) or (22) is clearly on the order of N^2, even after the required values of the complex exponential have been stored in a table. This makes the computation potentially burdensome.

Fortunately, there exists a class of algorithms that reduce the required number of operations to the order of $N \log_2(N)$ [2–6]. These are called *fast Fourier transform* (FFT) algorithms. N must be factorable into a product of small integers. Highest efficiency and the simplest implementation result when N is a power of 2 (i.e., $N = 2^p$ where p is an integer).

Notice that Eq. (21) can be written as the matrix product

$$\begin{bmatrix} F_0 \\ \vdots \\ F_{N-1} \end{bmatrix} = \begin{bmatrix} W_{0,0} & \cdots & W_{0,N-1} \\ \vdots & \ddots & \vdots \\ W_{N-1,0} & \cdots & W_{N-1,N-1} \end{bmatrix} \begin{bmatrix} f_0 \\ \vdots \\ f_{N-1} \end{bmatrix} \tag{23}$$

or

$$\mathbf{F} = \mathcal{W}\mathbf{f} \tag{24}$$

where

$$w_{n,i} = \frac{1}{\sqrt{N}} e^{-j2\pi\frac{ni}{N}} \tag{25}$$

Since the exponential function is periodic in the product of n and i, there is considerable symmetry in the matrix $\mathcal{W}$. The matrix can be factored into a product of N-by-N matrices that contain repeated values, including many zeros and ones [2]. If $N = 2^p$, $\mathcal{W}$ factors into p such matrices. The total number of operations required to implement p of those matrix products is substantially less than that required for Eq. (23).

The factor by which the FFT reduces the computational workload is

$$\frac{N^2}{N\log_2(N)} = \frac{N}{\log_2(N)} \tag{26}$$

This value increases with N, and for $N = 1{,}024$, the FFT is approximately 100 times as efficient as the direct implementation.

10.1.6 Fourier Transforms of Some Useful Functions

Table 10–1 lists the Fourier transforms of some common functions we will find useful.

TABLE 10–1 FOURIER TRANSFORMS OF SOME COMMON FUNCTIONS

Function	$f(t)$	$F(s)$
Gaussian	$e^{-\pi t^2}$	$e^{-\pi s^2}$
Rectangular pulse	$\Pi(t)$	$\frac{\sin(\pi s)}{\pi s}$
Triangular pulse	$\Lambda(t)$	$\frac{\sin^2(\pi s)}{(\pi s)^2}$
Impulse	$\delta(t)$	1
Unit step	$u(t)$	$\frac{1}{2}\left[\delta(s) - \frac{j}{\pi s}\right]$
Cosine	$\cos(2\pi f t)$	$\frac{1}{2}[\delta(s+f) + \delta(s-f)]$
Sine	$\sin(2\pi f t)$	$j\frac{1}{2}[\delta(s+f) - \delta(s-f)]$
Complex exponential	$e^{j2\pi f t}$	$\delta(s-f)$

10.2 PROPERTIES OF THE FOURIER TRANSFORM

10.2.1 Symmetry Properties

In the general case, a complex-valued function of a single real variable has a Fourier transform that is also a complex-valued function of a real variable. However, there are several restricted classes of functions that are of particular interest because of how their symmetry properties make them behave under the Fourier transformation.

10.2.1.1 Evenness and Oddness

A function $f_e(t)$ is even if and only if

$$f_e(t) = f_e(-t) \tag{27}$$

and a function $f_o(t)$ is odd if and only if

$$f_o(t) = -f_o(-t) \tag{28}$$

A function $f(t)$ that is neither even nor odd can be broken into even and odd components given, respectively, by

$$f_e(t) = \frac{1}{2}[f(t) + f(-t)] \tag{29}$$

and

$$f_o(t) = \frac{1}{2}[f(t) - f(-t)] \tag{30}$$

where

$$f(t) = f_e(t) + f_o(t) \tag{31}$$

We now investigate the effect of evenness and oddness on the Fourier transformation. Recall the Euler relation

$$e^{jx} = \cos(x) + j\sin(x) \tag{32}$$

We can rewrite the Fourier transform [Eq. (1)] as

$$F(s) = \int_{-\infty}^{\infty} f(t)e^{-j2\pi st}dt = \int_{-\infty}^{\infty} f(t)\cos(2\pi st)dt - j\int_{-\infty}^{\infty} f(t)\sin(2\pi st)dt \tag{33}$$

Expressing $f(t)$ as a sum of even and odd components [Eq. (31)] produces

$$\begin{aligned} F(s) = & \int_{\infty}^{\infty} f_e(t)\cos(2\pi st)\,dt + \int_{-\infty}^{\infty} f_o(t)\cos(2\pi st)\,dt \\ & -j\int_{-\infty}^{\infty} f_e(t)\sin(2\pi st)\,dt - j\int_{-\infty}^{\infty} f_o(t)\sin(2\pi st)\,dt \end{aligned} \tag{34}$$

Notice that the second and third terms are infinite integrals of the product of an even and an odd function. These terms evaluate to zero, and the Fourier transform reduces to

$$F(s) = \int_{-\infty}^{\infty} f_e(t)\cos(2\pi st)dt - j\int_{-\infty}^{\infty} f_o(t)\sin(2\pi st)dt = F_e(s) + jF_o(s) \tag{35}$$

Now we can list the symmetry properties of the Fourier transform:

1. An even component function produces an even component function in the transform.
2. An odd component function produces an odd component function in the transform.
3. An odd component function introduces the coefficient $-j$.
4. An even component function does not introduce a coefficient.

10.2.1.2 Real and Imaginary Components

We can use the preceding four rules to deduce the effect of the Fourier transformation on complex functions. If we express a general complex function as a sum of four components—an even and an odd real part, plus an even and an odd imaginary part—we can write the following four rules for the Fourier transformation:

1. The real even part produces a real even part.
2. The real odd part produces an imaginary odd part.
3. The imaginary even part produces an imaginary even part.
4. The imaginary odd part produces a real odd part.

Of particular interest is the case of input functions that are real, since we ordinarily use real functions to represent input images. Notice that a real function produces a transform that has an even real part and an odd imaginary part. This is referred to as a *Hermite* function, and it has the *conjugate symmetry* property

$$F(s) = F^*(-s) \tag{36}$$

where $*$ denotes the complex conjugate.

Table 10–2 lists the full expansion of the symmetry properties of the Fourier transform. Notice that the inverse transformation [Eq. (2)] differs from the direct transformation [Eq. (1)] only in the sign of the odd component. This tells us that the forward and inverse transforms of an even function are the same.

TABLE 10–2 SYMMETRY PROPERTIES OF THE FOURIER TRANSFORM

$f(t)$	$F(s)$
Even	Even
Odd	Odd
Real and even	Real and even
Real and odd	Imaginary and odd
Imaginary and even	Imaginary and even
Complex and even	Complex and even
Complex and odd	Complex and odd
Real	Hermite
Imaginary	Anti-Hermite
Real and even, plus imaginary and odd	Real
Real and odd, plus imaginary and even	Imaginary

10.2.2 The Addition Theorem

Suppose we have two Fourier transform pairs

$$\mathfrak{F}\{f(t)\} = F(s) \tag{37}$$

and

$$\mathfrak{F}\{g(t)\} = G(s) \tag{38}$$

If the two time functions are added, the Fourier transform of their sum is

$$\mathfrak{F}\{f(t)+g(t)\} = \int_{-\infty}^{\infty} [f(t)+g(t)]\, e^{-j2\pi st}dt \tag{39}$$

This may be rearranged to yield

$$\mathfrak{F}\{f(t)+g(t)\} = \int_{-\infty}^{\infty} f(t)e^{-j2\pi st}dt + \int_{-\infty}^{\infty} f(t)e^{-j2\pi st}dt = F(s)+G(s) \tag{40}$$

Thus, addition in the time or spatial domain corresponds to addition in the frequency domain, as illustrated in Figure 10–1. This fits well with the concept of linearity in a system. It follows from the addition theorem that

$$\mathfrak{F}\{cf(t)\} = cF(s) \tag{41}$$

where c is a rational constant. We take it as an axiom that Eq. (41) holds for any constant.

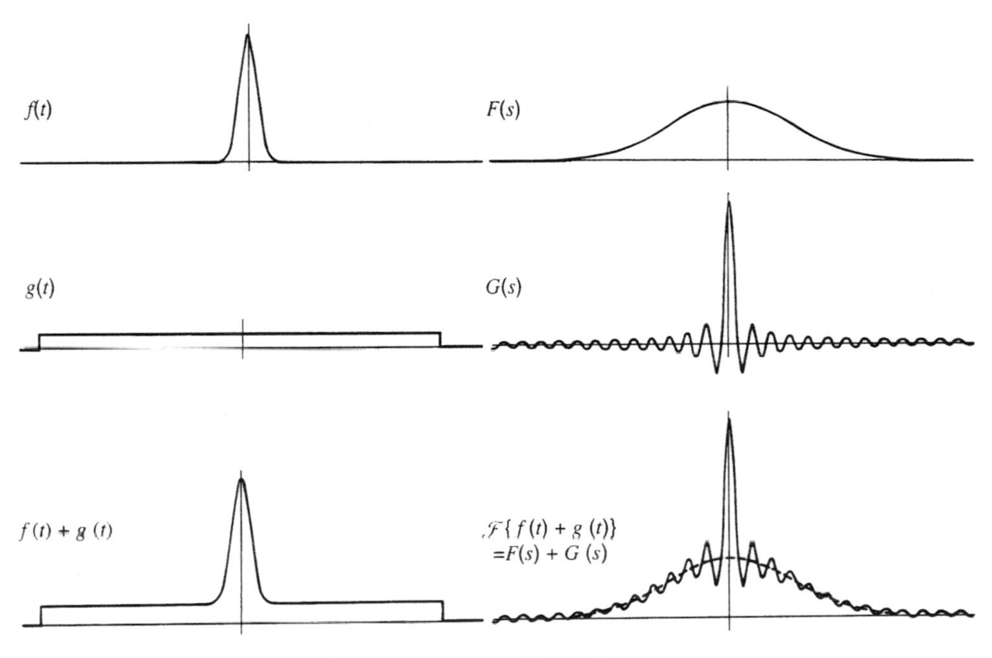

Figure 10–1 The addition theorem

10.2.3 The Shift Theorem

The shift theorem describes the effect that moving the origin of (shifting) a function has upon its transform. Using the function $f(t)$ as before, we can write

$$\mathfrak{F}\{f(t-a)\} = \int_{-\infty}^{\infty} f(t-a)e^{-j2\pi st}dt \tag{42}$$

where a is the amount of shift. Multiplying the right-hand side of the equation by

$$e^{j2\pi as}e^{-j2\pi as} = 1 \tag{43}$$

produces

$$\mathfrak{F}\{f(t-a)\} = \int_{-\infty}^{\infty} f(t-a)e^{-j2\pi s(t-a)}e^{-j2\pi as}dt \tag{44}$$

Next, we make the variable substitution

$$u = t-a \qquad du = dt \tag{45}$$

and move the second exponential outside the integral, leaving

$$\mathfrak{F}\{f(t-a)\} = e^{-j2\pi as}\int_{-\infty}^{\infty} f(u)e^{-j2\pi su}du = e^{-j2\pi as}F(s) \tag{46}$$

Thus, shifting a function introduces a complex exponential coefficient into its Fourier transform. Notice that if $a = 0$, this coefficient is unity. The complex coefficient

$$e^{-j2\pi as} = \cos(2\pi as) - j\sin(2\pi as) \tag{47}$$

has unit magnitude and revolves in the complex plane with increasing s. This means that shifting a function does not change the amplitude (modulus) of its Fourier transform, but does alter the distribution of energy between its real and imaginary parts. The result is a phase shift proportional to both frequency and a, the amount of shift.

10.2.4 The Convolution Theorem

Perhaps the most important theorem for linear system analysis is the convolution theorem. We can express the Fourier transform of the convolution of the functions given in Eqs. (37) and (38) as

$$\mathfrak{F}\{f(t) * g(t)\} = \int_{-\infty}^{\infty}\int_{-\infty}^{\infty} f(u)g(t-u)du\, e^{-j2\pi st}dt \tag{48}$$

which, after rearrangement, becomes

$$\mathfrak{F}\{f(t) * g(t)\} = \int_{-\infty}^{\infty} f(u)\int_{-\infty}^{\infty} g(t-u)e^{-j2\pi st}dt\, du \tag{49}$$

By the shift theorem, we can write

$$\mathfrak{F}\{f(t) * g(t)\} = \int_{-\infty}^{\infty} f(u)e^{-j2\pi su}G(s)du = G(s)\int_{-\infty}^{\infty} f(u)e^{-j2\pi su}du \tag{50}$$

This means that

$$\mathfrak{F}\{f(t) * g(t)\} = F(s)G(s) \tag{51}$$

and convolution in one domain corresponds to multiplication in the other domain. It follows that

$$\mathfrak{F}^{-1}\{F(s)G(s)\} = f(t) * g(t) \tag{52}$$

The convolution theorem points out a major benefit of the Fourier transform: Rather than performing convolution in one domain, which is complicated to visualize and expensive to implement, we can perform multiplication in the other domain for the same effect.

We can use the convolution theorem to derive the Fourier transform of the impulse. Recall that

$$f(t) * \delta(t) = f(t) \tag{53}$$

that is, the impulse is the identity under convolution. By the convolution theorem,

$$F(s)\mathfrak{F}\{\delta(t)\} = F(s) \tag{54}$$

Since this is true for any $f(t)$, we can choose one such that $F(s)$ has no zeros—for example, the Gaussian. Then we can divide by $F(s)$ to show that

$$\mathfrak{F}\{\delta(t)\} = 1 \tag{55}$$

proving that the Fourier transform of the impulse is unity.

10.2.5 The Similarity Theorem

The similarity theorem describes the effect that a change in scale of the abscissa has on the Fourier transform of a function.

Changing the abscissa's scale broadens or narrows a function. Thus, we can stretch or compress the function given in Eq. (37) by placing a coefficient in its argument. Its Fourier transform then becomes

$$\mathfrak{F}\{f(at)\} = \int_{-\infty}^{\infty} f(at)e^{-j2\pi st}dt \tag{56}$$

Multiplying both the integral and the exponent by a/a produces

$$\mathfrak{F}\{f(at)\} = \frac{1}{a}\int_{-\infty}^{\infty} f(at)e^{-j2\pi at(s/a)}a\,dt \tag{57}$$

We now make the variable substitution

$$u = at \qquad du = a\,dt \tag{58}$$

and write

$$\mathfrak{F}\{f(at)\} = \frac{1}{|a|}\int_{-\infty}^{\infty} f(u)e^{-j2\pi u(s/a)}du \tag{59}$$

which we recognize as

$$\mathfrak{F}\{f(at)\} = \frac{1}{|a|}F\left(\frac{s}{a}\right) \tag{60}$$

If the coefficient a is greater than unity, it contracts the function $f(t)$ horizontally, which, by Eq. (60), reduces the amplitude of the Fourier transform and expands it horizontally by the factor a. If a is less than unity, it has the opposite effect. This is illustrated in Figure 10–2. The similarity theorem implies that a narrow function has a broad Fourier transform and vice versa.

We can use the similarity theorem to derive a general expression for the Fourier transform of a Gaussian. Recall from Eqs. (5) and (12) that the Fourier transform of a Gaussian is also a Gaussian:

$$\mathfrak{F}\{e^{-\pi t^2}\} = e^{-\pi s^2} \tag{61}$$

By the similarity theorem,

$$\mathfrak{F}\{e^{-\pi(at)^2}\} = \frac{1}{a}e^{-\pi(s/a)^2} \tag{62}$$

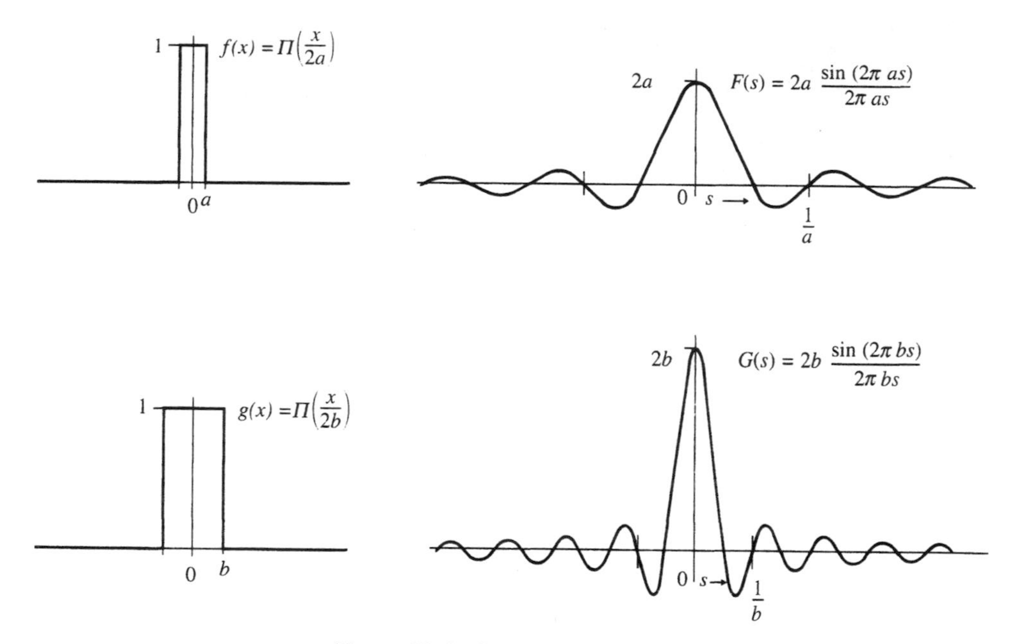

Figure 10–2 The similarity theorem

We now let

$$e^{-\pi(at)^2} = e^{-t^2/2\sigma^2} \tag{63}$$

and solve for

$$a = \frac{1}{\sqrt{2\pi\sigma^2}} \tag{64}$$

Now the transform is given by

$$\mathfrak{F}\{e^{-\pi(at)^2}\} = \sqrt{2\pi\sigma^2}e^{-2\pi^2\sigma^2s^2} \tag{65}$$

but since it, too, is a Gaussian, we can define a standard deviation α such that

$$e^{-2\pi^2\sigma^2s^2} = e^{-s^2/2\alpha^2} \tag{66}$$

This means that

$$2\pi^2\sigma^2s^2 = \frac{s^2}{2\alpha^2} \tag{67}$$

or

$$\alpha = \frac{1}{2\pi\sigma} \tag{68}$$

So the Fourier transform of a Gaussian of arbitrary standard deviation σ is

$$\mathfrak{F}\{e^{-t^2/2\sigma^2}\} = \sqrt{2\pi\sigma^2}e^{-s^2/2\alpha^2} \qquad \alpha = \frac{1}{2\pi\sigma} \tag{69}$$

Thus, the Fourier transform of a unit-amplitude Gaussian with standard deviation σ is another Gaussian with amplitude $\sqrt{2\pi}\sigma$ and standard deviation $1/(2\pi\sigma)$.

We can use the similarity theorem to illustrate again that the transform of the impulse is constant. Suppose that

$$f(t) = ae^{-\pi(at)^2} \tag{70}$$

and its transform is

$$F(s) = e^{-\pi(s/a)^2} \tag{71}$$

If we let a approach infinity, $f(t)$ narrows and grows in amplitude to approach an impulse, while $F(s)$ expands to approach constant unit amplitude. Thus, in the limiting case, the shrinking Gaussian approaches an impulse, and its expanding Gaussian transform approaches unity.

10.2.6 Rayleigh's Theorem

An important class of functions is those that are nonzero only over a finite portion of their domain. For such functions, we can discuss the total energy content. The energy of a function is defined as

$$\text{energy} = \int_{-\infty}^{\infty} |f(t)|^2 dt \tag{72}$$

provided that the integral exists. For transient functions, the integral in Eq. (72) exists, and the energy is a convenient parameter reflecting the total "size" of the function. Rayleigh's theorem states that

$$\int_{-\infty}^{\infty} |f(t)|^2 dt = \int_{-\infty}^{\infty} |F(s)|^2 ds \tag{73}$$

which means that the transform has the same energy as the original function.

The proof of Rayleigh's theorem is as follows. First we write

$$\int_{-\infty}^{\infty} |f(t)|^2 dt = \int_{-\infty}^{\infty} f(t)f^*(t)d(t) = \int_{-\infty}^{\infty} f(t)f^*(t)e^{j2\pi ut}dt \qquad u = 0 \tag{74}$$

that is, the second equality holds for $u = 0$. Again, we use the superscript asterisk to indicate the complex conjugate, since $f(t)$ is, in general, complex. We recognize Eq. (74) as the inverse Fourier transform of a product of two functions evaluated at the frequency $u = 0$. Since

$$\mathfrak{F}^{-1}\{f(t)f^*(t)\} = F(u) * F^*(-u) \qquad u = 0 \tag{75}$$

we can write the convolution integral as

$$\mathfrak{F}^{-1}\{f(t)f^*(t)\} = \int_{-\infty}^{\infty} F(s)F^*(s-u)ds \qquad u = 0 \tag{76}$$

Substituting $u = 0$ produces

$$\mathfrak{F}^{-1}\{f(t)f^*(t)\} = \int_{-\infty}^{\infty} F(s)F^*(s)ds \qquad u = 0 \tag{77}$$

which proves Eq. (73) and states that the energy is the same in both domains. If $f(t)$ is real and even, then $F(s)$ is also real and even, and

$$\int_{-\infty}^{\infty} f^2(t)dt = \int_{-\infty}^{\infty} F^2(s)ds \tag{78}$$

Notice how Rayleigh's theorem agrees with the similarity theorem: If we narrow a function at constant amplitude, we clearly reduce its energy. The similarity theorem states that narrowing a function broadens its transform, but also reduces its amplitude, keeping the energy equal in both domains.

10.3 LINEAR SYSTEMS AND THE FOURIER TRANSFORM

In this section, we examine the important role the Fourier transform plays in linear system analysis.

10.3.1 Linear System Terminology

Figure 10–3 shows, in both domains, the terminology commonly used for a linear system. In general, the Fourier transform of a signal is called the spectrum of that signal, and the inverse Fourier transform of a spectrum is a signal. Similarly, the impulse response and the transfer function form a Fourier transform pair.

10.3.2 Linear System Identification

Frequently, the impulse response and transfer function of a system are unknown and must be determined. This process is called *system identification.* For the linear system shown in Figure 10–3, the convolution theorem implies that

$$H(s) = F(s)G(s) \tag{79}$$

We can now write

$$G(s) = \frac{H(s)}{F(s)} \qquad F(s) \neq 0 \tag{80}$$

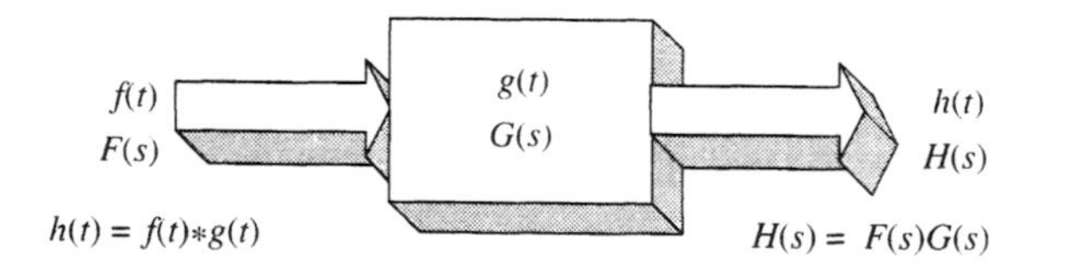

$f(t)$ = Input signal
$F(s)$ = Spectrum of input signal
$g(t)$ = Impulse response
$G(s)$ = Transfer function
$h(t)$ = Output signal
$H(s)$ = Spectrum of output signal

Figure 10–3 Linear system terminology

and therefore,

$$g(t) = \mathfrak{F}^{-1}\left\{\frac{\mathfrak{F}\{h(t)\}}{\mathfrak{F}\{f(t)\}}\right\} \tag{81}$$

This means that we can input a known $f(t)$, measure $h(t)$, and compute $g(t)$ by numerical integration. For instance, suppose $f(t)$ is an impulse. Then $h(t)$ is merely the impulse response, and no further action is necessary to identify the system.

As a more interesting example, assume that

$$f(t) = \Pi(t) \tag{82}$$

is the input, and

$$h(t) = \Lambda(t) \tag{83}$$

is measured at the output, as shown in Figure 10–4. Now

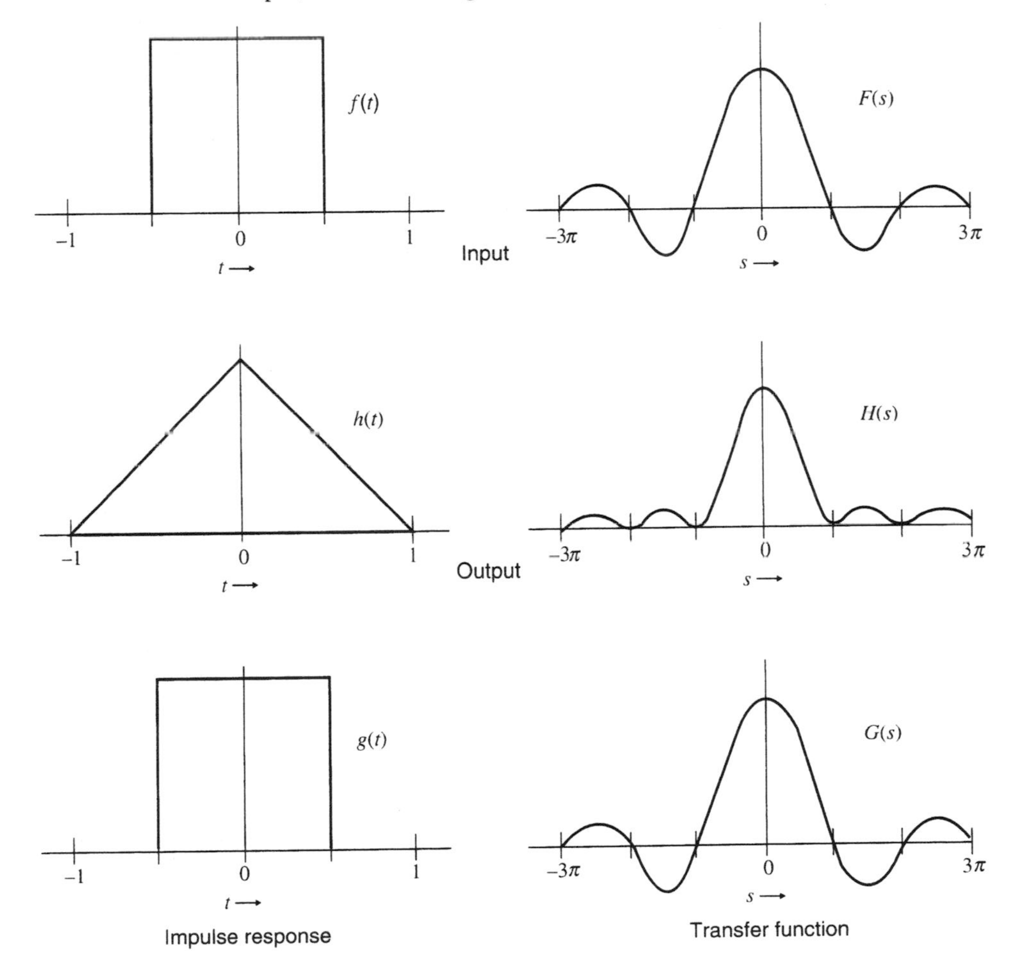

Figure 10–4 System identification, example 1

$$g(t) = \mathfrak{F}^{-1}\left\{\frac{\dfrac{\sin^2(\pi s)}{(\pi s)^2}}{\dfrac{\sin(\pi s)}{(\pi s)}}\right\} = \Pi(t) \tag{84}$$

is the impulse response.

As a second example, consider Figure 10–5. Suppose we choose as an input

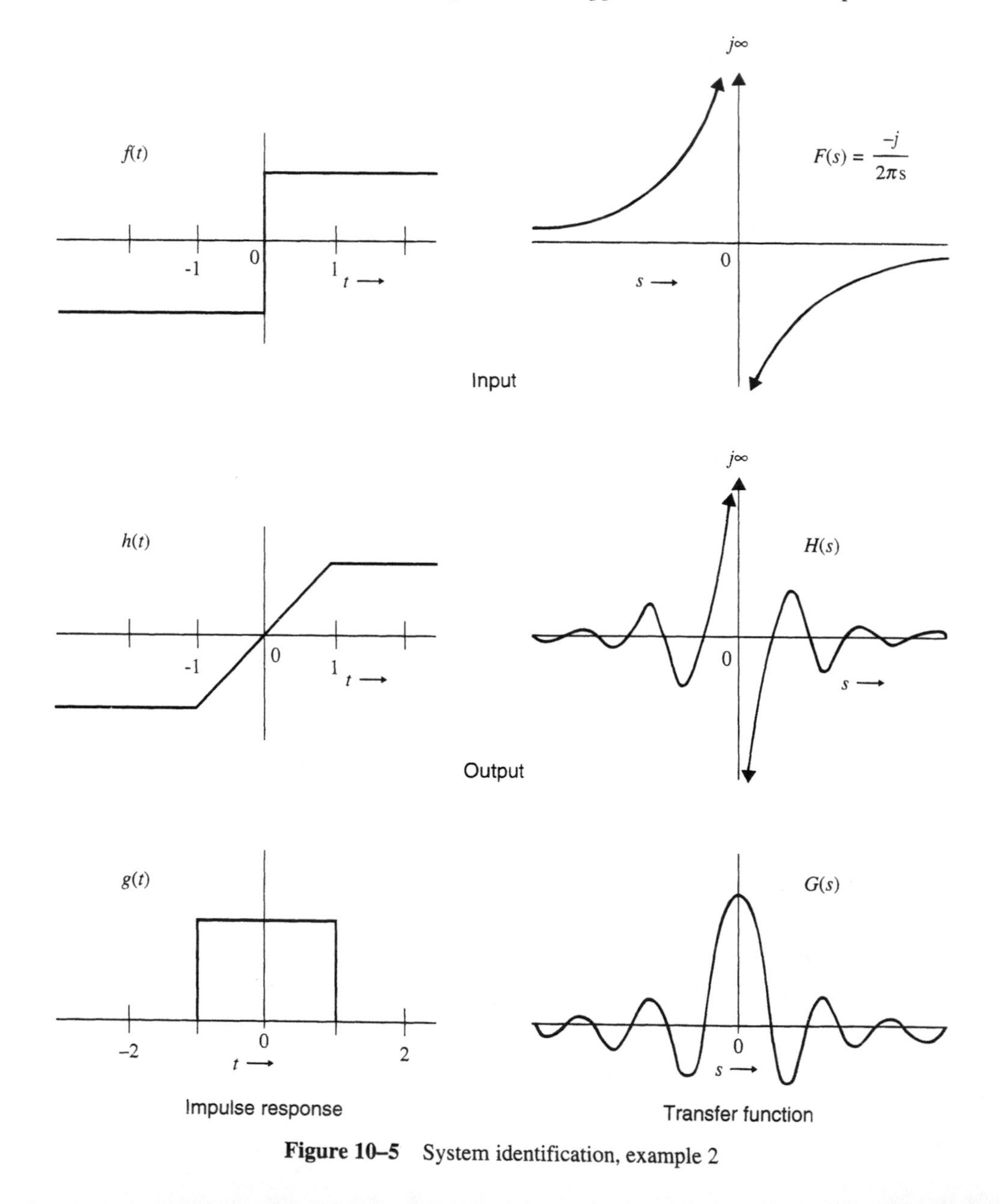

Figure 10–5 System identification, example 2

$$f(t) = u(t) - \frac{1}{2} = \begin{cases} -\frac{1}{2}, & t < 0 \\ 0, & t = 0 \\ +\frac{1}{2}, & t > 0 \end{cases} \tag{85}$$

which is an edge function having the spectrum

$$F(s) = \frac{-j}{2\pi s} \tag{86}$$

If the system's response is given by

$$h(t) = \begin{cases} -\frac{1}{2}, & t < -1 \\ t, & -1 \leq t \leq 1 \\ +\frac{1}{2}, & t > 1 \end{cases} \tag{87}$$

which has the spectrum

$$H(s) = -j\frac{\sin(\pi s)}{2(\pi s)^2} \tag{88}$$

we can write

$$G(s) = \frac{H(s)}{F(s)} = \frac{\sin(\pi s)}{\pi s} \tag{89}$$

which implies that the impulse response is

$$g(t) = \Pi(t) \tag{90}$$

In the preceding examples, the system output was expressed analytically and the problem solved directly. In the usual case, however, the process goes more like this: The output is digitized, both input and output are transformed by numerical integration, the ratio in Eq. (80) is computed directly, and the inverse Fourier transformation of Eq. (81) is performed by numerical integration. The fast Fourier transform, a computationally efficient algorithm for computing the Fourier transform, is most commonly used [3–10].

Notice that it is prudent to choose an input function whose spectrum does not have zeros. In the second example, we violate this constraint, but are fortunate enough to encounter an impulse response that also has zeros at those points in the frequency domain. If $F(s)$ has zero-crossings, $H(s)$ will as well, and $G(s)$ can be interpolated from surrounding values before the inverse transformation is performed numerically.

10.3.3 Sinusoidal Decomposition

The Fourier transform is a linear integral transform that uses the imaginary exponential as its kernel function. As shown in Eq. (33), the Fourier transform can be expressed as a sum of two transforms using the sine and cosine functions as kernels. Thus, it should come as no surprise that sine and cosine functions exhibit specialized behavior under Fourier transformation.

The following exercise yields insight into the relationship between the impulse response and the transfer function of a linear system. Consider again the linear system shown in Figure 10–3, and assume, for graphical convenience, that $f(t)$ and $g(t)$ are real and even. In Figure 10–6, the input and the impulse response are graphed in both domains.

For the input spectrum, let us divide the s-axis into small equal intervals Δs and divide $F(s)$ into narrow strips Δs wide. If Δs is sufficiently small, $F(s)$ is well approximated by a sum of rectangular pulses, as shown in Figure 10–7. Note that an approximation to $F(s)$ is given by an infinite summation of such pulse pairs:

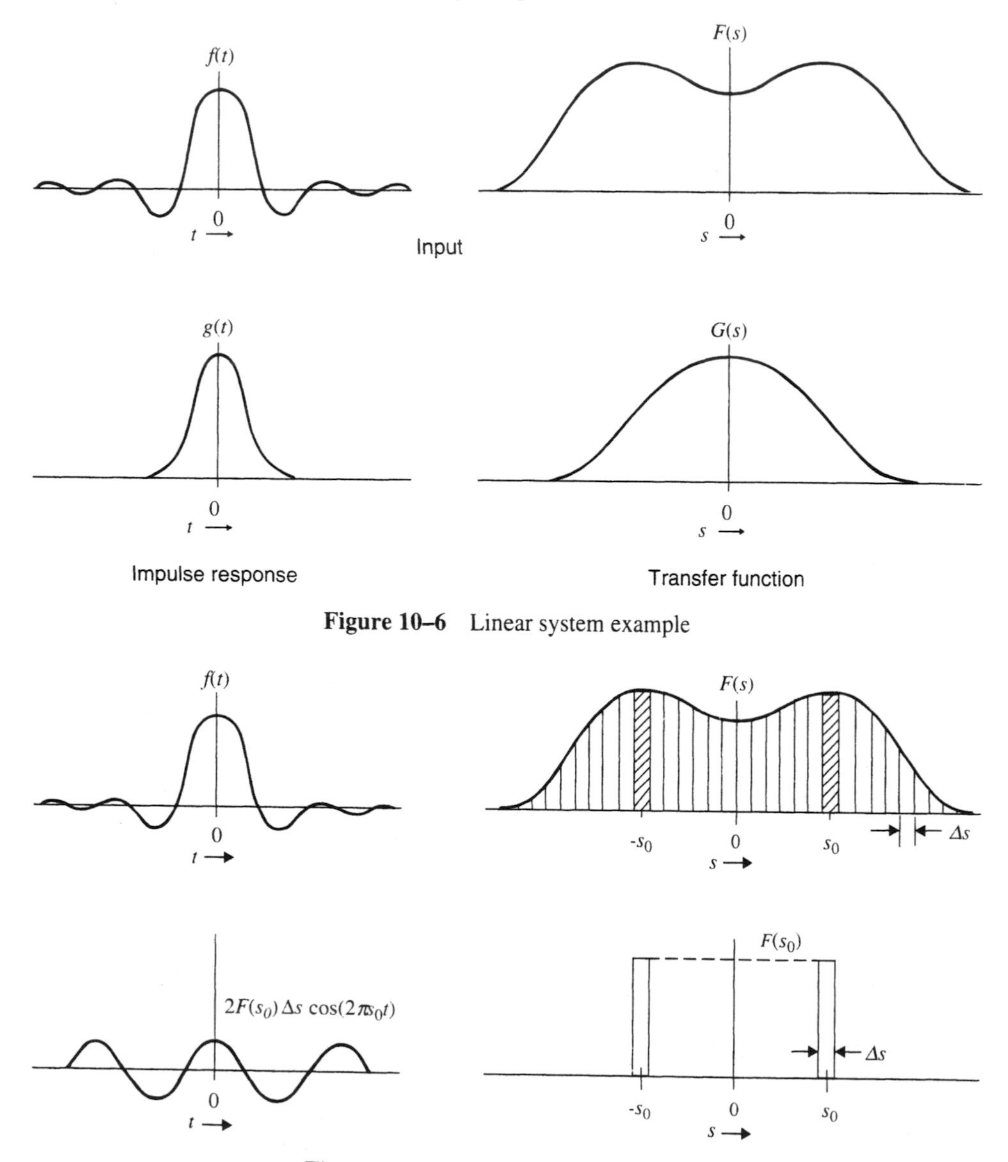

Figure 10–6 Linear system example

Figure 10–7 Sinusoidal decomposition

$$F(s) \approx \sum_{i=1}^{\infty} F(i\Delta s)\left[\Pi\left(\frac{s - i\Delta s}{\Delta s}\right) + \Pi\left(\frac{s + i\Delta s}{\Delta s}\right)\right] \tag{91}$$

Consider a particular pair of pulses, namely, those situated at $s = \pm s_0$ and having amplitude $F(s_0)$, width Δs, and area $F(s_0)\Delta s$. As Δs approaches zero, the pulse pair approaches an even impulse pair at $s = \pm s_0$, with infinitesimal strength $F(s_0)\Delta s$. The inverse transform of the even pulse pair approaches

$$2F(s_0)\Delta s \cos(2\pi s_0 t) \qquad s_0 = i\Delta s \tag{92}$$

Since $F(s)$ approaches a sum of even pulse pairs [Eq. (91)], $f(t)$ approaches a sum of cosines of the form of Eq. (92). This means that any even function can be decomposed into a sum of infinitely many cosines of infinitesimal amplitude.

Since the output spectrum is the product of the input spectrum and the transfer function, the output signal $h(t)$ can be expressed as a sum of cosines of the form

$$2G(s_0)F(s_0)\Delta s \cos(2\pi s_0 t) \tag{93}$$

We may now view the action of a linear filter as follows. The input signal $f(t)$ is first decomposed into a sum of cosines of all different frequencies. The amplitudes of the individual cosines are uniquely determined by $F(s)$, which in turn is the (unique) Fourier transform of $f(t)$.

Inside the linear system, each cosine of frequency s_0 is multiplied by $G(s_0)$, the amplitude of the transfer function evaluated at its frequency. Finally, all the cosines of modified amplitude are summed at the output of the filter to form the output signal $h(t)$.

Notice that this interpretation is consistent with two previously discussed properties of linear systems: (1) A sinusoidal input always produces a sinusoidal output at the same frequency, and (2) the transfer function at frequency s is the factor by which the amplitude of an input sinusoid of frequency s is multiplied.

If we had made $f(t)$ odd, $F(s)$ would have been imaginary and odd, the pulse pairs would have been imaginary and odd, and $f(t)$ would then decompose into sine functions. The remainder of the process would be identical, except that, at the output, the sine functions of modified amplitude would be summed to produce the odd output signal $h(t)$.

Similarly, if $f(t)$ were neither even nor odd, it could first be decomposed into even and odd component functions, each of which would then be decomposed as before into cosines and sines, respectively. The modified sines and cosines again would be summed at the output to produce the output signal $h(t)$.

The foregoing discussion assumes that the transfer function is real and even. Suppose instead that the input is real and even, but the impulse response $g(t)$ is real and odd. This makes the transfer function imaginary and odd. When the incoming even pulse pairs are multiplied by the imaginary odd transfer function, they are converted into imaginary odd impulse pairs. The process converts the incoming cosines into output sines. The output then becomes a summation of sine functions, and $g(t)$ is odd.

The preceding illustrates that convolving an even input function with an odd impulse response produces an odd function. From the graphical interpretation of the convolution integral, one can satisfy oneself that this is correct.

Consider now the case where the input function is a cosine, viz.,

$$f(t) = \cos(2\pi f_0 t) \qquad f_0 \geq 0 \tag{94}$$

and the impulse response is real, consisting of even and odd components, i.e.,

$$g(t) = g_e(t) + g_o(t) \tag{95}$$

The transfer function

$$G(s) = G_e(s) + jG_o(s) \tag{96}$$

is Hermite, which means that

$$G(f_0) = G_e(f_0) + jG_o(f_0) \qquad f_0 \geq 0 \tag{97}$$

and

$$G(-f_0) = G^*(f_0) = G_e(f_0) - jG_o(f_0) \qquad f_0 \geq 0 \tag{98}$$

Recall that the spectrum of the cosine is

$$F(s) = \frac{1}{2}[\delta(s - f_0) + \delta(s + f_0)] \tag{99}$$

We can now write the output spectrum as

$$H(s) = \frac{1}{2}G_e(f_0)[\delta(s - f_0) + \delta(s + f_0)] + j\frac{1}{2}G_o(f_0)[\delta(s - f_0) - \delta(s + f_0)] \tag{100}$$

which means that the output signal is

$$h(t) = G_e(f_0)\cos(2\pi f_0 t) + G_o(f_0)\sin(2\pi f_0 t) \tag{101}$$

This can be written as

$$h(t) = A\cos(2\pi f_0 t + \phi) \tag{102}$$

where

$$A = \sqrt{G_e^2(f_0) + G_o^2(f_0)} \quad \text{and} \quad \phi = \arctan\left[\frac{G_o(f_0)}{G_e(f_0)}\right] \tag{103}$$

This is an expected result in view of the property that a linear system can change the amplitude and phase of a sinusoidal input, but cannot change its frequency or functional form.

The foregoing exercise illustrates the relationship between the even and odd components of a real impulse response and the real and imaginary components of the transfer function. It shows how an odd component in the impulse response introduces an imaginary odd component into the transfer function. This produces a sine component output from a cosine component of the input and reflects itself in phase shift at the output. Finally, it illustrates that the amplitude of the output depends on the root-mean-square amplitude (modulus) of the complex transfer function.

Notice that we now have two equivalent ways of viewing the operation of a linear system: (1) We may visualize convolution, with functions being reflected, shifted, multiplied, and integrated, or (2) we may visualize sinusoidal decomposition followed by multiplication and resummation. We also understand the restrictions that evenness and oddness in one domain place on the functions in the other domain. Having these two options available affords us a very useful flexibility when approaching a problem with linear system analysis. It also illustrates the bilingual analogy mentioned at the beginning of this chapter.

10.3.4 Negative Frequency

Persons having prior experience with radio transmission or the use of a waveform analyzer or spectrum analyzer are sometimes uncomfortable with the concept of frequencies less than zero. Waveform and spectrum analyzers incorporate narrow bandpass filters that allow energy to pass only in a narrow range about certain sinusoidal frequencies. These filters act to select, out of a signal, the sinusoidal component at a particular frequency.

One can derive the spectrum of an electrical signal by tuning the narrow-band filter across the (positive) frequency range and plotting the amplitude of the output. Persons experienced in using this type of equipment may be unfamiliar with the concept of *negative frequency*.

Recall that the Fourier transform of the cosine is an even impulse pair and the transform of the sine is an imaginary odd impulse pair. Since the cosine is an even function, it must have an even spectrum, and similarly for oddness and the sine function.

For any real function, the spectrum is Hermite, and the left half is merely a complex conjugate reflection of the right half. For real functions, then, we are using a double-sided mathematical technique somewhat redundantly.

Since the left half of the spectrum is redundant for real functions, it could be ignored, as it implicitly is ignored in the use of a spectrum analyzer. However, we are using a somewhat more general mathematical approach to model physical processes, and the analysis is much simpler if we retain the left half of the functions.

Throughout Part 2 of the text, we graph double-sided spectra, although spectra are often plotted elsewhere only for positive frequency. We should keep in mind that, as long as we are using double-sided mathematics to model the operation of linear systems, the left half of the function, redundant though it may be, is a part of the analysis.

10.4 THE FOURIER TRANSFORM IN TWO DIMENSIONS

So far, we have considered the Fourier transform of one-dimensional functions of time. In digital image processing, and in the analysis of optical systems, the inputs and outputs are commonly two dimensional and, in some cases, higher dimensional. Our investment in the one-dimensional Fourier transform will not prove to be wasted effort, however, since the transform generalizes easily to higher dimensions.

10.4.1 Definition

For functions of two dimensions, the direct and inverse Fourier transforms are respectively defined as

$$F(u, v) = \int_{-\infty}^{\infty}\int_{-\infty}^{\infty} f(x, y)e^{-j2\pi(ux + vy)}dx\, dy \tag{104}$$

and

$$f(x, y) = \int_{-\infty}^{\infty}\int_{-\infty}^{\infty} F(u, v)e^{j2\pi(ux + vy)}du\, dv \tag{105}$$

where $f(x, y)$ is an image and $F(u, v)$ is its spectrum. $F(u, v)$ is, in general, a complex-valued function of two real frequency variables u and v. The variable u corresponds to frequency along the x-axis, and similarly for v and the y-axis.

Figure 10–8 shows an image and its two-dimensional amplitude spectrum. Gray level is scaled to represent the magnitude (square root of the sum of the squares of the real and imaginary parts) at each point u, v in two-dimensional frequency space. The origin is located at the center of the transform image. Periodic noise in the image produces the spikes in the transform.

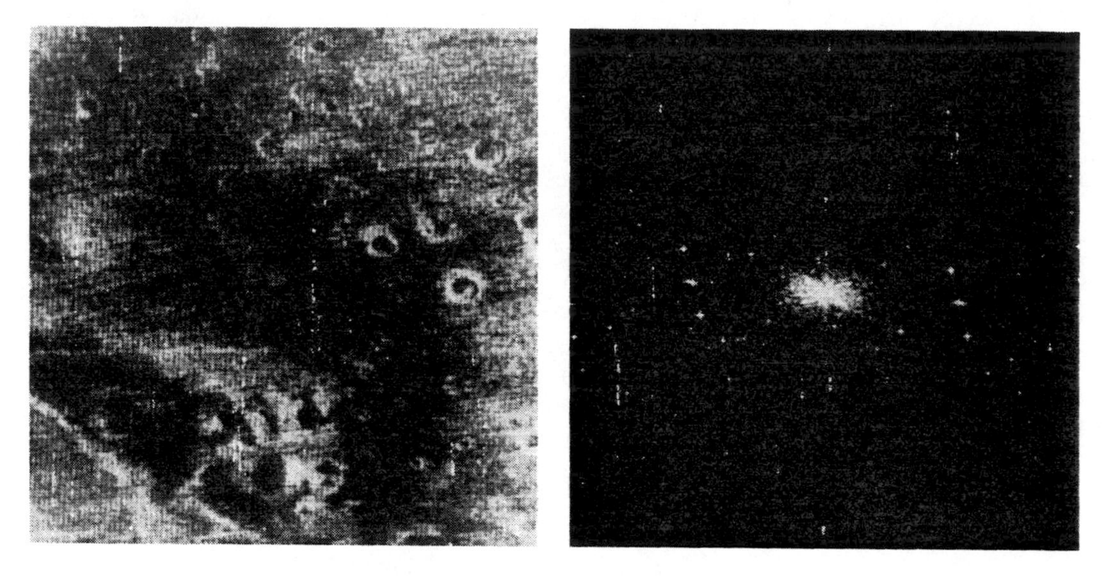

Figure 10–8 A two-dimensional Fourier transform

10.4.2 The Two-Dimensional DFT

If $g(i, k)$ is an N-by-N array, such as that obtained by sampling a continuous function of two dimensions at equal intervals on a rectangular grid, then its two-dimensional *discrete Fourier transform* (DFT) is the array given by

$$G(m, n) = \frac{1}{N}\sum_{i=0}^{N-1}\sum_{k=0}^{N-1} g(i, k) e^{-j2\pi\left(m\frac{i}{N} + n\frac{k}{N}\right)} \tag{106}$$

and the inverse DFT is

$$g(i, k) = \frac{1}{N}\sum_{m=0}^{N-1}\sum_{n=0}^{N-1} G(m, n) e^{j2\pi\left(i\frac{m}{N} + k\frac{n}{N}\right)} \tag{107}$$

As in one dimension, the DFT is quite similar to the continuous Fourier transform. And as before, the two-dimensional DFT of a bandlimited function sampled on a rectangular grid is a special case of the continuous Fourier transform.

Separability. The exponential in Eq. (106) can be factored, allowing us to write the transformation as

$$G(m, n) = \frac{1}{\sqrt{N}} \sum_{i=0}^{N-1} \left[\frac{1}{\sqrt{N}} \sum_{k=0}^{N-1} g(i, k) e^{-j2\pi\left(n\frac{k}{N}\right)} \right] e^{-j2\pi\left(m\frac{i}{N}\right)} \tag{108}$$

thereby separating the transformation into horizontal and vertical operations. Here, the term in brackets represents one-dimensional DFTs computed on the rows of the image. The outer summation then performs columnwise one-dimensional discrete Fourier transforms on the resulting array. Efficient implementations of the DFT in two dimensions use this approach along with the one-dimensional FFT. The inverse DFT is likewise separable.

10.4.3 Matrix Formulation

In matrix notation, the DFT can be written as

$$\mathbf{G} = \mathbf{FgF} \tag{109}$$

where

$$\mathbf{F} = [f_{ik}] = \left[\frac{1}{\sqrt{N}} e^{-j2\pi ik/N} \right] \tag{110}$$

is an N-by-N *kernel matrix* of complex coefficients.

F is a *unitary* matrix; that is, its inverse is the transpose of its complex conjugate. To invert a unitary matrix, one simply interchanges rows and columns and reverses the sign of the imaginary part of each element. Since **F** is also symmetric, the transposition is trivial.

Notice that row stacking to form a column vector and the use of a large block-circulant matrix, as was required for two-dimensional convolution (Sec. 9.3.4), is not necessary for computing the two-dimensional DFT. This is because the kernel function is separable into rowwise and columnwise operations, and **F** is unitary.

10.4.4 Properties of the Two-Dimensional Fourier Transform

The theorems of the two-dimensional Fourier transform are summarized in Table 10–3. Notice that the generalization from one dimension to two is quite direct.

The two-dimensional Fourier transform has several properties that have no one-dimensional counterpart. One is the property that if a two-dimensional image factors into a product of one-dimensional components, the same is true for the two-dimensional spectrum of the image. Another is the rotation property, which proves valuable in computerized axial tomography (CAT) scanners, discussed in Chapter 22.

The Laplacian is an omnidirectional second-derivative operator often used for edge detection and edge enhancement. Notice that using the Laplacian on a function multiplies its spectrum by a $u^2 + v^2$ term. Per the convolution theorem, then, the Laplacian corresponds to a linear system with a transfer function that increases as the square of frequency.

10.4.4.1 Separability

Suppose that

$$f(x, y) = f_1(x) f_2(y) \tag{111}$$

TABLE 10–3 PROPERTIES OF THE TWO-DIMENSIONAL FOURIER TRANSFORM

Property	Spatial domain	Frequency domain
Addition theorem	$f(x, y) + g(x, y)$	$F(u, v) + G(u, v)$
Similarity theorem	$f(ax, by)$	$\frac{1}{\lvert ab\rvert}F\left(\frac{u}{a}, \frac{v}{b}\right)$
Shift theorem	$f(x-a, y-b)$	$e^{-j2\pi(au+bv)}F(u, v)$
Convolution theorem	$f(x, y) * g(x, y)$	$F(u, v)G(u, v)$
Separable product	$f(x)g(y)$	$F(u)G(v)$
Differentiation	$\left(\frac{\partial}{\partial x}\right)^m\left(\frac{\partial}{\partial y}\right)^n f(x, y)$	$(j2\pi u)^m(j2\pi v)^n F(u, v)$
Rotation	$f(x\cos\theta + y\sin\theta,$ $-x\sin\theta + y\cos\theta)$	$F(u\cos\theta + v\sin\theta,$ $-u\sin\theta + v\cos\theta)$
Laplacian	$\nabla^2 f(x, y) = \left(\frac{\partial^2}{\partial x^2} + \frac{\partial^2}{\partial y^2}\right)f(x, y)$	$-4\pi^2(u^2 + v^2)F(u, v)$
Rayleigh's theorem	$\int_{-\infty}^{\infty}\int_{-\infty}^{\infty} \lvert f(x, y)\rvert^2 dx\, dy \quad =$	$\int_{-\infty}^{\infty}\int_{-\infty}^{\infty} \lvert F(u, v)\rvert^2 du\, dv$

Then

$$F(u, v) = \int_{-\infty}^{\infty}\int_{-\infty}^{\infty} f_1(x)f_2(y)e^{-j2\pi(ux+vy)}dx\, dy \tag{112}$$

can be rearranged to yield

$$F(u, v) = \int_{-\infty}^{\infty} f_1(x)e^{-j2\pi ux}dx \int_{-\infty}^{\infty} f_2(y)e^{-j2\pi vy}\, dy = F_1(u)F_2(v) \tag{113}$$

Thus, if a two-dimensional image factors into one-dimensional components, its spectrum does as well.

Consider as an example the elliptical two-dimensional Gaussian

$$e^{-(x^2/2\sigma_x^2 + y^2/2\sigma_y^2)} = e^{-x^2/2\sigma_x^2}e^{-y^2/2\sigma_y^2} \tag{114}$$

which factors into the product of two one-dimensional Gaussians. If the standard deviations of the two factors are equal, we have

$$e^{-(x^2+y^2)/2\sigma^2} = e^{-x^2/2\sigma^2}e^{-y^2/2\sigma^2} \tag{115}$$

which is the circular Gaussian. This function is extremely useful in the analysis of optical systems because it has circular symmetry and yet can be factored into one-dimensional components.

10.4.4.2 Similarity

The similarity theorem may be generalized to the case of two-dimensional transforms. We can write

$$\mathfrak{F}\{f(a_1x+b_1y, a_2x+b_2y)\}$$
$$= \iint_{-\infty}^{\infty} f(a_1x+b_1y, a_2x+b_2y)e^{-j2\pi(ux+vy)}dx\,dy \tag{116}$$

We make the substitutions

$$w = a_1x+b_1y \qquad z = a_2x+b_2y \tag{117}$$

in which case

$$x = A_1w+B_1z \qquad y = A_2w+B_2z \qquad dx = A_1dw+B_1dz \qquad dy = A_2dw+B_2dz \tag{118}$$

where

$$A_1 = \frac{b_2}{a_1b_2-a_2b_1} \qquad B_1 = \frac{-b_1}{a_1b_2-a_2b_1}$$
$$A_2 = \frac{-a_2}{a_1b_2-a_2b_1} \qquad B_2 = \frac{a_1}{a_1b_2-a_2b_1} \tag{119}$$

Then the Fourier transform becomes

$$\mathfrak{F}\{f(a_1x+b_1y, a_2x+b_2y)\}$$
$$= \int_{-\infty}^{\infty}\int_{-\infty}^{\infty} f(w,z)e^{-j2\pi\{(A_1u+A_2v)w+(B_1u+B_2v)z\}}dz\,dw(A_1B_2+A_2B_1) \tag{120}$$
$$= (A_1B_2+A_2B_1)F(A_1u+A_2v, B_1u+B_2v)$$

10.4.4.3 Rotation

From the two-dimensional similarity theorem, it follows that a rotation of $f(x, y)$ through an angle θ also rotates the spectrum of $f(x, y)$ by the same amount. We let

$$a_1 = \cos\theta \qquad b_1 = \sin\theta \qquad a_2 = -\sin\theta \qquad b_2 = \cos\theta \tag{121}$$

so that

$$A_1 = \cos\theta \qquad A_2 = \sin\theta \qquad B_1 = -\sin\theta \qquad B_2 = \cos\theta \tag{122}$$

and

$$\mathfrak{F}\{f(x\cos\theta+y\sin\theta, -x\sin\theta+y\cos\theta)\}$$
$$= F(u\cos\theta+v\sin\theta, -u\sin\theta+v\cos\theta) \tag{123}$$

10.4.4.4 Projection

Suppose we collapse a two-dimensional function $f(x, y)$ into a one-dimensional function by projection onto the x-axis to form

$$p(x) = \int_{-\infty}^{\infty} f(x, y)dy \tag{124}$$

Then the (one-dimensional) Fourier transform of $p(x)$ is

$$P(u) = \int_{-\infty}^{\infty}\int_{-\infty}^{\infty} f(x, y)dy\, e^{-j2\pi ux}dx \tag{125}$$

But $P(u)$ can be written as

$$P(u) = \int_{-\infty}^{\infty}\int_{-\infty}^{\infty} f(x, y)\, e^{-j2\pi(ux+0y)}dx\, dy = F(u, 0) \tag{126}$$

so the transform of the projection of $f(x, y)$ onto the x-axis is $F(u, v)$ evaluated along the u-axis. This combines with the rotation property to imply that the one-dimensional Fourier transform of $f(x, y)$ projected onto a line at an angle θ with the x-axis is just $F(u, v)$ evaluated along a line at an angle θ with the u-axis (Figure 10–9). The projection property forms the basis for system identification by line spread functions (Chapter 16) and for computerized axial tomography (Chapter 22).

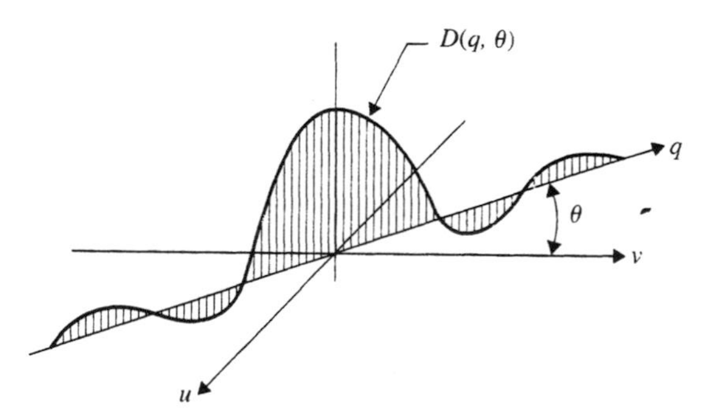

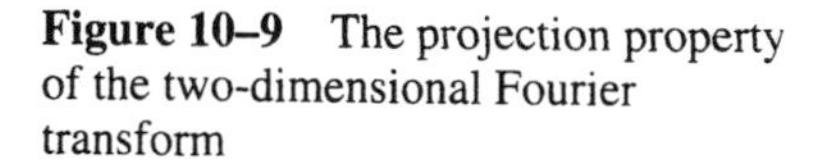
Figure 10–9 The projection property of the two-dimensional Fourier transform

10.4.5 Circular Symmetry and the Hankel Transform

Many important two-dimensional functions exhibit the property of circular symmetry. This means that the function can be expressed as a profile function of a single radial variable

$$f(x, y) = f_r(r) \tag{127}$$

where

$$r^2 = x^2 + y^2 \tag{128}$$

We now investigate the effect that circular symmetry has upon the two-dimensional Fourier transform. We can write the Fourier transform of $f(x, y)$ as

$$\int_{-\infty}^{\infty}\int_{-\infty}^{\infty} f(x, y)e^{-j2\pi(ux+vy)}dx\, dy = \int_{0}^{\infty}\int_{0}^{2\pi} f_r(r)e^{-j2\pi qr\cos(\theta-\phi)}r\, dr\, d\theta \tag{129}$$

where we have converted the integration from rectangular to annular and made the variable substitution

$$x + jy = re^{j\theta} \quad \text{and} \quad u + jv = qe^{j\phi} \tag{130}$$

We can now rearrange Eq. (129), dropping ϕ because the integral is taken over a full cycle of the cosine, to yield

$$\mathfrak{F}\{f(x, y)\} = \int_0^\infty f_r(r)\left[\int_0^{2\pi} e^{-j2\pi qr\cos(\theta)}d\theta\right] r\,dr \tag{131}$$

Now consider the integral in brackets, and recall the definition of the zero-order Bessel function of the first kind:

$$J_0(z) = \frac{1}{2\pi}\int_0^{2\pi} e^{-jz\cos(\theta)}d\theta \tag{132}$$

Recognizing Eq. (132) in Eq. (131) allows us to write

$$\mathfrak{F}\{f(x, y)\} = 2\pi\int_0^\infty f_r(r)J_0(2\pi qr)\,r\,dr \tag{133}$$

Notice that the Fourier transform of a circularly symmetric function is a function only of a single radial frequency variable q. This means that

$$F(u, v) = F_r(q) \tag{134}$$

where

$$q^2 = u^2 + v^2 \tag{135}$$

10.4.5.1 The Hankel Transform

For circularly symmetric functions, the direct transform is

$$F_r(q) = 2\pi\int_0^\infty f_r(r)J_0(2\pi qr)\,r\,dr \tag{136}$$

and the inverse transformation is

$$f_r(r) = 2\pi\int_0^\infty F_r(q)J_0(2\pi qr)\,q\,dq \tag{137}$$

These equations define a special case of the two-dimensional Fourier transform that is called the *Hankel transform of zero order.* This transform is a one-dimensional linear integral transform similar to the Fourier transform, except that the kernel is a Bessel function. Hence, two-dimensional functions with circular symmetry may be treated as one-dimensional functions of a single radial variable if the Hankel transform is substituted for the Fourier transform.

Hankel transforms of some familiar functions are listed in Table 10–4. Table 10–5 illustrates the theorems of the Hankel transform.

TABLE 10–4 HANKEL TRANSFORMS OF CERTAIN FUNCTIONS

Function	$f(r)$	$F(q)$
Reciprocal	$\frac{1}{r}$	$\frac{1}{q}$
Gaussian	$e^{-\pi r^2}$	$e^{-\pi q^2}$
Impulse	$\frac{\delta(r)}{\pi r}$	1
Rectangular pulse	$\Pi\left(\frac{r}{2a}\right)$	$\frac{aJ_1(2\pi aq)}{q}$
Triangular pulse	$\Lambda\left(\frac{r}{2a}\right)$	$\frac{2\pi}{ax^3}\int_0^x J_0(x)dx - \frac{2\pi}{ax^2}J_0(x)$
Shifted impulse	$\delta(r-a)$	$2\pi aJ_0(2\pi aq)$
Exponential delay	e^{-ar}	$\frac{2\pi a}{[(2\pi q)^2+a^2]^{3/2}}$
	$\frac{e^{-ar}}{r}$	$\frac{2\pi}{[(2\pi q)^2+a^2]^{1/2}}$
	$\pi r^2 e^{-\pi r^2}$	$\left(\frac{1}{\pi}-q^2\right)e^{-\pi q^2}$
	$\frac{\sin(2\pi ar)}{r}$	$\frac{\Pi(q/2a)}{\sqrt{a^2-q^2}}$

TABLE 10–5 PROPERTIES OF THE HANKEL TRANSFORM

Property	Spatial domain	Frequency domain
Addition theorem	$f(r)+g(r)$	$F(q)+G(q)$
Similarity theorem	$f(ar)$	$\frac{1}{a^2}F\left(\frac{q}{a}\right)$
Convolution theorem	$\int_0^\infty\int_0^{2\pi} f(\rho)g(r^2+\rho^2-2r\rho\cos\theta)\rho\, d\rho\, d\theta$	$F(q)G(q)$
Laplacian	$\nabla^2 f(r) = \frac{d^2f}{dr^2}+\frac{1}{r}\frac{df}{dr}$	$-4\pi^2q^2F(q)$
Rayleigh's theorem	$\int_0^\infty \lvert f(r)\rvert^2 r\, dr = E$	$\int_0^\infty \lvert F(q)\rvert^2 q\, dq = E$
Power theorem	$\int_0^\infty f(r)g^*(r)r\, dr = P$	$\int_0^\infty F(q)G^*(q)q\, dq = P$

10.4.5.2 Computing the Hankel Transform

The projection theorem gives us a simple way to compute the Hankel transform of a function, which is useful, for example, in the study of optical systems, which commonly have circularly symmetric impulse responses and transfer functions. Eqs. (124), (125), (126) and (134) allow us to write

$$F_r(q) = F(u, 0) = P(u) = \mathfrak{F}\{p(x)\} \tag{138}$$

and Eqs. (124), (127) and (128) imply that

$$p(x) = \int_{-\infty}^{\infty} f_r(\sqrt{x^2 + y^2})\, dy \tag{139}$$

So

$$F(q) = \mathfrak{F}\left\{\int_{-\infty}^{\infty} f_r(\sqrt{x^2 + y^2})\, dy\right\} \tag{140}$$

gives a two-step process for computing the Hankel transform: First project the function, and then compute its (one-dimensional) Fourier transform.

10.4.6 Interpretation

We conclude this introduction to the two-dimensional Fourier transform with Figure 10–10, which gives a bit of insight into the roles of amplitude and phase [11]. Parts (b) and (c) of the figure are displays of the amplitude and phase components, respectively, of the spectrum of the image in part (a).

One might be tempted to place more importance upon the amplitude spectrum, since it at least exhibits some recognizable structure, than upon the phase, which strikes the eye as essentially random. Eliminating the phase information, however, by setting the phase equal to zero and performing the inverse transformation yields part (d) of the figure—something bearing little resemblance to the original. On the other hand, eliminating the amplitude information (by setting the amplitude equal to a constant prior to the inverse transformation) yields part (e), a recognizable portrait.

While the amplitude spectrum specifies *how much* of each sinusoidal component is present, the phase information specifies *where* each of the sinusoidal components resides within the image. Figure 10–10 illustrates that disrupting this placement can create a devastating effect. As long as the components are kept in position, however, their amplitude appears to be less critical to the integrity of the image. For these reasons, most practical filters affect amplitude only, doing little or nothing to the phase information in the spectrum.

10.5 CORRELATION AND THE POWER SPECTRUM

In this section, we develop a series of analytical tools useful for studying the effects of noise in a linear system.

10.5.1 Autocorrelation

Recall that the self-convolution of a function is

$$f(t) * f(t) = \int_{-\infty}^{\infty} f(t) f(\tau - t) dt \tag{141}$$

If we do not reflect one term in the product, we form instead the autocorrelation function

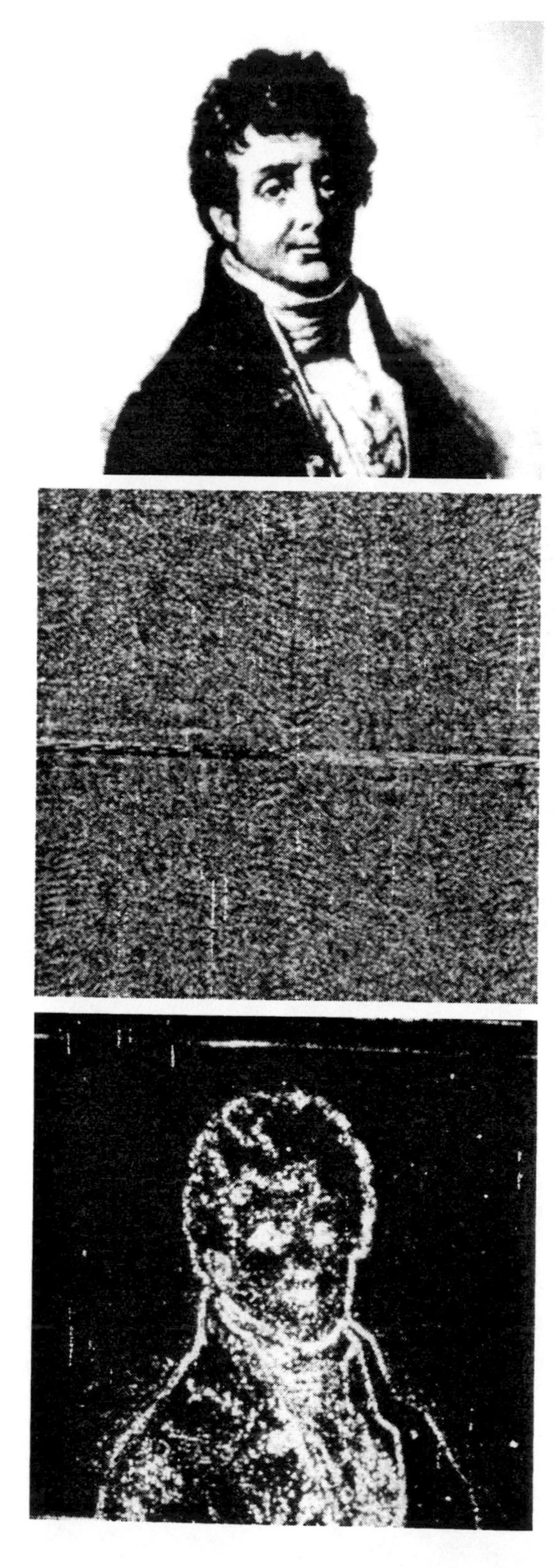

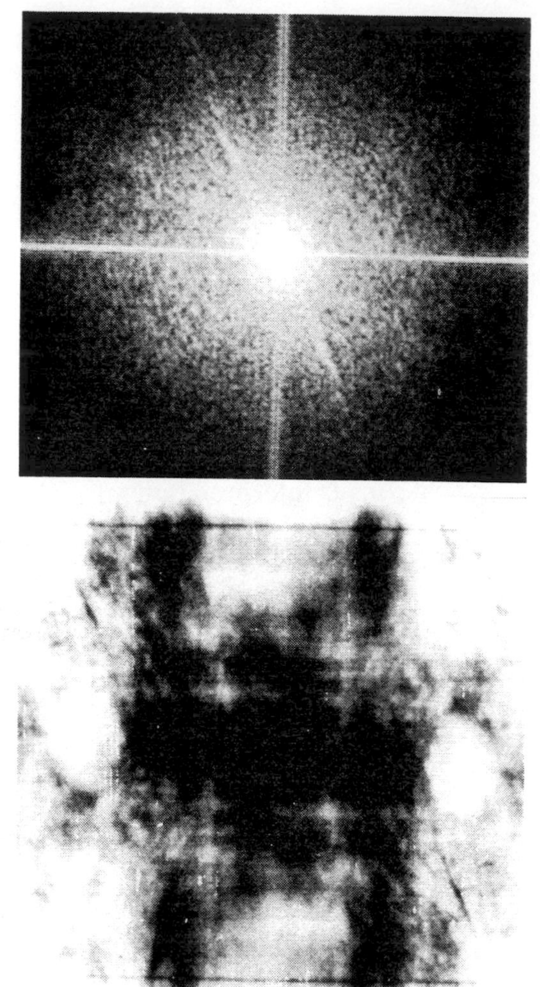

Figure 10–10 Jean Baptiste Joseph Fourier and his Fourier Transform (from [11]): (a) input image; (b) amplitude spectrum; (c) phase spectrum; (d) reconstruction from amplitude alone; (e) reconstruction from phase alone (Courtesy Prof. I. T. Young, Delft University of Technology).

$$R_f(\tau) = f(t) * f(-t) = \int_{-\infty}^{\infty} f(t) f(t+\tau) dt \tag{142}$$

The autocorrelation function is always even and has a maximum at $t = 0$. It has the property

$$\int_{-\infty}^{\infty} R_f(\tau) d\tau = \left[\int_{-\infty}^{\infty} f(t) dt \right]^2 \tag{143}$$

Every function has a unique autocorrelation function, but the converse is not true.

10.5.2 The Power Spectrum

The Fourier transform of the autocorrelation function is

$$\begin{aligned} P_f(s) = \mathfrak{F}\{R_f(\tau)\} = \mathfrak{F}\{f(t) * f(-t)\} &= F(s)F(-s) \\ &= F(s)F^*(s) = |F(s)|^2 \end{aligned} \tag{144}$$

and is called the *power spectral density function* or *power spectrum* of $f(t)$. If $f(t)$ is real, its autocorrelation function is real and even, and therefore, its power spectrum is real and even. Again, any $f(t)$ has a unique power spectrum, but the converse is not the case.

10.5.3 Cross-correlation

Given two functions $f(t)$ and $g(t)$, their cross-correlation function is given by

$$R_{fg}(\tau) = f(t) * g(-t) = \int_{-\infty}^{\infty} f(t) g(t+\tau) dt \tag{145}$$

In a sense, the cross-correlation function indicates the relative degree to which two functions agree for various amounts of misalignment (shifting).

The Fourier transform of the cross-correlation function is the *cross power spectral density function* or *cross power spectrum*

$$P_{fg}(s) = \mathfrak{F}\{R_{fg}(\tau)\} \tag{146}$$

10.6 SUMMARY OF FOURIER TRANSFORM PROPERTIES

In this chapter, we have developed a number of properties of the Fourier transform that will prove useful in subsequent analyses of image-processing systems. For convenience of reference, these properties are summarized in Table 10–6.

10.7 SUMMARY OF IMPORTANT POINTS

1. The Fourier transform is a linear integral transformation that establishes a unique correspondence between a complex-valued function (e.g., of time) and a complex-valued function of frequency.
2. The Fourier transform of a Gaussian function is another Gaussian.
3. Evenness and oddness are preserved by the Fourier transform.

TABLE 10–6 SUMMARY OF FOURIER TRANSFORM PROPERTIES

Property	Time (or Spatial) domain	Frequency domain
Terminology	Signal Impulse response Autocorrelation function Cross-correlation function $f(x)$	Spectrum Transfer function Power spectrum Cross power spectrum $F(s)$
Definition	$\int_{-\infty}^{\infty} F(s)e^{j2\pi xt}ds$	$\int_{-\infty}^{\infty} f(x)e^{-j2\pi xs}dx$
Addition theorem	$af(x)+bg(x)$	$aF(s)+bG(s)$
Similarity theorem	$f(ax)$	$\frac{1}{\lvert a\rvert}F\left(\frac{s}{a}\right)$
Shift theorem	$f(x-a)$	$e^{-j2\pi as}F(s)$
Convolution theorem	$f(x) * g(x)$	$F(s)G(s)$
Differentiation	$\frac{d}{dx}f(x)$	$j2\pi sF(s)$
Autocorrelation theorem	$R_f(\tau)=f(x) * f^*(-x)$	$\lvert F(s)\rvert^2 = P_f(s)$
Rayleigh's theorem	$\int_{-\infty}^{\infty} \lvert f(x)\rvert^2 dx = E$	$\int_{-\infty}^{\infty} \lvert F(s)\rvert^2 ds = E$
Power theorem	$\int_{-\infty}^{\infty} f(x)g^*(x)dx = P$	$\int_{-\infty}^{\infty} F(s)G^*(s)ds = P$

4. The Fourier transform of a real function is a Hermite function.
5. The Fourier transform of a sum of functions is the sum of their individual transforms (addition theorem).
6. Shifting the origin of a function introduces into its spectrum a phase shift that is linear with frequency and that alters the distribution of energy between the real and imaginary parts of the spectrum without changing the total energy (shift theorem).
7. Convolution of two functions corresponds to multiplication of their Fourier transforms (convolution theorem).
8. Narrowing a function broadens its Fourier transform and vice versa (similarity theorem).
9. The energy of a function (signal) is the same as that of its Fourier transform (spectrum).
10. The transfer function of a linear system can be determined as the ratio of its (measured) output spectrum to its (known) input spectrum.
11. The Fourier transform of a sinusoidal function is an equally spaced impulse pair.
12. An input signal can be decomposed into an infinite sum of infinitesimal sinusoids.
13. A linear system can be thought of as operating separately on the sinusoidal components of the input signal, which are summed at the output to form the output signal.

14. The Fourier transform generalizes readily to functions of two or more dimensions.
15. If a function of two variables can be separated into a product of two functions of a single variable, then so can its Fourier transform.
16. Rotating a function of two dimensions rotates its Fourier transform by the same amount.
17. Projecting (collapsing) a two-dimensional function onto a line at an angle θ to the x-axis and transforming the resulting one-dimensional function yields a profile of the two-dimensional spectrum taken along a line at an angle θ to the u-axis.
18. Circularly symmetric two-dimensional functions have circularly symmetric spectra.
19. The Hankel transform relates the profile function of a circularly symmetric function to that of its spectrum.
20. Autocorrelation is self-convolution without reflection of either function.
21. Cross-correlation is like convolution, except that neither function is reflected.
22. The Fourier transform of the autocorrelation function is the power spectrum.

PROBLEMS

1. Illustrate graphically that the convolution of an even and an odd function produces an odd function.
2. Use integration by parts to prove the differentiation property in Table 10–6.
3. Suppose you have a TV camera that you suspect has a barely perceptible interlace problem. You are convinced you can see, on hard-copy prints of digitized images, that every other line is slightly darker than the intervening lines. The manufacturer's representative says there's nothing wrong with the camera. How can you prove that there is a problem? You have a system capable of digitizing a TV image, averaging lines or columns of pixels and displaying a one-dimensional FFT. Describe the experiment and sketch the expected results.
4. Suppose you have two TV cameras that look identical, differing only in serial number. One is a special high-resolution model intended for a military customer, and the other is an economy model destined for a remote baby-sitting application. Due to a mix-up in shipping records, you don't know which is which. How can you identify the military camera? You have a system capable of digitizing a TV image, averaging lines or columns of pixels and displaying a one-dimensional FFT. Describe the experiment and sketch the expected results.
5. You have an RS-170 TV camera (see Figure 2-10) that has just been returned for repair. The customer says it has a problem with 60-Hz noise from the power line getting into the video signal. How can you verify that this is truly the problem before sending the camera out for repair? You have a system capable of digitizing a TV image, averaging lines or columns of pixels and displaying a one-dimensional FFT. Describe the experiment and sketch the expected results. Will the interlaced scan complicate the situation in this case, or not? Explain why or why not.
6. Suppose you have an RS-170 TV camera (see Figure 2-10) that has just been repaired. It had a problem with 40-kHz noise from the internal power supply getting into the video signal. How can you verify that the problem has indeed been fixed before placing the camera back into use? You have a system capable of digitizing a TV image, averaging lines or columns of pixels and displaying a one-dimensional FFT. Describe the experiment and sketch the expected results. Will the interlaced scan complicate the situation in this case? Explain why or why not.

PROJECTS

1. Develop a program that takes a single horizontal scan line out of a digital image and computes and displays a plot of the line's one-dimensional Fourier transform (amplitude and phase spectra). Use the program on a digital image of a tapered vertical bar to demonstrate the similarity theorem.
2. Develop a program as in Project 1, and add the capability to modify the amplitude spectrum (e.g., set a band of frequencies to zero), compute the inverse transform, plot the line, and reinsert it into the displayed image. Use the program to remove the high-frequency noise from a portion of a digital image.
3. Develop a program that can compute and display the two-dimensional Fourier transform (amplitude and phase spectra) of a digital image. Use the program on three digital images of the same scene taken through a wire screen held in front of the camera. Ensure that the screen is in focus well enough to be visible in the image. Rotate the screen 30° between scans. Identify the components of the amplitude spectrum that are due to the screen.
4. Develop a program as in Project 3, and add the capability to modify the amplitude spectrum (e.g., set an annular region of frequencies to zero), compute the inverse transform, and display the image. Use the program to remove the high-frequency noise from a portion of a digital image.
5. Use a program as in Project 4 to remove the shading from a digitized image.

REFERENCES

For references to additional material on the Fourier transform, see Appendix 2.

1. R. N. Bracewell, *The Fourier Transform and Its Applications* (2d revised ed.), McGraw-Hill, New York, 1986.
2. E. O. Brigham, *The Fast Fourier Transform,* Prentice-Hall, Englewood Cliffs, N.J., 1988.
3. J. W. Cooley and J. W. Tukey, "An Algorithm for the Machine Computation of Complex Fourier Series," *Math. Computation,* **19:**297–301, April 1965.
4. E. O. Brigham and R. E. Morrow, "The Fast Fourier Transform," *IEEE Spectrum,* **4:**63–70, December 1967.
5. G. D. Bergland, "A Guided Tour of the Fast Fourier Transform," *IEEE Spectrum,* **6:**41–52, July 1969.
6. D. F. Elliott and K. R. Rao, *Fast Transforms: Algorithms, Analyses, Applications,* Academic Press, New York, 1982.
7. B. Gold and C. M. Rader, *Digital Processing of Signals,* McGraw-Hill, New York, 1969.
8. H. J. Nussbaumer, *Fast Fourier Transform and Convolution Algorithms,* Springer-Verlag, Berlin, New York, 1981.
9. L. R. Rabiner and C. M. Rader, eds., *Digital Signal Processing,* IEEE Press, New York, 1972.
10. R. W. Ramirez, *The FFT, Fundamentals and Concepts,* Prentice-Hall, Englewood Cliffs, NJ, 1985.
11. A. V. Oppenheim, A. S. Willsky, and I. T. Young, *Signals and Systems,* Prentice-Hall, Englewood Cliffs, NJ, 1983.

CHAPTER 11

Filter Design

11.1 INTRODUCTION

In Chapters 9 and 10, we laid the groundwork for the analysis and design of linear filtering operations. In this chapter, we discuss techniques for designing filters to accomplish particular goals. To develop insight into the process, we first examine the time domain and frequency domain behavior of certain simple, but useful, filters. Later in the chapter, we approach the problem of designing filters that are optimal for doing a specific job.

As in Chapters 9 and 10, we perform the analysis with one-dimensional (time) signals, for simplicity of the graphics and mathematics. The generalization to two dimensions is straightforward. In the discussion of simple filters, we adhere to the linear system conventions introduced in the previous chapter. (Recall Figure 10–3.) A different set of variable names, however, is used in the discussion of optimal filters.

In the following section, we consider some conceptually simple filters in order to illustrate the time domain and frequency domain characteristics of filters and the effects they have upon the signals they process.

11.2 LOWPASS FILTERS

Very often, a signal or image has the majority of its energy in the low- and midfrequency range of its amplitude spectrum. At the higher frequencies, the information of interest is often buried by noise. Thus, a filter that reduces the amplitude of high-frequency components can reduce the visible effects of noise.

11.2.1 Simple Lowpass Filters

The Box Filter. A simple way to reduce high-frequency noise is with local averaging. This is implemented by convolving the signal with the rectangular pulse, $\Pi(x)$, as illustrated in Figure 9–16. This is called a *moving-average* filter. The gray level at each pixel is replaced with the average of the gray levels in a square or rectangular neighborhood.

Recall from Chapter 10 that the Fourier transform of the rectangular pulse has the form $\sin(x)/x$ (Figure 10–2). Figure 11–1 illustrates the effect of the negative side lobes of the box filter transfer function. The test target contains a vertical bar pattern of variable frequency. The impulse response is a horizontally oriented rectangular pulse of various widths. The outputs show black-for-white reversals of the polarity of the bars at frequencies corresponding to the negative lobes of the corresponding transfer functions.

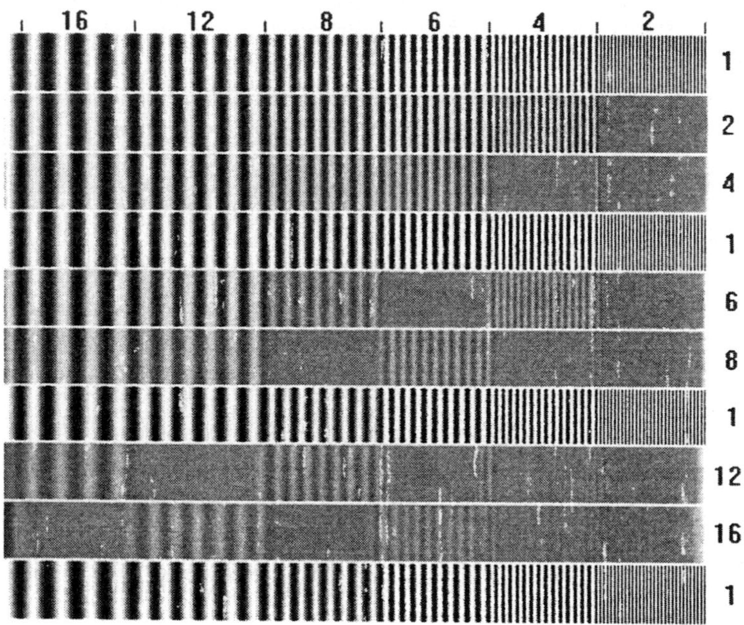

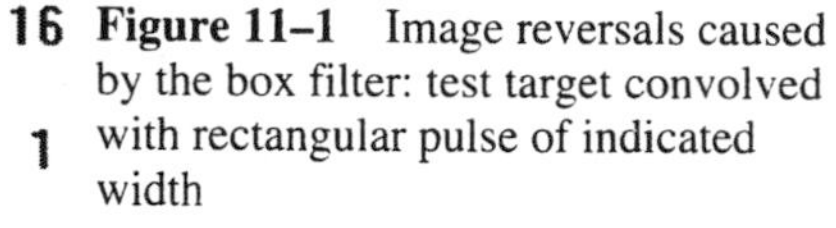
Figure 11–1 Image reversals caused by the box filter: test target convolved with rectangular pulse of indicated width

By the similarity theorem (Chapter 10), the width of the transfer function is inversely proportional to the width of the impulse response. As long as the box filter is no more than two pixels wide, the first zero-crossing of its transfer function falls at or above the highest frequency present in the sampled data (more on this in Chapter 12). If the box filter is more than two pixels wide, however, there is the danger of polarity reversal for small structures in the image, as seen in Figure 11–1.

The Triangular Filter. We can use the triangular pulse, $\Lambda(x)$, as a lowpass filter impulse response. This is sometimes called a *weighted-average* filter. In two dimensions, it takes on the appearance of a pyramid.

The spectrum of the triangular pulse has the form $[\sin(x)/x]^2$, which does not go negative and dies out with frequency much faster than that of the box filter. Thus, the smaller (positive) side lobes contribute less to the output image. This filter can be used safely in large sizes without fear of polarity reversal.

One can produce the same effect as a triangular filter by two successive applications of the rectangular filter. Because of the simplicity of the box filter, this may be more computationally efficient than using $\Lambda(x)$. In fact, using three or more successive applications of $\Pi(x)$ emulates filters that, like the Gaussian, have quite smooth behavior in the frequency domain.

High-Frequency Cutoff. A rather "brute force" lowpass filtering method that is sometimes used is to (a) compute the Fourier transform of the signal or image, (b) set the high-frequency portion of the amplitude spectrum to zero, and (c) compute the inverse Fourier transform of the result. This is equivalent to multiplying the spectrum by a rectangular pulse. This, in turn, is equivalent to convolving the signal or image with a $\sin(x)/x$ function.

Convolving with sin(x)/x causes *ringing* (recall Sec. 9.5.2) to appear in the vicinity of sharp peaks and edges. For this reason, sharp cutoff in the frequency domain is of limited usefulness.

11.2.2 The Gaussian Lowpass Filter

Since the Fourier transform of a Gaussian is also a Gaussian, this function yields a lowpass filter with smooth behavior in both domains. It can, of course, be implemented by convolution in the time or space domain, or by multiplication in the frequency domain.

11.3 BANDPASS AND BANDSTOP FILTERS

In some cases, the desired and undesired components of a signal or image occur predominantly in different frequency ranges of the spectrum. When the components are separable in this way, a transfer function that passes or stops particular frequencies can be useful.

11.3.1 The Ideal Bandpass Filter

Suppose we desire to implement, by convolution, a filter that passes energy only at frequencies between f_1 and f_2, where $f_2 > f_1$. The desired transfer function is given by

$$G(s) = \begin{cases} 1 & f_1 \le |s| \le f_2 \\ 0 & \text{elsewhere} \end{cases} \tag{1}$$

and is shown in Figure 11–2. Since $G(s)$ is an even rectangular pulse pair, it can be thought of as a rectangular pulse convolved with an even impulse pair. If we let

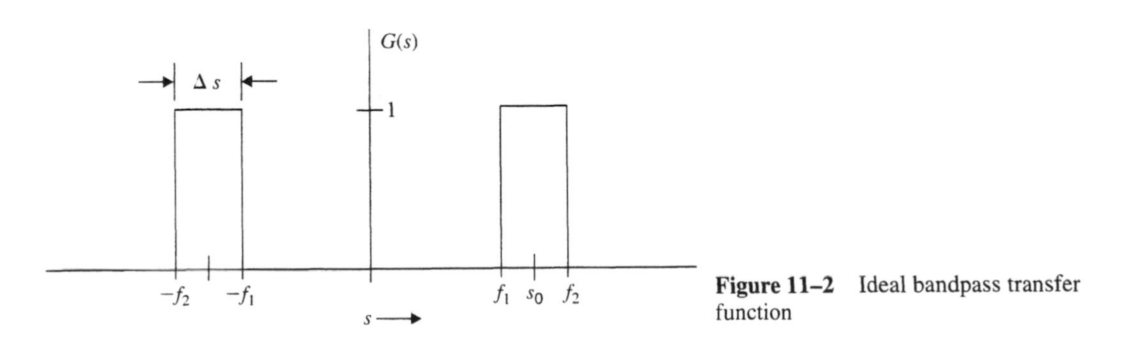

Figure 11–2 Ideal bandpass transfer function

$$s_0 = \frac{1}{2}(f_1 + f_2) \quad \text{and} \quad \Delta s = f_2 - f_1 \tag{2}$$

we can write the transfer function of the *ideal bandpass* filter as

$$G(s) = \Pi\left(\frac{s}{\Delta s}\right) * [\delta(s - s_0) + \delta(s + s_0)] \tag{3}$$

With the transfer function expressed in this form, we can easily write the impulse response:

$$g(t) = \Delta s \frac{\sin(\pi \Delta s t)}{\pi \Delta s t} 2\cos(2\pi s_0 t) = 2\Delta s \frac{\sin(\pi \Delta s t)}{\pi \Delta s t}\cos(2\pi s_0 t) \tag{4}$$

Since $\Delta s < s_0$, Eq. (4) describes a cosine of frequency s_0 enclosed in a $\sin(x)/x$ envelope having frequency $\Delta s/2$. This impulse response is graphed in Figure 11–3. The number of cosine cycles between envelope zero-crossings depends on the relationship between s_0 and Δs. Notice that if s_0 is held constant and Δs becomes small (i.e., a narrow passband), the envelope expands to include more and more cosine cycles between zero-crossings. As Δs approaches zero, the impulse response approaches a cosine. In the limiting case, the convolution actually becomes a cross-correlation of the input with the cosine at frequency s_0.

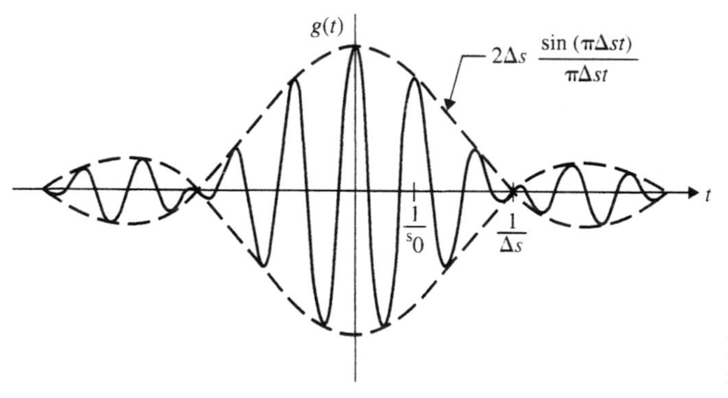

Figure 11–3 Ideal bandpass impulse response

11.3.2 The Ideal Bandstop Filter

The transfer function of a filter that passes energy at all frequencies except for a band between f_1 and f_2 is given by

$$G(s) = \begin{cases} 0 & f_1 \leq |s| \leq f_2 \\ 1 & \text{elsewhere} \end{cases} \tag{5}$$

and is graphed in Figure 11–4. For convenience, we again let s_0 be the center frequency and Δs be the *stopband* width [Eq. (2)]. Now we can write the transfer function as one minus a bandpass filter, i.e.,

$$G(s) = 1 - \Pi\left(\frac{s}{\Delta s}\right) * [\delta(s - s_0) + \delta(s + s_0)] \tag{6}$$

from which the impulse response is

$$g(t) = \delta(t) - 2\Delta s \frac{\sin(\pi \Delta s t)}{\pi \Delta s t}\cos(2\pi s_0 t) \tag{7}$$

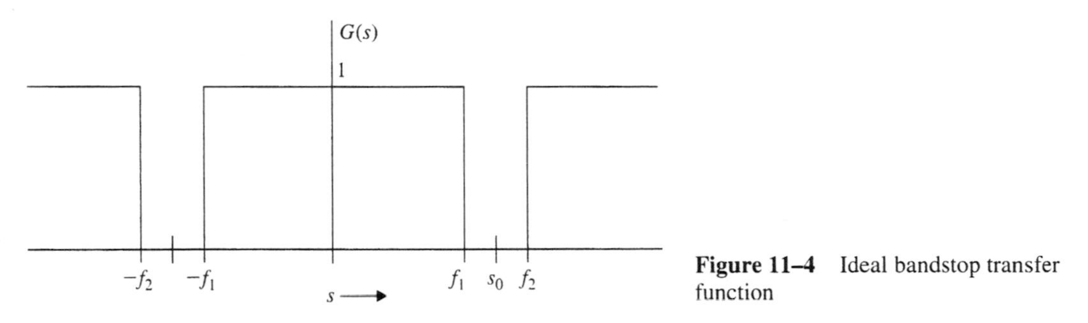

Figure 11–4 Ideal bandstop transfer function

This impulse response is graphed in Figure 11–5. Its behavior with changing bandwidth and center frequency is similar to that of the bandpass filter, which it resembles. If Δs is small, this filter is called a *notch filter*.

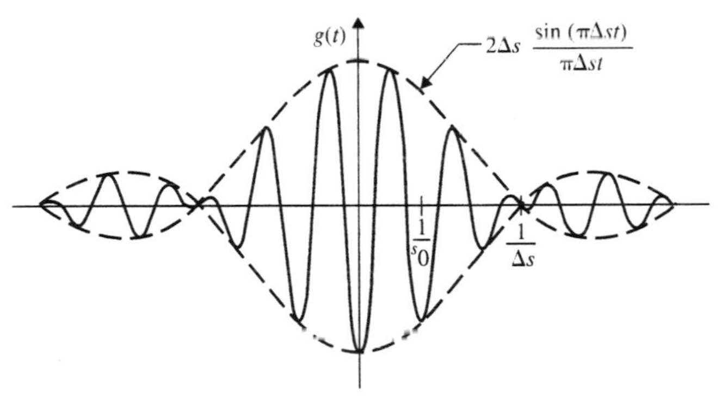

Figure 11–5 Ideal bandstop impulse response

11.3.3 The General Bandpass Filter

We now consider a class of bandpass filters constructed in the following way: We select a nonnegative unimodal function $K(s)$ and convolve it with an even impulse pair at frequency s_0. This yields a bandpass transfer function, as shown in Figure 11–6. That transfer function is given by

$$G(s) = K(s) * [\delta(s - s_0) + \delta(s + s_0)] \tag{8}$$

and the impulse response by

$$g(t) = 2k(t)\cos(2\pi s_0 t) \tag{9}$$

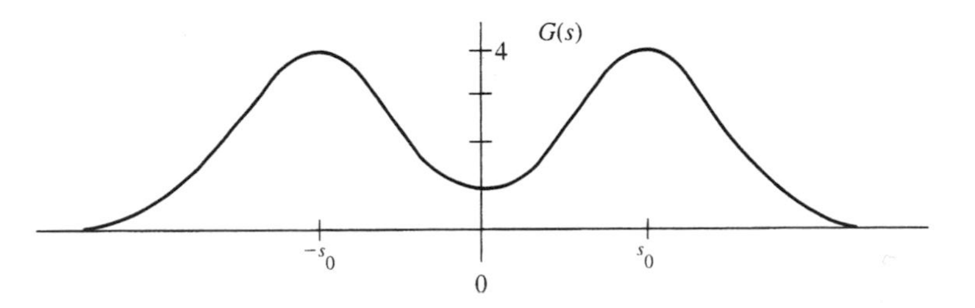

Figure 11–6 The general bandpass filter

This impulse response is a cosine of frequency s_0 in an envelope that is the inverse Fourier transform of $K(s)$.

Suppose, for example, that $K(s)$ is a Gaussian

$$G(s) = Ae^{-s^2/2\alpha^2} * [\delta(s - s_0) + \delta(s + s_0)] \tag{10}$$

Then the impulse response becomes

$$\sigma = \frac{1}{2\pi\alpha} \qquad g(t) = \frac{2A}{\sqrt{2\pi\sigma^2}} e^{-t^2/2\sigma^2} \cos(2\pi s_0 t) \tag{11}$$

This impulse response, a cosine in a Gaussian envelope, is graphed in Figure 11–7. Notice that we could easily generate a class of bandstop filters as well by this technique.

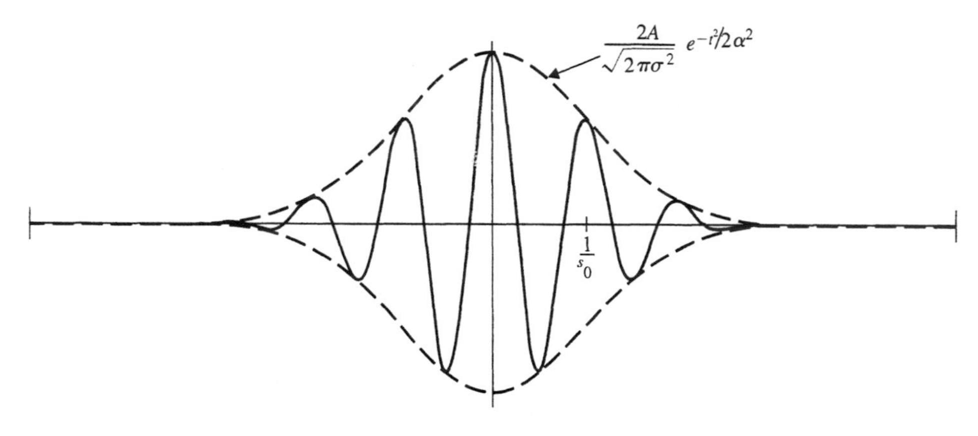

Figure 11–7 The Gaussian bandpass filter

11.4 HIGH-FREQUENCY ENHANCEMENT FILTERS

The term *high-frequency enhancement filter,* or *highpass filter,* is generally taken to describe a transfer function that is unity at zero frequency and increases with increasing frequency. Such a transfer function may either level off at some value greater than unity or, more commonly, fall back toward zero at higher frequencies. In the latter case, the high-frequency enhancement filter is actually a type of bandpass filter with the restriction of unity gain at zero frequency.

In practice, it is sometimes desired to have less than unity gain at zero frequency, so as to reduce the contrast of large, slowly varying components of the image. If the transfer function passes through the origin, it may be called a *Laplacian filter.*

11.4.1 The Difference-of-Gaussians Filter

We can produce a high-frequency enhancement transfer function by expressing it as the difference of two Gaussians of different widths:

$$G(s) = Ae^{-s^2/2\alpha_1^2} - Be^{-s^2/2\alpha_2^2} \qquad A \geq B,\ \alpha_1 > \alpha_2 \tag{12}$$

This is shown in Figure 11–8. The impulse response of such a filter is

$$g(t) = \frac{A}{\sqrt{2\pi\sigma_1^2}} e^{-t^2/2\sigma_1^2} - \frac{B}{\sqrt{2\pi\sigma_2^2}} e^{-t^2/2\sigma_2^2} \qquad \sigma_i = \frac{1}{2\pi\sigma_i} \tag{13}$$

and is graphed in Figure 11–9. Notice that the broad Gaussian in the frequency domain produces a narrow Gaussian in the time domain and vice versa. The impulse response shown in Figure 11–9 is typical of bandpass and highpass filters, having a positive pulse situated in a negative dish.

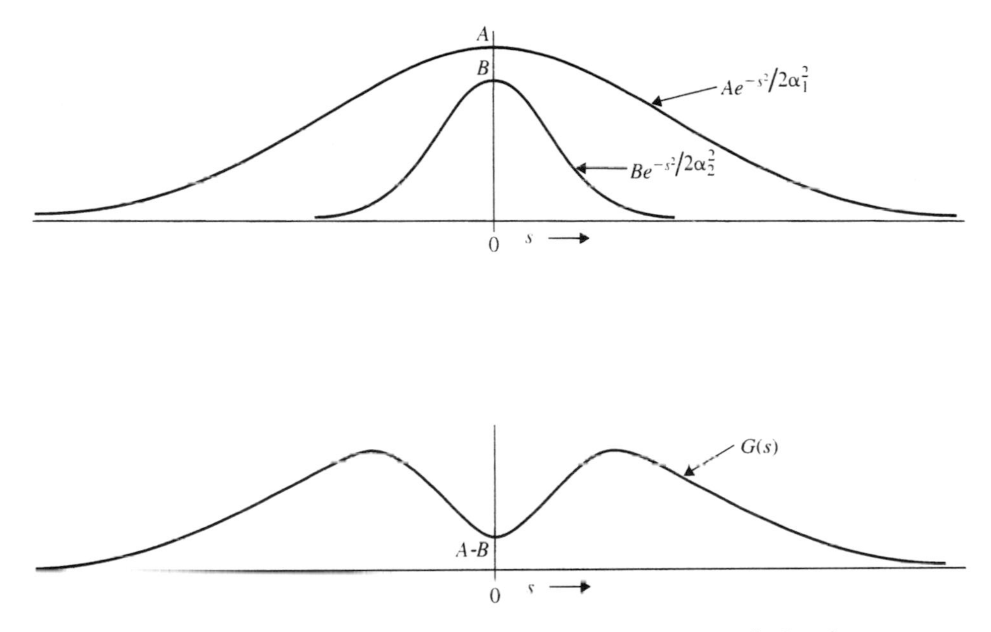

Figure 11–8 The Gaussian high-frequency enhancement transfer function

If we let α_1 approach infinity, the narrow Gaussian in the time domain narrows further to an impulse, and the filter has the form shown in Figure 11–10. Notice that the difference between a filter that rolls off (returns toward zero) at high frequencies and one that does not is the width of the central pulse in the time domain. In fact, the broader that central pulse, the faster the transfer function rolls off.

11.4.2 Rules of Thumb for Highpass Filter Design

In this section, we develop two rules that hold approximately for estimating the behavior of high-frequency enhancement filters. Suppose the impulse response of the filter is expressed as a narrow pulse minus a broad pulse, i.e.,

$$g(t) = g_1(t) - g_2(t) \tag{14}$$

as illustrated in Figure 11–11. We know that the transfer function $G(s)$ will have the general shape of a high-frequency enhancement filter. We would like to estimate the transfer function at zero frequency to determine its effect on the contrast of large objects within the

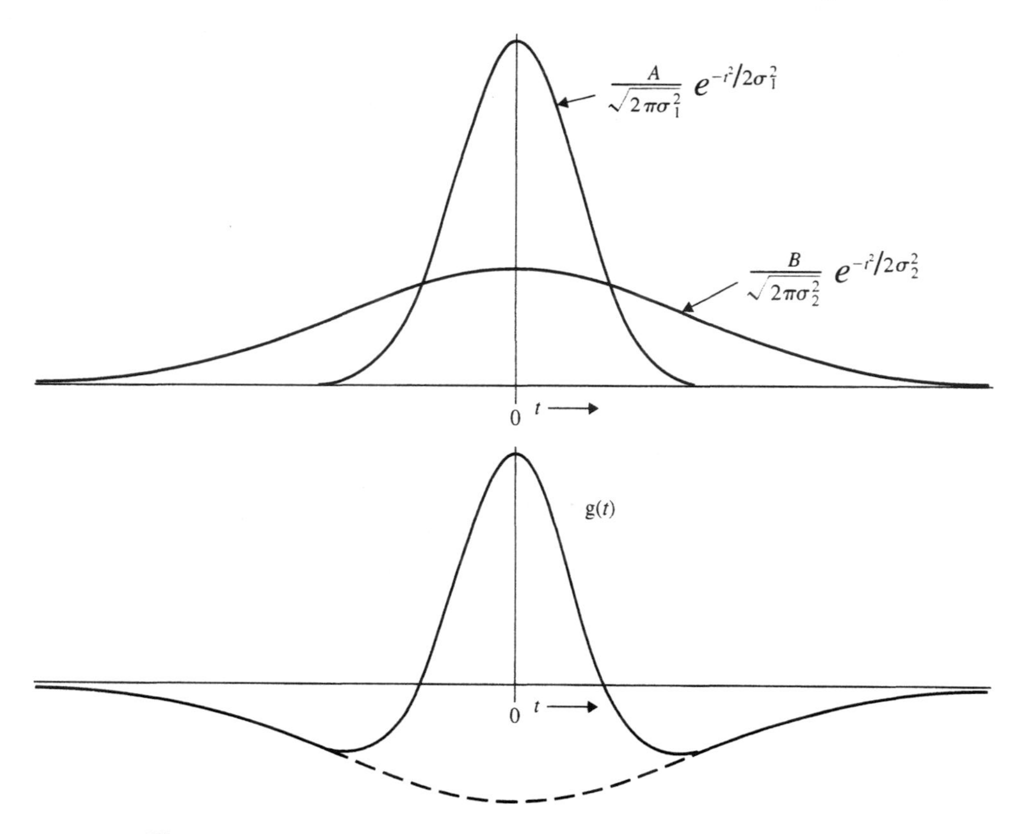

Figure 11–9 The Gaussian high-frequency enhancement impulse response

image. We also would like to estimate the maximum value the transfer function takes on at any frequency.

Maximum Value. If we write the Fourier transform of Eq. (14) and substitute the value $s = 0$, we obtain

$$G(0) = \int_{-\infty}^{\infty} g(t)dt = \int_{-\infty}^{\infty} g_1(t)dt - \int_{-\infty}^{\infty} g_2(t)dt = A_1 - A_2 \tag{15}$$

where A_1 and A_2 represent the areas under the two component functions.

We can place an upper bound on the magnitude of the transfer function if we assume that $G_2(s)$ goes to zero (dies out completely) before $G_1(s)$ decreases from its maximum value; that is,

$$G_{\max} \le G_1(0) = \int_{-\infty}^{\infty} g_1(t)dt = A_1 \tag{16}$$

We now have two rules of thumb for high-frequency enhancement filters composed of the difference of two pulses:

$$G(0) = A_1 - A_2 \quad \text{and} \quad G_{\max} \le A_1 \tag{17}$$

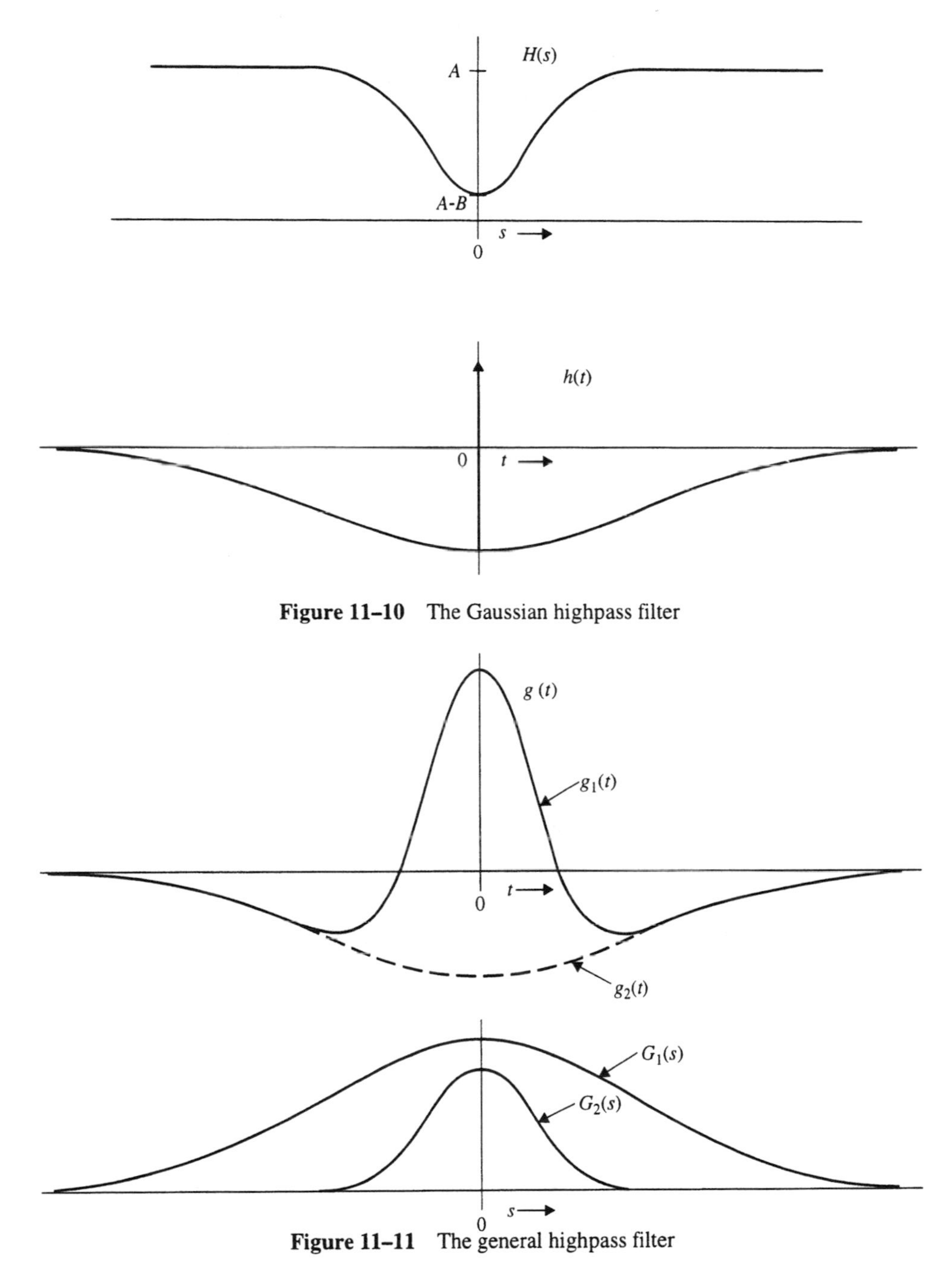

Figure 11–10 The Gaussian highpass filter

Figure 11–11 The general highpass filter

If $g_1(t)$ is an impulse (recall Figure 11–10), then equality holds for both rules in Eq. (17).

Low-Frequency Response. We now examine the effect a filter has upon large objects and areas of constant gray level within an image.

Assume the impulse response $g(t)$ is duration limited—that is, zero outside a finite interval. Assume also that the input signal $f(t)$ is constant over an interval larger than the duration of $g(t)$. This situation is shown in Figure 11–12. The output of the system is given by the convolution integral

$$h(x) = \int_{-\infty}^{\infty} f(\tau)g(x-\tau)d\tau \tag{18}$$

Over the interval of interest, however, the input signal is constant, and Eq. (18) becomes

$$h(x) = \int_{-\infty}^{\infty} cg(x-\tau)d\tau = c\int_{-\infty}^{\infty} g(\tau)d\tau \tag{19}$$

Notice that if we substitute $s = 0$ into the definition of the Fourier transform, we have

$$G(0) = \int_{-\infty}^{\infty} g(t)dt$$

which means that

$$h(x) = cG(0) \tag{20}$$

Thus, if $G(0) = 1$, the filter will not change the amplitude of large, constant areas of $f(x)$. Generalizing to two dimensions, this means that the filter does not change the contrast of large, flat areas within the input image. If $G(0) \neq 1$, it becomes a gain factor controlling the overall amplitude relationship between large components of $h(t)$ and $f(t)$.

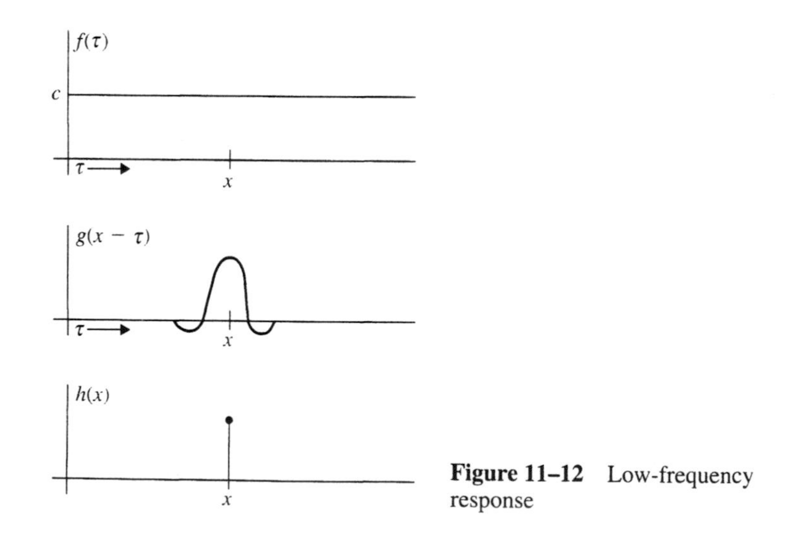

Figure 11–12 Low-frequency response

11.5 OPTIMAL LINEAR FILTER DESIGN

In this section, we develop techniques for designing filters that are, in some sense, optimal for doing a particular job. We do this by first establishing a criterion of performance and then maximizing that criterion by proper selection of the impulse response (or the transfer function) of the filter.

The history of digital image processing has seen considerable filter design done, as flying was done in World War I, "by the seat of the pants." Filters have been chosen for reasons of computational simplicity, past success, convenience, aesthetic appeal, rumor, and whim. Such filter design can prove successful, but it bears the unwholesome label *suboptimal.* It almost never produces the best filter for the job, and it can be downright dangerous.

Suboptimal filters—particularly those that are easy to implement by computer—can introduce artifacts into an image, usually without warning. Filters involving the rectangular pulse in the one domain, favorites of computer programmers, have an unsavory behavior in the opposite domain due to the infinite undulations of the $\sin(x)/x$ function.

Users of square-edged filters in one domain are often plagued by ringing and other artifactual phenomena in the other domain. They sometimes mistakenly regard these undesirable characteristics as inherent in digital processing, or they lament the lack of computer power necessary to do the job correctly.

In this section, we develop design techniques for optimal filters and show that they are, in general, quite well behaved. Armed with this knowledge, the user can intelligently trade off between optimality and computational simplicity without courting disastrous artifacts.

We first review the concept of a random variable and then develop design techniques for two optimal filters: the Wiener estimator [1–4], which is optimal for recovering an unknown signal from additive noise, and the matched detector [4–6], which is optimal for detecting a known signal buried in additive noise. Even if one never goes through the design process for an optimal filter, these two developments can sharpen one's insight into filter design considerably.

11.5.1 Random Variables

In previous chapters, we referred to the concept of a random variable, particularly for describing the noise that so often turns up in images. Since random variables play a major role in the development that follows, we discuss them here in more detail.

We use the term *random noise* to describe an unknown contaminating signal. The word *random* is actually a euphemism for our lack of knowledge. This ignorance results from dealing with a process, the physics of which is not well understood, or with a process too complicated to be analyzed in detail. Thus, if we have some general knowledge about a signal, but lack specific details, we describe the signal as random.

When we record a signal, we know that, during the recording process, an undesired contaminating signal will appear superimposed upon (added to) the desired signal. Although we might know the origin of the noise, we cannot express its functional form mathematically. After observing the noise for a period of time, we may develop a partial knowledge of it and be able to characterize some aspects of its behavior, even though we will never be able to predict that behavior in detail. Thus, the concept of a random variable becomes a useful tool in dealing with noise.

We may think of a random variable as follows: Consider an ensemble of infinitely many member functions. When we make our recording, one of those member functions emerges to contaminate our record, but we have no way of knowing which one. We can, however, make general statements about the ensemble as a group. In this way, we can express our partial knowledge of the contaminating signal.

11.5.1.1 Ergodic Random Variables

In the remainder of the book, it is sufficient to concern ourselves only with random variables that are *ergodic*. The definition of this term can be approached as follows.

There are two ways by which one can compute averages of a random variable. We can compute a *time average* by integrating a particular member function over all time, or we can average together the values of all member functions evaluated at some particular point in time. The latter technique produces an *ensemble average* at one point in time.

A random variable is ergodic if and only if (1) the time averages of all member functions are equal, (2) the ensemble average is constant with time, and (3) the time average and the ensemble average are numerically equal. Thus, for ergodic random variables, time averages and ensemble averages are interchangeable.

In Chapter 7, we introduced the expectation operator $\mathcal{E}\{x(t)\}$, which denotes the ensemble average of the random variable x computed at time t. Under the ergodicity property, $\mathcal{E}\{x(t)\}$ also denotes the value obtained when any particular sample of the random variable $x(t)$ is averaged over time; that is,

$$\mathcal{E}\{x(t)\} = \int_{-\infty}^{\infty} x(t)dt \tag{21}$$

Eq. (142) of Chapter 10 defines the autocorrelation function as a time average. For an ergodic random variable, the autocorrelation function is the same for all member functions, and it thus characterizes the ensemble. Therefore, when we say $n(t)$ is an ergodic random variable, we mean that it is an unknown function that has a known autocorrelation function. This represents the state of our partial knowledge of $n(t)$.

Since the autocorrelation function of $n(t)$,

$$R_n(\tau) = \int_{-\infty}^{\infty} n(t)n(t+\tau)dt \tag{22}$$

is known, its power spectrum,

$$P_n(s) = \mathfrak{F}\{R_n(\tau)\} \tag{23}$$

is also known. This means that we know the amplitude spectrum of $n(t)$, but do not know its phase spectrum. Indeed, the ensemble is composed of infinitely many functions that differ only in their phase spectra. Any real, even, nonnegative function can be the power spectrum of a random variable, and any real, even function that has a nonnegative spectrum can be the autocorrelation function of a random variable.

Fortunately, ergodic random variables model commonly encountered random signals quite well. For example, repeated observations of sources of "white noise" show that the measured power spectrum is, to a good approximation, constant with frequency.

11.5.2 The Wiener Estimator

The Wiener filter is the classic linear noise reduction filter. While there are simpler ways to derive the principal result pertaining to this filter, the development reproduced here points out the full power of the Wiener filter technique. The derivation is carried out here in one dimension for simplicity, and it is generalized to two dimensions in Chapter 16.

Suppose we have an observed signal $x(t)$, composed of a desired signal $s(t)$ contaminated by an additive noise function $n(t)$. We would like to design a linear filter to reduce the contaminative noise as much as possible and thus restore the signal as closely as possible to its original form. The filter is thus asked to "estimate" what the uncontaminated signal was.

The configuration is shown in Figure 11–13. The impulse response is $h(t)$, and the output of the filter is $y(t)$. Notice that we have now departed from the nomenclature used for linear systems in earlier sections.

Ideally, we would like $y(t)$ to be equal to $s(t)$, but in general, a linear filter is not powerful enough to recover a noise-contaminated signal exactly. What we shall do instead is select the impulse response $h(t)$ so that $y(t)$ will be as close as possible to $s(t)$.

Partial Knowledge. Before we begin, we must decide what knowledge we have about $s(t)$ and $n(t)$. If we know nothing at all about the signal or the noise, we cannot even get a start on the problem. At the other extreme, if we know one or both of the signals exactly, the solution is trivial.

For the purposes of the following analysis, we assume that both $s(t)$ and $n(t)$ are ergodic random variables and thus have known power spectra. This means that, although we do not know $n(t)$ exactly, we do know that it comes from an ensemble of functions, all having the same autocorrelation function and, hence, the same power spectrum. The same restriction applies to $s(t)$. Furthermore, we assume that either we know the power spectra *a priori* or we can capture samples of $s(t)$ and $n(t)$ and determine their power spectra, which are, in turn, representative of their respective ensembles.

11.5.2.1 Optimality Criterion

Before we begin the development of the optimal filter, we must establish an objective criterion of optimality. Since asking for $y(t) = s(t)$ is, in general, asking too much of a linear filter, we shall ask instead for the best job possible under the circumstances. As a criterion of optimality, we use the mean square error.

No matter what $h(t)$ is, optimal or not, we will obtain an output $y(t)$ in response to an input $s(t)$. We define the error signal at the output of the filter as

$$e(t) = s(t) - y(t) \tag{24}$$

that is, the amount by which the actual output differs from the desired output, as a function of time. If the impulse response, $h(t)$, is well chosen, the error signal will be, on the average, relatively small. A poor choice of $h(t)$ will produce a larger error signal.

As a measure of the average error, we use the *mean square error* given by

$$\text{MSE} = \varepsilon\{e^2(t)\} = \int_{-\infty}^{\infty} e^2(t)dt \tag{25}$$

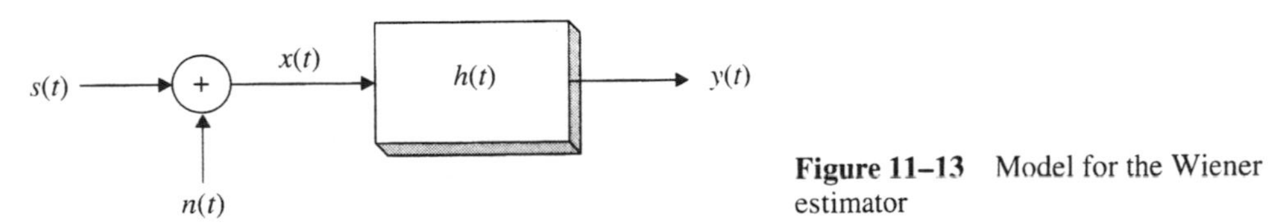

Figure 11–13 Model for the Wiener estimator

The latter equality holds because the error signal, itself a linear combination of ergodic random variables, is also an ergodic random variable.

Notice that $e^2(t)$ is positive for both positive and negative errors. Also, squaring the error causes large errors to be "penalized" more severely than small errors. For these reasons, minimizing the mean square error is an intuitively satisfactory choice for the optimality criterion. While other criteria (e.g., the average absolute error) could be used, they would complicate the analysis considerably and provide, for our purposes, little or no advantage.

11.5.2.2 The Mean Square Error

We now approach the problem as follows: Given the power spectra of $s(t)$ and $n(t)$, we must determine the impulse response $h(t)$ that minimizes the mean square error. Notice that the mean square error is a *functional* of $h(t)$, the impulse response, since a function, $h(t)$, maps into a real number, MSE.

The branch of mathematics concerned with functional minimization is the *calculus of variations,* which we employ here. In particular, we shall (1) obtain a functional expression for MSE in terms of $h(t)$, then (2) find an expression for the optimal (minimizing) impulse response, $h_0(t)$, in terms of known power spectra, and finally, (3) develop an expression for the MSE that results when $h_0(t)$ is used. The last step is done to indicate how well the optimal filter can be expected to work.

We begin by expanding the mean square error in Eq. (25):

$$\text{MSE} = \mathcal{E}\{e^2(t)\} = \mathcal{E}\{[s(t)-y(t)]^2\} = \mathcal{E}\{s^2(t)-2s(t)y(t)+y^2(t)\} \tag{26}$$

Since the expectation is an integral operator [Eq. (21)], we can write

$$\text{MSE} = \mathcal{E}\{s^2(t)\} - 2\mathcal{E}\{s(t)y(t)\} + \mathcal{E}\{y^2(t)\} = T_1 + T_2 + T_3 \tag{27}$$

where T_1, T_2, and T_3 are introduced so that we may consider the three terms separately. Writing T_1 as an integral, we have

$$T_1 = \mathcal{E}\{s^2(t)\} = \int_{-\infty}^{\infty} s^2(t)dt = R_s(0) \tag{28}$$

We recognize this as the $\tau = 0$ point on the (known) autocorrelation function of $s(t)$. Thus, its value is known from the outset.

Writing $y(t)$ as the convolution of $x(t)$ and $h(t)$ allows us to expand the second term as

$$T_2 = -2\mathcal{E}\left\{s(t)\int_{-\infty}^{\infty} h(\tau)x(t-\tau)d\tau\right\} \tag{29}$$

Since the expectation operator is actually an integral over time, we can rearrange Eq. (29) to produce

$$T_2 = -2\int_{-\infty}^{\infty} h(\tau)\mathcal{E}\{s(t)x(t-\tau)\}d\tau \tag{30}$$

Now we recognize the expectation inside the integral as the cross-correlation function of $s(t)$ and $x(t)$ and write

$$T_2 = -2\int_{-\infty}^{\infty} h(\tau)R_{xs}(\tau)d\tau \tag{31}$$

We can expand T_3 as the expectation of the product of two convolutions:

$$T_3 = \varepsilon\left\{\int_{-\infty}^{\infty} h(\tau)x(t-\tau)d\tau \int_{-\infty}^{\infty} h(u)x(t-u)du\right\} \tag{32}$$

This in turn may be rearranged as before to yield

$$T_3 = \int_{-\infty}^{\infty}\int_{-\infty}^{\infty} h(\tau)h(u)\varepsilon\{x(t-\tau)x(t-u)\}d\tau\, du \tag{33}$$

If we make the variable substitution $v = t - u$ inside the expectation operator, that factor becomes

$$\varepsilon\{x(t-\tau)x(t-u)\} = \varepsilon\{x(v+u-\tau)x(v)\} \tag{34}$$

which is simply the autocorrelation function of $x(t)$ evaluated at the point $u - \tau$. Now the third term can be written as

$$T_3 = \int_{-\infty}^{\infty}\int_{-\infty}^{\infty} h(\tau)h(u)R_x(u-\tau)d\tau\, du \tag{35}$$

The mean square error of Eq. (27) can now be written as

$$\text{MSE} = R_s(0) - 2\int_{-\infty}^{\infty} h(\tau)R_{xs}(\tau)d\tau + \int_{-\infty}^{\infty}\int_{-\infty}^{\infty} h(\tau)h(u)R_x(u-\tau)d\tau\, du \tag{36}$$

This is the mean square error in terms of the filter's impulse response and known autocorrelation and cross-correlation functions of the two input signal components. As expected, MSE is a functional of $h(t)$. We now wish to select the particular function $h_o(t)$ that causes MSE to take on its minimum value.

11.5.2.3 Minimizing MSE

We denote by $h_o(t)$ the particular function that minimizes MSE. In general, an arbitrary $h(t)$ will differ from the optimal $h_o(t)$, and we can define a function $g(t)$ to account for this variation from the optimal; that is,

$$h(t) = h_o(t) + g(t) \tag{37}$$

where $h(t)$ is an arbitrarily chosen (suboptimal) impulse response function and $g(t)$ is chosen to make the equality hold. The reason for this seemingly unnecessary complication is not obvious now, but it will allow us to establish a necessary condition upon $h_o(t)$.

If we substitute the definition of $g(t)$ in Eq. (37) into the equation for MSE [Eq. (36)], we obtain

$$\begin{aligned}\text{MSE} = {} & R_s(0) - 2\int_{-\infty}^{\infty} [h_o(\tau) + g(\tau)]\, R_{xs}(\tau)d\tau \\ & + \int_{-\infty}^{\infty}\int_{-\infty}^{\infty} [h_o(\tau) + g(\tau)]\, [h_o(u) + g(u)]\, R_x(u-\tau)d\tau\, du\end{aligned} \tag{38}$$

This expression can be expanded, producing seven terms:

$$\begin{aligned}\text{MSE} = & R_s(0) - 2\int_{-\infty}^{\infty} h_o(\tau)R_{xs}(\tau)d\tau + \int_{-\infty}^{\infty}\int_{-\infty}^{\infty} h_o(\tau)h_o(u)R_x(u-\tau)d\tau\,du \\ & + \int_{-\infty}^{\infty}\int_{-\infty}^{\infty} h_o(\tau)g(u)R_x(u-\tau)d\tau\,du + \int_{-\infty}^{\infty}\int_{-\infty}^{\infty} h_o(u)g(\tau)R_x(u-\tau)d\tau\,du \\ & -2\int_{-\infty}^{\infty} g(\tau)R_{xs}(\tau)d\tau + \int_{-\infty}^{\infty}\int_{-\infty}^{\infty} g(\tau)g(u)R_x(u-\tau)d\tau\,du\end{aligned} \tag{39}$$

Comparing the first three terms with Eq. (36), we see that their sum represents the mean square error that results when the optimal impulse response $h_o(t)$ is used. We denote this value by MSE_o. Since the autocorrelation function $R_x(u-\tau)$ is an even function, the fourth and fifth terms of Eq. (39) are equal. We can combine them with the sixth term and write the equation as

$$\begin{aligned}\text{MSE} = & \text{MSE}_o + 2\int_{-\infty}^{\infty} g(u)\left[\int_{-\infty}^{\infty} h_o(\tau)R_x(u-\tau)d\tau - R_{xs}(u)\right]du \\ & + \int_{-\infty}^{\infty}\int_{-\infty}^{\infty} g(u)g(\tau)R_x(u-\tau)du\,d\tau = \text{MSE}_o + T_4 + T_5\end{aligned} \tag{40}$$

where T_4 and T_5 are introduced for compactness of notation.

We shall now show that the term T_5 is nonnegative. Writing the autocorrelation function $R_x(u-\tau)$ as an integral produces

$$T_5 = \int_{-\infty}^{\infty}\int_{-\infty}^{\infty} g(u)g(\tau)\int_{-\infty}^{\infty} x(t-\tau)x(t-u)dt\,du\,d\tau \tag{41}$$

which may be rearranged to yield

$$T_5 = \int_{-\infty}^{\infty}\int_{-\infty}^{\infty} g(u)x(t-u)du\int_{-\infty}^{\infty} g(\tau)x(t-\tau)d\tau\,dt \tag{42}$$

If we define $z(t)$ as the function that results from convolving $g(t)$ with $x(t)$, we can recognize Eq. (42) as

$$T_5 = \int_{-\infty}^{\infty} z^2(t)dt \geq 0 \tag{43}$$

which can never be negative.

Returning now to the mean square error, we can write Eq. (40) as

$$\text{MSE} = \text{MSE}_o + 2\int_{-\infty}^{\infty} g(u)\left[\int_{-\infty}^{\infty} h_o(\tau)R_x(u-\tau)d\tau - R_{xs}(u)\right]du + T_5 \tag{44}$$

where MSE_o is the mean square error under optimal conditions and T_5 is independent of h_o and cannot be negative.

We wish to establish a condition on $h_o(\tau)$ that will ensure that MSE_o is the smallest value that MSE can have. One way to do this is to make the quantity in brackets be zero for all values of u. This makes T_4 drop out of Eq. (40) and guarantees that $\text{MSE}_o \leq \text{MSE}$. While imposing such a condition looks like the right thing to do, we still must make sure that it is both necessary and sufficient to optimize the filter.

We establish necessity by the following argument: Suppose that the term in brackets in Eq. (44) were nonzero for some values of u. Then, since $g(u)$ is an arbitrary function, it could take on large negative values where the bracketed term is positive, and vice versa. The integral in T_4 would then take on a large negative value, and MSE would become smaller than MSE_o. Since this would violate our definition, we conclude that it is necessary that the bracketed term in Eq. (44) be identically zero. This means that

$$R_{xs}(\tau) = \int_{-\infty}^{\infty} h_o(u) R_x(u - \tau) du \tag{45}$$

is a necessary condition for the mean square error to be minimized. Thus, the complication introduced in Eq. (37) has paid off by giving us a necessary condition for the optimal filter.

It is easy to see that Eq. (45) is also sufficient to optimize the filter—that is, that no additional conditions are required. Since the necessary condition causes T_4 to drop out of Eq. (40), the equation becomes

$$\text{MSE} = \text{MSE}_o + T_5 \qquad T_5 \geq 0 \tag{46}$$

from which it is clear that

$$\text{MSE} \geq \text{MSE}_o \tag{47}$$

Thus, Eq. (45) does, in fact, define the impulse response of the linear estimator that is optimal in the mean square sense.

It is easy to show that, for any linear system, the cross-correlation between input and output is given by

$$R_{xy}(\tau) = h(u) * R_x(u) \tag{48}$$

where $R_x(u)$ is the autocorrelation function of the input signal. (See Sec. 16.6.2.)

Notice now that the right-hand side of Eq. (45) is a convolution integral that can be written as

$$R_{xs}(\tau) = h_o(u) * R_x(u) = R_{xy}(\tau) \tag{49}$$

This relates the optimal impulse response to the autocorrelation of the input signal and the cross-correlation of the input and the desired signal. The second equality results from Eq. (48) and illustrates that the Wiener filter makes the input/output cross-correlation function equal to the signal/signal-plus-noise cross-correlation function.

Taking the Fourier transform of both sides of Eq. (49) leaves us with

$$P_{xs}(s) = H_o(s) P_x(s) = P_{xy}(s) \tag{50}$$

which implies that

$$H_o(s) = \frac{P_{xs}(s)}{P_x(s)} \tag{51}$$

is the frequency domain specification of the Wiener estimator.

11.5.2.4 Wiener Filter Design

Eq. (51) implies that we can design a Wiener estimator in the following way: (1) Digitize a sample of the input signal $s(t)$. (2) Autocorrelate the input sample to produce an estimate of $R_x(\tau)$. (3) Compute the Fourier transform of $R_x(\tau)$ to produce $P_x(s)$. (4) Obtain and digitize a sample of the signal in the absence of noise. (5) Cross-correlate the signal sample with the input sample to estimate $R_{xs}(\tau)$. (6) Compute the Fourier transform of $R_{xs}(\tau)$ to produce $P_{xs}(s)$. (7) Compute the transfer function of the optimal filter by Eq. (51). (8) If the filter is to be implemented by convolution, compute the inverse Fourier transform of $H_o(s)$ to produce the impulse response, $h_o(t)$, of the optimum linear estimator.

If it is impossible or impractical to obtain samples of the noise-free signal and the input signal, one could assume a functional form for the correlation functions or the power spectra required in Eq. (51). For example, "white noise" has a constant power spectrum, and some other functional form might be assumed for the desired signal or its power spectrum.

11.5.3 Examples of the Wiener Filter

11.5.3.1 Uncorrelated Signal and Noise

The autocorrelation functions in Eq. (49) and the power spectra in Eq. (51) are somewhat difficult to visualize and interpret. The situation is improved considerably, however, if we assume that the noise is uncorrelated with the signal. By definition, this means that

$$\varepsilon\{s(t)n(t)\} = \varepsilon\{s(t)\}\varepsilon\{n(t)\} \tag{52}$$

We can transform the numerator of $H_o(s)$ [Eq. (51)] and write

$$R_{xs}(\tau) = \varepsilon\{x(t)s(t+\tau)\} = \varepsilon\{[s(t)+n(t)]s(t+\tau)\} \tag{53}$$

or

$$R_{xs}(\tau) = \varepsilon\{s(t)s(t+\tau)\} + \varepsilon\{n(t)s(t+\tau)\} \tag{54}$$

In view of Eq. (52), we can write

$$R_{xs}(\tau) = R_s(\tau) + \varepsilon\{n(t)\}\varepsilon\{s(t+\tau)\} = R_s(\tau) + \int_{-\infty}^{\infty} n(t)dt \int_{-\infty}^{\infty} s(t+\tau)dt \tag{55}$$

or

$$R_{xs}(\tau) = R_s(\tau) + N(0)S(0) \tag{56}$$

A similar exercise in the denominator of Eq. (51) produces

$$R_x(\tau) = R_s(\tau) + R_n(\tau) + 2S(0)N(0) \tag{57}$$

Then Eq. (51) becomes

$$H_o(s) = \frac{P_s(s) + N(0)S(0)\delta(s)}{P_s(s) + P_n(s) + 2N(0)S(0)\delta(s)} \tag{58}$$

or, ignoring zero frequency,

$$H_o(s) = \frac{P_s(s)}{P_s(s) + P_n(s)} \qquad s \neq 0 \tag{59}$$

and we have the transfer function in terms of more easily computed spectra.

Notice that if either the signal or the noise has zero mean value, then Eq. (59) is valid for all frequencies, including zero. If both the signal and the noise have nonzero mean values, then

$$H_o(0) = \frac{1}{2} \tag{60}$$

Notice also that if there is no noise ($P_n(s) = 0$), then the transfer function takes on its maximum value of unity at all frequencies. Similarly, in the absence of a signal, it is everywhere zero.

11.5.3.2 Filter Performance

Recall that Eq. (36) gives the mean square error at the filter output. This quantity gives an indication of how well the filter will be able to recover the signal from the noise.

If we install the optimality condition of Eq. (45) in the third term of Eq. (36), it combines with the second term, leaving

$$\text{MSE}_o = R_s(0) - \int_{-\infty}^{\infty} h_o(\tau) R_{xs}(\tau) d\tau \tag{61}$$

a simple expression for the mean square error of the optimal filter. With uncorrelated zero mean noise, Eq. (56) suggests that we can replace $R_{xs}(\tau)$ with $R_s(\tau)$. But this is just the inverse Fourier transform of $P_s(s)$. So Eq. (61) becomes

$$\text{MSE}_o = R_s(0) - \int_{-\infty}^{\infty} h_o(\tau) \mathfrak{F}^{-1}\{P_s(s)\} d\tau \tag{62}$$

Writing out the inverse transformation and rearranging integrals produces

$$\text{MSE}_o = R_s(0) - \int_{-\infty}^{\infty} P_s(s) \int_{-\infty}^{\infty} h_o(\tau) e^{j2\pi s\tau} d\tau \, ds \tag{63}$$

Recognizing the first term and the second integral as Fourier transforms allows us to write

$$\text{MSE}_o = \int_{-\infty}^{\infty} P_s(s) ds - \int_{-\infty}^{\infty} P_s(s) H_o(-s) ds \tag{64}$$

Since the transfer function $H_o(s)$ is even, the minus sign in its argument can be ignored. We now substitute Eq. (59) into Eq. (64) and obtain

$$\text{MSE}_o = \int_{-\infty}^{\infty} P_s(s) ds - \int_{-\infty}^{\infty} P_s(s) \frac{P_s(s)}{P_s(s) + P_n(s)} ds \tag{65}$$

which may be rearranged to yield

$$\text{MSE}_o = \int_{-\infty}^{\infty} \frac{P_s(s) P_n(s)}{P_s(s) + P_n(s)} ds = \int_{-\infty}^{\infty} P_n(s) H_o(s) \, ds \tag{66}$$

the frequency domain expression for the mean square error in the case of uncorrelated signal and noise.

11.5.3.3 The Wiener Filter Transfer Function

Figure 11–14 illustrates the frequency domain behavior of the Wiener filter in the uncorrelated case.

At the low frequencies, where the signal power is much larger than that of the noise, the transfer function takes on values near 1, passing the energy in the signal. It then decreases to a value of 0.5 at the point where the signal and noise power are equal and declines toward zero at the higher frequencies, which are dominated by the noise.

When we assumed that our knowledge of $s(t)$ and $n(t)$ was limited to power spectra, we admitted that we had no information on the phase of the signal and noise. Notice that the transfer function $H_o(s)$ is real and even and thus introduces no phase shift.

The actual mean square error at the output, an indication of how successfully the filter is able to recover the signal from the contaminating noise, is given by Eq. (66). The integrand is plotted in Figure 11–14. Notice that the contributions to MSE occur only in

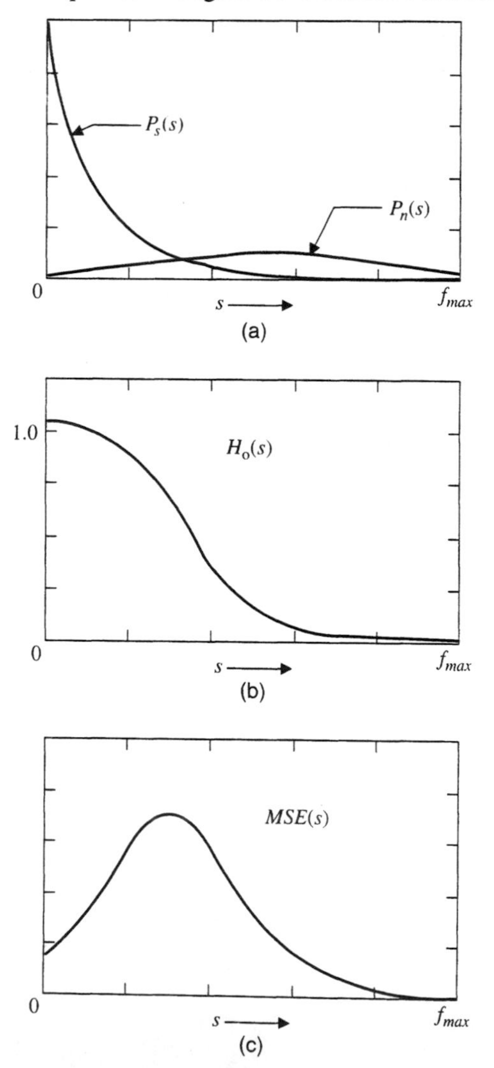

Figure 11–14 The Wiener filter transfer function

frequency bands where both the signal and noise power spectra are nonzero. The transfer function stops all noise energy in bands where the signal power is zero.

Figure 11–15 illustrates the case where the signal and the noise are separable in the frequency domain. In this case, the Wiener estimator passes the signal in its entirety and discriminates completely against the noise.

The case of a bandlimited signal imbedded in white noise is illustrated in Figure 11–16. Here, $H_o(s)$ is a bandpass filter. If the signal power spectrum is constant, the mean square error is proportional to its bandwidth.

If the signal-to-noise ratio is low, Eq. (66) reduces to approximately

$$\mathrm{MSE}_o \approx \int_{-\infty}^{\infty} P_s(s)\,ds = \int_{-\infty}^{\infty} |S(s)|^2\,ds \tag{67}$$

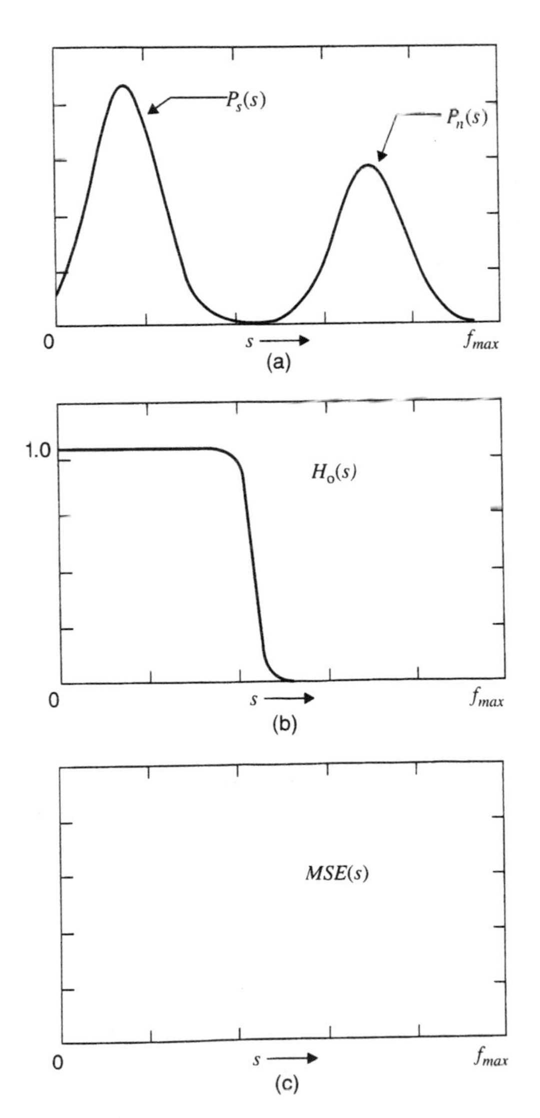

Figure 11–15 Separable signal and noise

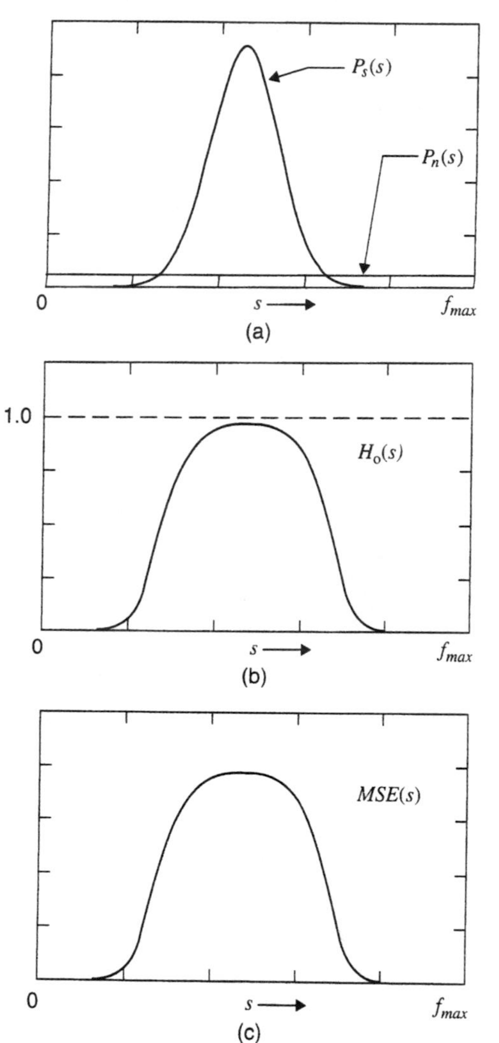

Figure 11–16 Bandlimited signal

which is, by Rayleigh's theorem,

$$\text{MSE}_o \approx \int_{-\infty}^{\infty} s^2(t)\,dt = R_s(0) = \text{energy} \tag{68}$$

Thus, in this case, the mean square error is, perhaps surprisingly, proportional to the energy in the signal.

11.5.4 Wiener Deconvolution

As previously discussed, ordinary deconvolution does not account for noise. Thus, deconvolution transfer functions, which often take on extremely large magnitudes at high frequencies, are not practical when noise is present.

Figure 11–17 illustrates the situation where deconvolution is followed by a Wiener filter. The desired signal $s(t)$ is first degraded by a linear system with impulse response $f(t)$. The output of the filter is then corrupted by an additive noise source $n(t)$ to form the observed signal $x(t)$.

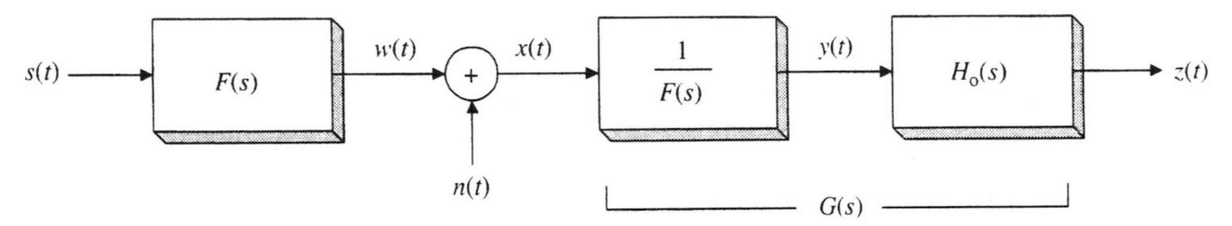

Figure 11–17 Wiener deconvolution

It is desirable to design a linear filter $g(t)$ that will simultaneously deconvolve the undesired impulse response $f(t)$ and discriminate against the noise. In Figure 11–17, $g(t)$ is illustrated as a concatenation of a deconvolution filter and a Wiener filter with impulse response $h_o(t)$.

Since the deconvolution filter is known, it remains only to determine the impulse response $h_o(t)$ before combining the two linear filters (by convolution) to produce $g(t)$.

The configuration in Figure 11–17 implies that the spectrum of the observed signal is

$$X(s) = F(s)S(s) + N(s) \tag{69}$$

Furthermore, assuming that $F(s)$ has no zeros, the spectrum of the input to the Wiener filter is

$$Y(s) = S(s) + \frac{N(s)}{F(s)} = S(s) + K(s) \tag{70}$$

Eq. (59) implies that, for uncorrelated signal and noise sources, the Wiener filter transfer function is

$$H_o(s) = \frac{P_s(s)}{P_s(s) + P_k(s)} = \frac{|S(s)|^2}{|S(s)|^2 + \left|\frac{N(s)}{F(s)}\right|^2} \tag{71}$$

Thus, the transfer function $G(s)$ of the optimal deconvolution filter in the mean square sense is

$$G(s) = \frac{H_o(s)}{F(s)} = \frac{1}{F(s)}\left[\frac{P_s(s)}{P_s(s) + P_k(s)}\right] = \frac{F^*(s)P_s(s)}{|F(s)|^2 P_s(s) + P_n(s)} \tag{72}$$

11.5.4.1 Examples

Figure 11–18 shows a one-dimensional example of a Wiener deconvolution filter. In this case, the signal has a Gaussian power spectrum, and the noise is white. The blurring function is the optical transfer function of a perfect lens. (See Chapter 15.)

Notice that, at low frequencies, $G(s)$ increases with frequency, to compensate for $F(s)$, which is decreasing. By the midrange, however, $G(s)$ begins to roll off toward zero to block the noise. In this example, the peak occurs at 40 percent of $f_{\max}$, where the signal power is still 14 times that of the noise. Thus, Wiener deconvolution is a rather conservative process, emphasizing noise reduction over reconstruction of the signal. This is a by-product

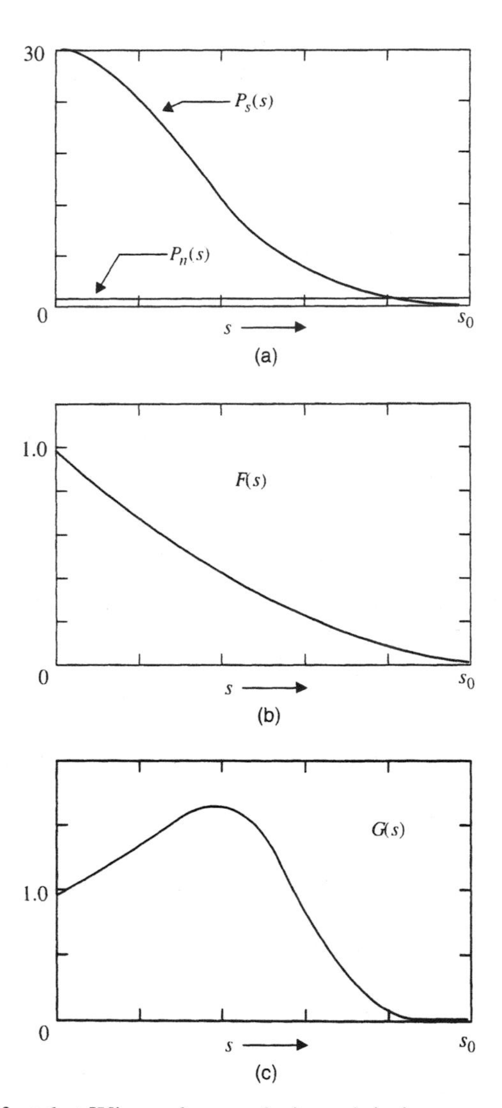

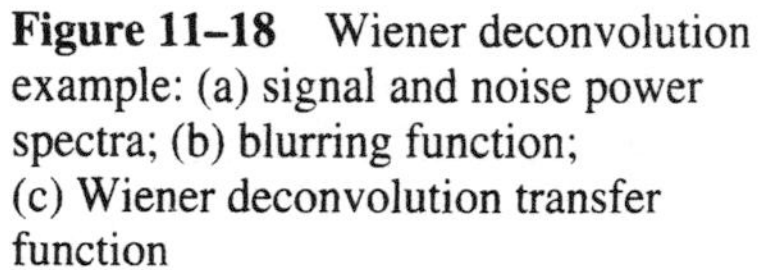

Figure 11–18 Wiener deconvolution example: (a) signal and noise power spectra; (b) blurring function; (c) Wiener deconvolution transfer function

of the fact that Wiener deconvolution minimizes mean square error. More aggressive filters for image restoration are discussed in Chapter 16.

Figure 11–19 shows an example of two-dimensional Wiener deconvolution in the frequency domain. Here, the blur is Gaussian, the signal power spectrum is 1/f, and the noise is white.

11.5.5 The Matched Detector

We now consider a filter that is optimal for a different purpose. Whereas the Wiener filter is designed to recover an unknown signal from noise, the matched detector is optimal for locating a known signal in a noisy background [4–6]. That is, the matched filter is designed to "detect" the occurrence of a signal of prescribed form in the presence of noise. (By contrast, the Wiener filter is designed to "estimate" what the signal was before it was contaminated with noise.)

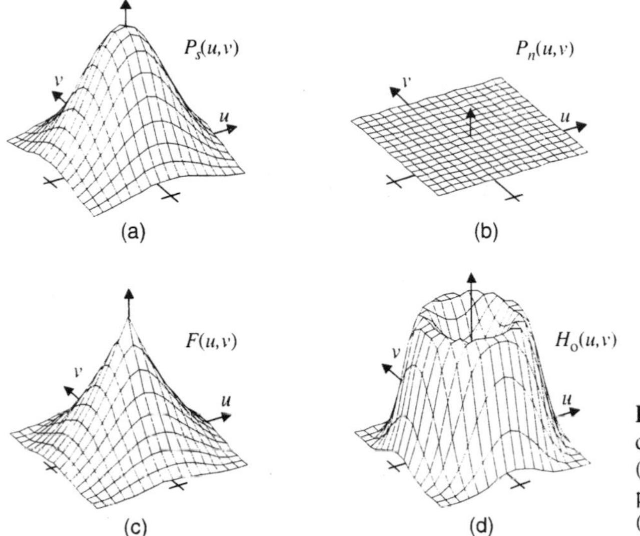

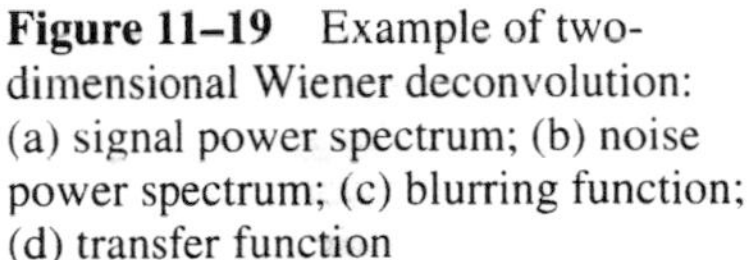
Figure 11–19 Example of two-dimensional Wiener deconvolution: (a) signal power spectrum; (b) noise power spectrum; (c) blurring function; (d) transfer function

The model for the development of the matched detector is shown in Figure 11–20. A signal $m(t)$ is contaminated by additive noise $n(t)$ to form the observed signal $x(t)$, which is input to the linear filter having impulse response $k(t)$, producing the output $y(t)$.

We wish to use the filter's output to detect the presence or absence of $m(t)$. That is to say, we shall monitor $y(t)$ to detect the occurrence of $m(t)$, a specified signal of known form. We wish to select the impulse response $k(t)$ that makes the job easy.

For the system in Figure 11–20,

$$y(t) = [m(t) + n(t)] * k(t) = m(t) * k(t) + n(t) * k(t) \tag{73}$$

which means that the system in Figure 11–21 is equivalent to that in Figure 11–20. In other words, it makes no difference whether $m(t)$ and $n(t)$ are summed before or after passing through the filter.

We define the component outputs as

$$u(t) = m(t) * k(t) \quad \text{and} \quad v(t) = n(t) * k(t) \tag{74}$$

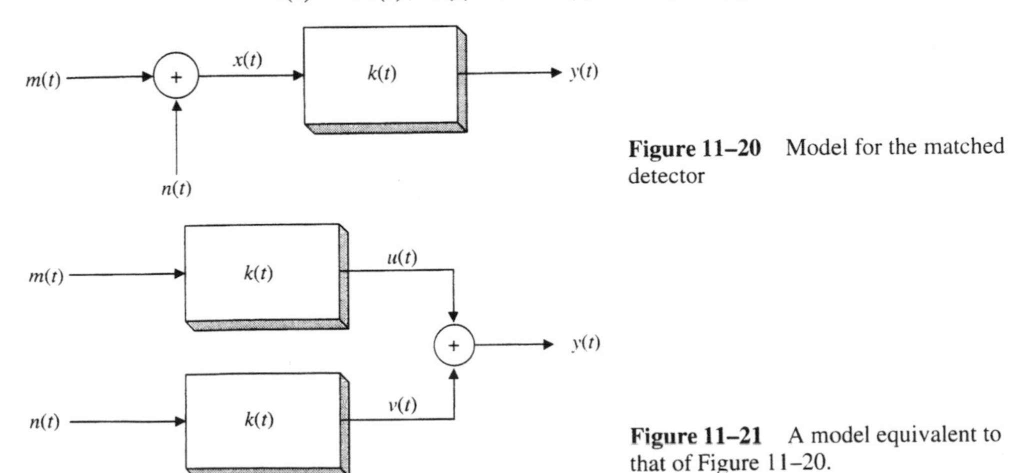

Figure 11–20 Model for the matched detector

Figure 11–21 A model equivalent to that of Figure 11–20.

Now $u(t)$ is the filtered signal and $v(t)$ is the filtered noise.

As with the Wiener filter, we must first stipulate what knowledge we have about the signal and noise, and establish a criterion of optimality. Suppose we know the functional form of $m(t)$, but we do not know at what point in time the signal occurs. The classical application of the matched detector has been the detection of reflected radar pulses. In this case, the reflected pulse, identical to the transmitted pulse, is known in form, but not in time of arrival. In digital image processing, the matched detector is useful for locating known features (calibration marks, alphabetic characters, etc.) in a noisy image.

As with the Wiener filter, we shall assume that the noise is an ergodic random variable with known power spectrum. We wish to design $k(t)$ so that, by observing the output, we may best be able to detect the signal when it occurs.

11.5.5.1 Optimality Criterion

As a measure of the performance of the filter, we shall use the average signal-to-noise power ratio at the output, evaluated at time zero:

$$\rho = \frac{\mathcal{E}\{u^2(0)\}}{\mathcal{E}\{v^2(0)\}} \tag{75}$$

The prototype signal, $m(t)$, is usually some relatively narrow function centered upon the origin. We want the output power to become large at $t = 0$, where the signal is located. Before and after, in the absence of signal, the output amplitude is relatively small.

By the shift-invariance property, if the signal, $m(t - t_1)$, arrives at some other time, t_1, then the amplitude of the filter output becomes large at t_1, thereby flagging the occurrence of the signal.

Clearly, if ρ is large, the amplitude of the output, $y(t)$, will be highly dependent on the presence or absence of $m(t)$, and it will be relatively insensitive to fluctuations in the noise $n(t)$. Thus, as a criterion for optimality of $k(t)$, we choose the maximization of ρ.

It is important to note that this criterion makes no guarantee that the output signal, $y(t)$, will resemble $m(t)$ in any way. However, since we already know the functional form of $m(t)$, we are not interested in fidelity of reproduction, as we were in the case of the Wiener filter. Instead, we want the output to be large when $m(t)$ is present and small when it is not.

Since $u(t)$ is deterministic, we can drop the expectation operator in the numerator and write Eq. (75) as

$$\rho = \frac{u^2(0)}{\mathcal{E}\{v^2(t)\}} = \frac{[m(t) * k(t)]^2}{\mathcal{E}\{[n(t) * k(t)]^2\}} = \frac{[\mathcal{F}^{-1}\{M(s) * K(s)\}]^2}{\mathcal{E}\{[n(t) * k(t)]^2\}} = \frac{\rho_n}{\rho_d} \tag{76}$$

where ρ_n and ρ_d allow us to consider the numerator and denominator separately.

We begin by expanding the denominator as a product of two convolution integrals:

$$\rho_d = \mathcal{E}\left\{\int_{-\infty}^{\infty} k(q)n(t-q)dq \int_{-\infty}^{\infty} k(\tau)n(t-\tau)d\tau\right\} \tag{77}$$

Since the expectation is an integral over time, and the impulse response $k(t)$ is not a random signal, we can rearrange the integrals in Eq. (77) to produce

$$\rho_d = \int_{-\infty}^{\infty}\int_{-\infty}^{\infty} k(q)k(\tau)\mathcal{E}\{n(t-q)n(t-\tau)\}dq\,d\tau \tag{78}$$

We recognize the expectation factor within the integral as the autocorrelation function $R_n(\tau - q)$ of the noise, which is, in turn, the inverse Fourier transform of $P_n(s)$, the noise power spectrum. Thus,

$$\varepsilon\{n(t-q)n(t-\tau)\} = R_n(\tau - q) = \int_{-\infty}^{\infty} P_n(s)e^{j2\pi s(\tau - q)}ds \tag{79}$$

which makes the denominator of ρ

$$\rho_d = \int_{-\infty}^{\infty}\int_{-\infty}^{\infty} k(q)k(\tau)\int_{-\infty}^{\infty} P_n(s)e^{j2\pi s(\tau - q)}ds\, dq\, d\tau \tag{80}$$

Now we can factor the exponential and rearrange the integrals to produce

$$\rho_d = \int_{-\infty}^{\infty} P_n(s)\left[\int_{-\infty}^{\infty} k(q)e^{-j2\pi sq}dq \int_{-\infty}^{\infty} k(\tau)e^{j2\pi s\tau}d\tau\right]ds \tag{81}$$

The term in brackets is the product of two inverse Fourier transforms, namely, $K(s)$ and $K(-s)$. Furthermore, since the impulse response $k(t)$ is a real function, the transfer function $K(s)$ is Hermite, and $K(-s) = K^*(s)$. Thus, the term in brackets reduces to

$$K(s)K(-s) = K(s)K^*(s) = |K(s)|^2 \tag{82}$$

Substituting this into Eq. (76) and writing out the Fourier transform in the numerator allows us to write the signal-to-noise power ratio as

$$\rho = \frac{\left[\int_{-\infty}^{\infty} K(s)M(s)ds\right]^2}{\int_{-\infty}^{\infty} |K(s)|^2 P_n(s)ds} \tag{83}$$

It is this expression that we wish to maximize. As with the Wiener filter, we must select a function (i.e., $K(s)$) to optimize a quantity.

11.5.5.2 The Schwartz Inequality

At this point, we make use of the Schwartz inequality. This is the mathematical result which states that

$$\int f^2(t)dt \int g^2(t)dt \geq \left[\int f(t)g(t)dt\right]^2 \tag{84}$$

where $f(t)$ and $g(t)$ are arbitrary real functions and the integration is performed between arbitrary limits. Our approach is to define the functions $f(t)$ and $g(t)$ in terms of factors appearing in Eq. (83) and obtain an inequality involving ρ. We shall then assume a form for the transfer function and show that it maximizes ρ. First, however, we shall prove the Schwartz inequality.

We begin by defining a nonnegative function of the variable λ by writing

$$Q(\lambda) = \int [\lambda f(t) + g(t)]^2 dt \geq 0 \tag{85}$$

Expanding the integrand and collecting terms produces

$$\int [\lambda f(t) + g(t)]^2 dt = \lambda^2 \int f^2(t)dt + 2\lambda \int f(t)g(t)dt + \int g^2(t)dt \geq 0 \tag{86}$$

Eq. (86) is a quadratic equation in the variable λ. Therefore,

$$\left[2\int f(t)g(t)dt\right]^2 - 4\int f^2(t)dt \int g^2(t)dt \leq 0 \tag{87}$$

or

$$\left[\int f(t)g(t)dt\right]^2 \leq \int f^2(t)dt \int g^2(t)dt \tag{88}$$

thus proving Eq. (84).

11.5.5.3 A Necessary Condition

We now use Schwartz's inequality to obtain a condition upon the signal-to-noise ratio ρ. First we define two functions

$$f(s) = K(s)\sqrt{P_n(s)} \tag{89}$$

and

$$g(s) = \frac{M(s)}{\sqrt{P_n(s)}} \tag{90}$$

Their product is

$$f(s)g(s) = K(s)M(s) \tag{91}$$

and their squared magnitudes are

$$|f(s)|^2 = |K(s)|^2 P_n(s) \tag{92}$$

and

$$|g(s)|^2 = \frac{|M(s)|^2}{P_n(s)} \tag{93}$$

If we substitute the functions defined in Eqs. (89) and (90) into Schwartz's inequality, using s as the variable of integration, we obtain

$$\left|\int_{-\infty}^{\infty} K(s)M(s)ds\right|^2 \leq \left[\int_{-\infty}^{\infty} |K(s)|^2 P_n(s)ds\right]\left[\int_{-\infty}^{\infty} \frac{|M(s)|^2}{P_n(s)}ds\right] \tag{94}$$

If we divide both sides by

$$\int_{-\infty}^{\infty} |K(s)|^2 P_n(s)ds \tag{95}$$

we are left with

$$\frac{\left|\int_{-\infty}^{\infty} K(s)M(s)ds\right|^2}{\int_{-\infty}^{\infty} |K(s)|^2 P_n(s)ds} \leq \frac{\int_{-\infty}^{\infty} |K(s)|^2 P_n(s)ds \int_{-\infty}^{\infty} \frac{|M(s)|^2}{P_n(s)}ds}{\int_{-\infty}^{\infty} |K(s)|^2 P_n(s)ds} \tag{96}$$

Recalling Eq. (83), we recognize the left side of the inequality as ρ. Furthermore, the denominator on the right-hand side cancels the first term of the numerator, leaving us with

$$\rho \leq \int_{-\infty}^{\infty} \frac{|M(s)|^2}{P_n(s)}ds \tag{97}$$

a relatively simple upper bound on ρ.

Thus, Schwartz's inequality has led us to Eq. (97), which states that ρ is less than or equal to an expression involving the power spectrum of the signal and that of the noise. Clearly, ρ will be maximized under the equality condition in Eq. (97). Since we want ρ to be as large as possible, we take

$$\rho_{\max} = \int_{-\infty}^{\infty} \frac{|M(s)|^2}{P_n(s)}ds \tag{98}$$

as a necessary condition for maximizing ρ.

11.5.5.4 The Transfer Function

Next, we assume a particular form for $K(s)$ and show that it does indeed maximize ρ. We assume that the optimal transfer function is

$$K_o(s) = C\frac{M^*(s)}{P_n(s)} \tag{99}$$

where C is an arbitrary constant. Substituting that assumed form into the general expression for ρ [Eq. (83)] produces

$$\rho = \frac{\left|\int_{-\infty}^{\infty} C\frac{M^*(s)}{P_n(s)}M(s)ds\right|^2}{\int_{-\infty}^{\infty} C^2\frac{M(s)^*M(s)}{P_n(s)^*P_n(s)}P_n(s)ds} \tag{100}$$

Canceling the constants and the $P_n(s)$'s in the denominator reduces the expression to

$$\rho = \frac{\left|\int_{-\infty}^{\infty} \frac{M^*(s)}{P_n(s)}M(s)ds\right|^2}{\int_{-\infty}^{\infty} \frac{M^*(s)M(s)}{P_n^*(s)}ds} \tag{101}$$

Since $P_n(s)$ is real and even, $P_n^*(s) = P_n(s)$, and the numerator is the square of the denominator. Now ρ reduces to

$$\rho = \int_{-\infty}^{\infty} \frac{|M(s)|^2}{P_n(s)} ds = \rho_{\max} \tag{102}$$

which satisfies the necessary condition for optimality of Eq. (98). This means that the transfer function assumed in Eq. (99) does indeed maximize the signal-to-noise power ratio at the output of the filter.

Notice that the magnitude of the transfer function

$$|K_o(s)| = |C| \frac{|M(s)|}{P_n(s)} \tag{103}$$

is proportional to the signal amplitude-to-noise power ratio as a function of frequency. The arbitrary constant C is not surprising, since we originally endeavored to maximize a ratio at the output.

11.5.6 Examples of the Matched Detector

To develop an insight into the operation of the matched detector, we consider some examples under particular conditions.

11.5.6.1 White Noise

In the first case, let us assume that the noise $n(t)$ is spectrally white; that is,

$$P_n(s) = N_0^2 \tag{104}$$

Since C in Eq. (99) is an arbitrary constant, we can set it equal to N_0^2, in which case the matched detector becomes

$$K_o(s) = M^*(s) \tag{105}$$

In the time domain, the impulse response is

$$k_o(t) = \mathfrak{F}^{-1}\{K_o(s)\} = \int_{-\infty}^{\infty} M^*(s) e^{-j2\pi st} ds \tag{106}$$

Since $m(t)$ is real, $M(s)$ is Hermite, and we can write

$$k_o(t) = \int_{-\infty}^{\infty} M(-s) e^{j2\pi(-s)(-t)} ds = m(-t) \tag{107}$$

Thus, the impulse response for the white noise case is merely a reflected version of the signal itself. This filter is said to be *matched* to the signal [5], and the term has become attached to the more general detector of Eq. (99).

The signal component of the output is given by

$$u(t) = m(t) * k_o(t) = \int_{-\infty}^{\infty} m(\tau) m(-t+\tau) d\tau = R_m(-t) \tag{108}$$

and the noise component by

$$v(t) = n(t) * k_o(t) = \int_{-\infty}^{\infty} n(\tau) m(-t+\tau) d\tau = R_{mn}(-t) \tag{109}$$

Since $k_o(t)$ in Eq. (107) is just the reflected signal we are trying to detect, the matched filter $k_o(t)$ is merely a cross-correlator, cross-correlating the incoming signal plus noise with the known form of the desired signal. The output is

$$y(t) = u(t) + v(t) = R_m(-t) + R_{mn}(-t) \tag{110}$$

which has a cross-correlation component everywhere, but has an autocorrelation component only where the signal is located.

If the correlation between the signal and noise is small, then $R_{mn}(\tau)$ is small for all values of τ, and the noise component at the output is small. Furthermore, the autocorrelation function $R_m(\tau)$ has a peak at $\tau = 0$. So,

$$\rho = \frac{u^2(0)}{\varepsilon\{v^2(t)\}} \tag{111}$$

is large at $t = 0$, or wherever the signal occurs, as desired.

11.5.6.2 The Rectangular Pulse Detector

Now, suppose, for example, that $m(t) = \Pi(t)$; that is, the matched filter is designed to detect a rectangular pulse in white noise. Suppose also that the input is $x(t) = s(t) + n(t)$, where $s(t) = \Pi(t - T)$ and $n(t)$ is white noise. Recall that the autocorrelation function of the rectangular pulse is given by

$$R_x(\tau) = \Pi(t) * \Pi(t) = \Lambda(\tau) \tag{112}$$

Now the output of the filter is

$$y(t) = R_{xm}(t) = R_{sm}(t) + R_{mn}(t) = \Lambda(t - T) + R_{mn}(t) \tag{113}$$

So, for the system shown in Figure 11–22, the components of the input and output are presented in Figure 11–23.

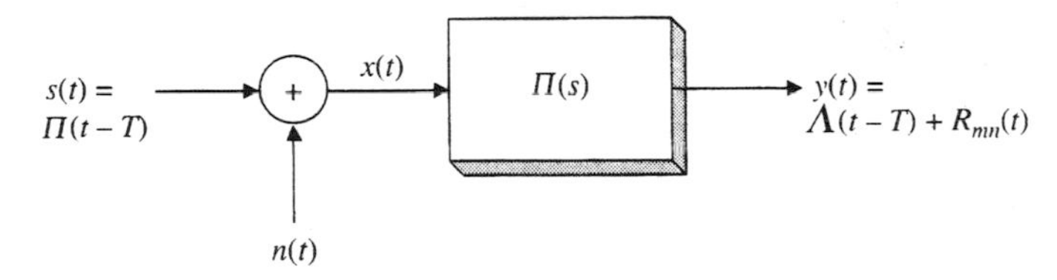

Figure 11–22 Rectangular pulse detector

From the latter figure, we see how the matched filter discriminates against the noise while responding to the signal. The output has a peak at $t = T$, the time at which the input pulse occurs, but takes on relatively small amplitude elsewhere. Thus, a simple examination of the output signal indicates when the input pulse occurs.

Notice that the form or shape of the signal is not preserved by the matched detector, as it was with the Wiener estimator. This is because we designed the filter to detect the presence or absence of a particular known input signal, rather than to estimate its noise-free shape.

11.5.6.3 Image Feature Detection

Figure 11–24 shows a matched filter that locates the grid intersections in a digitized graph. This information can be used, for example, to guide a geometric transformation

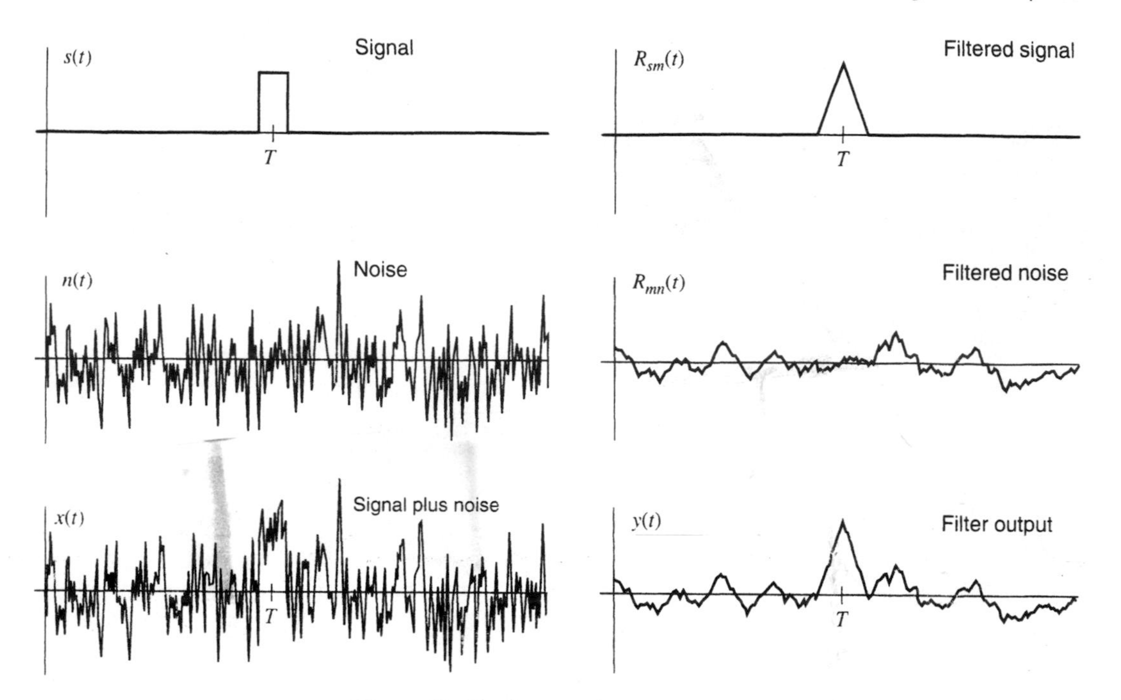

Figure 11–23 Input and output component signals

that rectifies the coordinates prior to automatic curve tracking. The convolution kernel (Figure 11–24a) matches what the image is expected to look like in the local area of a grid intersection.

11.5.7 Comparison of the Wiener Estimator and the Matched Detector

The Wiener estimator and the matched detector are each optimal filters designed to do a specific job. Although they were designed for different functions, it is instructive to compare the two filters.

Recall from Eq. (59) that for uncorrelated signal and noise the Wiener estimator transfer function is

$$H_o(s) = \frac{P_s(s)}{P_s(s) + P_n(s)} \tag{114}$$

and the mean square error one can expect when using this filter is, from Eq. (66),

$$\text{MSE}_o = \int_{-\infty}^{\infty} \frac{P_s(s)P_n(s)}{P_s(s) + P_n(s)} ds = \int_{-\infty}^{\infty} P_n(s)H_o(s)ds \tag{115}$$

If we let $C = 1$ in Eq. (99), the matched detector transfer function becomes

$$K_o(s) = \frac{S^*(s)}{P_n(s)} \tag{116}$$

and the signal-to-noise power ratio at its output is

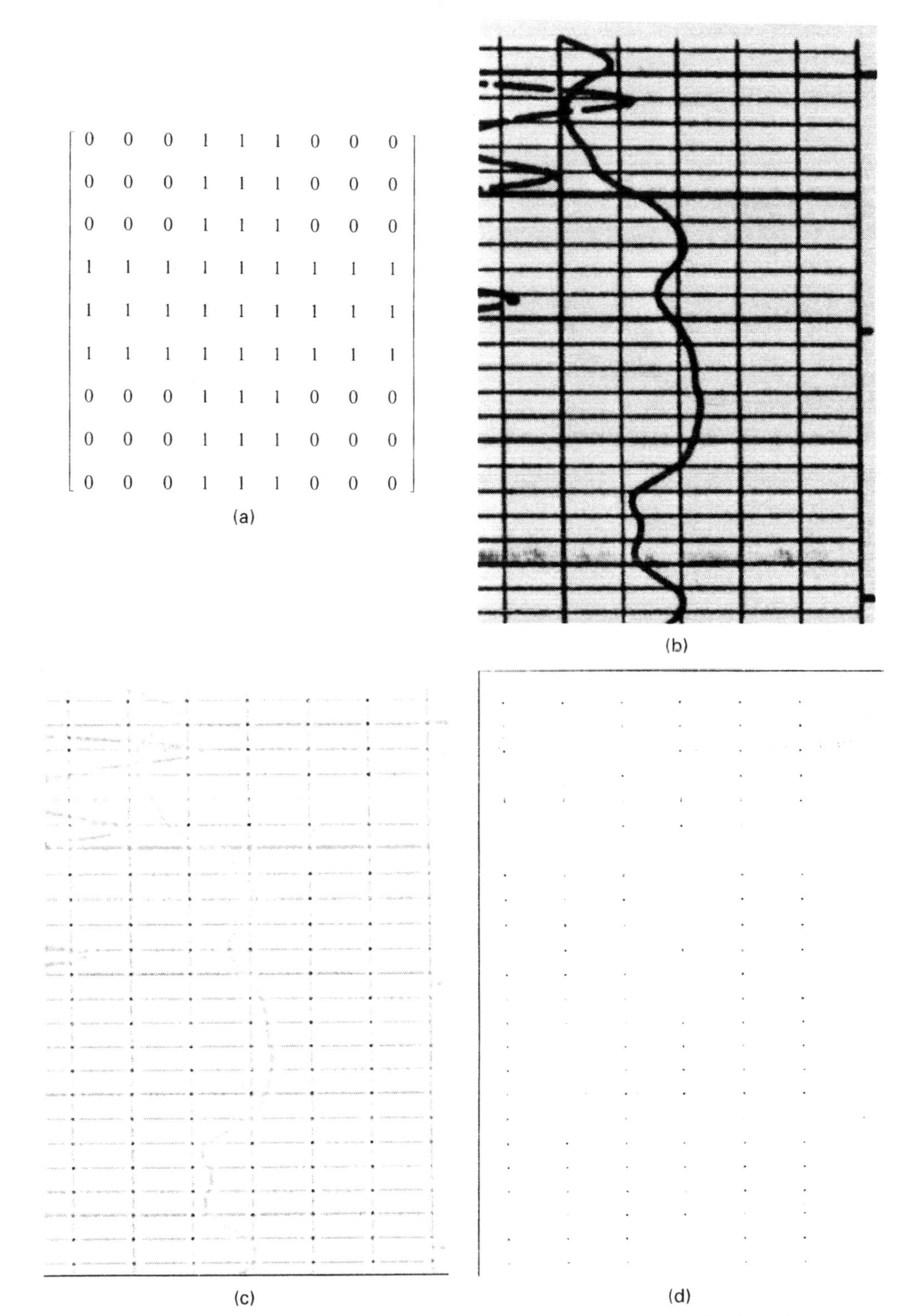

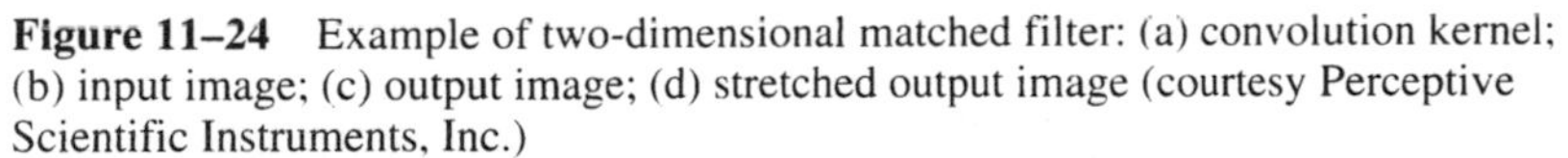

Figure 11–24 Example of two-dimensional matched filter: (a) convolution kernel; (b) input image; (c) output image; (d) stretched output image (courtesy Perceptive Scientific Instruments, Inc.)

$$\rho_{\max} = \int_{-\infty}^{\infty} \frac{P_s(s)}{P_n(s)} ds \tag{117}$$

First, notice that while $H_o(s)$ is real and even (and hence contains no phase information) $K_o(s)$ is Hermite and does contain phase information. Notice also that $H_o(s)$ is bounded between 0 and +1. This means that it can never amplify spectral components of the input signal. However, $K_o(s)$ has neither a positive nor a negative bound, so its frequency domain behavior is much less constrained.

Let us define the signal-to-noise power ratio as a function of frequency by

$$R(s) = \frac{|S(s)|^2}{|N(s)|^2} = \frac{P_s(s)}{P_n(s)} \tag{118}$$

In terms of this function, the magnitude of the matched detector transfer function is

$$|K_o(s)| = \frac{R(s)}{|S(s)|} = \frac{\sqrt{R(s)}}{|N(s)|} \tag{119}$$

and the signal-to-noise ratio is

$$\rho_{\max} = \int_{-\infty}^{\infty} R(s) ds \tag{120}$$

The Wiener filter transfer function is

$$|H_o(s)| = H_o(s) = \frac{R(s)}{1 + R(s)} \tag{121}$$

and the mean square error is given by

$$\text{MSE}_o = \int_{-\infty}^{\infty} \frac{R(s)P_n(s)}{1 + R(s)} \tag{122}$$

which is just that noise power that passes through the filter, accumulated over all frequencies.

Figure 11–25 shows an example of the frequency domain functions discussed in this section. For best performance of the matched detector, we want ρ to be large. This will occur if there are frequencies over which $P_s(s)$ is much larger than $P_n(s)$. On the other hand, in order for the Wiener filter to be successful, we want the area under the MSE integrand to be small. At frequencies where $P_s(s)$ and $P_n(s)$ are roughly equal, the contribution to MSE is maximum.

11.5.7.1 Practical Considerations

Estimation is a more difficult task than detection, for two reasons. First, we ask an estimator to recover the signal at all points in time, whereas we ask the detector only to determine when the signal occurs. Second, we have more *a priori* information in a detection problem in that we know the form of the signal exactly, instead of having only its power spectrum. Since we are asking a detector to do less with more information, we can expect better performance under the same conditions.

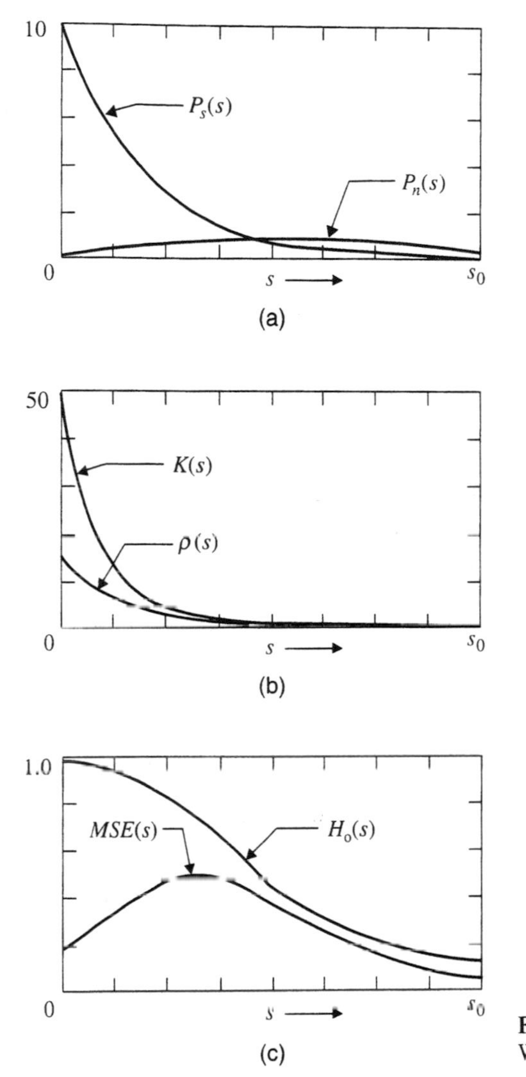

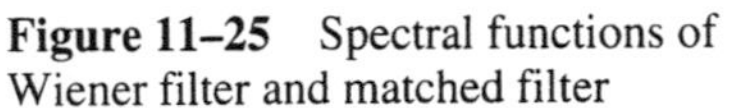
Figure 11–25 Spectral functions of Wiener filter and matched filter

Whether one uses a detector or an estimator is normally dictated by the problem. Since the two are designed for different jobs, they usually do not compete for consideration. Nevertheless, it is instructive to compare their behavior under similar conditions. Figure 11–26 presents a computer simulation that illustrates both the Wiener estimator and the matched detector when the signal is a Gaussian pulse embedded in white random noise. In this case, the signal-to-noise ratio is on the order of unity.

Both the estimator [Eq. (114)] and the detector [Eq. (116)] are lowpass filters in this situation, but they differ somewhat in form. The detector output clearly shows a peak at the point where the input pulse occurs. The estimator recovers the pulse from the noise, but not without residual error. The low-frequency components of the noise penetrate the Wiener filter and prevent exact recovery. One would expect better performance from both filters with improved signal-to-noise ratio, and conversely.

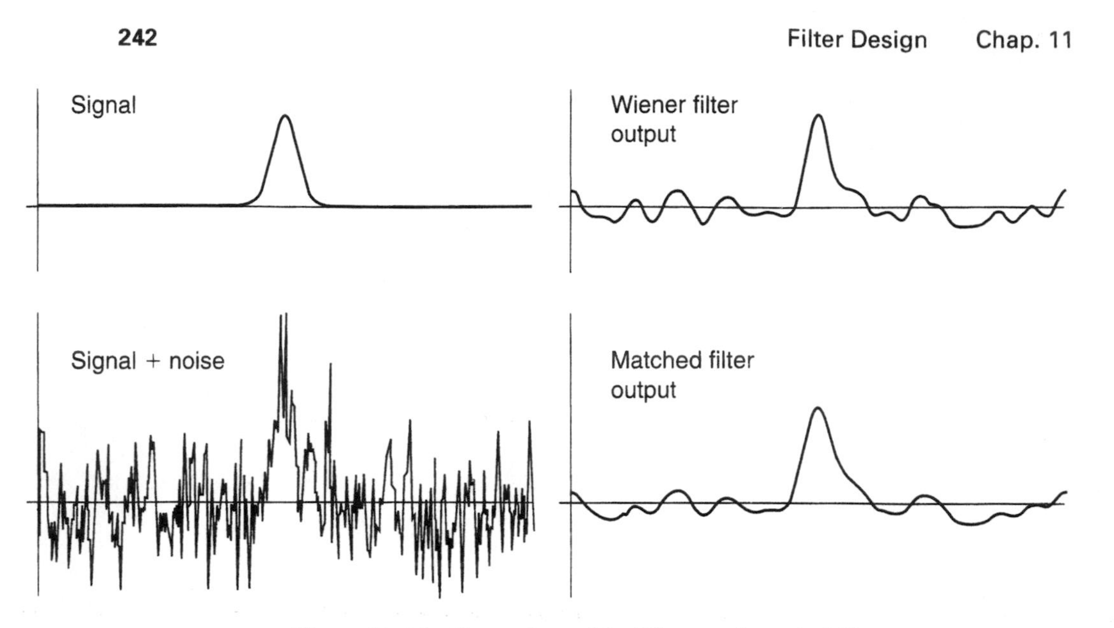

Figure 11–26 Comparison of the Wiener and matched filters

11.5.8 A Practical Example

We conclude the chapter with an example that illustrates how optimal filter theory can guide the design of practical filters. Figure 11–27 shows a digitized X ray of a tube filled with X-ray–absorbing dye. The image models angiography, a diagnostic technique in which dye is injected into blood vessels during X-ray exposure. Here, the smooth tube substitutes for the vessel.

The goal in this example is to develop a processing technique that will find the edges of the tube in the noisy image of Figure 11–27 and reliably measure the tube's diameter all along its length. Such a technique is useful for quantifying the narrowing of blood vessels that accompanies atherosclerosis and produces heart attacks [7].

Since the problem is one of edge detection, the matched detector would seem the natural choice. In this example, however, we pose the problem somewhat differently. We shall assume that the vessel's edges occur, on each image line, at the two points of steepest slope and attempt to locate these by differentiation. Before differentiating, however, we shall employ a Wiener filter to estimate the noise-free image. Furthermore, we shall process each horizontal scan line individually. This not only reduces the problem to a one-dimensional one, but also allows the procedure to respond to rapid changes in width, should they occur.

Figure 11–28 shows a gray-level plot of one line $f_i(x)$ from Figure 11–27. The evident noise is common in radiography, due primarily to film grain and photon statistics in the illuminating beam. Clearly, differentiating this curve would not produce reliable peaks at the inflection points, because of the noise.

Assuming uncorrelated signal $s(x)$ and noise $n(x)$, the specification of the Wiener filter [Eq. (59)] requires the power spectrum of the signal and that of the noise. We can estimate the signal's power spectrum by line averaging, since, with a smooth tube, all lines $f_i(x)$ should be identical in the absence of noise. Thus,

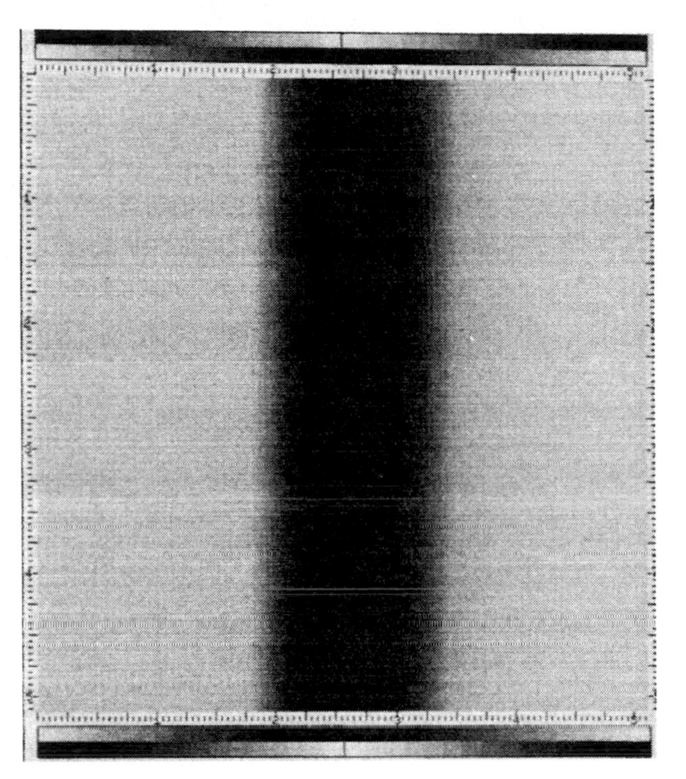

Figure 11–27 Digitized angiogram of a smooth tube

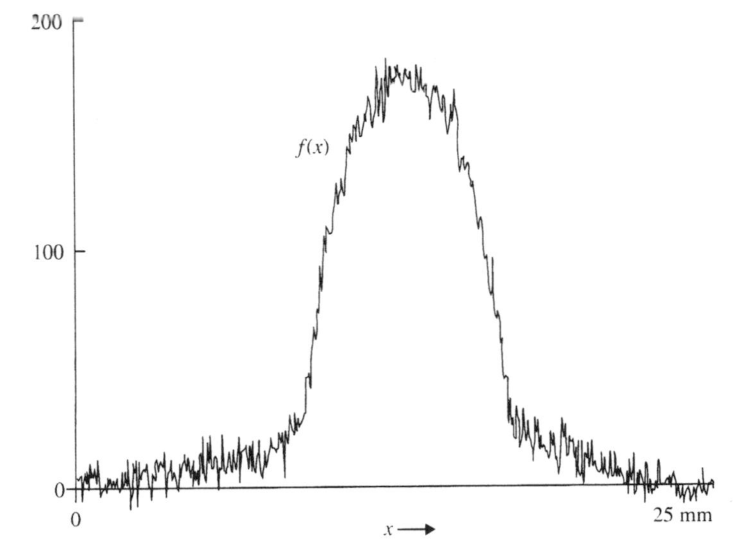

Figure 11–28 Line 100, Figure 11–27

$$P_s(s) = |\mathfrak{F}\{s(x)\}|^2 \approx \left|\mathfrak{F}\left\{\frac{1}{N}\sum_{i=1}^{N} f_i(x)\right\}\right|^2 \tag{123}$$

will reduce the noise by the factor $1/\sqrt{N}$. Figure 11–29 shows the result of averaging 60 lines in Figure 11–27 and the resulting amplitude spectrum of the signal.

Once the signal has been estimated, the power spectrum of the noise can be estimated from Figure 11–27 using line-by-line power spectrum averaging after subtraction of the signal; that is,

$$P_n(s) \approx \frac{1}{N}\sum_{i=1}^{N} |\mathfrak{F}\{f_i(x) - s(x)\}|^2 \tag{124}$$

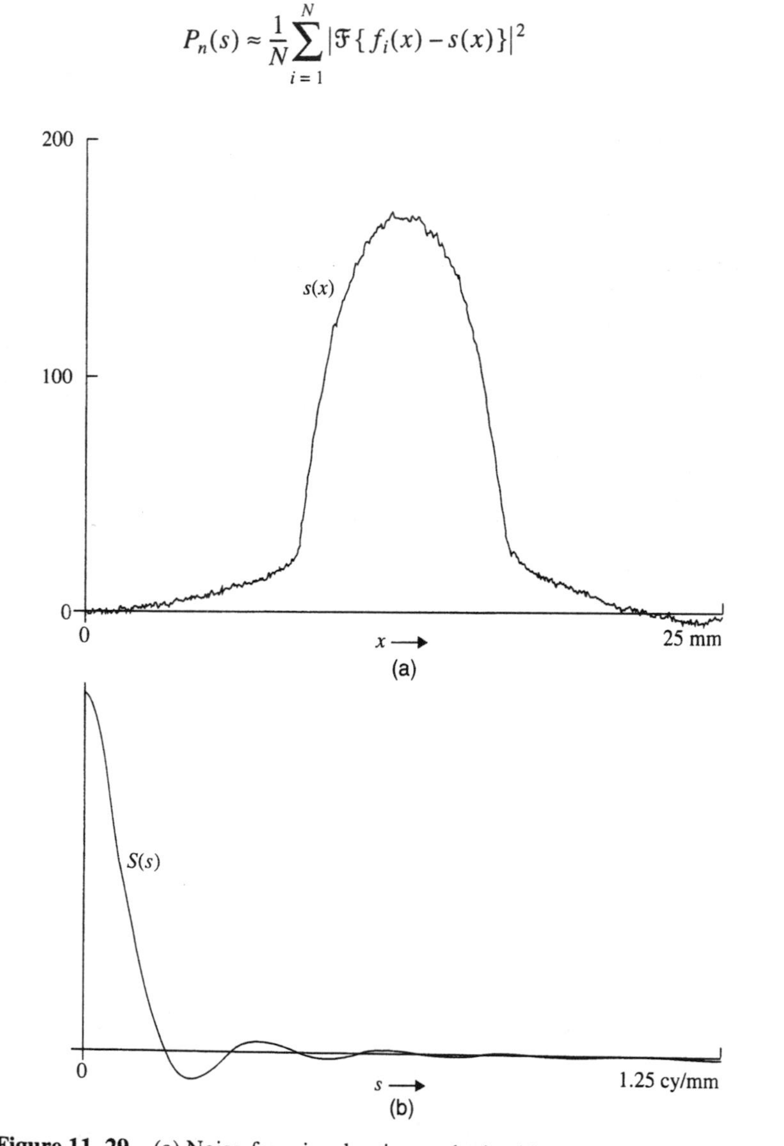

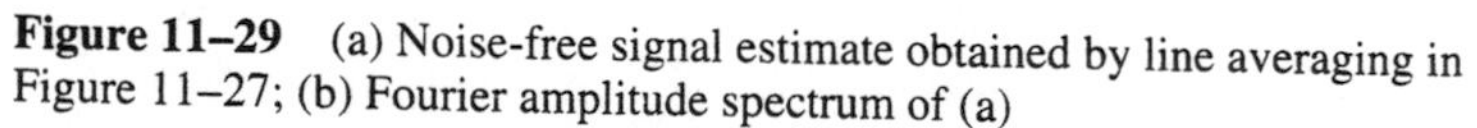

Figure 11–29 (a) Noise-free signal estimate obtained by line averaging in Figure 11–27; (b) Fourier amplitude spectrum of (a)

In this study, Eq. (124) showed the power spectrum of the noise to be essentially constant with frequency.

Figure 11–30(a) shows the Wiener filter transfer function $H_o(s)$ computed by Eq. (59). The transfer function takes on values near unity at the signal-dominated low frequencies and tends to zero at high frequencies.

We could inverse transform the transfer function in Figure 11–30(a) to obtain the impulse response for predifferentiation smoothing. There are, however, some practical considerations worthy of note.

The notches in the transfer function of Figure 11–30(a) are produced by the zero-crossings in the signal's spectrum [Figure 11–29(b)]. By the similarity theorem, the position of these notches will shift with changes in the width of the vessel.

This points up the fact that our signal is not actually an ergodic random process, as the Wiener filter development assumes. The member functions in the signal ensemble correspond to vessels of different width and thus do not all have identical power spectra. As it happens, we are forced to violate one of the assumptions on which the Wiener filter is based. We shall proceed nevertheless, acting in the belief that a "near-optimal" technique will prove an adequate substitute for true optimality, which is beyond our grasp.

If we were to include the troublesome notches in the design, our filter would be quite sensitive to slight changes in the vessel's width. It would be optimal only for the exact vessel width used in the design and would rapidly become suboptimal as the width varied. This is due to the rather abrupt frequency-domain behavior of the transfer function.

We choose instead to ignore the notches by fitting a smooth envelope to the transfer function. Figure 11–30(b) shows a smooth approximation, $\tilde{H}(s)$, to the Wiener filter transfer

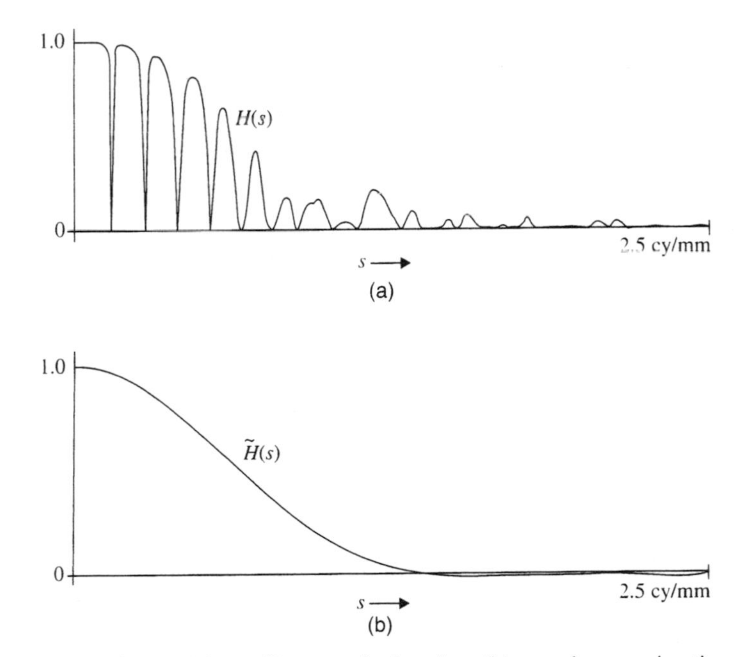

Figure 11–30 (a) Wiener filter transfer function; (b) smooth approximation to (a)

function. $\tilde{H}(s)$ was chosen because of two desirable properties: It is a reasonable approximation to the envelope of Figure 11–30(a), and its impulse response renders digital convolution quite an efficient computation.

Figure 11–31 shows the corresponding impulse response, $\tilde{h}(x)$, which is piecewise parabolic, and $\tilde{h}'(x)$, its first derivative, which is piecewise linear. Since differentiation commutes with convolution, using the latter function combines smoothing and differentiation into one step. Furthermore, digital convolution using a piecewise linear impulse response can be programmed to execute very efficiently [8].

Figure 11–32 shows the results of using the two impulse responses in Figure 11–31 on the image line in Figure 11–28. The first produces smoothing for noise reduction only, while the second combines smoothing with differentiation. In this case, the degree of noise reduction is gratifying. Notice also that the inflection points in the upper curve give rise to distinct peaks in the lower curve, suggesting that vessel edge detection is now a simple task.

The piecewise linear impulse response $\tilde{h}'(x)$ is a computationally efficient approximation to the differentiating Wiener filter for this application. Even though the signal is nonergodic, the notch-free transfer function $\tilde{H}(s)$ should be rather well behaved under suboptimal conditions, since it has no abrupt behavior in the frequency domain. Furthermore, Figure 11–32 strongly suggests that we have a comfortable solution to this edge detection

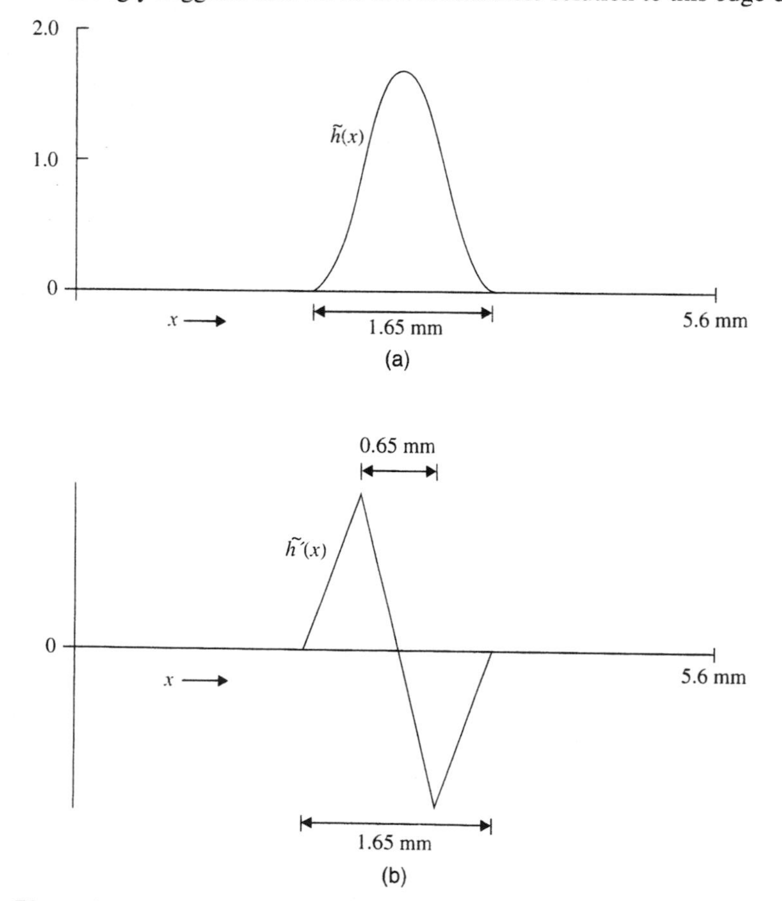

Figure 11–31 (a) Impulse response of Figure 11–30(b); (b) derivative of (a)

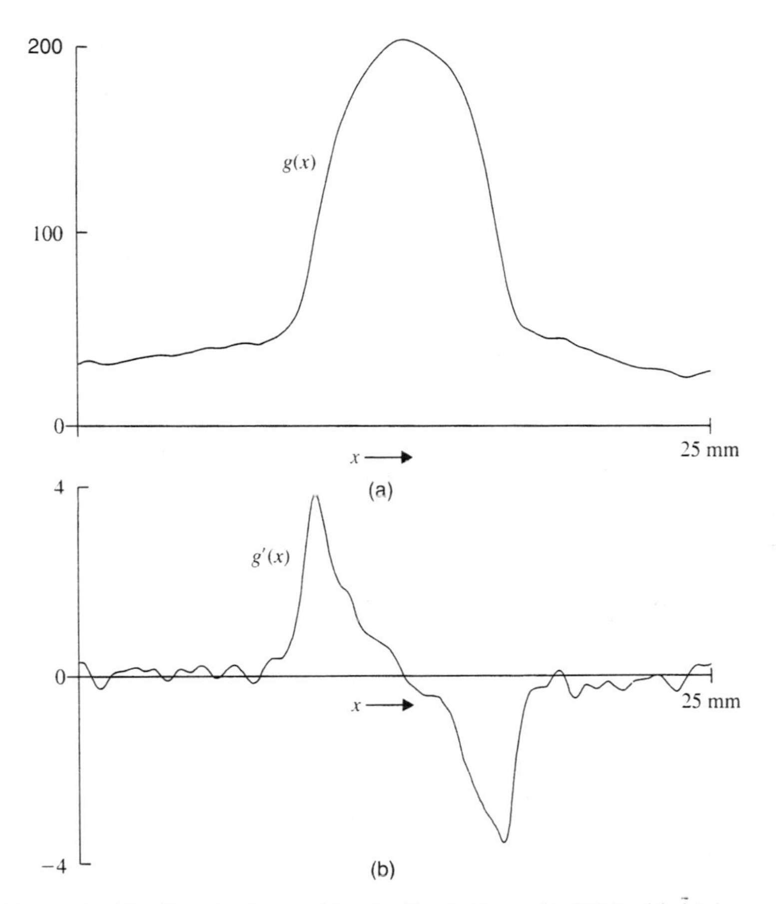

Figure 11–32 Results of smoothing the line in Figure 11–28(a) with $\bar{h}(x)$; (b) with $\bar{h}'(x)$

problem. The differentiating Wiener filter designed on the smooth tube has proved useful on routine angiograms [8].

11.6 ORDER-STATISTIC FILTERS

By definition, if a filter fails the test of linearity (Chapter 9), it is nonlinear. Many types of nonlinear filters have been described, tested, and used. Arguably, nonlinear approaches can solve certain types of image-processing problems better than linear filters can. They lack, however, the far-reaching and relatively straightforward theoretical background that underlies linear filters. For an introductory treatment, we address one of the most useful classes, *order-statistic filters,* so called because they are based on statistics derived from ordering (ranking) the elements of a set rather than computing means, etc. The median filter is one of these.

11.6.1 The Median Filter

The nonlinear filtering technique that has probably found most common usage is the median filter. It is a neighborhood operation, similar to convolution, except that the calculation is not a weighted sum. Instead, the pixels in the neighborhood are ranked in the order of their gray levels, and the midvalue of the group is stored in the output pixel. For an N-by-N median filter, where N is odd, the output gray level is the gray level of that input pixel which is greater than or equal to $(N^2 - 1)/2$ of the pixels in the neighborhood and less than or equal to $(N^2 - 1)/2$ of them.

Median filtering is normally a somewhat slower process than convolution, due to the requirement for sorting all the pixels in each neighborhood by gray level. There are, however, algorithms that speed up the process [9,10].

The median filter is popular because of its demonstrated ability to reduce random noise without blurring edges as much as a comparable linear lowpass filter. This is illustrated one dimensionally in Figure 11–33. Here, the signal is an edge plus a sinusoid at one-fourth the sampling frequency, and the median is computed over a three-point neighborhood. In this example, the median filter removes the sinusoid completely, while preserving the edge.

In general, light or dark objects having less than half the area of the median filter are essentially eliminated, while larger objects are preserved approximately intact. Thus, the spatial extent of the median filter must be "tuned" to the problem at hand. There is much less theory to guide the design of median filters than there is to guide linear filter design. Experimentation often substitutes for analysis.

The noise-reducing effect that a median filter has on an image depends on two related, but totally separate, things: the spatial extent of the neighborhood (mask), as mentioned

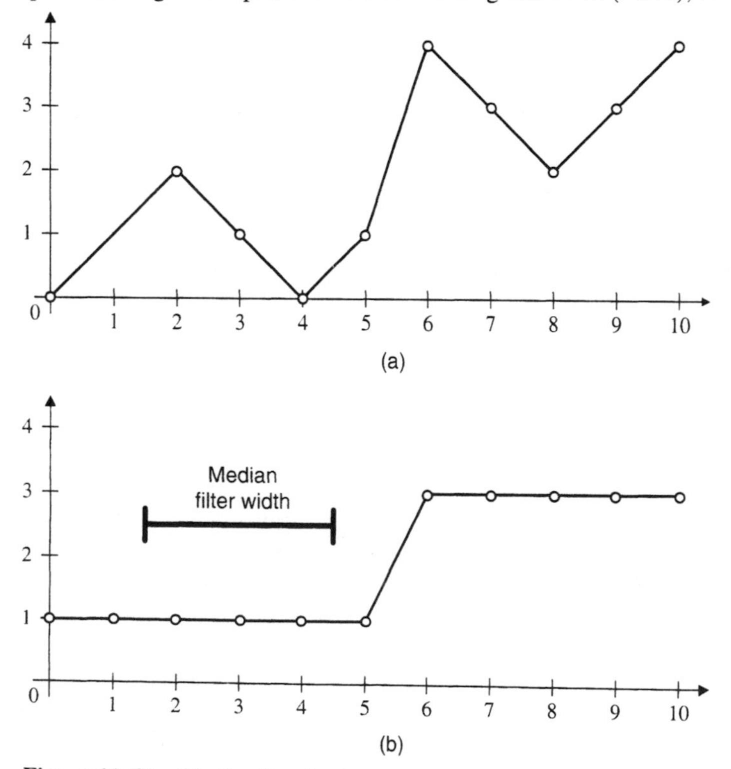

Figure 11–33 Median filtering in one dimension: (a) input, (b) output

above, and the number of pixels involved in the median computation. The simple case is an N-by-N square mask (where N is commonly odd), with all N^2 points used in the computation. One can, however, use a sparsely populated mask, as shown in Figure 11–34, to save time.

For large masks, the noise reduction effect of using more pixels in the computation of the median reaches a point of diminishing returns. Figure 11–35 shows how the noise reduction effect of a median filter depends on the number of pixels used in the computation. Here, different sparsely populated five-by-five median filter masks were used on an image containing white random noise. The standard deviation of the output image is plotted against the number of points used in the median computation. For more than 9 or 13 points, it is questionable whether the additional time required to rank the larger number of pixels is justified by the improvement in noise reduction. Thus, if the problem calls for a spatially large filter, one may be able to obtain the desired result with a sparsely populated median mask.

11.6.2 Other Order-Statistic Filters

The median filter is only one member of the class of order-statistic filters. If the input pixels in the neighborhood are ranked, the median represents the 50th percentile. Other percentiles can be used as well. Zero and 100 percent correspond to the minimum and maximum filters, respectively. Using percentiles other than 50 percent tends to darken or lighten the image. While these filters are less popular for general use, they are valuable in some applications.

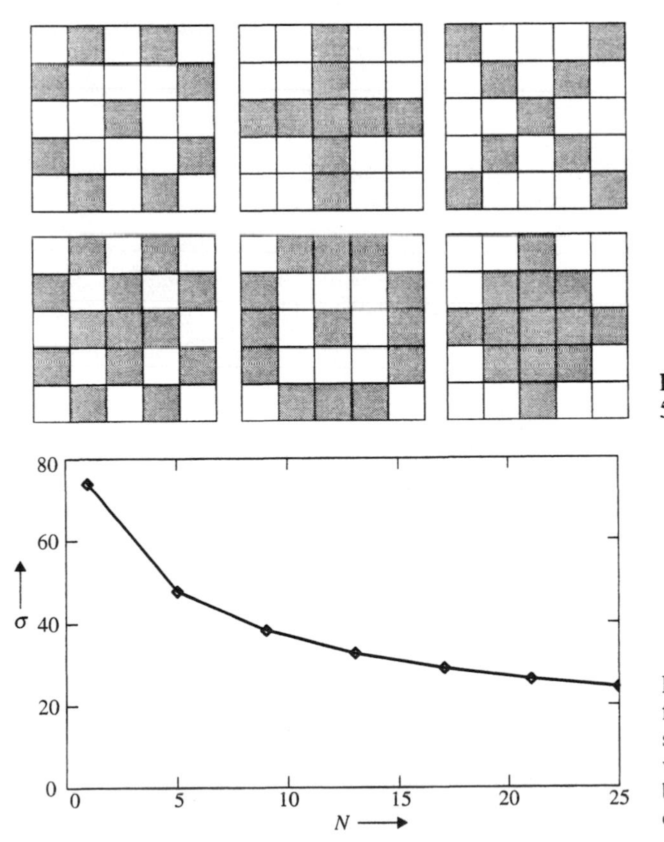

Figure 11–34 Sparsely populated 5 × 5 median filters

Figure 11–35 Effect of a five-by-five median filter on white noise: standard deviation of the output image versus the number of pixels in the five-by-five mask that are used in the computation of the median

11.7 SUMMARY OF IMPORTANT POINTS

1. A high-frequency enhancement-filter impulse response can be designed as a narrow positive pulse minus a broad negative pulse.
2. The transfer function of a high-frequency enhancement filter approaches a maximum value that is equal to the area under the narrow positive pulse.
3. The transfer function of a high-frequency enhancement filter has a zero frequency response equal to the difference of the areas under the two component pulses.
4. The zero frequency response of a filter determines how the contrast of large features is affected.
5. Filters designed for ease of computation rather than for optimal performance are likely to introduce artifacts into an image.
6. An ergodic random process is a signal whose known power spectrum and autocorrelation function represent all the available knowledge about the signal.
7. The Wiener estimator is optimal, in the mean square error sense, for recovering a signal of known power spectrum from additive noise of known power spectrum.
8. The Wiener filter transfer function takes on values near unity in frequency bands of high signal-to-noise ratio and near zero in bands dominated by noise.
9. The matched detector is optimal for detecting the occurrence of a known signal in a background of additive noise.
10. In the case of white noise, the matched filter correlates the input with the known form of the signal.
11. The Wiener filter transfer function is real, even, and bounded by zero and unity.
12. The matched filter transfer function is, in general, complex, Hermite, and unbounded.
13. Order-statistic filters are nonlinear and work by ranking the pixels in a neighborhood.
14. A median filter essentially eliminates objects less than half its size, while preserving larger objects. It is useful for noise reduction where edges must be preserved.
15. A sparsely populated mask can reduce computation time on spatially large median filters.

PROBLEMS

1. Prove Eq. (48).
2. A signal has power spectrum $P_s(s) = 10/|s|$, and the noise is white and uncorrelated with spectral amplitude 2. Sketch the Wiener filter transfer function, $H(s)$, and the signal-to-noise power ratio, $R(s)$, for $|s| < 20$. Is this a lowpass, bandpass or highpass filter?
3. A sample of the signal is approximately $s(x) = a\,\text{sech}(\pi a x)$, and the noise power spectrum is white with amplitude N_0. Sketch the Wiener filter transfer function for $0 < s < a$.
4. A sample of the signal is approximately $s(x) = a\,\text{sech}(\pi a x)$, and the noise amplitude spectrum is approximately $N(s) = \exp(-|s|/2a)$. Sketch the Wiener filter transfer function for $0 < s < f_{max} = a$.
5. The signal is $s(t) = 4\cos(2\pi f t)\exp(-t^2/2\sigma^2)$, where $f = 1/8$ and $\sigma = 12$. The noise is white with spectral amplitude 1. Design a Wiener filter to recover the signal. Sketch $s(t)$ for $-64 \le t \le 64$ and $P_s(s)$, $P_n(s)$, $H_o(s)$, and the integrand of the MSE integral for $0 \le s \le 0.5$.

6. The signal is $s(t) = \cos(2\pi ft)\,\text{sech}(\pi t/a)$, where $f = 1/8$ and $a = 6$. The noise has power spectrum $P_n(s) = 4\,\text{sech}(\pi s/0.3125)$. Design a Wiener filter to recover the signal. Sketch $s(t)$ for $-64 \leq t \leq 64$ and $P_s(s)$, $P_n(s)$, $H_0(s)$, and the integrand of the MSE integral for $0 \leq s \leq 0.5$.

PROJECTS

1. Develop a program for one-dimensional Wiener filter design. Use the program to estimate the waveshape of a short spoken word (or other brief sound) in a noisy digitized sound sequence.
2. Generate a digital signal 512 points long that contains a Gaussian pulse of amplitude 20 and standard deviation 5 points located at a noninteger position somewhere within. Add random numbers uniformly distributed between 0 and 20. Write down the exact location of the pulse, seal the information in an envelope and give the envelope to a New York accounting firm for safekeeping (or lock it in your desk). Exchange the locations of noisy pulses with another student who has done the same. Develop a program for one-dimensional matched filter design. Use the program to locate the exact position of the pulse obtained from your fellow student. Strive to locate the pulse more accurately than he or she can locate yours. Finally, open the envelopes and determine who has most closely located his or her pulse. Honor the victor with a suitable ritual, consistent with local custom.
3. Develop a program for two-dimensional Wiener filter design. Use the program to reduce the noise in a grainy photograph. Assume that the noise is white, and estimate its amplitude using a gray-level histogram computed in a flat area of the image.
4. Develop a program for two-dimensional matched filter design. Digitize an image of an assortment of pills, tablets, and capsules of different sizes and shapes on a contrasting background. Position the objects randomly, but not touching, and all aligned the same way. Use your program to pick out all the medications of one type.
5. Develop a program for two-dimensional Wiener deconvolution. Use the program to restore an image that has been blurred by a three-by-three box filter and has had random noise added.
6. Develop a program for two-dimensional Wiener deconvolution. Use the program to restore a digitized image that has been blurred by camera motion and has visible film grain noise. Estimate the blurring function from the profile of a sharp edge in the image, and estimate the amplitude of the noise from a gray-level histogram computed in a flat area of the image.
7. Use the convolution capability of an image-processing program as a matched detector to count the number of times the letter "A" (or your favorite letter) occurs on a page of text. Use a screen capture or an image from a paint program as a noise-free digitized page of text. Pick out one occurrence of the letter, and make a convolution kernel out of it. After the convolution, threshold the image and count the dots. If the threshold is set too low, which other letters start being counted? Why?
8. Do Project 7, but digitize an actual page of printed or typed text with a pixel spacing that makes the letters about 8 to 10 pixels high. Scale the image for good contrast of the print. Comment upon the performance of the technique.
9. Do Project 8 with a larger pixel spacing, one that makes the letters only about five pixels high. Comment upon the resulting performance of the technique.

REFERENCES

For additional references on filtering, see Appendix 2.

1. N. Wiener, *Extrapolation, Interpolation, and Smoothing of Stationary Time Series*, John Wiley & Sons, New York, 1949.

2. W. B. Davenport and W. L. Root, *An Introduction to the Theory of Random Signals and Noise,* McGraw-Hill, New York, 1958.
3. Y. W. Lee, *Statistical Theory of Communication,* John Wiley & Sons, New York, 1960.
4. L. A. Wainstein and V. D. Zubakov, *Extraction of Signals from Noise,* Prentice-Hall, Englewood Cliffs, NJ, 1962.
5. G. L. Turin, "An Introduction to Matched Filters," *IRE Transactions on Information Theory,* June 1960.
6. D. Middleton, "On New Classes of Matched Filters and Generalizations of the Matched Filter Concept," *IRE Transactions on Information Theory,* 349–360, June 1960.
7. E. S. Beckenbach, R. H. Selzer, D. W. Crawford, S. H. Brooks, and D. H. Blankenhorn, "Computer Tracking and Measurement of Blood Vessel Shadows from Arteriograms," *Medical Instrumentation,* **8,** No. 5, September–October, 1974.
8. K. R. Castleman, R. H. Selzer, and D. H. Blankenhorn, "Vessel Edge Detection in Angiograms: An Application of the Wiener Filter," in J. K. Aggarwal, ed., *Digital Signal Processing,* Point Lobos Press, No. Hollywood, CA, 1979.
9. T. S. Huang, G. T. Yang, and G. Y. Tang, "A Fast Two-Dimensional Median Filtering Algorithm," *IEEE Trans. Acoustics, Speech, and Signal Processing,* ASSP-27(1):13–18, 1979.
10. J. T. Astola and T. G. Campbell, "On Computation of the Running Median," *IEEE Trans. Acoustics, Speech, and Signal Processing,* ASSP-37(4):572–574, 1989.

CHAPTER 12

Processing Sampled Data

12.1 INTRODUCTION

In previous chapters, we have discussed digital image processing without particular attention to the effects of sampling. We have assumed that, done properly, sampling will not invalidate the results obtained from the analysis of continuous functions. But sampling is inherent in digital processing. Therefore, we shall use the tools we have developed in preceding chapters to approach sampling in a concise and effective manner in this chapter.

Chiefly, we investigate the ramifications of sampling continuous images and of processing sampled data. In particular, we address the following questions: (1) To what extent does sampling cause loss of information, and what is the nature of that loss? (2) Once a continuous function has been sampled, can it be recovered completely, and, if so, how? (3) How finely must we sample a function in order to preserve it? (4) What effect does sampling have upon the spectrum of a function? (5) If we treat a sampled function as if it were continuous, what assumptions, approximations, and errors are involved?

12.2 SAMPLING AND INTERPOLATION

Before we can describe quantitatively the effects of sampling, we must establish a mathematical procedure for modeling the process. To do this, we use a special function called the *Shah function.*

12.2.1 The Shah Function

A valuable tool for modeling the sampling process is the infinite impulse train, III (x), pronounced "Shah of x" and defined by

$$\mathrm{III}(x) = \sum_{n=-\infty}^{\infty} \delta(x-n) \tag{1}$$

III (x) is a series of unit-amplitude impulses that occur at unit spacing along the x-axis. Much to our good fortune, the Shah function is its own Fourier transform [1,2]; that is,

$$\mathfrak{F}\{\mathrm{III}(x)\} = \mathrm{III}(s) \tag{2}$$

We shall use this function to model the process of sampling a continuous signal.

12.2.1.1 Similarity

If we substitute the similarity theorem,

$$\mathfrak{F}\{f(ax)\} = \frac{1}{|a|}F\left(\frac{s}{a}\right) \tag{3}$$

into Eq. (2), we obtain

$$\mathfrak{F}\left\{\mathrm{III}\left(\frac{x}{\tau}\right)\right\} = \tau\mathrm{III}(\tau s) \tag{4}$$

where the spectrum is a train of impulses spaced every $1/\tau$ along the s-axis (Figure 12–1).

Recall that under similarity, the impulse has the curious property that

$$\delta(ax) = \frac{1}{|a|}\delta(x) \tag{5}$$

Since III (x) is an infinite train of equally spaced impulses [Eq. (1)], it also exhibits this behavior under stretching and compression. In particular,

$$\mathrm{III}(ax) = \sum_{n=-\infty}^{\infty} \delta(ax-n) = \sum_{n=-\infty}^{\infty} \delta\left[a\left(x-\frac{n}{a}\right)\right] \tag{6}$$

which means that

$$\mathrm{III}(ax) = \frac{1}{|a|}\sum_{n=-\infty}^{\infty} \delta\left(x-\frac{n}{a}\right) \tag{7}$$

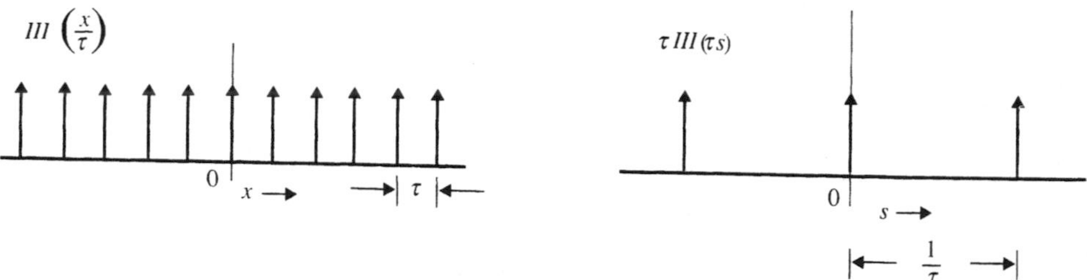

Figure 12–1 The Shah function and its spectrum

If we let $a = 1/\tau$, we have

$$\text{III}\left(\frac{x}{\tau}\right) = \tau \sum_{n=-\infty}^{\infty} \delta(x - n\tau) \tag{8}$$

or impulses spaced every τ. Notice that spacing the impulses every τ rather than at unit intervals multiplies the strength of the impulses by the factor τ. Transforming Eq. (8) yields

$$\mathfrak{F}\left\{\text{III}\left(\frac{x}{\tau}\right)\right\} = \tau\text{III}(\tau s) = \sum_{n=-\infty}^{\infty} \delta\left(s - \frac{n}{\tau}\right) \tag{9}$$

The last two equations indicate that a train of impulses of strength τ spaced every τ in the time domain produces a train of unit impulses spaced every $1/\tau$ in the frequency domain. We could, of course, divide Eq. (8) by τ to have impulses of unit strength in the time domain and, correspondingly, impulses of strength $1/\tau$ in the frequency domain.

12.2.2 Sampling with the Shah Function

Suppose a function $f(x)$ is bandlimited at a frequency s_0; that is,

$$F(s) = 0 \qquad |s| \geq s_0 \tag{10}$$

This is shown in Figure 12–2. If we sample $f(x)$ at equal intervals τ, we destroy $f(x)$ everywhere except at $x = n\tau$. We can model the sampling process as simply multiplying the function $f(x)$ by $\text{III}(x/\tau)$ to form $g(x)$, the sampled function. The process destroys the function between sample points by driving it to zero and yet preserves the value of the function at the sample points in the strength of the resulting impulses. The sampled function is illustrated in Figure 12–3. Mathematical convenience makes this model for sampling the method of choice.

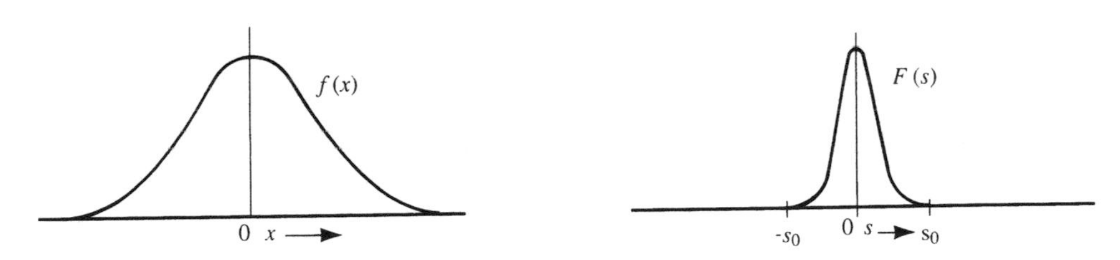

Figure 12–2 A bandlimited function

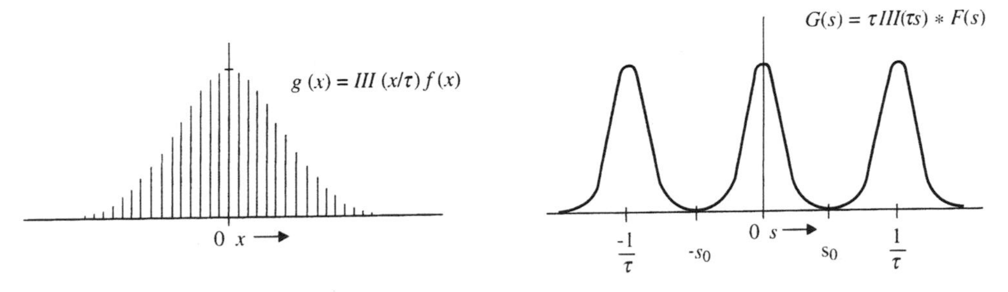

Figure 12–3 A sampled function

12.2.3 Sampling and the Spectrum

We now examine what sampling does to the spectrum of $f(x)$. The convolution theorem dictates that when we multiply $f(x)$ by $\mathrm{III}(x/\tau)$, we convolve $F(s)$ with $\tau\mathrm{III}(\tau s)$. Recall that $\tau\mathrm{III}(\tau s)$ is a series of unit-strength impulses spaced every $1/\tau$ along the s-axis. Recall also that convolution of a function with an impulse produces merely a copy of that function. Thus, the convolution in the frequency domain replicates $F(s)$ every $1/\tau$ along the s-axis.

As indicated in Figure 12–3, $G(s)$ consists of infinitely many copies of the spectrum $F(s)$ equally spaced along the s-axis from minus infinity to infinity. Notice that the spectrum $G(s)$ of the sampled function is periodic with frequency τ. Thus, any function sampled at equal intervals τ has a spectrum that is periodic with frequency τ.

12.2.4 The Sampling Theorem

Now that the function $f(x)$ has been sampled, the information between sample points has been lost. But can we recover the original function intact from the sample points? Clearly, we can reclaim $f(x)$ from $g(x)$ if we can reclaim $F(s)$ from $G(s)$. We can do the latter by merely eliminating all the replicas of $F(s)$, except the one that is centered upon the origin. One way to do this is to multiply $G(s)$ by $\Pi(s/2s_1)$, where

$$s_0 \le s_1 \le \frac{1}{\tau} - s_0 \tag{11}$$

Then

$$G(s)\Pi\left(\frac{s}{2s_1}\right) = F(s) \tag{12}$$

and we have recovered the spectrum of $f(x)$ from the spectrum of the sampled signal $g(x)$. The original function is given by

$$f(x) = \mathfrak{F}^{-1}\{F(s)\} = \mathfrak{F}^{-1}\left\{G(s)\Pi\left(\frac{s}{2s_1}\right)\right\} \tag{13}$$

Applying the convolution theorem to the right-hand side of Eq. (13) yields

$$f(x) = g(x) * 2s_1\frac{\sin(2\pi s_1 x)}{2\pi s_1 x} \tag{14}$$

which tells us how to reconstruct $f(x)$ from $g(x)$: We merely convolve the sampled function with an interpolating function of the form $\mathrm{sinc}(x) = \sin(x)/x$.

Eq. (14) shows us that we can indeed recover $f(x)$ from $g(x)$, and it tells us how to do it. This development, however, is subject to two restrictions. First, $f(x)$ must be bandlimited at s_0 [recall Eq. (10)], and second, the relationship between the sampling interval τ and the band limit s_0 must satisfy Eq. (11). What we have done is prove the well-known *sampling theorem* [3-7], which states that a function sampled at uniform spacing τ can be completely recovered from the sample values, provided that

$$\tau \le \frac{1}{2s_0} \tag{15}$$

where the function is bandlimited at s_0.

12.2.5 Interpolation

Convolving $g(x)$ with the interpolating function suggested in Eq. (14) in effect replicates a narrow $\sin(x)/x$ function at each sample point, as shown in Figure 12–4. Equation (14) guarantees that the summation of the overlapping $\sin(x)/x$ functions will add up to reproduce the original function exactly.

Figure 12–4 illustrates the case where $s_1 = 1/2\tau$, but Eq. (11) allows considerable arbitrariness in the frequency of the $\sin(x)/x$ function if the reciprocal of the sampling interval is considerably larger than the band limit, s_0. That equation allows us to place s_1 anywhere between s_0 and $1/\tau - s_0$. For convenience, we may place s_1 at the midway point:

$$s_1 = \frac{1}{2\tau} \tag{16}$$

Then the interpolating function becomes

$$\frac{1}{\tau}\frac{\sin\left(\pi\frac{x}{\tau}\right)}{\pi\frac{x}{\tau}} \tag{17}$$

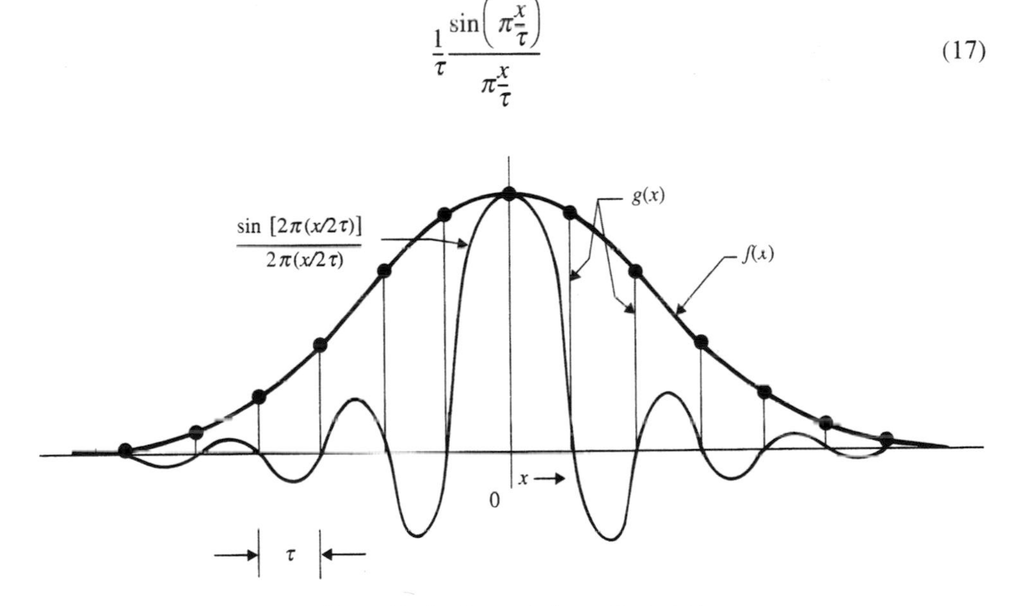

Figure 12–4 Interpolation with sin $(x)/x$

12.2.6 Undersampling and Aliasing

Equation (15) specifies how finely one must sample a function if it is to be totally recoverable from its sample values. We now examine what happens if that condition is not satisfied.

Suppose $\tau > 1/2s_0$. Then when $F(s)$ is replicated to form $G(s)$, the individual replicas will overlap and sum together (Figure 12–5). If we then interpolate, using the function in Eq. (17), we will not recover $f(s)$ exactly, because

$$G(s)\Pi\left(\frac{s}{2s_1}\right) \neq F(s) \tag{18}$$

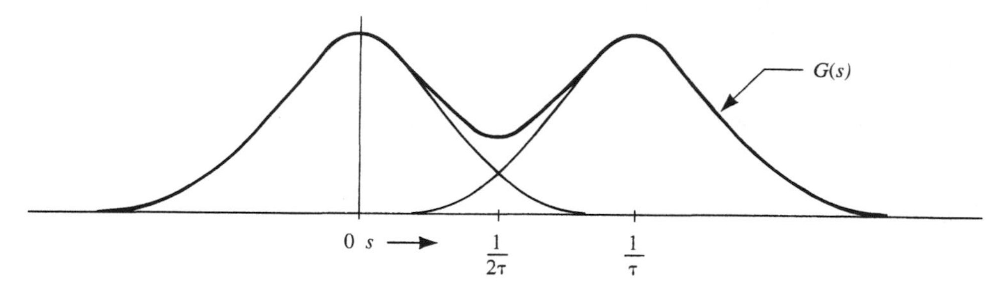

Figure 12–5 Overlap of replicated spectra

The effect of overlap of the spectral replicas can be viewed as follows. Energy above the frequency s_1 is folded back below s_1 and added to the spectrum. This folding back of energy is called *aliasing*, and the difference between $f(x)$ and the interpolated function is due to *aliasing error*.

As a general rule, the more energy that falls above s_1, the more energy will be folded down into the spectrum, and the worse will be the aliasing error. Notice that if $f(x)$ is even, then $F(s)$ is also even, and the aliasing effectively increases the energy in the spectrum. If $f(x)$ is odd, the opposite occurs, and the energy in the spectrum decreases. If $f(x)$ is neither even nor odd, then aliasing increases the even part and decreases the odd part, making the function and its spectrum more even than they were before.

12.2.7 Examples of Sampling

The following examples illustrate aliasing in the frequency domain and its effect in the time domain. Suppose that we have the function

$$f(t) = 2\cos(2\pi f_0 t) \tag{19}$$

which has the spectrum

$$F(s) = \delta(s + f_0) + \delta(s - f_0) \tag{20}$$

as shown in Figure 12–6. Suppose also that we sample $f(t)$ at equal intervals Δt. The period of $f(t)$ is $1/f_0$.

Oversampling. For case 1, suppose that

$$\Delta t = \frac{1}{4}\left(\frac{1}{f_0}\right) \tag{21}$$

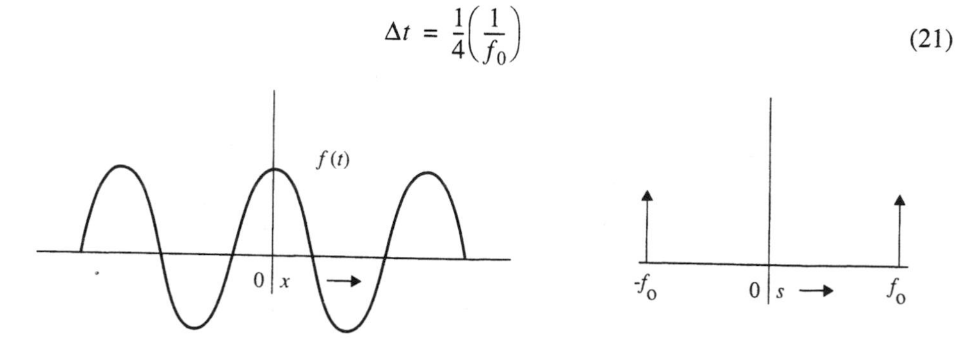

Figure 12–6 The cosine and its spectrum

which means that the folding frequency is

$$f_N = \frac{1}{2\Delta t} = 2f_0 \tag{22}$$

and we are taking four sample points per cycle of $f(t)$.

Figure 12–7 shows the sampled function and its spectrum. It also shows the interpolating function and its spectrum. Since $F(s)$ contains no energy above f_N, $f(t)$ can be completely recovered from its sample points.

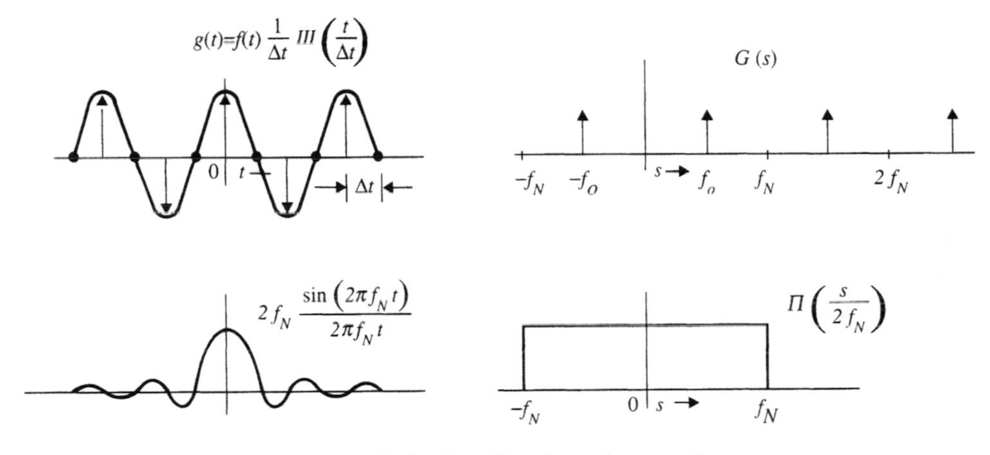

Figure 12–7 Sampling the cosine, case 1

Critical Sampling. In case 2, assume that

$$\Delta t = \frac{1}{2}\left(\frac{1}{f_0}\right) \tag{23}$$

which means that

$$f_N = f_0 \tag{24}$$

and we have two sample points per cycle. This case is illustrated in Figure 12–8. Here, we are sampling the cosine at its positive and negative peaks, and the function still can be completely recovered by interpolation, as in case 1. In the frequency domain, the impulses from adjacent replicas combine at $s = f_0$, but the spectrum of the interpolating function takes on the value 1/2 at that point, so the function is recovered intact.

Undersampling. For case 3, we let

$$\Delta t = \frac{2}{3}\left(\frac{1}{f_0}\right) \tag{25}$$

which means that

$$f_n = \frac{3}{4}f_0 \tag{26}$$

This case is illustrated in Figure 12–9. Here, the left-hand impulse from the spectral replicate centered upon $s = 2f_N$ falls between zero and f_N at the point $s = f_0/2$. Upon

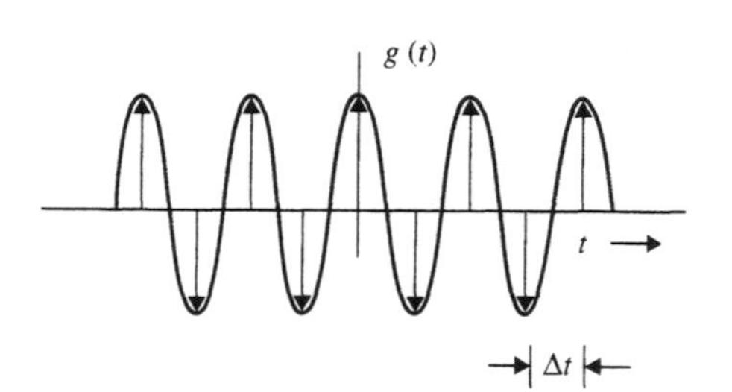

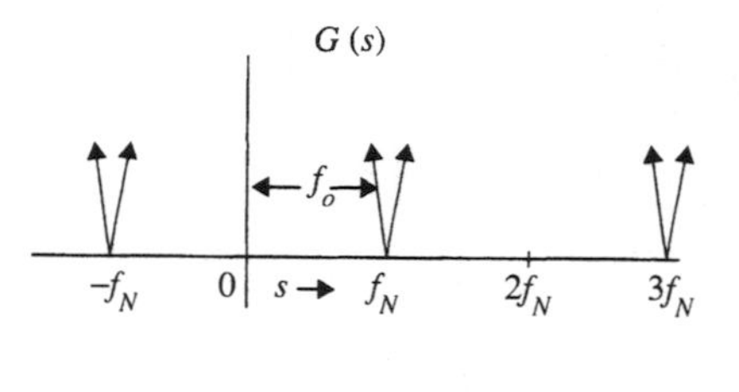

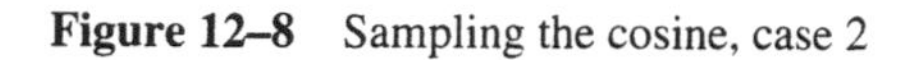

Figure 12–8 Sampling the cosine, case 2

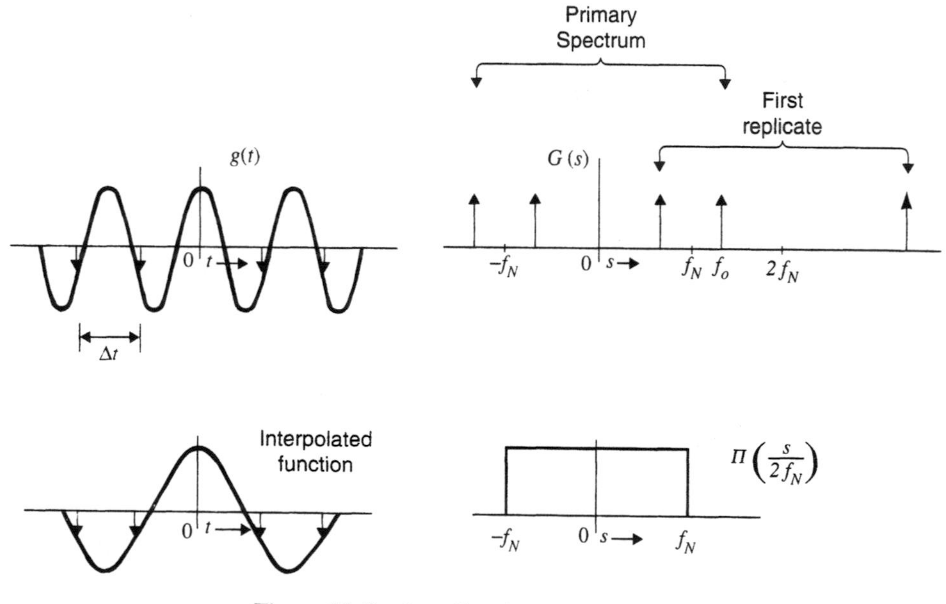

Figure 12–9 Sampling the cosine, case 3

interpolation, the energy at $s = f_0$ is aliased down to the frequency $f_0/2$. Figure 12–9 illustrates how interpolation fits a cosine of frequency $f_0/2$ through the sample points. This shows graphically how high-frequency information is aliased to appear as low-frequency information.

Severe Undersampling. In case 4, we let

$$\Delta t = \left(\frac{1}{f_0}\right) \tag{27}$$

so that

$$f_N = \frac{1}{2}f_0 \tag{28}$$

This case is illustrated in Figure 12–10. The energy at f_0 is aliased all the way down to zero

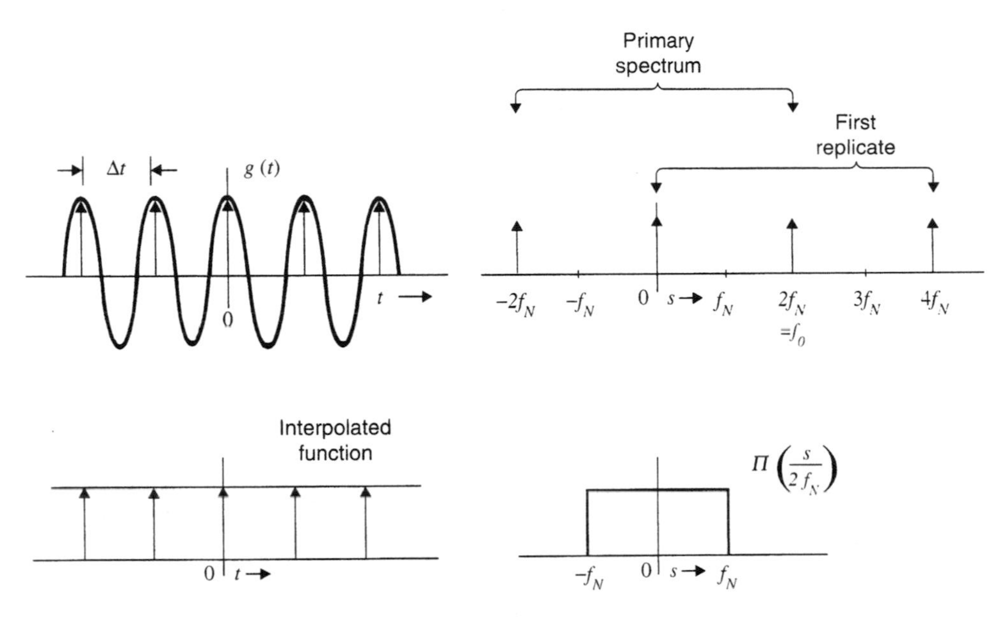

Figure 12–10 Sampling the cosine, case 4

frequency. The cosine is sampled only at its positive peaks, and when these sample points are interpolated, the resulting function is constant with unit amplitude.

Case 5 is the same as case 2, except that the function is

$$f(t) = 2 \sin(2\pi f_0 t) \tag{29}$$

as shown in Figure 12–11. Here, the odd impulse pairs from adjacent spectral replicas overlap at $s = f_N$, where they cancel. The figure illustrates why the interpolated function is zero. This case corresponds to sampling the sine at its zero crossings.

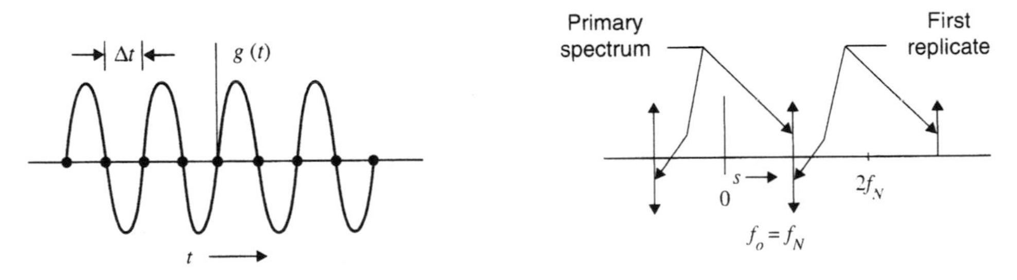

Figure 12–11 Sampling the sine, case 5

12.2.7.1 Aliasing in Image Digitization

Figure 12–12 shows an example of visible aliasing in a digitized image. This image is from a CCD camera with pixel width considerably smaller than pixel spacing. The shirt has a fine weave pattern that, in (a), is aliased down to lower frequencies, creating the Moiré effect. In (b), the camera was defocused very slightly to blur out the weave pattern, thereby removing the energy that is subject to aliasing.

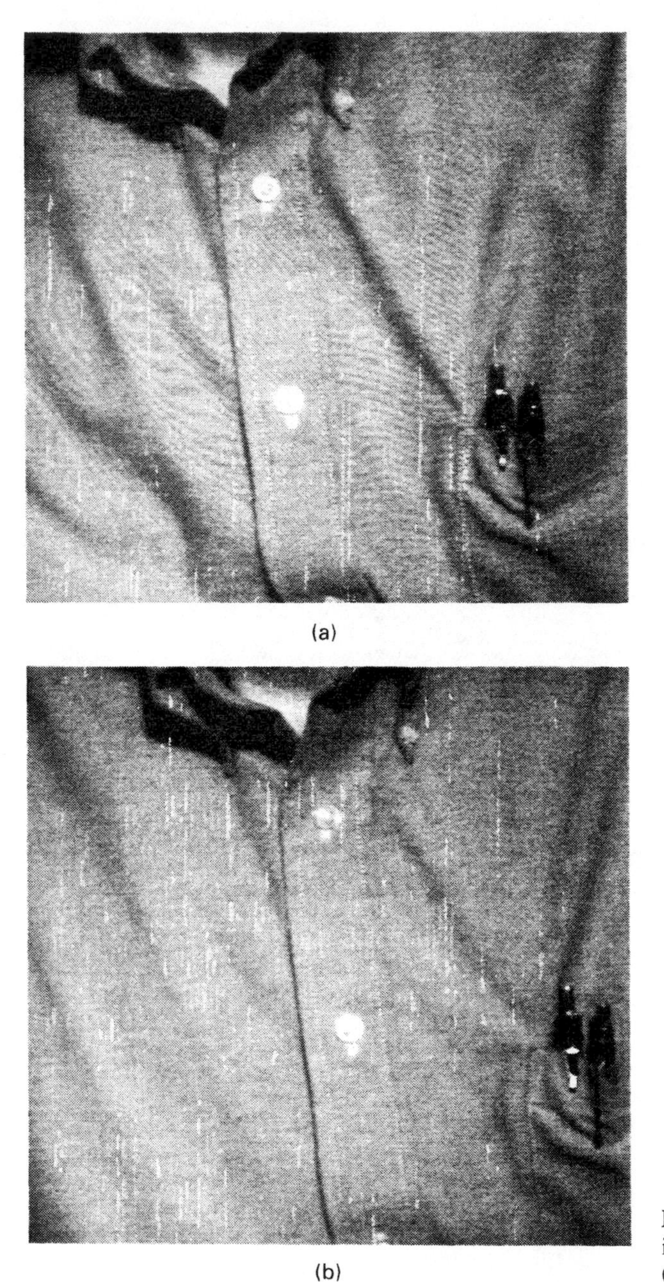

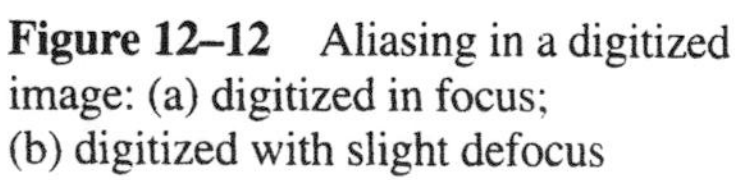

Figure 12–12 Aliasing in a digitized image: (a) digitized in focus; (b) digitized with slight defocus

12.3 COMPUTING SPECTRA

One important application of digital processing is merely to compute the spectrum of a signal or an image. In this section, we describe how to compute the spectrum of a signal and how the computed spectrum compares with the actual spectrum of the signal.

12.3.1 Truncation in the Time Domain

Suppose a signal $f(t)$ is represented by N sample points separated by constant spacing Δt, as shown in Figure 12–13. The total interval over which the signal is sampled is

$$T = N\Delta t \tag{30}$$

where T is the width of the *truncation window*. Since a signal can be sampled with only a finite number of points, the sampling process truncates the signal by ignoring it outside the truncation window. This amounts to setting the signal to zero outside the window.

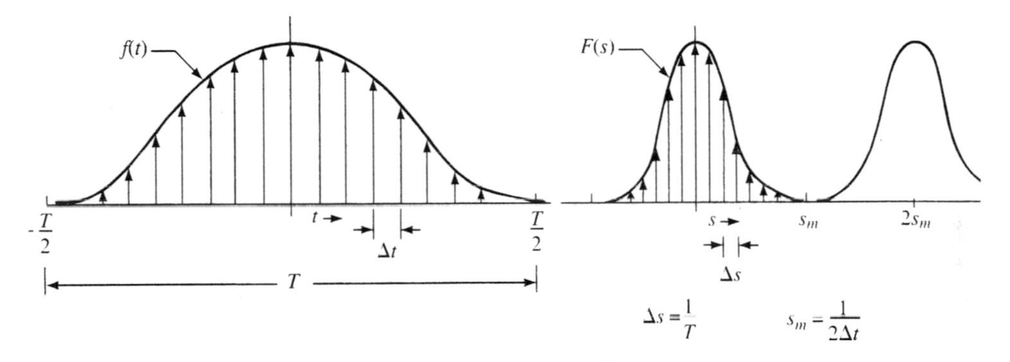

Figure 12–13 Computing spectra

We want to use the sample values of $f(t)$ to compute points on its spectrum $F(s)$. We may do this by programming the Fourier transform as a numerical integration. First, however, we must decide the number of points we shall compute on the spectrum, the spacing between those sample points, and the frequency range over which we shall compute the spectrum.

Since the sampled signal consists of N independent measurements, it is reasonable to compute a total of N points on the spectrum. Computing more points would introduce redundancy, while computing fewer points would not take advantage of all the information we have about $f(t)$. Thus, a general-purpose computer program for calculating the Fourier transform should take N (complex) sample points into N (complex) points on the spectrum. For convenience, the computed points are usually spaced equally along the s-axis.

12.3.2 Truncation in the Frequency Domain

Since $f(t)$ is a sampled function with sample spacing Δt, its spectrum $F(s)$ is periodic with period $1/\Delta t$. Clearly, we should confine our computation to cover only one cycle of $F(s)$. It is common practice to spread the N sample points evenly across that cycle of $F(s)$ which is centered upon the origin. This means that we compute points on $F(s)$ only over the range

$$-\frac{1}{2\Delta t} \leq s \leq \frac{1}{2\Delta t} \tag{31}$$

If we spread N equally spaced sample points over one cycle of $F(s)$, then

$$N\Delta s = \frac{1}{\Delta t} \tag{32}$$

where

$$\Delta s = \frac{1}{N\Delta t} = \frac{1}{T} \tag{33}$$

is the sample spacing in the frequency domain. Thus, for our purposes, the best choice for computing the spectrum of $f(t)$ is to compute points with equal spacing, given by Eq. (33), over a frequency range from $-s_m$ to s_m, where

$$s_m = \frac{1}{2\Delta t} \tag{34}$$

Notice that the maximum frequency we can compute is inversely related to the time domain sample spacing [Eq. (34)]. The frequency domain sample spacing, which determines how finely we can compute the spectrum, is inversely related to the width of the time domain truncation window [Eq. (33)].

12.3.3 Computing the Spectrum

In brief, the sample spacing in one domain dictates (or is dictated by) the truncation width in the other domain. If we desire to compute high-frequency components of the spectrum, then we must sample finely in the time domain. Furthermore, if we insist upon high resolution in the spectrum (small Δs), we must use a large truncation window in the time domain, even if the function is narrow. The relationships between the time and frequency domain sampling and truncation parameters are summarized in Table 12–1.

If $f(t)$ is complex and we compute its spectrum, the N real and N imaginary values are transformed to produce N real and N imaginary values of the spectrum. If $f(t)$ is real, then N real values and N zeros (the imaginary part) give rise to $N/2$ real and $N/2$ imaginary values in the right-hand half of the spectrum. Since $F(s)$ is Hermite, the left half of the spectrum is a mirror image of the right. Thus, the $N/2$ real and the $N/2$ imaginary values in the left half of the spectrum are, from the point of view of information content, redundant. Notice that, in both cases, the number of unconstrained sample points in the two domains is the same.

TABLE 12–1 SUMMARY OF SAMPLING AND TRUNCATION PARAMETERS

Parameter	Domain	Relations
Number of sample points	Both	$N = \frac{T}{\Delta T} = \frac{2s_m}{\Delta s}$
Sample spacing	Time	$\Delta t = \frac{T}{N} = \frac{1}{2s_m}$
Sample spacing	Frequency	$\Delta s = \frac{2s_m}{N} = \frac{1}{T}$
Truncation window width	Time	$T = N\Delta t$
Maximum computed frequency (also Nyquist or folding frequency)	Frequency	$s_m = \frac{1}{2\Delta t} = \frac{1}{2}N\Delta s$

12.4 ALIASING

We now take a closer look at the phenomena associated with aliasing to determine to what extent its detrimental effects can be controlled and how to do so. (See also [8–9].)

12.4.1 The Unavoidability of Aliasing

The sampling theorem indicates that a judicious choice of sample spacing can completely avoid aliasing when one is sampling a bandlimited function. Thus, if wise selection or good fortune allows us to work with bandlimited functions, then aliasing can be avoided. On the other hand, if we are forced to work with inherently non-bandlimited functions, then we are condemned to work in the shadow of unavoidable aliasing. Reality, unfortunately, works to our disadvantage here: Our plans are foiled by the process of truncation.

To see how this is so, suppose a bandlimited function is truncated to a finite duration T. The process may be modeled as multiplying the function by a rectangular pulse of width T. Recall that this has the effect of convolving the spectrum with a $\sin(x)/x$ function that has infinite duration in the frequency domain.

Since the convolution of two functions can be no narrower than either, we conclude that the spectrum of the truncated function is of infinite extent in the frequency domain. Thus, truncation destroys bandlimitedness and condemns digital processing to producing aliasing in all cases. Fortunately, while aliasing cannot be avoided totally, the resulting error can be bounded and reduced to the point of an approximation acceptable for practical use.

12.4.2 Bounding Aliasing Error

The following example illustrates how one can place a bound on aliasing error and select digitizing parameters to produce a desired accuracy in spite of unavoidable aliasing.

Suppose we wish to identify the linear system shown in Figure 12–14 by computing the spectrum of its response to a rectangular pulse. If $f(t)$ is the input pulse and $g(t)$ is the system's output, then the transfer function is

$$H(s) = \frac{G(s)}{F(s)} \tag{35}$$

Assume, for this case, that we know that the system is a lowpass filter, and thus its output is a rectangular pulse with slightly rounded corners.

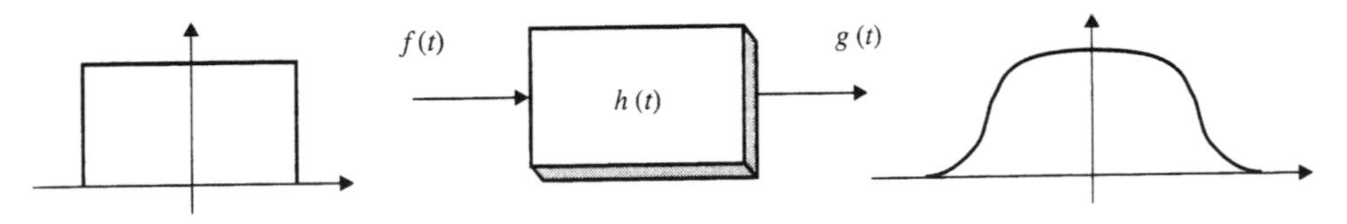

Figure 12–14 Linear system identification

If we are to evaluate Eq. (35) by digital computation, we must digitize $f(t)$ and $g(t)$ and compute their spectra. We must select the sample spacing Δt and the sampling period T so as to yield good spectral resolution with reasonably small aliasing error. To do this, we must define a measure of spectral resolution and a measure of aliasing error and relate the two quantities to the sampling parameters. Then we can make an intelligent choice of N, T, and Δt.

The input signal and its spectrum are shown in Figure 12–15. Since $F(s)$ extends from minus to plus infinity, no choice of Δt will completely avoid aliasing. $F(s)$ is enclosed in an

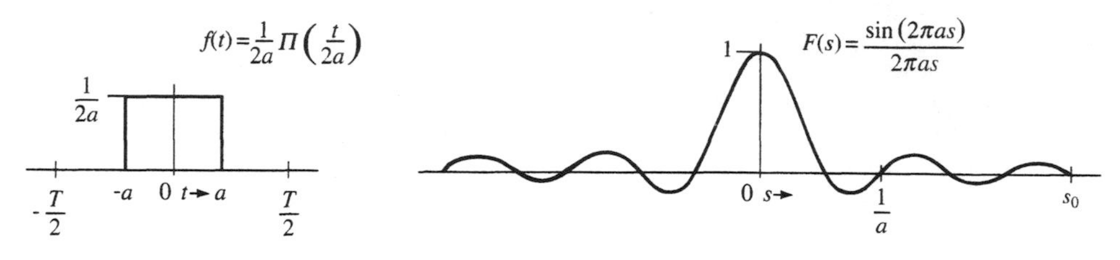

Figure 12–15 The input signal and its spectrum

envelope of the form $1/s$, however, and this assures that the peak amplitude of the function dies out with increasing frequency. If we ignore the sinusoidal variations and consider only the envelope, we note that the largest possible spectral amplitude to be aliased occurs at the frequency s_m. We can take this to be the worst case for aliasing and define, as a measure of aliasing error, the ratio of $F(s_m)$ to $F(0)$. Since $F(0)$ is unity and the envelope is $1/2\pi as$, we can write an upper bound on aliasing as

$$A \le \frac{1}{2\pi a s_0} = \frac{2\Delta t}{2\pi a} = \frac{\Delta t}{\pi a} \tag{36}$$

Notice that this bound on aliasing error, as we have defined it, is proportional to Δt, but independent of T. Thus, we can make the aliasing error as small as desired by making Δt small compared to the pulse width $2a$.

12.4.3 Spectral Resolution

$F(s)$ has sinusoidal variations of frequency a. Let us denote by M the number of sample points per cycle of $F(s)$ on the computed spectrum and use it as a measure of spectral resolution. The parameter M indicates how finely we are computing the sampled spectrum $F(s)$. The period of the sinusoidal variations of $F(s)$ is $1/a$, and

$$M\Delta S = \frac{1}{a} \tag{37}$$

or

$$M = \frac{1}{a\Delta s} = \frac{T}{a} \tag{38}$$

This means that we may have as many sample points per cycle of $F(s)$ as desired if we make the sampling period T large compared to the half-width of the pulse. Notice that if we insist upon both small aliasing error and high spectral resolution, then Δt is small, T is large, and the required number of sample points is very large. As it frequently happens, one must purchase accuracy with computer power.

12.5 TRUNCATION

Like sampling, truncation can cause a computed spectrum to differ from the actual spectrum of a function. Like the sample spacing, the truncation window must be selected wisely to produce suitably accurate results [10,11]. The next example illustrates the effect of truncation.

12.5.1 Computing the Spectrum of an Edge

Suppose we wish to calculate the spectrum of an edge (an approximate step function). This technique is often used to determine the transfer function of a filter that has already acted upon an image containing an edge. (See Sec. 16.6.) Since truncating an edge is quite a significant alteration, the following example illustrates the effect of truncation rather well.

In the example, we use the function sign(x) shown in Figure 12–16. In order to calculate the spectrum, we must first truncate $f(x)$ to a finite duration T. Since the sign(x) function goes to infinity with constant amplitude, we recognize that this example is sensitive to truncation.

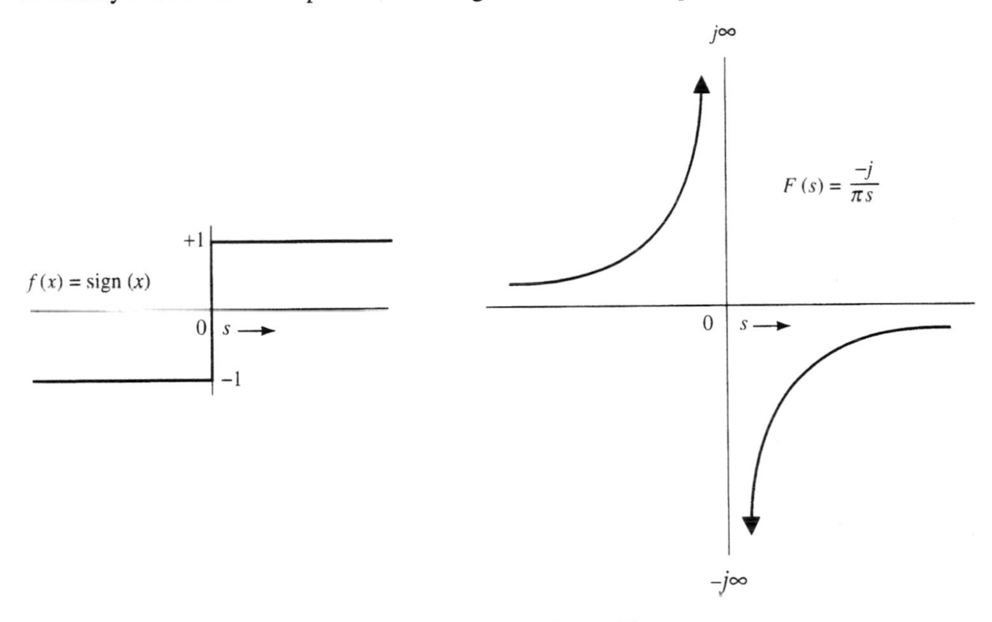

Figure 12–16 The step function and its spectrum

If we truncate the function with a truncation window of width T, the resulting function is given by

$$g(x) = f(x)\Pi\left(\frac{x}{T}\right) = \Pi\left(\frac{x}{T/2} - \frac{1}{2}\right) - \Pi\left(\frac{x}{T/2} + \frac{1}{2}\right) \tag{39}$$

as shown in Figure 12–17. Since the truncated function is an odd pair of rectangular pulses, it can be written as

$$g(x) = \Pi\left(\frac{x}{T/2}\right) * \left[\delta\left(x - \frac{T}{4}\right) - \delta\left(x + \frac{T}{4}\right)\right] \tag{40}$$

Transforming Eq. (40) produces the spectrum of the truncated edge function:

$$G(s) = -2j\sin\left(\pi s\frac{T}{2}\right)\frac{\sin(\pi sT/2)}{\pi s} \tag{41}$$

This may be rearranged to produce

$$G(s) = \frac{-2j}{\pi s}\sin^2\left(\frac{\pi sT}{2}\right) = 2F(s)\left[\frac{1}{2} - \frac{1}{2}\cos(\pi sT)\right] \tag{42}$$

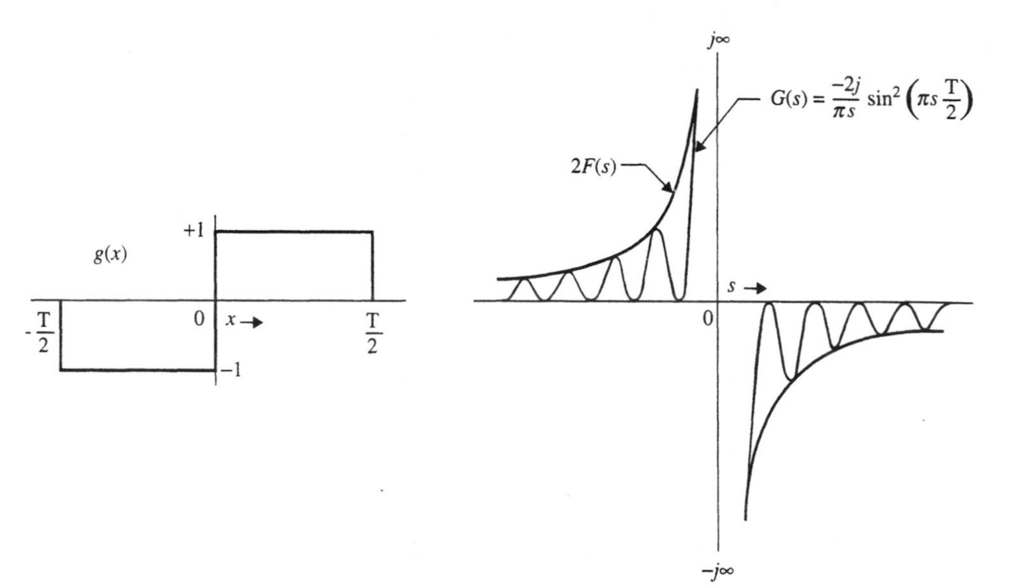

Figure 12–17 The truncated step function and its spectrum

a graph of which is shown in Figure 12–17. The spectrum of the truncated signal is a sinusoid enclosed under an envelope that is twice the desired spectrum $F(s)$. This considerable change in the nature of the spectrum is a result of truncation—in this case a relatively radical modification of the original function.

Since what we actually do is compute points on $G(s)$, we can ask where those points fall with respect to the sinusoidal variations in $G(s)$. The sample points on $G(s)$ will be computed at discrete frequencies

$$s_i = i\Delta s = \frac{i}{T} \qquad i = 0, 1, 2, \ldots, \frac{N}{2} \tag{43}$$

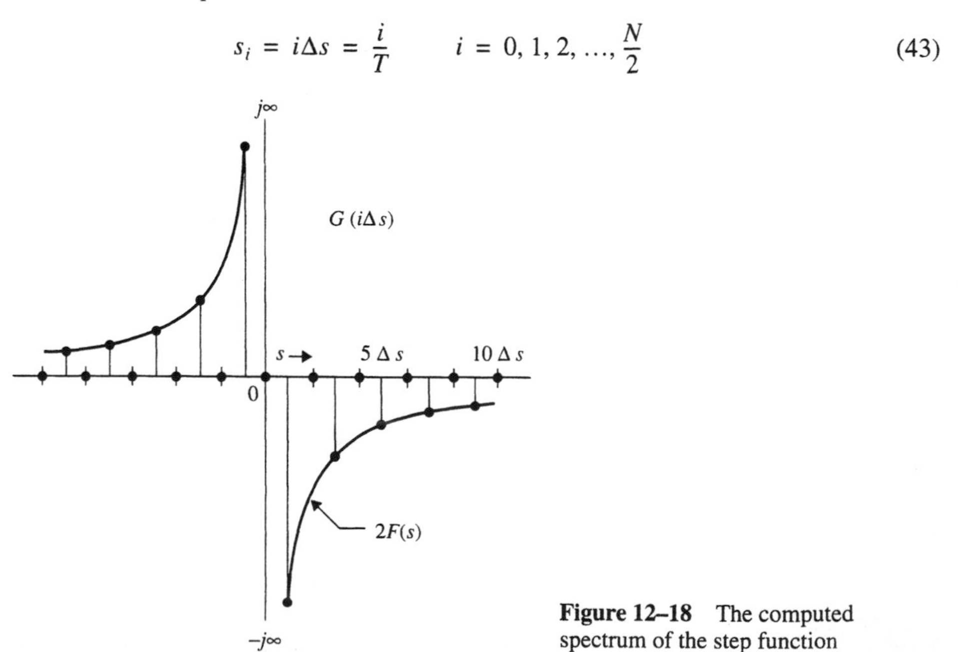

Figure 12–18 The computed spectrum of the step function

and the computed points will be

$$G(s_i) = 2F(s_i)\left[\frac{1}{2} - \frac{1}{2}\cos(i\pi)\right] \tag{44}$$

The cosine term takes on the value +1 for even i and −1 for odd i, so

$$G(s_i) = \begin{cases} 2F(s_i) & i \text{ odd} \\ 0 & i \text{ even} \end{cases} \tag{45}$$

This is shown in Figure 12–18.

12.5.2 Truncation Effects

Notice the curious effect of truncation in the preceding example: The odd-numbered points were correct, albeit twice normal size, while the even-numbered points were zero. It appears that truncation redistributed the energy among the odd and even points.

In this example, the edge was centered in the truncation window. The reader is invited to determine the effect upon the sample points of $G(s)$ if the edge is slightly off center in the truncation window.

One could obtain the expected result by convolving $G(i\Delta s)$ with a narrow, triangular local-averaging filter such as [1/4,1/2,1/4]. This would be equivalent to multiplying the truncated edge by a windowing function of the form $(\sin(x)/x)^2$. This, in turn, would avoid the discontinuities at $\pm T/2$ and prevent truncation error.

12.6 DIGITAL PROCESSING

We are now in a position to examine the overall, cumulative effects of digital processing upon a continuous signal or image. We consider the effects of sampling, truncation, interpolation, digitally implemented convolution, and Fourier transformation.

In this section, we desire only to digitize a function and then reconstruct it without processing. We begin with a continuous function $f(t)$, as shown in Figure 12–19. The function in this example has a triangular amplitude spectrum but random phase.

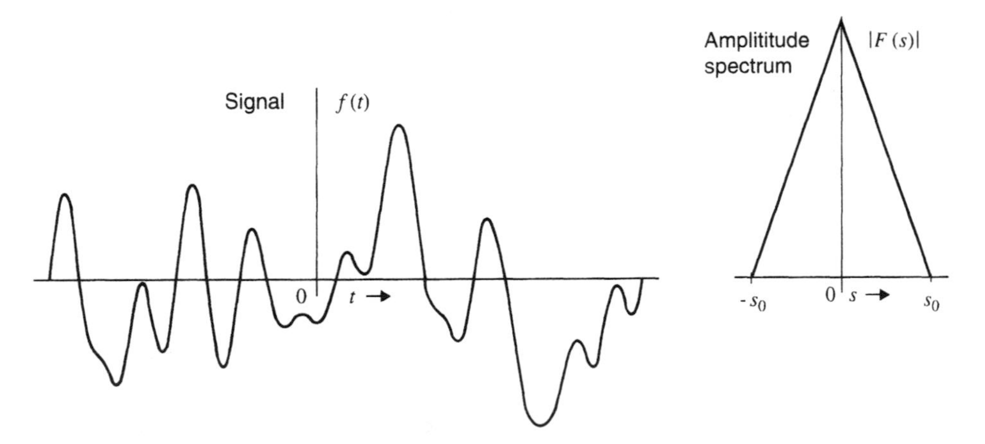

Figure 12–19 A signal and its spectrum

12.6.1 Truncation

When we digitize the signal, we must truncate it to a finite duration T. The truncation window $\Pi(t/T)$ and its spectrum are shown in Figure 12–20. Also shown are the truncated function and its spectrum. Truncating $f(t)$ convolves its spectrum with a narrow $\sin(x)/x$ function.

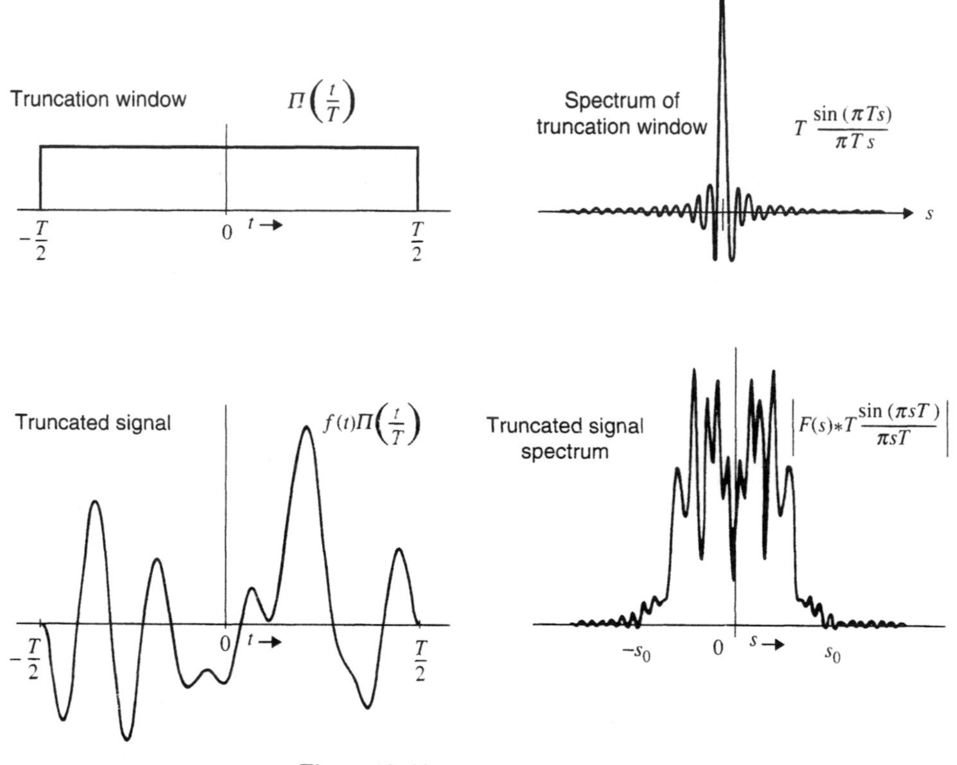

Figure 12–20 Truncating the signal

12.6.2 The Sampling Aperture

The digitizer will have a finite-width sampling aperture over which the signal is averaged at each sample point. As discussed in Chapter 9, this local averaging can be modeled by convolution with a suitable sampling aperture function. For an image digitizer, the sampling aperture function models the spatial sensitivity of the scanning spot. Electrical signals are usually sampled with a circuit that integrates over a fixed period.

In Figure 12–21, we model the sampling aperture with a small rectangular pulse of width τ. As shown in the figure, convolving the truncated signal with a sampling aperture function multiplies the spectrum by a broad $\sin(x)/x$ function.

If the sampling aperture were, for instance, a Gaussian, the spectrum of the truncated signal would be multiplied by a broad Gaussian. In either case, the effect of the sampling aperture is to reduce the high-frequency energy in the signal. Notice in Figure 12–21 that at frequencies beyond $s = 1/\tau$, the polarity of the energy will be reversed.

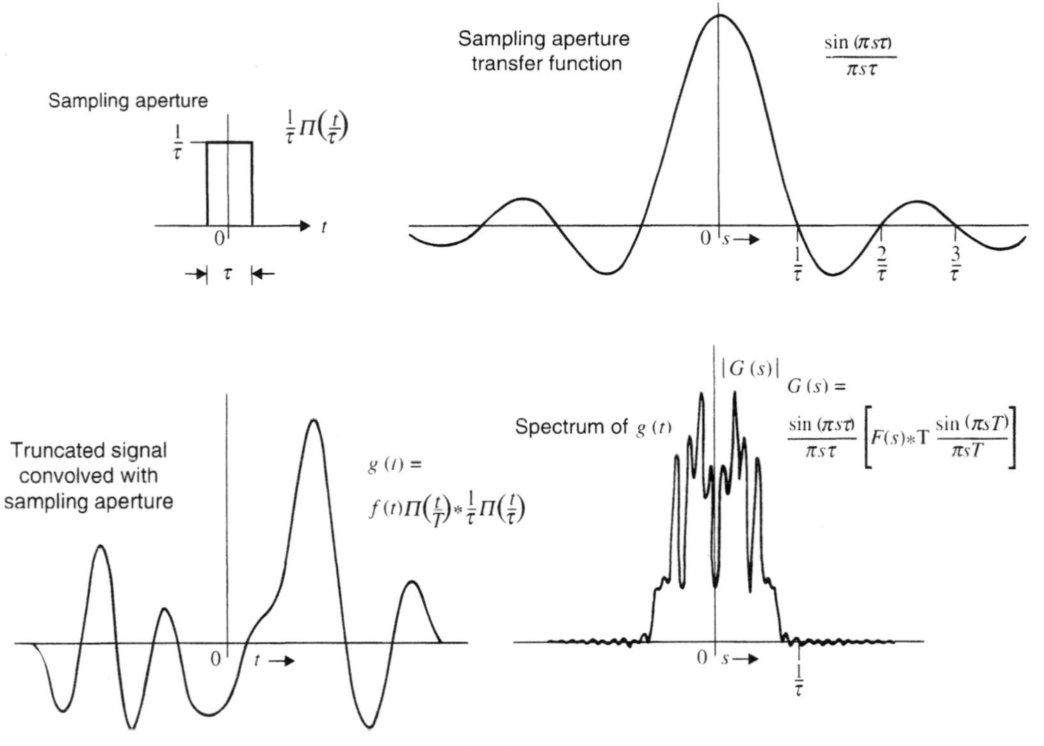

Figure 12–21 Convolving the sampling aperture

12.6.3 Sampling

The sampling process is illustrated in Figure 12–22. The truncated signal, smoothed by the sampling aperture, is multiplied by $\text{III}(t/\Delta t)$ to effect sampling. As illustrated, sampling the signal makes its spectrum periodic by replicating the original spectrum at intervals $1/\Delta t$.

12.6.4 Interpolation

Suppose we wish merely to interpolate the sampled function to regain $f(t)$ as well as possible. Figure 12–23 illustrates interpolation by convolution of the sampled function with a triangular pulse. In the figure, the width of the triangular pulse is $2t_0$.

Convolving the sampled function with the interpolating function multiplies its spectrum by a function of the form $\sin^2(x)/x^2$. Since this function generally decreases with increasing frequency, it tends to drive all replicas to zero, except for the primary replica located at $s = 0$.

Recall that the ideal interpolating function is $\sin(x)/x$, which multiplies the spectrum by a rectangular pulse centered on $s = 0$. However, the triangular pulse of Figure 12–23 produces approximately the same effect.

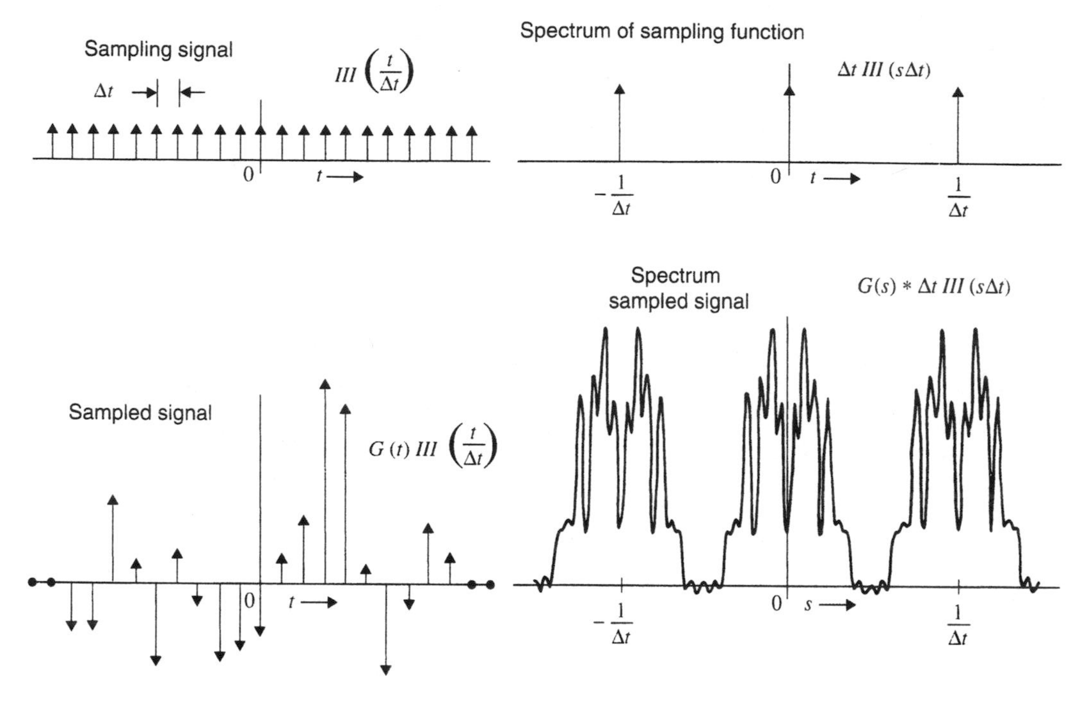

Figure 12–22 Sampling the signal

If we denote by $h(t)$ the function obtained by interpolating the truncated sampled function, then

$$h(t) = \left(\left\{\left[f(t)\Pi\frac{t}{T}\right] * \frac{1}{\tau}\Pi\left(\frac{t}{\tau}\right)\right\}\text{III}\left(\frac{t}{\Delta t}\right)\right) * \frac{1}{t_0}\Lambda\left(\frac{t}{t_0}\right) \tag{46}$$

and its spectrum is

$$H(s) = \left(\left\{\left[F(s) * T\frac{\sin(\pi sT)}{\pi sT}\right]\frac{\sin(\pi s\tau)}{\pi s\tau}\right\} * \Delta t\text{III}(s\Delta t)\right)\left[\frac{\sin(\pi st_0)}{\pi st_0}\right]^2 \tag{47}$$

12.6.5 The Effects of Digital Processing

Clearly, the question is not *whether* digital processing has an effect on the signal, but rather, *how much* effect it has.

In the foregoing example, the sampling aperture and interpolating function were chosen rather wide to demonstrate their effect. Specifically, $\tau = t_0 = 2\Delta t$. These parameters, while arbitrary, normally should be chosen in proper relationship to one another. For example, the sampling aperture should have width τ roughly equal to the sample spacing Δt. Also, for linear interpolation, $t_0 = \Delta t$.

Truncation convolves the spectrum with a narrow $\sin(x)/x$. If the truncation window is wide, its spectrum becomes narrow, approximating an impulse, and this reduces its effect. Also, if the function is already zero outside the window, truncation has no effect.

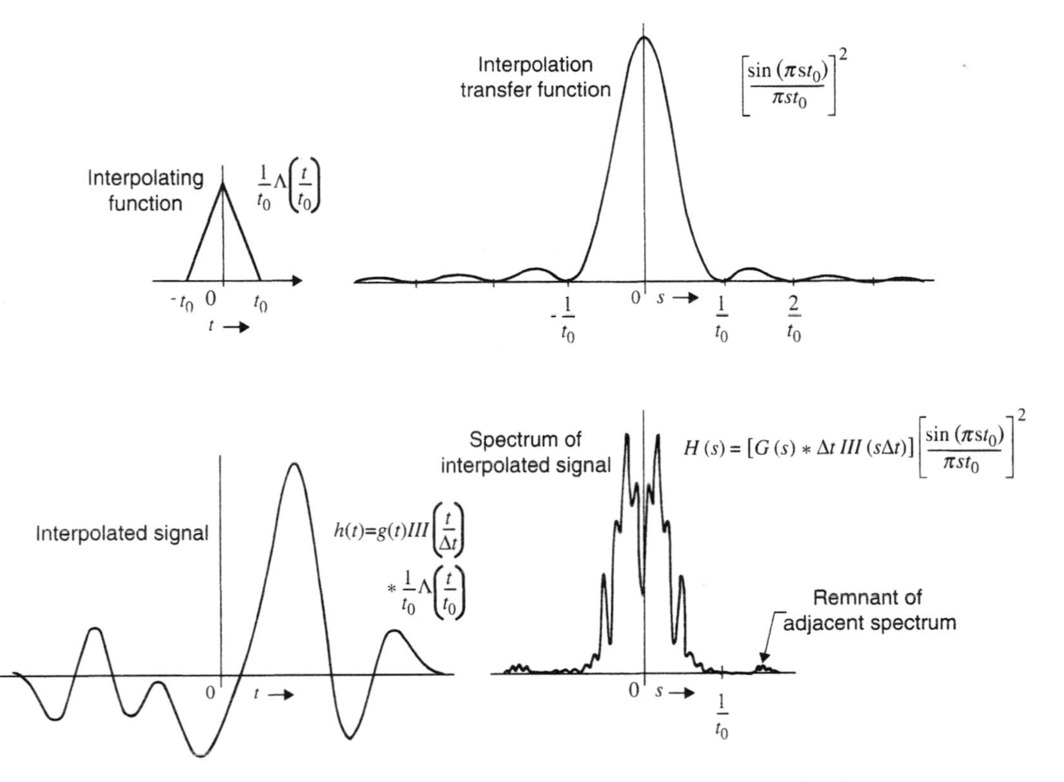

Figure 12–23 Interpolating the sampled signal

The sampling aperture, as illustrated in Figure 12–21, tends to reduce the high-frequency energy in the spectrum. In so doing, it can reduce subsequent aliasing. The sampling aperture can also reverse the polarity of the high-frequency energy if its transfer function goes negative.

Sampling, of course, makes the spectrum periodic. This produces aliasing of energy above the folding frequency, $1/2\Delta t$.

Interpolation restores the spectrum to a single replica centered upon the origin. This is done accurately, however, only if $\sin(x)/x$ is used as the interpolating function. Other interpolating functions remove spectral replicas incompletely, reduce the high-frequency energy content of the primary replica, or both.

The digitizing parameters usually result from the design of the digitizing equipment. The truncation window, for example, represents the maximum field of view of the image digitizer. The sampling aperture is merely the sensitivity function of the scanning spot. The sample spacing is often adjustable and should be set in relation to the spot diameter. For displaying an image, the interpolating function is the display spot itself.

12.7 CONTROLLING ALIASING ERROR

There are two parameters that we can use to prevent aliasing from corrupting the information that is of interest in the image: the sampling aperture and the sample spacing.

12.7.1 The Antialiasing Filter

Figure 12–24 illustrates how one can use a rectangular sampling aperture to reduce aliasing. The width of the aperture is twice the sample spacing. This places the first zero-crossing of its transfer function at $f_N = 1/2\Delta t$. Thus, energy at frequencies above f_N (which is subject to aliasing) will be attenuated severely.

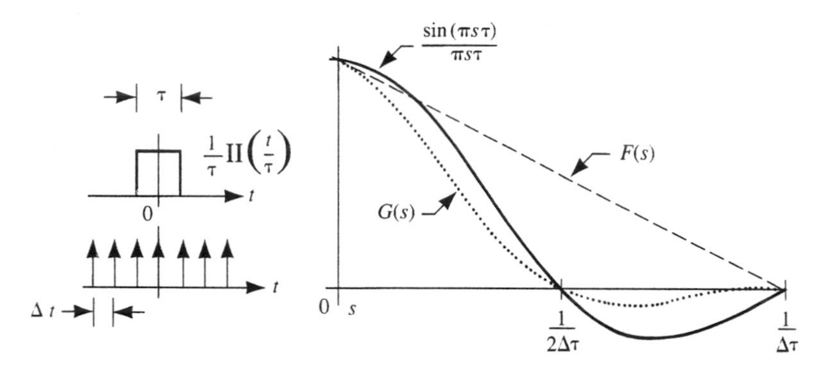

Figure 12–24 Reduction of aliasing with a rectangular aperture

The triangular sampling aperture used in Figure 12–25 is four sample points wide and also has its first zero-crossing at f_N. Since its spectrum dies out with frequency more rapidly than that of the rectangular pulse, it is more effective against aliasing. Like the rectangular pulse, however, it reduces the energy in $F(s)$ below f_N.

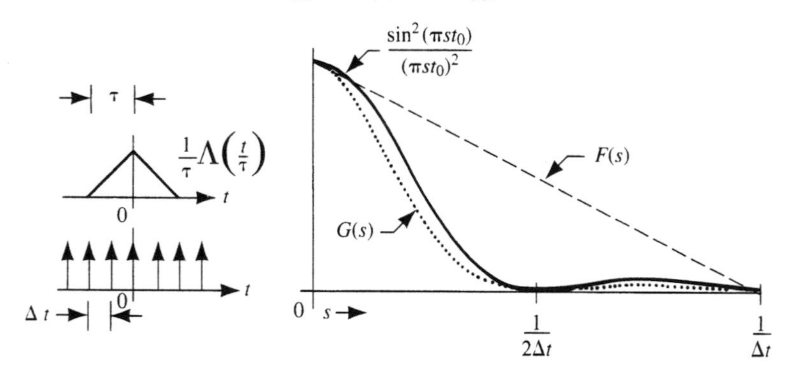

Figure 12–25 Reduction of aliasing with a triangular aperture

In Figure 12–12, aliasing occurred because the CCD camera had significant gaps between the pixels on its sensor chip. Thus, the sampling aperture (i.e., the sensor element) was too narrow to act as an antialiasing filter and remove the high-frequency information prior to sampling. In part (b), the camera was defocused slightly, and consequently the lens served as an antialiasing filter.

12.7.2 Oversampling

Eqs. (46) and (47) might appear to suggest that a continuous function cannot be processed digitally without severe distortion and that our previous development has been in vain. There is, however, a way out—by oversampling.

If we make the sample spacing small, we can place f_N far beyond the frequencies of interest in the spectrum. Then, when aliasing contaminates the upper part of the spectrum, it will have little or no effect upon the data of interest. As a rule of thumb, oversampling by a factor of two is adequate for most applications, although an analysis should be performed in each case.

Also, the truncation window should be large enough to produce minimum contamination of the signal's spectrum. By suitably oversampling, one can reduce aliasing and truncation effects to any desired order of magnitude. The piper, of course, must be paid—in this case with computer resources.

12.8 DIGITALLY IMPLEMENTED LINEAR FILTERING

Linear filtering can be implemented digitally in two different ways. First, the filtering operation implied in Figure 12–26 could be implemented by digital convolution of the sampled function $f(t)$ with $h(t)$ to produce $g(t)$.

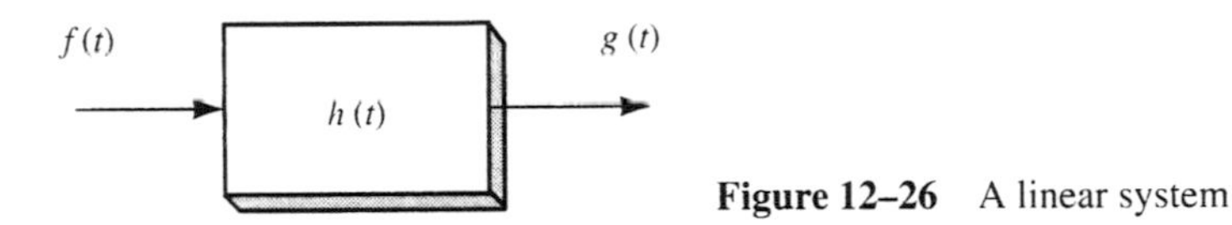

Figure 12–26 A linear system

Alternatively, one could transform $f(t)$ and $h(t)$ into the frequency domain with a Fourier transform algorithm implemented by numerical integration. Then the output spectrum $G(s)$ could be formed by multiplication and the output signal generated by an inverse transformation.

If one or both of the convolution input signals are of short duration, then the method of digital convolution is computationally simpler. Otherwise, efficient Fourier transform algorithms make the second method more practical. In this section, we compare the two approaches with respect to aliasing and truncation error.

12.8.1 Convolution Filtering

As noted before, sampling $f(t)$ and $h(t)$ makes their spectra periodic. If both signals are sampled at the same interval Δt, their spectra will be periodic with the same period, $1/\Delta t$. Convolution of the sampled signals multiplies the two spectra in the frequency domain to form $G(s)$, which is also periodic with frequency Δt. When $g(t)$ is interpolated, its spectrum is reduced to a single replica at the origin, as in the previous discussion.

If either $f(t)$ or h(t) is bandlimited below $s = 1/2\Delta t$, then $g(t)$ will be similarly bandlimited, and interpolation will reconstruct it exactly. Truncation, however, destroys bandlimitedness, and some aliasing is unavoidable. This aliasing will express itself in $g(t)$ in a straightforward manner. Thus, digital convolution introduces no new effects beyond those produced by sampling, truncation, and interpolation.

12.8.2 Frequency Domain Filtering

Figure 12–27 illustrates what happens when we compute a Fourier transform. The input signal $f(t)$ is sampled to form $x(t)$, which has a continuous, periodic spectrum. When we

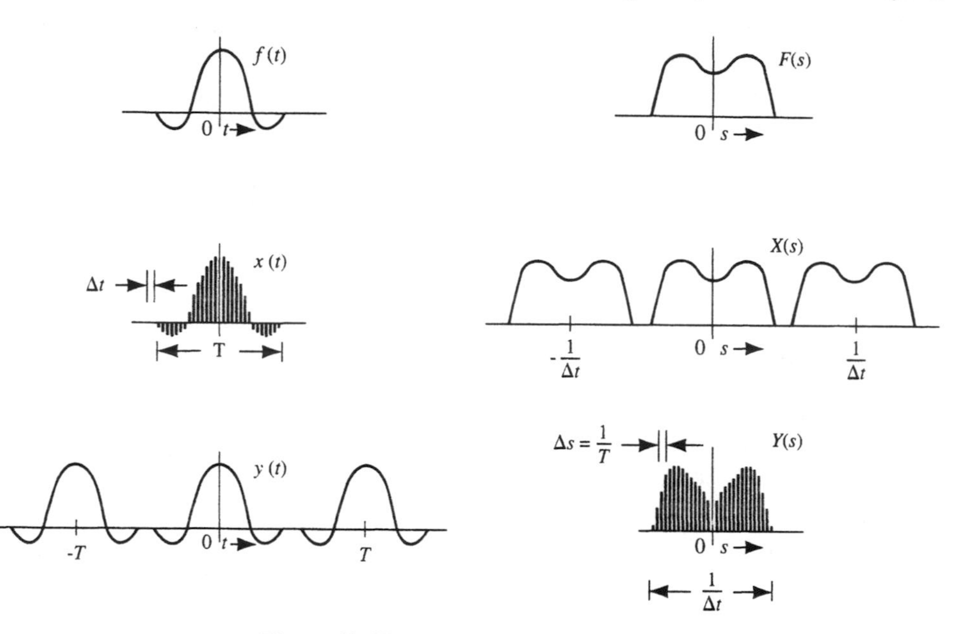

Figure 12–27 Frequency domain filtering

compute the Fourier transform of $x(t)$, we actually calculate equally spaced points on the primary cycle of its periodic spectrum, as illustrated in the figure.

We compute N points equally spaced every Δs over the frequency range from $-1/2\Delta t$ to $1/2\Delta t$. We denote the computed spectrum by $Y(s)$ because it is, in fact, not $X(s)$, the spectrum of $x(t)$.

Since $Y(s)$ is sampled, its inverse transform $y(t)$ is a continuous (unsampled) periodic function of infinite duration. Thus, the computed spectrum $Y(s)$ is not the spectrum of $x(t)$ or even that of $f(t)$, the underlying unsampled function. It is instead the spectrum of a continuous periodic function having period T. All the sample points of $x(t)$ fall exactly upon the primary cycle of $y(t)$, and barring aliasing, the primary cycle of $y(t)$ is exactly $f(t)$, the function that was sampled to form $x(t)$.

By computing the spectrum of $x(t)$ digitally, we have necessarily sampled that spectrum to produce $Y(s)$. This in turn is the spectrum of a continuous periodic function $y(t)$. We now have, in the frequency domain, the equivalent of spectral replication, which we saw before when we sampled in the time domain.

If we implement digitally the inverse transform, we can, of course, reclaim $x(t)$ from $Y(s)$. If we then interpolate $x(t)$, we can recover $f(t)$. The fact that $Y(s)$ corresponds to a periodic function produces no ill effect in this case. If we implement digital filtering by modifying the spectrum, however, the situation is not so simple.

Overlap of Replicated Spectra. Suppose we implement frequency domain filtering by multiplying $Y(s)$ by some transfer function $H(s)$. This convolves $y(t)$ with the impulse response $h(t)$. Since $y(t)$ is periodic, the convolution will tend to shift the adjacent cycles down into the primary cycle in the vicinity of $t = \pm T/2$.

If $h(t)$ is narrow and $y(t)$ is approximately constant in the area about $t = T/2$, then this overlap of adjacent cycles will have only a small effect. If $x(t)$ is not equal at each end of the truncation window, however, then $y(t)$ will have a discontinuity at $t = T/2$. This produces an artifactual discontinuity in the (periodic) function at each end of the truncation window. Convolution with the impulse response $h(t)$ then produces artifacts at both ends of the truncation window by smearing over the discontinuity.

While the smearing effect at the ends of the truncation window cannot be avoided completely, it can be reduced to tolerable levels (a) by making the truncation window wide with respect to the important components of the signal, so that nothing of interest is damaged, or (b) by arranging for $x(t)$ to have equal amplitude at each end of the truncation window, so that little or no discontinuity appears when it becomes periodic. One can do this by multiplying the truncated function by a *windowing function*. Such a function has unit amplitude over most of the window, but tapers to zero at each end.

The smearing effect at the ends of the truncation window that is encountered in frequency domain filtering is the frequency domain equivalent of the aliasing that results from sampling in the time domain. When implementing linear filtering by using computed spectra, one should perform an analysis to quantify the effects of the truncation.

12.9 SUMMARY OF IMPORTANT POINTS

1. The Shah function (impulse train) is its own Fourier transform [Eq. (2)].
2. Stretching and compressing the Shah function (similarity operations) alter the strength of impulses [Eq. (8)].
3. Sampling a continuous function can be modeled as multiplication by the Shah function.
4. A function that is bandlimited at frequency s_0 can be completely recovered from its sample values if they are taken no farther than $1/2s_0$ apart.
5. Undersampling causes aliasing, wherein energy above the folding frequency ($s - 1/2\Delta t$) appears an equal distance below the folding frequency.
6. Truncation destroys bandlimitedness and makes aliasing unavoidable in digital processing.
7. The effects of aliasing can be reduced to tolerable levels by oversampling, or by lowpass filtering prior to sampling.
8. Frequency domain filtering can produce a smearing effect near the ends of the truncation window (i.e., at the borders of an image).

PROBLEMS

1. Prove Eq. (2)
2. What would be the values of the sample points on the spectrum of the edge in Figure 12–18 if they were computed at $s_i = (i + ½)/T$ in Eq. (43)?
3. Sketch what Figure 12–18 would look like if $f(x) = \text{sign}(x - a)$ where $a = T/8$.
4. A signal is periodic with frequency $f_0 = 3$ Hz. You wish to compute its spectrum to determine how high in frequency its harmonics go. You know that it has already passed through a lowpass filter that stops all energy above 48 Hz. What is the minimum number of samples, taken over what period of time, that you could use to digitize this signal with critical sampling?

5. A signal is a cosine of frequency $f_0 = 0.22$ Hz in a Gaussian envelope of amplitude 4 and standard deviation $\sigma = 10$ seconds, centered on $t = 0$. For truncation purposes, assume that the signal is zero when its amplitude falls below 0.1 percent of its maximum value. How many samples over what period would you take to digitize this signal (a) with critical sampling? and (b) oversampling it by a factor of two? (c) If you use a digitizer that always takes 256 samples, will you have an aliasing problem?
6. A signal is a sine of frequency $f_0 = 430$ Hz in a Gaussian envelope of standard deviation $\sigma = 20$ msec, centered on $t = 0$. For truncation purposes, assume that the signal is zero when its amplitude falls below 0.1 percent of its maximum value. How many samples over what period would you take to digitize this signal, oversampling it by a factor of two? With critical sampling?
7. A signal is a sine of frequency $f_0 = 250$ Hz in an envelope of the form $4\text{sech}(\pi\alpha t)$, where $\alpha = 20$ msec, centered on $t = 0$. For truncation purposes, assume that the signal is zero when its amplitude falls below 0.1 percent of its maximum value. How many samples over what period would you take to digitize this signal, oversampling it by a factor of two? With critical sampling?
8. A signal is $\text{III}(x/\tau)$ in a Gaussian envelope of amplitude 2 and standard deviation σ, centered on $t = 0$. Here, $\tau = 100$ msec and $\sigma = 500$ msec. Sketch the signal and its spectrum.
9. A signal is $\text{III}(x/\tau)$ in a Gaussian envelope of amplitude 5 and standard deviation σ, centered on $t = 0$. Here, $\tau = 3$ msec and $\sigma = 2$ msec. Sketch the signal and its spectrum.
10. A 35-mm negative is 24 mm by 36 mm. It contains alternating black and white bars spaced D mm apart in the 36-mm direction. You have a 640-by-480 pixel digitizer. (a) What is the smallest pixel spacing with which you can digitize the entire negative? (b) If the bars are sinusoidal and $D = 0.15$ mm, can you digitize without aliasing problems? (c) If $D = 0.3$ mm, can you digitize with 2× oversampling? 3× oversampling? (d) If $D = 1$ mm, and the bars are nonsinusoidal, can you compute their spectrum to eight harmonics (i.e., $s_m = 8\times$ the frequency of the bars)?

PROJECTS

1. The marketing department of your company is proposing a new image-processing product design that reduces the size of digital images by simply discarding rows and columns. You know that the images will suffer from significant aliasing error. Your upper-level manager (who thinks *aliasing* means logging on under a phony user name) likes the earnings projections of the proposed new product. There is a new-product review meeting in a few days. You have but one opportunity to kill this ill-conceived design before its high-profile failure in the marketplace bankrupts your company. Most of your personal wealth is tied up in the company's stock and pension plans. You are the only one in the company who can see the danger. You must act quickly and be convincing.

   Digitize an image containing a strong high-frequency pattern. Demonstrate aliasing by resampling the image to half its size without using local averaging to prevent aliasing. Sketch the MTF of the image-digitizing system. On the same scale, mark the folding frequency before and after resampling. Also, mark the frequency of the pattern before and after resampling. Write a short report explaining the theory behind the demonstrated phenomenon, relating it to the observed effects of aliasing and discussing what can be done to correct the problem after it has occurred and how it can be prevented. Make a set of overhead projection transparencies, and present your report to your colleagues. Good luck!
2. Locate an image-digitizing system (film scanner, CCD camera, etc.) in which the scanning spot is, or can be set to be, significantly smaller than (roughly half of) the pixel spacing. Select an object (or an image of an object) that contains a strong high-frequency pattern. First compute the pixel spacing (at the object) at which aliasing of the pattern will just begin to occur. Then digitize

an image at 0.5, 1.0, and 2.0 times that pixel spacing. Write a short report presenting your results. Use the results to support a discussion of what pixel spacing should be used.

3. Develop a gallery of examples of aliasing (similar to Figure 12-12) by resampling digital images to smaller sizes by discarding rows and columns without local averaging. Make the best image into a photographic postcard, and send it to your friends. Write a brief report explaining what is required to generate a good example of digital image aliasing.
4. Locate an image-digitizing system (film scanner, CCD camera, etc.) in which the scanning spot is, or can be set to be, significantly smaller than the pixel spacing. Use the device to develop a gallery of examples of aliasing. Make the best image into a photographic Christmas card, and send it to the author. Write a brief report explaining what is required to generate a good example of digital image aliasing.
5. Use a mathematics program or write a program to implement frequency-domain lowpass filtering in one dimension. Use the program to demonstrate smearing at the ends of the truncation window on a function that differs in amplitude at each end of the window. Write a brief report describing your illustration of the phenomenon.
6. Select a digital image that exhibits significant differences in gray level between its right and left borders and/or between its top and bottom borders. Use an image-processing system to implement lowpass filtering in the frequency domain. Create three examples using progressively more severe lowpass filtering. Write a brief report illustrating the effect of smearing adjacent cycles.

REFERENCES

For additional reading, see Appendix 2.

1. R. N. Bracewell, *The Fourier Transform and Its Applications* (2d revised edition), McGraw-Hill, New York, 1986.
2. E. O. Brigham, *The Fast Fourier Transform and Its Applications,* Prentice-Hall, Englewood Cliffs, N.J., 1988.
3. C. E. Shannon, "A Mathematical Theory of Communication," *Bell System Technical Journal,* **XXVII**(3):379–423, 1948.
4. C. E. Shannon, "Communication in the Presence of Noise," *Proc. IRE,* **37:**10-31, 1949.
5. A. B. Jerri, "The Shannon Sampling Theorem—Its Various Extensions and Applications: A Tutorial Review," *Proc. IEEE,* 1565–1596, 1977.
6. A. Kohlenberg, "Exact Interpolation of Bandlimited Functions," *J. Appl. Physics,* 1432–1436, 1953.
7. H. Nyquist, "Certain Topics in Telegraph Transmission Theory," *AIEE Trans.,* p. 617, 1946.
8. R. R. Legault, "The Aliasing Problems in Two-Dimensional Sampled Imagery," *Perception of Displayed Information,* L. M. Biberman, ed., Plenum Press, New York, 1973.
9. H. J. Landau, "Sampling, Data Transmission, and the Nyquist Rate," *Proc. IEEE,* **55**(10):1701–1706, 1967.
10. J. L. Brown, Jr., "Bounds for Truncation Error in Sampling Expansions of Band-Limited Signals," *IEEE Trans. Inf. Theory,* **IT-15**(4):440–444, 1969.
11. J. L. Brown, Jr., "Mean-Square Truncation Error in Series Expansions of Random Functions," *J. SIAM,* **8,** 18–32, 1960.

CHAPTER 13

Discrete Image Transforms

13.1 INTRODUCTION

The discrete Fourier transform (DFT), introduced in Chapter 10, is but one of a number of discrete linear transformations that prove useful in digital image processing. In this chapter, we examine the topic more generally, developing several other transforms and some of their properties and applications as well.

Images of interest normally occur in continuous form and must be viewed that way as well. Since we are limited to working with a discrete representation of a continuous image, much of digital image processing requires that we keep sampling and interpolation considerations in mind while processing the discrete data. Some applications, however, allow us to treat the digital image as a discrete entity, without particular regard for the history of its origin or for the underlying continuous image.

One such application is image compression. Here, one wishes to encode an image into a more compact data format, either with no loss, or with only a tolerable loss of information content. Normally, considerations of optics, sampling, and interpolation, regarding the digitization and display of the image, are not of immediate concern, and the digital image can be treated merely as a data file.

A *representation* of an image is a particular embodiment of the data that defines the image. It is a presentation of the image data in a particular form or format. A digital image can be represented as a matrix or, with row stacking, as a vector.

13.2 LINEAR TRANSFORMATIONS

13.2.1 One-Dimensional Discrete Linear Transformations

Definition. If $\mathbf{x}$ is an N-by-1 vector and $\mathbf{T}$ is an N-by-N matrix, then

$$y_i = \sum_{j=0}^{N-1} t_{i,j} x_j \quad \text{or} \quad \mathbf{y} = \mathbf{Tx} \tag{1}$$

where $i = 0, \ldots, N-1$ defines a linear transformation of the vector $\mathbf{x}$. The matrix $\mathbf{T}$ is also called the *kernel matrix* of the transformation. Note that this use of the word *kernel* is different from its use in the term *convolution kernel* discussed in Sec. 9.3.4.

The result of the transformation is another N-by-1 vector, $\mathbf{y}$. The transformation is linear because $\mathbf{y}$ is formed by a first-order summation of the input elements. Each element y_i is the inner product of the input vector $\mathbf{x}$ with the ith row of $\mathbf{T}$.

Example. A simple example of a linear transformation is the rotation of a vector in a two-dimensional coordinate system. (See Chapter 8.) Here,

$$\begin{bmatrix} y_1 \\ y_2 \end{bmatrix} = \begin{bmatrix} \cos(\theta) & -\sin(\theta) \\ \sin(\theta) & \cos(\theta) \end{bmatrix} \begin{bmatrix} x_1 \\ x_2 \end{bmatrix} \tag{2}$$

rotates the vector $\mathbf{x}$ through the angle θ.

Inversion. After the transformation, the original vector can be recovered by the inverse transformation

$$\mathbf{x} = \mathbf{T}^{-1}\mathbf{y} \tag{3}$$

provided that $\mathbf{T}$ is nonsingular. As before, each element of $\mathbf{x}$ is an inner product, this time between $\mathbf{y}$ and a row of $\mathbf{T}^{-1}$. For the foregoing example, this amounts to a rotation through the same angle in the reverse direction.

13.2.1.1 Unitary Transforms

For a given vector length N, there are infinitely many transformation matrices $\mathbf{T}$ that could be used. The more useful ones, however, belong to a class having certain properties.

If $\mathbf{T}$ is a unitary matrix, then

$$\mathbf{T}^{-1} = \mathbf{T}^{*t} \quad \text{and} \quad \mathbf{TT}^{*t} = \mathbf{T}^{*t}\mathbf{T} = \mathbf{I} \tag{4}$$

where $*$ indicates complex conjugation of each of the elements of $\mathbf{T}$ and the ^{t} indicates the transpose operation. If $\mathbf{T}$ is unitary and has only real elements, then it is an orthogonal matrix, and it follows that

$$\mathbf{T}^{-1} = \mathbf{T}^{t} \quad \text{and} \quad \mathbf{TT}^{t} = \mathbf{T}^{t}\mathbf{T} = \mathbf{I} \tag{5}$$

Notice that the i, jth element of $\mathbf{TT}^t$ is the inner product of rows i and j of $\mathbf{T}$. Eq. (5) implies that this is zero unless $i = j$, in which case it is unity. Thus, the rows of $\mathbf{T}$ are a set of orthonormal vectors.

Example: The one-dimensional DFT. The one-dimensional DFT is an example of a unitary transform, since

$$\mathbf{F}_k = \frac{1}{\sqrt{N}} \sum_{i=0}^{N-1} f_i \exp\left(-j2\pi k \frac{i}{N}\right) \quad \text{or} \quad \mathbf{F} = \mathcal{W}\mathbf{f} \tag{6}$$

where $\mathcal{W}$ is a unitary (but not orthogonal) matrix with (complex) elements

$$w_{i,k} = \frac{1}{\sqrt{N}} \exp\left(-j2\pi k \frac{i}{N}\right) \tag{7}$$

Interpretation. Normally, the transform matrix $\mathbf{T}$ is non-singular (i.e., rank($\mathbf{T}$) = N), so as to make the transform invertible, as per Eq. (3). Then the rows of $\mathbf{T}$ form an orthonormal basis (a set of orthonormal basis vectors, or unit vectors) for the N-dimensional vector space of all N-by-1 vectors. This means that any N-by-1 sequence can be viewed as representing a vector from the origin to a point in N-dimensional space. Furthermore, any transform of the form of Eq. (1) can be viewed as a coordinate transformation, rotating the vector in N-space without changing its length.

In summary, then, a unitary linear transformation generates $\mathbf{y}$, a vector of N *transform coefficients*, each of which is computed as the inner product of the input vector $\mathbf{x}$ with one of the rows of the transform matrix $\mathbf{T}$. The inverse transform is computed similarly, as a set of inner products of the transform coefficient vector with the rows of the inverse transform matrix.

The forward transformation is generally considered to be a process of *analysis*, breaking the signal vector down into its elemental components. These fundamental components are naturally in the form of the basis vectors. The transform coefficients specify how much of each component is found to be present in the mixture that comprises the particular vector being decomposed.

The inverse transformation, on the other hand, is often considered a process of *synthesis*, reassembling the original vector from its components via summation. Here, the transform coefficients specify the proper amount of each basis vector that must be added to the mixture so as to reconstruct the input vector accurately and completely.

A key to this process is the principle that any vector can be uniquely decomposed into a set of normal basis vectors of the proper amplitude and later reconstituted by adding these components back together to reconstruct the original. It is significant that the number of transform coefficients is equal to the number of elements in the vector. Thus, the number of degrees of freedom is the same before and after the transformation, and information is neither created nor destroyed by the process.

A transformed vector is a representation of the original vector. Since it contains the same number of elements (and thus has the same number of degrees of freedom) as the original, and since the original can be recovered from it without error, it can be considered an alternative form of expressing the original vector. This chapter considers several alternative ways of representing digital signals and images, and the usefulness of each.

13.2.2 Two-Dimensional Discrete Linear Transformations

In two dimensions, the general linear transformation that takes the N-by-N matrix $\mathbf{F}$ into the transformed matrix $\mathbf{G}$ (also N by N) is

$$G_{m,n} = \sum_{i=0}^{N-1} \sum_{k=0}^{N-1} F_{i,k} \mathfrak{J}(i, k, m, n) \tag{8}$$

where i, k, m, and n are discrete variables that range from 0 to $N-1$ and $\mathfrak{I}(i, k, m, n)$ is the kernel function of the transformation.

$\mathfrak{I}(i, k, m, n)$ can be thought of as an N^2-by-N^2 block matrix having N rows of N blocks, each of which is an N-by-N matrix. The blocks are indexed by m, n and the elements of each N-by-N sub-matrix by i, k (See Figure 13–1.)

If $\mathfrak{I}(i, k, m, n)$ can be separated into the product of rowwise and columnwise component functions—that is, if

$$\mathfrak{I}(i, k, m, n) = T_r(i, m)T_c(k, n) \tag{9}$$

then the transformation is called *separable*. This means that it can be carried out in two steps—a rowwise operation followed by a columnwise operation (or vice versa):

$$G_{m,n} = \sum_{i=0}^{N-1}\left[\sum_{k=0}^{N-1} F_{i,k}T_c(k, n)\right]T_r(i, m) \tag{10}$$

Further, if the two component functions are identical, the transform is also called *symmetric* (not to be confused with a symmetric matrix). Then

$$\mathfrak{I}(i, k, m, n) = T(i, m)T(k, n) \tag{11}$$

and Eq. (8) can be written as

$$G_{m,n} = \sum_{i=0}^{N-1} T(i, m)\left[\sum_{k=0}^{N-1} F_{i,k}T(k, n)\right] \quad \text{or} \quad \mathbf{G} = \mathbf{TFT} \tag{12}$$

where $\mathbf{T}$ is a unitary matrix, called the *kernel matrix* of the transform, as before. We use this notation throughout the chapter, to signify a general, separable, symmetric unitary transform.

The inverse transform is

$$\mathbf{F} = \mathbf{T}^{-1}\mathbf{G}\mathbf{T}^{-1} = \mathbf{T}^{*t}\mathbf{G}\mathbf{T}^{*t} \tag{13}$$

and it recovers $\mathbf{F}$ exactly.

Example: The Two-dimensional DFT. The two-dimensional DFT is a separable and symmetric unitary transform. In this case, $\mathbf{T}$ in Eq. (12) becomes the matrix $\mathcal{W}$ from Eq. (7).

The inverse DFT uses $\mathcal{W}^{-1}$, which is simply the conjugate transpose of $\mathcal{W}$. The discrete Fourier transform pair is thus expressed as

$$\mathbf{G} = \mathcal{W}\mathbf{F}\mathcal{W} \quad \text{and} \quad \mathbf{F} = \mathcal{W}^{*t}\mathbf{G}\mathcal{W}^{*t} \tag{14}$$

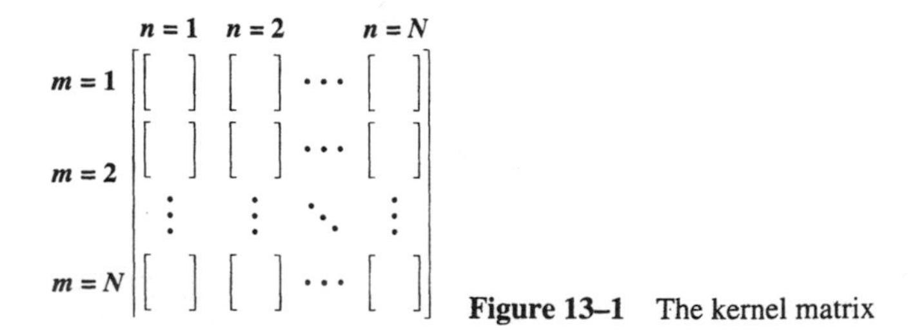

Figure 13–1 The kernel matrix

13.2.2.1 Orthogonal Transformations

Unlike the Fourier transform, many transforms have only real elements in their kernel matrix **T**. A unitary matrix with real elements is orthogonal, and the inverse transformation becomes simply

$$\mathbf{F} = \mathbf{T}^t\mathbf{G}\mathbf{T}^t \tag{15}$$

If **T** is a symmetric matrix, as is often the case, then the forward and inverse transforms are identical, so that

$$\mathbf{G} = \mathbf{TFT} \quad \text{and} \quad \mathbf{F} = \mathbf{TGT} \tag{16}$$

13.3 BASIS FUNCTIONS AND BASIS IMAGES

The primary difference between any two unitary transforms is the choice of basis functions, that is, the rows of **T**. Here, we examine basis functions in more detail.

13.3.1 Basis Functions

The rows of the kernel matrix form a set of basis vectors for an N-dimensional vector space. The rows are orthonormal; that is,

$$\mathbf{TT}^{*t} = \mathbf{I} \quad \text{or} \quad \sum_{i=0}^{N-1} T_{j,i}T^*_{k,i} = \delta_{j,k} \tag{17}$$

where $\delta_{j,k}$ is the Kronecker delta.

While any set of orthonormal vectors will serve for a linear transform, normally the entire set is derived from the same basic functional form. The Fourier transform, for example, uses the complex exponential as its prototypical basis function. The individual basis functions differ only in frequency.

Any vector in the space can be expressed as a weighted sum of unit-length basis vectors. Any one-dimensional (N-by-1) unitary transform, then, corresponds to a rotation of a vector in an N-dimensional vector space. Further, since an N-by-N image matrix can be row-stacked to form an N^2-by-1 vector, any two-dimensional, symmetric, separable unitary transform corresponds to a rotation of a vector in an N^2-dimensional vector space.

13.3.2 Basis Images

The inverse two-dimensional transform can be viewed as reconstructing the image by summing a set of properly weighted *basis images*. Each element in the transform matrix, **G**, is the coefficient by which the corresponding basis image is multiplied in the summation.

A basis image can be generated by inverse transforming a coefficient matrix containing only one nonzero element, which is set to unity. There are N^2 such matrices, and these produce N^2 basis images. Let one such coefficient matrix be

$$\mathbf{G}^{p,q} = \{\delta_{i-p,\,j-q}\} \tag{18}$$

where i and j are the row and column indices and p and q are integers that specify the location of the nonzero element. Then the inverse transform [Eq. (13)] is

$$F_{m,n} = \sum_{i=0}^{N-1} T(i,m)\left[\sum_{k=0}^{N-1} \delta_{i-p,k-q} T(k,n)\right] = T(p,m)T(q,n) \tag{19}$$

Thus, for a separable unitary transform, each basis image is the outer product of two rows of the transform matrix.

As with one-dimensional signals, the basis images can be thought of as a set of basic components into which any image can be decomposed. They are also the building blocks from which any image can be reassembled. The forward transform does the decomposition by determining the coefficients. The inverse transform does the reconstitution by summing the basis images, weighted by those coefficients.

Since infinitely many sets of basis images exist, infinitely many transforms exist as well. Thus, a particular set of basis images takes on profound importance only in the context of a particular transform.

13.4 SINUSOIDAL TRANSFORMS

For reasons mentioned in Chapter 10, the Fourier transform has emerged as the single most important transform in digital imaging. It has, however, several relatives that also use sinusoidal basis functions. These are introduced in this section, after a brief review of the discrete Fourier transform.

13.4.1 The Discrete Fourier Transform

Introduced in Chapter 10, the DFT is considered again here, in the context of separable unitary transforms, to enable us to draw comparisons between it and other transforms of the same type.

The kernel matrix for the DFT [recall Eqs. (6) and (7)] is

$$\mathcal{W} = \begin{bmatrix} w_{0,0} & \cdots & w_{0,N-1} \\ \vdots & \ddots & \vdots \\ w_{N-1,0} & \cdots & w_{N-1,N-1} \end{bmatrix} \tag{20}$$

where

$$w_{i,k} = \frac{1}{\sqrt{N}} e^{-j2\pi\frac{ik}{N}} \tag{21}$$

Because of the periodic nature of the imaginary exponential, $\mathcal{W}$ is unitary.

In one dimension, the forward and inverse DFTs are

$$\mathbf{F} = \mathcal{W}\mathbf{f} \quad \text{and} \quad \mathbf{f} = \mathcal{W}^{*t}\mathbf{F} \tag{22}$$

where $\mathbf{f}$ and $\mathbf{F}$ are N-by-1 signal and spectrum vectors, respectively. If $\mathbf{f}$ is real, $\mathbf{F}$ will, in general, have complex elements. Only if $\mathbf{f}$ has the proper symmetry (discussed next) will $\mathbf{F}$ be real.

13.4.1.1 The Spectrum Vector

Figure 13–2 shows where the different frequency components occur in the spectrum vector **F**, when **f** is real. The zero-frequency component and the highest frequency component (corresponding to the Nyquist frequency) appear only once. The remaining components are duplicated as complex conjugates. (Recall that the spectrum of a real function is a Hermite function.) If $\mathbf{F}^t$ is viewed as a row vector, the first $N/2 + 1$ elements are the right half of the spectrum, while the last $N/2 - 1$ elements are the left half. The frequency corresponding to the ith element of **F** is

$$s_i = \begin{cases} \frac{2i}{N} f_N & 0 \leq i \leq N/2 \\ -\frac{2(N-i)}{N} f_N & N/2 + 1 \leq i \leq N-1 \end{cases} \tag{23}$$

where f_N is the Nyquist (folding) frequency (half the sampling frequency). If the last $N/2 - 1$ elements of **f** form a mirror image of elements 1 through $N/2 - 1$, then **F** is even, and **F** will be real-valued.

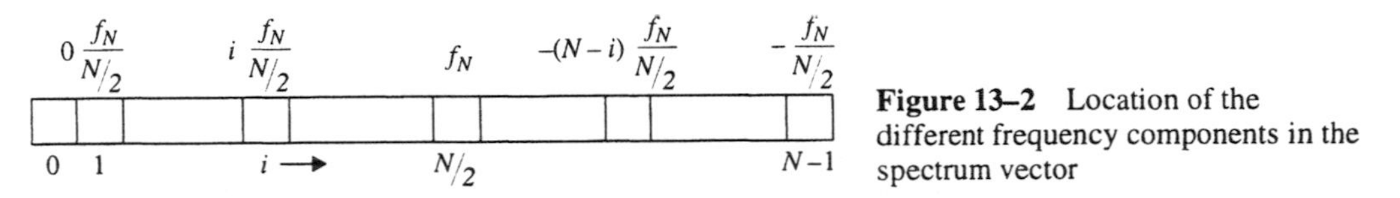

Figure 13–2 Location of the different frequency components in the spectrum vector

One can rotate the elements of **F** by the amount $N/2$, using a circular right (or left) shift operation, to produce a vector suitable for plotting the spectrum. In that case, the zero-frequency element is located at $N/2$, and frequency increases in both directions from there. The Nyquist frequency element appears only at F_0.

The shift theorem of the Fourier transform (Sec. 10.2.3) provides another way of achieving the same result. Applying the theorem to a shift in the frequency domain yields

$$F(u) \Leftrightarrow f(x) \Rightarrow F(u-u_0) \Leftrightarrow \exp\left(j2\pi x\frac{u_0}{N}\right)f(x)$$
$$= \exp(j\pi x)f(x) = (-1)^x f(x) \tag{24}$$

where the amount of shift is $u_0 = N/2$. This means that we have merely to change the signs of the odd-numbered elements of $f(x)$ prior to executing the DFT. Doing so leaves the spectrum properly shifted for plotting.

13.4.1.2 The Two-Dimensional DFT

In two dimensions, the forward and inverse DFTs are

$$\mathbf{G} = \mathcal{W}\mathbf{F}\mathcal{W} \quad \text{and} \quad \mathbf{F} = \mathcal{W}^{*t}\mathbf{G}\mathcal{W}^{*t} \tag{25}$$

where **F** is an image in matrix form and **G** is its spectrum matrix.

Figure 13–3 shows where the various spatial frequency terms are located in the spectrum matrix **G**. Rearrangement of the four quadrants, as shown in the figure, makes displaying the spectrum more convenient. That way, zero frequency falls at the center of

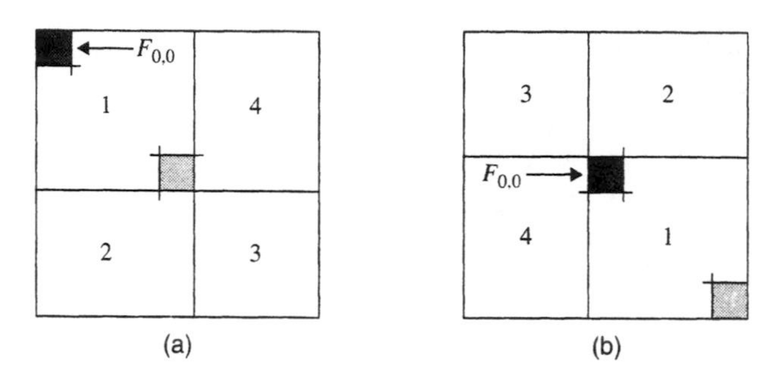

Figure 13–3 Location of the various spatial frequency terms in the spectrum matrix: (a) after transformation; (b) after rearrangement

the matrix, and frequency increases radially from there. In two dimensions, Eq. (24) generalizes to

$$F(u, v) \Leftrightarrow f(x, y) \Rightarrow F(u - N/2, v - N/2) \Leftrightarrow (-1)^{x+y} f(x, y) \tag{26}$$

and again, changing the sign of half the elements of the image matrix **F** effects the desired shift. If **F** has the symmetry shown in Figure 13–3(a), then **G** will be real valued.

13.4.2 The Discrete Cosine Transform

The discrete cosine transform (DCT) is defined in two dimensions as

$$G_c(m, n) = \alpha(m)\alpha(n)\sum_{i=0}^{N-1}\sum_{k=0}^{N-1} g(i, k)\cos\left[\frac{\pi(2i+1)m}{2N}\right]\cos\left[\frac{\pi(2k+1)n}{2N}\right] \tag{27}$$

and its inverse by

$$g(i, k) = \sum_{m=0}^{N-1}\sum_{n=0}^{N-1} \alpha(m)\alpha(n)G_c(m, n)\cos\left[\frac{\pi(2i+1)m}{2N}\right]\cos\left[\frac{\pi(2k+1)n}{2N}\right] \tag{28}$$

where the coefficients are

$$\alpha(0) = \sqrt{\frac{1}{N}} \quad \text{and} \quad \alpha(m) = \sqrt{\frac{2}{N}} \quad \text{for} \quad 1 \le m \le N \tag{29}$$

Like the DFT, the DCT can be expressed as a unitary matrix operation in the form

$$\mathbf{G_c} = \mathbf{CgC} \tag{30}$$

where the kernel matrix has elements

$$C_{i,m} = \alpha(m)\cos\left[\frac{\pi(2i+1)m}{2N}\right] \tag{31}$$

Also like the DFT, the DCT can be computed by a fast algorithm [1–3]. Unlike the DFT, the DCT is real valued. It has found wide usage in image compression, for reasons pointed out later in the chapter.

13.4.3 The Sine Transform

Jain [4] introduced the discrete sine transform (DST), defined as

$$G_s(m, n) = \frac{2}{N+1} \sum_{i=0}^{N-1} \sum_{k=0}^{N-1} g(i, k) \sin\left[\frac{\pi(i+1)(m+1)}{N+1}\right] \sin\left[\frac{\pi(k+1)(n+1)}{N+1}\right] \tag{32}$$

and

$$g(i, k) = \frac{2}{N+1} \sum_{m=0}^{N-1} \sum_{n=0}^{N-1} G_s(m, n) \sin\left[\frac{\pi(i+1)(m+1)}{N+1}\right] \sin\left[\frac{\pi(k+1)(n+1)}{N+1}\right] \tag{33}$$

The DST has unitary kernel matrix elements

$$T_{i,k} = \sqrt{\frac{2}{N+1}} \sin\left[\frac{\pi(i+1)(k+1)}{N+1}\right] \tag{34}$$

Unlike the other sinusoidal transforms, the DST is most conveniently computed for $N = 2^p - 1$, where p is an integer. Then it can be taken as the imaginary part of a specially constructed $(2N + 2)$-point FFT [5].

The DST has a fast implementation algorithm [6] and properties that prove useful in certain image compression problems, as discussed later in the chapter.

13.4.4 The Hartley Transform

In 1942, Hartley introduced a continuous integral transform as an alternative to the Fourier transform [7]. Bracewell later defined an analogous discrete unitary transform based on the Hartley transform [8]. The forward two-dimensional discrete Hartley transform (DHT)

$$G_{m,n} = \frac{1}{N} \sum_{i=0}^{N-1} \sum_{k=0}^{N-1} g_{i,k} \operatorname{cas}\left[\frac{2\pi}{N}(im + kn)\right] \tag{35}$$

and the inverse two-dimensional DHT

$$g_{i,k} = \frac{1}{N} \sum_{m=0}^{N-1} \sum_{n=0}^{N-1} G_{m,n} \operatorname{cas}\left[\frac{2\pi}{N}(im + kn)\right] \tag{36}$$

are identical and use the basis function

$$\operatorname{cas}(\theta) = \cos(\theta) + \sin(\theta) = \sqrt{2} \cos(\theta - \pi/4) \tag{37}$$

which is a cosine shifted 45 degrees to the right.

The kernel matrix of the Hartley transform has elements

$$T_{i,k} = \frac{1}{\sqrt{N}} \left[\operatorname{cas}\left(2\pi\frac{ik}{N}\right)\right] \tag{38}$$

Whereas the DFT transforms N real numbers into N complex numbers with conjugate symmetry, the discrete Hartley transform produces N real numbers.

As one might expect, the DHT is closely related to the DFT. In Chapter 10, we saw that the Hartley transform is simply the real part minus the imaginary part of the corresponding Fourier transform. Likewise, the Fourier transform is the even part minus j times the odd part of the Hartley transform.

The convolution theorem of the Hartley transform is only slightly more complicated than that of the Fourier transform. It is expressed as

$$g(x) = f(x) * h(x) \Leftrightarrow G(v) = F(v)H_e(v) + F(-v)H_o(v) \tag{39}$$

where $F(v)$ and $G(v)$ are the Hartley transforms of $f(x)$ and $g(x)$, respectively, and $H_e(v)$ and $H_o(v)$ are the even and odd components, respectively, of the Hartley transform of $h(x)$. (See Sec. 10.2.1 for a definition of even and odd components.)

In the common case where one of the functions is even, the second term of Eq. (39) drops out, and convolution corresponds to multiplication in the Hartley transform domain, just as it does with the Fourier transform in the frequency domain.

The DHT is a computational alternative to the DFT. There is a fast algorithm for the Hartley transform [9]. For linear filtering applications—particularly if the kernel is symmetric—the DHT can significantly reduce the computational work load, since it avoids complex arithmetic.

13.4.5 Other Sinusoidal Transforms

Jain [10] has introduced a family of unitary transforms having sinusoidal basis functions. The DFT, the DCT, and the DST belong to this family.

13.5 RECTANGULAR WAVE TRANSFORMS

Several transforms of interest in discrete image processing use basis functions that are variations of the square wave rather than sinusoids. In general, these are fast to compute, since many of the multiplication operations become trivial.

In this section, we introduce the Hadamard, Walsh, slant, and Haar transforms. The Haar transform differs fundamentally from the other three, and it is discussed further, in the context of wavelet transforms, in the next chapter.

13.5.1 The Hadamard Transform

The Hadamard transform [11–15] is a symmetric, separable unitary transformation that has only +1 and −1 as elements in its kernel matrix. It exists for $N = 2^n$, where n is an integer.

For the two-by-two case, the kernel matrix is

$$\frac{1}{\sqrt{2}}\mathbf{H}_2 = \frac{1}{\sqrt{2}}\begin{bmatrix} 1 & 1 \\ 1 & -1 \end{bmatrix} \tag{40}$$

and for successively larger N, these can be generated from the block matrix form

$$\frac{1}{\sqrt{N}}\mathbf{H}_N = \frac{1}{\sqrt{N}}\begin{bmatrix} \mathbf{H}_{N/2} & \mathbf{H}_{N/2} \\ \mathbf{H}_{N/2} & -\mathbf{H}_{N/2} \end{bmatrix} \tag{41}$$

For any size $N = 2^n$, the matrix contains only elements that are ±1, provided that the $N^{-1/2}$ factor is kept out in front. This makes the transform less expensive to compute.

For $N = 8$, for example, the Hadamard kernel matrix is

$$H_8 = \frac{1}{2\sqrt{2}} \begin{bmatrix} 1 & 1 & 1 & 1 & 1 & 1 & 1 & 1 \\ 1 & -1 & 1 & -1 & 1 & -1 & 1 & -1 \\ 1 & 1 & -1 & -1 & 1 & 1 & -1 & -1 \\ 1 & -1 & -1 & 1 & 1 & -1 & -1 & 1 \\ 1 & 1 & 1 & 1 & -1 & -1 & -1 & -1 \\ 1 & -1 & 1 & -1 & -1 & 1 & -1 & 1 \\ 1 & 1 & -1 & -1 & -1 & -1 & 1 & 1 \\ 1 & -1 & -1 & 1 & -1 & 1 & 1 & -1 \end{bmatrix} \begin{matrix} 0 \\ 7 \\ 3 \\ 4 \\ 1 \\ 6 \\ 2 \\ 5 \end{matrix} \qquad (42)$$

where the column to the right shows the number of sign changes along the corresponding row. Notice that these are different for each row. This sign change count is called the *sequency* of the row [16].

We can reorder the rows to make sequency increase uniformly with row number, much as frequency increases with the Fourier kernel. This yields a transform that is somewhat easier to interpret. The kernel of the *ordered Hadamard transform*, for $N = 8$, is thus

$$H_8 = \frac{1}{2\sqrt{2}} \begin{bmatrix} 1 & 1 & 1 & 1 & 1 & 1 & 1 & 1 \\ 1 & 1 & 1 & 1 & -1 & -1 & -1 & -1 \\ 1 & 1 & -1 & -1 & -1 & -1 & 1 & 1 \\ 1 & 1 & -1 & -1 & 1 & 1 & -1 & -1 \\ 1 & -1 & -1 & 1 & 1 & -1 & -1 & 1 \\ 1 & -1 & -1 & 1 & -1 & 1 & 1 & -1 \\ 1 & -1 & 1 & -1 & -1 & 1 & -1 & 1 \\ 1 & -1 & 1 & -1 & 1 & -1 & 1 & -1 \end{bmatrix} \begin{matrix} 0 \\ 1 \\ 2 \\ 3 \\ 4 \\ 5 \\ 6 \\ 7 \end{matrix} \qquad (43)$$

13.5.2 The Walsh Transform

The Hadamard transform basis functions are actually Walsh functions [17]. Thus, the Hadamard transform is also referred to as the Walsh transform.

13.5.3 The Slant Transform

The slant transform [18] was designed to have not only a constant first basis function, but a linear second basis function as well (Figure 13–4). The slanted second basis function matches the linearly sloping background that is present in many images.

The unitary kernel matrix for the slant transform is obtained by starting with the two-by-two Haar or Hadamard matrix

$$S_2 = \frac{1}{\sqrt{2}} \begin{bmatrix} 1 & 1 \\ 1 & -1 \end{bmatrix} \qquad (44)$$

and iterating it according to the schema

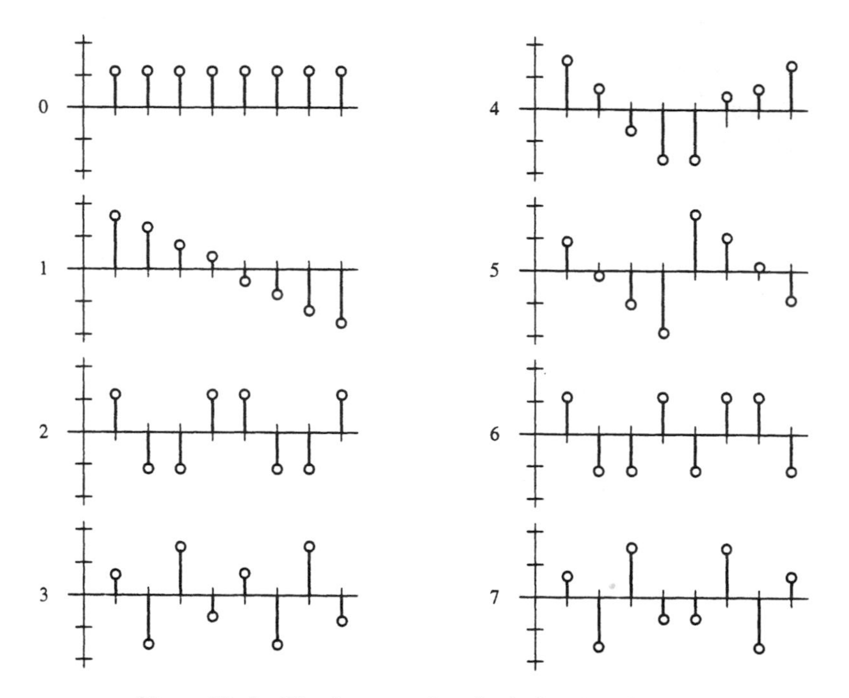

Figure 13–4 The slant transform basis functions for $N = 8$

$$S_N = \frac{1}{\sqrt{2}} \left[\begin{array}{cc|c|cc|c} 1 & 0 & \mathbf{0} & 1 & 0 & \mathbf{0} \\ a_N & b_N & & -a_N & b_N & \\ \hline \multicolumn{2}{c|}{\mathbf{0}} & \mathbf{I} & \multicolumn{2}{c|}{\mathbf{0}} & \mathbf{I} \\ \hline 0 & 1 & \mathbf{0} & 0 & -1 & \mathbf{0} \\ -b_N & a_N & & b_N & a_N & \\ \hline \multicolumn{2}{c|}{\mathbf{0}} & \mathbf{I} & \multicolumn{2}{c|}{\mathbf{0}} & -\mathbf{I} \end{array} \right] \left[\begin{array}{c|c} \mathbf{S}_{N/2} & \mathbf{0} \\ \mathbf{0} & \mathbf{S}_{N/2} \end{array} \right] \tag{45}$$

where **I** is the identity matrix of order $N/2 - 2$ and

$$a_{2N} = \sqrt{\frac{3N^2}{4N^2 - 1}} \quad \text{and} \quad b_{2N} = \sqrt{\frac{N^2 - 1}{4N^2 - 1}} \tag{46}$$

The slant transform basis functions occur in all sequencies from 0 through $N - 1$. The slant transform also has a fast transform algorithm and has been used for image compression [18].

13.5.4 The Haar Transform

The Haar transform is a symmetric, separable unitary transformation that uses Haar functions for its basis [19–21]. It exists for $N = 2^n$, where n is an integer.

Whereas the Fourier transform basis functions differ only in frequency, the Haar functions vary in both scale (width) and position. This gives the Haar transform a dual scale-position nature that is evident in its basis functions (Figure 13–5). Such a feature

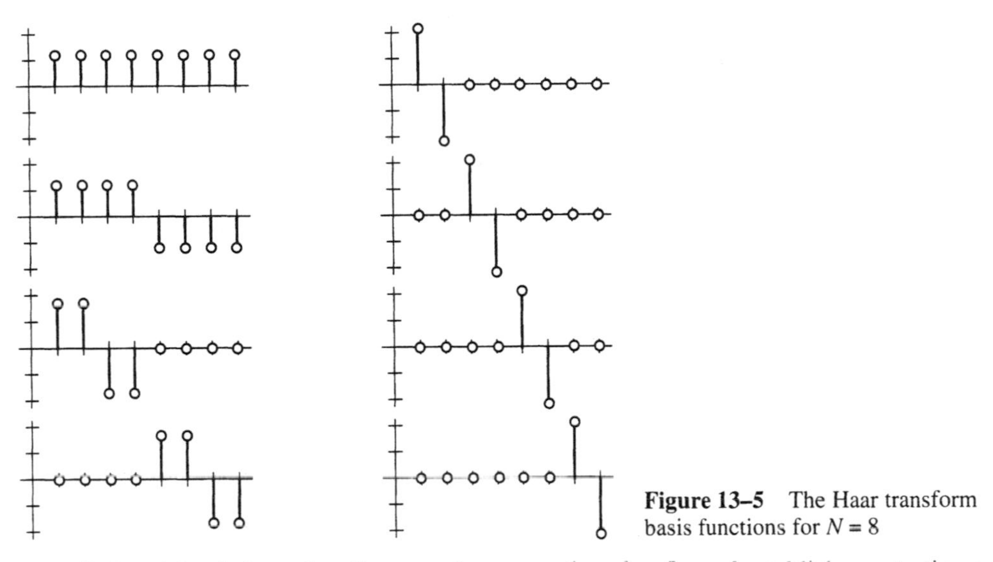

Figure 13–5 The Haar transform basis functions for $N = 8$

distinguishes it from the other transforms mentioned so far and establishes a starting point for wavelet transforms, which are introduced in the next chapter.

Basis Function Indexing. Since the Haar functions vary in two aspects (scale and position), they must be specified by a dual indexing scheme. The Haar functions are defined on the interval [0, 1] as follows. Let the integer $0 \le k \le N-1$ be specified (uniquely) by two other integers, p and q, as

$$k = 2^p + q - 1 \tag{47}$$

Notice that, under this construction, not only is k a function of p and q, but p and q are functions of k as well. For any value of $k > 0$, 2^p is the largest power of 2 such that $2^p \le k$, and $q - 1$ is the remainder.

The Haar functions are defined by

$$h_0(x) = \frac{1}{\sqrt{N}} \tag{48}$$

and

$$h_k(x) = \frac{1}{\sqrt{N}} \begin{cases} 2^{p/2} & \dfrac{q-1}{2^p} \le x < \dfrac{q-\frac{1}{2}}{2^p} \\ -2^{p/2} & \dfrac{q-\frac{1}{2}}{2^p} \le x < \dfrac{q}{2^p} \\ 0 & \text{otherwise} \end{cases} \tag{49}$$

If we let $x = i/N$ for $i = 0, 1, \ldots, N-1$, this gives rise to a set of basis functions, each of which is an odd rectangular pulse pair, except for $k = 0$, which, as in the case of many of the other transforms discussed here, is constant. Further, the basis functions vary in both scale (width) and position (Figure 13–5). The index p specifies the scale, while q determines the shift.

Whereas the transforms discussed so far use full-width basis functions, the Haar functions are all scaled, shifted versions of a single "prototype" function, the odd rectangular pulse pair. There are two major ramifications of this property.

First, although the basis functions are identified by the single index k, they have a dual scale-position nature that is specified by the indices p and q. Thus, it is less enlightening to plot the transform coefficients along the k-axis than it would be, for example, to plot a conventional frequency spectrum obtained with the Fourier transform.

Second, suppose a particular feature, such as an edge, is embedded in the signal at some position along the x-axis. The Fourier transform, for example, encodes this position into the phase spectrum in accordance with the shift theorem (Sec. 10.2.3). While the feature position is uniquely specified and can be recovered exactly via the inverse Fourier transform, it may not be particularly visible in any convenient display of the spectrum. (*Note:* If a single feature dominates the signal, then the phase plot will be linear, with slope related to feature position (as per the shift theorem), and this can be used to locate the feature. A multiplicity of features or the presence of noise, however, normally makes the phase plot so complicated as to be uninterpretable.)

By contrast, the Haar transform addresses lines and edges more directly, since its basis functions resemble these features. Recall that a signal, or a component thereof, which approximately matches one of the basis functions will produce, in the transform, a large coefficient corresponding to that basis function. Since the basis functions are orthonormal, that signal will produce small coefficients elsewhere. Thus, the Haar transform can call attention to specific line and edge features by their size and location.

The eight-by-eight unitary kernel matrix for the Haar transform is

$$\mathbf{Hr} = \frac{1}{\sqrt{8}}\begin{bmatrix} 1 & 1 & 1 & 1 & 1 & 1 & 1 & 1 \\ 1 & 1 & 1 & 1 & -1 & -1 & -1 & -1 \\ \sqrt{2} & \sqrt{2} & -\sqrt{2} & -\sqrt{2} & 0 & 0 & 0 & 0 \\ 0 & 0 & 0 & 0 & \sqrt{2} & \sqrt{2} & -\sqrt{2} & -\sqrt{2} \\ 2 & -2 & 0 & 0 & 0 & 0 & 0 & 0 \\ 0 & 0 & 2 & -2 & 0 & 0 & 0 & 0 \\ 0 & 0 & 0 & 0 & 2 & -2 & 0 & 0 \\ 0 & 0 & 0 & 0 & 0 & 0 & 2 & -2 \end{bmatrix} \tag{50}$$

and the same pattern holds for larger N. Because of the many constant and zero entries in the matrix, the Haar transform is very fast to compute.

The basis images for $N = 8$ appear in Figure 13–6. Notice that the lower right quadrant searches for small features at all different locations in the image.

13.6 EIGENVECTOR-BASED TRANSFORMS

Two important transforms use basis functions that are derived from eigenanalysis. (For a more complete summary of eigenanalysis, with numerical examples, see Appendix 3.)

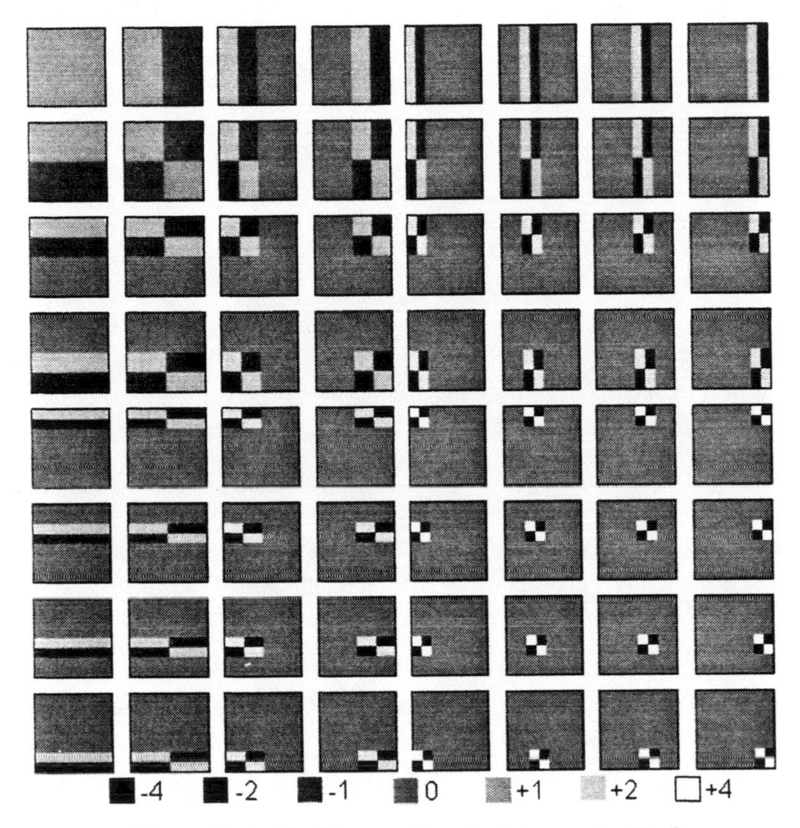

Figure 13–6 The Haar transform basis images for $N = 8$

13.6.1 Eigenanalysis

Recall that for an N-by-N matrix $\mathbf{A}$, there are N scalars, λ_k, $k = 0, \ldots, N - 1$, such that

$$|\mathbf{A} - \lambda_k \mathbf{I}| = 0 \tag{51}$$

The λ_k's are called the *eigenvalues* of the matrix. (See Appendix 3.) Further, the set of N vectors $\mathbf{v}_k$ such that

$$\mathbf{A}\mathbf{v}_k = \lambda_k \mathbf{v}_k \tag{52}$$

are called the *eigenvectors* of $\mathbf{A}$. They are N by 1, and each corresponds to one of the eigenvalues. The eigenvectors form an orthonormal basis set.

13.6.2 Principal-Component Analysis

Hotelling developed a linear transformation that removes the correlation among the elements of a random vector and called it "the method of principal components" [22]. Later, Karhunen [23] and Loéve [24] developed an analogous transformation for continuous signals. This approach leads to, among other things, a discrete image transform.

Suppose $\mathbf{x}$ is an N-by-1 random vector; that is, each element x_i of $\mathbf{x}$ is a random variable. The mean vector of $\mathbf{x}$ can be estimated from a sample of L such vectors by

$$\mathbf{m_x} \approx \frac{1}{L}\sum_{l=1}^{L}\mathbf{x}_l \tag{53}$$

and its covariance matrix by

$$\mathbf{C_x} = \mathcal{E}\{(\mathbf{x}-\mathbf{m_x})(\mathbf{x}-\mathbf{m_x})^t\} \approx \frac{1}{L}\sum_{l=1}^{L}\mathbf{x}_l\mathbf{x}_l^t - \mathbf{m_x}\mathbf{m_x}^t \tag{54}$$

The covariance matrix is N by N, real, and symmetric. The diagonal elements are the variances of the individual random variables, while the off-diagonal elements are their covariances.

Now let the matrix $\mathbf{A}$ define a linear transformation that generates a new vector $\mathbf{y}$ from any vector $\mathbf{x}$ by

$$\mathbf{y} = \mathbf{A}(\mathbf{x}-\mathbf{m_x}) \tag{55}$$

where $\mathbf{A}$ is constructed so that its rows are the eigenvectors of $\mathbf{C_x}$. For convenience, we arrange the rows in order of decreasing magnitude of the corresponding eigenvalues.

The transformed vector, $\mathbf{y}$, is a random vector with zero mean. Its covariance matrix is related to that of $\mathbf{x}$ by

$$\mathbf{C_y} = \mathbf{A}\mathbf{C_x}\mathbf{A}^t \tag{56}$$

Since the rows of $\mathbf{A}$ are eigenvectors of $\mathbf{C_x}$, $\mathbf{C_y}$ is a diagonal matrix having the eigenvalues of $\mathbf{C_x}$ along its diagonal. (This is a result of Eq. (52).) Thus,

$$\mathbf{C_y} = \begin{bmatrix} \lambda_1 & & 0 \\ & \ddots & \\ 0 & & \lambda_N \end{bmatrix} \tag{57}$$

and the λ_k are the eigenvalues of $\mathbf{C_y}$ as well.

Because the off-diagonal elements of $\mathbf{C_y}$ are zero, the elements of $\mathbf{y}$ are uncorrelated. Thus, the linear transformation $\mathbf{A}$ removes the correlation among the variables. Furthermore, each λ_k is the variance of y_k, the kth transformed variable.

Notice that the transform of Eq. (55) is invertible; that is, we can reconstruct a vector $\mathbf{x}$ from its transformed vector $\mathbf{y}$ by

$$\mathbf{x} = \mathbf{A}^{-1}\mathbf{y} + \mathbf{m} = \mathbf{A}^t\mathbf{y} + \mathbf{m} \tag{58}$$

The latter equality holds because $\mathbf{A}$ is unitary and real, and thus orthogonal.

13.6.2.1 Dimension Reduction

We can reduce the dimensionality of the $\mathbf{y}$ vectors by ignoring one or more of the eigenvectors that have small eigenvalues. Let $\mathbf{B}$ be the M-by-N matrix ($M < N$) formed by discarding the lower $N - M$ rows of $\mathbf{A}$, and assume, for simplicity, that $\mathbf{m} = \mathbf{0}$. Then the transformed vectors are smaller (i.e., M by 1) and are given by

$$\hat{\mathbf{y}} = \mathbf{B}\mathbf{x} \tag{59}$$

but the $\mathbf{x}$ vectors can still be reconstructed (approximately) by

$$\hat{\mathbf{x}} = \mathbf{B}^t\hat{\mathbf{y}} \tag{60}$$

The mean square error of this approximation is

$$MSE = \sum_{k=M+1}^{N} \lambda_k \tag{61}$$

that is, simply the sum of the eigenvalues corresponding to the discarded eigenvectors. Normally the eigenvalues vary considerably in magnitude, and the smaller ones can be ignored without the introduction of significant error.

13.6.3 The Karhunen-Loéve Transform

Eq. (55) defines a (one-dimensional) discrete transform. It is variously called the Karhunen-Loéve (or K-L) transform, the Hotelling transform, the eigenvector transform, or the method of principal components. We adhere to the common practice in the literature of calling it the K-L transform.

The dimension-reducing capability of the K-L transform makes it quite useful for image compression. Multispectral images, for example, have many gray-level values at every pixel, each gray-level corresponding to a different spectral band. Thus, a 1,000-by-1,000 24-channel multispectral image can be viewed as a set of one million 24-element random vectors (i.e., the pixels).

The K-L dimension-reducing technique can be applied to this set of vectors. Since the correlation between the different spectral bands of a multispectral image is commonly rather high, many of the 24 eigenvalues will be small. This means that the stack of 24 monochrome images can be represented with small error by only a few principal component images. Each of these is computed as a weighted sum of the original 24. Further, each image in the original set can be reconstructed, approximately, as a linear combination of the few principal-component images. This greatly simplifies the storage and distribution of, for example, images taken from Earth satellites.

In general, the basis images of the two-dimensional K-L transform depend upon the statistics of the particular image being transformed and cannot be written explicitly. If the image is a first-order Markov process, however, where the correlation between pixels decreases linearly with their separation distance, then the basis images for the K-L transform can be written explicitly [5,25]. The Markov assumption often fits commonly encountered images quite well. Further, as the correlation between adjacent pixels approaches unity, the K-L basis functions approach those of the discrete cosine transform [1,26]. Thus, the DCT, which is easily computed, approximates the K-L transform for commonly encountered images.

13.6.4 The SVD Transform

Any N-by-N matrix $\mathbf{A}$ can be expressed as

$$\mathbf{A} = \mathbf{U}\Lambda\mathbf{V}^t \tag{62}$$

where the columns of $\mathbf{U}$ and $\mathbf{V}$ are the eigenvectors of $\mathbf{AA}^t$, and $\mathbf{A}^t\mathbf{A}$ respectively, and Λ is an N-by-N diagonal matrix containing the *singular values* of $\mathbf{A}$ along its diagonal. (See Appendix 3 for more complete coverage of the topic.) Since $\mathbf{U}$ and $\mathbf{V}$ are orthogonal,

$$\Lambda = \mathbf{U}^t\mathbf{A}\mathbf{V} \tag{63}$$

Eq. (63) is thus the forward, and Eq. (62) the inverse, of a unitary transform pair. This transform is called *singular value decomposition* (SVD) transform [27]. If $\mathbf{A}$ is symmetric, $\mathbf{U} = \mathbf{V}$.

Notice that, unlike the transforms discussed in earlier sections, the kernel matrices $\mathbf{U}$ and $\mathbf{V}$ depend on the image $\mathbf{A}$ being transformed. In general, one must compute the eigenvectors of $\mathbf{A}\mathbf{A}^t$ and $\mathbf{A}^t\mathbf{A}$ for each image undergoing the transformation.

Notice also that since Λ is a diagonal matrix, it has at most N nonzero elements. Thus, we get lossless compression by at least a factor of N, and it will be greater than that if $\mathbf{A}$ has some zero (or negligible) singular values. Hence, the additional computation brings with it significant data compression.

Normally, several of the singular values are small enough to be ignored with little error. Thus "lossy" compression is achieved by ignoring the smaller $\Lambda_{i,i}$ values. The mean square error that results from this truncation is simply the sum of those singular values that are ignored.

The apparently miraculous compression power of the SVD transform is somewhat misleading. Although the entire image can be compressed into the diagonal elements of Λ, the kernel matrices $\mathbf{U}$ and $\mathbf{V}$ are unique for the image being compressed. These would have to be transmitted, along with the image, before reconstruction could occur at the receiving end. Possibly, however, one pair of kernal matrices could serve (approximately) for a group of similar images.

A Numerical Example. The SVD transform is illustrated in Figure 13–7, using a symmetric five-by-five pixel image.

$$A = \begin{bmatrix} 0 & 1 & 2 & 1 & 0 \\ 1 & 3 & 4 & 3 & 1 \\ 2 & 4 & 5 & 4 & 2 \\ 1 & 3 & 4 & 3 & 1 \\ 0 & 1 & 2 & 1 & 0 \end{bmatrix} \quad A \cdot A^t = \begin{bmatrix} 6 & 14 & 18 & 14 & 6 \\ 14 & 36 & 48 & 36 & 14 \\ 18 & 48 & 65 & 48 & 18 \\ 14 & 36 & 48 & 36 & 14 \\ 6 & 14 & 18 & 14 & 6 \end{bmatrix} \quad \lambda = \begin{bmatrix} 147.07 \\ 1.872 \\ 0.058 \\ 0 \\ 0 \end{bmatrix} \quad U = \begin{bmatrix} 0.186 & 0.638 & 0.241 & -0.695 & -0.695 \\ 0.476 & 0.058 & -0.52 & -0.133 & -0.128 \\ 0.691 & -0.422 & 0.587 & 0 & 0 \\ 0.476 & 0.058 & -0.52 & 0.133 & 0.128 \\ 0.186 & 0.638 & 0.241 & 0.695 & 0.695 \end{bmatrix}$$

$$\Lambda = U^tAU = \begin{bmatrix} 12.585 & 0 & 0 & 0 & 0 \\ 0 & -1.142 & 0 & 0 & 0 \\ 0 & 0 & 0.557 & 0 & 0 \\ 0 & 0 & 0 & 0 & 0 \\ 0 & 0 & 0 & 0 & 0 \end{bmatrix} \qquad A = U\Lambda U^t = \begin{bmatrix} 0 & 1 & 2 & 1 & 0 \\ 1 & 3 & 4 & 3 & 1 \\ 2 & 4 & 6 & 4 & 2 \\ 1 & 3 & 4 & 3 & 1 \\ 0 & 1 & 2 & 1 & 0 \end{bmatrix}$$

Forward transform | Inverse transform

Figure 13–7 The SVD transform of a symmetric five-by-five pixel image

13.7 TRANSFORM DOMAIN FILTERING

In Chapter 10, we saw that linear filtering—the action of a linear, shift-invariant system—can be modeled as a multiplication of the Fourier spectrum of an image by a transfer function defined in the frequency (i.e., transform) domain. While this important result is true only for the Fourier transform, analogous image-filtering operations can be defined for other transforms as well.

Like the Fourier transform, the general unitary transform expands an image as a weighted sum of basis images. The forward transformation process determines the weighting coefficients, while the inverse transformation reassembles the image from the expansion of the basis images.

Transform domain filtering involves modification of the weighting coefficients prior to reconstruction of the image via the inverse transform. With linear filtering, the transform is the Fourier transform, and the modification is effected by multiplying the spectrum by a transfer function. In the more general filtering case, the coefficient matrix is modified (by multiplication or other means) and the inverse transform produces the filtered image.

Clearly, it is the nature of the basis vectors (and of the resulting basis images) that establishes the different behavior of the various transforms. For example, sinusoidal noise contamination appears very compactly in the transform domain of a sinusoidal transform (recall Figure 10–8) and is thus easily removed by setting the corresponding coefficients to zero. The rectangular-wave transforms would be less well suited for this noise removal problem, since the contamination would not be as separable from the signal in their transform domains.

In general, if either the (desirable) signal components or the (undesirable) noise components of the image resemble one or a few of the basis images of a particular transform, then that transform will be useful in separating the two. This is because those components will be represented compactly in the transform domain. The general statement applies to problems of noise removal and signal detection as well.

The Haar transform, for example, is a good candidate for detecting vertical and horizontal lines and edges, since several of its basis images specifically match such features.

13.7.1 Edge, Line, and Spot Detection

Figure 13–8 illustrates the edge-detecting ability of the Haar transform on an eight-by-eight image. Since the transform is separable, an image feature that is a vertical or horizontal line

$$\begin{bmatrix} 1 & 1 & 1 & 1 & 1 & 1 & 1 & 1 \\ 1 & 1 & 1 & 1 & 1 & 1 & 1 & 1 \\ 0 & 0 & 0 & 0 & 0 & 0 & 0 & 0 \\ 0 & 0 & 0 & 0 & 0 & 0 & 0 & 0 \\ 0 & 0 & 0 & 0 & 0 & 0 & 0 & 0 \\ 0 & 0 & 0 & 0 & 0 & 0 & 0 & 0 \\ 0 & 0 & 0 & 0 & 0 & 0 & 0 & 0 \\ 0 & 0 & 0 & 0 & 0 & 0 & 0 & 0 \end{bmatrix} \longrightarrow \begin{bmatrix} 2 & 0 & 0 & 0 & 0 & 0 & 0 & 0 \\ 2 & 0 & 0 & 0 & 0 & 0 & 0 & 0 \\ 2.83 & 0 & 0 & 0 & 0 & 0 & 0 & 0 \\ 0 & 0 & 0 & 0 & 0 & 0 & 0 & 0 \\ 0 & 0 & 0 & 0 & 0 & 0 & 0 & 0 \\ 0 & 0 & 0 & 0 & 0 & 0 & 0 & 0 \\ 0 & 0 & 0 & 0 & 0 & 0 & 0 & 0 \\ 0 & 0 & 0 & 0 & 0 & 0 & 0 & 0 \end{bmatrix}$$

Image Harr transform

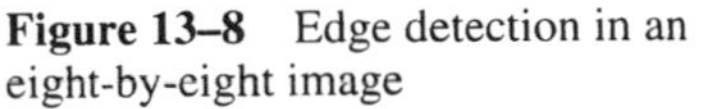

Figure 13–8 Edge detection in an eight-by-eight image

or edge produces nonzero entries in only the first row and the first column of the transform image, respectively.

In the Haar transform, the feature produces at most $N/2$ non-zero entries. The position of the feature determines which (and how many) of the entries are nonzero. In the other transforms, all N entries of the first row or column are, in general, nonzero.

Figure 13–9 shows several transforms of an image containing a single-pixel spike (impulse). All N^2 elements of these transforms are nonzero except for those of the Haar transform, which has only $2N$ nonzero entries. Again, the location of the nonzero entries is determined by the position of the spike.

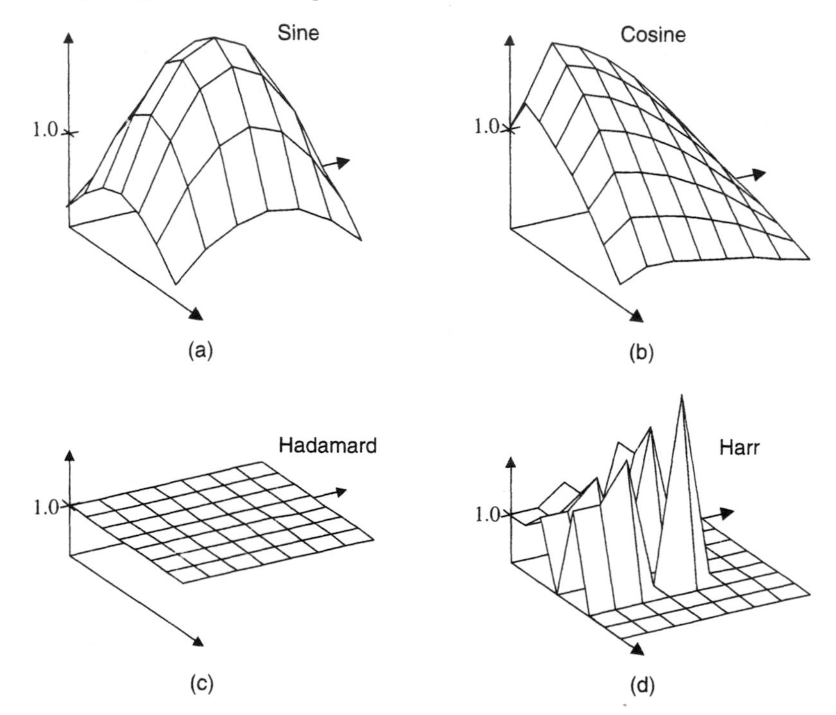

Figure 13–9 Transforms of an image containing an impulse: (a) DST; (b) DCT; (c) Hadamard: (d) Haar. The input is an eight-by-eight matrix, zero everywhere except the upper left element, which has value eight

13.7.2 Filter Design

Because of its close association with shift-invariant linear systems, the Fourier transform has a well-developed theoretical background to guide its use in image-filtering applications. The other transforms are less well supported in theory, and their use is often more experimental. An understanding of the similarities and differences among these transforms helps guide the search for workable solutions.

13.8 SUMMARY OF IMPORTANT POINTS

1. The rows of an N-by-N transformation matrix are a set or orthonormal basis vectors for an N-dimensional vector space.

2. A unitary linear transformation generates a vector of *N transform coefficients*, each of which is the inner product of the input vector with one of the rows of the transform matrix.
3. The inverse transform is formed similarly, by inner products of the transform coefficient vector with the rows of the inverse transform matrix.
4. The inverse transform can also be viewed as forming a weighted summation of the basis vectors, where the transform coefficients are the weights.
5. For a two-dimensional symmetric, separable unitary transformation, the basis images are the outer products of the rows of the transform matrix.

PROBLEMS

1. The eigenvalues of an eight-channel multispectral image are [6.1 168 0.08 13 64 214 1.2 0.2]. What will be the RMS error if you use principal component analysis for 2:1 data compression?
2. Design an 8 by 8 Haar transform filter mask that will remove small horizontal edges from an image.

PROJECTS

1. Develop a program that implements the discrete cosine transform, and use the program to demonstrate highpass filtering for image enhancement.
2. Develop a program that implements the discrete Hartley transform, and use the program to demonstrate lowpass filtering for noise reduction.
3. Develop a program that uses principal-component analysis to reduce a 24-bit-per-pixel color image to a 16-bit-per-pixel representation and back. Produce demonstration images, and comment upon the resulting degradation.
4. Develop a program that implements the slant transform, and use the program to demonstrate the removal of linear shading.
5. Develop a program that implements the Haar transform, and use the program to show the edges in an image.

REFERENCES

For further reading on topics relating to image transforms, see Appendix 2.

1. N. Ahmed, T. Natarajan, and K. R. Rao, "Discrete Cosine Transforms," *IEEE Trans. Comp.*, **C-23**:90–93, 1974.
2. M. J. Narasimha and A. M. Peterson, "On the Computation of the Discrete Cosine Transform," *IEEE Trans. Commun.*, **COM-26,** 6:934–936, 1978.
3. W. H. Chen, C. H. Smith, and S. C. Fralick, "A Fast Computational Algorithm for the Discrete Cosine Transform," *IEEE Trans. Commun.*, **COM-25,** 1004–1009, 1977.
4. A. K. Jain, "A Fast Karhunen-Loéve Transforms for a Class of Random Processes," *IEEE Trans. Commun.*, **COM-24,** 1023–1029, 1975.
5. A. K. Jain, *Fundamentals of Digital Image Processing,* Prentice-Hall, Englewood Cliffs, NJ, 1989.
6. P. Yip and K. R. Rao, "A Fast Computational Algorithm for the Discrete Sine Transform," *IEEE Trans. Commun.*, **COM-28**(2), 304–307, 1980.

7. R. V. L. Hartley, "A More Symmetrical Fourier Analysis Applied to Transmission Problems," *Proc. IRE,* **30:**144–150, 1942.

8. R. M. Bracewell, "The Discrete Hartley Transform," *J. Opt. Soc. Am.,* **73**(12):1832–1835, 1983.

9. R. M. Bracewell, *The Fourier Transform and Its Applications* (2d ed.), McGraw-Hill, New York, 1986.

10. A. K. Jain, "A Sinusoidal Family of Unitary Transforms," *IEEE Trans. Pattern Anal. Machine Intell.,* **PAMI-1**(4):356–365, 1979.

11. J. Hadamard, "Resolution d'une Question Relative aux Determinants," *Bull. Sci. Math.,* Ser. 2, **17,** Part I, 240–246, 1893.

12. J. E. Whelchel, Jr., and D. F. Guinn, "The Fast Fourier-Hadamard Transform and its Use in Signal Representation and Classification," *EASCON 1968 Convention Record,* 561–573, 1968.

13. W. K. Pratt, H. C. Andrews, and J. Kane, "Hadamard Transform Image Coding," *Proc. IEEE,* **57**(1):58–68, 1969.

14. H. Kitajima, "Energy Packing Efficiency of the Hadamard Transform," *IEEE Trans. Comm.* (correspondence), **COM-24,** 1256–1258.

15. J. Williamson, "Hadamard's Determinant Theorem and the Sum of Four Squares," *Duke Math. J.,* **11:**65–81, 1944.

16. H. F. Harmuth, "A Generalization Concept of Frequency and Some Applications," *IEEE Trans. Info. Theory,* **IT-14**(3):375–382, 1968.

17. J. L. Walsh, "A Closed Set of Normal Orthogonal Functions," *Am. J. Math.,* **45**(1):5–24, 1923.

18. W. K. Pratt, W. H. Chen, and L. R. Welch, "Slant Transform Image Coding," *IEEE Trans. Comm.,* **COM-22**(8):1075–1093, 1974.

19. A. Haar, "Zur Theorie der Orthogonalen Funktionen-System," Inaugural Dissertation, *Math. Annalen,* **5**:17–31, 1955.

20. H. C. Andrews, *Computer Techniques in Image Processing,* Academic Press, New York, 1970.

21. J. E. Shore, "On the Application of Haar Functions," *IEEE Trans. Comm.,* **COM-21,** 209–216, 1973.

22. H. Hotelling, "Analysis of a Complex of Statistical Variables into Principal Components," *J. Educ. Psychol.,* 24, 417–441, 498–520, 1933.

23. K. Karhunen, "Über Lineare Methoden in der Wahrscheinlich-Keitsrechnung," *Ann. Acad. Sci. Fennicae,* Ser. A.I.37 (English translation by I. Selin, "On Linear Methods in Probability Theory," Doc. T-131, The RAND Corp., Santa Monica, CA, 1960), 1947.

24. M. Loéve, "Fonctions Aléatoires de Second Ordre," in P. Lévy, *Processus Stochastiques et Mouvement Brownien,* Hermann, Paris, 1948.

25. W. K. Pratt, *Digital Image Processing* (2d ed.), John Wiley & Sons, New York, 1991.

26. R. J. Clark, *Transform Coding of Images,* Academic Press, New York, 1985.

27. G. H. Golub and C. Reinsch, "Singular Value Decomposition and Least Squares Solutions," *Numer. Math.,* **14,** 403–420, 1970.

CHAPTER 14

Wavelet Transforms

14.1 INTRODUCTION

Considerable interest has arisen in recent years regarding new transform techniques that specifically address the problems of image compression, edge and feature detection, and texture analysis. These techniques come under the headings of multiresolution analysis, time-frequency analysis, pyramid algorithms, and wavelet transforms [1].

In this chapter, we review some of the limitations of the traditional Fourier and similar transforms and define three types of wavelet transforms that promise improved performance for certain applications. We trace some of the developments that have led to the current state of wavelet analysis, noting the similarities that tend to unify these different approaches under the banner of *wavelet transforms*. Later in the chapter, we illustrate some of the applications of wavelet transforms.

We restrict ourselves to transforming real-valued, measurable, square-integrable functions of one and two dimensions, since these encompass the signals and images that are of interest to us. As before, we introduce each concept in one dimension for simplicity and then generalize it to two dimensions for application to images. We begin by introducing the three basic types of wavelet transforms. Then we illustrate some particular wavelets and some applications of wavelet transforms.

14.1.1 Waves and Wavelets

Recall that the Fourier transform uses, as its orthonormal basis functions, sinusoidal *waves*, so called because they resemble the waves of the ocean and propagating waves in other media. For the integral transform, these functions extend to infinity in both directions. The basis vectors of the discrete Fourier transform are also nonzero over their entire domain; that is, they do not have *compact support.*

By contrast, *transient* signal components are nonzero only during a short interval. Likewise, many important features in images (edges, for example) are highly localized in spatial position. Such components do not resemble any of the Fourier basis functions, and they are not represented compactly in the transform coefficients (i.e., the frequency spectrum), as discussed subsequently. This makes the Fourier and other wave transforms, such as those mentioned in the previous chapter, less than optimal representations for compressing and analyzing signals and images containing transient or localized components.

In fairness, we note that the Fourier transform can represent any analytic function—even a narrow transient signal—as a sum of sinusoids. It does this, however, by intricately arranging for the cancellation of sine waves (by destructive interference) to create a function that is zero over most of the interval. This is, of course, a valid way for an invertible transform to behave, but it leaves the spectrum a rather confusing picture of the function.

To combat such a deficiency, mathematicians and engineers have explored several approaches using transforms having basis functions of limited duration. These basis functions vary in position as well as frequency. They are waves of limited duration and are referred to as *wavelets.* Transforms based on them are called *wavelet transforms.* They are also called *ondelettes* in the considerable amount of French-language literature on the subject.

Figure 14–1 illustrates the difference between waves and wavelets. The top two curves are cosine waves that differ in frequency, but not in duration. The lower two are wavelets that differ in both frequency and position along the axis.

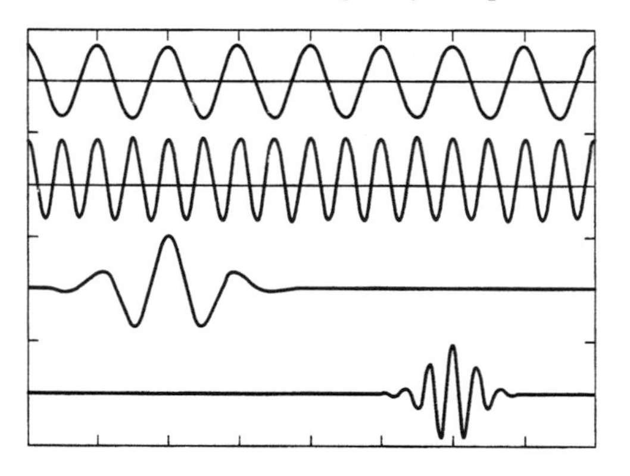

Figure 14–1 Waves and wavelets

The Haar transform (see Sec. 13.5.4) is the earliest example of what we now call a wavelet transform [2]. It differs from the other transforms in Chapter 13 in that its basis vectors are all generated by translations and scalings of a single function. The Haar function, which is an odd rectangular pulse pair, is the oldest and simplest wavelet.

14.1.2 Time-Frequency Analysis

The literature on signal processing includes considerable work regarding analyzing signals in terms of a two-dimensional *time-frequency* space. This approach actually preceded wavelet transforms, but it now fits into the same modern framework. According to it, each transient component of a signal maps to a position in the time-frequency plane that corresponds to that component's predominant frequency and time of occurrence (Figure 14–2).

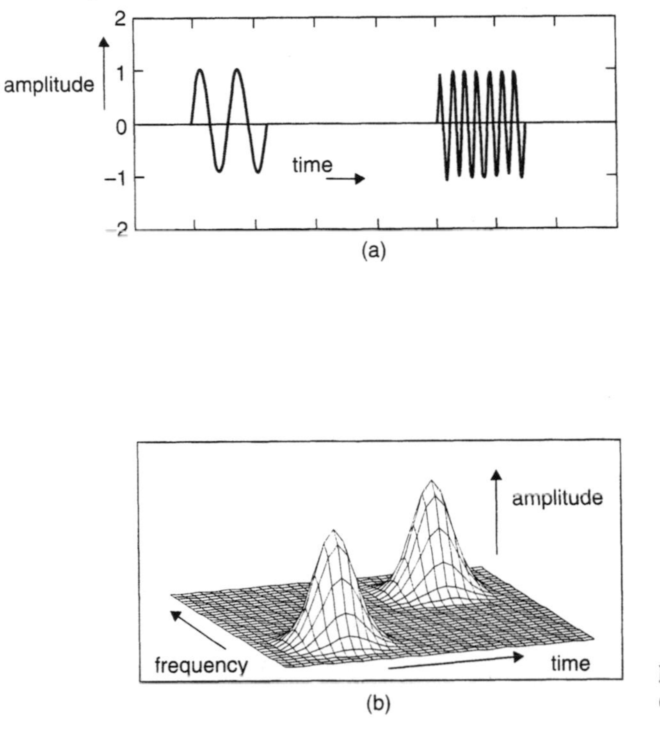

Figure 14–2 Time frequency space: (a) signal; (b) representation

In image analysis, the space is three dimensional and can be viewed as an image stack. A localized component will appear primarily at the level in the stack that corresponds to the component's predominant frequency. Figure 14–3 shows an image containing two localized components being submitted to two bandpass filters. In this case the two filters almost completely isolate the two components.

This approach began with Gabor's [3] *windowed Fourier transform,* and led to the *short-time Fourier transform* (STFT) and then to *subband coding.*

14.1.2.1 Wavelets and Music

Consider the musical notation shown in Figure 14–4. It can be viewed as depicting a two-dimensional time-frequency space. Frequency (pitch) increases from the bottom of the scale to the top, while time (measured in beats) advances to the right. Each note on the sheet music corresponds to one wavelet component (tone burst) that would appear in the recording of a performance of the song. The duration of each wavelet is coded by the type of note (e.g., quarter note, half note, etc.), rather than by its horizontal extent.

If we were to analyze a recorded musical performance and write out the corresponding score, we would have a type of wavelet transform. Similarly, a recording of a musician's performance of a song can be viewed as an inverse wavelet transform, since it reconstructs the signal from a time-frequency representation.

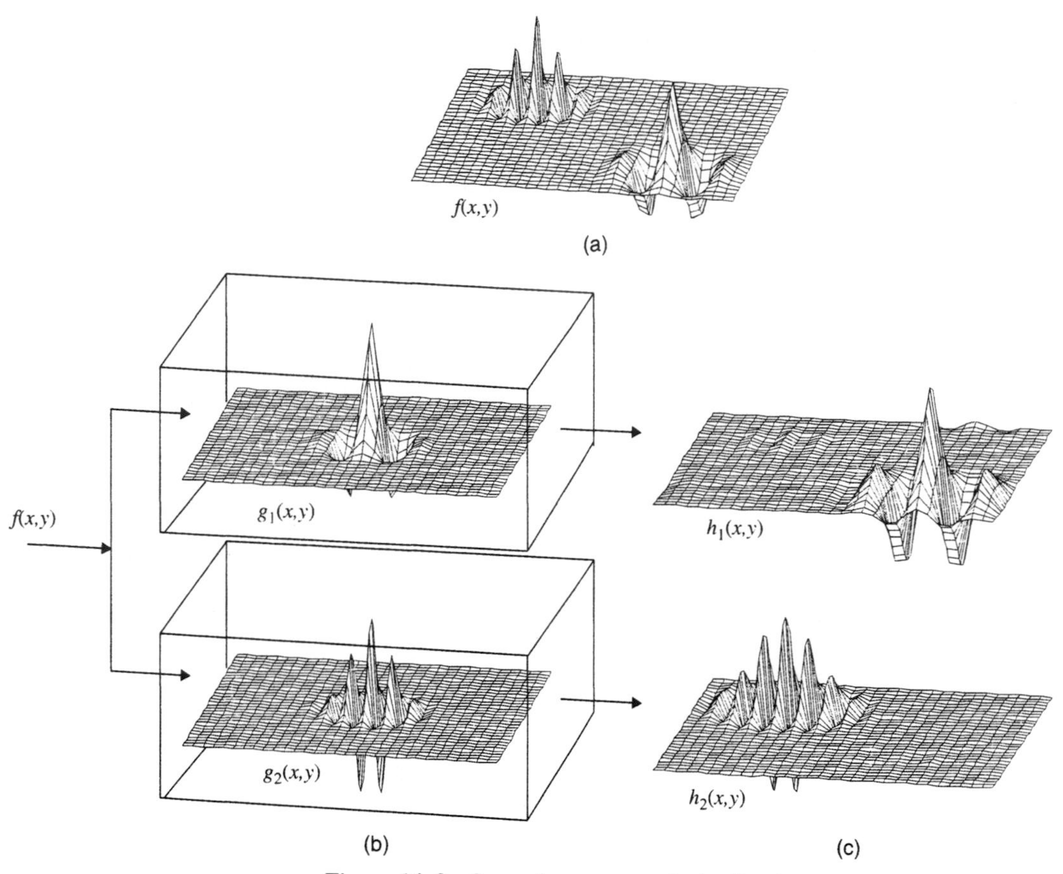

Figure 14–3 Space-frequency analysis of an image

Figure 14–4 Musical notation as a time-frequency plane

14.1.3 Transforms

Recall that each of the coefficients in a transform is determined by taking an inner product between the input function and one of the basis functions. This value represents, in some sense, the degree of similarity between the input function and that particular basis function. If the basis functions are orthogonal (or orthonormal), then an inner product taken between two basis functions is zero, indicating that these are all completely dissimilar. So if the signal or image is made up of components that are similar to one, or a few, of the basis functions, then all but one or a few of the coefficients will be small.

Similarly, the inverse transform can be viewed as reconstructing the original signal or image by summing basis functions that are weighted in amplitude by the transform coefficients. So if the signal or image is made up of components that are similar to one or a few of the basis functions, then this summation needs to have only a few terms of significant amplitude. Many of the terms can then be ignored, and the signal or image can be represented compactly by only a few transform coefficients.

Further, if the components of interest in the signal or image are similar to one or a few of the basis functions, then those components will manifest themselves in large coefficients for those (and only those) basis functions. They will thus be "easy to find" in the transform. Finally, if an undesirable (noise) component is similar to one or a few basis functions, then it, too, will be easy to find. It will be also easy to remove, simply by reducing (or setting to zero) the corresponding transform coefficients.

We conclude from all of this that there is potential value in using transforms with basis functions that are similar to the expected components of the signals or images to be transformed. We also note that transient components cannot be similar to the basis functions of the Fourier or other wave-type transforms.

14.1.3.1 Types of Transforms

Recall from Chapter 10 that there are three different, but related Fourier transformation techniques: the Fourier integral transform, the Fourier series expansion, and the DFT.

The Fourier integral transform associates two continuous functions (a signal and its spectrum). It and its inverse are given in one dimension by

$$F(s) = \int_{-\infty}^{\infty} f(x)e^{-j2\pi(xs)}dx \quad \text{and} \quad f(x) = \int_{-\infty}^{\infty} F(s)e^{j2\pi(xs)}ds \tag{1}$$

The Fourier series expansion represents a periodic function (or a transient function that can be considered to be one cycle of a periodic function) as a (finite or infinite) sequence of Fourier coefficients. It and its inverse are obtained by making $s = n\Delta s$ a discrete variable, so that

$$F_n = F(n\Delta s) = \int_0^L f(x)e^{-j2\pi(n\Delta sx)}dx \quad \text{and} \quad f(x) = \Delta s\sum_{n=0}^{\infty} F_n e^{j2\pi(n\Delta sx)} \tag{2}$$

where L is the period and $\Delta s = 1/L$.

The DFT represents a sampled function by a sampled spectrum, and the number of independent samples (degrees of freedom) is the same in both domains. It is obtained by making $x = i\Delta x$ a discrete variable as well. If $g(x)$ is bandlimited and sampled as required by the sampling theorem (Sec. 12.2.4), then $g_i = g(i\Delta x)$, and

$$G_k = \frac{1}{\sqrt{N}}\sum_{i=0}^{N-1} g_i e^{-j2\pi k\frac{i}{N}} \quad \text{and} \quad g_i = \frac{1}{\sqrt{N}}\sum_{k=0}^{N-1} G_k e^{j2\pi i\frac{k}{N}} \tag{3}$$

In all three transformation techniques, sines and cosines of different frequencies form a set of orthonormal basis functions. Also, each transform coefficient is determined by an inner product of the function being transformed and one of the basis functions. A discrete inner product and discrete basis functions are used for the DFT, while an integral inner product and continuous basis functions serve for the other two transforms. In each case, the inverse transform consists of summing basis functions whose amplitudes are weighted by the transform coefficients. This summation becomes an integral for the continuous Fourier transform.

The discrete transforms discussed in the previous chapter also use discrete orthonormal basis functions. Thus, they behave in a manner generally similar to the way the DFT behaves. For most of them, the basis functions are real and the forward and inverse transforms are identical.

14.1.3.2 Types of Wavelet Transforms

As with the Fourier transform, the same three possibilities exist for wavelet transforms: a continuous wavelet transform (CWT), a wavelet series expansion, and a discrete wavelet transform (DWT). The situation is slightly more complex, however, since the wavelet basis functions may or may not be orthonormal.

A set of wavelet basis functions can support a transform even if the functions are not orthonormal. This means, for example, that a wavelet series expansion might represent a bandlimited function by infinitely many coefficients. If this sequence of coefficients is truncated to finite length, then we can reconstruct only an approximation of the original function. Likewise, a discrete wavelet transform might require more coefficients than the original function has sample points in order to reconstruct it exactly, or even to an acceptable approximation.

14.1.3.3 Notation and Definitions

Next, we introduce some definitions to clarify the concept of a wavelet transform. For the present, we restrict the discussion primarily to transforming functions of one dimension.

In order to conform with the bulk of the literature on wavelets we use j as an integer index in this chapter. As elsewhere in the book, we also use j to represent the imaginary unit $\sqrt{-1}$, taking care not to use it both ways in the same equation. The distinction should be clear from the context.

The class of functions we seek to represent by a wavelet transform is those that are square integrable on the real line (i.e., the set of all real numbers—the x-axis). This class is denoted as $L^2(R)$. Thus, the notation $f(x) \in L^2(R)$ means

$$\int_{-\infty}^{\infty} |f(x)|^2 dx < \infty \tag{4}$$

In wavelet analysis, we generate a set of basis functions by dilating and translating a single prototype function, $\psi(x)$, which we call a *basic wavelet.* This is some oscillatory function, usually centered upon the origin, that dies out rapidly as $|x| \to \infty$. Thus, $\psi(x) \in L^2(R)$.

14.2 THE CONTINUOUS WAVELET TRANSFORM

The continuous wavelet transform (also called the integral wavelet transform) was introduced by Grossman and Morlet [4].

14.2.1 Definition

If $\psi(x)$ is a real-valued function whose Fourier spectrum, $\Psi(s)$, satisfies the *admissibility criterion* [4,5]

$$C_\psi = \int_{-\infty}^{\infty} \frac{|\Psi(s)|^2}{|s|} ds < \infty \tag{5}$$

then $\psi(x)$ is called a *basic wavelet.* Notice that, due to the s in the denominator of the integrand, it is necessary that

$$\Psi(0) = 0 \Rightarrow \int_{-\infty}^{\infty} \psi(x) dx = 0 \tag{6}$$

Furthermore, since $\Psi(\infty) = 0$ as well, we can see that the amplitude spectrum of an admissible wavelet is similar to the transfer function of a bandpass filter. In fact, any bandpass filter impulse response with zero mean [Eq. (6)] that decays to zero fast enough with increasing frequency [Eq. (5)] can serve as a basic wavelet for this transform.

A set of wavelet basis functions, $\{\psi_{a,b}(x)\}$, can be generated by translating and scaling the basic wavelet, $\psi(x)$, as

$$\psi_{a,b}(x) = \frac{1}{\sqrt{a}} \psi\left(\frac{x-b}{a}\right) \tag{7}$$

where $a > 0$ and b are real numbers. The variable a reflects the scale (width) of a particular basis function, while b specifies its translated position along the x-axis.

Normally the basic wavelet, $\psi(x)$, is centered at the origin, so that $\psi_{a,b}(x)$ is centered at $x = b$. Figure 14–5 shows an example of such a wavelet. This particular one is given by

$$\psi(x) = \frac{2}{\sqrt{3\sqrt{\pi}}}(1 - x^2)e^{-x^2/2} \tag{8}$$

The *continuous wavelet transform* of $f(x)$ with respect to the wavelet $\psi(x)$ is then [4,5]

$$W_f(a, b) = \langle f, \psi_{a,b} \rangle = \int_{-\infty}^{\infty} f(x) \psi_{a,b}(x) dx \tag{9}$$

The wavelet transform coefficients are once again given as inner products of the function being transformed with each of the basis functions.

Grossman and Morlet [4] showed that the inverse continuous wavelet transform is

$$f(x) = \frac{1}{C_\psi} \int_0^{\infty} \int_{-\infty}^{\infty} W_f(a, b) \psi_{a,b}(x) db \frac{da}{a^2} \tag{10}$$

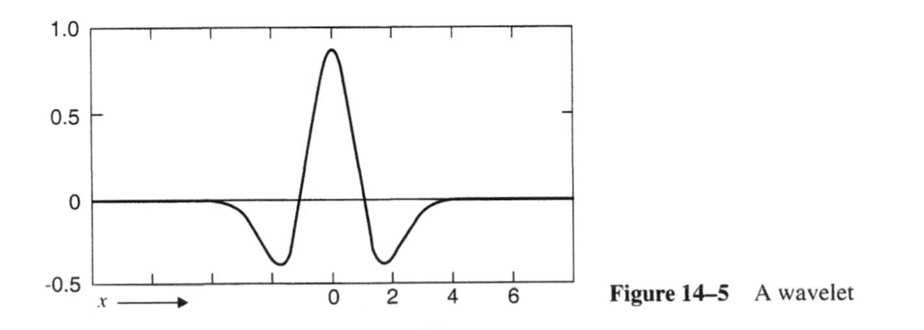

Figure 14–5 A wavelet

The scale factor in front of the right-hand side of Eq. (7) ensures that the norms of the wavelet basis functions are all equal, since

$$\left\| f\left(\frac{x-b}{a}\right) \right\| = \sqrt{\int_{-\infty}^{\infty} \left| f\left(\frac{x-b}{a}\right) \right|^2 dx} = \sqrt{a} \| f(x) \| \tag{11}$$

Since the basic wavelet has zero mean [Eq. (6)], all scalings and translations of it [Eq. (7)] will likewise have zero mean, and the mean of $f(x)$ must be accounted for separately.

14.2.2 The Two-Dimensional CWT

The continuous wavelet transform $W(a,b)$ of a one-dimensional function $f(x)$ is a function of two variables, one more than $f(x)$. The CWT is said to be *overcomplete,* as it represents a considerable increase in information content and in the volume required for data storage. For functions of more than one variable, this transform also increases the dimensionality by one.

If $f(x, y)$ is a function of two dimensions, its continuous wavelet transform is

$$W_f(a, b_x, b_y) = \int_{-\infty}^{\infty} \int_{-\infty}^{\infty} f(x, y) \psi_{a, b_x, b_y}(x, y) dx\, dy \tag{12}$$

where b_x and b_y specify the translation in two dimensions. The inverse two-dimensional continuous wavelet transform is

$$f(x, y) = \frac{1}{C_\psi} \int_0^{\infty} \int_{-\infty}^{\infty} \int_{-\infty}^{\infty} W_f(a, b_x, b_y) \psi_{a, b_x, b_y}(x, y)\, db_x db_y \frac{da}{a^3} \tag{13}$$

where

$$\psi_{a, b_x, b_y}(x, y) = \frac{1}{|a|} \psi\left(\frac{x-b_x}{a}, \frac{y-b_y}{a}\right) \tag{14}$$

and $\psi(x, y)$ is a two-dimensional basic wavelet. The same generalization extends to cover functions of more than two variables.

14.2.3 The Filter Bank Interpretation

The following exercise illustrates one way of viewing the continuous wavelet transform. We first define the general wavelet basis function at scale a as

$$\psi_a(x) = \frac{1}{\sqrt{a}} \psi\left(\frac{x}{a}\right) \tag{15}$$

This is the basic wavelet scaled by a and normalized by $a^{-1/2}$. It defines a set of functions that become broader with increasing a. We also define

$$\breve{\psi}_a(x) = \psi_a^*(-x) = \frac{1}{\sqrt{a}} \psi^*\left(-\frac{x}{a}\right) \tag{16}$$

which is the reflected complex conjugate of the scaled wavelet. If $\psi(x)$ is real and even, as is often the case, the reflection and conjugation have no effect.

Now we can write the continuous wavelet transform [Eq. (9)] as

$$W_f(a, b) = \int_{-\infty}^{\infty} f(x)\breve{\psi}_a(b - x)dx = f * \breve{\psi}_a \tag{17}$$

For fixed a, then, $W_f(a, b)$ is the convolution of $f(x)$ with the reflected conjugate wavelet at scale a.

Figure 14–6 shows the integral wavelet transform as a bank of linear (convolution) filters acting upon $f(x)$. Each value of a defines a different bandpass filter, and the outputs of all the filters, taken together, comprise the wavelet transform. Further, Eq. (10) becomes

$$f(x) = \frac{1}{C_\psi}\int_0^{\infty}\int_{-\infty}^{\infty}[f * \breve{\psi}_a](b)\psi_a(b - x)db\frac{da}{a^2} = \frac{1}{C_\psi}\int_0^{\infty}[f * \breve{\psi}_a * \psi_a](x)\frac{da}{a^2} \tag{18}$$

which implies that the filter outputs, each filtered again by $\psi_a(x)$ and properly scaled, combine to reconstruct $f(x)$. This is a statement of Calderon's identity [6,7], which predates Grossman and Morlet by 20 years.

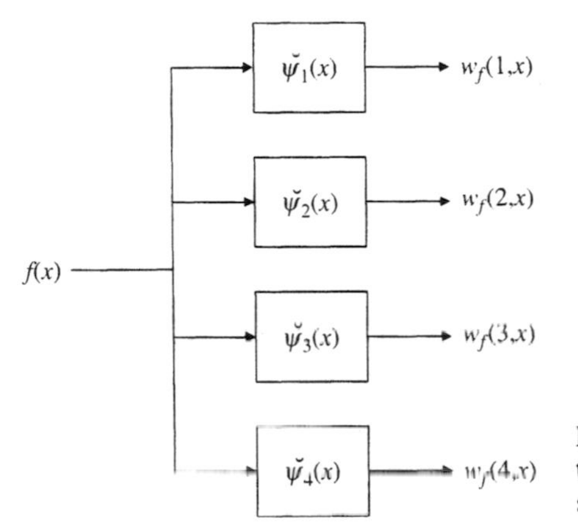

Figure 14–6 Filter bank analogy for the integral wavelet transform of a signal

Recall from the similarity theorem (Sec. 10.2.5) that

$$\mathfrak{F}\{f(ax)\} = \frac{1}{|a|}F\left(\frac{s}{a}\right) \tag{19}$$

This means that

$$\Psi_a(s) = \mathfrak{F}\{\psi_a(x)\} = \sqrt{a}\,\Psi(as) \tag{20}$$

and the center frequencies of the bandpass filters decrease as the transfer functions become more narrow with increasing a.

14.2.4 Two Dimensional Filter Banks

Figure 14–7 illustrates the filter bank approach in two dimensions. Here, each filter $\psi_a(x,y)$ is a two-dimensional impulse response, and its output is a bandpass-filtered version of the image. (Recall Figure 14–3). The stack of filtered images comprises the wavelet transform.

Again, the redundancy is considerable. In fact, if $\Psi(u,v)$, the transfer function of $\psi(x, y)$, is nonzero everywhere except at the origin, one could, theoretically, recover the

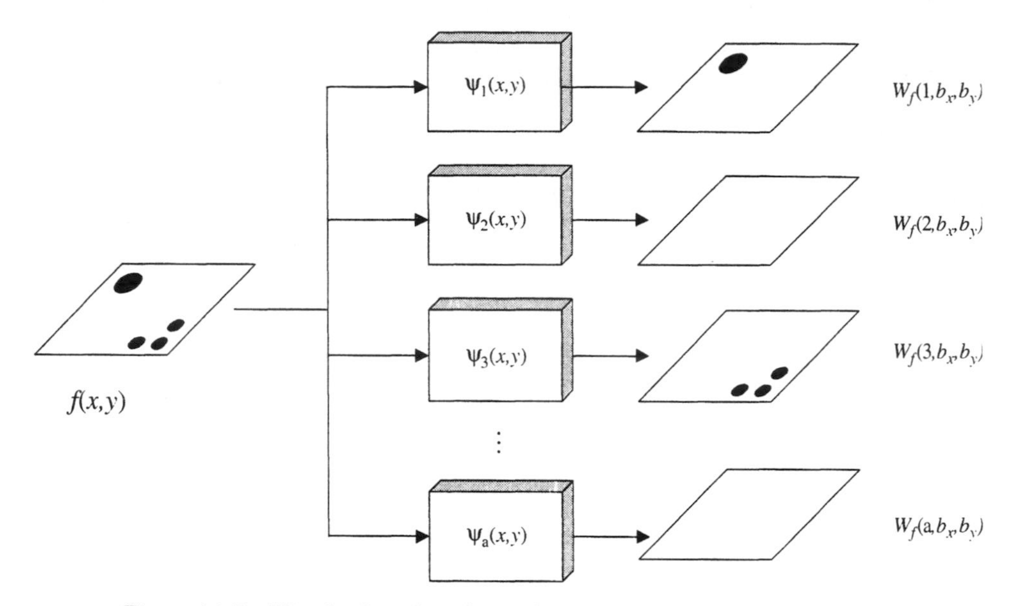

Figure 14–7 Filter bank analogy for the integral wavelet transform of an image

original image from *any one* of the filter outputs by inverse filtering (e.g., by deconvolution). Alternatively, if the image is bandlimited to an interval over which at least one $\Psi_a(u, v)$ is nonzero, then $f(x, y)$ could be recovered from that filter output alone. The conclusion, then, is that the potential value of the integral wavelet transform lies not in a compact representation, but in decomposition and analysis of signals and images.

To illustrate this, suppose that the image in Figure 14–7 contained, for example, circular objects of different sizes and that the basic wavelet were selected to respond only (or primarily) to circular objects of unit radius. Then an examination of the output image stack would reveal the locations of the objects. Further, each object would appear only (or primarily) in the specific output image that corresponded to its particular size.

14.3 THE WAVELET SERIES EXPANSION

14.3.1 Dyadic Wavelets

The second type of wavelet transform is somewhat more restrictive than the first. Again, a basic wavelet is scaled and translated to form a set of basis functions. Here, however, the scaling and translation are specified by integers rather than real numbers.

In this second definition, we restrict ourselves to forming the basis functions by *binary scalings* (shrinking by factors of two) and *dyadic translations* of the basic wavelet, $\psi(x)$. A dyadic translation is a shift by the amount $k/2^j$, which is an integer multiple of the binary scale factor and thus of the width of the wavelet as well. Binary scalings and dyadic translations are illustrated in Figure 14–8.

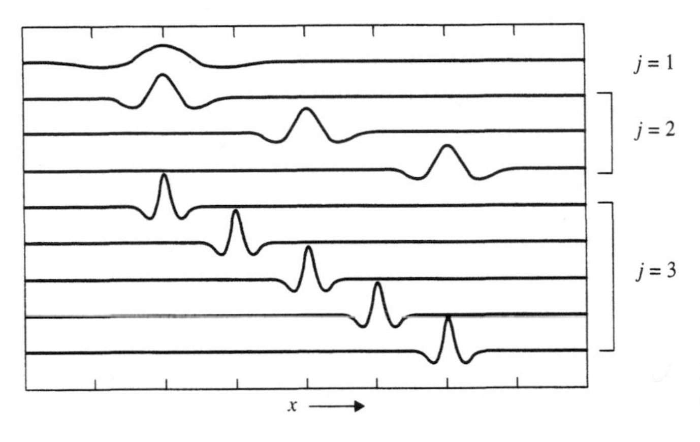

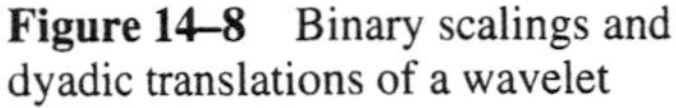
Figure 14–8 Binary scalings and dyadic translations of a wavelet

14.3.2 Definition

A function $\psi(x)$ is an *orthogonal wavelet* if the set $\{\psi_{j,k}(x)\}$ of functions defined by

$$\psi_{j,k}(x) = 2^{j/2}\psi(2^j x - k) \tag{21}$$

where $-\infty < j,k < \infty$ are integers, forms an orthonormal basis of $L^2(R)$ [5]. The integer j determines the dilation, while k specifies the translation.

The preceding wavelet set forms an orthonormal basis if, first,

$$\langle \psi_{j,k}, \psi_{l,m} \rangle = \delta_{j,l}\delta_{k,m} \tag{22}$$

where l and m are integers, $\delta_{j,k}$ is the Kronecker delta function, and $\langle \cdot, \cdot \rangle$ indicates the inner product; and second, if any function $f(x) \in L^2(R)$ can be written as

$$f(x) = \sum_{j=-\infty}^{\infty} \sum_{k=-\infty}^{\infty} c_{j,k}\psi_{j,k}(x) \tag{23}$$

where the transform coefficients are again given by inner products; that is,

$$c_{j,k} = \langle f(x), \psi_{j,k}(x) \rangle = 2^{j/2}\int_{-\infty}^{\infty} f(x)\psi(2^j x - k)dx \tag{24}$$

Eqs. (23) and (24) specify a *wavelet series expansion* of $f(x)$ relative to the wavelet $\psi(x)$ [5].

Notice that here a continuous function is represented by a doubly infinite sequence, and, in general, the transform is again overcomplete. Since the basis functions commonly extend to infinity in both directions, a complete reconstruction must include all terms.

If $\psi(x)$ is properly chosen, however, one might be able to truncate the series without serious approximation error. If $f(x)$ is of finite duration, and the basic wavelet is well localized (i.e., it approaches zero rapidly away from the origin), then many of the coefficients with large $|k|$ will be negligible. Likewise, coefficients with large $|j|$ will usually be small as well, since the wavelet basis function then becomes extremely broad or narrow.

14.3.3 Compact Dyadic Wavelets

If we further restrict $f(x)$ and the basic wavelet to functions that are zero outside the interval $[0,1]$, then the family of orthonormal basis functions can be specified by a single index, n; that is,

$$\psi_n(x) = 2^{j/2}\psi(2^j x - k) \tag{25}$$

where j and k are actually functions of n, as follows:

$$n = 2^j + k \quad \text{for} \quad j = 0, 1, \ldots \quad k = 0, 1, \ldots, 2^j - 1 \tag{26}$$

For any n, j is the largest integer such that $2^j \le n$, and $k = n - 2^j$.

Now the inverse transform is

$$f(x) = \sum_{n=0}^{\infty} c_n \psi_n(x) \tag{27}$$

where it is assumed that $\psi_0(x) = 1$. The transform coefficients are given by the inner product

$$c_n = \langle f(x), \psi_n(x) \rangle = 2^{j/2}\int_{-\infty}^{\infty} f(x)\psi(2^j x - k)dx \tag{28}$$

Here, a continuous function is being represented by a single infinite sequence, as with a Fourier series representation. The tremendous redundancy of the integral wavelet transform is absent. In fact, if one or a few of the $\psi_n(x)$ are similar to $f(x)$ (or its major components), then one might be able to truncate the series to a relatively few terms without appreciable approximation error.

We have here, as well, the basis of the discrete wavelet transform. If $f(i\Delta t)$ is a discrete function sampled with N points, where N is a power of two, and if $\psi(x)$ is a compact dyadic wavelet, then we can compute a discrete wavelet transform using discrete versions of Eqs. (27) and (28). Both equations become summations of N terms. The Haar transform offers an example of this.

14.3.3.1 Example: The Haar Transform

The Haar transform [2,8,9] is one of the earliest examples of what we now call a compact, dyadic, orthonormal wavelet transform. It differs from the other transforms mentioned in Chapter 13 in that its basis functions are all generated by translations and dilations of a basic wavelet. The Haar function, which is an odd rectangular pulse pair, is the simplest and oldest orthonormal wavelet with compact support.

The basic wavelet is progressively narrowed (reduced in scale) by powers of two. Each smaller wavelet is then translated by increments equal to its width, so that the complete set of wavelets at any scale completely covers the interval. As the basic wavelet is scaled down by powers of two, its amplitude is scaled up by powers of $\sqrt{2}$, to maintain orthonormality. The result of all this is a set of orthonormal basis functions (Figure 14–9). The basis function index, as defined in Eq. (26), differs slightly from that used in Sec. 13.5.4.

14.4 THE DISCRETE WAVELET TRANSFORM

The DWT most closely resembles the unitary transforms discussed in the previous chapter. It promises to be the most useful for image compression, processing, and analysis. Given a set of orthonormal basis functions, one can compute the discrete wavelet transform just as one does any other unitary transform, such as the Haar transform. Obtaining a suitable basic wavelet, however, requires further background material.

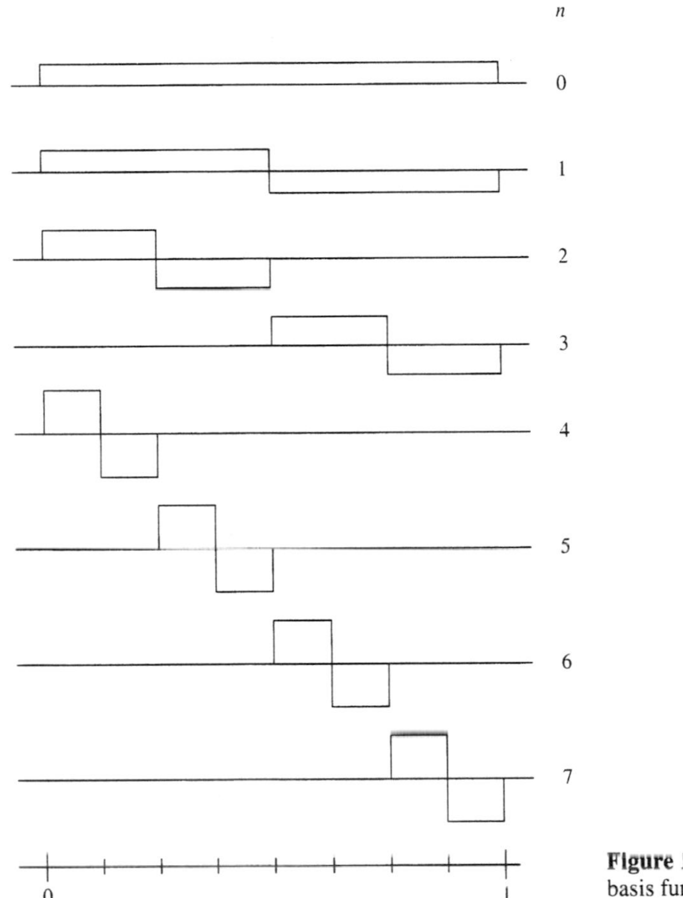

Figure 14–9 The Haar transform basis functions

In this section, we first review three techniques that have led to the development of the discrete wavelet transform: (1) filter bank theory, (2) multiresolution or time-scale analysis, particularly using pyramid representations, and (3) subband coding. This discussion is followed by an introduction to the discrete wavelet transform.

14.4.1 Filter Bank Theory

Workers in the area of speech analysis and acoustic signal processing have long used the concept of a bank of bandpass filters for decomposing a signal into components at different frequencies. Indeed, the method is a precursor to *time-frequency analysis,* in which the signal's components are displayed in a two-dimensional space whose dimensions are time of occurrence and frequency of oscillation. Here, we review the basics of that approach as a step leading toward a discussion of the discrete wavelet transform.

Suppose we have a signal composed of two *tone bursts* (sinusoids of short duration) embedded in random noise, as illustrated in Figure 14–10a. Suppose further that we wish to analyze this signal to detect the number, frequency, and position of the tone bursts.

The Fourier transform will, of course, reflect the entire content of the signal, but often not in a way that is easily interpreted. Position information, for example, is encoded in the

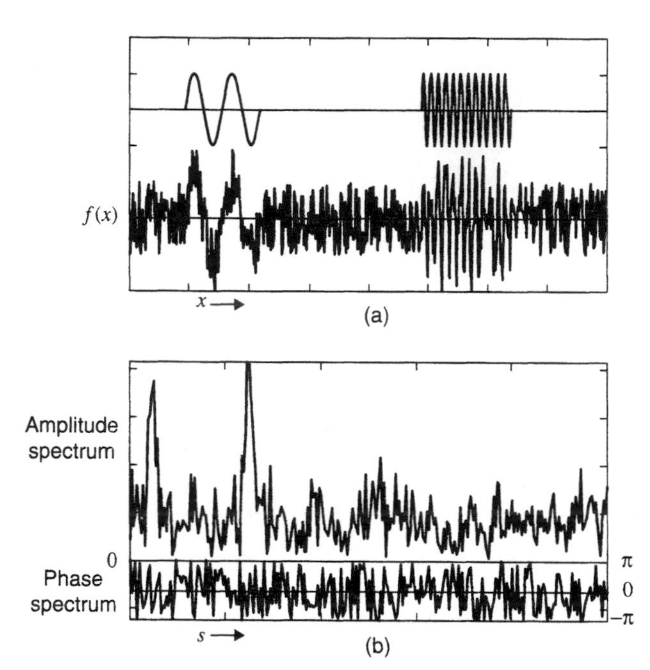

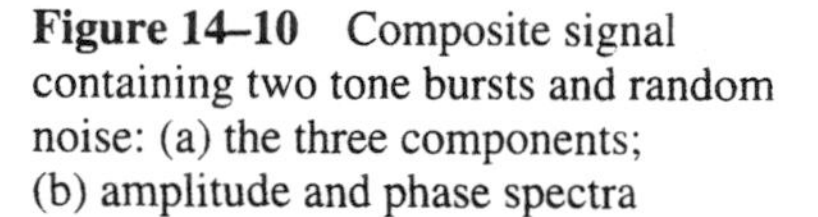
Figure 14–10 Composite signal containing two tone bursts and random noise: (a) the three components; (b) amplitude and phase spectra

phase spectrum in a complicated way. (Recall Figure 10–10.) While the amplitude spectrum may show distinct peaks due to each of the transient signal components, this is reliable only for transient detection when those components are large enough in amplitude and duration to dominate the spectrum. Figure 14–10b, for example, does manifest distinct peaks at the frequencies of the two tone bursts. The phase spectrum, however, gives little insight into the location of these components in time. Often, the uninteresting components of the signal (e.g., noise) complicate the spectrum to the point that a simple frequency analysis is insufficient to resolve the signal's components.

14.4.1.1 Ideal Bandpass Filters

Suppose we partition the frequency axis into a set of disjoint (adjacent, nonoverlapping) intervals and use this partitioning to define a set of ideal bandpass transfer functions, as shown in Figure 14–11b. The corresponding impulse responses appear in Figure 14–11a. Figure 14–12 shows the implementation of a bandpass filter bank. The input signal is fed into each of the bandpass filters in parallel. The corresponding outputs are $g_i(x)$. The $H_i(s)$ are constructed so that they sum to 1 for all frequencies, and thus, the $g_i(x)$ will sum to form $f(x)$. That is,

$$\sum_{i=1}^{\infty} H_i(s) = 1 \Rightarrow \sum_{i=1}^{\infty} g_i(x) = f(x) \tag{29}$$

Figure 14–13 shows the output of three of the bandpass filters shown in Figure 14–12. Notice that the two tone burst signals (recall Figure 14–10a) emerge from separate filters. Further, their locations along the time axis are evident in those outputs. Thus, we have an approach to decomposing the composite signal and identifying the components of interest.

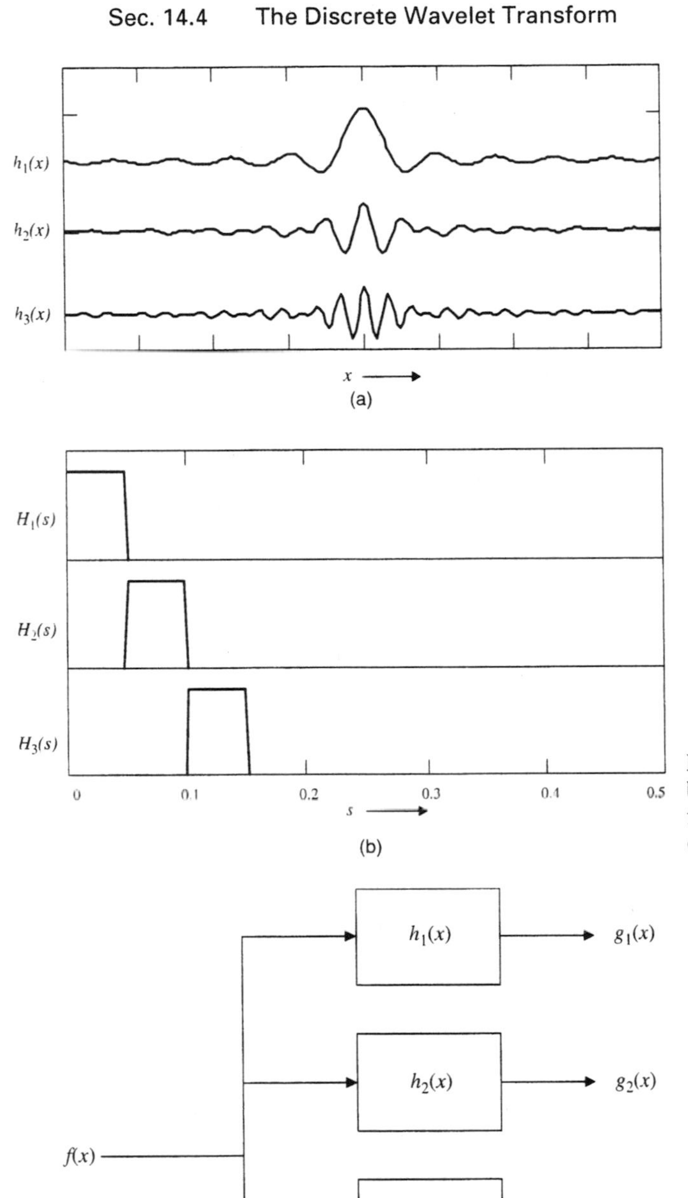

Figure 14–11 Generating a series of bandpass filters by partitioning the frequency axis: (a) impulse responses; (b) transfer functions

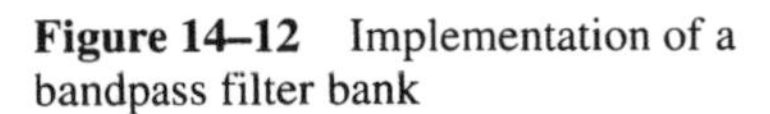

Figure 14–12 Implementation of a bandpass filter bank

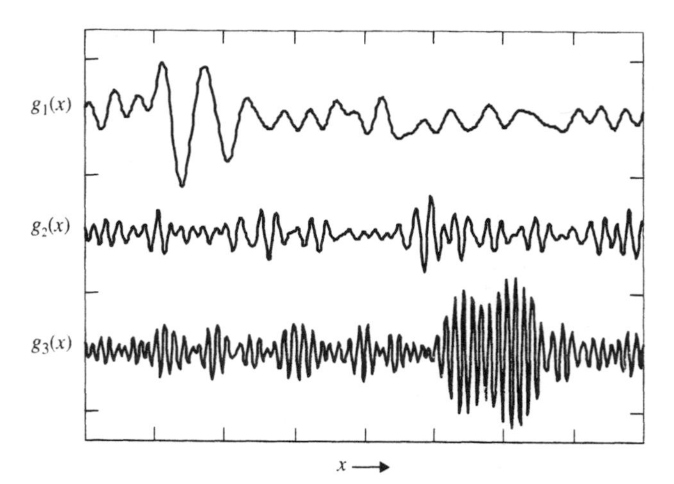

Figure 14–13 Bandpass filter outputs

Each of the bandpass filter outputs is formed by the convolution

$$g_i(x) = \int_{-\infty}^{\infty} f(t)h_i(x-t)dt \tag{30}$$

Since $H_i(s)$ is real and even, $h_i(x)$ will be as well. Then the reflection in the convolution integral has no effect, and the filter outputs can be written as

$$g_i(x) = \int_{-\infty}^{\infty} f(t)h_i(t-x)dt = \langle f(t), h_i(t-x)\rangle \tag{31}$$

Hence, each point on $g_i(x)$ is the inner product of $f(t)$ with a version of $h_i(t)$ that has been shifted to location x. We can also view $\{g_i(x)\}$ as a (two-dimensional) set of wavelet transform coefficients, where $\{h_i(x)\}$ is the set of wavelets. Further, $\{g_i(x)\}$ is sufficient to reconstruct $f(x)$ exactly, in view of Eq. (29).

The message borne by Eq. (31) is a significant one. The similarity between convolution, on the one hand, and taking inner products with shifted basis functions, on the other, is what brings the disparate pieces of the wavelet transform together into a unified whole.

14.4.1.2 Smooth Bandpass Filters

The functions $h_i(x)$ in Figure 14–11a lack one of the characteristics that good wavelet basis functions should have: They are not well localized. That is, they do not die out quickly away from their central region. This means that $h_i(x - x_0)$ will respond to strong components that are located distant from x_0. It is the sharp edges of $H_i(s)$ that give rise to the undesirable width of $h_i(x)$.

Designing the $H_i(s)$ functions to have smoother edges will reduce the width of the $h_i(x)$. Since the $H_i(s)$ must still sum to unity everywhere, the resulting bandpass transfer functions will overlap at their edges. One such construction is shown in Figure 14–14. Here, the passband edges are each a raised half-cycle of the cosine. The resulting narrowing of the impulse responses is evident.

Figure 14–15 shows the filter bank outputs with the signal of Figure 14–10a as input and smooth bandpass filters. Notice the improvement in localization. We have thus taken a

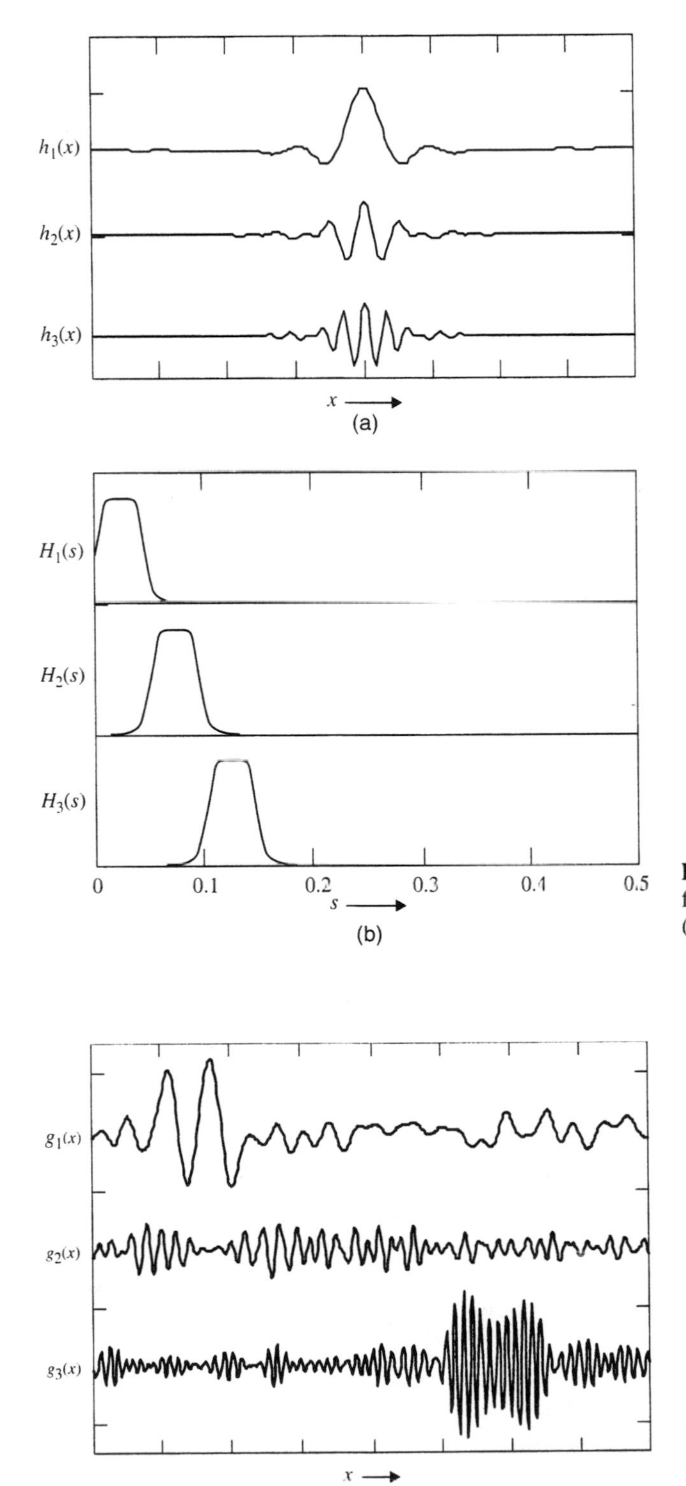

Figure 14–14 Smooth bandpass filters: (a) impulse responses; (b) transfer functions

Figure 14–15 Smooth bandpass filter bank output

step toward a *time-frequency* analysis of the composite signal. That is, we have means of localizing the transient components of the signal in both time (or position) and frequency.

14.4.2 Multiresolution Analysis

Many of the developments preceding wavelet analysis came in a field generally called *multi-resolution analysis*. These developments were intended to combat the limitations of the Fourier transform mentioned at the beginning of the chapter. We now summarize this approach as groundwork leading to modern wavelet analysis.

Filter bank theory offers a convenient means of representing signals composed of oscillatory components, such as musical notes and tone bursts. These components include several (or many) cycles of the oscillation within their duration. In image analysis, however, the localized components of interest often are not truly oscillatory, in that they include only one cycle or even just part of a cycle. Examples include lines, edges, and spots.

The objects in an image are observed to occur at different size scales. An edge, for example, can be either a sharp transition from black to white or one that occurs gradually over a considerable distance. In general, a multiresolution approach to image representation or analysis seeks to exploit this idea.

Cartography illustrates the approach. Maps are commonly drawn at different scales. The *scale* of a map is the ratio of the size of an actual territory to that of its representation on the map. At large scales, as on a globe, major features such as continents and oceans are visible, while details such as individual city streets fall below the resolution of the map. At smaller scales, the details become visible and the larger features are lost. Thus, to be able to navigate to a point at a distant location, one needs a set of maps drawn at different scales.

Wavelet transforms have developed along these multiresolution lines. As with time-frequency analysis, a signal is represented in a two-dimensional space, but here the vertical axis is scale rather than frequency. Scaling is achieved by dilating and contracting the basic wavelet to form a set of basis functions.

The basic wavelet, $\psi(x)$, is scaled as $\psi(x/a)$ (which is broadened if $a > 1$ and narrowed if $a < 1$) to form a set of basis functions. At large scale a, the dilated basis functions search for large features, while for small a, they seek out fine detail.

14.4.2.1 Pyramid Algorithms

Suppose we generated, from one 1,024-by-1,024–pixel digital image, 10 additional images by successively averaging 2-by-2–pixel blocks, each time discarding every second row and column of pixels. We would be left with images of 512 by 512, 256 by 256, etc., down to 1 by 1. If we then performed edge detection, for example, on each image, using one of the 3-by-3 edge detection operators mentioned in Chapter 18, we would find small edges in the original image, somewhat larger edges in the 512-by-512 and 256-by-256–pixel images, and only the very large edges in the 16-by-16–pixel and smaller images.

The Haar transform represents the dawn of this approach from almost a century ago. In its basis images (Figure 13–6), we see the concept of searching the image with edge detectors of different scales. The principle of binary dilation is evident there as well.

One might be tempted to observe that all edges, large and small, appear in the original 1,024-by-1,024–pixel image and that no change of resolution is required to locate them. The problem is that large edges—those manifesting a transition in gray level that spans a considerable distance—are difficult to detect with conventional (small) neighborhood operators such as the ones discussed in Chapter 18. One could scale the operators up to detect the larger edges, but it is more efficient to scale the image down. Using a large operator to search a high-resolution image for large edges is computational overkill.

Several forms of multiresolution analysis have been studied under different names over the years. It is only in recent years, however, that the basic similarity between multiresolution and filter bank approaches has been recognized, and these have been unified under the heading of wavelet transforms.

14.4.2.2 Laplacian Pyramid Coding

Burt and Adelson [10] introduced a pyramid coding scheme based on the Gaussian function. The image is lowpass filtered with a Gaussian impulse response, and the result is subtracted from the original image. The high-frequency detail in the image is retained in this difference image. The lowpass filtered image can then be subsampled without loss of detail. The process is illustrated as follows.

Let $f_0(i, j)$ be the original image, and let $g(i, j)$ be a Gaussian-shaped lowpass filter impulse response. Then, at each step of the encoding process, the image is decomposed into half-resolution low-frequency and full-resolution high-frequency components, $f_1(i, j)$ and $h_1(i, j)$, respectively for the first step, by

$$f_1(i, j) = [f_0 * g](2i, 2j) \quad \text{and} \quad h_1(i, j) = f_0(i, j) - [f_0 * g](i, j) \tag{32}$$

This process is iterated each time on the subsampled image. After n iterations of an N-by-N image, where $N = 2^n$, $f_n(i, j)$ is a single point. The encoded image pyramid consists of the $h_k(i, j)$'s and the final low-frequency image $f_n(i, j)$. This is shown in Figure 14–16.

Image decoding is done in the reverse order. *Upsampling* is the process of inserting zeros between sample points. Each subsampled image, $f_k(i, j)$, beginning with the last one, $f_n(i, j)$, is upsampled and interpolated by convolution with $g(i, j)$. Then the result is added to the next (previous) image $f_{k-1}(i, j)$, and the process is repeated on the resulting image. This reconstructs the original image without error [10].

Each $h_k(i, j)$ is the difference of two images obtained by convolving a single image with Gaussians of single and double width. This is equivalent to convolving the image with

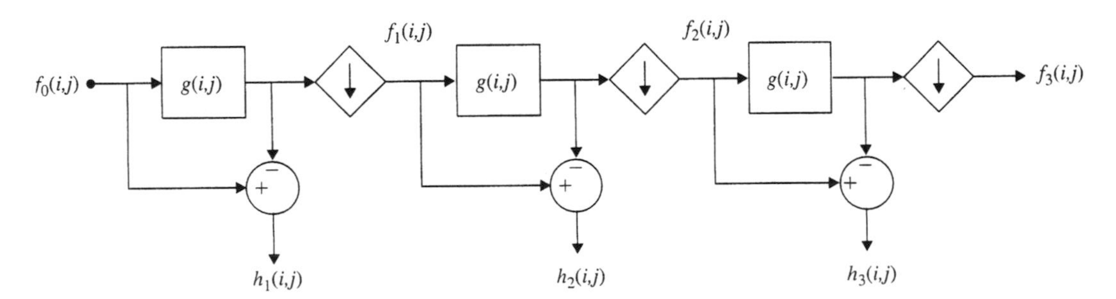

Figure 14–16 The Laplacian pyramid coding scheme

the difference of two Gaussians, which, in turn, approximates the "Laplacian of a Gaussian" highpass filter; hence the name chosen for this pyramid coding algorithm.

Although Laplacian pyramid coding increases the number of pixels required to represent the image by 33 percent, it can nevertheless accomplish a significant degree of image compression [10]. This occurs because the $h_k(i, j)$ images have significantly reduced correlation and dynamic range and are thus amenable to coarse quantization and even to setting some of the pixel values to zero. Further, the design of the Laplacian pyramid provided the inspiration that later led to the discrete wavelet transform.

14.4.3 Subband Coding

As further background leading to the discrete wavelet transform, we now describe a time-frequency technique called *subband coding*. Originally developed for compact coding of digitized audio signals, subband coding seeks to decompose a signal (or an image) into narrow-band (bandpass-filtered) components and represent these, without redundancy, in such a way that it is possible to reconstruct the original signal without error [11–13].

Given a bandlimited signal $f(t)$, that is,

$$\mathfrak{F}\{f(t)\} = F(s) = 0 \quad \text{for} \quad |s| \geq s_{\max} \tag{33}$$

we can sample the signal with uniform sample spacing Δt to form

$$f(i\Delta t) \qquad i = 0, 1, \ldots, N-1 \qquad s_{\max} \leq s_N = \frac{1}{2\Delta t} \tag{34}$$

(Figure 14–17a), where s_N is the Nyquist (folding) frequency. (Recall Chapter 12, Eq. 22.)

We begin the analysis by partitioning the frequency axis into disjoint subintervals. While any subinterval length could be used, we now choose $s_N/2$, as shown in Figure 14–17b, for reasons that will become clear later. Here, the spectrum $F(s)$ is periodic with period $2s_N$.

14.4.3.1 The Lower Halfband

Figure 14–17b shows an ideal halfband lowpass filter, $h_0(i\Delta t)$, so called because it passes only the frequency band $[-s_N/2, s_N/2]$, which is the low-frequency half of the total frequency band $[-s_N, s_N]$. The impulse response and transfer function of h_0 are

$$h_0(t) = \text{sinc}\left(\pi\frac{t}{2\Delta t}\right) \quad \text{and} \quad H_0(s) = \Pi\left(\frac{s}{s_N}\right) \tag{35}$$

where the rectangular pulse is

$$\Pi(x) = \begin{cases} 1 & |x| < \frac{1}{2} \\ \frac{1}{2} & |x| = \frac{1}{2} \\ 0 & |x| > \frac{1}{2} \end{cases} \tag{36}$$

and

$$\text{sinc}(x) = \frac{\sin(x)}{x} \tag{37}$$

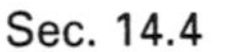

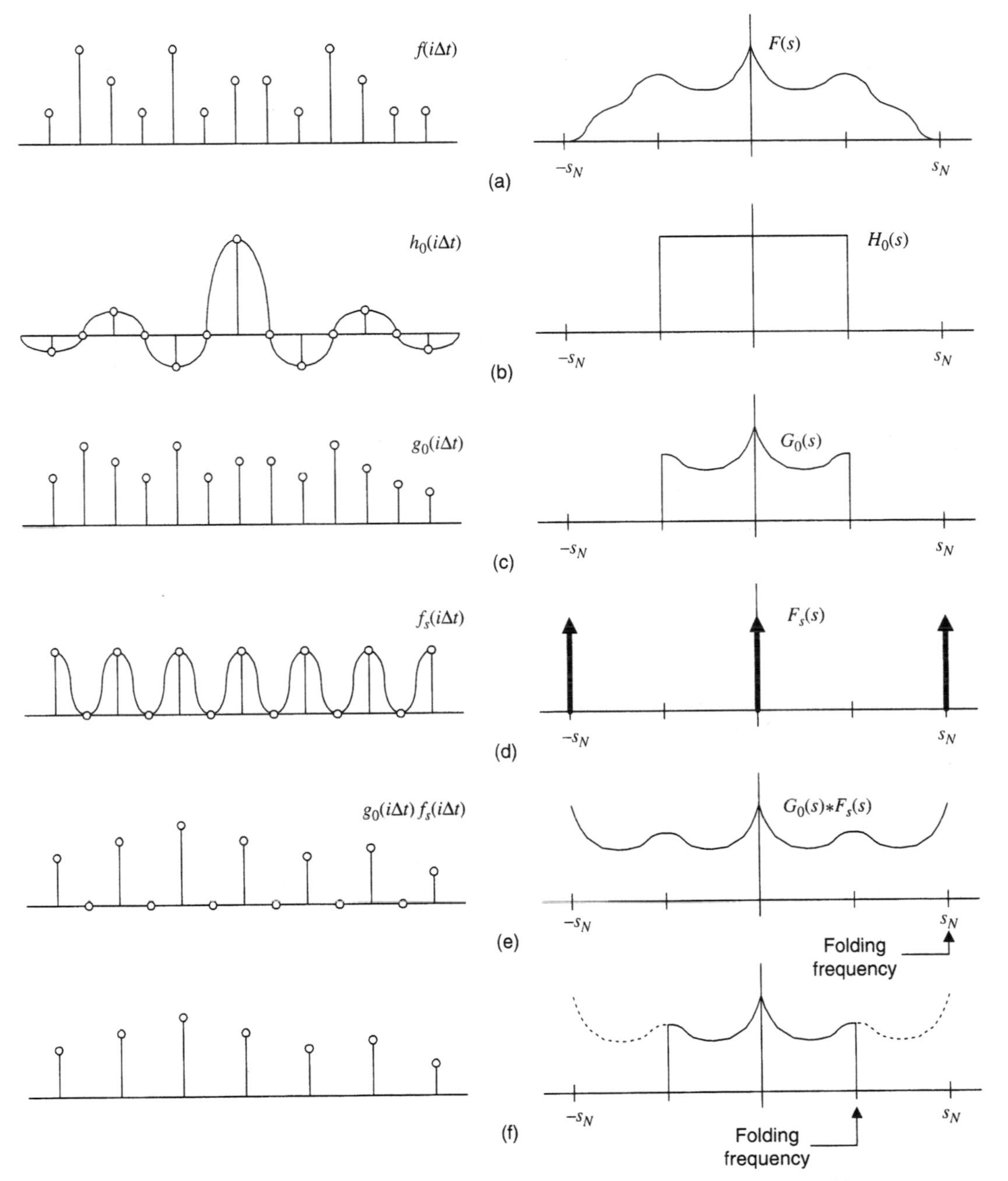

Figure 14–17 Subband coding, the lower halfband: (a) a sampled signal and its bandlimited spectrum; (b) the ideal halfband lowpass filter; (c) the lowpass filtered signal; (d) the subsampling function; (e) odd sample points replaced with zeros; (f) odd sample points discarded

Applying this filter to $f(i\Delta t)$ (Figure 14–17a) yields the signal $g_0(i\Delta t)$ (Figure 14–17c), which is bandlimited at $s = s_N/2$. This is a low-resolution (blurred) version of $f(i\Delta t)$. It retains the basic shape of $f(i\Delta t)$, but has lost the details.

Since $g_0(i\Delta t)$ has no energy above $s_N/2$, it could be sampled with sample spacing as large as $2\Delta t$ without introducing aliasing. In fact, we can discard every second sample and represent g_0 with only the remaining $N/2$ samples (Figure 14–17f). This process is called *subsampling* or *decimation.*

We can model subsampling as first multiplying the signal by a subsampling function that drives the odd-numbered samples to zero and then discarding the odd-numbered samples. Such a subsampling function

$$f_s(i\Delta t) = \frac{1}{2}[1 + \cos(2\pi s_N i\Delta t)] \tag{38}$$

and its spectrum

$$F_s(s) = \frac{1}{2}[\delta(s) + \delta(s - s_N) + \delta(s + s_N)] \tag{39}$$

are shown in Figure 14–17d.

When we multiply the signal $g_0(i\Delta t)$ by $f_s(i\Delta t)$, we convolve its spectrum with $F_s(s)$. The result is to make the spectrum symmetric in such a way that its period is reduced from $2s_N$ to s_N, as shown in Figure 14–17e. Its amplitude is also cut in half; we write

$$F_s(s) * G_0(s) = \frac{1}{2}G_0(s) + \frac{1}{2}G_0(s + s_N) + \frac{1}{2}G_0(s - s_N) \tag{40}$$

Clearly, we can now discard the odd-numbered sample points without loss of information (Figure 14–17f). This reduces the folding frequency to $s_N/2$ and leaves us with a signal that is properly sampled with sample spacing $2\Delta t$.

No information has been lost in the process of subsampling $g_0(i\Delta t)$. To see this, notice that we could recover $g_0(i\Delta t)$ from the subsampled signal in Figure 14–17f simply by (1) computing its ($N/2$-point) discrete spectrum, (2) padding it with zeros from $s_N/2$ to s_N to reconstruct $G_0(s)$ (Figure 14–17c), and (3) taking the inverse (N-point) DFT of $G_0(s)$ to reconstruct $g_0(i\Delta t)$, the signal shown in Figure 14–17c. While this is not the preferred method, it argues that subsampling $g_0(i\Delta t)$ produces no loss of information.

A simpler way to recover $g_0(i\Delta t)$ can also be seen in Figure 14–17. We first upsample the encoded lowband signal (Figure 14–17f) by inserting the zero-valued odd-numbered samples (to form Figure 14–17e). Then we filter that signal with $2h_0(i\Delta t)$, the ideal halfband lowpass filter (Figure14–17b). This will reconstruct the spectrum, and hence the signal, in Figure 14–17c, thereby recovering $g_0(i\Delta t)$.

In the frequency domain, we write

$$F_s(s) * G_0(s) \times H_0(s) =$$

$$\left[\frac{1}{2}G_0(s) + \frac{1}{2}G_0(s + s_N) + \frac{1}{2}G_0(s - s_N)\right] \times \Pi\left(\frac{s}{s_N}\right) = \frac{1}{2}G_0(s) \tag{41}$$

Notice that the lowpass filter impulse response, $h_0(i\Delta t)$, is $\mathrm{sinc}(\pi x/2\Delta t)$, which has zero-crossings at even multiples of the sample spacing, except at zero (Figure14–17b). Thus, it interpolates the intermediate (odd-numbered) values of $g_0(i\Delta t)$, where the zeros are located, and leaves the even-numbered samples alone.

14.4.3.2 The Upper Halfband

Turning now to the upper halfband of $f(i\Delta t)$ (Figure 14–18a), we can isolate the energy there with an ideal halfband bandpass filter (Figure 14–18b). This filter's impulse response and transfer function are, respectively,

$$h_1(t) = \delta(t) - \mathrm{sinc}\left(\pi\frac{t}{2\Delta t}\right) \quad \text{and} \quad H_1(s) = 1 - \Pi\left(\frac{s}{s_N}\right) \tag{42}$$

where $\Pi(x)$ is as in Eq. (36).

The filter produces a signal, $g_1(i\Delta t)$, whose spectrum is nonzero only in the upper halfband (Figure 14–18c). This signal contains exactly the high-frequency information that was eliminated from $f(i\Delta t)$ by the lowpass filter in Figure 14–17b. Thus, $g_0(i\Delta t)$ and $g_1(i\Delta t)$, taken together, contain all the information that was present in the original signal, $f(i\Delta t)$. In fact,

$$f(i\Delta t) = g_0(i\Delta t) + g_1(i\Delta t) = f(i\Delta t) * h_0(i\Delta t) + f(i\Delta t) * h_1(i\Delta t) \tag{43}$$

since

$$H_0(s) + H_1(s) = 1 \tag{44}$$

Figure 14–18d shows the subsampling function $f_s(i\Delta t)$ that was used in the analysis in Sec. 14.4.3.1. When $g_1(i\Delta t)$ (Figure 14–18c) is subsampled by $f_s(i\Delta t)$, its spectrum is convolved with $F_s(s)$. This fills the interval $[-s_N/2, s_N/2]$ with a replicate of its spectrum and produces the spectrum shown in Figure 14–18e. We write

$$F_s(s) * G_1(s) = \frac{1}{2}G_1(s) + \frac{1}{2}G_1(s + s_N) + \frac{1}{2}G_1(s - s_N) \tag{45}$$

This spectrum is now periodic with period $s_N/2$ and could be sampled at spacing $2\Delta t$ without aliasing. Thus, we now have another signal that is confined to the lower halfband, and it can be subsampled as before (Figure 14–18f).

This leaves the N-point signal $f(i\Delta t)$ encoded into two $N/2$-point signals. We have seen that $g_0(i\Delta t)$ can be recovered from the encoded lowband signal. It remains only to show that $g_1(i\Delta t)$ can be recovered from the encoded highband signal to see that $f(i\Delta t)$ [and hence $f(t)$] can be reconstructed without error.

Figure 14–18e shows the upsampled highband signal. Its spectrum is identical to that in Figure 14–18f, except that, after upsampling, the folding frequency is once again s_N. We can reconstruct $G_1(s)$, and thus $g_1(i\Delta t)$ (Figure 14–18c), simply by filtering this upsampled signal with $2h_1(i\Delta t)$ (Figure 14–18b) to eliminate the low-frequency energy. We write

$$F_s(s) * G_1(s) \times H_1(s) =$$
$$\left[\frac{1}{2}G_1(s) + \frac{1}{2}G_1(s + s_N) + \frac{1}{2}G_1(s - s_N)\right] \times \left[1 - \Pi\left(\frac{s}{s_N}\right)\right] = \frac{1}{2}G_1(s) \tag{46}$$

Thus, we have, in two-channel subband coding, an invertible representation of the signal in terms of two subsampled discrete filter outputs, and it is without redundancy (i.e., not overcomplete).

14.4.3.3 Aliasing the Upper Halfband

Clearly, subsampling $g_1(i\Delta t)$ by discarding every other sample point will result in aliasing. The energy at frequencies between $s_N/2$ and s_N will be aliased down to the interval $[0, s_N)$, as indicated in Figure 14–19a. This process, however, is nondestructive, since that interval is

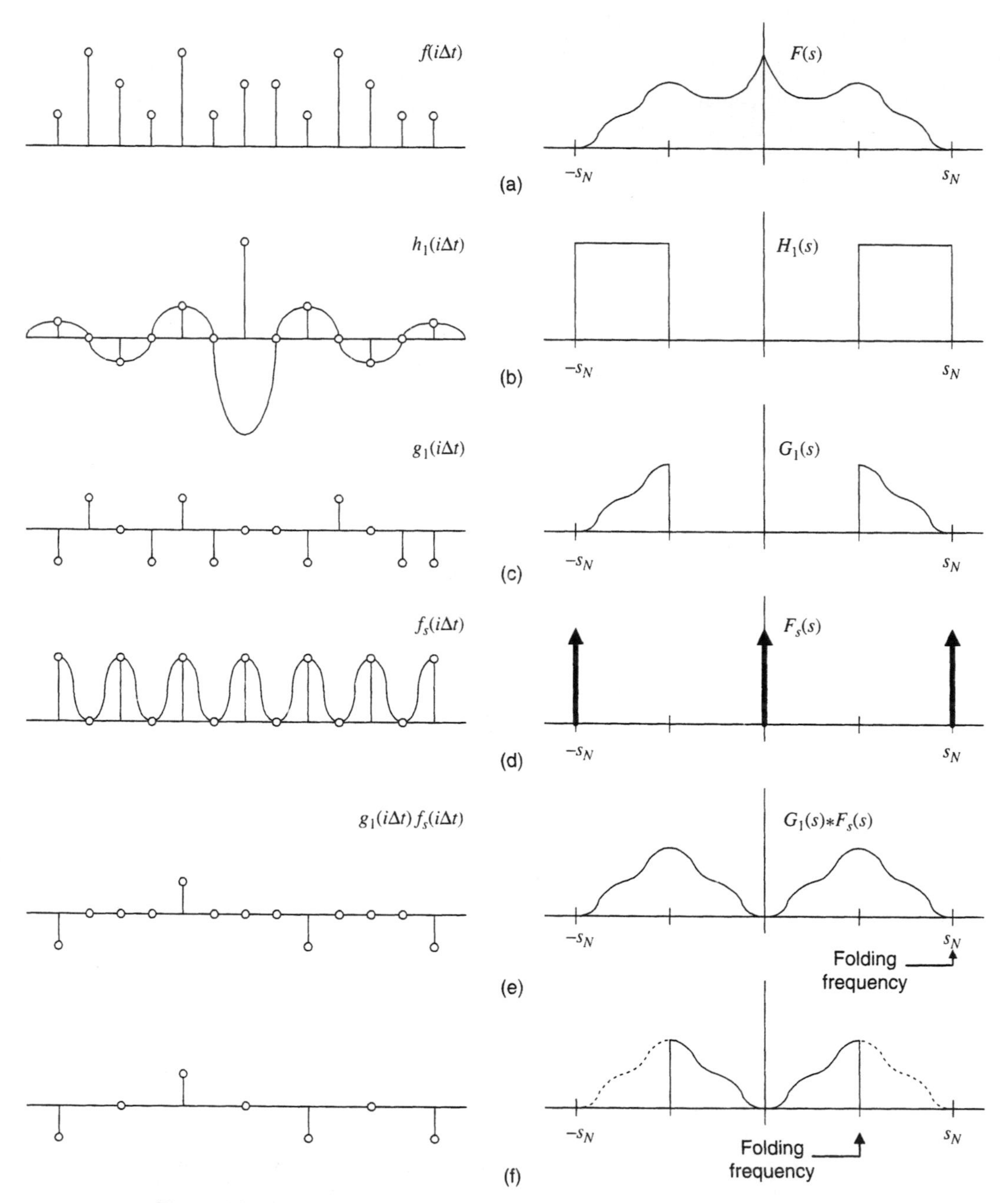

Figure 14–18 Subband coding, the upper halfband: (a) a sampled signal and its bandlimited spectrum; (b) the ideal halfband highpass filter; (c) the highpass filtered signal; (d) the subsampling function; (e) odd sample points replaced with zeros; (f) odd sample points discarded

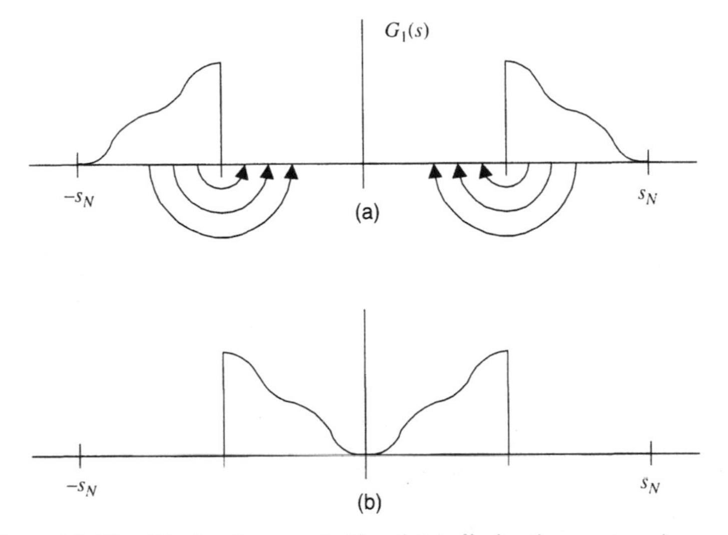

Figure 14–19 Aliasing the upper halfband: (a) aliasing the spectrum in Figure 14–18(c); (b) the result of aliasing

already vacant. It produces the spectrum shown in Figure 14–19b, which is bandlimited at $s_N/2$ and contains all the energy of $g_1(i\Delta t)$.

Ironically, aliasing, the bugaboo that usually threatens our ability to process continuous signals and images digitally, now comes to our aid. It is only necessary to subsample $g_1(i\Delta t)$ to obtain the upper subband coded signal. Furthermore, upsampling followed by filtering with $2h_1(i\Delta t)$, recovers $g_1(i\Delta t)$.

14.4.3.4 Subband Coding and Decoding

Two-channel subband coding, then, requires only filtering $f(i\Delta t)$ with $h_0(i\Delta t)$ and $h_1(i\Delta t)$, followed by subsampling each output. This yields the two half-length subband signals

$$g_0(k\Delta t) = \sum_i f(i\Delta t)h_0((-i+2k)\Delta t) \tag{47}$$

and

$$g_1(k\Delta t) = \sum_i f(i\Delta t)h_1((-i+2k)\Delta t) \tag{48}$$

Reconstruction is effected by upsampling the lower and upper subband signals, interpolating them with $2h_0(i\Delta t)$ and $2h_1(i\Delta t)$, respectively, and adding them together. This is given by

$$f(i\Delta t) = 2\sum_k [g_0(k\Delta t)h_0((-i+2k)\Delta t) + g_1(k\Delta t)h_1((-i+2k)\Delta t)] \tag{49}$$

and is illustrated in Figure 14–20.

We have a slight problem at the midfrequency point $s = s_N/2$, since encoding and decoding entails filtering $f(i\Delta t)$ twice, once with $h_0(i\Delta t)$ and once with $h_1(i\Delta t)$, and since $H_0(s_N/2) = 1/2$ and $H_1(s_N/2) = 1/2$. This problem could be avoided by using $\Pi(\pm\frac{1}{2}) = \sqrt{\frac{1}{2}}$ in Eq. (36). In the next section, where we use more general bandpass filters, we handle the situation explicitly.

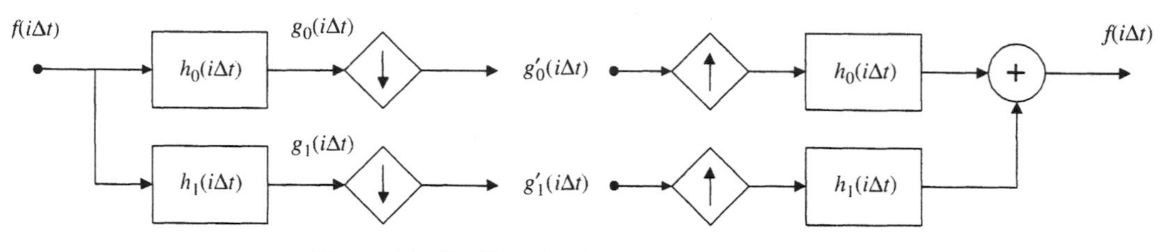

Figure 14–20 Two-band subband coding and reconstruction

We could have chosen to partition the frequency axis into M shorter intervals of length $2s_N/M$, producing M subband signals of N/M points each, as is commonly done in subband coding. Different frequency components then show up in separate subband channels. Since we are moving toward the DWT, however, we stick with the choice of two subbands ($M = 2$).

14.4.4 The Fast Wavelet Transform Algorithm

Mallat [14] defined a discrete wavelet transform algorithm that is more efficient than computing a full set of inner products. It applies two-band subband coding in an iterative fashion and builds the wavelet transform from the bottom up, that is, computing small-scale coefficients first.

After the first step of subband coding, as outlined in Sec. 14.4.3, the lower subband signal, $g_0(i\Delta t)$, is once again subjected to halfband subband coding. This leaves us with the $N/2$-point upper halfband signal and two $N/4$-point subband signals corresponding to the first and second quarters of the interval $[0, s_N]$.

The process is continued, at each step retaining the upper halfband signal and further encoding the lower halfband signal, until a one-point lowband signal is obtained. The transform coefficients are then the lowband point and the collection of subband-coded upper halfband signals. This is shown in Figure 14–21. The first $N/2$ coefficients come from the upper halfband of $F(s)$, the next $N/4$ points from the second quarterband, etc.

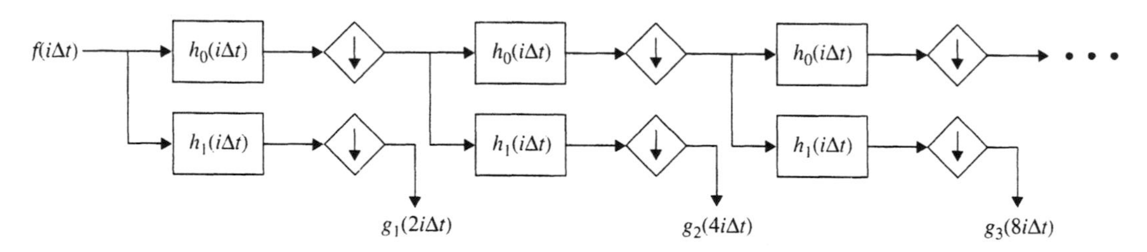

Figure 14–21 The discrete wavelet transform algorithm

The impulse response, h_j, doubles in scale at each iteration. Thus, we have an orthonormal wavelet transform. The basic wavelet is $h(t) = \delta(t) - \mathrm{sinc}(at)$, and the basis functions are $\{2^{-j/2}h(2^j t - n)\}$ [15]. Thus, subband coding, which is basically a time-frequency transform technique, has been employed to define a time-scale wavelet transform.

The foregoing algorithm is sometimes referred to as the *fast wavelet transform* (FWT), or Mallat's *herringbone algorithm,* due to the appearance of the diagram in Figure 14–21. The inverse transform is obtained by reversing the process, as shown in Figure 14–22.

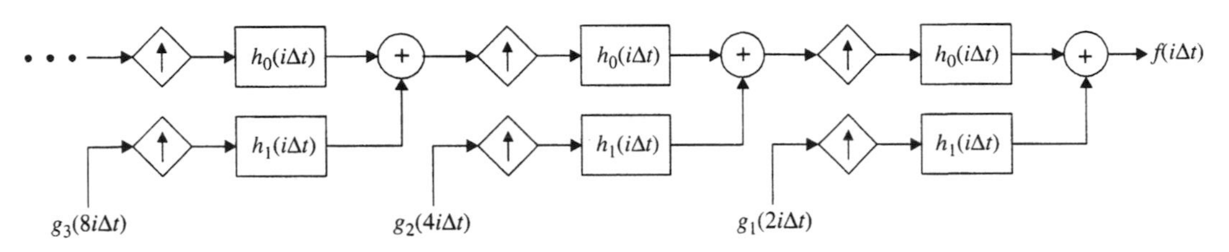

Figure 14–22 The inverse discrete wavelet transform

14.4.4.1 Basis Functions

We see in Figure 14–21 that each set of transform coefficients is obtained by convolving $f(i\Delta t)$ repeatedly with $h_0(i\Delta t)$ and then once with $h_1(i\Delta t)$. Thus, the basis functions of this wavelet transform are $h_1(i\Delta t)$ and other functions derived by convolving $h_1(i\Delta t)$ repeatedly with $h_0(i\Delta t)$. This is explored in more detail next.

14.4.5 Discrete Wavelet Transform Design

We are now prepared to approach the design of a basic wavelet for use in a discrete wavelet transform. As we saw in Sec. 14.4.1, it is not necessary that the filters in a filter bank implementation be ideal lowpass and bandpass filters. Similarly, for the DWT, we can use any pair of subband coding filters that allows Eq. (49) to hold.

Writing Eq. (49) in the frequency-domain, we have

$$F(s) = 2\left[\frac{1}{2}G_0(s)H_0(s) + \frac{1}{2}G_1(s)H_1(s)\right]$$
$$= 2\left[\frac{1}{2}F(s)H_0(s)H_0(s) + \frac{1}{2}F(s)H_1(s)H_1(s)\right] \tag{50}$$

which means that

$$F(s) = F(s)\,[H_0^2(s) + H_1^2(s)] \tag{51}$$

and the two filter transfer functions must satisfy the condition

$$H_0^2(s) + H_1^2(s) = 1 \quad \text{for} \quad 0 \le |s| \le s_N \tag{52}$$

The transfer functions are squared here because $f(t)$ is convolved twice with each filter, once during coding and once during decoding. This resolves the problem that was noted in Sec. 14.4.3.4.

Suppose $H_0(s)$ is a smooth-edged lowpass transfer function that we wish to use in a wavelet transform. Clearly, the corresponding $H_1(s)$ is given by

$$H_1^2(s) = 1 - H_0^2(s) \tag{53}$$

Thus, a well-selected lowpass filter is all that is required to design a discrete wavelet transform.

14.4.5.1 Mirror Filters

Comparing Figures 14–17b and 14–18b, we see that, for the case of the ideal bandpass filter, $h_1(i\Delta t)$ can be viewed as $h_0(i\Delta t)$, shifted by an amount s_N along the frequency axis. According to the shift theorem (Sec. 10.2.3)

$$\mathfrak{F}^{-1}\{H(s-a)\} = e^{j2\pi at}h(t) \Rightarrow \mathfrak{F}^{-1}\{H(s-s_N)\}$$
$$= e^{j2\pi\left(\frac{1}{2\Delta t}\right)i\Delta t}h(i\Delta t) = (-1)^i h(i\Delta t) \quad (54)$$

and such a half-period shift of the spectrum can be effected simply by changing the sign of the odd-numbered samples of the signal. Note the use of the imaginary unit in Eq. (54).

We can use this approach in the design of more general subband filters. Selecting $h_1(i\Delta t)$ so that

$$h_1((N-1-i)\Delta t) = (-1)^i h_0(i\Delta t) \quad (55)$$

where N is the length of $h_0(i\Delta t)$, we obtain the corresponding highpass filter. The filter $h_1(i\Delta t)$ is called the *mirror filter* of $h_0(i\Delta t)$. If $h_0(i\Delta t)$ is of short duration, we can be assured that $h_1(i\Delta t)$ will be short as well.

The symmetry property that $H_0(s)$ must have in order for Eq. (53) to hold, and for this entire approach to work, is

$$H_0^2\left(\frac{s_N}{2}+s\right) = 1 - H_0^2\left(\frac{s_N}{2}-s\right) \quad (56)$$

14.4.5.2 The Scaling Vector

To develop a discrete wavelet transform, then, we need only a discrete lowpass filter impulse response $h_0(k)$ that meets certain conditions [16]. This impulse response is sometimes called a *scaling vector.*

From $h_0(k)$ we can generate a related function $\phi(t)$, called the *scaling function.* We can also generate $h_1(k)$ and, from it and $\phi(t)$, the basic wavelet, $\psi(t)$. If the scaling vector has only a finite number of nonzero entries, then $\phi(t)$, $\psi(t)$, and the resulting wavelets will all have compact support [16]. That is, they will be zero outside a relatively short interval on the t-axis.

Actually, if we have either $h_0(k)$ or $\phi(t)$, we can use it to generate the other. It is usually easier to start with $h_0(k)$, which must satisfy Eq. (56). Let the scaling vector be a sequence such that

$$\sum_k h_0(k) = \sqrt{2} \quad \text{and} \quad \sum_k h_0(k)h_0(k+2l) = \delta(l) \quad (57)$$

Then there exists a scaling function

$$\phi(t) = \sum_k h_0(k)\phi(2t-k) \quad (58)$$

that can be built as a weighted sum of half-scale copies of itself, using $h_0(k)$ as the weights. From the observation in Sec. 14.4.4.1, $\phi(t)$ can also be computed numerically [16] by repeated convolution of $h_0(k)$ with scaled versions of the rectangular pulse function (Figure 14–23); that is,

$$\phi(x) = \lim_{i\to\infty} \eta_i(x) \quad (59)$$

where

$$\eta_i(x) = \sqrt{2}\sum_n h_0(n)\eta_{i-1}(2x-n) \quad (60)$$

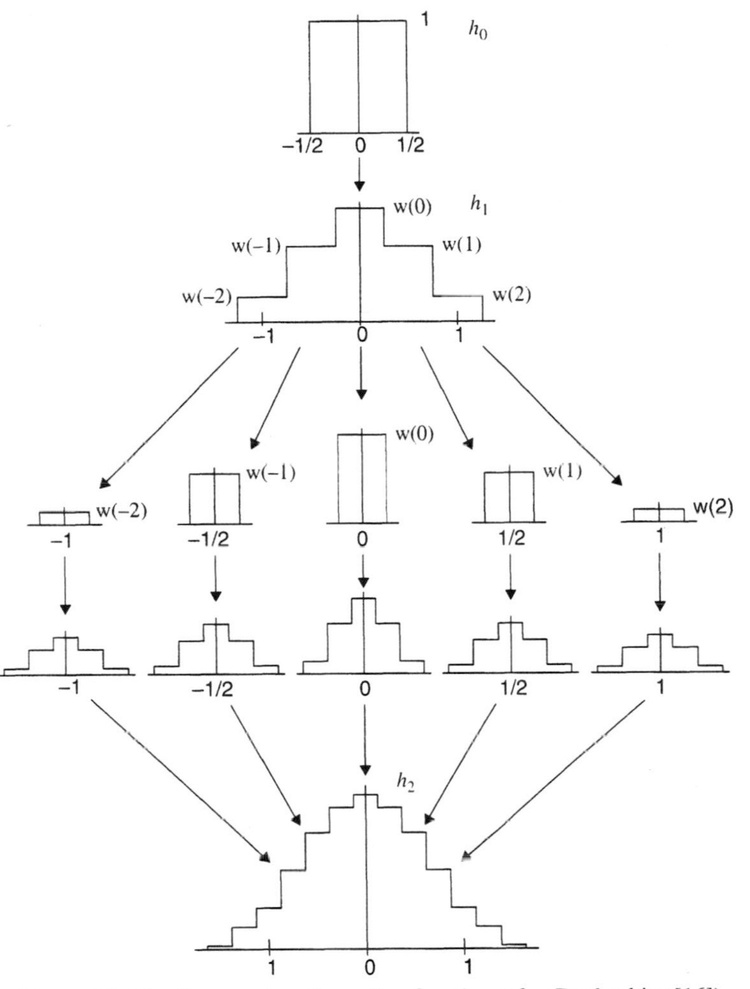

Figure 14–23 Constructing the scaling function (after Daubechies [16])

is a piecewise constant approximation to $\phi(t)$ and

$$\eta_0(x) = \Pi(x) = \begin{cases} 1 & |x| < \frac{1}{2} \\ \frac{1}{2} & |x| = \frac{1}{2} \\ 0 & |x| > \frac{1}{2} \end{cases} \tag{61}$$

Notice that the first iteration creates a piecewise constant function having the values of $h_0(k)$. Further, the resolution of the approximation doubles, and the approximation becomes smoother, with each iteration. Nine iterations, for example, will take a four-point sequence into a 1,024-point sampled function, and this is adequate for most digital implementations. The scaling function $\phi(t)$ is, then, a continuous function that has the same general shape as the discrete lowpass filter impulse response $h_0(k)$.

If, on the other hand, we start with a scaling function $\phi(t)$, it must be orthonormal under unit shifts; that is,

$$\langle \phi(t-m), \phi(t-n)\rangle = \delta_{m,n} \tag{62}$$

Then $h_0(k)$ can be computed from

$$h_0(k) = \langle \phi_{1,0}(t), \phi_{0,k}(t)\rangle \tag{63}$$

where

$$\phi_{j,k}(t) = 2^{j/2}\phi(2^j t - k) \qquad j = 0, 1, \ldots \qquad k = 0, 1, \ldots, 2^j - 1 \tag{64}$$

If the scaling vector has only a finite number of nonzero entries, then the resulting wavelets will have compact support [16].

If a desired scaling function $\hat{\phi}(t)$ is not orthonormal, it can be used to generate one that is orthonormal by proper normalization of its spectrum, $\hat{\Phi}(s)$ [7]. That is,

$$\Phi(s) = \frac{C\hat{\Phi}(s)}{\sqrt{\sum_{n=-\infty}^{\infty} \hat{\Phi}(s - 2\pi n)}} \tag{65}$$

where C is a constant.

14.4.5.3 The Wavelet Vector

Once we have both $\phi(t)$ and $h_0(k)$ in hand, we continue the development by defining a discrete highpass impulse response called the *wavelet vector* as

$$h_1(k) = (-1)^k h_0(-k+1) \tag{66}$$

and, from that, a basic wavelet

$$\psi(t) = \sum_k h_1(k)\phi(2t - k) \tag{67}$$

from which an orthonormal wavelet set

$$\psi_{j,k}(t) = 2^{j/2}\psi(2^j t - k) \tag{68}$$

follows.

14.4.5.4 Computing the Wavelet Transform

Given the set of orthonormal wavelets, the wavelet series expansion of the bandlimited continuous function $f(t)$ is

$$c_{j,k} = \int_{-\infty}^{\infty} f(t)\psi_{j,k}(t)dt \quad \text{and} \quad f(t) = \sum_{j,k} c_{j,k}\psi_{j,k}(t) \tag{69}$$

and the discrete wavelet transform of the sampled function is

$$c_{j,k} = \sum_i f(i\Delta t)\psi_{j,k}(i\Delta t) \quad \text{and} \quad f(i\Delta t) = \sum_{j,k} c_{j,k}\psi_{j,k}(i\Delta t) \tag{70}$$

The coefficients and summations can also be indexed by the single integer $n = 0, 1, \ldots, N-1$, where

$$n = 2^j + k \quad \text{for} \quad j = 0, 1, \ldots, \log_2(N) - 1 \qquad k = 0, 1, \ldots, 2^j - 1 \tag{71}$$

We refer to this as the *top-down* algorithm, since it computes large-scale coefficients first. By contrast, Mallat's herringbone algorithm computes small-scale coefficients first.

The design task, then, involves first finding a sequence $h_0(k)$ that satisfies Eq. (56) and then constructing the corresponding scaling function, or choosing an orthonormal scaling function and determining $h_0(k)$ from Eq. (63). A scaling function can be made orthonormal by Eq. (65). Then the wavelet vector, $h_1(k)$, is obtained from Eq. (66) and the basic wavelet from Eq. (67).

The discrete wavelet transform can be implemented either directly, by Eq. (70), or with the FWT herringbone algorithm. The latter does not require explicit construction of the scaling function and wavelet, and it is more computationally efficient.

To be mathematically precise, the conditions in Eq. (57) establish that the wavelets $\{\psi_{j,k}(t)\}$ constitute a *tight frame* and thus will support an invertible transform. They are not, however, adequate to guarantee that these basis functions will always be orthonormal. Lawton [17,18] and Cohen [19] give strict orthonormality conditions on $h_0(k)$, but the differences between a tight frame and an orthonormal transform are so slight that digital implementations are not affected. Thus, we can be satisfied using Eq. (57).

14.4.5.5 Examples

We illustrate the construction of a wavelet transform with three examples.

Example 1. Using ideal lowpass and bandpass filters, we have [15]

$$h_0(k) = \frac{1}{\sqrt{2}}\operatorname{sinc}\left(\pi\frac{k}{2}\right) \quad \text{and} \quad h_1(k) = \sqrt{2}\,\delta(k) - h_0(k) \tag{72}$$

and

$$\phi(t) = \operatorname{sinc}(\pi t) \quad \text{and} \quad \psi(t) = 2\phi(2t) - \phi(t) \tag{73}$$

This gives a discrete wavelet transform based on *sinc wavelets* (Figure 14–11). Notice that these wavelets do not have compact support.

Example 2. If we let

$$h_0(k) = \begin{cases} \dfrac{1}{\sqrt{2}} & k = 0, 1 \\ 0 & \text{otherwise} \end{cases} \quad \text{and} \quad h_1(k) = \begin{cases} \dfrac{1}{\sqrt{2}} & k = 0 \\ \dfrac{-1}{\sqrt{2}} & k = 1 \\ 0 & \text{otherwise} \end{cases} \tag{74}$$

then $\psi(t)$ is the Haar function, and we are led to the Haar transform. This scaling vector has two nonzero entries, and, as expected, the Haar transform does have compact support.

Example 3. The sequence $h_0(k)$, having four nonzero elements and given by

$$4\sqrt{2}h_0(k) = \begin{cases} (1+\sqrt{3}) & k=0 \\ (3+\sqrt{3}) & k=1 \\ (3-\sqrt{3}) & k=2 \\ (1-\sqrt{3}) & k=3 \\ 0 & \text{otherwise} \end{cases} \tag{75}$$

satisfies Eq. (56) and is thus a scaling vector [16]. Its scaling function and wavelet, constructed by the procedure outlined in Figure 14–23, are shown in Figure 14–24. This is one of a family of finite-length sequences that give rise to orthonormal wavelets having compact support. The family is discussed further in the following section.

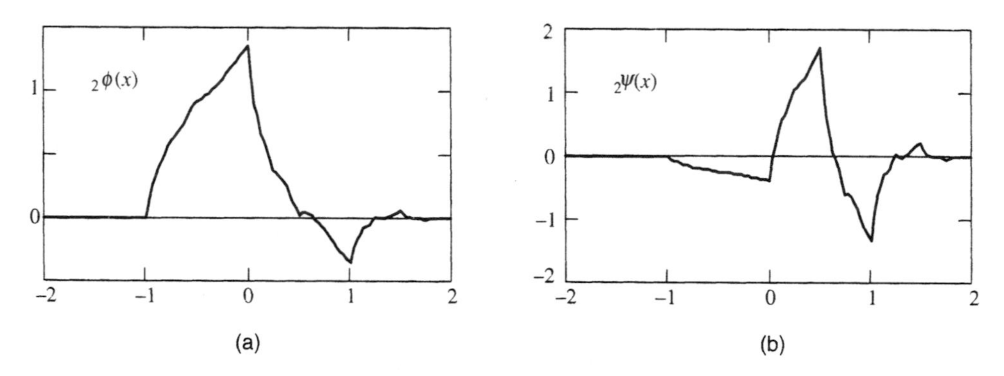

Figure 14–24 Daubechies' (a) scaling function and (b) wavelet for $r = 2$ (after [16])

14.4.5.6 Orthonormal Wavelets with Compact Support

Daubechies [16] has constructed a family, $\{_r\psi(x)\}$, of orthonormal wavelets having compact support. For each integer value of the index r, the set of wavelets

$$\{_r\psi_{j,k}(x)\} = \{2^{j/2}{}_r\psi(2^j x - k)\} \tag{76}$$

where j and k are integers, forms an orthonormal basis. Further, $_r\psi(x)$ is zero outside the interval $[0, 2r-1]$, its first r moments vanish, that is,

$$\int_{-\infty}^{\infty} x^n{}_r\psi(x)dx = 0 \qquad n = 0, 1, \ldots, r \tag{77}$$

and its number of continuous derivatives is approximately r/5. This describes a rather well-behaved, or *regular*, group of functions. Interestingly, $_1\psi(x)$ is the basic wavelet of the Haar transform.

Table 14–1 shows the sequences $h_0(k)$ that generate the orthonormal wavelets for $r = 3,5,7$, and 9. The construction technique was outlined in Sec. 14.4.5. Figure 14–25 shows plots of the corresponding wavelets. Notice that these functions become both broader and more regular with increasing r.

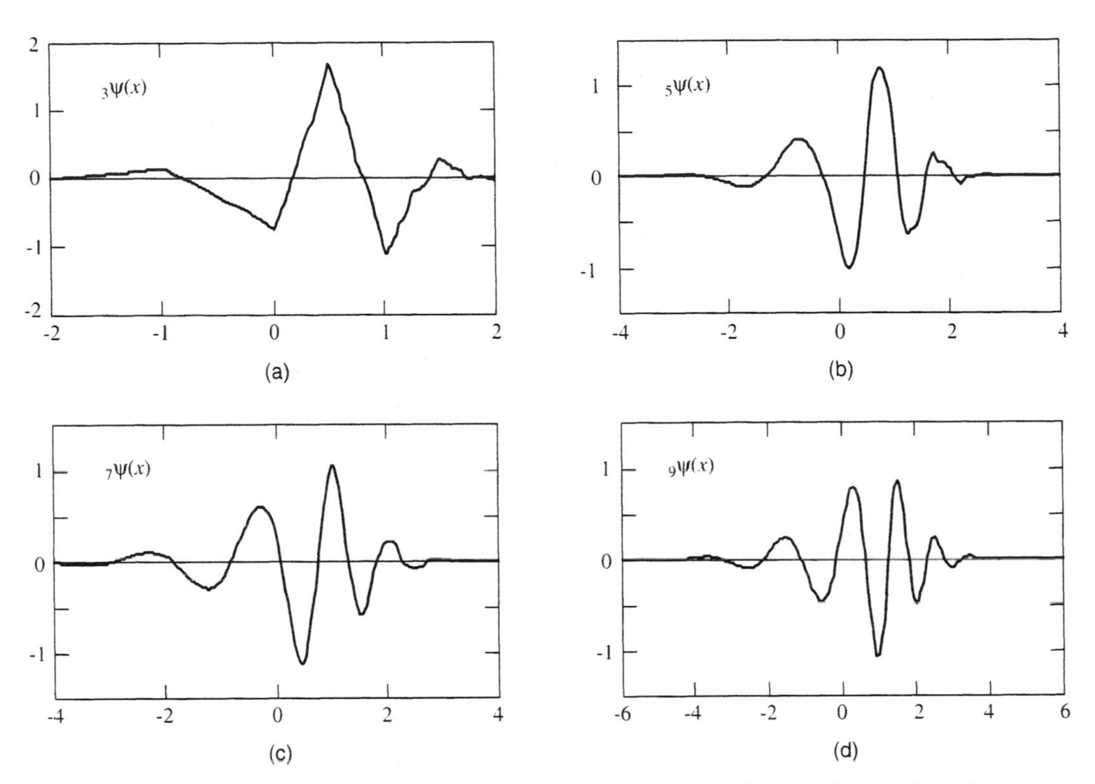

Figure 14–25 Orthonormal wavelets for (a) $r = 3$, (b) $r = 5$, (c) $r = 7$, and (d) $r = 9$ (after [16])

TABLE 14–1 DISCRETE FILTER SEQUENCES FOR THE ORTHONORMAL WAVELETS IN FIGURE 14–25 (r = 3, 5, 7 AND 9; FROM [16])

.3327	.8069	.4599	−.1350	−.0854	.0352				
.1601	.6083	.7243	.1384	−.2423	−.0322	.0776	−.0062	−.0126	.0033
.0779	.3965	.7291	.4698	−.1439	−.2240	.0713			
.0806	−.0380	−.0166	.0126	.0004	−.0018	.0004			
.0381	.2438	.6048	.6573	.1332	−.2933	−.0968	.1485	.0307	
−.0676	.0003	.0224	−.0047	−.0043	.0018	.0002	−.0003	.0000	

14.4.6 The Two-Dimensional Discrete Wavelet Transform

The concepts developed for the representation of one-dimensional signals generalize easily to two dimensions [5,7,14,16]. As with unitary image transforms, we consider the case where the two-dimensional scaling function is *separable;* that is,

$$\phi(x, y) = \phi(x)\phi(y) \tag{78}$$

where $\phi(x)$ is a one-dimensional scaling function. If $\psi(x)$ is its companion wavelet (Eq. 67), then the three two-dimensional basic wavelets

$$\psi^1(x, y) = \phi(x)\psi(y) \qquad \psi^2(x, y) = \psi(x)\phi(y) \qquad \psi^3(x, y) = \psi(x)\psi(y) \tag{79}$$

establish the foundation for a two-dimensional wavelet transform. Note that the superscript is used here as an index rather than an exponent. In particular, the set of functions

$$\{\psi^l_{j,m,n}(x, y)\} = \{2^j \psi^l(x - 2^j m, y - 2^j n)\} \qquad j \geq 0 \qquad l = 1, 2, 3 \tag{80}$$

where j, l, m, and n are integers, is an orthonormal basis for $L^2(R^2)$.

14.4.6.1 The Forward Transform

We begin with an N-by-N image, $f_1(x, y)$, where the subscript indicates scale and N is a power of two. For $j = 0$, the scale is $2^j = 2^0 = 1$, and this is the scale of the original image. Each larger integer value of j doubles the scale and halves the resolution. Some of the literature uses j to index the resolution rather than the scale. In that case $j \leq 0$, and its sign in the equations that follow is reversed.

The image can be expanded in terms of the two-dimensional wavelets as follows. At each stage of the transform, the image is decomposed into four quarter-size images, as shown in Figure 14–26. Each of the four images is formed by inner products with one of the wavelet basis images, followed by subsampling in x and y by a factor of two. For the first stage ($j = 1$), we write

$$\begin{aligned}
f_2^0(m, n) &= \langle f_1(x, y), \phi(x - 2m, y - 2n)\rangle \\
f_2^1(m, n) &= \langle f_1(x, y), \psi^1(x - 2m, y - 2n)\rangle \\
f_2^2(m, n) &= \langle f_1(x, y), \psi^2(x - 2m, y - 2n)\rangle \\
f_2^3(m, n) &= \langle f_1(x, y), \psi^3(x - 2m, y - 2n)\rangle
\end{aligned} \tag{81}$$

For subsequent stages ($j > 1$), $f^0_{2^j}(x, y)$ is decomposed in exactly the same way to form four smaller images at scale 2^{j+1} [Figure 14–26(c)]. The final result is an arrangement like that of the Haar transform, as shown in Figure 14–26(d).

Writing the inner products as convolutions, we have

$$\begin{aligned}
f^0_{2^{j+1}}(m, n) &= \left\{\left[f^0_{2^j}(x, y) * \phi(-x, -y)\right](2m, 2n)\right\} \\
f^1_{2^{j+1}}(m, n) &= \left\{\left[f^0_{2^j}(x, y) * \psi^1(-x, -y)\right](2m, 2n)\right\} \\
f^2_{2^{j+1}}(m, n) &= \left\{\left[f^0_{2^j}(x, y) * \psi^2(-x, -y)\right](2m, 2n)\right\} \\
f^3_{2^{j+1}}(m, n) &= \left\{\left[f^0_{2^j}(x, y) * \psi^3(-x, -y)\right](2m, 2n)\right\}
\end{aligned} \tag{82}$$

and the same four subsampled filtering operations are required at each stage.

Since the scaling and wavelet functions are separable, each convolution breaks down into one-dimensional convolutions on the rows and columns of $f^0_{2^j}(x, y)$. Figure 14–27 shows this in diagram form.

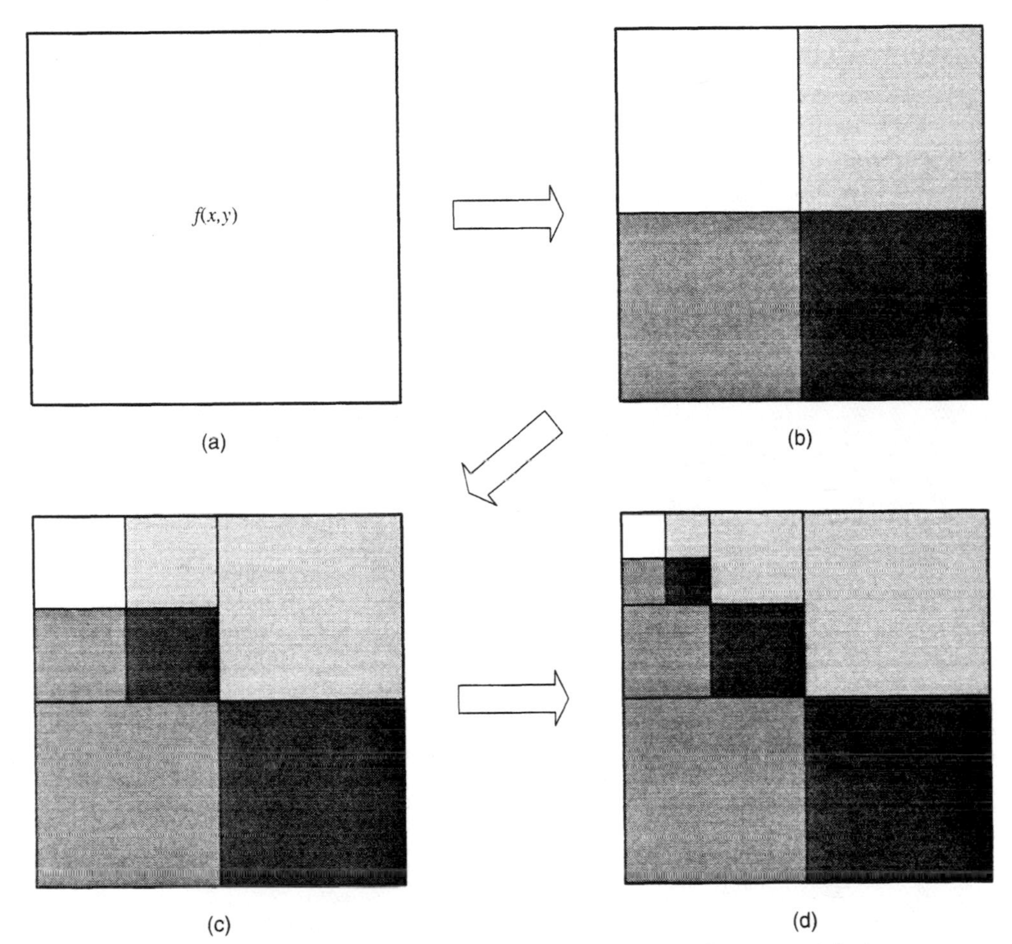

Figure 14–26 The two dimensional discrete wavelet transform: (a) original; (b) first, (c) second, (d) third step

At stage 1, for example, we first convolve the rows of the image $f_1(x, y)$ with $h_0(-x)$ and with $h_1(-x)$ and discard the odd-numbered columns (counting the leftmost as zero) of the two resulting arrays. The columns of each of the $N/2$-by-N arrays is then convolved with $h_0(-x)$ and with $h_1(-x)$, and the odd-numbered rows are discarded (counting the top row as zero). The result is the four $N/2$-by-$N/2$ arrays required for that stage of the transform.

The two-dimensional separable wavelet transform thus can be computed quickly. The transform process can be carried to J stages, where the integer $J \leq \log_2(N)$ for an N-by-N pixel image. If the transform coefficients are computed with floating-point accuracy, the inverse transform can reconstruct the original image with little degradation.

Figure 14–28 shows from where in the frequency plane each of the four next-higher scale images come, if we were to use sinc wavelets (that is, ideal halfband lowpass and bandpass filters). At each scale, $f^0_{2^j}(x, y)$ contains the low-frequency information from the previous stage, while $f^1_{2^j}(x, y)$, $f^2_{2^j}(x, y)$, and $f^3_{2^j}(x, y)$ contain the horizontal, vertical, and diagonal edge information, respectively.

rows
columns
columns
rows
$h_0(-x)$
$h_1(-x)$
$h_0(-x)$
$h_1(-x)$
$h_0(-x)$
$h_1(-x)$
$f^0_{2^{j-1}}(x,y)$
$f^0_{2^j}(x,y)$
$f^1_{2^j}(x,y)$
$f^2_{2^j}(x,y)$
$f^3_{2^j}(x,y)$

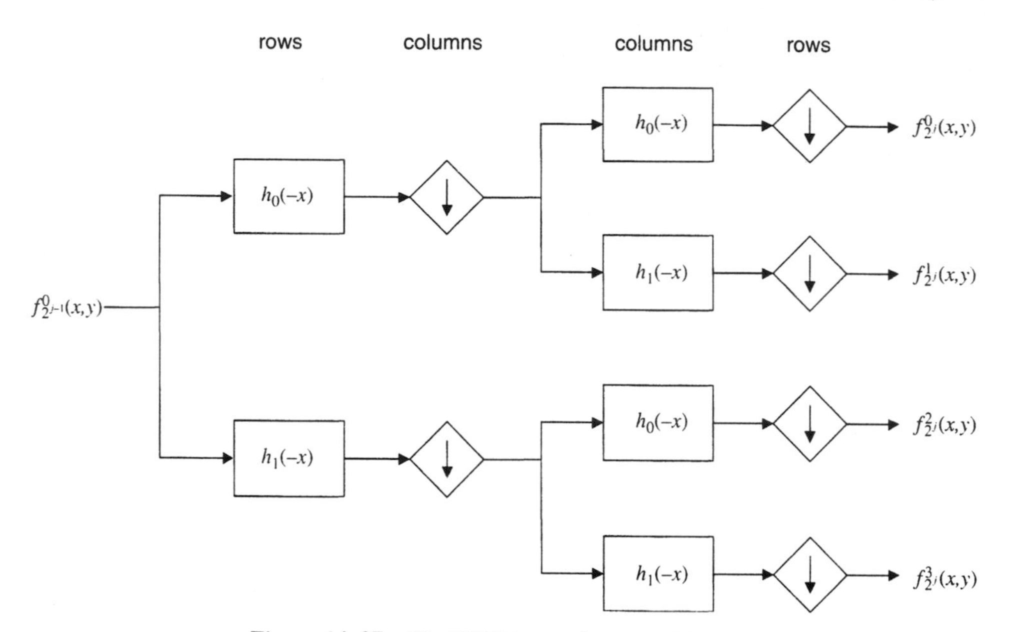

Figure 14–27 The DWT image decomposition step

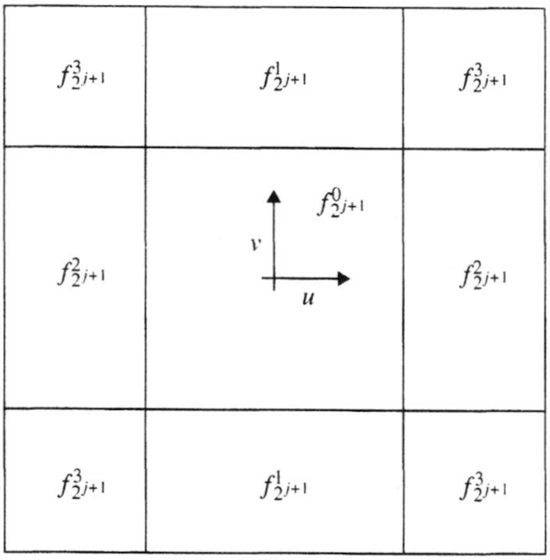

$f^3_{2^{j+1}}$
$f^1_{2^{j+1}}$
$f^3_{2^{j+1}}$
$f^0_{2^{j+1}}$
v
$f^2_{2^{j+1}}$
u
$f^2_{2^{j+1}}$
$f^3_{2^{j+1}}$
$f^1_{2^{j+1}}$
$f^3_{2^{j+1}}$

Figure 14–28 DWT decomposition in the frequency domain

14.4.6.2 The Inverse Transform

Inversion of the transform is done by a process similar to that just outlined [5,7,14,16]. This process is diagrammed in Figure 14–29.

At each stage (e.g., the last), we upsample each of the four previous stage arrays by inserting a column of zeros to the left of each column. Then we convolve the rows either with $h_0(x)$ or with $h_1(x)$, as shown in the figure, and add the $N/2$-by-N arrays together in pairs. The two resulting arrays are then upsampled to size N by N by adding a row of zeros above each row. The columns of these two arrays are then convolved with $h_0(x)$ and with $h_1(x)$, as shown. The sum of the two resulting arrays is the result for that stage of the reconstruction.

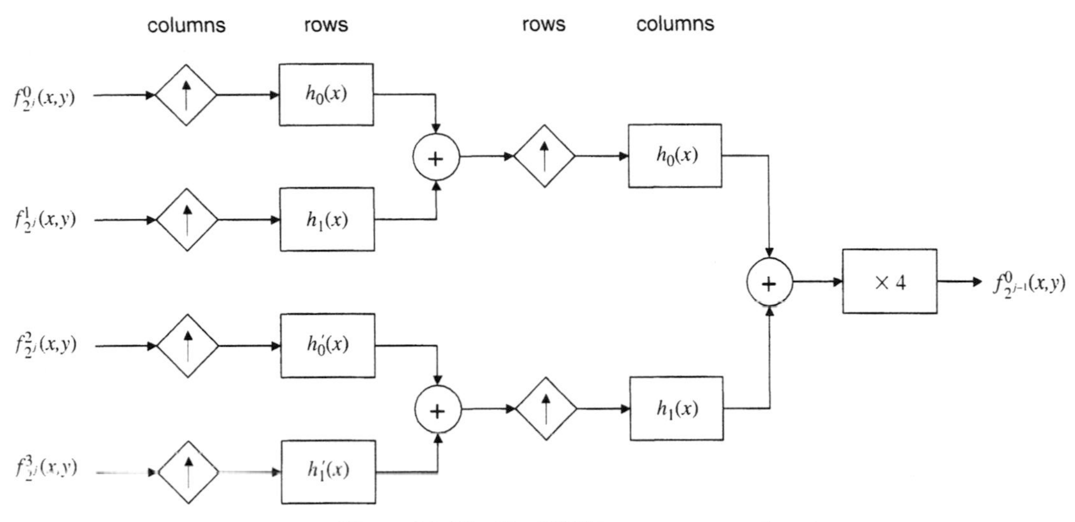

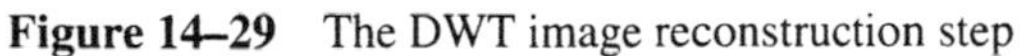
Figure 14–29 The DWT image reconstruction step

14.4.6.3 Examples

Figure 14–30 shows a numerical example of computing the first stage of the two-dimensional discrete wavelet transform. The figure depicts an eight-by-eight pixel image of a

$$\mathbf{f}=\begin{bmatrix}0&0&0&0&0&0&0&0\\0&0&0&1&1&0&0&0\\0&0&2&4&4&2&0&0\\0&1&4&8&8&4&1&0\\0&1&4&8&8&4&1&0\\0&0&2&4&4&2&0&0\\0&0&0&1&1&0&0&0\\0&0&0&0&0&0&0&0\end{bmatrix}\quad \mathbf{f}_{1,0}=\begin{bmatrix}0&0&0&0&0&0&0&0\\0&0&1&1&1&0&0&0\\0&2&4&5&4&2&0&0\\1&3&8&11&8&3&1&0\\1&3&8&11&8&3&1&0\\0&2&4&5&4&2&0&0\\0&0&1&1&1&0&0&0\\0&0&0&0&0&0&0&0\end{bmatrix}\quad \mathbf{f}_{1,1}=\begin{bmatrix}0&0&0&0&0&0&0&0\\0&0&0&0&0&0&0&0\\0&1&1&0&-1&-1&0&0\\1&2&3&0&-3&-2&-1&0\\1&2&3&0&-3&-2&-1&0\\0&1&1&0&-1&-1&0&0\\0&0&0&0&0&0&0&0\\0&0&0&0&0&0&0&0\end{bmatrix}$$

$$\mathbf{f}_{2,0}=\begin{bmatrix}0&0&0&0\\0&1&1&0\\0&4&4&0\\1&8&8&1\\1&8&8&1\\0&4&4&0\\0&1&1&0\\0&0&0&0\end{bmatrix}\quad \mathbf{f}_{2,1}=\begin{bmatrix}0&0&0&0\\0&0&0&0\\0&1&-1&0\\1&3&-3&-1\\1&3&-3&-1\\0&1&-1&0\\0&0&0&0\\0&0&0&0\end{bmatrix}\quad \mathbf{f}_{3,0}=\begin{bmatrix}0&1&1&0\\0&4&4&0\\1&9&9&1\\1&11&11&1\\1&9&9&1\\0&4&4&0\\0&1&1&0\\0&0&0&0\end{bmatrix}\quad \mathbf{f}_{3,1}=\begin{bmatrix}0&1&1&0\\0&2&2&0\\0&3&3&0\\0&0&0&0\\0&-3&-3&0\\0&-2&-2&0\\0&-1&-1&0\\0&0&0&0\end{bmatrix}\quad \mathbf{f}_{3,2}=\begin{bmatrix}0&0&0&0\\0&1&-1&0\\1&3&-3&1\\1&4&-4&-1\\1&3&-3&-1\\0&1&-1&0\\0&0&0&0\\0&0&0&0\end{bmatrix}\quad \mathbf{f}_{3,3}=\begin{bmatrix}0&0&0&0\\0&1&-1&0\\0&1&-1&0\\0&0&0&0\\0&-1&1&0\\0&-1&1&0\\0&0&0&0\\0&0&0&0\end{bmatrix}$$

$$\mathbf{f}_{4,0}=\begin{bmatrix}0&1&1&0\\1&9&9&1\\1&9&9&1\\0&1&1&0\end{bmatrix}\quad \mathbf{f}_{4,1}=\begin{bmatrix}0&1&1&0\\0&3&3&0\\0&-3&-3&0\\0&-1&-1&0\end{bmatrix}\quad \mathbf{f}_{4,2}=\begin{bmatrix}0&0&0&0\\1&3&-3&-1\\1&3&-3&-1\\0&0&0&0\end{bmatrix}\quad \mathbf{f}_{4,3}=\begin{bmatrix}0&0&0&0\\0&1&-1&0\\0&-1&1&0\\0&0&0&0\end{bmatrix}$$

Figure 14–30 Example of computing the two-dimensional discrete wavelet transform

Gaussian-like pulse. Figure 14–31 shows the corresponding (last) stage of the inverse discrete wavelet transform of the same image. (*Note:* Optionally, one can reverse the order of processing rows and columns in both the forward and inverse transforms.)

$$
g_{4,0}=\begin{bmatrix}0&0&0&0\\0&1&1&0\\0&0&0&0\\1&9&9&1\\0&0&0&0\\1&9&9&1\\0&0&0&0\\0&1&1&0\end{bmatrix}\quad
g_{4,1}=\begin{bmatrix}0&0&0&0\\0&1&1&0\\0&0&0&0\\0&3&3&0\\0&0&0&0\\0&-3&-3&0\\0&0&0&0\\0&-1&-1&0\end{bmatrix}\quad
g_{4,2}=\begin{bmatrix}0&0&0&0\\0&0&0&0\\0&0&0&0\\1&3&-3&-1\\0&0&0&0\\1&3&-3&-1\\0&0&0&0\\0&0&0&0\end{bmatrix}\quad
g_{4,3}=\begin{bmatrix}0&0&0&0\\0&0&0&0\\0&0&0&0\\0&1&-1&0\\0&0&0&0\\0&-1&1&0\\0&0&0&0\\0&0&0&0\end{bmatrix}
$$

$$
g_{3,0}=\begin{bmatrix}0&1&1&0\\0&1&1&0\\1&6&6&1\\1&6&6&1\\1&6&6&1\\1&6&6&1\\0&1&1&0\\0&1&1&0\end{bmatrix}\quad
g_{3,1}=\begin{bmatrix}0&0&0&0\\0&0&0&0\\0&-2&-2&0\\0&2&2&0\\0&2&2&0\\0&-2&-2&0\\0&0&0&0\\0&0&0&0\end{bmatrix}\quad
g_{3,2}=\begin{bmatrix}0&0&0&0\\0&0&0&0\\0&2&-2&0\\0&2&-2&0\\0&2&-2&0\\0&2&-2&0\\0&0&0&0\\0&0&0&0\end{bmatrix}\quad
g_{3,3}=\begin{bmatrix}0&0&0&0\\0&0&0&0\\0&-1&1&0\\0&1&-1&0\\0&1&-1&0\\0&-1&1&0\\0&0&0&0\\0&0&0&0\end{bmatrix}
$$

$$
g_{2,0}=\begin{bmatrix}0&0&0&0\\0&1&1&0\\0&4&4&0\\1&8&8&1\\1&8&8&1\\0&4&4&0\\0&1&1&0\\0&0&0&0\end{bmatrix}\quad
g_{2,1}=\begin{bmatrix}0&0&0&0\\0&0&0&0\\0&1&-1&0\\1&3&-3&-1\\1&3&-3&-1\\0&1&-1&0\\0&0&0&0\\0&0&0&0\end{bmatrix}\quad
g_{1,0}=\begin{bmatrix}0&0&0&0&0&0&0&0\\0&0&0&1&0&1&0&0\\0&0&0&4&0&4&0&0\\0&1&0&8&0&8&0&1\\0&1&0&8&0&8&0&1\\0&0&0&4&0&4&0&0\\0&0&0&1&0&1&0&0\\0&0&0&0&0&0&0&0\end{bmatrix}\quad
g_{1,1}=\begin{bmatrix}0&0&0&0&0&0&0&0\\0&0&0&0&0&0&0&0\\0&0&0&1&0&-1&0&0\\0&1&0&3&0&-3&0&-1\\0&1&0&3&0&-3&0&-1\\0&0&0&1&0&-1&0&0\\0&0&0&0&0&0&0&0\\0&0&0&0&0&0&0&0\end{bmatrix}
$$

$$
g_{0}=\begin{bmatrix}0&0&0&0&0&0&0&0\\0&0&1&1&1&1&0&0\\0&0&3&3&3&3&0&0\\1&1&6&6&6&6&1&1\\1&1&6&6&6&6&1&1\\0&0&3&3&3&3&0&0\\0&0&1&1&1&1&0&0\\0&0&0&0&0&0&0&0\end{bmatrix}\quad
g_{1}=\begin{bmatrix}0&0&0&0&0&0&0&0\\0&0&0&0&0&0&0&0\\0&0&-1&1&1&-1&0&0\\0&0&-2&2&2&-2&0&0\\0&0&-2&2&2&-2&0&0\\0&0&-1&1&1&-1&0&0\\0&0&0&0&0&0&0&0\\0&0&0&0&0&0&0&0\end{bmatrix}\quad
g=\begin{bmatrix}0&0&0&0&0&0&0&0\\0&0&0&1&1&0&0&0\\0&0&2&4&4&2&0&0\\0&1&4&8&8&4&1&0\\0&1&4&8&8&4&1&0\\0&0&2&4&4&2&0&0\\0&0&0&1&1&0&0&0\\0&0&0&0&0&0&0&0\end{bmatrix}
$$

Figure 14–31 Example of computing the two-dimensional inverse discrete wavelet transform

Figure 14–32 shows an example of separable two-dimensional wavelets [20]. These were constructed from Daubechies' $r = 2$ wavelet and scaling function (Figure 14–24) by Eqs. (78) and (79).

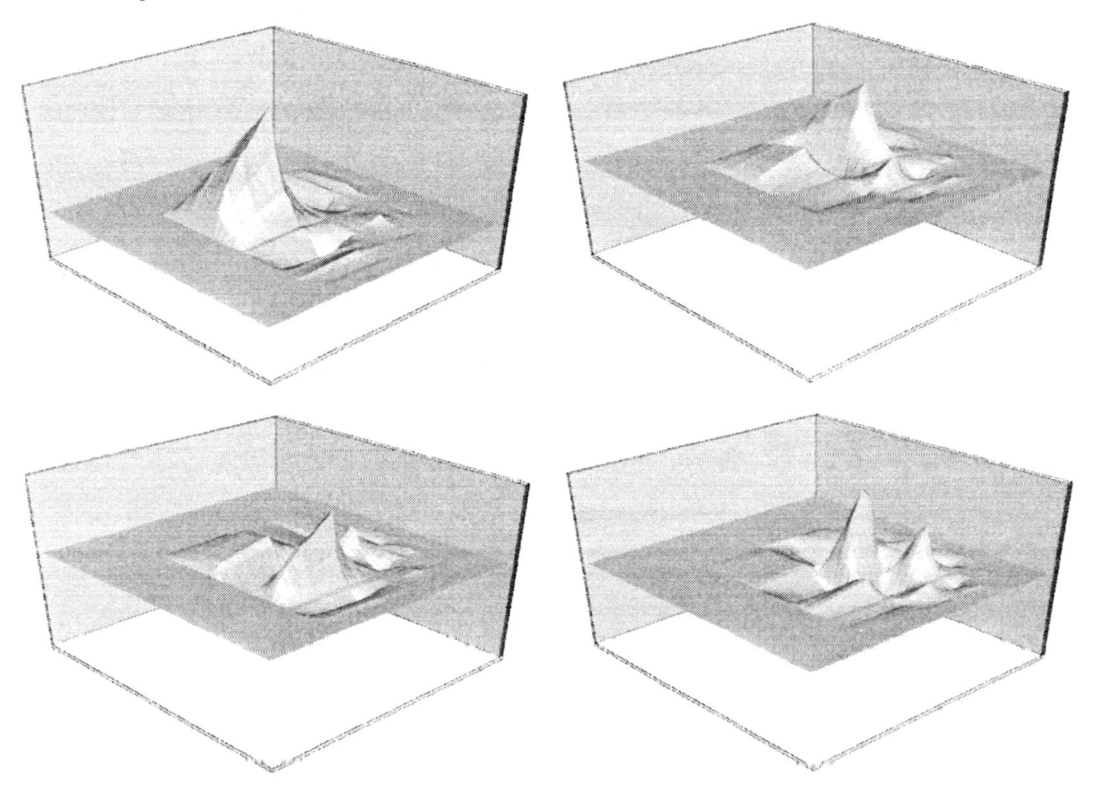

Figure 14–32 Separable two-dimensional wavelets constructed from Daubechies' $r = 2$ wavelet and scaling function (Courtesy Marcus Gross and Lars Lippert, reprinted by permission from [20])

14.4.7 Biorthogonal Wavelet Transforms

The functions that qualify as orthonormal wavelets with compact support lack desirable symmetry properties. It would be convenient, for example, if $\psi(t)$ could be an even or an odd function. By using two different wavelet bases, $\psi(x)$ and $\tilde{\psi}(x)$—one for decomposition (analysis) and the other for reconstruction (synthesis)—we can have symmetrical wavelets with compact support [5,7,21,22,23]. The two wavelets are *duals* of each other, and the wavelet families $\{\psi_{jk}(x)\}$ and $\{\tilde{\psi}_{jk}(x)\}$ are *biorthogonal;* that is,

$$\langle \psi_{j,k}, \tilde{\psi}_{l,m} \rangle = \delta_{j,l}\delta_{k,m} \tag{83}$$

Then we have

$$c_{j,k} = \langle f(x), \tilde{\psi}_{j,k}(x) \rangle \quad \text{and} \quad d_{j,k} = \langle f(x), \psi_{j,k}(x) \rangle \tag{84}$$

for the decomposition, and

$$f(x) = \sum_{j,k} c_{j,k}\psi_{j,k}(x) = \sum_{j,k} d_{j,k}\tilde{\psi}_{j,k}(x) \tag{85}$$

for the reconstruction. Either wavelet can be used for the decomposition, provided that the other one is used for the reconstruction. The biorthogonal wavelet transform allows the use of symmetric (even or odd) wavelets having compact support.

14.4.7.1 Implementation

The one-dimensional biorthogonal wavelet transform requires four discrete filters (impulse response vectors). We must choose two lowpass filters (scaling vectors), $h_0(n)$ and $\tilde{h}_0(n)$, whose transfer functions satisfy

$$H_0(0) = \tilde{H}_0(0) = 1 \quad \text{and} \quad H_0(s_N) = \tilde{H}_0(s_N) = 0 \tag{86}$$

where $s_N = 1/2\Delta x$ is the folding frequency. From these, we generate two bandpass filters (wavelet vectors), as before, by half-period shifts of their transfer functions [recall Eq. (54)]:

$$h_1(n) = (-1)^n h_0(1-n) \qquad \tilde{h}_1(n) = (-1)^n \tilde{h}_0(1-n) \tag{87}$$

Now we can implement the FWT herringbone algorithm using these four filters, as shown in Figure 14–33.

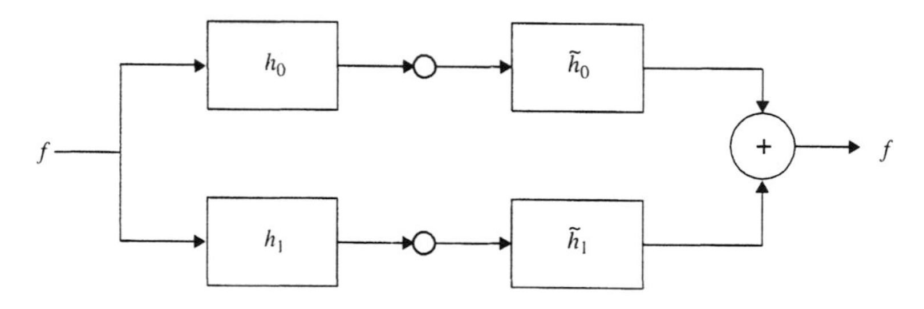

Figure 14–33 One decomposition step and one reconstruction step of the biorthogonal wavelet transform

14.4.7.2 Biorthogonal Wavelets

The conditions upon biorthogonal wavelet filters are

$$\sum_n h_0(n) = \sum_n \tilde{h}_0(n) = \sqrt{2} \quad \text{and} \quad \sum_n h_1(n) = \sum_n \tilde{h}_1(n) = 0 \tag{88}$$

and the perfect reconstruction property requires that

$$H_0(s)\tilde{H}_0(s) + H_1(s)\tilde{H}_1(s) = H_0(s)\tilde{H}_0(s) + H_0(s-s_N)\tilde{H}_0(s-s_N) = 1 \tag{89}$$

The two scaling functions are given, in the frequency domain, by

$$\Phi(2s) = \tilde{H}_0(s)\Phi(s) = \prod_{n=0}^{\infty} \tilde{H}_0(s/2^n) \quad \text{and} \quad \tilde{\Phi}(2s) = H_0(s)\tilde{\Phi}(s) = \prod_{n=0}^{\infty} H_0(s/2^n) \tag{90}$$

and the wavelets are then

$$\psi(x) = \sqrt{2}\sum_n h_1(n+1)\phi(2x-n) \quad \text{and} \quad \tilde{\psi}(x) = \sqrt{2}\sum_n \tilde{h}_1(n+1)\tilde{\phi}(2x-n) \tag{91}$$

14.4.7.3 Constructing Biorthogonal Wavelets

Biorthogonal wavelet design requires developing discrete impulse responses (scaling vectors) $h_0(n)$ and $\tilde{h}_0(n)$ whose transfer functions satisfy Eq. (86) and (89). This is an active area of research, and several authors have catalogued such filters and the corresponding biorthogonal wavelets.

Cohen, Daubechies, and Feauveau [21], for example, select $\phi(x)$ as a B-spline function (e.g., the triangle function) and develop $H_0(s)$ as a polynomial in $\cos(s)$. Vetterli and Herley [22] present approaches based on the theory of diophantine equations and on the theory of continued fractions. Generally, using longer impulse responses gives rise to more regular wavelets, that is, those having a larger number of derivatives and vanishing moments. Table 14–2 presents three pairs of scaling vectors, and Figure 14–34 shows the corresponding biorthogonal wavelets, constructed by the procedure outlined in Figure 14–23.

TABLE 14–2 DISCRETE FILTER SEQUENCES FOR THE BIORTHOGONAL WAVELETS IN FIGURE 14–33 (FROM[21] AND [22]).

Laplacian analysis filter:	$h_0 = \sqrt{2}[-.05\ \ .25\ \ .6\ \ .25\ \ -.05]^t$
Laplacian synthesis filter:	$\tilde{h}_0 = \sqrt{2}[-.0107\ \ -.0536\ \ .2607\ \ .6071\ \ .2607\ \ -.0536\ \ -.0107]^t$
Spline 2 filter:	$h_0 = \sqrt{2}[.25\ \ .5\ \ .25]^t$
Spline 4 filter:	$\tilde{h}_0 = \frac{\sqrt{2}}{128}[3\ \ -6\ \ -16\ \ 38\ \ 90\ \ 38\ \ -16\ \ -6\ \ 3]^t$
18-point analysis filter:	$h_0 = [.0012\ \ -.0007\ \ -.0118\ \ .0117\ \ .0713\ \ -.0310\ \ -.2263\ \ .0693\ \ .7318$ $.7318\ \ .0693\ \ -.2263\ \ -.0310\ \ .0713\ \ .0117\ \ -.0118\ \ -.0007\ \ .0012]^t$
18-point synthesis filter:	$\tilde{h}_0 = [.0012\ \ .0007\ \ -.0113\ \ -.0114\ \ .0235\ \ .0017\ \ -.0444\ \ .2044\ \ .6479$ $.6479\ \ .2044\ \ -.0444\ \ .0017\ \ .0235\ \ -.0114\ \ -.0113\ \ .0007\ \ .0012]^t$

14.4.7.4 Two-dimensional Biorthogonal Wavelets

The biorthogonal wavelets for the forward two-dimensional transform are given by Eq. (79), as before. For the inverse transform, they are

$$\tilde{\psi}^1(x, y) = \tilde{\phi}(x)\tilde{\psi}(y) \qquad \tilde{\psi}^2(x, y) = \tilde{\psi}(x)\tilde{\phi}(y) \qquad \tilde{\psi}^3(x, y) = \tilde{\psi}(x)\tilde{\psi}(y) \tag{92}$$

The implementation of the two-dimensional biorthogonal FWT is a straightforward extension of the orthonormal case.

14.5 WAVELET SELECTION

The ideal basic wavelet would be an oscillatory function of brief duration (i.e., having compact support or small amplitude outside a short interval) where all dyadic translations of binary scalings of the function are orthonormal. The Haar function illustrates this. Other available wavelet functions may fail to meet all these criteria.

First, while the basic wavelet must go to zero as $|x| \to \infty$ at least as fast as $1/x$ in order to meet the admissibility criterion, many wavelets still have infinite, rather than compact, support. This means that they are nonzero over the entire real line, except for their zero-crossings. It may be that dyadic translations of the wavelet at each scale are orthogonal, but

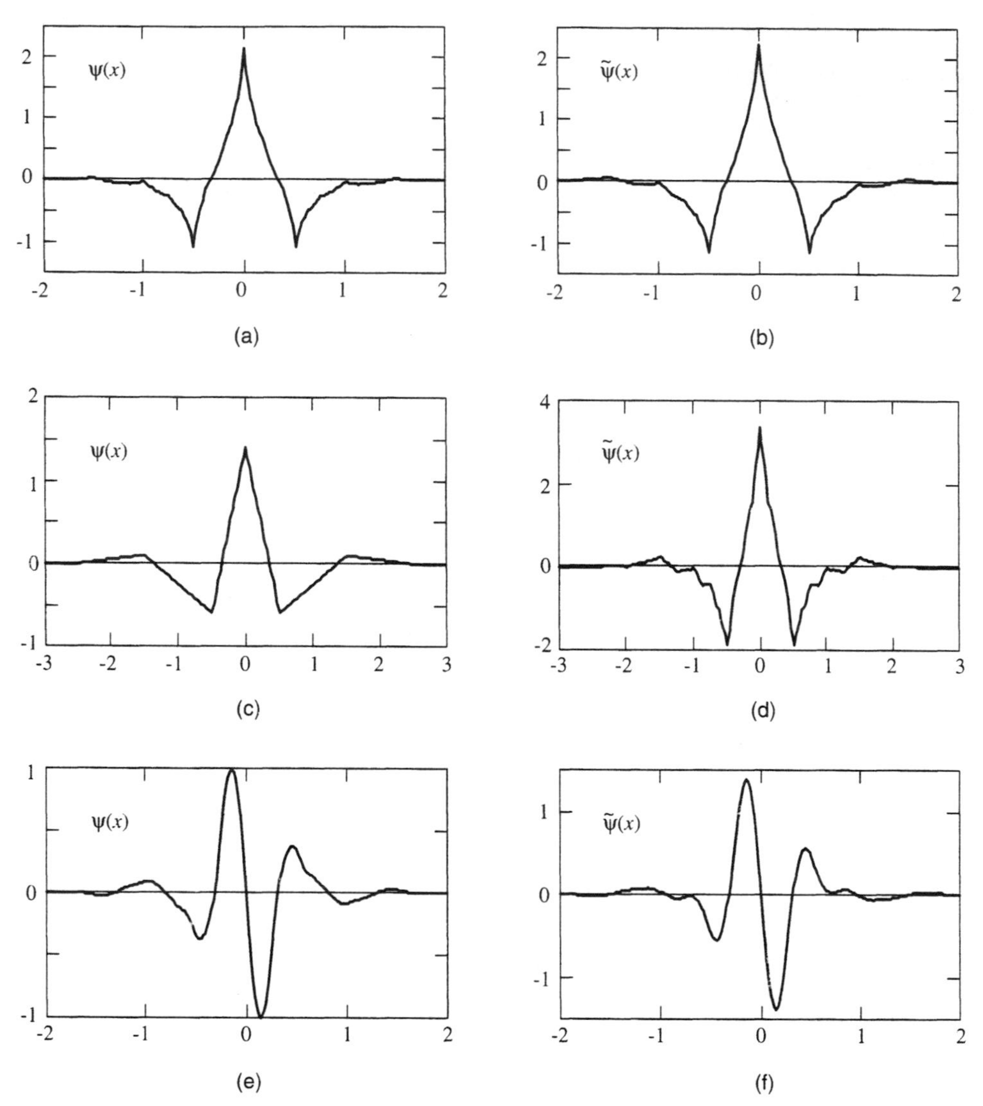

Figure 14–34 Examples of biorthogonal wavelets: (a) Laplacian pyramid wavelet [21]; (b) linear spline function wavelet [21]; (c) 18-point linear phase wavelet [22]

wavelets at different scales are not. Similarly, it may be that different scales of the wavelet are orthogonal, but some or all dyadic translations at the same scale are not.

Notice that some wavelet transforms (e.g., the CWT) are overcomplete, while others (e.g., the DWT) are not. For overcomplete transforms, the restrictions on the basis functions are relatively mild. For transforms involving little or no redundancy, such as the orthonormal discrete wavelet transform, the restrictions placed on basis functions are much more severe.

The biorthogonal DWT requires two scaling vectors and two wavelet vectors rather than one each, but this does not increase the computational burden of the process. The biorthogonal transform, however, affords a much wider choice of wavelet shape than the orthonormal transform, so it is preferable in many applications.

The choice of a basic wavelet is usually governed by the application. For lossless compression, for example, an orthonormal or biorthogonal basis is desirable or required, since the objective is to represent the function exactly and compactly. An overcomplete transform increases the amount of data required to represent the function exactly. If, on the other hand, the goal is lossy compression, the detection of specific components such as edges in an image, or noise removal, then it is more important to select a wavelet that is similar to the components of interest.

Wavelet transforms offer the promise of compact representation and efficient detection of image components that match the waveshape of the chosen wavelet. The orthonormal wavelet transform is inherently compact, but it does not behave well under slight shifts of the image components [24]. An image component that matches a wavelet will appear compactly in the transform if it happens to align with one of the dyadic positions of the wavelet, but not otherwise. For this reason, non-orthonormal transforms often perform better in detection tasks.

14.6 APPLICATIONS

Although wavelet transforms are relatively new on the image processing scene, they have already begun to see application in practice.

14.6.1 Image Compression

The discrete wavelet transform decomposes an image into a set of successively smaller orthonormal images. Further, while the gray-level histogram of the original image can be of any shape, those of the wavelet transform images are commonly unimodal and symmetrical about zero [14]. This simplifies an analysis of the statistical properties of the image.

Often, one can either coarsely quantize or eliminate entirely those coefficients having small value. Mallat and others have studied the possibility of reconstructing an image from only the zero-crossing locations of its wavelet transform [25]. While perfect reconstruction is generally impossible [7], many images can be adequately approximated by this highly compact coding.

14.6.2 Image Enhancement

The DWT decomposes an image into components of different size, position, and orientation. As with linear filtering in the Fourier frequency domain, one can alter the amplitude of coefficients in the wavelet transform domain prior to obtaining the inverse transform. This can selectively accentuate interesting components at the expense of undesirable ones. Figure 14–35 shows an example of edge-specific contrast enhancement [26,27]. Notice how the four peaks in the histogram are separated by the process.

14.6.3 Image Fusion

Image fusion combines two or more registered images of the same object into a single image that is more easily interpreted than any of the originals. This technique finds application in

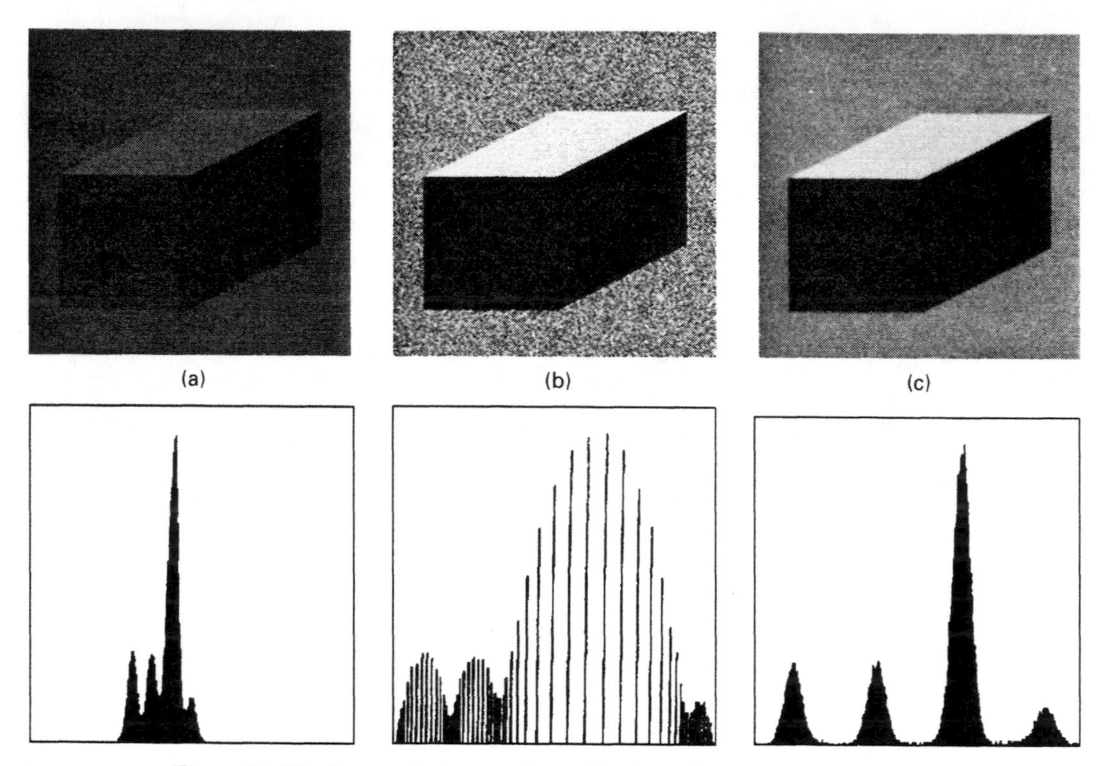

Figure 14–35 Image enhancement by multiscale gradient: (a) original; (b) enhanced by histogram equalization; (c) enhanced by scale-variable edge stretching. Gray-level histograms appear below each image (Courtesy Jian Lu, reprinted by permission from [26])

multispectral image interpretation, as well as medical imaging, where images of the same body part are obtained by several different imaging modalities.

Figure 14–36 shows two examples of image fusion using a wavelet transform [28]. In each case, the two images were combined in the transform domain by taking the maximum-amplitude coefficient at each coordinate. An inverse DWT of the resulting coefficients then reconstructed the fused image. In the first case, the process combined the in-focus information from the two input images. In the second case, the anatomic information of the MRI image was combined with the functional information of the PET scan to produce a convenient composite.

14.7 SUMMARY OF IMPORTANT POINTS

1. A basic wavelet is an oscillatory function that dies out as $|x| \to \infty$. Its spectrum resembles the transfer function of a bandpass filter.
2. A set of basis functions for a wavelet transform can be generated from dilations and translations of a basic wavelet.
3. The continuous wavelet transform represents a signal as a function of two variables: time and scale. It represents an image as a function of three variables: two for spatial position and one for scale.

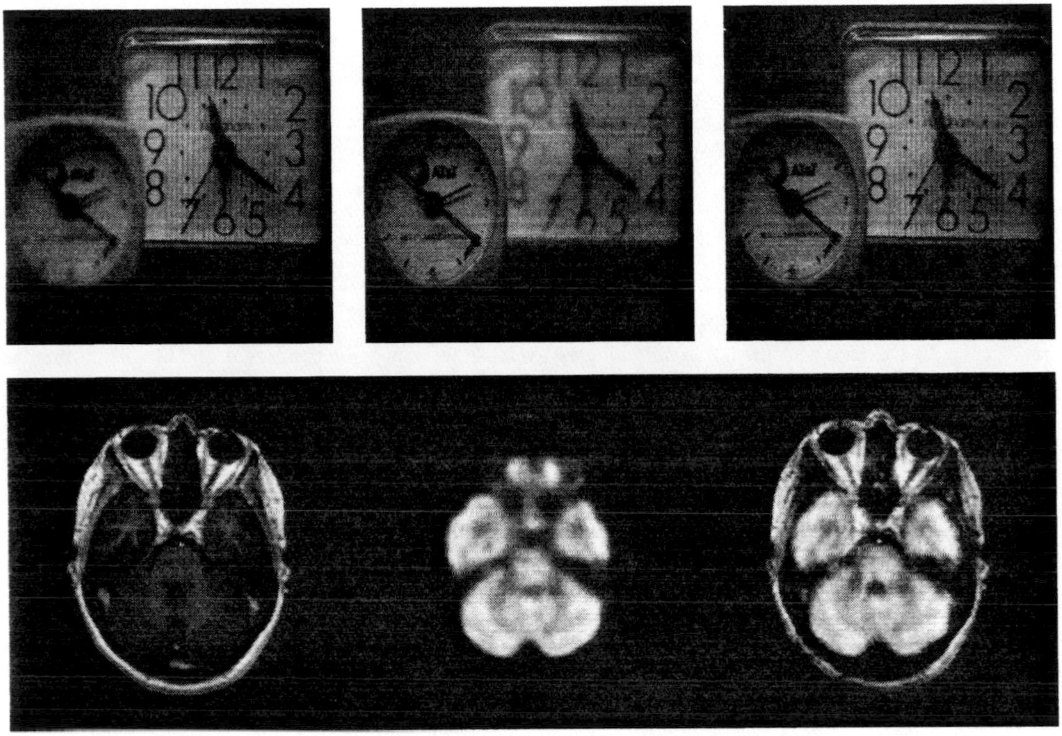

Figure 14–36 Wavelet transform image fusion: (a), (b) images taken at different focus settings; (c) fused image; (d) MRI image; (e) PET image; (f) fused image (Courtesy Henry Hui Li, reprinted by permission from [28])

4. The wavelet series expansion represents a periodic or finite-length signal with a series of coefficients.
5. The discrete wavelet transform represents an N-point signal with N coefficients. It represents an N-by-N image with N^2 coefficients.
6. The Haar transform is the simplest discrete wavelet transform.
7. The DWT can be implemented directly or, indirectly, by the fast wavelet transform (FWT, or herringbone) algorithm.
8. The separable two-dimensional DWT can also be implemented by the FWT algorithm.
9. Biorthogonal wavelet systems permit the DWT to use less restricted (e.g., symmetric) wavelets with compact support.

PROBLEMS

1. Which wavelet transform would you expect to perform best in detecting lines in an engineering drawing? Why?
2. Which wavelet transform would you expect to perform best in compressing fingerprint images? Why?

3. Which wavelet transform would you expect to perform best in image fusion? Why?
4. Which wavelet transform would you expect to perform best in detecting stars in a telescope image? Why?
5. Which wavelet transform would you expect to perform best in segmenting aerial photographs on the basis of texture? Why?

PROJECTS

1. Develop a program implementing the continuous wavelet transform, and use the program to locate the notes in a digitized recording of a simple song.
2. Develop a program for computing a wavelet series expansion of a signal, and use the program to compress a signal.
3. Develop a program for computing the discrete wavelet transform of a signal, and use the program to locate transient components in a signal.
4. Develop a program for computing a continuous wavelet transform of an image, and use the program to locate the spots in a simple image.
5. Develop a program for computing a wavelet series expansion of an image, and use the program to compress an image.
6. Develop a program for computing the discrete wavelet transform of an image, and use the program to locate edges in an image.

REFERENCES

1. S. Pittner, J. Schneid, and C. W. Ueberhuber, *Wavelet Literature Survey,* Technical University of Vienna, Vienna, Austria, 1993.
2. A. Haar, "Zur Theorie der Orthogonalen Funktionen-System," Inaugural Dissertation, *Math. Annalen,* **5:**17–31, 1955.
3. D. Gabor, "Theory of Communication," *IEEE Proc.,* **93:**429–441, 1946.
4. A. Grossman and J. Morlet, "Decomposition of Hardy Functions into Square Integrable Wavelets of Constant Shape," *SIAM J. Appl. Math.,* **15:**723–736, 1984.
5. C. K. Chui, *An Introduction to Wavelets,* Academic Press, San Diego, 1992.
6. A. P. Calderon, "Intermediate Spaces and Interpolation, the Complex Method," *Studia Math,* **24:**113–190, 1964.
7. Y. Meyer (transl. by R. D. Ryan), *Wavelets: Algorithms and Applications,* Society for Industrial and Applied Mathematics, Philadelphia, 1993.
8. H. C. Andrews, *Computer Techniques in Image Processing,* Academic Press, New York, 1970.
9. J. E. Shore, "On the Application of Haar Functions," *IEEE Trans. Comm.,* **COM-21,** 209–216, 1973.
10. P. J. Burt and E. H. Adelson, "The Laplacian Pyramid as a Compact Image Code," *IEEE Trans.,* **C-31:**532–540, 1983.
11. J. W. Woods and S. D. O'Neill, "Subband Coding of Images," *IEEE Trans.,* **ASSP-34:**1278–1288, 1986.
12. D. Esteban and C. Galand, "Application of Quadrature Mirror Filters to Split-Band Voice Coding Systems," *Int. Conf. on Acoustics, Speech and Signal Processing,* Washington, DC, pp. 191–195, 1977.

13. A. Croisier, D. Esteban, and C. Galand, "Perfect Channel Splitting by use of Interpolation, Decimation, Tree Decomposition Techniques," *Int. Conf. on Information Sciences and Systems,* pp. 443–446, 1976.

14. S. Mallat, "A Theory for Multiresolution Signal Decomposition: The Wavelet Representation," *IEEE Trans.,* **PAMI-11:**674–693, 1989.

15. R. A. Gopinath and C. S. Burrus, "Wavelet Transforms and Filter Banks," *Wavelets—A Tutorial in Theory and Applications* (C. K. Chui, ed.), pp. 603–654, Academic Press, 1992.

16. I. Daubechies, "Orthonormal Bases of Compactly Supported Wavelets," *Commun. on Pure and Appl. Math.,* **41:**909–996, 1988.

17. W. M. Lawton, "Tight Frames of Compactly Supported Wavelets," *J. Math. Phys.,* **31:**1898–1900, 1990.

18. W. M. Lawton, "Necessary and Sufficient Conditions for Existence of ON Wavelet Bases," *J. Math. Phys.,* **32:**57–61, 1991.

19. L. Cohen, "Time-Frequency Distributions—A Review," *Proc. IEEE,* **77**(7):941–981, 1989.

20. M. H. Gross, R. Koch, L. Lippert, and A. Dreger, "Multiscale Image Texture Analysis in Wavelet Spaces," *Proc. ICIP '94,* **III:**412–416, IEEE Computer Society Press, Los Alamitos, CA, 1994.

21. A. I. Cohen, I. Daubechies, and J. C. Feauveau, "Bi-Orthogonal Bases of Compactly Supported Wavelets," *Comm. Pure and Applied Math.,* **45:**485–560, 1992.

22. M. Vetterli and C. Herley, "Wavelets and Filter Banks: Theory and Design," *IEEE Trans.,* **SP-40**(9):2207–2232, 1992.

23. J. C. Feauveau, P. Mathieu, M. Barlaud, and M Antonini, "Recursive Biorthogonal Wavelet Transform for Image Coding," *ICASSP '91: 1991 Int. Conf. on Acoustics, Speech and Signal Processing,* IEEE Press, New York, **4:**2649–2652, 1991.

24. E. P. Simoncelli, W. T. Freeman, E. H. Adelson, and D. J. Heeger, "Shiftable Multiscale Transforms," *IEEE Trans.,* **IT-38**(2):587–607, 1992.

25. S. Mallat, "Zero-Crossings of a Wavelet Transform," *IEEE Trans.,* **IT-37**(4):1019–1033, 1991.

26. J. Lu, D. M. Healy, and J. B. Weaver, "Contrast Enhancement of Medical Images Using Multiscale Edge Representation," *Optical Engineering,* **33**(7):2151–2161, 1994.

27. J. Lu and D. M. Healy, "Contrast Enhancement via Multiscale Gradient Transformation," *Proc. ICIP '94,* **II:**482–486, IEEE Computer Society Press, Los Alamitos, CA, 1994.

28. H. Hui Li, B. S. Manjunath, and S. K. Mitra, "Multi-Sensor Image Fusion Using the Wavelet Transform," *Proc. ICIP '94,* **I:**51–55, IEEE Computer Society Press, Los Alamitos, CA, 1994.

CHAPTER 15

Optics and System Analysis

15.1 INTRODUCTION

So far in Part 2, we have developed a set of analytical tools that will allow us to analyze the components commonly used in digital imaging. Now we apply those tools to develop ways to quantify the performance of digital image-processing systems.

Two circumstances often arise that require a workable method for system analysis. One is when we are called upon to select or configure a digital imaging system for a particular type of use. Here, a suitable set of components or an entire system must be selected from a set of alternatives, usually in light of cost constraints.

The other circumstance arises each time a system user approaches a new problem. Normally, the user has control over only one link in the image-processing chain: the computer program that performs the digital processing operations. The performance of the other system components, from the digitizer to the display, is usually preset by hardware design, although selection options may be available. Proper maintenance is also required for best performance.

One must be able to specify what effect the hardware portion of the system will have upon an image, so as to compensate for these effects in software. In this way, the processing program can be fashioned to accomplish a given goal, without having concomitant degradations spoil the project.

Before a particular digital imaging problem can be approached properly, one must confirm that the instrumentation in use is adequate for the task. In particular, the resolution, magnification, number of pixels, pixel size, and pixel spacing must be appropriate for the tasks at hand. There should be a balance among the optics (camera, telescope, microscope, etc.), the image sensor (camera), the image digitization, storage and display hardware, and the algorithms used for processing and quantitative analysis of the digital images. In this chapter, we seek a set of workable guidelines for establishing such a balance.

A detailed analysis of all aspects of an image-processing system can become quite complex, and this extends beyond our scope. The approach used here is to make a few well-founded assumptions that lead to simple and broadly applicable rules of thumb. If necessary, a margin of safety can be added to guard against error in the underlying assumptions. In most cases of practical interest, the resulting accuracy will prove adequate.

15.1.1 Performance Analysis of a Digital Imaging System

The question we address here is, How can one analyze a system to determine whether it is adequate and cost effective for carrying out the image processing and quantitative image analysis projects for which it is intended? We seek to establish a balance among the various components in the imaging chain, so that the overall performance is adequate for the task and none of the components represents overkill compared to what is required to do the job.

We address the topics of spatial resolution and image sampling, with the goal of establishing a balance between the performance of each of the system components and that of the overall system. The aim is to relate the performance of the various components to that of the system as a whole.

Resolution. Considerable confusion often arises around the concept of resolution. To avoid this confusion, one needs a clear definition of what resolution is and a clear understanding of the goal of any analysis of the resolving power of an imaging instrument.

For our purposes, the key resolution question is: Will the system adequately reproduce the small detail in the objects of interest? This question can be answered readily if we first have a concise, quantitative answer to another question: How well does the system reproduce objects of different sizes? Then, assuming that we know the size of the detail of interest, we can obtain an answer to the key question of resolution.

To approach the latter question, we apply the tools of linear system theory (Chapter 9) to those components of the system that precede the actual sampling (i.e., the conversion from analog to digital form). These components can be assumed to behave as linear, shift-invariant system components, in which case linear system theory is applicable.

In particular, we analyze the image-forming optics and the image sensor (camera) to determine the effective size and shape of the scanning spot. From this come the imaging system point-spread function and its equivalent, the imaging system MTF. The latter forms the quantitative specification of resolution we require for the resolution portion of the analysis.

Sampling. The key question regarding the parameters of the sampling process can be stated as: How many pixels are required, and what must their spacing be, to ensure that the digitized image adequately represents the content of the optical image? This involves an entirely different set of considerations from those associated with resolution. Sampling is an extremely nonlinear process, and failing to distinguish between sampling and resolution considerations can create considerable confusion.

To approach the sampling question, we apply the sampling theorem (Chapter 12) to the analog-to-digital conversion step. This yields a simple way to determine whether the pixel spacing is small enough, and it describes what happens if it is not.

Image Display. The third key question in digital imaging system analysis can be stated as: Will the displayed image adequately represent the objects of interest? In applications involving only quantitative analysis, image display may be of little consequence or even unnecessary. In other applications—particularly those involving image processing and human interpretation—it is a vital element. As before, image display involves considerations different from those of resolution and sampling, and it deserves a separate analysis.

We consider the image display process to be an interpolation step and again apply the sampling theorem. This yields a way to determine whether the display process is adequate and gives guidelines for improvement when it is not.

Practical Considerations. Once each of the three aforementioned basic processes has been analyzed, one can combine the three results to determine whether the overall system design is balanced and adequate for the specific applications for which it is intended. Finally, one must assess the effect of each of the assumptions and approximations that have been made in the analysis and the effect that noise in the system will have.

In earlier chapters, we developed tools to describe the effects of sampling, interpolation, and linear filtering. Before we can analyze complete systems, we need a method to describe the effects of the lenses that are usually a part of the system. In the following section we develop techniques for analyzing the performance of optical systems, and in the remainder of the chapter we apply a collection of techniques to the analysis of complete digital imaging systems.

15.2 OPTICS AND IMAGING SYSTEMS

Optical imaging systems play an important role in digital imaging because they almost always appear at the front end (and frequently at both ends) of an image-processing system. If photography is involved prior to scanning, then another lens system must be included in the analysis.

Optical systems produce two effects upon an image: projection, as discussed in Chapter 2, and a degradation due to the effects of diffraction and lens aberrations. Projection accounts for inversion of the image in its coordinate system (i.e., a 180-degree rotation) and for magnification. The field of physical optics—particularly, diffraction theory—provides the tools to describe image degradation that is due to (1) the wave nature of light and (2) the aberrations of imperfectly designed and manufactured optical systems. Accordingly, we next present a brief development of important points from physical optics. For a more detailed treatment of optical system analysis, the reader should consult an optics text. (See Appendix 2.)

15.2.1 Basics of Optical Systems

Figure 15–1 shows an optical system consisting of a simple lens. A point source at the origin of the focal (object) plane produces a spot image at the origin of the image plane. The image

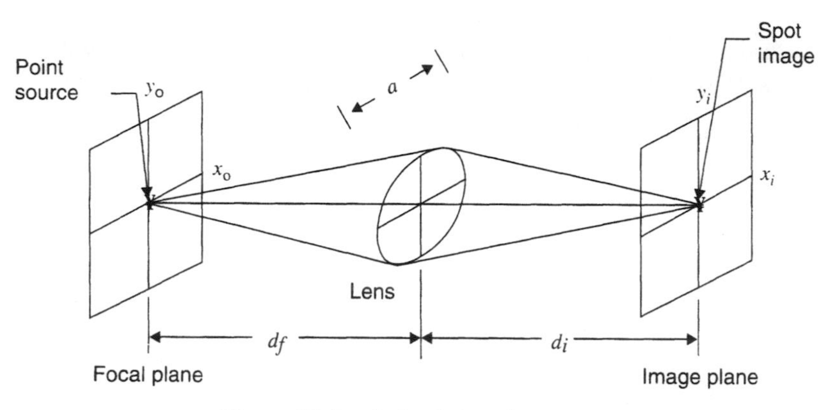

Figure 15–1 A simple imaging system

produced by a point source is called the *point-spread function* (PSF) in optical terms. It will take on its smallest possible size if the system is in focus, that is, if

$$\frac{1}{d_f} + \frac{1}{d_i} = \frac{1}{f} \tag{1}$$

where f is the focal length of the lens. By this nomenclature, the focal plane is that plane in the object space that forms an in-focus image on the image plane. This differs from the term *focal plane shutter* that is used in photography to describe a shutter located at the film (image) plane.

It is intuitively clear that increasing the intensity of the point source causes a proportional increase in the intensity of the spot image. This means that the lens is a two-dimensional linear system. It follows that two point sources produce an image in which the two spots combine by addition.

If the point source moves off the z-axis to a position (x_o, y_o), then the spot image moves to a new position given by

$$x_i = -Mx_o \qquad y_i = -My_o \tag{2}$$

where

$$M = \frac{d_i}{d_f} \tag{3}$$

is the *magnification* of the system.

For reasonably small off-axis distances in well-designed optical systems, the shape of the spot image undergoes essentially no change. Thus, the system can be assumed to be shift invariant (or, in optics terminology, *isoplanatic*), as well as linear, and the PSF is then its impulse response.

15.2.1.1 Linearity

An opaque object illuminated from the front (epiilluminated) or a light-absorbing object illuminated from behind (transilluminated) can be thought of as a two-dimensional distribution of point sources of light. The image of such an object is a summation of spatially distributed psf spots. This means that the image can be described as a convolution of the object with the PSF of the optical system.

Furthermore, an isoplanatic optical system can be completely specified by either its two-dimensional psf or its two-dimensional *optical transfer function* (OTF). The OTF is the two-dimensional Fourier transform of the PSF. Eq. (2) accounts for the projection performed by the optical system, while convolution with the PSF accounts for the loss of detail that is inherent in the imaging process.

15.2.1.2 Shift Invariance

Physical lens systems are not truly shift invariant. Typically, image sharpness degrades (i.e., the PSF expands) as one moves off the axis, but the shift variance is a gradual phenomenon. For a high-quality lens, the PSF, though not an impulse, at least is nonzero only over a small region. Since the shift variance is a gradual phenomenon, we can assume that each point is surrounded by a neighborhood of shift invariance. In the field of optics, these neighborhoods are called *isoplanatic patches*. Thus, if not globally shift invariant, the optical system at least can be assumed locally shift invariant over the small extent of the PSF, and convolution is still a valid model locally.

To an approximation that we can use routinely, an optical imaging system is a two-dimensional, shift-invariant linear system. If necessary, we can model the system with a PSF having a spatially variant parameter. While this technique can account for most typically encountered anisoplanatism, it is usually unnecessary in the analysis of high-quality lens systems.

15.2.1.3 Basic Relations

Eqs. (1) and (3) give rise to a set of formulas that are useful in the analysis of optical systems. In particular,

$$f = \frac{d_i d_f}{d_i + d_f} = \frac{d_i}{M+1} = d_f \frac{M}{M+1} \tag{4}$$

$$d_i = \frac{f d_f}{d_f - f} = f(M+1) \tag{5}$$

and

$$d_f = \frac{f d_i}{d_i - f} = f\frac{(M+1)}{M} \tag{6}$$

15.2.2 Coherent and Incoherent Illumination

In Figure 15–1, the point source emits a spherical light wave. The E-field amplitude as a function of time and space can be written as

$$u(x, y, z, t) = \frac{a}{r}\cos\left[-2\pi\frac{r}{\lambda} + 2\pi\left(\frac{c}{\lambda}t + \frac{\phi(t)}{\lambda}\right)\right] \tag{7}$$

where

$$r = \sqrt{x^2 + y^2 + z^2} \tag{8}$$

λ is the mean wavelength of the light, c is the speed of light, and $\phi(t)$ accounts for the phase fluctuation with time. Usually, this is random. Note that $\phi(t)$ also accounts for the bandwidth of quasi-monochromatic light. For convenience, we define the *wave number,* which is actually a frequency variable, as

$$k = \frac{2\pi}{\lambda} \tag{9}$$

and move to complex exponentials as before. Now Eq. (7) becomes

$$u(x, y, z, t) = \mathcal{R}e\left\{\frac{A}{r}e^{-jkr}e^{jk[ct + \phi(t)]}\right\} \tag{10}$$

In this section, we are concerned with the spatial distribution of light intensity in the spot image. We shall, for the time being, drop the $\mathcal{R}e\{\ \}$ and the time-varying components as being understood.

Under monochromatic illumination, the object is a spatial distribution of point sources at the same temporal frequency c/λ. If all the point sources have a fixed phase relationship, the illumination is called *coherent.* They may still fluctuate randomly, but they remain in synchrony, preserving fixed relative phase. If, on the other hand, the point sources vary in phase independently of each other, the illumination is called *incoherent.* In that case, the phase of each point source varies independently of its neighbors.

In most instances, the human eye or some other time-averaging sensor makes ultimate use of the image. Under time averaging, the random fluctuations of $\phi(t)$ are averaged out.

In coherent illumination, since the point sources fluctuate in unison, the fixed phase relationship permits stable patterns of constructive and destructive interference to exist among the point images. These stable patterns of interference are apparent to a time-averaging sensor. Thus, for coherent illumination, the convolution operation must be performed on the complex amplitude of the electromagnetic waves.

In incoherent illumination, the random relative phase relationships cause interference phenomena to average out to no net effect. Thus, the point images add statistically. This behavior is modeled accurately if the convolution is performed on an intensity (amplitude squared, or power) basis. Hence, in coherent illumination an optical system is linear in complex amplitude, while in incoherent light the system is linear in intensity.

15.2.3 Image Quality Factors

The two factors that limit the image quality of an optical system are lens aberrations and diffraction effects. Careful lens design can minimize, although never completely eliminate, aberrations. Diffraction effects result from the wave nature of light and the finite size of the lens. Since image-processing equipment usually employs high-quality optics with relatively low aberration levels, it is often diffraction that places the upper limit on image quality. In the next section, we derive the PSF of an aberration-free (diffraction-limited) optical system and indicate how to account for aberrations. We will be able to specify an optical system by its diffraction-limited PSF, by manufacturer-supplied PSF data, or by an experimentally determined PSF.

15.3 DIFFRACTION-LIMITED OPTICAL SYSTEMS

Since we have argued that, to a reasonable approximation, an optical system is a shift-invariant linear system, we need only to find an expression for either the PSF or the transfer function of the system. In Figure 15–1, the point source emits an expanding spherical wave, part of which enters the lens. The high refractive index of the lens slows the wave. Since the lens is thicker near the axis than near the edges, axial rays are slowed more than peripheral rays. In the ideal case, the variation in thickness is just right to convert the expanding spherical wave into another spherical wave converging toward the image point. Any deviation of the exit wave from spherical form is, by definition, due to aberration. Thus, a diffraction-limited optical system produces a converging spherical exit wave in response to the diverging spherical entrance wave of a point source.

15.3.1 Lens Shape

For a thin, double-convex lens having a diameter that is small compared to its focal length, the surfaces of the lens must be spherical to produce a spherical exit wave. Furthermore, the focal length f of the lens is given by the equation

$$\frac{1}{f} = (n-1)\left(\frac{1}{R_1} + \frac{1}{R_2}\right) \tag{11}$$

where n is the refractive index of the glass and R_1 and R_2 are the radii of the front and rear spherical surfaces of the lens [1].

For lens diameters that are not small in comparison to f, spherical lens surfaces are not adequate to produce a spherical exit wave. Such lenses do not converge peripheral rays to the same point on the z-axis as they do near-axial rays. This phenomenon is called spherical aberration, since it is an aberration resulting from the (inappropriate) spherical shape of the lens surfaces. High-quality optical systems employ aspheric surfaces and multiple lens elements to reduce spherical aberration.

15.3.2 Apertures and the Pupil Function

In Figure 15–1, the spot image formed by the truncated converging spherical wave is exactly the PSF of the system. Figure 15–2 shows a different, but equivalent, way to create the same image. Here, a converging spherical wave is truncated by an opaque screen containing an aperture. The aperture represents the extent of the lens in Figure 15–1. More complicated optical systems may contain several lenses and apertures, or *stops*. All apertures, however, can be projected through to the exit pupil to establish an effective exit aperture of the system. In Figure 15–2, the aperture represents the effective exit aperture of any aberration-free lens system.

The spatial distribution of transmittance in the screen containing the aperture is the pupil function. Thus, for a circular aperture of diameter a centered on a coordinate system (x_a, y_a), the pupil function is

$$p(x_a, y_a) = \Pi\left(\frac{\sqrt{x_a^2 + y_a^2}}{a}\right) \tag{12}$$

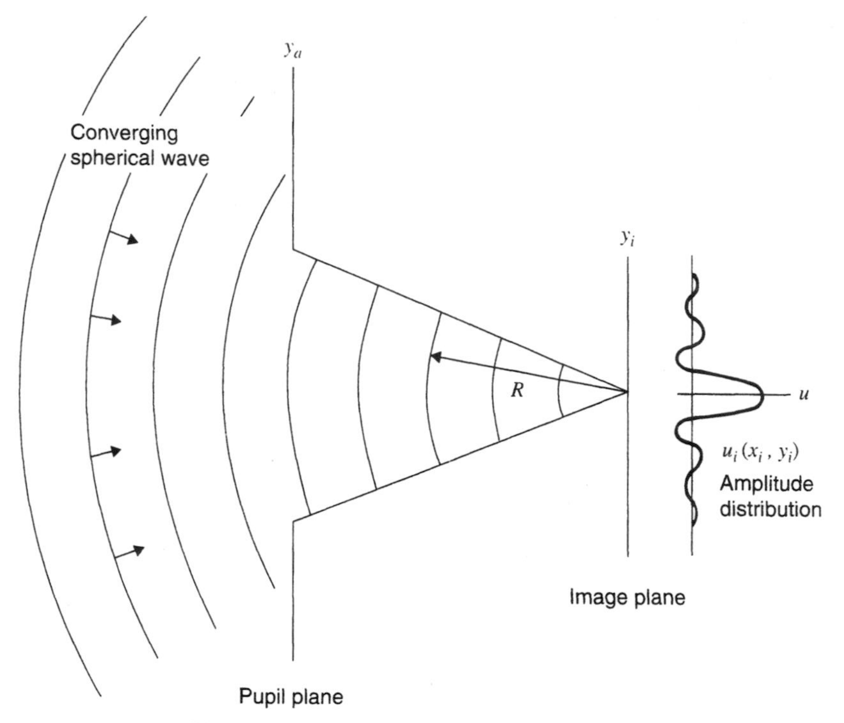

Figure 15–2 The truncated spherical exit wave

For ordinary apertures, the pupil function assumes only the values 0 and 1. It is possible, however, to implement variable transmittance pupils using photographic or metal film deposition techniques.

For aberration-free systems, the pupil function is real valued; otherwise it would disturb the spherical shape of the exit wave. Complex-valued pupil functions are used to model optical systems with aberrations.

While the analysis that follows permits the use of arbitrary pupil functions, the case of most practical importance is the circular aperture.

The E-field of the unit-amplitude converging spherical wave in Figure 15–2 can be written as

$$u(x_i, y_i, z_i) = \frac{1}{R}e^{-jkR} \tag{13}$$

using the conventions described in connection with Eq. (10). R is the distance of the point (x_i, y_i, z_i) from the origin of the image plane. In order to determine the distribution of light on the image plane, we shall make use of an important principle of wave motion.

15.3.3 The Huygens-Fresnel Principle

One of the most interesting and useful properties of optical wave propagation is embodied in the Huygens-Fresnel principle. This principle states that the field produced by a propagating wave front is the same as that which would be produced by an infinity of *secondary* point sources distributed all along that wave front [1]. In the case of a wave propagating through an aperture, the field at any point behind the aperture is the same as that which would be produced by filling the aperture with secondary point sources of the proper amplitude and phase. Mathematically, the Huygens-Fresnel principle says that the field at the point (x_i, y_i) in the image plane is given by

$$u_i(x_i, y_i) = \frac{1}{j\lambda} \iint_A u_a(x_a, y_a) \frac{1}{r} e^{jkr} \cos(\theta) dx_a\, dy_a \tag{14}$$

(See Figure 15–3.) The term $u_a(x_a, y_a)$ is the field in the aperture, and the integration is performed over the aperture. The distance from the point of interest at (x_i, y_i) to the point (x_a, y_a) in the aperture is r, while θ is the angle between the line connecting those two points and the normal to the plane of the aperture.

For our purposes, θ is small enough that $\cos(\theta)$ can be assumed to be unity. We can extend the integration limits of Eq. (14) to infinity if we multiply the converging wave by the pupil function. This effects truncation by driving the field to zero everywhere in the pupil plane except inside the aperture. Under these conditions, Eq. (14) becomes

$$u_i(x_i, y_i) = \frac{1}{j\lambda} \int_{-\infty}^{\infty} \int_{-\infty}^{\infty} p(x_a, y_a) \frac{1}{R} e^{-jkR} \frac{1}{r} e^{jkr} dx_a dy_a \tag{15}$$

This distance from the convergence point at the origin of the image plane to the point (x_a, y_a) in the aperture is

$$R = \sqrt{x_a^2 + y_a^2 + d_i^2} \tag{16}$$

and the distance from (x_a, y_a) to (x_i, y_i) is

$$r = \sqrt{(x_i - x_a)^2 + (y_i - y_a)^2 - d_i^2} \tag{17}$$

In Eq. (15), the terms $1/R$ and $1/r$ are well approximated by $1/d_i$. In the exponentials, however, the terms R and r have the large coefficient k, and we must use a better approximation.

15.3.4 The Fresnel Approximation

We can factor d_i out of Eqs. (16) and (17) and write them as

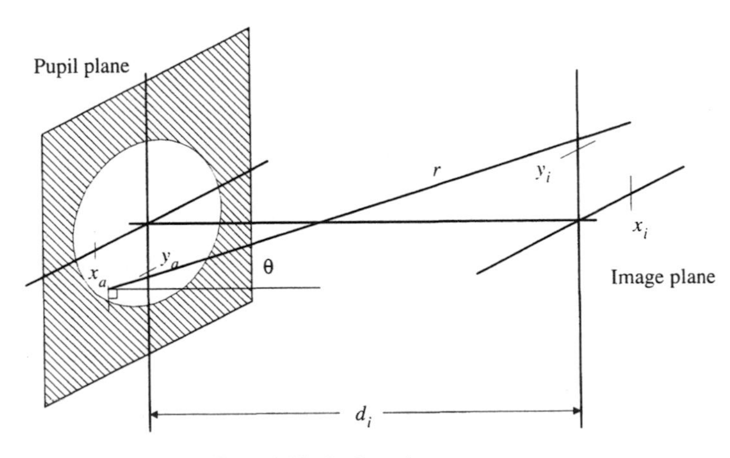

Figure 15–3 Imaging geometry

$$R = d_i\sqrt{1 + \left(\frac{x_a}{d_i}\right)^2 + \left(\frac{y_a}{d_i}\right)^2} \tag{18}$$

and

$$r = d_i\sqrt{1 + \left(\frac{x_i - x_a}{d_i}\right)^2 + \left(\frac{y_i - y_a}{d_i}\right)^2} \tag{19}$$

The binomial series expansion of the square root is

$$\sqrt{1+q} = 1 + \frac{q}{2} - \frac{q^2}{8} + \cdots \qquad |q| < 1 \tag{20}$$

If we use only the first two terms of the expansion, we produce the Fresnel approximations [1] to the distances in Eqs. (18) and (19):

$$R \approx d_i\left[1 + \frac{1}{2}\left(\frac{x_a}{d_i}\right)^2 + \frac{1}{2}\left(\frac{y_a}{d_i}\right)^2\right] \tag{21}$$

$$r \approx d_i\left[1 + \left(\frac{x_i - x_a}{d_i}\right)^2 + \frac{1}{2}\left(\frac{y_i - y_a}{d_i}\right)\right]^2 \tag{22}$$

15.3.5 The Coherent Point Spread Function

Substituting the foregoing approximations into Eq. (15) produces

$$\begin{aligned} u_i(x_i, y_i) = {} & \frac{1}{j\lambda d_i^2}\int_{-\infty}^{\infty}\int_{-\infty}^{\infty} p(x_a, y_a)e^{-jkd_i\left[1 + \frac{1}{2}\left(\frac{x_a}{d_i}\right)^2 + \left(\frac{y_a}{d_i}\right)\right]^2} \\ & \times e^{jkd_i\left[1 + \frac{1}{2}\left(\frac{x_i - x_a}{d_i}\right)^2 + \left(\frac{y_i - y_a}{d_i}\right)\right]^2} dx_a\, dy_a \end{aligned} \tag{23}$$

After expanding the exponents and collecting terms, we can write Eq. (23) as

$$u_i(x_i, y_i) = \frac{e^{(jk/2d_i)(x_i^2 + y_i^2)}}{j\lambda d_i^2}\int_{-\infty}^{\infty}\int_{-\infty}^{\infty} p(x_a, y_a)e^{(-j2\pi/\lambda d_i)(x_i x_a + y_i y_a)}dx_a\, dy_a \tag{24}$$

If we make the variable substitutions

$$x_a' = \frac{x_a}{\lambda d_i} \qquad y_a' = \frac{y_a}{\lambda d_i} \tag{25}$$

then Eq. (24) becomes

$$u_i(x_i, y_i) = \frac{\lambda}{j}e^{(jk/2d_i)(x_i^2 + y_i^2)}\int_{-\infty}^{\infty}\int_{-\infty}^{\infty} p(\lambda d_i x_a', \lambda d_i y_a')e^{-j2\pi(x_i x_a' + y_i y_a')}dx_a'\, dy_a' \tag{26}$$

We now have the extremely important result that the coherent PSF is, aside from a complex coefficient, merely the two-dimensional Fourier transform of the pupil function.

The complex exponential coefficient in Eq. (26) affects only the phase in the image plane, and this is ignored by commonly used image sensors. Thus, for our purposes, the term in front of the integral is merely a complex constant.

In Figure 15–2, the point source is on the z-axis. The preceding development can be done with the source located off the axis, and it produces the same result, although shifted as dictated by Eq. (2). This means that, under our assumptions, the system is indeed shift invariant. As the image point moves off the axis, however, the assumptions begin to break down. Thus, the PSF of an imaging system does indeed change (for the worse) in the periphery of the field. It is customary, however, to specify an imaging system by its on-axis PSF.

Eq. (26) gives the amplitude distribution in the image plane produced in response to a point source at the origin of the focal plane. The complex terms in front of the integral relate the brightness of the image to that of the point source and describe the phase variations in the image plane. Since typical image sensors ignore phase information, it is of little interest to us here. Furthermore, the overall brightness of the image is most easily determined by a separate analysis, taking into account that portion of the source radiation intercepted by the lens. Thus, the only parameters of interest to us are those that affect the quality of the image—namely, the shape of the PSF.

We can simplify the notation considerably if we give up absolute amplitude calibration and ignore the terms in front of the integral. Then we can write the convolution relation between the object (subscript o) and the image (subscript i)as

$$u_i(x_i, y_i) = \int_{-\infty}^{\infty}\int_{-\infty}^{\infty} h(x_i - x_o, y_i - y_o)u_o(Mx_o, My_o)dx_o\, dy_o \tag{27}$$

where the impulse response is given by

$$h(x, y) = \mathfrak{F}\{p(\lambda d_i x_a, \lambda d_i y_a)\} \tag{28}$$

In Eq. (27), the term $u_o(x_o, y_o)$ is the amplitude distribution of the object, and $u_o(Mx_o, My_o)$ is the object after projection without degradation into the image plane. Thus, we can consider imaging as a two-step process: geometrical projection, followed by convolution in the image plane with the PSF. The magnification factor M is negative unless the coordinate axes in the image plane and focal plane are rotated 180 degrees with respect to each other.

Frequently, it is most convenient to perform our analysis in the focal (object) plane. In that case, we can assume that convolution with the psf occurs in the focal plane and merely substitute df for di in Eq. (28). We then convolve the resulting psf with the unprojected object $u_o(x_o, y_o)$.

15.3.6 The Coherent Optical Transfer Function

The transfer function of an optical system is merely the Fourier transform of the impulse response in Eq. (28). This, however, is itself a Fourier transform—that of the pupil function. Transforming a function twice merely reflects it about the origin, so the coherent transfer function is given by

$$H(u, v) = p(-\lambda d_i u, -\lambda d_i v) \tag{29}$$

In the common case of symmetrical apertures, the 180-degree rotation has no effect. Thus, the pupil function, properly scaled, is the coherent OTF.

15.3.7 The Incoherent Point-Spread Function

A distribution of point sources described by Eq. (10) is adequate to model three kinds of illumination: monochromatic, narrow-band spatially coherent, and narrow-band incoherent. For monochromatic illumination, $\phi(t)$ is constant. If the light is spatially coherent, $\phi(t)$ is random, but bears a fixed relationship to all other points in the image. In the case of incoherent light, $\phi(t)$ is random at each point and independent of its neighbors. In this case, the observed intensity at a point (x_i, y_i) is

$$I_i(x_i, y_i) = \mathcal{E}\{u_i(x_i, y_i)u_i^*(x_i, y_i)\} \tag{30}$$

where the expectation operator $\mathcal{E}\{\ \}$ represents the time average over a period that is long compared with the vibration period of the light source. Since the $u_i(x_i, y_i)$ that results from a point source at the origin of the focal plane is given by Eq. (27), we can substitute into Eq. (30) to obtain

$$I_i(x_i, y_i) = \mathcal{E}\left\{\int_{-\infty}^{\infty}\int_{-\infty}^{\infty} h(x_i - x_1, y_i - y_1)u_o(Mx_1, My_1)dx_1\, dy_1 \times \int_{-\infty}^{\infty}\int_{-\infty}^{\infty} h^*(x_i - x_2, y_i - y_2)u_o^*(Mx_2, My_2)dx_2\, dy_2\right\} \tag{31}$$

Since $h(x, y)$ is independent of time, we can rearrange Eq. (31) to yield

$$I_i(x_i, y_i) = \int_{-\infty}^{\infty}\int_{-\infty}^{\infty}\int_{-\infty}^{\infty}\int_{-\infty}^{\infty} h(x_i - x_1, y_i - y_1)h^*(x_i - x_2, y_i - y_2) \times \mathcal{E}\{u_o(Mx_1, My_1)u_o^*(Mx_2, My_2)\}dx_1\, dy_1\, dx_2\, dy_2 \tag{32}$$

The expectation term is merely the temporal cross-correlation function of u_o at the points (x_1, y_1) and (x_2, y_2). Since, in the case of incoherent illumination, the cross-correlation of distinct image point sources is zero, this is a spatial impulse. Furthermore, if $x_1 = x_2$ and $y_1 = y_2$, the value of the expectation term is merely the intensity of the image at that point. This means that

$$\mathcal{E}\{u_o(Mx_1, My_1)u_o^*(Mx_2, My_2)\} = I_o(Mx_1, My_1)\delta(x_1 - x_2, y_1 - y_2) \tag{33}$$

Substituting this into Eq. (32) and carrying out the integration to eliminate the variables x_2 and y_2 produces

$$I_i(x_i, y_i) = \iint |h(x_i - x_o, y_i - y_o)|^2 I_o(Mx_o, My_o)dx_o,\, dy_o \tag{34}$$

where the variables x_o and y_o have been substituted for x_1 and y_1.

Eq. (34) is a two-dimensional convolution integral. It indicates that, under incoherent illumination, the system is linear in intensity, and the PSF is the squared modulus of $h(x,y)$, the coherent PSF. This, in turn, is the inverse Fourier transform of the pupil function, given by Eq. (29). Thus, the incoherent PSF is the power spectrum of the pupil function.

15.3.7.1 Circular Aperture

For a lens with a circular aperture of diameter a in narrow-band incoherent light having center wavelength λ, the PSF is

$$h(r) = \left[2 \frac{J_1\left(\pi\left[\frac{r}{r_0}\right]\right)}{\pi\left[\frac{r}{r_0}\right]} \right]^2 \quad (35)$$

where $J_1(x)$ is the first-order Bessel function of the first kind [1]. The constant r_0, a dimensional scale factor, is

$$r_0 = \frac{\lambda d_i}{a} \quad (36)$$

and r is radial distance measured from the optical axis of the image plane; that is,

$$r = \sqrt{x_i^2 + y_i^2} \quad (37)$$

15.3.8 The Incoherent Optical Transfer Function

The normalized Fourier transform of the incoherent PSF is called the *incoherent* OTF. Since the incoherent PSF is the power spectrum of the pupil function, the autocorrelation theorem implies that the incoherent OTF is the normalized autocorrelation function of the pupil function:

$$\mathrm{OTF}(u, v) = \frac{R_p(u, v)}{R_p(0, 0)} = \frac{\int_{-\infty}^{\infty}\int_{-\infty}^{\infty} p(\lambda d_i x, \lambda d_i y)\, p(\lambda d_i x - u, \lambda d_i y - v)\, dx\, dy}{\int_{-\infty}^{\infty}\int_{-\infty}^{\infty} p^2(\lambda d_i x, \lambda d_i y)\, dx\, dy} \quad (38)$$

15.3.8.1 Circular Aperture

For a lens with a circular aperture of diameter a in narrow-band incoherent light having center wavelength λ, the OTF is [1]

$$H(q) = \frac{2}{\pi - 2}\left\{ \cos^{-1}\left[\frac{q}{f_c}\right] - \sin\left[\cos^{-1}\left(\frac{q}{f_c}\right)\right]\right\} \quad (39)$$

where q is the spatial frequency variable, measured radially in two-dimensional frequency space. It is given by

$$q = \sqrt{u^2 + v^2} \quad (40)$$

where u and v are spatial frequencies in the x and y directions, respectively. The parameter f_c, called the *optical cutoff frequency*, is determined from

$$f_c = \frac{1}{r_0} = \frac{a}{\lambda d_i} \quad (41)$$

Figure 15–4 illustrates, for circular and rectangular apertures, the relationships among the pupil function and the coherent and incoherent point-spread and transfer functions. Notice that under coherent illumination the OTF is flat out to the cutoff frequency, while under incoherent illumination it drops off monotonically. Notice also that the cutoff frequency in incoherent light is twice as high as it is in coherent light.

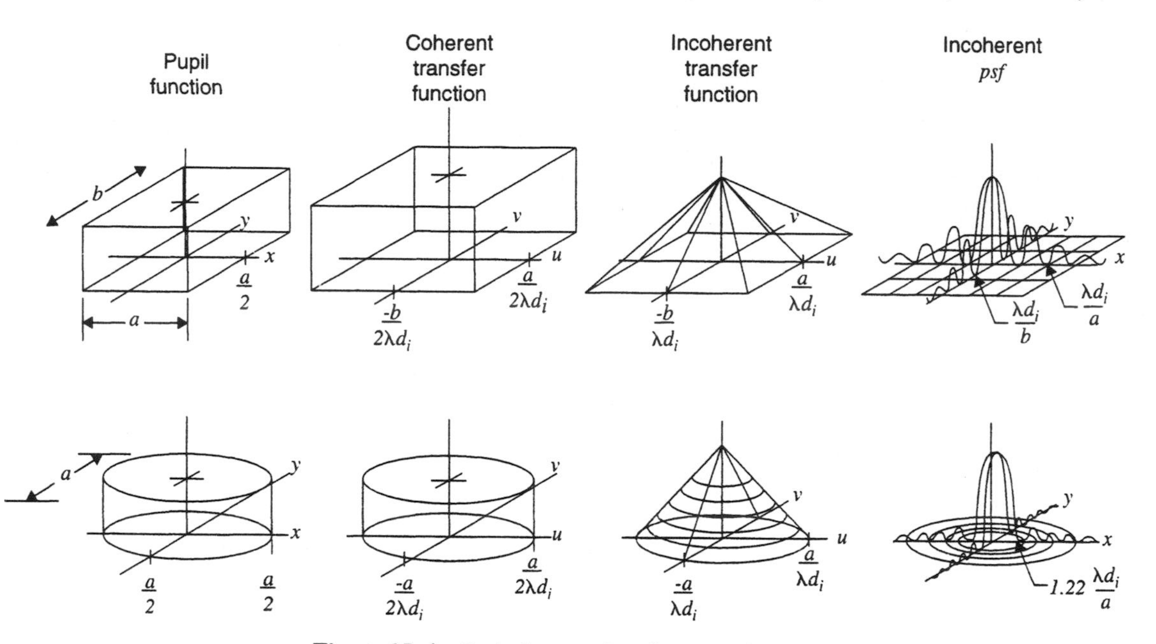

Figure 15–4 Optical properties of rectangular and circular apertures

15.3.9 Optical Transfer Function Design

If the exit pupil of an optical system is an aperture, the pupil function $p(x, y)$ takes on only the values 0 and 1. We can thus exert some control over the OTF by careful selection of the aperture. In fact, since photographic or metal film deposition techniques can be used to implement pupil functions that take on intermediate values, we can exert *considerable* control over the OTF.

For example, Frieden [2] has computed the circular pupil functions that maximize the OTF at particular frequencies. Several of these functions and the corresponding OTFs are shown in Figure 15–5. Notice that the circular aperture is very nearly optimal for maximizing the OTF at midrange frequencies, and little improvement by control of the pupil function is possible. To maximize the OTF at lower frequencies, we let the transmittance of the pupil fall off with increasing radius. This is called *apodization.* A central stop of appropriate diameter is nearly optimal for maximizing the OTF at frequencies above the midrange.

15.3.10 The Optical Transfer Function and the Modulation Transfer Function

The complex-valued OTF specifies how well the lens can reproduce, in the image plane, sinusoidal features that occur in the focal plane. The modulus (magnitude) of the OTF is the modulation transfer function (MTF) discussed in Chapter 2.

High-quality lenses are designed to introduce a minimum of phase shift and often can be assumed to be phaseless. This means that the OTF reduces to a (real-valued) MTF. For many purposes, then, one can use the terms *OTF* and *MTF* more or less interchangeably. As

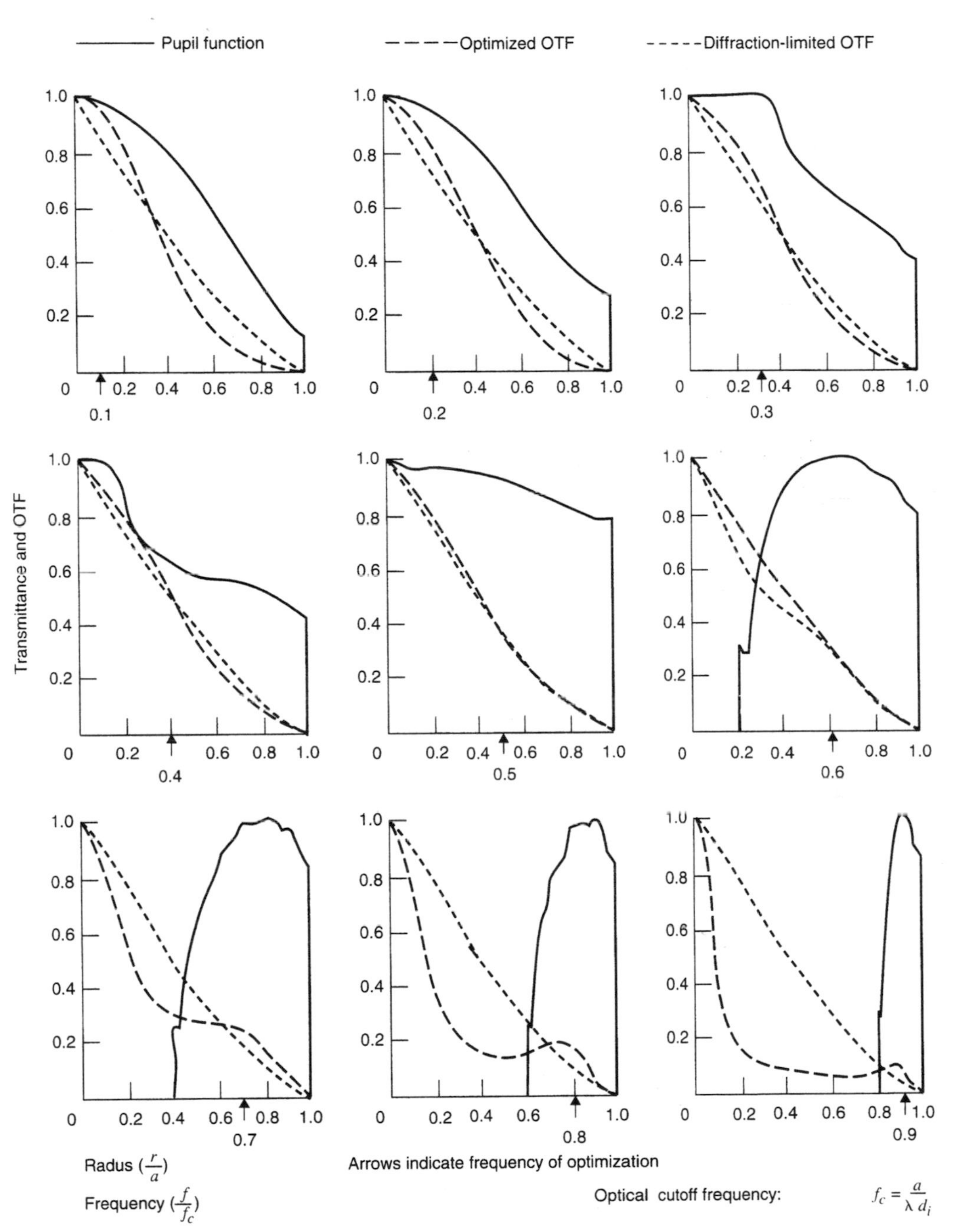

Figure 15–5 Optimal pupil functions (after Frieden [2])

stated before, the value of the MTF at a particular frequency is the factor by which the contrast of sinusoidal features in the image at that frequency is multiplied in the imaging process.

Symmetry. Since the OTF is the two-dimensional Fourier transform of the PSF, then if the PSF is an even function (i.e., symmetrical about the x- and y-axes), the OTF will be real valued and, likewise, an even function. Since the lens is circular, the image it forms of a point source is likewise circularly symmetrical. Thus, a phaseless system, a circular PSF and a circular, real-valued OTF go hand in hand.

In the equation in Figure 15–5, it is evident that the cutoff frequency can be improved (increased) by going to a larger aperture or a shorter wavelength.

Since the PSF and the OTF are related by the two-dimensional Fourier transform, having either enables one to obtain the other.

15.4 IMAGING SYSTEM ABERRATIONS

In earlier discussions, it was mentioned that an aberration-free optical system produces a spherical exit wave. Aberrations in the optical system cause the exit wave to depart from its ideal spherical shape. This can be modeled as before, using Figure 15–2, if we generalize the pupil function by defining it as

$$p(x, y) = T(x, y)e^{jkW(x, y)} \tag{42}$$

where $T(x, y)$ is, as before, the transmittance of the pupil and $W(x, y)$ accounts for the aberrations. $W(x, y)$ is the path length difference, in wavelengths, between the actual and the ideal (spherical wave) propagation paths from the point (x, y) in the aperture to the origin of the image plane.

15.4.1 Lens Aberrations

Proper choice of the aberration function $W(x, y)$ allows one to model the effects of spherical aberration, defocus, astigmatism, coma, field curvature, and image distortion [3]. *Field curvature* refers to the situation in which the surface of proper focus is a curved surface rather than the (flat) image plane. *Astigmatism* refers to the condition wherein rays coming through the exit pupil on the x_a-axis are not focused to the same point as those coming through on the y_a-axis. *Distortion* causes straight lines in the focal plane to be imaged as curved lines in the image plane. *Coma* refers to the situation in which rays from a single point in the focal plane, but passing through opposite sides of the aperture, converge to different points in the image plane.

While a complete study of optical aberrations is beyond our scope, two results from that field are of interest. First, there exists no transmittance function $T(x, y)$ that can drive the OTF negative. Second, no aberration function $W(x, y)$ can increase the OTF at any frequency, but aberrations can indeed drive the OTF negative [3].

Figure 15–6 illustrates the effect of spherical aberration on the OTF [4]. In this case, there is a path length difference of λ between axial and marginal rays. The image plane is located midway between the marginal and axial focal distances.

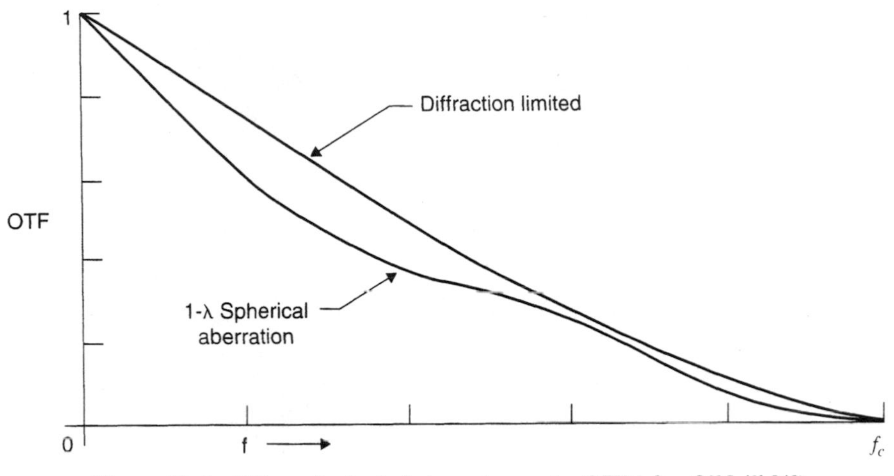

Figure 15–6 Effect of spherical aberration on the OTF (after O'Neill [4])

15.4.2 Defocus

Figure 15–7 illustrates the effect of various amounts of defocus [5,6]. Here defocus is measured in units of wavelengths of *defocus error* (path length difference between axial and marginal rays), not by the out-of-focus distance itself. The defocus OTF is symmetrical in defocus error; that is, an equal amount of positive and negative defocus produces the same OTF. However, since defocus error is monotonic, but not linear, with defocus distance, the OTF is not the same for equal distances in front of and behind the image plane.

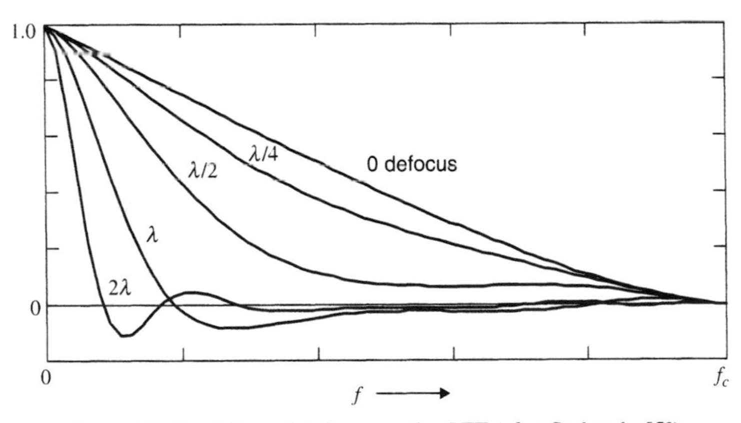

Figure 15–7 Effect of defocus on the OTF (after Stokseth, [5])

Notice that, for the larger amounts of defocus, the OTF goes negative at some frequencies. The effect of that is a black-for-white reversal of structures of that frequency in the image. This is illustrated in Figure 15–8. Frequency increases toward the center of the *spoke target* (a) and the *phase reversals* are evident in the defocused image (b). The phenomena of defocus and depth of field are discussed in more detail in Sec. 22.2.5.

Figure 15–8 Phase reversals due to defocus: (a) in-focus image of a spoke target; (b) defocused image (courtesy Prof. I. T. Young, from [7])

15.5 IMAGING SYSTEM RESOLUTION

Figure 15–9 illustrates, in more detail than Figure 15–4, the point spread function of diffraction-limited optical systems with circular and rectangular exit pupils.

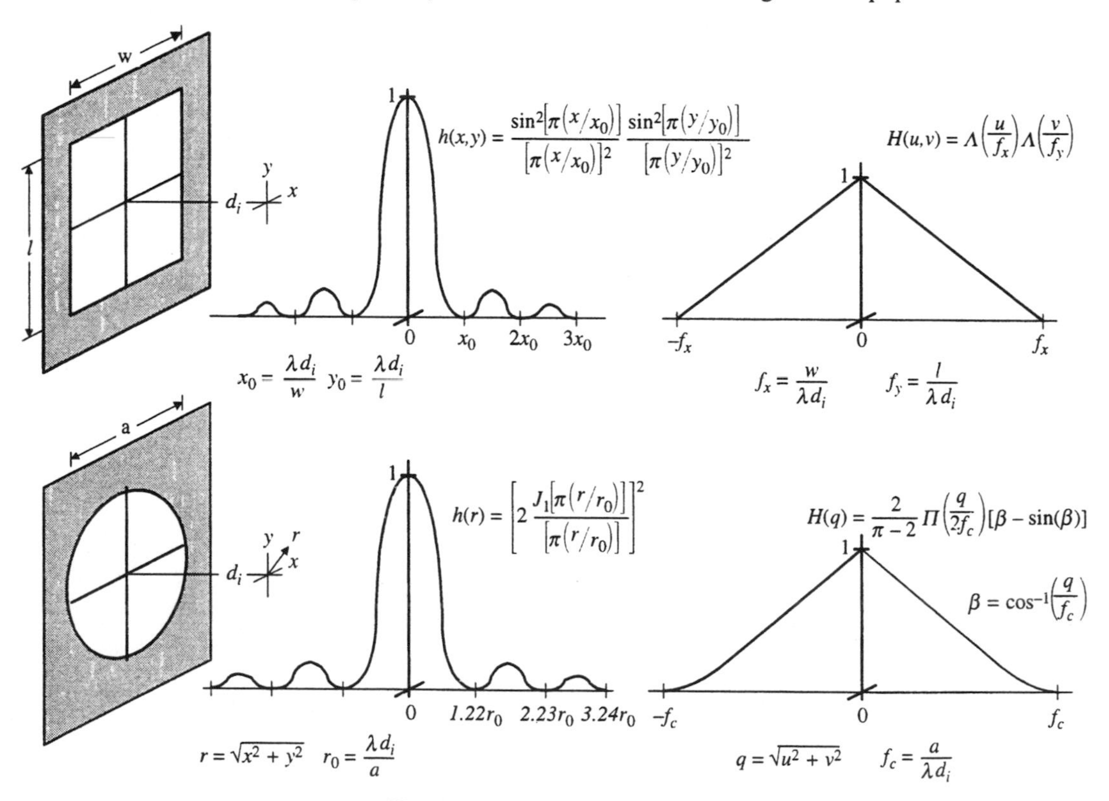

Figure 15–9 Summary of aperture properties

The Rayleigh Distance. For a lens with a circular aperture, the first zero of the image plane PSF occurs at a radius

$$\delta = 1.22\frac{\lambda d_i}{a} \tag{43}$$

which is called the *radius of the Airy disk* (after G. B. Airy [8]). According to the Rayleigh criterion of resolution (after Lord Rayleigh [9]), two point sources can just be resolved if they are separated, in the image, by the distance δ. (See Figure 15–10.)

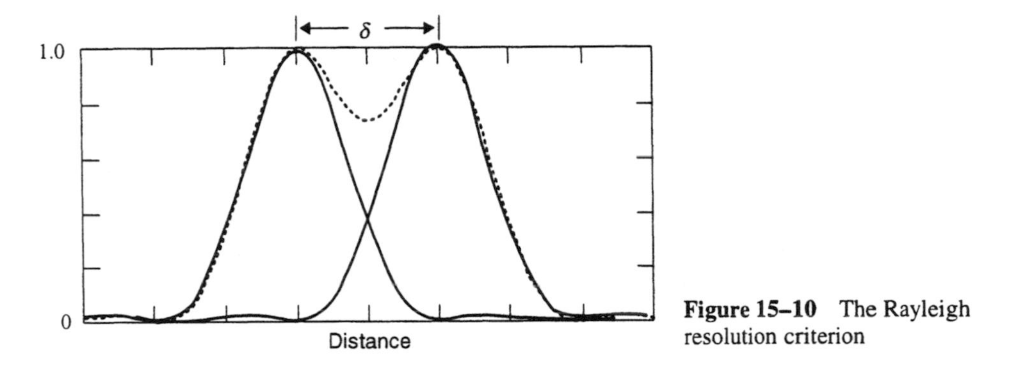

Figure 15–10 The Rayleigh resolution criterion

In the terminology of optics, the Rayleigh distance defines circular *resolution cells* in the image, since two point sources can be resolved if they do not fall within the same resolution cell.

The Abbe Distance. To a good approximation, the half-amplitude diameter of the central peak of the image plane PSF is given by the *Abbe distance* (after Ernst Abbe),

$$r_0 = \frac{\lambda d_i}{a} \tag{44}$$

With cameras imaging approximately planar objects, as in aerial photography and satellite imaging, and in microscopy, it is convenient to perform size calculations in the focal plane, rather than the image plane as above, since that is where the objects of interest reside. This involves a 180-degree rotation and a scaling by the factor M (Eq. (3)). The pixel spacing and resolution can then be specified in units of meters on the Earth's surface, micrometers at the specimen, etc. Spatial frequencies can then be specified in cycles per meter, cycles per micrometer, etc., respectively, in the focal plane.

15.5.1 Cameras

When working with camera lenses, normally $d_f >> d_i \approx f$, and the magnification $M << 1$ (Eq. (3)). It is conventional to specify the aperture diameter by using the *f-number*:

$$f\# = f/a \tag{45}$$

The *f*-number, or f-*stop*, of a lens is often written as *f*/5.6, for example, which means that $a = f/5.6$. The *f*-stop settings on camera lenses are commonly marked off in powers of the square root of two. This way, a one-stop change either doubles or halves the aperture area and, thus, the light intensity at the film (i.e., the *exposure*).

The incoherent optical cutoff frequency in the image plane coordinate system of a camera is

$$f_c = a/\lambda d_i \approx 1/(\lambda f\#) \tag{46}$$

The Abbe distance in the image plane is

$$r_0 = \lambda d_i/a \approx \lambda f\# \tag{47}$$

and the Rayleigh distance (resolution cell diameter) in the image plane is

$$\delta = 1.22\lambda d_i/a \approx 1.22\,\lambda f\# \tag{48}$$

These approximations usually serve well, except in the case of macro (close-up) photography, where d_i becomes significantly greater than f.

15.5.2 Telescopes

A telescopic imaging system aimed at a planet's surface may be treated as a camera system using the preceding formulation, although the surface may have to be modeled as spherical rather than planar. (See Chapter 8.) In stellar astronomy, however, the separation between objects is commonly specified in angular units (degrees, minutes, and seconds) rather than in linear measure.

Stars are, for practical purposes, point sources. That is, the image size of a star is many times smaller than the PSF of even the best telescope optics. Thus, each star produces in the image plane, not its own image, but a copy of the optical system's PSF. It is then the size of the PSF that determines how close together two stars can be (in angular measure) and still be resolved in the image as separate entities.

It is conventional to specify telescopes by their aperture diameter and f-number (Eq. (45)). As with camera systems, $d_f >> d_i \approx f$, and this approximation is almost always valid. Under these conditions, the incoherent optical cutoff frequency in the angular coordinate system centered on the telescope (in cycles per radian) is

$$f_c = a/\lambda \tag{49}$$

while the angular Abbe distance (in radians) is

$$r_0 = \lambda/a \tag{50}$$

and the angular Rayleigh distance (in radians) is

$$\delta = 1.22\lambda/a \tag{51}$$

15.5.3 Microscopes

In optical microscopes, d_i is fixed by the *optical tube length* of the microscope. The *mechanical tube length*—the distance from the mounting flange of the objective lens to the image plane—is commonly 160 mm. The optical tube length, however, is usually between 190 and 210 mm, depending upon the manufacturer. In any case, $d_i >> d_f \approx f$ and $M >> 1$, except when a low-magnification objective lens (less than 10×) is in use. Normally, it is the objective that determines the quality of the image, provided that the remaining optical components in the instrument are clean and properly aligned.

It is customary to specify the objective, not by focal length and aperture diameter, but by *power* (i.e., magnification, Eq. (3)) and *numerical aperture*, which is defined as

$$\mathrm{NA} = n\sin(\alpha) \approx a/2d_f \approx a/2f \tag{52}$$

where n is the refractive index of the medium (air, water, or immersion oil) located between the specimen and the lens, and $\alpha = \arctan(a/2d_f)$ is the angle between the optical axis and a marginal ray from the origin of the focal plane to the edge of the aperture. The approximations in Eq. (52) assume small aperture and high magnification, respectively. Microscope manufacturers commonly engrave the magnification power and numerical aperture on their objective lenses, and the actual focal length and aperture diameter are little used.

Often, the objective lens forms an image directly on the image sensor, and the pixel spacing scales down from the sensor to the specimen by a factor approximately equal to the objective power. In other cases, additional magnification is introduced by intermediate lenses located between the objective and the camera. The microscope eyepieces, which figure into conventional computations of "magnification," have no effect on pixel spacing. Ideally, one would measure, rather than calculate, pixel spacing in a digital imaging microscope.

Since $d_f \approx f$, the resolution parameters are simpler if we scale them to the focal (specimen) plane rather than working in the image plane. For a microscope objective, the incoherent optical cutoff frequency in the focal plane coordinate system is

$$f_c = Ma/\lambda d_i = a/\lambda d_f \approx 2\mathrm{NA}/\lambda \tag{53}$$

the Abbe distance is

$$r_0 = \frac{1}{M}\lambda\frac{d_i}{a} = \lambda\frac{d_f}{a} \approx \frac{\lambda}{2\mathrm{NA}} \tag{54}$$

and the Rayleigh distance (resolution cell diameter) is

$$\delta = 1.22r_0 = 0.61\lambda/\mathrm{NA} \tag{55}$$

The foregoing approximations begin to break down at low power and high NA, which normally do not occur together. One can compute and compare f and a, or the angles $\arctan(a/2d_f)$ and $\arcsin(\mathrm{NA}/n)$, to quantify the degree of approximation.

15.6 THE ANALYSIS OF COMPLETE SYSTEMS

We now have the tools to describe the effects of optics, sampling, filtering, and interpolation. In the remainder of this chapter, we apply this collection of techniques to the analysis of complete digital imaging systems.

In this context, we seek methods to determine whether a particular system is adequate and cost effective for carrying out the image-processing and quantitative image analysis projects for which it is intended. We seek, as well, a balance among subsystem components so that the overall performance of the system is adequate and no component represents serious overkill.

15.6.1 Resolution

Before we can develop a coherent approach to specifying the resolution of an imaging system, we must state some definitions. These are by no means standard in the field, but they form a workable basis upon which we can proceed.

15.6.1.1 Definitions

By *resolution,* we mean the ability of the imaging system to reproduce the contrast of objects of various sizes. Of particular interest are the smaller objects, since they are frequently the most troublesome. The term *contrast* refers to the differences in intensity within an object or between the object and the surrounding background. If an object were to lose contrast as a result of the imaging process, it would appear fainter in the image than it actually was in real life. If its contrast were reduced to zero, it would disappear.

The most useful way to quantify the concept of object size is by spatial frequency, in cycles or line pairs per unit of length. For our purposes, the most convenient expression of the resolution of an imaging system is its MTF. Since this is a real-valued function, it accounts only for the loss of contrast of objects during the imaging process, and not for any positional (phase) shift. The complex-valued transfer function accounts for both and can be used if necessary.

Commonly, however, the components of a digital imaging system can reasonably be assumed to be phaseless, shift-invariant, linear systems. The transfer function of a phaseless component is real valued (rather than complex valued) and is simply the MTF. Thus, the MTF tells all there is to know about a phaseless, shift-invariant, linear system, and it serves as a very convenient specification of resolution.

15.6.1.2 The Imaging System MTF

Digital imaging systems usually consist of a cascade of components through which the image passes sequentially. The MTFs of these subsystems combine by multiplication to form the overall MTF of the system. Thus, if the MTFs of the individual components are known, the MTF of the entire imaging system can be determined by multiplying the individual MTFs together.

The individual MTFs usually take on values less than unity over most of the frequency range. Hence, their product will be everywhere less than the smallest MTF, and the overall resolution of the system will be (perhaps considerably) worse than the weakest link in the imaging chain.

Often, the components that are critical to resolution are those located between the objects of interest and the analog-to-digital converter. For this reason, we use the *imaging system MTF* as the basic specification for the resolution of a digital imaging system. By definition, this is the composite MTF of all the linear components in front of the analog-to-digital converter.

The imaging system MTF of a digital imaging system is often determined principally by two components: the primary imager (lens or mirror) and the image sensor (camera). The primary imager is the main camera lens, telescope or microscope objective lens, or telescope mirror. In general, there may be several lenses, filters, mirrors, and beam splitters in the optical path from object to sensor. The primary imager, however, together with the camera, is ordinarily the component that limits resolution and determines the overall quality of the image.

Ideally (for best resolution), the PSF would be extremely narrow and without side lobes. From Eq. (35), we see that the scale factor r_0 is a specification of the PSF width. It becomes smaller with larger aperture, and it takes on smaller values at shorter illumination wavelengths (Eq. (36)). The side lobes cannot be eliminated.

15.6.1.3 Aperture, Wavelength, and Resolution

In Figures 15–4 and 15–9, the PSF has its first zero at a radius of $1.22r_0$. According to the *Rayleigh criterion* of resolution, two point sources can just be distinguished if they are separated, in the focal plane, by that distance. (Recall Section 15.5.) Thus, a common way to specify the resolution of an imaging system is the Rayleigh criterion. Notice that resolution improves (r_0 becomes smaller) at shorter wavelength and with larger aperture.

Another way to specify the resolution of a lens is by the diameter of the central peak of the PSF. To a good approximation, the equivalent diameter of the PSF is also given by the Abbe distance. Thus, like resolution, the PSF diameter becomes smaller at shorter wavelength and with larger aperture.

To understand better how a larger aperture improves resolution, consider the operation of a microscope. As light parallel to the optical axis enters the specimen from below, the small structures therein cause the light to be bent, due to the phenomenon of diffraction. The smaller the structures, the greater is the angle of diffraction. For structures below some limiting size, the light diffracted by them will exit the specimen at such an angle that it will not enter the lens aperture and thus will not contribute to the formation of the image. Increasing the diameter of the aperture will allow light diffracted by smaller structures to contribute to the image.

15.6.2 Pixel Spacing

We have covered separate analytical techniques for the separate considerations of resolution, sampling, and display. Now we combine these to specify the complete digital imaging system.

For microscopes, as well as for cameras imaging two-dimensional objects, it is most convenient to refer all measurements to the focal (object) plane. This is easily done if the appropriate magnification factors are known. These factors can be calculated or measured with the aid of a calibration standard. Angular measure is most convenient for telescopes.

Figure 15–11 shows the three parameters that should be well matched at the focal plane. Here, $F = 1/T$ represents the highest spatial frequency of interest that is present in the specimen. T is the period of the smallest detail of interest in the specimen. In the figure, noise dominates the spectrum at frequencies above F. $F_s = 1/\Delta x$ is the sampling frequency, where Δx is the sample spacing, and f_c is the cutoff frequency of the imaging system MTF.

As a rule of thumb, the diameter W of the scanning spot (the imaging system PSF), referred to the focal plane, should be no larger than one-half of T. This means that one scanning spot would fit within one half-cycle of the highest frequency sine wave. A larger

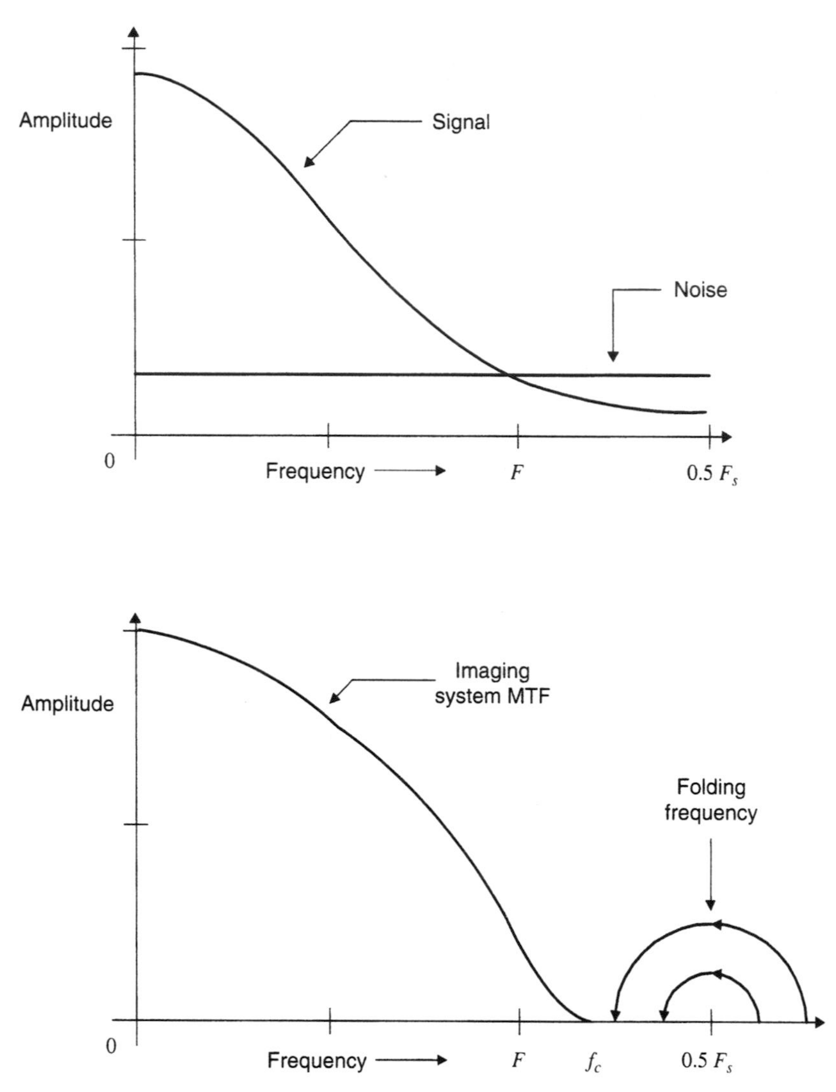

Figure 15–11 Resolution and sampling parameters in the frequency domain

scanning spot is prone to reduce the contrast of the image detail, due to its action as a low-pass filter.

15.6.2.1 The Nyquist Sampling Criterion

No matter how high the frequencies present in the object, no information above the cutoff frequency of the imaging system MTF will be presented to the digitizer. This frequency, in turn, can be no higher than the cutoff frequency of the OTF of the primary imaging lens or mirror. Thus, if we set the folding frequency (half the sampling frequency) equal to the OTF cutoff frequency, aliasing will be avoided, and proper interpolation can reconstruct the image from its sample points without error. Setting the folding frequency at the highest frequency present in the image is called sampling according to the *Nyquist criterion.* This places the pixel spacing at $\lambda f\#/2$ for cameras, at $\lambda/2a$ (in radians) for telescopes, and at $\lambda/4\text{NA}$ for microscopes.

15.6.2.2 The Rayleigh Sampling Criterion

The Rayleigh resolution criterion yields a slightly relaxed specification for pixel spacing. If the sample spacing is one-half the Rayleigh distance, then pixels will fall alternately upon and between (just resolvable) point sources separated by that distance in the image. In this case, the point sources can be resolved in the digital image. The pixel spacing will be $0.61\lambda f\#$ for cameras, $0.61\lambda/a$ (in radians) for telescopes, and $0.305\lambda/\text{NA}$ for microscopes. This value is 22 percent larger than the Nyquist criterion. It places the folding frequency at 82 percent of the OTF cutoff frequency. Aliasing is possible in this case, but given the low magnitude of the upper 18 percent of the OTF (particularly if aberration is present), it is unlikely to be significant in many practical cases.

15.6.2.3 Oversampling and Resampling

Oversampling can be used as a remedy for display with a suboptimal spot shape (Chapter 3) and for object measurement errors that result from making the image discrete. To display good-quality detail (with an inherently Gaussian display spot), it may be necessary to oversample the image by a suitable factor or to resample the image by digital interpolation prior to displaying it. (See Chapter 3.) In addition, to obtain accurate measurement data from the objects in the digitized image, it may likewise be necessary to oversample or resample the image prior to the analysis, or to build resampling or curve fitting into the measurement algorithms.

As an example of the latter, consider the problem of measuring the perimeter of an object in a digitized image of a microscopic specimen. If one programs a straightforward perimeter-tracking algorithm that merely sums the center-to-center distances of adjacent pixels on the boundary, one obtains, in actuality, the perimeter of a polygon that approximates the shape of the object. If the pixel spacing is chosen merely to satisfy the Rayleigh criterion or the Nyquist criterion, this approximation may lead to unacceptable errors. The problem can be overcome if the algorithm instead fits arcs of curves (e.g., quadratics or cubics) through the boundary points and measures perimeter distance along these. This topic is addressed in Chapter 19.

15.6.3 The System MTF

Figure 15–12 shows a linear system model of a typical digital image-processing system. If we assume that each link in the chain is a shift-invariant linear system, then the entire process can be modeled with a single PSF or transfer function. The MTFs combine by multiplication, and the PSFs combine by convolution. The accuracy of the analysis will depend on how well the assumptions of linearity and shift invariance fit each component.

The PSF or the transfer function of each component can be modeled analytically, determined experimentally, or taken from manufacturers' specifications. The lenses, for example, can be assumed diffraction limited, the display spot can be assumed Gaussian, and the MTF of the film is supplied by the manufacturer. The computer operation may or may

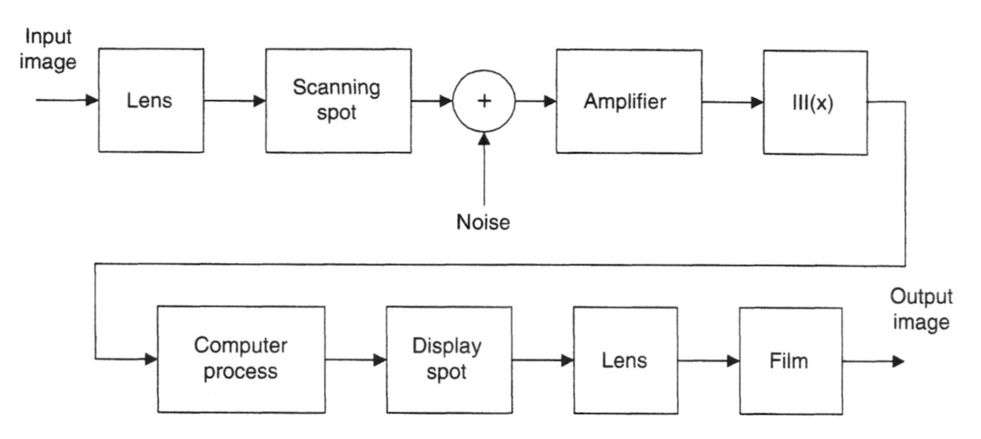

Figure 15–12 The elements of an image processing system

not be linear, but this is the only subsystem in Figure 15–12 that is directly under the user's control.

Frequently, it is useful to reduce the system in Figure 15–12 to that shown in Figure 15–13. Here, all subsystems not under user control have been combined into an overall system PSF, corresponding to the overall system MTF.

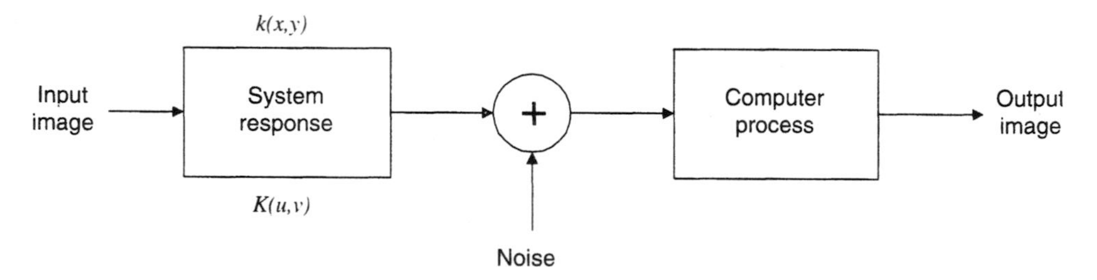

Figure 15–13 An equivalent system to that in Figure 15–12

Component MTFs commonly take on values that decline (below unity) with increasing frequency. When they combine, by multiplication, into the overall system MTF, the result will normally be narrower than the MTF of any single component. When the component PSFs combine, by convolution, the result will normally be broader than the PSF of any single component. Thus, a collection of components, all having acceptable-looking PSFs and transfer functions, may well combine to produce a system with disappointing performance.

15.6.4 Noise Considerations

In Figure 15–13, the computer processes not the original input image, but that image degraded by the system characteristics and contaminated with noise. In fact, noise is introduced at every step in the process. Image sensor noise is usually the prime offender, excluding noise that may already be present in the input image. We can assume that the noise is introduced at any position in Figure 15–12, provided that we account for the modification of its power spectrum as it is filtered by the various linear subsystems.

In Figure 15–11, the amplitude of the specimen is shown to fall off with increasing frequency, while that of noise does not. This is typical of actual specimens and the common noise sources, most of which can be assumed to be white noise. Thus, there are three ways to lose the fine detail in a specimen: to have it attenuated by the imaging system MTF (too low resolution), to have it corrupted by aliasing (too coarse sampling), and to have it buried in noise. In the last case, it is necessary to eliminate the offending sources of noise before proceeding with the design.

One potentially devastating noise source is the analog video recorder. The best situation is to avoid recording altogether and digitize the analog signal as close to the image sensor as possible. A second choice is to use a video recorder of instrumentation quality. Only when it is absolutely necessary or when image quality requirements are not critical should one consider the use of a videocassette recorder. Such a device alters the video signal in ways that severely degrade the quality of the digital image that can be obtained.

Noise reduction techniques are treated in Chapters 11 and 16. For now, it suffices to say that it serves no purpose to accurately image, sample, and display frequencies at which the signal is buried by noise. One should, however, ensure that high-frequency noise not be present in instances where it can be aliased down to frequencies at which signal information is present.

15.6.5 System Design

In a well-balanced system, (1) the noise will dominate only at frequencies above the highest frequency of interest in the image, and (2) the imaging system MTF will pass information at frequencies where the subject has content that is of interest and attenuate information at frequencies where the subject's detail is buried by noise. Following that, (3) the sampling frequency will be chosen to be high enough to prevent aliasing.

This principle can also be stated in the spatial domain: In a well-balanced system, (1) the size scale of the noise will be smaller than the smallest detail that is of interest in the subject, and (2) the imaging system PSF will be smaller than the detail that is of interest in the subject, but larger than the size scale of the noise. Following that, (3) the sample spacing will be chosen to be small enough to prevent aliasing.

15.7 EXAMPLES

In the remainder of this chapter, we consider two examples of image-processing systems and determine their overall PSFs and MTFs. For this exercise, we ignore the effects of sampling and truncation.

15.7.1 A Film-to-Film System

Figure 15–14 diagrams an image-processing system that uses photographic film for both input and output. We reduce the system in this figure to the system in Figure 15–13 by combining all the transfer functions, except the computer process, into a single equivalent transfer function. We assume that the input and output lens systems are diffraction limited, the sampling aperture is square, the amplifier has a single-pole lowpass characteristic, the display spot is Gaussian, and the MTF of the film is supplied by the manufacturer. The overall

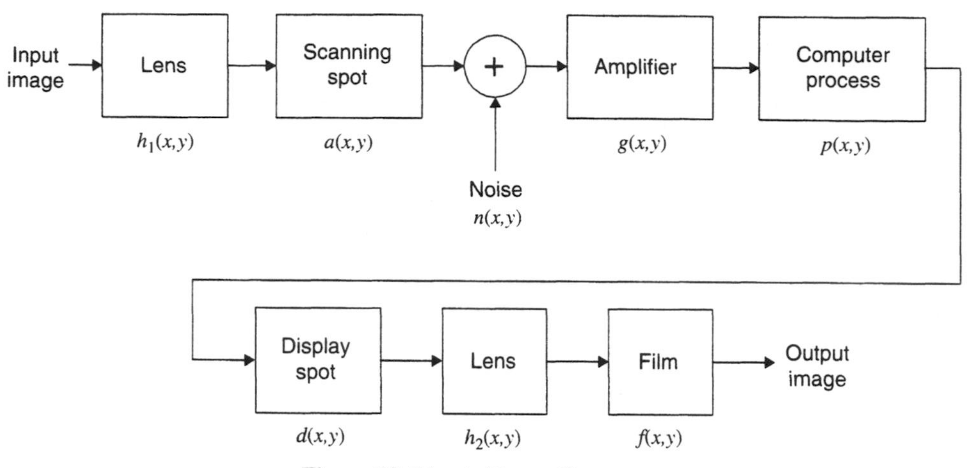

Figure 15–14 A film-to-film system

transfer function $K(u, v)$ is merely the product of the individual transfer functions, and the overall PSF $k(x, y)$ is its inverse Fourier transform.

Figure 15–15 shows the component PSFs and transfer functions and the overall PSF and transfer function. The equations for the component PSFs and transfer functions are listed in Table 15–1. Notice that the system PSF is broader, and the MTF narrower, than the respective PSFs and MTFs of any of the components.

The PSFs, and thus the transfer functions, of the two lenses and the display spot are circularly symmetric. We assume that the MTF of the film can be approximated by a product of hyperbolic secant functions. The sampling aperture and the amplifier are characterized by impulse responses separable in the x- and y-directions. Since the image is scanned in the x-direction, $g(x, y)$ is a lowpass filter in the x-direction and an impulse in the y-direction.

TABLE 15–1 POINT SPREAD FUNCTIONS AND TRANSFER FUNCTIONS

Point-spread functions	Transfer functions
$h_1(r) = \left[2\dfrac{J_1(\pi r/r_1)}{\pi r/r_1}\right]^2 \quad r_1 = \dfrac{\lambda d_1}{a_1}$	$H_1(q) = \dfrac{1}{\pi}\Pi\left(\dfrac{q}{2f_1}\right)[\beta_1 - \sin(\beta_1)] \quad \beta_1 = \cos^{-1}\left(\dfrac{q}{f_1}\right) \quad f_1 = \dfrac{a_1}{\lambda d_1}$
$a(x, y) = \dfrac{1}{w^2}\Pi\left(\dfrac{x}{w}\right)\Pi\left(\dfrac{y}{w}\right)$	$A(u, v) = \dfrac{\sin(\pi wu)}{\pi wu}\dfrac{\sin(\pi wv)}{\pi wv}$
$g(x, y) = \dfrac{f_o}{2}e^{-\lvert f_o x\rvert}$	$G(u, v) = \dfrac{\delta(v)}{1 + (2\pi u/f_o)^2}$
$d(r) = [2\pi\sigma^2]^{-1/2}e^{-r^2/2\sigma^2}$	$D(q) = e^{-q^2/2\alpha^2} \quad \alpha = \dfrac{1}{2\pi\sigma}$
$h_2(r) = \left[2\dfrac{J_1(\pi r/r_2)}{\pi r/r_2}\right]^2 \quad r_2 = \dfrac{\lambda d_2}{a_2}$	$H_2(q) = \dfrac{1}{\pi}\Pi\left(\dfrac{q}{2f_2}\right)[\beta_2 - \sin(\beta_2)] \quad \beta_2 = \cos^{-1}\left(\dfrac{q}{f_2}\right) \quad f_2 = \dfrac{a_2}{\lambda d_2}$
$f(x, y) = \dfrac{1}{c^2}\operatorname{sech}\left(\pi\dfrac{x}{c}\right)\operatorname{sech}\left(\pi\dfrac{y}{c}\right)$	$F(u, v) = \operatorname{sech}(\pi cu)\operatorname{sech}(\pi cv)$

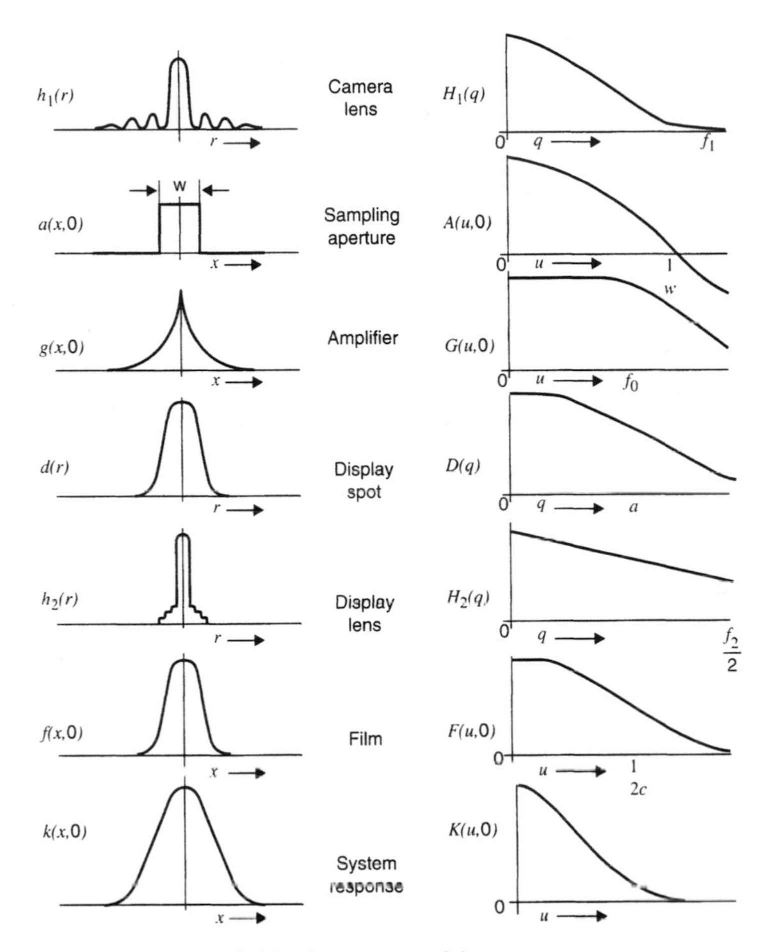

Figure 15–15 Components of the system response

Before the transfer functions and PSFs of the various components can be compared, they must be projected into a consistent frame of reference. Figure 15–16 illustrates how the various intermediate image planes can be projected back into the input plane. Magnification factors, based on the overall size of the image, allow projection of the PSFs into the image plane. Since the amplifier processes an electrical signal, its magnification factor reflects a change from time to space. If the scanning mechanism operates at 1 line per millisecond, then every second at the amplifier corresponds to 50 meters at the input plane.

Using the magnification factors in Figure 15–16 to project the assumed PSFs and transfer functions into the image plane produces the functions summarized in Figure 15–15. As that figure shows, the transfer function of the complete system is narrower, and the PSF broader, than their counterparts for any system component.

In Figure 15–15, the OTF of the entire system is the product of the component transfer functions. It is obvious, for example, that while the camera lens plays a significant role in limiting the overall frequency response, the display lens does not. Also, the amplifier, which has a small effect in the x-direction, need not appear at all in an analysis of the y-direction.

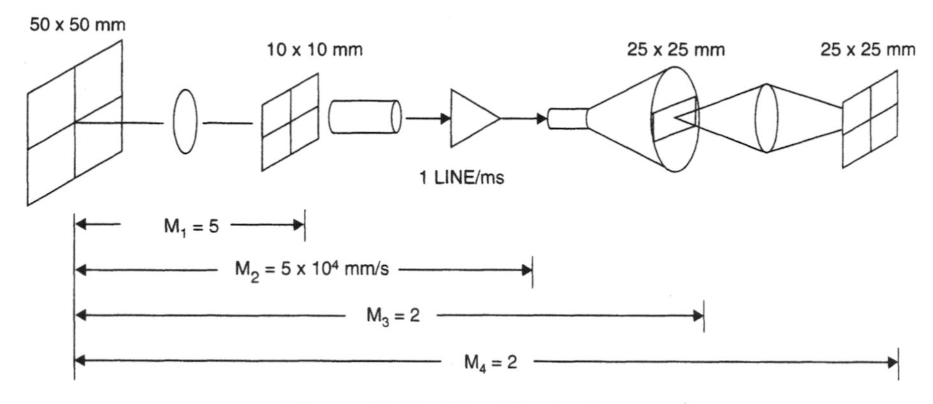

Figure 15–16 Magnification factors

15.7.2 A Microscope Digitizing System

As a second example, consider the system shown in Figure 15–17. This system consists of a digitizing television camera mounted on a microscope and can be modeled as in Figure 15–18. The specimen is imaged by a 100× microscope objective with numerical aperture 1.25.

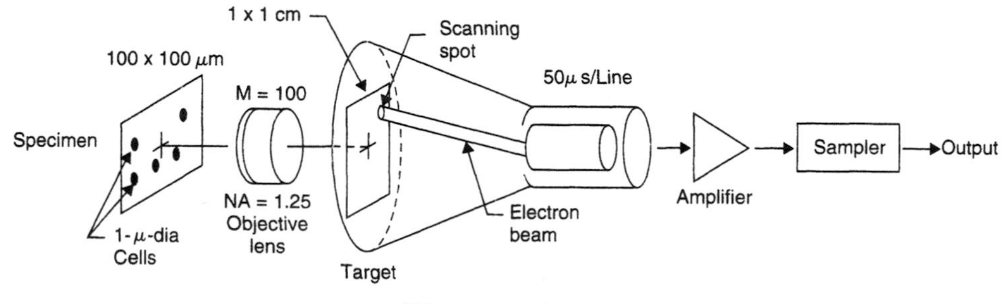

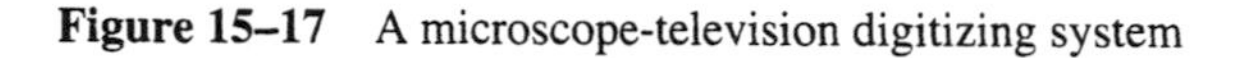

Figure 15–17 A microscope-television digitizing system

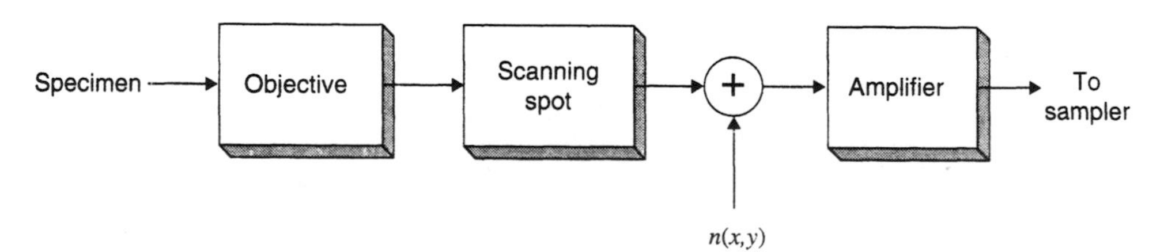

Figure 15–18 Linear components of the microscope digitizer

Figure 15–19 shows a two-dimensional analysis producing the overall PSF and transfer function of the system. If noise is introduced at the sensor, its power spectrum will be modified by the transfer function of the amplifier.

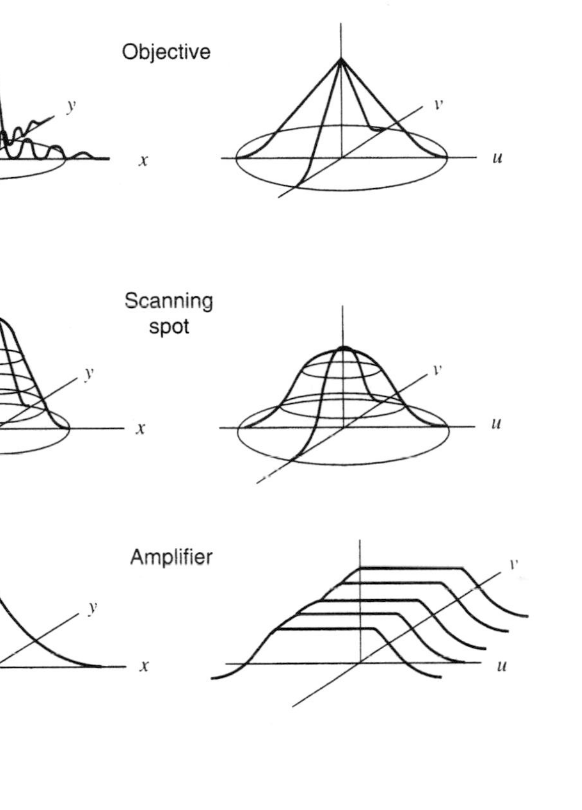

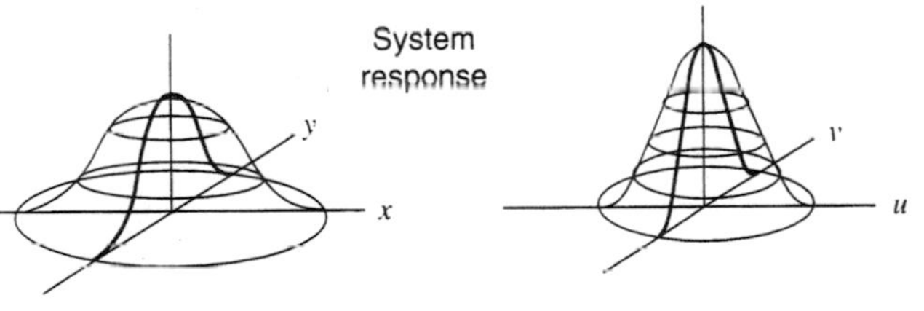

Figure 15–19 Components of the microscope digitizer response

Figure 15–20 shows the u-axis components of the various transfer functions in the microscope digitizing system. If the specimens of interest are circular spots that can be modeled by a 1-micron-diameter Gaussian spot, their spectrum is shown in the figure as $S(u)$. Since the transfer function of the system stays above 0.5 out to f_s, the frequency limit of the specimen, we would conclude that this system is probably adequate to digitize these specimens.

15.8 SUMMARY OF IMPORTANT POINTS

1. Lenses and other optical imaging systems can be treated as two-dimensional shift-invariant linear systems.

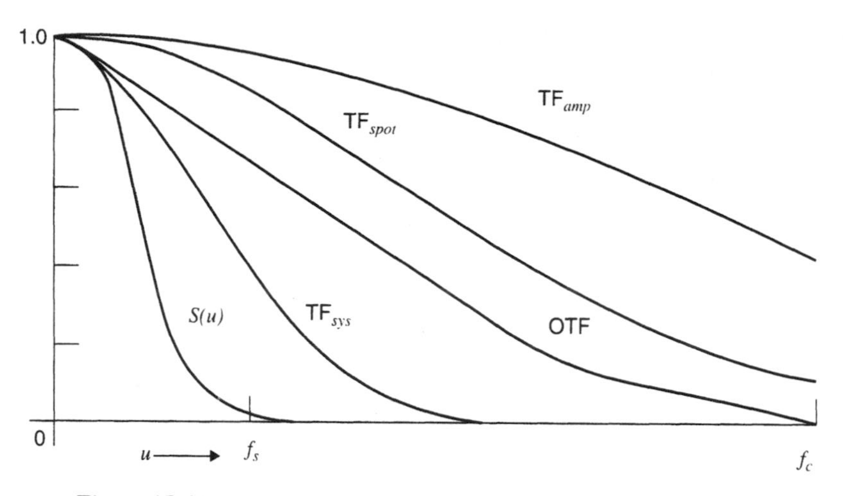

Figure 15–20 A one-dimensional analysis of the microscope digitizer

2. The assumptions involved in the linear analysis of optical systems begin to break down as one moves off the axis, particularly for wide-aperture or poorly designed optical systems.
3. Coherent illumination can be thought of as a distribution of point sources whose amplitudes maintain fixed phase relationships among themselves.
4. Incoherent illumination may be viewed as a distribution of point sources, each having random phase that is uncorrelated with its neighbors.
5. Under coherent illumination, an optical system is linear in complex amplitude.
6. Under incoherent illumination, an optical system is linear in intensity (amplitude squared).
7. The point-spread function of an optical system is finitely broad because of two effects: aberrations in the optical system and the wave nature of light.
8. An optical system having no aberrations is called diffraction-limited because its resolution is limited only by the wave nature of light (diffraction effects).
9. A diffraction-limited optical system transforms a diverging spherical entrance wave into a converging spherical exit wave.
10. The pupil function gives the transmittance of the plane containing the aperture of the optical system.
11. The coherent point-spread function is merely the Fourier transform of the pupil function [Eq. (28)].
12. The coherent transfer function has the same shape as the pupil function [Eq. (29)].
13. The incoherent PSF is the power spectrum of the pupil function [Eq. (34)].
14. The optical transfer function is the autocorrelation function of the pupil function [Eq. (38)].
15. A diffraction-limited optical system has a real-valued pupil function.
16. Aberrations in an optical system can be modeled by introducing a complex component into the pupil function [Eq. (42)].

17. Careful selection of the pupil function can increase the transfer function at specific spatial frequencies (Figure 15–5).
18. The transfer function of a diffraction-limited optical system can never go negative.
19. Aberrations in an optical system can never increase the modulation transfer function, but can drive the optical transfer function negative.
20. Complete image-processing systems may be modeled as a cascade of linear subsystems, each having an assumed or experimentally determined PSF.
21. The Guassian display spot is improperly shaped for image display. This can be overcome by resampling to simulate a $\sin(x)/x$-shaped display spot.
22. The Nyquist criterion sets the pixel spacing so that the folding frequency is at the highest frequency present in the image. This is typically taken as the optical transfer function cutoff frequency.
23. The Rayleigh criterion sets the sample spacing at half the resolution cell diameter.
24. In a well-balanced system, the modulation transfer function will pass the frequencies corresponding to image detail of interest, while blocking high frequencies that are dominated by noise. The sample spacing will be small enough to avoid aliasing.

PROBLEMS

1. A reconnaissance aircraft flying at an altitude of 10,000 meters carries a camera with an $f\# = 5.6$, 150-mm focal length lens pointing vertically downward. The image falls on a 2.0-cm-square, 1,024-by-1,024 CCD image-sensing array with square, full area pixels. Sketch the lens OTF and the sensor MTF on the same image-plane frequency axis, and mark the folding frequency. Sketch the lens and sensor PSFs on the same focal-plane axis. According to the Rayleigh criterion, could this lens resolve red ($\lambda = 0.65\ \mu$) campfires separated by 2 meters? 4 meters? 8 meters? In the digitized image, could you resolve and count campfires separated by 2 meters? 4 meters? 8 meters? If you replaced the CCD chip with one that sampled according to the Nyquist criterion, what would its pixel spacing have to be?
2. An astronaut orbiting at an altitude of 320 miles uses a camera with an $f/16$, 100-mm focal length lens and a blue ($\lambda = 0.45\ \mu$) filter pointing vertically downward. The 24-mm–by–36-mm film image is digitized to 682 by 1,024 pixels. Sketch the lens OTF on the focal-plane frequency axis, and mark the folding frequency. Sketch the lens PSF on the image-plane axis. According to the Rayleigh criterion, could this lens resolve oil well fires separated by 200 meters? 400 meters? 1,000 meters? In the digitized image, could you resolve and count oil well fires separated by 200 meters? 400 meters? 1,000 meters? If you rescanned the film according to the Nyquist criterion, what would the pixel spacing be?
3. A microscope uses a 100×, 1.2-NA objective lens. A 10-μm-long test target covers a distance of 80 pixels in the digitized image. What is the pixel spacing at the specimen? Using green ($\lambda = 0.55$ μm) incoherent light, what is the Rayleigh resolution limit? What is the OTF cutoff frequency? Will the pixel spacing permit resolving objects at the Rayleigh limit? What maximum pixel spacing (at the specimen) would? Will this pixel spacing avoid aliasing? What maximum pixel spacing (at the specimen) would? Sketch the OTF, and mark the cutoff frequency and the sampling and folding frequencies corresponding to the three pixel spacings mentioned above. Sketch the PSF, and show the three pixel spacings on the same scale.
4. Using the microscope objective mentioned in Problem 3, could you resolve micronuclei (tiny dots) separated by 0.1 micron? by 0.2 micron? by 0.4 micron? By approximately what factor

would the lens attenuate the contrast of rod-shaped bacteria 0.1 micron in diameter, separated by 0.1 micron? Capillaries 0.2 micron in diameter, separated by 0.2 micron? Arterioles 1 micron in diameter separated by 1 micron? Veins 50 microns in diameter separated by 50 microns?

5. A microscope uses a 10×, 0.45-NA objective lens. It has a 1,024-by-1,024 CCD camera with 6.5-micron pixel spacing. What is the pixel spacing at the specimen? Using red ($\lambda = 0.65$ μm) light, what is the Rayleigh resolution limit? What is the OTF cutoff frequency? Will the pixel spacing permit resolving objects at the Rayleigh limit? What is the maximum pixel spacing (at the specimen) that would? Will this pixel spacing avoid aliasing? What is the maximum pixel spacing (at the specimen) that would? Sketch the OTF, and mark the cutoff frequency and the sampling and folding frequencies corresponding to the three pixel spacings mentioned above. Sketch the PSF, and show the three pixel spacings on the same scale.
6. Using the objective mentioned in Problem 5, could you resolve micronuclei (tiny dots) separated by 0.2 micron? by 0.5 micron? by 1.0 micron? By approximately what factor would this lens attenuate the contrast of rod-shaped bacteria 0.1 micron in diameter, separated by 0.1 micron? Capillaries 0.2 micron in diameter, separated by 0.2 micron? Arterioles 1 micron in diameter separated by 1 micron? Veins 50 microns in diameter separated by 50 microns?
7. Suppose you have a 35-mm slide that shows the White House Christmas tree at night. The slide was taken with a 135-mm *f*/3.5 lens from a distance of 200 meters. You wish to digitize the film without aliasing any information in the image. What is the maximum pixel spacing you can use when scanning the film? If the tree is 30 meters tall, how large must the (square) digital image be? Assuming no image degradation due to the film or image motion, how close together can lights on the Christmas tree be and still be counted as separate?
8. Suppose you have a 3-inch *f*/11 telescope. Can you split (resolve) Alpha Centauri? Zeta Aquarii? The double, Epsilon in Lyra? Eta in Orion? Tau Cygni? Lambda in Cassiopeia? Lambda Lupi? Epsilon Ceti? (See table below)
9. Suppose you borrow an 8-inch *f*/8 telescope from a friend. Which of the double stars mentioned in Problem 8 can you now split?
10. Which of the double stars mentioned in Problem 8 can the 100-inch telescope at Lowell Observatory split?
11. Which of the double stars mentioned in Problem 8 can the 200-inch telescope at Palomar Observatory split?
12. Suppose a colleague of yours visited Palomar Observatory, attached a CCD camera to the 200-inch telescope, and digitized images of the star field near the Horsehead Nebula in Orion. In one of the images, you notice the A and B stars of the trapezium, Theta Orionis, at (x,y) locations (235,416) and (565,676), respectively. You wish to map the positions of stars in that region of Orion to the full resolution of the Palomar telescope. Compare the pixel spacing to the Rayleigh and Nyquist criteria. Can you use the digital images supplied by your friend in your research?
13. The Hubble Space Telescope has a primary mirror diameter of 2.4 meters. It has four wide-field cameras, all with a pixel spacing of 1.0 arc second, and four planetary cameras, all with a pixel spacing of 0.0436 arc second. Prior to its repair, the telescope had 0.5λ of spherical aberration and 1.2λ of defocus, where $\lambda = 0.547$ μ is the reference wavelength. (Recall Figure 15–7.) The net effect of these flaws was to increase the diameter of the telescope's PSF approximately five times. Which of the double stars mentioned in Problem 8 were the Hubble telescope optics capable of splitting? Which ones could be split in a digitized wide-field image? In a planetary camera image with 4-by-4 binning (pixel averaging)? With 2-by-2 binning? Without binning? Sketch the PSF of the lens and the binning processes on the same scale.
14. Repeat Problem 13 for the situation subsequent to repair of the Hubble Space Telescope optics. Assume diffraction-limited conditions.

Stellar Object	Angular Separation (arc-seconds)
Alpha Centauri	15
Theta Orionis	A–B:8.7, B–D:19.2, C–D:13.2, C–A: 12.9
Epsilon in Lyra	2.2, 3.0, 3.5'
Zeta Aquarii	1.7
Eta in Orion	1.4
Tau Cygni	0.9
Lambda in Cassiopeia	0.5
Lambda Lupi	0.2
Epsilon Ceti	0.1

PROJECTS

1. Generate an image of uncorrelated, random noise using a random number generator to assign gray levels to pixels. Compute the autocorrelation function and power spectrum of the noise.
2. Generate an image of uncorrelated, random white noise using a random number generator to assign phase values to the complex spectrum of the noise. Compute the autocorrelation function and power spectrum of the noise.
3. Use the image of Project 1 or 2 to identify a digital filter.
4. Use the image of Project 1 or 2 to identify an imaging system.
5. Generate an image of a horizontal frequency sweep target.
6. Generate an image of an omnidirectional (circular) frequency sweep target.
7. Use the image of Project 5 or 6 to identify a digital filter.
8. Use the image of Project 5 or 6 to identify an imaging system.
9. Use an image of an edge to determine the MTF of a telescope, camera, or microscope objective lens.
10. Use an image of an edge to determine the defocus MTF of a telescope, camera, or microscope objective lens, for several values of defocus.
11. Design a digital filter to deconvolve the effects of a 50-mm, *f*/8 camera lens when the pixel spacing is 25 microns at the image sensor. Limit the gain of the filter to 8.0.
12. Design a digital filter to deconvolve the effects of a 100×, 1.2-NA microscope objective lens when the pixel spacing is 15 microns at the image sensor. Assume incoherent green ($\lambda = 0.55$ micron) light. Limit the gain of the filter to 5.0.
13. Develop and test an autofocus algorithm. Use a convolution filter to simulate different amounts of defocus on a test image, and plot your focal sharpness parameter versus the amount of defocus.
14. Develop and test an autofocus algorithm. Digitize a scene with a camera, telescope, or microscope, with different amounts of defocus, and plot your focal sharpness parameter versus the amount of defocus.

REFERENCES

For further reading on optics and related topics, see Appendix 2.

1. J. W. Goodman, *Introduction to Fourier Optics,* McGraw-Hill, 1968 (reissued 1988).

2. B. R. Frieden, "Maximum Attainable MTF of Rotationally Symmetric Lens Systems," *Journal of the Optical Society of America,* **59:**402–406, 1969.

3. M. Born and E. Wolf, *Principles of Optics: Electromagnetic Theory of Propagation, Interference and Diffraction of Light* (6th ed.), Pergamon Press, Oxford, 1980.

4. E. L. O'Neill, *Introduction to Statistical Optics,* Addison-Wesley, Reading, MA, 1963.

5. P. A. Stokseth, "Properties of a Defocused Optical System," *Journal of the Optical Society of America,* **59:**1314–1321, 1969.

6. H. H. Hopkins, "The Frequency Response of a Defocused Optical System," *Proceedings of the Royal Society* (London), **A231:**91–103, 1955.

7. I. T. Young, "Image Fidelity: Characterizing the Imaging Transfer Function," *Methods in Cell Biology,* **30:**1–45, Academic Press, New York, 1989.

8. E. Abbe, *Archiv. Mikroscopische Anat.* **9:**413, 1873.

9. Lord Rayleigh, "On the Theory of Optical Images, with Special Reference to the Microscope," *Phil Mag.,* **42**(5):167, 1896.

Part 3

CHAPTER 16

Image Restoration

16.1 INTRODUCTION

Historically, a large portion of digital image-processing activity has been devoted to image restoration. This work includes both research in algorithm development and routine, goal-directed image processing. Many noteworthy contributions in digital image processing have been made in the latter area as well as the former. In this chapter, we address some of the more useful techniques.

By *image restoration,* we mean the removal or reduction of degradations that were incurred while the digital image was being obtained. These degradations include the blurring that can be introduced by optical systems, image motion, and the like, as well as noise from electronic and photometric sources. While image restoration could be defined to include many of the techniques discussed in Part 1, we take it to signify a more restricted class of operations.

The aim of image restoration is to bring the image toward what it would have been if it had been recorded without degradation. Each element in the imaging chain (lenses, film, digitizer, etc.) contributes to the degradation. Partial restoration of the lost image quality can serve as anything from a cosmetic frill to a matter of vital importance, depending upon the application. An example of the latter case is the lunar and planetary imaging missions of the space program.

In this chapter, we consider several approaches to image restoration. We also consider the system identification and noise-modeling problems. For a more thorough coverage of these subjects, the reader should consult a textbook or survey in the field [1–7,17].

16.1.1 Approaches and Models

The task of restoring a degraded image can be approached in one of two basic ways. If little is known about the image, one can attempt to model and characterize the sources of degradation (blurring and noise) and implement a process designed to remove or reduce their effects. This is an estimation approach, since one attempts to estimate what the image must have been before it was degraded by relatively well-characterized processes.

If, on the other hand, a great deal of prior knowledge of the image is available, it might be more fruitful to develop a mathematical model of the original image and fit the model to the observed image. As an example of this case, assume that the image is known to contain only circular objects of fixed size (e.g., stars, grains, cells, etc.). Here, the task is one of detection, since only a few parameters of the original image are unknown (number, position, amplitude, etc.).

Approaching the image restoration problem presents several other choices as well. First, the development can be done using either continuous or discrete mathematics. Second, the development can be carried out in either the spatial or frequency domain. Finally, while the implementation must be done digitally, the restoration can be effected in either the spatial domain (e.g., via convolution) or the frequency domain (via multiplication).

Fortunately, we have now identified a set of conditions that, if maintained, render the various approaches essentially equivalent. Thus, we can use whichever approach best suits our requirements and constraints, as long as we are mindful of the underlying assumptions.

Often, two or more approaches lead to the same restoration technique. The methods that perform well in practice are basic to this problem. One of them always seems to be waiting for us at the end of each journey, no matter in which direction we start or what kind of map and compass we use.

In this chapter, we review several of the more important image restoration techniques that have proved useful in practice. We begin with classical, continuous frequency domain approaches in roughly the chronological order of their development and application to digital imaging. We follow that examination with a discrete spatial domain approach that tends to unify the preceding results into a common framework. Next, we consider the practical aspects of dealing with space-variant blurring and nonstationary noise. Then we look at restoring bandlimited images beyond their cutoff frequencies and conclude with a discussion of ways to determine the parameters of the degradation and to implement the restoration.

16.2 CLASSICAL RESTORATION FILTERS

In this section, we use the system shown in Figure 16–1 to model image degradation and restoration. The image $f(x, y)$ is blurred by a linear operation $h(x, y)$, and noise $n(x, y)$ is added to form the degraded image $w(x, y)$. This is convolved with the restoration filter $g(x, y)$ to produce the restored image $\hat{f}(x, y)$.

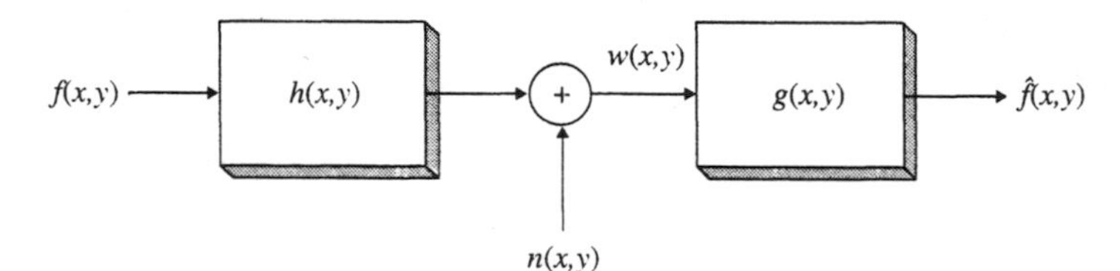

Figure 16–1 Continuous image restoration model

Linear system theory was used routinely in electrical filter design for many years before digital image processing became popular. It was applied widely to optics, digital signal processing, and other fields. Deconvolution, for example, has long been known in electrical filter design and time series analysis. Even the minimum mean-square estimator (Sec. 11.5.2) was worked out by Norbert Wiener in 1942 [8]. Thus, many of the techniques first applied to digital image restoration were generalizations of one-dimensional methods already in use in analog and digital signal processing. Even when specialized, new techniques were developed, they drew upon the classical frequency domain approach.

16.2.1 Deconvolution

In the mid-1960s, deconvolution (inverse filtering) began to be applied broadly to digital image restoration. Nathan used two-dimensional deconvolution to restore images from the early Ranger, Surveyor, and Mariner planetary exploration missions [9]. Since the signal spectrum normally dies out with frequency faster than that of the noise, the high frequencies are often dominated by noise. Nathan's approach was to limit the deconvolution transfer function to some maximum value (Figure 16–2).

During the same period, Harris deconvolved the blurring due to atmospheric turbulence in telescope images using an analytical model for the PSF [2], and McGlamery

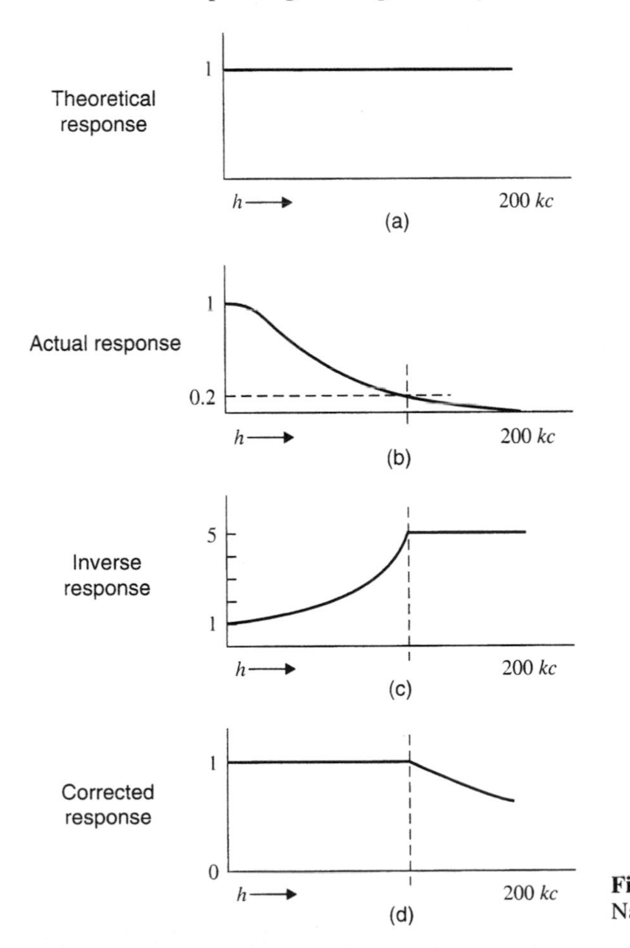

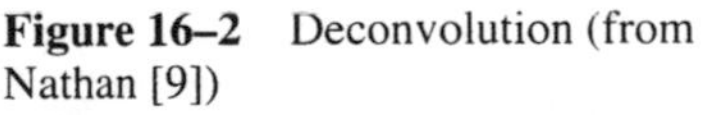
Figure 16–2 Deconvolution (from Nathan [9])

deconvolved atmospheric turbulence using an experimentally determined PSF [10]. Since then, deconvolution has become a standard technique for image restoration. Figure 16–3 illustrates the improvement that is possible in an image when this technique is carefully implemented.

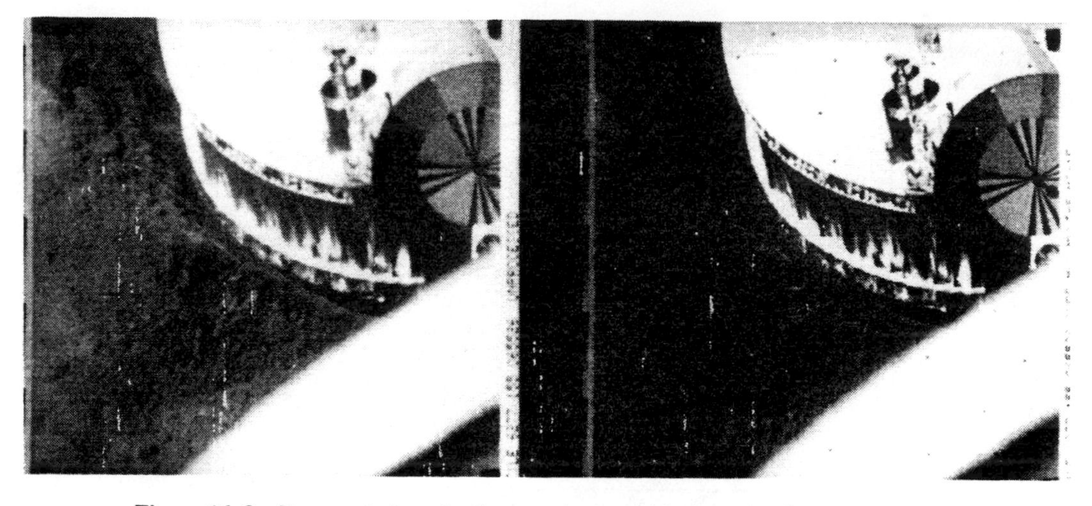

Figure 16–3 Deconvolution of a *Surveyor* image: (a) before; (b) after (Courtesy NASA-JPL)

16.2.2 Wiener Deconvolution

In most images, adjacent pixels are highly correlated, while the gray levels of widely separated pixels are only loosely correlated. From this, we can argue that the autocorrelation function of typical images generally decreases away from the origin (Figure 16–4). Since the power spectrum of an image is the (real and even) Fourier transform of its autocorrelation function, we can argue that the power spectrum of an image generally decreases with frequency.

Typical noise sources have either a flat power spectrum or one that decreases with frequency more slowly than typical image power spectra. Thus, the expected situation is for the signal to dominate the spectrum at low frequencies while the noise dominates at high frequencies. Since the magnitude of the deconvolution filter generally increases with frequency, the filter enhances high-frequency noise. The early attempts at deconvolution handled the noise problem by *ad hoc* and intuitive methods.

Helstrom [11] adopted the minimum mean-square error estimation procedure and presented the Wiener deconvolution filter, which has the two-dimensional transfer function

$$G(u, v) = \frac{H^*(u, v)P_f(u, v)}{|H(u, v)|^2 P_f(u, v) + P_n(u, v)} \tag{1}$$

and can also be written as

$$G(u, v) = \frac{H^*(u, v)}{|H(u, v)|^2 + P_n(u, v)/P_f(u, v)} \tag{2}$$

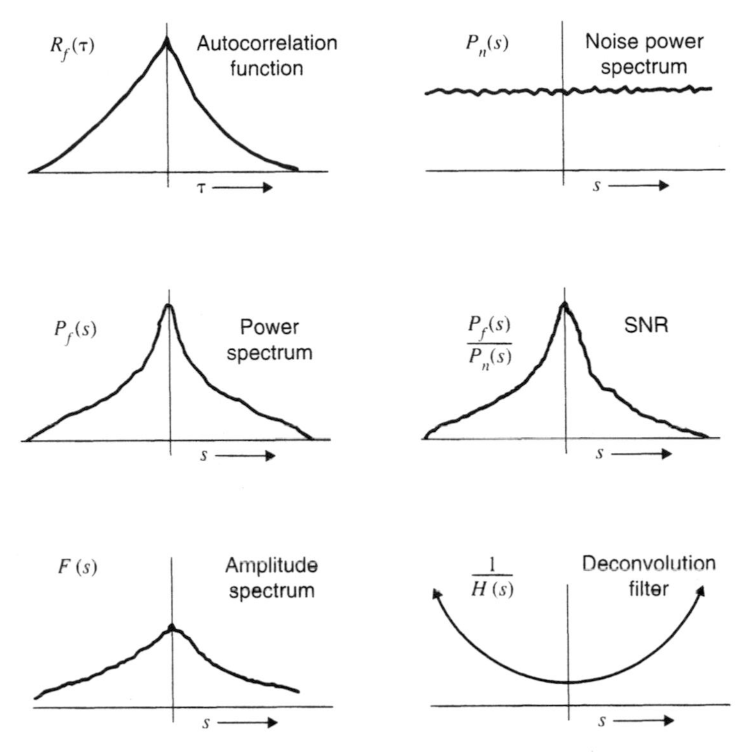

Figure 16–4 The noise problem in deconvolution

where P_f and P_n are the power spectra of the signal and noise, respectively. This filter was developed in Chapter 11 for one dimension.

Slepian [12] extended Wiener deconvolution to account for a stochastic PSF (e.g., due to atmospheric turbulence). Later, Pratt [13] and Habibi [14] developed means to increase the computational efficiency of Wiener deconvolution. (See [4] for a review of deconvolution techniques.)

Wiener deconvolution affords an optimal method for rolling off the deconvolution transfer function in the presence of noise, but it is plagued with three problems that limit its effectiveness. First, the mean square error (MSE) criterion of optimality is not particularly good if the image is being restored for the human eye [4,15]. The problem is that the MSE criterion weights all errors equally, regardless of their location in the image, while the eye is considerably more tolerant of errors in dark areas and high-gradient areas than elsewhere. In minimizing the mean square error, the Wiener filter also tends to smooth the image more than the eye would prefer.

Second, classical Wiener deconvolution cannot handle a spatially variant blurring PSF. This occurs with coma, astigmatism, curvature of field, and with motion blur that involves rotation.

Finally, the technique cannot handle the common case of nonstationary signals and noise. Most images are highly nonstationary, having large flat areas separated by sharp transitions (edges). Furthermore, several important noise sources are highly dependent on local gray level (signal-dependent noise). In the next two sections, we examine alternatives to and improvements upon Wiener deconvolution.

16.2.3 Power Spectrum Equalization

Cannon [16] showed that the filter which restores the power spectrum of the degraded image to its original amplitude is

$$G(u, v) = \left[\frac{P_f(u, v)}{|H(u, v)|^2 P_f(u, v) + P_n(u, v)}\right]^{1/2} \tag{3}$$

Like the Wiener filter, this *power spectrum equalization* (PSE) filter is phaseless (real and even). It is applicable for phaseless blurring functions, or phase may be determined by other methods [17].

The similarity between the PSE filter [Eq. (3)] and the Wiener deconvolution filter [Eq. (1)] is clear. Both filters reduce to straight deconvolution in the absence of noise, and both cut off completely in the absence of signal. The PSE filter, however, does not cut off at zeros in the blurring transfer function $F(u, v)$.

The image restoration power of the PSE filter is quite good, and in some cases the PSE filter may be preferable to Wiener deconvolution. The PSE filter is sometimes called a *homomorphic filter* [18].

16.2.4 Geometric Mean Filters

Consider the restoration filter transfer function given by

$$G(u, v) = \left[\frac{H^*(u, v)}{|H(u, v)|^2}\right]^{\alpha}\left[\frac{H^*(u, v)}{|H(u, v)|^2 + \gamma P_n(u, v)/P_f(u, v)}\right]^{1-\alpha} \tag{4}$$

where α and γ are positive real constants. This filter is a generalization of the filters previously discussed. The transfer function is parameterized in α and γ. Notice that if $\alpha = 1$, Eq. (4) reduces to a deconvolution filter. Also, if $\alpha = \frac{1}{2}$ and $\gamma = 1$, it reduces to the PSE filter of Eq. (3).

Notice in addition that if $\alpha = \frac{1}{2}$, Eq. (4) defines a filter that is the geometric mean between ordinary deconvolution and Wiener deconvolution. Thus, a third name for the filter in Eq. (3) is the geometric mean filter. It is common practice, however, to refer to the more general filter in Eq. (4) as the *geometric mean filter.*

If $\alpha = 0$ in Eq. (4), the result is the *parametric Wiener filter*

$$G(u, v) = \left[\frac{H^*(u, v)}{|H(u, v)|^2 + \gamma P_n(u, v)/P_f(u, v)}\right] \tag{5}$$

If $\gamma = 1$, this becomes the Wiener deconvolution filter of Eq. (2), while $\gamma = 0$ reduces it to straight deconvolution. In general, γ may be selected for any desired amount of Wiener-type smoothing.

Eq. (4) represents a very general class of restoration filters applicable in cases involving linear, space-invariant blurring functions and additive, uncorrelated noise. Andrews and Hunt [17] have examined the restoration power of the filter in Eq. (4) under conditions of slight blurring and moderate noise. They show that, under these conditions, straight deconvolution is least desirable, and Wiener deconvolution produces lowpass filtering more severe that the human eye desires. The parametric Wiener filter with γ less than unity and the geometric mean filter with the same constraint seem to produce more pleasing results.

16.3 LINEAR ALGEBRAIC RESTORATION

Andrews and Hunt [17,19,20] advanced an approach to the image restoration problem that is based on linear algebra. This approach may be more appealing to persons who prefer matrix algebra to integral calculus and discrete mathematics to the analysis of continuous functions. It offers a unified development of restoration filters, including those previously mentioned, and it yields insight into the numerical aspects of the image restoration problem.

Because of the size of the vectors and matrices involved, the linear algebraic approach may not lead to an efficient implementation. Instead, a restoration technique developed by this approach may be most efficiently implemented by other means.

16.3.1 The Discrete Restoration Model

Figure 16–5 shows the model we shall use in the development of discrete spatial restoration techniques. The top row indicates the desired (but impossible) situation, that is, an ideal

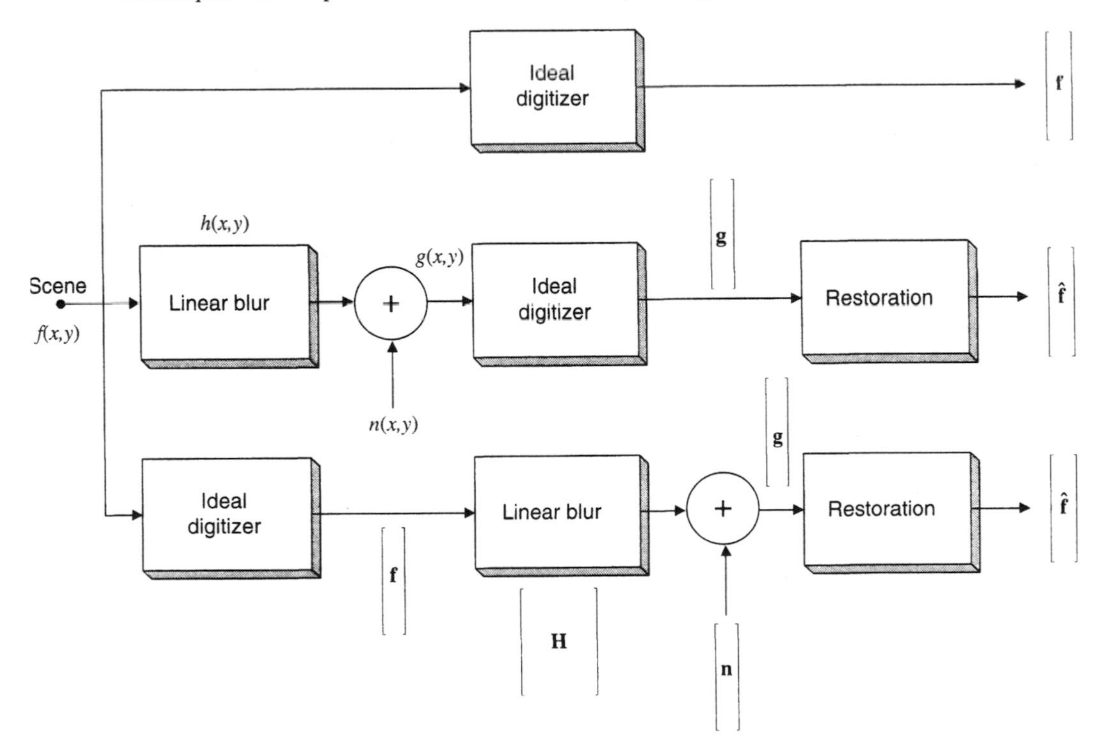

Figure 16–5 Model for linear algebraic restoration

digitizer operating on $f(x, y)$, the undegraded continuous function that represents the physical scene that gives rise to the image. This produces the padded, row-stacked N^2-by-1 column vector **f**, containing the desired (N-by-N) digital image. This column vector format for storage of a digital image was discussed in Sec. 9.3.4.

The second row of the figure models what actually happens when an image is digitized and restored. The scene function $f(x, y)$ is blurred by a linear operation $h(x, y)$, and then a two-dimensional noise image $n(x, y)$ is added, forming $g(x, y)$. Then an ideal digitizer forms the padded, row-stacked column vector **g**, which contains the observed (recorded) N-by-N digital image. This is then subjected to a restoration operation that produces $\hat{\mathbf{f}}$, which is an approximation to **f**, the desired result.

While the blur is linear, it may or may not be shift invariant. If it is, it amounts to a convolution of $f(x, y)$ with the PSF $h(x, y)$. If there is actually more than one blurring operator in the imaging chain, as is normally the case, these operators are assumed to be combined into $h(x, y)$. Likewise, multiple noise sources are assumed to be combined into $n(x, y)$. This model still is not all encompassing, since it does not account for nonlinearities or signal-dependent noise.

The third row of the figure shows the model that we analyze here. An ideal digitizer forms **f**, as before, but this is subjected to a discrete linear operation **H**. A discrete noise image, encoded in the padded, row-stacked column vector **n**, is added, producing the observed image **g**, likewise in vector form. A discrete restoration operation again produces the estimate $\hat{\mathbf{f}}$.

The formation of the observed image vector now can be expressed compactly as

$$\mathbf{g} = \mathbf{Hf} + \mathbf{n} \tag{6}$$

where **g**, **f**, and **n** are N^2-by-1 column vectors and **H** is an N^2-by-N^2 matrix. If the blur is shift invariant, **H** is a block-circulant matrix. Again, the digital images of interest are N by N after padding with zeros as required.

Notice that we are now modeling with discrete operations the degradations that took place before the image was converted into digital form. This has two ramifications. First, we should be able to create very impressive simulated examples with this model, since we can design the degradation process and implement it with precision. Restoration becomes merely a numerical exercise, for example, if we select an invertible degradation process. We do it, we undo it, and we recover the original to within round-off error.

Second, we now have the task of modeling the (continuous) degradation processes with discrete operations. This is similar to the earlier situation in which we had to ensure that our discrete processing of sampled data preserved the integrity of the underlying continuous functions. The effectiveness of an image restoration endeavor hinges upon the accuracy with which the degradation process is modeled.

16.3.2 Unconstrained Restoration

If $\mathbf{n} = \mathbf{0}$ or if we know nothing about the noise, we can set up the restoration as a least squares minimization problem in the following way. Let $\mathbf{e}(\hat{\mathbf{f}})$ be a vector of residual errors that result from using $\hat{\mathbf{f}}$ as an approximation to **f**. Eq. (6) then becomes

$$\mathbf{g} = \mathbf{Hf} = \mathbf{H}\hat{\mathbf{f}} + \mathbf{e}(\hat{\mathbf{f}}) \quad \text{or} \quad \mathbf{e}(\hat{\mathbf{f}}) = \mathbf{g} - \mathbf{H}\hat{\mathbf{f}} \tag{7}$$

and we seek to minimize the objective function

$$W(\hat{\mathbf{f}}) = \|\mathbf{e}(\hat{\mathbf{f}})\|^2 = \|\mathbf{g} - \mathbf{H}\hat{\mathbf{f}}\|^2 = (\mathbf{g} - \mathbf{H}\hat{\mathbf{f}})'(\mathbf{g} - \mathbf{h}\hat{\mathbf{f}}) \tag{8}$$

where $\|\mathbf{a}\| = \sqrt{\mathbf{a}'\mathbf{a}}$ denotes the Euclidean norm of a vector, that is, the square root of the sum of the squares of its elements.

This means that we wish to select $\hat{\mathbf{f}}$ so that if it is blurred by **H**, the result will differ from the observed image **g** by as little as possible in the mean square sense. Since **g** itself is simply **f** blurred by **H**, this is a satisfying approach. If **f** and $\hat{\mathbf{f}}$, both having been blurred by **H**, are nearly equal, then $\hat{\mathbf{f}}$ may be a good approximation to **f**.

Notice that this formulation is somewhat different from that used in the development of the Wiener filter in Sec. 11.5.2. There, we sought to minimize the difference between the restored signal and the original. Here, we are satisfied to minimize the difference between the blurred original and a similarly blurred estimate of the original. We cannot expect the results of these two formulations to be the same.

Setting to zero the derivative of $W(\hat{\mathbf{f}})$ with respect to $\hat{\mathbf{f}}$ produces

$$\frac{\partial W(\hat{\mathbf{f}})}{\partial \hat{\mathbf{f}}} = -2\mathbf{H}'(\mathbf{g} - \mathbf{H}\hat{\mathbf{f}}) = 0 \tag{9}$$

and solving for $\hat{\mathbf{f}}$ yields

$$\hat{\mathbf{f}} = (\mathbf{H}'\mathbf{H})^{-1}\mathbf{H}'\mathbf{g} = \mathbf{H}^{-1}\mathbf{g} \tag{10}$$

where the latter equality holds because **H** is a square matrix.

Eq. (10) identifies the inverse filter. With shift-invariant blur, **H** is block circulant, and this can be shown to specify deconvolution, given in the frequency domain by

$$\hat{F}(u, v) = \frac{G(u, v)}{H(u, v)} \tag{11}$$

If $H(u, v)$ has zeros, **H** is singular, and neither $\mathbf{H}^{-1}$ nor $(\mathbf{H}'\mathbf{H})^{-1}$ exists.

16.3.3 Constrained Least Squares Restoration

We can rearrange Eq. (6) as

$$\mathbf{g} - \mathbf{H}\mathbf{f} = \mathbf{n} \tag{12}$$

One way to account for the noise term is to introduce into the minimization the constraint that the norms of each side of Eq. (12) be the same; that is,

$$\|\mathbf{g} - \mathbf{H}\hat{\mathbf{f}}\|^2 = \|\mathbf{n}\|^2 \tag{13}$$

Now we can set up the problem as the minimization of

$$W(\hat{\mathbf{f}}) = \|\mathbf{Q}\hat{\mathbf{f}}\|^2 + \lambda(\|\mathbf{g} - \mathbf{H}\hat{\mathbf{f}}\|^2 - \|\mathbf{n}\|^2) \tag{14}$$

where **Q** is a matrix we select to define some linear operator on $\hat{\mathbf{f}}$ and λ is a constant called a *Lagrange multiplier*. The ability to specify **Q** gives us flexibility in setting the goal of the restoration.

As before, we set to zero the derivative of $W(\hat{\mathbf{f}})$ with respect to $\hat{\mathbf{f}}$:

$$\frac{\partial W(\hat{\mathbf{f}})}{\partial \hat{\mathbf{f}}} = 2\mathbf{Q}'\mathbf{Q}\hat{\mathbf{f}} - 2\lambda\mathbf{H}'(\mathbf{g} - \mathbf{H}\hat{\mathbf{f}}) = 0 \tag{15}$$

Solving for $\hat{\mathbf{f}}$ then yields

$$\hat{\mathbf{f}} = (\mathbf{H}'\mathbf{H} + \gamma\mathbf{Q}'\mathbf{Q})^{-1}\mathbf{H}'\mathbf{g} \tag{16}$$

where $\gamma = 1/\lambda$ is a constant that must be adjusted so that the constraint of Eq. (13) is satisfied. This is the general equation for the solution to constrained least squares restoration.

16.3.3.1 The Pseudoinverse Filter

If we let $\mathbf{Q} = \mathbf{I}$, the N^2-by-N^2 identity matrix, then we are seeking to minimize the norm of $\mathbf{f}$ subject to the noise constraint of Eq. (13). Eq. (16) then becomes

$$\hat{\mathbf{f}} = (\mathbf{H}'\mathbf{H} + \gamma\mathbf{I})^{-1}\mathbf{H}'\mathbf{g} \tag{17}$$

Notice that if we set $\gamma = 0$, this reduces to the inverse filter of Eq. (10).

16.3.3.2 The Parametric Wiener Filter

We can treat $\mathbf{f}$ and $\mathbf{n}$ as random vectors and select $\mathbf{Q}$ to be the noise-to-signal ratio

$$\mathbf{Q} = \mathbf{R}_f^{-1/2}\mathbf{R}_n^{1/2} \tag{18}$$

where $\mathbf{R}_f = \mathcal{E}\{\mathbf{f}\mathbf{f}'\}$ and $\mathbf{R}_n = \mathcal{E}\{\mathbf{n}\mathbf{n}'\}$ are the signal and noise covariance matrices, respectively. Then the solution [Eq. (16)] becomes

$$\hat{\mathbf{f}} = (\mathbf{H}'\mathbf{H} + \gamma\mathbf{R}_f^{-1}\mathbf{R}_n)^{-1}\mathbf{H}'\mathbf{g} \tag{19}$$

By assuming shift invariance and stationarity, and by using the matrix Fourier transform, one can easily show that this leads to the parametric Wiener filter of Eq. (5). While γ is an adjustable parameter, notice that with $\gamma = 1$, we have the classical Wiener filter that was shown in Sec. 11.5.2 to minimize the mean square difference between the original and restored images.

The foregoing linear algebraic development, using the minimization of Eq. (14) with the criterion of Eq. (18) for the case of shift-invariant blurring, has led us back to the same frequency domain specification for the Wiener filter that we developed in Chapter 11. Notice, however, that it is that earlier development, and not the one presented here, that shows this filter to be the one that makes the restored image look most like the original (in the mean square sense). While the latter development yields the same answer more quickly, it does not speak as strongly for the resulting optimal filter.

16.3.3.3 Smoothness Constraints

Restoration commonly involves inverse filtering a noisy, blurred image. Inverse filtering often emphasizes small details. Frequently, the blur matrix suffers from ill conditioning and may even be singular. Minimization seeks to create a restored image that, when blurred, resembles the noisy, blurred original. [c.f., e.g., Eq. (8)]. For these reasons, the restored image can suffer from large artifactual oscillations. One way to combat this is to select $\mathbf{Q}$ so as to enforce some degree of smoothness on the restored image. Then Eq. (14) seeks an estimate that is smooth, unblurred, and noise free.

Let **Q** correspond to a highpass convolution filtering operation, such as the Laplacian, which is a spatial second derivative; that is,

$$\nabla^2 f(x, y) = \left[\frac{\partial^2}{\partial x^2} + \frac{\partial^2}{\partial y^2}\right] f(x, y) \tag{20}$$

In Eq. (14), the term

$$\|\mathbf{Q}\hat{\mathbf{f}}\|^2 = \hat{\mathbf{f}}'\mathbf{Q}'\mathbf{Q}\hat{\mathbf{f}} \tag{21}$$

is the average of the squared, highpass–filtered estimate. The block-circulant matrix **Q** embodies the appropriate highpass convolution kernel, such as

$$p(x, y) = \begin{bmatrix} 0 & -1 & 0 \\ -1 & 4 & -1 \\ 0 & -1 & 0 \end{bmatrix} \tag{22}$$

which is a discrete approximation to the Laplacian. Then, from Eq. (16), the frequency domain specification of the (shift-invariant) restoration is

$$\hat{F}(u, v) = \left[\frac{H^*(u, v)}{|H(u, v)|^2 + \gamma|P(u, v)|^2}\right] G(u, v) \tag{23}$$

where $P(u, v)$ is the transfer function of the highpass filter implemented by **Q**. For the Laplacian, this is

$$P(u, v) = -4\pi^2(u^2 + v^2) \tag{24}$$

but other highpass transfer functions could be used as well. The value of γ controls how strongly the constraint enforces smoothness upon the estimate, and the shape of $P(u, v)$ determines how strongly the different frequencies are affected by the smoothness constraint.

16.4 RESTORATION OF LESS RESTRICTED DEGRADATIONS

In this section, we consider situations that are not restricted to shift-invariant blurring and stationary signals and noise.

16.4.1 Spatially Variant Blurring

While optical defocus and linear motion blur are spatially invariant linear operations, astigmatism, coma, curvature of field, and rotary motion blur are spatially variant. A direct and effective restoration method for correcting these degradations is *coordinate transformation restoration.* The approach involves using a geometric transformation on the degraded image that makes the resultant blurring function spatially invariant. This is followed by an ordinary spatially invariant restoration technique and then by a geometric transformation that inverts the first such operation and puts the image back into its original format.

Robbins and Huang [21,22] have applied this technique to coma, and Sawchuk has applied it to nonlinear motion blur [23,24] and to astigmatism and curvature of field [25]. For these spatially variant degradation sources, the required geometric transformations are known, and the restoration is quite effective.

16.4.2 Temporally Variant Blurring

The diffraction-limited resolution of a 200-inch telescope is approximately 0.05 second of arc. Under unfavorable conditions, however, atmospheric turbulence can reduce this resolution to about 2 sec of arc. Viewing stars through a turbulent atmosphere is similar to watching a point source of light through a moving textured-glass shower door.

With short exposures, atmospheric turbulence produces a speckle pattern due to phase distortion in the nonuniform atmosphere above the telescope. With longer exposures, atmospheric turbulence causes the speckle pattern to "dance" as the atmosphere undergoes change. Thus, long exposures integrate the dancing speckles to produce a large blur, much larger than the diffraction-limited PSF of the telescope. Since long exposures are required for photographing faint stars, atmospheric blurring (the so-called *seeing conditions*) place a limit on Earth-based astronomical resolution.

Time averaging in the spatial domain is equivalent to averaging complex spectra in the frequency domain. The time-averaged transfer function so obtained goes to zero at frequencies well below the diffraction limit of the telescope. Thus, in the presence of random phase distortion, time averaging does more harm than good.

Labeyrie [26,27] has shown experimentally that the time-averaged power spectrum of a point star image goes out to the diffraction limit. This means that the random phase fluctuations in the atmosphere average out in the power spectrum of the image. His restoration technique (*speckle interferometry*) consists of obtaining time-averaged power spectra of both the astronomical object of interest and a reference point star. He effects deconvolution by dividing the object's power spectrum by that of the point star. The result is an estimate of the diffraction-limited power spectrum of the unknown object. This can be inverse transformed to obtain the autocorrelation function of the object. Since phase information has been lost in the power spectrum, the object cannot be reconstructed exactly, but the autocorrelation function is adequate for identifying double stars and some other bodies that may be of interest.

Knox extended Labeyrie's technique to recover the phase information and obtain diffraction-limited images even under relatively poor seeing conditions [28,29]. Like Labeyrie, he used an ensemble average of short-exposure spectra to determine the power spectrum of the object. Phase information is obtained from the ensemble autocorrelation of the instantaneous power spectra [29,30].

16.4.3 Nonstationary Signals and Noise

The filters discussed earlier in this section all involve the assumption of stationary signals and noise. For an image to be stationary, the locally computed power spectrum would have to be the same (or approximately so) over the entire image. Unfortunately, this is often not the case. Most images are, in fact, highly nonstationary. Consider, for example, a photograph of the human face. The power spectrum of a local area containing the forehead would show much less high-frequency energy than the power spectrum of an area containing the eyes. A very large class of images can be modeled as a collection of regions of relatively constant gray level, separated by boundaries with relatively high gradient. Aerial photographs of farmland are but one example.

Several common noise sources cannot be modeled accurately as stationary random processes. Film grain noise, for example, is almost nonexistent in the low-density (least exposed) areas of a photographic negative, but the noise level increases with increasing density. Density digitizers, which follow an intensity detector with a logarithmic amplifier, produce a higher noise level in dark areas, where the small-signal gain of the logarithmic amplifier is greatest.

It is clear that, while the generalized Wiener filter is superior to straight deconvolution, it does not represent an upper limit on accuracy in image restoration.

16.4.3.1 Matrix Formulation

In Chapter 9, imposing the constraint of shift invariance allowed us to reduce the superposition integral to a simple convolution. If we do not impose shift invariance, the superposition that models image degradation can be written in matrix notation as

$$\mathbf{W} = \mathbf{FS} + \mathbf{N} \tag{25}$$

where the model of Figure 16–1 has been made discrete [17]. For digital images of N-by-N pixels, the matrices $\mathbf{W}$, $\mathbf{S}$, and $\mathbf{N}$ are N^2-by-1 column vectors formed by padding and row stacking (Sec. 9.3.4). The degradation matrix $\mathbf{F}$ is N^2 by N^2. It is an N-by-N block matrix composed of N-by-N blurring functions. This means that each pixel of $S(i,k)$ is degraded by convolution with a separate N-by-N blurring function. If the blurring function is shift invariant, then $\mathbf{F}$ is block circulant.

A minimum mean square estimator can be derived for this matrix formulation. For the generalized geometric mean filter, the restored image is given by

$$\mathbf{Z} = [(\mathbf{F}^{*t}\mathbf{F})^{-1}\mathbf{F}^{*t}]^{\alpha}[(\mathbf{F}^{*t}\mathbf{F} + \gamma[\boldsymbol{\phi}_{\mathbf{s}}]^{-1}[\boldsymbol{\phi}_{\mathbf{n}}])^{-1}\mathbf{F}^{*t}]^{1-\alpha}\mathbf{W} \tag{26}$$

where $\boldsymbol{\phi}_{\mathbf{s}}$ and $\boldsymbol{\phi}_{\mathbf{n}}$ are the covariance matrices of the signal and noise, respectively.

Notice that Eq. (26) is the matrix algebraic equivalent of Eq. (4). Notice also that if $N = 1{,}000$, the matrix $\mathbf{F}$ has a trillion (10^{12}) elements. Furthermore, if the degrading function has zeros, $\mathbf{F}$ will be singular. Clearly, Eq. (26) represents a formidable computational task. Under certain simplifying assumptions, it can be reduced to manageable computations, and some impressive examples have been generated [17]. However, the full power of this formulation has yet to be exploited in routine applications.

16.4.3.2 Local Stationarity

While images are seldom stationary in a global sense, they frequently can be assumed locally stationary. This means that the local power spectrum (computed over a small window) changes slowly as one moves the window within the image. In certain images this assumption might be quite good and in others marginal or questionable, but it represents a significant improvement over the assumption of global stationarity.

In most practical image restoration applications, the restoring PSF is relatively small compared to the size of the image. If the image is generally stationary in regions covering at least the extent of this PSF, then the assumption of local stationarity may well be justified.

One way to implement restoration under a model of local stationarity is to use the Wiener filter or its generalization [Eq. (4)], where the power spectra of the signal and/or the noise are functions of position in the image. However, unless these power spectra can be modeled by simple formulas having few spatially variant parameters, the computational expense will be relatively high. Furthermore, it is necessary to determine the local power spectrum throughout the image before the filter can be spatially parameterized.

A simple approach is to use the generalized geometric mean filter of Eq. (4), where the parameters γ and α are spatially variant and derived from the image. However, that equation is written in the frequency domain. If the restoration is implemented by convolution, α and γ do not appear as simple parameters in the convolution kernel.

A simpler method is to specify analytically a convolution kernel having one or more image-derived spatially variant parameters. This represents a computational simplification, since only a new convolution kernel needs to be computed, from a stored equation, at each pixel position.

16.4.3.3 Power Spectrum Parameters

Let us model the signal and noise as being space variant but locally stationary. By this, we mean that there are two scales in the image: On a small scale the image is stationary, but on a large scale it is not.

To illustrate, suppose we estimate the local power spectrum of the image at the point (x_1, y_1) by computing the squared magnitude of the two-dimensional Fourier transform of a relatively small rectangular piece of the image centered on (x_1, y_1). Suppose we then do the same thing using an identical window centered on a second point (x_2, y_2). If the two points are relatively close together, the estimated power spectra will be approximately equal, even if the two windows do not overlap. On the other hand, if the two points are widely separated in the image, the estimated power spectra will not necessarily agree. While this concept involves some approximations, it does allow us to extend previously developed techniques to account for common forms of space variance.

If the signal and noise are uncorrelated, then the local variance of the observed image is the sum of the signal and noise component variances; that is,

$$\sigma_w^2(x, y) = \sigma_s^2(x, y) + \sigma_n^2(x, y) \tag{27}$$

where the variances are computed over a relatively small local window centered on (x, y).

Let us assume that the noise is locally white with zero mean and power (mean square amplitude or variance) proportional to local mean gray level. Then the noise power spectrum and variance are related by

$$P_n(u, v, x, y) = P_n(0, 0, x, y) = \sigma_n^2(x, y) = N_0\mu_w(x, y) \tag{28}$$

where N_0 is a constant and $\mu_w(x, y)$ is the average gray level computed over some local window centered on (x, y).

Let us also assume that the signal power spectrum is separable into a prototype power spectrum $P_0(u, v)$ times a spatially variant factor; that is,

$$P_s(u, v, x, y) = f(x, y)P_0(u, v) \tag{29}$$

The resulting signal variance is

$$\sigma_s^2(x, y) = R_s(0, 0, x, y) = \int_{-\infty}^{\infty}\int_{-\infty}^{\infty} f(x, y)P_0(u, v)du\,dv = f(x, y)R_0 \tag{30}$$

where R_0 is the volume under the prototype power spectrum.

Solving for the space-variant factor produces

$$f(x, y) = \frac{\sigma_s^2(x, y)}{R_0} = \frac{\sigma_w^2(x, y) - N_0\mu_w(x, y)}{R_0} \tag{31}$$

where Eqs. (27) and (28) have been used. The signal power spectrum can now be written in terms of the local mean and variance of the observed image:

$$P_s(u, v, x, y) = \frac{P_0(u, v)}{R_0}[\sigma_w^2(x, y) - N_0\mu_w(x, y)] \tag{32}$$

We can now write a signal-dependent spatially variant generalized Wiener filter by substituting Eqs. (28) and (32) into

$$G(u, v, x, y) = \left[\frac{F^*(u, v)}{|F(u, v)|^2}\right]^{\alpha}\left[\frac{F^*(u, v)P_s}{|F(u, v)|^2P_s + \gamma P_n}\right]^{1-\alpha} \tag{33}$$

The spatially variant parameters $\mu_w(x, y)$ and $\sigma_w^2(x, y)$ must be computed from the input image. This means that the restoration must be preceded by a step that computes a mean image and a variance image from the input image. To implement Eq. (33) directly still would represent considerable computational expense.

16.4.3.4 Image Partitioning

A more practical solution is to produce a two-dimensional histogram of $\mu_w(x, y)$ versus $\sigma_s^2(x, y)$ and look for clusters of pixels in mean versus variance space. The space can then be partitioned into areas containing these clusters. The resulting regions could be mapped back into the image to define regions of relatively constant mean and variance. Then a restoration filter can be designed and implemented on each such region. In this way, spatially variant restoration would be only a few times more expensive than simple stationary restoration.

For example, one could partition the degraded image into disjoint regions having four types of content. The four regions would correspond to the four possible combinations of high and low mean gray levels with high and low signal variance. Four image restoration filters would be used, each in its appropriate region. If the filters' zero frequency responses were all equal, the boundaries between the regions would have, at most, slope discontinuities. This means that the boundaries would not be highly visible in the processed image.

Where more exact restoration is required, one can divide the range of mean and signal variance into smaller intervals. While this technique is several steps removed from full-fledged spatially variant restoration, it can produce a significant improvement over using the assumption of global stationarity.

16.4.3.5 Noise Power Ratio

Recall from Eq. (4) that the generalized Wiener filter responds only to the ratio of noise-to-signal power. The signal and noise power spectra do not appear independently in the filter equation. A simplified restoration procedure results if we assume that, throughout the image, the signal and noise power spectra change in amplitude, but not in functional form. This means that the SNR function (of spatial frequency) also changes only in amplitude throughout the image.

If the noise is locally white, and its signal-dependent amplitude is given by Eq. (28), we can write the ratio of the noise-to-signal power spectra as

$$\frac{P_n(u, v, x, y)}{P_s(u, v, x, y)} = \frac{R_0 N_0}{P_0(u, v)}\left[\frac{\mu_w(x, y)}{\sigma_w^2(x, y) - N_0\mu_w(x, y)}\right] = \frac{R_0 N_0}{P_0(u, v)}\mathrm{NPR}(x, y) \tag{34}$$

where $\mathrm{NPR}(x, y)$, which is the term in brackets, is called the *noise power ratio.* It represents the spatial variability of the ratio of power spectra and is easily computed from the mean and variance images of the degraded image. Note that Eq. (34) is written as a product of frequency-dependent and position-dependent terms.

The function $\mathrm{NPR}(x, y)$ can be viewed as an image itself. Its gray level represents the spatially variant noise-to-signal power ratio. This, in turn, is sufficient to specify the spatial variation of a restoration filter, under the current set of assumptions. One could use thresholds on $\mathrm{NPR}(x, y)$ at several gray levels to partition the degraded image into regions of roughly similar SNRs. A different restoration filter could then be used in each of these regions.

16.4.3.6 Linear Combination Filters

There is another way to use the NPR image to guide spatially variant restoration. This technique is relatively inexpensive and implements a smoothly space-variant restoration PSF. Suppose we generate a *mask* function $m(x, y)$ by normalizing $\mathrm{NPR}(x, y)$ to the range [0,1]. Then the value zero corresponds to the minimum, and unity to the maximum, noise-to-signal power ratio in the image. Next we design two restoration filters, $g_1(x, y)$ and $g_2(x, y)$ that correspond to the cases of low and high $\mathrm{NPR}(x, y)$, respectively.

We now convolve the image with the two restoration filters. These operations are given by

$$z_1(x, y) = w(x, y) * g_1(x, y) \tag{35}$$

and

$$z_2(x, y) = w(x, y) * g_2(x, y) \tag{36}$$

where $g_1(x, y)$ and $g_2(x, y)$ are the stationary restoration filters resulting from Eq. (4) under high noise and low noise conditions, respectively. The restored image is

$$z(x, y) = m(x, y)z_1(x, y) + [1 - m(x, y)]z_2(x, y) \tag{37}$$

The final restoration can also be written as

$$z(x, y) = w(x, y) * \{m(x, y)g_1(x, y) + [1 - m(x, y)]g_2(x, y)\} \tag{38}$$

If $m(x, y)$ is slowly varying compared to the extent of the restoration filter impulse responses, it may be assumed locally constant. Under this assumption, multiplication approximately commutes with convolution, and the equivalent space-variant restoration PSF is

$$g(x, y) = m(x, y)\,[g_1(x, y) - g_2(x, y)] + g_2(x, y) \tag{39}$$

Linear combination restoration consists of the following steps. First, the degraded image is processed to obtain a local mean gray-level image and a local variance image. Next, the mask function $m(x, y)$ is formed by normalizing NPR(x, y). [See Eq. (34).] Then, stationary filters $g_1(x, y)$ and $g_2(x, y)$ are designed for the two cases corresponding to the lowest and highest SNRs existing in the image. Two partially restored images $z_1(x, y)$ and $z_2(x, y)$ are formed by convolving the input image with each of the restoration filters. The final restored output is formed by

$$z(x, y) = m(x, y)\,[z_1(x, y) - z_2(x, y)] + z_2(x, y) \tag{40}$$

Linear combination restoration implements the smoothly spatially variant impulse response of Eq. (39) and avoids partitioning the image and the accompanying risk of visible region boundaries. Somewhat more complex than globally stationary restoration, linear combination restoration involves four local operations (calculating the mean, calculating the variance, and two convolutions) and the algebraic operations of Eqs. (34) and (40). Although not an optimal filter, a linear combination restoration filter exhibits the desired behavior. That is, it smooths most in areas of low SNR ratio and least where the SNR is high.

16.5 SUPERRESOLUTION

In Chapter 15, we saw that the incoherent transfer function of an optical system is the autocorrelation function of the pupil function. This implies that the transfer function is necessarily bandlimited; that is, it goes to zero for all frequencies above some cutoff frequency established by the diffraction limit of resolution.

Clearly, deconvolution could hope to restore the spectrum of an object only out to, but not beyond, the diffraction limit. Energy at frequencies beyond the diffraction limit, it would appear, is hopelessly lost. Resolution beyond the diffraction limit is theoretically possible, however, due to a useful property of the Fourier transform. Restoration procedures that seek to recover information beyond the diffraction limit are referred to as *superresolution* techniques. The method they employ is also called the *extrapolation of bandlimited functions.*

16.5.1 Analytic Continuation

If a function $f(x)$ is spatially bounded (that is, is zero outside some finite interval), then its spectrum $F(s)$ is an analytic function. Being analytic imposes a severe constraint upon how "wiggly" a function can be. A well-known property of analytic functions is that if such a function is known over a finite interval, then it is known everywhere [31]. This means that if two analytic functions agree exactly over any given interval, then they must agree everywhere and must be the same function. Stated in yet a different way, given a curve defined over a particular interval, no more than one analytic function can be fitted exactly to the given curve over that interval. The process of reconstructing an analytic function in its entirety, given the values of the function over a specified interval, is called *analytic continuation.*

Since an image is necessarily spatially bounded, its spectrum must be analytic. Ignoring noise for the moment, the spectrum of an image can be determined over the interval from zero to the diffraction limit. Thus, it is theoretically possible to reconstruct the analytic spectrum everywhere, or at least at some frequencies above the diffraction limit.

It was pointed out in Chapter 12 that a truncated (spatially bounded) function cannot be bandlimited. However, diffraction-limited optical systems attempt to enforce band-limitedness upon truncated functions. It is this incompatibility between spatial bounding and bandlimiting that superresolution techniques attempt to exploit.

16.5.2 Harris' Technique

Harris [32] questioned whether the diffraction limit is a theoretical upper limit on resolution or merely a practical limitation. He showed that no two spatially bounded objects produce identical images unless the objects themselves are identical. From this, it follows that, under noiseless conditions, any recorded image can correspond to one and only one object. Thus, it should be possible to reconstruct that object in infinite detail from its diffraction-limited image.

In this section, we present the superresolution technique advanced by Harris [32] and restated by Goodman [33]. The technique involves applying the sampling theorem, with domains reversed, to obtain a system of linear equations that can be solved for values of the signal spectrum outside the diffraction-limited passband. It also yields further insight into the effects of sampling and truncation.

Figure 16–6 shows a function and its spectrum. Since $f(x)$ is spatially bounded, we can apply the sampling theorem as before, but with the time and frequency domains reversed. The sampling theorem states that $F(s)$ can be completely reconstructed from a series of equally spaced sample points provided that they are taken no more that $1/2T$ apart. The reconstruction can be expressed as

$$F(s) = [\text{III}(2sT)F(s)] * \frac{\sin(2\pi sT)}{2\pi sT} \tag{41}$$

which accounts for sampling $F(s)$ every $1/2T$ and then interpolating to recover the function.

Writing the Shah function as an infinite sum of impulses, we obtain

$$F(s) = \left[\sum_{n=-\infty}^{\infty} \delta(s-2nT)F(s)\right] * \frac{\sin(2\pi sT)}{2\pi sT} \tag{42}$$

and exploiting the sifting property of the impulse produces

$$F(s) = \sum_{n=-\infty}^{\infty} F(2nT)\frac{\sin(2\pi sT-2nT)}{2\pi sT-2nT} \tag{43}$$

Suppose $f(x)$ is passed through a linear system that passes no energy above some frequency s_m. Deconvolution can recover the signal such that the spectrum is known exactly for frequencies out to s_m. Thus, direct measurement followed by deconvolution (if necessary) recovers the spectrum for frequencies less than s_m.

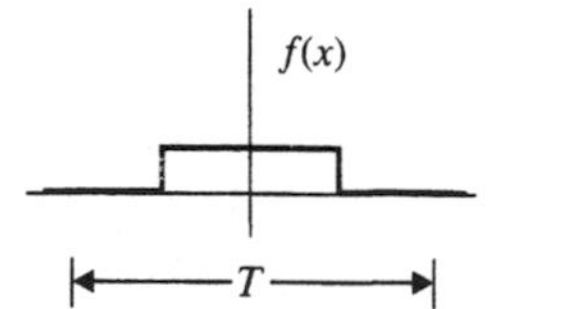

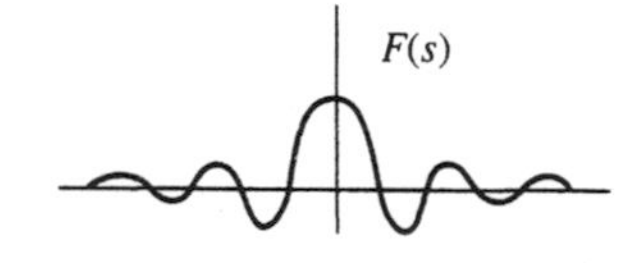

Figure 16–6 A spatially bounded function and its spectrum

Suppose that $F(s)$ is sampled so that M sample points fall within the passband $-s_m \leq s \leq s_m$ (Figure 16–7). Suppose further that we desire to determine $F(s)$ over the range $-s_n$ to s_n, where n implies some larger number N of sample points. Then an estimate of the spectrum, bandlimited at s_n (which is larger than s_m) can be computed from

$$F(s) \approx \hat{F}(s) = \sum_{n=-N}^{N} F(2nT) \frac{\sin(2\pi sT - 2nT)}{2\pi sT - 2nT} \tag{44}$$

If we compute $\hat{F}(s)$, we have successfully extended the band limit of the function from s_m out to s_n.

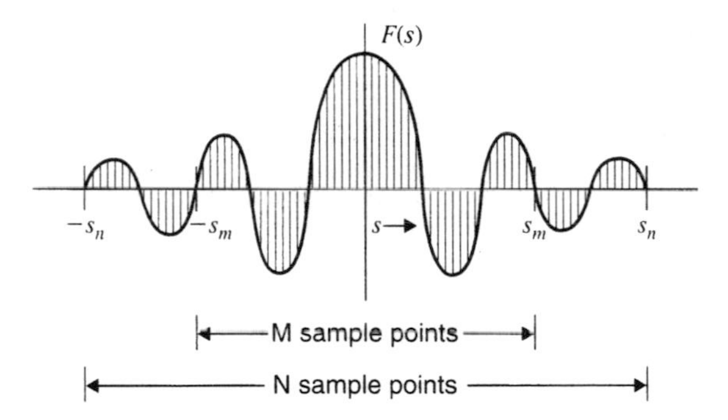

Figure 16–7 Sampled spectrum representation

Eq. (44) may be viewed as a linear equation in $2N + 1$ unknowns. The unknowns are the values of $F(2nT)$ at the sample points. Since the spectrum in known for $|s| \leq s_m$, we can generate a system of $2N + 1$ linear equations in $2N + 1$ unknowns by selecting $2N + 1$ frequencies within the passband and substituting the known values of $F(s)$ into Eq. (44).

Classical techniques can be used to solve the system of linear equations for the unknown values of the spectrum. These values can then be substituted into Eq. (44) to generate an estimate of the spectrum that is bandlimited at a frequency higher than the diffraction limit of the imaging system.

In practical cases, N may be relatively large and the linear equation solution computationally expensive. Since the spectrum of real functions is Hermite (the left half is the complex conjugate of the right half; see Chapter 10), this cuts the number of equations in half. Furthermore, since the spectrum is already known below the diffraction limit, only those points falling between s_m and s_n must be computed.

16.5.3 Successive Energy Reduction

There is an iterative, and possibly more practical, approach to recovering the high-frequency portion of the spectrum of a spatially bounded image. It involves successively enforcing space-limitedness upon the image, while keeping the known low-frequency portion of the spectrum intact.

Figure 16–8 illustrates the process in one dimension. We begin with $f(x)$, a triangular pulse (a) that represents the actual object and (b) its true spectrum, $F(s)$, out to some frequency s_n. In (d), $G_0(s)$ is the spectrum of $F(s)$ after it has been lowpass filtered by the transfer function of the imaging system, which is bandlimited at $s_m > s_n$. For this example, we assume an ideal lowpass transfer function. Figure 16–8(c) shows $g_0(x)$, which corresponds

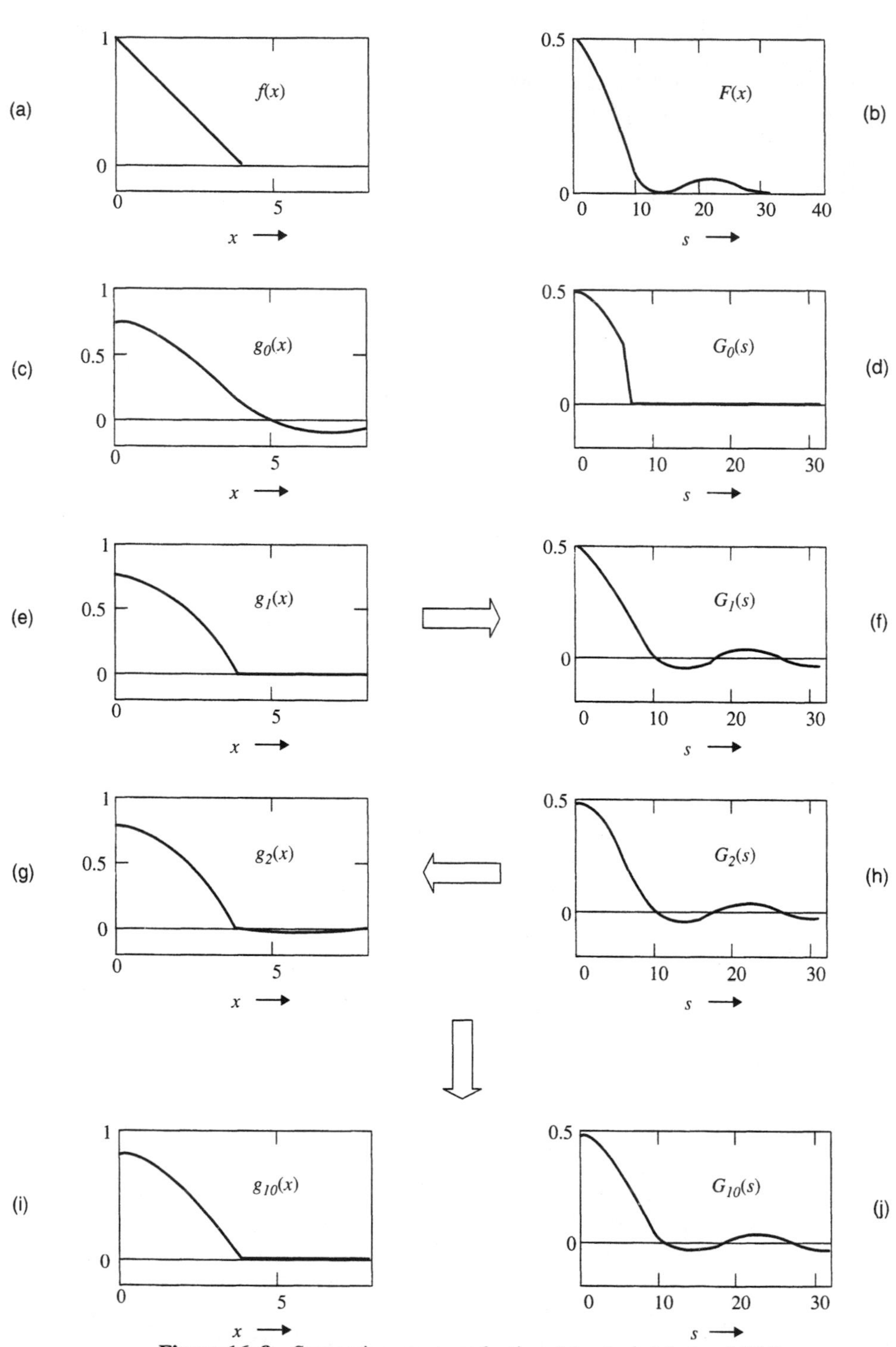

Figure 16–8 Successive energy reduction: (a) actual object and (b) its spectrum; (c) recorded image with (d) spectrum that has been bandlimited by the imaging system; (e) space-limited image; (h) spectrum restored to match (d) within the passband; (i) image and (j) spectrum after five iterations.

to the recorded image. The only thing we know with a high degree of accuracy, then, is $G_0(s)$ within the passband $|s| \le s_m$.

Notice that bandlimiting the spectrum causes $g_0(x)$ no longer to be space limited. The first step of the restoration is enforcing space-limitedness upon $g_0(x)$ by setting it to zero outside the domain of the pulse. This forms $g_1(x)$, shown in (e), and $G_1(s)$ is its spectrum (f). $G_1(s)$ looks more like $F(s)$, but it no longer conforms to $G_0(s)$ within the passband.

The second step involves replacing the values of $G_1(s)$ with those of $G_0(s)$ inside the passband, to form $G_2(s)$, shown in (h). This further improves the approximation. An inverse transform yields $g_2(x)$, shown in (g), which is a better approximation to $f(x)$, but is no longer space limited.

The two steps of (1) enforcing space-limitedness upon $g_i(x)$ and then (2) restoring the correct values to $G_{i+1}(s)$ within the passband (using $G_0(s)$) are repeated alternately. Figure 16–8 (i) and (j) show the results after five iterations. Each step reduces the energy of the error [34:8.18] given by

$$E = \int_{-\infty}^{\infty} |f(x) - g_i(x)|^2 dx \tag{45}$$

Figure 16–9 shows how $g_i(x)$ and $G_i(s)$ converge toward $f(x)$ and $F(s)$, respectively. The convergence generally becomes rather slow after the first few steps.

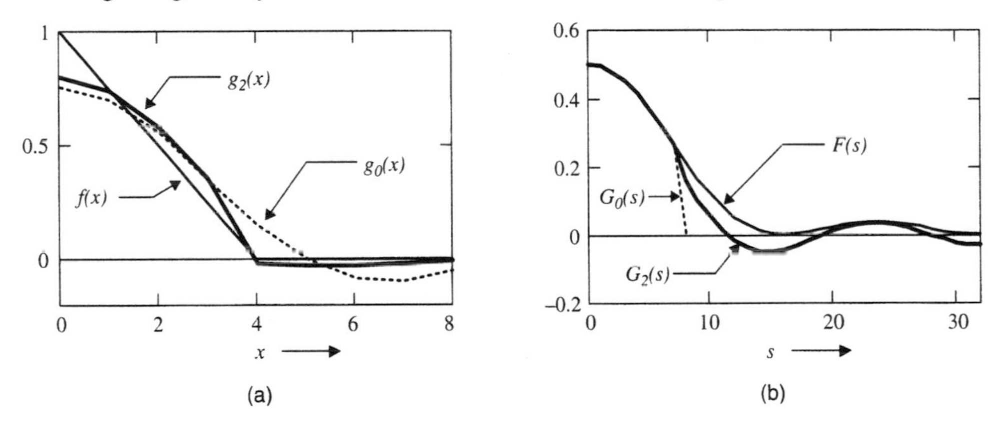

Figure 16–9 Convergence of successive energy reduction: $g_i(x)$ and $G_i(s)$ converge to $f(x)$ and $F(s)$, respectively, with increasing i

16.5.4 Practical Considerations

Any digital implementation of the extrapolation of an analytic function must be done carefully. The original image must be digitized with a very low noise level. It also must be oversampled by at least the factor by which its bandwidth is to be extended, and probably considerably more. In order to calculate the spectrum with fine resolution, one must compute the Fourier transforms over a domain much larger than the extent of the image. Finally, to avoid accumulating errors in the many forward and inverse transforms, one must employ a high degree of numerical precision.

There are various other approaches to reconstructing an imaged object with resolution beyond the diffraction limit. These include the use of prolate spheroidal wave functions [35–40], linear mean square extrapolation [34], and superimposed sinusoidal masks [41]. Several researchers have considered the effect of noise on the reconstruction process [38–40].

While some authors present impressive one-dimensional simulations of these techniques, practical examples have been rare. Whereas only one analytic function can exactly match a given function over a specified interval, many different analytic functions can approximate the given function very closely within the interval and then diverge significantly from it outside the interval. Andrews and Hunt [17] refer to "the myth of superresolution" and argue that noise constraints preclude any practical extension of resolution beyond the diffraction limit. Only with very high quality (low-noise) image digitization and careful computation can significant improvement be expected.

16.6 SYSTEM IDENTIFICATION

Before image restoration can be accomplished, the PSF of the blurring function must be known. In some cases, it is known in advance, but in others it must be determined experimentally from the degraded image. In this section, we consider methods for determining the PSF and MTF of an imaging system.

16.6.1 System Identification by Calibration Targets

In many cases, the transfer function of a system can be measured directly, once and for all, before the system is put into use. Suppose that for the system in Figure 16–10, the impulse response $h(x, y)$ is unknown and must be determined. We can find the transfer function directly from

$$H(u, v) = \frac{G(u, v)}{F(u, v)} \tag{46}$$

if $f(x, y)$ is a suitable test signal. Ideally, $F(u, v)$ should not have zeros. If it does, and if $H(u, v)$ can be assumed relatively smooth, we can still solve Eq. (46) by numerical techniques.

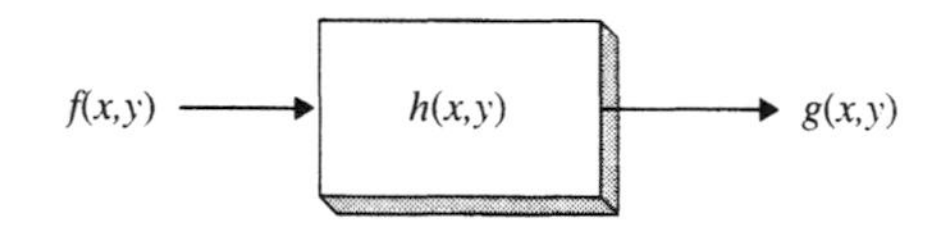

Figure 16–10 A linear system

16.6.1.1 Point Source Targets

If it were possible to input an impulse (or point source), then the output would be the impulse response (i.e., the PSF). While an impulse is physically impossible, we could get by with a pulse that is narrow compared to the PSF itself. Stars can be used to measure the PSF of a telescope, except that blurring by the atmosphere makes the PSF appear larger than it is. A bright point source LED can be employed with camera lenses, and small fluorescent beads are a possibility for identifying a microscope objective. In general, however, direct measurement of the PSF of optical systems—particularly bright-field microscopes—with point source targets is impractical, and other means must be employed.

16.6.1.2 Sine Wave Targets

Perhaps the most reliable means for determining the transfer function involves the use of sinusoidal input functions. Suppose the input is

$$f(x, y) = \cos(2\pi s_0 x) \tag{47}$$

which is a vertical bar pattern with a sinusoidal profile. (Recall Figure 11–1.) Since this input is also constant in the y-direction, the output is

$$g(x, y) = H(s_0, 0)\cos(2\pi s_0 x) \tag{48}$$

and the output spectrum is given by

$$G(u, v) = H(s_0, 0)\,[\delta(u - s_0) + \delta(u + s_0)]\,\delta(v) \tag{49}$$

This is an even impulse pair located on the u-axis at $u = \pm s_0$.

By repeating this procedure with many different frequencies at many different orientations, one can determine the transfer function to any desired degree of accuracy. Again, for circularly symmetric or separable transfer functions, the required amount of work is considerably reduced. In fact, the entire job can be done with one input image containing vertically and horizontally oriented sinusoidal bar patterns at several different frequencies. Such an input image is called a *sine wave target.* Since such targets are difficult to generate, particularly in small sizes required for measuring the PSF of a microscope, bar targets are sometimes used to measure the square wave response of the system, and this in turn is used to approximate the transfer function.

16.6.1.3 Line Targets

Suppose the input to the system is a line of infinitesimal width lying along the y-axis. We can express this as

$$f(x, y) = \delta(x) \tag{50}$$

which may be thought of as the product of a delta function in the x-direction and a constant (unity) in the y-direction. Then the output is given by the convolution

$$g(x, y) = \int_{-\infty}^{\infty}\int_{-\infty}^{\infty} h(p, q)\,\delta(x - p)\,dp\,dq = \int_{-\infty}^{\infty} h(x, y)\,dy \tag{51}$$

and the output spectrum is

$$G(u, v) = H(u, v)\,\delta(v) = H(u, 0)\,\delta(v) \tag{52}$$

Thus, the line input function has the effect of integrating out the y-component of the impulse response. By the projection property of the two-dimensional Fourier transform mentioned in Chapter 10, the spectrum of the output is merely the transfer function evaluated along the u-axis.

If $h(x, y)$ has circular symmetry, then the transfer function $H(u, v)$ can be completely determined from the line-spread function produced by an input line at any orientation. If $h(x, y)$ is separable into a product of a function of x times a function of y, then the vertical and horizontal line-spread functions of the system are adequate to determine the transfer function.

If $h(x, y)$ is asymmetrical, the rotation property of the two-dimensional Fourier transform implies that we can take line-spread functions at every angle of orientation, transform them to obtain profiles of $H(u, v)$ at every angle, and thus reconstruct the transfer function. This technique forms the basis of computerized axial tomography, discussed in Chapter 22.

16.6.1.4 Edge Targets

Suppose the input contains an abrupt transition from low to high amplitude along the y-axis. This input can be expressed as a step function in the x-direction times a constant in the y-direction and can be written as

$$f(x, y) = u(x) \tag{53}$$

where $u(x)$ is the unit step function introduced in Chapter 9. Since the edge function is the integral of the line input, and convolution commutes with differentiation and integration, the edge-spread function is the integral of the line-spread function. Thus, one can differentiate the edge-spread function and proceed as before. Alternatively, we can make use of the property that integration merely introduces a coefficient $1/j2\pi s$ into the Fourier transform. Thus,

$$G(u, v) = \frac{H(u, 0)\delta(v)}{j2\pi u} \tag{54}$$

from which the transfer function may be determined for nonzero u.

16.6.1.5 Frequency Sweep Targets

Another input that, like the sine wave target, avoids the necessity of transforming the output to determine the transfer function is the frequency sweep target. For purposes of illustration, consider the one-dimensional linear system in Figure 16–11.

The input is a harmonic signal whose frequency increases linearly with distance from the origin. A harmonic signal with frequency ax is given by

$$f(x) = e^{j2\pi ax^2} \tag{55}$$

The output signal is given by the convolution

$$g(x) = \int_{-\infty}^{\infty} h(\tau)e^{j2\pi a(x-\tau)^2}d\tau = e^{j2\pi ax^2}\int_{-\infty}^{\infty} h(\tau)e^{j2\pi a\tau^2}e^{-j4\pi ax\tau}d\tau \tag{56}$$

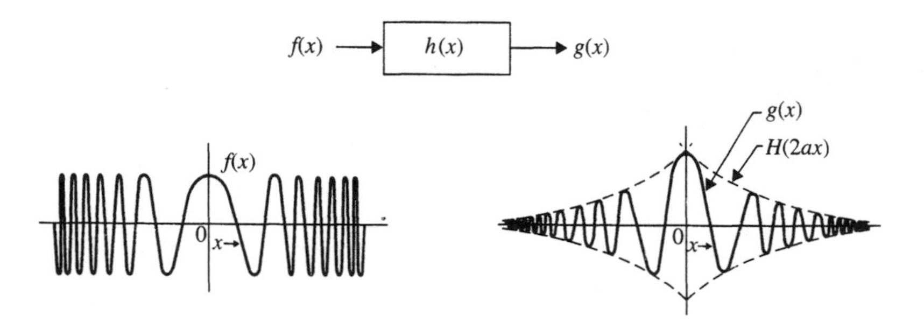

Figure 16–11 System identification with a frequency sweep input

where the second form is obtained by expanding the square in the exponential. If we make the substitution

$$s = 2a\tau \qquad ds = 2a\,d\tau \qquad \tau = \frac{s}{2a} \qquad d\tau = \frac{1}{2a}ds \tag{57}$$

and recognize the input signal in front of the integral sign, we obtain

$$g(x) = \frac{1}{2a}f(x)\int_{-\infty}^{\infty} h\left(\frac{s}{2a}\right)e^{j\pi s^2/2a}e^{-j2\pi sx}ds \tag{58}$$

We can now recognize the integral in Eq. (58) as the Fourier transform of a product. This can be written

$$g(x) = \frac{1}{2a}f(x)\mathfrak{F}\left\{h\left(\frac{s}{2a}\right)e^{j\pi s^2/2a}\right\} \tag{59}$$

If the impulse response goes to zero outside the interval $-T$ to T, then

$$h\left(\frac{s}{2a}\right) \approx 0 \qquad |s| > 2aT \tag{60}$$

Furthermore, if

$$\frac{(2aT)^2}{2a} = 2aT^2 \ll 1 \tag{61}$$

then

$$e^{j\pi s^2/2a} \approx 1 \qquad |s| \leq 2aT \tag{62}$$

and the output reduces to

$$g(x) = \frac{1}{2a}f(x)2aH(2ax) = f(x)H(2ax) \tag{63}$$

which is merely the input in an envelope that is the transfer function.

The assumption in Eq. (61) can be interpreted in two ways. First, it implies that the impulse response is narrow compared to the first cycle of the frequency sweep. By the similarity theorem, this is equivalent to assuming that the transfer function is broad compared to the first cycle of the frequency sweep. If this second condition were not true, it would be difficult to observe the envelope of the output.

Notice that using a frequency sweep target under the assumption of Eq. (61) allows us to determine the transfer function without having to compute a Fourier transform. If, on the other hand, we are willing to compute a Fourier transform, we can avoid making this assumption. Returning to Eq. (59), if we divide both sides by $f(x)$ and take the inverse Fourier transform, we obtain

$$\mathfrak{F}^{-1}\left\{\frac{g(x)}{f(x)}\right\} = \frac{1}{2a}h\left(\frac{s}{2a}\right)e^{j\pi s^2/2a} \tag{64}$$

If we take the magnitude of both sides of Eq. (64), the complex exponential disappears, and

$$\left|\mathfrak{F}^{-1}\left\{\frac{g(x)}{f(x)}\right\}\right| = \frac{1}{2a}h\left(\frac{s}{2a}\right) \tag{65}$$

which is easily solved for the impulse response $h(x)$. It is curious that transforming the ratio of the output to the input produces the impulse response rather than the transfer function.

16.6.2 System Identification by Cross-Correlation

Suppose we cross-correlate the output of a linear system with its input, as shown in Figure 16–12. The spectrum of the output of the cross-correlation is

$$Z(s) = G(s)F^*(s) = H(s)F(s)F^*(s) = H(s)P_f(s) \tag{66}$$

where $P_f(s)$ is the power spectrum of the input signal. If $f(x)$ is uncorrelated white noise, then $P_f(s)$ is a constant, and the output of the cross-correlator is merely the impulse response of the system. Thus, one can use a random noise image as input to a system and cross-correlate it with the system's output to obtain the PSF of the system. In addition, the spectrum of the output is the transfer function of the system.

One can generate an uncorrelated white noise image by first generating a two-dimensional spectrum that has constant amplitude and random phase and then computing its inverse Fourier transform.

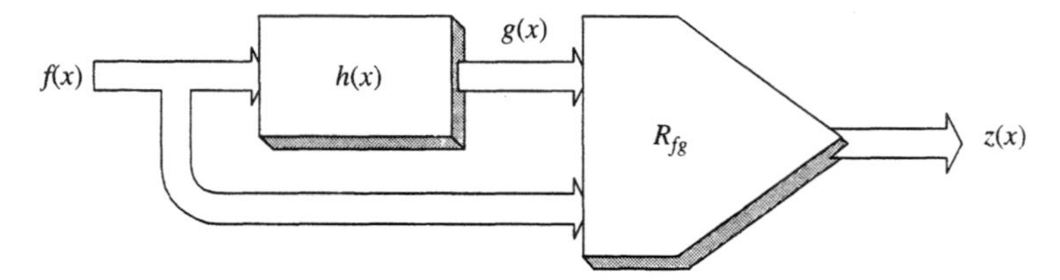

Figure 16–12 System identification by cross-correlation

16.6.3 Identifying the System from the Image

In some cases, it is impractical or impossible to calibrate the imaging system under the same conditions in which a particular degraded image was recorded. This is true for motion blur and stochastic degradation such as atmospheric turbulence, and when a photograph is to be restored and the original camera system is unavailable. In such instances, one must attempt to determine the degrading PSF from the image itself.

If the image contains any feature that can be modeled analytically, then, theoretically, the PSF can be obtained by deconvolution of the model.

16.6.3.1 Point Sources

If one can arrange for the degraded image to include a point source of light or a vanishingly small dark spot on a white background, then the PSF is available directly. If the point source or spot is of nonnegligible extent, then it can be modeled with a Gaussian, a flat-topped circular pulse, or some other suitable function that can be deconvolved to yield the PSF.

This technique is perhaps most valuable in astronomical photographs severely degraded by atmospheric turbulence. Here, point sources (stars) are readily available, and the degradation is severe enough that deconvolution can be a great help. In high-quality images, such as diffraction-limited camera images, it is difficult to find a point source or speck small enough to show the PSF and still large enough to come through the system with sufficient energy to be measured accurately. Since the PSF occupies a very small portion of the image, it is particularly vulnerable to corruption by system noise. For this reason, direct measurement of the PSF using a point source in the image is of limited use.

16.6.3.2 Lines

Under the projection theorem of the two-dimensional Fourier transform, the Fourier transform of the line-spread function gives a one-dimensional component of the two-dimensional transfer function. The line-spread function approach has the advantage that a line source in the image can be averaged along its extent to generate a relatively noise-free estimate. For high-quality systems, however, the line object in the image must be extremely thin. Therefore, it must be extremely bright (or dark) relative to its background in order to come through with sufficient amplitude.

16.6.3.3 Edges

Most images of ordinary scenes contain features that can be modeled as ideal edges. Such an edge can be averaged along its extent to produce a relatively noise-free estimate of the system edge-spread function in a particular direction. This can then be differentiated to produce the line-spread function, and that can be transformed to produce a component of the transfer function [17,42,43].

If the PSF is known to be circularly symmetric, the one-dimensional PSF derived from the line-spread function may simply be rotated to produce the two-dimensional PSF. If the PSF and, hence, the transfer function are separable into a product of functions, then one vertical and one horizontal edge are sufficient to determine the transfer function. In the general case, however, edges at many different orientations are required to determine the transfer function adequately.

Since differentiation is a highpass filter type of operation, noise in the edge-spread function will appear amplified in the resulting line-spread function. Thus, averaging along the edge should be employed wherever possible. If the edge is not perfectly straight and parallel to the sampling raster, however, averaging will blur the edge and make the transfer function appear to be more of a lowpass filter than it really is.

A skewed linear edge may be brought parallel to the sampling raster by a geometric transformation that effects rotation. Unless the scene is considerably oversampled, however, the interpolation inherent in rotation will also tend to blur the edge.

Another problem with the edge-spread function occurs when one considers using it over too narrow a region in the vicinity of the edge. Rabedeau [44] shows that for a diffraction-limited system, the edge-spread function must be considered over a width of almost 10 Airy disk diameters before the transfer function errors due to truncation drop below 2 percent.

Proper use of the edge-spread function is not as simple as it might seem, and accurate determination of the transfer function requires considerable care. In general, any determination of the PSF from the degraded imaged should be done very carefully.

16.6.4 Determining the OTF from the Degraded Image Spectrum

Ordinarily, images of complex scenes have reasonably smooth amplitude spectra. If the degrading transfer function has zeros (as in the case of linear motion blur, for example), these zeros will tend to force the spectrum of the degraded image to zero at specific frequencies. If the blurring function is adequately modeled, the locations of the zeros (or near-zeros) in the spatial frequency plane allow one to determine the unknown parameters of the blurring OTF. Visualization of the zeros in the spectrum is sometimes aided by preprocessing with a highpass filter [45].

By taking the logarithm of the power spectrum of the degraded image, one can enhance the amplitude of the dips due to zeros in the degrading transfer function. If the zeros are equally spaced, they produce a series of periodic spikes in the logarithm of the power spectrum. The power spectrum of the logarithm of the power spectrum, sometimes called the *cepstrum* [18], is useful for determining the exact spacing of the spikes and, consequently, the zeros of the degrading transfer function [16,46].

A perhaps more powerful technique involves segmenting the degraded image into square regions that are large compared to the extent of the degrading PSF [47] and averaging the logarithm of the power spectrum of all such regions [48]. For complex scenes, the signal components tend to average out in the average log spectrum, whereas the degrading transfer function, which is constant throughout the image, does not. The average log power spectrum converges approximately to the logarithm of the squared magnitude of the degrading transfer function [17].

16.7 NOISE MODELING

Those noise sources that commonly corrupt images can be divided into three categories. First, images originally recorded on photographic film are subject to degradation by film grain noise. Second, the conversion of an image from optical to electrical form is a statistical process, since, in reality, each picture element receives a finite number of photons. Finally, electronic amplifiers that process a signal introduce thermal noise. Considerable effort has been devoted to modeling noise from these three sources.

16.7.1 Electronic Noise

Electronic noise due to the random thermal motion of electrons in resistive circuit elements is the simplest of the three sources to model. This type of noise has been successfully modeled by circuit designers for a long time. It is usually modeled as spectrally white Gaussian noise with zero mean value. Thus, it has a Gaussian histogram and a flat power spectrum. It is completely specified by its RMS value (standard deviation). Sometimes, electronic circuits exhibit so-called *one-over-*f noise. This is random noise with an intensity that dies out inversely with frequency. However, image-processing problems seldom require modeling of the $1/f$ component of the noise [49].

16.7.2 Photoelectronic Noise

Photoelectronic noise is due to the statistical nature of light and of the photoelectronic conversion process that takes place in image sensors. At low light levels, where the effect is relatively severe, photoelectronic noise is often modeled as random with a Poisson density function [17]. The standard deviation of this distribution is equal to the square root of the mean.

At high light levels, the Poisson distribution approaches the Gaussian, which is simpler to model. Again, the standard deviation (RMS amplitude) is equal to the square root of the mean. This implies that the noise amplitude is signal-dependent.

16.7.3 Film Grain Noise

As described in Chapter 2, a photographic emulsion consists of silver halide crystals suspended in gelatin. Photographic exposure is a binary process, with each grain being either totally exposed or unexposed. During development, exposed grains are reduced to opaque grains of pure silver, while unexposed grains are washed off. Thus, the variable density of a photographic negative is due to variations in the concentration of silver grains. Under microscopic examination, the smooth tones of a photographic image assume a random grainy appearance. Randomness is further introduced by the variable number of photons required to expose a particular grain and by the varying size of the grains themselves. The subjective appearance of these factors is termed *graininess*.

For most practical purposes, film grain noise can be effectively modeled as a Gaussian process (white noise). Like photoelectronic noise, the underlying distribution is Poisson. Since the mean grain diameter for specific films is published by the manufacturer, only the standard deviation of film grain noise as a function of grain size and the local image density remain to be determined.

In 1913, Nutting modeled the photographic emulsion as a sandwich of layers approximately one grain diameter in thickness. He showed that the measured optical density is

$$D = 0.43\frac{na}{A} \tag{67}$$

where a is the cross-sectional area of a single grain, A is the area of the aperture used to measure optical density, and n is the total number of grains that fall within the aperture [50]. For fixed values of a and A, n is a random variable with a binomial distribution. Taking the expectation of Eq. (67) produces

$$\mathcal{E}\{D\} = 0.43\frac{\mathcal{E}\{n\}a}{A} \tag{68}$$

and since Eq. (67) is linear, the variance is given by

$$\sigma_D^2 = 0.43\frac{\sigma_n^2 a}{A} \tag{69}$$

If a is small compared to A, the binomial distribution of n can be modeled by a Poisson distribution, and hence, the variance is equal to the mean [51]. Making this substitution produces

$$\sigma_D = \sqrt{0.43\frac{a}{A}}\,[\mathcal{E}\{D\}]^{1/2} \tag{70}$$

This equation indicates that film grain noise is worse with large-grain (high-speed) emulsions and small scanning apertures and in dense areas of the image. Thus, film grain noise is also signal-dependent.

The preceding analysis assumes uniform grain size. Haugh [52] showed that if the grain size is distributed, the exponent in Eq. (70) should be somewhat less than one-half.

Using sensitometric data from Higgins and Stultz [53], Naderi [54] showed, that the exponent lies between 0.3 and 0.4 for a reasonably small aperture. Thus, film grain noise can be modeled as a zero-mean white Gaussian process with RMS amplitude (standard deviation) proportional to the cube root of the local average density.

We have seen that, of the three common noise sources, two are signal-dependent. This signal dependence may be ignored for common restoration work, but for high levels of accuracy, it must be taken into account.

16.8 IMPLEMENTATION

In this section we consider alternative ways to implement the restoration of an image after the required operation has been identified [55].

16.8.1 Transform Domain Filtering

If the restoration operation is linear and shift invariant, it can be implemented by multiplication in the Fourier transform frequency domain. This involves first a two-dimensional DFT, followed by point-by-point multiplication of the spectrum by the transfer function, and then an inverse DFT. For an N-by-N image, this requires $N \log_2(N)$ multiply-add operations for each transform if the FFT is used and N^2 multiplications to implement the filter. This approach is useful when the restoration transfer function is developed in the frequency domain.

In some cases, the restoration is better done using a discrete transform other than the Fourier transform. Most of the transforms mentioned in this text have fast implementation algorithms similar to the FFT. The required modification in the transform domain then depends on the nature of the restoration. That is, it may be something other than multiplication by a transfer function.

16.8.2 Large-Kernel Convolution

If the restoration is a linear, shift-invariant operation, it can be implemented by convolution in the spatial domain. Discrete convolution with the restoration PSF is numerically equivalent to the DFT method above, provided that both the image and the PSF array are N by N. The convolution of two N-by-N arrays requires N^4 operations, significantly more than the FFT method, making this approach much less practical for images of reasonable size.

16.8.3 Small-Kernel Convolution

Unless the image is severely oversampled, the signal spectrum, and consequently the restoration MTF, will normally extend most of the way to the folding frequency before it dies out. From the similarity theorem of the Fourier transform, we know that if the transfer function is broad, the impulse response will be narrow. Thus, the convolution kernel for implementing a restoration PSF might well be zero, or approximately so, except within a reasonably small radius about the origin. In that case, the majority of the operations required for an N-by-N convolution (those distant from the origin) will contribute little or nothing to the restoration.

A properly designed small kernel (M by M, where $M < N$) of perhaps nine by nine, or even as small as three by three, pixels might then produce an acceptable approximation to the result of convolution with the full N-by-N array. Convolving an M-by-M kernel with an N-by-N image requires M^2N^2 multiply-add operations. Hence, we now address ways to derive compact restoration kernels.

16.8.3.1 Subsampling the Transfer Function

The inverse two-dimensional DFT can compute an M-by-M PSF from an M-by-M transfer function. The N-by-N restoration MTF can be subsampled to size M-by-M. This way, it is properly scaled, in that it covers the frequency range from zero to the Nyquist freqency, and yet the resulting kernel has the desired size.

The restoration MTF may have to be smoothed to avoid aliasing in the subsampling process. If so, the small kernel will then implement the smoothed MTF and thus will not match the full-sized, original MTF. Smoothing the MTF tends to narrow the PSF, thereby making it more space-limited. This is simply lowpass filtering with the domains reversed.

Figure 16–13 illustrates the approach in one dimension. A 28-point discrete Gaussian lowpass transfer function vector, **F**, was subsampled by a factor of four, producing a 7-point vector. The inverse DFT of the latter, properly scaled, yields the 7-point kernel, $\hat{\mathbf{f}}$. The graph in the figure shows the effect that the approximation has on the transfer function.

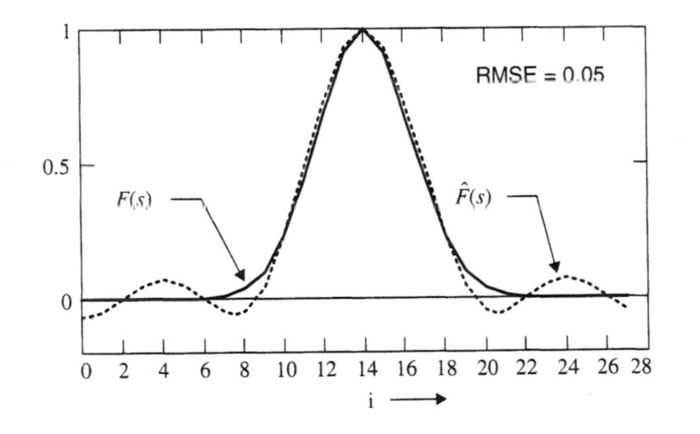

$\mathbf{F} = [\cdots\ 0\ \ .01\ \ .04\ \ .1\ \ .23\ \ .44\ \ .69\ \ .91\ \ 1\ \ .91\ \ .69\ \ .44\ \ .23\ \ .1\ \ .04\ \ .01\ \ 0\ \cdots]^t$

$\mathbf{f} = [\cdots\ 0\ \ 0\ \ .01\ \ .02\ \ .06\ \ .12\ \ .18\ \ .21\ \ .18\ \ .12\ \ .06\ \ .02\ \ .01\ \ 0\ \ 0\ \cdots]^t$

$\hat{\mathbf{F}} = [0\ \ 0\ \ .23\ \ 1\ \ .23\ \ 0\ \ 0]^t$ $\hat{\mathbf{f}} = [.08\ \ .13\ \ .18\ \ .21\ \ .18\ \ .13\ \ .08]^t$

Figure 16–13 Subsampling the MTF: **F** is a 28-element vector specifying the desired MTF and **f** is the corresponding 28-point impulse response vector. $\hat{\mathbf{F}}$ is the MTF subsampled to 7 points, and $\hat{\mathbf{f}}$ is the corresponding 7-point kernel. The graph shows the actual and approximate MTFs

16.8.3.2 Truncating the Kernel

A simpler approach to small-kernel convolution is merely to truncate the PSF array to some acceptably small size. Multiplying the PSF by a square pulse convolves the MTF with a $\sin(x)/x$ function. Unless the PSF is spatially bounded (essentially zero outside the truncation window), this can alter its transfer function significantly. The transfer function of the truncated kernel can be computed and compared with the complete restoration MTF to determine whether the effects of truncation are acceptable.

Truncating the kernel reduces the "detail" in the transfer function, just as eliminating high-frequency components from a spectrum reduces the detail in the corresponding signal or image. Thus, the transfer function of a truncated kernel can follow the basic shape of the desired MTF, but, being inherently smoother, it cannot conform to local variations.

The inverse DFT, like the forward DFT, is an orthonormal transform. Hence, each basis function is orthogonal to every other. This means that no modification of the remaining kernel elements can replace any of the detail that was lost by truncating the kernel. In other words, the MTF of the truncated kernel is the best approximation to that of the large kernel, in the mean squares sense.

Computing the Kernel. Recall from Sec. 10.1.4 that the discrete Fourier transform

$$F_k = \frac{1}{\sqrt{N}}\sum_{i=0}^{N-1} f_i \exp\left(-j2\pi k\frac{i}{N}\right) \qquad i, k = 0, 1, \ldots, N-1 \tag{71}$$

expresses the relationship between an N-point convolution kernel $\{f_i\}$ and its (N-point) transfer function $\{F_k\}$. In matrix form, this is

$$\mathbf{F} = \mathcal{W}\mathbf{f} \quad \text{and} \quad \mathbf{f} = \mathcal{W}^{-1}\mathbf{F} \tag{72}$$

where $\mathcal{W}$ is an N-by-N unitary matrix with elements

$$w_{i,k} = \frac{1}{\sqrt{N}}\exp\left(-j2\pi k\frac{i}{N}\right) \tag{73}$$

and its inverse is merely its conjugate transpose. Since $0 \le k \le N-1$, the elements of $\mathbf{F}$ represent N points in the transfer function that are equally spaced in the interval $[-s_N, s_N]$, where

$$s_N = \frac{1}{2\Delta t} \tag{74}$$

is the Nyquist frequency.

Sec. 13.4.1.1 pointed out that the DFT requires a somewhat awkward arrangement of the elements in the signal and spectrum vectors. (Recall Figure 13–2.) If the signal and spectrum are centered, not at element 0, but at element a of their vectors, then the one-dimensional DFT equation becomes

$$F_k = \frac{1}{\sqrt{N}}\sum_{i=0}^{N-1} f_i \exp\left[-j2\pi(k-a)\frac{(i-a)}{N}\right] \tag{75}$$

and similarly for the inverse transform. Normally a would specify the central element of the vector, that is,

$$a = \begin{cases} N/2 & N \text{ even} \\ (N-1)/2 & N \text{ odd} \end{cases} \tag{76}$$

This formulation can be more convenient for kernel computation than the standard DFT. We lose the computational advantage of the FFT implementation, but this is seldom a significant factor with kernels of ordinary size. Further, it is often convenient to use kernels of odd length (so that there is a central element), but the FFT requires even length.

Now, suppose that g is an M-by-1 kernel vector, and we wish to compute from it an N-by-1 spectrum vector, where $N > M$. The larger number of points are to be spread across the same frequency range, $[-s_N, s_N]$, so their spacing will be closer than it would be in an M-point spectrum. In this case we can write

$$F_k = \frac{1}{\sqrt{M}} \sum_{m=0}^{M-1} g_m \exp\left[-j2\pi \frac{(k-a)}{N}(m-b)\right] \tag{77}$$

where $0 \le m \le M-1$, $0 \le k \le N-1$, a is as above and

$$b = \begin{cases} M/2 & M \text{ even} \\ (M-1)/2 & M \text{ odd} \end{cases} \tag{78}$$

This equation computes an N-point spectrum from an M-point signal. In matrix form, it is

$$\mathbf{F} = \mathbf{Wg} \tag{79}$$

where $\mathbf{W}$ is an N-by-M matrix having elements

$$w_{k,m} = \frac{1}{\sqrt{M}} \exp\left[-j2\pi \frac{(k-a)}{N}(m-b)\right] \tag{80}$$

A 56-point spectrum vector, plotted as $\hat{F}(s)$ in Figure 16–13, was computed with this method from the 7-point kernel, $\hat{\mathbf{f}}$ shown. This approach of computing a long spectrum or signal vector from a short signal or spectrum vector, respectively, makes it convenient to visualize the smooth (bandlimited, analytic) function that underlies a discrete signal or spectrum vector.

Now, suppose $\mathbf{F}$ is a specified N-point transfer function, and let $\mathbf{g}$ be a corresponding, but unknown, M-point kernel intended to approximate it. Then Eq. (79) represents N equations in M unknowns. This is an overconstrained system of equations, and it cannot be solved for exact values of g_m. It is, however, amenable to a minimum mean square error solution by the pseudoinverse method [56]. (See Sec. 19.5 and Appendix 3.) This yields

$$\mathbf{g} = [\mathbf{W}^*\mathbf{W}]^{-1}\mathbf{W}^*\mathbf{F} \tag{81}$$

where the * indicates the conjugate transpose. Thus, $\mathbf{g}$ is an M-point vector containing the kernel elements that minimize the mean square error

$$MSE = \|\mathbf{F} - \mathbf{Wg}\|^2 = \sum_{i=0}^{N-1} |F_k - G_k|^2 \tag{82}$$

where $\mathbf{G} = \mathbf{Wg}$ is the actual transfer function of the small kernel, $\mathbf{g}$, computed to N points.

As a numerical example, suppose $N = 14$, $M = 7$, and the desired transfer function (specified as a 14-element vector), is

$$\mathbf{F} = [0\ 0\ 0\ 0\ .01\ .14\ .61\ 1\ .61\ .14\ .01\ 0\ 0\ 0]'$$

This is a Gaussian lowpass filter corresponding to the kernel

$$\mathbf{f} = [.01\ .02\ .05\ .13\ .27\ .45\ .61\ .67\ .61\ .45\ .27\ .13\ .05\ .02]'$$

If we use $a = 3$ and $b = 7$ in Eq. (80), we obtain, from Eq. (81),

$$\mathbf{g} = [.27\ .45\ .61\ .67\ .61\ .45\ .27]'$$

which is merely the truncated kernel, as expected, since the MMSE approximate kernel is simply the truncation of the larger kernel.

We can use $\mathbf{G} = \mathbf{Wg}$ to compute the 14-point transfer function of the small kernel. This yields

$$\mathbf{G} = [-.05\ 0\ .05\ -.02\ -.05\ .2\ .65\ .89\ .65\ .2\ -.05\ -.02\ .05\ 0]'$$

The two transfer functions are graphed in Figure 16–14.

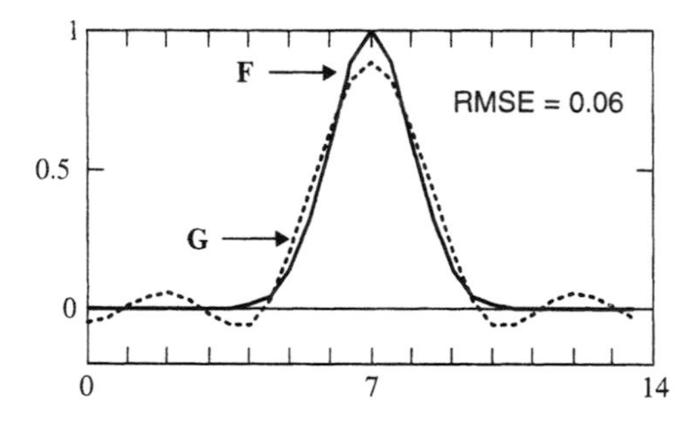

Figure 16–14 The effect of truncating the kernel: **F** is the transfer function of a 14-point Gaussian lowpass filter kernel, and **G** is the transfer function of a seven point truncation of the kernel

While the preceding discussion applies to one dimension, the generalization to two dimensions is straightforward. One merely employs row stacking to format the two-dimensional transfer function into a vector representation. The kernel likewise emerges in row-stacked format.

16.8.4 Kernel Decomposition

Modern image-processing systems often incorporate special hardware for high-speed convolution with a small (typically, three-by-three) kernel. This hardware becomes useful when an M-by-M kernel is decomposed into a set of smaller (e.g., three-by-three) kernels that are then applied sequentially. For example, $(M - 1)/2$ kernels of size three by three will implement an M-by-M convolution. While this cannot substitute exactly for an arbitrary M-by-M kernel, the result is often a good approximation. In this section, we discuss the decomposition of large kernels into sets of smaller ones.

16.8.4.1 SVD Convolution

Singular-value decomposition (SVD; see Sec. 13.6.4 and Appendix 3) expresses an M-by-M matrix of rank R as a sum of R M-by-M matrices of rank 1. Further, each such matrix is an outer product of two M-by-1 eigenvectors, and each is weighted, in the summation, by one of the singular values of the matrix. Since convolution commutes with addition, this can be implemented as a sum of R images, each obtained by convolution with one of the matrices in the sum.

This would appear to increase, rather than decrease, the computational load of the process. Each of the convolutions, however, can be implemented as an M-by-1 convolution on each row of the image, followed by a 1-by-M convolution on each column. This requires only $2MN^2$ multiply-add operations (rather than M^2N^2) for each matrix in the summation. The complete convolution can be done in $2RMN^2$ operations, which will be less than M^2N^2 if $R < M/2$. If the kernel exhibits circular symmetry, the rows below the center row are identical to those above, and the rank can be no greater than $(M + 1)/2$. Also, these one-dimensional rowwise and columnwise convolutions can be performed by high-speed hardware in many image-processing systems.

As a numerical example, consider the three-by-three convolution kernel

$$\mathbf{F} = \begin{bmatrix} 1 & 2 & 1 \\ 2 & 3 & 2 \\ 1 & 2 & 1 \end{bmatrix} \tag{83}$$

Its singular-value decomposition is simplified because the kernel is square and symmetric. The unitary matrices (see Appendix 3) are equal, i.e.,

$$\mathbf{U} = \mathbf{F}\mathbf{F}' = \mathbf{V} = \mathbf{F}'\mathbf{F} = \begin{bmatrix} 6 & 10 & 6 \\ 10 & 17 & 10 \\ 6 & 10 & 6 \end{bmatrix} \tag{84}$$

and they have eigenvalues

$$\begin{bmatrix} \lambda_1 \\ \lambda_2 \\ \lambda_3 \end{bmatrix} = \begin{bmatrix} 28.86 \\ 0.14 \\ 0 \end{bmatrix} \tag{85}$$

and eigenvectors

$$\mathbf{u}_1 = \mathbf{v}_1 = \begin{bmatrix} 0.454 \\ 0.766 \\ 0.454 \end{bmatrix} \quad \mathbf{u}_2 = \mathbf{v}_2 = \begin{bmatrix} 0.542 \\ -0.643 \\ 0.542 \end{bmatrix} \quad \text{and} \quad \mathbf{u}_3 = \mathbf{v}_3 = \begin{bmatrix} -0.707 \\ 0 \\ 0.707 \end{bmatrix} \tag{86}$$

U and **V** are matrices of rank 2, since one eigenvalue is zero. The singular values are on the diagonal of

$$\Lambda = \mathbf{U}'\mathbf{F}\mathbf{V} = \begin{bmatrix} 5.37 & 0 & 0 \\ 0 & -0.372 & 0 \\ 0 & 0 & 0 \end{bmatrix} \tag{87}$$

and the SVD summation is

$$\mathbf{F} = \sum_{j=1}^{2} \Lambda_{j,j} \mathbf{u}_j \mathbf{v}_j^t \tag{88}$$

which, in this case, has only two terms.

The ramification of this result for convolution purposes is that we can convolve the rows and columns of the image with $\mathbf{u}_1$, then separately with $\mathbf{u}_2$, and then add the two resulting images, properly scaled, to obtain the desired result, without error.

Notice that the second singular value is much smaller than the first. Thus, we can neglect the second term in the summation without introducing much error of approximation. Using the first term alone, we have

$$\mathbf{F} \approx \Lambda_{1,1} \mathbf{u}_1 \mathbf{u}_1^t = \begin{bmatrix} 1.11 & 1.87 & 1.11 \\ 1.87 & 3.15 & 1.87 \\ 1.11 & 1.87 & 1.11 \end{bmatrix} \tag{89}$$

which may be an acceptable approximation to the kernel in Eq. (83). This operation can be implemented as convolutions of $\mathbf{u}_1$ first with the rows and then with the columns of the image (or vice versa).

A second example makes the point more strongly if we change the central element of $\mathbf{F}$ to 4. This reduces the rank of the matrix to 1, since all three rows are then identical to within a scale factor. In that case

$$\mathbf{F} = \begin{bmatrix} 1 & 2 & 1 \\ 2 & 4 & 2 \\ 1 & 2 & 1 \end{bmatrix} \quad \lambda = \begin{bmatrix} 36 \\ 0 \\ 0 \end{bmatrix} \quad \Lambda = \begin{bmatrix} 36 & 0 & 0 \\ 0 & 0 & 0 \\ 0 & 0 & 0 \end{bmatrix} \quad \text{and} \quad \mathbf{u}_1 = \begin{bmatrix} 0.408 \\ 0.816 \\ 0.408 \end{bmatrix} \tag{90}$$

The SVD summation now has only one term, which is

$$\mathbf{F} = \Lambda_{1,1} \mathbf{u}_1 \mathbf{u}_1^t = \sqrt{\Lambda_{1,1}} \mathbf{u}_1 \sqrt{\Lambda_{1,1}} \mathbf{u}_1^t = \begin{bmatrix} 1 \\ 2 \\ 1 \end{bmatrix} \begin{bmatrix} 1 & 2 & 1 \end{bmatrix} \tag{91}$$

Thus, singular-value decomposition has factored the three-by-three kernel into the product of identical three-by-one and one-by-three vectors. These can then be convolved with the rows and columns of the image sequentially, requiring six (rather than nine) multiply-add operations per pixel.

16.8.4.2 SGK Decomposition

Using SVD in combination with the *small generating kernel* (SGK) decomposition technique [57,58:9.6], we can decompose any M-by-M kernel into a set of smaller kernels that can be applied sequentially. For example, an M-by-M kernel can be decomposed into $(M-1)/2$ kernels of size three by three to implement approximately the same convolution.

As shown in the previous subsection, each of the separable matrices in an SVD summation is an outer product of two M-by-1 eigenvectors [e.g., Eq. (88)]. These vectors, in turn, can be expanded by SGK decomposition as a sequential convolution of three-by-one kernels [59]. With this approach, $R(M-1)$ convolutions with three-by-one kernels are required to implement convolution with an M-by-M matrix of rank R.

Suppose an M-by-M kernel has been decomposed into one or more pairs of M-by-1 vectors by SVD, as illustrated before. We now seek to decompose each of these pairs into $(M-1)/2$ kernels of size three by one. To illustrate the technique, we decompose a five-by-five kernel into two three-by-three component kernels.

SVD shows that the kernel in Figure 16–15 is a matrix of rank 1 that is the outer product of the vector $\mathbf{h} = (1,3,4,3,1)^t$ with itself. We now seek to decompose the five-by-one kernel $\mathbf{h}$ into two three-by-one components, $\mathbf{f}$ and $\mathbf{g}$.

Since convolution is associative,

$$\mathbf{y} = \mathbf{h}*\mathbf{x} = \mathbf{f}*[\mathbf{g}*\mathbf{x}] \text{ implies } \mathbf{h} = \mathbf{f}*\mathbf{g} \tag{92}$$

and, in the frequency domain,

$$H(s) = F(s)G(s) \tag{93}$$

Thus, the challenge is to factor the transfer function $H(u, v)$ into two transfer functions that are suitable for three-by-one convolution sequences.

From the definition of the one-dimensional discrete Fourier transform, we can write

$$H(s) = \sum_{i=0}^{M-1} h_i e^{-j2\pi s\frac{i}{M}} \tag{94}$$

Switching to the notation of the z-transform, we let

$$z = e^{j2\pi\frac{s}{M}} \tag{95}$$

and we can write Eq. (94) as

$$H(z) = \sum_{i=0}^{M-1} h_i z^{-i} = h_0 + h_1 z^{-1} + h_2 z^{-2} + h_3 z^{-3} + h_4 z^{-4} \tag{96}$$

Factoring out h_0 and z^{-4} yields

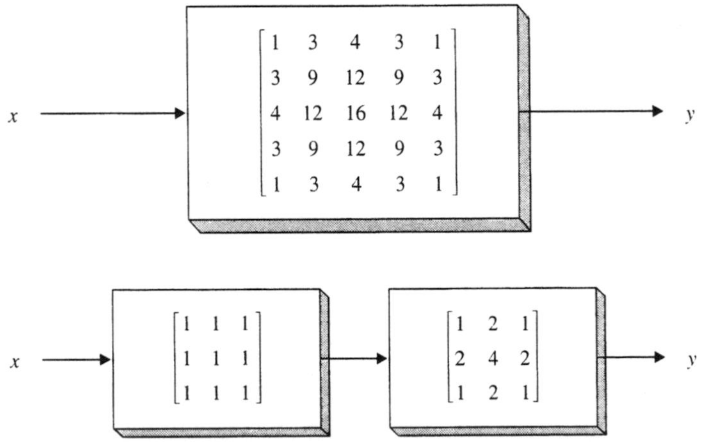

$x \rightarrow \begin{bmatrix} 1 & 3 & 4 & 3 & 1 \\ 3 & 9 & 12 & 9 & 3 \\ 4 & 12 & 16 & 12 & 4 \\ 3 & 9 & 12 & 9 & 3 \\ 1 & 3 & 4 & 3 & 1 \end{bmatrix} \rightarrow y$

$x \rightarrow \begin{bmatrix} 1 & 1 & 1 \\ 1 & 1 & 1 \\ 1 & 1 & 1 \end{bmatrix} \rightarrow \begin{bmatrix} 1 & 2 & 1 \\ 2 & 4 & 2 \\ 1 & 2 & 1 \end{bmatrix} \rightarrow y$

Figure 16–15 Small generating kernel decomposition

$$H(z) = h_0 z^{-4}\left[z^4 + \frac{h_1}{h_0}z^3 + \frac{h_2}{h_0}z^2 + \frac{h_3}{h_0}z + \frac{h_4}{h_0}\right] \tag{97}$$

which has a polynomial in z inside the brackets.

Using this same technique on f and g, we can write Eq. (93) as

$$\begin{aligned} H(z) &= h_0 z^{-4}\left[z^4 + \frac{h_1}{h_0}z^3 + \frac{h_2}{h_0}z^2 + \frac{h_3}{h_0}z + \frac{h_4}{h_0}\right] = \\ F(z)G(z) &= f_0 z^{-2}\left[z^2 + \frac{f_1}{f_0}z + \frac{f_2}{f_0}\right] g_0 z^{-2}\left[z^2 + \frac{g_1}{g_0}z + \frac{g_2}{g_0}\right] \end{aligned} \tag{98}$$

Canceling z^{-4} on both sides, and substituting the h_i values for the example in Figure 16–14 gives

$$[z^4 + 3z^3 + 4z^2 + 3z + 1] = f_0 g_0\left[z^2 + \frac{f_1}{f_0}z + \frac{f_2}{f_0}\right]\left[z^2 + \frac{g_1}{g_0}z + \frac{g_2}{g_0}\right] \tag{99}$$

The polynomial on the left side can be factored into the product of four terms of the form $(z - r_i)$, where each r_i is one of the four (possibly complex) roots of the polynomial.

If complex roots exist, they usually occur as complex conjugate pairs. (In this example, two of the roots are $-0.5 \pm j\sqrt{3/2}$.) The roots are then paired and multiplied, yielding real quadratic terms.

Several mathematics software packages incorporate symbolic processing engines with the capability to find the roots of and factor polynomials. The left-hand side of Eq. (99) factors into quadratic terms, and we obtain

$$(z^2 + z + 1)(z^2 + 2z + 1) = f_0 g_0\left[z^2 + \frac{f_1}{f_0}z + \frac{f_2}{f_0}\right]\left[z^2 + \frac{g_1}{g_0}z + \frac{g_2}{g_0}\right] \tag{100}$$

from which we can solve for $\mathbf{f} = (1,1,1)^t$ and $\mathbf{g} = (1,2,1)^t$.

Notice that one arbitrary choice had to be made: The constraint was $f_0 g_0 = 1$, and we chose $f_0 = g_0 = 1$.

The two three-by-three kernels are $\mathbf{ff}^t$ and $\mathbf{gg}^t$. The result of this SGK decomposition example, then, is

$$\begin{bmatrix} 1 & 3 & 4 & 3 & 1 \\ 3 & 9 & 12 & 9 & 3 \\ 4 & 12 & 16 & 12 & 4 \\ 3 & 9 & 12 & 9 & 3 \\ 1 & 3 & 4 & 3 & 1 \end{bmatrix} = \begin{bmatrix} 1 & 1 & 1 \\ 1 & 1 & 1 \\ 1 & 1 & 1 \end{bmatrix} * \begin{bmatrix} 1 & 2 & 1 \\ 2 & 4 & 2 \\ 1 & 2 & 1 \end{bmatrix} \tag{101}$$

Normally, SGK decomposition cannot reconstruct the original kernel without error, as we have been fortunate enough to do in this example. The error, however, is introduced in the SVD step, where those terms in the summation having the smaller singular values are ignored. Error is not introduced by factoring the z-transform. Thus, one has some control over the approximation by deciding how many singular values to include.

Symmetry in the kernel matrix tends to concentrate magnitude into one or a few of the singular values. The trade-off between accuracy and computational efficiency can be guided by the fact that the mean square error is equal to the sum of the singular values that are discarded.

16.8.5 Matrix Filtering

The restoration techniques developed with the linear algebraic approach can be implemented by multiplication of an N^2-by-1 row-stacked image vector by an N^2-by-N^2 restoration matrix. This amounts to convolving the image with a separate N-by-N kernel for each of the N^2 output pixels. For images of normal size, this implementation has severe practical limitations.

If the restoration is shift invariant, the restoration matrix will be block circulant, and it can be diagonalized by the Fourier matrix [20,60:5.2]. In that case, it reduces to the equivalent of ordinary frequency-domain restoration.

16.9 SUMMARY OF IMPORTANT POINTS

1. Spatially invariant restoration can be accomplished with deconvolution, Wiener deconvolution, power spectrum equalization (PSE), or geometric mean filters.
2. The geometric mean filter [Eq. (4)] includes the Wiener deconvolution and PSE filters as special cases.
3. Noise usually restricts the degree of restoration of an image that is possible, particularly at high spatial frequencies.
4. Coordinate transformation restoration (CTR) is useful with known spatially variant blurring functions.
5. Speckle interferometry can reduce the effects of temporally variant blurring functions.
6. While most images are generally nonstationary, many can be assumed locally stationary.
7. One can partition an image into regions based on SNR and restore each region with a separate filter.
8. The linear combination filter produces a smoothly space-variant impulse response with modest computational complexity.
9. Superresolution techniques exploit the incompatibility between spatial bounding and bandlimiting in order to reconstruct the spectrum beyond the diffraction limit.
10. The blurring function can be determined from features in the image or from the degraded image spectrum.
11. A linear system can be identified with an input that is an impulse, a line, an edge, a sine wave target, or a frequency sweep target.
12. A linear system can be identified by cross-correlating a white random noise input signal with the system output.
13. Electronic noise is white with a Gaussian histogram.
14. Photoelectronic noise can be modeled as white and Gaussian, with RMS amplitude equal to the square root of the mean.

15. Film grain noise can be modeled as white and Gaussian, with RMS amplitude proportional to the cube root of the local average density.
16. Kernel truncation produces a small kernel that best approximates a larger transfer function in the mean square sense.
17. Singular-value decomposition can decompose a two-dimensional convolution kernel into a set of one-dimensional kernels.
18. The small generating kernel (SGK) technique can factor a large convolution kernel matrix into a set of smaller kernels that can be applied sequentially.

PROBLEMS

1. Suppose you have two microscope objectives marked only as 100×, 1.2 NA. One is supposed to be quite expensive. When they are tested in green ($\lambda = 0.55$ μm) incoherent light, a black-to-white transition in a digitized image has the gray-level values given below. The pixel spacing is 0.10 micron at the specimen. Sketch the edge-spread function, line-spread function, and MTF of each objective and the diffraction-limited PSF and OTF for such a lens. Which objective lens costs $226, and which one sells for $1,834? Do you see any evidence of inaccuracy in this method at low frequencies? If so, what could it be due to?

   Objective A:

   [35 36 38 40 43 49 65 92 125 152 168 175 177 179 181 182]

   Objective B:

   [25 27 29 33 40 53 73 99 128 154 175 188 195 198 201 203]

2. A pawn shop has two highly rated camera lenses for sale at a low price because one has a scratch on the glass surface, while the other has a small bubble inside the glass. You borrow the lenses and digitize a distant edge at *f*/4 through a green ($\lambda = 0.55$ μm) filter with a pixel spacing of 0.6 micron at the image sensor. The gray levels across the edge are given below for each lens. Sketch the edge-spread function, line-spread function, and OTF of each objective and the diffraction-limited PSF and OTF. Is either lens a bargain? If so, which one? Would you buy both?

   Scratch: [4 4 5 7 11 15 22 30 39 49 60 70 79 87 94 99 103 105 106 106]

   Bubble: [82 82 82 82 81 77 70 61 51 42 35 31 30 30 30 30 30 30 30 30]

3. A colleague borrowed your expensive 1.0-NA, 63× microscope objective because his identical lens had been seriously damaged when some experimental animals (spider monkeys) got loose in the lab. After he returned the lens, you wondered whether he may have mistakenly given you back the damaged lens instead of your own. Not wanting to create a flap in the department, you quietly scanned an edge in red ($\lambda = 0.65$ μm) light with 5.7-micron pixel spacing at the sensor, obtaining the edge-spread function below. Sketch the edge-spread function, line-spread function, and OTF of the objective and the diffraction-limited PSF and OTF for that lens. What is your next step? Do you confront your colleague with his error or thank him for returning your lens?

   ESF: [40 40 40 41 45 52 61 71 80 87 91 92 92 92]

4. A friend offers to sell you his expensive 6-inch, *f*/8 telescope, which he says has hardly been used. The condition of the case indicates otherwise. The price is a good one, provided that the instrument is not damaged. You digitize a distant blue ($\lambda = 450$ nm) star on a clear night at 0.3-arc-second

pixel spacing and obtain the spot profile given below. Sketch the actual and diffraction-limited PSFs for this telescope. Would you buy the telescope? Why or why not?

[123 123 123 123 124 127 130 132 133 132 130 127 124 123 123 123]

5. Find the 8-point discrete impulse response that best implements the transfer function given by the spectrum vector:

$F = [1.25\ 1.07\ 0.6\ .09\ -.25\ -.29\ -.1\ .14\ .25\ .14\ -.1\ -.29\ -.25\ .09\ 0.6\ 1.07]'$

6. What is the 7-point discrete impulse response that best implements the transfer function given by this spectrum vector?

$F = [1.0\ 1.2\ 1.6\ 2.0\ 1.8\ 1.4\ 1.0\ 0.5\ 0\ 0.5\ 1.0\ 1.4\ 1.8\ 2.0\ 1.6\ 1.2]'$

7. Decompose the following (rank one) five-by-five convolution kernel into an equivalent pair of five-by-one kernels. Decompose each of those into an equivalent pair of three-by-one kernels. From those, generate an equivalent pair of three-by-three kernels, as in Figure 16–15.

$$\begin{bmatrix} 1 & 2 & 3 & 2 & 1 \\ 2 & 4 & 6 & 4 & 2 \\ 3 & 6 & 9 & 6 & 3 \\ 2 & 4 & 6 & 4 & 2 \\ 1 & 2 & 3 & 2 & 1 \end{bmatrix}$$

8. Decompose the following (rank one) five-by-five convolution kernel into an equivalent pair of five-by-one kernels. Decompose each of those into an equivalent pair of three-by-one kernels. From those, generate an equivalent pair of three-by-three kernels, as in Figure 16–15.

$$\begin{bmatrix} 1 & -2 & -6 & -2 & 1 \\ -2 & 4 & 12 & 4 & -2 \\ -6 & 12 & 36 & 12 & -6 \\ -2 & 4 & 12 & 4 & -2 \\ 1 & -2 & -6 & -2 & 1 \end{bmatrix}$$

9. Decompose the following (rank one) five-by-five convolution kernel into an equivalent pair of five-by-one kernels. Decompose each of those into an equivalent pair of three-by-one kernels. From those, generate an equivalent pair of three-by-three kernels, as in Figure 16–15.

$$\begin{bmatrix} 1 & -1 & -4 & -1 & 1 \\ -1 & 1 & 4 & 1 & -1 \\ -4 & 4 & 16 & 4 & -4 \\ -1 & 1 & 4 & 1 & -1 \\ 1 & -1 & -4 & -1 & 1 \end{bmatrix}$$

10. Decompose the following (rank two) five-by-five convolution kernel into a pair of three-by-three kernels, which, if applied sequentially, will produce approximately the same effect.

$$\begin{bmatrix} 1 & 4 & 5 & 4 & 1 \\ 4 & 16 & 20 & 16 & 4 \\ 5 & 20 & 20 & 20 & 5 \\ 4 & 16 & 20 & 16 & 4 \\ 1 & 4 & 5 & 4 & 1 \end{bmatrix}$$

PROJECTS

1. Generate an image of a horizontal frequency sweep target or an omnidirectional (circular) frequency sweep target.
2. Generate an image of uncorrelated, white random noise using a random number generator to assign phase values to its complex spectrum. Compute the autocorrelation function and power spectrum of the image.
3. Use the image of Project 1 or 2 to identify an imaging system. Assume white noise, and estimate its RMS level in that system. Design and test a Wiener deconvolution filter.
4. Use an image of an edge to determine the MTF of a telescope, camera, or microscope objective lens. Estimate the noise power spectrum from an image of a flat area. Design and test a Wiener deconvolution filter.
5. Use an image of a point or an edge to determine the MTF of a defocused telescope, camera, or microscope objective lens. Sketch the MTF and the diffraction-limited OTF on the same graph. Design and test a deconvolution filter.
6. Digitize a camera, telescope, or microscope image so that it exhibits motion blur in one direction. Use an image of an edge perpendicular to the direction of motion to determine the MTF of the imaging system with motion blur. Sketch the line-spread function and MTF of the imaging system. Sketch the diffraction-limited OTF and compare it with the MTF. Design and test a deconvolution filter.
7. Design a digital convolution filter to deconvolve the effects of a 50-mm, *f*/8 camera lens when the pixel spacing is 25 microns at the image sensor. Limit the gain of the filter to 8.0.
8. Design a digital convolution filter to deconvolve the effects of a 100×, 1.2-NA microscope objective lens when the pixel spacing is 15 microns at the image sensor. Assume incoherent green ($\lambda = 0.55$ micron) light. Limit the gain of the filter to 5.0.

REFERENCES

1. H. C. Andrews, "Digital Image Restoration: A Survey," *IEEE Computer,* **7**(5):36–45, May 1974.
2. J. L. Harris, Sr., "Image Evaluation and Restoration," *J. Opt. Soc. Amer.,* **56**:569–574, May 1966.
3. B. R. Hunt, "Digital Signal Processing," *Proc. IEEE,* **63**(4):693–708, April 1975.
4. M. M. Sondhi, "Image Restoration: The Removal of Spatially Invariant Degradations," *Proc. IEEE,* **60**(7):842–853, July 1972.
5. R. H. Bates and M. J. McDonnell, *Image Restoration and Reconstruction,* Oxford University Press, Oxford, UK, 1989.
6. A. K. Katsaggelos, ed., *Digital Image Restoration,* Springer-Verlag, Berlin, New York, 1991.
7. I. Sezan and A. M. Tekalp, *Image Restoration,* Prentice Hall, Inc., Englewood Cliffs, NJ, 1992.
8. N. Wiener, *Extrapolation, Interpolation, and Smoothing of Stationary Time Series,* MIT Press, Cambridge, MA, 1942.
9. R. Nathan, *Digital Video Handling,* Technical Report 32-877, Jet Propulsion Laboratory, Pasadena, CA, January 5, 1966.
10. B. L. McGlamery, "Restoration of Turbulence Degraded Images," *J. Opt. Soc. Amer.,* **57**(3):293–297, March 1967.
11. C. W. Helstrom, "Image Restoration by the Method of Least Squares," *J. Opt. Soc. Amer.,* **57**(3):297–303, March 1967.

12. D. Slepian, "Linear Least-Squares Filtering of Distorted Images," *J. Opt. Soc. Amer.*, **57**(7):918–922, July 1967.
13. W. K. Pratt, "Generalized Wiener Filter Computation Techniques," *IEEE Trans. Computers*, 636–641, July 1972.
14. A. Habibi, *Fast Suboptimal Wiener Filtering of Markov Processes*, University of Southern California, USCIPI Report 530, Los Angeles, 75–80, March 1974.
15. T. N. Cornsweet, *Visual Perception*, Academic Press, New York, 1970.
16. T. M. Cannon, *Digital Image Deblurring by Nonlinear Homomorphic Filtering*, Ph.D. Thesis, Computer Science Department, University of Utah, Salt Lake City, 1974.
17. H. C. Andrews and B. R. Hunt, *Digital Image Restoration*, Prentice-Hall, Inc., Englewood Cliffs, NJ, 1977.
18. A. V. Oppenheim, R. W. Schafer, and T. G. Stockman, "Nonlinear Filtering of Multiplied and Convolved Signals," *Proc. IEEE*, **56:**1264–1291, August 1968.
19. B. R. Hunt, "A Matrix Theory Proof of the Discrete Convolution Theorem," *IEEE Trans.* **AU-19**(4):285–288, 1971.
20. B. R. Hunt, "The Application of Constrained Least Squares Estimation to Image Restoration by Digital Computer," *IEEE Trans.* **C-22**(9):805–812, 1973.
21. G. M. Robbins and T. S. Huang, "Image Restoration for a Class of Linear Spatially-Variant Degradation," *Pattern Recognition*, **2**(2):91–105, 1970.
22. G. M. Robbins and T. S. Huang, "Inverse Filtering for Linear Shift-Variant Imaging Systems," *Proc. IEEE*, **60**(7):862–872, July 1972.
23. A. A. Sawchuk, "Space-Variant Image Motion Degradation and Restoration," *Proc. IEEE*, **60**(7):854–861, July 1972.
24. A. A. Sawchuk and M. J. Peyrovian, "Space-Variant Image Restoration by Coordinate Transformations," *J. Opt. Soc. Amer.*, **64**(2):138–144, February 1974.
25. A. A. Sawchuk and M. J. Peyrovian, "Restoration of Astigmatism and Curvature of Field," *J. Opt. Soc. Amer.*, **65**(6):712–715, June 1975.
26. A. Labeyrie, "Attainment of Diffraction Limited Resolution in Large Telescopes by Fourier Analysis Speckle Patterns in Star Images," *Astron. & Astrophys.*, **6**(1):85–87, 1970.
27. D. Y. Gezari, A. Labeyrie, and R. V. Stachnik, "Speckle Interferometry: Diffraction-Limited Measurements of Nine Stars with the 200-Inch Telescope," *Astrophys. J.*, **173**(1):L1–L5, April 1, 1972.
28. K. T. Knox and B. J. Thompson, "Recovery of Images from Atmospherically Degraded Short-Exposure Photographs," *Astrophys. J.*, **193:**L45–L48, October 1, 1974.
29. K. T. Knox, "Image Retrieval from Astronomical Speckle Patterns," *J. Opt. Soc. Amer.*, **66**(11):1236–1239, November 1976.
30. K. T. Knox, *Diffraction Limited Imaging of Astronomical Telescopes*, Ph.D. Thesis, University of Rochester, Rochester, NY, 1975.
31. H. Cartan, *Elementary Theory of Analytic Functions of One or Several Complex Variables*, Addison Wesley, Reading, MA, 1963.
32. J. L. Harris, "Diffraction and Resolving Power," *J. Opt. Soc. Amer.*, **54**(7):931–936, July 1964.
33. J. W. Goodman, *Introduction to Fourier Optics*, McGraw-Hill, New York, 1968 (reissued 1988).
34. A. K. Jain, *Fundamentals of Digital Image Processing*, Prentice-Hall, Englewood Cliffs, NJ, 1989.
35. C.W. Barnes, "Object Restoration in a Diffraction-Limited Imaging System," *J. Opt. Soc. Amer.*, **56**(5):575–578, May 1966.

36. H. A. Brown, "Effect of Truncation on Image Enhancement by Prolate Spheroidal Functions," *J. Opt. Soc. Amer.*, **59:**228–229, 1969.

37. C. Pask, "Simple Optical Theory of Super-Resolution," *JOSA Letters, J. Opt. Soc. Amer.*, **66**(1):68–70, January 1976.

38. B. R. Frieden, "Band-Unlimited Reconstruction of Optical Objects and Spectra," *J. Opt. Soc. Amer.*, **57**(8):1013–1019, August 1967.

39. C. K. Rushforth, "Restoration, Resolution, and Noise," *J. Opt. Soc. Amer.*, **58**(4):539–545, April 1968.

40. C. L. Rino, "Bandlimited Image Restoration by Linear Mean-Square Estimation," *J. Opt. Soc. Amer.*, **59**(5):547–553, May 1969.

41. S. Wadaka and T. Sato, "Superresolution in Incoherent Imaging System," *J. Opt. Soc. Amer.*, **65**(3):354–355, March 1975.

42. B. Tatian, "Method for Obtaining the Transfer Function from the Edge Response Function," *J. Opt. Soc. Amer.*, **55:**1014–1019, August 1965.

43. A. G. Tescher, "Data Compression and Enhancement of Sampled Images," *Applied Optics*, **11**(4):919–925, April 1972.

44. M. E. Rabedeau, "Effect of Truncation of Line-Spread and Edge-Response Functions on the Computed Optical Transfer Function," *J. Opt. Soc. Amer.*, **59**(10):1309–1314, October 1969.

45. D. B. Gennery, "Determination of Optical Transfer Function by Inspection of Frequency-Domain Plot," *J. Opt. Soc. Amer.*, **63**(12):1571–1577, December 1973.

46. E. R. Cole, *The Removal of Unknown Image Blurs by Homomorphic Filtering*, Ph.D. Thesis, Department of Electrical Engineering, University of Utah, Salt Lake City, 1973.

47. T. S. Huang, W. F. Scheiber, and O. J. Tretiak, "Image Processing," *Proc. IEEE*, **59**(11):1586–1609, 1971.

48. T. R. Stockham, T. M. Cannon, and R. B. Ingebretsen, "Blind Deconvolution by Digital Signal Processing," *Proc. IEEE*, **63:**679–692, April 1975.

49. W. B. Davenport and W. L. Root, *An Introduction to the Theory of Random Signals and Noise*, McGraw-Hill, New York, 1958.

50. J. C. Dainty and R. Shaw, *Image Science*, Academic Press, London, 1974.

51. D. G. Falconer, "Image Enhancement and Film-Grain Noise," *Optica Acta*, **17:**693–705, 1970.

52. E. F. Haugh, "A Structural Theory for the Selwyn Granularity Coefficient," *J. Photo. Soc.*, **11:**65, 1963.

53. G. C. Higgins and K. F. Stultz, "Experimental Study of RMS Granularity as a Function of Scanning Spot Size," *J. Opt. Soc. Amer.*, **49:**925, 1959.

54. F. Naderi, *Estimation and Detection of Images Degraded by Film-Grain Noise*, University of Southern California, USCIPI Report 690, Los Angeles, California, September 1976.

55. E. L. Hall, "A Comparison of Computations for Spatial Frequency Filtering," *Proc. IEEE*, **60**(7):887–891, 1972.

56. R. W. Schutten and G. F. Vermeij, "The Approximation of Image Blur Restoration Filters by Finite Impulse Responses," *IEEE Trans.*, **PAMI-2**(2):176–180, 1980.

57. J. F. Abramatic and O. D. Faugeras, "Design of Two-Dimensional FIR Filters from Small Generating Kernels," *Proc. IEEE Conf. Pat. Rec. and Image Processing*, Chicago, May, 1978.

58. W. K. Pratt, *Digital Image Processing*, John Wiley & Sons, Inc., New York, 1991.

59. W. K. Pratt, "Intelligent Image Processing Display Terminal," *Proc. SPIE*, **199:**189–194, 1979.

60. R. C. Gonzalez and R. E. Woods, *Digital Image Processing*, Addison-Wesley, Reading, MA, 1992.

CHAPTER 17

Image Compression

17.1 INTRODUCTION

As an activity, digital image processing generally creates significant numbers of large files containing digital image data. Very often, these must be archived or exchanged among different users and systems. This calls for efficient methods for the storage and transfer of digital image data files [1].

Since digital images, by their nature, are quite data intensive, reducing their size can produce solutions that are more ambitious than would otherwise be practical. By eliminating redundant or unnecessary information, *image compression* is the activity that addresses this aim.

17.1.1 Redundant and Irrelevant Information

Image data files commonly contain a considerable amount of information that is *redundant* and much that is *irrelevant*, making them prime candidates for modern data compression techniques. The distinction between redundancy and irrelevancy can be illustrated by an example.

Suppose a traveling businessman who has not yet arranged transportation from the airport to his home in Boston at the end of the trip receives the following message at his hotel in Amsterdam:

> Your wife, Helen, will meet you at Logan Airport in Boston at 5 minutes past 6:00 P.M. tomorrow night.

We ask how that message might be shortened and still serve its purpose. First, it contains information that is already known to the traveler. Surely, he already knows that Logan Airport is located in Boston, and he does not need to be reminded of his wife's name. Eliminating the redundant information, we can write:

> Your wife will meet you at Logan Airport at 5 minutes past 6:00 P.M. tomorrow night.

Here, we have compressed the message without any loss of information. Pressing the point further, we ask whether we can squeeze it even more without serious damage. We trim the note to:

> Helen will meet you at Logan at 6:00 P.M. tomorrow night.

Accuracy has suffered a bit, but probably not in a significant way. The traveler will have to guess that *Helen* refers to his wife (and not, for example, to his great-aunt Helen who lives in a suburb of Phoenix) and that *Logan* refers to the airport in Boston (and not to Logan's Pub in London or the main character in the film *Logan's Run*). There is the further risk that he will spend an anxious 5 minutes waiting and wondering whether Helen has had a traffic accident, since her arrival time has been rounded off to the nearest hour (quantized). Nevertheless, if paper and ink are at a premium, the abbreviated message will serve its purpose.

17.1.2 Data Compression

Data compression techniques exploit inherent redundancy and irrelevancy by transforming a data file into a smaller file from which the original image file can later be reconstructed, exactly or approximately. The ratio of the two file sizes (the *compression ratio*) specifies the degree of compaction.

Some data compression algorithms are *lossless,* while others are not. A lossless algorithm eliminates only redundant information, so that one can recover the image exactly upon *decompression* of the file. A *lossy* compression algorithm eliminates irrelevant information as well, and thus permits only an approximate reconstruction of the original, rather than an exact duplicate. As one might expect, lossy compression algorithms achieve higher compression ratios. For images, a slight loss of fidelity is often an acceptable trade-off for a much higher degree of compaction. Some images, and all executable program files, can tolerate no alteration of data at all. Lossless compression must be used in these cases.

The times required for file compression and decompression are not negligible. The algorithms that achieve the densest compaction are not usually the fastest, so choices must be made for each application. Some file compression programs offer the user choices of lossless versus lossy compression and options regarding the trade-off of speed versus compression ratio. Lossy algorithms usually offer choices regarding the trade-off between fidelity of reconstruction and degree of compaction.

17.2 LOSSLESS COMPRESSION TECHNIQUES

Lossless data compression algorithms fall into two broad categories: dictionary-based techniques and statistical methods. Dictionary-based techniques generate a compressed file containing fixed-length codes (usually 12 to 16 bits), each of which represents a particular sequence of values in the original file.

Statistical methods implement data compression by representing frequently occurring characters in the file with fewer bits than they do less commonly occurring ones [2]. This is the approach Samuel F. B. Morse used when he defined the international telegraph code. The often used letter *e*, for example, is represented by a single dot, whereas the much less common *z* is coded as dash, dash, dot, dot.

17.2.1 Dictionary-Based Techniques

17.2.1.1 Run-Length Encoding

The simplest dictionary-based data compression technique is *run length encoding* (RLE). Images—particularly those having few gray levels—often contain regions of adjacent pixels, all with the same gray level or color. In an image being stored line by line, a series of pixels having the same gray-level value is called a *run*. One can store a code specifying that value, followed by the length of the run, rather than simply storing the same value many times over. This is run-length encoding. It achieves considerable compaction, for example, with graphics and with images of objects residing upon a constant background. Other types of images compress poorly. Under worst case conditions (for example, where every pixel differs from its neighbors) RLE can actually double the size of the file.

17.2.1.2 LZW Encoding

LZ coding is a lossless technique first described by Lemple and Ziv [3,4]. It was extended by Welch [5] to form the widely used, proprietary *LZW algorithm* [6]. Like RLE, it effects compression by encoding strings of characters. However, unlike RLE, it builds up a table of strings (particular sequences of bytes) and their corresponding codes as it encodes the file. A file of 8-bit bytes can be encoded, for example, into 12-bit codes. Of the 4,096 possible codes, 256 of them represent all possible single bytes. The remaining 3,840 are assigned to strings as they are encountered in the data during compression.

The first time a string not already in the table occurs, it is stored in full, along with the code that is assigned to it. Thereafter, when that string occurs again, only its code is stored. This squeezes redundancy out of the file. Not only is the string table built dynamically during compression, but it need not be stored with the compressed file: The decompression algorithm can reconstruct it from the information in the compressed file.

17.2.2 Statistical Encoding Methods

17.2.2.1 The Information Content of a Message

Before discussing statistical coding techniques, we consider the classical theory of information content. Suppose we have a memoryless source of messages that uses an *alphabet* $\{a_k\}$, $k = 0,1,\ldots,K-1$. Here the a_k are the symbols of that alphabet. Suppose further that the probability of occurrence of each symbol is known and denoted as $P(a_k)$. In a message from a memoryless source, the ordering of the symbols in the message is unimportant; only their presence in the message matters.

Shannon [7,8] defined a measure of the information imparted by the occurrence of the symbol a_k in a message as

$$I(a_k) = -\log[P(a_k)] \tag{1}$$

This measure is satisfying because (a) the more unlikely a symbol is, the more information its presence contributes to the message, and (b) the information in a message is the sum of the information contributed by the symbols that comprise it. Notice that a symbol that always appears in every message (i.e., $P(a_i) = 1$) conveys no information ($I(a_i) = 0$). An example of such a noninformative symbol is the word *Dear* in the salutation of a letter.

The *entropy* of the message source, defined by

$$H = E\{I(a_k)\} = -\sum_{k=0}^{K-1} P(a_k)\log[P(a_k)] \tag{2}$$

specifies the average information content (per symbol) of the messages generated by the source. The entropy of a message source is nonnegative and takes on its maximum value when all symbols are equally likely. If we choose 2 as the base for the logarithm, the units of entropy are *bits per symbol.*

The redundancy remaining in a message after encoding it by a particular coding scheme is the difference between the average word length of the code and the entropy of the source; that is,

$$R = E\{L_{w}(a_k)\} - H \tag{3}$$

where $L_w(a_k)$ is the length (in bits, for binary coding) of the code word used to represent the symbol a_k. A coding scheme removes all redundancy if it produces an average word length that is equal to the entropy of the message source. This can be achieved if one can design the code so that the word lengths are

$$L_w(a_k) = -\log[P(a_k)] \tag{4}$$

and this formula represents a lower bound on average word length. For binary coding, this is possible only if the probabilities of all the symbols are negative integer powers of two (e.g., 0.5, 0.25, etc.).

17.2.2.2 Huffman Coding

Huffman coding [2], introduced in the 1950s, is a lossless statistical method that always finds a variable-length code with minimum redundancy. It uses a binary encoding tree for representing commonly occurring values in few bits and less common values in more bits. Static Huffman coding uses an encoding tree constructed in advance of compression from a table of probabilities of occurrence of the possible data values. Dynamic Huffman coding constructs the encoding tree on the fly, during the compression process [9].

More advanced statistical methods [10–16] can achieve higher compression ratios, but at the cost of increased encoding and decoding times. Special-purpose hardware designed to implement compression and decompression can dramatically reduce the overhead associated with compressing image files.

17.2.3 Binary Image Compression Standards

Two standards, originally established for facsimile transmission by the Consultative Committee of the International Telephone and Telegraph (CCITT), have come into common use for binary image compression. The *Group 3* standard is based on horizontal RLE using a Huffman code to specify the run lengths [17].

In RLE, it is the locations of the white-to-black and black-to-white transitions that are important. In some cases in Group 3, and exclusively in the newer *Group 4* encoding, transitions on the current line are encoded with respect to prior transitions on either the current or the previous line. This is done in a manner designed to reduce the size of the encoded image file.

On typical documents, these encoding methods achieve compression ratios of about 15. Some types of images, however (such as halftone images, which are composed of tiny dots), actually become larger after encoding.

17.3 LOSSY IMAGE CODING

17.3.1 Scalar Quantization

One of the simplest ways to reduce data volume is to quantize the image to a smaller number of gray levels. Figure 17–1 shows the gray-scale transformation function (see Chapter 6) of a quantizer. When the input falls between two *decision thresholds,* the output is set to the corresponding *representative level.*

Lloyd [18] and Max [19] showed that, for an image having a given pdf, as evidenced by its gray-level histogram, the quantization scheme that minimizes the mean square error introduced by quantization has the following two interdependent properties: (1) Each decision threshold falls exactly midway between two adjacent representative levels, and (2) each representative level falls at the centroid of the section of the pdf between two successive decision thresholds. This establishes a system of equations that normally must be solved iteratively to determine the decision thresholds and representative levels.

17.3.2 Rate Distortion Theory

Rate distortion theory [20] seeks to relate the *distortion* (reconstruction error) of a fixed-word-length coding scheme to the *data rate* (e.g., number of bits per pixel) used in the

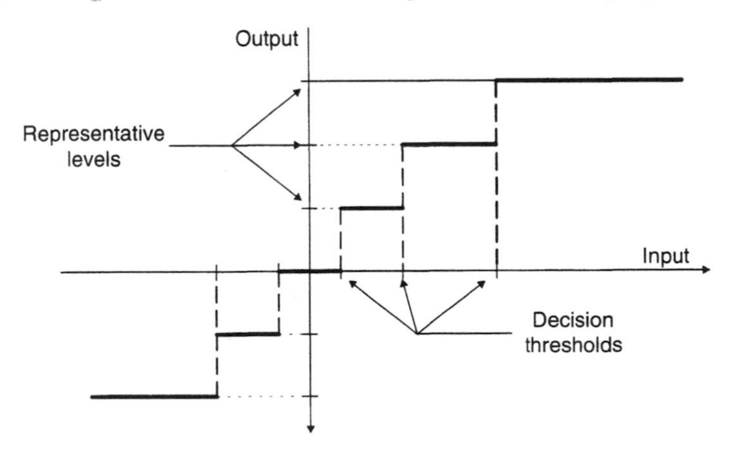

Figure 17–1 Scalar Quantization (after Girod, et. al., [20])

scheme. Since the theory assumes that the input image is continuous, the distortion can never be zero with a finite data rate, because of quantization error. While it does not specify the form of optimal coders, rate distortion theory does present guidelines about the conditions under which the best performance is achieved.

When a lossy compression scheme is used, the reconstructed image $g(x, y)$ differs from the original $f(x, y)$. This difference (the distortion) is conveniently quantified by the mean square error of reconstruction:

$$D = E\{[f(x, y) - g(x, y)]^2\} \tag{5}$$

If we establish a maximum allowable amount of distortion D^*, the corresponding lower bound $R(D^*)$ on the bit rate required in the coding scheme is a monotonically decreasing function of D^* [21,22]. $R(D^*)$ is called the *rate distortion function* (Figure 17–2). The inverse function $D(R)$ (the likewise monotonic *distortion rate function*) is sometimes used instead.

The entropy of the reconstruction error is bounded by [20,23]

$$H[f(x, y) - g(x, y)] \le \frac{1}{2}\log(2\pi e D^*) \tag{6}$$

Equality holds in this relation if the difference image has statistically independent pixels and a Gaussian pdf. This tells us that the best encoding scheme will produce an error image that contains only white, Gaussian noise. Thus, one can subjectively evaluate an image coder by examining the difference between the original and the decoded image. Any recognizable structure in that difference image (see Figure 17–4d, for example) is evidence of the suboptimality of the coder.

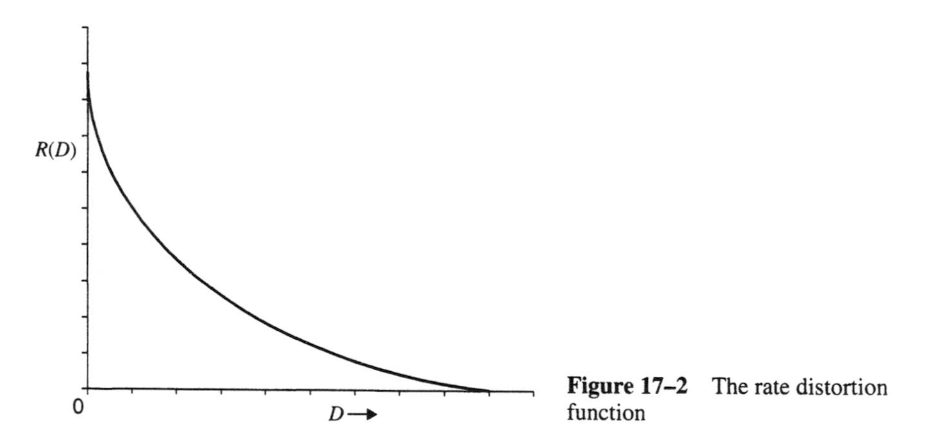

Figure 17–2 The rate distortion function

17.3.2.1 Uncorrelated Gaussian Images

Suppose the image $f(x, y)$, to be encoded has statistically independent pixels and a Gaussian pdf with variance σ^2. For this case, the rate distortion function is [20]

$$R(D) = \frac{1}{2}\max\left[\log_2\left(\frac{\sigma^2}{D}\right), 0\right] \tag{7}$$

in bits per pixel. We can define the SNR (in decibels) of the coding scheme as

$$SNR = 10 \cdot \log_{10}\left(\frac{\sigma^2}{D}\right) \tag{8}$$

As shown in Figure 17–3, this is a straight line relationship with a slope of 6 dB per bit. That is, each additional bit of code word length adds 6 dB to the SNR.

While most images have neither Gaussian histograms nor uncorrelated pixels, this case represents the most difficult encoding situation. That is, the bit rate required for non-Gaussian and for correlated sources is always lower for the same level of distortion [20].

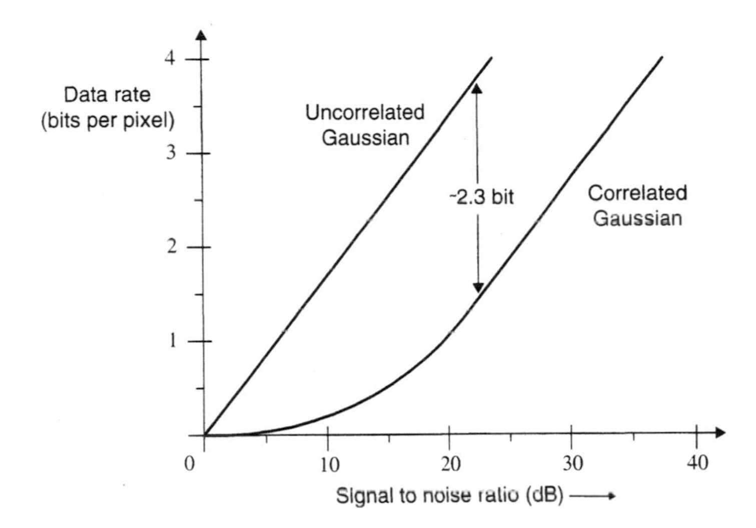

Figure 17–3 Rate distortion SNR curves for images with Gaussian pdfs (after Girod, et. al. [20]).

17.3.2.2 Correlated Gaussian Images

The correlation among neighboring pixels in an image is specified by the autocorrelation function of the image and, equivalently, by its power spectrum (the Fourier transform of the autocorrelation function; see Chapter 10). While the rate distortion function for correlated Gaussian images cannot be written in closed form, both distortion and rate can be written as functions of another parameter, θ:

$$D(\theta) = \frac{1}{4\pi^2}\int_{-\infty}^{\infty}\int_{-\infty}^{\infty} \min[\theta, P_f(u, v)]du\, dv \tag{9}$$

$$R(\theta) = \frac{1}{8\pi^2}\int_{-\infty}^{\infty}\int_{-\infty}^{\infty} \max\left[0, \log\left(\frac{P_f(u, v)}{\theta}\right)\right] du\, dv \tag{10}$$

Here, $P_f(u, v)$ is the power spectrum of the image, $f(x, y)$. As $\theta \geq 0$ sweeps through its range, it specifies the rate distortion function.

For example, if the image has a Gaussian pdf and an exponentially decaying autocorrelation function, then its rate distortion SNR curve falls about 2.3 bits below that of the uncorrelated case for the higher bit rates [20], as shown in Figure 17–3. Here, the correlation between adjacent pixels can be exploited to reduce the bit rate by more than two bits per pixel. Regrettably, rate distortion theory fails to specify how this should be done.

17.4 TRANSFORM IMAGE CODING

One of the most useful applications of discrete image transforms (Chapter 13) is in image compression. Combined with other compression techniques, they allow the transmission, storage, and display of images and video sequences that otherwise would be impractical.

17.4.1 Introduction

Suppose we have an ensemble of images to be encoded into a compact data representation. We can transform the images, discard those coefficients that are near zero, and coarsely quantize those that are small, thereby concentrating our data transmission and storage resources upon the coefficients that contain the most information about the image. When the image is reconstructed later, little important content will have been lost. This approach is called *transform image coding* [24].

Block Encoding. Often the image is divided into blocks of typically 8 by 8 or 16 by 16 pixels, and each of these is transformed separately. This simplifies the transformation process, particularly if eigenvectors must be computed. The subsequent elimination of some transform coefficients and the coarse quantization of others, however, can cause noticeable changes in gray level at the edges of the blocks. This is called *blocking artifact,* and it can make the boundaries of the block obtrusive (see Figure 17–4c).

Bit Allocation. One must establish how many bits will be used to code each of the coefficients that result from transforming an image block. Using rate distortion theory and the assumption that the block is a Gaussian random variable yields

$$r_{i,j} = \frac{1}{2}\max\left[\log_2\left(\frac{\sigma_{i,j}^2}{D}\right), 0\right] \tag{11}$$

as the number of bits required for the i, jth coefficient, where $\sigma_{i,j}^2$ is the variance of that coefficient and D is the maximum allowable distortion, in the mean square error sense [20].

Image Quality Considerations. There is always a trade-off between the compression ratio achieved and the amount of information lost to the encoding. Normally, the human eye is the ultimate judge of whether the information loss is acceptable or annoying. Thus, there is a subjective as well as an objective component to the design process. Often, the quantitative measures of image degradation (e.g., mean square error) do not agree well with the preferences of the human eye.

Transform Selection. To what extent a particular transform will support data compression depends on both the transform and the nature of the images being compressed. The practicality of an image coding scheme depends on the computational work load of the encoding and decoding steps, as well as the degree of compression obtained. The availability of a fast implementation algorithm can greatly enhance the appeal of a particular transform.

Figure 17–4 Examples of image compression: (a) original 560-by-764 pixel, eight-bit image; (b) JPEG compression at 0.5 bit per pixel; (c) JPEG compression at 0.2 bit per pixel; (d) difference image between (a) and (c), contrast times eight.

17.4.2 Image Coding with Eigenvector-Based Transforms

SVD Transform. The SVD transform (Sec. 13.6.4) is capable of the most data compression, since its basis functions are customized for the image being transformed. That is, its columns are the eigenvectors of the image matrix times its transpose. The computational load, however, is severe for this transform. Not only does no fast transform exist, but the eigenvectors of each N-by-N matrix must be computed in advance of the transformation itself. With block encoding, this becomes more practical, but nevertheless, burdensome.

As an approximation, for a group of similar images or for the blocks in an image, one can use the SVD transform kernel matrix of a typical image or block to transform a set of images and hope that the off-diagonal elements of the transformed matrix will be, if not zero, at least small. Clearly, the various blocks in an image will vary greatly in content. Experience shows, similarly, that images of the same subject matter usually have radically different SVD basis functions as well. Thus, this technique sees little actual use.

K-L Transform. Like the SVD transform, the K-L transform (Sec. 13.6.3) is capable of considerable data compression, since its basis functions are customized for the covariance matrix of the class of images being transformed. The basis images depend upon the statistics of the image being transformed, rather than the image itself. Thus, it is reasonably likely that a group of images will have statistics similar enough that they can be successfully encoded by the same kernel matrix.

Recall that in the development of the Wiener filter (Sec. 11.5.2), we assumed that the signal and noise, while unknown in detail, had known power spectra. This allowed us to develop a noise reduction filter that was optimum for all such instances of signals and noise.

We can make a similar assumption regarding the images to be compressed. If they all have, or can be assumed to have, the same covariance matrix, then one K-L kernel matrix will be suitable for all. Furthermore, if we make certain assumptions about the nature of the covariance matrix, we can achieve additional simplification.

Markov Processes. A stationary random sequence is called a *first-order Markov sequence* if the conditional probability of each element in the sequence depends only upon the value of the immediately preceding element. The covariance matrix for an N-by-1 Markov sequence has the form

$$\mathbf{C} = \begin{bmatrix} 1 & \rho & \rho^2 & \cdots & \rho^{N-1} \\ \rho & 1 & \rho & \cdots & \rho^{N-2} \\ \rho^2 & \rho & 1 & \ddots & \vdots \\ \vdots & \vdots & \ddots & \ddots & \rho \\ \rho^{N-1} & \rho^{N-2} & \cdots & \rho & 1 \end{bmatrix} \tag{12}$$

where $0 \leq \rho \leq 1$. The eigenvalues of this covariance matrix are

$$\lambda_k = \frac{1-\rho^2}{1-2\rho\cos(\omega_k)+\rho^2} \tag{13}$$

and its eigenvectors are

$$v_{m,k} = \sqrt{\frac{2}{N+\lambda_k}} \sin\left[\omega_k\left(m - \frac{N-1}{2}\right) + (k+1)\frac{\pi}{2}\right] \tag{14}$$

for $0 \leq m, k \leq N-1$ [25:8.5,26:5.11]. The ω_k are roots of the transcendental equation

$$\tan(N\omega) = -\frac{(1-\rho^2)\sin(\omega)}{\cos(\omega) - 2\rho + \rho^2\cos(\omega)} \tag{15}$$

Thus, the basis vectors of the K-L transform can be computed once a value for ρ is determined.

DCT Approximation to the K-L Transform. For $\rho \approx 1$, as is often the case with images of natural scenes, the basis vectors of the DCT offer a good approximation to those of the K-L transform [24,27]. For this reason, the DCT is often used as a substitute for the K-L transform, as in the JPEG algorithm mentioned in Sec. 17.5, for example. While the DCT provides significantly lower spectral decorrelation efficiency than the K-L transform [28], its basis vectors are fixed.

17.4.3 Image Coding with Other Transforms

The rectangular wave transforms (Sec. 13.5) have a preponderance of constant-valued basis vector elements, which make them more efficient for computation than sinusiodal or (especially) eigenvector-based transforms. For this reason, they are appealing for use in transform image coding.

In general, the rectangular wave transforms do not pack the energy of commonly encountered images into a few transform coefficients quite as effectively as do sinusoidal or (especially) eigenvector transforms. Thus, somewhat less effective compression accompanies their computational simplicity. The Hadamard and slant transforms have nevertheless proven themselves useful for image compression. The image compression capability of wavelet transforms (discussed in Chapter 14) often proves superior to that of other transforms [20,28,29,30].

17.5 IMAGE COMPRESSION STANDARDS

The Joint Photographics Experts Group (JPEG), sponsored jointly by the International Standards Organization (ISO) and the CCITT, has established an open (published, nonproprietary) algorithm for compression of still images [31–34]. It achieves compression ratios of 15 to 25 without a significant loss of visual quality. With a slight sacrifice of quality, 40-to-1 compression, or more, is possible. (See Figure 17–4.) Table 17–1 compares the compression capability of JPEG with several other image file formats.

If the image is in color, the JPEG algorithm first converts from RGB components to luminance and chrominance components (see Chapter 21) and discards half the chrominance information. Then it uses the DCT (see Chapters 10 and 13) for block transform coding, discards high-frequency coefficients, and quantizes the remaining coefficients to reduce the data volume further. Finally, it applies RLE and Huffman coding to finish the compression task. JPEG decompression is simply the reverse of JPEG compression, making the algorithm symmetrical.

TABLE 17–1 COMPRESSION STATISTICS FOR FIGURE 17–4

File Format (560 by 764)	File Size (kbytes)	Bit Rate (bits/pixel)	Compression Ratio
BMP	427,840	8.0	1:1
PCX	427,021	8.0	1:1
TIF (uncomp.)	431,947	8.08	1:1
GIF*	265,366	4.96	1.6:1
JPEG	27,285	0.50	16:1
JPEG	10,914	0.20	40:1

*Lossless

Another open algorithm, developed by the Motion Picture Experts Group (MPEG), compresses full-motion video (motion pictures with sound). It is similar in concept to the JPEG algorithm, except that it also exploits the redundancy between consecutive video frames. The resulting compression ratios of 100:1 make it practical for transmitting color video with sound over one-megabit-per-second channels and storing digital video clips of reasonable duration on disk drives.

High-speed hardware for JPEG and MPEG compression and decompression significantly reduces the computational overhead of these techniques.

17.6 SUMMARY OF IMPORTANT POINTS

1. Image compression reduces the storage requirement for digital imaging and the time required for image transfer, but at the cost of compression and decompression time.
2. Lossy compression can achieve higher compression ratios than lossless compression, which preserves the integrity of the data.
3. The SVD transform gives the best image compression, but at prohibitive computational cost.
4. The K-L transform is optimal for coding images from a stationary ensemble of images, but requires laborious computation of eigenvectors.
5. For images that can be modeled as first-order Markov processes, the DCT is a good approximation to the K-L transform, especially if ρ is near unity.
6. Image compression based on rectangular wave transforms is more computationally efficient, but generally less effective than DCT coding.
7. The Lloyd-Max quantizer (Sec. 17.3.1) minimizes the mean square error introduced by quantization.
8. Rate distortion theory provides guidelines about the conditions under which the best performance of fixed-word-length image coding is achieved.
9. The rate distortion function gives a lower bound on the bit rate required to obtain fixed-word-length coding with a specified maximum level of distortion.
10. The best encoding scheme will produce an error image that contains only white, Gaussian noise.

11. For encoding an uncorrelated image having a Gaussian histogram, the reconstruction SNR is roughly six times the number of bits per pixel.
12. The required bit rate for encoding correlated and non-Gaussian images is always less than that required for uncorrelated Gaussian images, for a fixed level of distortion.
13. Modern image and video compression standards utilize combinations of data compression techniques to achieve effective and robust results.
14. The image quality that results from lossy compression depends upon both the compression ratio and the content of the image. Evaluation should include side-by-side comparison on high-quality display devices, using images that are representative of those to be compressed.

PROBLEMS

1. Given 640-by-480-by-8–bit digitized television frames, each with a 1,024-byte label, and a lossless compression algorithm having a compression ratio of 4.25, how many seconds of (30 frame-per-second) video can you store on a disk drive with 220 megabytes of available space without compression? With compression?
2. Suppose you have two image compressors: "RLE," which averages 3.8:1 compression and takes :02 (sec) per megabyte for compression and :03 per megabyte for decompression; and "Statistical," which averages 6:1 compression and takes :08 per megabyte for compression and :12 per megabyte for decompression. Which, if any, would you use to send 240-by-320–pixel-by-1-bit images over a 9,600-baud (960-byte-per-second) telephone line? How many images per minute could you transfer and decompress? Assume that the receiving computer cannot receive and decompress simultaneously.
3. Given the conditions in Problem 2, which compressor, if any, would you use to send 3,000-by-4,000–pixel-by-12-bit X-ray images over a 400-kilobit-per-second microwave link? How many images per minute could you transfer and decompress?
4. Given the conditions in Problem 2, which compressor, if any, would you use to send 480-by-640-by-8-bit images over a 1.2-megabit-per-second satellite link? How many images per minute could you transfer and decompress?

PROJECTS

1. Implement a lossless image compression algorithm, and quantify its compression and decompression times and compression ratio on two particular types of images (e.g., digitized documents and satellite images).
2. Implement a lossy image compression algorithm, and quantify its compression and decompression times, compression ratio, and fidelity on two particular types of images (e.g., portraits and X ray images).
3. Use a lossy algorithm to compress and decompress an image, and subtract the decompressed image from the original. Use the resulting difference image to support quantitative and qualitative arguments about the acceptability, or lack thereof, of the information loss for a particular imaging application.
4. Write a justification to convince a radiologist to use a particular lossy compression algorithm for digital archiving of X ray films. Illustrate your argument with original and decompressed images.
5. Write a justification to convince a radiologist not to use a particular lossy compression algorithm for digital archiving of X ray films. Illustrate your argument with original and decompressed images.

REFERENCES

For additional reading on image compression, see Appendix 2.

1. D. C. Kay and J. R. Levine, *Graphics File Formats*, Windcrest/McGraw-Hill, Blue Ridge Summit, PA, 1992.
2. D. A. Huffman, "A Method for the Construction of Minimum Redundancy Codes," *Proc. IRE*, **40**(10):1098–1101, 1952.
3. J. Ziv and J. Lempel, "A Universal Algorithm for Sequential Data Compression," *IEEE Trans. Info. Theory*, **IT-23**(3):337–343, 1977.
4. J. Ziv and J. Lempel, "A Universal Algorithm for Sequential Data Compression," *IEEE Trans. Info. Theory*, **IT-24**(5):530–537, 1977.
5. T. A. Welch, "A Technique for High-Performance Data Compression," *IEEE Computer*, **17**(6):8–19, 1984.
6. T. A. Welch, "High Speed Data Compression and Decompression Apparatus and Method," United States Patent No. 4,558,302, Dec. 19, 1985 (assigned to Unisys Corporation, PO Box 500, Blue Bell, PA 19424-0001).
7. C. E. Shannon, "A Mathematical Theory of Communication," *Bell System Tech. Journal*, 27:379–423, 623–656, 1948.
8. N. J. A. Sloane and A. D. Wyner, eds., *Claude Elwood Shannon, Collected Papers,* IEEE Press, New York, 1993.
9. J. S. Vitter, "Design and Analysis of Dynamic Huffman Codes," *Journal of the ACM*, October 1987.
10. R. K. Miller and T. C. Walker, *Image Compression*, SEAI Technical Publications, 1991.
11. M. R. Nelson, "Arithmetic Coding and Statistical Modeling," *Dr. Dobbs' Journal*, February 1991.
12. T. C. Bell, J. G. Cleary, and I. H. Witten, *Text Compression*, Prentice-Hall, Englewood Cliffs, NJ, 1990.
13. J. A. Storer, *Data Compression*, Computer Science Press, Rockville, MD, 1988.
14. G. Held and T. R. Marshall, *Data Compression: Techniques and Applications, Hardware and Software Considerations*, Wiley, New York, 1991.
15. I. H. Witten, R. M. Neal, and J. G. Cleary, "Arithmetic Coding for Data Compression," *Communications of the ACM*, **30**(6):520–540, 1987.
16. M. Rabbani and P. W. Jones, *Digital Image Compression Techniques*, SPIE—International Society for Optical Engineering, 1991.
17. R. Hunter and A. H. Robinson, "International Digital Facsimile Coding Standards," *Proc. IEEE*, **68**(7):854–867, 1980.
18. S. P. Lloyd, "Least Squares Quantization in PCM," Proc. Institute of Mathematical Statistics Meeting, Atlantic City, NJ, September 1957.
19. J. Max, "Quantizing for Minimum Distortion," *IRE Trans. Info. Theory,* **IT-6**:7–12, March 1960.
20. B. Girod, F. Hartung, and U. Horn, "Subband Image Coding" (Chapter 7), in A. Akansu and J. K. Smith, eds., *Design and Application of Subband and Wavelets,* Kluwer Academic Publishers, Dordrecht, Boston, London, 1995.
21. R. G. Gallager, *Information Theory and Reliable Communication,* John Wiley and Sons, New York, 1968.
22. T. Berger, *Rate Distortion Theory*, Prentice-Hall, Englewood Cliffs, NJ, 1971.

23. R. E. Blahut, "Computation of Channel Capacity and Rate Distortion Functions," *IEEE Trans.*, **IT-18**:460–473, 1972.
24. R. J. Clark, *Transform Coding of Images*, Academic Press, New York, 1985.
25. W. K. Pratt, *Digital Image Processing*, John Wiley & Sons, New York, 1991.
26. A. K. Jain, *Fundamentals of Digital Image Processing*, Prentice-Hall, Englewood Cliffs, NJ, 1989.
27. N. Ahmed, T. Natarajan, and K. R. Rao, "Discrete Cosine Transforms," *IEEE Trans. Comp.*, **C-23**:90–93, 1974.
28. J. A. Saghri, A. G. Tescher, and J. T. Reagan, "Practical Transform Coding of Multispectral Imagery," *IEEE Signal Processing Magazine,* **12**(1):32–43, 1995.
29. J. W. Woods and S. D. O'Neill, "Subband Coding of Images," *IEEE Trans.*, **ASSP-34**:1278–1288, 1986.
30. M. E. Blain and T. R. Fischer, "A Comparison of Vector Quantization Techniques in Transform and Subband Coding of Imagery," *Signal Processing: Image Communication*, **3**(1):91–105, 1991.
31. N. Baran, "Putting the Squeeze on Graphics," *Byte*, p. 289, December 1990.
32. P. H. Ang, P. A. Ruetz, and D. Auld, "Video Compression Makes Big Gains," *IEEE Spectrum*, **28**(10):16–19, 1991.
33. E. A. Fox, "Advances in Interactive Digital Multimedia Systems," *Computer*, **24**(10):9–21, 1991.
34. W. Penebaker and J. Mitchell, *JPEG Still Image Compression Standard*, Van Nostrand Reinhold, New York, 1992.
35. N. S. Jayant and P. Noll, *Digital Coding of Waveforms*, Prentice-Hall, New York, 1984.
36. A. N. Netravali and B. G. Haskell, *Digital Pictures—Representation and Compression*, Plenum Press, New York and London, 1988.

CHAPTER 18

Pattern Recognition: Image Segmentation

18.1 INTRODUCTION

So far in this book, we have primarily considered ways to improve images for display. In Chapter 16, our ambition was to retrieve an image that more closely resembled the original, undegraded scene.

In this chapter and the next two, we address some aspects of analyzing the content of an image. This means that we endeavor to find out what is in the picture. We examine two approaches, statistical pattern recognition and neural networks, each as applied to digital images. Volumes have been written on both of these topics, much to the benefit of the reader who wishes to go beyond this introduction to the field.

In these three chapters on pattern recognition, we address a collection of topics from the field. In particular, we consider statistical pattern recognition, implemented by digital image-processing techniques. This involves first locating and isolating the objects in an image and then identifying (classifying) those objects using techniques from the field of statistical decision theory. We also look at the use of artificial neural networks for pattern recognition.

18.1.1 Statistical Pattern Recognition

The computer vision branch of the field of artificial intelligence is concerned with developing algorithms for analyzing the content of an image. A variety of approaches toward *image understanding* have been employed, and we now consider one: statistical pattern recognition. Not only is this the most widely used approach, but an understanding of it is fundamental to a complete comprehension of the pattern recognition process, however it may be implemented.

Statistical pattern recognition assumes that the image may contain one or more objects and that each object belongs to one of several predetermined types, categories, or *pattern classes.* While pattern recognition can be implemented in several ways, we are concerned only with its implementation by digital image-processing techniques.

Given a digitized image containing several objects, the pattern recognition process consists of three major phases. (See Figure 18–1.) The first phase is called *image segmentation* or *object isolation,* in which each object is found and its image is isolated from the rest of the scene.

The second phase is called *feature extraction.* This is where the objects are measured. A *measurement* is the value of some quantifiable property of an object. A *feature* is a function of one or more measurements, computed so that it quantifies some significant characteristic of the object. The feature extraction process produces a set of features that, taken together, comprise the *feature vector.* This drastically reduced amount of information (compared to the original image) represents all the knowledge upon which the subsequent classification decisions must be based. It is productive to conceptualize an n-dimensional space in which all possible n-element feature vectors reside. Thus, any particular object corresponds to a point in *feature space.*

The third phase of pattern recognition is *classification.* Its output is merely a decision regarding the class to which each object belongs. Each object is recognized as being of one particular type, and the recognition is implemented as a classification process. Each object is assigned to one of several preestablished groups (classes) that represent all the possible types of objects expected to exist in the image. A *misclassification error* occurs if the assignment is to an inappropriate class. The probability of this occurring is the *misclassification error rate.*

Classification is based solely on the feature vector. In the next two chapters, we consider classification techniques derived from the fields of statistical decision theory and neural networks.

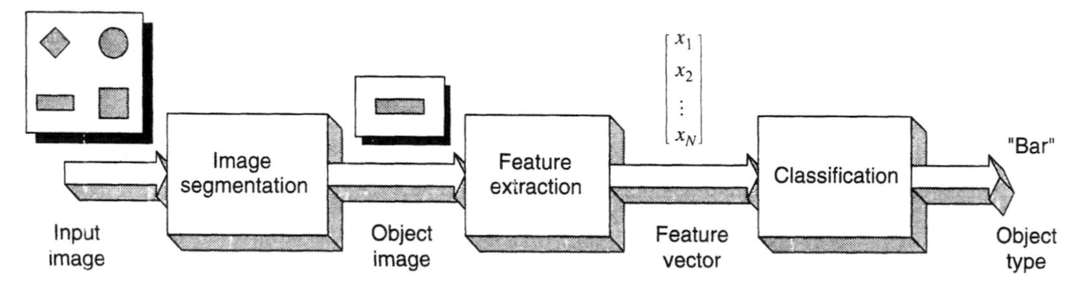

Figure 18–1 The three phases of pattern recognition

18.1.2 An Example of Pattern Recognition

The basic concepts of statistical pattern recognition can best be illustrated by an example. Suppose we desire to implement a sorting system for fruit coming down a conveyor belt. The actual sorting can be effected by movable partitions that drop down and deflect the various fruit items off the conveyor belt and into the appropriate shipping box, as illustrated in Figure 18–2. Let us suppose that the fruits of interest are cherries, apples, lemons, and grapefruits. What we need is an image-processing system that can observe the approaching fruits, classify each one, and drop the appropriate partition in time to box the fruit properly.

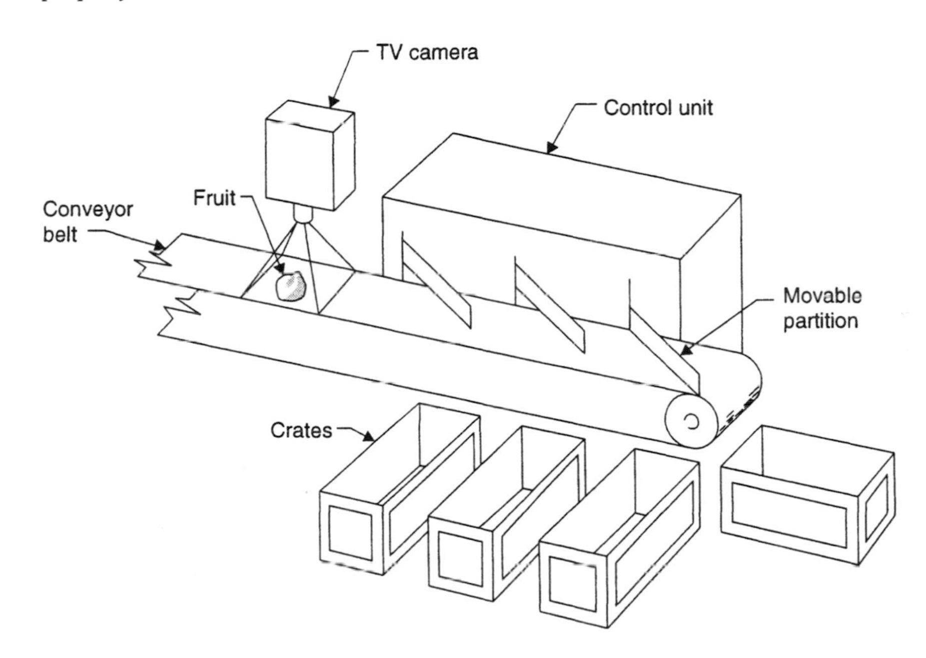

Figure 18–2 The fruit sorting system

We can install a digitizing television camera above the conveyor belt and implement the classification decision in a computer. For this example, let us measure two things about each piece of fruit: its diameter and its color. The computer program will process each digitized image and compute both the diameter of the fruit in millimeters and a parameter indicative of color.

Suppose we use a color TV camera, and the program computes each object's brightness in the red, green, and blue channels. (See Chapter 21.) It can then derive a feature (such as the red-to-green brightness ratio) that takes on low values for yellow fruit and high values for red fruit. We can call this parameter the *redness measure.*

Figure 18–3 shows the two-dimensional feature space defined by the two parameters, diameter and redness, and the expected clusters produced by each of the four classes of fruit. By placing appropriate decision lines in the feature space, we can partition it into one region per class and, in so doing, establish a *classification rule.*

When any fruit approaches the TV camera, it is measured, and its features specify a point in the two-dimensional feature space. Depending on where this point falls in that space, the fruit is assigned to one of the four classes. As soon as the classification decision is made, the mechanism drops the partition that will then deflect the fruit into the appropriate shipping container.

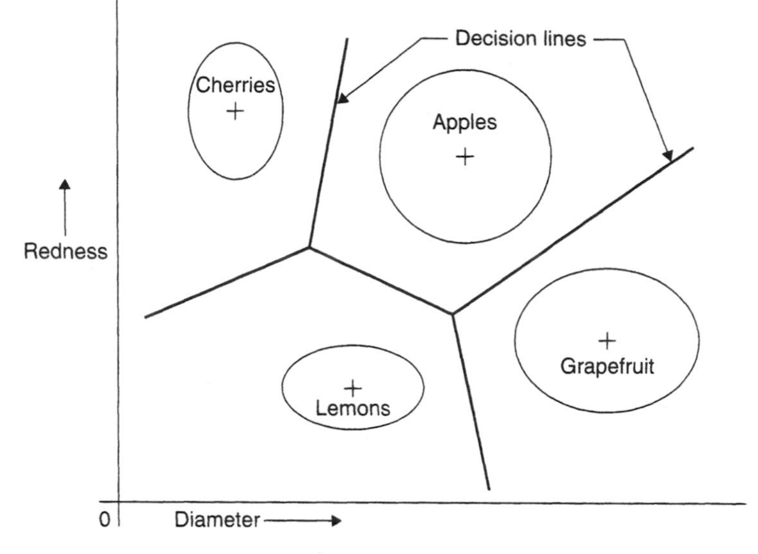

Figure 18–3 The feature space

While the preceding system has not yet found wide usage in the fruit-packing industry, it serves to illustrate statistical pattern recognition. The role that statistics plays in the design and operation of the system will become more clear in the next two chapters. For now, it suffices to say that each class of fruit produces a PDF in the feature space. The decision lines can be determined, from the interaction of these PDFs, in such a way as to avoid, or at least minimize, misclassification errors.

18.1.3 Pattern Recognition System Design

The design of a pattern recognition system is usually done in the five steps listed in Table 18–1: object locator design, feature selection, classifier design, classifier training, and performance evaluation.

The *object locator* is the algorithm that isolates the images of the individual objects in the complex scene. This isolation of objects is called image segmentation or scene segmentation, the topic addressed in this chapter. *Feature selection* involves deciding which properties of the object (size, shape, etc.) best distinguish among the various classes of objects and thus should be computed. *Classifier design* consists of establishing a mathematical basis for the classification procedure. The various adjustable parameters of the classifier itself (decision thresholds, etc.) are pinned down in the *classifier training* stage. Finally, it is usually desirable to estimate the misclassification error rates that can be expected when the system is put into operation. This constitutes the *performance evaluation* step.

18.2 THE IMAGE SEGMENTATION PROCESS

We can define the image segmentation process as one that partitions a digital image into disjoint (nonoverlapping) regions [1]. For our purposes, a *region* is a connected set of pixels—

TABLE 18–1 PATTERN RECOGNITION SYSTEM DESIGN

Step	Function
1. Object locator design	Select the scene segmentation algorithm that will isolate the individual objects in the image.
2. Feature selection	Decide which properties of the objects best distinguish the object types and how to measure these.
3. Classifier design	Establish the mathematical basis of the classification algorithm, and select the type of classifier structure to be used.
4. Classifier training	Fix the various adjustable parameters (decision boundaries, etc.) in the classifier to suit the objects being classified.
5. Performance evaluation	Estimate the expected rates of the various possible misclassification errors.

that is, a set in which all the pixels are adjacent or touching [2]. The formal definition of *connectedness* is as follows: Between any two pixels in a connected set, there exists a connected path wholly within the set, where a *connected path* is a path that always moves between neighboring pixels. Thus, in a connected set, you can trace a connected path between any two pixels without ever leaving the set.

There are two rules of *connectivity,* and either one can be adopted. If only laterally adjacent pixels (up, down, right, left) are considered to be connected, this is *four-connectivity,* and the objects are *four-connected.* Thus, each pixel has only four neighbors to which it can be connected. If, in addition, diagonally adjacent (45-degree neighbor) pixels are also considered to be connected, we have *eight-connectivity,* and the objects are *eight-connected.* Each pixel would then have eight neighbors to which it could be connected. Either connectivity rule can be used, as long as one is consistent. Often eight-connectivity yields results that lie closer to one's intuition.

When a human observer views a scene, the processing that takes place in the visual system essentially segments the scene for him or her. This is done so effectively that one sees not a complex scene, but rather something one thinks of as a collection of objects. With digital processing, however, we must laboriously isolate the objects in an image by breaking up the image into sets of pixels, each of which is the image of one object. While the task of image segmentation hardly has a counterpart in human visual experience, it is a nontrivial task in digital image analysis.

Image segmentation can be approached from three different philosophical perspectives. In the case we call the *region approach,* one assigns each pixel to a particular object or region. In the *boundary approach,* one attempts only to locate the boundaries that exist between the regions. In the *edge approach,* one seeks to identify edge pixels and then link them together to form the required boundaries. All three approaches are useful for visualizing the problem.

In this chapter, we examine several techniques for isolating the objects in a digital image. Once isolated, the objects can be measured and classified. Techniques for these activities are addressed in the next two chapters.

18.3 IMAGE SEGMENTATION BY THRESHOLDING

Thresholding is a particularly useful region-approach technique for scenes containing solid objects resting upon a contrasting background. It is computationally simple and never fails to define disjoint regions with closed, connected boundaries.

When using a threshold rule for image segmentation, one assigns all pixels at or above the threshold gray level to the object. All pixels with gray level below the threshold fall outside the object. The boundary is then that set of interior points, each of which has at least one neighbor outside the object.

Thresholding works well if the objects of interest have uniform interior gray level and rest upon a background of different, but uniform, gray level. If the objects differ from their background by some property other than gray level (texture, etc.), one can first use an operation that converts that property to gray level. Then gray-level thresholding can segment the processed image.

18.3.1 Global Thresholding

In the simplest implementation of boundary location by thresholding, the value of the threshold gray level is held constant throughout the image. If the background gray level is reasonably constant throughout, and if the objects all have approximately equal contrast above the background, then a fixed global threshold will usually work well, provided that the threshold gray level is properly selected.

18.3.2 Adaptive Thresholding

In many cases, the background gray level is not constant, and the contrast of objects varies within the image. In such cases, a threshold that works well in one area of the image might work poorly in other areas. In these cases, it is convenient to use a threshold gray level that is a slowly varying function of position in the image.

Figure 18–4 shows a microscope image of the chromosomes from a single human blood cell. In this image, the background gray level varies due to nonuniform illumination, and contrast varies from one chromosome to the next. In Figure 18–4(a), a constant threshold gray level has been used throughout the image to isolate the chromosomes. Each chromosome was given a boundary and a sequence number. In Figure 18–4(b), the threshold was varied from one chromosome to the next commensurately with local background and the contrast of the chromosomes [3,4]. This produced fewer segmentation errors—cases where multiple chromosomes were stuck together or individual chromosomes were broken up. A similar study showed that accuracy of measurement of the areas of the chromosomes was improved by adaptive thresholding. In Figure 18–4(b), the threshold for each chromosome was set approximately midway between its mean interior gray level and the local background gray level [3,5].

18.3.3 Optimal Threshold Selection

Unless the object in the image has extremely steep sides, the exact value of the threshold gray level can have considerable effect on the boundary position and overall size of the extracted object. This means that subsequent size measurements—particularly area—are sensitive to the threshold gray level. For this reason, we need an optimal, or at least consistent, method to establish the threshold.

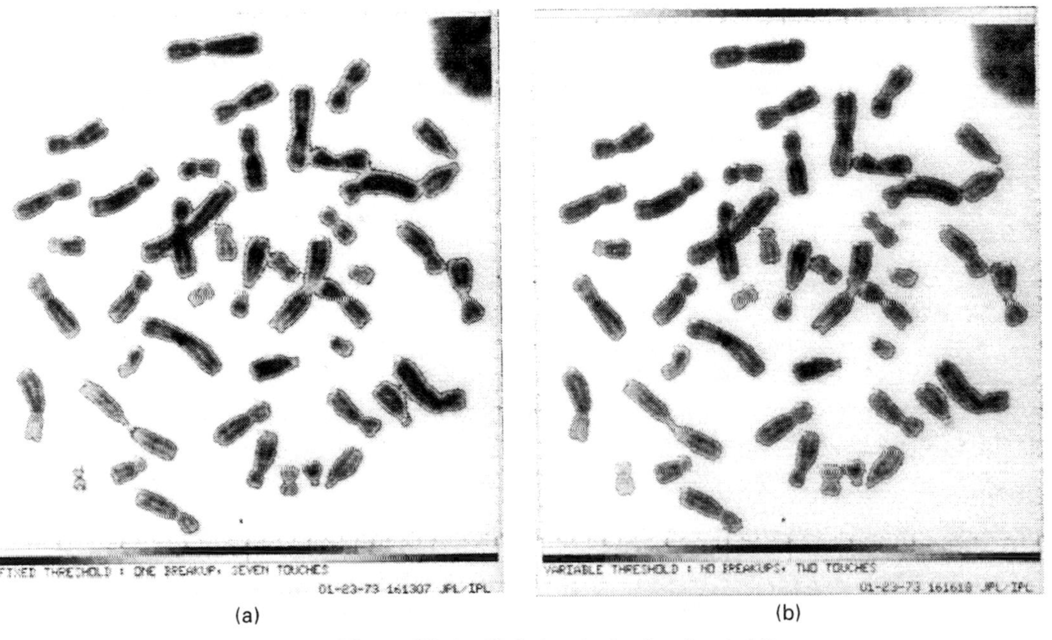

(a) (b)

Figure 18–4 Global and adaptive thresholding

18.3.3.1 Histogram Techniques

An image containing an object on a contrasting background has a bimodal gray-level histogram (Figure 18–5). The two peaks correspond to the relatively large numbers of points inside and outside the object. The dip between the peaks corresponds to the relatively few points around the edge of the object. In cases like this, the histogram is commonly used to establish the threshold gray level [6–9].

Recall from Chapter 5 that the area of an object defined by a gray-level threshold T is

$$A = \int_{T}^{\infty} H(D)dD \qquad (1)$$

Notice that increasing the threshold from T to $T + \Delta T$ causes only a slight decrease in area if the threshold corresponds to the dip in the histogram. Therefore, placing the threshold at the dip in the histogram minimizes the sensitivity of the area measurement to small errors in threshold selection.

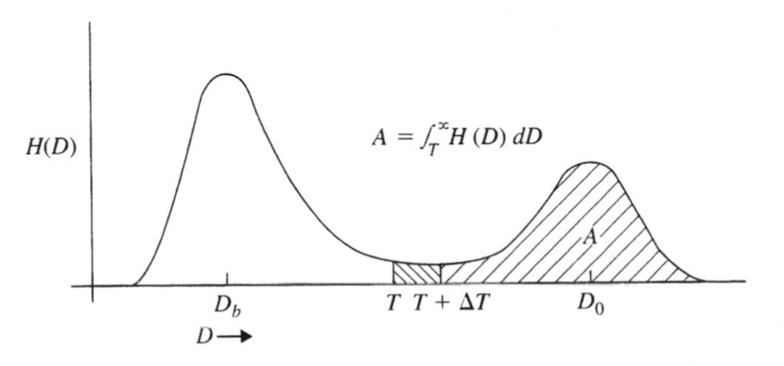

Figure 18–5 The bimodal histogram

If the image or the region of the image containing the object is noisy and not large, the histogram itself will be noisy. Unless the dip is uncommonly sharp, the noise will make its location obscure, or at least unreliable from one image to the next. This can be overcome to some extent by smoothing the histogram, using either convolution or a curve-fitting procedure. If the two peaks are of unequal size, smoothing may tend to shift the position of the minimum. The peaks, however, are easy to locate and relatively stable under reasonable amounts of smoothing. A more reliable method is to place the threshold at some fixed position relative to the two peaks—perhaps midway [5]. The two peaks represent the modal (most commonly occurring) gray levels of the interior and exterior points of the objects. In general, these parameters can be more reliably estimated than the least commonly occurring gray level—that is, the dip in the histogram.

One can form a histogram of only those pixels having a relatively high gradient magnitude [9]—for example, the highest 10 percent [10]. This eliminates the large number of interior and exterior pixels from consideration and may make the dip in the histogram more accessible. One can also divide the histogram by the average gradient of pixels at each gray level to further enhance the dip [9], or average the gray level of high-gradient pixels to determine a threshold [10,11].

The Laplacian filter is a two-dimensional second derivative operator. Laplacian filtering, followed by smoothing and thresholding at a gray level of zero or slightly above, tends to segment objects at zero-crossings of the second derivative, which correspond to inflection points on the edges of the objects [12]. The two-dimensional histogram of gray level vs. gradient can also be used to establish segmentation criteria [13].

18.3.3.2 Adaptive Thresholding

The adaptive segmentation technique of Figure 18–4(b) was implemented as a two-pass technique [3,5]. Before the first pass, the image was divided into sectors of 100 by 100 pixels. From the gray-level histogram of each sector, a threshold was determined midway between the background peak and the data peak. Sectors containing unimodal histograms were ignored.

In the first pass, the boundaries of the object were defined using a gray-level threshold that was constant within sectors, but different for the various sectors. The objects so defined were not extracted from the image, but the interior mean gray level of each object was computed.

On the second pass, each object was given its own threshold that lay midway between its interior gray level and the background gray level of its principal sector. Examination of Figure 18–4 indicates that the number of touches dropped from seven to two, while the number of breakups dropped from one to none.

18.3.4 The Analysis of Spots

In many important cases, it is necessary to find objects that are roughly circular in shape. The development that follows is aimed primarily at circular objects. Restricting ourselves to circular objects allows us to pursue optimal threshold selection considerably further than we could otherwise. The concepts developed are nonetheless useful for more general cases as well.

18.3.4.1 Definitions

Suppose an image $B(x, y)$ contains a single *spot*. By definition, this image contains a point (x_0, y_0) of maximum gray level. If we establish polar coordinates centered upon (x_0, y_0), so that the image is given by $B_p(r, \theta)$, then

$$B_p(r_1, \theta) \geq B_p(r_2, \theta) \qquad \text{if } r_2 > r_1 \tag{2}$$

for all values of θ. We call $B(x, y)$ a *monotone spot* if equality is not allowed in Eq. (2). This means that gray level strictly decreases along a line extending out in any direction from the center point (x_0, y_0). For monotone spots, a flat top is not allowed, and (x_0, y_0) is unique.

An important special case occurs if all contours of a monotone spot are circles centered on (x_0, y_0). We call this special case a *concentric circular spot* (CCS). To a good approximation, this usually describes the noise-free images of stars in a telescope, certain cells in a microscope, and many other important types of images. Noise will usually cause real images to deviate from these definitions, but the theory can prove useful anyway [10,12].

For a CCS, the function $B_p(r, \theta)$ is independent of θ, and we call it the *spot profile function.* This curve is useful for threshold selection. For example, we could locate the inflection point and select the gray-level threshold so as to place the boundary at the point of maximum slope. This is approximately where the human eye places the boundary when viewing an image containing a smooth edge, and it is reasonably stable under smoothing and the addition of noise. This boundary may tend to underestimate the actual size of objects [10]. Other unique points on the profile, such as the maximum magnitude of the second derivative [10], can be used as well.

If we threshold a monotone spot at a gray level T, we define an object having a certain area and perimeter. As we vary T throughout the range of gray levels, we generate the threshold area function $A(T)$ and the perimeter function $p(T)$. Both of these functions are unique for any spot. Both are continuous for monotone spots, and either is sufficient to specify a CCS completely. As a matter of definition, two spots are p-*equivalent* if they have identical perimeter functions and H-*equivalent* if they have identical histograms. It follows that H-equivalent spots have identical threshold area functions.

18.3.4.2 The Histogram and the Profile

Suppose a CCS image $B(x, y)$ is given by its profile function $B_p(r)$. We now seek an expression for the spot histogram in terms of the profile function. Suppose we threshold $B(x, y)$ at gray level D and again at gray level $D + \Delta D$. This defines two circular contours of radius r and $r + \Delta r$, respectively, as shown in Figure 18–6. The area of the annular ring between the contours is

$$\Delta A = \pi r^2 - \pi(r + \Delta r)^2 \approx -2\pi r \Delta r \tag{3}$$

where the approximation is obtained by assuming Δr small and neglecting Δr^2.

Eq. (3) can be rearranged as

$$\frac{\Delta A}{\Delta r} \approx -2\pi r \tag{4}$$

The histogram of the image is, by definition,

$$H_B(D) = \mathop{\mathcal{L}}_{\Delta D \to 0} \frac{\Delta A}{\Delta D} \tag{5}$$

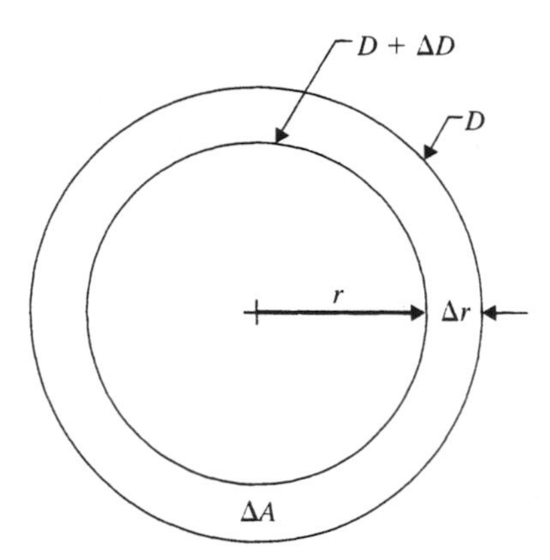

Figure 18–6 Thresholding a concentric circular spot

We can divide the numerator and denominator by Δr and substitute Eq. (4) into the numerator to produce

$$H_B(D) = \mathop{\mathcal{L}}_{\Delta D \to 0} \frac{\Delta A/\Delta r}{\Delta D/\Delta r} = \frac{-2\pi r}{d/dr B_p(r)} \tag{6}$$

To obtain the rightmost equality, we note that both Δr and ΔD approach zero, and we recognize the derivative of the profile function in the denominator.

We are not through yet, since the right side of Eq. (6) is a function of r instead of a function of D. Since $B(x, y)$ is the image of a monotone spot, $B_p(r)$ is a monotonically decreasing function, and hence, its inverse function

$$r(D) = B_p^{-1}(D) \tag{7}$$

exists. We can now substitute this into the numerator and denominator of Eq. (6) to make the histogram a function of gray level, as desired. Notice that, since the profile function $B_p(r)$ decreases monotonically with r, the denominator of Eq. (6) is negative. This cancels the minus sign in the numerator to make the histogram positive, as expected.

18.3.4.3 The Area-Derived Profile

We now seek an expression for the profile of a CCS in terms of its histogram. The radius of the circular object obtained by thresholding a CCS at gray level T is

$$R(T) = \left[\frac{1}{\pi}A(T)\right]^{1/2} = \left[\frac{1}{\pi}\int_T^{\infty} H_B(D)dD\right]^{1/2} \tag{8}$$

For a monotone spot, the histogram $H_B(D)$ is nonzero between its minimum and maximum gray levels. This means that the area function $A(T)$ is monotonically increasing, and consequently, so is $R(T)$. Thus, the inverse function of Eq. (8) exists, and it is the profile. Hence, we can compute the area-derived profile of a CCS by integrating the histogram to obtain the area function, taking first the square root and then the inverse function.

18.3.4.4 The Perimeter-Derived Profile

Thresholding a CCS at gray level T produces a circular object of radius

$$R(T) = \frac{1}{2\pi}P(T) \tag{9}$$

where $p(T)$ is the perimeter function. As with the previous technique, the profile is merely the inverse function of Eq. (9). Thus, if the perimeter function is known, the profile may be obtained by the inverse of Eq. (9).

18.3.4.5 Noncircular and Noisy Spots

We can most easily obtain the profile of an image containing a noise-free CCS simply by taking the gray levels along the scan line that contains the peak. For noncircular spots and noisy spots, however, the foregoing techniques can be useful. For example, one can use the histogram of a noncircular spot to obtain the profile of the H-equivalent CCS and select the threshold gray level that maximizes the slope at the boundary. In other cases, it is useful to measure the perimeter function and determine the profile of the p-equivalent CCS. Either of these techniques could produce thresholds suitable for the image at hand.

In digitized images of natural scenes, the noise level is frequently so high that differentiating a single scan line cannot reliably identify the inflection point on the profile. However, the area-derived and perimeter-derived profiles are computed using most or all of the edge pixels in the object. This process employs inherent noise reduction by averaging. Further noise reduction can be effected by smoothing the histogram or perimeter function before computing the profile, or by smoothing the profile function itself. The area-derived profile is the easier to compute, and it has superior noise discrimination properties.

Random noise in the image usually makes the threshold boundary jagged. While this may have little effect on the area function, it tends to make the perimeter function erroneously large. Even though the error can be reduced by boundary smoothing built into the perimeter measurement routine, computational simplicity is still on the side of the area-derived profile.

Sieracki, Reichenbach, and Webb [10] compared nine methods of threshold selection, including two based on the area-derived profile (maximum magnitude of the first derivative and maximum magnitude of the second derivative) for measuring the diameter of fluorescent microspheres. Generally speaking, they found the latter method to be the most accurate of the nine for spheres of different sizes and intensities. It also performed well for cells in tissue culture [10,12]. Finding the maximum of the first derivative, like the other methods tested, tended to underestimate the sizes of objects.

18.3.5 Average Boundary Gradient

For highly noncircular spots, the H-equivalent and p-equivalent CCS profiles may not be acceptable for placing the gray-level threshold. For objects of arbitrary shape, we can examine the average gradient around the boundary as a function of the threshold gray level that defines the boundary [3].

Suppose a noncircular monotone spot is thresholded at gray levels of D and $D + \Delta D$, as shown in Figure 18–7. At some point a on the outer boundary, Δr is the perpendicular distance to the inner boundary. Since Δr is perpendicular to a contour line, it lies in the

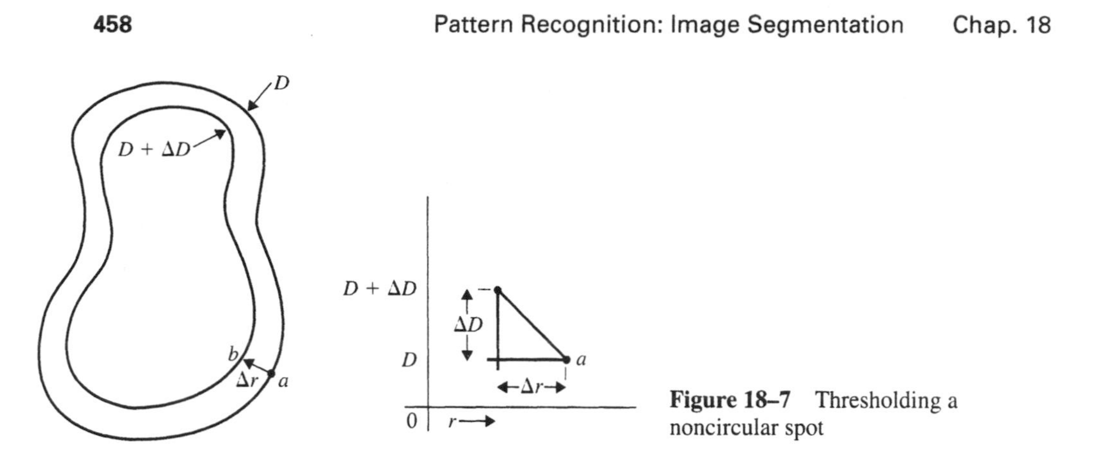

Figure 18–7 Thresholding a noncircular spot

direction of the gradient vector at point a. The magnitude of the gradient vector at point a on the outer boundary is

$$|\nabla \mathbf{B}| = \mathcal{L}_{\Delta D \to 0} \frac{\Delta D}{\Delta r} \tag{10}$$

Since we are interested in the average gradient around the boundary, we can simply average $|\nabla B|$ around the outer boundary. If Δr is small with respect to the perimeter, the area between the two boundaries is merely

$$\Delta A = p(D)\overline{\Delta r} \tag{11}$$

where $\overline{\Delta r}$ is the average perpendicular distance from the outer to the inner boundary and $p(D)$ is the perimeter function. To obtain the average gradient around the boundary, we need merely to substitute $\overline{\Delta r}$ for Δr in Eq. (10). This produces

$$|\overline{\nabla \mathbf{B}}| = \mathcal{L}_{\Delta D \to 0} \frac{\Delta D}{\Delta A} p(D) = \frac{p(D)}{H_B(D)} \tag{12}$$

which indicates that the average boundary gradient is merely the ratio of the perimeter function to the histogram.

The average boundary gradient function is not difficult to compute, and it readily identifies the threshold gray level that maximizes the slope at the boundary. For noisy images, the perimeter function and the histogram may require smoothing before computing the average boundary gradient function.

18.3.6 Objects of General Shape

Although some of the foregoing results were developed primarily for restricted types of objects, they are nonetheless useful for more general cases. Suppose an image contains objects of a general shape on a low gray-level background. While the objects may be relatively flat on top, nonmonotonic, and without a unique peak, they usually have sides that slope uniformly down toward the background. The PSF of optical systems forbids sides of infinite slope in real images. On the sides of the objects, contour lines are closed and generally convex curves that may have local concavities.

We can assume that each threshold gray level defines a single closed curve for each object. Under these conditions, we need to consider only the range of gray levels corresponding to the sloping sides of the object. We now have four ways to establish the maximum-slope threshold gray level, T:

1. We can select T at a local minimum in the histogram. This is the easiest technique, and it minimizes the sensitivity of the area measurement to small variations in T.
2. We can select T corresponding to the inflection point in the H-equivalent CCS profile function. This is a simple computation, and it involves considerable averaging for noise reduction.
3. We can select T to maximize the average boundary gradient. This involves computing the perimeter function, but requires no approximation regarding equivalent spot images.
4. We can select T corresponding to the inflection point in the p-equivalent CCS profile function.

Any one of the foregoing methods can be implemented for routine use. For large-scale studies, one might use one of these methods to characterize the objects under study. Then a shortcut method could be implemented for routine use. If a profile analysis showed, for example, that the optimal threshold gray level for isolated star images in telescope pictures occurs midway between the peak and the background gray level, then this simplified method could be employed for routine use.

18.3.7 The Watershed Algorithm

A relative of adaptive thresholding is the watershed algorithm. Figure 18–8 illustrates how this approach works. We assume that the objects in the figure are of low gray level, on a high-gray-level background. The figure shows the gray levels along one scan line that cuts through two objects that are close together.

The image is initially thresholded at a low gray level, one that segments the image into the proper number of objects, but with boundaries that are too small. Then the threshold is raised gradually, one gray level at a time. The objects' boundaries will expand as the threshold increases. When they touch, however, the objects are not allowed to merge. Thus, these points of first contact become the final boundaries between adjacent objects. The process is terminated before the threshold reaches the gray level of the background—that is, at the point when the boundaries of well-isolated objects are properly set.

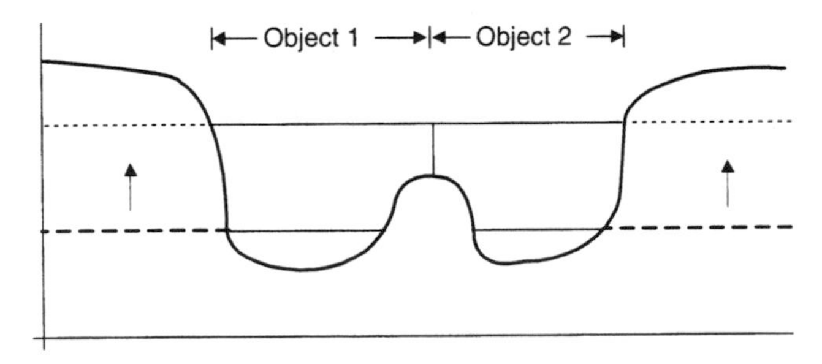

Figure 18–8 The watershed algorithm

Rather than simply thresholding the image at the optimum gray level, then, the watershed approach begins with a threshold that is too low, but that properly isolates the individual objects. Then as the threshold is gradually raised to the optimum level, merging of objects is not allowed. This can solve the problem posed by objects that are too close together for global thresholding to work. The final segmentation will be correct (i.e., there will be one boundary per actual object in the image) if and only if the segmentation at the initial threshold is correct.

Both the initial and final threshold gray levels must be well chosen. If the initial threshold is too low, then low-contrast objects will be missed at first and then merged with nearby objects as the threshold increases. If the initial threshold is too high, objects will be merged from the start. The final threshold value determines how well the final boundaries fit the objects. The threshold selection methods discussed in this chapter can be useful in setting these two values.

18.4 GRADIENT-BASED SEGMENTATION METHODS

The preceding region approaches accomplish segmentation by partitioning the image into sets of interior and exterior points. By contrast, boundary approaches attempt to find the edges directly by their high gradient magnitudes. In this section, we discuss three such methods.

18.4.1 Boundary Tracking

Suppose we start with the gradient magnitude image (Figure 7–5) computed from an image containing a single object on a contrasting background. We can start the boundary-tracking process by identifying the pixel of the highest gray level (i.e., the pixel with the highest gradient in the original image) as the first boundary point, since it certainly must be on the boundary. If several points have the maximum gray level, then we choose arbitrarily.

Next we search the three-by-three neighborhood centered on the first boundary point and take the neighbor with the maximum gray level as the second boundary point. If two neighbors have the same maximum gray level, we choose arbitrarily. At this point, we begin the iterative process of finding the next boundary point, given the current and previous boundary points. Working in the three-by-three neighborhood centered on the current boundary point, we examine the neighbor diametrically opposite the previous boundary point and the neighbors on each side of it (Figure 18–9). The next boundary point is one of those three that has the highest gray level. If all three or two adjacent boundary points share the highest gray level, then we choose the middle one. If the two nonadjacent points share the highest gray level, we choose arbitrarily.

In the noise-free image of a monotone spot, this algorithm will trace out the maximum gradient boundary; however, even small amounts of noise can send the tracking temporarily or hopelessly off the boundary. Noise effects can be reduced by smoothing the gradient image before tracking or by implementing a *tracking bug*. Even so, boundary tracking does not guarantee closed boundaries, and the tracking algorithm can get lost and run off the border of the image.

A tracking bug is an algorithmic "insect" that works as follows. First we define a rectangular averaging window (the bug), usually having uniform weights (Figure 18–10). The

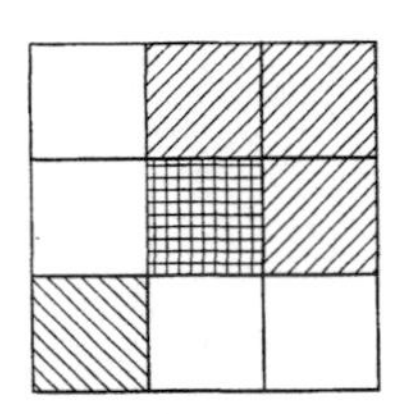

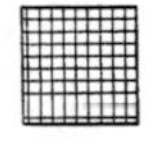
Current boundary point

Last boundary point

Candidates for next boundary point

Figure 18–9 Boundary tracking

last two or last few boundary points define the current direction of the boundary. The rear portion of the bug is centered on the current boundary point, with its axis oriented along the current direction. The bug is subsequently oriented at an angle θ to either side.

In each position, the average gradient under the bug is computed. The next boundary point is taken as one of the pixels under the front portion of the bug when it is in the highest average gradient position. Clearly, the tracking bug is a spatially larger implementation of the boundary-tracking procedure described earlier. The larger size of the bug implements smoothing of the gradient image and makes it less susceptible to noise. It also limits how sharply the boundary can change directions.

The size and shape of the bug may be altered to achieve the best performance. The "inertia" of the bug can be increased by reducing the side-looking angle θ. In practice, the exact shape of the bug appears to have little effect on its performance. Gradient-tracking

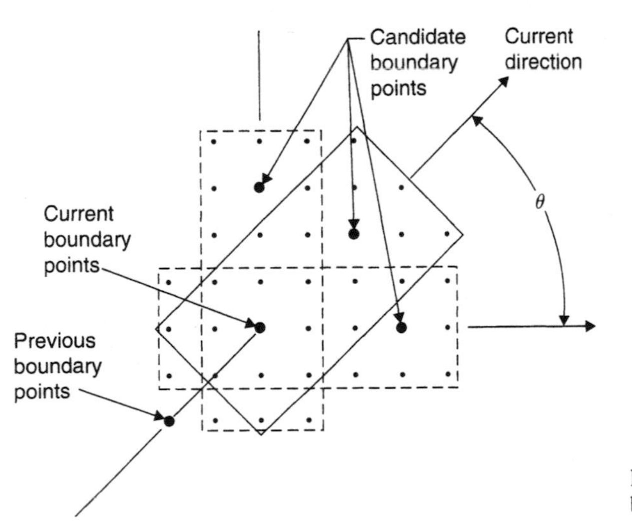

Figure 18–10 The boundary tracking bug

bugs are usually useful only in extremely low-noise images or in situations where human intervention can prevent catastrophic derailments.

18.4.2 Gradient Image Thresholding

If we threshold a gradient image at moderate gray level, we find both object and background below the threshold and most edge points above it (Figure 18–11). Kirsch's segmentation method makes use of this phenomenon [14]. In this technique, one first thresholds the gradient at a moderately low level to identify the object and the background, which are separated by bands of edge points that are above the threshold. Then the threshold is gradually increased. This causes both the object and the background to grow. When they touch, they are not allowed to merge, but rather, the points of contact define the boundary. This is an application of the watershed algorithm to the gradient image.

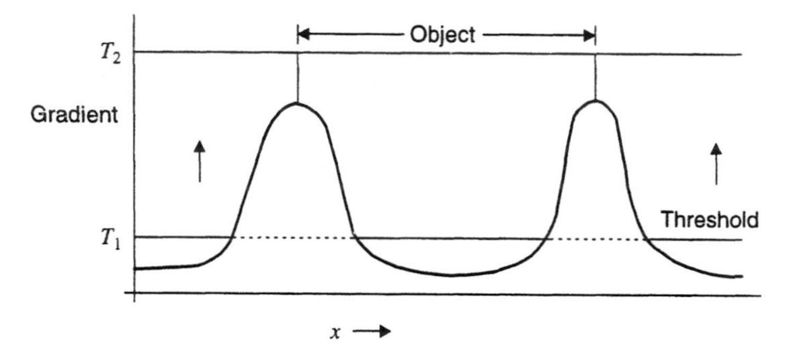

Figure 18–11 Kirsch's segmentation algorithm

While Kirsch's method is more computationally expensive than thresholding, it tends to produce maximum gradient boundaries, and it avoids many of the problems of gradient-tracking bugs. For multiple object images, the segmentation is correct if and only if it is done correctly by the initial thresholding step. Smoothing the gradient image beforehand produces smoother boundaries.

18.4.3 Laplacian Edge Detection

The Laplacian is a scalar second-derivative operator for functions of two dimensions. It is defined as

$$\nabla^2 f(x, y) = \frac{\partial^2}{\partial x^2} f(x, y) + \frac{\partial^2}{\partial y^2} f(x, y) \tag{13}$$

It is commonly implemented digitally by either of the convolution kernels shown in Figure 18–12.

Since it is a second derivative, the Laplacian will produce an abrupt zero-crossing at an edge (Figure 18–13). The Laplacian is a linear, shift-invariant operator, and its transfer function is zero at the origin of frequency space. (See Table 10-3.) Thus, a Laplacian-filtered image will have zero mean gray level.

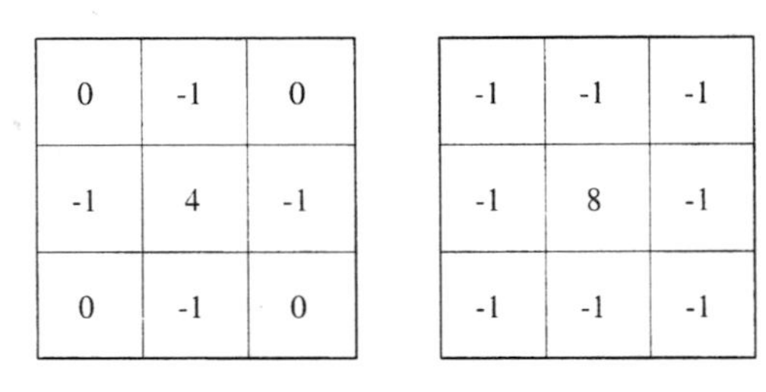

0	-1	0
-1	4	-1
0	-1	0

-1	-1	-1
-1	8	-1
-1	-1	-1

Figure 18–12 Laplacian convolution kernels

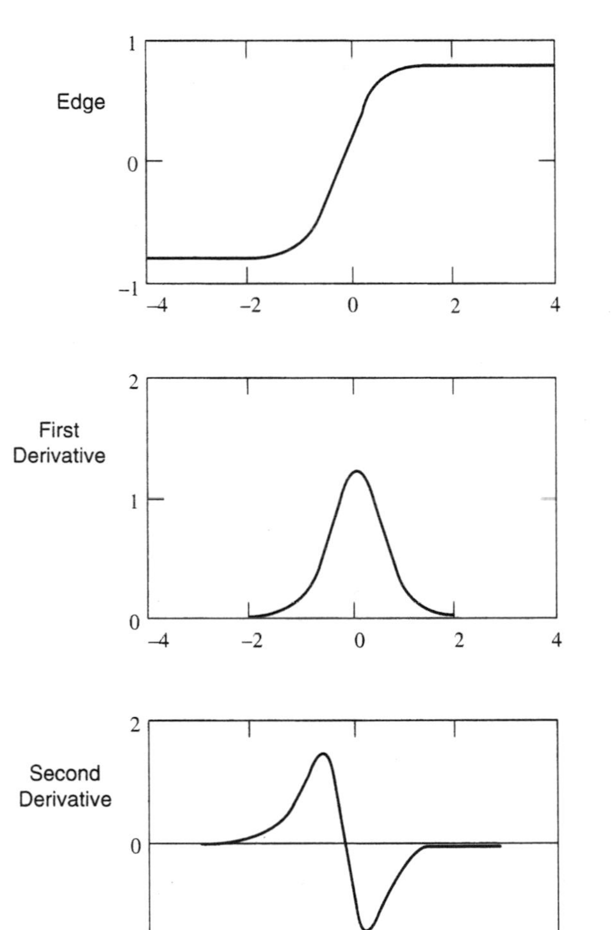

Figure 18–13 Derivatives of an edge

If a noise-free image has sharp edges, the Laplacian can find them. The binary image that results from thresholding a Laplacian-filtered image at zero gray level will produce closed, connected contours when interior points are eliminated. (See Sec. 18.7.) The presence of noise, however, imposes a requirement for lowpass filtering prior to using the Laplacian.

A Gaussian lowpass filter is a good choice for this pre-smoothing. Since convolution is associative [Chapter 9, Eq. (39)] we can combine the Laplacian and Gaussian impulse responses into a single *Laplacian of Gaussian* kernel [15,16]:

$$-\nabla^2 \frac{1}{2\pi\sigma^2} e^{-\frac{x^2+y^2}{2\sigma^2}} = \frac{1}{\pi\sigma^4}\left[1 - \frac{x^2+y^2}{2\sigma^2}\right] e^{-\frac{x^2+y^2}{2\sigma^2}} \quad (14)$$

This impulse response is separable in x and y and thus can be implemented efficiently. It has the shape of the general bandpass filter impulse response discussed in Chapter 11, namely a positive peak in a negative dish (Figure 18–14). The parameter σ controls the width of the central peak and, thus, the amount of smoothing. In fact, it is well approximated by the difference of Gaussians filter of Sec. 11.4.1 (Chapter 11, Eq. (12)) when the ratio of standard deviations is $\sigma_2 = 1.6\sigma_1$ [15].

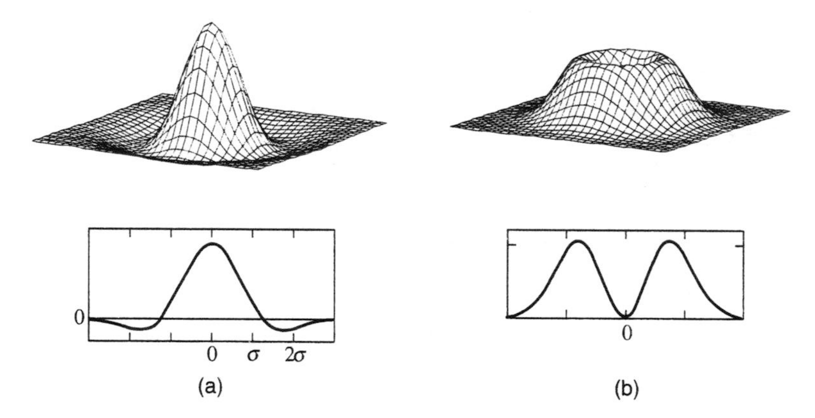

Figure 18–14 The Laplacian-of-Gaussian filter: (a) impulse response, (b) transfer function

18.5 EDGE DETECTION AND LINKING

Another approach to establishing the boundaries of the objects in an image is first to examine each pixel and its immediate neighborhood to determine whether that pixel is, in fact, on the boundary of an object. Pixels exhibiting the required characteristics are labeled *edge points*. An image in which gray level reflects how strongly each corresponding pixel meets the requirements of an edge pixel is called an *edge image* or *edge map*. This can also be displayed as a *binary edge image* showing only the location (not the magnitude) of the edge points. An image that encodes the direction of the edge, instead of (or in addition to) the magnitude, is a *directional edge image*.

An edge image normally shows each object outlined in edge points, but these seldom form the closed, connected boundaries that are required for image segmentation. Thus, another step is required before extraction of the object is complete. *Edge point linking* is the process of associating nearby edge points so as to create a closed, connected boundary. This process fills in the gaps left by noise and shading effects.

18.5.1 Edge Detection

If a pixel falls on the boundary of an object in an image, then its neighborhood will be a zone of gray-level transition. The two characteristics of principal interest are the slope and direction of that transition. These are the magnitude and direction, respectively, of the gradient vector.

Edge detection operators examine each pixel neighborhood and quantify the slope, and often the direction as well, of the gray-level transition. There are several ways to do this, most of which are based upon convolution with a set of directional derivative masks.

The Roberts Edge Operator. One local differential operator for finding edges is the *Roberts edge detector* [17]. It is given by

$$g(x, y) = \{[\sqrt{f(x, y)} - \sqrt{f(x+1, y+1)}]^2 + [\sqrt{f(x+1, y)} - \sqrt{f(x, y+1)}]^2\}^{1/2} \quad (15)$$

where $f(x, y)$ is the input image with integer pixel coordinates (x, y). The inner square roots make the operation resemble the processing that takes place in the human visual system.

The Sobel Edge Operator. The two convolution kernels shown in Figure 18–15 form the *Sobel edge operator* [18]. Each point in the image is convolved with both kernels. One kernel responds maximally to a generally vertical edge and the other to a horizontal edge. The maximum value of the two convolutions is taken as the output value for that pixel. The result is an edge magnitude image.

-1	-2	-1
0	0	0
1	2	1

-1	0	1
-2	0	2
-1	0	1

Figure 18–15 The Sobel edge operator

The Prewitt Edge Operator. The two convolution kernels shown in Figure 18–16 form the *Prewitt edge operator* [7]. As with the Sobel operator, each point in the image is convolved with both kernels, and the maximum determines the output. The Prewitt operator likewise produces an edge magnitude image.

-1	-1	-1
0	0	0
1	1	1

1	0	-1
1	0	-1
1	0	-1

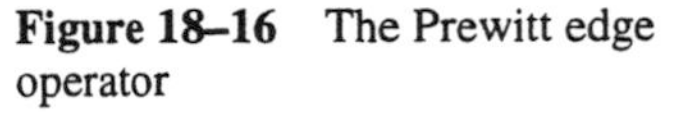

Figure 18–16 The Prewitt edge operator

The Kirsch Edge Operator. The eight convolution kernels shown in Figure 18–17 make up the *Kirsch edge operator* [14]. Each point in the image is convolved with all

+5	+5	+5
−3	0	−3
−3	−3	−3

−3	+5	+5
−3	0	+5
−3	−3	−3

−3	−3	+5
−3	0	+5
−3	−3	+5

−3	−3	−3
−3	0	+5
−3	+5	+5

−3	−3	−3
−3	0	−3
+5	+5	+5

−3	−3	−3
+5	0	−3
+5	+5	−3

+5	−3	−3
+5	0	−3
+5	−3	−3

+5	+5	−3
+5	0	−3
−3	−3	−3

Figure 18–17 The Kirsch edge operator

eight masks. Each mask responds maximally to an edge oriented in a particular general direction. The maximum value over all eight orientations is the output value for the edge magnitude image. The index of the maximally responding mask encodes the direction of the edge.

Edge Detector Performance. Visually, the edge images produced by the foregoing edge operators appear rather similar. They generally look like the line drawing a draftsman would make from the picture. The Roberts operator, being two by two, responds best on sharp transitions in low-noise images. The other three operators, being three by three, handle more gradual transitions and noisier images better.

Normally, for the two-mask edge detectors, the larger magnitude is taken as the output value. This makes them somewhat sensitive to the orientation of the edge. More consistent omnidirectional response can be obtained by taking the square root of the sum of the squares [19]. This approximates the true gradient magnitude better.

Notice that the Sobel and Prewitt three-by-three edge operators can be generalized to eight orientations and used like the Kirsch operator to obtain edge orientation images [20].

18.5.2 Edge Linking

If the edges are reliably strong, and the noise level is low, one can threshold an edge image (recall Figure 7–7, for example) and thin the resulting binary image (see Sec. 18.7.4.2) down to single-pixel-wide closed, connected boundaries. Under less than ideal conditions, however, such an edge image will have gaps that must be filled.

Small gaps can be filled simply by searching a five-by-five or larger neighborhood, centered on an endpoint, for other endpoints and then filling in boundary pixels as required to connect them. In complex scenes with lots of edge points, however, this can oversegment the image. To combat oversegmentation, one can require that the two endpoints agree in edge strength and orientation, to within specified tolerances, before they are connected.

18.5.2.1 Heuristic Search

Suppose we have what appears to be a gap in a boundary in an edge image, but it is too long to fill accurately with a straight line, it may not really be a gap in the same boundary, or perhaps both. We can establish, as a quality measure, a function that can be computed for every connected path between the two endpoints, which we call A and B. This edge quality function could include the average of the edge strengths of the points, perhaps minus some measure of their average disagreement in orientation angles [17,21,22].

We start by evaluating the neighbors of A as candidates for taking the first step toward B. Normally, only the three neighbors of A that lie in the general direction of B would be considered. We select the one that maximizes the edge quality function from A to that point. Then it becomes the starting point for the next iteration. When we finally reach B, the edge quality function over the newly created path is compared to a threshold. If the newly created edge is insufficiently strong, it is discarded.

Heuristic search techniques become computationally expensive if the edge quality function is complex and the gaps to be evaluated are many and long. Such techniques perform well in relatively simple images, but they do not necessarily converge upon the globally optimal path between endpoints.

18.5.2.2 Curve Fitting

If the edge points are generally sparse, it might be desirable to fit a piecewise linear or higher order spline curve through them to establish a boundary suitable for extracting objects. General curve-fitting techniques are discussed in Sec. 19.5. Here, we mention the piecewise linear method called *iterative endpoint fitting* [23].

Suppose we have a group of edge points lying scattered between two particular edge points A and B, and we wish to select a subset of these to form the nodes of a piecewise linear path from A to B. We begin by establishing a straight line from A to B. Then we compute the perpendicular distance from that line to each of the remaining edge points. The furthest one becomes the next node on the path, which now has two branches. The process is repeated on each new branch of the path, until no remaining edge point lies more than some fixed distance away from the nearest branch. When this is done for pairs of points (A, B) all around the object, it produces a polygonal approximation to the boundary.

18.5.2.3 Hough Transform

The straight line $y = mx + b$ can be expressed in polar coordinates as [23]

$$\rho = x\cos(\theta) + y\sin(\theta) \tag{16}$$

where (ρ, θ) defines a vector from the origin to the nearest point on the line (Figure 18–18a). This vector will be perpendicular to the line.

We can consider a two-dimensional space defined by the two parameters ρ and θ. Any line in the x, y-plane plots to a point in that space. Thus, the Hough transform of a straight line in x, y-space is a point in ρ, θ space.

Now consider a particular point (x_1, y_1) in the x, y-plane. There are many straight lines that pass through this point, and each of these lines plots to a point in ρ,θ-space. These points, however, must satisfy Eq. (16) with x_1 and y_1 as constants. Thus, the locus of all such lines in x, y-space is a sinusoid in parameter space, and any point in the x, y-plane (Figure 18–18b) corresponds to a sinusoidal curve in ρ, θ space (Figure 18–18c).

If we have a set of edge points x_i, y_i that lie on a straight line having parameters ρ_0 and θ_0, then each edge point plots to a curve in ρ, θ space. However, all these curves must intersect at the point (ρ_0, θ_0), since this is a line they all have in common (Figure 18–18c).

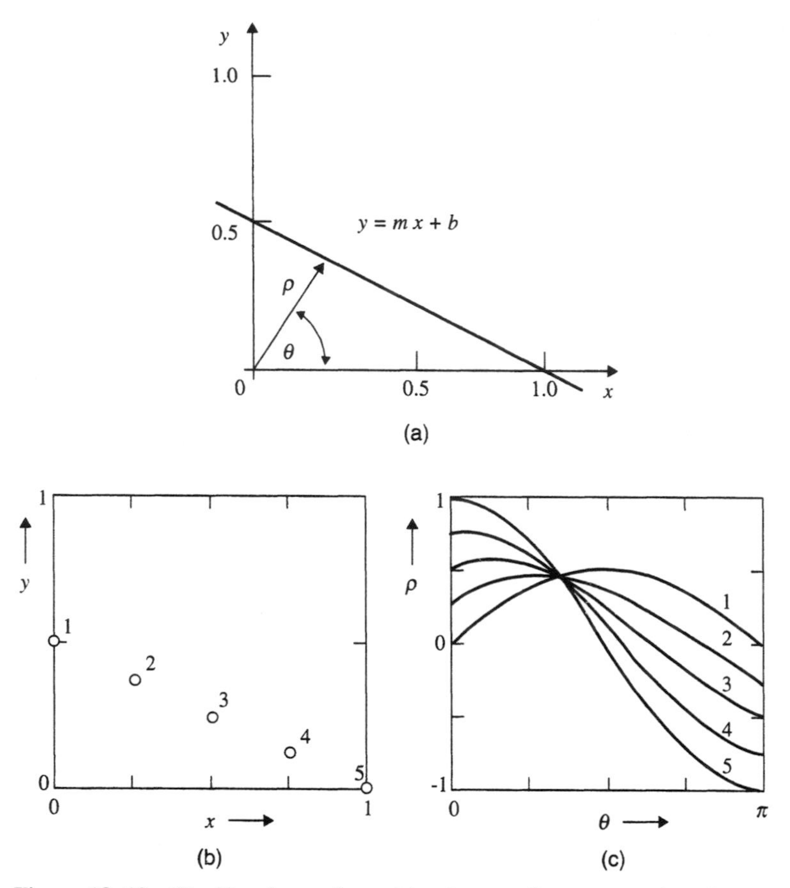

Figure 18–18 The Hough transform: (a) polar coordinate expression of a straight line; (b) x, y plane; (c) ρ, θ plane

Thus, to find the straight-line segment that the points fall upon, we can set up a two-dimensional histogram in ρ, θ space. For each edge point, (x_i, y_i), we increment all the histogram bins in ρ, θ space that correspond to the Hough transform (sinusoidal curve) for that point. When we have done this for all the edge points, the bin containing (ρ_0, θ_0) will be a local maximum. Thus, we search the ρ, θ space histogram for local maxima and obtain the parameters of linear boundary segments.

18.6 REGION GROWING

Region growing [24–27] is an approach to image segmentation that has received considerable attention in the computer vision segment of the artificial intelligence community. With this approach, one begins by dividing an image into many tiny regions. These initial regions may be small neighborhoods or even single pixels. In each region, suitably defined properties that reflect membership in an object are computed. The properties that distinguish the pixels inside the different objects might include average gray level, texture, or color information. Thus, the first step assigns to each region a set of parameters whose values reflect the object to which they belong.

Next, all boundaries between adjacent regions are examined. A measure of boundary strength is computed utilizing the differences of the averaged properties of the adjacent regions. A given boundary is *strong* if the properties differ significantly on either side of that boundary, and it is *weak* if they do not. Strong boundaries are allowed to stand, while weak boundaries are dissolved and the adjacent regions merged.

The process is iterated by alternately recomputing the object membership properties for the enlarged regions and then dissolving weak boundaries. The region-merging process is continued until a point is reached where no boundaries are weak enough to be dissolved. Then, image segmentation is complete. Monitoring this procedure gives one the impression of regions in the interior of objects growing until their boundaries correspond with the edges of the object.

Region-growing algorithms are computationally more expensive than the simpler techniques, but region growing is able to utilize several image properties directly and simultaneously in determining the final boundary location. Perhaps it shows greatest promise in the segmentation of natural scenes, where strong a priori knowledge is not available.

Figure 18–19 shows four stages in the region growing of one muscle fiber viewed on a microscope slide. In this example, low gradient was the sole region membership property. The lower right quadrant shows the final boundary.

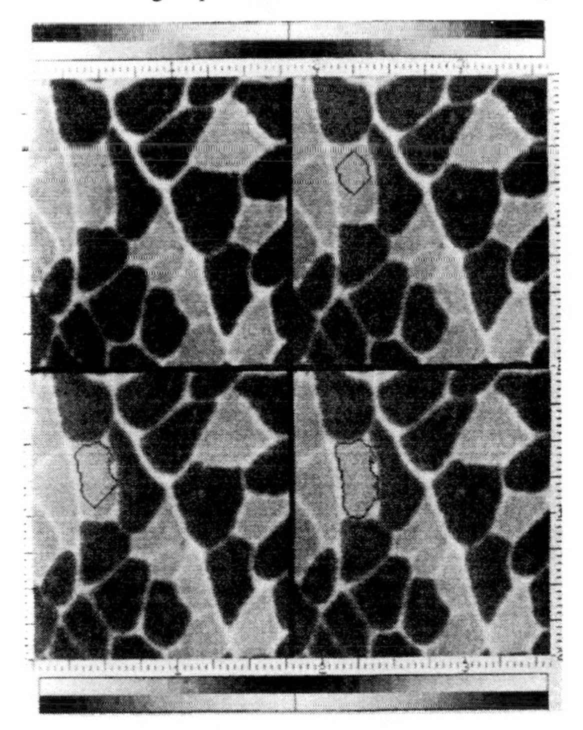

Figure 18–19 Region growing example

18.7 BINARY IMAGE PROCESSING

Binary images—those having only two gray levels—constitute an important subset of digital images. A binary image (e.g., a silhouette or an outline) normally results from an image segmentation operation. If the initial segmentation is not completely satisfactory, some form of processing done on the binary image can often improve the situation.

Recall that there are two rules of connectivity (four-connectivity and eight-connectivity), and one must use one or the other (Sec. 18.2). The four-connectivity approach acknowledges only vertically or horizontally adjacent pixels as neighbors, while eight-connectivity recognizes the eight nearest pixels as neighbors. For many applications, it is more productive to use eight-connectivity.

Many of the processes discussed in this section can be implemented as three-by-three neighborhood operations. In a binary image, any pixel, together with its eight neighbors, represents nine bits of information. Thus, there are only $2^9 = 512$ possible configurations for a three-by-three neighborhood in a binary image.

Convolution of a binary image with the three-by-three kernel in Figure 18–20 generates a nine-bit (512-gray-level) image in which the gray level of each pixel specifies the configuration of the three-by-three binary neighborhood centered on that point. Neighborhood operations thus can be implemented with a 512-entry look-up table with one-bit output. Whether the operation is implemented in software or in specially designed hardware, it is often much more efficient to use a look-up table than some other implementation.

16	8	4
32	1	2
64	128	256

Figure 18–20 Binary neighborhood encoding

This approach can be used to implement a logical operation called a *hit-or-miss transformation*. The look-up table is loaded to search for a particular pattern—for example, all nine pixels being black. The output is one or zero, depending on whether the neighborhood matches the mask. If, whenever the pattern is matched (a hit), the central pixel is set to white and the central pixel of all other configurations is left unchanged (a miss), the operation would reduce solid objects to their outlines by eliminating interior points.

18.7.1 Morphological Image Processing

A powerful set of binary image processing operations developed from a set-theoretical approach [28,29] comes under the heading of *mathematical morphology* [30–35]. Although the basic operations are simple, they and their variants can be concatenated to produce much more complex effects [36,37]. Furthermore, they are amenable to a look-up table implementation in relatively simple hardware for fast *pipeline processing* [38–40]. While commonly used on binary images, this approach can be extended to gray-scale images as well [34,41].

In the general case, morphological image processing operates by passing a *structuring element* over the image in an activity similar to convolution (Figure 18–21). Like the convolution kernel, the structuring element can be of any size, and it can contain any complement of 1's and 0's. At each pixel position, a specified logical operation is performed between the structuring element and the underlying binary image. The binary result of that logical operation is stored in the output image at that pixel position. The effect created depends upon the size and content of the structuring element and upon the nature of the logical operation.

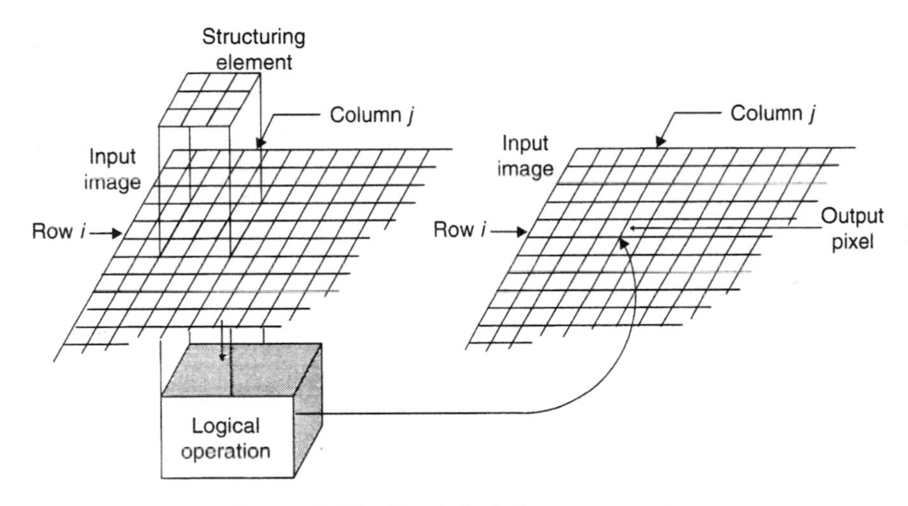

Figure 18–21 Morphological image processing

For this introduction to the subject, we concentrate on the simplest case, namely, the use of a basic three-by-three structuring element containing all 1's. With this restriction, it is the logical operation that determines the outcome.

18.7.1.1 Set Theory Nomenclature

In the language of morphological processing, both the binary image, **B**, and the structuring element, **S**, are sets defined on a two-dimensional Cartesian grid, where the 1's are the elements of those sets. For a summary of set theory definitions and results, see Appendix 3.

We denote by $\mathbf{S}_{xy}$ the structuring element after it has been translated so that its origin is located at the point (x, y). The output of a morphological operation is another set, and the operation can be specified by a set-theoretical equation.

18.7.2 Erosion and Dilation

The basic morphological operations are erosion and dilation, shown in Figure 18–22. By definition, a boundary point is a pixel that is located inside an object, but that has at least one neighbor outside the object.

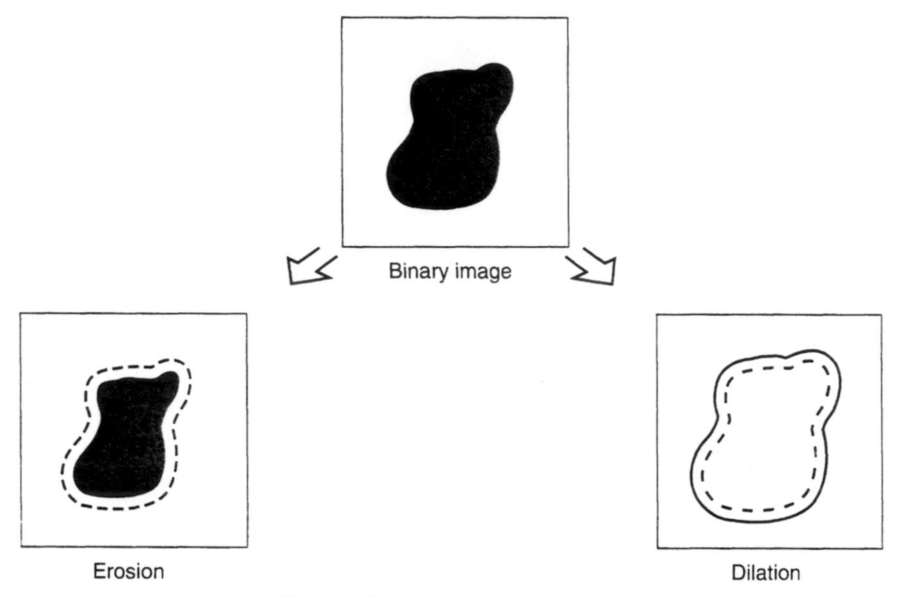

Figure 18–22 Erosion and dilation

18.7.2.1 Erosion

Simple erosion is the process of eliminating all the boundary points from an object, leaving the object smaller in area by one pixel all around its perimeter. If the object is circular, its diameter decreases by two pixels with each erosion. If it narrows to less than three pixels thick at any point, it will become disconnected (into two objects) at that point. Objects no more than two pixels thick in any direction are eliminated. Erosion is useful for removing from a segmented image objects that are too small to be of interest.

General erosion is defined by

$$\mathbf{E} = \mathbf{B} \otimes \mathbf{S} = \{x, y | \mathbf{S}_{xy} \subseteq \mathbf{B}\} \tag{17}$$

That is, the binary image **E** that results from eroding **B** by **S** is the set of points (x, y) such that if **S** is translated so that its origin is located at (x, y), then it is completely contained within **B**. With the basic three-by-three structuring element, general erosion reduces to simple erosion.

18.7.2.2 Dilation

Simple dilation is the process of incorporating into the object all the background points that touch it, leaving it larger in area by that amount. If the object is circular, its diameter increases by two pixels with each dilation. If two objects are separated by less than three pixels at any point, they will become connected (merged into one object) at that point. Dilation is useful for filling holes in segmented objects.

General dilation is defined by

$$\mathbf{D} = \mathbf{B} \oplus \mathbf{S} = \{x, y | \mathbf{S}_{xy} \cap \mathbf{B} \neq \varnothing\} \tag{18}$$

That is, the binary image **D** that results from dilating **B** by **S** is the set of points (x, y) such that if **S** is translated so that its origin is located at (x, y), then its intersection with **B** is not empty. With the basic three-by-three structuring element, this reduces to simple dilation.

18.7.3 Opening and Closing

Opening. The process of erosion followed by dilation is called *opening*. It has the effect of eliminating small and thin objects, breaking objects at thin points, and generally smoothing the boundaries of larger objects without significantly changing their area. Opening is defined by

$$\mathbf{B} \circ \mathbf{S} = (\mathbf{B} \otimes \mathbf{S}) \oplus \mathbf{S} \tag{19}$$

Closing. The process of dilation followed by erosion is called *closing*. It has the effect of filling small and thin holes in objects, connecting nearby objects, and generally smoothing the boundaries of objects without significantly changing their area. Closing is defined by

$$\mathbf{B} \bullet \mathbf{S} = (\mathbf{B} \oplus \mathbf{S}) \otimes \mathbf{S} \tag{20}$$

Often, when noisy images are segmented by thresholding, the resulting boundaries are quite ragged, the objects have false holes, and the background is peppered with small noise objects. Successive openings or closings can improve the situation markedly. Sometimes several iterations of erosion, followed by the same number of dilations, produces the desired effect.

18.7.4 Variants of Erosion and Dilation

Normally the erosion operation, repeatedly applied, will shrink an object out of existence. Dilation, similarly, will merge all the objects in an image into one. The processes can be altered, however, to produce other results that are more appropriate in some applications.

18.7.4.1 Shrinking

When erosion is implemented in such a way that single-pixel objects are left intact, the process is called *shrinking*. This is useful when the total object count must be preserved.

Shrinking can be used iteratively to develop a size distribution for a binary image containing approximately circular objects. It is run alternately with a three-by-three operator that counts the number of single-pixel objects in the image. With each pass, the radius is reduced by one pixel, and more of the objects shrink to single-pixel size. Recording the count at each iteration gives the cumulative distribution of object size. Highly noncircular objects (e.g., dumbbell-shaped objects) may break up while shrinking, so this technique has its restrictions.

18.7.4.2 Thinning

Erosion can be programmed as a two-step process that will not break objects. The first step is a normal erosion, but it is conditional; that is, pixels are marked as candidates for removal, but are not actually eliminated. In the second pass, those candidates that can be removed without destroying connectivity are eliminated, while those that cannot are retained. Each pass is a three-by-three neighborhood operation that can be implemented as a table-lookup operation [42–45].

Thinning reduces a curvilinear object to a single-pixel-wide line, showing its topology graphically. In Figure 18–23, thinning a group of chromosomes, some of which are touching, produces a graph with one segment for each chromosome. This can be used as the basis for a separation algorithm for objects that are in contact.

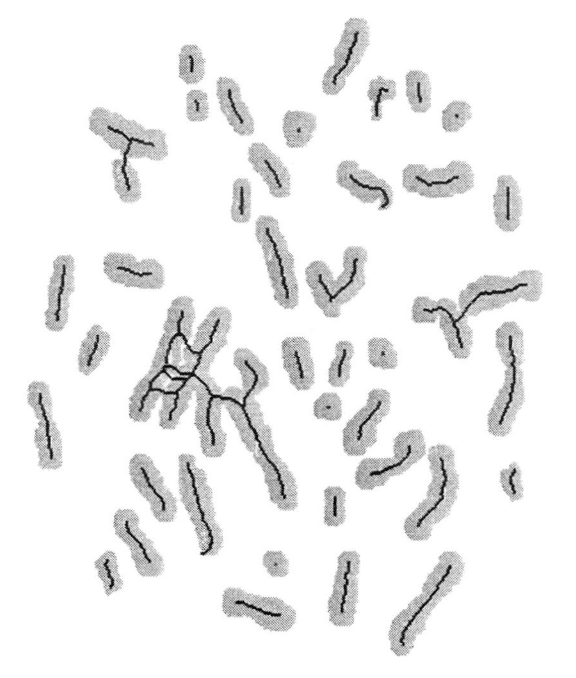

Figure 18–23 Thinning

18.7.4.3 Skeletonization

An operation related to thinning is *skeletonization,* also known as the *medial axis transform* or the *grass-fire technique* [46–50]. The medial axis is the locus of the centers of all the circles that are tangent to the boundary of the object at two or more disjoint points. Skeletonization is seldom implemented, however, by actually fitting circles inside the object.

Conceptually, the medial axis can be thought of as being formed in the following way. Imagine that a patch of grass, in the shape of the object, is set on fire all around the periphery at once. As the fire progresses inward, the locus of points where advancing fire lines meet is the medial axis.

Skeletonization can be implemented with a two-pass conditional erosion, as with thinning. The rule for deleting pixels, however, is slightly different. Figure 18–24 compares thinning with skeletonization. The primary difference is that the medial axis skeleton extends to the boundary at corners, while the skeleton obtained by thinning does not.

18.7.4.4 Pruning

Often, the thinning or skeletonizing process will leave *spurs* on the resulting figure. These are short branches having an endpoint located within three or so pixels of an intersection.

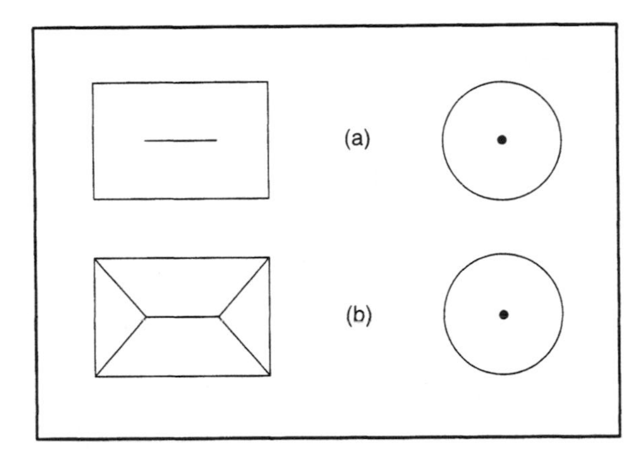

Figure 18–24 Thinning and skeletonization: (a) thinned skeleton; (b) medial axis

Spurs result from single-pixel-sized undulations in the boundary that give rise to a short branch. They can be removed by a series of three-by-three operations that remove endpoints (thereby shortening all the branches), followed by reconstruction of the branches that still exist. A three-pixel spur, for example, disappears after three iterations of removing endpoints. Not having an endpoint to grow back from, the spur is not reconstructed.

18.7.4.5 Thickening

Dilation can be implemented so as not to merge nearby objects. This can be done in two passes, similarly to thinning. An alternative is to complement the image and use the thinning operation on the background. In fact, each of the variants of erosion has a companion dilation-type operation obtained when it is run on a complemented image.

Some segmentation techniques tend to fit rather tight boundaries to objects so as to avoid erroneously merging them. Often, the best boundary for isolating objects is too tight for subsequent measurement. Thickening can correct this by enlarging the boundaries without merging separate objects.

18.7.4.6 An example

Figure 18–25 illustrates how morphological operations can be concatenated to implement a complex process. Here an image of a printed circuit board is analyzed to locate a break point in the traces.

18.7.5 The Distance Transformation

Another related operation that can be performed on binary images is the distance transformation. It results, however, not in another binary image, but in a gray-level image. The gray level at each pixel is the distance from that pixel to the nearest background pixel.

An approximate distance transformation can be computed by an erosion-like operation wherein, on each pass, pixels are labeled with the iteration number rather than being eliminated from the object. The so-called *chamfer algorithm* computes a distance transformation in only two passes over the image [51,52].

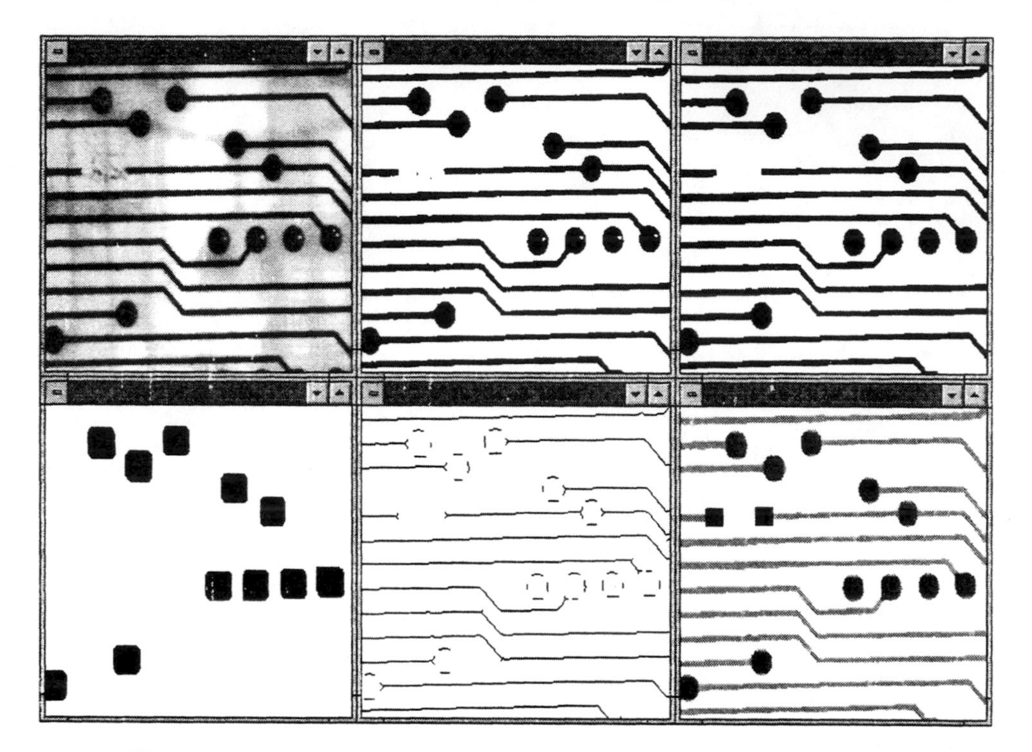

Figure 18–25 Morphological analysis of a printed circuit board image: (a) grayscale image; (b) thresholded image; (c) cleanup by opening; (d) isolation of pads by erosion and dilation; (e) isolation of traces by skeletonization; (f) final display of traces, pads and break points (Courtesy Luc Nocente, Noesis Vision)

Figure 18–26 illustrates the concept of the two-pass distance transformation in one dimension. Figure 18–26(a) is a one-dimensional binary image containing an object denoted by 1's on a background of 0's. Figure 18–26(b) is the result of the first (forward) pass, which is conducted from left to right. At each pixel, background points are left as zeros, but interior points are replaced with a count of how many steps have been taken since the last zero was encountered. In Figure 18–26(c), we see the result of the second (backward) pass, which is conducted from right to left. In this pass, each pixel is replaced with the minimum of (a) what it was or (b) the number of steps taken since a zero was last encountered. The result is an image in which gray level reflects distance to the nearest boundary.

In the two-dimensional distance transformation, a mask resembling a convolution kernel (see Figure 18–27) is passed over the image in a process reminiscent of the convolution operation. (Recall Sec. 9.3.4.) As with the one-dimensional distance transformation,

0	0	0	0	1	1	1	1	1	0	0	0	0	(a)

0	0	0	0	1	2	3	4	5	0	0	0	0	(b)

0	0	0	0	1	2	3	2	1	0	0	0	0	(c)

Figure 18–26 One-dimensional distance transformation: (a) binary image; (b) result of first (L→R) pass; (c) result of second (R→L) pass

there are two passes. The forward pass moves from left to right, working down the image from the top, while the backward pass moves from right to left, working up the image from the bottom. At each position, a set of two-term sums is formed by adding each element in the mask to the underlying pixel value. Where the mask is blank, nothing is done. The pixel under the center of the mask is replaced by the minimum of the sums.

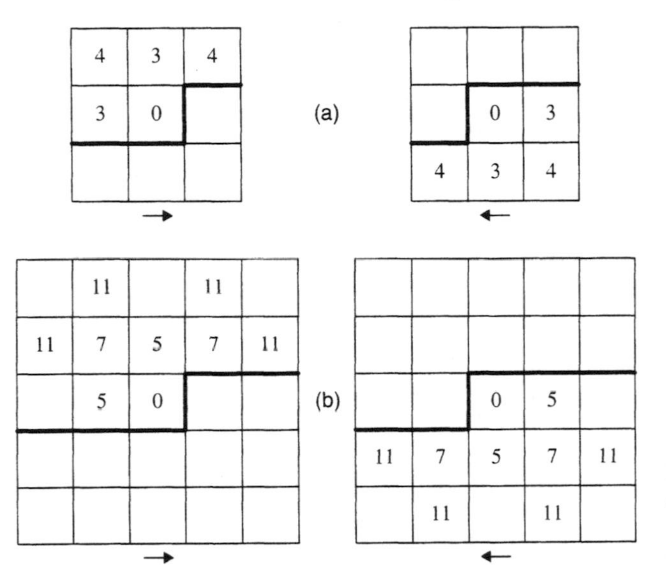

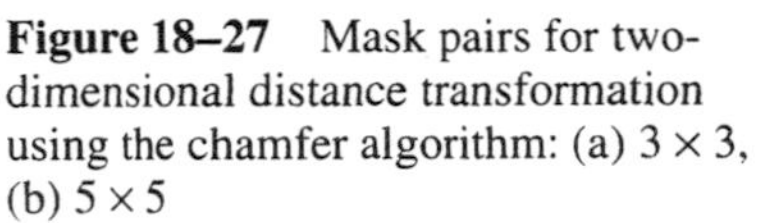

Figure 18–27 Mask pairs for two-dimensional distance transformation using the chamfer algorithm: (a) 3×3, (b) 5×5

The three-by-three masks in Figure 18–27 yield a distance image in which the gray levels are three times the Euclidian distance to the boundary. The maximum deviation from true Euclidian distance is 8 percent. The five-by-five masks yield a distance image that is scaled up by a factor of five, and their maximum error is only 2 percent [52].

The distance transform is useful, for example, in segmenting clusters of objects that are in contact. Each object in the cluster produces a local maximum (located roughly at its center) in the distance image. The watershed algorithm (decreasing from an initially high threshold) can then segment the distance image into the individual component objects, as shown in Figure 18–28. Using the watershed algorithm on the distance transformed image (Figure 18–28(b)) effectively breaks apart circular objects that are touching (Figure 18–28(c)).

18.7.6 Boundary Curvature Analysis

The curvature at a point on a curve is defined as the rate of change of the tangent angle at that point, as one traverses the curve. The curvature of an object's boundary is positive in regions where the object is convex and negative where it is concave.

In Figure 18–29, for example, a plot of the curvature of the boundary shown reveals two sharp negative peaks corresponding to the two concavities. If the objects are expected to be convex, this signals a segmentation error. A cutting line, drawn between the two points a and b, separates the two objects. Thus, the boundary curvature function can assist in the automatic detection and correction of segmentation errors.

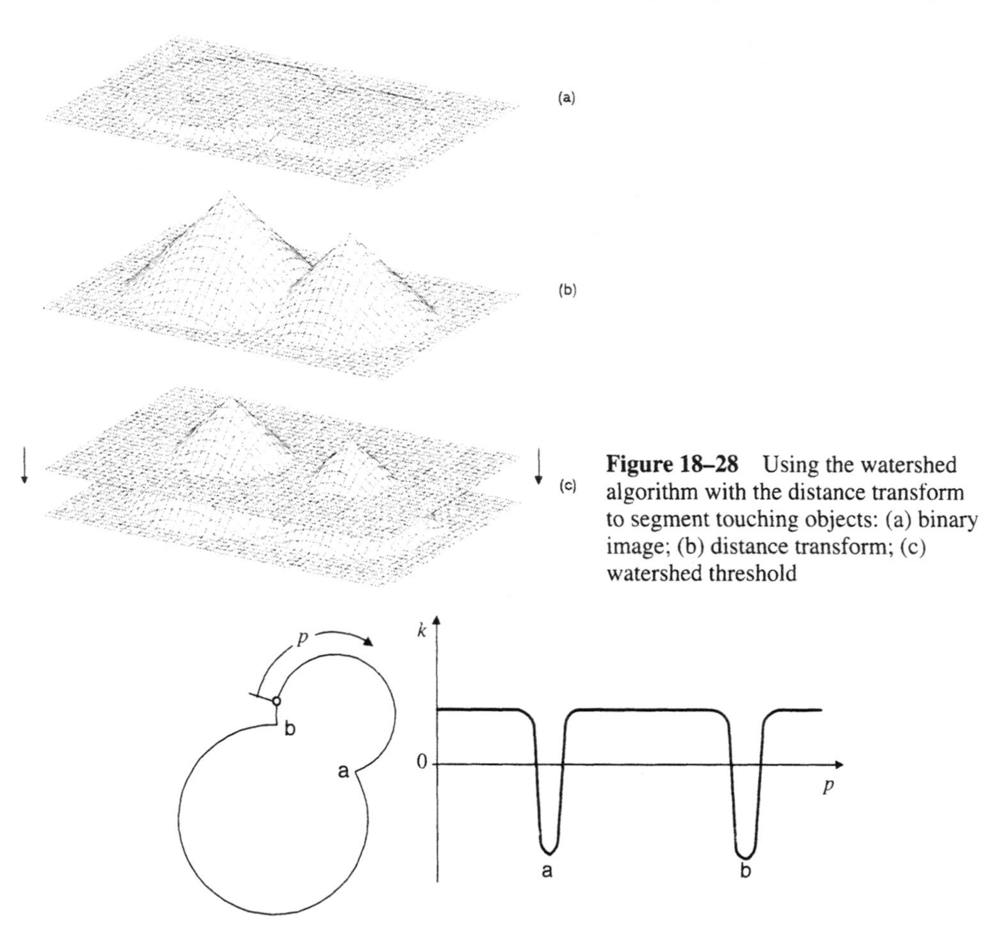

Figure 18–28 Using the watershed algorithm with the distance transform to segment touching objects: (a) binary image; (b) distance transform; (c) watershed threshold

Figure 18–29 The boundary curvature function

18.8 SEGMENTED IMAGE STRUCTURE

If only gross measurements of each object are required, it is not necessary to extract the objects from the original image. In other cases, we may wish to compose a new image showing the objects somehow rearranged, or we may wish to display each object in its own image. We may also wish to perform further measurement or other processing on the individual objects, one at a time. In these cases, it may be worthwhile to extract and store the individual objects in a more convenient format.

In general, each object should be assigned a sequence number as it is found. This object number can be used to identify and track the individual objects in the scene. In this section, we discuss three ways to structure the segmented image.

18.8.1 The Object Membership Map

One way to store segmentation information is to generate a separate image, the same size as the original, and encode object membership on a pixel-by-pixel basis. In the *object membership map,* the gray level of each pixel encodes the sequence number of the object to which the corresponding pixel in the original image belongs. For example, all pixels belonging to object 27 in the image will have a gray level of 27 in the membership map.

The membership map technique is perfectly general, but it is not a particularly compact way to store segmentation information. It requires an additional full-size digital image to describe a scene containing even one small object. It is, however, the type of image that will compress quite significantly, since it normally will contain large areas of constant "gray level."

If only the size and shape of objects are of interest, the original image may be discarded after segmentation. Further data reduction results if there is only one object or if the objects need not be differentiated. In either case, the membership map becomes a binary image.

The data requirements of image segmentation sometimes dictate that the process be done in several passes over the image. A binary or multilevel membership map is often useful as an intermediate step in a multiple-pass image segmentation procedure.

18.8.2 The Boundary Chain Code

A more compact format for storing the image segmentation information is the *boundary chain code* [49,53–55]. Since it is the boundary that defines an object, it is not necessary to store the location of interior points. Furthermore, the boundary chain code exploits the fact that boundaries are connected paths.

The chain code starts by specifying the (x, y)-coordinates of an arbitrarily selected starting point on the boundary of the object. The identified pixel has eight neighbors, and at least one of these must also be a boundary point. The boundary chain code specifies the direction in which a step must be taken to go from the present boundary point to the next one.

Since there are eight possible directions, they can be numbered, say, from 0 through 7. Figure 18–30 shows one conceivable assignment of the eight direction codes. The boundary chain code then consists of the coordinates of the starting point, followed by the sequence of direction codes that specify the path around the boundary.

With the boundary chain code, storing the segmentation of an object requires only one (x, y)-coordinate and then three bits for each boundary point. This is considerably less storage space than that required for the object membership map. When a complex scene is segmented, the program can store each object boundary as a single record consisting of the object number, the perimeter (number of boundary points), and the chain code. In addition, there are several size and shape features that can be extracted directly from the boundary chain code, as is shown in the next chapter.

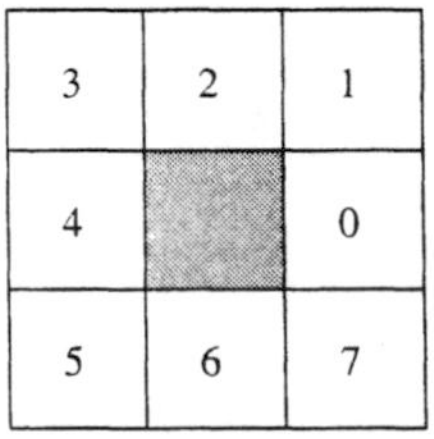

3	2	1
4		0
5	6	7

Figure 18–30 The boundary direction code

Generation of the boundary chain code usually requires random access to the input image, since the boundary must be tracked through the image. With boundary-tracking techniques of image segmentation, generation of the chain code is a natural adjunct. With boundary location by thresholding, the chain code usually must be generated in a subsequent step. Generation of the boundary chain code does not fit quite as well into line-by-line processing of images stored on disk. Since interior points are discarded, the chain code is less useful when further processing of the individual object images is required.

18.8.3 Line Segment Encoding

Line segment encoding is a line-by-line technique for storing extracted objects. The process is best illustrated by the example shown in Figure 18–31. Suppose we wish to segment an image using a gray-level threshold T. The program examines the image, line by line, working down from the top, looking for pixels having gray level greater than or equal to T.

In the figure, the segment labeled 1–1 is a sequence of three adjacent pixels on line 100 having gray level at or above the threshold. Thus, segment 1–1 is the first line segment of the first object (object number 1) that is encountered by the program.

Upon examination of line 101, the program encounters two segments, 1–2 and 2–1, that are above the threshold. Since it is impossible to tell at this time that both segments actually belong to the same object, the program assumes that the second segment on line 101 is part of a second object, which it calls object number 2. Since segment 1–2 underlies segment 1–1, the program assumes that both of these segments are part of object number 1.

The process continues through line 102, but at line 103 only a single segment is found, and it underlies segments of both objects 1 and 2. The program now recognizes that objects 1 and 2 are the same, and segment numbering continues for object 1.

On line 105 the program again finds two segments. Since they both underlie segment 1–5, however, they obviously belong to object 1. On line 107, no segments that underlie

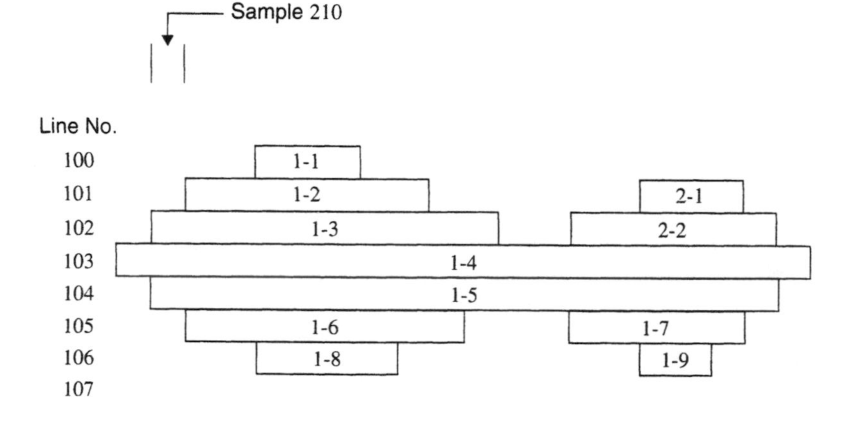

Figure 18–31 Object line segments

segment 1–8 or 1–9 are found, and the isolation of object 1 is complete. In this way, it is the line segments that, taken together, specify the object that has been isolated.

Figure 18–32 shows one way the object segment information can be organized for storage on disk. Each time a new object is located, the program generates a new object file. This file begins with an object label containing the object number and the number of segments in the object. The latter entry must be continually updated until segmentation of the object is complete.

Following the object label, the individual line segments are stored as records. In Figure 18–32, they are stored with a segment label, followed by the gray-level values of the pixels in that segment. The segment label contains the number of the line from which the segment was extracted, the coordinate of the first pixel on the line segment, and the number of pixels in the line segment.

For the object in Figure 18–31, two object segment files would be opened. After only two segments have been stored in object file 2, however, the program discovers that objects 1 and 2 are the same. Accordingly, further construction of object file 2 is discontinued. Either then, or after segmentation is complete for this object, the two object segment files may be merged.

The result of the single-pass line segment encoding technique is a set of segment files, one for each object. If each segment file is stored as a single record on a disk drive, only one revolution of the disk is required to read or write an entire object. An object image can easily be reconstructed in memory simply by unpacking the segment file. This is particularly useful when further processing of object images is desired.

For segmenting large images, the input image is read, line by line, from disk, and object segment files are assembled in memory. As soon as an object file is completed, its label is finalized, and that file is written to disk as one record. An advantage of this method is that the object's area, perimeter, IOD, and horizontal and vertical extent measurements are easily built into the object extraction step. In this way, several important object features are known by the time the segmentation step is complete.

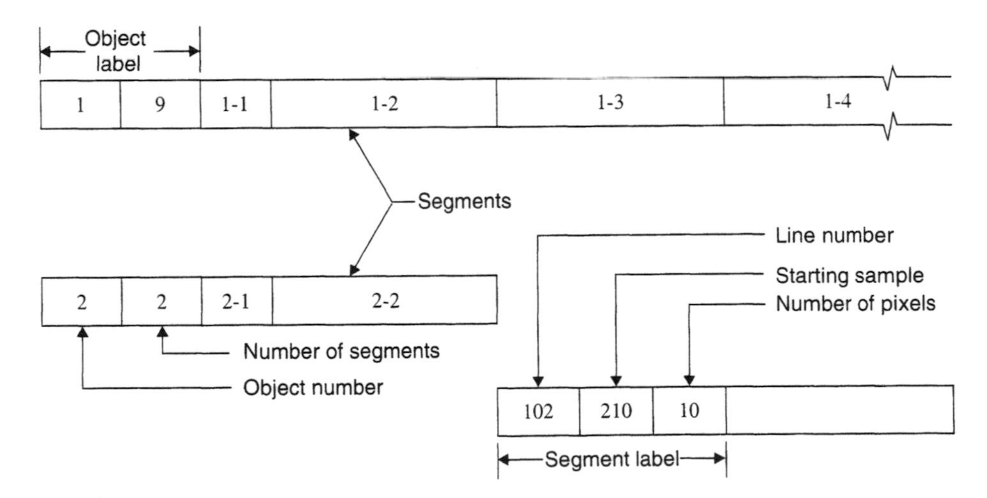

Figure 18–32 The object segment file

18.9 SUMMARY OF IMPORTANT POINTS

1. Image segmentation is the process of partitioning a digital image into disjoint, connected sets of pixels, one of which corresponds to the background and the remainder to the objects in the image.
2. Image segmentation can be approached as the process of either assigning pixels to objects or finding boundaries between objects (or between objects and the background).
3. Gray-level thresholding is a simple segmentation technique that always produces closed, connected boundaries.
4. Background flattening and noise removal processes, conducted prior to segmentation, can often improve performance during segmentation.
5. Unless background gray level and object contrast are relatively constant, it is often necessary to allow the threshold gray level to vary within the image.
6. For images of simple objects on a contrasting background, placing the threshold at the dip of the bimodal histogram minimizes the sensitivity of the measured area to threshold variations.
7. The profile function of a concentric circular spot may be derived from the histogram or the perimeter function of its image.
8. The average gradient around a contour line can be computed from the perimeter function and the histogram [Eq. (12)].
9. Object segmentation can be implemented by tracking the boundaries in, or by thresholding, the gradient image.
10. Region-growing techniques are useful for segmenting complex scenes using complex object definitions.
11. The segmentation of an image may be stored as a membership map, as a boundary chain code, or by line segment encoding.

PROBLEMS

1. Below is the histogram of a 20-gray-level image (zero is black) of one white billiard ball on a dark background. The ball is made of a material that weighs 1.5 grams per cm^3. The pixel spacing is 1 mm. How much does the ball weigh? (*Hint:* Plot the area-derived profile first.)

   [0 100 500 3,000 9,000 3,000 500 200 100 200 300 500 627 500 300 200 100 0 0 0]

2. Below is the histogram of a 20-gray-level image containing one fruit on a contrasting background. The pixel spacing is 2 mm. Is the fruit a cherry, a grapefruit, or a pumpkin?

   [0 100 200 300 500 600 500 300 200 100 200 500 3,000 8,000 20,000 8,000 3,000 500 100 0]

3. Below is the histogram of a 32-gray-level image (zero is black) containing one 12-inch-diameter black phonograph record with a white label, lying on a gray background. What is the pixel spacing? What is the diameter of the label?

   [0 0 0 0 100 200 2,000 6,000 2,000 200 100 0 0 200 3,000 9,000 3,000 200 0 0 50 100 400 100 50 0 0 0 0 0 0 0]

PROJECTS

1. Develop a program that will generate digital images of noisy Gaussian spots on a background of specified gray level. Include the capability to specify the position and x- and y-dimension (standard deviation) of the spot, and the RMS amplitude of the white, uniformly distributed noise. Generate an image of a 200-gray-level-tall, 15-pixel-by-20-pixel spot with 10-gray-level peak-amplitude noise.
2. Develop a program that will generate area- and perimeter-derived profiles for spots such as those described in Project 1, and form the first and second derivatives of those profiles. Define SNR as spot amplitude divided by RMS noise amplitude. For circular spots of radius 5, 10, and 20 pixels, with SNRs of 40, 20, 10, and 5, generate the area-derived profiles and locate the point of maximum slope. Determine empirically, for each size of spot, what is the minimum SNR required to locate the inflection point with no more than a one-pixel error.
3. Develop a program that will fit a two-dimensional Gaussian function to a noisy Gaussian spot on a zero-gray-level background (see Sec. 19.5.5). Use the program to determine the position, size, and amplitude of a noisy spot in an image generated by a program such as that described in Project 1 or obtained by digitizing an image of a round object.
4. Develop an adaptive thresholding program that can set the threshold for each object in a scene using one of the threshold selection techniques described in this chapter, and test the program on an image containing five objects of different contrast on an uneven background. Use either a digitized image or an image generated by a program such as the one described in Project 1.

REFERENCES

1. R. M. Haralick and L. G. Shapiro, "Survey: Image Segmentation," *Comput. Vision, Graphics, Image Proc.*, **29:**100–132, 1985.
2. A. Rosenfield, "Connectivity in Digital Pictures," *Journal of the ACM*, **17:**146–160, 1970.
3. R. J. Wall, *The Gray Level Histogram for Threshold Boundary Determination in Image Processing to the Scene Segmentation Problem in Human Chromosome Analysis*, Ph.D. Thesis, University of California at Los Angeles, 1974.
4. K. Castleman and R. Wall, "Automatic Systems for Chromosome Identification," in T. Caspersson, ed., *Nobel Symposium 23—Chromosome Identification*, Academic Press, New York, 1973.
5. K. Castleman and J. Melnyk, *An Automated System for Chromosome Analysis: Final Report*, Document No. 5040-30, Jet Propulsion Laboratory, Pasadena, CA, July 4, 1976.
6. J. Prewitt and M. Mendelsohn, "The Analysis of Cell Images," *Annals of the N.Y. Academy of Sciences*, 128,1035–1053, 1966.
7. J. Prewitt, "Object Enhancement and Extraction," in B. Lipkin and A., Rosenfeld, eds., *Picture Processing and Psychopictorics*, Academic Press, New York, 1970.
8. R. J. Wall, A. Klinger, and K. R. Castleman, "Analysis of Image Histograms," *Proc. 2nd. Int. Joint Conf. on Pattern Recognition* (IEEE Pub. 74CH-0885-4C), 341–344, Copenhagen, August 1974.
9. J. Weszka, "A Survey of Threshold Selection Techniques," *Computer Graphics and Image Processing*, 7, 259–265, 1978.
10. M. E. Sieracki, S. E. Reichenbach, and K. L. Webb, "Evaluation of Automated Threshold Selection Methods for Accurately Sizing Microscopic Fluorescent Cells by Image Analysis," *Applied and Environmental Microbiology*, **55,**11:2762–2772, November 1989.

11. Y. H. Katz, "Pattern Recognition of Meteorological Satellite Cloud Photography," *Proc. 3rd Symp. Remote Sensing of the Environment* (2d ed.), pp. 173–190, Univ. of Michigan, Ann Arbor, 1964.
12. C. L. Viles and M. E. Sieracki, "Measurement of Marine Picoplankton Cell Size by Using a Cooled, Charge-Coupled Device Camera with Image-Analyzed Fluorescence Microscopy," *Applied and Environmental Microbiology,* **58**(2):584–592, February 1992.
13. D. P. Panda and A. Rosenfeld, "Image Segmentation by Pixel Classification in (Gray level, Edge value) Space," *IEEE Trans. Comput.* **C-27**:875–879, 1978.
14. R. A. Kirsch, "Computer Determination of the Constituent Structure of Biological Images," *Computers in Biomedical Research,* **4,** 315–328, 1971.
15. D. Marr and E. Hildreth, "Theory of Edge Detection," *Proc. R. Soc. London, Ser. B,* **207:**187–217, 1980.
16. D. Marr, *Vision,* Freeman, San Francisco, 1982.
17. L. G. Roberts, "Machine Perception of Three-Dimensional Solids," in J.T. Tippett, ed., *Optical and Electro-Optical Information Processing,* 159–197, MIT Press, Cambridge, MA, 1965 (reprinted in [55]).
18. L. S. Davis, "A Survey of Edge Detection Techniques," *CGIP,* **4:**248–270, 1975.
19. I. E. Abdou and W. K. Pratt, "Quantitative Design and Evaluation of Enhancement/Thresholding Edge Detectors," *Proc. IEEE,* **67**(5):753–763, 1979.
20. G. S. Robinson, "Edge Detection by Compass Gradient Masks," *CGIP,* **6**(5):492–501, 1977.
21. R. Nevatia, "Locating Object Boundaries in Textured Environments," *IEEE Trans. Comp.* **C-25:**1170–1180, 1976.
22. J. M. Lester, H. A. Williams, B. A. Weintraub, and J. F. Brenner, "Two Graph Searching Techniques for Boundary Finding in White Blood Cell Images," *Computers in Biology and Medicine,* **8:**293–308, 1978.
23. R. E. Duda and P. E. Hart, *Pattern Classification and Scene Analysis,* Wiley, New York, 1973.
24. C. R. Brice and C.L. Fennema, "Scene Analysis Using Regions," *Artificial Intelligence,* **1,** 205–226, Fall 1970 (reprinted in [55]).
25. Y. Yakamovsky and J. A. Feldman, "A Semantics-Based Decision Theory Region Analyzer," *Proc. 3rd Int. Joint Conf. on Artificial Intelligence,* 580–588, August 1973 (reprinted in [55]).
26. S. L. Horowitz and T. Pavlidis, "Picture Segmentation by a Directed Split-and-Merge Procedure," *Proc. 2nd Int. Joint Conf. on Pattern Recognition* (IEEE Publ. 74CH-0885-4C), 424–433, August 1974 (reprinted in [55]).
27. S. Zucker, "Region Growing: Childhood and Adolescence," *Computer Graphics and Image Processing,* **5:**382–399, 1976.
28. H. Minkowski, "Volumen und Oberflache," *Math. Ann.,* **57:**447–459, 1903.
29. G. Matheron, *Random Sets and Integral Geometry,* Wiley, New York, 1975.
30. J. Serra, *Image Analysis and Mathematical Morphology, 1,* Academic Press, New York, 1982.
31. J. Serra, "Introduction to Mathematical Morphology," *Computer Vision, Graphics, and Image Processing,* **35**(3):283–305, 1986.
32. J. Serra, ed., *Image Analysis and Mathematical Morphology, 2,* Academic Press, New York, 1988.
33. C. R. Giardina and E. R. Dougherty, *Morphological Methods in Image and Signal Processing,* Prentice-Hall, Englewood Cliffs, NJ, 1988.
34. F. Meyer and S. Beucher, "Morphological Segmentation," *J. Visual Comm. and Image Representation,* **1**(1):21–46, 1990.

35. E. R. Dougherty, *An Introduction to Morphological Image Processing*, SPIE Press, Bellingham, WA, 1992.

36. R. M. Haralick, S. R. Sternberg, and X. Zhuang, "Image Analysis Using Mathematical Morphology," *IEEE Trans.*, **PAMI-9**(4):532–550, 1987.

37. P. Maragos, "Tutorial on Advances in Morphological Image Processing and Analysis," *Optical Engineering*, **26**(7):623–632, 1987.

38. S. R. Sternberg, "Parallel Architectures for Image Processing," *Proc. 3rd International IEEE Compsac*, Chicago, 1981.

39. S. R. Sternberg, "Biomedical Image Processing," *IEEE Computer*, 22–34, 1983.

40. R. M. Lougheed and D. L. McCubbrey, "The Cytocomputer: A Practical Pipelined Image Processor," *Proc. 7th Annual International Symposium on Computer Architecture*, 1980.

41. S. R. Sternberg, "Grayscale Morphology," *Computer Vision, Graphics, and Image Processing*, **35**(3):333–355, 1986.

42. A. Rosenfeld, "A Characterization of Parallel Thinning Algorithms," *Information and Control*, **29:**286–291, 1975.

43. T. Pavlidis, "A Thinning Algorithm for Discrete Binary Images," *Computer Graphics and Image Processing*, **13**(2):142–157, 1980.

44. W. K. Pratt and I. Kabir, "Morphological Binary Image Processing with a Local Neighborhood Pipeline Processor," *Computer Graphics*, Tokyo, 1984.

45. W. K. Pratt, *Digital Image Processing* (2d ed.), John Wiley & Sons, New York, 1991.

46. H. Blum, "A Transformation for Extracting New Descriptors of Shape," *Symposium Models for the Perception of Speech and Visual Form*, W. Wathen-Dunn, ed., MIT Press, Cambridge, MA, 1967.

47. J. C. Mott-Smith, "Medial Axis Transforms," *Picture Processing and Psychopictorics*, B. S. Lipkin and A. Rosenfeld, eds., Academic Press, New York, 1970.

48. C. Arcelli and G. Sanniti Di Baja, "On the Sequential Approach to Medial Line Thinning Transformation," *IEEE Trans. Systems, Man, and Cybernetics*, **SMC-8**(2):139–144, 1978.

49. H. Freeman, "On the Encoding of Arbitrary Geometric Configurations," *IRE Transactions on Electronic Computers*, **EC-10,** 260–268, June 1961 (reprinted in [55]).

50. H. Blum, "Biological Science and Visual Shape (Part I)," *J. Theor. Biol.*, **38:**205–287, 1973.

51. G. Borgefors, "Distance Transformations in Arbitrary Dimensions," *Comput. Vis., Graphics and Im. Proc.*, **27:**321–345, 1984.

52. G. Borgefors, "Distance Transformations in Digital Images," *Comput. Vis., Graphics and Im. Proc.*, **34:**344–371, 1986.

53. H. Freeman, "A Review of Relevant Problems in the Processing of Line-Drawing Data," in A. Grasselli, ed., *Automatic Interpretation and Classification of Images*, Academic Press, New York, 1969.

54. H. Freeman, "Boundary Encoding and Processing," in B. Lipkin and A. Rosenfeld, eds., *Picture Processing and Psychopictorics*, Academic Press, New York, 1970.

55. J. K. Aggarwal, R. O. Duda, and A. Rosenfeld, eds., *Computer Methods in Image Analysis*, IEEE Press, New York, 1977 (also available from John Wiley & Sons, New York).

CHAPTER 19

Pattern Recognition: Object Measurement

19.1 INTRODUCTION

In Chapter 18, we introduced pattern recognition and discussed the isolation and extraction of objects from a complex scene. In this chapter, we address the problem of measuring the objects, so that they can be identified by their measurements. Much has been written on this subject, and we can only introduce the basic concepts here. For a more detailed treatment, the reader should consult the literature on image analysis. (See Appendix 2.)

19.2 SIZE MEASUREMENTS

In this section, we consider several commonly used features that reflect the size of an object. These features have come into common usage because they are important in a variety of pattern recognition problems and they lend themselves well to digital image analysis.

It is convenient first to compute spatial measures in terms of pixels and photometric measures in terms of gray levels. Later, length and area measurements can be calibrated by multiplying them by the pixel spacing or the area of a pixel, as appropriate. The photometric calibration curve for the digitizer affords a means of converting gray levels to photometric units. Often, this is a simple linear equation. Any point operations (Chapter 6) that have been performed on the image must be accounted for in the photometric calibration as well.

19.2.1 Area and Perimeter

The area of an object is a convenient measure of the object's overall size. Dependent only on the boundary of the object, a measurement of area disregards gray-level variations inside. The perimeter of an object is particularly useful for discriminating between objects with simple and complex shapes. A simply shaped object uses less perimeter to enclose its area. Area and perimeter measurements are easily computed during the extraction of an object from a segmented image.

Boundary Definition. Before we can specify an algorithm for measuring the area or perimeter of an object, we must establish a definition regarding the boundary of the object. In particular, we must ensure that we are not measuring the perimeter of one polygon and the area of another. The question that must be resolved is, Are the boundary pixels completely or only partially contained in the object? In other words, does the actual boundary of the object pass through the centers of the boundary pixels or around their outside edges?

Pixel Count Area. The simplest (uncalibrated) area measurement is just a count of the number of pixels inside (and including) the boundary. The perimeter that corresponds to this definition is then the distance around the outside of all the pixels. Normally, measuring this distance involves a large number of 90° turns, thus producing an exaggerated value for the perimeter.

Perimeter of a Polygon. Perhaps a more satisfying approach to measuring an object's perimeter is to establish that the boundary of the object is the polygon having a vertex at the center of each boundary pixel. The perimeter, then, is a sum of lateral ($\Delta p = 1$) and diagonal ($\Delta p = \sqrt{2}$) steps. This sum can be accumulated either while the object is being extracted by line segment encoding (Sec. 18.8.3) or in one pass around the boundary while building a chain code (Sec. 18.8.2). The perimeter of an object is

$$p = N_e + \sqrt{2}N_o \tag{1}$$

where N_e is the number of even and N_o is the number of odd steps in the boundary chain code when the convention of Figure 18-30 is used. The perimeter is also simple to compute from the object segment file by summing the center-to-center distances between adjacent pixels on the boundary.

Area of the Polygon. The area of the polygon defined by pixel centers is the pixel count minus one more than half the number of boundary pixels; that is,

$$A = N_o - \left[\frac{N_b}{2} + 1\right] \tag{2}$$

where N_o and N_b are the numbers of pixels in the object (including boundary pixels) and in the boundary, respectively. This correction of the pixel-count area acknowledges that, on the average, a boundary pixel is half inside and half outside the object. Furthermore, when a closed curve is traversed, an additional pixel's worth of area falls outside, due to the net convexity of the object. Alternatively, one can correct the pixel-count-derived area measurement approximately by subtracting half the perimeter.

19.2.1.1 Computing Area and Perimeter

There is a computationally simple way to compute both the area and perimeter of a polygon in one traversal of the boundary of the polygon. Figure 19–1 illustrates the fact that the area of a polygon is the sum of the areas of all the triangles formed by lines connecting the vertices to an arbitrary point (x_0, y_0). Without loss of generality, we can let that point be the origin of the coordinate system of the image.

Figure 19–2 assists us in developing an equation for the area of a triangle having one vertex at the origin. The horizontal and vertical lines divide the region into rectangles, some of which have sides of the triangle as their diagonals. Thus, half the area of each such rectangle falls outside the triangle. By inspection of the figure, we can write

$$dA = x_2y_1 - \frac{1}{2}x_1y_1 - \frac{1}{2}x_2y_2 - \frac{1}{2}(x_2 - x_1)(y_1 - y_2) \quad (3)$$

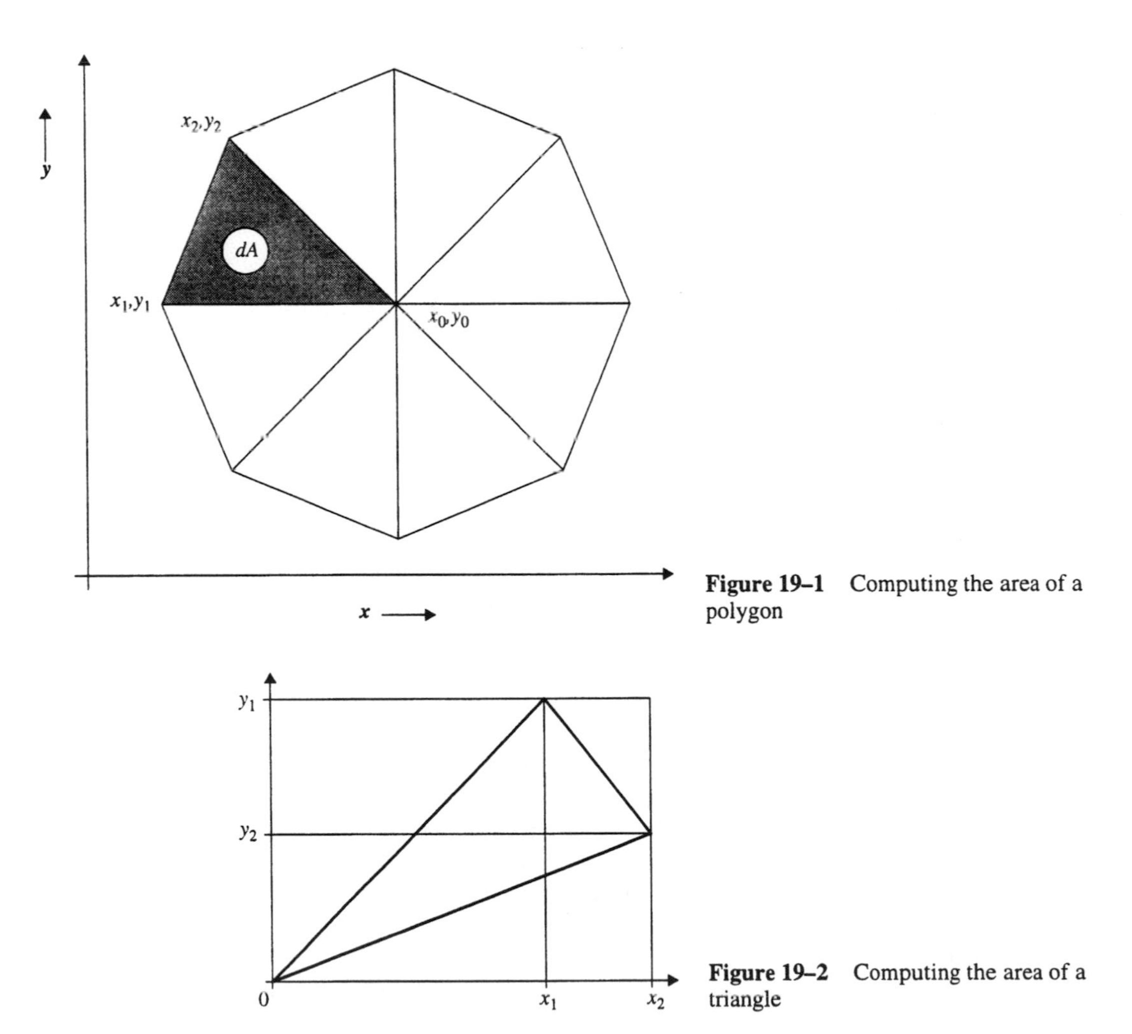

Figure 19–1 Computing the area of a polygon

Figure 19–2 Computing the area of a triangle

Expanding and collecting terms simplifies this expression to

$$dA = \frac{1}{2}(x_1 y_2 - x_2 y_1) \tag{4}$$

and the total area becomes

$$A = \frac{1}{2}\sum_{i=1}^{N_b} [x_i y_{i+1} - x_{i+1} y_i] \tag{5}$$

where N_b is the number of boundary points.

Notice that, if the origin lies outside the object, any particular triangle includes some area that is not inside the polygon. Notice also that the area of a particular triangle can be either positive or negative, depending on the direction in which the boundary is being traversed. By the time a complete circuit around the boundary is made, all the area that falls outside the object has been subtracted out.

A simpler approach yielding the same result makes use of Green's theorem. This result from integral calculus says that the area enclosed by a closed curve in the x, y-plane is given by the contour integral

$$A = \frac{1}{2}\oint (x dy - y dx) \tag{6}$$

where the integration is carried out around the closed curve. For discrete segments, Eq. (6) becomes,

$$A = \frac{1}{2}\sum_{i=1}^{N_b} [x_i(y_{i+1} - y_i) - y_i(x_{i+1} - x_i)] \tag{7}$$

which can be put into the form of Eq. (5).

The corresponding perimeter is the sum of lengths of the sides of the polygon. If all of the boundary points of the polygon are used as vertices, this will be a sum of all the lateral and diagonal measurements, as before.

19.2.1.2 Boundary Smoothing

Often, the perimeter measurement is artificially high because of noise in the image and because the boundary points are restricted to a rectangular sampling grid. Boundary smoothing with binary image processing (Sec. 18.7) can reduce the noise, but cannot alleviate the rectilinear sampling.

Further boundary smoothing, however, can be built into the measurement of area and perimeter by using only a subset of the boundary pixels as vertices. Particularly in areas of low curvature, one can simply skip boundary pixels. Too much of this, however, can obscure the true shape of the object and reduce the accuracy of the measurement.

Boundary smoothing can also be effected by representing the boundary in parametric form. If the object is sufficiently convex, the boundary can be expressed in polar coordinates about some point inside the object (Figure 19–3(a)). In this case, the boundary is specified by a function of the form $\rho(\theta)$. The only requirement is that ρ must be single valued for any θ.

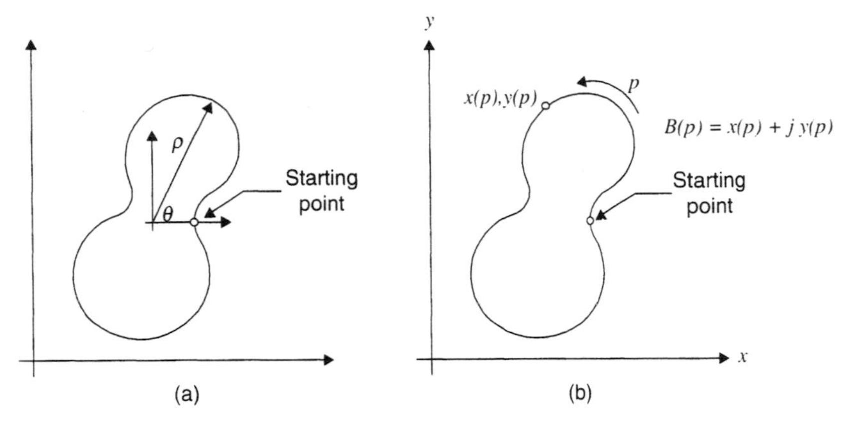

Figure 19–3 Parametric boundary representation: (a) the polar boundary function; (b) the complex boundary function

If the shape is so complex that no such point exists, the boundary can be represented by the more general complex-valued boundary function

$$B(p_i) = x_i + jy_i \tag{8}$$

where p_i is the distance along the boundary from an arbitrary starting point to the ith boundary point and $i = 1, \ldots, N_b$ is the index of boundary points (Figure 19–3(b)).

In either case, the parametric boundary function is periodic. One cycle of it can be lowpass filtered in the frequency domain by (1) a Fourier transform, (2) multiplication by a phaseless (real and even) lowpass transfer function, and (3) an inverse Fourier transform.

Points on the smoothed boundary function are no longer restricted to the sampling grid. All or a subset of such points can be used as vertices in the area and perimeter calculations. Again, one might use boundary vertices selected to be spaced inversely with curvature.

19.2.2 Average and Integrated Density

The IOD is the sum of the gray levels of all pixels in the object. It reflects the "mass" or "weight" of the object and is numerically equal to the area multiplied by the mean interior gray level of the object. Computation of the IOD is covered in Chapter 5. The average density is merely IOD divided by area.

19.2.3 Length and Width

It is easy to compute the horizontal and vertical extent of an object while it is being extracted from an image. One needs only the minimum and maximum row number and column number for this computation. For objects of random orientation, however, horizontal and vertical may not be the directions of interest. In this case, it is necessary to locate the major axis of the object and measure length and width relative to it.

There are several ways to establish the principal axis of an object once the boundary of the object is known. One can compute a best fit straight (or curved) line through the points in the object [1,2]. The principal axis can also be computed from moments, as discussed in the next section. A third way uses the minimum enclosing rectangle (MER) around the object [1].

With the MER technique, the boundary of the object is rotated through 90° in steps of 3° or so. After each incremental rotation, a horizontally oriented MER is fit to the boundary. Computationally, this involves merely keeping track of the minimum and maximum x and y values of the rotated boundary points. At some angle of rotation, the area of the MER goes through a minimum. The dimension of the MER at that point can be taken to be the length and width of the object. The angle at which the MER is minimized gives the principal axis of the object, at least as determined by this method. This technique is particularly useful for rectangular objects, but it gives satisfactory results for more general shapes as well.

19.3 SHAPE ANALYSIS

Frequently, the objects of one class can be distinguished from other objects by their shape. Shape features can be used independently of, or in combination with, size measurements. In this section, we consider some commonly used shape parameters.

19.3.1 Rectangularity

A measurement that reflects the rectangularity of an object is the *rectangle fit factor*

$$R = \frac{A_o}{A_R} \tag{9}$$

where A_o is the object's area and A_R is the area of the object's MER. R represents how well an object fills its MER. It takes on a maximum value of 1.0 for rectangular objects, assumes the value $\pi/4$ for circular objects, and becomes small for slender, curved objects. The rectangle fit factor is bounded between 0 and 1.

Another related shape feature is the *aspect ratio*

$$A = \frac{W}{L} \tag{10}$$

which is the ratio of width to length of the MER. This feature can distinguish slender objects from roughly square or circular objects.

19.3.2 Circularity

A group of shape features are called *circularity measures* because they are minimized by the circular shape. Their magnitude tends to reflect the complexity of the boundary being measured. The most commonly used circularity measure is

$$C = \frac{P^2}{A} \tag{11}$$

the ratio of perimeter squared to area. This feature takes on a minimum value of 4π for a circular shape. More complex shapes yield higher values. The circularity measure C is roughly correlated with the subjective concept of complexity of the boundary.

A related circularity measurement is the *boundary energy* [3]. Suppose an object has perimeter P and we measure distance around the boundary from some starting point with the variable p. At any point, the boundary has an instantaneous radius of curvature $r(p)$. That is the radius of the circle tangent to the boundary at that point (Figure 19–4). The curvature function at point p is

$$K(p) = \frac{1}{r(p)} \tag{12}$$

The function $K(p)$ is periodic with period P. We can compute the average energy per unit length of boundary as

$$E = \frac{1}{P}\int_0^P |K(p)|^2 dp \tag{13}$$

For fixed area, the circle has minimum boundary energy

$$E_0 = \left(\frac{2\pi}{P}\right)^2 = \left(\frac{1}{R}\right)^2 \tag{14}$$

where R is the radius of the circle. Curvature and, hence, boundary energy are easily computed from the chain code [3]. Young has shown that the boundary energy reflects the perceptual concept of boundary complexity better than the circularity measure of Eq. (11) [3].

A third circularity measure makes use of the average distance from an interior point to the boundary object [4]. This distance is

$$\bar{d} = \frac{1}{N}\sum_{i=1}^{N} x_i \tag{15}$$

where x_i is the distance from the ith pixel to the nearest boundary point in an object of N points. The shape measure is

$$g = \frac{A}{\bar{d}^2} = \frac{N^3}{\left(\sum_{i=1}^{N} x_i\right)^2} \tag{16}$$

The sum in the denominator of Eq. (16) is the IOD of the distance-transformed image. The distance transformation was introduced in Sec. 18.7.5. The gray-level value of a pixel in a

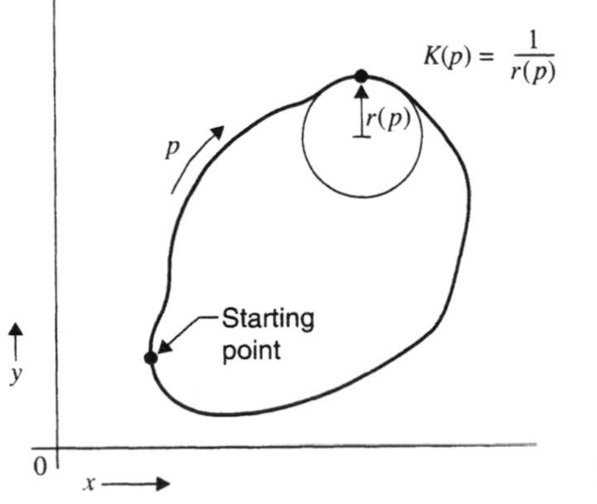

Figure 19–4 Radius of curvature

distance-transformed image reflects the distance of that pixel from the nearest boundary. Figure 19–5 shows a binary image and its distance transform.

For circles and regular polygons, Eq. (16) gives the same value as Eq. (11); however, the discriminatory power of Eq. (16) may be superior for the more complex shapes.

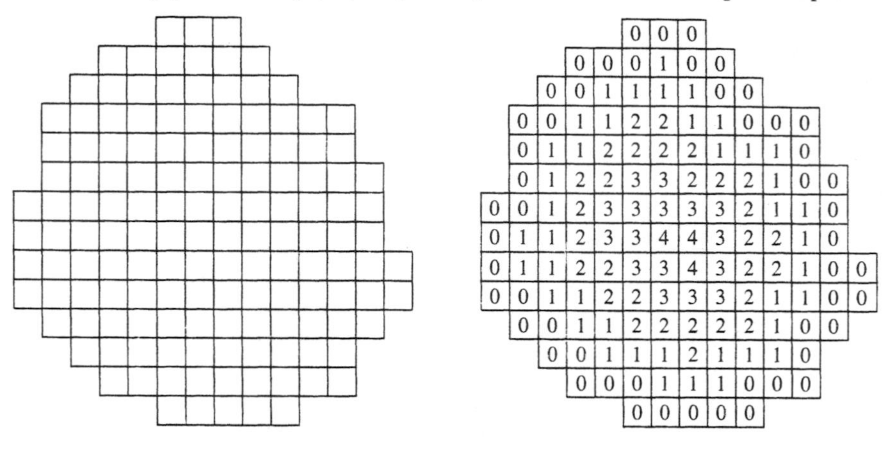

Figure 19–5 The distance transform

19.3.3 Invariant Moments

The moments of a function are commonly used in probability theory [5,6]. However, several desirable properties that can be derived from moments are also applicable to shape analysis.

Definition. The *set of moments* of a bounded function $f(x, y)$ of two variables is defined by

$$M_{jk} = \int_{-\infty}^{\infty}\int_{-\infty}^{\infty} x^j y^k f(x, y)dx\,dy \qquad (17)$$

where j and k take on all nonnegative integer values. The moments of PDFs are widely used in probability theory.

As j and k take on all nonnegative integer values, they generate an infinite set of moments. Furthermore, this set is sufficient to specify the function $f(x, y)$ completely. In other words, the set $\{M_{jk}\}$ is unique for the function $f(x, y)$, and only $f(x, y)$ has that particular set of moments.

For shape-descriptive purposes, suppose $f(x, y)$ takes on the value 1 inside the object and 0 elsewhere. This silhouette function reflects only the shape of the object and ignores internal gray-level detail. Every unique shape corresponds to a unique silhouette and, furthermore, to a unique set of moments.

The parameter $j + k$ is called the *order* of the moment. There is only one zero-order moment,

$$M_{00} = \int_{-\infty}^{\infty}\int_{-\infty}^{\infty} f(x, y)dx\,dy \qquad (18)$$

and it is clearly the area of the object. There are two first-order moments and correspondingly more moments of higher orders. We can make all first- and higher-order moments invariant with respect to the size of the object by dividing them by M_{00}.

19.3.3.1 Central Moments

The coordinates of the center of gravity of an object are

$$\bar{x} = \frac{M_{10}}{M_{00}} \qquad \bar{y} = \frac{M_{01}}{M_{00}} \tag{19}$$

The so-called *central moments* are computed using the center of gravity as the origin:

$$\mu_{jk} = \int_{-\infty}^{\infty}\int_{-\infty}^{\infty} (x-\bar{x})^j (y-\bar{y})^k f(x,y)\,dx\,dy \tag{20}$$

The central moments are position invariant.

19.3.3.2 Principal Axes

The angle of rotation θ that causes the second-order central moment μ_{11} to vanish may be obtained from

$$\tan 2\theta = \frac{2\mu_{11}}{\mu_{20} - \mu_{02}} \tag{21}$$

The coordinate axes x', y' at an angle θ from the x, y axes are called the *principal axes* of the object. The 90° ambiguity in Eq. (21) can be resolved if we specify that

$$\mu_{20} < \mu_{02} \qquad \mu_{30} > 0 \tag{22}$$

If the object is rotated through the angle θ before moments are computed, or if the moments are computed relative to the x', y' axes, then the moments are rotation invariant.

19.3.3.3 Invariant Moments

The area-normalized central moments computed relative to the principal axis are invariant under magnification, translation, and rotation of the object. Only moments of third order and higher are nontrivial after such normalization. The magnitudes of these moments reflect the shape of the object and can be used in pattern recognition. Invariant moments and combinations thereof have been applied to the recognition of the shapes of printed letters [7,8] and to chromosome analysis [9].

While invariant moments definitely have some of the properties that good shape features must have, they may or may not have all of them in any particular instance. The uniqueness of the shape of an object is spread out over an infinite set of moments. Thus, a large set of features may be required to distinguish similar shapes. The resulting high-dimensional classifier may become quite sensitive to noise and to intraclass variations. In some cases, a few relatively low-order moments may reflect the distinguishing shape characteristics of an object. Usually, some experimentation will suggest which, if any, of the invariant moments are both reliable and discriminating shape features.

Gray-Level Images. If we let $f(x, y)$ be the gray-level image of an object, rather than a binary-valued silhouette function, we can compute invariant moments as before. The zero-order moment [Eq. (18)] becomes the integrated optical density, rather than the area. However, the preceding development applies in a similar manner. For gray-level images, the invariant moments reflect not just the shape of the object, but also the density distribution within it. As before, it must be shown, for each object recognition problem, that a reasonably small number of invariant moments can reliably distinguish among the different objects.

19.3.4 Shape Descriptors

Sometimes it is useful to describe the shape of an object in more detail than that offered by a single parameter but more compactly than is reflected in the object image itself. A *shape descriptor* is a compact representation of an object's shape.

19.3.4.1 The Differential Chain Code

One shape descriptor is the boundary chain code discussed in the previous chapter. Figure 19–6 shows a simple object with its boundary chain code and the derivative of the boundary chain code. The *differential chain code* reflects the curvature of the boundary, and convexities and concavities show up as peaks, while the boundary chain code shows the boundary tangent angle as a function of distance around the object. Both functions can be further analyzed to obtain measures of shape.

Polygonal shapes have one sharp convexity per vertex and are thus separable in the differential chain code. For example, a measure of triangularity might be the amplitude of the third harmonic of a Fourier series expansion of the differential chain code. One might

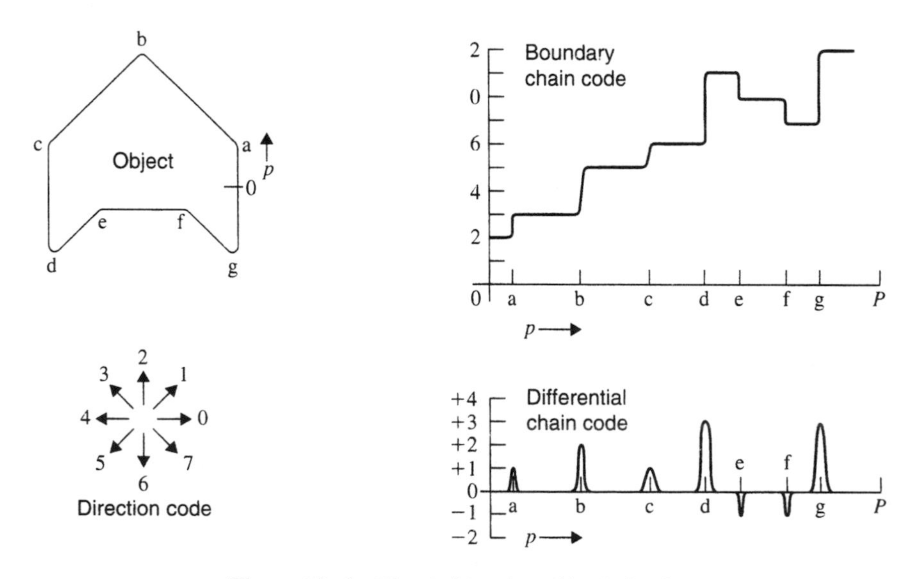

Figure 19–6 The chain code and its derivative

then distinguish between triangles and squares by using the ratio of the third to the fourth harmonic amplitude. Smoothing of the boundary chain code is usually required before differentiation.

19.3.4.2 Fourier Descriptors

We have examined three different periodic functions that completely describe an object's shape: the boundary chain code, the polar boundary function (Figure 19–3(a)), and the complex boundary function (Figure 19–3(b)). Since each of these is periodic, the Fourier transform of one cycle of any of them is an alternative representation of the associated object's shape [10].

Again because it is periodic, each of these boundary functions has a discrete (sampled) spectrum. The strengths of the impulses in the spectrum correspond to the coefficients of the Fourier series expansion of the (periodic) function. In many cases, one can lowpass filter the boundary function spectrum without destroying the characteristic shape of the object. This means that only the amplitudes and phases of the low-frequency impulses in the spectrum (i.e., the low-order Fourier coefficients) are required to characterize the basic shape of the object. These values, then, are candidates for shape descriptors.

19.3.4.3 The Medial Axis Transform

Another data reduction technique that retains shape information is the *medial axis transformation* discussed in the previous chapter [11,12]. A point inside the object is on the medial axis if and only if it is the center of a circle that is tangent to the boundary of the object at two nonadjacent points. A value associated with each point on the medial axis is the radius of the circle just described. It represents the minimum distance to the boundary from that point.

One way to find the medial axis is by erosion. One successively removes the outer perimeter of points in a manner similar to peeling an onion. If removing a particular point would disconnect the object, then that point is on the medial axis. Its value is simply the number of layers that have been previously peeled.

For binary images, the medial axis transform retains the shape of the original object. This means that the transformation is invertible and the object can be reconstructed from its medial axis transform. When programmed on digital images using a rectangular sampling grid, the inversion may differ slightly from the original object [13]. Figure 19–7(a) is a digital image of a chromosome, of which Figure 19–7(b) shows the medial axis transform. The image in (a) was computed by an algorithm of R. J. Wall [13]. Figure 19–7(c) shows how the medial axis transform depends on the orientation of the object with respect to the sampling grid. The medial axis transform can also be computed for gray-level images [14].

The medial axis transform is useful for finding the central axis of long, narrow, curved objects such as bent chromosomes [13,15]. Frequently it is useful as a graph only, and the values it produces are ignored. Other shape descriptors, such as the number of branches the object has and the total length of the object, can be computed from the graph itself [16].

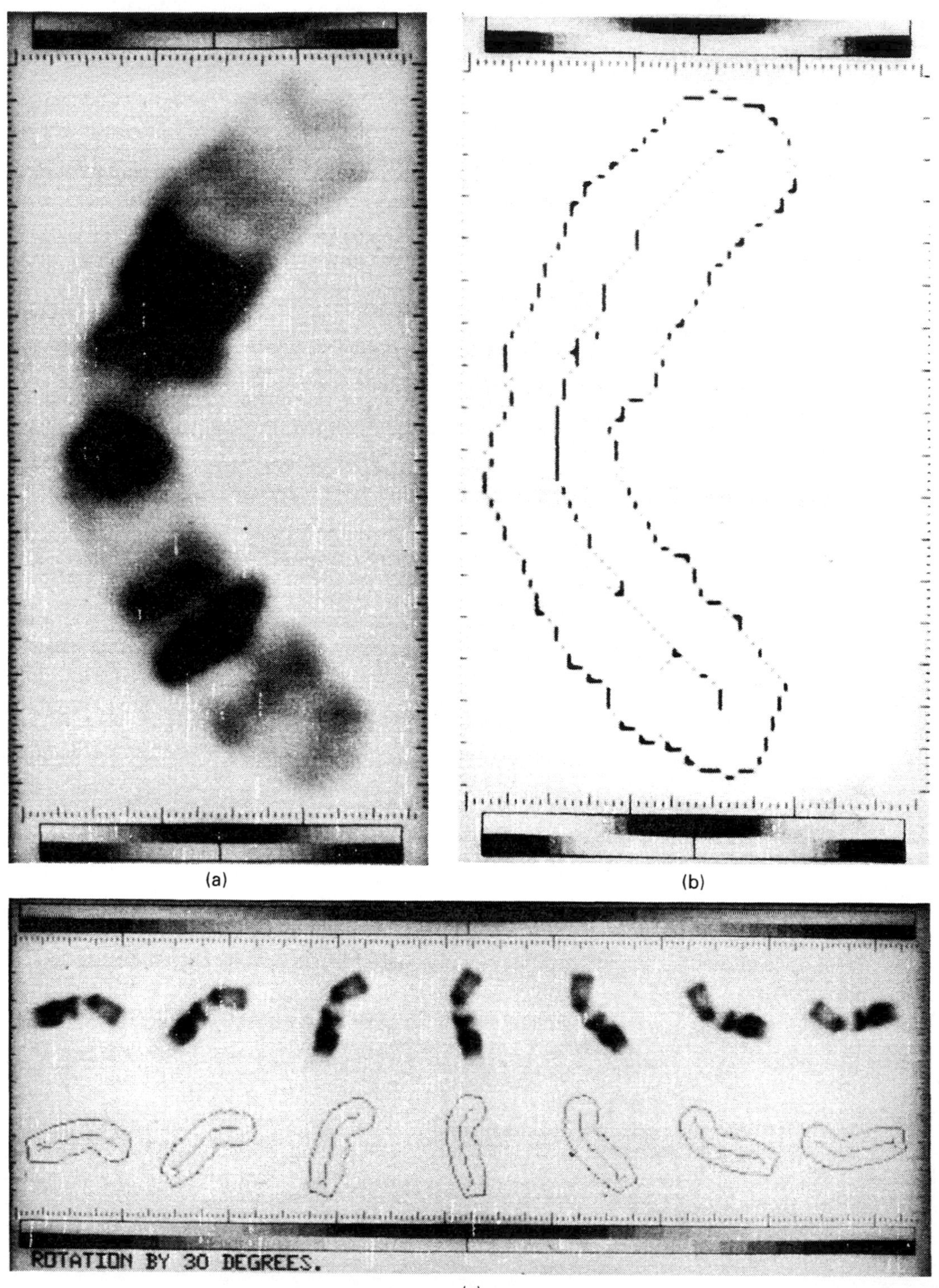

Figure 19–7 The medial axis transform: (a) digital image; (b) medial axis transform; (c) the effect of orientation

19.4 TEXTURE ANALYSIS

If you ask 10 people whether they know what texture is, almost certainly, each will say yes. However, you will most likely get 10 substantially different definitions from them.

19.4.1 Definitions

The word *texture* originally referred to the appearance of woven fabric, but a general definition is "the arrangement or characteristics of the constituent elements of anything, especially as regards surface appearance or tactile qualities" [17]. A more relevant definition for our purposes is "an attribute representing the spatial arrangement of the gray levels of the pixels in a region" [18].

Here, we are concerned with measuring the texture of an object in an image. If the gray level is constant everywhere in the object, or nearly so, we say that the object has no texture. If the gray level varies significantly within the object—apart from simple shading—then the object has texture. When we seek to measure texture, we attempt to quantify the nature of the variation in gray level within an object.

Electronic noise induced by a camera and film grain noise are examples of a *random texture*. In such cases, the variation in gray level in the object exhibits no recognizable pattern. By contrast, cross-hatching is a *pattern texture* that does exhibit a visible regularity.

Random textures are most commonly characterized by statistical properties such as standard deviation of gray level (for measuring the amplitude of texture) and autocorrelation width (for measuring the size of texture). Pattern textures can be additionally characterized by extracting measurements that quantify the nature and directionality (if any) of the pattern.

A *texture feature* is a value, computed from the image of an object, that quantifies some characteristic of the gray-level variation within the object. Normally, a texture feature is independent of the object's position, orientation, size, shape, and average gray level (brightness).

19.4.2 Texture Segmentation

Sometimes objects differ from the surrounding background, and each other, in texture but not in average brightness. In that case, image segmentation must be based on texture. This is done by first computing a texture image wherein the gray level of each pixel reflects some property of the texture in the local area of that pixel. In this image, then, objects differ by gray level, and the image can be segmented by conventional means. The texture measurement techniques discussed in this section map textural characteristics into gray-level values and can thus be used for texture segmentation as well.

19.4.3 Statistical Texture Features

Simple statistical measures of gray-level variation include standard deviation, variance, skewness, and kurtosis. These can be computed as moments of the gray-level histogram of the object, as can the *module* feature [19]

$$I = \sum_{i=1}^{N} \frac{H_i - M/N}{\sqrt{\dfrac{H_i(1 - H_i/M) + M(1 - 1/N)}{N}}} \tag{23}$$

where M is the number of pixels in the object and N the number of gray levels in the gray scale.

Research indicates that the human eye is insensitive to textural differences of order higher than the second (i.e., variance). This, however, does not preclude texture features from exploiting such quantifiable differences if they exist in particular objects. It merely suggests that visual classification of the training set may not be adequate.

19.4.3.1 The Co-Occurrence Matrix

Suppose that we establish a direction (horizontal, vertical, etc.) and a distance (one pixel, two pixels, etc.). in an image. Then the i, jth element of the *co-occurrence matrix* **P** for an object is the number of times, divided by M, that gray levels i and j occur in two pixels separated by that distance and direction in the object, where M is the number of pixel pairs contributing to **P**. The matrix **P** is N by N, where the gray scale has N shades of gray.

Separate co-occurrence matrices can be established for each combination of distance and direction. The total number of pixel pairs, M, contributing to the matrix is less than the number of pixels in the object, and it declines with increasing distance. Thus, the matrix can be rather sparse for small objects. For this reason, the gray scale N is often reduced—say, from 256 to 8 gray levels—for the computation of the co-occurrence matrix.

Once the co-occurrence matrix has been formed, texture features can be computed from it. A number of co-occurrence matrix–based features have been defined and tested [20–26]. Examples include *entropy*,

$$H = \sum_{i=1}^{N}\sum_{j=1}^{N} P_{ij}\log P_{ij} \tag{24}$$

inertia,

$$I = \sum_{i=1}^{N}\sum_{j=1}^{N} (i-j)^2 P_{ij} \tag{25}$$

and *energy*,

$$E = \sum_{i=1}^{N}\sum_{j=1}^{N} [P_{ij}]^2 \tag{26}$$

Some co-occurrence matrix–based texture features correspond to characteristics that are recognized by the eye [23], but many do not. In general, one must determine experimentally which of these features have discriminatory power.

19.4.4 Other Texture Features

Spectral Features. For a given image, the two-dimensional Fourier transform, of course, contains complete information on the image's texture. Thus, it may be useful to derive texture features from the spectrum, as well as from the object itself.

One can average the two-dimensional spectrum in annular rings to produce a one-dimensional function of frequency that ignores directionality. Similarly, one can average the spectrum in radial slices to produce a function of angle that shows *only* the directionality of the texture pattern. Each of these functions can be further reduced to scalar features that offer the desired discrimination ability. Normally, one would inspect these reduced-dimensional functions from different classes to determine how to reduce them further to scalars.

For a small, odd-shaped object, it may be a challenge to compute a two-dimensional spectrum. One can transform one or more squares that are completely enclosed in the object, averaging their spectra together. Otherwise one can pad a larger, square image with synthetic data outside the object to make it complete.

Structural Features. The structural approach to texture analysis assumes that the texture pattern is composed of a spatial arrangement of *texture primitives*. These are small objects that constitute, for example, one unit of a repeated pattern. Feature extraction then becomes the task of locating the primitives and quantifying their spatial arrangement.

As a simple example, consider an image of a section of liver tissue in which the cell nuclei have been stained dark. The primitives are the nuclei, and these are rather uniformly distributed throughout healthy tissue. Certain disease processes, however, cause random cell death, disrupting the spatial arrangement of the cells. Here, the mean and standard deviation of the neighboring cell separation distance are candidate structural texture features. Often, several such candidates must be evaluated to find a suitably strong performer.

19.5 CURVE AND SURFACE FITTING

Sometimes in image analysis it is useful to fit a one-dimensional function, such as a polynomial or Gaussian, through a set of data points. Polynomial warping (Sec. 8.3.4) requires this. In autofocus, for example (see Chapter 15), one can find the point of focus by first fitting a parabola or Gaussian through a plot of the focus parameter versus z-axis position and then solving for the location of the peak.

Sometimes it is useful to fit a two-dimensional surface, such as a two-dimensional polynomial or Gaussian, through an image or a portion thereof. This can be done for noise removal when the underlying (noise-free) image has a functional form that is known or assumed. The fitting process determines the parameters of the equation for the function, so that the image can be computed in noise-free form.

Surface fitting is also used for noise removal when one of the noise components (such as a shading pattern) can be fitted, computed, and subtracted out.

Surface fitting can also be done for purposes of measurement when the object of interest has a known or assumed functional form. Stars in an astronomical image, for example, can be modeled as two-dimensional Gaussians. Since the fitting procedure determines the values of the parameters that specify each object (e.g., position, size, shape, amplitude), it serves a measurement function as well.

19.5.1 Minimum Mean Square Error Fitting

Given a set of points (x_i, y_i), a commonly used fitting technique is to find the function $f(x)$ that minimizes the mean square error. This is given by

$$MSE = \frac{1}{N}\sum_{i=1}^{N}[y_i - f(x_i)]^2 \qquad (27)$$

where (x_i, y_i) are the data points, of which there are N.

If $f(x)$ is to be a parabola, for example, its equation is

$$f(x) = c_0 + c_1 x + c_2 x^2 \tag{28}$$

and the curve-fitting procedure is used to determine the best values of the coefficients c_0, c_1, and c_2. That is, we wish to determine the values of those coefficients that will make the parabola pass through the given points with minimum error, in the mean square sense.

19.5.2 Matrix Formulation

It is convenient to use matrix algebra (see Appendix 3 for a review) to develop the solution to the preceding problem. We begin by forming matrices **B** containing the given x-values, **Y** containing the given y-values, and **C** containing the coefficients that are to be determined:

$$\mathbf{Y} = \begin{bmatrix} y_1 \\ y_2 \\ \vdots \\ y_N \end{bmatrix} \qquad \mathbf{B} = \begin{bmatrix} 1 & x_1 & x_1^2 \\ 1 & x_2 & x_2^2 \\ \vdots & \vdots & \vdots \\ 1 & x_N & x_N^2 \end{bmatrix} \qquad \mathbf{C} = \begin{bmatrix} c_0 \\ c_1 \\ c_2 \end{bmatrix} \tag{29}$$

Now the column vector of error values (one element for each of the data points) can be written as

$$\mathbf{E} = \mathbf{Y} - \mathbf{BC} \tag{30}$$

where the matrix product **BC** is the column vector of y-values computed from Eq. (28).

Eq. (27) for the mean square error is now given by

$$\mathrm{MSE} = \frac{1}{N}\mathbf{E}^T\mathbf{E} \tag{31}$$

Substituting Eq. (30) into Eq. (31), differentiating with respect to the elements of **C**, and setting the derivative to zero leads to the solution [27,28]

$$\mathbf{C} = [\mathbf{B}^T\mathbf{B}]^{-1}[\mathbf{B}^T\mathbf{Y}] \tag{32}$$

which is the vector of coefficients that minimize the mean square error. The square matrix $[\mathbf{B}^T\mathbf{B}]^{-1}\mathbf{B}^T$ is called the *pseudoinverse* of **B**, and this solution is called the *pseudoinverse method.*

Notice that if the number of points is equal to the number of coefficients, **B** is a square matrix and can be inverted directly (provided that it is nonsingular). In this case, Eq. (32) reduces to

$$\mathbf{C} = \mathbf{B}^{-1}\mathbf{Y} \tag{33}$$

and we have the familiar problem of solving a set of linear equations in as many unknowns.

19.5.3 One-Dimensional Parabola Fit

As a numerical example, let us fit a parabola through a set of five points. The values are

$$\mathbf{X} = \begin{bmatrix} 0.9 \\ 2.2 \\ 3 \\ 4 \\ 5 \end{bmatrix} \qquad \mathbf{Y} = \begin{bmatrix} 1.8 \\ 3 \\ 2.5 \\ 3 \\ 2 \end{bmatrix} \qquad \mathbf{B} = \begin{bmatrix} 1 & 0.9 & 0.81 \\ 1 & 2.2 & 4.84 \\ 1 & 3 & 9 \\ 1 & 4 & 16 \\ 1 & 5 & 25 \end{bmatrix} \tag{34}$$

and Figure 19–8 shows the cluster of points and the best fitting parabola, determined by this method. The calculations produce

$$\mathbf{B}^T\mathbf{B} = \begin{bmatrix} 5 & 15 & 56 \\ 15 & 56 & 227 \\ 56 & 227 & 986 \end{bmatrix} \qquad \mathbf{B}^T\mathbf{Y} = \begin{bmatrix} 12.3 \\ 37.7 \\ 136.5 \end{bmatrix} \quad \text{and} \quad \mathbf{C} = \begin{bmatrix} 0.747 \\ 1.415 \\ -.230 \end{bmatrix} \tag{35}$$

We can compare the computed values with the observed data and view the error vector:

$$\mathbf{Y} = \begin{bmatrix} 1.8 \\ 3 \\ 2.5 \\ 3 \\ 2 \end{bmatrix} \qquad \mathbf{BC} = \begin{bmatrix} 1.83 \\ 2.75 \\ 2.92 \\ 2.73 \\ 2.07 \end{bmatrix} \qquad \mathbf{E} = \begin{bmatrix} -.03 \\ +.25 \\ -.42 \\ +.27 \\ -.07 \end{bmatrix} \tag{36}$$

If this were, for example, an autofocus application, we would want to solve for the position of the peak of the parabola. Setting the derivative of Eq. (28) to zero allows us to solve for

$$x_{\max} = \frac{-c_2}{2c_3} = 3.076 \quad \text{and} \quad f(x_{\max}) = 2.923 \tag{37}$$

If the points happen to be gray levels along a scan line, the x_i's are equally spaced, but there is, in general, no restriction on the arrangement of the points. They can be any scattered cluster of points. The only restriction is that $f(x)$ be, in fact, a function of x and thus be single valued for any x. That is, $f(x)$ cannot bend back upon itself to fit the data.

The first factor on the right side of Eq. (32) represents a matrix inversion, and this could present a computational barrier. The matrix is only three-by-three, however, no matter how many points are used in the fit. Thus, the computational complexity is not overly burdensome.

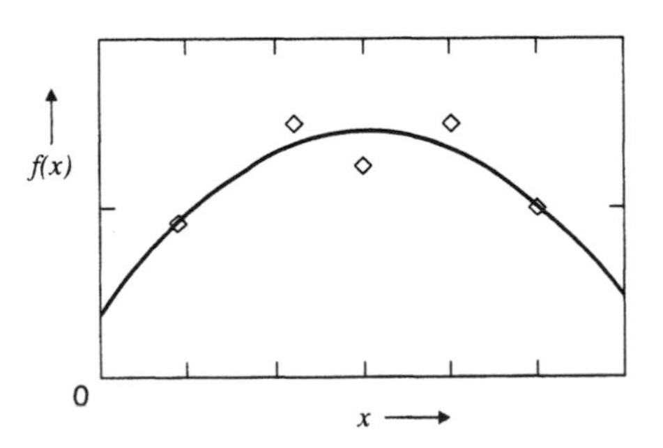

Figure 19–8 Fitting a parabola through five data points

19.5.4 Two-Dimensional Cubic Fit

One can generalize the foregoing technique to polynomials of order greater than two and to two-dimensional functions as well.

An effective background-flattening technique results from fitting a two-dimensional polynomial through a collection of background points that have been selected because of their low gray level. The resulting function is then subtracted from the image to flatten the background.

We illustrate this with the case of fitting a two-dimensional cubic. The function has 10 terms:

$$f(x, y) = c_0 + c_1 x + c_2 y + c_3 xy + c_4 x^2 + c_5 y^2 + c_6 x^2 y + c_7 xy^2 + c_8 x^3 + c_9 y^3 \quad (38)$$

The matrix **B** is N by 10:

$$\mathbf{B} = \begin{bmatrix} 1 & x_1 & y_1 & x_1 y_1 & x_1^2 & y_1^2 & x_1^2 y_1 & x_1 y_1^2 & x_1^3 & y_1^3 \\ \vdots & \vdots & \vdots & \vdots & \vdots & \vdots & \vdots & \vdots & \vdots & \vdots \end{bmatrix} \quad (39)$$

Hence, a 10-by-10 matrix inversion is required in Eq. (32). Figure 19–9 shows an example of background subtraction using the two-dimensional cubic fit.

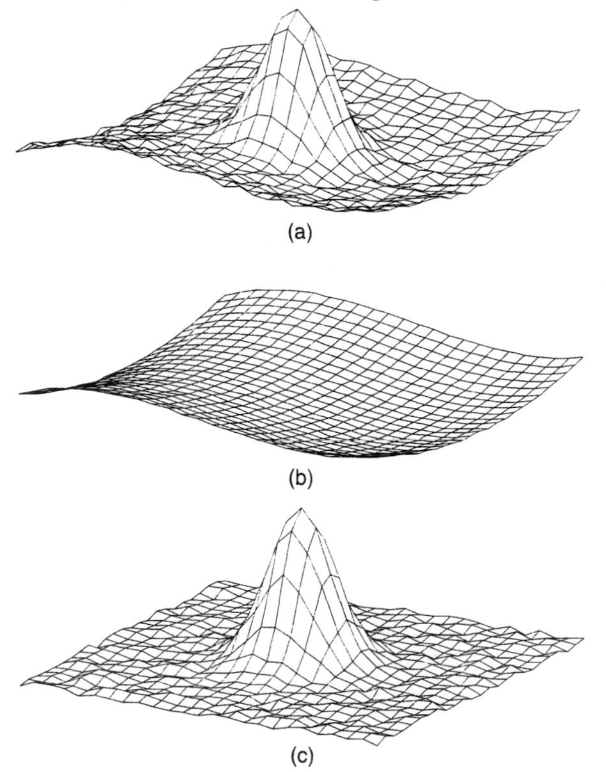

Figure 19–9 Fitting a two-dimensional cubic through the background of an image: (a) image containing one spot on a noisy, shaded background; (b) cubic fit through background points; (c) image after background subtraction

19.5.5 Two-Dimensional Gaussian Fit

One can measure a circular or elliptical object in an image by fitting a two-dimensional Gaussian surface through the image. The equation for the two-dimensional Gaussian is

$$z_i = Ae^{\left[-\frac{(x_i - x_o)^2}{2\sigma_x^2} - \frac{(y_i - y_o)^2}{2\sigma_y^2}\right]} \tag{40}$$

where A is the amplitude, (x_o, y_o) the position, and σ_x and σ_y the standard deviations (radii) in the two directions.

If we take the logarithm of both sides, expand the square, and collect terms, we are left with a quadratic in x and y. If we then multiply both sides by z_i, we have

$$z_i \ln(z_i) = \left[\ln(A) - \frac{x_o^2}{2\sigma_x^2} - \frac{y_o^2}{2\sigma_y^2}\right] z_i + \frac{x_o}{\sigma_x^2}[x_i z_i] + \frac{y_o}{\sigma_y^2}[y_i z_i] + \frac{-1}{2\sigma_x^2}[x_i^2 z_i] + \frac{-1}{2\sigma_y^2}[y_i^2 z_i] \tag{41}$$

which can be written in matrix form as

$$\mathbf{Q} = \mathbf{CB} \tag{42}$$

where $\mathbf{Q}$ is an N-by-1 vector with elements

$$q_i = z_i \ln(z_i) \tag{43}$$

$\mathbf{C}$ is a five-element vector composed entirely of Gaussian parameters

$$\mathbf{C}^T = \left[\ln(A) - \frac{x_o^2}{2\sigma_x^2} - \frac{y_o^2}{2\sigma_x^2} \quad \frac{x_o}{\sigma_y^2} \quad \frac{y_o}{\sigma_y^2} \quad \frac{-1}{2\sigma_x^2} \quad \frac{-1}{2\sigma_y^2}\right] \tag{44}$$

and $\mathbf{B}$ is an N-by-5 matrix with ith row

$$[b_i] = [z_i \quad z_i x_i \quad z_i y_i \quad z_i x_i^2 \quad z_i y_i^2] \tag{45}$$

The $\mathbf{C}$ matrix is computed by Eq. (32) as before, and we can recover the Gaussian parameters from it by

$$\sigma_x^2 = \frac{-1}{2c_4} \qquad \sigma_y^2 = \frac{-1}{2c_5} \tag{46}$$

$$x_0 = c_2\sigma_x^2 \qquad y_o = c_3\sigma_y^2 \tag{47}$$

and

$$A = e^{\left[c_1 + \frac{x_o}{2\sigma_x^2} + \frac{y_o}{2\sigma_y^2}\right]} \tag{48}$$

Only a five-by-five matrix must be inverted, regardless of N, the number of points used in the fit.

Figure 19–10(a) shows a Gaussian fitted to a noisy peak by this method. The raw image is a computed Gaussian with added random noise. Table 19–1 compares the parameters determined from the fit with those used to generate the image. The original Gaussian is not

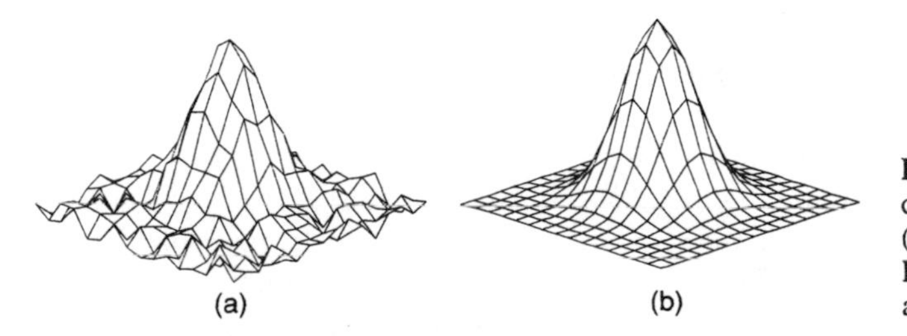

Figure 19–10 Fitting a two-dimensional Gaussian to a noisy peak: (a) raw image; (b) Gaussian fit. The RMS error is 6 percent of the peak amplitude

TABLE 19–1 ACTUAL VERSUS FITTED GAUSSIAN PARAMETERS

	A	x_o	y_o	σ_x	σ_y
Actual	10	4	4	2	2
Fitted	10.17	4.04	4.06	2.00	2.06

reconstructed exactly, because of the noise. Its parameters, however, are reasonably well estimated in the table, and Figure 19–10(b) is a reasonable facsimile of its noise-free form.

19.5.6 Ellipse Fitting

In many types of images, the objects of interest are circular, or at least elliptical. Thus, it is valuable to be able to fit an ellipse of arbitrary size, shape, and orientation to a collection of boundary points [29–32].

The general equation for a conic section is

$$ax^2 + bxy + cy^2 + dx + ey + f = 0 \tag{49}$$

and this will be an ellipse if

$$b^2 - 4ac < 0 \tag{50}$$

An ellipse is specified by five parameters: the x- and y-coordinates of its center, the lengths of its semimajor and semiminor axes, and the angle its major axis makes with the horizontal axis. We can fit an ellipse through five points by substituting their coordinates into Eq. (49) and solving the resulting five equations simultaneously. We can obtain a best fit through more points by fitting ellipses through five-point subsets and averaging (or taking the median of) their parameters [31].

Without loss of generality, we can normalize Eq. (49) by letting $a = 1$. We can then write the sum of squared errors as

$$\varepsilon^2 = \sum_i (x_i^2 + bx_iy_i + cy_i^2 + dx_i + ey_i + f)^2 \tag{51}$$

If we take partial derivatives of Eq. (51) with respect to the coefficients b, c, d, e, and f, and set each to zero, we obtain five equations in sums of powers and products of x_i and y_i that can be solved simultaneously for these coefficients [30]. The procedure can be implemented by the inversion of a five-by-five matrix as before.

19.5.7 Practical Considerations

If one repeatedly fits polynomials to successive scan lines in an image, the **B** matrix does not change from one line to the next, and the matrix inversion need be done only once.

It is important to select the points used in the fitting procedure so that they cover the entire area of interest. The behavior of the function can be quite unpredictable outside the area over which it has been constrained to fit actual data. When fitting an image, it is also important to cover the entire image with sample points, even if they are sparse (N is small).

If N is small, and the data points are not well scattered over the image, one can encounter ill-conditioning problems during matrix inversion. The number of points must be at least the number of columns in **B** and should be two to three times that.

One can fit a curve through a cluster of points in two-dimensional space. An example would be fitting an axis through the thinned skeleton of a curvilinear object. The fit is limited, however, by the fact that $f(x)$ is single valued for any x. This may prevent the curve from passing gracefully through the cluster of points. If the points are arranged more or less vertically, for example, it will be impossible to get an acceptable fit with $y = f(x)$. In that case, it would be better to fit $x = f(y)$ to the data.

In general, it might be worthwhile to determine the principal axis of the cluster of data points and rotate them so that the axis is horizontal prior to applying the curve-fitting procedure. Alternatively, one can fit the data points to a function defined in a rotated coordinate system.

With the two-dimensional Gaussian fit, it is essential that the sample points be spread all around the peak. Attempting to fit a two-dimensional Guassian to one side of a peak is courting disaster. If the data points happen to define a dip, rather than a peak, then the fitted Gaussian is upside down, c_4 and c_5 are positive, and the standard deviations (Eq. (46)) are imaginary. This situation can occur unexpectedly when the function is fitted to data points that are not well spread around all sides of the peak.

When fitting an ellipse to five points, one may find that the data points fit, instead, a parabola or hyperbola. Thus, it is necessary to impose logic upon the fitting exercise.

19.6 SUMMARY OF IMPORTANT POINTS

1. Object size is reflected in measurements of area, IOD, length, width, and perimeter, among other features.
2. Object shape is reflected in measurements of rectangle fit and circularity and in the invariant moments.
3. Object shape can be encoded in the chain code, the polar boundary function, the complex boundary function, and the medial axis transform.
4. Texture can be quantified by statistical measures, by features computed from the co-occurrence matrix, and by spectral and structural approaches.
5. Curve fitting can be used to estimate the function that underlies a noisy observation, provided that the form of the function is known or can be assumed.
6. A polynomial or Gaussian can be fitted to one- or two-dimensional data. While a matrix inversion is required, it is usually of relatively small size and reasonably well behaved.
7. When fitting a curve or a surface, it is vital to use a set of data points that span the entire region of interest.
8. Surface fitting can be used to extract an object of interest from an image or to estimate the object's amplitude, size, and shape parameters. Surface fitting can also estimate an unwanted component, such as background shading, so that it can be subtracted out.

PROBLEMS

1. Show that Eq. (7) leads to Eq. (5).
2. Show that Eq. (3) leads to Eq. (4).

3. Following are the boundary point coordinates of an object. Compute p^2/A to determine whether the object is a circle or a square.

   x: [97 85 66 42 22 10 9 21 40 64 84 96]

   y: [78 98 110 111 99 80 56 36 24 23 35 54]

4. Following are the boundary point coordinates of an object. Compute p^2/A to determine whether the object is a circle or a square.

   x: [460 580 560 540 520 380 240 100 120 140 160 300]

   y: [160 180 320 480 600 580 560 540 400 260 120 140]

5. Fit a straight line through the following set of points, and determine the x-value of the zero-crossing. Plot the points and the fitted line.

$$x = [0\ 1\ 2\ 3]$$
$$y = [.5\ .8\ 2.2\ 2.8]$$

6. Following are the values for the focus parameter at several z-axis positions. (See Chapter 15.) Fit a parabola through the points, and determine the z-axis position of the in-focus point. Plot the points and sketch the fitted parabola.

$$z = [0\ 2\ 3\ 5\ 7]$$
$$f = [445\ 620\ 710\ 580\ 390]$$

7. Following are the values for the focus parameter at several z-axis positions. (See Chapter 15.) Fit a Gaussian through the points, and determine the z-axis position of the in-focus point. Plot the points and sketch the fitted Gaussian.

$$z = [-8\ -3\ 2\ 6\ 12]$$
$$f = [41\ 62\ 58\ 60\ 38]$$

8. Following are several background points from a 480-by-512–pixel image $f(x, y)$ that has a shading problem. Fit a plane through the points, subtract it from those points, and calculate the RMS value of the surviving noise. (*Optional:* Plot the points and the fitted surface.)

   x: [1 100 200 300 1 100 200 300 1 100 200 300 1 100 200 300]

   y: [1 1 1 1 100 100 100 100 200 200 200 200 300 300 300 300]

   f: [18 26 39 47 37 36 39 40 58 48 43 44 75 63 53 39]

9. Repeat Problem 8, using a second-order (bilinear) surface

$$g(x, y) = c_0 + c_1x + c_2y + c_3xy$$

   Is the RMS noise reduced over what it was with the planar fit? If so, by what factor? (*Optional:* Plot the points and the fitted surface.)

10. Below are the gray levels at several pixels along a single (horizontal) scan line in an image taken with a camera having a left-to-right shading problem. Fit a straight line through the points, and plot the points and the fitted line. Subtract the line from those points, and calculate the RMS value of the surviving noise. Is it worth building this technique into your image-digitizing software? Assume that the additional complexity is justified only if the RMS background noise can be cut by half or more.

$$x = [1\ 100\ 200\ 300\ 400\ 500]$$
$$f = [27\ 46\ 63\ 69\ 68\ 63]$$

11. Repeat Problem 10 using a second-order (parabola) fit. Is it worth building this technique into your image-digitizing software? Assume that the additional complexity (above the linear fit) is justified only if the RMS background noise can be cut by half or more.

12. Repeat Problem 11 using a third-order (cubic) fit. Is it worth building this technique into your image-digitizing software? Assume that the additional complexity (above the parabola fit) is

justified only if the RMS background noise can be cut by half or more. Would it be productive to consider higher order fitting procedures? Why or why not?

13. Repeat Problem 10 using the following data:

    $x = [1\ 100\ 200\ 300\ 400\ 500]$

    $f = [24\ 39\ 32\ 18\ 15\ 27]$

14. Repeat Problem 11 using the data given in Problem 13.
15. Repeat Problem 12 using the data given in Problem 13.
16. Fit a conic section to the following six points. Sketch the curve. Is it a parabola, a hyperbola, or an ellipse?

    $x = [32\ 60\ 78\ 99\ 71\ 42]$, $y = [12\ 18\ 23\ 41\ 55\ 62]$

17. Fit a conic section to the following six points. Sketch the curve. Is it a parabola, a hyperbola, or an ellipse?

    $x = [28\ 41\ 55\ 61\ 46\ 33]$, $y = [23\ 21\ 30\ 40\ 41\ 33]$

18. Fit a conic section to the following six points. Sketch the curve. Is it a parabola, a hyperbola, or an ellipse?

    $x = [102\ 111\ 125\ 128\ 116\ 103]$, $y = [73\ 68\ 80\ 101\ 108\ 89]$

PROJECTS

1. Develop a program that can measure the area and perimeter of objects. Use circular objects of known diameter to test the program at different pixel spacings. Report on its accuracy.
2. Develop a program that can measure the average density or brightness of objects. Use objects of known density or brightness to test the program at different pixel spacings. Report on its accuracy.
3. Develop a program that can measure the shape of objects. Use circular, square, triangular, and rectangular objects of known dimension to test the program at different pixel spacings. Report on its accuracy.
4. Develop a program that can fit a two-dimensional cubic to the background of an image, compute the resulting function, and subtract it out of the image.
5. Develop a program that can locate the stars in a telescope image, fit a two-dimensional Gaussian to each star, and list the position, diameter, and brightness of each. Test the program on a digitized astronomical image.
6. Implement an autofocus program that can compute a focus parameter, fit a parabola or Gaussian to the resulting curve, and display the position of optimum focus.
7. Develop a program that can fit an ellipse to a collection of points (x, y). Test the program on images of coins and of thin sections of cylindrical objects cut at various angles. Report on its accuracy and any problems encountered with the fitting.

REFERENCES

For additional reading, see Appendix 2.

1. J. Hilditch and D. Rutovitz, "Chromosome Recognition," *Annals of the New York Academy of Science*, **157**:339–364, 1969.

2. H. A. Lubbs and R. S. Ledley, "Automated Analysis of Differentially Stained Human Chromosomes," in T. Caspersson and L. Zech, eds., *Nobel Symposium 23—Chromosome Identification,* Academic Press, New York, 61–76, 1973.
3. I. T. Young, J. E. Walker, and J. E. Bowie, "An Analysis Technique for Biological Shape. I," *Information and Control,* **25:**357–370, 1974.
4. P. E. Danielson, "A New Shape Factor," *Computer Graphics and Image Processing,* **7:**292–299, 1978.
5. A. Papoulis, *Probability, Random Variables, and Stochastic Processes,* McGraw-Hill, New York, 1965.
6. E. Kreyszig, *Introductory Mathematical Statistics,* John Wiley & Sons, Inc., New York, 1970.
7. M. K. Hu, "Visual Pattern Recognition by Moment Invariants," *IRE Trans. Info. Theory,* February 1962, 179–187.
8. F. L. Alt, "Digital Pattern Recognition by Moments," *JACM,* **9:**240–258, 1962.
9. J. W. Butler, M. K. Butler, and A. Stroud, "Automatic Classification of Chromosomes," in K. Enslein, ed., *Data Acquisition and Processing in Biology and Medicine,* **3,** Pergamon Press, New York, 1964.
10. C. T. Zahn and R. Z. Roskies, "Fourier Descriptors for Plane Closed Curves," *IEEE Trans. Computers,* **C-21:**269–281, 1972.
11. H. Blum, "Biological Science and Visual Shape (Part I)," *J. Theor. Biol.,* **38:**205–287, 1973.
12. H. Blum, "A Transformation for Extracting New Descriptors of Shape," in W. Wathen-Dunn, ed., *Models for the Perception of Speech and Visual Form,* MIT Press, Cambridge, MA, 1967.
13. R. J. Wall, A. Klinger, and S. Harami, "An Algorithm for Computing the Medial Axis Transform and Its Inverse," *Proceedings of the 1977 Workshop on Picture Data Description and Management,* 121–122, Proceedings 77CH1187-4C, IEEE Computer Society, Piscataway, NJ, 1977.
14. G. Levi and U. Montanari, "A Gray-Weighted Skeleton," *Information and Control,* **17:**62–91, 1970.
15. K. Castleman and R. Wall, "Automatic Systems for Chromosome Identification," in T. Caspersson, ed., *Nobel Symposium 23—Chromosome Identification,* Academic Press, New York, 77–84, 1973.
16. T. Pavlidis, "A Review of Algorithms for Shape Analysis," *Computer Graphics and Image Processing,* **7:**243–258, 1978.
17. S. I. Landau, editor-in-chief, *Webster Illustrated Contemporary Dictionary,* Doubleday, Garden City, NY.
18. IEEE Standard 610.4-1990, *IEEE Standard Glossary of Image Processing and Pattern Recognition Terminology,* IEEE Press, New York, 1990.
19. G. E. Lowitz, "Can a Local Histogram Really Map Texture Information?" *Pattern Recognition,* **16**(2):141–147, 1983.
20. T. R. Reed and J. M. H. du Buf, "A Review of Recent Texture Segmentation and Feature Extraction Techniques," *CVGIP: Image Understanding,* **57**(3):359–372, 1993.
21. R. M. Haralick, "Statistical and Structural Approaches to Texture," *Proc. IEEE,* **67:**786–804, 1979.
22. R. M. Haralick, K. Shanmugam, and I. Dinstein, "Textural Features for Image Classification," *IEEE Trans.* **SMC-3**(1):610–621, 1973.
23. H. Tamura, S. Mori, and T. Yamawaki, "Texture Features Corresponding to Visual Perception," *IEEE Trans.* **SMC-8:**460–473, 1978.

24. R. W. Conners, M. M. Trivedi, and C. A. Harlow, "Segmentation of a High-Resolution Urban Scene Using Texture Operators," *CVGIP,* **25:**273–310, 1984.

25. J. S. Weszka, C. R. Dyer, and A. Rosenfeld, "A Comparative Study of Texture Measures of Terrain Classification," *IEEE Trans.* **SMC-6**(4):269–285, 1976.

26. L. S. Davis, M. Clearman, and J. K. Aggarwal, "An Empirical Evaluation of Generalized Cooccurrence Matrices," *IEEE Trans.* **PAMI-2:**214–221, 1981.

27. D. H. Ballard and C. M. Brown, *Computer Vision,* Prentice-Hall, Englewood Cliffs, NJ, 1982.

28. J. Netter and W. Wesserman, *Applied Linear Statistical Models,* Richard D. Irvin, 1974.

29. J. P. P. Starink and I. T. Young, "Localization of Circular Objects," *Pat. Rec. Letters,* **14:**895–905, 1993.

30. W-Y. Wu and M-J. J. Wang, "Elliptical Object Detection by Using its Geometric Properties," *Pat. Rec.,* **26**(10):1499–1509, 1993.

31. P. L. Rosin, "Ellipse Fitting by Accumulating Five-Point Fits," *Pat. Rec. Letters,* **14:**661–669, 1993.

32. P. L. Rosin, "A Note on the Least Squares Fitting of Ellipses," *Pat. Rec. Letters,* **14:**799–808, 1993.

CHAPTER 20

Pattern Recognition: Classification and Estimation

20.1 INTRODUCTION

In Chapter 18, we introduced statistical pattern recognition and discussed the isolation and extraction of objects from a complex scene. Chapter 19 addressed ways to measure the characteristics of those objects. In this chapter, we approach the problem of identifying objects by classifying them into groups. Much has been written on this subject, and we can only introduce the basic concepts here. For a more complete treatment, the reader should consult a text on the subject. (See Appendix 2.)

20.2 CLASSIFICATION

20.2.1 Feature Selection

If we desire a system to distinguish objects of different types, we must first decide which characteristics of the objects should be measured to produce descriptive parameters. The particular characteristics that are measured are called the *features* of the object, and the resulting parameter values comprise the feature vector for each object. Proper selection of the features is important, since only these will be used to identify the objects.

There are few analytical means to guide the selection of features. Frequently, intuition guides the listing of potentially useful features. Feature-ordering techniques compute the relative power of the various features. This, in turn, allows the list to be pared to the best few features.

Good features have four characteristics:

1. *Discrimination.* Features should take on significantly different values for objects belonging to different classes. For example, diameter is a good feature in the fruit-sorting example of Chapter 18, since it takes on significantly different values for cherries and grapefruits.
2. *Reliability.* Features should take on similar values for all objects of the same class. For example, color may be a poor feature for apples if they occur in varying degrees of ripeness. That is, a green apple and a ripe (red) apple might differ significantly in color, even though they both belong to the class of apples.
3. *Independence.* The various features used should be uncorrelated with each other. The diameter and the weight of a fruit would constitute highly correlated features, since weight is approximately proportional to the cube of the diameter. The problem is that both diameter and weight essentially reflect the same property, namely, the size of the fruit. While highly correlated features might be combined (e.g., by averaging them together) to reduce sensitivity to noise, they generally should not be used as separate features.
4. *Small Numbers.* The complexity of a pattern recognition system increases rapidly with the *dimensionality* (number of features used) of the system. More importantly, the number of objects required to train the classifier and to measure its performance increases exponentially with the number of features [1]. In some cases, it may be impractical to acquire the amount of data required to train the classifier adequately. Finally, adding more features that are either noisy or highly correlated with existing features can actually degrade the performance of the classifier, particularly in view of the limited size of the training set [2–4].

In practice, the feature selection process usually involves testing a set of intuitively reasonable features and reducing the set to an acceptable number of the best ones. Frequently, few or none of the available features are ideal in terms of the foregoing characteristics.

20.2.2 Classifier Design

Classifier design consists of establishing the logical structure of the classifier and the mathematical basis of the classification rule. Commonly, for each object encountered, the classifier computes, for each of the classes, a value that indicates (by its magnitude) the degree to which that object resembles the objects that are typical of that class. This value is computed as a function of the features, and it is used to select the most appropriate class for assignment.

Most classifier decision rules reduce to a threshold rule that partitions the measurement space into disjoint regions, one (or perhaps more) for each class. Each region (range of feature values) corresponds to a single class. If the feature values fall within a particular region, then the object is assigned to the corresponding class. In some cases, one or more such regions may correspond to a class called "unknown."

20.2.3 Classifier Training

Once the basic decision rules of the classifier have been established, one must determine the particular threshold values that separate the classes. This is generally done by training the classifier on a group of known objects. The *training set* is a collection of objects from each class that have been previously identified by some accurate method. Objects in the training set are measured, and the measurement space is partitioned, by decision surfaces, into regions that maximize the accuracy of the classifier when it operates on the training set.

When training a classifier, one might use a simple rule, such as minimizing the total number of classification errors. If some misclassifications are more undesirable than others, one might establish a *cost function* that accounts for this by weighting the different errors appropriately. The decision lines are then placed to minimize the overall "cost" of operating the classifier.

If the training set is representative of the objects as a whole, then the classifier should perform about as well on new objects as it did on the training set. Obtaining a large enough training set is frequently a laborious task. In order to be representative, the training set should include examples of all types of objects that might be encountered, including those rarely seen. If the training set excludes certain uncommon objects, then it is *unrepresentative*. If it contains classification errors, it is *biased*.

20.2.4 Measurement of Performance

A classifier's accuracy can be directly estimated by tabulating its performance on a known test set of objects. If the test set is big enough to be representative of the objects at large, and if it is free of errors, the resulting estimate of performance can be quite useful.

An alternative method of estimating performance is to use a test set of known objects to estimate the PDFs of the features for objects belonging to each group. Given the underlying PDFs, one can use the classification parameters to calculate the expected error rates. If the general form of these PDFs is known, this technique can be superior to the use of a test set of marginal or inadequate size.

One is tempted to take the performance of the classifier on the training set as a measure of its overall performance, but this estimate is usually biased optimistically. A better approach is to use a separate test set for evaluating the performance of the classifier. This, however, increases significantly the requirement for preclassified data.

If previously classified objects are at a premium, one can use a round-robin procedure in which the classifier is trained on all but one of the available objects, and that object is then classified. When this is done for all of the objects, one has an estimate of the overall performance of the classifier.

20.3 FEATURE SELECTION

In a pattern recognition problem, one is usually faced with the task of selecting which of the many available features should actually be measured and presented to the classifier. The feature selection problem has received considerable attention in the literature, but no clear-cut solution to it has emerged. This section is intended to give the reader a flavor of the problem.

As mentioned before, one seeks a small set of reliable, independent, and discriminating features. In general, one expects the performance of the classifier to degrade as features are eliminated, at least if they are useful features. In fact, eliminating noisy or highly correlated features can actually improve performance.

Feature selection, then, may be viewed as the process of eliminating some features (starting with the poorest) and combining others that are related, until the feature set becomes manageable and performance is still adequate. If the feature set is to be reduced from M features to some smaller number N, we seek the particular set of N features that maximizes overall classifier performance.

A brute force approach to feature selection is as follows. For all possible subsets of N features, train the classifier, and quantify its performance by tabulating the misclassification rates of the classifier with respect to various groups. Then generate an overall performance index that is a function of the error rates. An example of this approach would be a linear sum of error probabilities, each weighted according to how serious an error it is. Finally, use that set of N features that produces the best performance index.

The problem with the brute force approach, of course, is the huge amount of work involved for all but the simplest of pattern recognition problems. In fact, frequently, only enough resources to train and evaluate the classifier once are available. In most practical problems, the brute force approach is impractical, and some less costly technique must be used to reach the same goal.

In the following discussion, we consider the simple case of reducing a two-feature problem to a one-feature problem. Suppose a training set is available that contains objects from M different classes. Let N_j be the number of objects from class j. The two features obtained when the ith object in class j is measured are x_{ij} and y_{ij}. We can start by computing the mean value of each feature for each class:

$$\hat{\mu}_{xj} = \frac{1}{N_j}\sum_{i=1}^{N_j} x_{ij} \quad (1)$$

and

$$\hat{\mu}_{yj} = \frac{1}{N_j}\sum_{i=1}^{N_j} y_{ij} \quad (2)$$

The carets on top of μ_{xj} and μ_{yj} remind us that these are estimates of the class means based upon the training set, rather than being the true class means.

20.3.1 Feature Variance

Ideally, the features should take on similar values for all objects within the same class. The estimated variance of the feature x within class j is

$$\hat{\sigma}_{xj}^2 = \frac{1}{N_j}\sum_{i=1}^{N_j} (x_{ij} - \hat{\mu}_{xj})^2 \quad (3)$$

and, for feature y it is

$$\hat{\sigma}_{yj}^2 = \frac{1}{N_j}\sum_{i=1}^{N_j} (y_{ij} - \hat{\mu}_{yj})^2 \quad (4)$$

20.3.2 Feature Correlation

The correlation of the features x and y in class j can be estimated by

$$\hat{\sigma}_{xyj} = \frac{\frac{1}{N_j}\sum_{i=1}^{N_j}(x_{ij} - \hat{\mu}_{xj})(y_{ij} - \hat{\mu}_{yj})}{\hat{\sigma}_{xj}\hat{\sigma}_{yj}} \tag{5}$$

This quantity is bounded by -1 and $+1$. A value of zero indicates that the two features are uncorrelated, while a value near $+1$ implies a high degree of correlation. A value of -1 implies that each variable is proportional to the negative of the other. If the magnitude of the correlation is near 1, the two features might well be combined into one, or one of them might be discarded.

20.3.3 Class Separation Distance

A relevant measure of the ability of a feature to distinguish between two classes is the variance-normalized distance between class means. For feature x, this is given by

$$\hat{D}_{xjk} = \frac{|\hat{\mu}_{xj} - \hat{\mu}_{xk}|}{\sqrt{\hat{\sigma}_{xj}^2 + \hat{\sigma}_{xk}^2}} \tag{6}$$

where the two classes are j and k. Clearly, the superior feature is the one producing the widest class separation.

20.3.4 Dimension Reduction

There are many ways to combine the two features x and y into a single feature z. A simple way is to use a linear function (see 13.6.2.1):

$$z = ax + by \tag{7}$$

Since classifier performance is not affected by scaling the magnitude of the features, we can impose a restriction on the magnitude, such as

$$a^2 + b^2 = 1 \tag{8}$$

This can be incorporated into Eq. (7) by writing

$$z = x\cos\theta + y\sin\theta \tag{9}$$

where θ is a new variable designating the proportions of x and y in the mixture.

If each object in the training set corresponds to a point in two-dimensional feature space (i.e., the xy-plane), then Eq. (9) describes the projection of all of the points onto the z-axis, which makes an angle θ with the x-axis. This is shown in Figure 20–1. Clearly, θ should be selected to maximize the class separation or some other criterion of the quality of a feature. For further discussion of dimension reduction, the reader should consult a textbook on pattern recognition. (See Appendix 2.)

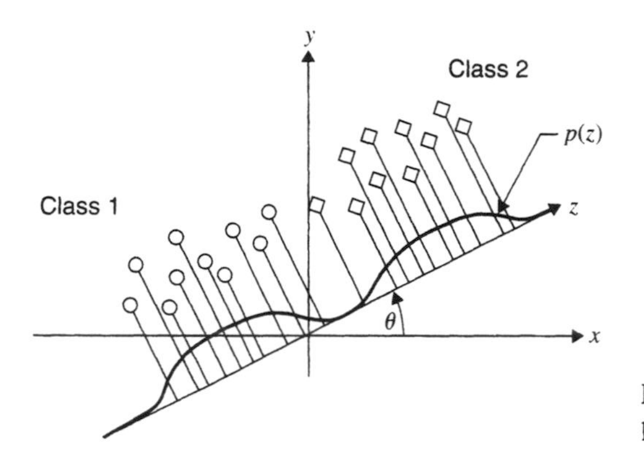

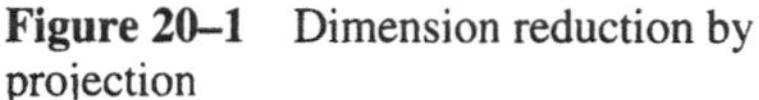
Figure 20–1 Dimension reduction by projection

20.4 STATISTICAL CLASSIFICATION

In this section, we consider some of the statistical methods commonly used for classification.

20.4.1 Statistical Decision Theory

Suppose we have a simplified fruit-sorting problem as in Chapter 18, but with only two classes and a single feature. This means that the objects that present themselves belong either to class 1 (cherries) or to class 2 (apples). For each object, we measure one property, diameter, and this is the feature we call x.

It may be that the PDF of the diameter measurement x is known for one or both classes of objects. For example, the Cherry Farmers' Association may issue a report stating that the mean diameter of cherries is 20 mm and the PDF is approximately Gaussian with a standard deviation of 4 mm. If the PDF of the diameter of apples is unknown, we might estimate it by measuring a large number of apples, plotting a histogram of their diameters, and computing the mean and variance. After normalization to unit area, and perhaps some smoothing, this histogram can be taken as an estimate of the corresponding PDF.

20.4.1.1 A Priori Probabilities

It may be that one class is, in general, more likely to occur than the order. For example, suppose that the conveyor belt in the fruit-sorting example is known to transport twice as many cherries as apples over any extended period. Thus, we can say that the a priori probabilities of the two classes are

$$P(C_1) = \frac{2}{3} \quad \text{and} \quad P(C_2) = \frac{1}{3} \tag{10}$$

These equations merely state that class 1 is twice as likely to occur as class 2. The a priori probabilities represent our knowledge about an object before it has been measured. In this example, we know that an unmeasured object is twice as likely to be a cherry as an apple.

Conditional Probabilities. Figure 20–2 shows what the two PDFs might look like. We denote the conditional PDF for cherry diameter as $p(x|C_1)$, which can be read as "the probability that diameter x will occur, given that the object belongs to class 1." Similarly, $p(x|C_2)$ is the probability of diameter x occurring, given class 2 (apples).

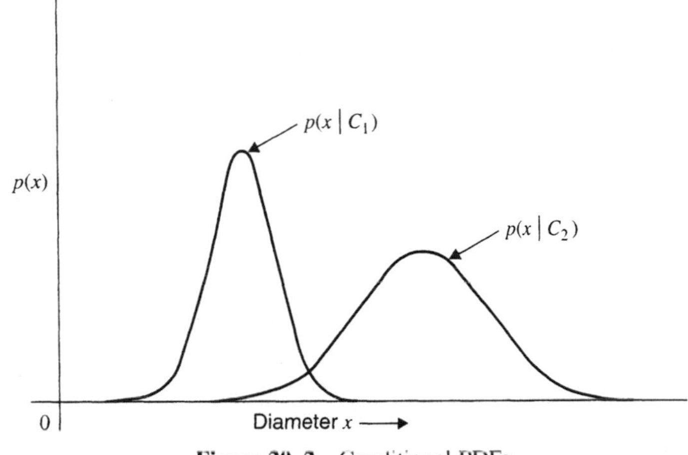

Figure 20–2 Conditional PDFs

20.4.1.2 Bayes' Theorem

Before an object has been measured, our knowledge of it consists merely of knowing the a priori probabilities of Eq. (10). After measurement, however, we should be able to use the measurement and the conditional PDFs to improve our knowledge of the object's class membership. After measurement, the so-called a posteriori probability that the object belongs to class i is given by Bayes' theorem; that is,

$$P(C_i|x) = \frac{p(x|C_i)P(C_i)}{p(x)} \tag{11}$$

where

$$p(x) = \sum_{i=1}^{2} p(x|C_i)P(C_i) \tag{12}$$

is the normalization factor required to make the set of a posteriori probabilities sum to unity.

Bayes' theorem allows us to combine the a priori probabilities of class membership, the conditional PDF, and the measurement made to compute, for each class, the probability that the measured object belongs to that class. Given this information, we might choose to assign each object to its most likely class. In our fruit-sorting example, we would assign the object to class 1 (i.e., we would call it a cherry) if

$$P(C_1|x) \geq P(C_2|x) \tag{13}$$

and assign it to class 2 (apples) otherwise. Substituting Bayes' theorem [Eq. (11)] into Eq. (13) and multiplying out the common denominator produces

$$p(x|C_1)P(C_1) \geq p(x|C_2)P(C_2) \tag{14}$$

as the condition for assignment to class 1 of a fruit having diameter x. At the decision threshold, where equality holds in Eq. (14), we may assign objects to classes arbitrarily. The classifier defined by this decision rule is a *maximum-likelihood* classifier.

The General Case. Suppose we make not one, but n, measurements on each object. Rather than a single feature value, we now have a feature vector $[x_1, x_2, \ldots, x_n]^T$, and each measured object corresponds to a point in n-dimensional feature space. Suppose also that there are not two, but m, classes of objects. Under these conditions, the a posteriori probability of membership in class i is, by Bayes' theorem,

$$p(C_i|x_1, x_2, \ldots, x_n) = \frac{p(x_1, x_2, \ldots, x_n|C_i)P(C_i)}{\sum_{i=1}^{m} p(x_1, x_2, \ldots, x_n|C_i)P(C_i)} \quad (15)$$

where the conditional PDFs are now n-dimensional.

20.4.1.3 Bayes' Risk

Every time we assign an object to a class, we risk making an error. In multiclass problems, some misclassifications may be more harmful than others. A quantitative way to account for this is with a cost function.

Let l_{ij} be the cost (or "loss") of assigning an object to class i when it really belongs in class j. Usually, l_{ij} will take on the value zero for correct decisions ($i = j$), small values for harmless errors, and larger values for more costly mistakes. Bayes' risk is the expected long-term cost of operating the classifier. The risk is evaluated by integrating the probability-weighted cost function.

Suppose we measure an object and assign it to class i. The expected loss resulting from this assignment is the conditional risk

$$R(C_i|x_1, x_2, \ldots, x_n) = \sum_{j=1}^{m} l_{ij} p(C_j|x_1, x_2, \ldots, x_n) \quad (16)$$

which is just the cost averaged over all m of the groups to which the object might actually belong. Thus, given the feature vector, there is a certain risk involved in assigning the object to any group.

20.4.1.4 Bayes' Rule

Bayes' decision rule states that each object should be assigned to the class that produces the minimum conditional risk. If we do this, we can then let $R_m(x_1, x_2, \ldots, x_n)$ be the resulting minimum risk corresponding to the feature vector $[x_1, x_2, \ldots, x_n]^T$. The overall long-term risk of operating the classifier with the Bayes' decision rule is called *Bayes' risk.* It is obtained by integrating the risk function over the entire feature space:

$$R = \int_{-\infty}^{\infty} R_m(x_1, x_2, \ldots, x_n) p(x_1, x_2, \ldots, x_n) dx_1, dx_2, \ldots, \quad dx_n \quad (17)$$

Clearly, no other decision rule can reduce $R_m(x_1, x_2, \ldots, x_n)$ at any point, and the overall risk is minimized by using Bayes' decision rule.

20.4.2 Classifier Types

It is useful to distinguish among different types of classifiers based upon what is known about the underlying statistics and what must be estimated.

Parametric and Nonparametric Classifiers. If the functional form of the conditional PDFs is known, but some parameters of the density function (mean value, variances, etc.) are unknown, then the classifier is called *parametric.* Since the a priori probabilities are also parameters, they may be unknown. With parametric classifiers, the functional form of the conditional PDFs is assumed, on the basis of some fundamental knowledge about the objects themselves. Frequently, functional forms are assumed for mathematical expediency, as well as for more intrinsic reasons.

If the functional form of some or all of the conditional PDFs is unknown, the classifier is termed *nonparametric.* This means that all conditional PDFs must be estimated from training set data. To do so requires considerably more data than merely estimating a few parameters in a PDF of known functional form. Thus, nonparametric techniques are used when suitable parametric models are unavailable and large amounts of training data are within reach.

20.4.3 Parameter Estimation and Classifier Training

The process of estimating the conditional PDFs or their parameters using object measurements is referred to as *training the classifier.*

20.4.3.1 Supervised and Unsupervised Training

If the objects have been previously classified by some error-free process, the process is referred to as *supervised training.* With *unsupervised training,* the conditional PDFs are estimated using samples whose class is unknown. The classes, and even the number thereof, must be determined by locating clusters of points in measurement space. This is called *cluster analysis.* Unsupervised training is normally used only when it is inconvenient or impossible to obtain a preclassified training set or when the number and characteristics of the classes have not been otherwise determined.

We concern ourselves here with two commonly used approaches to supervised training: the maximum-likelihood and Bayesian techniques. While the two techniques are philosophically different in their approach, they usually produce similar results. Which is more appropriate depends on the specific situation.

20.4.3.2 Maximum-Likelihood Estimation

The maximum-likelihood estimation approach assumes that the parameters to be estimated are fixed but unknown. A given sample (the training set) is drawn, and the estimate of the parameter is taken to be that value which makes the occurrence of the observed training set most likely.

For example, suppose that 100 samples are drawn from a normal distribution of unknown mean, but with a standard deviation of 2. Suppose further that the mean value of the 100 samples is 12. It is, of course, much more likely that the 100 samples came from a population having a mean value of 12 than from a population with a mean of 0, for example. Although the latter situation is possible, it requires a coincidence of highly unlikely events. It can be shown that the underlying population mean which makes that observed sample mean most likely is 12.

Maximum-likelihood estimation is a well-developed subject and considerably beyond our scope. We are content here to introduce the concept and quote the well-known result that the maximum-likelihood estimates of the mean and standard deviation of a normal distribution are the sample mean and sample standard deviation, respectively.

20.4.3.3 Bayesian Estimation

Unlike maximum-likelihood estimation, the Bayesian approach treats the unknown parameter as a random variable. Furthermore, it assumes that something is known about the unknown parameter in advance. Bayesian estimation assumes that the unknown parameter has a known, or assumed, a priori PDF before any samples are taken. After the training set has been measured, Bayes' theorem is used to allow the sample values to update, or refine, the a priori PDF. This results in an a posteriori PDF of the unknown parameter value. We hope that this PDF has a single narrow peak, centered on the true value of the parameter.

As an example of Bayesian estimation, suppose we wish to estimate the mean of a normal distribution with known variance. Before measuring the training set, we can use whatever knowledge is available to establish an a priori PDF on the unknown mean value. We call this a priori density function $p(\mu)$.

We denote the known functional form of the PDF of the unknown mean by $p(x|\mu)$. This states that, given a value for μ, we then know $p(x)$. If we let X represent the set of sample values obtained by measuring the training set, Bayes' theorem gives the a posteriori PDF of μ after the training set has been measured:

$$p(\mu|X) = \frac{p(X|\mu)p(\mu)}{\int p(X|\mu)p(\mu)d\mu} \tag{18}$$

What we really want is $p(x|X)$, the best estimate of the density $p(x)$, given the training set measurements X. One way to achieve this is to set up the joint (two-dimensional) PDF of both x and μ and then integrate out the μ-component; that is,

$$p(x|X) = \int_{-\infty}^{\infty} p(x, \mu|X)d\mu \tag{19}$$

The joint density in the integrand can be written as a product of two independent one-dimensional PDFs. Then Eq. (19) becomes

$$p(x|X) = \int_{-\infty}^{\infty} p(x|\mu)p(\mu|X)d\mu \tag{20}$$

This is the desired result, since $p(x|\mu)$ is the assumed functional form and $p(\mu|X)$ is the a posteriori PDF of the unknown mean from Eq. (18).

An Example. To see how $p(\mu|X)$ affects $p(x|X)$, suppose that $p(\mu|X)$ has a single sharp peak at $\mu = \mu_0$. This means that our a priori knowledge has combined with the training set to specify μ within narrow limits around the value μ_0. If the peak is sufficiently sharp, we can approximate $p(\mu|X)$ by an impulse at μ_0:

$$p(\mu|X) \approx \delta(\mu - \mu_0) \tag{21}$$

Then Eq. (20) becomes

$$p(x|X) = \int_{-\infty}^{\infty} p(x|\mu)\delta(\mu - \mu_0)d\mu \tag{22}$$

which, by the sifting property of the impulse, is

$$p(x|X) = p(x|\mu_0) \tag{23}$$

This says that μ_0 is the best estimate of the unknown mean.

Suppose, on the other hand, that the a posteriori distribution of the unknown mean, $p(\mu|X)$, has a relatively broad peak about μ_0. In this case, $p(x|X)$ becomes a weighted average of many PDFs, all having different means in the neighborhood of μ_0. This has the effect of smearing or broadening $p(x|X)$ to reflect our uncertainty about the mean value.

As mentioned earlier, maximum-likelihood and Bayesian estimation produce similar, if not identical, results in many common cases. For example, both approaches tend to establish the unknown mean at the mean of a large training set. Bayesian estimation allows us to combine any a priori knowledge we have with the quantitative data of the training set to estimate the unknown parameter. Furthermore, the width of $p(\mu|X)$ is an indication of how confidently we have estimated the unknown parameter.

Using Bayesian Estimation. To summarize, the steps involved in Bayesian estimation are as follows. First, we assume an a priori PDF for the unknown parameter or parameters. Second, we collect sample values from the population by measuring the training set. Third, we use Bayes' theorem to refine the a priori PDF into the a posteriori PDF, using the sample values. Finally, we form the joint density of x and the unknown parameter and integrate out the latter to leave the desired estimate of the PDF.

If we have strong ideas about the probable values of the unknown parameter, we may assume a narrow a priori PDF. If, on the other hand, we know little about the parameter, we should assume a relatively broad PDF.

The effect of using sample values to refine the a priori PDF is shown from

$$p(\mu|X) = \frac{1}{c}p(X|\mu)p(\mu) = \frac{1}{c}\prod_{i=1}^{n} p(x_i|\mu)p(\mu) \tag{24}$$

where c is the denominator of Eq. (18) and Π indicates an n-term product. Since the n samples are taken independently, the probability of pulling out the entire training set is merely the product of the individual probabilities of pulling out each sample.

If the samples are tightly clustered about the sample mean μ_s, then $p(X|\mu)$ has a sharp peak at or near $\mu = \mu_s$. If the assumed a priori density $p(\mu)$ is relatively flat in that area, then

$$p(x|X) = \int_{-\infty}^{\infty} p(x|\mu)p(X|\mu)p(\mu)d\mu \tag{25}$$

The function $p(x|\mu)$ is the assumed form of the PDF with μ as a parameter. As far as the integral in Eq. (25) is concerned, $p(x|\mu)$ is a function of x and μ. The function $p(X|\mu)$ is the probability that the sample set X would be drawn if the PDF indeed had the mean value μ. It is given by Eq. (24), is a function of μ, and becomes increasingly sharp as n increases. Our prior knowledge of the unknown parameter μ is given by $p(\mu)$, which is the assumed a priori PDF of the unknown mean.

Prior Knowledge. We now consider two cases that illustrate the role of prior knowledge and the training set in Bayesian estimation. In case 1, we have strong feelings about the value of μ, and we take a relatively small number of samples in the training set. This means that we would assume that $p(\mu)$ is narrow about μ_0, our preconceived idea of the mean value. If n is small, $p(X|\mu)$ is broad about the sample mean μ_s. Then Eq. (25) can be approximated by

$$p(x|X) \approx \int p(x|\mu)\delta(\mu - \mu_0)d\mu = p(x|\mu_0) \tag{26}$$

This indicates that the Bayesian estimate of the unknown PDF is basically of the assumed parametric form, with our preconceived value μ_0 substituted for the mean.

In the second case, suppose we do not have strong feelings about the mean value and that we employ a large training set. Thus, we assume a $p(\mu)$ that is broad about μ_s, the sample mean. Then the Bayesian estimate of the unknown PDF is

$$p(x|X) \approx \int p(x|\mu)\delta(\mu - \mu_s)d\mu = p(x|\mu_s) \tag{27}$$

In this case, the large training set has overpowered our timid a priori estimate and substituted the sample mean into the assumed form of the unknown PDF. Thus, as the number of samples increases, the final estimate of the mean moves from our initial estimate μ_0 toward the sample mean μ_s. Our a priori confidence is represented by the sharpness of $p(\mu)$: The sharper this function is, the more slowly the estimate moves toward μ_s with increasing n.

Maximum-likelihood estimation allows us to use the training set to estimate the unknown mean. Bayesian estimation allows us to combine our prior knowledge with the training set to estimate the unknown mean. If our prior knowledge is meager compared to the knowledge embodied in the training set, then both methods tend to converge toward the sample mean.

20.4.3.4 An Example of Classifier Training

We conclude our discussion of statistical classification with an example that illustrates training a classifier. The objects to be classified are the human chromosomes. Under the optical microscope, the 46 chromosomes from the nucleus of a human lymphocyte (white blood cell) appear in scattered disarray [Figure 20–3(a)]. The 46-chromosome complement is known to consist of 22 pairs of morphologically similar, *homologous* chromosomes and 2 sex-determinative chromosomes (XX for the female and XY for the male). The two long arms and the two short arms of each chromosome connect at the *centromere* of that chromosome.

For diagnostic purposes, it is customary to arrange the chromosome images into groups of similar morphology. This arrangement produces the *karyotype* of Figure 20–3(b). The groups are designated by the letters A through G, as indicated. This display format facilitates visual examination for abnormal or missing chromosomes. With modern specimen preparation techniques it is possible to stain the chromosomes so that all 24 types are distinguishable, but this example serves better to illustrate the points under discussion here.

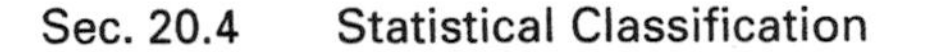

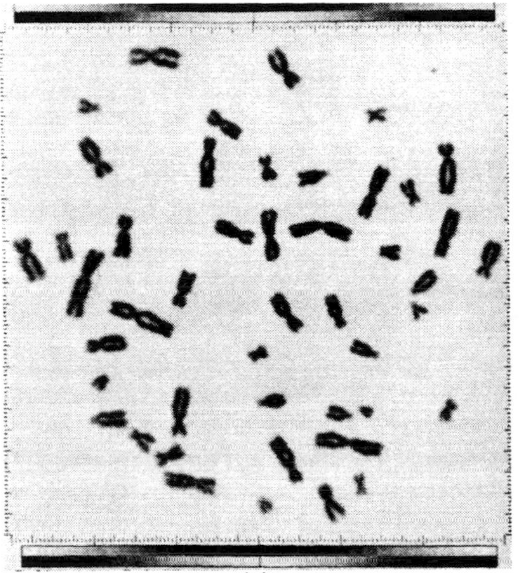

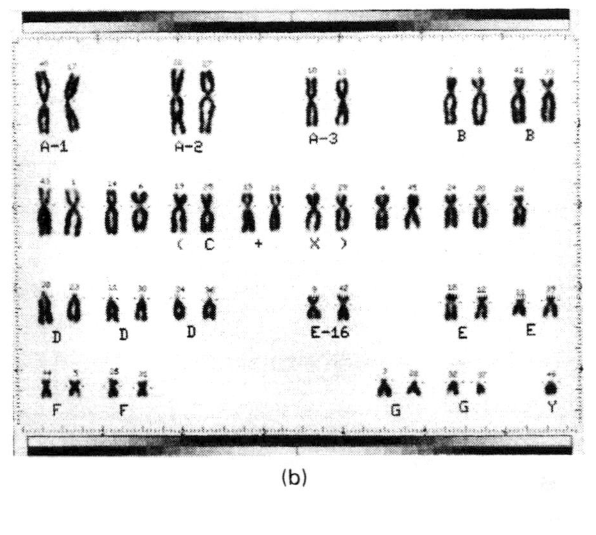

Figure 20–3 Human chromosomes: (a) digitized microscope image; (b) karyotype

As a pattern recognition task, our job is merely to assign each incoming chromosome to one of the seven groups, A through G. We shall measure two features of each chromosome: total length and arm length ratio. The latter feature is called the *centromeric index* and is the ratio of long-arm length to total length.

Figure 20–4(a) shows a two-dimensional histogram of the measurements from the 2,300 chromosomes found in a set of 50 normal cells. In the two-dimensional feature space, the abscissa is chromosome length, while the ordinate is centromeric index. Gray level is indicated by a combination of derivative shading and contour lines. The histogram has been smoothed slightly by convolution with a lowpass filter. Multiple clusters are clearly evident, indicating the morphological differences of the homologous pairs.

Figure 20–4(b) shows a similar histogram for only those chromosomes that belong to the C group. This subset of chromosomes was identified by an expert cytogeneticist. The histogram of all non-C group chromosomes appears in Figure 20–4(c).

Training the classifier in this case consists of partitioning the feature space into disjoint regions, one for each karyotype group. The smoothed histogram in Figure 20–4(b) can be viewed as an unnormalized estimate of the PDF for C-group chromosomes. It can be written as

$$f_c(x, y) = Np(C)p(x, y|C) \tag{28}$$

where N (= 50) is the number of cells in the training set, $p(\mathrm{C})$ is the a priori probability that an unmeasured chromosome belongs to the C group, and $p(x, y|C)$ is the PDF for C-group chromosomes. The normal male karyotype has 15 and the female karyotype 16 chromosomes in the C group, which includes the X chromosomes. Thus, if males and females are equally likely, the a priori probability is

$$p(C) = \frac{15.5}{46} \tag{29}$$

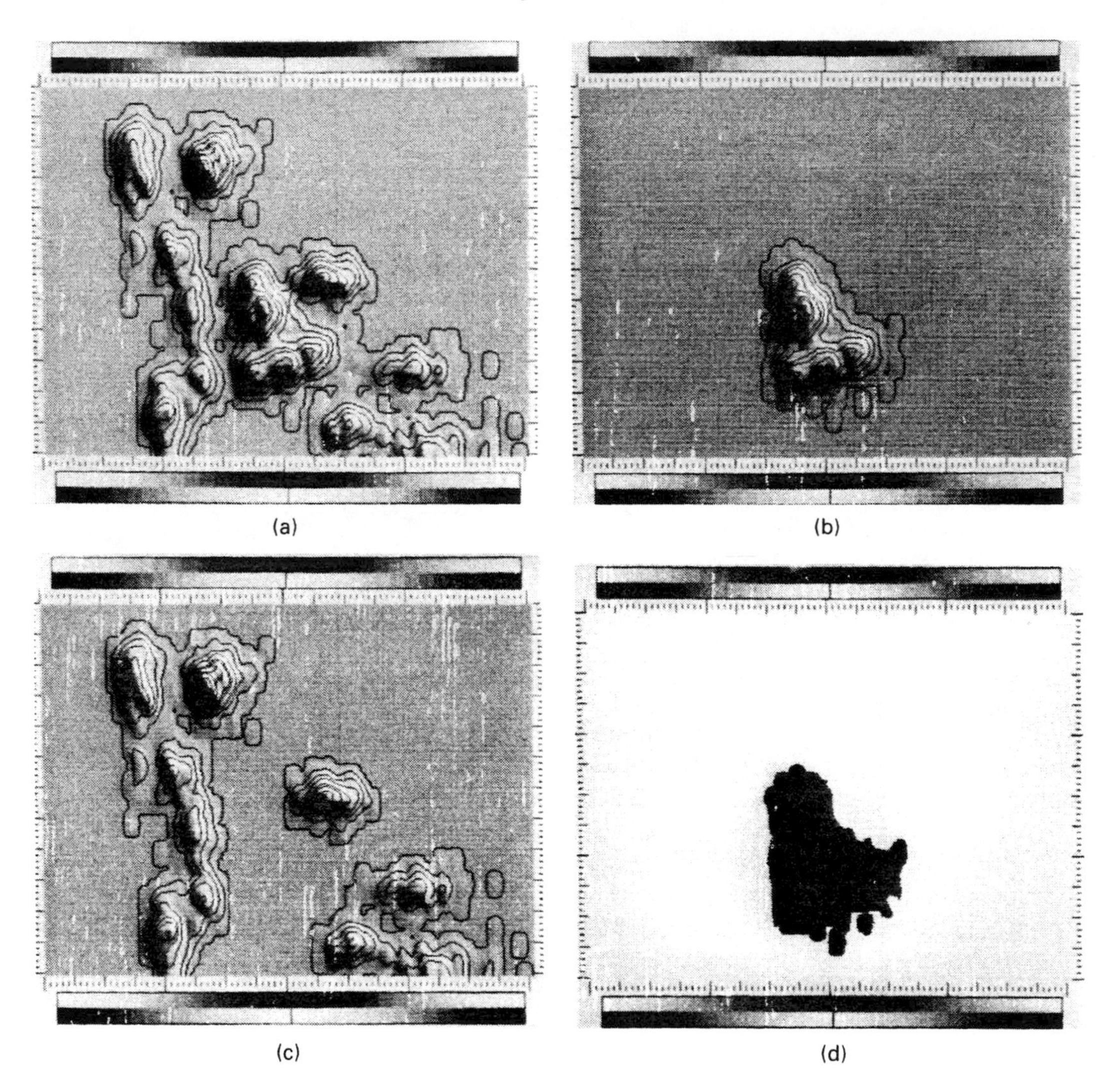

Figure 20–4 Chromosome PDFs: (a) all chromosomes; (b) C group only; (c) non-C group chromosomes; (d) C group decision region

Eq. (14) gives the decision rule for the maximum-likelihood classifier. This means that we should assign a chromosome with feature values (x, y) to the C group if the histogram of Figure 20–4(b) is greater at (x, y) than the histogram of Figure 20–4(c). We can identify this region of maximum likelihood by subtracting the digital image of Figure 20–4(c) from that of Figure 20–4(b). This region is shown in Figure 20–4(d) for the C group. A similar procedure for the other groups produces the classifier presented in Figure 20–5.

20.4.4 Classifier Performance

There are several ways to estimate the performance of a classifier after it has been designed and trained. If its dimensionality is low, and the PDFs are known or can be estimated, one

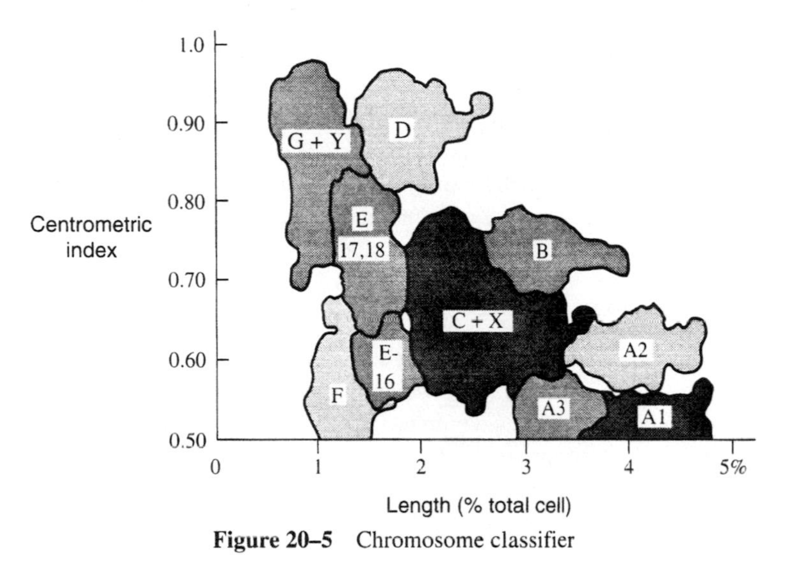

Figure 20–5 Chromosome classifier

can compute the probability of error as the area under the tails. Alternatively, one can run the classifier on a known test set, preferably one that is different from the training set.

As a general rule, in pattern recognition applied to digital images, the quality of the image limits the reliability of the measurements, and this in turn limits the accuracy of classification by causing overlap of the PDFs. The quality of the image is degraded by optics, noise, and distortion. These combine with the in-class variability of the objects to broaden the PDFs.

The classifier should be appropriate for the problem, but a more sophisticated classifier will not necessarily perform better than a simple one. Overlap of the classes in feature space establishes the fundamental limitation on a classifier's accuracy: No classifier, however sophisticated, can distinguish between two objects of a different type when they have the same measurement values.

20.5 NEURAL NETWORKS

A different approach to pattern recognition that has attracted considerable interest in recent years comes out of the field of artificial neural network technology. Initially inspired by biological nervous systems, the development of artificial neural networks has more recently been motivated by their applicability to certain types of problems and their potential for parallel-processing implementations. Out of these have emerged a number of network designs that are capable of both supervised and unsupervised training in pattern recognition problems.

20.5.1 Neural Network Architecture

A neural network is a collection of interconnected identical nodes, or *processing elements* (PEs), each of which is relatively simple in operation. Each PE receives inputs from several of the "upstream" PEs in the network, generates a scalar output, and sends it "downstream" to another group of PEs.

The interconnection scheme, or *network architecture,* is one of the major design choices. The PEs are commonly organized into layers. The number of PEs in each layer is a design choice. In some networks each PE in one layer receives input from every PE in the previous layer and sends its output to every PE in the subsequent layer. Some network architectures, however, permit communication among PEs within a layer, and *feedback architectures* even allow for communication to PEs in previous layers. The final layer is called the *output layer,* and all other layers are termed *hidden layers.*

20.5.2 The Processing Element

The basic processing element of a neural network operates rather simply. It merely sums the product of its input vector and a weight vector, transforms the result according to a sigmoid transformation function, and outputs the (scalar) result. This result then passes on to become the input of one or many other PEs through the network interconnections. Figure 20–6 depicts a typical processing element.

The actual processing done by such a PE can be described as a function of a dot product; that is,

$$O = g[\mathbf{X}^T \cdot \mathbf{W}] = g\left[\sum_{i=1}^{N} x_i w_i\right] = g[S] \tag{30}$$

where O is the (scalar) output, $\mathbf{X}$ is the input vector, and $\mathbf{W}$ is the weight vector associated with the given PE. The weights used in this summation are, in fact, the parameters that are adjusted during the training process, after which they remain fixed in ordinary usage.

The weighted sum is subjected to a nonlinear transformation by the *activation function,* $g[\cdot]$. This is a function with a sigmoid shape. It is monotonically increasing, is differentiable, and approaches 0 and 1 asymptotically at large negative and large positive values of its argument, respectively. Its primary purpose is to limit the output of the PE to the range [0,1]. The form of the function g is a design choice, and it can exert considerable influence on the behavior of the network. By convention, outputs are positive, but interconnection weights can be either positive (reinforcing) or negative (inhibiting).

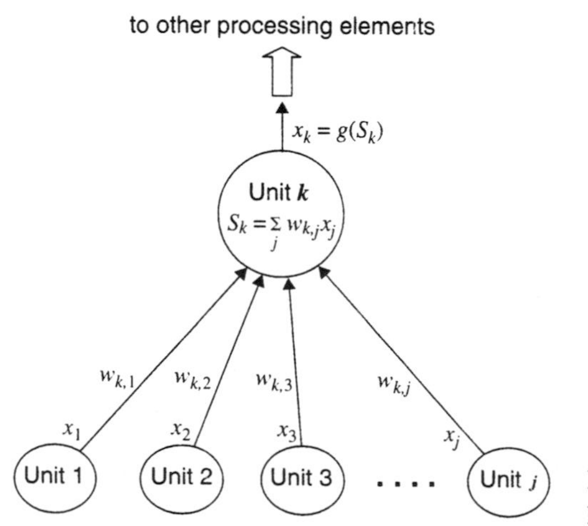

Figure 20–6 Schematic of a processing element

During a (supervised) training exercise, feature vectors of known objects from the training set are presented in random order to the network. The interconnection weights of the PEs are adjusted slightly each time, using a fixed training rule, to "nudge" the output of the network in the direction of the correct value. As training proceeds, performance improves, until the network has finally converged upon the proper set of weights for each PE.

20.5.3 Neural Network Operation

In a pattern recognition application, the input to the network is the feature vector of the unknown object. The feature vector is presented to each of the PEs in the first layer of the network. Often the feature vector is augmented by an additional element that is always unity. This provides for an additional weight in the summation that acts as an offset in the activation function. The input information then propagates through the various layers until an output vector appears at the output layer. The unknown object is assigned to the class somehow specified by the output vector. The network, then, accepts a feature vector as input and generates an output vector indicating a *membership value* corresponding to the class to which the unknown object belongs.

In a four-class problem, for example, when a class-2 object is presented to the network, the correct output vector (i.e., the *target vector*) is [0100]. In general, the result will not be so clear cut, but one hopes that the output of node 2 will at least exceed that of its competitors.

After the PE definition and interconnection architecture have been fixed, the behavior of the network is determined by the weights in the branches that connect the elements. Values for the connection weights are adjusted during the training of the network and are held constant when the network is operating in a production mode.

Most current applications of neural networks are implemented by digital simulation. They use either software or digital signal processing (DSP) chips to emulate parallel computation. Such an implementation generally involves configuring simulation software for the chosen network architecture and then training the network. A stripped-down version of the simulator is later embedded in the final application for use in a production environment.

In any digital simulation of a group of interconnected PEs, there is the question of the order of processing, that is, the sequence in which the elements are updated. Thus, the updating rule is an important design factor of a neural network.

20.5.4 Neural Network Performance

The advantages most often stated in favor of a neural network approach to pattern recognition are that (1) it requires less input of knowledge about the problem than other approaches, (2) it is capable of implementing more complex partitioning of feature space, and (3) it is amenable to high-performance parallel-processing implementations.

Advocates of this approach also point out the awesome pattern recognition capabilities of the human brain, suggesting that artificial neural networks have the potential perhaps to approach that level of performance. Pattern recognition implementations tested to date, however, generally tend to approach only the performance of well-designed statistical classifiers.

The disadvantages of neural network solutions, compared with statistical approaches, include (1) the extensive amount of training required, (2) slower operation when implemented as a simulation on a conventional computer, and (3) the unavailability of a detailed understanding of the decision-making process that is being used (e.g., the decision surfaces in feature space).

The underlying principles in play here are (1) that any classifier, however implemented, acts merely to partition feature space into regions corresponding to each class and assign objects accordingly, and (2) that the performance of a classifier is ultimately limited by the overlap of the classes in feature space. These combine with the practical difficulty of obtaining a representative training set and using it to establish optimum partition surfaces, to establish the ground rules for developing a classifier.

A neural network will excel only when it has been trained to carve up the feature space better than a comparable statistical classifier can do. Even so, its performance is fundamentally constrained by overlap of the classes.

We next introduce two networks that are amenable to pattern recognition: the backpropagation network [5,6] and the counterpropagation network [7]. Applications of neural networks to problems in fields other than pattern recognition are not addressed.

20.5.5 The Backpropagation Network

The standard configuration for a two-layer backpropagation network is shown in Figure 20–7. The number of PEs in each layer varies with the application. More hidden layers can be added between the input hidden layer and the output layer. We assume here that all input vectors have their values scaled between 0.1 and 0.9.

When the network is operating, each PE in the hidden layer forms a dot product of its weight vector and the input vector. The resulting weighted sum, S, is then transformed by the activation function

$$g(S) = \frac{1}{1 + e^{-S}} \tag{31}$$

This is a differentiable sigmoid function that approaches 0 and 1 at the two extremes of its argument.

The vector of results from the hidden layer is passed to the output layer, where the PEs process it in the same manner and produce the resultant vector.

20.5.5.1 Classifier Training

At the start of training, all connection weights in the network are set to random values in the range [–0.5, +0.5]. All input vectors are scaled so that the minimum and maximum values for any component are 0.1 and 0.9, respectively.

A *training pattern* is one particular input vector and its corresponding target vector. One of these is selected at random from the training set, and the input vector is propagated through the network. After the resulting output is compared to the target vector, the connection weights between the hidden and output layers are adjusted in such a manner as to make the output vector slightly nearer the target vector. After that, the hidden layer immediately below the output layer is similarly adjusted.

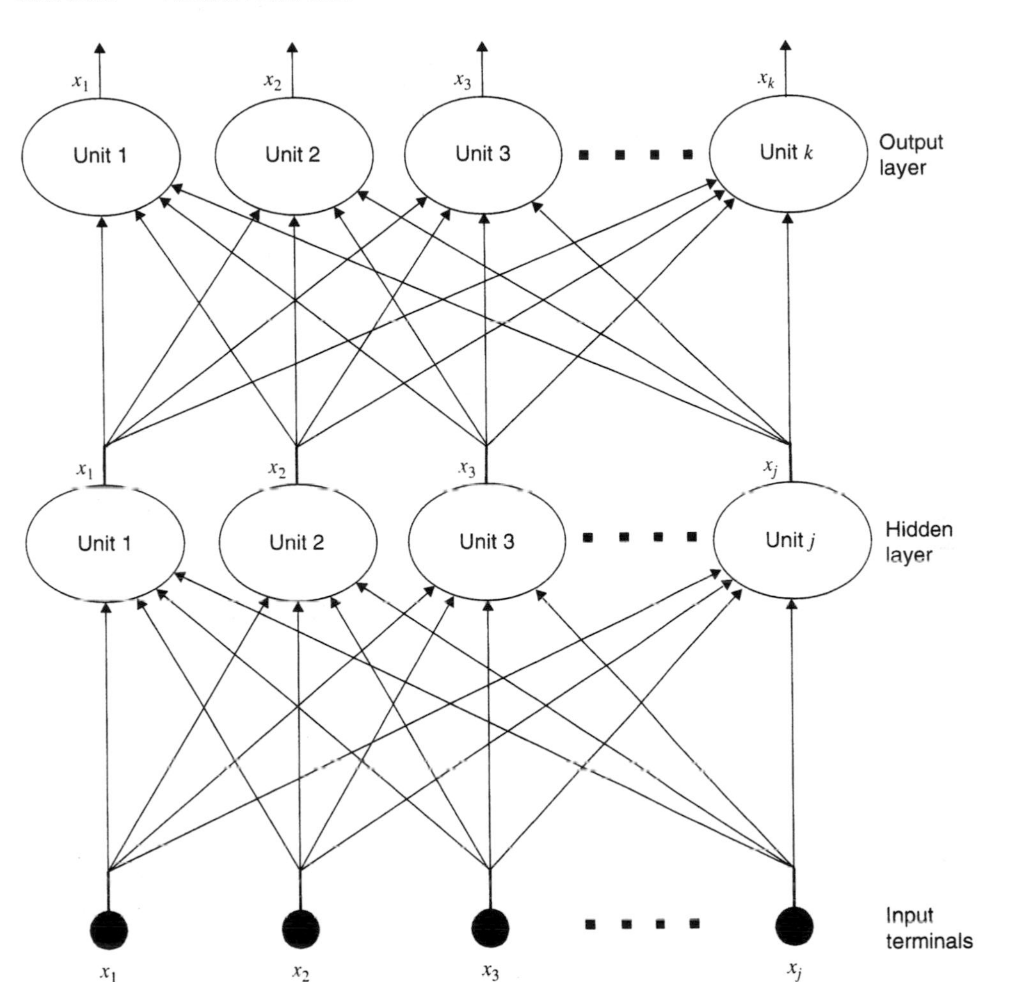

Figure 20–7 Backpropagation network

While Figure 20–7 shows only a two-layer network, in general any number of layers can be used. We use the more general nomenclature in Table 20–1 in the following discussion of backpropagation training.

The training proceeds from top to bottom, beginning with the PEs in the output layer. The amount of adjustment to the ith weight at the input of the jth output layer node ($k = N$) is

$$\Delta w_{ijN} = \eta \delta_{jN} g' [S_{jN}] O_{iN-1} \tag{32}$$

where the error

$$\delta_{jN} = t_j - O_{jN} \tag{33}$$

is the difference between the jth element of the target vector (i.e., the desired output value) and the actual output value of output layer node j.

Eq. (32) is known as the *generalized delta rule* [6]. It is based on the method of

TABLE 20–1 BACKPROPAGATION NETWORK NOMENCLATURE

N = number of layers
N_k = number of nodes in layer k
N_N = number of output nodes
$k = 1, \ldots, N$ = layer index
$j = 1, \ldots, N_k$ = node index for a particular layer k
$i = 1, \ldots, N_{k-1}$ = input index for a particular node in layer k
w_{ijk} = ith input weight of the jth node in layer k
S_{jk} = weighted sum of inputs to node j of layer k
O_{jk} = output value of node j of layer k
t_j = jth element of the target vector
δ_{jk} = error at the output of node j in layer k

gradient descent. The amount of adjustment [Eq. (32)] is some percentage η of the error δ_{jN}, at that output node, multiplied by the slope of the activation function $g'(S_{jN})$, times the ith element of the output vector coming from the previous hidden layer. The latter is just the input that this weight acts upon.

Next, the weights at the input of each hidden layer node are adjusted by an amount

$$\Delta w_{ijk} = \eta \delta_{jk} g'[S_{jk}] O_{ik-1} \tag{34}$$

This is similar to Eq. (32), except that now the error term, δ_{jk}, represents the error contributed by all the output nodes; that is,

$$\delta_{jk} = \sum_{i=1}^{N_{k+1}} w_{ijk+1} \delta_{ik+1} \tag{35}$$

If there are more than two layers, the training process continues from output toward input, layer by layer, using Eqs. (34) and (35). In the training process, then, the errors are *back-propagated* through the network in a manner similar to the forward propagation of input data that occurs during normal operation. The errors propagate in reverse, and the results of this propagation guide the adjustment of the interconnection weights.

The process is repeated for all remaining pairs of input and target vectors. It is then repeated for the whole training set a number of times, until the error over all input vectors falls below a preset threshold.

At any stage in the training, a global error measure is

$$E_{\text{RMS}} = \sqrt{\frac{\sum_{j=1}^{N_N} \sum_{p=1}^{P} \delta_{jp}^2}{P N_N}} \tag{36}$$

where P is the number of patterns in the training set, N_N is the number of output nodes, and $\delta_{jp} = t_{jp} - O_{jp}$ is the error, for the pth input pattern, between the jth elements of the target and output vectors.

The update equations (34) and (35) are obtained by differentiating this error measure with respect to the connection weights. The amount by which the weights are updated is simply taken to be proportional to the negative gradient of E_{RMS}. As a result, each update moves the network along an error surface, always in the direction of steepest descent.

The error surface "valley" into which the network eventually settles may not be the deepest one. That is, the network may converge to a local minimum of error instead of the global minimum, as desired. Nevertheless, if this error is low enough, the performance may still be acceptable.

If necessary, one can retrain the network using a different set of initial random weights to start the network at a different position on the error surface, thereby improving its chances of finding the global minimum, or at least a lower local minimum. One can also try training a redesigned network that uses a different number of hidden nodes.

During training, one can monitor the RMS error at the output layer (i.e., the difference from the target vector) for each input pattern. As a rule of thumb, training can be stopped after the RMS error falls below approximately 0.01. Once this is true, the network is said to have *converged* and has "learned the mapping." The connection weights then become fixed, the network's overall performance can be tested, and the network can be put into a production mode and used on real data.

20.5.5.2 Overtraining

The training process can be allowed to go on too long. Recall that any pattern recognition system, whether implemented by statistical, network, or other means, merely partitions the measurement space into regions corresponding to the different classes. With the Bayes classifier, designed assuming normal statistics, the partitioning is done by second-order hypersurfaces in n-dimensional feature space. The complexity of the partitioning is thus somewhat restricted by inherent limitations upon how convoluted a second-order hypersurface can be.

With a neural network, the decision surfaces that result from extensive training can be quite complex, particularly if the number of nodes and interconnections is large. If the size of the training set is not large, this can lead to a situation in which the network merely becomes tuned to ("memorizes") the particular training set, rather than adjusting itself to recognize all members of the classes at large.

One can envision a partitioning of the feature space wherein the network has placed a small hyperellipsoid around each point in a small training set. This will, of course, produce a low error on the training set, but poor performance in general.

Overtraining can be avoided by using a large training set and a test set that is distinct from the training set. When the error rate, measured on the test set, ceases to diminish and begins to increase, overtraining has commenced.

20.5.5.3 Design Considerations

The size of the network is an important consideration from both the performance and computational points of view. It has been shown [8,9] that one hidden layer is sufficient to approximate the mapping of any continuous function and that at most two hidden layers are required to approximate any function in general [10].

The number of PEs in the first hidden layer is usually dictated by the application. When a backpropagation network is used to classify objects, that number is equal to the length of the feature vector. Likewise, the number of nodes in the output layer is usually the same as the number of classes.

The number of subsequent hidden layers and the number of PEs in each such layer are design choices. In most applications, the latter number is a small fraction of the number of units in the input layer. It is usually desirable to keep this number small to reduce the danger of overtraining. On the other hand, too few PEs in the hidden layer may make it difficult for the network to converge to a suitable partitioning of a complex feature space. Once a network has converged, it can be shrunk in size and retrained, often with an improvement in overall performance.

As with statistical classifiers, data used for training must be representative of the population over the entire feature space in order for the network adequately to model the probability density function of each class. It is also important that the training patterns be presented randomly. The network must be able to generalize to the entire training set as a whole, not to individual classes one at a time. Presenting classes of vectors sequentially can result in poor convergence and unreliable class discrimination. Training on patterns randomly generates a type of noise that can help jog the network out of a local minimum. Noise is sometimes added to the training set for this purpose and has been found to assist convergence.

20.5.6 The Counterpropagation Network

The more recently developed counterpropagation architecture [7] differs conceptually from the architecture of the backpropagation network. Although the operation of a counterpropagation network is easier to comprehend, it generally requires of the designer more insight into the problem than does the backpropagation network.

The counterpropagation network is capable of unsupervised learning. That is, the training set need not be preclassified. As training advances, the network will locate naturally occurring clusters of points in feature space and make classes out of them. In applications where the data are expected or known to occur in separate classes, but suitable preclassified input data are unavailable, this can be quite useful.

The interconnection architecture for the forward-mapping counterpropagation network is the same as for the backpropagation network in Figure 20–7. However, whereas the backpropagation network can have many layers, the counterpropagation network is limited to two. Further, the activation function of each PE is linear (rather than sigmoidal), and its output is merely the dot product of Eq. 30.

The other important difference is the type of processing done in the hidden layer. That layer is called a *competitive layer* because its nodes compete to generate an output value. The hidden node computing the largest result wins the competition and outputs a value of 1. All other hidden nodes output a value of 0.

Since only one hidden node at a time is active, and it outputs a value of 1 to all the output layer nodes, the resulting network output is actually a vector of connection weights from the upper layer. Those connection weights that are connected to the output of the winning hidden layer node become the output vector. As a result, the weights of the output layer function as a type of lookup table, generating the desired output each time a class is recognized by one of the hidden nodes.

The counterpropagation network's pattern recognition capability is embodied in the computation done by the hidden layer's PEs. Because of the competitive nature of the hidden layer, that computation reflects the degree of similarity between the input vector and an ideal vector corresponding to the connection weight vector of each hidden layer node. The node computing the highest result will be the one having an input weight vector that is most similar to the input vector.

PEs can use either of two computation methods. The more common one, described earlier in reference to backpropagation, is the dot product. This is the magnitude of the projection of one vector onto another. Therefore, at any hidden layer node,

$$S_{j1} = \mathbf{X} \cdot \mathbf{W}_{j1} = \|\mathbf{X}\| \|\mathbf{W}_{j1}\| \cos(\theta) \tag{37}$$

where θ is the angle between the input vector $\mathbf{X}$ and the weight vector $\mathbf{W}_{j1}$.

Both the input vector and the output layer weight vector are normalized, so that the dot product at the hidden node is equal to the cosine of the angle between them. The result at each hidden node thus ranges from −1.0 for vectors that are exactly opposite each other to 1.0 for vectors pointing in the same direction. Accordingly, this computation considers objects to be similar if their angular direction from the origin of feature space is similar. It does not compute the distance between the two points in feature space. This suffices, however, for those pattern recognition problems where the class means surround the origin of feature space (or can be transformed to do so).

An alternative computation at the jth hidden layer node is

$$S_{j1} = \sqrt{\sum_{i=1}^{N_1} |w_{ij1} - x_i|^2} \tag{38}$$

where S_{j1} is now the distance between the input and weight vectors. The winning hidden node here is the one computing the minimum result.

Neither input nor weight vectors in this case are normalized, but it is useful to scale all components to the same range of values. This prevents numerically large parameters from dominating the computation.

20.5.6.1 Supervised Training

Without performing an actual training exercise, one could develop a forward-mapping counterpropagation network by calculating average (*prototype*) feature vectors for a number of different classes and setting the weights on the hidden layer interconnections to those values. Each hidden node would then compare the input vector against its prototype feature vector (encoded in its connection weights) by means of Eq. (37) or (38). The node computing the largest dot product result or the minimum distance result would be the one whose prototype feature vector most closely matched the input vector.

The number of hidden layer nodes must equal the number of classes, and the number of input terminals must equal the number of features. The output layer could be a single node that encodes the class number, with each input weight equal to the class number recognized by the corresponding hidden layer node. For example, if hidden layer node 1 wins when the input vector most closely matches the class-3 prototype vector, then the weight connecting that node and the output node would be 3. Since the winning node always outputs a 1 and all others output 0, the dot product computation at the output layer produces a value of 3, the winning class number.

20.5.6.2 Network Design

The number of hidden nodes should be comparable to the number of expected classes. Since one may not know this number in advance, the number of hidden nodes should be set somewhat greater than a best estimate of the number of classes. The computation method (angle or distance) for the hidden layer should be selected on the basis of which fits the distribution of classes in feature space better. If this is unknown, both methods may be tried.

20.5.6.3 Unsupervised Training

The "one-shot" training method presented in Sec. 20.5.6.1 shows the operation of a counterpropagation network in a production mode, but does not illustrate unsupervised training. The training in that section was supervised in that the network was developed using prototype weight vectors from classes already known to the network designer.

Whereas in the backpropagation network all layers are trained at once, in the counterpropagation network only the hidden layer is trained. Unsupervised training normally proceeds as follows. First, all connection weights are initialized by making them equal, random, or evenly spread about feature space.

As with the backpropagation network, input vectors are randomly selected from a training set, are preprocessed, and are presented to the network. Then, connection weights are modified according to an update rule. After each input vector is presented, the winning node is determined. Only the connection weights associated with the winning node are updated, and that is done according to the rule

$$\Delta w_{ij1} = \alpha(x_i - w_{ij1}) \tag{39}$$

where α is called the *learning rate*. Each weight vector component is adjusted by some proportion α of the difference between it and the corresponding input vector component.

Each adjustment nudges the weight vector of the winning node in the direction of the input vector, as depicted by simple vector addition in Figure 20–8. If the same input vector is presented again, the same node would win the competition and be nudged even closer. However, since input vectors are randomly presented, and no vector can be presented twice

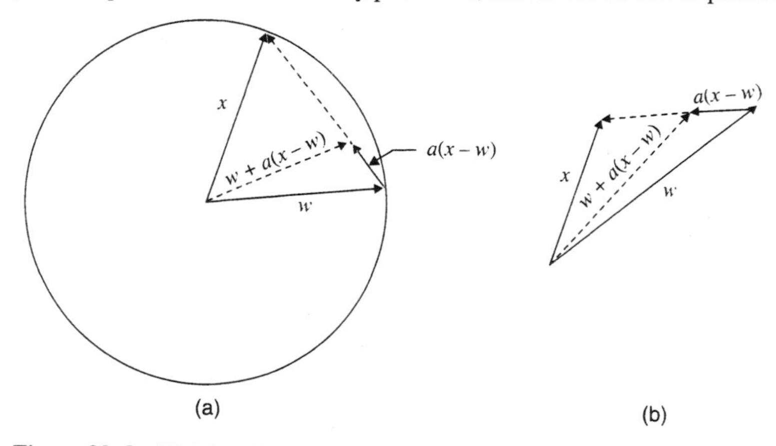

Figure 20–8 Weight adjustment: (a) normalized vectors; (b) unnormalized vectors

until all others have been presented at least once, the weight vectors for each node will be nudged in many directions during the training exercise.

By competing for the input vectors, an average prototype weight vector gradually develops for each cluster in feature space. For example, the weight vectors initially start off equal (Figure 20–9(a)) and gravitate toward the average vector for each of the clusters that exist in feature space (Figure 20–9(b)). Some network designers prefer to start with weight vectors that are random or that are uniformly spread about feature space.

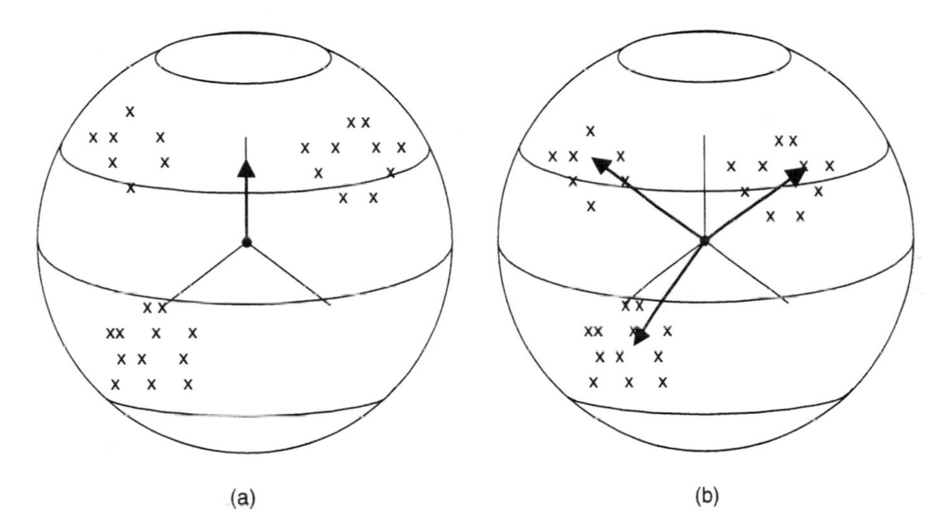

Figure 20–9 Prototype vectors: (a) initially equal; (b) gravitation toward the centroids of clusters in feature space

The hidden nodes are monitored during training to detect when a particular input vector causes the same node to win more than once. When this occurs for all training vectors, the network can be said to have converged. Many (but usually not all) of the nodes in the hidden layer become regular winners as their weight vectors converge toward the mean vectors of the classes.

As far as the network is concerned, there are only different classes of input vectors. It does not "know" what each of the classes should be called. Hence, the node–to–class number correspondence is generally established in supervised training, as described earlier.

Once all the weights have been determined, unknown input vectors can be presented to the network. A winning node will emerge, based on the similarity between the input vector and its weight vector, and the appropriate class number will appear at the output.

20.5.6.4 Design Considerations

The calculations involved in counterpropagation do not demand a neural network implementation, since the basic equations are derived from relatively simple algorithms and concepts. However, a network framework allows a possible parallel implementation for an accelerated hardware design, and it facilitates a number of interesting algorithm extensions that can greatly enhance its processing capabilities.

For example, a problem in counterpropagation is the *stability-plasticity dilemma.* As training proceeds, it is possible for hidden nodes to oscillate between two or more clusters, changing endlessly rather than converging. One solution is to start training with a high learning rate, to move the hidden node weight vectors quickly into the vicinity of clusters, and then to decrease the learning rate as training proceeds.

Another possibility is to initialize the hidden node weight vectors to individual input samples. In this way, candidate clusters are available from the start, and competition can often filter out the better ones. However, forcing the weight vectors to locations in the feature space too quickly can limit the network's ability to react to new data, thus reducing its plasticity.

Too few hidden nodes can also result in network instability, since there might be more classes than there are hidden nodes. On the other hand, too many hidden nodes can result in a system that attempts to draw meaningless distinctions.

20.6 PROPORTION ESTIMATION

In many applications, it is necessary to go a step beyond classification and tabulate the number of each type of object found. Frequently, what is needed is an estimate of one or more proportions—that is, what portion of the total population of objects falls into each class. For this, we draw upon the topic of proportion estimation from the field of statistics.

20.6.1 The Two-Class, Error-Free Case

Definitions. Suppose we wish to determine what proportion p of the students on a particular campus are female ($0 \le p \le 1$). We begin with the following definitions:

$$p = P\{\text{a randomly selected student is female}\} \tag{40}$$

$$q = P\{\text{a randomly selected student is called female}\} \tag{41}$$

Since we are now assuming that we can identify female students without error, p and q are identical in this case.

We next conduct an experiment by interviewing N randomly selected students on the subject of gender. We find n of them to be female, and $N - n$ of them male. It is natural to take the sample proportion,

$$\hat{q} = \frac{n}{N} \tag{42}$$

as an estimate of the proportion of female students. However, unless N is large enough to encompass the entire student body, it alone will be nothing better than an *estimate* of the true underlying proportion p. If N is small, it can be a rather poor estimate at that. The difference between the value of $\hat{q}$ from any particular experiment and the true proportion p can be attributed to *statistical sampling error.*

20.6.1.1 The Distribution of the Estimator

If we were to repeat the preceding experiment many times, we would observe different values for $\hat{q}$. In fact, $\hat{q}$ is a random variable with a binomial distribution. For large N (i.e., greater than about 24), this distribution is approximately Gaussian (normal), with respective mean and standard deviation [11]

$$q = p \quad \text{and} \quad \sigma_q = \sqrt{\frac{p(1-p)}{N}} \tag{43}$$

Recall that approximately 95 percent of the area of the normal distribution falls within two standard deviations on either side of the mean. Thus, we can say with 95-percent confidence that any one observed proportion $\hat{q}$ lies between $p - 2\sigma_q$ and $p + 2\sigma_q$.

As the sample size increases, the distribution becomes progressively more narrow about its mean p, which is the actual proportion of female students on campus. Thus, we can estimate p as accurately as desired by taking a large enough N.

Since we do not know what p is to begin with, it is difficult to calculate σ_q. At the outset, we can play it safe by assuming the worst case. Notice that $p = 0.5$ maximizes σ_q, so using that value gives a conservatively broad estimate for the width of the distribution. After the data are collected, we can substitute $\hat{q}$ for p in Eq. (43) to get a better estimate.

20.6.1.2 Example: Opinion Polls

As a numerical example, let $N = 1{,}000$. Assuming that $p = 0.5$, $\sigma_q = 1.58$ percent, and our confidence interval is approximately ±3 percent. This is a commonly used scenario for the political polls that are published in newspapers. They query a thousand people and claim 3-percent accuracy.

20.6.2 The Two-Class Case with Classification Error

The foregoing theory applies if we classify objects with an error-free, two-class classifier and use the results to estimate the proportion. Suppose now that our method for determining gender is less than foolproof. Here, we consider what effect classification error has on proportion estimation [12–14].

Let the two classifier error rates be

$$\varepsilon_1 = P\{\text{a female is called a male}\} \tag{44}$$

and

$$\varepsilon_2 = P\{\text{a male is called a female}\} \tag{45}$$

Again, $\hat{q} = n/\text{N}$ is (approximately, for large N) normally distributed, but the mean of that distribution is now

$$q = p(1-\varepsilon_1) + (1-p)\varepsilon_2 \tag{46}$$

This is just the probability that either a female will be classified correctly or a male classified incorrectly.

20.6.2.1 Estimator Bias

Notice that the mean of the distribution is no longer p, the true proportion, as it was in the error-free case. It can be higher or lower, depending on the relative values of two error rates. Here, classification error has introduced bias into our estimate of the proportion. Of course, if both error rates are zero, this case reduces to the previous one.

The standard deviation of the distribution of $\hat{q}$ is

$$\sigma_q = \sqrt{\frac{q(1-q)}{N}} \tag{47}$$

This tends to zero as the sample becomes larger. Like the mean, it can be either larger or smaller than in the error-free case. The distressing thing is that larger sample sizes cause the distribution of $\hat{q}$ to become narrow about the wrong answer. Left unchecked, this could seriously interfere with automatic proportion estimation.

20.6.2.2 Unbiasing the Estimator

Although the value $\hat{q}$ that results from any one experiment is a biased estimator of p, it is an unbiased estimator of q, the probability that a student will be classified as female (Eq. 41). If the error rates are known, we can compute an unbiased estimate of p from

$$\hat{p} = \frac{\hat{q} - \varepsilon_2}{1 - \varepsilon_1 - \varepsilon_2} \tag{48}$$

Here, we have solved Eq. (46) for p and substituted $\hat{q}$ for q. Now p is once again the mean of the distribution of our estimator $\hat{p}$, and we can estimate the proportion as accurately as we wish, provided that we are willing to collect enough data.

Notice that any error in the value of ε_1 or ε_2 will undermine the accuracy of this approach. Since these are classifier error rates, they usually must be estimated by experiment. The test set, then, must be of adequate size and representative of the entire population.

20.6.3 The Multiclass Case

We can extend the preceding development to cover the case where the population has more than two classes [15].

20.6.3.1 Definitions

Suppose there are K different types of objects in the population. Then we have a vector $\mathbf{p}$ of proportions, with elements

$$p_i = P\{\text{randomly selected object belongs to class } i\} \tag{49}$$

where $i = 1, \ldots, K$. The classifier error rates can be specified in the format of a confusion matrix $\mathbf{C}$ having elements

$$c_{ij} = P\{\text{object of class } i \text{ is assigned to class } j\} \tag{50}$$

where $j = 1, \ldots, K$. In these terms, the confusion matrix is an array of classification probabilities. Other authors often use the same name for an array of unnormalized classification results.

We let $\mathbf{q}$ be the vector of object classification probabilities with elements

$$q_j = P\{\text{randomly selected object belongs to class } j\} \tag{51}$$

given by

$$q_j = \sum_{i=1}^{K} p_i C_{ij} \quad \text{or} \quad \mathbf{q} = \mathbf{C}^T \mathbf{p} \tag{52}$$

If the classifier examines N objects and assigns n_j of them to class j, then the maximum likelihood estimator of $\mathbf{q}$ is the vector $\hat{\mathbf{q}}$, having elements

$$\hat{q}_j = \frac{n_j}{N} \tag{53}$$

20.6.3.2 The Estimator

In analogy to the two-class case, we now seek a vector $\hat{\mathbf{p}}$ that (a) is based on $\hat{\mathbf{q}}$, (b) is an unbiased estimator of $\mathbf{p}$, and (c) minimizes the mean square estimation error given by

$$\text{MSEE} = \frac{1}{N} \sum_{i=1}^{K} \lambda_i \mathcal{E}[(p_i - \hat{p}_i)^2] \tag{54}$$

where $\mathcal{E}[\ ]$ is the expectation operator and λ is a vector of non-negative weights which allows us to emphasize those classes in which errors are most costly. While the values of the λ_i's are arbitrary, we can, without loss of generality, scale them so that they sum to 1. If no relative weighting is desired, we can make all the elements of λ equal.

The unbiased estimator of $\mathbf{p}$ is [15]

$$\hat{\mathbf{p}} = [\mathbf{C}^T]^{-1} \hat{\mathbf{q}} \tag{55}$$

This is the multiclass generalization of Eq. (48). It says that multiplying the observed proportions by the inverse of the confusion matrix removes the bias introduced by misclassification errors. As before, the error rates must be known accurately.

20.6.3.3 The Befuddlement Matrix

The actual mean square estimation error is [15]

$$\text{MSEE} = \frac{1}{N} \sum_{i=1}^{K} \lambda_i p_i (1 - p_i) + \frac{1}{N} \mathbf{p}^T \mathbf{B} \lambda \tag{56}$$

where the matrix $\mathbf{B}$ has elements

$$B_{ml} = \sum_{i=1}^{K} C_{ml} [C_{li}^{-1}]^2 - \delta_{ml} \tag{57}$$

where δ_{ml} is the Kronecker delta function, i.e.,

$$\delta_{ml} = \begin{cases} 1, & m = l \\ 0, & m \neq l \end{cases} \tag{58}$$

Dependent only on the confusion matrix, $\mathbf{B}$ is an alternative expression of the classifier error rates. It is called the *befuddlement matrix* to avoid confusion. Its elements are non-negative. If the classifier is a good one (i.e., if the off-diagonal elements of $\mathbf{C}$ are small), then $\mathbf{B}$ is approximately the confusion matrix with $1 - c_{ij}$ substituted along the diagonal [15].

As with **B**, the elements of **p** and λ are nonnegative. Thus, the second term of Eq. (56) can never be negative and can never decrease the MSEE, no matter what values **p** and λ take on.

When the classifier is error free (i.e., when **C** = **I**), all the elements of **B** are zero, and the second term of Eq. (56) drops out. This leaves the first term as the estimation error that results only from limited sample size. The second term, then, represents the additional estimation error that results from misclassification.

Since the estimator is unbiased [thanks to Eq. (55)] both terms of Eq. (56) tend to zero with increasing sample size. Hence, one can, in theory, estimate the proportions to any desired degree of accuracy (even with a poor classifier) by examining a large enough number of objects.

Eq. (56) also allows us to compare different classifiers to select the one that best supports proportion estimation. Given the confusion matrix of a particular classifier, one can compute the befuddlement component of MSEE (i.e., $\mathbf{p}^T\mathbf{B}\lambda$) that the classifier will contribute. The classifier contributing the least befuddlement error is superior for the task of proportion estimation.

With a poor classifier, the befuddlement error term in Eq. (56) will be dominant, and many additional samples will be required to overcome misclassification effects. On the other hand, if the classifier is good enough that the befuddlement error term is significantly less than the sampling error term, then further improvement of the classifier may not be worth the effort.

20.6.3.4 Two-Class Befuddlement

Let us now return to the two-class case. If ε_1 and ε_2 are small, the befuddlement matrix is approximately [15]

$$\mathbf{B} = \begin{bmatrix} \varepsilon_1 & \varepsilon_1 \\ \varepsilon_2 & \varepsilon_2 \end{bmatrix} \tag{59}$$

and the befuddlement error is given by

$$\mathbf{p}^T\mathbf{B}\lambda = [\varepsilon_2 + p(\varepsilon_1 - \varepsilon_2)](\lambda_1 + \lambda_2) \tag{60}$$

Since the λ's appear only as a sum, they have merely a scaling effect in this case. Furthermore, if p is small (i.e., females are rare), then it is ε_2 (misclassifying a male) that contributes most to MSEE, and conversely if p is large. If the mix is approximately equal ($p \approx 0.5$), then both errors are equally troublesome.

Often a classifier has an adjustable parameter that controls a trade-off between ε_1 and ε_2. One can decrease one at the expense of increasing the other. In that case, Eq. (60) gives guidance on how to optimize the setting.

20.7 SUMMARY OF IMPORTANT POINTS

1. Features used for classification should be discriminative, reliable, independent, and few in number.
2. A training set used to establish classifier parameters should be representative and unbiased.

3. Classifier performance (error rates) can be estimated by classifying a known test set.
4. Effective features have small within-class variance, low correlation, and large variance-normalized separation between class means.
5. Bayes' theorem [Eq. (11)] gives the probability that a measured object belongs to a particular class.
6. Bayes' decision rule minimizes the risk of operating a classifier.
7. Unknown parameters may be estimated by maximum-likelihood or Bayesian techniques.
8. A neural network is a collection of interconnected identical processing elements arranged in layers. Each node computes a weighted sum of its inputs and passes its output on to the nodes in the next layer.
9. In a neural network used for pattern recognition, the feature vector is input to the first layer, and the last layer outputs a class assignment.
10. Neural networks are trained by repeated application of the training set, with small adjustments made in the interconnection weights at each step.
11. A neural network classifier is subject to overtraining, where it customizes itself to the training set.
12. The performance of a well-trained neural network classifier is usually similar to that of a well-designed statistical classifier. Less knowledge of the problem is required for the development of a neural network classifier, but less knowledge of the decision-making process is available.
13. Classification errors introduce bias into a proportion estimate. With a biased estimator, the estimate does not converge to the true underlying proportion as the sample size increases.
14. Bias can be removed from a proportion estimate by multiplying the vector of observed proportions by the inverse of the confusion matrix [Eq (55)]. Then a large sample size yields proportion estimates of arbitrarily good accuracy.
15. With an unbiased estimator, the mean square estimation error has two components, one due to sampling and one due to misclassification [Eq. (56)]. Both components approach zero for large sample size.
16. The better classifier for proportion estimation is the one that has the lower befuddlement error, $\mathbf{p}^T\mathbf{B}\boldsymbol{\lambda}$.

PROBLEMS

1. The mean weight of an orange is 100 grams, with a standard deviation of 25 grams. The mean weight of a grapefruit is 180 grams, with a standard deviation of 40 grams. Oranges are one and one-half times as common as grapefruits. The seven fruits in a particular box weigh 80, 100, 120, 140, 160, 180, and 200 grams. How many oranges are there in the box?
2. A particular campus has an approximately equal mix of male and female students. In a two-class student gender proportion estimator, the two misclassification errors are always equal, but they can be reduced by further refinement of the algorithm. What value of ε_1 and ε_2 will make the befuddlement error equal to the sampling error? How low do ε_1 and ε_2 have to go so that the befuddlement error is only one-eighth of the sampling error?

3. On a particular campus the student body is approximately three-quarters men. In an existing two-class student gender proportion estimator, the misclassification errors are both 0.25. How many students must be interviewed to reduce the MSEE to 1 percent? Either error rate can be reduced by further refinement of the algorithm. Which one should you endeavor to reduce in order to cut down the required sample size? If you reduce only that one, what values of ε_1 and ε_2 will make the befuddlement error equal to half the sampling error? Then how many students must be interviewed to reduce the MSEE to 1 percent?

PROJECTS

1. Develop a two-class, two-feature Bayes classifier and train it to identify male and female humans using height and body weight as features. Write a brief report describing the design, training, and performance of the classifier.
2. Develop a Bayes classifier program that can identify the suit of playing cards (i.e., diamonds, hearts, clubs, and spades) in digitized images of the suite symbol. Test the program on a poker hand.
3. Train a neural network to classify random vectors from three distributions. Using a small training set, plot the error on the training set and on a separate test set as a function of the amount of training. Carry the experiment out to the point of demonstrated overtraining.
4. Using the same classes, features, and training and test sets, compare the performance of a neural net and a Bayes classifier. Write a report summarizing the advantages and disadvantages of each.

REFERENCES

For additional reading, see Appendix 2.

1. W. Meisel, *Computer-Oriented Approaches to Pattern Recognition,* Academic Press, New York, 1972.
2. A. K. Jain and B. Chandrasekaran, "Dimensionality and Sample Size Considerations in Pattern Recognition Practice," *Handbook of Statistics,* (Vol. 2, pp. 835–855), North Holland Publishing Company, 1982.
3. L. Kanal, and B. Chandrasekaran, "On Dimensionality and Sample Size in Statistical Pattern Recognition," *Pat. Rec.,* **3**:225–234, 1971.
4. I. T. Young, "Further Considerations of Sample Size and Feature Size," *IEEE Trans.* **IT-24**(6):773–775, 1978.
5. A. E. Bryson and Y. Ho, *Applied Optimal Control,* Blaisdell, New York, 1969.
6. D. E. Rumelhart, J. L. McClelland, and the PDP Research Group, *Parallel Distributed Processing: Explorations in the Microstructure of Cognition,* Vols. 1 & 2, MIT Press, Cambridge MA, 1986.
7. R. Hecht-Nielsen, "Applications of Counterpropagation Networks," *Neural Networks,* **1**:131–139, 1988.
8. G. Cybenko, "Approximation by Superpositions of a Sigmoidal Function," *Mathematics of Control, Signals, and Systems,* **2**:303–314, 1989.
9. K. M. Hornik, M. Stinchcombe, and H. White, "Multilayer Feedforward Networks Are Universal Approximators," *Neural Networks,* **2,** 359–366, 1989.
10. G. Cybenko, *Continuous Valued Neural Networks with Two Hidden Layers Are Sufficient,* Technical Report, Dept. of Computer Science, Tufts University, Bedford, MA, 1988.

11. L. Ott and W. Mendenhall, *Understanding Statistics* (5th ed.), PWS-KENT, Boston, 1990.
12. K. R. Castleman and B. S. White, "Optimizing Cervical Cell Classifiers," *Analytical and Quantitative Cytology,* **2**(2):117–122, 1980.
13. K. R. Castleman and B. S. White, "The Tradeoff of Cell Classifier Error Rates," *Cytometry,* **1**(2):156–160, 1980.
14. K. R. Castleman and B. S. White, "The Effect of Abnormal Cell Proportion on Specimen Classifier Performance," *Cytometry,* **2**(4):155–158, 1981.
15. B. S. White and K. R. Castleman, "Estimating Cell Populations," *Pattern Recognition,* **13**(5):365–370, 1981.

CHAPTER 21

Color and Multispectral Image Processing

21.1 INTRODUCTION

In previous chapters, we discussed two-dimensional digital images. Such images can be thought of as having a gray level that is a function of two spatial variables. A straightforward generalization to three dimensions would leave us with images having a gray level that is a function of two spatial variables and one spectral variable. These are called *multispectral images*. When the spectral sampling is restricted to three bands, and these correspond to the red, green, and blue spectral bands to which the human visual system responds, we call the procedure *color image processing*.

A three-dimensional image can be formed by sampling not only the two spatial coordinates of an optical image, but also the wavelength spectrum of the light at each point. Thus, instead of quantizing the total light intensity falling upon each pixel, one samples and quantizes the electromagnetic spectrum of that illumination. This forms a three-dimensional image in which gray level is a function of two spatial variables and a third variable, optical wavelength.

The discipline concerned with processing such images is commonly called *multispectral image analysis*. The resulting images are sometimes referred to as *multidigital images*. They are usually organized as a series of two-dimensional digital images, each of which was obtained by digitizing the original image in a narrow spectral band.

21.2 MULTISPECTRAL IMAGE ANALYSIS

Perhaps the greatest effort devoted to multispectral analysis has been in the field of remote sensing [1]. Multispectral images are obtained from aircraft or spacecraft that overfly a region of interest on the earth's surface. Each pixel of the image is sensed by a battery of narrow-band light-measuring devices. Thus, the image is digitized with multivalued pixels. Twenty-four or more spectral channels are commonly used. The resulting image is processed as a set of 24 or so two-dimensional digital images. Each two-dimensional image shows the object as it would appear through a narrow-band optical filter. The spectral range covered by multispectral analysis need not be limited to the visible spectrum. Commonly, the range of interest extends from the infrared through the visible spectrum and into the ultraviolet.

A considerable portion of multispectral analysis is devoted to *pixel classification.* In this process, the image is partitioned into regions that correspond to different types of surfaces, such as lakes, fields, forests, and residential and industrial areas. Each multivalued pixel is classified as to the surface type using its set of spectral intensity measurements. The classification is accomplished with techniques similar to those discussed in Chapter 20. Frequently, algebraic operations such as subtraction and forming ratios are performed on the set of images to enhance surface differences. While the image taken in any particular spectral band will suffer from shading due to illumination effects, ratio images show surface properties more reliably. The interested reader should consult the literature on remote sensing for an introduction to this subject [1].

21.3 COLOR IMAGE PROCESSING

21.3.1 Color Vision

The most familiar form of multispectral imaging is normal color vision. The retina of the human eye is covered with photoreceptor cells (Figure 21–1) that are functionally analogous to the receptor sites (pixels) on a CCD chip. The photoreceptor cells absorb light from the image that is focused on the retina by the lens and cornea. They generate nerve impulses that travel to the brain, via approximately a million fibers in the optic nerve. The frequency of these impulses encodes the brightness of the incident light.

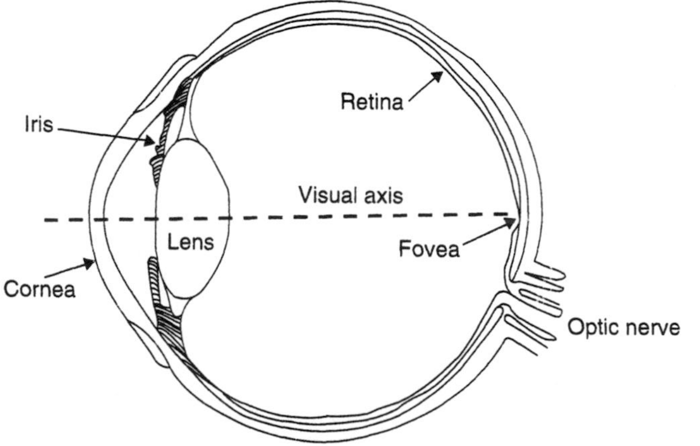

Figure 21–1 The human eye (right eye, from above)

The photoreceptor cells are a mixture of two types, rods and cones, so called for their physical shape. The rod cells are the more sensitive, providing us with very light-sensitive, monochromatic night vision. The cones afford color vision, but only at higher light levels.

The cones occur in three types, differing mainly in the photochemistry they employ to convert light into nerve impulses. The cones divide the visible portion of the electromagnetic spectrum into three bands: red, green, and blue. For this reason, these three colors are referred to as the *primary colors* of human vision. Figure 21–2 shows the sensitivity spectra of the three types of cones in the human visual system [2].

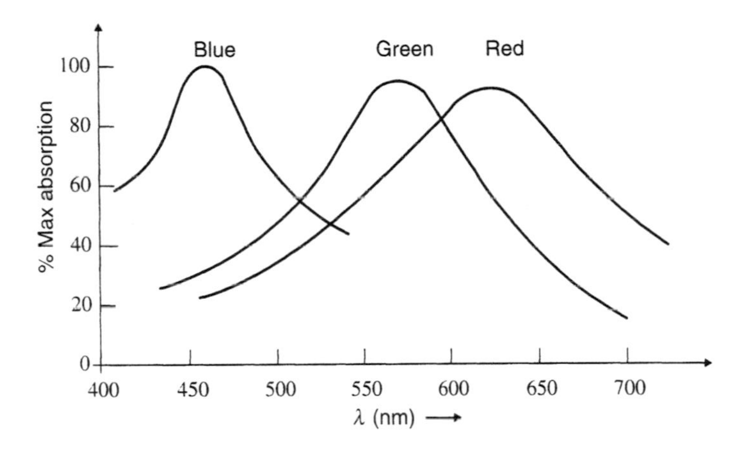

Figure 21–2 Sensitivity spectra of human photoreceptor cells

The nerve impulses generated by the photoreceptor cells in response to light pass through a layer of bipolar cells and a layer of ganglion cells. The artificial neural networks described in Chapter 20 are modeled after the architecture and operation of these retinal cells. The axon fibers of the million or so ganglion cells form the optic nerve, which conducts the image data to the brain.

21.3.2 Tricolor Imaging

Because of the nature of the human visual system, the bulk of product development effort and expense in electronic imaging has been devoted to tricolor systems, particularly television cameras, digitizers, displays, and printers. Thus, the three-color model takes on a special importance. Not only is color image enhancement a tricolor exercise, but quantitative color image analysis is also commonly done on tricolor equipment, since it is produced in high volume at relatively low cost.

Common examples of tricolor imaging systems include color photography and color television (Chapters 2, 3). In both cases, the visible spectrum is divided into three bands—red, green, and blue—approximating the spectral quantization employed by the human eye. In color photography, separate images are developed on three sandwiched photographic emulsions. In color television, three image sensors are employed, one each behind red, green, and blue optical filters. For display purposes, red, green, and blue images are superimposed, either on the color print or on the color display screen. This overlay produces approximately the same effect on the retina as the original scene and thus looks normal.

While a tricolor digital image can be thought of as a scalar function of three coordinates (two spatial and one spectral), it is usually more convenient to treat it as an ordinary (two-dimensional) image having three gray levels (red, green, and blue) at each pixel. In other contexts, it is more useful to consider it an overlay of three monochrome digital images. Color image processing and analysis remain simple if one is able to visualize these two alternatives clearly. Then, many of the concepts discussed in previous chapters can be applied with little modification.

21.3.3 Color Specification

RGB Format. There are several ways one can quantitatively specify a color, such as that of a pixel in a color digital image. The most straightforward way is to use the red, green, and blue brightness values, scaled between, for example, zero and one. We call this convention the *RGB format.* Each pixel—and, indeed, any color it is possible to visualize—can be represented by a point in the first quadrant of three-space, as shown by the color cube in Figure 21–3. The gray level histogram of a tri-color image is a scatter of points in RGB-space.

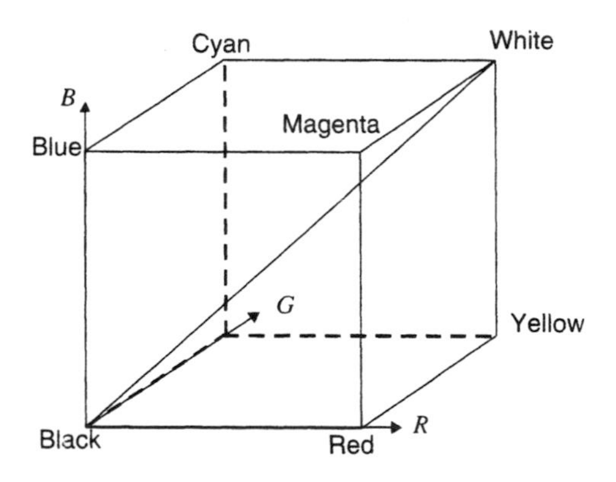

Figure 21–3 Rectangular color space

The origin of the RGB color space represents no brightness of any of the primary colors and is thus the color black. Full brightness of all three primaries together appears as white. Equal amounts of the three color components at lesser brightness produces a shade of gray. The locus of all such points falls on the diagonal of the color cube and is called the *gray line.* Three of the corners of the color cube correspond to the primary colors—red, green, and blue. The remaining three corners correspond to the secondary colors—yellow, cyan (blue-green), and magenta (purple).

HSI Format. Another useful specification scheme, called *HSI format,* is a formalization of the color system developed by Munsell and commonly used by artists [3,4]. Its design reflects the way humans see color, and it offers advantages for image processing as well.

In HSI format, *I* stands for *intensity,* or brightness. It is, for our purposes, just the average of the R, G, and B gray-level values, although different schemes with unequal weighting of the colors are also used [5]. The intensity value specifies the overall brightness of the pixel, without regard to what its color is. One can convert a color image to monochrome by averaging the RGB components together, thereby discarding the color information.

The two parameters that contain the color information are the *hue* (*H*) and *saturation*

(S), although equivalent terms are sometimes used. These two parameters are illustrated by the color circle in Figure 21–4. Hue is expressed as an angle. The hue of a color refers to which spectral wavelength (i.e., which color of the rainbow) it most closely matches. Arbitrarily, a hue of 0° is red, 120° is green, and 240° is blue. Hue traverses the colors of the visible spectrum as it goes from 0 to 240°. Between 240° and 360° fall the nonspectral (purple) colors that the eye perceives.

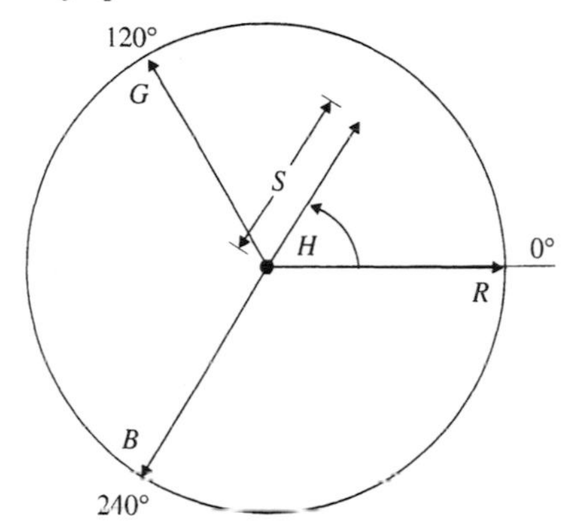

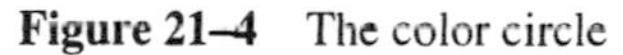

Figure 21–4 The color circle

The saturation parameter is the radius of the point from the origin of the color circle. Around the periphery of the circle fall the *pure,* or *saturated,* colors, and their saturation values are unity. At the center lie neutral (gray) shades, that is, those with zero saturation.

The concept of saturation can be illustrated as follows. If you had a bucket of bright red paint, it would correspond to a hue of 0° and saturation 1. Mixing in white paint makes the red less intense, reducing its saturation, but without making it darker. Pink would correspond to a saturation of 0.5 or so. As more white is added to the mixture, the red becomes paler and the saturation decreases, eventually approaching zero (white). If, on the other hand, you mixed black paint with the bright red, its intensity would decrease (toward black), while its hue (red) and saturation (1.0) remained constant.

Taken together, the three color coordinates define a cylindrical color space (Figure 21–5). The gray shades fall along the axis from black at the bottom to white at the top. The fully bright, fully saturated colors fall on the perimeter of the circular top surface.

There are many other color coordinate systems that are used. Those established by the Commission Internationale de l'Éclairage (CIE), an international standards committee for light and color, are perhaps the most widely used. They are based on experimental data from color-matching experiments conducted on human observers.

21.3.4 Color Coordinate Conversion

For image-processing purposes, it is useful to be able to convert between RGB and HSI color coordinates. Some processes are naturally more successful when carried out in one system or the other.

21.3.4.1 RGB-to-HSI Conversion

The conversion from RGB to HSI format can be approached as follows. Recall that the gray line is the diagonal of the color cube in RGB space, and it is the vertical axis in cylindrical

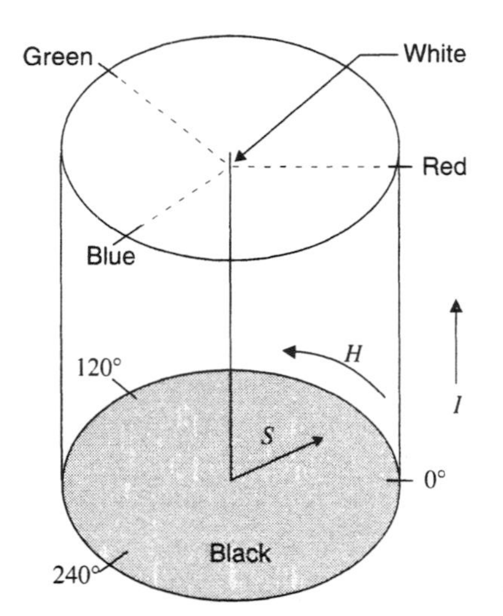

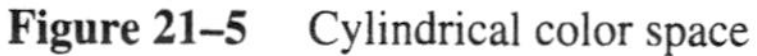

Figure 21–5 Cylindrical color space

HSI space. Thus, we can begin by establishing an (x, y, z) coordinate system in which the RGB cube is rotated so that its diagonal lies along the z-axis and its R-axis lies in the xz-plane (Figure 21–6 [6]). This rotation is given by

$$x = \frac{1}{\sqrt{6}}[2R - G - B] \qquad y = \frac{1}{\sqrt{2}}[G - B] \qquad z = \frac{1}{\sqrt{3}}[R + G + B] \tag{1}$$

Next, we convert to cylindrical coordinates by defining polar coordinates in the xy-plane. We have

$$\rho = \sqrt{x^2 + y^2} \qquad \phi = \text{ang}(x, y) \tag{2}$$

where $\text{ang}(x, y)$ is the angle a line from the origin to the point (x, y) makes with the x-axis. This is basically the arc tangent, but with attention paid to which quadrant the point is in.

We now have cylindrical coordinates, where (ϕ, ρ, z) corresponds to (H, S, I), but there are two problems with saturation: It is not independent of intensity, as we would like

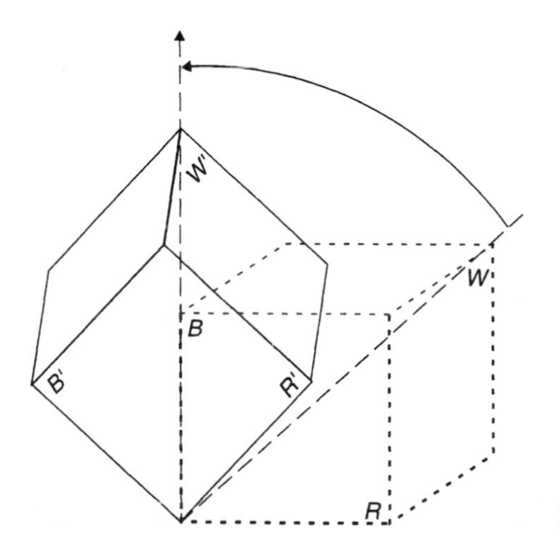

Figure 21–6 Rotating the RGB cube

it to be, and the fully saturated colors (those having no more than two of the primary colors present) fall on a hexagon in the *xy*-plane (Figure 21–7(a)), rather than on a circle. The remedy is to normalize ρ by dividing by its maximum for that value of ϕ. This leads to the saturation formula [6]

$$S = \frac{\rho}{\rho_{\max}} = 1 - \frac{3\min(R, G, B)}{R + G + B} = 1 - \frac{\sqrt{3}}{I}\min(R, G, B) \tag{3}$$

The fully saturated colors are now on a unit-radius circle in the *xy*-plane (Figure 21–7(b)).

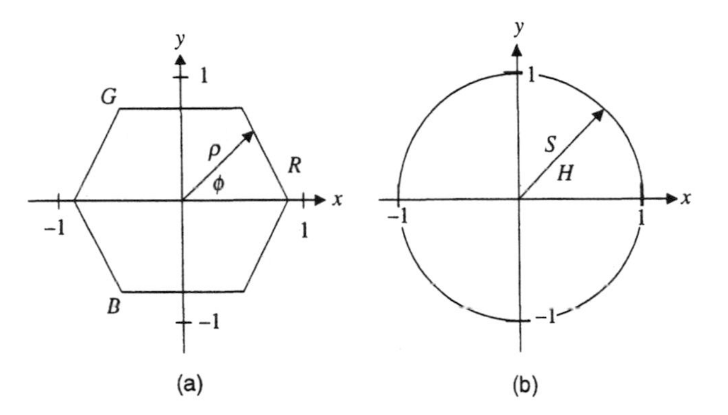

Figure 21–7 The *x*, *y* plane of color space: (a) unnormalized polar coordinates; (b) normalized saturation

While the hue can be taken to be ϕ in equation (2), an equivalent method is to compute the angle

$$\theta = \cos^{-1}\left[\frac{\frac{1}{2}[(R-G)+(R-B)]}{\sqrt{(R-G)^2+(R-B)(G-B)}}\right] \tag{4}$$

and the hue is then

$$H = \begin{cases} \theta & G \geq B \\ 2\pi - \theta & G \leq B \end{cases} \tag{5}$$

21.3.4.2 HSI-to-RGB Conversion

The formulas for converting from HSI to RGB take on slightly different form, depending upon the sector of the color circle in which the point to be converted falls [7]. For $0° \leq H < 120°$,

$$R = \frac{I}{\sqrt{3}}\left[1 + \frac{S\cos(H)}{\cos(60° - H)}\right] \qquad B = \frac{I}{\sqrt{3}}(1 - S) \qquad G = \sqrt{3}I - R - B \tag{6}$$

while for $120° \leq H < 240°$,

$$G = \frac{I}{\sqrt{3}}\left[1 + \frac{S\cos(H - 120°)}{\cos(180° - H)}\right] \qquad R = \frac{I}{\sqrt{3}}(1 - S) \qquad B = \sqrt{3}I - R - G \tag{7}$$

and for $240° \leq H < 360°$,

$$B = \frac{I}{\sqrt{3}}\left[1 + \frac{S\cos(H - 240°)}{\cos(300° - H)}\right] \qquad G = \frac{I}{\sqrt{3}}(1 - S) \qquad R = \sqrt{3}I - G - B \tag{8}$$

There are several variations of HSI conversion [5,8]. From a color image-processing point of view, the specific choice may not materially affect the result, as long as hue is an angle, saturation is independent of intensity, and the transformation is invertible.

21.3.5 Color Image Enhancement

21.3.5.1 Color Balance

Often when a color image is digitized, it will not appear properly when displayed. Different sensitivities, gain factors, offsets (black levels), etc., in the three color channels perform different linear transformations on the three component images during digitizing. The result is an image with its primary colors "out of balance." All the objects in the scene are shifted in color from how they should appear. Most noticeably, objects that should be gray take on color.

The first test of color balance is whether all the gray objects indeed appear gray. The second test is if the highly saturated colors have the proper hue. If the image has a prominent black or white background, this will produce a discernible peak in the histograms of the RGB component images. If these peaks occur at different gray levels, it signals color imbalance.

The remedy for color imbalance of this type is to use linear gray-scale transformations on each of the individual R, G, and B images. Normally, only two of the component images need to be transformed to match the third. The simplest way to design the required gray-scale transformation function is to (1) select relatively uniform light gray and dark gray areas of the image, (2) compute the mean gray level of both areas in all three component images, and (3) use a linear contrast stretch on two of the component images that will make them match the third. If each of the two areas has the same gray level in all three component images, color balance has been achieved.

If the camera and digitizing system are stable, the required transformations can be determined before the digitizing session by digitizing a black-and-white step-wedge test target. By using several steps of the wedge, any nonlinearity present can be detected and removed. The process is similar to standard photometric calibration (Chapter 6), except that the output gray levels should match in all three component images.

21.3.5.2 Contrast and Color Enhancement

In working with the RGB components of a tricolor digital image, one must be careful to avoid upsetting the color balance. Essentially all of the image-processing techniques previously discussed will produce very predictable results if applied to the intensity component of an image in HSI format. In many ways, the intensity component can be treated as a monochrome image. The color information, embedded in the hue and saturation components, will usually tag along without protest. Any geometric operations, of course, must be carried out in exactly the same way on all three components, whether these are in RGB or HSI format.

Saturation Enhancement. One can make the colors in an image more bold by multiplying the saturation at each pixel by a constant greater than 1. Likewise, a constant less than 1 reduces the apparent intensity of the colors. A nonlinear point operation can be used on the saturation image, as long as the transformation function is zero at the origin. Changing the saturation of pixels with near-zero saturation can upset the color balance.

Hue Alteration. Since hue is an angle, one logical thing to do is add a constant to the hue of each pixel. This has the effect of shifting the color of each object up or down the rainbow. If the angle added or subtracted is only a few degrees, the process will "cool" or "warm" the color image respectively. Larger angles will drastically alter its appearance. A general point operation performed on the hue image will exaggerate color differences between objects in portions of the spectrum where the slope of the transformation function is greater than 1, and conversely. Since hue is an angle, operations processing the hue component image must treat the gray scale as periodic, recognizing that, for eight bits, for example, $255 + 1 = 0$, and $0 - 1 = 255$.

21.3.5.3 Color Image Restoration

One can apply the techniques discussed in Chapter 16 to the R, G, and B images individually in a straightforward extension to color. There are, however, some special considerations that apply to tricolor images.

If an image is being restored or enhanced for the sake of its appearance, one does well to take note of the strengths and weaknesses of the human eye. Detail, for example, is much more visible in intensity than in color. Blurring of edges, then, is much more disturbing if it affects intensity rather than hue or saturation. Similarly, graininess (random noise) of a reasonable amplitude is more apparent in intensity than in color. Finally, the eye is much more sensitive to graininess in flat areas than in busy areas containing high-contrast detail. This applies to both intensity and color (hue and saturation) noise.

With the foregoing in mind, we can construct a general outline for approaching a color image enhancement or restoration project:

1. Use a linear point operation to ensure that the RGB image fits properly within the gray scale and is in color balance.
2. Convert to HSI format.
3. Use a lowpass filter or, perhaps better, a median filter on the hue and saturation images to reduce the random color noise within objects. Some blurring of edges in these images will not be noticeable in the final product, so this step can involve significant noise reduction. The filter used must preserve the average gray level (i.e., $\mathrm{MTF}(0,0) = 1$).
4. Use a space-variant approach (e.g., linear combination filters; see Chapter 16) to restore the intensity image. This step sharpens edges and enhances detail, while reducing graininess in flat areas. Again, $\mathrm{MTF}(0,0) = 1$.
5. Use linear point operations on all three components, as required, to ensure proper utilization of the gray scale.
6. Convert to RGB format, and display or print the image.

Beginning with a good-quality digitized image, the amount of visible improvement possible with this approach can be quite striking.

21.3.5.4 Pseudocolor

The term *pseudocolor* refers to generating a color image from a monochrome image by mapping each of the gray levels (located along the axis of the color cylinder) to a point in color space. This is simply assigning a color to each gray level by some rule that can be stored in a lookup table.

The attraction of pseudocolor stems from the fact that the human eye can reliably discern many more different colors than it can different shades of gray. Thus, while one might be able to appreciate only 40 or so of 256 gray levels on a monochrome display, many more shades might be visible when mapped to different colors. There are, however, monochrome techniques (e.g., contour lines, gradient shading, etc.) that can render subtle variations more visible. (Recall Figure 20-4.)

A pseudocolor mapping is usually more satisfactory if it employs some pattern, rather than a random assignment of colors. Normally, the grayscale axis maps to a continuous line that curves its way through color space. Mapping the black and white points onto themselves is often useful. In general, the more conservative mappings are the more successful, since substantial visual agony can result from the more ambitious color assignment schemes.

Basically a detail of the image display process, pseudocolor has been glorified with terms like *pseudocolor processing,* and *pseudocolor analysis.* A favorite tool of salespeople, it finds frequent use in system demonstrations. It can bring a glaze over a customer's eyes more quickly than any other known display technique.

My own searchings have produced a painfully short list of demonstrably productive pseudocolor applications. In one, developed by Donald Winkler at the NASA Johnson Space Center, a real-time pseudocolor display was used to assist operators in setting the light level on a digitizing microscope. The entire gray scale was mapped onto itself with the exception of level 255, which was mapped to a bright red. The operators' instructions were "Increase the lamp current until you see red, and then decrease it until the red goes away." This application resulted in thousands of properly digitized images. It also completes the aforementioned list.

21.3.6 Color Image Analysis

Much of the previous discussion of monochrome image analysis also can be applied directly to color images. There are, however, some differences worthy of note.

21.3.6.1 Color Compensation

In some applications, the goal is to isolate various types of objects that differ primarily or exclusively in color. In fluorescence microscopy, for example, different constituents of a biological specimen (e.g., different components of cells) are stained with different colored fluorescent dyes. The analysis often involves being able to visualize these objects separately, but in correct spatial relationship to each other.

If the preparation procedure stains three chemical components of the specimen, for example, with red, green, and blue fluorescent dyes, one can digitize and display the specimen as a normal tricolor image. The RGB component images are then registered monochrome images, each showing objects of a specific type. This paves the way for image segmentation and object measurement using techniques previously discussed.

Given the broad and overlapping sensitivity spectra of commonly used color image digitizers, as well as the varied emission spectra of available fluorescent dyes (*fluorophores*), one seldom obtains complete isolation of the three types of objects in the three component images. Normally, each type of object will be visible in all three of the color component images, although at reduced contrast in two of them. We refer to this phenomenon as *color spread.*

We can model the color spread effect as a linear transformation [9,10]. Let the matrix **C** specify how the colors are spread among the three channels. Then each element c_{ij} is the proportion of the brightness from fluorophore j that appears in color channel i of the digitized image. Let **x** be the three-by-one vector of actual fluorophore brightness values at a particular pixel, scaled as gray levels that would be produced by an ideal digitizer (one with no color spread or black-level offset). Then

$$\mathbf{y} = \mathbf{C}\mathbf{x} + \mathbf{b} \tag{9}$$

is the vector of RGB gray levels recorded at that pixel by the digitizer. **C** accounts for the color spread, while the vector **b** accounts for the black-level offset of the digitizer. That is, b_i is the gray level that corresponds to black (zero brightness) in channel i.

Eq. (9) is easily solved for the true brightness:

$$\mathbf{x} = \mathbf{C}^{-1}[\mathbf{y} - \mathbf{b}] \tag{10}$$

Color spread can thus be eliminated by premultiplying the RGB gray-level vector for each pixel by the inverse of the color spread matrix, after the black level has been subtracted from each channel.

The foregoing analysis assumes that the exposure time is the same for each color channel, or at least that it is the same as that used in the calibration study that determined the color spread matrix. Sometimes it is necessary to use different exposure times to compensate for large differences in brightness among the three color components of the specimen. We can account for this in the following way.

Let the diagonal matrix **E** specify the relative exposure time used in each channel in a particular digitization. That is, e_{ii} is the ratio of the current exposure time for color channel i to the exposure time used for the color spread calibration image. Then Eq. (9) becomes

$$\mathbf{y} = \mathbf{E}\mathbf{C}\mathbf{x} + \mathbf{b} \tag{11}$$

which can be solved for

$$\mathbf{x} = \mathbf{C}^{-1}\mathbf{E}^{-1}[\mathbf{y} - \mathbf{b}] \tag{12}$$

Since **E** is a diagonal matrix, its inverse is diagonal as well, having diagonal elements that are simply the reciprocals of the corresponding elements of **E**. Further, $\mathbf{C}^{-1}\mathbf{E}^{-1}$ can be thought of as a modified color compensation matrix: It is merely $\mathbf{C}^{-1}$ after each ith column has been divided by e_{ii}. Thus, there is a simple way to modify the color compensation matrix to account for variation in exposure time.

The preceding development assumes that gray levels are linear with brightness. For some cameras, an RGB point operation might be required to establish this condition prior to color compensation.

21.3.6.2 Example of Color Compensation

Figure 21–8 shows an RGB image of human bone marrow cells that have been stained with DAPI, a blue fluorescent dye. The image was digitized by a color television camera mounted on a fluorescence microscope. In this preparation, cells that are in the process of dividing also absorb FITC, a green fluorescent dye. Finally, the DNA located at the centromeres of the two number-8 chromosomes is labeled with Texas Red, a red fluorescent dye.

Ideally, all the cells would be visible in the blue channel, dividing cells would be visible in the green channel as well, and two dots per cell, corresponding to the number-8 chromosomes, would appear in the red channel. In the figure, however, all components appear in all channels due to overlapping sensitivity spectra of the three color channels.

The color spread matrix for the instrument that recorded the image in Figure 21–8 appears in Table 21-1. The matrix states that, for example, only 44 percent of a DAPI molecule's brightness is recorded in the blue channel, while 32 percent of it shows up in the

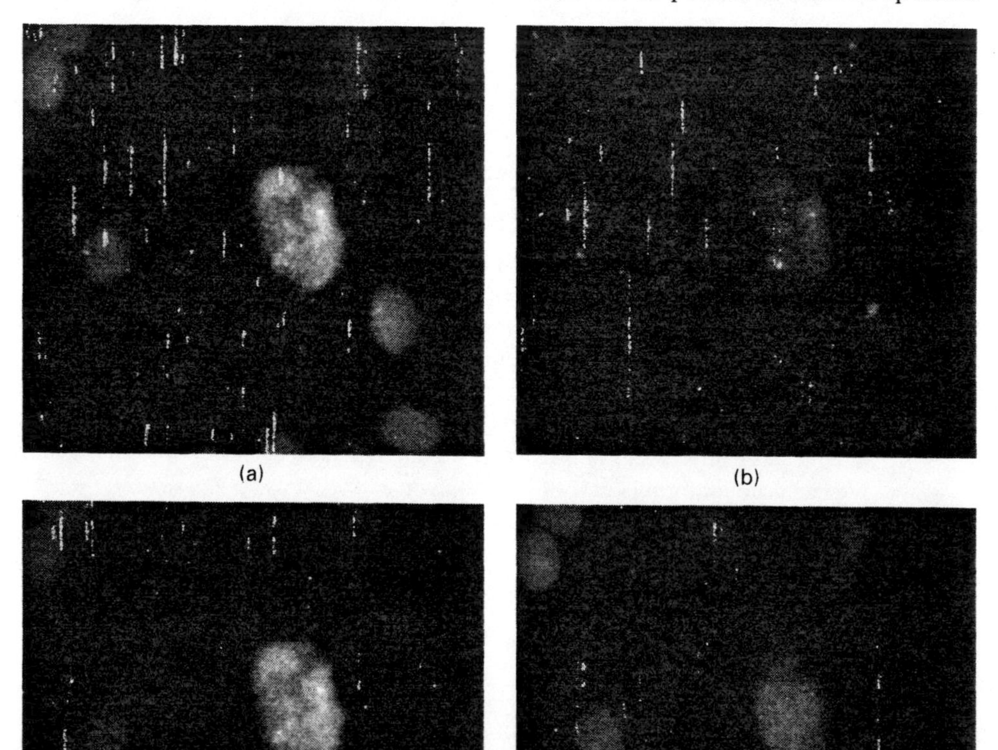

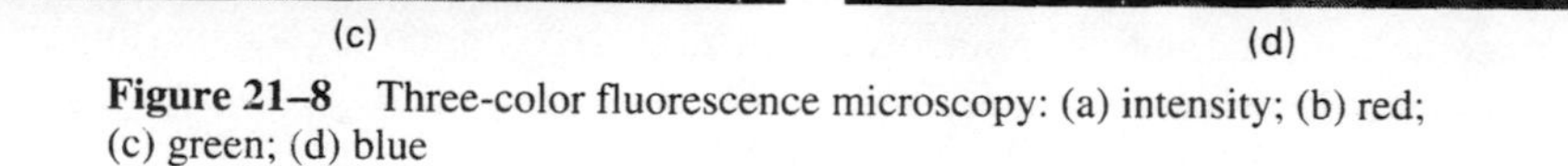

Figure 21–8 Three-color fluorescence microscopy: (a) intensity; (b) red; (c) green; (d) blue

TABLE 21–1 COLOR SPREAD MATRIX

	Texas Red	FITC	DAPI
Red	0.85	0.26	0.24
Green	0.05	0.65	0.32
Blue	0.10	0.09	0.44

green channel and 24 percent finds its way into the red channel. The values in this matrix were determined experimentally from digitized images of cells stained with single fluorophores, and they would be different for other combinations of dyes, camera, and optics.

The color compensation matrix $\mathbf{C}^{-1}$ specifies what must be done to correct the color spread. The inverse of the matrix in Table 21–1 is

$$\mathbf{C}^{-1} = \begin{bmatrix} 1.24 & -.45 & -.35 \\ 0.05 & 1.69 & -1.26 \\ -.29 & -.24 & 2.61 \end{bmatrix} \tag{13}$$

Thus, to correct the red channel image, one should, at each pixel, take 124 percent of the gray level in the red channel image, add 5 percent of the green channel value, and subtract 29 percent of the blue. The second and third rows likewise specify how to correct the green and blue channel images, respectively.

A numerical example illustrates how the computation proceeds at each pixel in the RGB image. Using the color spread matrix in Table 21–1 and illustrative values for $\mathbf{x}$ and $\mathbf{b}$, Eq. (11) gives the resulting recorded gray level values:

$$\mathbf{y} = \mathbf{ECx} + \mathbf{b} = \begin{bmatrix} 1 & 0 & 0 \\ 0 & 1 & 0 \\ 0 & 0 & 2 \end{bmatrix} \begin{bmatrix} .85 & .26 & .24 \\ .05 & .65 & .32 \\ .10 & .09 & .44 \end{bmatrix} \begin{bmatrix} 201 \\ 143 \\ 104 \end{bmatrix} + \begin{bmatrix} 18 \\ 22 \\ 20 \end{bmatrix} = \begin{bmatrix} 251 \\ 158 \\ 178 \end{bmatrix} \tag{14}$$

Here we have assumed that twice the normal exposure time was used in the blue channel. Then Eq. (12) recovers the true brightness values:

$$\mathbf{x} = \mathbf{C}^{-1}\mathbf{E}^{-1}(\mathbf{y} - \mathbf{b}) = \begin{bmatrix} 1.24 & -0.45 & -0.35 \\ 0.05 & 1.69 & -1.26 \\ -0.29 & -0.24 & 2.61 \end{bmatrix} \begin{bmatrix} 1 & 0 & 0 \\ 0 & 1 & 0 \\ 0 & 0 & 0.5 \end{bmatrix} \left(\begin{bmatrix} 251 \\ 158 \\ 178 \end{bmatrix} - \begin{bmatrix} 18 \\ 22 \\ 20 \end{bmatrix} \right) = \begin{bmatrix} 201 \\ 143 \\ 104 \end{bmatrix} \tag{15}$$

The matrix product in Eq. (15) is simply

$$\mathbf{C}^{-1}\mathbf{E}^{-1} = \begin{bmatrix} 1.24 & -0.45 & -0.18 \\ 0.05 & 1.69 & -0.63 \\ -0.29 & -0.24 & 1.31 \end{bmatrix} \tag{16}$$

which is the same as $\mathbf{C}^{-1}$, except that the elements in the third column have been halved to account for the longer exposure in the blue channel. Since the matrix is the same for all pixels in the image, it can be computed once and used repeatedly.

Figure 21–9 shows the result of color compensation applied to the image in Figure 21–8.

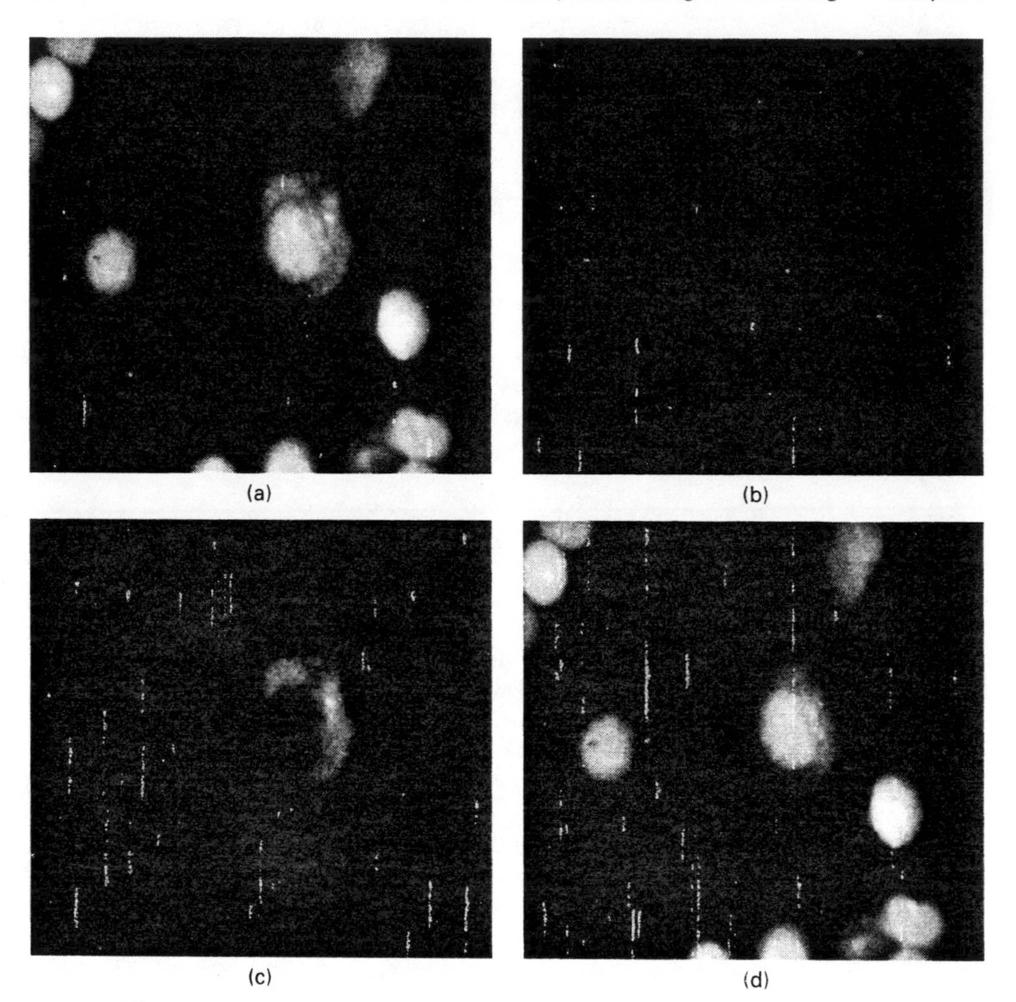

Figure 21–9 The result of color compensation: (a) intensity; (b) red; (c) green; (d) blue

Here, the three differently stained types of objects have been effectively isolated to the three color component images. This makes image segmentation and measurement a much simpler task. Color compensation also increases the saturation of the displayed color image, since color spread tends to desaturate the image.

21.3.6.3 Color Image Segmentation

Segmenting a color image by thresholding becomes a process of partitioning color space. The different objects in the image often correspond to separate clusters of points in a three-dimensional histogram defined in RGB or HSI space. A three-feature Bayes classifier design can prove helpful in partitioning the space.

The hue and saturation of an object are normally dictated by the light-absorbing or -reflecting properties of the material of which the object is made. The intensity of the object, however, is seriously affected by illumination and viewing angle. A shadow, for example, falling across an object will normally have much more effect on the intensity of the pixels therein than on the two color parameters. Thus, it may be productive to segment the image in the hue-saturation plane (i.e., on the color circle rather than in three-dimensional color space), thereby ignoring intensity completely. Some noise reduction by smoothing or median filtering the two color parameters may prove helpful as well.

21.3.6.4 Color Image Measurement

Once segmentation is complete, measurements of size and shape are the same as with a monochrome image. Brightness, however, now includes the added aspect of color. One can compute the average hue and average saturation of each object, as well as its average intensity. Classification proceeds as before.

21.4 SUMMARY OF IMPORTANT POINTS

1. Multispectral images are digitized functions of x, y, and optical wavelength that show the reflectance spectrum of the object at each pixel.
2. Normally, in tricolor image processing, the color balance should be achieved with the image in RGB format and the bulk of the processing or analysis performed in HSI format.
3. Most of the techniques developed for monochrome images are applicable to the intensity component of a tricolor digital image.
4. The spreading of primary-colored objects to other color channels can be compensated for by multiplying the RGB values by the inverse of the color spread matrix.

PROBLEMS

1. Suppose you have a test target that is a black square within a white square. When you digitize the target with a particular RGB tricolor system, you get bimodal histograms in all three channels. The peaks are located as follows: $R = [62,242]$, $G = [31,251]$, $B = [12,238]$. Does this system require color balance? If so, design a color point operation that will do the job. Make it so that black has gray level 16 and white has gray level 242.
2. Suppose you digitize a test target consisting of four gray bars uniformly spaced in brightness from black to white. The average HSI values of the four bars are $[H, S, I] = [259,0.571,32]$, $[90,0.024,145]$, $[82,0.116,259]$, $[81,0.152,372]$. Plot the four points in HS space. What is the color appearance of each of the four bars? Is the digitizer color balanced? If not, will a linear point operation put it in color balance? If so, design such an operation. If not, design a piecewise linear point operation that will.
3. Suppose you digitize a test target consisting of four gray bars uniformly spaced in brightness from black to white. The average HSI values of the four bars are $[H, S, I] = [0,0.25,23]$, $[101,0.16,144]$, $[199,0.192,300]$, $[300,0.083,416]$. Plot the four points in HS space. What is the color appearance of each of the four bars? Is the digitizer color balanced? If not, will a linear point operation put it in color balance? If so, design such an operation. If not, design a piecewise linear point operation that will.

PROJECTS

1. Develop a program for RGB-to-HSI and HSI-to-RGB color image conversion. Test the program on an image containing all extreme values of R, G, and B. Subtract an RGB image that has been converted to HSI and back from the original image, and describe the contents of the difference image.
2. Perform an image restoration on a digitized color image using the outline in Sec. 21.3.5.3, but only stationary (non-space-variant) filtering. Report on the practical limits of each of the enhancement steps and the amount of improvement attained.
3. Perform an image restoration on a digitized color image using the outline in Sec. 21.3.5.3 and space-variant filtering (e.g., linear combination filters). Report on the practical limits of each of the enhancement steps and the amount of improvement attained.
4. Develop a program that can manipulate an HSI image as described in Sec. 21.3.5.3, and use the program to improve the image of a friend. Report on the methods and results.
5. Develop a demonstrably productive pseudocolor application. Publish the method and its results in a prestigious journal. Send me a Christmas card with the pseudocolor image on the front and the reprint attached. Include comments relevant to the situation.

REFERENCES

1. R. G. Greeves, A. Anson, and D. Landen, eds., *Manual of Remote Sensing* (Vol. I), American Society of Photogrammetry, Falls Church, VA 1975.
2. G. Wald, "The Receptors for Human Color Vision," *Science,* **145**(3636):1007–1017, 1964.
3. A. H. Munsell, *A Color Notation* (8th ed.), Munsell Color Company, Boston, 1939.
4. A. H. Munsell, *A Grammar of Color,* Van Nostrand-Reinhold, New York, 1969.
5. W. K. Pratt, *Digital Image Processing,* John Wiley & Sons, Inc., New York, 1991.
6. R. S. Ledley, M. Buas, and T. J. Golab, "Fundamentals of True-Color Image Processing," *Proc. 10th Int. Conf. Pat. Rec.,* IEEE Comp. Soc. Press, Los Alamitos, CA (Cat. No. 90CH2898-5) **1**:791–795, 1990.
7. R. C. Gonzalez and R. E. Woods, *Digital Image Processing,* Addison-Wesley, Reading, MA, 1992 (Sec. 4.6.2).
8. A. K. Jain, *Fundamentals of Digital Image Processing,* Prentice Hall, Englewood Cliffs, NJ, 1989.
9. K. R. Castleman, "Color Compensation for FISH Image Processing," *Bioimaging,* **1**(3):159–165, 1993.
10. K. R. Castleman, "Color Compensation with Unequal Integration Periods," *Bioimaging,* **2**(3):160–162, 1994.

CHAPTER 22

Three-Dimensional Image Processing

22.1 INTRODUCTION

In previous chapters, we discussed two-dimensional digital images. Such images can be thought of as having gray levels that are a function of two spatial variables. The most straightforward generalization to three dimensions would have us deal with images having gray levels that are a function of three spatial variables. We call these images *spatially three dimensional*. Several examples are ocean water temperature as a function of x, y, and depth; atmospheric pollution levels as a function of x, y, and altitude; and gravity field strength as a function of three dimensions in outer space. Perhaps more common examples are three-dimensional images of transparent microscope specimens or of larger objects viewed with X-ray illumination. In these images, the gray level represents some local property, such as optical density per millimeter of path length.

Most common in human experience is the ordinary three-dimensional world in which we live. Indeed, most of the two-dimensional images we see have been derived from this three-dimensional world by camera systems that employ a perspective projection to reduce the dimensionality from three to two. By modeling this projection, one can implement the inverse projection to learn more about the three-dimensional object that produced a given image in the first place. Similarly, given a mathematical description of a three-dimensional object, one can compute the image that would be obtained by a camera at a specified location. Thus, another topic deserving of the name *three-dimensional image processing* concerns the simulation of image-forming projections and their inverses.

We address five topics in three-dimensional image processing in this chapter. These topics are appropriate for treatment using hardware and software oriented toward two-dimensional digital image processing. Logically, then, these applications build upon the techniques discussed in previous chapters. By contrast, three-dimensional computer graphics has a different hardware and software emphasis. For an introduction to this fascinating field, the interested reader should consult a textbook on the subject [1]. The following subsections introduce the five topics treated in this chapter.

22.1.1 Spatially Three-Dimensional Images

Consider a three-dimensional object that is not perfectly transparent, but that does allow light to pass through. We can think of a local property that is distributed throughout the object in three dimensions. This property is the *local optical density*. It might be specified in units of optical density per millimeter of path length. For example, if the object were a slab of uniform local property oriented perpendicular to the illuminating beam, the measured optical density of the slab would be proportional to both the value of the local property and the slab thickness.

Thin specimens of biological tissue appear transparent under a microscope. In this chapter, we discuss how three-dimensional imaging can be performed using optical microscopy.

22.1.2 CAT Scanners

In the X-ray portion of the electromagnetic spectrum, many materials, including the human body, are transparent. Computerized axial tomography (CAT) is an X-ray technique that produces three-dimensional images of a solid object. The technique is used in medical diagnosis, for viewing structures deep inside the human body. It is also used in nondestructive testing (NDT), for examining critical parts for evidence of internal flaws. NDT is used on aircraft engine parts, aerospace components, nuclear reactor pressure vessels, and a variety of metal and composite components having a high-reliability requirement.

CAT scanners have made a significant impact on the fields of health care and NDT in the past two decades. CAT is a discipline that requires digital image processing for its very existence: The recorded data must undergo significant processing before any image is visible.

22.1.3 Stereometry

When a camera forms an image of a three-dimensional scene, it necessarily discards certain information about that scene. This loss of information is a direct result of the perspective projection that reduces the dimensionality from three to two. For example, a feature of a certain size in the image could result from either a large distant object or a small nearby object. This *range ambiguity* is a result of the information loss in the imaging projection.

When a three-dimensional scene is photographed by a pair of cameras located at slightly different positions, the range ambiguity can be resolved. The two images produced are called a *stereoscopic image pair.* A range image is an image in which gray level represents not brightness, but rather the distance from the camera to the reflecting surface in the scene that gives rise to the corresponding pixel brightness. Each pixel in a digitized image can be viewed as projecting a slender cone out through the imaging lens (Figure 22–1). In the brightness image, the gray level of a particular pixel indicates the amount of light

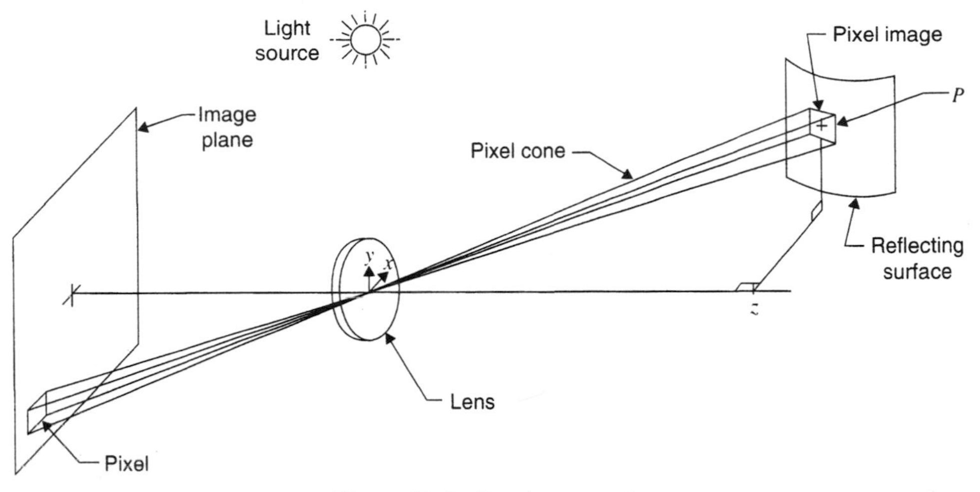

Figure 22–1 Imaging geometry

reflected off the first surface intersected by the pixel cone. In the range image, the gray level represents the length of the pixel cone.

The combination of a brightness image and a range image restores much of the information lost in the imaging projection. It is not, however, a complete description of the original scene, since surfaces may be obscured in the image. Nonetheless, for many purposes, the range image is a useful adjunct to the brightness image. Stereometry is the technique of deriving a range image from a stereo pair of brightness images. It has long been used as a manual technique for creating elevation maps of the earth's surface. Later in this chapter, we discuss computer-implemented stereometry.

22.1.4 Stereoscopic Display

If it is possible to compute a range image from a stereo pair, then it should be possible to generate a stereo pair given a single brightness image and a range image. In fact, this technique makes it possible to generate stereoscopic displays that give the viewer a sensation of depth. If a stereoscopic image pair is presented to a viewer in such a way that each eye sees one of the two images, the resulting visual sensation of depth can duplicate that of viewing the original scene. Stereo display techniques can increase the available information in a computer-driven display.

22.1.5 Shaded Surface Display

It is frequently desirable to generate either monocular or stereo pair images of a three-dimensional object that exists only as a mathematical description. By modeling the imaging system, one can compute the digital image that would result if the object existed and if it were digitized by conventional means. Shaded surface display grew out of the domain of computer graphics and has developed rapidly in the past few years. It is commonly done on hardware systems designed for two-dimensional digital image processing and is thus appropriate for discussion here.

22.2 THREE-DIMENSIONAL IMAGING

In this section, we discuss images defined in three-dimensional space. The local property (*e.g.*, brightness, density) is defined throughout a solid volume. The generalization from two to three dimensions is quite direct, but the data-handling requirements are considerably more severe in three dimensions.

22.2.1 Optical Sectioning

The optical microscope is a commonly used tool in histology and microanatomy. These disciplines are concerned with the structure and function of physiological specimens on a microscopic scale. The specimens, however, are three dimensional, and this presents problems for analysis with a conventional optical microscope. First, only those structures in or near the plane of focus are visible. Furthermore, structures just outside the focal plane are visible, but they appear blurred. Structures farther away from the focal plane are not visible, but they contribute to the recorded image as well.

The effect of three-dimensionality can be overcome by *serial sectioning,* a technique that involves slicing the specimen to produce a series of thin sections that may be studied individually to develop an understanding of the three-dimensional structure of the specimen. Serial sectioning has two major disadvantages: a loss of registration that occurs when the sections become separated after slicing, and an unavoidable geometric distortion as the slices are processed. The latter includes stretching, curling, folding, and tearing of the thin sections.

In many applications, it would be advantageous to obtain a three-dimensional display of the biological specimen. A three-dimensional display is important because improper interpretation of two-dimensional section images has led to a variety of misunderstandings of structure [2]. A three-dimensional display can be produced by digitizing the specimen with the focal plane situated at various levels along the optical axis (optical sectioning) and then processing each resulting image to remove or reduce the defocused information from structures located in neighboring planes. In this section, we address the use of digital image processing for deblurring optical section images and for three-dimensional display of the optically sectioned specimen.

22.2.2 Thick Specimen Imaging

Figure 22–2 diagrams the optical system of a microscope imaging a specimen of thickness T. The three-dimensional coordinate system has its origin at the bottom of the specimen, and the z-axis coincides with the optical axis of the microscope. The lens–to–image-plane distance d_i is fixed, and the in-focus plane falls at $z = z'$, a distance d_f below the center of the lens. The image plane has its own coordinate system (x', y'), with its origin on the z-axis.

The focal length of the objective lens determines the distance d_f to the focal plane from the lens equation

$$\frac{1}{d_i} + \frac{1}{d_f} = \frac{1}{f} \qquad (1)$$

This, in turn, determines the magnification, or power, of the objective:

$$M = \frac{d_i}{d_f} \qquad (2)$$

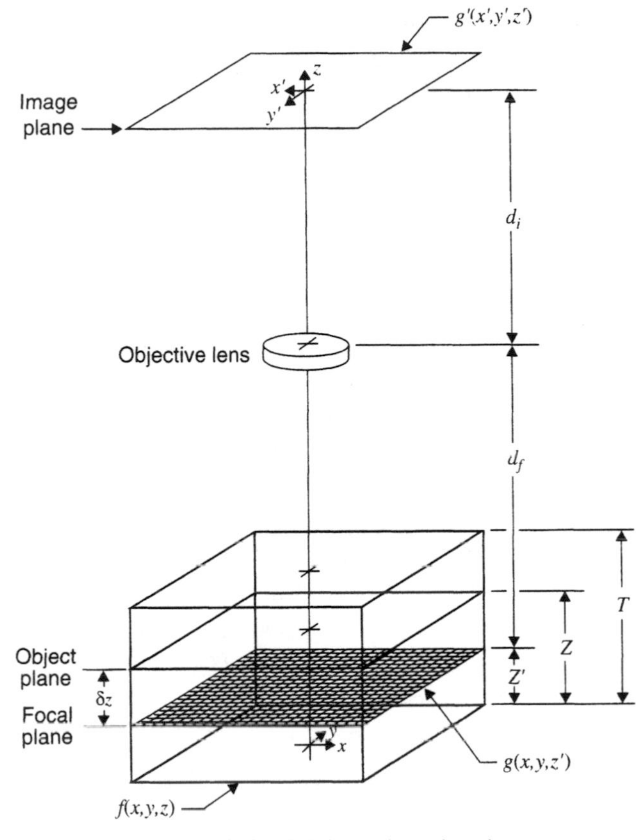

Figure 22–2 Thick specimen imaging

Since the image distance d_i and the focal length f are fixed, the focal plane may be placed anywhere within the specimen simply by moving the specimen up and down as a unit. Thus, we can place the focal plane at any desired level z'. The focal length of the objective is related to the other microscope parameters by

$$f = \frac{d_i}{M+1} = \frac{M}{M+1}d_f = \frac{d_i d_f}{d_i + d_f} \tag{3}$$

and the distance from the center of the lens to the focal plane is

$$d_f = \frac{d_i}{M} = \frac{M+1}{M}f = \frac{f d_i}{d_i - f} \tag{4}$$

For this analysis, we assume that the specimen has been stained with a fluorescent dye, and this produces a three-dimensional distribution of brightness throughout the specimen. The analysis of a light-absorbing specimen is similar.

We can describe the intensity (brightness or optical density) distribution by the function $f(x, y, z)$. We denote the (two-dimensional) image that results when the focal plane is located at level z' by $g'(x', y', z')$.

The dimensions of interest are those of the specimen, not those of the magnified image. Since we are processing a digital image anyway, it is more convenient to refer all scale factors (pixel spacing, spatial frequency, etc.) to the coordinate system of the specimen rather than that of the image plane. This also simplifies the notation.

We define an ideal (distortion-free) projection from the image plane back into the focal plane. This projection of $g'(x', y', z')$ to form $g(x, y, z')$ counteracts the magnification and 180° rotation introduced by the imaging projection, and it places the image back into the coordinate system of the specimen. Thus, a point at x, y, z in the specimen volume images to a point at x, y, z' in the focal plane. We are ignoring the slight change in magnification that is produced by defocus.

We now wish to establish the relationship between the image $g(x, y, z')$ and the specimen function $f(x, y, z)$. Figure 22–3 illustrates the simplified case, where the specimen has zero intensity, except in the object plane located at $z = z_1$; that is,

$$f(x, y, z) = f_1(x, y)\delta(z - z_1) \tag{5}$$

This corresponds to two-dimensional imaging with the object out of focus by the amount $z_1 - z'$. Since a defocused lens is still a linear system, we can write the convolution relation

$$g_1(x, y, z') = f(x, y, z_1) * h(x, y, z_1 - z') \tag{6}$$

where $h(x, y, z_1 - z')$ is the PSF of the optical system, defocused by the amount $z_1 - z'$.

We can model the three-dimensional specimen as a stack of object planes located at small intervals Δz along the z-axis, that is,

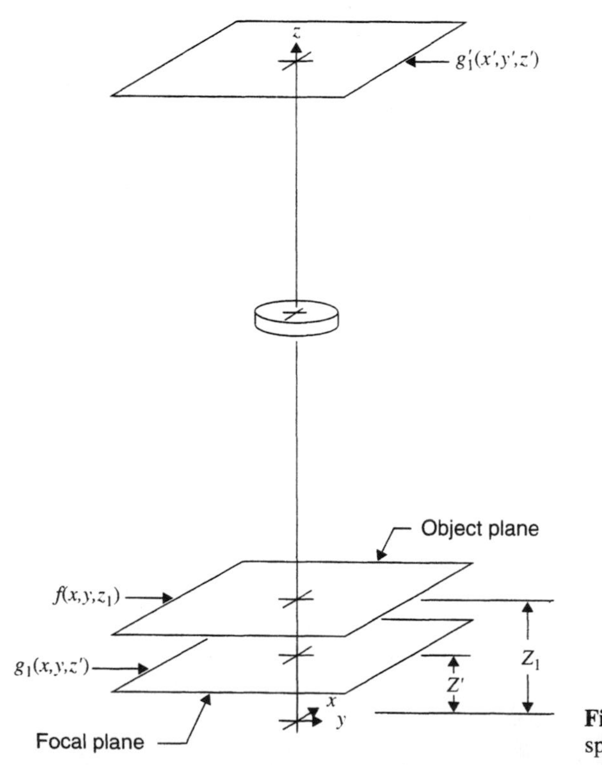

Figure 22–3 Imaging a planar specimen

$$\sum_{i=1}^{N} f(x, y, i\Delta z)\Delta z \tag{7}$$

where

$$N = \frac{T}{\Delta z} \tag{8}$$

The image of this stack obtained with the focal plane located at z' is the sum of the individual plane images; that is,

$$g(x, y, z') = \sum_{i=1}^{N} f(x, y, i\Delta z) * h(x, y, z' - i\Delta z)\Delta z \tag{9}$$

If we substitute $z = i\Delta z$ and take the limit as Δz approaches zero (and N approaches infinity), the summation becomes an integration, and Eq. (9) reduces to

$$g(x, y, z') = \int_{0}^{T} f(x, y, z) * h(x, y, z' - z)dz \tag{10}$$

If we specify that $f(x, y, z)$ is zero outside the field of view and outside the range $0 \leq z \leq T$, and write out the two-dimensional convolution, we are left with

$$g(x, y, z') = \int_{-\infty}^{\infty}\int_{-\infty}^{\infty}\int_{-\infty}^{\infty} f(x', y', z)h(x - x', y - y', z' - z)dx'\, dy'\, dz \tag{11}$$

Thus, microscope imaging of a thick specimen involves a three-dimensional convolution of the specimen function with the PSF.

22.2.3 Deblurring Optical Section Images

We now seek a means of removing the defocused information from optical section images. In other words, we wish to recover the function $f(x, y, z)$ from a series of images $g(x, y, z')$ taken at different focal plane levels z'. While this approach faces theoretical limitations [3,4], it can be done well enough to make it an important tool in biological research, particularly fluorescence microscopy.

22.2.3.1 Deconvolution

We could recover the specimen function by three-dimensional deconvolution, subject to the restrictions imposed by zeros in the transfer function. Transforming Eq. (11) yields the frequency domain relation

$$G(u, v, w) = F(u, v, w)H(u, v, w) \tag{12}$$

where u, v, and w are frequency variables in the x-, y-, and z-directions, respectively. The spectrum of the specimen function is

$$F(u, v, w) = G(u, v, w)H'(u, v, w) \tag{13}$$

where

$$H'(u, v, w) = \frac{1}{H(u, v, w)} \tag{14}$$

is the inverse three-dimensional OTF.

Transforming back to the spatial domain yields

$$f(x, y, z) = g(x, y, z) * h'(x, y, z) \tag{15}$$

Writing out the z-component of the convolution integral produces

$$f(x, y, z) = \int_{-\infty}^{\infty} g(x, y, z') * h'(x, y, z-z')dz' \tag{16}$$

where z' is now a dummy variable of integration.

If we make the z-axis discrete by dividing it into intervals Δz by letting $z = j\Delta z$, $z' = i\Delta z$, and $dz' = \Delta z$, Eq. (16) becomes

$$f(x, y, j\Delta z) = \sum_{i=-\infty}^{\infty} g(x, y, i\Delta z) * h'(x, y, j\Delta z - i\Delta z)\Delta z \tag{17}$$

When the focal plane moves outside the specimen ($i < 0$ or $i > N$), the information content of the resulting image becomes rather meager (except at low frequencies, as discussed later). Thus, we can approximate Eq. (17) by the finite summation

$$f(x, y, j\Delta z) \approx \sum_{i=-M}^{N+M} g(x, y, i\Delta z) * h'(x, y, j\Delta z - i\Delta z)\Delta z \tag{18}$$

where M is some positive integer. This reduces the restoration of each object plane to a finite summation of two-dimensional convolutions.

While three-dimensional deconvolution might result in restoration of the specimen function $f(x, y, z)$, it is fraught with difficulties. First, there is the complexity of computing the spectrum of the three-dimensional PSF. Second, there is the computation of $h'(x, y, z)$, the inverse three-dimensional transform of Eq. (14). Finally, Eq. (18) also represents considerable computational effort, especially if Δz is small and if $N + 2M$ must be large in order to enclose the specimen.

22.2.3.2 Simultaneous Equations

For a second approach, let us again approximate the specimen by a stack of object planes separated at equal intervals Δz along the z-axis. We generate a series of optical section images by digitizing the specimen repeatedly while moving the focal plane up the z-axis in the same increments Δz. We make the substitutions

$$z' = j\Delta z \qquad 1 \le j \le N \qquad dz = \Delta z \tag{19}$$

and the jth section image is obtained from Eq. (9); that is,

$$g(x, y, j\Delta z) = \sum_{i=1}^{N} f(x, y, i\Delta z) * h(x, y, i\Delta z - j\Delta z)\Delta z \tag{20}$$

where $h(x, y, z)$ is assumed to be approximately symmetric in z.

We can simplify the notation by temporarily dropping x, y, and the constant Δz as understood and writing i and j as subscripts. With these changes, Eq. (20) becomes

$$g_j = \sum_{i=1}^{N} f_i * h_{i-j} = \sum_{i=1-j}^{N-j} f_{i+j} * h_i \tag{21}$$

This states simply that the jth section image is a sum of convolutions of the various specimen planes with the appropriate defocus PSFs. (Recall that $(i-j)\Delta z$ is the defocus distance.)

We can simplify the situation by taking the two-dimensional Fourier transform of Eq. (21). This moves us from the spatial to the frequency domain, where convolution corresponds to multiplication. By definition,

$$G_j = \mathfrak{F}\{g(x, y, j\Delta z)\} \qquad F_i = \mathfrak{F}\{f(x, y, i\Delta z)\} \qquad H_i = \mathfrak{F}\{h(x, y, i\Delta z)\} \tag{22}$$

and Eq. (21) becomes

$$G_j = \sum_{i=1-j}^{N-j} f_{i+j} H_i \tag{23}$$

Given a set of optical section images, G_j, for $1 \le j \le N$, Eq. (23) represents a set of N simultaneous linear equations in N unknowns. Thus, we have a second possibility for recovering the specimen function $f(x, y, z)$: We could use Cramer's rule or some other such technique to solve the system of equations represented by Eq. (23) for the F_j's. The computational complexity of this task, however, is formidable. In reality, F_j, G_j, and H_j are two-dimensional functions of frequency. Hence, the system of equations would have to be solved for every sample point in the (two-dimensional) frequency domain. While this could be done (provided that a solution exists), it is questionable whether the results would justify the computational expense.

22.2.3.3 An Approximate Method

Rather than an exact solution, which recovers the specimen function completely, what may be of more practical use is an approximate method that significantly improves the situation at reasonable expense [5,6]. We now abandon the notion of an exact (and consequently simultaneous) solution and seek instead to develop a simpler technique that yields good performance.

Let us pull the $i = 0$ term out of Eq. (21), leaving two summations, one for positive i and one for negative i. We have

$$g_j = f_j * h_0 + \sum_{i=1-j}^{-1} f_{i+j} * h_i + \sum_{i=1}^{N-j} f_{i+j} * h_i \tag{24}$$

which may be rearranged as

$$f_j * h_0 = g_j - \sum_{i=1-j}^{-1} f_{i+j} * h_i - \sum_{i=1}^{N-j} f_{i+j} * h_i \tag{25}$$

where h_0 is the in-focus PSF of the microscope. This equation states that the specimen at level j, convolved with the in-focus PSF, is given by the image at level j minus a sum of adjacent specimen planes that have been blurred by out-of-focus PSFs h_i. In this summation, i represents the distance between the focal plane and the object plane.

Eq. (25) suggests that we can recover the specimen at level j by subtracting, from the image at level j, a series of adjacent specimen planes blurred by the defocus transfer function. We do not have available the adjacent specimen planes f_{i+j}, but we do have access to the adjacent plane images g_{i+j}.

We see from Eq. (24) that each image contains the corresponding specimen plane plus a sum of defocused adjacent specimen planes. Since the defocus transfer function tends to discriminate against high spatial frequencies (fine detail), but passes low-frequency information, we can make the general statement that the image spectrum G_j contains the specimen spectrum F_j plus excess low-frequency information from adjacent planes. The farther away the planes are, the less medium-frequency information they contribute, but the very lowest frequencies accumulate, in the image, from all the planes.

We can approximate the specimen f_j by a highpass-filtered version of the image g_j; that is,

$$f_j \approx g_j * k_0 \tag{26}$$

where k_0 is some heuristically determined highpass filter with a transfer function that takes on the value zero at zero frequency and unity at the high frequencies of interest. This will remove the large amount of excess low-frequency information and make the approximation reasonable. If, furthermore, we ignore the blurring effect of the in-focus PSF, we can write the following approximation to Eq. (25):

$$f_j \approx g_j - \sum_{i=1-j}^{-1} g_{i+j} * k_0 * h_i - \sum_{i=1}^{N-j} g_{i+j} * k_0 * h_i \tag{27}$$

It may be necessary to use only some small number M of adjacent planes to remove most of the troublesome defocused information. Eq. (27) then becomes

$$f_j \approx \bar{f}_j = g_j - \sum_{i=1}^{M} (g_{j-i} * h_{-i} + g_{j+i} * h_i) * k_0 \tag{28}$$

This suggests that we can partially remove the defocused structures by subtracting $2M$ adjacent plane images that have been convolved with the appropriate defocus PSF and a highpass filter k_0. The filter and the number M of adjacent planes must be selected to give reasonable results. While we cannot expect this technique to recover the specimen function exactly, it does improve optical section images at modest expense.

Figure 22–4 illustrates the results of the foregoing simple deblurring algorithm for optical sections. The algorithm involves only the two adjacent plane images ($M = 1$) and is [5]

$$\hat{f}_j = 5g_j - 2(g_{j-1} + g_{j+1}) * h_1 \tag{29}$$

where h_1 is a PSF that approximates the blurring due to defocus by the amount Δz.

Figures 22–4(a) through (c) show three digitized optical section images of a Golgi stained (silver-impregnated) horizontal cell in the catfish retina ($\Delta z = 5\ \mu$). The blurred upper and lower plane images appear in Figure 22–4(d) and (f). The result of deblurring Figure 22–4(b) with Eq. (20) is shown in Figure 22–4(e). Notice that structures which appear only in Figure 22–4(b) are preserved at full contrast, while defocused structures from adjacent planes are removed. Structures visible in all three planes have lost some of their contrast because the excess low-frequency information was not removed from adjacent plane images (i.e. Eq. (26) was not used).

Extensions of this technique [7] have come into relatively common usage and are available on several commercial systems. Their main advantage is that they yield significantly improved three-dimensional images with only about one second of processing time required [7].

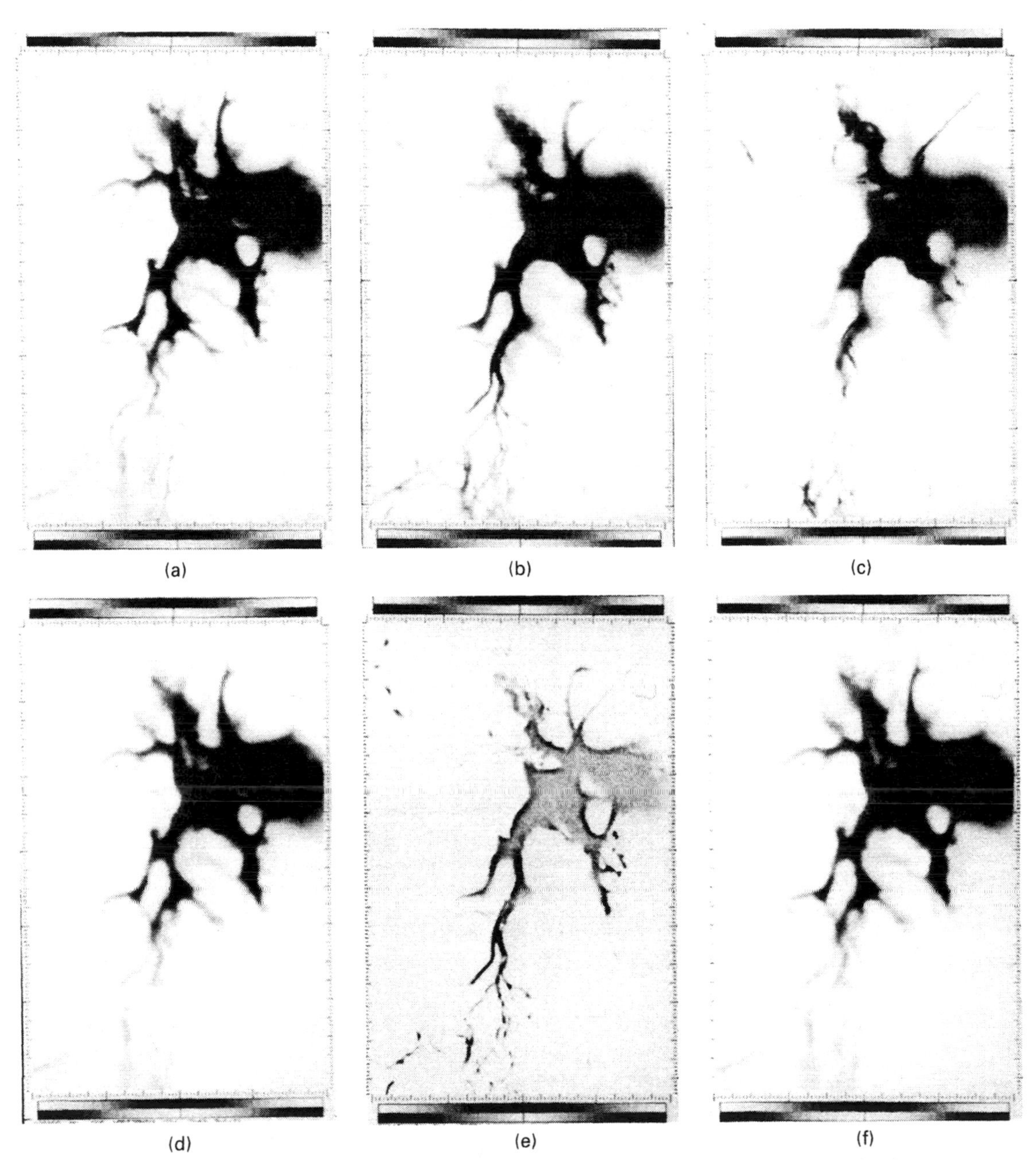

Figure 22–4 Deblurring optical sections: (a), (b), (c) digitized optical section images; (d), (f) blurred adjacent plane images; (e) deblurred image (from [5])

22.2.3.4 Constrained Iterative Deconvolution

The three-dimensional reconstruction problem can be approached in yet another way: iteratively reconstructing a synthetic specimen function that, when blurred by the three-dimensional

PSF, yields approximately the recorded image [7]. The convergence of the technique is improved if one or more constraints are imposed upon the solution. The most common constraint is that the specimen function must be nonnegative. Here, we no longer have a linear system, and enforcement of such constraints can possibly lead to resolution beyond the diffraction limit. (Recall Sec.16.3.)

Starting from an initial approximation, $\hat{f}_0(x, y, z)$, the error that remains after the ith iteration is (Recall Eq. (21))

$$e_i(x, y, z) = g(x, y, z) - \hat{f}_i(x, y, z) * h(x, y, z) \tag{30}$$

where $\hat{f}_i(x, y, z)$ is the ith approximation of the specimen function, $g(x, y, z)$ is the recorded image, and $h(x, y, z)$ is the (known) three-dimensional PSF.

After each iteration, the estimate is updated by some process based on the error function. For example, an additive correction is

$$\hat{f}_{i+1}(x, y, z) = \hat{f}_i(x, y, z) + \delta_{i+1}(x, y, z) \tag{31}$$

where $\delta_{i+1}(x, y, z)$ is the update. Then the constraints are imposed. In this case,

$$\hat{f}_{i+1}(x, y, z) \geq 0 \tag{32}$$

is an appropriate restriction for the estimate of the specimen function.

Agard, et al. [7] have used

$$\delta_{i+1}(x, y, z) = \gamma(x, y, z) e_i(x, y, z) \tag{33}$$

for the update, where

$$\gamma_i(x, y, z) = 1 - \frac{[\hat{f}_i(x, y, z) * h(x, y, z) - A]^2}{A^2} \tag{34}$$

is a scaling function and A is a constant.

Faster convergence results, however, when a highpass–filtered version of e_i is used for the update in Eq. (33) [7]. We can see why this is true by switching to the frequency domain and setting the error after the i+1st iteration to zero. We have

$$E_{i+1}(u, v, w) = G(u, v, w) - [\hat{F}_i(u, v, w) + \Delta_{i+1}(u, v, w)]H(u, v, w) = 0 \tag{35}$$

which can be solved for

$$\Delta_{i+1}(u, v, w) = \frac{E_i(u, v, w)}{H(u, v, w)} \tag{36}$$

This is just a deconvolved version of the previous step's residual error function. Of course, deconvolving the error function is no easier than solving the original problem. But the result indicates that judicious use of highpass filtering, which can approximate the required deconvolution, will reduce the number of times the correction must be applied.

This method has produced good reconstructions in a variety of biological investigations [8]. It requires processing times on the order of one hour.

Constrained iterative least squares deconvolution. A natural way to pose the three-dimensional reconstruction problem is to find the specimen function $\hat{f}(x, y, z)$ that minimizes

$$\sum_{i,j,k} \left| g_{ijk} - [\hat{f} * h]_{ijk} \right|^2 \tag{37}$$

where i, j, and k are the pixel coordinates of the recorded three-dimensional image data and $*$ represents three-dimensional convolution. As before, the function $\hat{f}(x, y, z)$ is refined iteratively.

Three-dimensional imaging is essentially a noisy lowpass filtering (blurring) process, with the noise introduced after the blurring. Image noise sources may well introduce high-frequency components that do not correspond to any (blurred) physically possible component of the specimen. This situation can force the iterative process to include artifactual high-frequency components in the reconstructed specimen. Impulse noise in $g(x, y, z)$, for example, might correspond to physically impossible high-frequency components in $\hat{f}(x, y, z)$. Combined with truncation (and often undersampling)—particularly in the z-direction—least squares reconstruction can lead to inaccurate results. Remedies for these problems include smoothing $\hat{f}(x, y, z)$ between iterations [7] and terminating the reconstruction process before the high-frequency artifacts build up.

Constrained iterative regularization. A *well-posed* estimation problem is an estimation problem in which a solution (a) exists, (b) is unique, and (c) depends on the input data in a continuous fashion. For the reasons just mentioned, the least squares reconstruction problem is ill posed [9].

Regularization is a procedure that seeks a solution which approaches the true input distribution as the amount of noise is reduced and as the image is sampled more finely and over a larger volume. Applied to the problem under consideration here, it seeks the nonnegative function $\hat{f}(x, y, z)$ that minimizes

$$\sum_{i,j,k} \left| g_{ijk} - [\hat{f} * h]_{ijk} \right|^2 + \alpha \iiint |f(x, y, z)|^2 dx\, dy\, dz \tag{38}$$

where α is a constant. The second term enforces smoothness on $\hat{f}(x, y, z)$ to prevent noise in g_{ijk} from introducing unwarranted oscillations. The value of α determines the amount of smoothing. If α is too small, we face the same problems as with least squares deconvolution. If it is too large, $\hat{f}(x, y, z)$ will be too smooth to show the detail of interest.

Carrington [9] presents an iterative numerical method for minimizing Eq. (38) that produces impressive reconstructions [9–12]. Required processing time on a graphics workstation is on the order of an hour.

22.2.4 The Defocus OTF

The preceding deblurring techniques require a knowledge of the three-dimensional PSF of the imaging system. We now investigate the behavior of the transfer function of a defocused optical system.

22.2.4.1 Square Aperture

Recall from Chapter 15 that the OTF of an optical system under incoherent illumination is the autocorrelation of its pupil function. For a square aperture of width l, the pupil function with defocus becomes [13]

$$P(x, y) = \Pi\left(\frac{x}{l}\right)\Pi\left(\frac{y}{l}\right)e^{j\pi(\varepsilon/\lambda)(x^2+y^2)} \tag{39}$$

where the complex exponential represents the phase disturbance due to the optical path length error that results from defocus.

The defocus error is [13]

$$\varepsilon = \frac{1}{d_i} + \frac{1}{d_o} - \frac{1}{f} = \frac{\delta z}{d_f(d_f - \delta z)} \tag{40}$$

The u-axis component of the image plane OTF is [13]

$$T(u, 0) = \Lambda\left(\frac{u}{f_c}\right)\text{sinc}\left[l^2\frac{\varepsilon}{\lambda}\left(1 - \frac{|u|}{f_c}\right)\frac{u}{f_c}\right] \tag{41}$$

where

$$f_c = \frac{l}{\lambda d_i} \quad \text{and} \quad \text{sinc}(x) = \frac{\sin(x)}{x} \tag{42}$$

The object plane OTF results if we substitute d_f for d_i in Eq. (42).

Notice that Eq. (41) is a sinc function in an envelope that is the in-focus OTF. For $\varepsilon = 0$ (no defocus), the argument of the sinc is zero, and we are left with the in-focus OTF. Notice also that the argument is quadratic in the frequency variable u. This effects frequency modulation of the sinc. The "frequency" of the sinc decreases linearly to zero as u goes from zero to f_c.

22.2.4.2 Circular Aperture

For an optical system with a circular aperture of radius A, the pupil function with defocus becomes

$$P(r) = \Pi\left(\frac{r}{2A}\right)e^{jkwr^2/A^2} \qquad k = \frac{2\pi}{\lambda} \qquad r^2 = x^2 + y^2 \tag{43}$$

where the defocus is specified by the maximum path length error [14]

$$w = -d_i - \delta z\cos\alpha + (d_i^2 + 2d_i\delta z + \delta z^2\cos^2\alpha)^{1/2} \qquad \alpha = \arctan\frac{A}{d_i} \tag{44}$$

and the image is recorded on a plane located $d_i + \delta z$ behind the lens. Hopkins [15] showed that the recording plane OTF of a defocused optical system is given by

$$\begin{aligned} T_H(s) = {} & \frac{4}{\pi a}\cos\left(\frac{1}{2}as\right)\left\{\beta J_1(a) + \sum_{n=1}^{\infty}(-1)^{n+1}\frac{\sin(2n\beta)}{2n}\left[J_{2n-1}(a) - J_{2n+1}(a)\right]\right\} \\ & -\frac{4}{\pi a}\sin\left(\frac{1}{2}as\right)\sum_{n=0}^{\infty}(-1)^n\frac{\sin[(2n+1)\beta]}{2n+1}\left[J_{2n}(a) - J_{2n+2}(a)\right] \end{aligned} \tag{45}$$

where

$$a = 2kws \qquad \beta = \cos^{-1}\frac{q}{f_c} \qquad s = \frac{2q}{f_c} \qquad q^2 = u^2 + v^2 \qquad f_c = \frac{2A}{\lambda d_i} \tag{46}$$

Stokseth [14] derived an approximation of the form

$$T_i(s) = (1 - 0.69s + 0.0076s^2 + 0.043s^3)\,\text{jinc}\left[4kw\left(1 - \frac{|s|}{2}\right)\frac{s}{2}\right] \tag{47}$$

where

$$\text{jinc}\,(x) = 2\frac{J_1(x)}{x} \quad \text{and} \quad |s| < 2 \tag{48}$$

The coefficients of the third-order polynomial in Eq. (47) were selected to make the approximation accurate at large values of defocus ($w \geq 5\lambda$). At zero defocus ($w = 0$), the jinc term is unity, and the polynomial differs only slightly from the in-focus OTF.

In deblurring optical sections, we are interested primarily in the adjacent planes, where defocus is relatively small. We can make the approximation more accurate for small defocus by substituting the in-focus OTF for the polynomial [16]. This produces

$$H(w, q) \approx \frac{1}{\pi}(2\beta - \sin 2\beta)\,\text{jinc}\left[4kw\left(1 - \frac{|q|}{f_c}\right)\frac{q}{f_c}\right] \tag{49}$$

Note the similarity between the approximate OTF for a circular aperture in Eq. (49) and the OTF for a square aperture in Eq. (41). This approximation is accurate at zero defocus and differs less than 1 percent from Stokseth's approximation at $w = 5\lambda$.

Figure 22–5 illustrates the effect of defocus on the OTF. Curves were computed from Eq. (49) for several amounts of defocus w. As expected, the OTF narrows markedly with defocus. The circularly symmetric OTFs may be inverse Fourier transformed to produce the defocus PSFs required for three-dimensional reconstruction. Using the Hankle transform (see Sec. 10.4.5) simplifies this task.

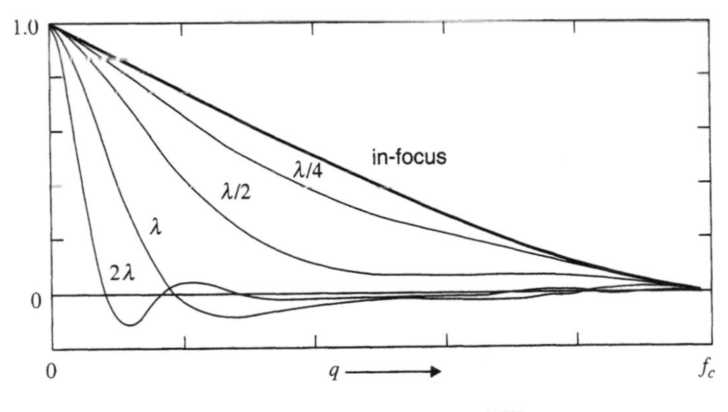

Figure 22–5 The defocus OTF

22.2.5 Microscope Defocus

Eq. (49) allows us to calculate the microscope OTF for various amounts of defocus. Figure 22–6 shows an out-of-focus point source located a distance Δz beyond the focal plane of a microscope. While it casts an out-of-focus image on the image plane, it produces an in-focus

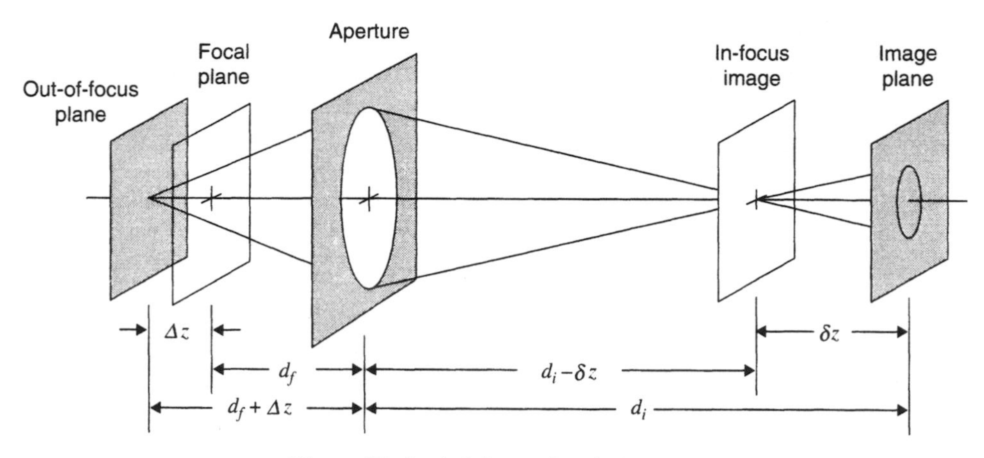

Figure 22–6 A defocused optical system

image at a point δz in front of the image plane. Like d_i and d_f, these two distances must satisfy the lens equation

$$\frac{1}{f} = \frac{1}{d_f + \Delta z} + \frac{1}{d_i + \delta z} \tag{50}$$

Therefore,

$$\delta z = d_i - \frac{f(d_f + \Delta z)}{d_f + \Delta z - f} \tag{51}$$

and

$$\Delta z = \frac{f\,(d_i - \delta z)}{d_i - \delta z - f} - d_f \tag{52}$$

relate the out-of-focus distances on both sides of the lens. Given a specimen-space defocus value Δz, we can calculate the corresponding δz to use in Eq. (44). We must also substitute $d_i - \delta z$ for d_i in Eq. (44), since it is now the location of the in-focus image plane. Then Eq. (49) gives the defocus OTF. The defocus PSF can be obtained with an inverse Fourier transformation.

22.2.5.1 High Magnification

Working with high magnification ($M >> 1$) and small defocus ($\delta z << d_i$), one can make some approximations that simplify some of the preceding formulas significantly. In Eq. (44) α is a small angle, and the third term in parentheses is by far the smallest of the three. Thus, we can replace $\cos^2(\alpha)$ with 1, and that equation simplifies to

$$w = \delta z[1 - \cos(\alpha)] \tag{53}$$

The double-angle formula for the cosine allows us to write

$$w = 2\delta z \sin^2\left(\frac{\alpha}{2}\right) \tag{54}$$

and since, for angles less than about 0.2 radian, the sine and the arc tangent are approximately equal to the angle,

$$w \approx \delta z \frac{\alpha^2}{2} = \frac{\delta z}{2} \arctan^2\left(\frac{NA}{M}\right) \approx \delta z \frac{NA^2}{2M^2} \tag{55}$$

Moving now to object space, expanding Eq. (52) over a common denominator yields

$$\Delta z = \frac{f d_i - f\delta z - d_i d_f + \delta z d_f + f d_f}{d_i - \delta z - f} \tag{56}$$

The denominator is dominated by d_i, so we can neglect the other two terms. When we do, the result can be written as

$$\Delta z \approx \delta z \left[\frac{d_f}{d_i} - \frac{f}{d_i}\right] + f + \frac{f d_f}{d_i} - d_f \tag{57}$$

Using the relations in Sec. 15.2.1, one can show that the last three terms of Eq. (57) sum to zero, while the first reduces to $\delta z[1/M - 1/(M+1)]$, so that

$$\Delta z \approx \delta z \left[\frac{1}{M} - \frac{1}{M+1}\right] = \frac{\delta z}{M(M+1)} \tag{58}$$

or, since M is large,

$$\Delta z \approx \frac{\delta z}{M^2} \tag{59}$$

We now have simple expressions relating the object-plane and image-plane defocus distances [Eq. (59)] and the defocus path length error to the image-plane defocus distance [Eq. (55)]. Substituting Eq. (59) into Eq. (53) yields

$$w = \Delta z \frac{NA^2}{2} \tag{60}$$

which relates the defocus path length error to the specimen-space defocus distance. Note that the approximations involved in this development introduce errors on the order of $1/M$, or about one percent at 100×. The exception is the approximation that leads to Eq. (53). Its effect is illustrated next.

22.2.5.2 An Example

Consider a 100×, 1.2*NA* oil immersion ($n = 1.6$) objective in green ($\lambda = 0.55\ \mu$) light. We seek to determine the object-space defocus distance that produces a quarter-wavelength defocus error and to determine the resulting defocus OTF and PSF.

Assuming that the optical tube length d_i is 200 mm, and using equations from Sec. 15.5.3, we find the values shown in Table 22–1. One-quarter wavelength of focus error ($w = \lambda/4$) yields $\Delta z = 0.191\ \mu$ for the corresponding defocus distance. Figure 22–7 shows how quarter-wave defocus affects the OTF and the PSF.

Figure 22–8 shows, under this set of conditions, the relationship between the specimen-space defocus distance Δz and the defocus error w, using both the exact [Eq. (44)] and the approximate [Eq. (60)] expressions for w. Although w is negative for negative Δz, the defocus

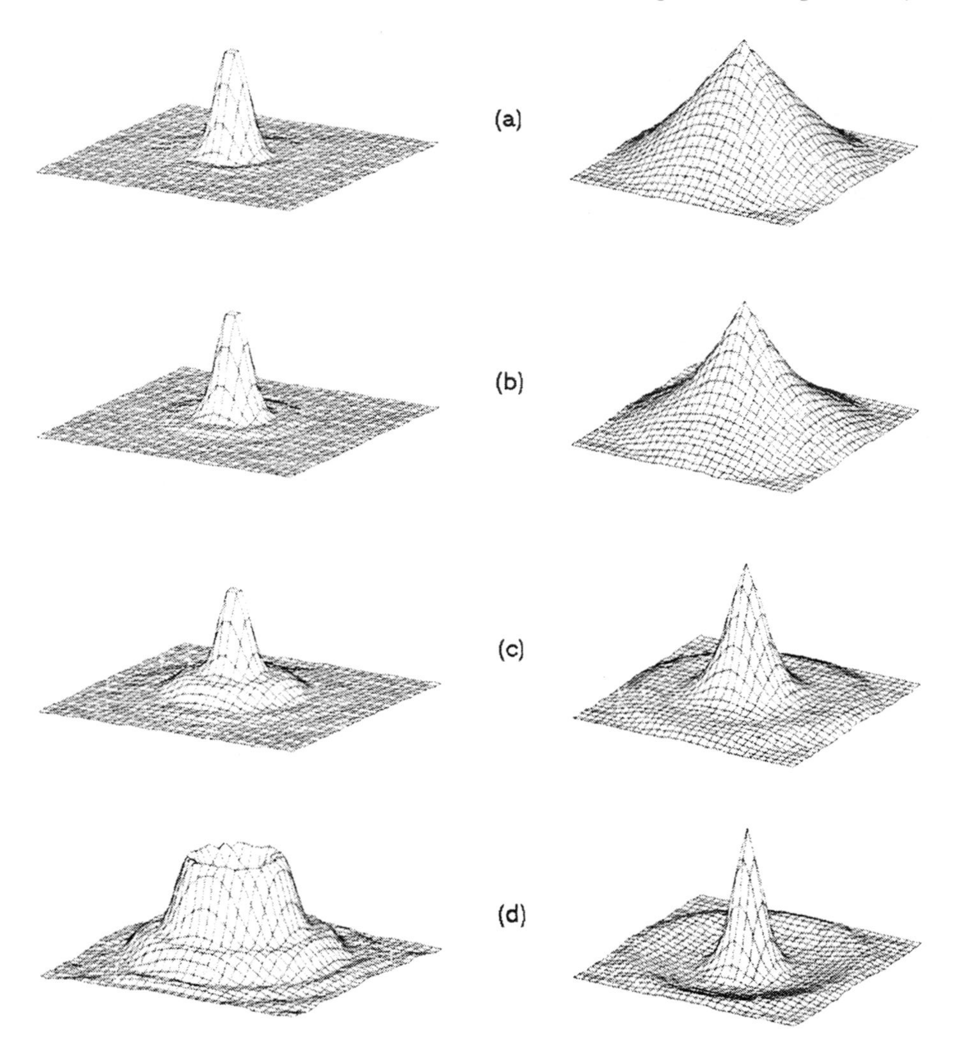

Figure 22–7 The effect of defocus on the psf and OTF: (a) in focus; (b) 1/4-wave defocus; (c) 1/2-wave defocus; (d) 3/4-wave defocus

TABLE 22–1 CALCULATIONS FOR THE MICROSCOPE DEFOCUS EXAMPLE

$d_f = \frac{d_i}{M} = 2$ mm	$f = \frac{d_i}{M+1} = 1.98$ mm
$\theta = \tan^{-1}(NA) = 50.2°$	$A = d_f \tan(\theta) = 2.4$ mm
$\alpha = \tan^{-1}\left[\frac{A}{d_i}\right] = 0.69°$	$f_c = \frac{2NA}{\lambda} = 4.36$ cp μ
$\delta z = \frac{2wM^2}{NA^2} = \frac{2\frac{\lambda}{4}M^2}{NA^2} = 1.91$ mm	$\Delta z = \frac{\delta z}{M^2} = 0.191$ μ

OTF [Eq. (49)] is symmetrical in w, and the sign has no effect. Notice that the approximate expression for w is symmetrical in Δz, whereas the exact expression is not. This is the result of the approximation [Eq. (53)] that paved the way for significant simplification of the exact expression. Notice also that, for small amounts of defocus (in this example), there is roughly one wavelength of defocus error per micron of specimen-space defocus distance.

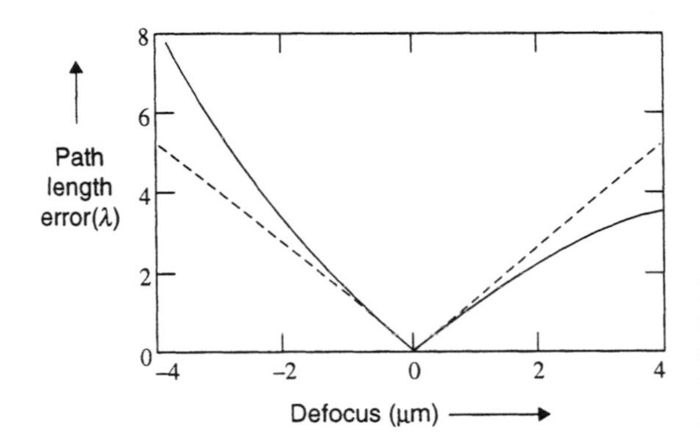

Figure 22–8 Defocus path length error versus defocus distance in specimen space, exact and approximate formulas (100×, 1.2*NA* objective, green light)

22.2.5.3 Depth of Focus

The quarter-wave defocus OTF in Figure 22–5 can be taken to be the limit of useful resolution of the defocused microscope. If we establish one-quarter wavelength of defocus error as the limit of the focal depth of the objective [17], then the depth of focus is, from Eq. (60),

$$DOF = \Delta z\left(\frac{\lambda}{4}\right) = \frac{\lambda}{2NA^2} \tag{61}$$

22.2.5.4 Practical Considerations

Notice in Eq. (49) and Figure 22–5 that the OTF becomes narrower with increasing amounts of defocus, but does not lose amplitude at zero frequency. Thus, as a point source goes out of focus, its image becomes larger and dimmer, but its integrated brightness remains approximately the same. This can be demonstrated in the fluorescence microscope with subresolution fluorescent beads [7,11]. The phenomenon gives rise to a z-axis truncation problem that affects low spatial frequencies. If the series of optical sections is taken through less than the entire specimen block, then structures outside the imaged area will contribute (low-frequency) information to the image. The reconstruction algorithm may be affected by this information. For many applications the lowest frequencies are of little interest, and such errors in the reconstruction are tolerable. Since noise tends to dominate the highest frequencies, it is the medium-frequency information that is reconstructed most accurately.

One can also determine the three-dimensional PSF experimentally in the fluorescence light microscope by digitizing a series of defocus images of a subresolution fluorescent bead [7,11,18]. While this is subject to noise and sampling constraints, it avoids the approximations inherent in diffraction theory, and it accounts for any asymmetry and aberrations in the optical system. Done carefully, such an approach can yield superior reconstruction performance [7].

22.3 COMPUTERIZED AXIAL TOMOGRAPHY

Biological tissue, including the human body, is opaque to light in the visible spectrum, except in very thin sections. Biological tissue does, however, transmit X rays. Some structures in the body—bones, for example—absorb X rays more heavily than other structures. Conventional radiography (Figure 22–9) produces an image in which the three-dimensional structures in the body are projected onto a plane and superimposed upon each other. In radiography, no lens is involved, but rather, the subject stands between a point source and the recording film. The structures in the body cast superimposed shadows on the film. This creates difficulty in interpreting the multiple overlapping images of different structures. Radiologists frequently use multiple views (X rays taken at different angles) to resolve ambiguities.

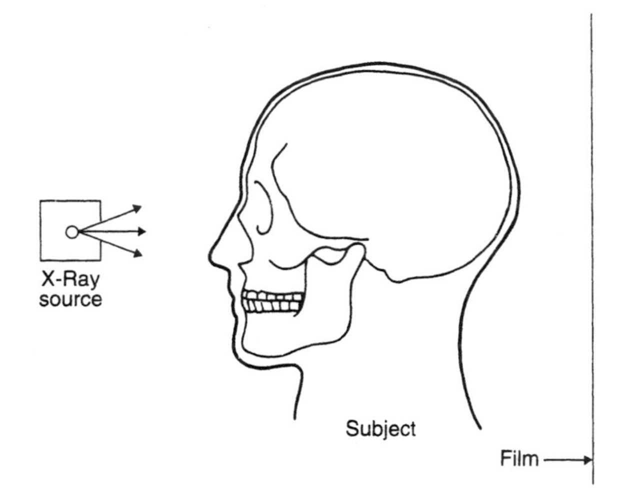

Figure 22–9 Conventional radiography

22.3.1 Tomography

Conventional tomography is an X-ray technique that isolates objects in a particular plane of interest (Figure 22–10). Tomography employs a source and film that move during the exposure. In Figure 22–10, the source moves down while the film moves up in such a way that any point P in the plane of interest always lies on a line connecting the source with the corresponding point P' on the film. Structures outside the plane of interest become blurred because their images on the film move during the exposure. Objects near the plane of interest are blurred less than remote objects. The technique is useful where image detail is required in deeply imbedded structures, such as those of the middle ear. One disadvantage is that the required X-ray dosage is usually higher than in normal radiography.

22.3.2 Axial Tomography

Computerized axial tomography (CAT) is a technique that incorporates digital image processing to obtain three-dimensional images [19–24]. The devices involved, commonly called CAT scanners, reconstruct the three-dimensional image of the X ray–absorbing object.

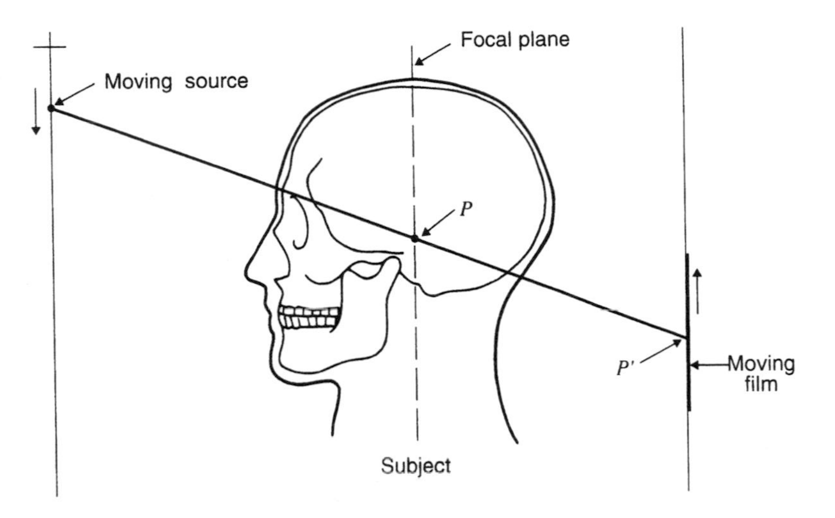

Figure 22–10 Conventional tomography

The technique is illustrated in Figure 22–11. A planar X-ray beam penetrates the object, and the transmitted beam intensity is measured by a linear array of X-ray detectors. This produces the transmitted intensity function shown in the figure. A series of these intensity functions is recorded as the apparatus rotates about the object through a small angle between each exposure. A complete series would cover 180° of rotation in steps of from 2° to 6°.

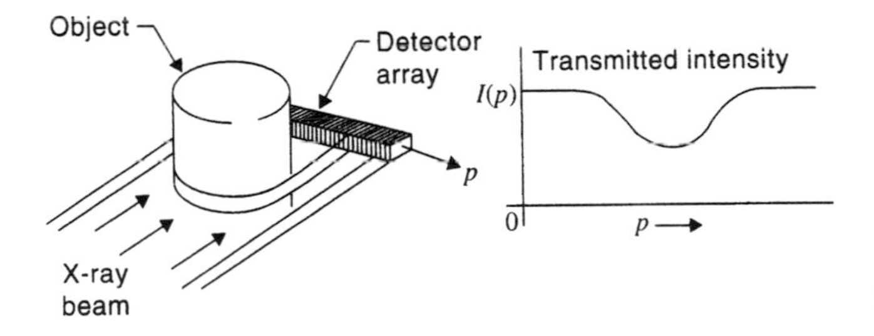

Figure 22–11 Axial tomography

The resulting set of one-dimensional intensity functions is used to compute a two-dimensional cross-sectional image of the object at the level of the beam. This process is repeated as the beam-detector unit is moved down the object in small steps, producing a set of cross-sectional images that can be "stacked" to form a three-dimensional image of the object.

The projection process is described analytically by the *Radon transform* [25], given by

$$d_r(p, \theta) = \int_{-\infty}^{\infty}\int_{-\infty}^{\infty} d(x, y)\delta[x\cos(\theta) + y\sin(\theta) - s]dx\,dy \tag{62}$$

where $d(x, y)$ is the density distribution of the object in the plane at level z and the beam direction forms an angle θ with the y-axis (Figure 22–12). For any p and θ, the value of $d_r(p, \theta)$

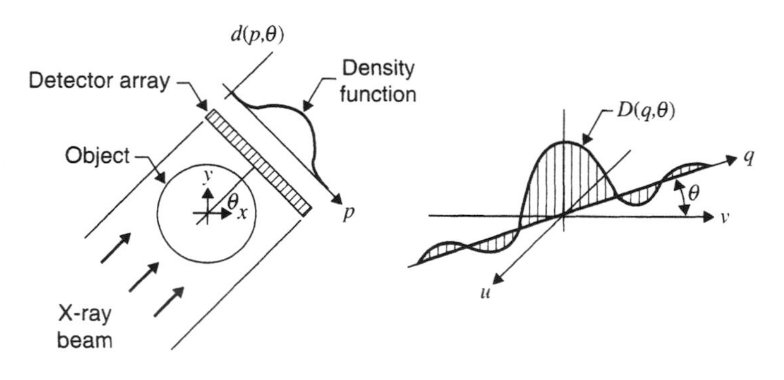

Figure 22–12 CAT reconstruction

is the amount of density that falls along the line that passes within a distance p of the origin and is oriented at an angle θ with the y-axis. For any θ, $d_r(p, \theta)$ is the (one-dimensional) projection of $d(x, y)$ onto a line oriented at an angle θ with the x-axis.

22.3.3 Image Reconstruction

Figure 22–12 illustrates the Fourier transform technique for CAT image reconstruction. The transmitted intensity function is used to compute the projected density function $d(p, \theta)$ using

$$d_r(p, \theta) = \log\left[\frac{I_o}{I(p, \theta)}\right] \tag{63}$$

where I_0 is the incident beam intensity and $I(p, \theta)$ is the transmitted intensity at position p along the linear detector array.

Under the similarity properties of the two-dimensional Fourier transform (see Chapter 10), we can write

$$\mathfrak{F}\{d_r(p, \theta)\} = D_r(q, \theta) \tag{64}$$

where θ is an angle measured with respect to the u-axis,

$$q = \sqrt{u^2 + v^2} \tag{65}$$

and

$$D(u, v) = \mathfrak{F}\{d(x, y)\} \tag{66}$$

Thus, each projected density function $d_r(p, \theta)$ yields a function $D_r(q, \theta)$ that is a radial slice through the two-dimensional Fourier transform of the object. A set of $D_r(q, \theta_i)$, where θ_i covers 180° in small steps, can be interpolated to determine $D(u,v)$ approximately. This, in turn, can be inverse transformed, yielding $d(x, y)$. Performed over a range of z, the technique produces $d(x, y, z)$, the three-dimensional X-ray density image of the object.

Some CAT scanners use simpler, though less exact, reconstruction algorithms to reduce the computational load. The simplest such algorithm is *back projection.* The back projection operation [25] is

$$b(x, y) = \int_0^{\pi} d_r[x\cos(\theta) + y\sin(\theta), \theta]\, d\theta \tag{67}$$

With this technique, each projected density function $d_r(\theta, p)$ is expanded (projected back) along the beam axis to form a two-dimensional image containing bars parallel to the axis. When all such images at one z-level are superimposed (summed), one obtains an approximate reconstruction of a cross section at that level. The reconstructed function $b(x, y)$ is actually $d(x, y)$ blurred by a PSF having the form

$$h(x, y) = \frac{1}{\sqrt{x^2 + y^2}} \tag{68}$$

While simple back projection was used in early CAT scanners, modern instruments use more accurate methods. These methods are commonly implemented by highpass filtering each (one-dimensional) projection prior to back projection. Using a filter with an MTF that increases with frequency linearly from zero produces the inverse Radon transform [25], which reconstructs $d(x, y)$.

The accuracy or resolution obtained by a CAT scanner depends on several parameters, including (1) how finely the projected density function is sampled, (2) how finely it is quantized, (3) the reconstruction algorithm used, (4) the interpolation method used, (5) the beam thickness, and (6) the sample spacing in the z-direction.

As in other radiography techniques, noise presents a problem in axial tomography. The principal noise source is due to the random distribution of photons in the illuminating beam. This effect is called *quantum mottle* in radiology. It is a result of the necessarily low exposure dosage to the patient and is similar to photoelectronic noise, discussed in Chapter 16.

Lowpass or median filtering of the reconstructed cross-sectioned image discriminates against the random noise, but at the expense of resolution. Thus, in each case, there is a trade-off between noise and resolution. The techniques discussed in Chapter 16 are generally applicable. The noise situation can also be improved by higher beam energy. However, while this is practical in nondestructive testing of mechanical components, there is a clinical trade-off between image noise and X-ray dosage to human subjects.

22.4 STEREOMETRY

Stereometry is a technique by which one can deduce the three-dimensional shape of an object from a stereoscopic image pair. To do this, one must model the geometry of image formation. Figure 22–1 diagrams an object, a light source, and a camera system. We establish a three-dimensional coordinate system centered upon the optical center of the lens system. The optical axis of the camera coincides with the z-axis.

The object of interest is an opaque surface in front of the camera. Depending on the reflectance of that surface, a portion of the light striking it is reflected, scattering in all directions. Some portion of the scattered light passes through the lens aperture and forms an image of the object at the image plane of the camera.

If the image is to be digitized, we can think of the image plane as being covered with an array of pixels. In Figure 22–1, one of the pixels is projected back through the lens to form an image of that pixel on the object. The projection of the pixel forms a *pixel cone,* extending out from its apex at the center of the lens until it encounters the first opaque surface.

The pixel cone's intersection with the object defines that region of the object to which the pixel corresponds. A portion of the light incident upon the pixel's image is scattered back into the lens aperture. All of this light is converged by the lens to fall upon the given pixel and thus to determine its gray level.

In addition to brightness, we can associate another value with the pixel in question. The distance from the center of the lens to the point p defines the *range* of this pixel. Notice that if other surfaces lie behind the object, they are obscured. Thus, the range of a pixel is the distance along its pixel cone from the center of the lens to the first opaque surface encountered. We can generate a *range image* by assigning each pixel a gray level proportional, not to its brightness, but to the length of its pixel cone.

22.4.1 Stereoscopic Imaging

Figure 22–13 diagrams a dual camera configuration suitable for stereoscopic imaging. A three-dimensional coordinate system has its origin at the center of the lens of the left camera. In this example, the optical axes of the two cameras are parallel and lie in the XZ-plane. Under these conditions, the cameras are said to be *boresighted.* The Z-axis coincides with the optical axis of the left camera. Both camera lenses have focal length f, and they are separated by the distance d.

22.4.1.1 Range Equations

Suppose the point P, with coordinates (X_o, Y_o, Z_o), is situated in front of the cameras, casting an image on both image planes. Then, using similar triangles in the XZ-plane and in the YZ-plane, we can show that a line from P through the center of the left camera lens will intersect the $Z = -f$ (image) plane at

$$X_l = -X_o\frac{f}{Z_o} \qquad Y_l = -Y_o\frac{f}{Z_o} \tag{69}$$

Similarly, a line from P through the center of the right camera lens will intersect the image plane at

$$X_r = -(X_o + d)\frac{f}{Z_o} - d \qquad Y_r = -Y_o\frac{f}{Z_o} \tag{70}$$

We now set up a two-dimensional coordinate system in each image plane. It is convenient to have each of them rotated 180° from the main coordinate system, so as to counteract the rotation that is intrinsic to the imaging process. Thus,

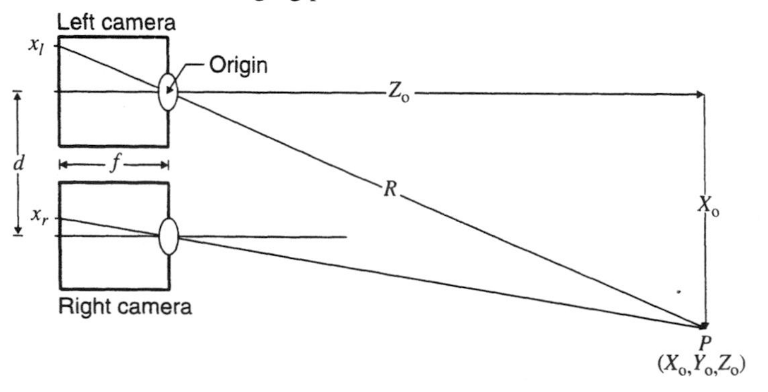

Figure 22–13 Stereoscopic imaging

$$x_l = -X_l \qquad y_l = -Y_l \qquad x_r = -X_r - d \qquad y_r = -Y_r \tag{71}$$

Now the coordinates of the point images are

$$x_l = X_o \frac{f}{Z_o} \qquad y_l = Y_o \frac{f}{Z_o} \tag{72}$$

and

$$x_r = (X_o + d) \frac{f}{Z_o} \qquad y_r = Y_o \frac{f}{Z_o} \tag{73}$$

Notice that the y-coordinate of the point is the same in both images.

Rearranging Eqs. (72) and (73) allows us to write

$$X_o = x_l \frac{Z_o}{f} = x_r \frac{Z_o}{f} - d \tag{74}$$

Solving this for Z_o produces

$$Z_o = \frac{fd}{x_r - x_l} \tag{75}$$

the *normal-range* equation. This equation relates the normal component Z_o of range to the amount of pixel shift between the two images. Notice that in Eq. (75) Z_o is a function only of the difference between x_r and x_l, and not their individual magnitudes. Since Z_o must be positive, $x_r \geq x_l$. Notice also that the numerator may be rather small compared to Z_o. This implies that the denominator (the pixel shift) will be extremely small for large Z_o. Thus, small inaccuracies in determining the position of a feature in the two images can produce large errors in range calculations.

Again using similar triangles, this time in three-space, we can write

$$\frac{R}{Z_o} = \frac{\sqrt{f^2 + x_l^2 + y_l^2}}{f} \tag{76}$$

Rearranging and substituting Eq. (75) for Z_o produces

$$R = \frac{d\sqrt{f^2 + x_l^2 + y_l^2}}{x_r - x_l} \tag{77}$$

which is the *true-range* equation. This gives the total distance from the origin to the point P. For narrow-angle (telephoto) systems, $X_o, Y_o << Z_o$, and x_l and y_l are small compared to f. Then Eq. (77) can be approximated by Eq. (75).

Given corresponding pixels in the left and right images, one can calculate either the normal range from Eq. (75) or the true range from Eq. (77). However, it is a nontrivial task to find the value of x_r that corresponds to each x_l, particularly in view of the high level of accuracy required.

22.4.1.2 Range Calculations

Stereometric ranges can be calculated in the following way. First, for each pixel in the left image, determine what pixel position in the right image corresponds to the same point on the object. For a boresighted system, as diagrammed in Figure 22–13, this can be accomplished on a line-by-line basis, since any point on the object maps to the same vertical position (and hence to the same scan line) on both images. Next, calculate the difference $x_r - x_l$ to produce a *displacement image*, in which gray level (properly scaled) represents pixel shift. Then, using the displacement image, calculate Z_o at each pixel by Eq. (75) to produce a normal-range image. Finally, calculate the X-coordinate and Y-coordinate of each point by

$$X_o = x_l \frac{Z_o}{f} \qquad Y_o = y_l \frac{Z_o}{f} \tag{78}$$

The foregoing procedure allows us to calculate the X,Y,Z-coordinates of every point on the object that maps to a pixel in the camera. Using Eq. (77) to compute R as a function of X and Y produces a true-range image. In either case, we have succeeded in mapping the visible surface of the object in three dimensions.

In Figure 22–13, the cameras are boresighted. Except in cases where Z_o is much larger than d, it may be necessary to *converge* the cameras to ensure that their fields of view overlap to include objects in the near field. In a converged system, the camera axes are not parallel, but converge to some point in the XZ-plane. In this case, the same techniques apply, but the range equations are slightly more complex. If the two camera axes do not even lie in the same plane, the situation is even more complex [26]. Sometimes it is necessary to determine the camera geometry from a stereo image pair. This can be done by a least squares fitting procedure that uses six or more points of known X,Y,Z-position to determine the imaging geometry of each camera [26–28].

22.4.2 Stereo Matching

Figure 22–14 illustrates a technique that can be used to locate the right image pixel position that corresponds to a particular left image pixel. To obtain accurate range information, one may have to do this with sub-pixel accuracy. Suppose the given pixel in the left image has coordinates x_l, y_l. We fit imaginary windows around that pixel and the pixel having the same coordinates in the right image. Next, we compute a measure of the agreement between the images inside the two windows. This can be calculated using cross-correlation, a sum of squared differences, or a similar technique. In any case, the image agreement measure should reach a maximum when the two windows contain the same features.

We repeat the process as the window in the right image moves toward the right. At some point, the moving window will be centered at x_r, y_l and will contain essentially the same

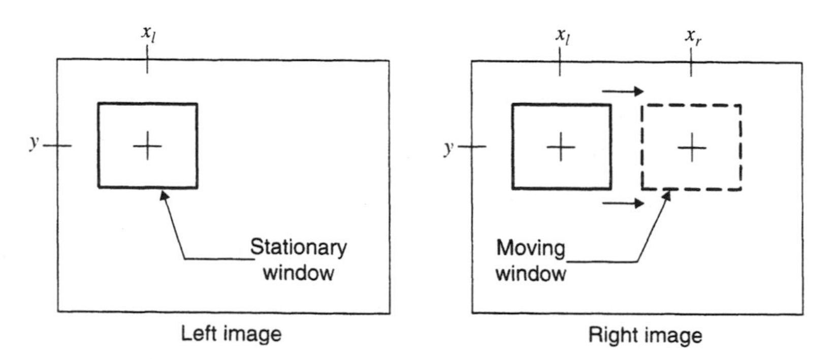

Figure 22–14 Pixel shift calculation

detail as the fixed window in the left image. When this happens, the image content in the two windows is approximately the same, and the measure of image agreement is maximized.

Noise in the images tends to corrupt the image agreement measure. The situation can be improved somewhat by increasing the size of the correlation window. Doing so reduces the resolution of the resulting range image, however, since large windows tend to smear over abrupt changes in range. Thus, the window size should be as small as possible, consistent with maintaining a low probability of miscalculating the pixel shift. The pixel shift calculation is also more reliable if the surface of the object exhibits considerable texture or high-frequency detail. It is very difficult to determine the range of a smooth surface. Sometimes it is helpful to project a random texture pattern onto such a surface to achieve an accurate range measurement.

22.4.3 Stereometry with Wide-Angle Cameras

The Viking Mars Lander spacecraft employed stereoscopic imaging. Each Lander had two digitizing cameras spaced 1 meter apart. In these angle-scanning cameras, however, the pixels were equally spaced in azimuth and elevation angle, rather than being equally spaced in the image plane. Thus, the coordinates of a pixel are given by the azimuth and elevation angles of the centerline of its pixel cone. As illustrated in Figure 22–15, the azimuth is the angle between the yz-plane and a vertical plane containing the pixel cone axis. The elevation angle is the angle between the xz-plane and a plane containing the x-axis and the pixel cone axis. The reference axes (zero azimuth, zero elevation) of the two cameras lie parallel to each other in the xz-plane.

Using the geometry in Figure 22–15, we can write the normal-range component in terms of the two camera azimuth coordinates θ_l and θ_r as

$$z = \frac{d}{\tan\theta_l \quad \tan\theta_r} \tag{79}$$

The two remaining coordinates of the point P are given by

$$x = z\tan\theta_l \tag{80}$$

and

$$y = z\tan\phi_l \tag{81}$$

where ϕ_l is the elevation coordinate and is the same for both cameras.

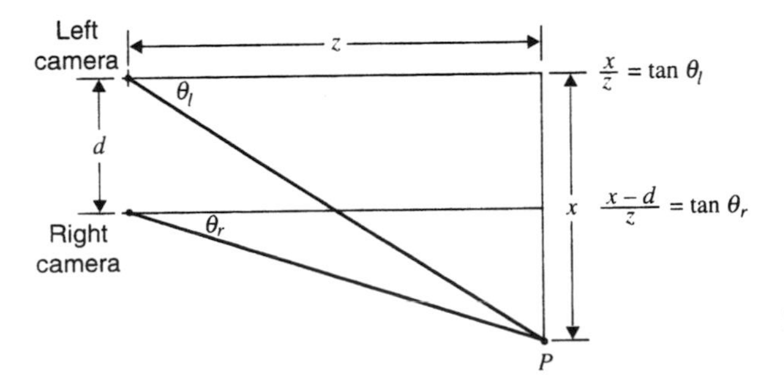

Figure 22–15 Stereoscopic angle-scanning camera

Figure 22–16 shows a stereo pair from the Viking Lander. Stereometry was used in the near field to establish a set of grid lines on the surface.

Figure 22–16 Stereo pair of images from Viking Lander camera (courtesy NASA/JPL)

Stereoscopic camera systems for robots sometimes employ fish-eye lenses which cover a wide angular field of view, but produce distorted images. (See Sec. 8.4.2.) Here it is necessary to rectify the images prior to stereometry [29,30].

22.5 STEREOSCOPIC IMAGE DISPLAY

A three-dimensional scene can be re-created for a viewer through stereoscopic display techniques. This is the basis of the "3–D" movies and stereoscopic photography that have been popular since the beginning of the twentieth century. It also provides a means of displaying three-dimensional digital images, such as biological cells [8].

22.5.1 Display Geometry

Figure 22–17 illustrates the viewing geometry for stereoscopic display. The stereoscopic image pair is positioned a distance D in front of the viewer's eyes, which are separated by the interocular distance S. A small feature located at coordinates x_l, y_l in the left image and x_r, y_l in the right image will appear to the observer as if it were located at point P.

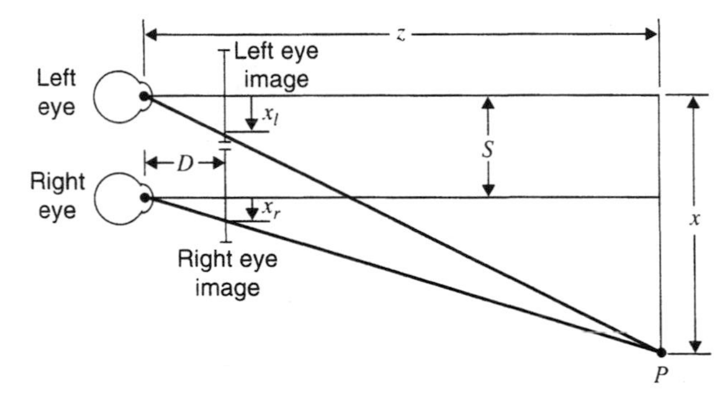

Figure 22–17 Stereoscopic display

A geometric development similar to that surrounding Figure 22–13 produces a range relation

$$z = \frac{DS}{x_l - x_r} \tag{82}$$

which is reminiscent of Eq. (75). The x-coordinates of corresponding points in the two images are related by

$$x_r = x_l - \frac{DS}{z} \tag{83}$$

This implies that for distant objects ($z = \infty$), the right- and left-eye coordinates are identical. As an object is shifted left in the right-eye image, its apparent position moves toward the observer.

Stereoscopic photography is a technique that uses a camera configuration similar to that shown in Figure 22–13 and a viewing apparatus similar to that of Figure 22–17 to reproduce three-dimensional scenes. Suppose that the two cameras in Figure 22–13 produce positive transparencies at the image plane. These transparencies can be rotated 180° about the z-axis and positioned in front of the observer, as in Figure 22–17. If the relationship

$$DS = fd \tag{84}$$

is satisfied, the scene will appear as if the observer had viewed it firsthand.

Two conditions must be satisfied to obtain accurate reproduction of a three-dimensional scene. First, there should be converging lenses in front of each of the viewer's eyes so that the viewer can focus his or her eyes at infinity and still see the two transparencies in focus. Positive lenses with focal length equal to D are commonly used. Without these lenses, the viewer must uncouple the learned connection that exists between the focus and the convergence of the eyes. While one can learn to do this, it is unnatural and uncomfortable.

Second, the viewing geometry is exact only when the viewer's line of sight falls along the z-axis. If the viewer fixes his or her gaze on other points in the image, the original scene is not reproduced exactly. Normally, this approximation is not distracting.

22.5.2 Stereo Display Generation

Suppose the left-eye image and the normal-range image are given, and it is desired to produce the right-eye image for stereoscopic display. This requires only a geometric transformation of the form

$$x_r = x_l - \frac{DS}{z} \qquad y_r = y_l \tag{85}$$

which is merely a copying operation with variable horizontal shift.

The transformation for a single line of the image is illustrated in Figure 22–18. The right-eye image is generated by copying the gray level at coordinate x_l into the pixel located at x_r. At each point (x_l, y), the amount of shift is a reciprocal function of the range.

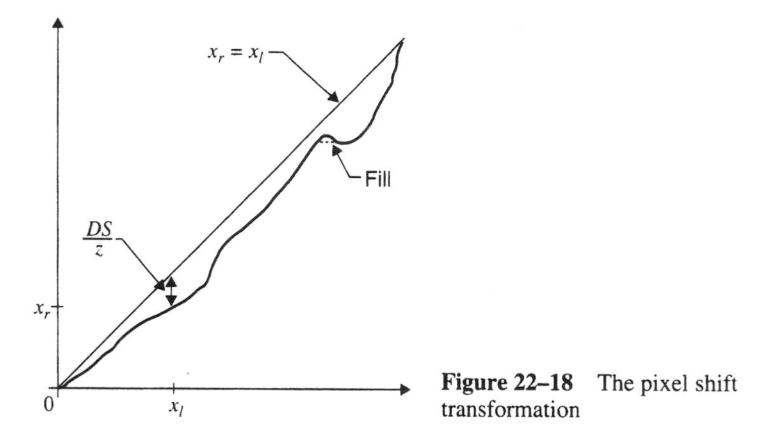

Figure 22–18 The pixel shift transformation

It is desirable that x_r be a nondecreasing function of x_l. If this function had negative slope over some interval, it would produce a right-for-left reversal in the generated image. As illustrated in Figure 22–18, we can use a horizontal fill technique to remove any local areas of negative slope.

In areas of zero slope, features of finite size in the left image become compressed to a point in the right image. This occurs, for example, when the right eye is looking directly along a surface that is visible to the left eye. Negative slope in the pixel shift transformation corresponds to the case in which the two eyes are looking at opposite sides of the same surface. In normal scenes, both of these conditions are rare.

For proper stereoscopic effect and comfortable viewing, one should keep the maximum pixel shift to no more than about 5 percent of the image width. In this case, the occurrence of zero or negative slope in the pixel shift function is quite rare.

Given a monocular brightness image and a range image of a particular scene, one might obtain a more pleasing stereo display by generating both right-eye and left-eye images. The right-eye image is generated by Eq. (85), but using only half the prescribed amount of shift. The left-eye image is generated by shifting an equal amount in the opposite direction. This technique can produce a superior display for an image containing nearby objects with considerable shape-related detail.

Figure 22–19 illustrates a stereoscopic image pair produced by a transformation of the form of Eq. (85). The left-eye image is a grid pattern, and the normal-range image is a Gaussian function. The right-eye image is the one produced by Eq. (85).

22.5.3 Display Quality

The surfaces displayed by stereoscopic techniques should have an abundance of fine detail or texture to assist the viewer's eye in the matching process. The human visual system executes a process that is apparently similar in effect to that described earlier for stereometric

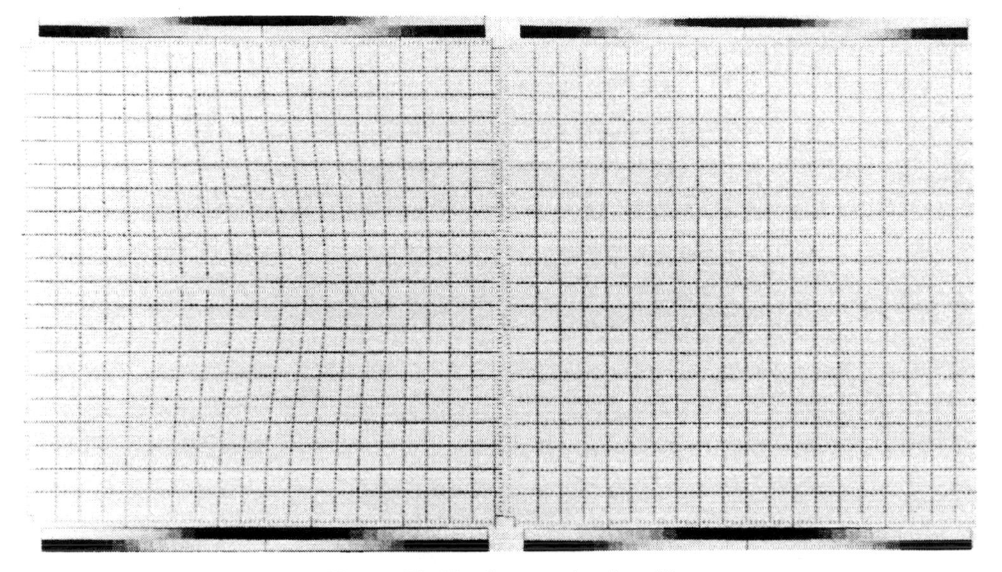

Figure 22–19 Stereo pair of a grid

ranging. Thus, smooth (untextured) surfaces are usually difficult to view properly in a stereoscopic display. Artificially introduced surface texture can help.

In stereo work, it is important that the display pixels not be visible. If they are, the viewer's eyes will be confused in attempting to cross-correlate the pixel patterns in the two images. This can create visual discomfort and destroy depth perception in the display. Reproduction of the picture by a screening process can also introduce conflicting texture. For further discussions of the human visual system in this regard, the interested reader should consult a text on the subject [31,32].

22.5.4 Display of Optical Section Stacks

A series of optical section images can be displayed as shown in Figure 22–20. The stack of transparent sections can be observed from any viewpoint specified by an azimuth, elevation, and range. The section images are projected onto an imaginary viewing screen, where they are superimposed by summation. The projection is accomplished by a geometric operation and is illustrated in Figure 22–21. A computer-generated rectangular grid image was projected with azimuth 60°, elevation 45°.

Figure 22–22 shows two stereo image pairs, each generated by projecting a stack of retinal cell images for two viewpoints.

22.6 SHADED SURFACE DISPLAY

Shaded surface display is a technique used to generate an image of a three-dimensional object that exists only as a mathematical description. Although the discipline is usually thought of in connection with computer graphics [1], it requires a digital image display system. Therefore, we introduce this related subject here.

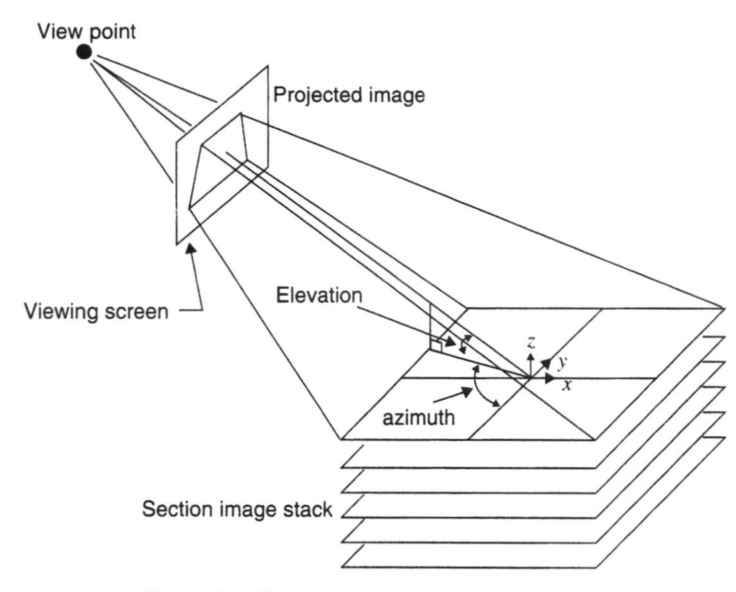

Figure 22–20 Image stack projection geometry

Figure 22–21 Projection of a grid image

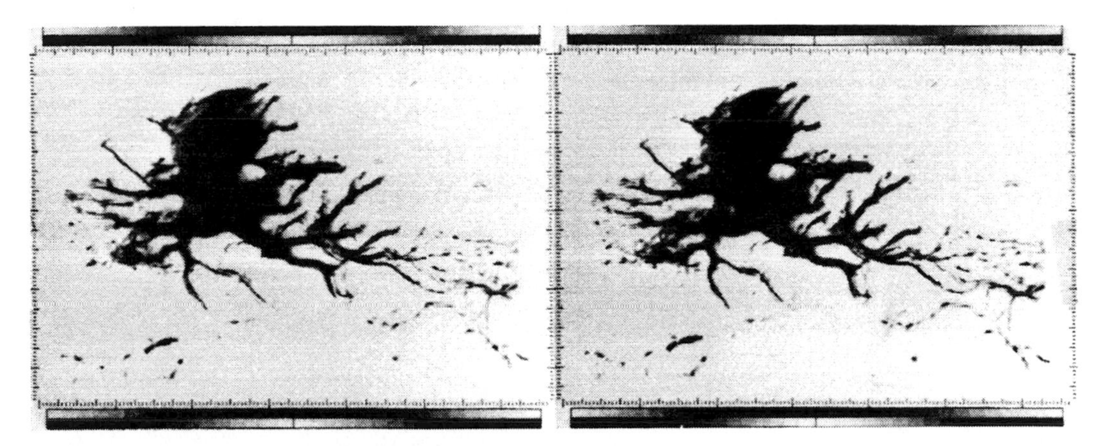

Figure 22–22 Stereo pair of image stacks

The object of interest is given by a mathematical description, in a three-dimensional coordinate system, of its opaque outer surface. The user specifies the location of all light sources and of the imaginary camera that is to generate the image. The latter position is called the *viewpoint*. The display algorithm then computes the image that the imaginary camera would make of the object.

Surface display requires modeling of three things: the spatial description of the surface, the light-reflecting phenomenon at the surface, and the geometry of the light sources and the imaging projection.

22.6.1 Surface Description

The three-dimensional surface of the object is ordinarily described by a polyhedral approximation [33]. Selected points on the object's surface form the vertices of the polygonal faces of the polyhedron. Triangles are commonly used for the faces, since it is always possible to pass a plane through three points. A planar quadrilateral cannot always connect four points on a surface. Figure 22–23 shows an image generated using a polyhedral approximation employing rectangles.

The description of the surface may be in the form of a list describing each polygon by the three-dimensional coordinates of its vertex points. Such a description is somewhat redundant, however, since each point is actually the vertex of several adjacent polygons and thus will appear in the list more than once. The actual format of the file containing the description of the surface (the *polygon file*) involves a trade-off between compact storage and ease of access while computing the projected image. Clearly, the more polygons used to define the surface, the more accurate the representation will be.

22.6.2 Surface Reflection Phenomena

Figure 22–24 illustrates the reflection of light from a flat surface. A point source at distance r provides incident light that makes an angle θ with the normal to the surface. A camera is located on a line that makes an angle ϕ with the normal. The light intensity falling upon the surface is proportional to $\cos(\theta)/r^2$.

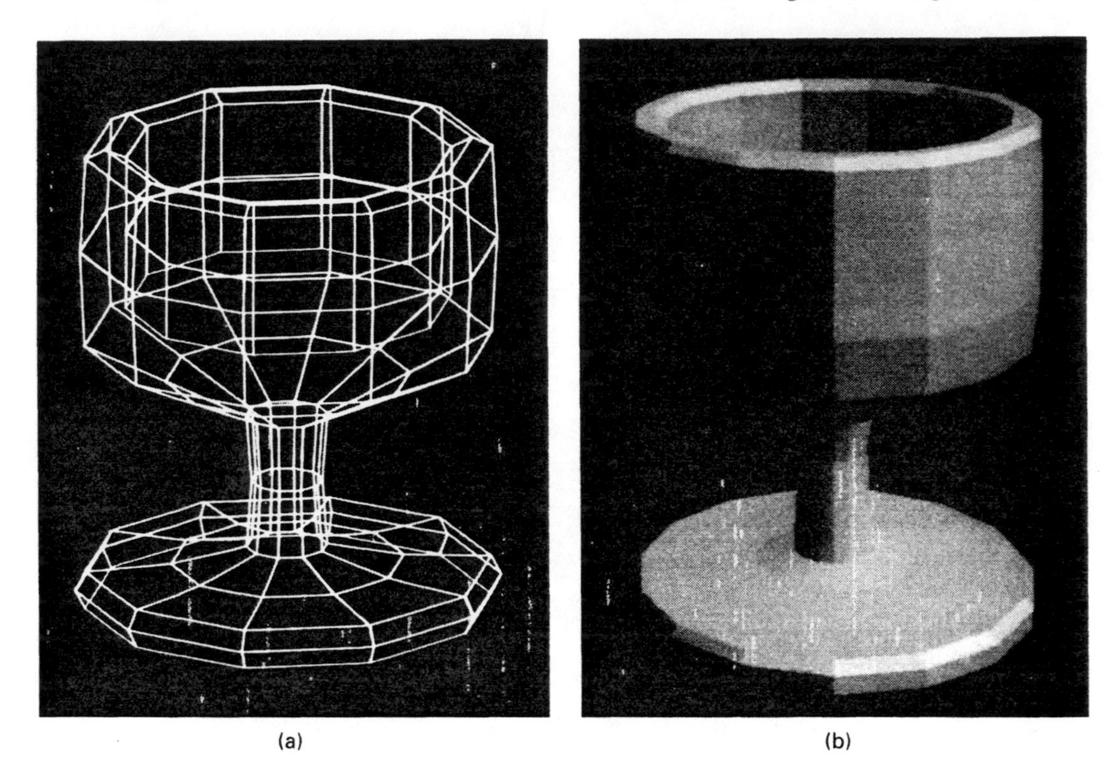

Figure 22–23 (a) Graphic (wire grid) display; (b) shaded surface display (courtesy James Blinn, NASA/JPL)

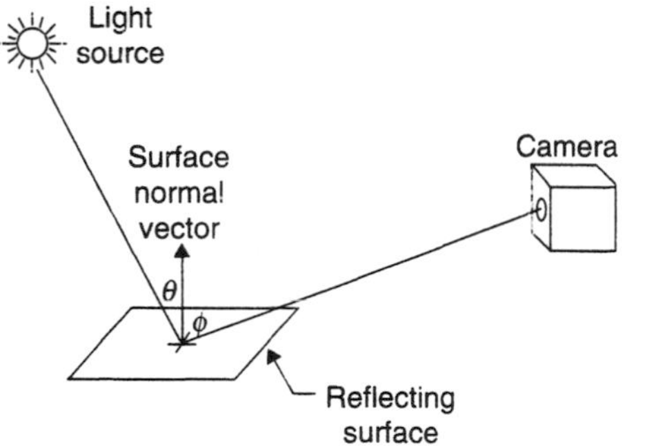

Figure 22–24 Surface reflection

There are two important types of reflection: diffuse scattering and specular reflection. Diffuse scattering is characteristic of matte or chalky surfaces, and reflected intensity on these surfaces can be modeled as proportional to $\cos(\phi)$. Specular reflection is characteristic of shiny or metallic surfaces. The intensity due to specular reflection can be modeled as proportional to $[\cos(\theta - \phi)]^n$, where n is between 0.5 and 10. The larger values of n make the surface appear more shiny.

The apparent brightness of a uniformly radiating surface varies as $1/\cos(\phi)$ because, as the viewer moves away from the normal (increasing ϕ), the same amount of energy from the surface projects into a smaller area of his or her retina. We can now write the reflected intensity equation as

$$I = A\frac{\cos(\theta)}{r^2}\frac{1}{\cos(\phi)}\{B\cos(\phi) + (1-B)[\cos(\theta+\phi)]^n\} \qquad 0 \le B \le 1 \tag{86}$$

where B and n are surface reflectance parameters and A is a constant of proportionality.

The parameter B determines how the incident light is divided between diffuse and specular reflection. For a purely diffusing surface, we can let $B = 1$. If r is very large, it can be assumed constant over the extent of the object and can be absorbed into the proportionality constant. Then Eq. (86) reduces to

$$I = C\cos(\theta) \tag{87}$$

a computationally simple surface brightness rule.

22.6.3 Imaging Geometry

Figure 22–25 shows the model for computing the image of the object's surface. The cone from any pixel p projects through the lens, and its axis intersects the surface at some point P that falls on a particular polygon. Thus, the gray level (brightness) of pixel p can be computed from Eq. (86) if the normal vector to the surface of the polygon at P is known. The image is generated, pixel by pixel, by first determining upon which polygon the pixel cone axis falls and then computing the light intensity reflected into the camera using the geometry of Figure 22–25.

Perhaps the most challenging aspect of shaded surface display is the organization of, and search algorithm for, the polygon file. The generation of such images can be quite slow and expensive, particularly if file management is not handled efficiently. Image generation for real-time display usually requires special-purpose high-speed image-processing hardware.

The image is ordinarily generated in the conventional line-by-line digital image-processing fashion. Any image line intersects only a limited number of polygons. Thus, the search algorithm needs to work with only a few active polygons at a time. If one pixel on the line does not fall on an active polygon, the previously unused polygons are searched to find

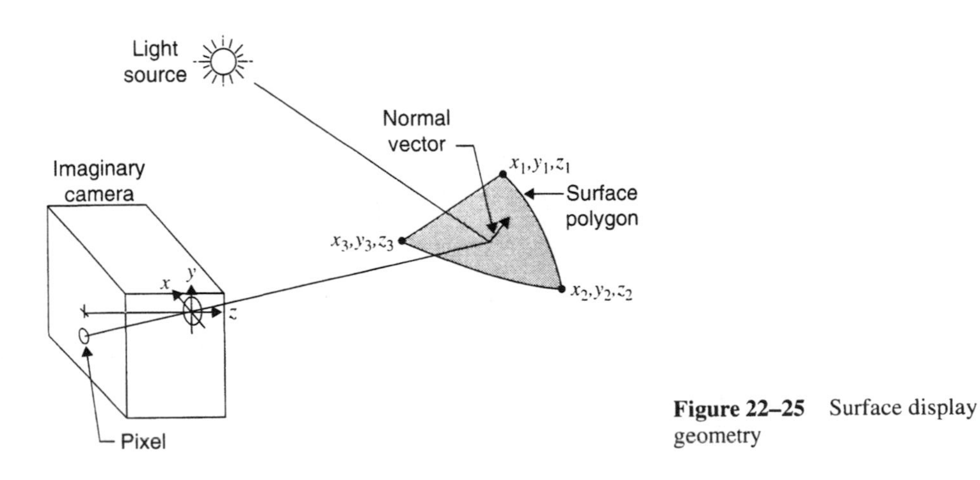

Figure 22–25 Surface display geometry

which one should be activated. If no pixel on the line falls on a particular active polygon, that polygon becomes inactive. Some pixels may fall on no polygon at all (outside the object), and these can be set to black or some other background gray level. For more information on search algorithms, the interested reader can consult a textbook [1] or the literature on computer graphics.

22.6.4 Smooth Shading

The polyhedral approximation to a curved surface produces an artificial appearance in the computed image (Figure 22–23(b)). The polygon edges represent highly visible discontinuities in brightness. Using a larger number of polygons helps, but it is an expensive remedy.

Goroud [34] advanced a computationally simple method for achieving a smooth surface approximation. Each vertex on the surface is actually the vertex of several adjacent polygons. The *surface normal vector* at each vertex point is defined as the average of the normal vectors of the surrounding polygons. When a pixel cone axis intersects a surface polygon, the local surface normal vector is obtained by interpolation from the surrounding vertices, as illustrated in Figure 22–26. This technique causes the normal vector to vary smoothly rather than abruptly over the surface, and it produces a smooth surface appearance, as shown in Figure 22–27.

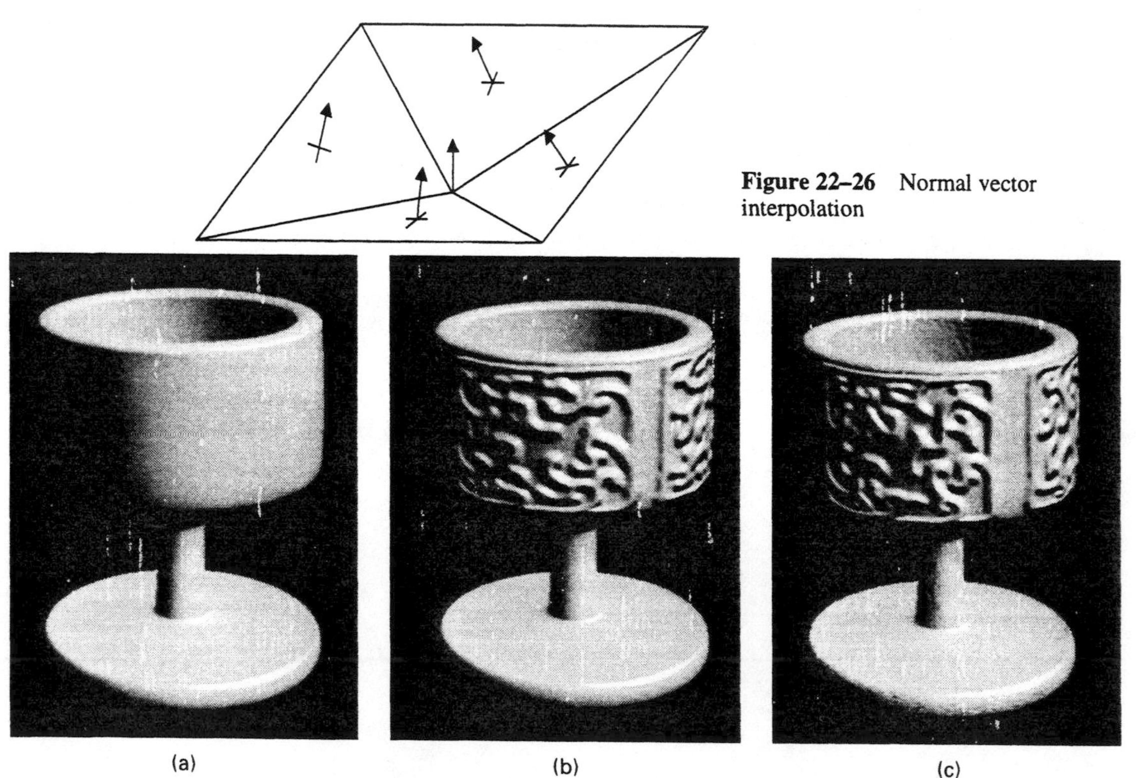

Figure 22–26 Normal vector interpolation

(a) (b) (c)

Figure 22–27 Surface display: (a) smooth shading; (b) relief pattern added; (c) random surface texture added (courtesy James Blinn, NASA/JPL)

22.7 SUMMARY OF IMPORTANT POINTS

1. Thick specimen imaging involves a three-dimensional convolution of the specimen function with the defocus PSF.
2. Theoretically, optical section images can be deblurred exactly by three-dimensional deconvolution or by a simultaneous linear equation approach.
3. Practically, optical section images can be deblurred approximately by subtraction of blurred neighboring plane images.
4. The defocus OTF of a circular lens is given by Eq. (49).
5. Computerized axial tomography uses the projection property of the two-dimensional Fourier transform to reconstruct an image from a set of its projections.
6. A range image can be computed from a stereo pair [Eq. (75)].
7. A stereo pair can be generated from a brightness image and a range image [Eq. (85)].
8. Surface texture is helpful in stereometry and stereoscopic display.
9. Shaded surface display techniques produce images of objects that exist only as a description of a mathematical surface.

PROBLEMS

1. How many calibration points (known X, Y, Z) do you need to determine the imaging geometry (f, d) of a boresighted stereo camera system? What are the restrictions on the position of the points?
2. How many calibration points do you need to determine the imaging geometry of a stereo camera system when the cameras have the same focal length, but are not boresighted? Assume that the cameras are mounted on a bar such that the lens center of the right camera is at $Z = 0$ in the coordinate system of the left camera.
3. Suppose you have two pictures of a scene taken with the same camera, but from slightly different, and unknown, positions. Assuming that nothing has changed in the scene between exposures, how many calibration points do you need to establish the imaging geometry of this system?
4. Suppose you have a boresighted stereoscopic camera system (Figure 22–13) with 50-mm lenses separated by 70 mm. Where on each sensor plane will the image of a small object located at $(X, Y, Z) = (3\text{ m}, 2\text{ m}, 6\text{ m})$ fall? What is the true range to the object?
5. Suppose you have a boresighted stereoscopic camera system (Figure 22–13) with 135-mm lenses separated by 100 mm. Where is an object (X, Y, Z = ?) that falls on the sensor planes at x_l = 51.9231 mm, x_r = 52.4423 mm, and y = 20.7692 mm? What is the true range to the object?
6. Suppose you have a boresighted stereoscopic camera system (Figure 22–13) with focal length by 60 mm. An object at $Y = 0.4$ meter falls on the sensor planes at $x_l = -14.5833$ mm, $x_r = -12.8333$ mm, and $y = 11.6667$ mm. What is the separation of the lenses? What is the true range to the object?
7. Suppose you are calibrating a boresighted stereoscopic camera system (Figure 22–13) with lenses of unknown focal length and unknown camera separation. An object at $(X, Y, Z) = (0, 0, 2\text{ m})$ falls on the sensor planes at $(x_l, x_r, y) = (0, 10\text{ mm}, 0)$, and another object at $(X, Y, Z) = (0, 0, 10\text{ m})$ falls on the sensor planes at $(x_l, x_r, y) = (0, 2\text{ mm}, 0)$. Can you determine f and d from those measurements? If so, do so; if not, please explain your failure to do so.

8. Suppose you are calibrating a boresighted stereoscopic camera system (Figure 22–13) with lenses of unknown focal length and unknown camera separation. An object at $(X, Y, Z) = (1\text{ m}, 0\text{ m}, 10\text{ m})$ falls on the sensor planes at $(x_l, x_r, y) = (10\text{ mm}, 12\text{ mm}, 0)$. Can you determine f and d from those measurements? If so, do so; if not, please explain your failure to do so.
9. Suppose you have a boresighted stereoscopic camera system (Figure 22–13) with 200-mm lenses separated by 250 mm. The image of an object falls on the sensor planes at $(x_l, x_r, y) = (3.3333\text{ mm}, 3.5000\text{ mm}, 1.0000\text{ mm})$. You have a one-pixel (±10-micron) uncertainty in the sensor plane measurements. What is the most likely true range to the object? How close might the object be? How far could it be?
10. A boresighted stereoscopic camera system has been dropped from the cargo hold of a DC-9 by the overnight shipping company. You aim the camera at a star and get $(x_l, x_r, y_l, y_r) = (17.6654, 17.6654, -2.0504, -2.0405)$ mm. Has the instrument been damaged? How do you know?
11. Suppose your artillery position is under attack from four enemy armored tanks. You have an Acme high-resolution battlefield stereoscope (see Figure 22–13) with boresighted 500-mm lenses 1 meter apart. You click on each tank and get the following sensor plane position data:

    Tank No. 1 $x_l = -70.0000$ mm, $x_r = -69.6667$ mm, $y = 1.3333$ mm
    Tank No. 2 $x_l = -5.0000$ mm, $x_r = -4.5000$ mm, $y = 1.5000$ mm
    Tank No. 3 $x_l = 150.0000$ mm, $x_r = 151.0000$ mm, $y = 2.0000$ mm
    Tank No. 4 $x_l = 75.0000$ mm, $x_r = 75.1667$ mm, $y = 0.2500$ mm

    The tanks have a gun range of 1,000 m, and your gun range is 2,000 m. The tanks are not moving, but tanks 1 and 3 have their guns facing your direction. Which tanks would you fire on, and in what sequence?
12. Below are single scan lines (starting at $x = 0$) from each of a stereo pair of digital images. The cameras are boresighted, with $f = 100$ mm and $d = 300$ mm, and both lines are at $y = 0$. The pixel spacing is 15 microns. The image shows an enemy tank on a battlefield, with a wooded area behind. What is the true range to the tank? How far away are the woods? (*Hint*: Start by plotting the two scan lines on the same graph.)

    Left:

    [25,30,26,32,25,31,25,31,26,29,25,31,31,26,26,31,25,29,24,28,25,31,25,30,25,33,26,30,25,29,26]

    Right:

    [33,36,32,37,33,39,32,38,32,38,33,36,32,36,32,38,38,33,33,36,31,35,32,38,32,37,32,40,33,37,32]
13. Develop the stereo equations (analogous to Eq. 75) for the case where the stereo camera axes converge to a point $(X, Y, Z) = (0, 0, Z_c)$.

PROJECTS

1. Develop a program to locate corresponding points in a stereo image pair and generate a displacement image.
2. Develop a program to compute a normal-range image from a displacement image, given the imaging geometry.
3. Develop a program to compute a true-range image from a displacement image, given the imaging geometry.

4. Develop a program to determine the imaging geometry for a stereometric camera system, given pixel coordinates and ranges of several calibration points in space.
5. Develop a program to generate random dot stereograms, given the normal range $z(x, y)$ in functional form.
6. Develop a program to generate random dot stereograms, given the normal range $z(x, y)$ as a digital image.
7. Develop a program to deblur optical section images, and test the program on a biological specimen.

REFERENCES

1. W .M. Newman and R. F. Sproull, *Principles of Interactive Computer Graphics,* McGraw-Hill Book Company, New York, 1973.
2. H. Elias, "Three-Dimensional Structure Identified from Single Sections," *Science,* **174:**993–1000, December 1971.
3. T. Tommasi, A. Diaspro, and B. Bianco, "3-D Reconstruction in Optical Microscopy by a Frequency-Domain Approach," *Signal Processing,* **32**(3):357–366, 1993.
4. T. Wilson and J. B. Tan, "Three Dimensional Image Reconstruction in Conventional and Confocal Microscopy," *Bioimaging,* **1**(3):176–185, 1993.
5. M. Weinstein and K. R. Castleman, "Reconstructing 3-D Specimens from 2-D Section Images," *Proceedings of the SPIE,* **26:**131–138, 1971.
6. D. A. O'Handley, E. S. Beckenbach, K. R. Castleman, R. H. Selzer, and R. J. Wall, "Picture Analysis Applied to Biomedicine," *Computer Graphics and Image Processing,* **2:**417–432, 1973.
7. D. A. Agard, Y. Hiraoka, P. Shaw, and J. W. Sedat, "Fluorescence Microscopy in Three-Dimensions," *Methods in Cell Biology,* **30:**353–377, 1989.
8. M. R. Paddy, A. S. Belmont, H. Saumweber, D. A. Agard, and J. W. Sedat, "Interphase Nuclear Envelope Lamins form a Discontinuous Network That Interacts with Only a Fraction of the Chromatin in the Nuclear Periphery," *Cell,* **62:**89–106, 1990.
9. W. Carrington, "Image Restoration in 3D Microscopy with Limited Data," *Proceedings of the SPIE,* **1205:**72–83, 1990.
10. W. Carrington, K. E. Fogarty, and F. S. Fay, "3D Fluorescence Imaging of Single Cells Using Image Restoration," in K. Fosbett and S. Grinstein, eds., *Noninvasive Techniques in Cell Biology,* 53–72, Wiley-Liss, New York, 1990.
11. F. S. Fay, W. Carrington, and K. E. Fogarty, "Three-Dimensional Molecular Distribution in Single Cells Analyzed Using the Digital Imaging Microscope," *Journal of Microscopy,* **153**(2):133–149, 1989.
12. L. M. Loew, R. A. Tuft, W. Carrington, and F. S. Fay, "Imaging in Five Dimensions: Time-Dependent Membrane Potentials in Individual Mitochondria," *Biophysical Journal,* **65:**2396–2407, 1993.
13. J. W. Goodman, *Introduction to Fourier Optics,* McGraw-Hill Book Company, New York, 1968.
14. P. A. Stokseth, "Properties of a Defocused Optical System," *J. Optical Soc. Amer.,* **59**(10): 1314–1321, October 1969.
15. H. H. Hopkins, "The Frequency Response of a Defocused Optical System," *Proc. Royal Soc.* (London), **A231:**91–103, 1955.
16. K. R. Castleman, *Digital Image Processing,* Prentice-Hall, Englewood Cliffs, NJ, 1979.
17. M. Born and E. Wolf, *Principles of Optics: Electromagnetic Theory of Propagation, Interference and Diffraction of Light* (6th ed.), Pergamon Press, Oxford, 1980.

18. Y. Hiraoka, J. W. Sedat, and D. A. Agard, "Determination of Three-Dimensional Imaging Properties of a Light Microscope System," *Biophysical Journal,* **57**:325–333, 1990.

19. R. Gordon and G. T. Herman, "Reconstruction of Pictures from Their Projections," *Comm. ACM,* **14**(12):759–768, December 1971.

20. R. Gordon and G. T. Herman, "Three-Dimensional Reconstruction from Projections," *International Review of Cytology,* **38**:111–151, 1974.

21. Z. H. Cho, ed., "Special Issue on Three-Dimensional Image Reconstruction," *IEEE Transactions on Nuclear Science,* **NS-21**(3), June 1974.

22. R. Gordon, G. T. Herman, and S. A. Johnson, "Image Reconstruction from Projections," *Scientific American,* **233**(4):56–68, October 1975.

23. R. N. Bracewell and S. J. Wernecke, "Image Reconstruction over a Finite Field of View," *J. Opt. Soc. Amer.,* **65**(11):1342–1346, November 1975.

24. J. T. Payne and E. C. McCullough, "Basic Principles of Computer-Assisted Tomography," *Applied Radiology,* **103**:53–60, March/April 1976.

25. A. K. Jain, *Fundamentals of Digital Image Processing,* Prentice Hall, Englewood Cliffs, NJ, 1989.

26. Y. Yakimovsky and R. Cunningham, "A System for Extracting Three-Dimensional Measurements from a Stereo Pair of TV Cameras," *Computer Graphics and Image Processing,* **7**:195–210, 1978.

27. W. K. Pratt, *Digital Image Processing,* John Wiley & Sons, Inc., New York, 1991.

28. D. H. Ballard and C. M. Brown, *Computer Vision,* Prentice-Hall, Englewood Cliffs, NJ, 1982 (Section A1.8).

29. S. Shah and J. K. Aggarwal, "A Simple Calibration Procedure for Fish-Eye (High Distortion) Lens Camera," *Proc. IEEE Int. Conf. on Robotics and Automation,* 3422–3427, 1994.

30. S. Shah and J. K. Aggarwal, "Depth Estimation Using Stereo Fish-Eye Lenses," *ICIP-94, Proc. IEEE Int. Conf. on Image Processing,* **2**:740–744, 1994.

31. T. N. Cornsweet, *Visual Perception,* Academic Press, New York, 1970.

32. B. Julesz, *Foundations of Cyclopean Perception,* University of Chicago Press, Chicago, 1971.

33. H. Fuchs, Z. Kedem, and S. Uselton, "Optimal Surface Reconstruction from Planar Contours," *Comm. ACM,* **20**:693–702, 1977.

34. H. Goroud, "Continuous Shading of Curved Surfaces," *IEEE Trans. on Computers,* **C-20**(6): 623–629, June 1971.

APPENDIX 1

Glossary of Digital Image-Processing Terms

This glossary is provided to help the reader avoid confusion brought about by the specialized usage of common words in this book. The following definitions conform roughly to general usage in digital image processing, but by no means constitute a standard in the field. They tend to agree, but not exactly, with definitions in glossaries published in the fields of image processing [1–3] and computer technology [4–6].

Algebraic operation - an image-processing operation involving the pixel-by-pixel sum, difference, product, or quotient of two images.

Aliasing - an artifact produced when the pixel spacing is too large in relation to the detail in an image (Chapter 12).

Arc - (1) a continuous portion of a circle; (2) a connected set of pixels representing a portion of a curve.

Binary image - a digital image having only two gray levels (usually zero and one, black and white).

Blur - a loss of image sharpness, introduced by defocus, lowpass filtering, camera motion, etc.

Border - the first and last row and column of a digital image.

Boundary chain code - a sequence of directions specifying the boundary of an object.

Boundary pixel - an interior pixel that is adjacent to at least one background pixel (contrast with *interior pixel, exterior pixel*).

Boundary tracking - an image segmentation technique in which arcs are detected by searching sequentially from one arc pixel to the next.

Brightness - the value, associated with a point in an image, that represents the amount of light emanating or reflected from the object at that point.

Change detection - an image-processing technique in which the pixels of two registered images are compared (e.g. by subtraction) to detect differences in the objects therein.

Class - see *pattern class*.

Closed curve - a curve whose beginning and ending points are at the same location.

Cluster - a set of points located close together in a space (e.g., in feature space).

Cluster analysis - the detection, measurement and description of clusters in a space.

Concave - the characteristic of an object whereby at least one straight-line segment between two interior points of the object is not entirely contained within the object (contrast with *convex*).

Connected - the characteristic of the pixels of an object or curve whereby any two points within the object can be joined by an arc made up entirely of adjacent pixels also contained within the object.

Contour encoding - an image compression technique in which a region that has a constant gray level is encoded by specifying only its boundary.

Contrast - the amount of difference between the average brightness (or gray level) of an object and that of the surrounding background.

Contrast stretch - a linear gray-scale transformation.

Convex - the characteristic of an object whereby all straight-line segments between two interior points of the object are entirely contained within the object (contrast with *concave*).

Convolution - a mathematical process for combining two functions to produce a third function. Convolution models the operation of a shift-invariant linear system (Sec. 9.3).

Convolution kernel - (1) the two-dimensional array of numbers used in convolution filtering of a digital image; (2) the function with which a signal or image is convolved.

Curve - (1) a continuous path through space; (2) a connected set of pixels representing a path (see *arc, closed curve*).

Deblurring - (1) an image-processing operation designed to reduce blurring and sharpen the detail in an image; (2) removing or reducing the blur in an image, often one step of image restoration or reconstruction.

Decision rule - in pattern recognition, a rule or algorithm used to assign an object in an image to a particular class. The assignment is based on measurements of the features of the object.

Digital image - (1) an array of integers representing an image of a scene; (2) a sampled and quantized function of two or more dimensions, generated from and representing a continuous function of the same dimensionality; (3) an array generated by sampling a continuous function on a rectangular (or other) grid and quantizing its value at the sample points.

Digital image processing - digital processing of images, the manipulation of pictorial information by computer.

Digitization - the process of converting an image of a scene into digital form.

Edge - (1) a region of an image in which the gray level changes significantly over a short distance; (2) a set of pixels belonging to an arc and having the property that pixels on opposite sides of the arc have significantly different gray levels.

Edge detection - an image segmentation technique in which edge pixels are identified by examining neighborhoods.

Edge enhancement - any image-processing technique in which edges are made to appear sharper by increasing the contrast between the gray levels of the pixels located on opposite sides of the edge.

Edge image - an image in which each pixel is labeled as either an edge pixel or a nonedge pixel.

Edge linking - an image-processing technique in which neighboring edge pixels in an edge image are connected to form an edge.

Edge operator - a neighborhood operator that labels the edge pixels in an image.

Edge pixel - a pixel that lies on an edge.

Enhance - to increase the contrast or subjective visibility of.

Exterior pixel - a pixel that falls outside all the objects in a binary image (contrast with *interior pixel*).

False negative - in two-class pattern recognition, a misclassification error in which a positive object is labeled negative.

False positive - in two-class pattern recognition, a misclassification error in which a negative object is labeled positive.

Feature - a characteristic of an object, something that can be measured and that assists in classification of the object (e.g., size, texture, shape).

Feature extraction - a step in the pattern recognition process in which measurements of the objects are computed.

Feature selection - a step in the pattern recognition system development process in which measurements or observations are studied to identify those that can be used to assign objects to classes.

Feature space - see *measurement space.*

Fourier transform - a linear transformation that uses the complex exponential $e^{-j2\pi sx} = \cos(2\pi sx) + j\sin(2\pi sx)$ as the kernel function.

Geometric correction - an image restoration technique in which a geometric transformation is used to remove geometric distortion.

Gray level - (1) the value, associated with a pixel in a digital image, representing the brightness of the original scene at the point represented by that pixel; (2) a quantized measurement of the local property of the image at a pixel location.

Gray scale - the set of all possible gray levels in a digital image.

Gray-scale transformation - the function, employed in a point operation, that specifies the relationship between input and corresponding output gray-level values.

Hankel transform - a linear transformation, similar to the Fourier transform, that relates the (one-dimensional) profile of a circularly symmetric function of two dimensions to the (one-dimensional) profile of the function's two-dimensional (also circularly symmetric) Fourier transform (Sec. 10.4.5).

Harmonic signal - a complex-valued signal composed of a cosine real part plus an imaginary sine part at the same frequency (Sec. 9.2.1).

Hermite function - a complex-valued function having an even real part and an odd imaginary part (Sec. 10.2.1).

Highpass filtering - an image enhancement (usually convolution) operation in which the high-frequency components are emphasized relative to the low frequency components.

Hole - in a binary image, a connected region of background points that is completely surrounded by interior points.

Image - any representation of a physical scene or of another image.

Image compression - any process that eliminates redundancy from or approximates an image, in order to represent it in a more compact form.

Image coding - translating image data into another form from which it can be recovered (e.g., compression).

Image enhancement - any process intended to improve the visual appearance of an image.

Image matching - any process involving quantitative comparison of two images in order to determine their degree of similarity.

Image-processing operation - a series of steps that transforms an input image into an output image.

Image reconstruction - the process of constructing or recovering an image from data that occurs in nonimage form.

Image registration - a geometric operation intended to position one image of a scene with respect to another image of the same scene so that the objects in the two images coincide.

Image restoration - any process intended to return an image to its original condition by reversing the effects of prior degradations.

Image segmentation - (1) the process of detecting and delineating the objects of interest in an image; (2) the process of subdividing an image into disjoint regions. Normally, these regions correspond to objects and the background upon which the objects reside.

Interior pixel - in a binary image, a pixel that falls inside an object (contrast with *boundary pixel, exterior pixel*).

Interpolation - the process of determining the value of a sampled function between its sample points.

Kernel - see convolution kernel.

Line detection - an image segmentation technique in which line pixels are identified by examining neighborhoods.

Line pixel - a pixel contained in an arc that approximates a straight line.

Local operation - an image-processing operation that assigns a gray level to each output pixel on the basis of the gray levels of pixels located in a neighborhood of the corresponding input pixel. A neighborhood operation (contrast with *point operation*).

Local property - the interesting characteristic that varies with position in an image (e.g., brightness or color for optical images; elevation, temperature, population density, etc., for nonoptical images).

Lossless image compression - any image compression technique that permits exact reconstruction of the original image.

Lossy image compression - any image compression technique that inherently involves approximation and does not permit exact reconstruction of the image.

Matched filtering - using a matched filter (Chapter 11) to detect the presence and location of specific objects in an image.

Measurement space - in pattern recognition, an n-dimensional vector space containing all possible measurement vectors.

Misclassification - in pattern recognition, the assignment of an object to any class other than its true class.

Multispectral image - a set of images of the same scene, each formed by radiation from a different wavelength band of the electromagnetic spectrum.

Neighborhood - a set of pixels located near a given pixel.

Neighborhood operation - an image-processing operation that assigns a gray level to each output pixel on the basis of the gray levels of pixels located in a neighborhood of the corresponding input pixel (see *local operation,* contrast with *point operation*).

Noise - irrelevant components of an image that hamper recognition and interpretation of the data of interest.

Noise reduction - any process that reduces the undesirable effects of noise in an image.

Object - in pattern recognition, a connected set of pixels in a binary image, usually corresponding to a physical object in the scene represented by the image.

Optical image - the result of projecting light emanating from a scene onto a surface, as with a lens.

Pattern - a meaningful regularity that members of a pattern class express in common and that can be measured and used to classify objects of interest.

Pattern class - one of a set of mutually exclusive, pre-established categories to which an object can be assigned.

Pattern classification - the process of assigning objects to pattern classes.

Pattern recognition - the detection, measurement, and classification of objects in an image by automatic or semiautomatic means.

Pel - contraction of *picture element.*

Perimeter - the circumferential distance around the boundary of an object.

Picture element - the smallest element of a digital image. The basic unit of which a digital image is composed.

Pixel - contraction of *picture element.*

Point operation - an image-processing operation that assigns a gray level to each output pixel on the basis of only the gray level of the corresponding input pixel (contrast with *neighborhood operation*).

Quantitative image analysis - any process that extracts quantitative data from a digital image.

Quantization - the process by which the local property of an image, at each pixel, is assigned one of a finite set of gray levels.

Region - a connected subset of an image.

Region growing - an image segmentation technique in which regions are formed by repeatedly taking the union of adjacent subregions that are similar in gray level or texture.

Registered - (1) the condition of being in alignment; (2) when two or more images are in geometric alignment with each other and the objects therein coincide.

Registered images - two or more images of the same scene that have been positioned with respect to one another so that the objects in the scene occupy the same positions.

Resolution - (1) in optics, the minimum separation distance between distinguishable point objects; (2) in image processing, the degree to which closely spaced point objects in an image can be distinguished from one another.

Run - in image coding, a sequence of consecutive pixels that all have the same gray level.

Run length - the number of pixels in a run.

Run-length encoding - an image compression technique in which the rows of an image are represented as sequences of runs, each specified by a given run length and gray level.

Sampling - the process of dividing an image into pixels (according to a sampling grid) and measuring the local property (e.g., brightness or color) at each pixel.

Scene - a particular arrangement of physical objects.

Sharp - pertaining to the detail in an image, well defined and readily discernible.

Sharpening - any image-processing technique intended to enhance the detail in an image.

Sigmoid function - a function having a shape that resembles the letter *S*. The sigmoid is one type of gray-scale transformation function. Sigmoid functions are also used in the processing elements of a neural network.

Sinusoidal - having the shape of the sine function.

Smoothing - any image-processing technique intended to reduce the amplitude of small detail in an image. Smoothing is often used for noise reduction.

Statistical pattern recognition - an approach to pattern recognition that uses probability and statistical methods to assign objects to pattern classes.

Structural pattern recognition - an approach to pattern recognition in which objects are represented in terms of primitives and relationships among primitives in order to describe and classify the objects.

Syntactic pattern recognition - a type of structural pattern recognition that identifies primitives and relationships according to natural or artificial language patterns.

System - anything that accepts an input and produces an output in response.

Texture - in image processing, an attribute representing the amplitude and spatial arrangement of the local variation of gray level in an image.

Thinning - a binary image-processing technique that reduces objects to sets of thin (one-pixel-wide) curves.

Threshold - a specified gray level used for producing a binary image.

Thresholding - the process of producing a binary image from a gray-scale image by assigning each output pixel the value 1 if the gray level of the corresponding input pixel is at or above the specified threshold gray level, and the value 0 if the input pixel is below that level.

Transfer function - for a linear, shift-invariant system, the function of frequency that specifies the factor by which the amplitude of a sinusoidal input signal at each frequency is multiplied to form the output signal.

REFERENCES

1. R.M. Haralick, "Glossary and Index to Remotely Sensed Image Pattern Recognition Concepts," *Pattern Recognition*, **5**:391–403, 1973.
2. IEEE Std 610.4–1990, *IEEE Standard Glossary of Image Processing and Pattern Recognition Terminology*, IEEE, New York, 1990.
3. R. M. Haralick and L. G. Shapiro, "Glossary of Computer Vision Terms," *Pattern Recognition*, **24**:69–93, 1991.
4. L. Darcy and L. Boston, *Webster's New World Dictionary of Computer Terms* (3d ed.), Prentice-Hall, New York, 1988.
5. B. Pfaffenberger, *Que's Computer User's Dictionary* (2d ed.), Que Corporation, Carmel, Indiana, 1991.
6. C. J. Sippl and R. J. Sippl, *Computer Dictionary* (3d ed.), Howard W. Sams & Co., Indianapolis, IN, 1980.

APPENDIX 2

Bibliography

This appendix contains references for further reading on selected topics. The first section lists books, the second journal articles and conference papers. The subsections are arranged by topic, with entries alphabetized by first author.

A2.1 BOOKS

A2.1.1 Visual and Color Perception

G. A. AGOSTON, *Color Theory and Its Applications in Art and Design*, Springer-Verlag, Berlin, 1979.

T. N. CORNSWEET, *Visual Perception*, Academic Press, New York, 1970.

R. A. ENYORD, ed., *Color: Theory and Imaging Systems*, Society of Photographic Scientists and Engineers, Washington, DC, 1973.

R. M. EVANS, *An Introduction to Color*, John Wiley & Sons, New York, 1959.

C. H. GRAHAM, ed., *Vision and Visual Perception*, John Wiley & Sons, New York, 1965.

B. JULESZ, *Foundations of Cyclopean Perception*, University of Chicago Press, Chicago, 1971.

Munsell Book of Color, Munsell Color Co., 2441 North Calvert St., Baltimore, MD.

W. OSTWALD, *The Color Primer*, Van Nostrand-Reinhold, New York, 1969.

M. H. PIRENNE, *Vision and the Eye* (2d ed.), Associated Book Publishers, London, 1967.

J. J. SHEPPARD, JR., *Human Color Perception*, Elsevier, New York, 1968.

A2.1.2 Optics

M. BORN AND E. WOLF, *Principles of Optics: Electromagnetic Theory of Propagation, Interference and Diffraction of Light* (6th ed.), Pergamon Press, Oxford, 1980.

M. H. FREEMAN, *Optics* (10th ed.), Butterworths, London, 1990.

J. W. GOODMAN, *Introduction to Fourier Optics*, McGraw-Hill, New York, 1968.

J. W. GOODMAN, *Statistical Optics*, Wiley, New York, 1985.

R. D. GUENTHER, *Modern Optics*, Wiley, New York, 1990.

O. S. HEAVENS AND R. W. DITCHBURN, *Insight into Optics*, Wiley, New York, 1991.

E. HECHT AND A. ZAJAC, *Optics* (2d ed.), Addison-Wesley, Reading, MA, 1987.

K. IIZUKA, *Engineering Optics*, Springer-Verlag, Berlin & New York, 1985.

S. INOUE, *Video Microscopy*, Plenum Press, New York, 1986.

M. P. KEATING, *Geometric, Physical, and Visual Optics*, Butterworth's, Boston, 1988.

R. KINGSLAKE, *Optical System Design*, Academic Press, London & New York, 1983.

M. V. KLEIN AND T. E. FURTAK, *Optics* (2d ed.), Wiley, New York, 1986.

E. H. LINFOOT, *Fourier Methods in Optical Image Evaluation*, Focal Press, London & New York, 1964.

J. R. MEYER-ARENDT, *Introduction to Classical and Modern Optics* (2d ed.), Prentice-Hall, Englewood Cliffs, NJ, 1984.

K.D. MOLLER, *Optics*, University Science Books, Mill Valley, CA, 1988.

E. L. O'NEILL, *Introduction to Statistical Optics*, Addison-Wesley, Reading, Massachusetts, 1963.

S. P. PARKER, ed., *Optics Source Book*, McGraw-Hill, New York, 1988.

F. G. SMITH AND J.H. THOMSON, *Optics* (2d ed.), Wiley, New York, 1988.

E. G. STEWARD, *Fourier Optics*, Prentice-Hall, Englewood Cliffs, NJ, 1990.

W.T. WELFORD, *Optics* (3d ed.), Oxford University Press, Oxford & New York, 1988.

C. S. WILLIAMS AND O. A. BECKLUND, *Introduction to the Optical Transfer Function*, Wiley, New York, 1989.

A2.1.3 Television and Image Display

K. B. BENSON, *Television Engineering Handbook: Featuring HDTV Systems* (rev. ed.), McGraw-Hill, New York, 1992.

I. P. CSORBA, ed., *Selected Papers on Image Tubes*, SPIE Press, Bellingham, WA, 1990.

D. G. FINK ed., *Television Engineering Handbook,* McGraw-Hill, New York, 1957.

D. G. FINK AND D. CHRISTIANSEN, *Electronics Engineer's Handbook*, McGraw-Hill, New York, 1989.

G. HUTSON, P. SHEPHERD, AND J. BRICE, *Colour Television Theory: System Principles, Engineering Practice & Applied Technology*, McGraw-Hill, New York, 1990.

A. F. INGLIS, *Video Engineering: NTSC, EDTV, & HDTV Systems*, McGraw-Hill, New York, 1992.

M.S. KIVER, *Color Television Fundamentals*, McGraw-Hill, New York, 1965.

H. R. LUXENBERG AND R. L. KUEHN, eds., *Display Systems Engineering*, McGraw-Hill, New York, 1968.

I. NEIDHARDT, *Technical Dictionary of TV Engineering: TV Electronics in Four Languages* (English, German, French, and Russian), Franklin, 1964.

J. I. PANKOVE, ed., *Display Devices* (Topics in Applied Physics Series, Vol. 40), Springer-Verlag, New York, 1980.

H. POOLE, *Fundamentals of Display Systems*, MacMillan and Company, London, 1966.

WHARTON, S. METCALFE, AND G. C. PLATTS, *Broadcast Transmission Engineering Practice*, Focal Press, 1992.

A2.1.4 Mathematical Background

N. AHMED AND K.R. RAO, *Orthogonal Transforms for Digital Signal Processing*, Springer-Verlag, New York, 1975.

R. BELLMAN, *Introduction to Matrix Analysis* (2d ed.), McGraw-Hill, New York, 1970.

I. DAUBECHIES, *Ten Lectures on Wavelets*, Society for Industrial and Applied Mathematics, Philadelphia, PA, 1992.

R. DEUTSCH, *Estimation Theory*, Prentice-Hall, Englewood Cliffs, NJ, 1965.

T. N. E. GREVILLE, ed., *Theory and Applications of Spline Functions*, Academic Press, New York, 1969.

B. JACOB, *Linear Algebra*, W. H. Freeman and Company, New York, 1990.

D. N. LAWLEY AND A. E. MAXWELL, *Factor Analysis as a Statistical Method*, Butterworth, London, 1963.

B. NOBLE, *Applied Linear Algebra*, Prentice-Hall, Englewood Cliffs, NJ, 1969.

A. PAPOULIS, *Probability, Random Variables, and Stochastic Processes*, McGraw-Hill, New York, 1965.

A. PAPOULIS, *Systems and Transforms with Applications in Optics*, McGraw-Hill, New York, 1968.

W. H. PRESS, S. A. TEUKOLSKY, W. T. VETTERING, AND B. P. FLANNERY, *Numerical Recipes in C* (2d ed.), Cambridge University Press, Cambridge, U.K., 1992.

C.R. RAO AND S.K. MITRA, *Generalized Inverse of Matrices and Its Applications*, Wiley, New York, 1971.

D.F. ROGERS AND J.A. ADAMS, *Mathematical Elements for Computer Graphics*, McGraw-Hill, New York, 1976.

B.W. RUST AND W.R. BURRUS, *Mathematical Programming and the Numerical Solution of Linear Equations*, American Elsevier, New York, 1972.

I. SELIN, *Detection Theory*, Princeton University Press, Princeton, NJ, 1965.

J. B. THOMAS, *Statistical Communication Theory*, John Wiley & Sons, New York, 1969.

J. B. THOMAS, *An Introduction to Applied Probability Theory and Random Processes*, Wiley, New York, 1971.

A2.1.5 The Fourier Transform

R. N. BRACEWELL, *The Fourier Transform and Its Applications* (2d revised ed.), McGraw-Hill, New York, 1986.

R. N. BRACEWELL, *The Hartley Transform*, Oxford University Press, Oxford, U.K., 1986.

E. O. BRIGHAM, *The Fast Fourier Transform,* Prentice-Hall, Englewood Cliffs, NJ, 1974.

E. O. BRIGHAM, *The Fast Fourier Transform and Its Applications*, Prentice-Hall, Englewood Cliffs, NJ, 1988.

D. C. CHAMPENEY, *Fourier Transforms and Their Physical Applications*, Academic Press, New York, 1973.

P. M. DUFFIEUX, *The Fourier Transform and Its Applications to Optics*, Books on Demand, 1983.

D. F. ELLIOTT AND K. R. RAO, *Fast Transforms: Algorithms and Applications*, Academic Press, New York, 1983.

J. R. HANNA AND J. H. ROWLAND, *Fourier Series, Transforms, and Boundary Value Problems* (2d ed.), John Wiley and Sons, New York, 1990.

R. D. HARDING, *Fourier Series and Transforms*, IOP Publishing, 1985.

A. G. MARSHALL AND F. R. VERDUN, *Fourier Transforms in NMR, Optical, and Spectrometry: A User's Handbook*, Elsevier Science Publishing Company, Amsterdam, 1990.

H. J. NUSSBAUMER, *Fast Fourier Transform and Convolution Algorithms*, Springer-Verlag, Berlin & New York, 1981.

R. PALEY AND N. WIENER, *Fourier Transforms in the Complex Domain,* American Mathematical Society, 1987.

A. PAPOULIS, *The Fourier Integral and Its Applications*, McGraw-Hill, New York, 1962.

B. E. PETERSEN, *Introduction to the Fourier Transform and Pseudo-Differential Operators*, Pitman Advanced Publishing Program, Boston, 1983.

R. W. RAMIREZ, *The FFT, Fundamentals and Concepts*, Prentice-Hall, Englewood Cliffs, NJ, 1985.

R. TOLIMIERI, *Algorithms for Discrete Fourier Transform and Convolution*, Springer-Verlag, New York, 1989.

J. S. WALKER, *Fourier Analysis*, Oxford University Press, Oxford, U.K., 1988.

A2.1.6 Digital Signal Processing

N. AHMED AND K. R. RAO, *Orthogonal Transforms for Digital Signal Processing*, Springer-Verlag, New York, 1975.

R. E. CROCHIERE AND L. R. RABINER, *Multirate Digital Signal Processing,* Prentice-Hall, Englewood Cliffs, NJ, 1983.

W. B DAVENPORT AND W. L ROOT, *An Introduction to the Theory of Random Signals and Noise*, McGraw-Hill, New York, 1958.

H. F. HARMUTH, *Transmission of Information by Orthogonal Signals*, Springer-Verlag, New York, 1970.

H. S. MALVAR, *Signal Processing with Lapped Transforms*, Artech House, Norwood, MA, 1991.

A. V. OPPENHEIM, A. S. WILLSKY, AND I. T. YOUNG, *Signals and Systems*, Prentice-Hall, Englewood Cliffs, NJ, 1983.

A. PAPOULIS, *Signal Analysis*, McGraw-Hill, New York, 1977.

L. R. RABINER AND B. GOLD, *Theory and Application of Digital Signal Processing*, Prentice-Hall, Englewood Cliffs, NJ, 1975.

R. E. SCHWARTZ AND B. FRIEDLAND, *Linear Systems*, McGraw-Hill, New York, 1965.

T. J. TERRELL, *Introduction to Digital Filters*, Macmillan, London, 1980.

B. WIDROW AND S. D. STEARNS, *Adaptive Signal Processing,* Prentice-Hall, Englewood Cliffs, NJ, 1985.

A2.1.7 Digital Image Processing

J. K. AGGARWAL, R. O. DUDA, AND A. ROSENFELD, eds., *Computer Methods in Image Analysis*, IEEE Press, New York, 1977.

H. C. ANDREWS (with contributions by W.K. Pratt and K. Caspari), *Computer Techniques in Image Processing*, Academic Press, New York, 1970.

H. C. ANDREWS, ed., *Digital Image Processing*, IEEE Press, 1978.

G. A. BAXES, *Digital Image Processing: A Practical Primer*, Prentice-Hall, Englewood Cliffs, NJ, 1984.

G. A. BAXES, *Digital Image Processing: A Practical Primer* (reprint of 1984 edition), Cascade Press, Denver, CO, 1988.

G. A. BAXES, *Digital Image Processing: Principles and Applications*, John Wiley and Sons, New York, 1994.

R. BERNSTEIN, ed., *Digital Image Processing for Remote Sensing*, IEEE Press, Wiley, New York, 1978.

L. BOLC AND Z. KULPA, *Digital Image Processing Systems*, Springer-Verlag, Berlin, 1981.

K. R. CASTLEMAN, *Digital Image Processing*, Prentice-Hall, Englewood Cliffs, NJ, 1979.

R. CHELLAPPA, *Digital Image Processing* (2d ed.), IEEE Computer Society Press, Los Alamitos, CA, 1992.

C. DE JAGER AND H. NIEUWENHUIJZEN, eds., *Image Processing Techniques in Astronomy*, Kluwer Academic Publishers, Dordrect Boston London, 1975.

DIGITAL EQUIPMENT STAFF, *Image Processing, Video Terminals, and Printer Technologies*, Vol. 3, No. 4. Prentice-Hall, Englewood Cliffs, NJ, 1992.

E. R. DOUGHERTY AND C. R. GIARDINA, *Image Processing—Continuous to Discrete,* Vol. I: *Geometric, Transform, and Statistical Methods,* Prentice-Hall, Englewood Cliffs, NJ, 1987.

E. R. DOUGHERTY AND C. R. GIARDINA, *Matrix-Structured Image Processing*, Prentice-Hall, Englewood Cliffs, NJ, 1987.

E. R. DOUGHERTY, *Digital Image Processing Methods*, Marcel Dekker, 1994.

D. E. DUDGEON AND R. M. MERSEREAU, *Multidimensional Digital Signal Processing*, Prentice-Hall, Englewood Cliffs, NJ, 1984.

M. J. B. DUFF, ed., *Computing Structures for Image Processing*, Academic Press, London, 1983.

M. P. EKSTROM, *Digital Image Processing Techniques*, Academic Press, New York, 1984.

J. D. FOLEY AND A. VAN DAM, *Fundamentals of Interactive Computer Graphics*, Addison-Wesley, Reading, MA, 1982.

R. GONZALEZ AND P. WINTZ, *Digital Image Processing* (2d ed.), Addison-Wesley, Reading, MA, 1987.

R. C. GONZALEZ AND R. E. WOODS, *Digital Image Processing*, Addison-Wesley, Reading, MA, 1992.

W. B. GREEN, *Digital Image Processing: A Systems Approach* (2d ed.), Van Nostrand Reinhold, New York, 1989.

E. L. HALL, *Computer Image Processing and Recognition*, Academic Press, New York, 1979.

R. M. HORD, *Digital Image Processing of Remotely Sensed Data*, Academic Press, New York, 1982.

T. S. HUANG, *Picture Processing and Digital Filtering*, Springer-Verlag, New York, 1975.

T. S. HUANG, *Image Sequence Analysis*, Springer-Verlag, New York, 1981.

T. S. HUANG, *Image Sequence Processing and Dynamic Scene Analysis*, Springer-Verlag, New York, 1983.

Z. HUSSAIN, *Digital Image Processing: Practical Applications of Parallel Processing Techniques*, E. Horwood, New York, 1991.

B. JAHNE, *Digital Image Processing: Concepts, Algorithms, and Scientific Applications* (2d ed.), Springer-Verlag, New York, 1993.

A. K. JAIN, *Fundamentals of Digital Image Processing*, Prentice-Hall, Englewood Cliffs, NJ, 1989.

H. KERZNER, *Image Processing in Well Log Analysis*, Prentice-Hall, Englewood Cliffs, NJ, 1988.

J. KITTLER AND M. J. DUFF, *Image Processing System Architectures*, John Wiley and Sons, New York, 1985.

R. LEWIS, *Practical Digital Image Processing*, Ellis Horwood, New York, 1990.

B. S. LIPKIN AND A. ROSENFELD, eds., *Picture Processing and Psychopictorics*, Academic Press, New York, 1970.

D. MARR, *Vision*, W. H. Freeman, San Francisco, 1982.

J. P. MULLER, ed., *Digital Image Processing in Remote Sensing*, Taylor and Francis, 1988.

W. NIBLACK, *An Introduction to Digital Image Processing*, Prentice-Hall, Englewood Cliffs, NJ, 1986.

T. PAVLIDIS, *Algorithms for Graphics and Image Processing*, Computer Science Press, Rockville, MD, 1982.

D. E. PEARSON, *Image Processing*, McGraw-Hill, New York, 1991.

I. PITAS, *Digital Image Processing Algorithms*, Prentice-Hall, Englewood Cliffs, NJ, 1993.

W. K. PRATT, *Digital Image Processing* (2d ed.), John Wiley & Sons, New York, 1991.

K. PRESTON, Jr., and L. Uhr, *Multicomputers and Image Processing, Algorithms and Programs*, Academic Press, New York, 1982.

A. ROSENFELD, *Picture Processing by Computer*, Academic Press, New York, 1969.

A. ROSENFELD, ed., *Digital Picture Analysis*, Springer-Verlag, New York, 1976.

A. ROSENFELD AND A.C. KAK, *Digital Picture Processing* (2d ed.), Academic Press, New York, 1982.

J. C. RUSS, *The Image Processing Handbook*, CRC Press, Boca Raton, FL, 1992.

R. J. SCHALKOFF, *Digital Image Processing and Computer Vision*, John Wiley & Sons, New York, 1989.

R. A. SCHOWENGERDT, *Techniques for Image Processing and Classification in Remote Sensing*, Academic Press, New York, 1983.

J. C. SIMON AND A. ROSENFELD, eds., *Digital Image Processing and Analysis* (No. 22), Kluwer Academic Publishers, Dordrect Boston London, 1978.

J. C. SIMON AND R. M. HARALICK, eds., *Digital Image Processing*, Kluwer Academic Publishers, Dordrect Boston London, 1981.

P. STUCKI, ed., *Advances in Digital Image Processing: Theory, Application, Implementation*, Plenum Press, New York, 1979.

J. TEUBER, *Digital Image Processing*, Prentice-Hall, Englewood Cliffs, NJ, 1992.

F. M. WAHL, *Digital Image Signal Processing*, Artech House, Boston, 1987.

G. WOLBERG, *Digital Image Warping*, IEEE Computer Society Press, Los Alamitos, CA, 1990.

A2.1.8 Morphological Image Processing

C. R. GIARDINA AND E. R. DOUGHERTY, *Morphological Methods in Image and Signal Processing*, Prentice-Hall, Englewood Cliffs, NJ, 1988.

G. MATHERON, *Random Sets and Integral Geometry*, Wiley, New York, 1975.

J. SERRA, *Image Analysis and Mathematical Morphology*, 1, Academic Press, New York, 1982.

J. SERRA, ed., *Image Analysis and Mathematical Morphology*, 2, Academic Press, New York, 1988.

A2.1.9 Image Restoration

H. C. ANDREWS AND B. R. HUNT, *Digital Image Restoration*, Prentice-Hall, Englewood Cliffs, NJ, 1977.

R. H. BATES AND M. J. MCDONNELL, *Image Restoration and Reconstruction,* Oxford University Press, Oxford, U.K., 1989.

A. K. KATSAGGELOS, T. S. HUANG, T. KOHONEN, AND M. R. SCHROEDER, eds., *Digital Image Restoration*, Springer-Verlag, New York, 1991.

I. SEZAN AND A. M. TEKALP, *Image Restoration*, Prentice-Hall, Englewood Cliffs, NJ, 1992.

H. STARK, ed., *Image Recovery: Theory and Application,* Academic Press, New York, 1987.

A2.1.10 Pattern Recognition

H. C. ANDREWS, *Introduction to Mathematical Techniques in Pattern Recognition*, Wiley-Interscience, New York, 1972.

G. C. CHENG, ed., *Pictorial Pattern Recognition*, Thompson, Washington, DC, 1968.

R. O. DUDA AND P. E. HART, *Pattern Classification and Scene Analysis*, John Wiley & Sons, New York, 1973.

K. S. FU, *Sequential Methods in Pattern Recognition and Machine Learning*, Academic Press, New York, 1968.

K. S. FU, *Syntactic Pattern Recognition and Applications*, Prentice-Hall, Englewood Cliffs, NJ, 1982.

K. FUKUNAGA, *Introduction to Statistical Pattern Recognition*, Academic Press, New York, 1972.

R. C. GONZALEZ AND M. G. THOMASON, *Syntactic Pattern Recognition: An Introduction*, Addison-Wesley, Reading, MA, 1978.

A. GRASSELLI, *Automatic Interpretation and Classification of Images*, Academic Press, New York, 1969.

W. MEISEL, *Computer-Oriented Approaches to Pattern Recognition*, Academic Press, New York, 1972.

Y. H. PAO, *Adaptive Pattern Recognition and Neural Networks*, Addison-Wesley, Reading, MA, 1989.

E. A. PATRICK, *Fundamentals of Pattern Recognition*, Prentice-Hall, Englewood Cliffs, NJ, 1972.

T. PAVLIDIS, *Structural Pattern Recognition*, Springer-Verlag, New York, 1977.

R. SCHALKOFF, *Pattern Recognition: Statistical, Structural and Neural Approaches*, John Wiley & Sons, New York, 1992.

J. C. SIMON, *Patterns and Operators: The Foundations of Data Representations,* McGraw-Hill, New York, 1986.

J. T. TOU AND R. C. GONZALEZ, *Pattern Recognition Principles,* Addison-Wesley, Reading, MA, 1974.

T. Y. YOUNG AND K. S. FU, eds., *Handbook of Pattern Recognition and Image Processing*, Academic Press, San Diego, 1986.

A2.1.11 Computer Vision and Artificial Intelligence

D. H. BALLARD AND C. M. BROWN, *Computer Vision*, Prentice-Hall, Englewood Cliffs, NJ, 1982.

G. G. DODD AND L. ROSSOL, eds., *Computer Vision and Sensor-Based Robots*, Plenum Press, New York, 1979.

O. D. FAUGERAS, *Fundamentals in Computer Vision*, Cambridge Univ. Press, Cambridge, U.K., 1983.

K. S. FU, R. C. GONZALES, AND C. S. G. LEE, *Robotics: Control, Sensing, Vision, and Intelligence*, McGraw-Hill, New York, 1987.

A. R. HANSON AND E. M. RISEMAN, eds., *Computer Vision Systems*, Academic Press, New York, 1978.

B. K. P. HORN, *Robot Vision*, McGraw-Hill, New York, 1986.

M. D. LEVINE, *Vision in Man and Machine*, McGraw-Hill, New York, 1985.

R. NEVATIA, *Machine Perception*, Prentice-Hall, Englewood Cliffs, NJ, 1982.

N. J. NILSSON, *Principles of Artificial Intelligence*, Tioga, Palo Alto, CA, 1980.

R. J. SCHALKOFF, *Digital Image Processing and Computer Vision*, John Wiley & Sons, New York, 1989.

A2.1.12 Data Compression

A. GERSHO AND R. M. GRAY, *Vector Quantization and Signal Compression,* Kluwer Academic Publishers, Boston, MA, 1992.

G. HELD AND T. R. MARSHALL, *Data Compression: Techniques and Applications, Hardware and Software Considerations* (3d ed.), Wiley, Chichester, New York, 1991.

N. S. JAYANT AND P. NOLL, *Digital Coding of Waveforms*, Prentice-Hall, Englewood Cliffs, NJ, 1984.

T. J. LYNCH, *Data Compression Techniques and Applications*, Lifetime Learning Publications, Belmont, CA, 1985.

M. NELSON, *The Data Compression Book: Featuring Fast, Efficient Data Compression Techniques in C,* M&T Books, Redwood City, CA, 1992.

J. A. STORER, *Data Compression: Methods and Theory*, Computer Science Press, Rockville, MD, 1988.

R. N. WILLIAMS, *Adaptive Data Compression*, Kluwer Academic Publishers, Boston, 1991.

A2.1.13 Image Compression

R. J. CLARK, *Transform Coding of Images*, Academic Press, New York, 1985.

R. K. MILLER AND T. C. WALKER, *Image Compression*, SEAI Technical Publications, 1991.

W. K. PRATT, *Image Coding*, John Wiley, New York, 1978.

M. RABBANI AND P. W. JONES, *Digital Image Compression Techniques*, SPIE Press, Bellingham, WA, 1991.

A2.1.14 Three-Dimensional Image Processing

A. K. JAIN AND P. J. FLYNN, eds., *Three-Dimensional Object Recognition Systems,* Elsevier Science Publishers, Amsterdam, 1993.

A. C. KAK AND M. SLANEY, *Principles of Computerized Tomographic Imaging*, IEEE Press, New York, 1988.

A2.1.15 Software Development

R. M. BAECKEER, A. MARCUS, ET AL., *Human Factors and Typography for More Readable Programs*, Addison-Wesley, Reading, MA, 1990.

D. BERKELEY, R. DE HOOG, AND P. HUMPHREYS, *Software Development Project Management: Process and Support*, E. Horwood, New York, 1990.

C. M. BROWN, *Human-Computer Interface Design Guidelines*, Ablex Publishing Corp., Norwood, NJ, 1988.

CHANTICO PUBLISHING COMPANY, *CASE: The Potential and the Pitfalls*, QED Information Sciences, Wellesley, MA, 1989.

T. DE MARCO, *Structured Analysis and System Specification*, Prentice-Hall, Englewood Cliffs, NJ, 1978.

J. R. JOHNSON, *The Software Factory: Managing Software Development and Maintenance* (2d ed.), QED Information Sciences, Wellesley, MA, 1991.

R. A. MCGRATH, *Where's the Manual? Preparing and Producing the Software User's Manual*, Van Nostrand Reinhold, New York, 1991.

R. O. PETERSON, *Managing the Systems Development Function*, Van Nostrand Reinhold, New York, 1987.

R. S. PRESSMAN, *Software Engineering, A Practitioner's Approach*, McGraw-Hill, New York, 1987.

R. S. PRESSMAN, *Making Software Engineering Happen: A Guide for Instituting the Technology*, Prentice-Hall, Englewood Cliffs, NJ, 1988.

N. WHITTEN, *Managing Software Development Projects: Formula for Success,* Wiley, New York, 1990.

G. P. WILHELMIJ, *Symbolic Software for Interactive Descriptions of Dynamic Systems*, Pitman, London & Morgan Kaufmann, San Mateo, CA, 1991

R. T. YEH, *CASE Technology*, Kluwer Academic Publishers, Boston, 1992.

E. YOURDON, *Decline & Fall of the American Programmer*, Prentice-Hall, Englewood Cliffs, NJ, 1992.

A2.1.16 User Interface Design

N. S. BORENSTEIN, *Programming as if People Mattered: Friendly Programs, Software Engineering, and Other Noble Delusions,* Princeton University Press, Princeton, NJ, 1991.

J. R. BROWN AND S. CUNNINGHAM, *Programming the User Interface: Principles and Examples,* Wiley, New York, 1989.

B. LAUREL, ed., *The Art of Human-Computer Interface Design,* Addison-Wesley, Reading, MA, 1990.

D. J. MAYHEW, *Principles and Guidelines in Software User Interface Design,* Prentice-Hall, Englewood Cliffs, NJ, 1992.

MICROSOFT CORPORATION, *The Windows Interface: An Application Design Guide,* Microsoft Press, Redmond, WA, 1992.

J. E. POWELL, *Designing User Interfaces,* Microtrend Books, San Marcos, CA, 1990.

S. RIMMER, *Graphical User Interface Programming,* Windcrest, Blue Ridge Summit, PA, 1992.

T. RUBIN, *User Interface Design for Computer Systems,* E. Horwood, Chichester & Halsted Press, New York, 1988.

B. SHNEIDERMAN, *Designing the User Interface: Strategies for Effective Human-Computer Interaction* (2d ed.), Addison-Wesley, Reading, MA, 1992.

SUN MICROSYSTEMS, INC., *OPEN LOOK Graphical User Interface Application Style Guidelines,* Addison-Wesley, Reading, MA, 1990.

H. THIMBLEBY, *User Interface Design,* ACM Press, New York, Wokingham, UK & Addison-Wesley, Reading, MA, 1990.

A2.1.17 Visual Languages

S. K. CHANG, ed., *Principles of Visual Programming Systems*, Prentice-Hall, Englewood Cliffs, NJ, 1990.

S. K. CHANG, ed., *Visual Languages and Visual Programming*, Plenum Press, New York, 1990.

E. JUNGERT AND R. R. KORFHAGE, eds., *Visual Languages and Applications,* Plenum Press, New York, 1990.

R. RUCKER, *Mind Tools*, Houghton-Mifflin Company, Boston, 1987.

N. C. SHU, *Visual Programming*, Van Nostrand Reinhold Co., New York, 1988.

A2.2 RESEARCH PAPERS

A2.2.1 Sampling, Aliasing, and Truncation

J. L. BROWN, JR., "Bounds for Truncation Error in Sampling Expansions of Band-Limited Signals," *IEEE Trans. Inf. Theory* **IT-15**(4):440–444, 1969.

K. R. CASTLEMAN, "Spatial and Photometric Resolution and Calibration Requirements for Cell Image Analysis," *Applied Optics,* **26**(16):3338–3342, 1987.

K. R. CASTLEMAN, "Resolution and Sampling Requirements for Digital Image Processing, Analysis and Display," in D. Shotton, ed., *Electronic Light Microscopy*, Wiley-Liss, New York, 1993, chapter 3.

H. HARMS AND H. M. AUS, "Estimation of the Sampling Error in a High Resolution TV Microscope Image Processing System," *Cytometry*, **5**:228–235, 1984.

H. D. HELMS AND J. B. THOMAS, "Truncation Error of Sampling Theory Expansions," *Proc. IRE*, **50**(2):179–184, 1962.

S. J. KATZBERG, F. O. HUCK, AND S. D. WALL, "Photosensor Aperture Shaping to Reduce Aliasing in Optical-Mechanical Line-Scan Imaging Systems," *Applied Optics*, **12**(5), 1973.

H. J. LANDA, "Sampling, Data Transmission, and the Nyquist Rate," *Proc. IEEE*, **55**(10):1701–1706, 1967.

R. R. LEGAULT, "The Aliasing Problems in Two-Dimensional Sampled Imagery," in L.M. Biberman, ed., *Perception of Displayed Information*, Plenum Press, New York, 1973.

S. P. LLOYD, "A Sampling Theorem for Stationary (Wide Sense) Stochastic Processes," *Trans. Am. Math. Soc.*, **92**(1):1–12, 1959.

A. PAPOULIS, "Error Analysis in Sampling Theory," *Proc. IEEE*, **54**:(6)947–955, 1966.

J. M. S. PREWITT, "The Selection of Sampling Rate for Digital Scanning," *IEEE Trans. Biomed. Eng.* **BME-12**:14–21, 1965.

H. S. SHAPIRO AND R. A. SILVERMAN, "Alias-Free Sampling of Random Noise," *J. SIAM*, **8**(2):225–248, 1960.

B. TATIAN, "Asymptotic Expansions for Correcting Truncation Error in Transfer-Function Calculations," *J. Opt. Soc. Am.*, **61**(9):1214–1224, 1971.

J. M. WHITTAKER, "Interpolatory Function Theory," *Cambridge Tracts in Mathematics and Mathematical Physics*, Cambridge University Press, Cambridge, U.K., 1935, chapter 4.

I. T. YOUNG, "Sampling Density and Quantitative Microscopy," *Analytical and Quantitative Cytology and Histology*, **10**(4):269–275, 1988.

I. T. YOUNG, "Image Fidelity: Characterizing the Imaging Transfer Function," *Methods in Cell Biology*, **30**:1–45, 1989.

A2.2.2 Geometric Operations

D. I. BARNEA AND H. F. SILVERMAN, "A Class of Algorithms for Fast Image Registration," *IEEE Trans. Computers* **C-21**(2):179–186, 1972.

E. CATMULL AND A. R. SMITH, "3-D Transformation of Images in Scanline Order," *Computer Graphics (SIGGRAPH '80 Proc.)*, **14**(3):279–285, 1980.

W. K. PRATT, "Correlation Techniques of Image Registration," *IEEE Trans. Aerospace and Elec. Syst.* **AES-10**(3):353–358, 1974.

Q. TIAN AND M.N. HUHNS, "Algorithms for Subpixel Registration," *Computer Graphics, Vision, and Image Processing*, **35**(2):220–233, 1986.

A2.2.3 The Fourier Transform

W. T. COCHRAN, et al., "What Is the Fast Fourier Transform?" *IEEE Trans. Audio and Electroacoustics* **AU-15**(2):45–55, 1967.

W. T. COCHRAN, et al., "What Is the Fast Fourier Transform?" *Proc. IEEE*, **55**(10): 1664–1674, 1967.

J. W. COOLEY, P. A. W. LEWIS, AND P. D. WELCH, "Historical Notes on the Fast Fourier Transform," *IEEE Trans. Audio and Electroacoustics*, **AU-15**(2):76–79, 1967.

J. W. COOLEY, P. A. W. LEWIS, AND P. D. WELCH, "Application of the Fast Fourier Transform to Computation of Fourier Integrals," *IEEE Trans. Audio and Electroacoustics* **AU-15**(2):79–84, 1967.

J. W. COOLEY, P. A. W. LEWIS, AND P. D. WELCH, "The Fast Fourier Transform and Its Applications," *IEEE Trans. Educ.* **E-12**(1):27–34, 1969.

J. W. COOLEY AND J. W. TUKEY, "An Algorithm for the Machine Calculation of Complex Fourier Series," *Math. of Comput.*, **19**, 297–301, 1965.

W. M. GENTLEMAN AND G. SANDE, "Fast Fourier Transform for Fun and Profit," *Fall Joint Computer Conf.*, **29**, 563–578, Spartan, Washington, DC, 1966.

W. M. GENTLEMAN, "Matrix Multiplication and Fast Fourier Transformations," *Bell System Tech. J.*, **47**, 1099–1103, 1968.

D. K. KAHANER, "Matrix Description of the Fast Fourier Transform," *IEEE Trans. Audio Electroacoustics* **AU-18**(4):442–450, 1970.

A2.2.4 Image Transforms

N. AHMED, T. NATARAJAN, AND K.R. RAO, "Discrete Cosine Transforms," *IEEE Trans. Comp.* **C-23**, 90–93, 1974.

V. R. ALGAZI AND D. J. SAKRISON, "On the Optimality of Karhunen-Loeve Expansion" (Correspondence), *IEEE Trans. Information Theory*, 319–321, March 1969.

H. C. ANDREWS, "Two Dimensional Transforms," *Topics in Applied Physics: Picture Processings and Digital Filtering*, **6**, T.S. Huang, ed., Springer-Verlag, New York, 1975.

J. L. BROWN, JR., "Mean-Square Truncation Error in Series Expansions of Random Functions," *J. SIAM*, **8**:18–32, 1960.

N. J. FINE, "On the Walsh Functions," *Trans. Am. Math. Soc.*, **65**, 373–414, 1949.

N. J. FINE, "The Generalized Walsh Functions," *Trans. Am. Math. Soc.*, **69**, 66–77, 1950.

A. HAAR, "Zur Theorie der Orthogonalen Funktionen-System," Inaugural Dissertation, *Math. Annalen*, **5**:17–31, 1955.

J. L. HAMMOND AND R. S. JOHNSON, "Orthogonal Square-Wave Functions," *J. Franklin Inst.*, **273**, 211–225, 1962.

K. W. HENDERSON, "Some Notes on the Walsh Functions, " *IEEE Trans. Electronic Computers* **EC-13**(1):50–52, 1964.

J. J. Y. HUANG AND P. M. SCHULTHEISS, "Block Quantization of Correlated Gaussian Random Variables," *IEEE Trans. Commun. Syst.* **CS-11**(3):289–296, 1963.

A. K. JAIN AND E. ANGEL, "Image Restoration, Modelling, and Reduction of Dimensionality," *IEEE Trans. Computers* **C-23**, 470–476, 1974.

A. KOSCHMAN, "On the Filtering of Nonstationary Time Series," *Proc. 1954 Natl. Electron. Conf.*, **126**, 1954.

H. P. KRAMER AND M. V. MATHEWS, "A Linear Coding for Transmitting a Set of Correlated Signals," *IRE Trans. Info. Theory* **IT-12**, 41–46, 1956.

R. E. A. C. PALEY, "A Remarkable Series of Orthogonal Functions," *Proc. London Math. Soc.*, **34**:241–279, 1932.

W. K. PRATT, H. C. ANDREWS, AND J. KANE, "Hadamard Transform Image Coding," *Proc. IEEE*, **57**(1):58–68, 1969.

W. K. PRATT, W. H. CHEN, AND L. R. WELCH, "Slant Transform Image Coding," *IEEE Trans. Comm.* **COM-22**(8):1075–1093, 1974.

W. K. PRATT, "Vector Formulation of Two Dimensional Signal Processing Operations," *Computer Graphics and Image Processing*, **4**(1):1–24, 1975.

W. D. RAY AND R. M. DRIVER, "Further Decomposition of the Karhunen-Loeve Series Representation of a Stationary Random Process," *IEEE Trans. Inf. Theory* **IT-16** (6):663–668, 1970.

J. A. ROESE, W. K. PRATT, AND G. S. ROBINSON, "Interframe Cosine Transform Image Coding," *IEEE Trans. Comm.* **COM-25**, 1329–1339, 1977.

J. E. SHORE, "On the Application of Haar Functions," *IEEE Trans. Comm.* **COM-21**, 209–216, 1973.

S. WATANABE, "Karhunen-Loeve Expansion and Factor Analysis, Theoretical Remarks and Applications," *Trans. Fourth Prague Conf. Inform. Theory, Statist. Decision Functions,* Random Processes, Prague, 635–660, 1965.

A2.2.5 Image Compression

S. APIKI, "Lossless Data Compression," *Byte*, p. 309, March 1991.

A. K. JAIN, "Image Data Compression: A Review," *Proc. IEEE*, **69**:349–389, 1981.

M. R. NELSON, "LZW Data Compression," *Dr. Dobbs' Journal*, October 1989.

A. N. NETRAVALI AND J. O. LIMB, "Picture Coding: A Review," *Proc. IEEE*, **68**(3):366–406, 1980.

A2.2.6 Image Restoration and Filtering

J. F. ABRAMATIC AND O. D. FAUGERAS, "Design of Two-Dimensional FIR Filters from Small Generating Kernels," *Proc. IEEE Conference on Pattern Recognition and Image Processing*, Chicago, 1978.

J. F. ABRAMATIC AND O. D. FAUGERAS, "Sequential Convolution Techniques for Image Filtering," *IEEE Trans. Acoustics, Speech, and Signal Processing* **ASSP-30**(1):1–10, 1982.

J. F. ABRAMATIC AND O. D. FAUGERAS, "Correction to 'Sequential Convolution Techniques for Image Filtering,'" *IEEE Trans. Acoustics, Speech, and Signal Processing* **ASSP-30**(2):346, 1982.

G. L. ANDERSON AND A.N. NETRAVALI, "Image Restoration Based on a Subjective Criterion," *IEEE Trans. Syst. Man. Cyb.* **SMC-6**(12):845–853, 1976.

H. C. ANDREWS, "Digital Image Restoration: A Survey," *Computer J.*, **7**(5):36–45, 1974.

B. R. FRIEDEN, "Restoring with Maximum Likelihood and Maximum Entropy," *J. Opt. Soc. Am.*, **62**(4):511–518, 1972.

B. R. FRIEDEN, "Image Restoration by Discrete Deconvolution of Minimal Length," *J. Opt. Soc. Am.*, **64**, 682–686, 1974.

B. R. FRIEDEN, "Image Enhancement and Restoration," in T.S. Huang, ed., *Picture Processing and Digital Filtering*, Springer-Verlag, New York, 1975.

J. L. HARRIS, "Resolving Power and Decision Theory," *J. Opt. Soc. Am.*, **54**, 606–611, 1964.

J. L. HARRIS, SR., "Image Evaluation and Restoration," *J. Opt. Soc. Am.*, **56**(5):569–574, 1966.

C. W. HELSTROM, "Image Restoration by the Method of Least Squares," *J. Opt. Soc. Am.*, **57**(3):297–303, 1967.

J. L. HORNER, "Optical Restoration of Images Blurred by Atmospheric Turbulence Using Optimum Filter Theory," *Appl. Opt.*, **9**(1):167–171, 1970.

H. S. HOU AND H. C. ANDREWS, "Cubic Splines for Image Interpolation and Digital Filtering," *IEEE Trans. Acoustics, Speech, and Signal Processing* **ASSP-26**(6):508–517, 1978.

J. V. HU AND L. R. RABINER, "Design Techniques for Two-Dimensional Digital Filters," *IEEE Trans. Audio and Electroacoustics* **AU-20**(4):249–257, 1972.

T. S. HUANG, D. S. BAKER, AND S. P. BERGER, "Iterative Image Restoration," *Appl. Opt.*, **14**(5):1165–1168, 1975.

T. S. HUANG AND P. M. NARENDRA, "Image Restoration by Singular Value Decomposition," *Appl. Opt.*, **14**(9):2213–2216, 1975.

T. S. HUANG, G. T. YANG, AND G. Y. TANG, "A Fast Two-Dimensional Median Filtering Algorithm," *IEEE Trans. Acoust., Speech, Sig. Proc.* **ASSP-27**(1):13–18, 1979.

B. R. HUNT, "A Matrix Theory Proof of the Discrete Convolution Theorem," *IEEE Trans. Audio and Electroacoust.* **AU-19**(4):285–288, 1971.

B. R. HUNT, "The Application of Constrained Least Squares Estimation to Image Restoration by Digital Computer," *IEEE Trans. Comput.* **C-22**(9):805–812, 1973.

A. K. JAIN AND E. ANGEL, "Image Restoration, Modelling, and Reduction of Dimensionality," *IEEE Trans. Computers* **C-23**, 470–476, 1974.

J-S. LEE, "Digital Image Enhancement and Noise Filtering by Use of Local Statistics," *IEEE Trans. Pattern Analysis and Machine Intelligence* **PAMI-2**(2):165–168, 1980.

D. P. MACADAM, "Digital Image Restoration by Constrained Deconvolution," *J. Opt. Soc. Am.*, **60**(12):1617–1627, 1970.

N. D. A. MASCARENHAS AND W. K. PRATT, "Digital Image Restoration Under a Regression Model," *IEEE Trans. Circuits and Systems* **CAS-22**(3):252–266, 1975.

B. L. MCGLAMERY, "Restoration of Turbulence-Degraded Images," *J. Opt. Soc. Am.*, **57**(3):293–297, 1967.

P. F. MUELLER AND G. O. REYNOLDS, "Image Restoration by Removal of Random Media Degradations," *J. Opt. Soc. Am.*, **57**(11):1338–1344, 1967.

R. NATHAN, "Picture Enhancement for the Moon, Mars, and Man," in G.C. Cheng, ed., *Pictorial Pattern Recognition*, Thompson, Washington, DC, 235–239, 1968.

R. NATHAN, "Spatial Frequency Filtering," in B.S. Lipkin and A. Rosenfeld, eds., *Picture Processing and Psychopictorics*, Academic Press, New York, 151–164, 1970.

T. A. NODES AND N. C. GALLAGHER, JR., "Median Filters: Some Manipulations and Their Properties," *IEEE Trans. Acoustics, Speech, and Signal Processing* **ASSP-30**(5):739–746, 1982.

D. A. O'HANDLEY AND W. B. GREEN, "Recent Developments in Digital Image Processing at the Image Processing Laboratory of the Jet Propulsion Laboratory," *Proc. IEEE*, **60**(7):821–828, 1972.

A. PAPOULIS, "Approximations of Point Spreads for Deconvolution," *J. Opt. Soc. Am.*, **62**(1):77–80, 1972.

W. K. PRATT, "Generalized Wiener Filtering Computation Techniques," *IEEE Trans. Computers* **C-21**(7):636–641, 1972.

W. K. PRATT, "Pseudoinverse Image Restoration Computational Algorithms," in G.W. Stroke, Y. Nesterikhin, and E.S. Barrekette, eds., *Optical Information Processing,* Vol. II, Plenum Press, New York, 1977.

W. K. PRATT AND F. DAVARIAN, "Fast Computational Techniques from Pseudoinverse and Wiener Image Restoration," *IEEE Trans. Computers* **C-26**(6):571–580, 1977.

C. L. RINO, "Bandlimited Image Restoration by Linear Mean-Square Estimation," *J. Opt. Soc. Am.*, **59**, 547–553, 1969.

G. M. ROBBINS AND T. S. HUANG, "Inverse Filtering for Linear Shift-Variant Imaging Systems," *Proc. IEEE*, **60**, 862–872, 1972.

C. K. RUSHFORTH AND R. W. HARRIS, "Restoration, Resolution, and Noise," *J. Opt. Soc. Am.*, **58**, 539–545, 1968.

A. A. SAWCHUK, "Space-Variant Image Motion Degradation and Restoration," *Proc. IEEE*, **60**, 854–861, 1972.

R. W. SCHUTTEN AND G. F. VERMEIJ, "The Approximation of Image Blur Restoration Filters by Finite Impulse Responses," *IEEE Trans. Pattern Anal. Mach. Intell.* **PAMI-2**(2):176–180, 1980.

J. L. SHANKS, "Computation of the Fast Walsh-Fourier Transform," *IEEE Trans. Comput.*, **C-18**(5):457–459, 1969.

J. L. SHANKS, S. TREITEL, AND J. H. JUSTICE, "Stability and Synthesis of Two-Dimensional Recursive Filters," *IEEE Trans. Audio and Electroacoustics* **AU-20**(2):115–128, 1972.

C. E. SHANNON, "A Mathematical Theory of Communication," *The Bell Sys. Tech. J.*, **XXVII**(3):379–423, 1948.

C. E. SHANNON, "Communication in the Presence of Noise," *Proc. IRE*, **37**(1):10–21, 1949.

D. SLEPIAN, "Linear Least-Squares Filtering of Distorted Images," *J. Opt. Soc. Am.*, **57**, 918–922, 1967.

D. SLEPIAN, "Restoration of Photographs Blurred by Image Motion," *BSTJ*, **46**(10):2353–2362, 1967.

M. M. SONDHI, "Image Restoration: The Removal of Spatially Invariant Degradations," *Proc. IEEE*, **60**(7):842–853, 1972.

T. G. STOCKMAN, JR., T. M. CANNON, AND P. B. INGEBRETSEN, "Blind Deconvolution through Digital Signal Processing," *Proc. IEEE*, **63**(4):678–692, 1975.

J. TSUJIUCHI, "Correction of Optical Images by Compensation of Aberrations and by Spatial Frequency Filtering," in E. Wolf, ed., *Progress in Optics*, **2**, Wiley, New York, 131–180, 1963.

G. L. TURIN, "An Introduction to Matched Filters," *IRE Trans. Inf. Theory*, **IT-6**(3):311–329, 1960.

J. S. WIEJAK, H. BUXTON, AND B. F. BUXTON, "Convolution with Separable Masks for Early Image Processing," *Computer Vision, Graphics, and Image Processing*, **32**(3):279–290, 1985.

P. A. WINTZ, "Transform Picture Coding," *Proc. IEEE*, **60**(7):809–820, 1972.

G. J. WOLFE AND J.L. MANNOS, "Fast Median Filter Implementation," *Proc. Soc. Photo-Optical Inst. Eng.*, **207**, 154–160, 1979.

A2.2.7 Image Segmentation and Edge Detection

I. ABDOU, *Quantitative Methods of Edge Detection*, University of Southern California, Image Processing Institute, USCIPI Report 830, 1973.

I. ABDOU AND W. K. PRATT, "Quantitative Design and Evaluation of Enhancement/Thresholding Edge Detectors," *Proc. IEEE*, **67**(5):753–763, 1979.

E. ARGYLE, "Techniques for Edge Detection," *Proc. IEEE*, **59**(2):285–287, 1971.

D. H. BALLARD, "Generalizing the Hough Transform to Detect Arbitrary Shapes," *Pattern Recognition*, **13**(2):111–122, 1981.

V. BERZINS, "Accuracy of Laplacian Edge Detectors," *Computer Vision, Graphics, and Image Processing*, **27**(2):195–210, 1984.

J. CANNY, "A Computational Approach to Edge Detection," *IEEE Trans. Pattern Analysis and Machine Intelligence* **PAMI-8**(6):679–698, 1986.

A. E. COWART, W. E. SNYDER, AND W. H. RUEDGER, "The Detection of Unresolved Targets Using the Hough Transform, " *Comput. Vision Graph Image Proc.*, **21**, 222–238, 1983.

L. S. DAVIS, "A Survey of Edge Detection Techniques," *Comput. Graphics Image Proc.*, **4**, 248–270, 1975.

L. S. DAVIS, "Hierachical Generalized Hough Transforms and Line-Segment Based Generalized Hough Transforms," *Pattern Recog.*, **15**(4):277–285, 1982.

R. O. DUDA AND P. E. HART, "Use of the Hough Transformation to Detect Lines and Curves in Pictures," *Comm. ACM*, **15**(1):11–15, 1972.

C. R DYER, "Gauge Inspection Using Hough Transforms," *IEEE Trans. Pattern Anal. Machine Intell.* **PAMI-5**(6):621–623, 1983.

K. S. FU AND J. K. MUI, "A Survey of Image Segmentation," *Pattern Recog.*, **13**(1):3–16, 1981.

R. M. HARALICK AND J. S. J. LEE, "Context Dependent Edge Detection and Evaluation," *Pattern Recog.*, **23**(1–2):1–20, 1990.

R. M. HARALICK AND L. G. SHAPIRO, "Survey: Image Segmentation," *Comput. Vision, Graphics, Image Proc.*, **29**, 100–132, 1985.

C. C. HSU AND J. S. HUANG, "Partitioned Hough Transform for Ellipsoid Detection," *Pattern Recognition*, **23**(3–4):275–282, 1990.

J. ILLINGWORTH AND J. KITTLER, "A Survey of the Hough Transform," *Computer Vision, Graphics, and Image Processing*, **44**(1):87–116, 1976.

R. KIRSCH, "Computer Determination of the Constituent Structure of Biological Images," *Comput. Biomed. Res.*, **4**, 315–328, 1971.

S. U. LEE, S. Y. CHUNG, AND R. H. PARK, "A Comparative Performance Study of Several Global Thresholding Techniques for Segmentation," *Comput. Vision, Graphics, Image Proc.*, **52**(2):171–190, 1990.

A. MARTELLI, "Edge Detection Using Heuristic Search Methods," *Comput. Graphics Image Proc.*, **1**, 169–182, 1972.

A. MARTELLI, "An Application of Heuristic Search Methods to Edge and Contour Detection," *Comm. ACM*, **19**(2):73–83, 1976.

F. MEYER AND S. BEUCHER, "Morphological Segmentation," *J. Visual Comm. and Image Representation*, **1**(1):21–46, 1990.

V. S. NALWA AND T. O. BINFORD, "On Detecting Edges," *IEEE Trans. Pattern Analysis and Machine Intelligence* **PAMI-6**, 699–714, 1986.

R. B. OHLANDER, K. PRICE, AND D. R. READY, "Picture Segmentation Using a Recursive Region Splitting Method," *Computer Graphics and Image Processing*, **8**(3):313–333, 1978.

Y. OHTA, T. KANADE, AND T. SAKI, "Color Information for Region Segmentation," *Computer Graphics and Image Processing*, **13**(3):222–241, 1980.

T. PAVLIDIS AND S. L. HOROWITZ, "Segmentation of Plane Curves," *IEEE Trans. Computers* **C-23**(8):860–870, 1974.

T. PAVLIDIS AND Y. T. LIOW, "Integrating Region Growing and Edge Detection," *IEEE Trans. Pattern Anal. Mach. Intell.*, **12**(3):225–233, 1990.

A. PEREZ AND R. C. GONZALEZ, "An Iterative Thresholding Algorithm for Image Segmentation," *IEEE Trans. Pattern Anal. Machine Intell.* **PAMI-9**(6):742–751, 1987.

P. PERONA AND J. MALIK, "Scale-Space and Edge Detection Using Anisotropic Diffusion," *IEEE Trans. Pattern Anal. Machine Intell.*, **12**(7):629–639, 1990.

M. PETROU AND J. KITTLER, "Optimal Edge Detector for Ramp Edges," *IEEE Trans. Pattern Anal. Machine Intell.*, **13**(5):483–491, 1991.

J. M. S. PREWITT AND M. L. MENDELSOHN, "The Analysis of Cell Images," *Ann. N.Y. Acad. Sci.*, **128**, 1036–1053, 1966.

J. M. S. PREWITT, "Object Enhancement and Extraction," in B.S. Lipkin and A. Rosenfeld, eds., *Picture Processing and Psychopictorics*, Academic Press, New York, 1970.

G. S. ROBINSON, "Edge Detection by Compass Gradient Masks," Note, *Computer Graphics and Image Processing*, **6**(5):492–501, 1977.

A. ROSENFELD, "Connectivity in Digital Pictures," *JACM*, **17**(1):146–160, 1970.

A. ROSENFELD AND M. THURSTON, "Edge and Curve Detection for Visual Scene Analysis," *IEEE Trans. Computers* **C-20**(5):562–569, 1971.

A. ROSENFELD, M. THURSTON, AND Y. H. LEE, "Edge and Curve Detection: Further Experiments," *IEEE Trans. Computers* **C-21**(7):677–715, 1972.

P. K. SAHOO, S. SOLTANI, A. K. C. WONG, AND Y. C. CHAN, "A Survey of Thresholding Techniques," *Comput. Vision, Graphics, Image Proc.*, **4**, 233–260, 1988.

N. SAITO AND M. A. CUNNINGHAM, "Generalized E-Filter and Its Application to Edge Detection," *IEEE Trans. Pattern Anal. Machine Intell.*, **12**(8):814–817, 1990.

V. TORRE AND T.A. POGGIO, "On Edge Detection," *IEEE Trans. Pattern Analysis and Machine Intelligence* **PAMI-8**(2):147–163, 1986.

J. S. WESZKA, R. N. NAGEL, AND A. ROSENFELD, "A Threshold Selection Technique," *IEEE Trans. Computers,* **C-23**(12):1322–1326, 1974.

J. S. WESZKA, "A Survey of Threshold Selection Techniques," *Comput. Graphics Image Proc.,* **7**(2):259–265, 1978.

S. D. YANKOWITZ AND A. M. BRUCKSTEIN, "A New Method for Image Segmentation," *Computer Vision, Graphics, and Image Processing*, **46**(1):82–95, 1989.

S. W. ZUCKER, "Region Growing: Childhood and Adolescence," *Comput. Graphics Image Proc.*, **5**, 382–389, 1976.

A2.2.8 Shape

F. L. ALT, "Digital Pattern Recognition by Moments," *JACM*, **9**(2):240–258, 1962.

J. E. BOWIE AND I. T. YOUNG, "An Analysis Technique for Biological Shape. II," *Acta Cytologica*, **21**(3):455–464, 1977.

L. CALABI AND W. E. HARNETT, "Shape Recognition, Prairie Fires, Convex Deficiencies and Skeletons," *Am. Math. Monthly*, **75**(4):335–342, 1968.

R. L. COSGRIFF, *Identification of Shape,* Ohio State University Research Foundation, Columbus, OH, Report 820–11, 1960.

T. R. CRIMMINS AND W. R. BROWN, "Image Algebra and Automatic Shape Recognition," *IEEE Trans. Aerospace and Electron Syst.* **AES-21**, 60–69, 1985.

M. K. HU, "Visual Pattern Recognition by Moment Invariants," *IRE Trans. Info. Theory* **IT-8**, 179–187, 1962.

Z. KULPA, "Area and Perimeter Measurements of Blobs in Discrete Binary Pictures," *Computer Graphics and Image Processing*, **6**:434–451, 1977.

H. MINKOWSKI, "Volumen und Oberfläche," *Math. Ann.*, **57**, 447–459, 1903.

J. C. MOTT-SMITH, "Medial Axis Transforms," in B.S. Lipkin and A. Rosenfeld, eds., *Picture Processing and Psychopictorics*, Academic Press, New York, 1970.

T. PAVLIDIS, "A Thinning Algorithm for Discrete Binary Images," *Computer Graphics and Image Processing*, **13**(2):142–157, 1980.

E. PERSOON AND K. S. FU, "Shape Discrimination Using Fourier Descriptors," *IEEE Trans. Systems Man. Cyb.* **SMC-7**(2):170–179, 1977.

A. ROSENFELD AND J. L. PFLATZ, "Distance Functions on Digital Pictures," *Pattern Recognition*, **1**, 33–62, 1968.

E. SALARI AND P. SIY, "The Ridge-Seeking Method for Obtaining the Skeleton of Digital Images," *IEEE Trans. Syst. Man Cyb.* **SMC-14**(3):524–528, 1984.

J. SKLANSKY, R. L. CHAZIN, AND B. J. HANSEN, "Minimum-Perimeter Polygons of Digitized Silhouettes," *IEEE Trans. Comput.* **C-21**(3):260–268, 1972.

G. Y. TANG, "A Discrete Version of Green's Theorem," *IEEE Trans. Pattern Analysis and Machine Intelligence*, **PAMI-7**(3):338–344, 1985.

C.-H. TEH AND R. T. CHIN, "On Digital Approximation of Moment Invariants," *Computer Vision, Graphics, and Image Processing*, **33**(3):318–326, 1986.

C. H. TEH AND R. T. CHIN, "On the Detection of Dominant Points on Digital Curves," *IEEE Trans. Pattern Anal. Machine Intell.*, **11**(8):859–872, 1989.

R. Y. WONG AND E. L. HALL, "Scene Matching with Invariant Moments," *Comput. Graph. Image Proc.*, **8**(1):16–24, 1978.

I. T. YOUNG, J. E. WALKER, AND J. E. BOWIE, "An Analytical Technique for Biological Shape, I," *Info. and Control*, **25**:357–370, 1974.

S. S. YU AND W. H. TSAI, "A New Thinning Algorithm for Gray-Scale Images," *Pattern Recog.*, **23**(10):1067–1076, 1990.

C. T. ZAHN AND R. Z. ROSKIES, "Fourier Descriptors for Plane Closed Curves," *IEEE Trans. Comput.* **C-21**(3):269–281, 1972.

T. Y. ZHANG AND C.Y. SUEN, "A Fast Parallel Algorithm for Thinning Digital Patterns," *Comm. ACM*, **27**(3):236–239, 1984.

A2.2.9 Color

O. D. FAUGERAS, "Digital Color Image Processing within the Framework of a Human Visual Model," *IEEE Trans. Acoustics, Speech, and Signal Processing* **ASSP-27**(4):380–393, 1979.

A. K. JAIN, "Color Distance and Geodesics in Color 3 Space," *J. Opt. Soc. Am.*, **62**(11):1287–1290, 1972.

G. H. JOBLOVE AND D. GREENBERG, "Color Spaces for Computer Graphics," *Computer Graphics*, **12**(3):20–25, 1978.

D. B. JUDD, "Hue, Saturation, and Lightness of Surface Colors with Chromatic Illumination," *J. Opt. Soc. Am.*, **30**(1):2–32, 1940.

D. B. JUDD, "Standard Response Functions for Protanopic and Deuteranopic Vision," *J. Opt. Soc. Am.*, **35**(3):199–221, 1945.

E. H. LAND, "Experiments in Color Vision," *Scientific American*, **200**(5):84–99, 1959.

H. LEVKOWITZ AND G. T. HERMAN, "GLHS: A Generalized Lightness, Hue and Saturation Color Model," *CVGIP; Graphical Models and Image Processing*, **55**(4):271–285, 1993.

J. J. MCCANN, IN R.A. ENYARD, ed., "Human Color Perception," *Color: Theory and Imaging Systems*, Society of Photographic Scientists and Engineers, Washington, DC, 1–23, 1973.

M. W. SCHWARTZ, W. B. COWAN, AND J. C. BEATTY, "An Experimental Comparison of RGB, YIQ, LAB, HSV and Opponent Color Models," *ACM Trans. Graphics*, **6**(2):123–158, 1987.

J. J. SHEPPARD, JR., R. H. STRATTON, AND C. GAZLEY, JR., "Pseudocolor as a Means of Image Enhancement," *Am. J. Optom. Arch. Am. Acad. Optom.*, **46**, 735–754, 1969.

G. WALD, "Human Vision and the Spectrum," *Science*, **101**(2635):653–658, 1945.

G. WALD, "The Receptors for Human Color Vision," *Science*, **145**(3636):1007–1017, 1964.

C. WARE AND W. B. COWAN, "The RGBY Color Geometry," *ACM Trans. Graphics*, **9**(2):226–232, 1990.

W. T. WINTRINGHAM, "Color Television & Colorimetry," *Proc. IRE*, **39**(10):1135–1172, 1951.

W. D. WRIGHT, "The Sensitivity of the Eye to Small Colour Differences," *Proc. Phys. Soc. (London)*, **53**, 93, 1941.

A2.2.10 Texture

R. M. HARALICK, R. SHANMUGAN, AND I. DINSTEIN, "Textural Features for Image Classification," *IEEE Trans. Syst. Man Cyb.* **SMC-3**(6):610–621, 1973.

R. M. HARALICK, "Statistical and Structural Approach to Texture," *Proc. IEEE*, **67**(5):786–804, 1979.

B. JULESZ, et al., "Inability of Humans to Discriminate between Visual Textures That Agree in Second-order Statistics—Revisited," *Perception*, **2**, 391–405, 1973.

B. JULESZ, "Experiments in the Visual Perception of Texture," *Scientific American*, **232**(4):2–11, 1975.

R. NEVATIA, "Locating Object Boundaries in Textured Environments," *IEEE Trans. Computers* **C-25**(11):1170–1175, 1976.

W. K. PRATT, O. D. FAUGERAS, AND A. GAGALOWICZ, "Visual Discrimination of Stochastic Texture Fields," *IEEE Trans. Systems, Man, and Cybernetics* **SMC-8**(11):796–804, 1978.

F. TOMITA, Y. SHIRAI, AND S. TSUJI, "Description of Texture by a Structural Analysis," *IEEE Trans. Pattern Anal. Mach. Intell.* **PAMI-4**(2):183–191, 1982.

F. TOMITA, M. YACHIDA, AND S. TSUJI, "Detection of Homogeneous Regions by Structural Analysis," *Proc. International Joint Conference on Artificial Intelligence*, Stanford, CA, 564–571, 1973.

WECHSLER, "Texture Analysis—A Survey," *Signal Processing*, **2**, 271–280, 1980.

S. W. ZUCKER, A. ROSENFELD, AND L. S. DAVIS, "Picture Segmentation by Texture Discrimination," *IEEE Trans. Computers* **C-24**(12):1228–1233, 1975.

A2.2.11 Windowed Fourier Transform

A. C. Bovic, M. Clark, and W. S. Geisler, "Multichannel Texture Analysis Using Localized Spatial Filters," *IEEE Trans.* **PAMI-12**:55–73, 1990.

D. Gabor, "Theory of Communication," *IEEE Proc.*, **93**:429–441, 1946.

G. H. Granlund, "In Search of a General Picture Processing Operator," *CGIP*, 8:155–173, 1978.

H. E. Knutsson and G. H. Granlund, "Fourier Domain Design of Line and Edge Detectors," *Proc. IEEE Conf. on Pat. Rec.*, Miami, 1980.

M. Porat and Y. Y. Zeevi, "The Generalized Gabor Scheme of Image Representation in Biological and Machine Vision," *IEEE Trans.* **PAMI-10**:452–468, 1988.

M. R. Portnoff, "Time-Frequency Representation of Digital Signals and Systems Based on Short-Time Fourier Analysis," *IEEE Trans. ASSP*-28:55–69, 1980.

A2.2.12 Subband Coding

R. E. Crochière, S. A. Weber, and J. L. Flanagan, "Digital Coding of Speech in Subbands," *Bell System Technical Journal*, **55**:1069–1085, 1976.

A. Croisier, D. Esteban, and C. Galand, "Perfect Channel Splitting by Use of Interpolation, Decimation, Tree Decomposition Techniques," *Int. Conf. of Information Sciences and Systems*, 443–446, 1976.

D. Esteban and C. Galand, "Application of Quadrature Mirror Filters to Split-Band Voice Coding Systems," *Int. Conf. on Acoustics, Speech and Signal Processing*, Washington, DC, 191–195, 1977.

F. Minzer, "Filters for Distortion-Free Two-Band Multirate Filter Banks," *IEEE Trans.* **ASSP-33**:626–630, 1985.

M. J. T. Smith and T. P. Barnwell, "Exact Reconstruction for Tree-Structured Subband Coders," *IEEE Trans.* **ASSP-34**:434–441, 1986.

M. Vetterli, "Filter Banks Allowing Perfect Reconstruction," *Signal Processing*, **10**(3):219–244, 1986.

M. Vetterli, "A Theory of Multirate Filter Banks," *IEEE Trans.;* **ASSP-35**(3):356–372, 1987.

M. Vetterli and D. Le Gall, "Perfect Reconstruction FIR Filter Banks: Some Properties and Factorizations," *IEEE Trans.* **ASSP-37**(7):1057–1071, 1989.

M. Vetterli and C. Herley, "Wavelets and Filter Banks: Theory and Design," *IEEE Trans.* **SP-40**(9):2207–2232, 1992.

J. W. Woods and S. D. O'Neill, "Subband Coding of Images," *IEEE Trans.* **ASSP-34**:1278–1288, 1986.

A2.2.13 Wavelet Transforms

G. Battle, "Block Spin Construction of Ondelettes, Part I: Lemarie Functions," *Comm. Math. Phys.*, **110**:601–615, 1987.

G. Beylkin, R. Coifman, and V. Rokhlin, "Fast Wavelet Transforms and Numerical Algorithms I," *Comm. Pure and Appl. Math.*, **44**:141–183, 1991.

A. P. CALDERON, "Intermediate Spaces and Interpolation, the Complex Method," *Studia Math.*, **24**:113–190, 1964.

A. I. COHEN, I. DAUBECHIES, AND J. C. FEAUVEAU, "Bi-Orthogonal Bases of Compactly Supported Wavelets," *Comm. Pure and Applied Math.*, **45**:485–560, 1992.

L. COHEN, "Time-Frequency Distributions—A Review," *Proc. IEEE*, **77**(7):941–981, 1989.

R. COIFMAN AND Y. MEYER, "Remarques sur l'analyse de Fourier à Fenêtre," *C. R. Acad. Sci. Paris*, **1**:961–1005, 1991.

I. DAUBECHIES, A. GROSSMAN, AND Y. MEYER, "Painless Non-orthogonal Expansions," *J. Math. Phys.*, **27**:1271–1283, 1986.

I. DAUBECHIES, "Orthonormal Bases of Compactly Supported Wavelets," *Commun. on Pure and Appl. Math.*, **41**:909–996, 1988.

I. DAUBECHIES, "The Wavelet Transform, Time-Frequency Localization and Fourier Analysis," *IEEE Trans.* **IT-36**:961–1004, 1990.

W. T. FREEMAN AND E. H. ADELSON, "The Design and Use of Steerable Filters," *IEEE Trans.* **PAMI-13**:891–906, 1991.

R. A. GOPINATH AND C. S. BURRUS, "Wavelet Transforms and Filter Banks," in C. K. Chui, ed.,*Wavelets—a Tutorial in Theory and Applications*, pp. 603–654, Academic Press, Boston, 1992.

A. GROSSMAN AND J. MORLET, "Decomposition of Hardy Functions into Square Integrable Wavelets of Constant Shape," *SIAM J. Appl. Math.*, **15**:723–736, 1984.

C. HERLEY AND M. VETTERLI, "Wavelets Generated by IIR Filter Banks," *Proc. ICASSP-92*, **4**:601–604, 1992.

W. M. LAWTON, "Tight Frames of Compactly Supported Wavelets," *J. Math. Phys.*, **31**:1898–1900, 1990.

W. M. LAWTON, "Necessary and Sufficient Conditions for Existence of ON Wavelet Bases," *J. Math. Phys.*, **32**:57–61, 1991.

P. G. LEMARIE AND Y. MEYER, "Ondelettes et Bases Hilbertiennes," *Rev. Mat. Iberoamericana*, **2**:1–18, 1986.

S. MALLAT, "A Theory for Multiresolution Signal Decomposition: The Wavelet Representation," *IEEE Trans.* **PAMI-11**:674–693, 1989.

H. S. MALVAR AND D. H. STAELIN, "The LOT (Lapped Orthogonal Transform): Transform Coding without Blocking Effects," *IEEE Trans.* **ASSP-37**:553–559, 1989.

H. S. MALVAR, "Lapped Transforms for Efficient Transform/Subband Coding," *IEEE Trans.* **ASSP-38**:969–978, 1990.

H. S. MALVAR, "Fast Algorithm for Modulated Lapped Transform," *Electronics Letters*, **27**:775–776, 1991.

O. RIOUL AND P. DUHAMEL, "Fast Algorithms for Discrete and Continuous Wavelet Transforms," *IEEE Trans.* **IT-38**(2):568–586, 1992.

M. J. SHENSA, "The Discrete Wavelet Transform: Wedding the *à trous* and Mallat Algorithms," *IEEE Trans.* **SP-40**:2464–2482, 1992.

E. P. SIMONCELLI, W. T. FREEMAN, E. H. ADELSON, AND D. J. HEEGER, "Shiftable Multiscale Transforms," *IEEE Trans.* **IT-38**:587–607, 1992.

R. WILSON, A. D. CALWAY, AND E. R. S. PEARSON, "A Generalized Wavelet Transform for Fourier Analysis: The Multiresolution Fourier Transform and Its Application to Image and Audio Signal Analysis," *IEEE Trans.* **IT-38**:674–690, 1992.

A2.2.14 Wavelet Image Compression

M. ANTONINI, M. BARLAUD, P. MATHIEU, AND I. DAUBECHIES, "Image Coding Using Vector Quantization in the Wavelet Transform Domain," *Proc. ICASSP-90,* **4**:2297–2300, IEEE Press, New York, 1990.

M. ANTONINI, M. BARLAUD, P. MATHIEU, AND I. DAUBECHIES, "Image Coding Using Wavelet Transform," *IEEE Trans.* **IP-1**(2):205–220, 1992.

J. FROMENT AND S. MALLAT, "Second Generation Compact Image Coding with Wavelets," in C. K. Chui, ed.,*Wavelets—a Tutorial in Theory and Applications*, pp. 655–678, Academic Press, Boston, 1992.

R. HUMMEL AND R. MONIOT, "Reconstruction from Zero-Crossings in Scale-Space," *IEEE Trans.* **ASSP-37**(12), 1989.

A. S. LEWIS AND G. KNOWLES, "Image Compression Using the 2-D Wavelet Transform," *IEEE Trans.* **IP-1**(2):244–250, 1992.

S. MALLAT AND S. ZHONG, "Compact Image Coding from Edges with Wavelets," *Proc. ICASSP-91,* **4**:2745–2748, IEEE Press, New York, 1991.

S. MALLAT, "Zero-Crossings of a Wavelet Transform," *IEEE Trans.* **IT-37**(4):1019–1033, 1991.

S. MALLAT AND S. ZHONG, "Characterization of Signals from Multiscale Edges," *IEEE Trans.* **PAMI-14**(7):710–732, 1992.

N. MOAYERI, I. DAUBECHIES, Q. SONG, AND H. S. WANG, "Wavelet Transform Image Coding Using Trellis Coded Vector Quantization," *Proc. ICASSP-92,* **4**:405–408, IEEE Press, New York, 1992.

M. V. WICKERHAUSER, "Acoustic Signal Compression with Wavelet Packets," in C. K. Chui, ed., *Wavelets—A Tutorial in Theory and Applications*, pp. 679–700, Academic Press, Boston, 1992.

S. ZHONG AND S. MALLAT, "Compact Image Representation from Multiscale Edges," *Proc. 3d Int. Conf. on Comp. Vision,* 522–525, IEEE Comp. Soc. Press, Los Alamitos, CA, 1990.

A2.2.15 Wavelet Filtering

C. H. CHEN, W-L SHU, AND S-K SIN, "A Comparison of Wavelet Deconvolution Techniques for Ultrasonic NDT," *1988 IEEE Int. Conf. on Acoustics, Speech and Signal Processing,* **2**:867–870, 1988.

I. DAUBECHIES, "Time-Frequency Localization Operators: A Geometric Phase Space Approach," *IEEE Trans.* **IT-34**(4):605–612, 1988.

A. R DAVIES AND R. WILSON, "Curve and Corner Extraction Using the Multiresolution Fourier Transform," *Proc. Int. Conf. on Image Proc. and Applic.* (No. 354), 282–285, IEEE, London, 1992.

D. GARREAU, "Multiscale Inverse Filtering," *Proc. ICASSP-90* **5**:2495–2498, 1990.

S. MALLAT AND W. L. HWANG, "Singularity Detection and Processing with Wavelets," *IEEE Trans.* **IT-38**:617–643, 1992.

A. P. PETROPULU, "Detection of Transients Using Discrete Wavelet Transform," *Proc. ICASSP-92,* **2**:477–480, IEEE Press, New York, 1992.

K. E. PRAGER AND P. F. SINGER, "Image Enhancement and Filtering Using Wavelets," *Conf. Record of the 25th Asilomar Conf. on Signals, Systems and Computers*, IEEE Computer Society Press, Los Alamitos, CA, 1991.

A2.2.16 Three-Dimensional Microscopy

D. A. AGARD, "Optical Sectioning Microscopy: Cellular Architecture in Three Dimensions," *Annual Reviews in Biophysics and Bioengineering,* **13**:191–219, 1984.

M. AGUILAR, E. ANGUIANO, A. DIASPRO, AND M. PANCORBO, "Digital Filters to Restore Information from Fast Scanning Tunneling Microscopy Images," *Journal of Microscopy*, **165**(2):311–324, 1991.

B. BIANCO AND A. DIASPRO, "Analysis of Three-Dimensional Cell Imaging Obtained with Optical Microscopy Techniques Based on Defocusing," *Cell Biophysics*, **15**(3):189–199, 1989.

A. DIASPRO, M. SARTORE, AND C. NICOLINI, "3D Representation of Biostructures Imaged with an Optical Microscope," *Image and Vision Computing*, **8**(2):130–141, 1990.

A. DIASPRO, "3-D Reconstruction and Lateral Views of Biological Specimens," *Microscopy and Analysis*, 29–31, July 1993.

A. ERHARDT, G. ZINZER, D. KOMITOWSKI, AND J. BILLE, "Reconstructing 3-D Light-Microscopic Images by Digital Image Processing," *Applied Optics,* **24**:194–200, 1985.

F. S. FAY, W. CARRINGTON, L. M. LIFSHITZ, AND K. E. FOGARTY, "Three-Dimensional Analysis of Molecular Distribution in Single Cells Using the Digital Imaging Microscope," *Proceedings of the SPIE*, **1161**:12–23, 1989.

H. FREEMAN, "On the Encoding of Arbitrary Geometric Configurations," *IEEE Trans. Elec. Computers*, **EC-10,** 260–268, 1961.

H. FREEMAN, "Boundary Encoding and Processing," in B.S. Lipkin and A. Rosenfeld, eds., *Picture Processing and Psychopictorics*, Academic Press, New York, 241–266, 1970.

H. FREEMAN, "Computer Processing of Line Drawings," *Comput. Surveys*, **6**, 57–97, 1974.

H. FREEMAN AND R. SHAPIRO, "Determining the Minimum-Area Enclosing Rectangle for an Arbitrary Closed Curve," *Comm. ACM*, **18**(7):409–413, 1975.

S. FRISKIN GIBSON AND F. LANNI, "Measured and Analytical Point Spread Functions of the Optical Microscope for Use in 3-D Optical Serial Sectioning Microscopy," in *Optical Microscopy for Biology*, 109–118, Wiley-Liss, New York, 1990.

Y. HIRAOKA, J. R. SWEDLOW, M. R. PADDY, D. A. AGARD, AND J. W. SEDAT, "Three-Dimensional Multiple Wavelength Fluorescence Microscopy for the Structural Analysis of Biological Phenomena," *Seminars in Cell Biology,* **2**:153–165, 1991.

S. INOUE AND T. D. INOUE, "Computer-Aided Stereoscopic Video Reconstruction and Serial Display from High-Resolution Light-Microscope Optical Sections, *Annals of the New York Academy of Science,* **483**:392–404, 1986.

S. KAWATA AND S. MINAMI, "The Principle and Applications of Optical Microscope Tomography," *Acta Histochem. Cytochem.*, **19**(1):73–81, 1986.

C. PREZA, et al., "Regularized Linear Method for Reconstruction of Three-Dimensional Microscopic Objects from Optical Sections," *Journal of the Optical Society of America*, **9**(2):219–228, 1992.

P. J. SHAW, D. A. AGARD, Y. HIRAOKA, AND J. W. SEDAT, "Tilted View Reconstruction in Optical Microscopy: Three-Dimensional Reconstruction of *Drosophila Melanogaster* Embryo Nuclei," *Biophysics Journal,* **55**:101–110, 1988.

N. STREIBL, "Three Dimensional Imaging by a Microscope," *Journal of the Optical Society of America,* **2:**121–127, 1985.

A2.2.17 Visual Languages

S. K. CHANG, "Visual Languages: A Tutorial and Survey," *IEEE Software*, **4**:29-39, 1987.

E. A. FOX, "Advances in Interactive Digital Multimedia Systems," *Computer*, **24**(10):9–21, 1991.

D. D. MCCRACKEN, "Revolution in Programming: An Overview," *Datamation,* **19**(12): 50–52, 1973.

J. RASURE, D. ARGIRO, T. SAUR, AND C. WILLIAMS, "Visual Language and Software Development Environment for Image Processing," *International Journal of Imaging Systems and Technology*, **2:**183–199, 1990.

J. R. RASURE AND C. S. WILLIAMS, "An Integrated Data Flow Visual Language and Software Development Environment," *Journal of Visual Languages and Computing*, **2**:217–246, 1991.

APPENDIX 3

Mathematical Background

This appendix lists some of the definitions and results from several fields that are relevant to the material developed in the text. They are presented in summary form, without derivation. Only those results directly supporting the concepts covered in the text are mentioned. For an in-depth coverage of these topics, the reader should consult an appropriate textbook [1–3].

A3.1 LINEAR ALGEBRA

A3.1.1 Vectors and Matrices

Definitions. A *matrix* is an ordered rectangular array of numbers. The M-by-N matrix $\mathbf{A}$ has M rows and N columns and is denoted by

$$\mathbf{A} = [a_{i,j}] = \begin{bmatrix} a_{1,1} & a_{1,2} & \cdots & a_{1,N} \\ a_{2,1} & a_{2,2} & \cdots & a_{2,N} \\ \vdots & \vdots & \ddots & \vdots \\ a_{M,1} & a_{M,2} & \cdots & a_{M,N} \end{bmatrix} \tag{1}$$

where $a_{i,j}$ are the *elements,* or *entries,* of $\mathbf{A}$ and $i = 1, 2, \ldots M$, $j = 1, 2, \ldots N$ are indices.

The *transpose* of a matrix $\mathbf{A}$ is another matrix, denoted $\mathbf{A}^T$ and obtained by interchanging the rows and columns of $\mathbf{A}$. For example, if

$$\mathbf{A} = \begin{bmatrix} 1 & 3 & 5 \\ 8 & 2 & 7 \end{bmatrix} \quad \text{then} \quad \mathbf{A}^T = \begin{bmatrix} 1 & 8 \\ 3 & 2 \\ 5 & 7 \end{bmatrix} \tag{2}$$

A *column vector* is an M-by-1 matrix. A *row vector* is a 1-by-N matrix. Respectively, these are

$$\mathbf{b} = [b_i] = \begin{bmatrix} b_1 \\ b_2 \\ \vdots \\ b_N \end{bmatrix} \quad \text{and} \quad \mathbf{b}^T = [b_1 \; b_2 \cdots b_N] \tag{3}$$

where b_i are the elements of the vector. Unless otherwise specified, the term *vector* refers to a column vector.

A matrix is a *square matrix* if $M = N$. A square matrix $\mathbf{A}$ is a *symmetric matrix* if $a_{i,j} = a_{j,i}$. For example,

$$\mathbf{A} = \begin{bmatrix} 1 & -1 & 2 \\ -1 & 3 & 4 \\ 2 & 4 & 0 \end{bmatrix} \tag{4}$$

is a symmetric square matrix.

A *diagonal matrix* is a square matrix having zero elements everywhere except on the diagonal; that is, $a_{i,j} = 0$ for $i \neq j$.

The *identity matrix* $\mathbf{I}$ is a diagonal matrix having 1's on the diagonal (i.e., $a_{i,i} = 1$). For example, the three-by-three identity matrix is

$$\mathbf{I} = \begin{bmatrix} 1 & 0 & 0 \\ 0 & 1 & 0 \\ 0 & 0 & 1 \end{bmatrix} \tag{5}$$

The *trace* of a square matrix is a scalar that is the sum of its diagonal elements:

$$\text{tr}[\mathbf{A}] = \sum_{i=1}^{N} a_{i,i} \tag{6}$$

The *scalar product* (a constant times a matrix) is defined by

$$c\mathbf{A} = \mathbf{A}c = c[a_{i,j}] = [ca_{i,j}] \tag{7}$$

where c is a constant.

Scalar addition of a matrix and a constant is defined by

$$c + \mathbf{A} = \mathbf{A} + c = [a_{i,j}] + c = [a_{i,j} + c] \tag{8}$$

Matrix addition of two M-by-N matrices is defined by

$$\mathbf{A} + \mathbf{B} = \mathbf{B} + \mathbf{A} = [a_{i,j} + b_{i,j}] \tag{9}$$

Matrix addition is defined only for the matrices of the same size.

The *matrix product* of an M-by-P matrix and a P-by-N matrix is the M-by-N matrix

$$\mathbf{AB} = \mathbf{D} = [d_{i,j}] = \left[\sum_{k=0}^{P-1} a_{i,k} b_{k,j}\right] \tag{10}$$

The matrix product is defined only for matrices in which the number of columns of the left-hand matrix equals the number of rows of the right-hand matrix.

For vectors of equal length, the *outer product* is the (rank 1) matrix

$$\mathbf{ab}^T = \begin{bmatrix} a_1 \\ a_2 \\ \\ a_N \end{bmatrix} [b_1\ b_2 \cdots b_N] = \begin{bmatrix} a_1 b_1 & a_1 b_2 & \cdots & a_1 b_N \\ a_2 b_1 & a_2 b_2 & \cdots & a_2 b_N \\ \vdots & \vdots & \ddots & \vdots \\ a_N b_1 & a_N b_2 & \cdots & a_N b_N \end{bmatrix} \tag{11}$$

and the *inner product* is the scalar

$$\mathbf{a}^T\mathbf{b} = [a_1\ a_2 \cdots a_N] \begin{bmatrix} b_1 \\ b_2 \\ \vdots \\ b_N \end{bmatrix} = c \tag{12}$$

The *Euclidean norm* of a vector is defined as the scalar

$$\|\mathbf{a}\| = \sqrt{\mathbf{a}^T\mathbf{a}} = \sqrt{\sum_{i=0}^{N-1} a_i^2} \tag{13}$$

If $\mathbf{a}$ contains the coordinates of a point in an N-dimensional Euclidean space, then the norm of $\mathbf{a}$ is the distance from the origin to that point. As another example, suppose $\mathbf{a}^T = \lfloor x_1, y_1, z_1 \rfloor$ and $\mathbf{b}^T = \lfloor x_2, y_2, z_2 \rfloor$ are vectors representing the positions of two points in three-dimensional space. Then their separation distance is

$$d = \|\mathbf{a} - \mathbf{b}\| = \sqrt{(x_1 - x_2)^2 + (y_1 - y_2)^2 + (z_1 - z_2)^2} \tag{14}$$

Matrix Inversion. The *inverse* of a square matrix $\mathbf{A}$ is another matrix, $\mathbf{A}^{-1}$, of the same size such that

$$\mathbf{AA}^{-1} = \mathbf{A}^{-1}\mathbf{A} = \mathbf{I} \tag{15}$$

where $\mathbf{I}$ is the identity matrix of the same size. The inverse is unique, provided that it exists. If no such matrix exists, then $\mathbf{A}$ is a *singular matrix.* If $\mathbf{A}$ is nonsingular, but so close to singular that computing its inverse is fraught with numerical problems, then it is called *ill conditioned.*

The *determinant* $|\mathbf{A}|$ of a square matrix $\mathbf{A}$ is a (unique) scalar-valued function of the elements of $\mathbf{A}$. It has the properties that (a) $|\mathbf{I}| = 1$, (b) if $\mathbf{A}$ has two identical rows (or columns), then $|\mathbf{A}| = 0$, (c) if $\mathbf{B}$ is obtained by multiplying a single row (or column) of $\mathbf{A}$ by a constant k then $|\mathbf{B}| = k|\mathbf{A}|$, and (d) if $\mathbf{A}$, $\mathbf{B}$, and $\mathbf{C}$ are N-by-N matrices that are identical except for the ith row, and for the ith row, $c_{i,j} = a_{i,j} + b_{i,j}$, then $|\mathbf{C}| = |\mathbf{A}| + |\mathbf{B}|$.

From the foregoing, it follows that (a) the matrix **A** is singular if $|A| = 0$, (b) the matrix **A** is singular if any row can be obtained by multiplying any other row by a constant (and likewise for columns), (c) $|\mathbf{A}^T| = |\mathbf{A}|$, (d) $|\mathbf{A}^{-1}| = 1/|\mathbf{A}|$, and (e) $|\mathbf{AB}| = |\mathbf{BA}| = |\mathbf{A}||\mathbf{B}|$.

The *rank* R of an N-by-N matrix **A** is an integer, $1 \le R \le N$. If A is nonsingular, then $R = N$. R is the size of the largest nonsingular R-by-R submatrix that can be formed by discarding rows and columns of **A**. $N - R$ is the number of rows that are linear combinations of other rows.

If **A** is an M-by-N matrix, then its *pseudoinverse*, $\mathbf{A}^-$, is the matrix product

$$\mathbf{A}^- = (\mathbf{A}^T\mathbf{A})^{-1}\mathbf{A}^T \quad \text{and} \quad \mathbf{A}^-\mathbf{A} = \mathbf{I} \tag{16}$$

provided that $(\mathbf{A}^T\mathbf{A})^{-1}$ exists.

Properties. Table A3–1 lists some of the properties of matrices and matrix algebraic operations.

TABLE A3--1 MATRIX PROPERTIES

Matrix	$\mathbf{A} = [a_{ij}]$
Transpose	$\mathbf{A}^T = [a_{ji}]$
Symmetric	$a_{ji} = a_{ij}$; $\mathbf{A}^T = \mathbf{A}$
Unitary	$\mathbf{A}^{-1} = \mathbf{A}^T$
Orthogonal	$\mathbf{AB} = \mathbf{I}$

A3.1.2 Eigenvalues and Eigenvectors

Eigenvalues. For an N-by-N matrix, there are N scalars λ_k, $k = 1,\ldots N$, such that

$$|\mathbf{A} - \lambda_k\mathbf{I}| = 0 \tag{17}$$

The λ_k's are the (unique) set of *eigenvalues* or *characteristic values* of the matrix.

Each eigenvalue can be thought of as an amount which, when subtracted from each diagonal element, makes the matrix singular. Since there is no ordering of the eigenvalues implied by this definition, we can arrange them arbitrarily. It is most convenient to index them from largest to smallest in magnitude; that is, $|\lambda_k| \ge |\lambda_{k+1}|$.

If the matrix is singular to begin with, then at least one of its N eigenvalues is zero. The *rank* of the matrix is the number of nonzero eigenvalues. The *condition number* of the matrix is the ratio of its largest to its smallest eigenvalue. If this is large (but finite), the matrix is *ill conditioned,* and inversion may be a numerically challenging process.

Eigenvectors. The N-by-1 vectors $\mathbf{v}_k$ such that

$$\mathbf{A}\mathbf{v}_k = \lambda_k\mathbf{v}_k \tag{18}$$

are called the *eigenvectors* or *characteristic vectors* of **A**. There are N of them, and each corresponds to one of the eigenvalues. If **A** is real and symmetric, then the λ_k's are real.

For example, suppose

$$\mathbf{A} = \begin{bmatrix} 1 & 2 \\ 2 & 1 \end{bmatrix} \tag{19}$$

Then

$$\mathbf{A}\begin{bmatrix}1\\1\end{bmatrix} = \begin{bmatrix}1 & 2\\2 & 1\end{bmatrix}\begin{bmatrix}1\\1\end{bmatrix} = \begin{bmatrix}3\\3\end{bmatrix} = 3\begin{bmatrix}1\\1\end{bmatrix} \tag{20}$$

and

$$\mathbf{A}\begin{bmatrix}1\\-1\end{bmatrix} = \begin{bmatrix}1 & 2\\2 & 1\end{bmatrix}\begin{bmatrix}1\\-1\end{bmatrix} = \begin{bmatrix}-1\\1\end{bmatrix} = -1\begin{bmatrix}1\\-1\end{bmatrix} \tag{21}$$

Thus, 3 is an eigenvalue of this matrix, with $[1, 1]^T$ as the corresponding eigenvector, and likewise for -1 and $[1, -1]^T$.

A3.1.3 Singular-Value Decomposition

Any M-by-N matrix, $\mathbf{A}$ ($M \geq N$) can be written as

$$\mathbf{A} = \mathbf{U}\boldsymbol{\Lambda}\mathbf{V}^T \tag{22}$$

where $\mathbf{U}$ and $\mathbf{V}$ are M-by-N and N-by-N matrices, respectively, with orthonormal columns, and $\boldsymbol{\Lambda}$ is an N-by-N diagonal matrix containing the *singular values* of $\mathbf{A}$ along its diagonal. In particular, the columns of $\mathbf{U}$ are the eigenvectors of $\mathbf{A}\mathbf{A}^T$, and the columns of $\mathbf{V}$ are the eigenvectors of $\mathbf{A}^T\mathbf{A}$. Then, since $\mathbf{U}$ and $\mathbf{V}$ are unitary,

$$\boldsymbol{\Lambda} = \mathbf{U}^T\mathbf{A}\mathbf{V} \tag{23}$$

Sum of Unit-Rank Matrices. Since $\boldsymbol{\Lambda}$ is a diagonal matrix, singular-value decomposition allows us to express an M-by-M matrix of rank R as a sum of R M-by-M matrices of rank 1. Each such matrix is an outer product of two M-by-1 eigenvectors and is weighted, in the summation, by one of the singular values. Specifically,

$$\mathbf{A} = \mathbf{U}\boldsymbol{\Lambda}\mathbf{V}^T = \sum_{j=1}^{R} \boldsymbol{\Lambda}_{j,j}\mathbf{u}_j\mathbf{v}_j^T \tag{24}$$

where R is the rank of $\mathbf{A}$ and $\mathbf{u}_j$ and $\mathbf{v}_j$ are the jth columns of $\mathbf{U}$ and $\mathbf{V}$, respectively.

As a numerical example, consider the three-by-three matrix

$$\mathbf{A} = \begin{bmatrix}1 & 2 & 1\\2 & 3 & 2\\1 & 2 & 1\end{bmatrix} \tag{25}$$

Its singular-value decomposition is simplified because the matrix is square and symmetric. The unitary matrices are equal; therefore,

$$\mathbf{A}\mathbf{A}^T = \mathbf{A}^T\mathbf{A} = \begin{bmatrix}6 & 10 & 6\\10 & 17 & 10\\6 & 10 & 6\end{bmatrix} \tag{26}$$

And they have eigenvalues

$$\begin{bmatrix}\lambda_1\\\lambda_2\\\lambda_3\end{bmatrix} = \begin{bmatrix}28.86\\0.14\\0\end{bmatrix} \tag{27}$$

and eigenvectors

$$\mathbf{u}_1 = \mathbf{v}_1 = \begin{bmatrix} 0.454 \\ 0.766 \\ 0.454 \end{bmatrix} \quad \mathbf{u}_2 = \mathbf{v}_2 = \begin{bmatrix} 0.542 \\ -0.643 \\ 0.542 \end{bmatrix} \quad \text{and} \quad \mathbf{u}_3 = \mathbf{v}_3 = \begin{bmatrix} -0.707 \\ 0 \\ -0.707 \end{bmatrix} \tag{28}$$

U is a matrix of rank 2, since one of its eigenvalues is zero. The singular values are on the diagonal of

$$\boldsymbol{\Lambda} = \mathbf{U}^T\mathbf{A}\mathbf{V} = \begin{bmatrix} 5.37 & 0 & 0 \\ 0 & -0.372 & 0 \\ 0 & 0 & 0 \end{bmatrix} \tag{29}$$

and the expansion of the singular-value decomposition is

$$\mathbf{A} = \sum_{j=1}^{3} \Lambda_{j,j}\mathbf{u}_j\mathbf{v}_j^T \tag{30}$$

which, in this case, has only two nonzero terms.

Notice that the second singular value is much smaller than the first. Thus, we can neglect the second term in the summation without introducing much error of approximation. Using the first term alone, we have

$$\mathbf{A} \approx \Lambda_{1,1}\mathbf{u}_1\mathbf{v}_1^T = \begin{bmatrix} 1.11 & 1.87 & 1.11 \\ 1.87 & 3.15 & 1.87 \\ 1.11 & 1.87 & 1.11 \end{bmatrix} \tag{31}$$

which may be an acceptable approximation to the matrix in Eq. (25).

Matrix inversion. If the M-by-M matrix **A** is singular, then one or more of its singular values will be zero. If it is ill conditioned, one or more will be small, and inversion by ordinary numerical means will be difficult. Singular-value decomposition gives us a way to handle either case.

Taking the inverse of Eq. (22) yields

$$\mathbf{A}^{-1} = \mathbf{U}^T\boldsymbol{\Lambda}^{-1}\mathbf{V} \tag{32}$$

where $\boldsymbol{\Lambda}^{-1}$ is a diagonal matrix with elements $1/\Lambda_{ij}$ on the diagonal. Singular values (Λ_{ij}) that are small or zero make it difficult or impossible, respectively, to compute Eq. (32), but setting the corresponding diagonal elements of $\boldsymbol{\Lambda}^{-1}$ to zero often yields a usable approximation.

A3.1.4 Systems of Equations

Suppose we have a set of N equations in M variables, having the form

$$\begin{aligned} a_{1,1}x_1 + a_{1,2}x_2 + \cdots + a_{1,N}x_N &= c_1 \\ a_{2,1}x_1 + a_{2,2}x_2 + \cdots + a_{2,N}x_N &= c_2 \\ &\vdots \\ a_{M,1}x_1 + a_{M,2}x_2 + \cdots + a_{M,N}x_N &= c_M \end{aligned} \tag{33}$$

This can be written in matrix form as

$$\begin{bmatrix} a_{1,1} & a_{1,2} & \cdots & a_{1,N} \\ a_{2,1} & a_{2,2} & \cdots & a_{2,N} \\ \vdots & \vdots & \ddots & \vdots \\ a_{M,1} & a_{M,2} & \cdots & a_{M,N} \end{bmatrix} \begin{bmatrix} x_1 \\ x_2 \\ \vdots \\ x_N \end{bmatrix} = \begin{bmatrix} c_1 \\ c_2 \\ \vdots \\ c_M \end{bmatrix} \quad \text{or} \quad \mathbf{Ax} = \mathbf{c} \tag{34}$$

where $\mathbf{x} = [x_i]$ is an N-by-1 column vector of variables, $\mathbf{c} = [c_j]$ is an M-by-1 column vector of constants, and $\mathbf{A} = [a_{i,j}]$ is the M-by-N matrix of coefficients. Normally, $\mathbf{A}$ and $\mathbf{c}$ are known and $\mathbf{x}$ is to be solved for.

The solution to this system of equations is that particular set of x_i values that make all the equations hold simultaneously. If $M = N$ this is

$$\mathbf{x} = \mathbf{A}^{-1}\mathbf{c} \tag{35}$$

provided that A is nonsingular.

For example, suppose we have two equations in two variables:

$$\begin{aligned} x_1 - 2x_2 &= 0 \\ 2x_1 - 3x_2 &= 7 \end{aligned} \tag{36}$$

This can be written as

$$\begin{bmatrix} 1 & -2 \\ 2 & 3 \end{bmatrix} \begin{bmatrix} x_1 \\ x_2 \end{bmatrix} = \begin{bmatrix} 0 \\ 7 \end{bmatrix} \quad \text{or} \quad \mathbf{Ax} = \mathbf{c} \tag{37}$$

The Eqs. (36) specify two straight lines in two-dimensional x_1, x_2-space (Figure A3–1). The solution of this system of two simultaneous equations is the particular vector $\mathbf{x}$ that specifies the point where the lines cross. This is

$$\mathbf{x} = \mathbf{A}^{-1}\mathbf{c} = \begin{bmatrix} .429 & .286 \\ -.286 & .143 \end{bmatrix} \begin{bmatrix} 0 \\ 7 \end{bmatrix} = \begin{bmatrix} 2 \\ 1 \end{bmatrix} \tag{38}$$

In Figure A3–1, we see that the two lines do indeed cross at $x_1 = 2$, $x_2 = 1$. If the two lines were parallel, then A would be singular, and no solution would exist.

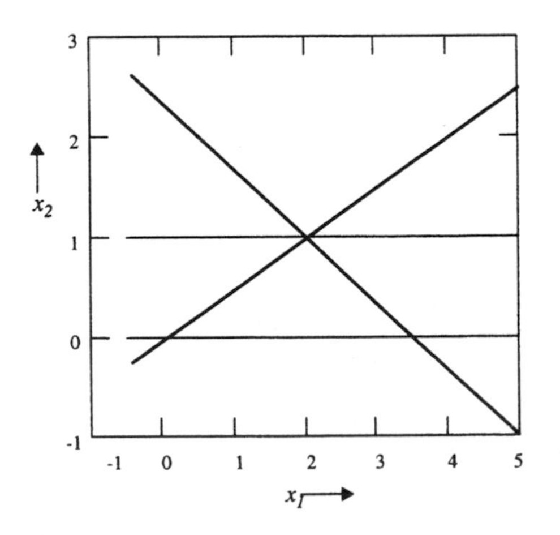

Figure A3–1 Two equations in two variables

If A is ill conditioned or singular, we can use singular-value decomposition to obtain a solution that is usually workable. We substitute Eq. (32) into Eq. (35) to get

$$\mathbf{x} = \mathbf{U}^T \Lambda^{-1} \mathbf{V} \mathbf{c} \tag{39}$$

As above, Λ^{-1} is a diagonal matrix with elements $1/\Lambda_{ij}$ on the diagonal. Where diagonal elements of Λ are either small or zero, correponding elements are set to zero in Λ^{-1}. This yields the solution that minimizes $|\mathbf{Ax} - \mathbf{c}|$.

A3.1.5 Least Squares Solutions

When the number of equations exceeds the number of unknowns, the system of equations is *overconstrained,* and (in general) no single solution will satisfy all the equations exactly. What is required is a best overall solution that satisfies all the equations approximately. One commonly used approach is to find the solution that minimizes the mean square error of all the equations.

For example, suppose the system has three equations in two variables:

$$\mathbf{Ax} = \mathbf{c} \quad \text{or} \quad \begin{bmatrix} a_{1,1} & a_{1,2} \\ a_{2,1} & a_{2,2} \\ a_{3,1} & a_{3,2} \end{bmatrix} \begin{bmatrix} x_1 \\ x_2 \end{bmatrix} = \begin{bmatrix} c_1 \\ c_2 \\ c_3 \end{bmatrix} \tag{40}$$

Then $\mathbf{A}$ is not square and thus has no inverse. In general, there will be no vector $\mathbf{x}$ that satisfies all the equations simultaneously. Thus, we seek instead a vector $\hat{\mathbf{x}}$ that satisfies them all approximately. In particular, we seek the vector that minimizes

$$\|\mathbf{A}\hat{\mathbf{x}} - \mathbf{c}\|^2 = (\mathbf{A}\hat{\mathbf{x}} - \mathbf{c})^T(\mathbf{A}\hat{\mathbf{x}} - \mathbf{c}) \tag{41}$$

Pseudoinverse Solution. By setting to zero the derivative with respect to $\hat{\mathbf{x}}$ of Eq. (41), we can solve for $\hat{\mathbf{x}}$ and obtain

$$\hat{\mathbf{x}} = (\mathbf{A}^t\mathbf{A})^{-1}\mathbf{A}^T\mathbf{c} = \mathbf{A}^{-}\mathbf{c} \tag{42}$$

Thus, the pseudoinverse of $\mathbf{A}$ yields the least squares solution, provided that $(\mathbf{A}^T\mathbf{A})^{-1}$ exists.

To illustrate, suppose we add one more equation to the previous example. Eq. (40) then becomes

$$\begin{bmatrix} -1 & 2 \\ 2 & 3 \\ 2 & -1 \end{bmatrix} \begin{bmatrix} x_1 \\ x_2 \end{bmatrix} = \begin{bmatrix} 0 \\ 7 \\ 5 \end{bmatrix} \tag{43}$$

Now

$$\hat{\mathbf{x}} = (\mathbf{A}^T\mathbf{A})^{-1}\mathbf{A}^T\mathbf{c} = \mathbf{A}^{-}\mathbf{c} = \begin{bmatrix} -.148 & .180 & .246 \\ .164 & .189 & -.107 \end{bmatrix} \begin{bmatrix} 0 \\ 7 \\ 5 \end{bmatrix} = \begin{bmatrix} 2.492 \\ 0.787 \end{bmatrix} \tag{44}$$

is the least squares solution. Figure A3–2 shows the three lines that correspond to the three equations, as well as the point that represents $\hat{\mathbf{x}}$, the least squares solution. In this example, the mean square error (Eq. 41) is 1.607.

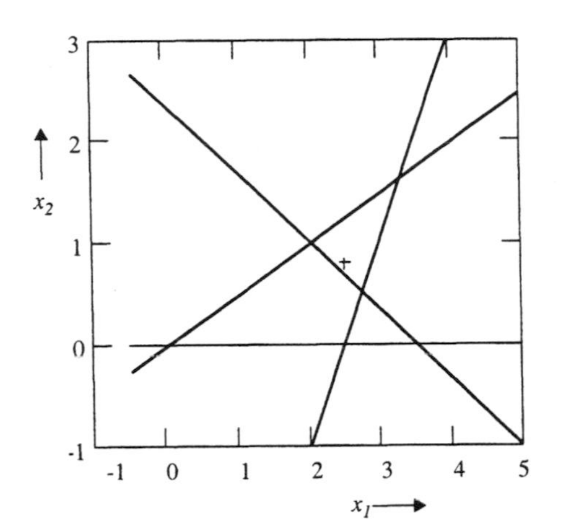

Figure A3–2 Three equations in two variables

If we were to change the third element of **c** to 3, then the third line would move to the left, and all three lines would intersect at the point $(x_1, x_2) = (1, 2)$. In this case, $\hat{\mathbf{x}}^T = (1, 2)$, and the mean square error is zero.

Singular-Value Decomposition Solution. If $\mathbf{A}^T\mathbf{A}$ is ill conditioned or singular, we can use singular-value decomposition to obtain a least squares solution. We simply use Eq. (39), again setting troublesome elements of Λ^{-1} to zero.

A3.1.6 Linear Transformations

If **x** is an N-by-1 vector and **A** is an N-by-N matrix, then

$$y_i = \sum_{j=1}^{N} a_{i,j} x_j \quad \text{or} \quad \mathbf{y} = \mathbf{A}\mathbf{x} \tag{45}$$

where $i = 1,\ldots,N$ defines a linear transformation of the vector **x**. The result is another N-by-1 vector, **y**.

A simple example of this is the rotation of a two-dimensional coordinate system (Chapter 8). Here,

$$\begin{bmatrix} y_1 \\ y_2 \end{bmatrix} = \begin{bmatrix} \cos(\theta) & -\sin(\theta) \\ \sin(\theta) & \cos(\theta) \end{bmatrix} \begin{bmatrix} x_1 \\ x_2 \end{bmatrix} \tag{46}$$

rotates the vector **x** through the angle θ.

After the transformation, the original vector can be recovered, if necessary, by the inverse transformation

$$\mathbf{x} = \mathbf{A}^{-1}\mathbf{y} \tag{47}$$

provided that **A** is nonsingular.

For a given vector length N, there are infinitely many transformation matrices **A**. The more commonly used ones, however, belong to a class having certain useful properties.

If **A** is a unitary matrix, then

$$\mathbf{A}^{-1} = \mathbf{A}^{*T} \quad \text{and} \quad \mathbf{A}\mathbf{A}^{*T} = \mathbf{I} \tag{48}$$

and the rows (and columns) of **A** form a set of orthonormal basis vectors (unit vectors) for an N-dimensional vector space. Thus, any such transformation can be viewed as a coordinate rotation in N-dimensional space.

The one-dimensional discrete Fourier transform is an example of a unitary linear transformation, since

$$F_k = \frac{1}{\sqrt{N}} \sum_{i=0}^{N-1} f_i \exp(-j2\pi ki) = \mathcal{W}\mathbf{f} \tag{49}$$

where $\mathcal{W}$ is a unitary matrix with elements

$$w_{i,k} = \frac{1}{\sqrt{N}} \exp\left(-j2\pi k\frac{i}{N}\right) \tag{50}$$

In two dimensions, the general linear transformation that takes the N-by-N matrix **F** into the transformed matrix **G** (also N by N) is

$$G_{m,n} = \sum_{i=0}^{N-1} \sum_{k=0}^{N-1} F_{i,k} \mathfrak{I}(i, k, m, n) \tag{51}$$

where i, k, m, and n are discrete variables that range from 0 to $N-1$ and $\mathfrak{I}(i, k, m, n)$ is the kernel function of the transformation.

If $\mathfrak{I}(i, k, m, n)$ can be separated into the product of rowwise and columnwise component functions—that is, if

$$\mathfrak{I}(i, k, m, n) = T_r(i, m) T_c(k, n) \tag{52}$$

then the transformation is called *separable*. Further, if the two component functions are identical, it is also called *symmetric*. Then

$$\mathfrak{I}(i, k, m, n) = T(i, m) T(k, n) \tag{53}$$

and Eq. (51) can be written as

$$G_{m,n} = \sum_{i=0}^{N-1} \sum_{k=0}^{N-1} F_{i,k} T(i, m) T(k, n) \quad \text{or} \quad \mathbf{G} = \mathbf{TFT} \tag{54}$$

The inverse transformation is

$$\mathbf{F} = \mathbf{T}^{-1}\mathbf{G}\mathbf{T}^{-1} \tag{55}$$

The two-dimensional discrete Fourier transform is an example of a symmetric, separable unitary transformation. In this case, **T** becomes the matrix $\mathcal{W}$ from Eq. (50). The inverse discrete Fourier transform uses $\mathcal{W}^{-1}$, which is simply the conjugate transpose of $\mathcal{W}$. The discrete Fourier transform pair is thus

$$\mathbf{G} = \mathcal{W}\mathbf{F}\mathcal{W} \quad \text{and} \quad \mathbf{F} = \mathcal{W}^{*T}\mathbf{G}\mathcal{W}^{*T} \tag{56}$$

Unlike the Fourier transform, many transformations have elements of **T** that are real. A unitary matrix with real elements is also orthogonal, and the inverse transformation becomes simply

$$\mathbf{F} = \mathbf{T}^T\mathbf{G}\mathbf{T}^T \tag{57}$$

If **T** is also a symmetric matrix, as is often the case, then the forward and inverse transforms are identical; that is,

$$\mathbf{G} = \mathbf{TFT} \quad \text{and} \quad \mathbf{F} = \mathbf{TGT} \tag{58}$$

A3.1.7 Principal-Component Analysis

Suppose **x** is an N-by-1 random vector; that is, each element x_i of **x** is a random variable. The mean vector can be estimated from a sample of L such vectors by

$$\mathbf{m}_x \approx \frac{1}{L}\sum_{l=1}^{L} \mathbf{x}_l \tag{59}$$

and its covariance matrix by

$$\mathbf{C}_x = E\{(\mathbf{x}-\mathbf{m}_x)(\mathbf{x}-\mathbf{m}_x)^T\} \approx \frac{1}{L}\sum_{l=1}^{L} \mathbf{x}_l\mathbf{x}_l^T - \mathbf{m}_x\mathbf{m}_x^T \tag{60}$$

The covariance matrix is real and symmetric. The diagonal elements are the variances of the individual random variables, while the off-diagonal elements are their covariances.

We now define a linear transformation that generates a new vector **y** from any **x** by

$$\mathbf{y} = \mathbf{A}(\mathbf{x}-\mathbf{m}_x) \tag{61}$$

where **A** is a matrix constructed so that its rows are the eigenvectors of $\mathbf{C}_x$. For convenience, we arrange the rows in order of decreasing magnitude of the corresponding eigenvalue.

The transformed vector **y** is also a random vector, with zero mean. Its covariance matrix can be determined from that of **x** by

$$\mathbf{C}_y = \mathbf{A}\mathbf{C}_x\mathbf{A}^T \tag{62}$$

Since the rows of **A** are eigenvectors of $\mathbf{C}_x$, $\mathbf{C}_y$ is a diagonal matrix having the eigenvalues of $\mathbf{C}_x$ along its diagonal (as a result of Eq. (18)). Hence,

$$\mathbf{C}_y = \begin{bmatrix} \lambda_1 & & 0 \\ & \ddots & \\ 0 & & \lambda_N \end{bmatrix} \tag{63}$$

These are also the eigenvalues of $\mathbf{C}_y$.

This means that the random vector **y** is composed of uncorrelated random variables. Thus, the linear transformation **A** removes the correlation among the variables. Furthermore, each λ_k is the variance of y_k, the kth transformed variable. Eq. (61) is referred to as the *Hotelling transform.* (See Chapter 13.)

Notice that this transformation is invertible; that is, we can reconstruct a vector **x** from its transformed vector **y** by

$$\mathbf{x} = \mathbf{A}^{-1}\mathbf{y} = \mathbf{A}^T\mathbf{y} \tag{64}$$

The latter equality holds because **A** is symmetric.

As a numerical example, suppose a three-by-one random vector **x** has the covariance matrix

$$\mathbf{C}_x = \begin{bmatrix} 6 & 2 & 0 \\ 2 & 2 & -1 \\ 0 & -1 & 1 \end{bmatrix} \tag{65}$$

which has eigenvalues and eigenvectors

$$\lambda = \begin{bmatrix} 6.854 \\ 2 \\ 0.146 \end{bmatrix} \quad \mathbf{v}_1 = \begin{bmatrix} 0.918 \\ 0.392 \\ -0.067 \end{bmatrix} \quad \mathbf{v}_2 = \begin{bmatrix} 0.333 \\ -0.667 \\ 0.667 \end{bmatrix} \quad \mathbf{v}_3 = \begin{bmatrix} -0.217 \\ 0.634 \\ 0.742 \end{bmatrix} \tag{66}$$

Then, for one particular zero-mean vector $\mathbf{x}^T = (2, 1, -0.1)$,

$$\mathbf{y} = \mathbf{A}\mathbf{x} = \begin{bmatrix} 0.918 & 0.392 & -0.067 \\ 0.333 & -0.667 & 0.667 \\ -0.217 & 0.634 & 0.742 \end{bmatrix} \begin{bmatrix} 2 \\ 1 \\ -0.1 \end{bmatrix} = \begin{bmatrix} 2.234 \\ -0.067 \\ 0.127 \end{bmatrix} \tag{67}$$

From Eq. (62), the covariance matrix of the transformed random vector $\mathbf{y}$ is

$$\mathbf{C}_y = \mathbf{A}\mathbf{C}_x\mathbf{A}^T = \begin{bmatrix} 6.854 & 0 & 0 \\ 0 & 2 & 0 \\ 0 & 0 & 0.146 \end{bmatrix} \tag{68}$$

which has the eigenvalues on its diagonal, as expected. Thus, Eq. (64) allows us to recover $\mathbf{x}$ from $\mathbf{y}$.

Dimension Reduction. We can reduce the dimensionality of the $\mathbf{y}$ vectors by ignoring one or more of the eigenvectors that have small eigenvalues. Let $\mathbf{B}$ be the M-by-N matrix ($M < N$) formed by discarding the lower $N - M$ rows of $\mathbf{A}$. Then the transformed vectors are smaller (i.e., M-by-1) and are given by

$$\hat{\mathbf{y}} = \mathbf{B}\mathbf{x} \tag{69}$$

but the $\mathbf{x}$ vectors can still be reconstructed (approximately) by

$$\hat{\mathbf{x}} = \mathbf{B}^T\hat{\mathbf{y}} \tag{70}$$

The mean square error of this approximation is

$$\text{MSE} = \sum_{k=M+1}^{N} \lambda_k \tag{71}$$

that is, simply the sum of the eigenvalues corresponding to the discarded eigenvectors.

Considering again the preceding numerical example, suppose we reduce $\mathbf{y}$ to two dimensions by discarding the third row of the transformation matrix $\mathbf{A}$, since λ_3 is considerably smaller than the other two eigenvalues. Then we have

$$\hat{\mathbf{y}} = \mathbf{B}\mathbf{x} = \begin{bmatrix} 0.918 & 0.392 & -0.067 \\ 0.333 & -0.667 & 0.667 \end{bmatrix} \begin{bmatrix} 2 \\ 1 \\ -0.1 \end{bmatrix} = \begin{bmatrix} 2.234 \\ -0.067 \end{bmatrix} \tag{72}$$

We can reconstruct the original vector, approximately, by

$$\hat{\mathbf{x}} = \mathbf{B}^T\hat{\mathbf{y}} = \begin{bmatrix} 0.918 & 0.333 \\ 0.392 & -0.667 \\ -0.667 & 0.667 \end{bmatrix} \begin{bmatrix} 2.234 \\ -0.067 \end{bmatrix} = \begin{bmatrix} 2.027 \\ 0.920 \\ -0.194 \end{bmatrix} \tag{73}$$

Notice that $\hat{\mathbf{x}}$ differs slightly from $\mathbf{x}$. In this case, the mean square error is just $\lambda_3 = 0.146$, the eigenvalue of the discarded eigenvector. Perhaps more enlightening, the root mean square error (i.e., $\sqrt{\text{MSE}}$) is 0.382. Assuming Gaussian statistics, the elements of $\hat{\mathbf{x}}$ will differ from those of $\mathbf{x}$ by less than that value about 60 percent of the time.

If $\mathbf{C}_x$ is singular, its rank R is less than N, and it will have $N - R$ zero eigenvalues. Principal-component analysis gracefully reduces the dimensionality from N to R, yielding a more tractable problem.

A3.2 SET THEORY

A3.2.1 Definitions

Sets and Elements. A *set* is a collection of objects, called the *elements* of the set. In this discussion, elements are symbolized by lowercase letters and sets by uppercase letters. The set **S** is termed the *universal set,* containing all the objects of interest in any problem, or *universe of discourse.*

The notation $\mathbf{a} \in \mathbf{A}$ means that the element **a** is a member of the set **A**, and $\mathbf{a} \notin \mathbf{B}$ means that **a** is not a member of set **B**. For any object **a** and set **C**, either $\mathbf{a} \in \mathbf{C}$ or $\mathbf{a} \notin \mathbf{C}$. The notation $\mathbf{C} = \{\mathbf{a}, \mathbf{b}, \mathbf{c}\}$ means that **a**, **b**, and **c** are the elements of **C**. The set denoted by $\varnothing$ and having no elements is called the *null* or *empty* set.

Subsets. If a set **A** contains all the elements of another set **B**, then **B** is a *subset* of **A** (written $\mathbf{B} \subseteq \mathbf{A}$) and **A** is a *superset* of **B** (written $\mathbf{A} \supseteq \mathbf{B}$). A set is both a subset and a superset of itself. If **A** and **B** contain exactly the same elements, they are the same set (written $\mathbf{A} = \mathbf{B}$). If **B** is a subset of **A** and **A** contains at least one element that is not in **B**, then **B** is a *proper subset* of **A**.

Union and Intersection. If **A** and **B** are each subsets of **S**, then the set **C** made up of all the elements of **A** and all the elements of **B** forms a subset of **S** called the *union* of **A** and **B** (written $\mathbf{C} = \mathbf{A} \cup \mathbf{B}$). The elements that are common to **A** and **B** form a subset **D** of **S** called the *intersection* of **A** and **B** (written $\mathbf{D} = \mathbf{A} \cap \mathbf{B}$). If **A** and **B** have no elements in common, then their intersection is empty ($\mathbf{A} \cap \mathbf{B} = \varnothing$).

Difference and Complement. The elements that are in **A** but not in **B** form a subset **E** of **S** that is called the *difference* between **A** and **B** (written $\mathbf{E} = \mathbf{A} - \mathbf{B}$). The set **A'** of elements that are in **S** but are not in **A** is called the *complement* of **A** with respect to **S** (written $\mathbf{A}' = \mathbf{S} - \mathbf{A}$).

A3.2.2 Properties

The following statements are directly derivable from the preceding definitions [4].

1. $\mathbf{A \cup A = A}$
2. $\mathbf{A \cap A = A}$
3. $\mathbf{A \cup S = S}$
4. $\mathbf{A \cap S = A}$
5. $\mathbf{A \cup \varnothing = A}$
6. $\mathbf{A \cap \varnothing = \varnothing}$
7. $\mathbf{(A')' = A}$
8. $\mathbf{A \cup A' = S}$
9. $\mathbf{A \cap A' = \varnothing}$
10. $\mathbf{A \cup B = B \cup A}$
11. $\mathbf{A \cap B = B \cap A}$
12. $\mathbf{(A \cup B) \cup C = A \cup (B \cup C)}$
13. $\mathbf{(A \cap B) \cap C = A \cap (B \cap C)}$
14. $\mathbf{A \cup (B \cap C) = (A \cup B) \cap (A \cup C)}$
15. $\mathbf{A \cap (B \cup C) = (A \cap B) \cup (A \cap C)}$
16. $\mathbf{(A \cup B)' = A' \cap B'}$
17. $\mathbf{(A \cap B)' = A' \cup B'}$
18. $\mathbf{A - B = A \cap B'}$
19. $\mathbf{(A - B) - C = A - (B \cup C)}$
20. If $\mathbf{A \cap B = \varnothing}$, then $\mathbf{(A \cup B) - B = A}$
21. $\mathbf{A - (B \cup C) = (A - B) \cap (A - C)}$

REFERENCES

1. R. Bellman, *Introduction to Matrix Analysis* (2d ed.), McGraw-Hill, New York, 1970.
2. B. Jacob, *Linear Algebra,* W. H. Freeman and Company, New York, 1990.
3. W. H. Press, S. A. Teukolsky, W. T. Vettering, and B. P. Flannery, *Numerical Recipes in C* (2d ed.), Cambridge University Press, 1992.
4. J. Singer and J. L. Berggren, "Set Theory," *Microsoft ® Encarta,* Microsoft Corporation, Redmond, WA, 1993.

Index

B

C

E

F

G

H

I

J

K

L

M

N

O

P

Q

R

S

T

U

V

W

X

Y